MyPsychLab VIDEO SERIES

TABLE OF CONTENTS

D0023110

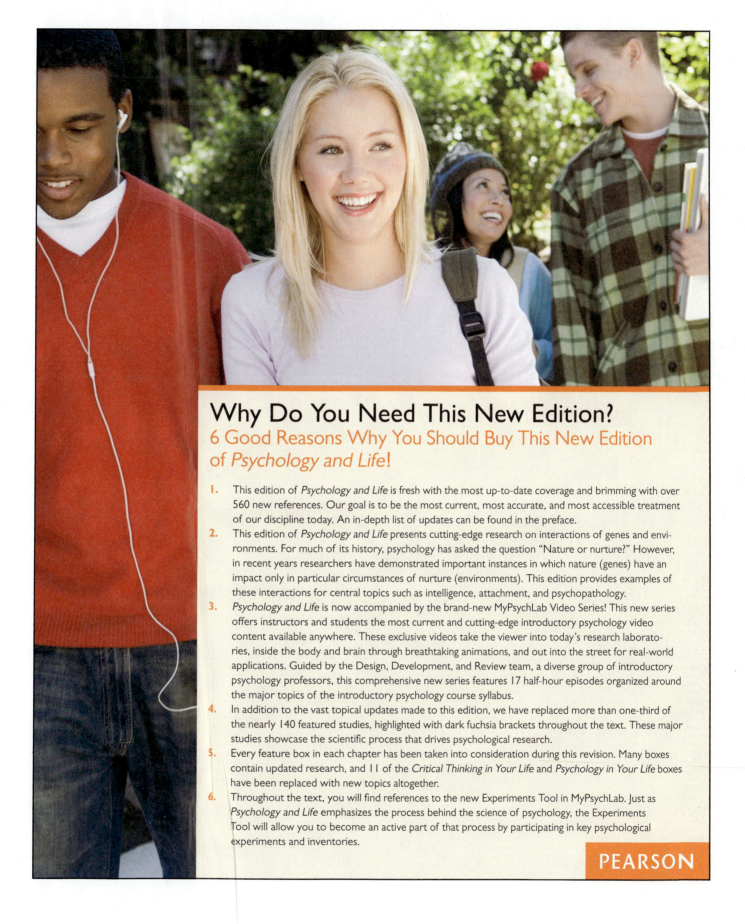

Why Do You Need This New Edition?

6 Good Reasons Why You Should Buy This New Edition of *Psychology and Life*!

1. This edition of *Psychology and Life* is fresh with the most up-to-date coverage and brimming with over 560 new references. Our goal is to be the most current, most accurate, and most accessible treatment of our discipline today. An in-depth list of updates can be found in the preface.

2. This edition of *Psychology and Life* presents cutting-edge research on interactions of genes and environments. For much of its history, psychology has asked the question "Nature or nurture?" However, in recent years researchers have demonstrated important instances in which nature (genes) have an impact only in particular circumstances of nurture (environments). This edition provides examples of these interactions for central topics such as intelligence, attachment, and psychopathology.

3. *Psychology and Life* is now accompanied by the brand-new MyPsychLab Video Series! This new series offers instructors and students the most current and cutting-edge introductory psychology video content available anywhere. These exclusive videos take the viewer into today's research laboratories, inside the body and brain through breathtaking animations, and out into the street for real-world applications. Guided by the Design, Development, and Review team, a diverse group of introductory psychology professors, this comprehensive new series features 17 half-hour episodes organized around the major topics of the introductory psychology course syllabus.

4. In addition to the vast topical updates made to this edition, we have replaced more than one-third of the nearly 140 featured studies, highlighted with dark fuchsia brackets throughout the text. These major studies showcase the scientific process that drives psychological research.

5. Every feature box in each chapter has been taken into consideration during this revision. Many boxes contain updated research, and 11 of the *Critical Thinking in Your Life* and *Psychology in Your Life* boxes have been replaced with new topics altogether.

6. Throughout the text, you will find references to the new Experiments Tool in MyPsychLab. Just as *Psychology and Life* emphasizes the process behind the science of psychology, the Experiments Tool will allow you to become an active part of that process by participating in key psychological experiments and inventories.

PEARSON

20TH EDITION

Psychology and Life

Richard J. Gerrig

Stony Brook University

Boston   Columbus   Indianapolis   New York   San Franciso   Upper Saddle River
Amsterdam   Cape Town   Dubai   London   Madrid   Milan   Munich   Paris   Montreal   Toronto
Delhi   Mexico City   São Paulo   Sydney   Hong Kong   Seoul   Singapore   Taipei   Tokyo

Editorial Director: Craig Campanella
Editor-in-Chief: Jessica Mosher
Acquisitions Editor: Amber Chow
Editorial Assistant: Diane Szulecki
Managing Editor, Editorial: Judy Casillo
Director of Marketing: Brandy Dawson
Marketing Manager: Brigeth Rivera
Senior Managing Editor: Maureen Richardson
Project Manager: Annemarie Franklin
Media Editor: Beth Stoner
Media Project Manager: Pam Weldin
Operations Supervisor: Mary Fischer

Operations Buyer: Diane Peirano
Creative Director: Blair Brown
Art Director: Leslie Osher
Interior/Cover Designer: Carmen DiBartolomeo
Cover Photos: iStockphoto/Shutterstock
Full-Service Project Management: S4Carlisle Publishing
    Services
Composition: S4Carlisle Publishing Services
Printer/Binder: Courier/Kendallville
Cover Printer: Lehigh-Phoenix Color/Hagerstown
Text Font: Minion Pro

Library of Congress Cataloging-in-Publication Data
Gerrig, Richard J.
    Psychology and life / Richard J. Gerrig. — 20th ed.
        p. cm.
    ISBN-13: 978-0-205-85913-9—ISBN-10: 0-205-85913-5   1. Psychology. I. Title.
    BF121.G47 2013
    150—dc23

                                                2012001117

10 9 8 7 6 5 4 3 2 1

Student Edition:
ISBN-10:   0-205-85913-5
ISBN-13: 978-0-205-85913-9

Instructor's Review Copy:
ISBN-10:   0-205-85914-3
ISBN-13: 978-0-205-85914-6

A la Carte:
ISBN-10:   0-205-86313-2
ISBN-13: 978-0-205-86313-6

PEARSON

To Phil Zimbardo, for entrusting me with *Psychology and Life*.

Brief Contents

Contents

Meet the Author

Richard J. Gerrig is a professor of psychology at Stony Brook University. Before joining the Stony Brook faculty, Gerrig taught at Yale University, where he was awarded the Lex Hixon Prize for teaching excellence in the social sciences. Gerrig's research on the cognitive psychological aspects of language use has been widely published. One line of work examines the mental processes that underlie efficient communication. A second research program considers the cognitive and emotional changes readers experience when they are transported to the worlds of stories. His book *Experiencing Narrative Worlds* was published by Yale University Press. Gerrig is a Fellow of the Society for Text & Discourse, the American Psychological Association, and the Association for Psychological Science. Gerrig is the proud father of Alexandra, who at age 21 provides substantial and valuable advice about many aspects of psychology and life. Life on Long Island is greatly enhanced by the guidance and support of Timothy Peterson.

Preface

Teaching introductory psychology is one of the greatest challenges facing any academic psychologist. Indeed, because of the range of our subject matter, it is probably the most difficult course to teach effectively in all of academia. The course must cover both the micro-level analyses of nerve cell processes and the macro-level analyses of cultural systems: both the vitality of health psychology and the tragedy of lives blighted by mental illness. The challenge in writing this text—like the challenge in teaching—is to give form and substance to all this information, to bring it to life for your students.

More often than not, students come into the course filled with misconceptions about psychology that they have picked up from the infusion of "pop psychology" into our society. They also bring with them high expectations about what they want to get out of a course in psychology—they want to learn much that will be personally valuable, that will help them improve their everyday lives. Indeed, that is a tall order for any teacher to fill. But I believe that *Psychology and Life* can help you to fill it.

The goal has been to design a text that students will enjoy reading as they learn what is so exciting and special about the many fields of psychology. The goal for every chapter, in every sentence, has been to ensure that students will want to go on reading. At the same time, I have focused on how the text will work within the syllabi of instructors who value a research-centered, applications-relevant approach to psychology.

This 20th edition of *Psychology and Life* has only a single author, but it retains the vision reflected in the collaboration between Richard Gerrig and Philip Zimbardo. That partnership was forged because of a shared a commitment to teaching psychology as a science relevant to human welfare. Phil Zimbardo and I brought our teaching experience to bear on a text that balances scientific rigor with psychology's relevance to contemporary life concerns. This latest edition continues the text's tradition of bringing the most important psychological insights to bear on your students' lives.

TEXT THEME: THE SCIENCE OF PSYCHOLOGY

The aim of *Psychology and Life* is to use solid scientific research to combat psychological misconceptions. In my experience as a teacher, one of the most reliable aspects of teaching introductory psychology is that students offer questions that are urgent for them:

My mother is taking Prozac: Will we learn what it does?
Are you going to teach us how to study better?

I need to put my son in day care to come back to school. Is that going to be all right for him?
What should I do if I have a friend talking about suicide?

It is comforting that each of these questions has been addressed by rigorous empirical research. *Psychology and Life* is devoted to providing students with scientific analyses of their foremost concerns. As a result, the features of *Psychology and Life* support a central theme: psychology as a science, with a focus on *applying* that science to your students' lives.

Critical Thinking in Your Life

An important goal of *Psychology and Life* is to teach the scientific basis of psychological reasoning. When students ask questions, they quite often have acquired partial answers based on the types of information that are available in the popular media. Some of that information is accurate, but often students do not know how to make sense of it. How do they learn to interpret and evaluate what they hear in the media? How can they become wiser consumers of the overabundance of research studies and surveys cited? How can they judge the credibility of these sources? To counteract this infusion of so-called reliable research, this text provides students with the scientific tools to think critically about the information with which they are surrounded and to draw generalizations appropriate to the goals and methods of research.

A feature called **Critical Thinking in Your Life** seeks to confront students directly with the experimental basis of critical conclusions. The intention is not to maintain that each of these boxes has the definitive answer to a particular research area, but to invite critical thinking and open the door for further questions.

Critical Thinking in Your Life

DOES "COMFORT FOOD" REALLY GIVE COMFORT?

An important goal of *Psychology and Life* is to improve your ability to think critically: The text should help you "reach intelligent decisions about what [you] should believe and how [you] should act" (Appleby, 2006, p. 61). To get started toward that goal, let's consider a real-world scenario. You're having a tough day, so you decide to indulge in some comfort food. Now take a step back. What evidence would you want to decide whether comfort food really makes you feel better? Let's see how researchers have approached this question.

If comfort food really gives comfort, people should consume more while experiencing emotional distress. To test that hypothesis, a team of researchers asked college women to watch a "brutal and violent" film excerpt (Evers et al., 2010). The researchers intended the excerpt to produce negative emotions—and it did. However, some of the women were told to suppress their emotional responses while they watched, "so that anybody looking at them would not be able to determine what kind of excerpt they were watching" (p. 797). A second group was not asked to hide their feelings. After watching the film, the students believed they were starting an unrelated study on taste. They were given the opportunity to eat both comfort food (for example, chocolate) and non-comfort food (for example, unsalted crackers). The women who had suppressed their emotions ate twice as much comfort food as the other group; they ate just about the same amount of non-comfort food. This pattern suggests that people actually do prefer comfort food when they are experiencing emotional turmoil.

But why does comfort food help with negative emotions? Another pair of researchers suggested that, across our lives, we mostly eat comfort food in the company of loved ones (Troisi & Gabriel, 2011). For that reason, we have associations built up in memory so that comfort food calls to mind the emotional warmth of those relationships. To test that hypothesis, the researchers assembled two groups of students: Some had previously reported that chicken soup was a comfort food; the second group did not have that association. The students then completed a task in which they were given word fragments (for example, *li—*) that could be completed as relationship words (for example, *like*). The researchers demonstrated that the students who consumed chicken soup—when it counted as a comfort food—produced the most relationship words. For that group, the experience of eating chicken soup made relationship associations easily accessible in memory.

These projects suggest that the memories associated with the consumption of comfort food help people deal with negative emotions. Now, use your critical thinking skills. What else would you like to know before you indulge in your own comfort food binge? 👁

- In the first study, why might the researchers have kept their sample to just one sex?
- With respect to the researchers' theory, why would chicken soup not be comfort food for everyone?

Psychology in Your Life

The questions I cited earlier are real questions from real students, and your students will find the answers throughout the book. These questions represent data collected from students over the years. The text uses the students' own questions—what they've said they need to know about psychology—in the form of the popular **Psychology in Your Life** sections. The hope is that your students will see, in each instance, exactly why psychological knowledge is directly relevant to the decisions they make every day of their lives.

Psychology in Your Life

IN WHAT WAYS DO PSYCHOLOGISTS PARTICIPATE IN THE LEGAL SYSTEM?

An important lesson of *Psychology and Life* is that empirical research provides psychologists with a broad range of expertise. As the text unfolds, you'll have a good many opportunities to see how research results apply to important issues in everyday life. You'll also see how psychological expertise functions in the public forum. As an initial example, let's consider how *forensic psychologists* become involved in important legal decisions.

The legal system relies on forensic psychologists to provide assessments for both civil and criminal proceedings (Packer, 2008). On the civil side, for example, forensic psychologists provide evidence that influences decisions about child custody in divorce hearings. They might also testify about the potential psychological harm workers have sustained in a particular place of employment. On the criminal side, forensic psychologists evaluate people's capacity to understand the acts they have committed and their competence to stand trial. Forensic psychologists also assess whether individuals are a danger to themselves or others. Let's examine that last role more closely.

Suppose that a person is sent to prison for committing a violent crime. After having served some time, he or she arrives at a parole hearing. An important consideration at that hearing will be what lies in the prisoner's future. What is the likelihood that violent acts will occur again?

In recent years, psychologists have attempted to provide increasingly research-based answers to that question (Fabian, 2006). This research often begins with a theoretical analysis of the life factors that make violence more or less likely. Researchers make an important distinction between *static* and *dynamic* factors (Douglas & Skeem, 2005). Static factors are those that are relatively stable over time (such as gender and age at first conviction); dynamic variables are those that may change over time (such as emotional control and substance abuse). The inclusion of dynamic factors suggests how risk changes over time. Past history alone does not provide a valid indication of how a person will behave in the future. It's also important to measure the trajectory of a person's life.

Researchers must provide evidence that risk assessment devices are successful at predicting future violence (Singh et al., 2011; Yang et al., 2010). To do so, researchers often follow groups of individuals over time. For example, Wong and Gordon (2006) evaluated 918 adult male offenders who were incarcerated in the Canadian provinces of Alberta, Saskatchewan, and Manitoba. Each participant was evaluated with the Violence Risk Scale (VRS), which measures six static and 20 dynamic variables. To evaluate the validity of the VRS, the researchers followed their participants over several years, to see how often they were convicted of new crimes after they had been released into the community. In both the short term (after 1 year) and the longer term (after 4.4 years), men who had obtained higher ratings on the VRS were more likely to be convicted of additional violent crimes.

Research results of this sort are quite important because they help forensic psychologists provide more accurate guidance for legal judgments.

Featured Studies

These major studies showcase the *how* and *why* behind key psychological research. These studies have been integrated into the text itself, allowing students to understand their full impact within the context of their reading. Example topics include plasticity in the visual cortex of adult rats, the impact of meditation on brain structure, the impact of culture on judgments of which category members are typical, the impact of emotional arousal on memory, self-handicapping in academic contexts, family therapy for children's anxiety disorders, cross-cultural differences in cognitive dissonance, and consequences of implicit prejudice. Many of the nearly 120 featured studies throughout the text are new or have been revised for this edition.

Pedagogical Features

Psychology and Life has maintained a reputation for presenting the science of psychology in a way that is challenging, yet accessible, to a broad range of students, and the 20th edition is no exception. To enhance students' experience, the book includes several pedagogical features:

- *Stop and Review.* This feature appears at the end of every major section and provides students with thought-provoking questions to test their mastery of material before moving on. Answers to these questions can be found in the Answer Appendix at the back of the book.
- *Recapping Main Points.* Each chapter concludes with a chapter summary, *Recapping Main Points,* which summarizes the chapter content and is organized according to major section headings.
- *Key Terms.* Key terms are boldfaced in the text as they appear with their definitions at the bottom of each page and are listed, with page references, at the end of each chapter for quick review.
- *Practice Test.* Each chapter concludes with a practice test with 15 multiple-choice questions based on the material in both the main text and the boxes. In addition, the practice test provides sample essay questions that allow students to think more broadly about the content of each chapter. Multiple-choice answers can be found in the Answer Appendix.
- *MyPsychLab Resources.* Throughout the chapters, valuable video clips, audio files, and simulations are referred to that will help you understand the concepts in each chapter. In the eText, they are hyperlinked to take you directly to the resource in MyPsychLab.

NEW IN THE 20TH EDITION

Selected Chapter-by-Chapter Changes

Chapter 1

- New Critical Thinking in Your Life: Does "Comfort Food" Really Give Comfort?
- Updated discussion of structuralism and functionalism.
- Updated figures on distributions of degrees and work settings for psychologists.

Chapter 2

- New Psychology in Your Life: Does Wishful Thinking Affect How You Evaluate Information?
- Updated Critical Thinking in Your Life: Why Is Skill with Numbers Important?

- Updated example of the process of research: "Language style matching predicts relationship initiation and stability" (Ireland et al., 2011)
- New featured studies:
  - "The invisible benefits of exercise" (Ruby et al., 2011)
  - "Media use and child sleep: The impact of content, timing, and environment" (Garrison et al., 2011)
  - "Birds of a feather sit together: Physical similarity predicts seating choice" (Mackinnon et al., 2011)

Chapter 3

- New Critical Thinking in Your Life: How Does Culture Become "Embrained"?
- New section on the interaction of genes and environments
- New discussion of mirror neurons
- Expanded discussion of H. M.
- New featured studies:
  - "A genetic analysis of coffee consumption in a sample of Dutch twins" (Vink et al., 2009)
  - "Children's genotypes interact with maternal responsive care in predicting children's competence: Diathesis-stress or differential susceptibility?" (Kochanska et al., 2011)
  - "Attention and memory in aged rats: Impact of lifelong environmental enrichment" (Harati et al., 2011)

Chapter 4

- New Psychology in Your Life: Does a Painful Break-up Really Hurt?
- New research study: "Differential neuronal responses to the self and others in the extrastriate body area (EBA) and the fusiform body area" (Vocks et al., 2010)
- New figure and discussion of the thalamus and lateral geniculate nucleus

Chapter 5

- Revised section on unattended information
- Update on paradoxical insomnia
- Update on properties of dreams
- New featured studies:
  - "Sleep selectively enhances memory expected to be of future relevance" (Wilhelm et al., 2011)
  - "Effect of hypnosis on pain and blink reflexes in patients with painful temporomandibular disorders" (Abrahamsen et al., 2011)
  - "Impact of mindfulness-based stress reduction training on intrinsic brain connectivity" (Kilpatrick et al., 2011)

Chapter 6

- New Critical Thinking in Your Life: When Do "Time Outs" Change Children's Behavior?
- Updated research added to Psychology in Your Life: How Does Classical Conditioning Affect Cancer Treatment?
- Biological constraints integrated into sections on classical and operant conditioning
- New featured studies:
  - "Interactions of temperatures and taste in conditioned aversions" (Smith et al., 2010)
  - "Testing pigeon memory in a change detection task" (Wright et al., 2010)

Chapter 7

- New Psychology in Your Life: How Can You Benefit from the "Testing Effect"?
- New research on working memory capacity (Kleider et al., 2010; Sörqvist et al., 2010)
- Revised section on processes and implicit memory with updated research (Eich & Metcalfe, 2009)
- New material on judgments of learning
- Revised discussion of Alzheimer's disease
- New featured studies:
  - "Writing about testing worries boosts exam performance in the classroom" (Ramirez & Beilock, 2011)
  - "Long-term conceptual implicit memory: A decade of evidence" (Thomson et al., 2010)
  - "Combating co-witness contamination: Attempting to decrease the negative effects of discussion on eye-witness memory" (Paterson et al., 2011)
  - "Faces are special but not too special: Spared face recognition in amnesia is based on familiarity" (Aly et al., 2010)

Chapter 8

- Updated research in Critical Thinking in Your Life: Why and How Do People Lie?
- New discussion of the Pirahã people with respect to language and thought
- New research on the belief-bias effect (Dube et al., 2010)
- Section on creativity moved to this chapter
- New research on the anchoring heuristic (Adaval & Wyer, 2011)
- New featured studies:
  - "Attenuating information in spoken communication: For the speaker, or for the addressee?" (Galati & Brennan, 2010)
  - "Who dunnit? Cross-linguistic differences in eye-witness memory" (Fausey & Boroditsky, 2011)
  - "Ending on a high note: Adding a better end to effortful study" (Finn, 2010)
  - "Ventral striatal signal changes represent missed opportunities and predict future choice" (Büchel et al., 2011)

Chapter 9

- New Critical Thinking in Your Life: Why Do Intelligent People Have Longer Lives?
- New Psychology in Your Life: What Brain Differences Accompany Higher Intelligence?
- Updated information on intellectual disabilities
- Critiques of Sternberg's and Gardner's theories of intelligence
- New research on interactions of genetics and environment (Tucker-Drob et al., 2011)
- New research on assessment of early childhood interventions (Lee, 2011; Zhai et al., 2011)
- New featured studies:
  - "The practical intelligence of entrepreneurs: Antecedents and a link with new venture growth" (Baum et al., 2011).
  - "Trait emotional intelligence in sports: A protective role against stress through heart rate variability?" (Laborde et al., 2011)

Chapter 10

- New Psychology in Your Life: What Happens When Children Become Bilingual?
- Updated research in Critical Thinking in Your Life: How Does Day Care Affect Children's Development?
- Discussion of ethical concerns for developmental research
- Discussion of critical periods versus sensitive periods
- Discussion of the cephalocaudal and proximodistal principles
- New research on infant cognition (Jowkar-Baniani & Schmuckler, 2011; Newman et al., 2010)
- New section on theory of mind
- New research on the long-term impact of infant temperament (Degnan et al., 2011).
- New discussion of Marcia's concept of identity status
- Revised discussion of prenatal hormones and sex differences
- New research on gender differences in moral reasoning (Mercadillo et al., 2011; You et al., 2011)
- New featured studies:
  - "The association between computer use and cognition across adulthood: Use it so you won't lose it?" (Tun & Lachman, 2010)
  - "The association between parenting and attachment security is moderated by a polymorphism of the mineralocorticoid receptor gene: Evidence for differential susceptibility" (Luijk et al., 2011)
  - "The effect of passengers and risk-taking friends on risky driving and crashes/near crashes among novice teenagers" (Simons-Morton et al., 2011)
  - "Establishing the next generation at work: Leader generativity as a moderator of the relationship between leader age, leader-member exchange, and leadership success" (Zacher et al., 2011)
  - "Gender differences in the neural correlates of humor processing: Implications for different processing modes" (Kohn et al., 2011)

Chapter 11

- Updated research in Critical Thinking in Your Life: How Does Motivation Affect Academic Achievement?
- Revised discussion of hormones and the regulation of eating
- Updated discussion on obesity, including interactions of genes and environment that may predispose some individuals to obesity (Gautron & Elmquist, 2011)
- Revised discussion of racial differences in body dissatisfaction
- New research on power and cheating in relationships (Lammers et al., 2011)
- New research on sexual norms in the United States
- New research on the consequences of need for achievement
- New featured studies:
  - "Getting a bigger slice of the pie. Effects on eating and emotion in restrained and unrestrained eaters" (Polivy et al., 2010)
  - "Sperm competition risk affects male mate choice copying" (Bierbach et al., 2011)
  - "Mating interest improves women's accuracy in judging male sexual orientation" (Rule et al., 2011)

Chapter 12

- Expanded section on culture and facial expressions
- Revised section on culture and emotional expression
- Revised section on the impact of moods and emotions
- New research examining the long-term impact of 9/11/01 (DiGrande et al., 2011)
- Revised discussion of the impact of socioeconomic factors on physical psychological health
- Revised discussion of psychoneuroimmunology
- New research on an intervention for Type A behavior (Wright et al., 2011)
- New featured studies:
  - "The weapon focus effect on memory for female versus male perpetrators" (Pickel, 2009)
  - "The development and initial validation of a brief daily hassles scale suitable for use with adolescents" (Wright et al., 2010)
  - "Preventing children's stress after disaster with teacher-based intervention: A controlled study" (Wolmer et al., 2011)
  - "Spousal support and changes in distress over time in couples coping with cancer: The role of personal control" (Dagan et al., 2011)
  - "Benefit finding, affective reactions to diabetes stress, and diabetes management among early adolescents" (Tran et al., 2011)
  - "Patient and physician beliefs about control over health: Association of symmetrical beliefs with medication regimen" (Christensen et al., 2010)

Chapter 13

- New Psychology in Your Life: Do You Believe That Personality Can Change?
- New discussion of Carl Rogers's view of the self
- New discussion of terror management theory
- New featured studies:
  - "Sources of cumulative continuity in personality: A longitudinal multiple-rater twin study" (Kandler et al., 2010)
  - "What it pays to know about a close other: The value of if-then personality knowledge in close relationships" (Friesen & Kammrath, 2011)
  - "The effects of self-efficacy on academic success of first-generation college sophomore students" (Vuong et al., 2010)
  - "Culturally divergent responses to mortality salience" (Ma-Kellams & Blascovich, 2011)

Chapter 14

- Updated research added to Psychology in Your Life: How Can We Pinpoint Interactions of Nature and Nurture?
- New research on the prevalence of PTSD (DiGrande et al., 2011; Fan et al., 2011)
- New research on cognitive biases and anxiety disorders (Taylor et al., 2010)
- Revised discussion of behavioral approaches to mood disorders
- New research on adolescent sexuality and suicide (Marshal et al., 2011)
- Revised section on the stigma of mental illness

- New featured studies:
  - "The moderational role of anxiety sensitivity in flight phobia" (Vanden Bogaerde & De Raedt, 2011)
  - "Motor inhibition in hysterical conversion disorder" (Cojan et al., 2010)
  - "The rejection-rage contingency in borderline personality disorder" (Berenson et al., 2011)
  - "The relationship of multiple aspects of stigma and personal contact with someone hospitalized for mental illness, in a nationally representative sample" (Boyd et al., 2010)

Chapter 15

- New Critical Thinking in Your Life: Can Internet-Based Therapies Be Effective?
- Revised discussion of diversity issues in psychotherapy
- Revised discussion of mental illness and homelessness
- Excerpts from transcripts of psychodynamic, cognitive behavioral, and client-centered therapy
- Updated information on drug therapies and ECT
- New section on common factors in psychotherapy, including a discussion of the therapeutic alliance
- New discussion of community psychology
- New featured studies:
  - "Treating cockroach phobia with augmented reality" (Botella et al., 2010)
  - "Amount of earnings during prize contingency management treatment is associated with posttreatment abstinence outcomes" (Petry & Roll, 2011)
  - "Mothers and fathers in family cognitive-behavioral therapy for anxious youth" (Podell & Kendall, 2011)

Chapter 16

- New research on culture and self-serving biases (Imada & Ellsworth, 2011)
- Revised discussion of conformity in everyday life
- New discussion of jigsaw classrooms
- New discussion of evolutionary analyses of facial attractiveness
- New research on culture and love (Riela et al., 2010)
- Reassessment of the facts of Kitty Genovese's murder and expanded discussion of contemporary research on bystander intervention
- New featured studies:
  - "They say a triple lutz: Bias and perception in American and Russian newspaper coverage of the 2002 Olympic figure skating scandal" (Stepanova et al., 2009)
  - "Self-verification as a mediator of mothers' self-fulfilling effects on adolescents' educational attainment" (Scherr et al., 2011)
  - "Why do people get phished? Testing individual differences in phishing vulnerability within an integrated information processing model" (Vishwanath et al., 2011)
  - "'I hope I'm not disturbing you, am I?' Another operationalization of the foot-in-the-mouth paradigm" (Meineri & Guéguen, 2011).
  - "We must not be enemies: Interracial contact and the reduction of prejudice among authoritarians" (Dhont & Van Hiel, 2009)

- "What is beautiful is good because what is beautiful is desired: Physical attractiveness stereotyping as projection of personal goals" (Lemay et al., 2010)
- "This is your brain on violent video games: Neural desensitization to violence predicts increased aggression following violent video game exposure" (Engelhardt et al., 2011)

THE *PSYCHOLOGY AND LIFE* TEACHING AND LEARNING PROGRAM

A good textbook is only one part of the package of educational materials that makes an introductory psychology course valuable for students and effective for instructors. A number of valuable ancillary materials in both electronic and print form will make the difficult task of teaching introductory psychology easier for you and more interesting for your students.

The **Instructor's Manual (IM)**, authored by David Ward (Arkansas Tech University), gives you unparalleled access to a huge selection of classroom-proven assets. Each chapter offers integrated teaching outlines to help instructors seamlessly incorporate all the ancillary materials for this book into their lectures. Instructors will also find an extensive bank of lecture launchers, handouts, activities, crossword puzzles, suggestions for integrating third-party videos and web resources, and cross-references to the hundreds of multimedia and video assets found in the MyPsychLab course. The Instructor Manual is available for download from the Instructor's Resource Center at http://www.pearsonhighered.com/irc or from the Instructor's DVD (ISBN 0-205-89877-7).

The **Test Bank**, authored by Jason Spiegelman (Community College of Baltimore County) contains, for each chapter, **multiple-choice** questions, some of which address myths or factoids from the text, along with **true/false** questions and **fill-in-the-blank** questions. Each conceptual and applied multiple-choice question has an answer justification, and all questions include a page reference, a difficulty rating (easy/medium/difficult), and skill type (conceptual/factual/applied). **Essay** questions which deal specifically with critical-thinking skills, have also been included, along with sample answers for each. The TIF is available for download from the Instrutor's Resource Center at http://www.pearsonhighered.com/irc or from the Instructor's DVD (ISBN 0-205-89877-7).

The test bank is available in a computerized format called **Pearson MyTest**. It is a powerful assessment generation program that helps instructors easily create and print quizzes and exams. Questions and tests can be authored online, allowing instructors ultimate flexibility and the ability to efficiently manage assessments anytime, anywhere. Instructors can easily access

existing questions, and edit, create, and store using simple drag-and-drop and Word-like controls. Data on each question provide information on difficulty level and page number. For more information, go to http://www.PearsonMyTest.com.

Power Point Presentations: Pearson is pleased to offer a unique and comprehensive collection of PowerPoint presentations, prepared by Christopher T. Arra (Northern Virginia Community College) for use in your classroom. The PowerPoints are available for download at the Instructor's Resource Center (http://www.pearsoned.com/IRC) or on the Instructor's Resource DVD (ISBN 0-205-89877-7). **Instructors can choose from a PowerPoint lecture presentation** that highlights major topics from the chapter, pairing them with select art images, or a **PowerPoint collection of the complete art files** from the text. Finally, Pearson has developed a set of **Interactive PowerPoints** (available only on the Instructor's Resource DVD) with embedded animations, videos, and activities. Many of the slides include layered art, allowing instructors the ability to highlight specific aspects of a figure, such as identifying each part of the brain.

Instructor's DVD (ISBN 0-205-89877-7): Bringing all of the 20th edition's instructor resources together in one place, the Instructor's Resource DVD offers all versions of the PowerPoint presentations, the electronic files for the Instructor's Manual materials, and the Test Bank to help you customize your lecture notes. (Note that these resources can also be downloaded from the Instructor Resource Center online by following the directions at **http://www.pearsonhighered.com/irc.**)

Online Options for Instructors and Students

MyPsychLab for *Psychology and Life*, 20th Edition

MyPsychLab

Personalize Learning with MyPsychLab

- The **new MyPsychLab** delivers proven results in helping students succeed, provides engaging experiences that personalize learning, and comes from a trusted partner with educational expertise and a deep commitment to helping students and instructors achieve their goals.
- The **new Experiments Tool** within MyPsychLab allows students to experience psychology by participating in key experiments, inventories, and surveys. All experiments in the Tool collect data, providing instructors with a valuable tool for illustrating the science behind core psychological concepts in their classroom.
- The **Pearson eText** lets students access their textbook anytime, anywhere, and in any way they want—including listening online or downloading to an iPad.
- A **personalized study plan** for each student, based on Bloom's Taxonomy, arranges content from less complex thinking—such as remembering and understanding—to more complex critical thinking—such as applying and analyzing. This layered approach promotes better critical-thinking skills and helps students succeed in the course and beyond.
- **Assessment** tied to every video, application, and chapter enables both instructors and students to track progress and get immediate feedback. With results feeding into

a powerful grade book, the assessment program helps instructors identify student challenges early—and find the best resources with which to help students.

- An **assignment calendar** allows instructors to assign graded activities, with specific deadlines, and measure student progress.
- New **MyClassPrep** collects the very best class presentation resources in one convenient online destination, so instructors can keep students engaged throughout every class.

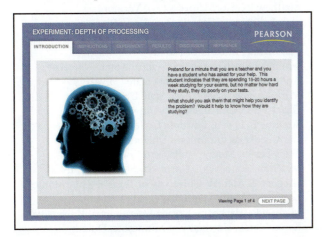

MyPsychLab for BlackBoard and MyPsychLab for WebCT: The customized BlackBoard cartridge and WebCT epack include the complete Test Item File, chapter Learning Objectives, Glossary Flashcards, Chapter Summaries, a link to MyPsychLab, and Chapter Exams. Ask your Pearson representative about custom offerings for other learning management systems.

New MyPsychLab Video Series

This new video series offers instructors and students the most current and cutting-edge introductory psychology video content available anywhere. These exclusive videos take the viewer into today's research laboratories, inside the body and brain through breathtaking animations, and out into the street for real-world applications. Guided by the Design, Development, and Review team, a diverse group of introductory psychology professors, this comprehensive new series features 17 half-hour episodes organized around the major topics of the introductory psychology course syllabus. The MyPsychLab video series was designed with flexibility in mind. Each half-hour episode in the MyPsychLab video series is made up of several five-minute clips that can be viewed separately or together:

- *The Big Picture* introduces the topic of the episode and draws in the viewer.
- *The Basics* uses the power of video to present foundational topics, especially those that students find difficult to understand.
- *Special Topics* dives deeper into high-interest and often cutting-edge topics, showing research in action.
- *Thinking Like a Psychologist* models critical thinking and explores research methods.
- *In the Real World* focuses on applications of psychological research.
- *What's in It for Me?* These clips show students the relevance of psychological research to their lives.

Students can access the videos anytime within MyPsychLab, and each clip is accompanied by enriching self-assessment quizzes. Instructors can access the videos for classroom presentation in MyPsychLab or on DVD.

ACCESSING ALL RESOURCES

For a list of all student resources available with *Psychology and Life,* go to www.mypearsonstore.com, enter the text ISBN (0-205-85913-5), and check out the "Everything That Goes with It" section under the book cover.

For access to all instructor supplements for Gerrig, *Psychology and Life,* **simply go to** http://pearsonhighered.com/irc and follow the directions to register (or log in if you already have a Pearson user name and password).

Once you have registered and your status as an instructor is verified, you will be e-mailed a login name and password. Use your login name and password to gain access to the catalogue. Click on the "online catalogue" link, click on "psychology" followed by "introductory psychology" and then the Gerrig, *Psychology and Life* text. Under the description of each supplement is a link that allows you to download and save the supplement to your desktop.

For technical support for any of your Pearson products, you and your students can contact http://247.pearsoned.com.

PERSONAL ACKNOWLEDGMENTS

Although the Beatles may have gotten by with a little help from their friends, I have survived the revision and production of this edition of *Psychology and Life* only with a great deal of help from many colleagues and friends. I especially thank Brenda Anderson, Ruth Beyth-Marom, Susan Brennan, Turhan Canli, Joanne Davila, Anna Floyd, Tony Freitas, Paul Kaplan, Daniel Klein, Anne Moyer, Timothy Peterson, Suzanne Riela, John Robinson, and Aimée Surprenant.

I would like to thank the following reviewers of both this edition and previous ones, who read drafts of the manuscript and provided valuable feedback:

Nancy Adams, Marshalltown Community College
Debra Ainbinder, Lynn University

Robert M. Arkin, Ohio State University
Trey Asbury, Campbell University
Gordon Atlas, Alfred University
Lori L. Badura, State University of New York at Buffalo
David Barkmeier, Northeastern University
Tanner Bateman, Virginia Tech
Darryl K. Beale, Cerritos College
N. Jay Bean, Vassar College
Susan Hart Bell, Georgetown College
Danny Benbassat, George Washington University
Stephen La Berge, Stanford University
Karl Blendell, Siena College
Michael Bloch, University of San Francisco
Richard Bowen, Loyola University
Mike Boyes, University of Calgary
Wayne Briner, University of Nebraska at Kearney
D. Cody Brooks, Denison University
Thomas Brothen, University of Minnesota
Christina Brown, Saint Louis University
Sarah A. Burnett, Rice University
Brad J. Bushman, Iowa State University
Jennifer L. Butler, Case Western Reserve University
James Calhoun, University of Georgia
Timothy Cannon, University of Scranton
Marc Carter, Hofstra University
John Caruso, University of Massachusetts–Dartmouth
Dennis Cogan, Texas Tech University
Sheree Dukes Conrad, University of
     Massachusetts–Boston
Randolph R. Cornelius, Vassar College
Leslie D. Cramblet, Northern Arizona University
Catherine E. Creeley, University of Missouri
Lawrence Dachowski, Tulane University
Mark Dombeck, Idaho State University
Wendy Domjan, University of Texas at Austin
Dale Doty, Monroe Community College
Victor Duarte, North Idaho College
Linda Dunlap, Marist College
Tami Egglesten, McKendree College
Kenneth Elliott, University of Maine at Augusta
Matthew Erdelyi, Brooklyn College, CUNY
Michael Faber, University of New Hampshire
Valeri Farmer-Dougan, Illinois State University
Trudi Feinstein, Boston University
Mark B. Fineman, Southern Connecticut State University
Diane Finley, Prince George Community College
Kathleen A. Flannery, Saint Anselm College
Lisa Fournier, Washington State University
Traci Fraley, College of Charleston
Rita Frank, Virginia Wesleyan College
Nancy Franklin, Stony Brook University
Ronald Friedman, University at Albany
Eugene H. Galluscio, Clemson University
Preston E. Garraghty, Indiana University
Adam Goodie, University of Georgia
Ruthanna Gordon, Illinois Institute of Technology
Peter Gram, Pensacola Junior College
Jeremy Gray, Yale University
W. Lawrence Gulick, University of Delaware
Pryor Hale, Piedmont Virginia Community College
Rebecca Hellams, Southeast Community College
Jacqueline L. Hess, University of Indianapolis

Dong Hodge, Dyersburg State Community College
Lindsey Hogan, University of North Texas
Rebecca Hoss, College of Saint Mary
Mark Hoyert, Indiana University Northwest
Herman Huber, College of St. Elizabeth
Richard A. Hudiburg, University of North Alabama
James D. Jackson, Lehigh University
Stanley J. Jackson, Westfield State College
Tim Jay, Massachusetts College of Liberal Arts
Matthew Johnson, University of Vermont
Seth Kalichman, Georgia State University
Colin Key, University of Tennessee at Martin
Mark Kline, Indiana University
Jennifer Trich Kremer, Pennsylvania State University
Andrea L. Lassiter, Minnesota State University
Mark Laumakis, San Diego State University
Charles F. Levinthal, Hofstra University
Suzanne B. Lovett, Bowdoin College
Carrie Lukens, Quinnipiac University
Tracy Luster, Mount San Jacinto College
M. Kimberley Maclin, University of Northern Iowa
Gregory G. Manley, University of Texas at San Antonio
Leonard S. Mark, Miami University
Michael R. Markham, Florida International University
Karen Marsh, University of Minnesota, Duluth
Kathleen Martynowicz, Colorado Northwestern
     Community College
Laura May, University of South Carolina–Aiken
Dawn McBride, Illinois State University
Michael McCall, Ithaca College
Mary McCaslin, University of Arizona
David McDonald, University of Missouri
Mark McKellop, Juniata College
Lori Metcalf, Gatson College
Greg L. Miller, Stanford University School of Medicine
Karl Minke, University of Hawaii–Honolulu
Charles D. Miron, Catonsville Community College
J. L. Motrin, University of Guelph
Anne Moyer, Stony Brook University
Eric S. Murphy, University of Alaska
Kevin O'Neil, Florida Gulf Coast University
Barbara Oswald, Miami University
William Pavot, Southwest State University
Amy R. Pearce, Arkansas State University
Kelly Elizabeth Pelzel, University of Utah
Linda Perrotti, University of Texas at Arlington
Brady J. Phelps, South Dakota State University
Gregory R. Pierce, Hamilton College
William J. Pizzi, Northeastern Illinois University
Mark Plonsky, University of Wisconsin–Stevens Point
Cheryl A. Rickabaugh, University of Redlands
Bret Roark, Oklahoma Baptist University
Rich Robbins, Washburn University
Daniel N. Robinson, Georgetown University
Michael Root, Ohio University
Nicole Ruffin, Hampton University
Nina Rytwinski, Case Western Reserve University
Bernadette Sanchez, DePaul University
Patrick Saxe, State University of New York at New Paltz
Mary Schild, Columbus State University
Katherine Serafine, George Washington University
Elizabeth Sherwin, University of Arkansas–Little Rock

Stu Silverberg, Westmoreland County Community College
Norman R. Simonsen, University of
     Massachusetts–Amherst
Peggy Skinner, South Plains College
R. H. Starr, Jr., University of Maryland–Baltimore
Weylin Sternglanz, Nova Southeastern University
Priscilla Stillwell, Black River Technical College
Charles Strong, Northwest Mississippi Community
     College
Dawn Strongin, California State University, Stanislaus
Walter Swap, Tufts University
Jeffrey Wagman, Illinois State University
David Ward, Arkansas Tech University
Douglas Wardell, University of Alberta
Linda Weldon, Essex Community College
Alan J. Whitlock, University of Idaho

Paul Whitney, Washington State University
Allen Wolach, Illinois Institute of Technology
John Wright, Washington State University
John W. Wright, Washington State University
Jim Zacks, Michigan State University

The enormous task of writing a book of this scope was possible only with the expert assistance of all these friends and colleagues and that of the editorial staff of Pearson. I gratefully acknowledge their invaluable contributions at every stage of this project, collectively and, now, individually. I thank the following people at Pearson: Amber Chow, Acquisitions Editor; Judy Casillo, Managing Editor—Editorial; Diane Szulecki, Editorial Assistant; Brigeth Rivera, Marketing Manager; Jeanette Koskinas, Executive Marketing Manager; and Annemarie Franklin, Production Project Manager.

Psychology
and Life

Psychology and Life

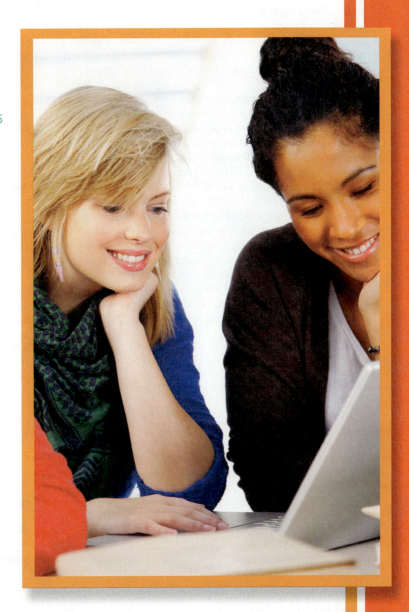

Why should you study psychology? The answer to that question is quite straightforward. Psychological research has immediate and crucial applications to important issues of everyday experience: your physical and mental health, your ability to form and sustain close relationships, and your capacity for learning and personal growth. One of the foremost goals of *Psychology and Life* is to highlight the personal relevance and social significance of psychological expertise. ◉

Every semester when I begin to teach, I am faced with students who enter an introductory psychology class with some very specific questions in mind. Sometimes those questions emerge from their own experience ("What should I do if I think my mother is mentally ill?" "Will this course teach me how to improve my grades?"); sometimes those questions emerge from the type of psychological information that is communicated through the media ("Should I worry when people use cell phones while they're driving?" "Is it possible to tell when people are lying?") The challenge of introductory psychology is to bring the products of scientific research to bear on questions that matter to you.

Research in psychology provides a continuous stream of new information about the basic mechanisms that govern mental and behavioral processes. As new ideas replace or modify old ideas, psychologists are continually intrigued and challenged by the many fascinating pieces of the puzzle of human nature. I hope that, by the end of this journey through psychology, you too will cherish your store of psychological knowledge.

Foremost in the journey will be a scientific quest for understanding. We will inquire about the how, what, when, and why of human behavior and about the causes and consequences of behaviors you observe in yourself, in other people, and in animals. We will consider why you think, feel, and behave as you do. What makes you uniquely different from all other people? Yet why do you often behave so much like others? Are you molded by heredity, or are you shaped more by personal experiences? How can aggression and altruism, love and hate, and mental illness and creativity exist side by side in this complex creature—the human animal? In this opening chapter, we ponder how and why all these types of questions have become relevant to psychology's goals as a discipline. ◉

WHAT MAKES PSYCHOLOGY UNIQUE?

To appreciate the uniqueness and unity of psychology, you must consider the way psychologists define the field and the goals they bring to their research and applications. By the end of the text, I hope you will think like a psychologist. This first section will give you a strong idea of what that might mean.

Definitions

Many psychologists seek answers to this fundamental question: What is human nature? Psychology answers this question by looking at processes that occur within individuals as well as forces that arise within the physical and social environment. In this light, we'll define **psychology** as the scientific study of the behavior of individuals and their mental processes. Let's explore the critical parts of this definition: *scientific, behavior, individual,* and *mental*.

The scientific aspect of psychology requires that psychological conclusions be based on evidence collected according to the principles of the scientific method. The **scientific method** consists of a set of orderly steps used to analyze and solve problems. This method uses objectively collected information as the factual basis for drawing conclusions. Chapter 2 will elaborate on the features of the scientific method more fully as we consider how psychologists conduct their research.

Behavior is the means by which organisms adjust to their environment. Behavior is action. The subject matter of psychology largely consists of the observable behavior of humans and other species of animals. Smiling, crying, running, hitting, talking, and touching are some obvious examples of behavior you can observe. Psychologists examine what the individual does and how the individual goes about doing it within a given behavioral setting and in the broader social or cultural context.

The subject of psychological analysis is most often an *individual*—a newborn infant, a college student adjusting to life in a dormitory, or a woman coping with the stress of her husband's deterioration from Alzheimer's disease. However, the subject might also be a chimpanzee learning to use symbols to communicate, a white rat navigating a maze, or a sea slug responding to a danger signal. An individual might be studied in its natural habitat or in the controlled conditions of a research laboratory.

Many researchers in psychology also recognize that they cannot understand human actions without also understanding *mental processes,* the workings of the human mind. Much human activity takes place as private, internal events—thinking, planning, reasoning, creating, and dreaming. Many psychologists believe that mental processes represent the most important aspect of psychological inquiry. As you shall soon see, psychological investigators have devised ingenious techniques to study mental events and processes—to make these private experiences public.

The combination of these concerns defines psychology as a unique field. Within the *social sciences,* psychologists focus largely on the behavior of individuals in various settings, whereas sociologists study social behavior of groups or institutions, and anthropologists focus on the broader context of behavior in different cultures. Even so, psychologists draw broadly from the insights of other scholars. Psychologists share many interests with researchers in *biological sciences,* especially with those who study brain processes and the biochemical bases of behavior. As part of *cognitive science,*

....

◉ **Watch** the **Video** *The Big Picture: Asking the Tough Questions* on **MyPsychLab**

◉ **Watch** the **Video** *How Much Do You Know About Psychology?* on **MyPsychLab**

psychology The scientific study of the behavior of individuals and their mental processes.

scientific method The set of procedures used for gathering and interpreting objective information in a way that minimizes error and yields dependable generalizations.

behavior The actions by which an organism adjusts to its environment.

Most psychological study focuses on individuals—usually human ones, but sometimes those of other species. Is there anything happening in your life that might make you want to conduct a research study?

psychologists' questions about how the human mind works are related to research and theory in computer science, philosophy, linguistics, and neuroscience. As a *health science*—with links to medicine, education, law, and environmental studies—psychology seeks to improve the quality of each individual's and the collective's well-being.

Although the remarkable breadth and depth of modern psychology are a source of delight to those who become psychologists, these same attributes make the field a challenge to the student exploring it for the first time. There is so much more to the study of psychology than you might expect initially—and, because of that, there will also be much of value that you can take away from this introduction to psychology. The best way to learn about the field is to learn to share psychologists' goals. Let's consider those goals. ◉

The Goals of Psychology

The goals of the psychologist conducting basic research are to describe, explain, predict, and control behavior. These goals form the basis of the psychological enterprise. What is involved in trying to achieve each of them?

Describing What Happens   The first task in psychology is to make accurate observations about behavior. Psychologists typically refer to such observations as their *data* (*data* is the plural, *datum* the singular). **Behavioral data** are reports of observations about the behavior of organisms and the conditions

under which the behavior occurs. When researchers undertake data collection, they must choose an appropriate *level of analysis* and devise measures of behavior that ensure *objectivity*.

To investigate an individual's behavior, researchers may use different *levels of analysis*—from the broadest, most global level down to the most minute, specific level. Suppose, for example, you were trying to describe a painting you saw at a museum (see **Figure 1.1** on page 4). At a global level, you might describe it by title, *Bathers,* and by artist, Georges Seurat. At a more specific level, you might recount features of the painting: Some people are sunning themselves on a riverbank while others are enjoying the water, and so on. At a very specific level, you might describe the technique Seurat used—tiny points of paint—to create the scene. The description at each level would answer different questions about the painting.

Different levels of psychological description also address different questions. At the broadest level of psychological analysis, researchers investigate the behavior of the whole person within complex social and cultural contexts. At this level, researchers might study cross-cultural differences in violence, the origins of prejudice, and the consequences of mental illness. At the next level, psychologists focus on

. . . .

◉ **Watch** the **Video** *Thinking Like a Psychologist: Debunking Myths* on **MyPsychLab**

behavioral data   Observational reports about the behavior of organisms and the conditions under which the behavior occurs or changes.

What Makes Psychology Unique?   **3**

FIGURE 1.1 Levels of Analysis
Suppose you wanted a friend to meet you in front of this painting. How would you describe it? Suppose your friend wanted to make an exact copy of the painting. How would you describe it?

narrower, finer units of behavior, such as speed of reaction to a stop light, eye movements during reading, and children's grammatical errors while acquiring language. Researchers can study even smaller units of behavior. They might work to discover the biological bases of behavior by identifying the places in the brain where different types of memories are stored, the biochemical changes that occur during learning, and the sensory paths responsible for vision or hearing. Each level of analysis yields information essential to the final composite portrait of human nature that psychologists hope ultimately to develop.

However tight or broad the focus of the observation, psychologists strive to describe behavior *objectively*. Collecting the facts as they exist, and not as the researcher expects or hopes them to be, is of utmost importance. Because every observer brings to each observation his or her *subjective* point of view—biases, prejudices, and expectations—it is essential to prevent these personal factors from creeping in and distorting the data. As you will see in the next chapter, psychological researchers have developed a variety of techniques to maintain objectivity.

Explaining What Happens Whereas *descriptions* must stick to perceivable information, *explanations* deliberately go beyond what can be observed. In many areas of psychology, the central goal is to find regular patterns in behavioral and mental processes. Psychologists want to discover *how* behavior works. Why do you laugh at situations that differ from your expectations of what is coming next? What conditions could lead someone to attempt suicide or commit rape?

Explanations in psychology usually recognize that most behavior is influenced by a combination of factors. Some factors operate within the individual, such as genetic makeup, motivation, intelligence level, or self-esteem. These inner determinants tell something special about the organism. Other factors, however, operate externally. Suppose, for example, that a child tries to please a teacher to win a prize or that a motorist trapped in a traffic jam becomes frustrated and hostile. These behaviors are largely influenced by events outside the person. When psychologists seek to explain behavior, they almost

always consider both types of explanations. Suppose, for example, psychologists want to explain why some people start smoking. Researchers might examine the possibility that some individuals are particularly prone to risk taking (an internal explanation) or that some individuals experience a lot of peer pressure (an external explanation)—or that both a disposition toward risk taking and situational peer pressure are necessary (a combined explanation).

Often a psychologist's goal is to explain a wide variety of behavior in terms of one underlying cause. Consider a situation in which your professor says that, to earn a good grade, each student must participate regularly in class discussions. Your roommate, who is always well prepared for class, never raises his hand to answer questions or volunteer information. Your professor chides him for being unmotivated and assumes he is not bright. That same roommate also goes to parties but speaks only to people he knows, doesn't openly defend his point of view when it is challenged by someone less informed, and rarely engages in small talk at the dinner table. What is your analysis? What underlying cause might account for this range of behavior? How about *shyness*? Like many other people who suffer from intense feelings of shyness, your roommate is unable to behave in desired ways (Zimbardo & Radl, 1999). We can use the concept of shyness to explain the full pattern of your roommate's behavior.

To forge such causal explanations, researchers must often engage in a creative process of examining a diverse collection of data. Master detective Sherlock Holmes drew shrewd conclusions from scraps of evidence. In a similar fashion, every researcher must use an informed imagination, which creatively *synthesizes* what is known and what is not yet known. A well-trained psychologist can explain observations by using her or his insight into the human experience along with the facts previous researchers have uncovered about the phenomenon in question. Much psychological research is an attempt to give accurate explanations for different behavioral patterns.

Predicting What Will Happen Predictions in psychology are statements about the likelihood that a certain behavior will occur or that a given relationship will be found. Often an accurate explanation of the causes underlying some form of behavior will allow a researcher to make accurate predictions about future behavior. Thus, if we believe your roommate to be shy, we could confidently predict that he would be uncomfortable when asked to give a speech in front of a large class. When different explanations are put forward to account for some behavior or relationship, they are usually judged by how well they can make accurate and comprehensive predictions. If your roommate was to speak happily to the class, we would be forced to rethink our diagnosis.

Just as observations must be made objectively, scientific predictions must be worded precisely enough to enable them to be tested and then rejected if the evidence does not support them. Suppose, for example, a researcher predicts that the presence of a stranger will reliably cause human and monkey babies, beyond a certain age, to respond with signs of anxiety. We might want to bring more precision to this prediction by examining the dimension of "stranger." Would fewer signs of anxiety appear in a human or a monkey baby if the stranger were also a baby rather than an adult, or if the stranger were of the same species rather than of a different one? To improve future predictions, a researcher would create systematic variations in environmental conditions and observe their influence on the baby's response.

A psychological prediction.

Controlling What Happens   For many psychologists, control is the central, most powerful goal. Control means making behavior happen or not happen—starting it, maintaining it, stopping it, and influencing its form, strength, or rate of occurrence. A causal explanation of behavior is convincing if it can create conditions under which the behavior can be controlled.

The ability to control behavior is important because it gives psychologists ways of helping people improve the quality of their lives. Throughout *Psychology and Life,* you will see examples of the types of *interventions* psychologists have devised to help people gain control over problematic aspects of their lives. Chapter 15, for example, discusses treatments for mental illness. You will see how people can harness psychological forces to eliminate unhealthy behaviors like smoking and initiate healthy behaviors like regular exercise (see Chapter 12).

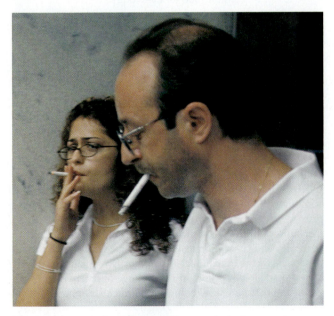

What causes people to smoke? Can psychologists create conditions under which people will be less likely to engage in this behavior?

You will learn what types of parenting practices can help parents maintain solid bonds with their children (Chapter 10); you will learn what forces make strangers reluctant to offer assistance in emergency situations and how those forces can be overcome (Chapter 16). These are just a few examples of the broad range of circumstances in which psychologists use their knowledge to control and improve people's lives. In this respect, psychologists are a rather optimistic group; many believe that virtually any undesired behavior pattern can be modified by the proper intervention. *Psychology and Life* shares that optimism.

Stop *and* Review

1. What are the four components of the definition of psychology?
2. What four goals apply to psychologists who conduct research?
3. Why is there often a close relationship between the goals of explanation and prediction?

✓• Study and Review on MyPsychLab

THE EVOLUTION OF MODERN PSYCHOLOGY

Today, it is relatively easy to define psychology and to state the goals of psychological research. As you begin to study psychology, however, it is important to understand the many forces that led to the emergence of modern psychology. At the core of this historical review is one simple principle: *Ideas matter.* Much of the history of psychology has been characterized by heated debates about what constitutes the appropriate subject matter and methodologies for a science of mind and behavior.

This historical review will be carried out at two levels of analysis. The first section will consider the period of history in which some of the critical groundwork for modern psychology was laid down. This focus will enable you to witness at close range the battle of ideas. The second section will describe in a broader fashion seven perspectives that have emerged in the modern day. For both levels of focus, you should allow yourself to imagine the intellectual passion with which the theories evolved. 🔍

Psychology's Historical Foundations

In 1908, **Hermann Ebbinghaus** (1858–1909), one of the first experimental psychologists, wrote "Psychology has a long past, but only a short history" (Ebbinghaus, 1908/1973). Scholars had long asked important questions about human nature—about how people perceive reality, the nature of consciousness, and the origins of madness—but they did not possess the means to answer them. Consider the fundamental questions posed in the

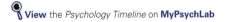

🔍 **View** the *Psychology Timeline* on **MyPsychLab**

Critical Thinking in Your Life

DOES "COMFORT FOOD" REALLY GIVE COMFORT?

An important goal of *Psychology and Life* is to improve your ability to think critically: The text should help you "reach intelligent decisions about what [you] should believe and how [you] should act" (Appleby, 2006, p. 61). To get started toward that goal, let's consider a real-world scenario. You're having a tough day, so you decide to indulge in some comfort food. Now take a step back. What evidence would you want to decide whether comfort food really makes you feel better? Let's see how researchers have approached this question.

If comfort food really gives comfort, people should consume more while experiencing emotional distress. To test that hypothesis, a team of researchers asked college women to watch a "brutal and violent" film excerpt (Evers et al., 2010). The researchers intended the excerpt to produce negative emotions—and it did. However, some of the women were told to suppress their emotional responses while they watched, "so that anybody looking at them would not be able to determine what kind of excerpt they were watching" (p. 797). A second group was not asked to hide their feelings. After watching the film, the students believed they were starting an unrelated study on taste. They were given the opportunity to eat both comfort food (for example, chocolate) and non-comfort food (for example, unsalted crackers). The women who had suppressed their emotions ate twice as much comfort food as the other group; they ate just about the same amount of non-comfort food. This pattern suggests that people actually do prefer comfort food when they are experiencing emotional turmoil.

But why does comfort food help with negative emotions? Another pair of researchers suggested that, across our lives, we mostly eat comfort food in the company of loved ones (Troisi & Gabriel, 2011). For that reason, we have associations built up in memory so that comfort food calls to mind the emotional warmth of those relationships. To test that hypothesis, the researchers assembled two groups of students: Some had previously reported that chicken soup was a comfort food; the second group did not have that association. At the start of the experiment, some students ate chicken soup and others did not. The students then completed a task in which they were given word fragments (for example, *li—*) that could be completed as relationship words (for example, *like*). The researchers demonstrated that the students who consumed chicken soup—when it counted as a comfort food—produced the most relationship words. For that group, the experience of eating chicken soup made relationship associations easily accessible in memory.

These projects suggest that the memories associated with the consumption of comfort food help people deal with negative emotions. Now, use your critical thinking skills. What else would you like to know before you indulge in your own comfort food binge? 👁

- In the first study, why might the researchers have kept their sample to just one sex?
- With respect to the researchers' theory, why would chicken soup not be comfort food for everyone?

4th and 5th centuries B.C. by the classical Greek philosophers **Plato** (427–347 B.C.) and **Aristotle** (384–322 B.C.): How does the mind work? What is the nature of free will? What is the relationship of individual citizens to their community or state? Although forms of psychology existed in ancient Indian Yogic traditions, Western psychology traces its origin to the writings of these philosophers. Plato and Aristotle defined opposing views that continue to have an impact on contemporary thinking. Consider how people come to know about the world. In the *empiricist* view, people begin life with their mind as a blank tablet; the mind acquires information through experiences in the world. **John Locke** (1632–1704) articulated this position at length in the 17th century; its roots can be traced to Aristotle. In the *nativist* view, people begin life with mental structures that provide constraints on how they experience the world. **Immanuel Kant** (1724–1804) fully developed this position in the 18th century; its roots can be traced to Plato. (In later chapters, we revisit this theoretical debate in the form of "nature versus nurture.") The French philosopher **René Descartes** (1596–1650) provided another important step toward contemporary psychology. Descartes proposed what, in his time, was a

very new and very radical idea: The human body is an "animal machine" that can be understood scientifically—by discovering natural laws through empirical observation. Toward the end of the 19th century, psychology began to emerge as a discipline when researchers applied the laboratory techniques from other sciences—such as physiology and physics—to the study of such fundamental questions from philosophy.

A critical figure in the evolution of modern psychology was **Wilhelm Wundt**, who, in 1879 in Leipzig, Germany, founded the first formal laboratory devoted to experimental psychology. Although Wundt had been trained as a physiologist, over his research career his interest shifted from questions of body to questions of mind: He wished to understand basic processes of sensation and perception as well as the speed of simple mental processes. By the time he established his psychology laboratory, Wundt had already accomplished a range of research and published the first of several editions of *Principles of Physiological*

👁 **Watch** the **Video** *How to Be a Critical Thinker* on **MyPsychLab**

In 1879, Wilhelm Wundt founded the first formal laboratory devoted to experimental psychology. Suppose you decided to found your own psychology laboratory. What one area in your life would you study if you could?

Psychology (King et al., 2009). Once Wundt's laboratory was established at Leipzig, he began to train the first graduate students specifically devoted to the emerging field of psychology. Those students often became founders of their own psychology laboratories around the world.

As psychology became established as a separate discipline, psychology laboratories began to appear in universities throughout North America, the first at Johns Hopkins University in 1883. These early laboratories often bore Wundt's impact. For example, after studying with Wundt, **Edward Titchener** became one of the first psychologists in the United States, founding a laboratory at Cornell University in 1892. However, at around the same time, a young Harvard philosophy professor who had studied medicine and had strong interests in literature and religion developed a uniquely American perspective. **William James**, brother of the great novelist Henry James, wrote a two-volume work, *The Principles of Psychology* (1890/1950), which many experts consider to be the most important psychology text ever written. Shortly after, in 1892, G. Stanley Hall founded the American Psychological Association. By 1900 there were more than 40 psychology laboratories in North America (Benjamin, 2007).

Almost as soon as psychology emerged, a debate arose about the proper subject matter and methods for the new discipline. This debate isolated some of the issues that still loom large in psychology. Let's consider the tension between structuralism and functionalism.

Structuralism: The Elements of the Mind Psychology's potential to make a unique contribution to knowledge became apparent when psychology became a laboratory science organized around experiments. In Wundt's laboratory, experimental participants made simple responses (saying yes or no, pressing a button) to stimuli they perceived under conditions varied by laboratory instruments. Because the data were collected through systematic, objective procedures, independent observers could replicate the results of these experiments. Emphasis on the

scientific method (see Chapter 2), concern for precise measurement, and statistical analysis of data characterized Wundt's psychological tradition.

When Titchener brought Wundt's psychology to the United States, he advocated that such scientific methods be used to study consciousness. Titchener's goal was to uncover the underlying structure of the human mind by defining the component elements of an individual's mental life. In fact, he conceived his research program in analogy to the work of chemists (1910, p. 49): "The psychologist arranges the mental elements precisely as the chemist classifies his elementary substances." Titchener's approach came to be known as **structuralism**, the study of the basic structural components of mind and behavior.

To discover the basic elements. Titchener relied on the technique of **introspection**, the systematic examination by individuals of their own thoughts and feelings about specific sensory experiences. Consider the domain of taste: Based on his introspections, Titchener suggested that all taste experiences emerge from combinations of the basic sensations of salty, sweet, sour, and bitter. In Chapter 4, you'll learn that Titchener's analysis was missing only one basic element. However, instrospection functioned less well in other domains of human experience: Titchener and his followers identified more than 44,000 distinct elements of sensory experiences (Benjamin, 2007)! Structuralism attracted many critics because it was impossible to confirm that the products of each individual's introspections were general aspects of human psychology.

One important alternative to structuralism, pioneered by the German psychologist **Max Wertheimer**, focused on the way in which the mind understands many experiences as *gestalts*—organized wholes—rather than as the sums of simple parts: Your experience of a painting, for example, is more than the sum of the individual daubs of paint. As you will see in Chapter 4, **Gestalt psychology** continues to have an impact on the study of perception.

A second major opposition to structuralism came under the banner of *functionalism.*

Functionalism: Minds With a Purpose William James agreed with Titchener that consciousness was central to the study of psychology. However, James focused his attention not on the elements of mental processes, but on their purpose. James wished to understand the ways in which consciousness functions to help people adapt effectively to their environments. James's approach became known as **functionalism**.

For functionalists, the key question to be answered by research was "What is the function or purpose of any behavioral act?" For example, a structuralist might look at a *reflex* and try to identify its basic components. By contrast, a theorist like

structuralism The study of the structure of mind and behavior; the view that all human mental experience can be understood as a combination of simple elements or events.

introspection Individuals' systematic examination of their own thoughts and feelings.

Gestalt psychology A school of psychology that maintains that psychological phenomena can be understood only when viewed as organized, structured wholes, not when broken down into primitive perceptual elements.

functionalism The perspective on mind and behavior that focuses on the examination of their functions in an organism's interactions with the environment.

Classroom practices in the United States were changed through the efforts of the functionalist John Dewey. As a student, what classroom experiences have you experienced that encouraged your "intellectual curiosity"?

John Dewey focused on the functions of reflexes, which he described as "a continuously ordered sequence of acts, all adapted in themselves and in the order of their sequence, to reach a certain objective end, the reproduction of the species, the preservation of life, locomotion to a certain place" (1896, p. 366). Dewey's concern for the practical uses of mental processes led to important advances in education. His theorizing provided the impetus for *progressive education* in his own laboratory school and more generally in the United States: "Rote learning was abandoned in favor of learning by doing, in expectation that intellectual curiosity would be encouraged and understanding would be enhanced" (Kendler, 1987, p. 124).

Although James believed in careful observation, he put little value on the rigorous laboratory methods of Wundt. In James's psychology, there was a place for emotions, self, will, values, and even religious and mystical experience. His "warm-blooded" psychology recognized a uniqueness in each individual that could not be reduced to formulas or numbers from test results. For James, explanation rather than experimental control was the goal of psychology.

The Legacy of These Approaches   Despite their differences, the insights of the practitioners of both structuralism and functionalism created an intellectual context in which contemporary psychology could flourish. Psychologists currently examine *both* the structure and the function of behavior. Consider the process of speech production. Suppose you want to invite a friend over to watch the Superbowl. To do so, the words you speak must serve the right function—*Superbowl, with me, today*—but also have the right structure: It wouldn't do to say, "Would watch Superbowl me the with today you to like?" To understand how speech production works, researchers study the way that speakers fit meanings (functions) to the grammatical structures of their languages (Bock, 1990). (Chapter 8 will describe some of the processes of language production.) *Psychology and Life* will emphasize both structure and function as we review both classic and contemporary research. Psychologists continue to employ a great variety of methodologies to study the general forces that apply to all humans as well as unique aspects of each individual.

Women as Pioneering Researchers

It probably won't surprise you to learn that, early in its history, research and practice in psychology were dominated by men. Even when they were still few in numbers, however, women made substantial contributions to the field (Benjamin, 2007). Let's consider four women who were pioneers in different areas of psychological research.

Mary Whiton Calkins (1863–1930) studied with William James at Harvard University. However, because she was a woman she was allowed to participate only as a "guest" graduate student. Although she completed all the requirements for a PhD with an exceptional record, the Harvard administration refused to grant a PhD to a woman. Despite this insult, Calkins established one of the first psychology laboratories in the United States and invented important techniques for studying memory. In 1905, she became the first woman president of the American Psychological Association.

In 1894, **Margaret Floy Washburn** (1871–1939) graduated from Cornell University to become the first woman to receive a PhD in psychology. She went on to write an influential early textbook, *The Animal Mind,* which was published in 1908. The book provided a review of research on perception, learning, and memory across animal species. In 1921, Washburn became the second woman to lead the American Psychological Association.

In 1894, Margaret Washburn became the first woman to receive a PhD in psychology. She went on to write an influential textbook, *The Animal Mind* (1908). What challenges might she have faced as a pioneer woman researcher?

Helen Thompson Wooley (1874–1947) accomplished some of the earliest research that examined differences between the sexes (Maracek et al., 2003; Milar, 2000). For her PhD research at the University of Chicago in 1900, Wooley compared the performance of 25 men and 25 women on a battery of tests, including tests of intelligence and emotions. The research led her to the conclusion that differences between the sexes arose not from natural ability but rather from differences in men and women's social experiences across their life spans. Wooley also offered a famous critique of "the flagrant personal bias, logic martyred in the cause of supporting a prejudice, unfounded assertions, and even sentimental rot and drivel" (Wooley, 1910, p. 340) that characterized research, largely by men, on differences between the sexes.

Leta Stetter Hollingworth (1886–1939) was inspired by Wooley to bring research data to bear on claims about gender differences (Maracek et al., 2003). In particular, Hollingworth attacked the claim that women were genetically inferior to men with respect to their levels of creativity and intelligence. Hollingworth also conducted some of the earliest research on children who tested at the extremes of intelligence—both those who had mental retardation and those who were gifted. She invented a curriculum to help nurture the talents of gifted children that she was able to implement in school settings in New York City.

Since the days in which these women were pioneers, the field of psychology has changed in the direction of far greater diversity. In fact, in recent years more women than men have earned PhDs in the field (National Science Foundation, 2010). I will highlight the work of diverse researchers throughout *Psychology and Life*. As psychology continues to contribute to the scientific and human enterprise, more people—women and men, and members of all segments of society—are being drawn to its richness.

Perspectives on Psychology

Suppose your friend accepts the invitation to join you for the Superbowl. What *perspective* does each of you bring to your viewing of the game? Suppose one of you played football in high school, whereas the other did not. Or suppose one of you has rooted from birth for one of the competing teams, whereas the other has no prior commitments. You can see how these different perspectives would affect the way in which you evaluate the game as it unfolds.

In a similar fashion, psychologists' perspectives determine the way in which they examine behavior and mental processes. The perspectives influence what psychologists look for, where they look, and what research methods they use. This section defines seven perspectives—psychodynamic, behaviorist, humanistic, cognitive, biological, evolutionary, and sociocultural. As you read the section, note how each perspective defines the causes and consequences of behavior. ◉

....

◉ **Watch** the **Video** *The Basics: Diverse Perspectives* on **MyPsychLab**

psychodynamic perspective A psychological model in which behavior is explained in terms of past experiences and motivational forces; actions are viewed as stemming from inherited instincts, biological drives, and attempts to resolve conflicts between personal needs and social requirements.

A word of caution: Although each perspective represents a different approach to the central issues of psychology, you should come to appreciate why most psychologists borrow and blend concepts from more than one of these perspectives. Each perspective enhances the understanding of the entirety of human experience.

The Psychodynamic Perspective According to the **psychodynamic perspective**, behavior is driven, or motivated, by powerful inner forces. In this view, human actions stem from inherited instincts, biological drives, and attempts to resolve conflicts between personal needs and society's demands. Deprivation states, physiological arousal, and conflicts provide the power for behavior. According to this model, the organism stops reacting when its needs are satisfied and its drives reduced. The main purpose of action is to reduce tension.

Psychodynamic principles of motivation were most fully developed by the Viennese physician **Sigmund Freud** (1856–1939) in the late 19th and early 20th centuries. Freud's ideas grew out of his work with mentally disturbed patients, but he believed that the principles he observed applied to both normal and abnormal behavior. Freud's psychodynamic theory views a person as pulled and pushed by a complex network of inner and outer forces. Freud's model was the first to recognize that human nature is not always rational and that actions may be driven by motives that are not in conscious awareness.

Many psychologists since Freud have taken the psychodynamic model in new directions. Freud himself emphasized early childhood as the stage in which personality is formed. Neo-Freudian theorists have broadened psychodynamic theory to include social influences and interactions that occur over the individual's entire lifetime. Psychodynamic ideas have had a

Sigmund Freud, photographed with his daughter, Anna, on a trip to the Italian Alps in 1913. Freud suggested that behavior is often driven by motives outside of conscious awareness. What implications does that perspective have for the ways in which you make life choices?

great influence on many areas of psychology. You will encounter different aspects of Freud's contributions as you read about child development, dreaming, forgetting, unconscious motivation, personality, and psychoanalytic therapy.

The Behaviorist Perspective Those who take the **behaviorist perspective** seek to understand how particular environmental stimuli control particular kinds of behavior. First, behaviorists analyze the *antecedent* environmental conditions—those that precede the behavior and set the stage for an organism to make a response or withhold a response. Next, they look at the *behavioral response,* which is the main object of study—the action to be understood, predicted, and controlled. Finally, they examine the observable *consequences* that follow from the response. A behaviorist, for example, might be interested in the way in which speeding tickets of varying penalties (the consequences of speeding) change the likelihood that motorists will drive with caution or abandon (behavioral responses).

The behaviorist perspective was pioneered by **John Watson** (1878–1958), who argued that psychological research should seek the laws that govern observable behavior across species. **B. F. Skinner** (1904–1990) extended the influence of behaviorism by expanding its analyses to the consequences of behaviors. Both researchers insisted on precise definitions of the phenomena studied and on rigorous standards of evidence. Both Watson and Skinner believed that the basic processes they investigated with nonhuman animals represented general principles that would hold true for humans as well.

Behaviorism has yielded a critical practical legacy. Its emphasis on the need for rigorous experimentation and carefully defined variables has influenced most areas of psychology. Although behaviorists have conducted much basic research with nonhuman animals, the principles of behaviorism have been widely applied to human problems. Behaviorist principles have yielded a more humane approach to educating children (through the use of positive reinforcement rather than punishment), new therapies for modifying behavior disorders, and guidelines for creating model utopian communities.

The Humanistic Perspective Humanistic psychology emerged in the 1950s as an alternative to the psychodynamic and the behaviorist models. According to the **humanistic perspective**, people are neither driven by the powerful, instinctive forces postulated by the Freudians nor manipulated by their environments, as proposed by the behaviorists. Instead, people are active creatures who are innately good and capable of choice. Humanistic psychologists study behavior, but not by reducing it to components, elements, and variables in laboratory experiments. Instead, they look for patterns in people's life histories.

The humanistic perspective suggests that the main task for humans is to strive for positive development. For example, **Carl Rogers** (1902–1987) emphasized that individuals have a natural tendency toward psychological growth and health—a process that is aided by the positive regard of those who surround them. **Abraham Maslow** (1908–1970) coined the term *self-actualization* to refer to each individual's drive toward the fullest development of his or her potential. In addition, Rogers, Maslow, and their colleagues defined a perspective that strives to deal with the whole person, practicing a *holistic* approach to human psychology. They believed that true understanding requires integrating knowledge of the individual's mind, body, and behavior with an awareness of social and cultural forces.

The humanistic approach expands the realm of psychology to include valuable lessons from the study of literature, history, and the arts. In this manner, psychology becomes a more complete discipline. Humanists suggest that their view is the yeast that helps psychology rise above its focus on negative forces and on the animal-like aspects of humanity. As we shall see in Chapter 15, the humanistic perspective had a major impact on the development of new approaches to psychotherapy.

The Cognitive Perspective The cognitive revolution in psychology emerged as another challenge to the limits of behaviorism. The centerpiece of the **cognitive perspective** is human

John Watson was an important pioneer of the behaviorist perspective. Why did he find it necessary to research behaviors of both humans and nonhuman animals?

....

behaviorist perspective The psychological perspective primarily concerned with observable behavior that can be objectively recorded and with the relationships of observable behavior to environmental stimuli.

behaviorism A scientific approach that limits the study of psychology to measurable or observable behavior.

humanistic perspective A psychological model that emphasizes an individual's phenomenal world and inherent capacity for making rational choices and developing to maximum potential.

cognitive perspective The perspective on psychology that stresses human thought and the processes of knowing, such as attending, thinking, remembering, expecting, solving problems, fantasizing, and consciousness.

Carl Rogers provided foundational ideas for the humanistic perspective. Why did Rogers place an emphasis on positive regard?

Within the cognitive perspective, an individual responds to reality not as it is in the objective world of matter but as it is in the *subjective reality* of the individual's inner world of thoughts and imagination. Because of its focus on mental processes, many researchers see the cognitive perspective as the dominant approach in psychology today.

The Biological Perspective The **biological perspective** guides psychologists who search for the causes of behavior in the functioning of genes, the brain, the nervous system, and the endocrine system. An organism's functioning is explained in terms of underlying physical structures and biochemical processes. Experience and behaviors are largely understood as the result of chemical and electrical activities taking place within and between nerve cells.

Researchers who take the biological perspective generally assume that psychological and social phenomena can be ultimately understood in terms of biochemical processes: Even the most complex phenomena can be understood by analysis, or reduction, into ever smaller, more specific units. They might, for example, try to explain how you are reading the words of this sentence with respect to the exact physical processes in cells in your brain. According to this perspective, behavior is determined by physical structures and hereditary processes. Experience can modify behavior by altering these underlying biological structures and processes. Researchers might ask, "What changes in your brain occurred while you learned to read?" The task of psychobiological researchers is to understand behavior at the most precise level of analysis.

Many researchers who take the biological perspective contribute to the multidisciplinary field of **behavioral neuroscience**. Neuroscience is the study of brain function; behavioral neuroscience attempts to understand the brain processes underlying behaviors such as sensation, learning, and emotion. The advances in the brain-imaging techniques highlighted in Chapter 3 have led to dramatic breakthroughs in the field of **cognitive neuroscience**. Cognitive neuroscience trains a multidisciplinary research focus on the brain bases of higher cognitive functions such as memory and language. As you shall see, brain-imaging techniques allow the biological perspective to be extended into a broad range of human experience. ◉

The Evolutionary Perspective The **evolutionary perspective** seeks to connect contemporary psychology to a central idea of the life sciences, Charles Darwin's theory of evolution by natural selection. The idea of natural selection is quite simple:

thought and all the processes of knowing—attending, thinking, remembering, and understanding. From the cognitive perspective, people act because they think, and people think because they are human beings, exquisitely equipped to do so.

According to the cognitive model, behavior is only partly determined by preceding environmental events and past behavioral consequences, as behaviorists believe. Some of the most significant behavior emerges from totally novel ways of thinking, not from predictable ways used in the past. Consider how children learn their native language. In his book *Verbal Behavior* (1957), B. F. Skinner suggested that children acquire language through ordinary processes of learning. **Noam Chomsky** (b. 1928) helped originate the cognitive perspective by arguing forcefully against Skinner's claim. Chomsky asserted that even children are able to produce utterances that fall outside the bounds of their previous experience. In his own research with children, the Swiss researcher **Jean Piaget** (1896–1980) used a series of mental tasks to demonstrate qualitative changes over the course of cognitive development. To explain children's growing sophistication, Piaget made reference to children's inner cognitive states.

Cognitive psychologists study higher mental processes such as perception, memory, language use, thinking, problem solving, and decision making at a variety of levels. Cognitive psychologists view thoughts as both results and causes of overt actions. Feeling regret when you've hurt someone is an example of thought as a result. But apologizing for your actions after feeling regret is an example of thought as a cause of behavior.

···

◉ **Watch** the **Video** *Developmental Cognitive Neuroscience: Adele Diamond* on **MyPsychLab**

biological perspective The approach to identifying causes of behavior that focuses on the functioning of genes, the brain, the nervous system, and the endocrine system.

behavioral neuroscience A multidisciplinary field that attempts to understand the brain processes that underlie behavior.

cognitive neuroscience A multidisciplinary field that attempts to understand the brain processes that underlie higher cognitive functions in humans.

evolutionary perspective The approach to psychology that stresses the importance of behavioral and mental adaptiveness, based on the assumption that mental capabilities evolved over millions of years to serve particular adaptive purposes.

Those organisms that are better suited to their environments tend to produce offspring (and pass on their genes) more successfully than those organisms with poorer adaptations. Over many generations, the species changes in the direction of the privileged adaptation. The evolutionary perspective in psychology suggests that *mental abilities* evolved over millions of years to serve particular adaptive purposes, just as physical abilities did.

To practice evolutionary psychology, researchers focus on the environmental conditions in which the human brain evolved. Humans spent 99 percent of their evolutionary history as hunter–gatherers living in small groups during the Pleistocene era (the roughly 2-million-year period ending 10,000 years ago). Evolutionary psychology uses the rich theoretical framework of evolutionary biology to identify the central adaptive problems that faced this species: avoiding predators and parasites, gathering and exchanging food, finding and retaining mates, and raising healthy children. After identifying the adaptive problems that these early humans faced, evolutionary psychologists generate inferences about the sorts of mental mechanisms, or psychological adaptations, that might have evolved to solve those problems.

Evolutionary psychology differs from other perspectives most fundamentally in its focus on the extremely long process of evolution as a central explanatory principle. Evolutionary psychologists, for example, attempt to understand the different sex roles assumed by men and women as products of evolution, rather than as products of contemporary societal pressures. Because evolutionary psychologists cannot carry out experiments that vary the course of evolution, they must be particularly inventive to provide evidence in favor of their theories.

The Sociocultural Perspective Psychologists who take a **sociocultural perspective** study *cross-cultural* differences in the causes and consequences of behavior. The sociocultural perspective is an important response to the criticism that psychological research has too often been based on a Western conception of human nature and had as its subject population mostly white middle-class Americans (Arnett, 2008; Gergen et al., 1996). A proper consideration of cultural forces may involve comparisons of groups within the same national boundaries. For example, researchers may look within the United States to compare the prevalence of eating disorders for women of different races (see Chapter 11). Cultural forces may also be assessed across nationalities, as in comparisons of media reports in the United States and Japan (see Chapter 16). Cross-cultural psychologists want to determine whether the theories researchers have developed apply to all humans, or only to more narrow, specific populations.

A cross-cultural perspective can be brought to bear on almost every topic of psychological research: Are people's perceptions of the world affected by culture? Do the languages people speak affect the way they experience the world? How does culture affect the way children develop toward adulthood? How do cultural attitudes shape the experience of old age? How

does culture affect our sense of self? Does culture influence an individual's likelihood to engage in particular behaviors? Does culture affect the way individuals express emotions? Does culture affect the rates at which people suffer from psychological disorders?

By asking these types of questions, the sociocultural perspective often yields conclusions that directly challenge those generated from the other perspectives. Researchers have claimed, for example, that many aspects of Freud's psychodynamic theories cannot apply to cultures that are very different from Freud's Vienna. This concern was raised as early as 1927 by the anthropologist Bronislaw Malinowski (1927), who soundly critiqued Freud's father-centered theory by describing the family practices of the Trobriand Islanders of New Guinea, for whom family authority resided with mothers rather than with fathers. The sociocultural perspective, therefore, suggests that some universal claims of the psychodynamic perspective are incorrect. The sociocultural perspective poses a continual, important challenge to generalizations about human experience that ignore the diversity and richness of culture.

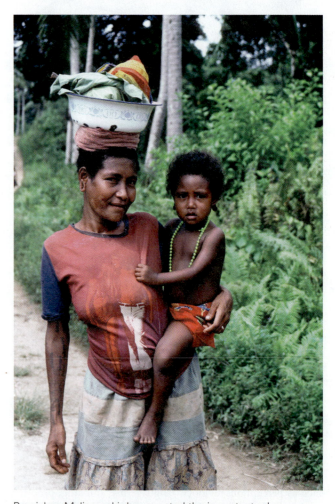

Bronislaw Malinowski documented the important roles women play in the culture of the Trobriand Islands. Why is cross-cultural research critical to the search for universal psychological principles?

....

sociocultural perspective The psychological perspective that focuses on cross-cultural differences in the causes and consequences of behavior.

Table 1.1 • Comparison of Seven Perspectives on Psychology

Perspective	Focus of Study	Primary Research Topics
Psychodynamic	Unconscious drives Conflicts	Behavior as overt expression of unconscious motives
Behaviorist	Specific overt responses	Behavior and its stimulus causes and consequences
Humanistic	Human experience and potentials	Life patterns Values Goals
Cognitive	Mental processes Language	Inferred mental processes through behavioral indicators
Biological	Brain and nervous system processes	Biochemical basis of behavior and mental processes
Evolutionary	Evolved psychological adaptations	Mental mechanisms in terms of evolved adaptive functions
Sociocultural	Cross-cultural patterns of attitudes and behaviors	Universal and culture-specific aspects of human experience

Comparing Perspectives: Focus on Aggression   Each of the seven perspectives rests on a different set of assumptions and leads to a different way of looking for answers to questions about behavior. **Table 1.1** summarizes the perspectives. As an example, let's briefly compare how psychologists using these models might deal with the question of why people act aggressively. All of the approaches have been used in the effort to understand the nature of aggression and violence. For each perspective, here are examples of the types of claims researchers might make and experiments they might undertake:

- *Psychodynamic.* Analyze aggression as a reaction to frustrations caused by barriers to pleasure, such as unjust authority. View aggression as an adult's displacement of hostility originally felt as a child against his or her parents.
- *Behaviorist.* Identify reinforcements of past aggressive responses, such as extra attention given to a child who hits classmates or siblings. Assert that children learn from physically abusive parents to be abusive with their own children.
- *Humanistic.* Look for personal values and social conditions that foster self-limiting, aggressive perspectives instead of growth-enhancing, shared experiences.
- *Cognitive.* Explore the hostile thoughts and fantasies people experience while witnessing violent acts, noting both aggressive imagery and intentions to harm others. Study the impact of violence in films and videos, including pornographic violence, on attitudes toward gun control, rape, and war.
- *Biological.* Study the role of specific brain systems in aggression by stimulating different regions and then recording any destructive actions that are elicited. Also analyze the brains of mass murderers for abnormalities; examine female aggression as related to phases of the menstrual cycle.
- *Evolutionary.* Consider what conditions would have made aggression an adaptive behavior for early humans. Identify psychological mechanisms capable of selectively generating aggressive behavior under those conditions.

- *Sociocultural.* Consider how members of different cultures display and interpret aggression. Identify how cultural forces affect the likelihood of different types of aggressive behavior.

From this example of aggression, you can see how the different perspectives conspire to provide a full understanding of particular domains of psychological research. In contemporary psychology, most research is informed by multiple perspectives. Throughout *Psychology and Life,* you will see how new theories often emerge from combinations of different perspectives. In addition, technological advances have made it easier for researchers to combine perspectives. For example, the innovative brain-imaging techniques you'll learn about in Chapter 3 allow researchers to bring a biological perspective to topics as varied as language processing (Chapter 8) and personality differences (Chapter 13). Moreover, developments such as the Internet have made it easier for researchers to collaborate across the globe. They can bring a sociocultural perspective to topics as diverse as moral reasoning (Chapter 10) and people's body images (Chapter 11). Psychology's diversity of perspectives helps researchers think creatively about core topics of human experience.

Stop *and* Review

1. What are the central concerns of the structuralist and functionalist approaches?
2. What conclusions did Helen Thompson Wooley draw about differences between the sexes?
3. How do the psychodynamic and behaviorist perspectives conceptualize the forces that shape people's actions?
4. What is the purpose of cognitive neuroscience?
5. How do the evolutionary perspective and sociocultural perspective complement each other?

✓—[**Study** and **Review** on **MyPsychLab**

WHAT PSYCHOLOGISTS DO

You now know enough about psychology to formulate questions that span the full range of psychological inquiry. If you prepared such a list of questions, you would be likely to touch on the areas of expertise of the great variety of individuals who call themselves psychologists. **Table 1.2** provides my own version of such questions and indicates what sort of psychologist might address each one.

As you examine the table, you will note the great many subfields within the profession of psychology. Some of the labels the field uses tell you about the major content of a psychologist's expertise. For example, *cognitive psychologists* focus on basic cognitive processes such as memory and language; *social psychologists* focus on the social forces that shape people's attitudes and behavior. Some of the labels identify the domains in which psychologists apply their expertise. For example, *industrial–organizational psychologists* focus their

Table 1.2 • The Diversity of Psychological Inquiry

The Question	Who Addresses It?	Focus of Research and Practice
How can people cope better with day-to-day problems?	Clinical psychologists Counseling psychologists Community psychologists Psychiatrists	Study the origins of psychological disorders and day-to-day problems to evaluate treatment options; provide diagnosis and treatment of psychological disorders and other issues of personal adjustment
How can I cope with the aftereffects of a stroke?	Rehabilitation psychologists	Provide assessment and counseling for people with illnesses or disabilities; offer coping strategies and education to affected individuals, caretakers, employers, and community members
How do memories get stored in the brain?	Biological psychologists Psychopharmacologists	Study the biochemical bases of behavior, feelings, and mental processes
How can you teach a dog to follow commands?	Experimental psychologists Behavior analysts	Use laboratory experiments, often with nonhuman participants, to study basic processes of learning, sensation, perception, emotion, and motivation
Why can't I always recall information I'm sure I know?	Cognitive psychologists Cognitive scientists	Study mental processes such as memory, perception, reasoning, problem solving, decision making, and language use
What makes people different from one another?	Personality psychologists Behavioral geneticists	Develop tests and theories to understand differences in personalities and behaviors; study the influence of genetics and environments on those differences
How does peer pressure work?	Social psychologists	Study how people function in social groups as well as the processes by which people select, interpret, and remember social information
What do babies know about the world?	Developmental psychologists	Study the changes that occur in the physical, cognitive, and social functioning of individuals across the life span; study the influence of genetics and environments on those changes
Why does my job make me feel so depressed?	Industrial–organizational psychologists Human factors psychologists	Study the factors that influence performance and morale in the general workplace or on particular tasks; apply those insights in the workplace
How should teachers deal with disruptive students?	Educational psychologists School psychologists	Study how to improve aspects of the learning process; help design school curricular, teaching–training, and child-care programs
Why do I get sick before every exam?	Health psychologists	Study how different lifestyles affect physical health; design and evaluate prevention programs to help people change unhealthy behaviors and cope with stress
Was the defendant insane when she committed the crime?	Forensic psychologists	Apply psychological knowledge to human problems in the field of law enforcement
Why do I always choke during important basketball games?	Sports psychologists	Assess the performance of athletes and use motivational, cognitive, and behavioral principles to help them achieve peak performance levels
How can I make sense of all the numbers people throw at me?	Quantitative psychologists Psychometricians	Develop and evaluate new statistical methods; construct and validate measurement tools
How accurately can psychologists predict how people will behave?	Mathematical psychologists	Develop mathematical expressions that allow for precise predictions about behavior and tests of contrasting psychological theories

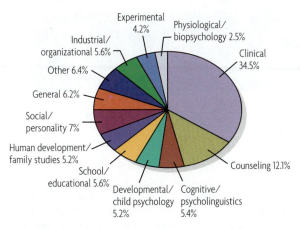

FIGURE 1.2 Distribution of Degrees to Subfields of Psychology

In 2009, roughly 3,500 people received PhDs in the many subfields of psychology (National Science Foundation, 2010). Although the largest percentage of those degrees went to individuals pursuing careers in clinical psychology, students also received advanced training in several other areas of basic and applied research.

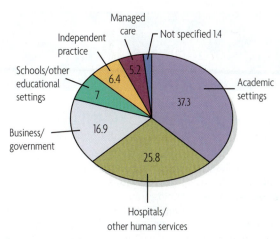

FIGURE 1.3 Work Settings for Psychologists

Shown are percentages of psychologists working in particular settings, according to a survey of American Psychological Association (APA) members holding doctoral degrees in psychology.

efforts on improving people's adjustment in the workplace; *school psychologists* focus on students' adjustment in educational settings.

Each type of psychologist achieves a balance between *research*—seeking new insights—and *application*—putting those insights to use in the world. There's a necessary relationship between those two types of activities. For example, we often think of *clinical psychologists* largely as individuals who apply psychological knowledge to better people's lives. However, as you will see in Chapters 14 and 15, clinical psychologists also have important research functions. Contemporary research continues to improve our understanding of the distinctions among psychological disorders and the treatments that best ease patients' distress. **Figure 1.2** provides information about

the numbers of people who pursue PhDs across psychology's many subfields.

Take a look back at Table 1.2. This list of questions illustrates why psychology has so many divisions. Did these questions capture your own concerns? If you have the time, make a list of your own questions. Cross off each question as *Psychology and Life* answers it. If, at the end of the course, you still have unanswered questions, please contact me! (My e-mail address can be found in the preface.) ✳

Have you begun to wonder exactly how many practicing psychologists there are in the world? Surveys suggest the number is well over 500,000. **Figure 1.3** gives you an idea of the distribution of settings in which psychologists function. Although the percentage of psychologists in the population is greatest in Western industrialized nations, interest in psychology continues to increase in many countries. The International Union of Psychological Science draws together member organizations from 71 countries (Ritchie, 2010). The American Psychological Association (APA), an organization that includes psychologists from all over the world, has over 150,000 members. A second international organization, the Association for Psychological Science (APS), with about 23,000 members, focuses more on scientific aspects of psychology and less on the clinical, or treatment, side.

Stop *and* Review

① What is the relationship between research and application?

② In what two settings are most psychologists employed?

✓─[Study and Review on MyPsychLab

Developmental psychologists may use puppets or other toys in their study of how children behave, think, or feel. Why might it be easier for a child to express his or her thoughts to a puppet than to an adult?

✳ Explore the Concept *Psychologists at Work* on MyPsychLab

Psychology in Your Life

IN WHAT WAYS DO PSYCHOLOGISTS PARTICIPATE IN THE LEGAL SYSTEM?

An important lesson of *Psychology and Life* is that empirical research provides psychologists with a broad range of expertise. As the text unfolds, you'll have a good many opportunities to see how research results apply to important issues in everyday life. You'll also see how psychological expertise functions in the public forum. As an initial example, let's consider how *forensic psychologists* become involved in important legal decisions.

The legal system relies on forensic psychologists to provide assessments for both civil and criminal proceedings (Packer, 2008). On the civil side, for example, forensic psychologists provide evidence that influences decisions about child custody in divorce hearings. They might also testify about the potential psychological harm workers have sustained in a particular place of employment. On the criminal side, forensic psychologists evaluate people's capacity to understand the acts they have committed and their competence to stand trial. Forensic psychologists also assess whether individuals are a danger to themselves or others. Let's examine that last role more closely.

Suppose that a person is sent to prison for committing a violent crime. After having served some time, he or she arrives at a parole hearing. An important consideration at that hearing will be what lies in the prisoner's future. What is the likelihood that violent acts will occur again?

In recent years, psychologists have attempted to provide increasingly research-based answers to that question (Fabian, 2006). This research often begins with a theoretical analysis of the life factors that make violence more or less likely. Researchers make an important distinction between *static* and *dynamic* factors (Douglas & Skeem, 2005). Static factors are those that are relatively stable over time (such as gender and age at first conviction); dynamic variables are those that may change over time (such as emotional control and substance abuse). The inclusion of dynamic factors suggests how risk changes over time. Past history alone does not provide a valid indication of how a person will behave in the future. It's also important to measure the trajectory of a person's life.

Researchers must provide evidence that risk assessment devices are successful at predicting future violence (Singh et al., 2011; Yang et al., 2010). To do so, researchers often follow groups of individuals over time. For example, Wong and Gordon (2006) evaluated 918 adult male offenders who were incarcerated in the Canadian provinces of Alberta, Saskatchewan, and Manitoba. Each participant was evaluated with the Violence Risk Scale (VRS), which measures six static and 20 dynamic variables. To evaluate the validity of the VRS, the researchers followed their participants over several years, to see how often they were convicted of new crimes after they had been released into the community. In both the short term (after 1 year) and the longer term (after 4.4 years), men who had obtained higher ratings on the VRS were more likely to be convicted of additional violent crimes.

Research results of this sort are quite important because they help forensic psychologists provide more accurate guidance for legal judgments.

HOW TO USE THIS TEXT

You are about to embark on an intellectual journey through the many areas of modern psychology. As you begin, I want to share with you some important information that will help guide your adventures. "The journey" is a metaphor used throughout *Psychology and Life*; your teacher serves as the tour director, the text as your tour book, and your author as your personal tour guide. The goal of this journey is for you to discover what is known about the most incredible phenomena in the entire universe: the brain, the human mind, and the behavior of all living creatures. Psychology is about understanding the seemingly mysterious processes that give rise to your thoughts, feelings, and actions.

This guide offers general strategies and specific suggestions about how to use this book to get the quality grade you deserve for your performance and to get the most from your introduction to psychology.

Study Strategies

1. *Set aside sufficient time* for your reading assignments and review of class notes. This text contains much new technical information, many principles to learn, and a new glossary of terms to memorize. To master this material, you will need at least three hours of reading time per chapter.

2. *Keep a record of your study time* for this course. Plot the number of hours (in half-hour intervals) you study at each reading session. Chart your time investment on a cumulative graph. Add each new study time to the previous total on the left-hand axis of the graph and each study session on the baseline axis. The chart will provide visual feedback of your progress and show you when you have not been hitting the books as you should.

3. *Be an active participant.* Optimal learning occurs when you are actively involved with the learning materials. That means reading attentively, listening to lectures mindfully,

paraphrasing in your own words what you are reading or hearing, and taking good notes. In the text, underline key sections, write notes to yourself in the margins, and summarize points that you think might be included on class tests.

4. *Space out your studying.* Research in psychology tells us that it is more effective to do your studying regularly rather than cramming just before tests. If you let yourself fall behind, it will be difficult to catch up with all the information included in introductory psychology at last-minute panic time.

5. *Get study-centered.* Find a place with minimal distractions for studying. Reserve that place for studying, reading, and writing course assignments—and do nothing else there. The place will come to be associated with study activities, and you will find it easier to work whenever you are seated at your study center.

Take the teacher's perspective, anticipating the kinds of questions she or he is likely to ask and then making sure you can answer them. Find out what kinds of tests you will be given in this course—essay, fill-in, multiple-choice, or true/false. That form will affect the extent to which you focus on the big ideas and/or on details. Essays and fill-ins ask for recall-type memory; multiple-choice and true/false tests ask for recognition-type memory.

Study Techniques

This section gives you specific advice about a technique you can use to learn the material for this course and your other courses. The technique emerged from principles of human memory you will encounter in Chapter 7. It is called *PQ4R* from the initials of the six phases it suggests for effective study: Preview, Question, Read, Reflect, Recite, and Review (Thomas & Robinson, 1972).

1. *Preview.* Skim through the chapter to get a general sense of the topics the chapter will discuss. Make yourself aware of the organization and major topics. Read the section headings and scan the photos and figures. In fact, your first stop for each chapter should be the section "Recapping Main Points." There you will find the main ideas of the chapter organized under each of the first-level headings, which will give you a clear sense of what the chapter covers.

2. *Question.* For each section, make up questions. You should use the section headings and key terms to help you. For example, you might transform the heading "The Goals of Psychology" into the question "What are the goals of psychology?" You might use the key term *biological perspective* to generate the question, "What is the major focus of the biological perspective?" These questions will help direct your attention as you read.

3. *Read.* Read the material carefully so that you are able to answer the questions you invented.

4. *Reflect.* As you read the text, reflect on it to relate the material to your prior knowledge about the topics. Think of extra examples to enrich the text. Try to link the ideas together across the subsections.

5. *Recite.* After you have read and reflected on a section, try to demonstrate your recall of the material as concretely as possible. For example, answer the questions you invented earlier by producing the material out loud. For later review, write down the ideas you find difficult to remember.

6. *Review.* After you have read the entire chapter, review the key points. If you are unable to recall important points, or you cannot answer the questions you invented, consult the book and repeat the earlier phases (read, reflect, and recite).

Take a moment now to use PQ4R for one of the earlier sections of this chapter to see how each phase works. It will take you some time to master the flow of PQ4R. Make that investment at the beginning of the semester.

You are now prepared to take full advantage of *Psychology and Life.* Let's make your journey through this text worthwhile, full of memorable moments and unexpected pleasures!

Stop *and* Review

① What does it mean to be an active participant in a course?
② What is the relationship between the *Question* and *Read* phases of PQ4R?
③ What is the purpose of the *Recite* phase of PQ4R?
✓—Ⓔ **Study** and **Review** on **MyPsychLab**

Recapping Main Points

What Makes Psychology Unique?

- Psychology is the scientific study of the behavior and the mental processes of individuals.
- The goals of psychology are to describe, explain, predict, and help control behavior.

The Evolution of Modern Psychology

- Structuralism emerged from the work of Wundt and Titchener. It emphasized the structure of the mind and behavior built from elemental sensations.

- Functionalism, developed by James and Dewey, emphasized the purpose behind behavior.
- Taken together, these theories created the agenda for modern psychology.
- Women made substantial research contributions in psychology's early history.
- Each of the seven perspectives on psychology differs in its view of human nature, the determinants of behavior, the focus of study, and the primary research approach.

- The psychodynamic perspective looks at behavior as driven by instinctive forces, inner conflicts, and conscious and unconscious motivations.
- The behaviorist perspective views behavior as determined by external stimulus conditions.
- The humanistic perspective emphasizes an individual's inherent capacity to make rational choices.
- The cognitive perspective stresses mental processes that affect behavioral responses.
- The biological perspective studies relationships between behavior and brain mechanisms.
- The evolutionary perspective looks at behavior as having evolved as an adaptation for survival in the environment.
- The sociocultural perspective examines behavior and its interpretation in cultural context.

What Psychologists Do

- Psychologists work in a variety of settings and draw on expertise from a range of specialty areas.
- Almost any question that can be generated about real-life experiences is addressed by some member of the psychological profession.

How to Use This Text

- Devise concrete strategies for determining how much study time you need and how to distribute the time most efficiently.
- Take an active approach to your lectures and the text. The PQ4R method provides six phases—Preview, Question, Read, Reflect, Recite, and Review—for enhanced learning.

KEY TERMS

behavior (p. 2)
behavioral data (p. 3)
behavioral neuroscience (p. 11)
behaviorism (p. 10)
behaviorist perspective (p. 10)
biological perspective (p. 11)

cognitive neuroscience (p. 11)
cognitive perspective (p. 10)
evolutionary perspective (p. 11)
functionalism (p. 7)
Gestalt psychology (p. 7)
humanistic perspective (p. 10)

introspection (p. 7)
psychodynamic perspective (p. 9)
psychology (p. 2)
scientific method (p. 2)
sociocultural perspective (p. 12)
structuralism (p. 7)

1. The definition of psychology focuses on both
   _____ and _____.
   a. behaviors; structures
   b. behaviors; mental processes
   c. mental processes; functions
   d. mental processes; structures

2. To what goal of psychology is "level of analysis" most
   relevant?
   a. explaining what happens
   b. describing what happens
   c. predicting what will happen
   d. controlling what happens

3. If you want to _____ what will happen, you first
   must be able to _____ what will happen.
   a. describe; explain   c. control; predict
   b. describe; control   d. explain; predict

4. While watching a horror film, Betty suppressed her
   emotions but Hilda did not. You would expect Betty
   to eat _____ comfort food than Hilda and
   _____ non-comfort food.
   a. more; the same amount of
   b. more; less
   c. the same amount of; more
   d. less; more

5. Who founded the first laboratory that was devoted to
   experimental psychology?
   a. William James   c. Max Wertheimer
   b. Wilhelm Wundt   d. John Dewey

6. A researcher tells you that her main goal is to understand
   mental experiences as the combination of basic
   components. It is most likely that she finds the historical
   roots of her research in
   a. functionalism.
   b. the humanist perspective.
   c. structuralism.
   d. the evolutionary perspective.

7. Who was the first woman to serve as president of the
   American Psychological Association?
   a. Margaret Washburn   c. Jane Goodall
   b. Anna Freud   d. Mary Calkins

8. Two professors at universities in Boston and Mumbai
   are collaborating on a research project to determine how
   their students in the United States and India respond to
   the same reasoning problems. It's likely that they take a
   _____ perspective in their research.
   a. humanistic   c. biological
   b. sociocultural   d. psychodynamic

9. The _____ perspective draws on the ways in
   which human mental abilities serve adaptive purposes.
   a. cognitive   c. evolutionary
   b. humanistic   d. sociocultural

10. When you're home with the flu, you spend a lot of
    time watching CourtTV. You weren't surprised to see a
    _____ psychologist testifying during a trial.
    a. health   c. forensic
    b. social   d. developmental

11. What type of question would a cognitive psychologist be
    likely to ask?
    a. Why do children sometimes have imaginary friends?
    b. Why do some students get sick every time they have a
       major exam?
    c. How can we design a keyboard for a computer that
       allows people to type more quickly?
    d. How are bilingual individuals able to switch between
       their two languages?

12. Which type of psychologist is *least* likely to focus on
    genetic aspects of human psychology?
    a. industrial–organizational psychologists
    b. developmental psychologists
    c. personality psychologists
    d. biological psychologists

13. Individuals with advanced degrees in psychology are most
    likely to be working in
    a. academic settings.
    b. hospitals and clinics.
    c. business and government.
    d. independent practice.

14. In assessments of violence risk, _____ counts as
    a dynamic factor.
    a. gender
    b. substance abuse
    c. stability of family upbringing
    d. age at first conviction

15. In what phase of P4QR should you try to relate the
    textbook material to your prior knowledge about a topic?
    a. Reflect   c. Review
    b. Recite   d. Question

ESSAY QUESTIONS

1. With respect to the goals of psychology, why is it
   appropriate to characterize psychologists as "rather
   optimistic"?

2. Why is it often good to consider the same research
   question from several of psychology's seven perspectives?

3. Why does the field of psychology include both research
   and application?

2

Research Methods in Psychology

You may recall that in Chapter 1 I asked you to compose a list of questions that you would like to have answered by the end of *Psychology and Life*. Students who have used the book in the past responded to this request with a range of interesting concerns. Here are some of their questions:

- Should I use my cell phone while I drive?
- Can memory research help me study for exams?
- How can I become more creative?
- Is it okay to put kids in day care?

In this chapter, we consider how psychologists generate answers to questions that matter most to students. The focus will be on the special way in which psychology applies the scientific method to its domain of inquiry. By the end of the chapter, you should understand how psychologists design their research: How can solid conclusions ever be drawn from the complex and often fuzzy phenomena that psychologists study—how people think, feel, and behave? Even if you never do any scientific research in your life, mastering the information in this section will be useful. The underlying purpose here is to help improve your *critical thinking skills* by teaching you how to ask the right questions and evaluate the answers about the causes, consequences, and correlates of psychological phenomena. The mass media constantly release stories that begin with, "Research shows that. . . ." By sharpening your intelligent skepticism, this chapter will help you become a more sophisticated consumer of the research-based conclusions that confront you in everyday life.

THE PROCESS OF RESEARCH

The research process in psychology can be divided into several steps that usually occur in sequence (see **Figure 2.1**). The process typically begins with *Step 1,* in which observations, beliefs, information, and general knowledge lead someone to come up with a new idea or a different way of thinking about a phenomenon. Where do researchers' questions originate? Some come from direct observations of events, humans, and nonhumans in the environment. Other research addresses traditional parts of the field: Some issues are considered to be "great unanswered questions" that have been passed down from earlier scholars. Researchers often combine old ideas in unique ways that offer an original perspective. The hallmark of the truly creative thinker is the discovery of a new truth that moves science and society in a better direction.

As psychologists accumulate information about phenomena, they create theories that become an important context to formulate research questions. A **theory** is an organized set of concepts that *explains* a phenomenon or set of phenomena. At the common core of most psychological theories is the assumption of **determinism,** the idea that all events—physical, mental,

....

 Watch the **Video** *The Big Picture: How to Answer Psychological Questions?* on **MyPsychLab**

theory An organized set of concepts that explains a phenomenon or set of phenomena.

determinism The doctrine that all events—physical, behavioral, and mental—are determined by specific causal factors that are potentially knowable.

Step 1 Initial observation or question

Similarity plays a large role in relationships, as does conversation. Perhaps conversation provides a context for couples to gauge similarity.

Step 2 Form a hypothesis

Couples whose style of language use is more similar will show more stability in their relationships.

Step 3 Design the study

Couples' instant messages for a 10-day period were assessed on a variety of linguistic features yielding an index of *language style* matching.

Three months later, couples indicated whether they were still dating.

Step 4 Analyze the data and draw conclusions

The data revealed that couples with more language style matching were more likely to still be dating.

Step 5 Report the findings

The article appeared in the prestigious journal *Psychological Science.*

Step 6 Consider open questions

The discussion in the article acknowledges that the direction of the effect remains open: More language style matching might lead to better relationships or might lead to more language style matching.

Step 7 Act on open questions

These or other researchers can undertake new research to answer the open questions.

FIGURE 2.1 Steps in the Process of Conducting and Reporting Research

To illustrate the steps in the scientific process, consider a study that examined the relationship between couples' language styles and the stability of their relationships (Ireland et al., 2011).

and behavioral—are the result of, or determined by, specific causal factors. These causal factors are limited to those in the individual's environment or within the person. Researchers also assume that behavior and mental processes follow *lawful patterns* of relationships, patterns that can be discovered and revealed through research. Psychological theories are typically claims about the causal forces that underlie such lawful patterns.

When a theory is proposed in psychology, it is generally expected both to account for known facts and, as *Step 2* in the research process, generate new hypotheses. A **hypothesis** is a tentative and testable statement about the relationship between causes and consequences. Hypotheses are often stated as if–then predictions, specifying certain outcomes from specific conditions. We might predict, for example, that *if* children view a lot of violence on television, *then* they will engage in more aggressive acts toward their peers. Research is required to verify the if–then link. For *Step 3,* researchers rely on the *scientific method* to put their hypotheses to the test. The scientific method is a general set of procedures for gathering and interpreting evidence in ways that limit sources of errors and yield dependable conclusions. Psychology is considered a science to the extent that it follows the rules established by the scientific method. Much of this chapter is devoted to describing the scientific method. Once researchers have collected their data, they proceed to *Step 4,* in which they analyze those data and generate conclusions.

If researchers believe that their data will have an impact on the field, they will move on to *Step 5* and submit the paper for publication in a journal. For publication to be possible, researchers must keep complete records of observations and data analyses in a form that other researchers can understand and evaluate. Secrecy is banned from the research procedure because all data and methods must eventually be open for *public verifiability;* that is, other researchers must have the opportunity to inspect, criticize, replicate, or disprove the data and methods.

Much psychological research appears in journals that are published by organizations such as the American Psychological Association or the Association for Psychological Science. When research manuscripts are submitted to most journals, they undergo a process of *peer review.* Each manuscript is typically sent to two to five experts in the field. Those experts provide detailed analyses of the manuscript's rationale, methodology, and results. Only when those experts have been sufficiently satisfied do manuscripts become journal articles. This is a rigorous process. For example, in 2010, journals published by the American Psychological Association (2011) rejected, on average, 71 percent of the manuscripts submitted to them. The process of peer review isn't perfect—no doubt some worthy research projects are overlooked and some uneven ones slip through—but, in general, this process ensures that the research you read in the vast majority of journals has met high standards.

At Step 5, psychologists also often try to disseminate their results to a wider public. In a presidential address to the American

Psychological Association, George Miller (1969) reached the celebrated conclusion that the responsibility of professional psychologists "is less to assume the role of experts and try to apply psychology ourselves than to give it away to the people who really need it—and that includes everyone" (p. 1071). Individual psychologists often write books and give lectures that are directed toward broad audiences. Major professional organizations, such as the American Psychological Association and Association for Psychological Science, also issue press releases and create public forums in which researchers can give psychology away.

At *Step 6* of the research process, the scientific community reflects on the research and identifies questions the work leaves unresolved. Most research articles start this process in a *discussion* section in which the researchers lay out the implications and limitations of their work. They might explicitly describe the type of future research they consider desirable. When the data do not fully support a hypothesis, researchers must rethink aspects of their theories. Thus there is continual interaction between theory and research. At *Step 7,* the original researchers or their peers might act on open questions and begin the research cycle again.

This research process is centered around appropriate uses of the scientific method. The goal of the scientific method is to allow researchers to draw conclusions with maximum objectivity. Conclusions are *objective* when they are uninfluenced by researchers' emotions or personal biases. Each of the next two sections begins with a *challenge to objectivity* and then describes the *remedy* prescribed by the scientific method. ⊙

Observer Biases and Operational Definitions

When different people observe the same events, they don't always "see" the same thing. This section describes the problem of *observer bias* and the steps researchers take as remedies.

The Challenge to Objectivity   An **observer bias** is an error due to the personal motives and expectations of the viewer. At times, people see and hear what they expect rather than what is. Consider a rather dramatic example of observer bias. Around

Participants, as well as spectators and broadcast viewers, are subject to observer bias. How can you determine what really happened?

⊙ **Watch** the **Video** *What Do You Think About Psychological Research?* on **MyPsychLab**

hypothesis A tentative and testable explanation of the relationship between two (or more) events or variables; often stated as a prediction that a certain outcome will result from specific conditions.

observer bias The distortion of evidence because of the personal motives and expectations of the viewer.

the beginning of the 20th century, a leading psychologist, Hugo Munsterberg, gave a speech on peace to a large audience that included many reporters. He summarized the news accounts of what they heard and saw in this way:

> The reporters sat immediately in front of the platform. One man wrote that the audience was so surprised by my speech that it received it in complete silence; another wrote that I was constantly interrupted by loud applause and that at the end of my address the applause continued for minutes. The one wrote that during my opponent's speech I was constantly smiling; the other noticed that my face remained grave and without a smile. The one said that I grew purple-red from excitement; and the other found that I grew chalk-white. (1908, pp. 35–36)

It would be interesting to go back to the original newspapers, to see how the reporters' accounts were related to their political views—then we might be able to understand why the reporters supposedly saw what they did.

You can look for examples of observer biases in your day-to-day life. Suppose, for example, you are in a close relationship. How might the motives and expectations you bring to that relationship affect the way you view your partner's behavior? Let's consider a study of 125 married couples.

Featured Study

The couples were videotaped while they had two different 10-minute conversations (Knobloch et al., 2007). For one conversation, the couples discussed a positive aspect of their relationship; for the other, they discussed a recent unexpected event that had changed how sure they were (for better or for worse) about the future of their relationship. After each conversation, the two spouses gave individual ratings about the quality of the interactions along dimensions such as how warm or cold they thought their partner had been and how much their partner attempted to dominate the conversation. The researchers also asked neutral raters—people who had no connections to the couples—to watch and evaluate the conversations. Against the baseline provided by those neutral ratings, the couples' ratings displayed consistent observer bias. The direction of the bias was determined by how certain each member reported him- or herself to be about the future of the relationship. The researchers noted, for example, that "participants who were sure about their marriage had strong positive reactions to conversations that seemed normal to the naked eye" (p. 173).

This study demonstrates how expectations can lead different observers to reach different conclusions. The biases of the observers act as *filters* through which some things are noticed as relevant and significant and others are ignored as irrelevant and not meaningful.

Let's apply this lesson to what happens in psychology experiments. Researchers are often in the business of making observations. Given that every observer brings a different set of prior experiences to making those observations—and often those experiences include a commitment to a particular theory—you can see why observer biases could pose a problem. Researchers must work hard to ensure that they are viewing behavior with a "naked eye," free of biases. What can

researchers do to ensure that their observations are minimally affected by prior expectations?

The Remedy To minimize observer biases, researchers rely on standardization and operational definitions. **Standardization** means using uniform, consistent procedures in all phases of data collection. All features of the test or experimental situation should be sufficiently standardized so all research participants experience exactly the same experimental conditions. Standardization means asking questions in the same way and scoring responses according to preestablished rules. Having results printed or recorded helps ensure their comparability across different times and places and with different participants and researchers.

Observations themselves must also be standardized: Scientists must solve the problem of how to translate their theories into concepts with consistent meaning. The strategy for standardizing the meaning of concepts is called *operationalization*. An **operational definition** standardizes meaning within an experiment, by defining a concept in terms of specific operations or procedures used to measure it or to determine its presence. All the variables in an experiment must be given operational definitions. A **variable** is any factor that varies in amount or kind. Recall the experiment in Figure 2.1. The researchers assessed the variable *language style matching*, which could take on any value between 0 and 1.

In experimental settings, researchers most often wish to demonstrate a cause-and-effect relationship between two types of variables. Imagine, for example, that you wished to test the hypothesis we considered earlier: that children who view a lot of violence on television will engage in more aggressive acts toward their peers. To test that hypothesis, you might devise an experiment in which you manipulated the amount of violence each participant viewed. That factor you manipulate would be the **independent variable;** it functions as the causal part of the relationship. For each level of violence viewed, you could then assess how much aggression each participant displayed. Aggression is the effect part of the cause-effect relationship; it is the **dependent variable,** which is what the experimenter measures. If researchers' claims about cause and effect are correct, the value of the dependent variable will *depend* on the value of the independent variable. 👁

Let's take a moment to put these new concepts to use in the context of a real experiment. The research project we consider begins with a great philosophical question: Do people have free will, or is their behavior determined by forces of genetics and environment outside their control? The study didn't attempt to answer that question. Rather, the researchers argued that the

....

👁 **Watch** the **Video** *Distinguishing Independent and Dependent Variables* on **MyPsychLab**

standardization A set of uniform procedures for treating each participant in a test, interview, or experiment, or for recording data.

operational definition A definition of a variable or condition in terms of the specific operation or procedure used to determine its presence.

variable In an experimental setting, a factor that varies in amount and kind.

independent variable In an experimental setting, a variable that the researcher manipulates with the expectation of having an impact on values of the dependent variable.

dependent variable In an experimental setting, a variable that the researcher measures to assess the impact of a variation in an independent variable.

Is violent behavior caused by viewing violence on television? How could you find out?

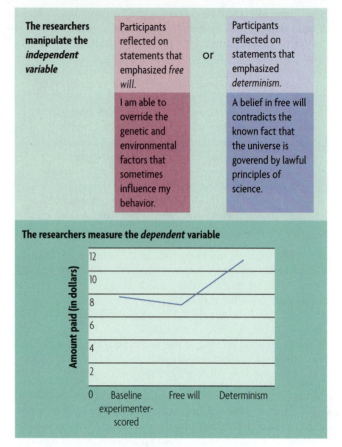

FIGURE 2.2 Elements of an Experiment

To test their hypotheses, researchers create operational definitions for the independent and dependent variables.

Data from Kathlee D. Vohs and Jonathan W. Schooler, The value of believing in free will: Encouraging a belief in determinism increases cheating, *Psychological Science*, January 1, 2008, pages 49–54. © 2008 by the Association for Psychological Science.

way in which different individuals answer this question—their beliefs in *free will* versus *determinism*—has an impact on how they behave (Vohs & Schooler, 2008). The researchers reasoned that people who are guided by a worldview of determinism would feel less personal responsibility for bad behavior because they'd consider it out of their control. To test this hypothesis, the researchers gave students an opportunity to cheat!

Figure 2.2 presents important aspects of the experiment. The researchers recruited roughly 120 college undergraduates to serve as participants. The independent variable for the study was participants' beliefs in free will versus determinism. To manipulate this variable, the researchers presented students with a series of 15 statements and asked them to think about each statement for one minute. As you might expect, those statements were different for the free will and determinism conditions. Figure 2.2 provides examples.

To test their hypothesis, the researchers needed to provide the students with an opportunity to cheat. During the experiment, the students attempted to answer 15 problems from Graduate Record Examination (GRE) practice tests. They could earn $1 for each correct answer. Participants scored their own answers in the absence of the experimenter. That provided the context for cheating: The experimenter would never know if a participant paid him- or herself more money than was due. The dependent variable for the experiment was the amount of money participants paid themselves.

Figure 2.2 provides the results of the experiment. To determine how average students would actually score on the 15 GRE questions, the researchers had an extra condition in which they scored participants' performance themselves to see how much money the students would earn. The bar labeled "Baseline experimenter-scored" provides that information. As you can see from the other two bars in Figure 2.2, the independent variable had the effect on the dependent variable that the researchers expected. Those students who had been prompted to take the perspective of determinism paid themselves about $4 more than those students who focused on free will. Because of the experimenter-scored baseline—which shows free-will students at the same level as experimenter-scored students—we can infer that the determinism students were cheating. Take a moment to think about other ways in which you might operationalize the experimental variables, to test the same hypothesis by other means. You might, for example, want to measure cheating in some other fashion, to show that the results generalize to other

life circumstances. This type of concern provides a transition to an exploration of experimental methods.

Experimental Methods: Alternative Explanations and the Need for Controls

You know from day-to-day experience that people can suggest many causes for the same outcome. Psychologists face this same problem when they try to make exact claims about causality. To overcome causal ambiguity, researchers use **experimental methods:** They manipulate an independent variable to look for an effect on a dependent variable. The goal of this method is to make strong causal claims about the impact of one variable on the other. In this section, let's review the problem of *alternative explanations* and some steps researchers take to counter the problem.

The Challenge to Objectivity When psychologists test a hypothesis, they most often have in mind an explanation for

....

experimental method Research methodology that involves the manipulation of independent variables to determine their effects on the dependent variables.

why change in the independent variable should affect the dependent variable in a particular way. For example, you might predict, and demonstrate experimentally, that the viewing of television violence leads to high levels of aggression. But how can you know that it was precisely the viewing of *violence* that produced aggression? To make the strongest possible case for their hypotheses, psychologists must be very sensitive to the existence of possible *alternative explanations*. The more alternative explanations there might be for a given result, the less confidence there is that the initial hypothesis is accurate. When something other than what an experimenter purposely introduces into a research setting changes a participant's behavior and adds confusion to the interpretation of the data, it is called a **confounding variable.** When the real cause of some observed behavioral effect is *confounded,* the experimenter's interpretation of the data is put at risk. Suppose, for example, that violent television scenes are louder and involve more movement than do most nonviolent scenes. In that case, the superficial and violent aspects of the scenes are confounded. The researcher is unable to specify which factor uniquely produces aggressive behavior.

Although each different experimental method potentially gives rise to a unique set of alternative explanations, there are two types of confounds that apply to almost all experiments, which researchers call *expectancy effects* and *placebo effects.* Unintentional **expectancy effects** occur when a researcher or observer subtly communicates to the research participants the behaviors he or she expects to find, thereby producing the desired reaction. Under these circumstances, the experimenter's expectations, rather than the independent variable, actually help trigger the observed reactions.

In an experiment, 12 students were given groups of rats that were going to be trained to run a maze (Rosenthal & Fode, 1963). Half of the students were told their rats were from a special maze-bright breed. The other students were told their rats were bred to be maze-dull. As you might guess, their rats were actually all the same. Nonetheless, the students' results corresponded with their expectations for their rats. The rats labeled bright were found to be much better learners than those that had been labeled as dull.

How do you suppose the students communicated their expectations to their rats? Do you see why you should worry even more about expectancy effects when an experiment is carried out within species—with a human experimenter and human participants? Expectation effects distort the content of discovery.

A **placebo effect** occurs when experimental participants change their behavior in the *absence* of any kind of experimental manipulation. This concept originated in medicine to account for cases in which a patient's health improved after he or she had received medication that was chemically inert or a treatment that was nonspecific. The placebo effect refers to an improvement in health or well-being related to the individual's *belief* that the treatment will be effective. Some treatments with no genuine medical effects have been shown to produce good or excellent outcomes for patients on whom they were used (Colloca & Miller, 2011).

In a psychological research setting, a placebo effect has occurred whenever a behavioral response is influenced by a person's expectation of what to do or how to feel rather than by the specific intervention or procedures employed to produce that response. Recall the experiment relating television viewing to later aggression. Suppose we discovered that experimental participants who hadn't watched any television at all also showed high levels of aggression. We might conclude that these individuals, by virtue of being put in a situation that allowed them to display aggression, would expect they were *supposed* to behave aggressively and would go on to do so. Experimenters must always be aware that participants change the way they behave simply because they are aware of being observed or tested. For example, participants may feel special about being chosen to take part in a study and thus act differently than they would ordinarily. Such effects can compromise an experiment's results.

The Remedy: Control Procedures Because human and animal behaviors are complex and often have multiple causes, good research design involves anticipating possible confounds and devising strategies for eliminating them. Similar to defensive strategies in sports, good research designs anticipate what the other team might do and make plans to counteract it. Researchers' strategies are called **control procedures**—methods that attempt to hold constant all variables and conditions other than those related to the hypothesis being tested. In an experiment, instructions, room temperature, tasks, the way the researcher is dressed, time allotted, the way the responses are recorded, and many other details of the situation must be similar for all participants, to ensure that their experience is the same. The only differences in participants' experiences should be those introduced by the independent variable. Let's look at remedies for the specific confounding variables, expectancy and placebo effects.

Imagine, for example, that you enriched the aggression experiment to include a treatment group that watched comedy programs. You'd want to be careful not to treat your comedy and violence participants in different ways based on your expectations. Thus, in your experiment, we would want the research assistant who greeted the participants and later assessed their aggression to be unaware of whether they had watched a violent program or a comedy: We would keep the research assistant *blind* to the assignment of participants to conditions. In the best circumstances, bias can be eliminated by keeping *both* experimental assistants and participants blind to which

---

confounding variable A stimulus other than the variable an experimenter explicitly introduces into a research setting that affects a participant's behavior.

expectancy effect Result that occurs when a researcher or observer subtly communicates to participants the kind of behavior he or she expects to find, thereby creating that expected reaction.

placebo effect A change in behavior in the absence of an experimental manipulation.

control procedure Consistent procedure for giving instructions, scoring responses, and holding all other variables constant except those being systematically varied.

participants get which treatment. This technique is called a **double-blind control.** In our prospective aggression experiment, we couldn't keep participants from knowing whether they had watched comedy or violence. However, we would take great care to ensure that they couldn't guess that our later analyses would focus on their subsequent aggression.

To account for placebo effects, researchers generally include an experimental condition in which the treatment is not administered. This is a **placebo control.** Placebo controls fall into the general category of controls by which experimenters assure themselves they are making appropriate comparisons. Suppose you see a late-night TV commercial that celebrates the herbal supplement ginkgo biloba as an answer to all your memory problems. What might you expect if you buy a supply of ginkgo and take it weekly? One study demonstrated that university students who took ginkgo every morning for six weeks did, in fact, show improvements in their performance on cognitive tasks (Elsabagh et al., 2005). On one task, people were asked to view a series of 20 pictures on a computer screen, name them, and later recall those names. The participants were 14 percent better at this task after six weeks of ginkgo. However, participants who took a placebo—a pill with no active ingredients—also improved by 14 percent. The placebo control suggests that improvement on the task was the result of practice from the initial session. The data from control conditions provide an important baseline against which the experimental effect is evaluated.

The Remedy: Research Designs To implement control conditions, researchers make decisions about what type of research design best suits their goals. In some research designs, which are referred to as **between-subjects designs,** different groups of participants are *randomly assigned,* by chance procedures, to an experimental condition (exposed to one or more experimental treatments) or to a control condition (not exposed to an experimental treatment). **Random assignment** is one of the major steps researchers take to eliminate confounding variables that relate to individual differences among potential research participants. This is the procedure you'd want to use for the aggression experiment. The random assignment to experimental and control conditions makes it quite likely that the two groups will be similar in important ways at the start of an experiment because each participant has the same probability of being in a treatment condition as in a control condition. We shouldn't have to worry, for example, that everyone in the **experimental group** loves violent television and everyone in the **control group** hates it. Random assignment should mix both types of people together in each group. If outcome differences are found between conditions, we can be more confident that the differences were caused by a treatment or intervention rather than by preexisting differences.

Researchers also try to approximate randomness in the way they bring participants into the laboratory. Suppose you would like to test the hypothesis that 6-year-old children are more likely to lie than 4-year-old children. At the end of your experiment, you'd like your conclusions to apply to the whole **population** of 4-year-olds and 6-year-olds. However, you can bring only a very small subset—a **sample**—of the world's 4- and 6-year-olds into your laboratory. Typically, psychology experiments use from 20 to 100 participants. How should you choose your group of children? Researchers attempt to construct a **representative sample,** which is a sample that closely

matches the overall characteristics of the population with respect, for example, to the distribution of males and females, racial and ethnic groups, and so on. For example, if your study of children's lying included only boys, we wouldn't consider that a representative sample of the full population of 4- and 6-year-olds. To achieve a representative sample, researchers often use the procedure of **random sampling,** which means that every member of a population has an equal likelihood of participating in the experiment. (In the Statstical Supplement that follows this chapter, we describe the procedures researchers use to determine whether experimental results can be generalized beyond a particular sample. Please read the Supplement in conjunction with this chapter.)

Another type of experimental design—a **within-subjects design**—uses each participant as his or her own control. For example, each participant might experience more than one level of the independent variable. Or, the behavior of an experimental participant before getting the treatment might be compared with behavior after. Consider an experiment that examined the accuracy of people's judgments about future exercise.

Suppose you are contemplating a visit to the gym. You're probably more likely to go if you think that you're going to enjoy the workout. But how accurate are your predictions about your future enjoyment? A team of researchers tested the hypothesis that people habitually underestimate the extent to which they'll enjoy their exercise (Ruby et al., 2011). To test their hypothesis, the researchers approached people who attended fitness classes regularly. Before a class began, they asked the participants to predict how much they

Featured Study

---

double-blind control An experimental technique in which biased expectations of experimenters are eliminated by keeping both participants and experimental assistants unaware of which participants have received which treatment.

placebo control An experimental condition in which treatment is not administered; it is used in cases where a placebo effect might occur.

between-subjects design A research design in which different groups of participants are randomly assigned to experimental conditions or to control conditions.

random assignment A procedure by which participants have an equal likelihood of being assigned to any condition within an experiment.

experimental group A group in an experiment that is exposed to a treatment or experiences a manipulation of the independent variable.

control group A group in an experiment that is not exposed to a treatment or does not experience a manipulation of the independent variable.

population The entire set of individuals to which generalizations will be made based on an experimental sample.

sample A subset of a population selected as participants in an experiment.

representative sample A subset of a population that closely matches the overall characteristics of the population with respect to the distribution of males and females, racial and ethnic groups, and so on.

random sampling A procedure that ensures that every member of a population has an equal likelihood of participating in an experiment.

within-subjects design A research design that uses each participant as his or her own control; for example, the behavior of an experimental participant before receiving treatment might be compared to his or her behavior after receiving treatment.

thought they would enjoy the class on a scale ranging from 1 (not at all) to 10 (very much). People, on average, gave a rating of 7.6. After the class, the people rated their actual enjoyment. They gave consistently higher ratings, with an average of 8.2 on the 10-point scale.

Because this study used a within-subjects design, the researchers could draw the strong conclusion that the participants were underestimating their future enjoyment. You might wonder why. The researchers suggested that people contemplating exercise are too focused on the beginning of the workout—which is often the worst part. In a later between-subjects experiment, they asked participants to imagine doing either the best part of their workout routine either first or last. Those people who imagined doing the best part first gave consistently higher average ratings (8.0 on the 10-point scale) than people who imagined doing the best part last (7.0). Do you see how you can harness this result the next time you contemplate getting some exercise?

The research methodologies we have considered so far all involve the manipulation of an independent variable to look for an effect on a dependent variable. Although this experimental method often allows researchers to make the strongest claims about causal relations among variables, several conditions can make this method less desirable. First, during an experiment, behavior is frequently studied in an artificial environment, one in which situational factors are controlled so heavily that the environment may itself distort the behavior from the way it would occur naturally. Critics claim that much of the richness and complexity of natural behavior patterns is lost in controlled experiments, sacrificed to the simplicity of dealing with only one or a few variables and responses. Second, research participants typically know they are in an experiment and are being tested and measured. They may react to this awareness by trying to please the researcher, attempting to "psych out" the research purpose, or changing their behavior from what it would be if they were unaware of being monitored. Third, some important research problems are not amenable to ethical experimental treatment. We could not, for example, try to discover whether the tendency toward child abuse is transmitted from generation to generation by creating an experimental group of children who would be abused and a control group of

children who would not be. The next section turns to a type of research method that often addresses these concerns.

Correlational Methods

Is intelligence associated with how long people live? Are optimistic people healthier than pessimists? Is there a relationship between experiencing child abuse and later mental illness? These questions involve variables that a psychologist could not easily or ethically manipulate. To answer these questions, researchers carry out studies using **correlational methods.** Psychologists use correlational methods when they want to determine to what extent two variables, traits, or attributes are related.

To determine the precise degree of correlation that exists between two variables, psychologists compute a statistical measure known as the **correlation coefficient (r).** This value can vary between $+1.0$ and -1.0, where $+1.0$ indicates a perfect positive correlation, -1.0 indicates a perfect negative correlation, and 0.0 indicates no correlation at all. A positive correlation coefficient means that as one set of scores increases, a second set also increases. The reverse is true with negative correlations; the second set of scores goes in the opposite direction to the values of the first scores (see **Figure 2.3** on page 28). Correlations that are closer to zero mean that there is a weak relationship or no relationship between scores on two measures. As the correlation coefficient gets stronger, closer to the ± 1.0 maximum, predictions about one variable based on information about the other variable become increasingly more accurate.

Throughout *Psychology and Life,* you will see many correlational studies that have led to important insights. To whet your appetite, let's consider one example here.

A team of researchers wished to determine whether children's media habits (television, video games, and computer usage) had an impact on the likelihood that they would have sleep problems (Garrison et al., 2011). To address this question, the researchers asked the parents of 3- to 5-year-old children to keep "media diaries" (in which they recorded the children's media usage) for one week. The parents also completed a Sleep Habits Questionnaire that assessed how long it took children to fall asleep as well as the frequency of "repeated night wakings, nightmares, difficulty waking in the morning, and daytime tiredness" (p. 30). The data analyses indicated that each extra hour of nighttime media use resulted in more sleep problems. In addition, daytime consumption of violent media (but not other types of content) also predicted more sleep problems.

Featured Study

Can you see why a correlational design is appropriate to address this issue? You can't randomly assign children to watch lots of television or none at all. You must wait to see what patterns emerge from families' actual habits. Do these results suggest decisions you might make if you become a parent?

correlational method Research methodology that determines to what extent two variables, traits, or attributes are related.

correlation coefficient (r) A statistic that indicates the degree of relationship between two variables.

Why do people underestimate how much they will enjoy an exercise session?

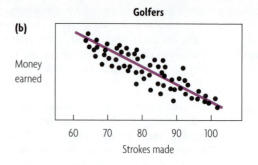

FIGURE 2.3 Positive and Negative Correlations

These imaginary data display the difference between positive and negative correlations. Each point represents a single bowler or golfer. (a) In general, the more points a professional bowler scores, the more money he or she will earn. Thus, there is a positive correlation between those two variables. (b) The correlation for golf is negative, because golfers earn more money when they make fewer strokes.

When we interpret correlational data, we always need to take care before we make causal claims. Let's stay with the topic of sleep. Research suggests that students who are at risk for sleep disorders are also more likely to have particularly low GPAs (Gaultney, 2010). Based on this result, you might want to take the next step and say that the way to improve students' GPAs would be to force them to sleep more. This intervention is misguided. A strong correlation indicates only that two sets of data are related in a systematic way; the correlation does not ensure that one causes the other. *Correlation does not imply causation.* The correlation could reflect any one of several cause-and-effect possibilities. Many of those possibilities involve a *third variable* that works in the background to bring about the correlation. Suppose, for example, that people both sleep better and get higher grades when they take easy courses. Under those circumstances, the difficulty of students' courses would be a third variable that would bring about a positive correlation between amount of sleep and GPA. It could also be that case people who study more efficiently get to bed sooner or that people who experience anxiety about schoolwork cannot fall asleep. You can see from these three possibilities that correlations most often require researchers to probe for deeper explanations. 👁

Let's consider a couple more examples of the difficulty of making causal claims from correlations. Recall the study we outlined in Figure 2.1. The main result was that couples with more language style matching were more likely to have relationships that endured over time (Ireland et al., 2011). The researchers acknowledged that the design was correlational: They couldn't be sure whether more language style matching leads to better relationships or better relationships lead to more language style matching. As a second example, consider a study that asked participants to examine photographs of the CEOs of Fortune 500 companies (Rule & Ambady, 2008). Based just on the photographs, participants indicated how good they thought each person would be at leading a company. On the whole, the CEOs who got the highest leadership ratings—again, based only on their photographs—led the most profitable companies. Why might this positive correlation emerge? The researchers were careful to acknowledge that more than one causal pathway

is possible: "Of course, we cannot draw any causal inferences as to whether more successful companies choose individuals with a particular appearance to be their CEOs or whether individuals with a particular appearance emerge as more successful in their work as CEOs" (p. 110). For each of these cases, you can see why correlation does not imply causation. You can also see how correlational research can call attention to intriguing patterns in the world.

We've already given you several examples of the outcomes of experiments. The next section fills in more about how psychologists measure important processes and dimensions of experience.

Stop *and* Review

① What is the relationship between theories and hypotheses?
② What steps can researchers take to overcome observer biases?
③ Why do researchers use double-blind controls?
④ What is meant by a within-subjects design?
⑤ Why does correlation not imply causation?

CRITICAL THINKING Consider the study in which participants predicted their future enjoyment for exercise. Why might the researchers have used people who exercise regularly as participants?

✓•—▯ **Study** and **Review** on **MyPsychLab**

PSYCHOLOGICAL MEASUREMENT

Because psychological processes are so varied and complex, they pose major challenges to researchers who want to measure them. Although some actions and processes are easily seen, many, such as anxiety or dreaming, are not. Thus one task for a

....

👁 **Watch** the **Video** *Correlations Do Not Show Causation* on **MyPsychLab**

Psychology in Your Life

DOES WISHFUL THINKING AFFECT HOW YOU EVALUATE INFORMATION?

In the discussion of challenges to objectivity, observer biases loomed large: Scientists need to take careful measures to ensure that they don't see just what they want to see. However, the concern with observer bias is equally pressing in the real world. Think about all the information you have available through the wonders of the Internet. How do you evaluate all that information when you make important decisions? Researchers have demonstrated that people often engage in wishful thinking. Let's review one study that reached that conclusion.

To begin the study, the researchers defined two populations of participants by their attitudes toward day care (Bastardi et al., 2011). All the participants indicated that they planned to have children in the future. They also indicated that they thought home care was superior to day care. One group, which the researchers called the *unconflicted* group, said that they planned to use home care for their (future) children. The second group, which the researchers called the *conflicted* group, said that they planned to put their children in day care (even though they thought home care was better).

Next, the researchers described two studies to the participants about the relative effectiveness of the two types of child care. The studies differed in their conclusions: One favored day care and the other favored home care. They also differed in their methods: In one study the children were randomly assigned to the two types of care; in the other, the students were matched so that the children in each setting were highly similar.

The researchers asked the participants to indicate how valid and convincing they found each study. For example, the participants judged which study they thought would yield higher-quality conclusions on a scale that ranged from "random assignment much more valid" to "statistical matching much more valid." How would we see an impact of wishful thinking? Recall that the conflicted participants forecasted a future in which they would put their children in day care. As a consequence, they evaluated a study much more positively when it indicated the superiority of day care over home care. Note, of course, that the description of the study hadn't changed—the only thing that was different was the conclusion the participants wished the study to reach.

The researchers also asked the participants to rate the relative superiority of day care versus home care. Recall that both groups had initially rated home care as better. However, after learning about studies that provided balanced information, the conflicted group changed their attitudes dramatically in the direction of thinking that day care was better.

You can imagine yourself in the situation of the participants in the conflicted group. They are eager to find information that supports the difficult decision they foresee in their future. The study demonstrates how that eagerness—that wishful thinking—affects how they assess the information available to them. As you go through life making judgments about how to assess information, think what you might do to keep wishful thinking out of the process.

What procedures might you follow to determine the correlation between students' sleep habits and their success in college? How would you evaluate potential causal relationships underlying any correlation?

psychological researcher is to make the unseen visible, to make internal events and processes external, and to make private experiences public. You have already seen how important it is for researchers to provide operational definitions of the phenomena they wish to study. Those definitions generally provide some procedure for assigning numbers to, or *quantifying,* different levels, sizes, intensities, or amounts of a variable. Many measurement methods are available, each with its particular advantages and disadvantages. ◉

This review of psychological measurement begins with a discussion of the distinction between two ways of gauging the accuracy of a measure: reliability and validity. I then review different measurement techniques for data collection. By whatever means psychologists collect their data, they must use appropriate statistical methods to verify their hypotheses. A description of how psychologists analyze their data is given in the Statistical Supplement, which follows this chapter.

◉ **Watch** the **Video** *Research Methods* on **MyPsychLab**

Achieving Reliability and Validity

The goal of psychological measurement is to generate findings that are both reliable and valid. **Reliability** refers to the consistency or dependability of behavioral data resulting from psychological testing or experimental research. A reliable result is one that will be repeated under similar conditions of testing at different times. A reliable measuring instrument yields comparable scores when employed repeatedly (and when the thing being measured does not change). Consider the experiment that manipulated participants' beliefs about free will. That experiment used 122 participants. The experimenters' claim that the result was "reliable" means that they should be able to repeat the experiment with any new group of participants of comparable size and generate the same pattern of data.

Validity means that the information produced by research or testing accurately measures the psychological variable or quality it is intended to measure. A valid measure of *happiness,* for example, should allow us to predict how happy you are likely to be in particular situations. A valid experiment means that the researcher can generalize to broader circumstances, often from the laboratory to the real world. Suppose a professor instructs his class to meditate on free will just before an exam. That professor likely accepts as valid the idea that belief in free will lowers students' impulse to cheat. Tests and experiments can be reliable without being valid. We could, for example, use your shoe size as an index of your happiness. This would be reliable (we'd always get the same answer), but not valid (we'd learn very little about your day-to-day happiness level).

As you now read about different types of measures, try to evaluate them in terms of reliability and validity.

Self-Report Measures

Often researchers are interested in obtaining data about experiences they cannot directly observe. Sometimes these experiences are internal psychological states, such as beliefs, attitudes, and feelings. At other times, these experiences are external behaviors but—like sexual activities or criminal acts—not generally appropriate for psychologists to witness. In these cases, investigations rely on self-reports. **Self-report measures** are verbal answers, either written or spoken, to questions the researcher poses. Researchers devise reliable ways to quantify these self-reports so they can make meaningful comparisons between different individuals' responses.

Self-reports include responses made on questionnaires and during interviews. A *questionnaire* or *survey* is a written set of questions, ranging in content from questions of fact ("Are you a registered voter?"), to questions about past or present behavior ("How much do you smoke?"), to questions about attitudes and feelings ("How satisfied are you with your present job?"). *Open-ended* questions allow respondents to answer freely in their own words. Questions may also have a number of *fixed alternatives* such as *yes, no,* and *undecided.*

An *interview* is a dialogue between a researcher and an individual for the purpose of obtaining detailed information. Instead of being completely standardized, like a questionnaire, an interview is *interactive.* An interviewer may vary the questioning to follow up on something the respondent said. Good interviewers are also sensitive to the process of the social interaction as well as to the information revealed. They are trained to establish *rapport,* a positive social relationship with the respondent that encourages trust and the sharing of personal information.

Although researchers rely on a wide variety of self-report measures, there are limits to their usefulness. Obviously, many forms of self-report cannot be used with preverbal children, illiterate adults, speakers of other languages, some mentally disturbed people, and nonhuman animals. Even when self-reports can be used, they may not be reliable or valid. Participants may misunderstand the questions or not remember clearly what they actually experienced. Furthermore, self-reports may be influenced by social desirability. People may give false or misleading answers to create a favorable (or, sometimes, unfavorable) impression of themselves. They may be embarrassed to report their true experiences or feelings.

Behavioral Measures and Observations

As a group, psychological researchers are interested in a wide range of behaviors. They may study a rat running a maze, a child drawing a picture, a student memorizing a poem, or a worker repeatedly performing a task. **Behavioral measures** are ways to study overt actions and observable and recordable reactions.

One of the primary ways to study what people do is *observation.* Researchers use observation in a planned, precise, and systematic manner. Observations focus on either the *process* or the

By watching from behind a one-way mirror, a researcher can make observations of a child without influencing or interfering with the child's behavior. Have you ever changed your behavior when you knew you were being watched?

....

reliability The degree to which a test produces similar scores each time it is used; stability or consistency of the scores produced by an instrument.

validity The extent to which a test measures what it was intended to measure.

self-report measure A self-behavior that is identified through a participant's own observations and reports.

behavioral measure Overt actions or reaction that is observed and recorded, exclusive of self-reported behavior.

products of behavior. In an experiment on learning, for instance, a researcher might observe how many times a research participant rehearsed a list of words (process) and then how many words the participant remembered on a final test (product). For *direct observations,* the behavior under investigation must be clearly visible and overt and easily recorded. For example, in a laboratory experiment on emotions, a researcher could observe a participant's facial expressions as the individual looked at emotionally arousing stimuli.

A researcher's direct observations are often augmented by technology. For example, contemporary psychologists often rely on computers to provide very precise measures of the time it takes for research participants to perform various tasks, such as reading a sentence or solving a problem. Although some forms of exact measurement were available before the computer age, computers now provide extraordinary flexibility in collecting and analyzing precise information. Chapter 3 will describe the newest types of technologies that allow researchers to produce behavioral measures of a remarkable kind: pictures of the brain at work.

In **naturalistic observation,** some naturally occurring behavior is viewed by a researcher, who makes no attempt to change or interfere with it. In some cases, the observation takes place in a laboratory. For instance, a researcher behind a one-way mirror might observe how children use their verbal abilities to persuade their friends to help with tasks (McGrath & Zook, 2011). In other cases, researchers go out into the world to observe behavior.

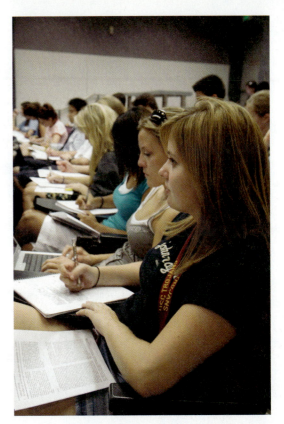

When you enter a college classroom, do you notice people sitting together based on their physical similarity?

Featured Study

Consider this scenario: You enter a crowded classroom and you need to choose a seat. What factors influence your choice? A team of researchers suggested that "birds of a feather sit together": Specifically, they hypothesized that students choose to sit near people with whom they shared physical similarity (Mackinnon et al., 2011). To test this hypothesis, the researchers took digital photographs of 14 university classrooms with 2,228 students. You probably won't be surprised to learn that students were more likely to sit near other students of the same sex and race. However, the researchers' analyses also revealed that people were more likely to sit together based on whether they were wearing glasses as well as similarity in their hair length and hair color.

Do you see why naturalistic observation provides an excellent method to test the hypothesis? Meanwhile, it's very unlikely that students scan a classroom and think, "I'm going sit next to him because we both have long blond hair." This study allows you to reflect on ways in which physical similarity influences your behavior outside of your awareness.

Naturalistic observation is especially useful in the early stages of an investigation. It helps researchers discover the extent of a phenomenon or to get an idea of what the important variables and relationships might be. The data from naturalistic observation often provide clues for an investigator to use in formulating a specific hypothesis or research plan.

When they wish to test hypotheses with behavioral measures, researchers sometimes turn to *archival data.* Imagine all the types of information you might find in a library or on the Web: birth and death records, weather reports, movie attendance figures, legislators' voting patterns, and so on. Any of those types of information could become valuable to test the right hypothesis. Consider a study that examined whether men and women differ in their level of *heroism* (Becker & Eagly, 2004). To address this question, the researchers couldn't create a laboratory test; they couldn't set a building on fire to see whether more men or women rushed in. Instead, they defined behaviors out in the world that were arguably heroic and then looked to archival records to assess the relative contributions of men and women. For example, the researchers examined participation in "Doctors of the World," an organization that sends medical personnel to all corners of the globe. Personnel in this program assume a "nonnegligible risk [by] delivering health and medical services in environments marked by local violence and unsanitary conditions" (Becker & Eagly, 2004, p. 173). What did the archival data show? More than half of the participants in Doctors of the World (65.8 percent) were women. You can see why archival data are essential to address certain types of questions.

Before we leave the topic of psychological measurement, you should be aware that many research projects combine both self-report measures and behavioral observations. Researchers may, for example, specifically look for a relationship between how people report they will behave and how they actually behave. In addition, rather than involving large numbers of participants, some research projects will focus all their measures on a single individual or small group in a **case study.** Intensive analyses of particular individuals can sometimes yield

naturalistic observation A research technique in which unobtrusive observations are made of behaviors that occur in natural environments.

case study Intensive observation of a particular individual or small group of individuals.

Table 2.1 • What's in a Name? Methods and Measures

Research Goal	Dependent Measure	
	Self-Report	**Observation**

Correlational Methods

To assess the correlation between the frequency of people's names and their experience of happiness.	Each participant's assessment of his or her own happiness.	
To assess the correlation between the frequency of children's names and their acceptance by peers.		Children's amount of social interaction on the playground.

Experimental Methods

To determine if people judge identical photos differently when different names are assigned to them.	Participants' ratings of baby pictures to which random names have been assigned.	
To determine if people's actual social interactions change because of name-based expectations.		The number of positive facial expressions people produce in conversation with a stranger who has introduced himself as *Mark* or *Marcus*.

important insights into general features of human experience. For example, in Chapter 3 you will learn that careful observations of single patients with brain damage provided the basis for important theories of the localization of language functions in the brain.

You have now seen several types of procedures and measures that researchers use. Before we move on, let's see how the same issue can be addressed in different research designs. Consider Shakespeare's question, "What's in a name?" In *Romeo and Juliet,* Juliet asserts, "That which we call a rose by any other name would smell as sweet." But is that correct? Do you think your name has an impact on the way other people treat you? Is it better to have a common, familiar name or a rare, distinctive one? Or does your name not matter at all? **Table 2.1** gives examples of combinations of measures and methods that researchers might use to answer those questions. As you read through Table 2.1, ask yourself how willing you would be to participate in each type of study. The next section discusses the ethical standards that govern psychological research.

Stop *and* Review

① Why can some measures be reliable but not valid?
② Why is it important for interviewers to establish rapport?

③ Suppose a researcher spends time observing children's behavior on a playground. What kind of measure would that be?

✓● Study and Review on MyPsychLab

ETHICAL ISSUES IN HUMAN AND ANIMAL RESEARCH

Respect for the basic rights of humans and animals is a fundamental obligation of all researchers (Bersoff, 2008). All research is conducted with respect to a critical question: How should the *potential gains* of a research project be weighed against the *costs* it incurs to those who are subjected to procedures that are risky, painful, stressful, or deceptive? For example, Chapter 16 describes classic experiments on *obedience to authority*. In those experiments, participants were deceived into believing that they were giving dangerous electric shocks to total strangers. Evidence from the experiments suggests that the participants were experiencing severe emotional distress. Although the research may be quite important to an understanding of human nature, it is difficult to assert that this gain in knowledge offsets the emotional costs to the participants.

Beginning in 1953, the American Psychological Association published guidelines for ethical standards for researchers. Current research practice is governed by the 2002 revision of those guidelines (including a series of amendments made through 2010). To guarantee that these and other ethical principles are honored, special committees oversee every research proposal, imposing strict guidelines issued by the U.S. Department of Health and Human Services. Universities and colleges, hospitals, and research institutes each have *review boards* that approve and reject proposals for human and animal research. Let's review some of the factors those review boards consider.

Informed Consent

At the start of nearly all laboratory research with human subjects, participants undergo a process of **informed consent.** They are *informed* about the procedures they will experience as well as the potential risks and benefits of participation. Given that information, participants are asked to sign a statement indicating that they *consent* to continue. Participants are also assured that their privacy is protected: All records of their behavior are kept strictly confidential; they must approve any public sharing of them. In addition, participants are told in advance that they may leave an experiment any time they wish, without penalty, and they are given the names and phone numbers of officials to contact if they have any grievances.

Risk/Gain Assessment

Most psychology experiments carry little risk to the participants, especially where participants are merely asked to perform routine tasks. However, some experiments that study more personal aspects of human nature—such as emotional reactions, self-images, conformity, stress, or aggression—can be upsetting or psychologically disturbing. Therefore, whenever a researcher conducts such a study, risks must be minimized, participants must be informed of the risks, and suitable precautions must be taken to deal with strong reactions. Where any risk is involved, it is carefully weighed by each institutional review board in terms of its necessity for achieving the benefits to the participants of the study, to science, and to society.

Intentional Deception

For some kinds of research, it is not possible to tell the participants the whole story in advance without biasing the results. If you were studying the effects of violence on television on aggression, for example, you would not want your participants to know your purpose in advance. But is your hypothesis enough to justify the deception?

The American Psychological Association's (2002) ethical principles give explicit instructions about the use of deception. The APA provides several restrictions: (1) The study must have sufficient scientific and educational importance to warrant deception; (2) researchers must not deceive participants about research that has a high likelihood of causing physical pain or severe emotional distress; (3) researchers must demonstrate that no equally effective procedures excluding deception

are available; (4) the deception must be explained to the participants by the conclusion of the research; and (5) participants must have the opportunity to withdraw their data once the deception is explained. In experiments involving deception, a review board may impose constraints, insist on monitoring initial demonstrations of the procedure, or deny approval.

Debriefing

Participation in psychological research should always be a mutual exchange of information between researcher and participant. The researcher may learn something new about a behavioral phenomenon from the participant's responses, and the participant should be informed of the purpose, hypothesis, anticipated results, and expected benefits of the study. At the end of an experiment, each participant must be given a careful **debriefing,** in which the researcher provides as much information about the study as possible and makes sure that no one leaves feeling confused, upset, or embarrassed. If it was necessary to mislead the participants during any stage of the research, the experimenter carefully explains the reasons for the deception. Finally, participants have the right to withdraw their data if they feel they have been misused or their rights abused in any way.

Issues in Animal Research

Should animals be used in psychological and medical research? This question has often produced very polarized responses. On one side are researchers who point to the very important breakthroughs research with animals has allowed in several areas of behavioral science (Carroll & Overmier, 2001: Mogil et al., 2010). The benefits of animal research have included discovery and testing of drugs that treat anxiety and mental illnesses as well as important knowledge about drug addiction. Animal research benefits animals as well. For example, veterinarians are able to provide improved treatments that emerged through animal research.

For defenders of animal rights, "ethical concerns about compromised animal welfare cannot be eased by human benefits alone" (Olsson et al., 2007, p. 1680). Ethicists encourage researchers to adhere to the three *Rs:* Researchers should devise tests of their hypothesis that enable them to *reduce* the number of animals they require or to *replace* the use of animals altogether; they should *refine* their procedures to minimize pain and distress (Ryder, 2006). Each animal researcher must judge his or her work with heightened scrutiny.

The American Psychological Association (APA) provides firm ethical guidelines for researchers who use nonhuman animals in their research (APA, 2002). The APA expects

....

 Watch the **Video** *Special Topics: Ethics* on **MyPsychLab**

 Watch the **Video** *Before Informed Consent: Robert Guthrie* on **MyPsychLab**

informed consent The process through which individuals are informed about experimental procedures, risks, and benefits before they provide formal consent to become research participants.

debriefing A procedure conducted at the end of an experiment in which the researcher provides the participant with as much information about the study as possible and makes sure that no participant leaves feeling confused, upset, or embarrassed.

Researchers who use animal subjects are required to provide a humane environment. Do you think scientific gains justify the use of nonhuman animals in research?

researchers who work with animals to have received specific training to ensure the comfort and health of their subjects. Researchers must enforce humane treatment and take reasonable measures to minimize discomfort and pain. Psychologists may use procedures "subjecting animals to pain, stress, or privation only when an alternative procedure is unavailable and the goal is justified by its prospective scientific, educational, or applied value" (p. 1070). If you become a researcher, how might you make decisions about the costs and benefits of animal research?

Stop *and* Review

① What is the purpose of informed consent?
② What is the purpose of debriefing?
③ What are the three Rs of animal research?

✓ **Study** and **Review** on **MyPsychLab**

BECOMING A CRITICAL CONSUMER OF RESEARCH

The final section of this chapter focuses on the kinds of critical thinking skills you need to become a wiser consumer of psychological knowledge. Honing these thinking tools is essential for any responsible person in a dynamic society such as ours. Psychological claims are an ever-present aspect of the daily life of any thinking, feeling, and acting person in this psychologically sophisticated society. Unfortunately, much information on psychology does not come from the books, articles, and reports of accredited practitioners. Rather, this information comes from newspaper and magazine articles, TV and radio shows, pop psychology, and self-help books. To be a *critical thinker* is to go beyond the information as given and to delve

....

⊙ **Watch** the **Video** *Thinking Like a Psychologist: Critical Thinking* on **MyPsychLab**

beneath slick appearances, with the goal of understanding the substance without being seduced by style and image. ⊙

Studying psychology will help you make wiser decisions based on scientific evidence. Always try to apply the insights you derive from your formal study of psychology to the informal psychology that surrounds you: Ask questions about your own behavior or that of other people, seek answers to these questions with respect to rational psychological theories, and check out the answers against the evidence available to you.

Here are some general rules to keep in mind to be a more sophisticated shopper as you travel through the supermarket of knowledge:

- Avoid the inference that correlation is causation.
- Ask that critical terms and key concepts be defined operationally so that there can be consensus about their meanings.
- Consider first how to disprove a theory, hypothesis, or belief before seeking confirming evidence, which is easy to find when you're looking for a justification.
- Always search for alternative explanations to the obvious ones proposed, especially when the explanations benefit the proposer.
- Recognize how personal biases can distort perceptions of reality.
- Be suspicious of simple answers to complex questions or single causes and cures for complex effects and problems.
- Question any statement about the effectiveness of some treatment, intervention, or product by finding the comparative basis for the effect: compared to what?
- Be open-minded yet skeptical: Recognize that most conclusions are tentative and not certain; seek new evidence that decreases your uncertainty while keeping yourself open to change and revision.
- Challenge authority that uses personal opinion in place of evidence for conclusions and is not open to constructive criticism.

As you read *Psychology and Life,* try to apply open-minded skepticism. You shouldn't view your study of psychology as the acquisition of a list of facts. Instead, strive to participate in the joy of observing and discovering and putting ideas to the test.

A news interview with an expert may include misleading sound bites taken out of context or oversimplified "nutshell" descriptions of research conclusions. How could you become a wiser consumer of media reports?

Critical Thinking in Your Life

WHY IS SKILL WITH NUMBERS IMPORTANT?

Imagine that you've become a clinical psychologist. You are called upon to make an important judgment (Slovic et al., 2000):

Mr. James Jones has been evaluated for discharge from a mental health facility where he has been treated for the past several weeks. A prominent psychologist has reached this conclusion: Of every 100 patients similar to Mr. Jones, 10 percent are estimated to commit an act of violence to others during the first several months of discharge.

You must judge whether Mr. Jones is high, medium, or low risk for violent acts following discharge. What judgment would you make? Now consider a slightly different version of the scenario:

Of every 100 patients similar to Mr. Jones, 10 are estimated to commit an act of violence to others during the first several months of discharge.

Once again, what risk judgment would you make? Look closely: The two versions of the scenario describe exactly the same mathematical situation; 10 percent out of 100 equals 10 out of 100. Even so, people give quite different judgments. In one study, Mr. Jones was rated as "low risk" by 30.3 percent of participants who got "10 percent out of 100"; he was rated as "low risk" by just 19.4 percent of participants who got "10 out of 100" (Slovic et al., 2000). The researchers suggested that the difference arises from the "frightening images evoked by the frequency format" (p. 290). Specifically, it's relatively hard to form a firm mental image of 10 percent, whereas you can easily imagine surveying a room of 100 people and finding 10 who might be dangerous.

An important first lesson here is that a statistic's format can have a major impact on how people act on information.

But here's a second important lesson: People who have better numerical skills are less likely to be influenced by a statistic's presentation. In one study, researchers measured students' *numeracy* (a term that parallels *literacy*) by having them answer questions that captured knowledge of probability concepts (Peters et al., 2006). The researchers used the students' scores to divide them into *high numerate* and *low numerate* groups. In response to the scenario with Mr. Jones, the low-numerate students gave quite different risk ratings for the two versions. However, the high-numerate students gave virtually identical ratings. Numeracy also has an impact in real-world settings (Galesic & Garcia-Retamero, 2011). For example, as people make critical decisions about medical care, they must often evaluate data about factors such as hospital performance and costs. More-numerate people show better comprehension of such complex data and make higher-quality decisions (Reyna et al., 2009).

The good news is that college provides you with ample opportunities to become more numerate. Your coursework should lay the groundwork for you to make better data-based decisions well beyond your college years.

- In the scenario with Mr. Jones, people perceive more risk when they read "20 out of 100" versus "2 out of 10." Why might that be?
- How might you choose a statistic's format to influence public opinion?

Recapping Main Points

The Process of Research

- In the initial phase of research, observations, beliefs, information, and general knowledge lead to a new way of thinking about a phenomenon. The researcher formulates a theory and generates hypotheses to be tested.
- To test their ideas, researchers use the scientific method, a set of procedures for gathering and interpreting evidence in ways that limit errors.
- Researchers combat observer biases by standardizing procedures and using operational definitions.
- Experimental research methods determine whether causal relationships exist between variables specified by the hypothesis being tested.

- Researchers rule out alternative explanations by using appropriate control procedures.
- Correlational research methods determine if and how much two variables are related. Correlations do not imply causation.

Psychological Measurement

- Researchers strive to produce measures that are both reliable and valid.
- Psychological measurements include self-reports and behavioral measures.

Ethical Issues in Human and Animal Research

- Respect for the basic rights of human and animal research participants is the obligation of all researchers. Various safeguards have been enacted to guarantee ethical and humane treatment.

Becoming a Critical Consumer of Research

- Becoming a wise research consumer involves learning how to think critically and knowing how to evaluate claims about what research shows.

KEY TERMS

behavioral measure (p. 30)
between-subjects design (p. 26)
case study (p. 31)
confounding variable (p. 25)
control group (p. 26)
control procedure (p. 25)
correlation coefficient (*r*) (p. 27)
correlational method (p. 27)
debriefing (p. 33)
dependent variable (p. 23)
determinism (p. 21)
double-blind control (p. 26)

expectancy effect (p. 25)
experimental group (p. 26)
experimental method (p. 24)
hypothesis (p. 22)
independent variable (p. 23)
informed consent (p. 33)
naturalistic observation (p. 31)
observer bias (p. 22)
operational definition (p. 23)
placebo control (p. 26)
placebo effect (p. 25)
population (p. 26)

random assignment (p. 26)
random sampling (p. 26)
reliability (p. 30)
representative sample (p. 26)
sample (p. 26)
self-report measure (p. 30)
standardization (p. 23)
theory (p. 21)
validity (p. 30)
variable (p. 23)
within-subjects design (p. 26)

1. A(n) _____ is an organized set of concepts that explains a phenomenon or set of phenomena.
- a. theory
- b. hypothesis
- c. operational definition
- d. correlation

2. When articles are submitted to most journals, they are sent out to experts for detailed analyses. This process is known as
- a. debriefing.
- b. informed consent.
- c. peer review.
- d. control procedures.

3. Professor Peterson is testing the hypothesis that people will cooperate less when a lot of people are in a group. In the experiment he plans, he will vary the number of people in each group. That will be his
- a. placebo control.
- b. independent variable.
- c. double-blind control.
- d. dependent variable.

4. Rahul is serving as a research assistant. In the first phase of the experiment, Rahul gives each participant a can of cola or a can of caffeine-free cola. In the second phase of the experiment, Rahul times the participants with a stopwatch while they play a video game. It sounds like this study is lacking a(n)
- a. placebo control.
- b. correlational design.
- c. operational definition.
- d. double-blind control.

5. Matt is participating in a two-day experiment. On Day 1, he takes a memory test after running on a treadmill for 2 minutes. On Day 2, he takes a similar test after running for 10 minutes. The experimenters plan to compare Matt's performance on the two tests. This sounds like a
- a. within-subjects design.
- b. double-blind control.
- c. between-subjects design.
- d. correlational design.

6. Shirley visits an antique store. The owner explains to her that the smaller an object is, the more he can charge for it. This is an example of a
- a. correlation coefficient.
- b. negative correlation.
- c. positive correlation.
- d. placebo effect.

7. Sally is about to travel from New York to Chicago. Although she prefers to drive, she has decided to get on an airplane. Sally reads a pair of articles about the relative safety of the two types of travel. She concludes that the one that favors air travel is considerably more valid. This sounds like an example of
- a. determinism.
- b. expectancy effects.
- c. informed consent.
- d. wishful thinking.

8. Dr. Paul is developing a new measure of hunger. He says, "I need a measure that will accurately predict how much food people will eat in their next meal." Dr. Paul's statement is about the _____ of the measure.
- a. operational definition
- b. standardization
- c. validity
- d. reliability

9. Giovanna is worried that the results of her experiment may be affected by her participants' desire to provide favorable impressions of themselves. It sounds as if she might be using _____ measures.
- a. valid
- b. self-report
- c. reliable
- d. operational

10. Ben believes that men are more likely to arrive late to classes than are women. To test this hypothesis most effectively, Ben should use
- a. a within-subjects design.
- b. a correlational design.
- c. self-report measures.
- d. naturalistic observation.

11. Andrew wishes to test the hypothesis that people give more freely to charities when the weather is pleasant. To test this hypothesis, Andrew is likely to make use of
- a. double-blind controls.
- b. expectancy effects.
- c. laboratory observation.
- d. archival data.

12. Before you participate in an experiment, the researcher should provide you with information about procedures, potential risks, and expected benefits. This process is called
- a. a risk/gain assessment.
- b. informed debriefing.
- c. informed consent.
- d. operational definitions.

13. Which one of these is *not* among the three Rs that ethicists suggest should guide research using nonhuman animals?
- a. relate
- b. refine
- c. reduce
- d. replace

14. Always search for _____ explanations to the obvious ones proposed.
- a. optimistic
- b. alternative
- c. negative
- d. opposite

15. You ask people to respond to scenarios that describe the risk associated with excess cell-phone usage. You expect people to give the highest risk estimates when they read that "_____ people suffer serious vocal chord damage."
- a. 10 of every 100
- b. 10 percent of
- c. 20 of every 100
- d. 20 percent of

ESSAY QUESTIONS

1. Why is it so important that research procedures be open for public verifiability?

2. Suppose you wanted to measure "happiness." What might you do to assess the validity of your measure?

3. With respect to ethical principles, how are risks and gains defined in the context of psychological research?

Statistical Supplement

Understanding Statistics: Analyzing Data and Forming Conclusions

As Chapter 2 noted, psychologists use statistics to make sense of the data they collect. They also use statistics to provide a quantitative basis for the conclusions they draw. Knowing something about statistics, therefore, can help you appreciate the process by which psychological knowledge is developed. To demonstrate this point, I will follow a single project from its real-world inspiration to the statistical arguments the researchers used to draw conclusions.

The project began in response to the types of stories that appear on newspaper front pages, about shy individuals who became *sudden murderers*. Here's an example:

> *Fred Cowan was described by relatives, co-workers, and acquaintances as a "nice, quiet man," a "gentle man who loved children," and a "real pussycat." The principal of the parochial school Cowan had attended as a child reported that his former student had received A grades in courtesy, cooperation, and religion. According to a co-worker, Cowan "never talked to anybody and was someone you could push around." Cowan, however, surprised everyone who knew him when, one Valentine's Day, he strolled into work toting a semiautomatic rifle and shot and killed four co-workers, a police officer, and, finally, himself.*

This story has a common plot: A shy, quiet person suddenly becomes violent, shocking everyone who knows him. What did Fred Cowan have in common with other people who are suddenly transformed from gentle and caring into violent and ruthless? What personal attributes might distinguish them from us?

A team of researchers had a hunch that there might be a link between shyness and other personal characteristics and violent behavior (Lee et al., 1977). They began to collect some data that might reveal such a connection. The researchers reasoned that seemingly nonviolent people who suddenly commit murders are probably typically shy, nonaggressive individuals who keep their passions in check and their impulses under tight control. For most of their lives, they suffer many silent injuries. Seldom, if ever, do they express anger, regardless of how angry they really feel. On the outside, they appear unbothered, but on the inside they may be fighting to control furious rages. Because they are shy, they probably do not let others get close to them, so no one knows how they really feel. Then, suddenly, something explodes. At the slightest provocation—one more small insult, one more little rejection, one more bit of social pressure—the fuse is lit, and they release the suppressed violence that has been building up for so long. Because they did not learn to deal with interpersonal conflicts through discussion and verbal negotiation, these sudden murderers act out their anger physically.

The researchers' reasoning led them to the hypothesis that shyness would be more characteristic of *sudden murderers*— people who had engaged in homicide without any prior history of violence or antisocial behavior—than it would of *habitual criminal murderers*—those who had committed homicide but had had a previous record of violent criminal behavior. In addition, sudden murderers should have higher levels of control over their impulses than habitually violent people. Finally, their passivity and dependence would be manifested in more feminine and androgynous (both male and female) characteristics, as measured on a standard sex-role inventory, than those of habitual criminals.

To test their ideas about sudden murderers, the researchers obtained permission to administer psychological questionnaires to a group of inmates serving time for murder in California prisons. Nineteen inmates (all male) agreed to participate in the study. Prior to committing murder, some had committed a series of crimes, whereas the other part of the sample had had no previous criminal record. The researchers collected three kinds of data from these two types of participants: shyness scores, sex-role identification scores, and impulse control scores.

Shyness scores were collected using the Stanford Shyness Survey. The most important item on this questionnaire asked if the individual was shy; the answer could be either yes or no. The second questionnaire was the Bem Sex-Role Inventory (BSRI), which presented a list of adjectives, such as *aggressive* and *affectionate,* and asked how well each adjective described the individual (Bem, 1974, 1981). Some adjectives were typically associated with being "feminine," and the total score of these adjectives was an individual's femininity score. Other adjectives were considered "masculine," and the total score of those adjectives was an individual's masculinity score. The final sex-role score, which reflected the difference between an individual's femininity and masculinity, was calculated by subtracting the masculinity score from the femininity score. The third questionnaire was the Minnesota Multiphasic Personality Inventory (MMPI), which was designed to measure many different aspects of personality (see Chapter 13). The study used only the "ego-overcontrol" scale, which measures the degree to which a person acts out or controls impulses. The higher the individual's score on this scale, the more ego overcontrol the individual exhibits.

The researchers predicted that, compared with murderers with a prior criminal record, sudden murderers would (1) more often describe themselves as shy on the shyness survey, (2) select more feminine traits than masculine ones on the sex-role scale, and (3) score higher in ego overcontrol. What did they discover?

Before you find out, you need to understand some of the basic procedures that were used to analyze these data. The actual sets of data collected by the researchers are used here as the source material to teach you about some of the different types of statistical analyses and also about the kinds of conclusions they make possible.

Table S.1 • Raw Data from the Sudden Murderers Study

		BSRI	MMPI
Inmate	Shyness	Femininity–Masculinity	Ego Overcontrol
Group 1: Sudden Murderers			
1	Yes	+5	17
2	No	−1	17
3	Yes	+4	13
4	Yes	+61	17
5	Yes	+19	13
6	Yes	+41	19
7	No	−29	14
8	Yes	+23	9
9	Yes	−13	11
10	Yes	+5	14
Group 2: Habitual Criminal Murderers			
11	No	−12	15
12	No	−14	11
13	Yes	−33	14
14	No	−8	10
15	No	−7	16
16	No	+3	11
17	No	−17	6
18	No	+6	9
19	No	−10	12

ANALYZING THE DATA

For most researchers in psychology, analyzing the data is an exciting step. Statistical analysis allows researchers to discover if their predictions were correct. In this section, we will work step by step through an analysis of some of the data from the Sudden Murderers Study.

The *raw data*—the actual scores or other measures obtained—from the 19 inmates in the Sudden Murderers Study are listed in **Table S.1**. As you can see, there were 10 inmates in the sudden murderers group and 9 in the habitual criminal murderers group. When first glancing at these data, any researcher would feel what you probably feel: confusion. What do all these scores mean? Do the two groups of murderers differ from one another on these various personality measures? It is difficult to know just by examining this disorganized array of numbers.

Psychologists rely on two types of statistics to help draw meaningful conclusions from the data they collect: descriptive and inferential. **Descriptive statistics** use mathematical procedures in an objective, uniform way to describe different aspects of numerical data. If you have ever computed your GPA, you already have used descriptive statistics. **Inferential statistics** use probability theory to make sound decisions about which results might have occurred simply through chance variation.

. . . .

descriptive statistics Statistical procedures that are used to summarize sets of scores with respect to central tendencies, variability, and correlations.

inferential statistics Statistical procedures that allow researchers to determine whether the results they obtain support their hypotheses or can be attributed just to chance variation.

Descriptive Statistics

Descriptive statistics provide a summary picture of patterns in the data. They are used to describe sets of scores collected from one experimental participant or, more often, from different groups of participants. They are also used to describe relationships among variables. Thus, instead of trying to keep in mind all the scores obtained by each of the participants, researchers get indexes of the scores that are most *typical* for each group. They also get measures of how *variable* the scores are with respect to the typical score—whether the scores are spread out or clustered closely together. Let's see how researchers derive these measures.

Frequency Distributions How would you summarize the data in Table S.1? To present a clear picture of how the various scores are distributed, we can draw up a **frequency distribution**—a summary of how frequently each of the various scores occurs. The shyness data are easy to summarize. Of the 19 scores, there are 9 *yes* and 10 *no* responses; almost all the *yes* responses are in Group 1, and almost all the *no* responses are in Group 2. However, the ego-overcontrol and sex-role scores do not fall into easy *yes* and *no* categories. To see how frequency distributions of numerical responses can allow informative comparisons between groups, we will focus on the sex-role scores.

Consider the sex-role data in Table S.1. The highest score is +61 (most feminine) and the lowest is −33 (most masculine). Of the 19 scores, 9 are positive and 10 negative. This means that 9 of the murderers described themselves as relatively feminine and 10 as relatively masculine. But how are these scores distributed between the groups? The first step in preparing a frequency distribution for a set of numerical data is to *rank-order* the scores from highest to lowest. The rank ordering for the sex-role scores is shown in **Table S.2**. The second step is to group these rank-ordered scores into a smaller number of categories called *intervals*. In this study, 10 categories were used, with each category covering 10 possible scores. The third step is to construct a frequency distribution table, listing the intervals from highest to lowest and noting the *frequencies*, the number of scores within each interval. Our frequency distribution shows us that the sex-role scores are largely between −20 and +9 (see **Table S.3**). The majority of the inmates' scores did not deviate much from zero. That is, they were neither strongly positive nor strongly negative.

The data are now arranged in useful categories. The researchers' next step was to display the distributions in graphic form.

Graphs Distributions are often easier to understand when they are displayed in graphs. The simplest type of graph is a *bar graph*. Bar graphs allow you to see patterns in the data. We can use a bar graph to illustrate how many more sudden murderers than habitual criminal murderers described themselves as shy (see **Figure S.1**).

Table S.3 • Frequency Distribution of Sex-Role Difference Scores

Category	Frequency
+60 to +69	1
+50 to +59	0
+40 to +49	1
+30 to +39	0
+20 to +29	1
+10 to +19	1
0 to +9	5
−10 to −1	4
−20 to −11	4
−30 to −21	1
−40 to −31	1

Table S.2 • Rank Ordering of Sex-Role Difference Scores

Highest	+61	−1	
	+41	−7	
	+23	−8	
	+19	−10	
	+6	−12	
	+5	−13	
	+5	−14	
	+4	−17	
	+3	−29	
		−33	**Lowest**

Note: + scores are more feminine; − scores are more masculine.

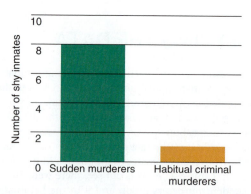

FIGURE S.1 Shyness for Two Groups of Murderers (a Bar Graph)

frequency distribution A summary of how frequently each score appears in a set of observations.

For more complex data, such as the sex-role scores, we can use a *histogram*, which is similar to a bar graph except that the categories are intervals—number categories instead of the name categories used in the bar graph. A histogram gives a visual picture of the number of scores in a distribution that are in each interval. It is easy to see from the sex-role scores shown in the histograms (in **Figure S.2**) that the distributions of scores are different for the two groups of murderers.

You can see from Figures S.1 and S.2 that the overall distributions of responses conform to two of the researchers' hypotheses. Sudden murderers were more likely to describe themselves as shy and were more likely to use feminine traits to describe themselves than were habitual criminal murderers.

Measures of Central Tendency So far, we have formed a general picture of how the scores are *distributed*. Tables and graphs increase our general understanding of research results, but we want to know more—for example, the one score that

is most typical of the group as a whole. This score becomes particularly useful when we compare two or more groups; it is much easier to compare the typical scores of two groups than their entire distributions. A single *representative* score that can be used as an index of the most typical score obtained by a group of participants is called a **measure of central tendency.** (It is located in the center of the distribution, and other scores tend to cluster around it.) Typically, psychologists use three different measures of central tendency: the *mode*, the *median*, and the *mean*.

The **mode** is the score that occurs more often than any other. For the measure of shyness, the modal response of the sudden murderers was *yes*—8 out of 10 said they were shy. Among habitual criminal murderers, the modal response was *no*. The sex-role scores for the sudden murderers had a mode of +5. Can you figure out what the mode of their ego-overcontrol scores is? The mode is the easiest index of central tendency to determine, but it is often the least useful. You will see one reason for this relative lack of usefulness if you notice that only one overcontrol score lies above the mode of 17, and six lie below it. Although 17 is the score obtained most often, it may not fit your idea of "typical" or "central."

The **median** is more clearly a central score; it separates the upper half of the scores in a distribution from the lower half. The number of scores larger than the median is the same as the number that is smaller. When there is an odd number of scores, the median is the middle score; when there is an even number of scores, researchers most often average the two scores at the middle. For example, if you rank-order the sex-role scores of only the habitual criminal murderers on a separate piece of paper, you will see that the median score is −10, with four scores higher and four scores lower. For the sudden murderers, the median is +5—the average of the fifth and sixth scores, each of which happens to be +5. The median is not affected by extreme scores. For example, even if the sudden murderers' highest sex-role score had been +129 instead of +61, the median value would still have been +5. That score would still separate the upper half of the data from the lower half. The median is quite simply the score in the middle of the distribution.

The **mean** is what most people think of when they hear the word *average*. It is also the statistic most often used to describe a set of data. To calculate the mean, you add up all the scores in a distribution and divide by the total number of scores. The operation is summarized by the following formula:

$$M = \frac{(\Sigma X)}{N}$$

In this formula, M is the mean, X is each individual score, Σ (the Greek letter sigma) is the summation of what

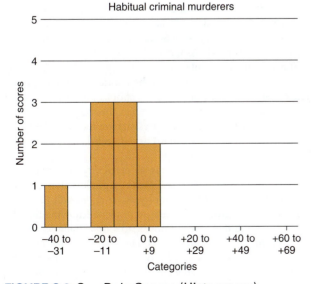

FIGURE S.2 Sex-Role Scores (Histograms)

measure of central tendency A statistic, such as a mean, median, or mode, that provides one score as representative of a set of observations.

mode The score appearing most frequently in a set of observations; a measure of central tendency.

median The score in a distribution above and below which lie 50 percent of the other scores; a measure of central tendency.

mean The arithmetic average of a group of scores; the most commonly used measure of central tendency.

immediately follows it, and N is the total number of scores. Because the summation of all the sex-role scores (ΣX) is 115, and the total number of scores (N) is 10, the mean (M) of the sex-role scores for the sudden murderers would be calculated as follows:

$$M = \frac{(115)}{10} = 11.5$$

Try to calculate their mean overcontrol scores yourself. You should come up with a mean of 14.4.

Unlike the median, the mean *is* affected by the specific values of all scores in the distribution. Changing the value of an extreme score does change the value of the mean. For example, if the sex-role score of inmate 4 were +101 instead of +61, the mean for the whole group would increase from 11.5 to 15.5.

Variability   In addition to knowing which score is most representative of the distribution as a whole, it is useful to know how representative that measure of central tendency really is. Are most of the other scores fairly close to it or widely spread out? **Measures of variability** are statistics that describe the distribution of scores around some measure of central tendency. Take a look back at Figure S.2. You can see that the sex-role scores for the habitual criminals seem to cluster more tightly together than do the scores for sudden murderers. That difference gives you a sense of what's meant by variability.

The simplest measure of variability is the **range,** the difference between the highest and the lowest values in a frequency distribution. For the sudden murderers' sex-role scores, the range is 90: (+61) – (–29). The range of their overcontrol scores is 10: (+19) – (+9). To compute the range, you need to know only two of the scores: the highest and the lowest.

The range is simple to compute, but psychologists often prefer measures of variability that are more sensitive and that take into account *all* the scores in a distribution, not just the extremes. One widely used measure is the **standard deviation (SD),** a measure of variability that indicates the *average* difference between the scores and their mean. To figure out the standard deviation of a distribution, you need to know the mean of the distribution and the individual scores. The general procedure involves subtracting the value of each individual score from the mean and then determining the average of those mean deviations. Here is the formula:

$$SD = \sqrt{\frac{\Sigma(X - M)^2}{N}}$$

You should recognize most of the symbols from the formula for the mean. The expression ($X – M$) means "individual score minus the mean" and is commonly called the *deviation score.* The mean is subtracted from each score, and each resulting score is squared (to eliminate negative values). Then the mean

....

measure of variability A statistic, such as a range or standard deviation, that indicates how tightly the scores in a set of observations cluster together.

range The difference between the highest and the lowest scores in a set of observations; the simplest measure of variability.

standard deviation (SD) The average difference of a set of scores from their mean; a measure of variability.

Table S.4 • Calculating the Standard Deviation of Sudden Murderers' Ego-Overcontrol Scores

Squared Score (X)	Deviation (score minus mean) (X − M)	Deviations Squared (score minus mean)^2 (X − M)^2
17	2.6	6.76
17	2.6	6.76
13	−1.4	1.96
17	2.6	6.76
13	−1.4	1.96
19	4.6	21.16
14	−0.4	0.16
9	−5.4	29.16
11	−3.4	11.56
14	−0.4	0.16

$$\text{Standard deviation} = SD = \sqrt{\frac{\Sigma(X - M)^2}{N}}$$

$$\Sigma(X - M)^2 = 86.40$$

$$\sqrt{\frac{86.40}{10}} = \sqrt{8.64} = 2.94$$

$$SD = 2.94$$

of these deviations is calculated by summing them up (Σ) and dividing by the number of observations (N). The symbol $\sqrt{}$ tells you to take the square root of the enclosed. The standard deviation of the overcontrol scores for the sudden murderers is calculated in **Table S.4**. Recall that the mean of these scores is 14.4. This, then, is the value that must be subtracted from each score to obtain the corresponding deviation scores.

The standard deviation tells us how variable a set of scores is. The larger the standard deviation, the more spread out the scores are. The standard deviation of the sex-role scores for the sudden murderers is 24.6, but the standard deviation for the habitual criminals is only 10.7. These standard deviations confirm your earlier observation of Figure S.2. They show that there was less variability in the habitual criminals group. Their scores clustered more closely about their mean than did those of the sudden murderers. When the standard deviation is small, the mean is a good representative index of the entire distribution. When the standard deviation is large, the mean is less typical of the whole group.

Can you see why measures of variability are important? An example may help. Suppose you are a grade-school teacher. It is the beginning of the school year, and you will be teaching reading to a group of 30 second graders. Knowing that the average child in the class can now read a first-grade-level book will help you to plan your lessons. You could plan better, however, if you knew how *similar* or how *divergent* the reading abilities of the 30 children were. Are they all at about the same level (low variability)? If so, then you can plan a fairly standard second-grade lesson. What if several can read advanced material and others can barely read at all (high variability)? Now the mean level is not so representative of the entire class, and you will have to plan a variety of lessons to meet the children's varied needs.

Correlation   Another useful tool in interpreting psychological data is the **correlation coefficient (*r*),** a measure of the nature and strength of the relationship between two variables (such as height and weight or sex-role score and ego-overcontrol score). It tells us the extent to which scores on one measure are associated with scores on the other. If people with high scores on one variable tend to have *high* scores on the other variable, then the correlation coefficient will be positive (greater than 0). If, however, most people with high scores on one variable tend to have *low* scores on the other variable, then the correlation coefficient will be negative (less than 0). If there is *no* consistent relationship between the scores, the correlation will be close to 0 (see also Chapter 2).

Correlation coefficients range from +1 (perfect positive correlation) through 0 to −1 (perfect negative correlation). The further a coefficient is from 0 in *either* direction, the more closely related the two variables are, positively or negatively. Higher coefficients permit better predictions of one variable, given knowledge of the other.

In the Sudden Murderers Study, the correlation coefficient (symbolized as *r*) between the sex-role scores and the overcontrol scores turns out to be +0.35. Thus the sex-role scores and the overcontrol scores are positively correlated. In general, individuals seeing themselves as more feminine also tend to be higher in overcontrol. However, the correlation is modest, compared with the highest possible value, +1.00, so we know that there are exceptions to this relationship.

Inferential Statistics

We have used a number of descriptive statistics to characterize the data from the Sudden Murderers Study, and now we have an idea of the pattern of results. However, some basic questions remain unanswered. Recall that the research team hypothesized that sudden murderers would be shyer, more overcontrolled, and more feminine than habitual criminal murderers. After we have used descriptive statistics to compare average responses and variability in the two groups, it appears that there are some differences between the groups. But how do we know if the differences are large enough to be meaningful? If we repeated this study, with other sudden murderers and other habitual criminal murderers, would we expect to find the same pattern of results, or could these results have been an outcome of chance? If we could somehow measure the entire population of sudden murderers and habitual criminal murderers, would the means and standard deviations be the same as those we found for these small samples?

Inferential statistics are used to answer these kinds of questions. They tell us which inferences we *can* make from our samples and which conclusions we can legitimately draw from our data. Inferential statistics use probability theory to determine the likelihood that a set of data occurred simply by chance variation.

The Normal Curve   To understand how inferential statistics work, we must look first at the special properties of a distribution called the *normal curve*. When data on a variable (for example, height, IQ, or overcontrol) are collected from a large number of individuals, the numbers obtained often fit a curve roughly similar to that shown in **Figure S.3** on page 44. Notice that the curve is symmetrical (the left half is a mirror image of the right) and bell shaped—high in the middle, where most scores are, and lower the farther you get from the mean. This type of curve is called a **normal curve,** or *normal distribution*. (A *skewed* distribution is one in which scores cluster toward one end instead of around the middle.)

In a normal curve, the median, mode, and mean values are the same. A specific percentage of the scores can be predicted to fall under different sections of the curve. Figure S.3 shows IQ scores on the Stanford-Binet Intelligence Test. These scores have a mean of 100 and a standard deviation of 15. If you indicate standard deviations as distances from the mean along the baseline, you find that a little over 68 percent of all the scores are between the mean of 100 and 1 standard deviation above and below—between IQs of 85 and 115. Roughly another 27 percent of the scores are found between the first and second standard deviations below the mean (IQ scores between 70 and 85) and above the mean (IQ scores between 115 and 130). Less than 5 percent of the scores fall in the third standard deviation above and below the mean, and very few scores fall beyond—only about one quarter of 1 percent. This normal distribution tells you how common or rare different outcomes would be (such as an individual having an IQ of 115 versus 170).

A normal curve is also obtained by collecting a series of measurements whose differences are due only to chance. Suppose you flip a coin 10 times in a row and record the number of heads and tails. If you repeat the exercise for a 100 sets of 10 tosses, you probably will get a few sets with all heads or no heads, more sets where the number is between these extremes, and, most typically, more sets where you get 5 heads and 5 tails. If you plotted your sets of tosses, you should get a graph that closely fits a normal curve with the mean at 5 heads and 5 tails.

Statistical Significance   But suppose you flipped the coin all those times, and you didn't get a mean of 5 heads and 5 tails. Suppose you plotted your data and, after all those sets of 10 tosses, the mean was 8 heads and 2 tails. You would almost certainly wonder if there were something dishonest about the coin. Here's the question you'd want to ask: Suppose the coin were in fact, a fair coin—what is the probability that you'd obtain an outcome as extreme as the one you got? That question is the core type of question addressed by inferential statistics. If the probability of getting 80% heads (just by random chance) was sufficiently low, then you could conclude that you hadn't been flipping a fair coin.

When researchers look at the outcomes of experiments, they ask how likely it is that whatever differences they obtained

....

correlational coefficient (*r*)   A statistic that indicates the degree of relationship between two variables.

normal curve   The symmetrical curve that represents the distribution of scores on many psychological attributes; allows researchers to make judgments of how unusual an observation or result is.

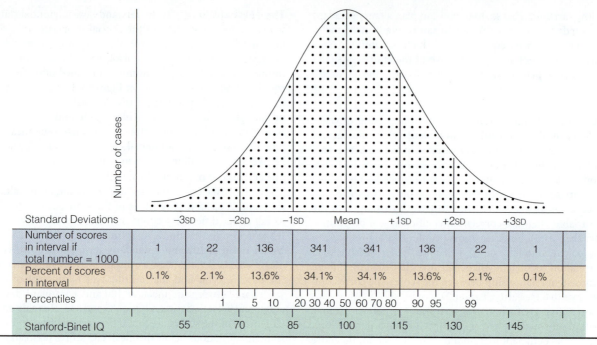

Standard Deviations		−3SD		−2SD		−1SD		Mean		+1SD		+2SD		+3SD	
Number of scores in interval if total number = 1000		1		22		136		341		341		136		22		1	
Percent of scores in interval		0.1%		2.1%		13.6%		34.1%		34.1%		13.6%		2.1%		0.1%	
Percentiles					1		5 10	20 30 40 50 60 70 80		90 95		99			
Stanford-Binet IQ		55		70		85		100		115		130		145		

FIGURE S.3 A Normal Curve

occurred simply by chance. Because chance differences have a normal distribution, a researcher can use the normal curve to answer this question. By common agreement, psychologists accept a difference as "real" when the probability that it might be due to chance is less than 5 in 100 (indicated by the notation $p < .05$). A **significant difference** is one that meets this criterion. However, in some cases, even stricter probability levels are used, such as $p < .01$ (less than 1 in 100) and $p < .001$ (less than 1 in 1,000). With a statistically significant difference, a researcher can draw a conclusion about the behavior that was under investigation.

There are many different types of tests for estimating the statistical significance of sets of data. The type of test chosen for a particular case depends on the design of the study, the form of the data, and the size of the groups. I will mention only one of the most common tests, the *t-test,* which may be used when an investigator wants to know if the difference between the means of two groups is statistically significant.

Let's return to the sex-role scores of the two groups of murderers. For the sudden murders, the scores had a mean of 11.5 and a standard deviation of 24.6; the habitual criminals had a mean of −10.2 and a standard deviation of 10.7. The *t-test* combines the information about the means and standard deviations to determine whether the scores of the sudden murderers are significantly different from those of the habitual criminal murderers. The *t-test* uses a mathematical procedure to confirm the conclusion you may have drawn from Figure S.2: The distributions of sex-role scores for the two groups is sufficiently different to be "real." If we carry out

the appropriate calculations—which evaluate the difference between the two means as a function of the variability around those two means—we find that there is a very slim chance, less than 5 in 100 ($p < .05$), of obtaining such a large *t* value if no true difference exists. The difference is, therefore, statistically significant, and we can feel more confident that there is a real difference between the two groups. The sudden murderers *did* rate themselves as more feminine than did the habitual criminal murderers.

On the other hand, the difference between the two groups of murderers in overcontrol scores turns out not to be statistically significant ($p < .10$), so we must be more cautious in making claims about this difference. There is a trend in the predicted direction—the difference is one that would occur by chance only 10 times in 100. However, the difference is not within the standard 5-in-100 range. (The difference in shyness, analyzed using another statistical test for frequency of scores, is in fact significant.)

So, by using inferential statistics, we are able to answer some of the basic questions with which we began, and we are closer to understanding the psychology of people who suddenly change from mild-mannered, shy individuals into murderers. Any conclusion, however, is only a statement of the *probable* relationship between the events that were investigated; it is never one of certainty. Truth in science is provisional, always open to revision by later data from better studies, developed from better hypotheses.

You might take a moment to consider what else you'd like to know, to put these data in a richer context. For example, you might want to know how both types of murderers differ from individuals who have never committed murders on measures such as their sex-role scores. If we collected new data we could use descriptive and inferential statistics to answer such questions as whether all murderers are, on such dimensions, different from those who don't commit murders. What might you expect?

....

significant difference A difference between experimental groups or conditions that would have occurred by chance less than an accepted criterion; in psychology, the criterion most often used is a probability of less than 5 times out of 100, or $p < .05$.

BECOMING A WISE CONSUMER OF STATISTICS

Now that we have considered what statistics are, how they are used, and what they mean, let's talk briefly about how they can be misused. Many people accept unsupported so-called facts that are bolstered by the air of authority of a statistic. Others choose to believe or disbelieve what the statistics say without having any idea of how to question the numbers that are presented in support of a product, politician, or proposal. At the end of Chapter 2, you saw some suggestions about how you can become a wiser research consumer. Based on this brief survey of statistics, we can extend that advice to situations in which people make specific statistical claims.

There are many ways to give a misleading impression using statistics. The decisions made at all stages of research—from who the participants are to how the study is designed, what statistics are selected, and how they are used—can have a profound effect on the conclusions that can be drawn from the data.

The group of participants can make a large difference that can easily remain undetected when the results are reported. For example, a survey of views on abortion rights will yield very different results if conducted in a small conservative community in the South rather than at a university in New York City. Likewise, a pro-life group surveying the opinions of its membership will very likely arrive at conclusions that differ from those obtained by the same survey conducted by a pro-choice group.

Even if the participants are randomly selected and not biased by the methodology, the statistics can produce misleading results if the assumptions of the statistics are violated. For example, suppose 20 people take an IQ test; 19 of them receive scores between 90 and 110, and 1 receives a score of 220. The mean of the group will be strongly elevated by that one outlying high score. With this sort of a data set, it would be much more accurate to present the median, which would accurately report the group's generally average intelligence, rather than the mean, which would make it look as if the average member of this group had a high IQ. This sort of bias is especially powerful in a small sample. If, however, the number of people in this group were 2,000 instead of 20, the one extreme outlier would make virtually no difference, and the mean would be a legitimate summary of the group's intelligence.

One good way to avoid falling for this sort of deception is to check on the size of the sample. Large samples are less likely to be misleading than small ones. Another check is to look at the median or the mode as well as the mean. The results can be interpreted with more confidence if they are similar than if they are different. Always closely examine the methodology and results of the research reported. Check to see if the experimenters report their sample size, measures of variability, and significance levels.

Statistics are the backbone of psychological research. They are used to understand observations and to determine whether the findings are, in fact, correct. Through the methods you've seen, psychologists can prepare a frequency distribution of data and find the central tendencies and variability of the scores. They can use the correlation coefficient to determine the strength and direction of the association between sets of scores. Finally, psychological investigators can find out how representative the observations are and whether they are significantly different from what would be observed among the general population. Statistics can also be used poorly or deceptively, misleading those who do not understand them. But when statistics are applied correctly and ethically, they allow researchers to expand the body of psychological knowledge.

KEY TERMS

correlation coefficient (*r*) (p. 43)
descriptive statistics (p. 39)
frequency distribution (p. 40)
inferential statistics (p. 39)
mean (p. 41)

measure of central tendency (p. 41)
measure of variability (p. 42)
median (p. 41)
mode (p. 41)
normal curve (p. 43)

range (p. 42)
significant difference (p. 44)
standard deviation (SD) (p. 42)

3

The Biological and Evolutionary Bases of Behavior

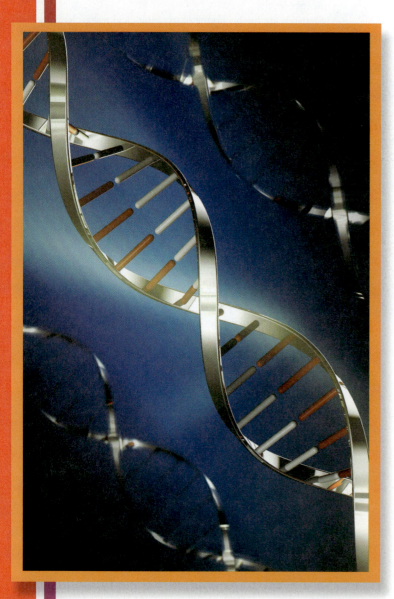

What makes you a unique individual? *Psychology and Life* provides many answers to this question, but in this chapter we will focus on the biological aspects of your individuality. To help you understand what makes you different from the people around you, we will consider the role that heredity plays in shaping your life and in forming the brain that controls your experiences. Of course, you can appreciate these differences only against the background of what you have in common with all other people. You might, therefore, think of this as a chapter about biological potential: What possibilities for behavior define the human species, and how do those possibilities emerge for particular members of that species?

In a way, this chapter stands as proof of one remarkable aspect of your biological potential: Your brain is sufficiently complex to carry out a systematic examination of its own functions. Why is this so remarkable? The human brain is sometimes likened to a spectacular computer: At only 3 pounds, your brain contains more cells than there are stars in our entire galaxy—over 100 billion cells that communicate and store information with astonishing efficiency. But even the world's mightiest computer is incapable of reflecting on the rules that guide its own operation. Thus you are much more than a computer; your consciousness allows you to put your vast computational power to work, trying to determine your species' own rules for operation. The research we examine in this chapter arose from the special human desire for self-understanding.

The goal for this chapter is to help you to understand how biology contributes to the creation of unique individuals against a shared background potential. To approach this goal, I first describe how evolution and heredity determine your biology and behavior. You'll then see how laboratory and clinical research provide a view into the workings of the brain, the nervous system, and the endocrine system. Finally, we'll consider the basic mechanisms of communication among cells in your nervous system that produce the full range of complex human behaviors.

Psychologists often wish to understand the separate impact of nature and nurture on individuals' courses through life. Why might it be easier to observe the impact of environments versus the impact of heredity?

Because the features of environments can be directly observed, it is often easier to understand how they affect people's behavior. You can, for example, actually watch a parent acting aggressively toward a child and wonder what consequences such treatment might have on the child's later tendency toward aggression; you can observe the overcrowded and impoverished settings in which some children grow up and wonder whether these features of the environment lead to aggressive behaviors. The biological forces that shape behavior, by comparison, are never plainly visible to the naked eye. To make the biology of behavior more understandable to you, the chapter will begin by reviewing some of the basic elements of the theory of evolution—the principles that shape a species' potential repertory of behaviors. We'll then consider how behavioral variation is passed from generation to generation.

HEREDITY AND BEHAVIOR

In Chapter 1, you learned that one of the major goals of psychology is to discover the causes underlying the variety of human behavior. An important dimension of causal explanation within psychology is defined by the end points of *nature* versus *nurture,* or *heredity* versus *environment.* Consider, as we did in Chapter 1, the question of the roots of aggressive behavior. You might imagine that individuals are aggressive by virtue of some aspect of their biological makeup: They may have inherited a tendency toward violence from one of their parents. Alternatively, you might imagine that all humans are about equally predisposed to aggression and that the degree of aggression individuals display arises in response to features of the environment in which they are raised. The correct answer to this question has a profound impact on how society treats individuals who are overly aggressive—by focusing resources on changing certain environments or on changing aspects of the people themselves. You need to be able to discriminate the forces of heredity from the forces of environment.

Evolution and Natural Selection

In 1831, **Charles Darwin** (1809–1882), fresh out of college with a degree in theology, set sail from England on HMS *Beagle,* an ocean research vessel, for a five-year cruise to survey the coast of South America. During the trip, Darwin collected everything that crossed his path: marine animals, birds, insects, plants, fossils, seashells, and rocks. His extensive notes became the foundation for his books on topics ranging from geology to emotion to zoology. The book for which he is most remembered is *The Origin of Species,* published in 1859. In this work, Darwin set forth science's grandest theory: the evolution of life.

Natural Selection Darwin developed his theory of evolution by reflecting on the species of animals he had encountered while on his voyage. One of the many places *Beagle* visited was the Galápagos Islands, a volcanic archipelago off the west coast of South America. These islands are a haven for diverse forms of wildlife, including 13 species of finches, now known as Darwin's finches. Darwin wondered how so many different species of finches could have come to inhabit the islands. He reasoned that they couldn't have migrated from the mainland because

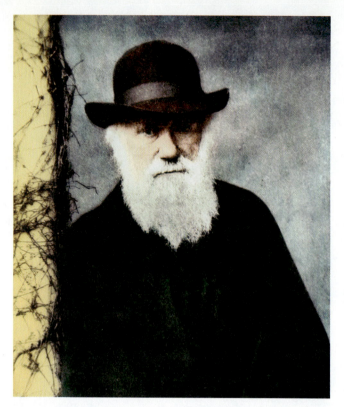

What observations ultimately led Charles Darwin to propose the theory of evolution?

In general, the theory of natural selection suggests that organisms well adapted to their environment, whatever it happens to be, will produce more offspring than those less well adapted. Over time, those organisms possessing traits more favorable for survival will become more numerous than those not possessing those traits. In evolutionary terms, an individual's success is measured by the number of offspring he or she produces.

Contemporary research has shown that natural selection can have dramatic effects, even in the short run. In a series of studies by **Peter** and **Rosemary Grant** (Grant & Grant, 2006, 2008), involving several species of Darwin's finches, records were kept of rainfall, food supply, and the population size of these finches on one of the Galápagos Islands. In 1976, the population numbered well over 1,000 birds. The following year brought a murderous drought that wiped out most of the food supply. The smallest seeds were the first to be depleted, leaving only larger and tougher seeds. That year the finch population decreased by more than 80 percent. However, smaller finches with smaller beaks died at a higher frequency than larger finches with thicker beaks. Consequently, as Darwin would have predicted, the larger birds became more numerous in the following years. Why? Because only they, with their larger bodies and thicker beaks, were fit enough to respond to the environmental change caused by the drought. Interestingly, in 1983, rain was plentiful, and seeds, especially the smaller ones, became abundant. As a result, smaller birds outsurvived larger birds, probably because their beaks were better suited for pecking the smaller seeds. The Grants' study shows that natural selection can have noticeable effects even over short periods. Researchers continue to document the impact of environments on natural selection in diverse species such as fruit flies, mosquitoes, flounders, and pygmy possums (Hoffmann & Willi, 2008).

Although Darwin provided the foundation for evolutionary theory, researchers continue to study mechanisms of evolutionary change that fell beyond the bounds of Darwin's ideas (Shaw & Mullen, 2011). For example, one important question that Darwin was unable to address fully was how populations with common ancestors evolve so that one species becomes two. As you have already seen in the Grants' research with Darwin's finches, species can change rapidly in response to local environments. One explanation for the appearance of new species is that they emerge when two populations from an original species become geographically separate—and

those species didn't exist there. He suggested, therefore, that the variety of species reflected the operation of a process he came to call **natural selection**.

Darwin's theory suggests that each species of finch emerged from a common set of ancestors. Originally, a small flock of finches found their way to one of the islands; they mated among themselves and eventually their number multiplied. Over time, some finches migrated to different islands in the archipelago. What happened next was the process of natural selection. Food resources and living conditions—*habitats*—vary considerably from island to island. Some of the islands are lush with berries and seeds, others are covered with cacti, and others have plenty of insects. At first, the populations on different islands were similar—there was *variation* among the groups of finches on each island. However, because food resources on the islands were limited, a bird was more likely to survive and reproduce if the shape of its beak was well suited to the food sources available on the island. For example, birds that migrated to islands rich in berries and seeds were more likely to survive and reproduce if they had thick beaks. On those islands, birds with thinner, more pointed beaks, unsuitable for crushing or breaking open seeds, died. The environment of each island determined which among the original population of finches would live and reproduce and which would more likely perish, leaving no offspring. Over time, this led to very different populations on each island and permitted the different species of Darwin's finches to evolve from the original ancestral group.

....

natural selection Darwin's theory that favorable adaptations to features of the environment allow some members of a species to reproduce more successfully than others.

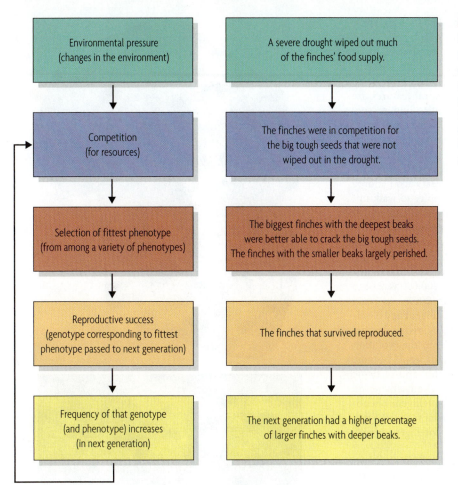

FIGURE 3.1 How Natural Selection Works

Environmental changes create competition for resources among species members. Only those individuals possessing characteristics instrumental in coping with these changes will survive and reproduce. The next generation will have a greater number of individuals possessing these genetically based traits.

therefore evolve in response to different environmental events. However, contemporary research on evolution has uncovered examples of new species that have emerged without that type of geographic isolation (Fitzpatrick et al., 2008). Researchers are pursuing a variety of explanations for how species arise under those circumstances. For example, some subsets of Darwin's finches are more likely to mate with finches that are physically similar to them. Such mating patterns may lead to the emergence of new species (Hendry et al., 2009).

Genotypes and Phenotypes   Let's return our focus to the forces that bring about change within an existing species. The example of the ebb and flow of finch populations demonstrates why Darwin characterized the course of evolution as *survival of the fittest*. Imagine that each environment poses some range of difficulties for each species of living beings. Those members of the species who possess the range of physical and psychological attributes best adapted to the environment are most likely to survive. To the extent that the attributes that foster survival can be passed from one generation to another—and stresses in the environment endure over time—the species is likely to evolve.

To examine the process of natural selection in more detail, I must introduce some of the vocabulary of evolutionary theory. Let us focus on an individual finch. At conception, that finch inherited a **genotype**, or genetic structure, from its parents. In the context of a particular environment, this genotype determined the finch's development and behavior. The

outward appearance and repertory of behaviors of the finch are known as its **phenotype**. For our finch, its genotype may have interacted with the environment to yield the phenotype of *small beak* and *ability to peck smaller seeds*.

If seeds of all types were plentiful, this phenotype would have no particular bearing on the finch's survival. Suppose, however, that the environment provided insufficient seeds to feed the whole population of finches. In that case, the individual finches would be in *competition* for resources. When species function in circumstances of competition, phenotypes help determine which individual members are better adapted to ensure survival. Recall our finch with a small beak. If only small seeds were available, our finch would be at a *selective advantage* with respect to finches with large beaks. If only large seeds were available, our finch would be at a disadvantage.

Only finches that survive can reproduce. Only those animals that reproduce can pass on their genotypes. Therefore, if the environment continued to provide only small seeds, over several generations the finches would probably come to have almost exclusively small beaks—with the consequence that they would be almost exclusively capable of eating only small seeds. In this way, forces in the environment can shape a species' repertory of possible behaviors. **Figure 3.1** provides a simplified

genotype The genetic structure an organism inherits from its parents.

phenotype The observable characteristics of an organism, resulting from the interaction between the organism's genotype and its environment.

model of the process of natural selection. Let us now apply these ideas to human evolution.

Human Evolution By looking backward to the circumstances in which the human species evolved, you can begin to understand why certain physical and behavioral features are part of the biological endowment of the entire human species. In the evolution of our species, natural selection favored two major adaptations—bipedalism and encephalization. Together, they made possible the rise of human civilization. *Bipedalism,* which refers to the ability to walk upright, emerged in our evolutionary ancestors 5 to 7 million years ago (Thorpe et al., 2007). As our ancestors evolved the ability to walk upright, they were able to explore new environments and exploit new resources. *Encephalization* refers to increases in brain size. Early human ancestors, who emerged about 4 million years ago (for example, *Australopithecus*), had brains roughly the same size as those of chimpanzees (see **Figure 3.2**). In the time from 1.9 million years ago *(Homo erectus)* to 200,000 years ago *(Homo sapiens),* brain size tripled (Gibbons, 2007). As brain size increased, our ancestors became more intelligent and developed capacities for complex thinking, reasoning, remembering, and planning (Sherwood et al., 2008). However, the evolution of a bigger brain did not guarantee that humans would become more intelligent—what was important was the kind of tissue that developed and expanded within the brain (Ramachandran, 2011). The genotype coding for mobile and intelligent phenotypes slowly squeezed out other, less well-adapted genotypes from the human gene pool, affording only intelligent bipeds the opportunity to reproduce.

After bipedalism and encephalization, perhaps the most important evolutionary milestone for our species was the advent of *language* (Sherwood et al., 2008). Think of the tremendous adaptive advantages that language conferred on early humans. Simple instructions for making tools, finding a good hunting or fishing spot, and avoiding danger would save time, effort, and lives. Instead of learning every one of life's lessons firsthand, by trial and error, humans could benefit from experiences shared by others. Conversation, even humor, would strengthen the social bonds among members of a naturally gregarious species. Most important, the advent of language would provide for the transmission of accumulated wisdom, from one generation to future generations.

Language is the basis for *cultural evolution,* which is the tendency of cultures to respond adaptively, through learning, to environmental change (Ramachandran, 2011). Cultural evolution has given rise to major advances in toolmaking, improved agricultural practices, and the development and refinement of industry and technology. Cultural evolution allows our species to make very rapid adjustments to changes in environmental conditions. Adaptations to the use of personal computers, for example, have arisen in only the past few decades. Even so, cultural evolution could not occur without genotype coding for the capacities to learn and to think abstractly. Culture—including art, literature, music, scientific knowledge, and philanthropic activities—is possible only because of the potential of the human genotype.

Variation in the Human Genotype

You have seen that the conditions in which humans evolved favored the evolution of important shared biological potential: for example, bipedalism and the capacity for thought and

FIGURE 3.2 Increases in Brain Size across Human Evolution

Early in human evolution, brain size doubled from *Australopithecus* (top) to *Homo erectus* (middle). Over the course of evolution, increases continued so that the brains of modern humans, *Homo sapiens* (bottom), are three times larger than those of *Australopithecus*.

FIGURE 3.3 Genetic Material

The nucleus of each cell in your body contains a copy of the chromosomes that transmit your genetic inheritance. Each chromosome contains a long strand of DNA arranged in a double helix. Genes are segments of the DNA that contain instructions for the production of the proteins that guide your individual development.

From Lefton, Lester A.; Brannon, Linda, *Psychology*, 8th Edition, © 2003. Printed and electronically reproduced by permission of Pearson Education Inc., Upper Saddle River, New Jersey.

Nucleus

A SINGLE CELL

A CHROMOSOME

A SEGMENT OF DNA

language. There remains, however, considerable variation within that shared potential. Your mother and father have endowed you with a part of what their parents, grandparents, and all past generations of their family lines have given them, resulting in a unique biological blueprint and timetable for your development. The study of the mechanisms of **heredity**—the inheritance of physical and psychological traits from ancestors—is called **genetics** (Carlson, 2004).

The earliest systematic research exploring the relationship between parents and their offspring was published in 1866 by **Gregor Mendel** (1822–1884). Mendel's studies were carried out on the humble garden pea. He was able to demonstrate that the physical features of peas that emerged from different seeds—for example, whether the peas appeared *round* or *wrinkled*—could be predicted from the physical features of the plants from which the seeds had been obtained. Based on his observations, Mendel suggested that pairs of "factors"—one inherited from each parent—determined the properties of the offspring (Lander & Weinberg, 2000). Although Mendel's work originally received little attention from other scientists, modern techniques have allowed researchers to visualize and study Mendel's "factors," which we now call *genes*.

Much of this section will focus on **human behavior genetics,** a research field that unites genetics and psychology to explore the causal link between inheritance and behavior (Kim, 2009). The study of human behavior genetics most often focuses on the origins of individual differences: What factors in your individual genetic inheritance help to explain the way you think and behave? To complement human behavior genetics, two other fields have emerged that take a broader focus on how forces of natural selection affected the behavioral repertory of humans and other species. Researchers in the field of **sociobiology** provide evolutionary explanations for the social behavior and social systems of humans and other animal species. Researchers in **evolutionary psychology** extend those evolutionary explanations to include other aspects of human experience, such as how the mind functions. This chapter focuses on individual differences. However, as *Psychology and Life* unfolds, we'll consider instances in which the evolutionary perspective sheds light on shared human experience.

These examples range from partner choices in relationships (Chapter 11) to emotional expression (Chapter 12).

Let's start with some basic principles of genetics.

Basic Genetics In the nucleus of each of your cells is genetic material called **DNA (deoxyribonucleic acid;** see **Figure 3.3**). DNA is organized into tiny units, called **genes**. Genes contain the instructions for the production of proteins. These proteins regulate the body's physiological processes and the expression of phenotypic traits: body build, physical strength, intelligence, and many behavior patterns.

Genes are found on rodlike structures known as *chromosomes*. At the very instant you were conceived, you inherited from your parents 46 chromosomes—23 from your mother and 23 from your father. Each of these chromosomes contains thousands of genes—the union of a sperm and an egg results in only one of many billion possible gene combinations. The **sex chromosomes** are those that contain genes coding for development of male or female physical characteristics. You inherited an X chromosome from your mother and either an X or a Y chromosome from your father. An XX combination codes for development of female characteristics; an XY combination codes for development of male characteristics.

....

heredity The biological transmission of traits from parents to offspring.

genetics The study of the inheritance of physical and psychological traits from ancestors.

human behavior genetics The area of study that evaluates the genetic component of individual differences in behaviors and traits.

sociobiology A field of research that focuses on evolutionary explanations for the social behavior and social systems of humans and other animal species.

evolutionary psychology The study of behavior and mind using the principles of evolutionary theory.

DNA (deoxyribonucleic acid) The physical basis for the transmission of genetic information.

gene The biological unit of heredity; discrete section of a chromosome responsible for transmission of traits.

sex chromosome Chromosome that contains the genes that code for the development of male or female characteristics.

Human chromosomes—at the moment of conception, you inherited 23 from your mother and 23 from your father.

The pairs of genes you inherited—one from your mother and one from your father—provide the genetic starting point for most physical and psychological attributes. In many cases, there are different versions of a particular gene. Your phenotype is determined by the versions you inherited. Consider what happens when people come in contact with poison ivy: One version of a gene makes them immune to its allergic effects; the other version of the same gene will have them breaking out in a rash. However, the gene that makes people immune is the *dominant* version of the gene, whereas the gene that makes people susceptible is the *recessive* version. When people inherit different versions of a gene, the dominant gene wins out. If your skin responds badly to poison ivy, you likely inherited two recessive genes. A range of other physical traits (such as the color of your eyes and hair or the breadth of your lips) is determined by dominant and recessive genes.

As we begin to consider the genetic basis of more complex aspects of human experience, it is important to note that more than one pair of genes contributes to a particular attribute. These characteristics are known as **polygenic traits** because more than one gene influences the phenotype. For example, Chapter 15 will discuss the genetic basis of psychological disorders. For each disorder, research suggests that more than one gene influences which individuals will be at risk (Keller & Miller, 2006).

Beginning in 1990, the U.S. government funded an international effort called the *Human Genome Project (HGP)*. The **genome** of an organism is the full sequence of genes found on the chromosomes with the associated DNA. In 2003, the HGP achieved the goal of providing a complete sequencing of the human genome. With that information in hand, researchers have now turned their attention to identifying all 20,500 human genes (Clamp et al., 2007). The ultimate goal is to provide a complete account of the location and functions of that full set of genes.

Heritability To achieve the goal of understanding the functions of genes, research in human behavior genetics often focuses on estimating the **heritability** of particular human traits and behaviors. Heritability is measured on a scale of 0 to 1. If an estimate is near 0, it suggests that the attribute is largely a product of environmental influences; if an estimate is near 1, it suggests that the attribute is largely a product of genetic influences.

To separate environmental influences from genetic influences, researchers often use *adoption studies* or *twin studies*. For adoption studies, researchers obtain as much information as possible about the birth parents of children who are raised in adoptive homes. As the children develop, researchers assess the relative similarity of children to their birth families—representing genetics—and their adoptive families—representing environment.

In twin studies, researchers examine the extent to which *monozygotic (MZ)* twins (also called *identical twins*) and *dizygotic (DZ)* twins (also called *fraternal twins*) show similarity within pairs on particular traits or behaviors. MZ twins arise from a single fertilized egg. Historically, researchers believed that MZ twins share 100 percent of their genetic material. However, recent evidence suggests that factors both before and after birth often make "identical" twins less than genetically identical (Silva et al., 2011). Even so, MZ twins have more genetic overlap than DZ twins, who share roughly 50 percent of their genetic material. (DZ twins are no more genetically alike than any other pair of brothers and sisters.) Researchers compute heritability estimates by determining how much more alike MZ twins are than DZ twins on a particular attribute. Consider a twin study that assessed genetic impact on people's coffee consumption.

Featured Study

The study focused on a large sample of 2,252 MZ twins and 2,243 DZ twins from the Netherlands (Vink et al., 2009). The twins completed a survey that asked them to estimate the number of cups of caffeinated coffee they drank each day and also the number of cups of tea. The researchers found that MZ twins were more similar in the habits: For each comparison, the correlations were higher for MZ twins than for DZ twins. The researchers' statistical analyses yielded a "moderate" heritability estimate of 0.39 for coffee consumption. In addition, the twins' preference for coffee over tea yielded a "rather large" estimate of 0.62.

Are you part of a family that starts each day with a large cup of coffee—and can hardly stand the thought of tea? These data support the idea that some part of that behavior is explained by genes. In fact, researchers have begun to take the next step, to try to identify the actual genes that influence coffee consumption. Two independent studies have converged on the conclusion that important variation occurs among genes that affect individuals' ability to metabolize caffeine (Cornelis et al., 2011; Sulem et al., 2011). One group of researchers speculated that some gene variants might allow people to consume more coffee because their body eliminates caffeine

----

polygenic trait Characteristic that is influenced by more than one gene.

genome The genetic information for an organism, stored in the DNA of its chromosomes.

heritability The relative influence of genetics—versus environment—in determining patterns of behavior.

more efficiently (Sulem et al., 2011). This example of the heritability of coffee consumption illustrates the evolution of contemporary research. Scientists try to move from a statement of fact (for example, "Coffee consumption is heritable") to an understanding of why that fact is true (for example, "Variation in particular genes affects individuals' ability to clear their bodies of caffeine").

The ability of researchers to associate genes with behavior points to some of the ethical issues that have arisen in the wake of the Human Genome Project's successes (Wilkinson, 2010). For example, a variety of techniques already allow prospective parents to choose to have a boy or a girl. Should they be willing and able to make that choice? How about choices with respect to a child's intelligence level, sports ability, or criminal inclinations? As the HGP and related efforts continue to yield new insights, such ethical questions will become increasingly prominent in debates over public policy.

You've learned that researchers are often able to estimate the heritability of important aspects of human experience. Let's now see why environments are critical as well.

Interactions of Genes and Environments This chapter began with a contrast between nature and nurture as causal forces in people's lives. However, researchers have increasingly come to document that both genetics and environments play critical roles to determine organisms' behaviors. Let's consider an example in which the circumstances in which children are raised have a major impact on the consequences of the genes they inherited.

The study followed a group of children from ages 15 months to 67 months (Kochanska et al., 2011). With respect to genetics, the study assessed differences in a gene that affects the neurotransmitter serotonin (see page 59). The gene comes in short (s) and long (l) forms. The study contrasted children who inherited two long versions (ll) to children who acquired at least one short version (sl and ss). With respect to environments, the study assessed differences in the way the mothers treated their children. When the children were ages 15, 25, 38, and 52 months, the researchers observed them interacting with their mothers in a variety of naturalistic settings (for example, daily chores and play). The main measure was how responsive the mothers were to their children's needs in each setting. At age 67 months, the researchers assessed the children's school competence (combining measures such as reading and math ability). Figure 3.4 demonsrates the joint impact of genes and environment. For children born with at least one short variant of the gene, the mothers' responsiveness had a considerable impact: More maternal responsiveness led to greater school competence. However, for children born with two long variants of the gene, the mothers' responsiveness had virtually no impact on the children's outcomes.

Suppose you want to predict a child's school competence. As you look at Figure 3.4, make sure you understand why it wouldn't be enough to have information just about genetics or just about the environment.

From this example you can see why researchers seek to understand how and why certain environments allow genes

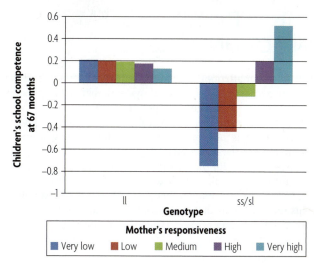

FIGURE 3.4 Genes and Environment Interact to Yield Children's School Competence

Children in this study inherited either two long versions (ll) of a gene or at least one short version (ss and sl). They also experienced varying levels of maternal responsiveness. The children's school competence is the product of both genetics and environment. For example, children with the ll genotype who experienced very low maternal responsiveness were equally as competent as children with an ss or sl genotype who experienced high maternal responsiveness.

Data from Grazyna Kochanska, Sanghag Kim, Robin A. Barry and Robert A. Philibert, Children's genotypes interact with maternal responsive care in predicting children's competence, *Development and Psychopathology*, May 23, 2011, pp. 605–616.

to be expressed and certain genes affect the importance of the environment. We are going to return to this important concept of interactions of genes and environments in later chapters. Here are two examples: In Chapter 9, you'll see how genes and environments interact with respect to intellectual abilities; in Chapter 10, you'll encounter another instance in which parenting and genes intereact to affect children's outcomes. As you encounter each of these examples, it should become increasingly clear to you that the answer is very rarely nature *or* nurture. Rather, you will see how behavior is often the joint product of nature *and* nurture.

Stop *and* Review

① How does the Grants' research on finches illustrate the role of genetic variation in the process of evolution?
② What is the difference between a genotype and a phenotype?
③ What were two evolutionary advances most critical in human evolution?
④ What is meant by heritability?

CRITICAL THINKING Consider the study that evaluated maternal responsiveness. Why might the researchers have sampled behavior at several points in time?

 Study and **Review** on **MyPsychLab**

THE NERVOUS SYSTEM IN ACTION

Let's turn our attention now to the remarkable products of the human genotype: the biological systems that make possible the full range of thought and performance. Researchers who pursue these natural laws are called *neuroscientists*. Today, **neuroscience** is one of the most rapidly growing areas of research. Important discoveries come with astonishing regularity. The objective for the remainder of this chapter is to explore how the information available to your senses is ultimately communicated throughout your body and brain by nerve impulses. This section begins that exploration by discussing the properties of the basic unit of the nervous system, the neuron.

The Neuron

A **neuron** is a cell specialized to receive, process, and/or transmit information to other cells within the body. Neurons vary in shape, size, chemical composition, and function, but all neurons have the same basic structure (see **Figure 3.5**). There are between 100 billion and 1 trillion neurons in your brain.

Neurons typically take in information at one end and send out messages from the other. The part of the cell that receives incoming signals is a set of branched fibers called **dendrites**, which extend outward from the cell body. The basic job of the dendrites is to receive stimulation from sense receptors or other neurons. The cell body, or **soma**, contains the nucleus of the cell and the cytoplasm that sustains its life. The soma integrates information about the stimulation received from the dendrites (or in some cases received directly from another neuron) and passes it on to a single, extended fiber, the **axon**. In turn, the axon conducts this information along its length—which, in the spinal cord, can be several feet and, in the brain, less than a millimeter. At the other end of axons are swollen, bulblike structures called **terminal buttons**, through which the neuron is able to stimulate nearby glands, muscles, or other neurons. Neurons generally transmit information in only one direction: from the dendrites through the soma to the axon to the terminal buttons (see **Figure 3.6**).

There are three major classes of neurons. **Sensory neurons** carry messages from sense receptor cells *toward* the central

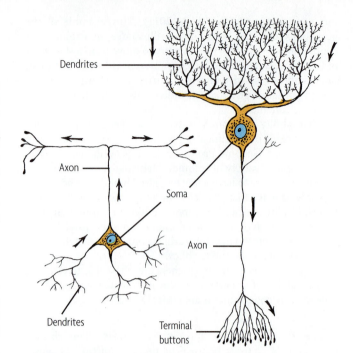

FIGURE 3.5 Two Types of Neurons
Note the differences in shape and dendritic branching. Arrows indicate directions in which information flows. Both cells are types of interneurons.

nervous system. Receptor cells are highly specialized cells that are sensitive, for example, to light, sound, and body position. **Motor neurons** carry messages *away* from the central nervous system toward the muscles and glands. The bulk of the neurons in the brain are **interneurons**, which relay messages from sensory neurons to other interneurons or to motor neurons. For every motor neuron in the body there are as many as 5,000 interneurons in the great intermediate network that forms the computational system of the brain.

As an example of how these three kinds of neurons work together, consider the pain withdrawal reflex (see **Figure 3.7**). When pain receptors near the skin's surface are stimulated by a sharp object, they send messages via sensory neurons to an

....

👁 **Watch** the **Video** *The Basics: How the Brain Works? Part 1* on **MyPsychLab**

neuroscience The scientific study of the brain and of the links between brain activity and behavior.

neuron A cell in the nervous system specialized to receive, process, and/or transmit information to other cells.

dendrite One of the branched fibers of neurons that receive incoming signals.

soma The cell body of a neuron, containing the nucleus and cytoplasm.

axon The extended fiber of a neuron through which nerve impulses travel from the soma to the terminal buttons.

terminal button A bulblike structure at the branched ending of an axon that contains vesicles filled with neurotransmitters.

sensory neuron Neuron that carries messages from sense receptors toward the central nervous system.

motor neuron Neuron that carries messages away from the central nervous system toward the muscles and glands.

interneuron Brain neuron that relays messages from sensory neurons to other interneurons or to motor neurons.

A neuron that affects contractions in the human intestine. What are the roles of the dendrites, soma, and axons in neural transmission?

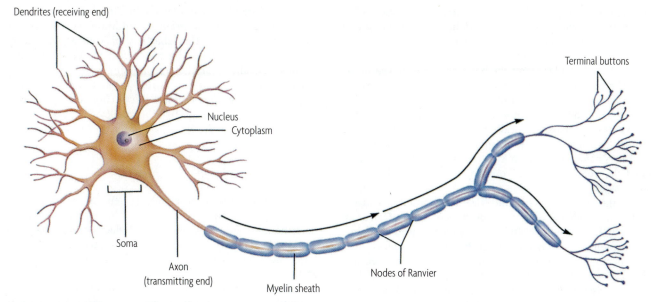

FIGURE 3.6 The Major Structures of the Neuron
The neuron receives nerve impulses through its dendrites. It then sends the nerve impulses through its axon to the terminal buttons, where neurotransmitters are released to stimulate other neurons.

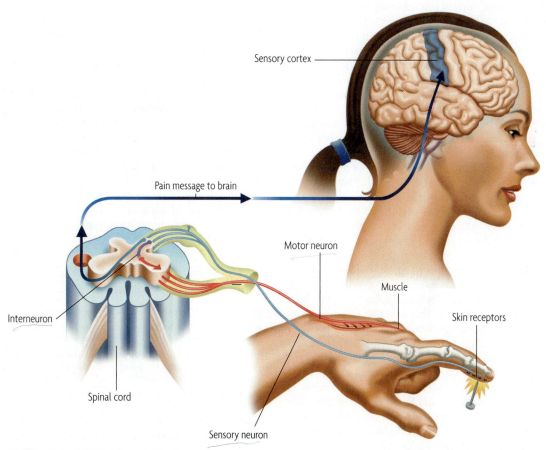

FIGURE 3.7 The Pain Withdrawal Reflex
The pain withdrawal reflex shown here involves only three neurons: a sensory neuron, a motor neuron, and an interneuron.

interneuron in the spinal cord. The interneuron responds by stimulating motor neurons, which, in turn, excite muscles in the appropriate area of the body to pull away from the pain-producing object. It is only *after* this sequence of neuronal events has taken place, and the body has been moved away from the stimulating object, that the brain receives information about the situation. In cases such as this, where survival depends on swift action, your perception of pain often occurs after you have physically responded to the danger. Of course, then the information from the incident is stored in the brain's memory system so that the next time you will avoid the potentially dangerous object altogether, before it can hurt you.

In the mid-1990s, **Giacomo Rizzolatti** and his colleagues made an accidental discovery of a new type of neuron (Rizolatti & Sinigaglia, 2010). The researchers were studying the function of motor neurons in the brains of macaques. Their work demonstrated that some neurons were active when the monkeys actually performed motor actions. However, they were surprised to discover that some neurons also fired when the monkeys only observed a researcher performing the same action! The researchers called these neurons **mirror neurons** because they respond when an individual observes another individual performing an action. Although the evidence is indirect (because researchers cannot conduct the same sorts of studies with humans that they conduct with monkeys), there is substantial evidence that mirror neurons are also at work in humans' brains. Mirror neurons may enable us to understand the *intentions* of other people's behavior. Imagine you see your friend Josh's hand moving toward a ball. As that happens, "your own ball-reaching neurons start firing. By running this virtual simulation of being Josh, you get the immediate impression that he is intending to reach for the ball" (Ramachandran, 2011, p. 128). Thus, mirror neurons allow you to use your own experiences to make sense of other people's behavior (Sinigaglia & Rizzolatti, 2011). These neurons may have afforded humans great ability to learn through imitation, which allowed for efficient cultural evolution. Such claims about the broad influence of mirror neurons on human achievement have led to an explosion of research.

Interspersed among the brain's vast web of neurons are about 5 to 10 times as many glial cells (**glia**). The word *glia* is derived from the Greek word for *glue*, which gives you a hint of one of the major duties performed by these cells: They hold neurons in place. In vertebrates, glial cells have several other important functions (Kettenmann & Verkhratsky, 2008). A first function applies during development. Glial cells help guide newborn neurons to appropriate locations in the brain. A second function is housekeeping. When neurons are damaged and die, glial cells in the area multiply and clean up the cellular junk left behind; they can also take up excess neurotransmitters and other substances at the gaps between neurons. A third function is insulation. Glial cells form an insulating cover, called a **myelin sheath**, around some types of axons. This fatty insulation greatly increases the speed of nerve signal conduction. A fourth function of glial cells is to prevent toxic substances in the blood from reaching the delicate cells of the brain. Specialized glial cells, called astrocytes, make up a *blood–brain barrier,* forming a continuous envelope of fatty material around the blood vessels in the brain. Substances that are not soluble in fat do not dissolve through this barrier, and because many poisons and other harmful substances are not fat soluble, they cannot penetrate the barrier to reach the brain. In addition, neuroscientists have come to believe that glia may play an active role in neural communication. Glia may affect the concentrations of ions that allow for the transmission of nerve impulses (Henneberger & Rusakov, 2010). In addition, some glia may generate the same types of electrochemical signals that neurons generate (Káradóttir et al., 2008). The next section discusses those signals. ✳

Action Potentials

So far, I have spoken loosely about neurons "sending messages" or "stimulating" each other. The time has come to describe more formally the kinds of electrochemical signals used by the nervous system to process and transmit information. These signals are the basis of all you know, feel, desire, and create.

This is the basic question asked of each neuron: Should it or should it not *fire*—produce a response—at some given time? In loose terms, neurons make this decision by combining the information arriving at their dendrites and soma (cell body) and determining whether those inputs are predominantly saying "fire" or "don't fire." More formally, each neuron will receive a balance of **excitatory**—fire!—and **inhibitory**—don't fire!—**inputs**. In neurons, the right pattern of excitatory inputs over time or space will lead to the production of an *action potential:* The neuron fires.

The Biochemical Basis of Action Potentials To explain how an **action potential** works, you need to appreciate the biochemical environment in which neurons draw together incoming information. All neural communication is produced by the flow of electrically charged particles, called *ions,* through the neuron's membrane, a thin "skin" separating the cell's internal and external environments. Think of a nerve fiber as a piece of macaroni, filled with salt water, floating in a salty soup. The soup and the fluid in the macaroni both contain ions—atoms of sodium ($Na+$), chloride ($Cl-$), and potassium ($K+$)—that have either positive ($+$) or negative ($-$) charges (see **Figure 3.8**). The membrane, or the surface of the macaroni, plays a critical role in keeping the ingredients of the two fluids in an appropriate balance. When a cell is inactive, or in a resting state, there is a greater concentration of potassium ions inside the axon and a greater concentration of sodium ions outside the

....

✳ **Explore** the **Concept** *Virtual Brain: Neural Conduction* on **MyPsychLab**

mirror neuron Neuron that responds when an individual observes another individual performing a motor action.

glia The cells that hold neurons together and facilitate neural transmission, remove damaged and dead neurons, and prevent poisonous substances in the blood from reaching the brain.

myelin sheath Insulating material that surrounds axons and increases the speed of neural transmission.

excitatory input Information entering a neuron that signals it to fire.

inhibitory input Information entering a neuron that signals it not to fire.

action potential The nerve impulse activated in a neuron that travels down the axon and causes neurotransmitters to be released into a synapse.

In a resting state, the fluid surrounding the axon has a different concentration of ions than the fluid inside the axon. For that reason, the fluid within the cell is *polarized* with respect to the exterior fluid, providing the neuron's resting potential.

When a nerve impulse arrives at a segment of the axon, positively charged sodium ions flow into the axon. The inflow of sodium causes the nerve cell to become *depolarized*. The nerve impulse is passed down the axon as each successive segment becomes depolarized.

Once the nerve impulse has been passed along, sodium ions flow back out of the axon to restore the resting potential.

Once the resting potential is restored, the segment of the axon is ready to transmit another impulse.

FIGURE 3.8 The Biochemical Basis of Action Potentials

Action potentials rely on an imbalance of the electrical charge of the ions present inside and outside of axons.

From Lefton, Lester A.; Brannon, Linda, *Psychology*, 8th Edition, © 2003. Printed and electronically reproduced by permission of Pearson Education Inc., Upper Saddle River, New Jersey.

axon. The membrane is not a perfect barrier; it "leaks" a little, allowing some sodium ions to slip in while some potassium ions slip out. To correct for this, nature has provided transport mechanisms within the membrane that pump out sodium and pump in potassium. Successful operation of these sodium-potassium pumps leaves the fluid inside a neuron with a slightly negative voltage (70/1,000 of a volt) relative to the fluid outside. This means that the fluid inside the cell is *polarized* with respect to the fluid outside the cell. This slight polarization is called the **resting potential**. It provides the electrochemical context in which a nerve cell can produce an action potential.

The nerve cell begins the transition from a resting potential to an action potential in response to the pattern of inhibitory and excitatory inputs. Each kind of input affects the likelihood that the balance of ions from the inside to the outside of the cell will change. They cause changes in the function of **ion channels**, excitable portions of the cell membrane that selectively permit certain ions to flow in and out. Inhibitory inputs cause the ion channels to work harder to keep the inside of the cell negatively charged—this will keep the cell from firing. Excitatory inputs cause the ion channels to begin to allow sodium ions to flow in—this will allow the cell to fire. Because sodium ions have a positive charge, their influx can begin to change the relative balance of positive and negative charges across the cell membrane. An action potential begins when the excitatory inputs are sufficiently strong with respect to inhibitory inputs to *depolarize* the cell from −70 millivolts to −55 millivolts: Sufficient sodium has entered the cell to effect this change.

Once the action potential begins, sodium rushes into the neuron. As a result, the inside of the neuron becomes positive relative to the outside, meaning the neuron has become fully depolarized. A domino effect now propels the action potential down the axon. The leading edge of depolarization causes ion channels in the adjacent region of the axon to open and allow sodium to rush in. In this way—through successive depolarization—the signal passes down the axon (see Figure 3.8).

How does the neuron return to its original resting state of polarization after it fires? When the inside of the neuron becomes positive, the channels that allow sodium to flow in close and the channels that allow potassium to flow out open. The outflow of potassium ions restores the negative charge of the neuron. Thus, even while the signal is reaching the far end of the axon, the portions of the cell in which the action potential originated are being returned to their resting balance, so that they can be ready for their next stimulation.

Properties of the Action Potential   The biochemical manner in which the action potential is transmitted leads to several important properties. The action potential obeys the **all-or-none law**: The size of the action potential is unaffected by increases in the intensity of stimulation beyond the threshold level. Once excitatory inputs sum to reach the threshold level, a uniform action potential is generated. If the threshold is not

resting potential The polarization of cellular fluid within a neuron, which provides the capability to produce an action potential.

ion channel A portion of neurons' cell membranes that selectively permits certain ions to flow in and out.

all-or-none law The rule that the size of the action potential is unaffected by increases in the intensity of stimulation beyond the threshold level.

FIGURE 3.9 **Timetable for Electrical Changes in the Neuron during an Action Potential**

Sodium ions entering the neuron cause its electrical potential to change from slightly negative during its polarized, or resting, state to slightly positive during depolarization. Once the neuron is depolarized, it enters a brief refractory period during which further stimulation will not produce another action potential. Another action potential can occur only after the ionic balance between the inside and the outside of the cell is restored.

reached, no action potential occurs. An added consequence of the all-or-none law is that the size of the action potential does not diminish along the length of the axon. In this sense, the action potential is said to be *self-propagating;* once started, it needs no outside stimulation to keep itself moving. It's similar to a lit fuse on a firecracker.

Different neurons conduct action potentials along their axons at different speeds; the fastest have signals that move at the rate of 200 meters per second, the slowest plod along at 10 centimeters per second. The axons of the faster neurons are covered with a tightly wrapped myelin sheath—consisting, as noted earlier, of glial cells—making this part of the neuron resemble short tubes on a string. The tiny breaks between the tubes are called *nodes of Ranvier* (see Figure 3.6). In neurons having myelinated axons, the action potential literally skips along from one node to the next—saving the time and energy required to open and close ion channels at every location on the axon. Damage to the myelin sheath throws off the delicate timing of the action potential and causes serious problems. Multiple sclerosis (MS) is a devastating disorder caused by deterioration of the myelin sheath. It is characterized by double vision, tremors, and eventually paralysis. In MS, specialized cells from the body's immune system actually attack myelinated neurons, exposing the axon and disrupting normal synaptic transmission (Wu & Alvarez, 2011).

After an action potential has passed down a segment of the axon, that region of the neuron enters a **refractory period** (see **Figure 3.9**). During the *absolute refractory period,* further stimulation, no matter how intense, cannot cause another action potential to be generated; during the *relative refractory period,*

the neuron will fire only in response to a stimulus stronger than what is ordinarily necessary. Have you ever tried to flush the toilet while it is filling back up with water? There must be a critical level of water for the toilet to flush again. Similarly, for a neuron to be able to generate another action potential, it must "reset" itself and await stimulation beyond its threshold. The refractory period ensures, in part, that the action potential will travel in only one direction down the axon: It cannot move backward because "earlier" parts of the axon are in a refractory state.

Synaptic Transmission

When the action potential completes its leapfrog journey down the axon to a terminal button, it must pass its information along to the next neuron. But no two neurons ever touch: They are joined at a **synapse**, with a small gap between the *presynaptic membrane* (the terminal button of the sending neuron) and the *postsynaptic membrane* (the surface of a dendrite or soma of a receiving neuron). When the action potential reaches the terminal button, it sets in motion a series of events called **synaptic transmission**, which is the relaying of information from one neuron to another across the synaptic gap (see **Figure 3.10**). Synaptic transmission begins when the arrival of the action potential at the terminal button causes small round packets, called *synaptic*

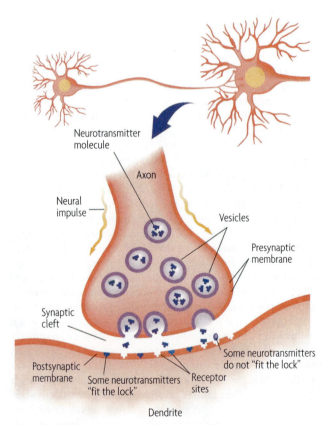

FIGURE 3.10 **Synaptic Transmission**

The action potential in the presynaptic neuron causes neurotransmitters to be released into the synaptic gap. Once across the gap, they stimulate receptor molecules embedded in the membrane of the postsynaptic neuron. Multiple neurotransmitters can exist within the same cell.

refractory period The period of rest during which a new nerve impulse cannot be activated in a segment of an axon.

synapse The gap between one neuron and another.

synaptic transmission The relaying information from one neuron to another across the synaptic gap.

vesicles, to move toward and affix themselves to the interior membrane of the terminal button. Inside each vesicle are **neurotransmitters**, biochemical substances that stimulate other neurons. The action potential also causes ion channels to open, allowing calcium ions into the terminal button. The influx of calcium ions causes the rupture of the synaptic vesicles and the release of whatever neurotransmitters they contain. Once the synaptic vesicles rupture, the neurotransmitters are dispersed rapidly across the *synaptic cleft,* the gap between the terminal button of one neuron and the cell membrane of the next. To complete synaptic transmission, the neurotransmitters attach to *receptor molecules* embedded in the postsynaptic membrane.

The neurotransmitters will bind to the receptor molecules under two conditions. First, no other neurotransmitters or other chemical substances can be attached to the receptor molecule. Second, the shape of the neurotransmitter must match the shape of the receptor molecule—as precisely as a key fits into a keyhole. If either condition is not met, the neurotransmitter will not attach to the receptor molecule. This means that it will not be able to stimulate the postsynaptic membrane. If the neurotransmitter does become attached to the receptor molecule, then it may provide "fire" or "don't fire" information to this next neuron. Once the neurotransmitter has completed its job, it detaches from the receptor molecule and drifts back into the synaptic gap. There it is either decomposed through the action of enzymes or reabsorbed into the presynaptic terminal button for quick reuse.

Depending on the receptor molecule, a neurotransmitter will have either an excitatory or an inhibitory effect. That is, the same neurotransmitter may be excitatory at one synapse but inhibitory at another. Each neuron integrates the information it obtains at synapses with between 1,000 and 10,000 other neurons to decide whether it ought to initiate another action potential. It is the integration of these thousands of inhibitory and excitatory inputs that allows all-or-none action potentials to provide the foundation for all human experience.

You may be wondering why we've taken this trip so deep into the nervous system. After all, this is a psychology course, and psychology is supposed to be about behavior and thinking and emotion. In fact, synapses are the biological medium in which all of these activities occur. If you change the normal activity of the synapse, you change how people behave, how they think, and how they feel. Understanding the functioning of the synapse has led to tremendous advances in the understanding of learning and memory, emotion, psychological disorders, drug addiction, and, in general, the chemical formula for mental health. You will use the knowledge you have acquired in this chapter throughout *Psychology and Life.*

Neurotransmitters and Their Functions

Dozens of chemical substances are known or suspected to function as neurotransmitters in the brain. The neurotransmitters that have been studied most intensively meet a set of technical criteria. Each is manufactured in the presynaptic terminal button and is released when an action potential reaches that terminal. The neurotransmitter's presence in the synaptic cleft produces a biological response in the postsynaptic membrane; and, if its release is prevented, no subsequent responses can occur. To give you a sense of the effects different neurotransmitters have on the regulation of behavior, I will discuss a set

that has been found to play an important role in the daily functioning of the brain. This brief discussion will also enable you to understand many of the ways in which neural transmission can go awry. 👁

Acetylcholine *Acetylcholine* is found in both the central and peripheral nervous systems. Memory loss among patients suffering from Alzheimer's disease, a degenerative disease that is increasingly common among older persons, is believed to be caused by the deterioration of neurons that secrete acetylcholine (Craig et al., 2011). Acetylcholine is also excitatory at junctions between nerves and muscles, where it causes muscles to contract. A number of toxins affect the synaptic actions of acetylcholine. For example, botulinum toxin, often found in food that has been preserved incorrectly, poisons an individual by preventing release of acetylcholine in the respiratory system. This poisoning, known as *botulism,* can cause death by suffocation. Curare, a poison Amazon Indians use on the tips of their blowgun darts, paralyzes lung muscles by occupying critical acetylcholine receptors, preventing the normal activity of the transmitter.

GABA *GABA* (gamma-aminobutyric acid) is the most common inhibitory neurotransmitter in the brain. GABA may be used as a messenger in as many as a third of all brain synapses. Neurons that are sensitive to GABA are particularly concentrated in brain regions such as the thalamus, hypothalamus, and occipital lobes (see pages 68–69). GABA appears to play a critical role in some forms of psychopathology by inhibiting neural activity. When levels of this neurotransmitter in the brain become low, people may experience anxiety or depression (Croarkin et al., 2011; Kalueff & Nutt, 2007). Anxiety disorders are often treated with *benzodiazepine* drugs, such as *Valium* or *Xanax,* that increase GABA activity. The *benzodiazepine* drugs do not attach directly to GABA receptors. Instead they allow GABA itself to bind more effectively to postsynaptic receptor molecules.

Glutamate Glutamate is the brain's most common excitatory neurotransmitter. Because glutamate helps transmit information within the brain, it plays a critical role in processes of emotional response, learning, and memory (Morgado-Bernal, 2011). Learning proceeds more slowly when glutamate receptors are not functioning properly. In addition, disruptions of brain levels of glutamate have been associated with various psychological disorders, including schizophrenia (Bustillo et al., 2011). Glutamate also plays a role in addictions to drugs, alcohol, and nicotine. Researchers are beginning to explore the possibilities of treatments for these addictions that alter the brain's use of glutamate (Markou, 2007; Myers et al., 2011).

Dopamine, Norepinephrine, and Serotonin The *catecholamines* are a class of chemical substances that include two important neurotransmitters, *norepinephrine* and *dopamine.* Both have been shown to play prominent roles in psychological

....

👁 **Watch** the **Video** *In the Real World: Too Much, or Too Little, of a Good Thing* on **MyPsychLab**

neurotransmitter Chemical messenger released from a neuron that crosses the synapse from one neuron to another, stimulating the postsynaptic neuron.

Roughly 1.5 million people in the United States, including the actor Michael J. Fox, are impaired by Parkinson's disease. Research on the neurotransmitter dopamine has led to advances in understanding this disease. How does basic research in neuroscience allow for improved treatments?

disorders such as anxiety disorders, mood disorders, and schizophrenia (Goddard et al., 2010; Keshavan et al., 2011). Drugs that increase brain levels of norepinephrine elevate mood and relieve depression. Conversely, higher-than-normal levels of dopamine have been found in persons with schizophrenia. As you might expect, one way to treat people with this disorder is to give them a drug that decreases brain levels of dopamine. We'll revisit these drug treatments in Chapter 15.

All the neurons that produce *serotonin* are located in the brain stem (see p. 67), which is involved in arousal and many autonomic processes. The hallucinogenic drug LSD (lysergic acid diethylamide) appears to produce its effects by suppressing the effects of serotonin neurons (Fantegrossi et al., 2008). These serotonin neurons normally inhibit other neurons, but the lack of inhibition produced by LSD creates vivid and bizarre sensory experiences, some of which last for hours. As we'll see in Chapter 14, abnormal levels of serotonin in the brain are associated with mood disorders. For example, reduced levels of serotonin may lead to depression. That's why many antidepressant drugs, such as *Prozac,* enhance the action of serotonin by preventing it from being removed from the synaptic cleft. 👁

....

👁 **Watch** the **Video** *What's In It For Me?: Your Brain on Drugs* on **MyPsychLab**

neuromodulator Any substance that modifies or modulates the activities of the postsynaptic neuron.

Endorphins The *endorphins* are a group of chemicals that are usually classified as neuromodulators. A **neuromodulator** is any substance that modifies or modulates the activities of the postsynaptic neuron. Endorphins (short for *endogenous morphines*) play an important role in the control of emotional behaviors (anxiety, fear, tension, pleasure) and pain—drugs like opium and morphine bind to the same receptor sites in the brain. Endorphins have been called the "keys to paradise" because of their pleasure–pain controlling properties. Researchers have examined the possibility that endorphins are at least partially responsible for the pain-reducing effects of acupuncture and placebos (Han, 2011; Pollo et al., 2011). Such tests rely on the drug *naloxone,* whose only known effect is to block morphine and endorphins from binding to receptors. Any procedure that reduces pain by stimulating release of endorphins becomes ineffective when naloxone is administered. With the injection of naloxone, acupuncture and placebos do, in fact, lose their power—suggesting that, ordinarily, endorphins help them do their work.

Stop *and* Review

① What is the pattern of information flow through the major parts of each neuron?
② What is meant by the "all-or-none law"?
③ How do neurotransmitters pass from one neuron to the next?
④ What chemical substance is the most common inhibitory neurotransmitter in the brain?

✔● **Study** and **Review** on **MyPsychLab**

BIOLOGY AND BEHAVIOR

You now have an understanding of the basic mechanisms that allow nerve cells to communicate. The time has come to assemble those neurons into the larger systems that guide your body and mind. This discussion begins with an overview of the techniques researchers use to hasten new discoveries. Next, we turn to a general description of the structure of the nervous system, followed by a more detailed look at the brain itself. I discuss the activity of the endocrine system, a second biological control system that works in cooperation with your nervous system and brain. Finally, we'll consider ways in which your life experiences continue to modify your brain.

Eavesdropping on the Brain

Neuroscientists seek to understand how the brain works at a number of different levels—from the operation of large structures visible to the naked eye to the properties of individual nerve cells visible only under powerful microscopes. The techniques researchers use are suited to their level of analysis. Here, you'll encounter the techniques that have been used most often to attribute functions and behaviors to particular regions of the brain.

Interventions in the Brain Several research methods in neuroscience involve direct intervention with structures in

HOW DOES YOUR BRAIN DETERMINE TRUST?

Suppose a friend makes you a promise and says, "Trust me!" Should you? In recent years, researchers have begun to understand how your brain responds when you have to make decisions about trust. Much of that research has concentrated on the hormone *oxytocin*. Oxytocin first became the focus of researchers who were interested in the biological mechanisms that prompt nonhuman animals to form social bonds. Contemporary research suggests that the hormone plays a broad role in personal and social processes (IsHak et al., 2011). Let's consider trust.

To document the dramatic impact of oxytocin, a team of researchers recruited participants to play a game that focused on trust (Baumgartner et al., 2008). The game required two players to distribute a pool of "money units." In each round, the *investor* had to decide how many money units, out of 12, to invest. The experimenters provided the *trustee* with returns on those investments. The trustee then had the opportunity to share those returns fairly with the investor or not. In fact, halfway through the game, the investors all got the same feedback: The experimenters told them that they were getting their fair share only about half the time. The trustees could not be trusted!

What happened in the second half of the game depended on the investors' levels of oxytocin. Before the game started, half the investors received a dose of the hormone through a nasal spray. (Once it is absorbed, the hormone is able to cross into the brain.) The other participants received a placebo. For the first half of the game, it made little difference what investors had inhaled. The figure plots the average number of money units participants invested in each round. As you can see, before the feedback, oxytocin participants invested nearly the same amount as placebo participants. You might expect that the dramatic feedback—Don't trust this person!—would prompt participants to reduce their investments. That's exactly what the placebo group did. Their investments fell for the second half of the game. However, the oxytocin group didn't reduce their investments. In fact, the trend was in the opposite

direction. Apparently, the preexperimental dose of oxytocin prevented participants from acting on the information that the other players had violated their trust.

There's one more element to this project: While the investors were making their decisions they were undergoing fMRI scans. Those brain data enabled the researchers to determine what brain areas the dose of oxytocin affected. The scans revealed that oxytocin participants showed less activity in regions of the brain, such as the amygdala, that are involved in fear responses. The researchers suggested that, by dampening fear responses, oxytocin increases participants' ability "to trust in situations characterized by the risk of betrayal" (Baumgartner et al., 2008, p. 645).

After reading about this study, you might wonder whether your brain chemistry predisposes you to trust or distrust your friend. Researchers are starting to consider exactly that question of how individual differences in oxytocin function may have an important impact on social behavior (Bartz et al., 2011).

Data from J. A. Bartz & E. Hollander, The neuroscience of affiliation: Forging links between basic and clinical research on neuropeptides and social behavior, *Hormones and Behavior, 50*, pp. 518–528.

the brain. These methods find their historical roots in circumstances like the story of railroad foreman Phineas Gage, who in September 1848 suffered an accident in which a 3-foot, 7-inch-long pole was blown, as the result of an unexpected explosion, clear through his head. Gage's physical impairment was remarkably slight: He lost vision in his left eye, and the left side of his face was partially paralyzed, but his posture, movement, and speech were all unimpaired. Yet, psychologically, he was a changed man, as his doctor's account made clear:

> The equilibrium or balance, so to speak, between his intellectual faculties and animal propensities seems to have been destroyed. He is fitful, irreverent, indulging at times in the grossest profanity (which was not previously his custom), manifesting but little deference for his fellows, impatient of restraint or advice when it conflicts with his desires. . . . Previous to his injury, though untrained in schools, he possessed a well-balanced mind, and was looked upon by those who knew him as a shrewd, smart businessman, very energetic and persistent in executing all his plans of operation. In this regard his mind was radically changed, so decidedly that his friends and acquaintances said he was "no longer Gage." (Harlow, 1868, pp. 339–340)

Phineas Gage is shown holding the pole that caused his injury. Why were doctors so fascinated by Gage's changes in personality?

application of intense heat, cold, or electricity. As you would guess, experimental work with permanent lesions is carried out exclusively with nonhuman animals. (Recall the discussion in Chapter 2 that the ethics of this type of animal research has now come under heightened scrutiny.) Our conception of the brain has been radically changed as researchers have repeatedly compared and coordinated the results of lesioning experiments on animals with the growing body of clinical findings on the effects of brain damage on human behavior.

In recent years, scientists have developed a procedure called **repetitive transcranial magnetic stimulation (rTMS)** that uses pulses of magnetic stimulation to create temporary, reversible "lesions" in human participants—without any damage being done to tissue, brain regions can be briefly inactivated. This new technique enables researchers to address a range of questions that would not have been possible with nonhuman experiments (Sandrini et al., 2011). Consider an application of rTMS to study how your brain responds to nouns and verbs.

If you've spent any time studying languages, you're likely aware that nouns and verbs serve very different functions. A team of researchers used rTMS to test the hypothesis that different brain regions are at work when you produce the two parts of speech (Cappelletti et al., 2008). In the experiment, participants completed simple phrases presented by computer. For example, participants would read, "today I walk," and then complete, "yesterday I . . ." Similarly, they would read "one child," and then complete "many. . . ." Under ordinary circumstances, participants should be relatively quick to respond "walked" and "children." Suppose, however, that the researchers are able to use rTMS to "lesion" brain regions that help make these responses possible. Then, we'd expect participants' responses to be slowed down. In fact, the researchers identified one brain region (in the vicinity of Broca's area) that, when stimulated by rTMS, yielded slower performance for verbs but not for nouns. These data support the hypothesis that your brain processes make distinctions between nouns and verbs.

Featured Study

Gage's injury came at a time when scientists were just beginning to form hypotheses about the links between brain functions and complex behavior. The behavioral changes following the dramatic piercing of his brain prompted his doctor to hypothesize brain bases for aspects of personality and rational behavior.

At about the same time that Gage was convalescing from his injury, **Paul Broca** was studying the brain's role in language. His first research in this area involved an autopsy of a man whose name was derived from the only word he had been able to speak, "Tan." Broca found that the left front portion of Tan's brain had been severely damaged. This finding led Broca to study the brains of other persons who suffered from language impairments. In each case, Broca's work revealed similar damage to the same area of the brain, a region now known as **Broca's area**. As you will see as *Psychology and Life* unfolds, contemporary researchers still attempt to correlate patterns of behavior change or impairment with the sites of brain damage.

The problem with studying accidentally damaged brains, of course, is that researchers have no control over the location and extent of the damage. To produce a well-founded understanding of the brain and its relationship to behavioral and cognitive functioning, scientists need methods that allow them to specify precisely the brain tissue that has been incapacitated. Researchers have developed a variety of techniques to produce **lesions**, highly localized brain injuries. They may, for example, surgically remove specific brain areas, cut the neural connections to those areas, or destroy those areas through

You can see why this experiment would not be possible with nonhuman participants: Humans are the only species that habitually produces nouns and verbs.

On other occasions, neuroscientists learn about the function of brain regions by directly *stimulating* them. For example, in the mid-1950s, **Walter Hess** (1881–1973) pioneered the use of electrical stimulation to probe structures deep in the brain. For example, Hess put electrodes into the brains of freely moving cats. By pressing a button, he could then send a small electrical current to the point of the electrode. Hess carefully recorded the behavioral consequences of stimulating each of 4,500 brain sites in nearly 500 cats. Hess discovered that, depending on the location of the electrode, sleep, sexual arousal, anxiety, or terror could be provoked by the flick of the switch—and turned off just as abruptly. For example, electrical stimulation of certain regions of the brain led the otherwise gentle cats to bristle with rage and hurl themselves on a nearby object.

Recording and Imaging Brain Activity Other neuroscientists map brain function by using electrodes to record the electrical activity of the brain in response to environmental

---

Broca's area The region of the brain that translates thoughts into speech or signs.

lesion Injury to or destruction of brain tissue.

repetitive transcranial magnetic stimulation (rTMS) A technique for producing temporary inactivation of brain areas using repeated pulses of magnetic stimulation.

stimulation. The brain's electrical output can be monitored at different levels of precision. At the most specific, researchers can insert ultrasensitive microelectrodes into the brain to record the electrical activity of a single brain cell. Such recordings can illuminate changes in the activity of individual cells in response to stimuli in the environment.

For human subjects, researchers often place a number of electrodes on the surface of the scalp to record larger, integrated patterns of electrical activity. These electrodes provide the data for an **electroencephalogram (EEG),** or an amplified tracing of the brain activity. EEGs can be used to study the relationship between psychological activities and brain response. For example, in one experiment, researchers used EEGs to demonstrate that people's brains respond differently when they view emotionally charged images (Hajcak & Olvet, 2008). While their brain activity was being recorded, participants viewed a series of pleasant (e.g., smiling faces), neutral (e.g., household objects), and unpleasant (e.g., violent images) pictures on a computer screen. The EEGs revealed distinct patterns for the neutral versus emotional pictures: Participants appeared to devote more attention to the pleasant and unpleasant pictures, and that greater attention lingered even after the pictures left the computer screen.

Some of the most exciting technological innovations for studying the brain are machines originally developed to help neurosurgeons detect brain abnormalities, such as damage caused by strokes or diseases. These devices produce images of the living brain without invasive procedures that risk damaging brain tissue.

To obtain three-dimensional images of the brain, researchers may use **computerized axial tomography (CT or CAT).** When an individual undergoes a CT scan, his or her head is placed in a doughnut-shaped ring that contains an X-ray source and an X-ray detector. During the scan, focused X-ray beams pass through the individual's head from several different angles. The computer assembles those separate X-ray images into coherent pictures of the brain. Researchers often

What can psychologists learn by looking at PET scans?

use CT scans to determine the location and extent of brain damage or brain abnormalities.

In research with **positron emission tomography,** or **PET,** subjects are given different kinds of radioactive (but safe) substances that eventually travel to the brain, where they are taken up by active brain cells. Recording instruments outside the skull can detect the radioactivity emitted by cells that are active during different cognitive or behavioral activities. This information is then fed into a computer that constructs a dynamic portrait of the brain, showing where different types of psychological activities are actually occurring.

Magnetic resonance imaging, or **MRI,** uses magnetic fields and radio waves to generate pulses of energy within the brain. As the pulse is tuned to different frequencies, some atoms line up with the magnetic field. When the magnetic pulse is turned off, the atoms vibrate (resonate) as they return to their original positions. Special radio receivers detect this resonance and channel information to a computer, which generates images of the locations of different atoms in areas of the brain. By looking at the image, researchers can link brain structures to psychological processes.

....

electroencephalogram (EEG) A recording of the electrical activity of the brain.

computerized axial tomography (CT or CAT) A technique that uses narrow beams of X-rays passed through the brain at several angles to assemble complete brain images.

positron emission tomography (PET) scan Brain image produced by a device that obtains detailed pictures of activity in the living brain by recording the radioactivity emitted by cells during different cognitive or behavioral activities.

magnetic resonance imaging (MRI) A technique for brain imaging that scans the brain using magnetic fields and radio waves.

How have new imaging techniques expanded the range of questions researchers can ask?

Magnetic resonance imaging (MRI) produces this color-enhanced profile of a normal brain. What is the purpose of trying to identify brain regions that underlie particular functions?

MRI is most useful for providing clear images of anatomical details; PET scans provide better information about function. A newer technique called **functional MRI**, or **fMRI**, combines some of the benefits of both techniques by detecting magnetic changes in the flow of blood to cells in the brain; fMRI allows more precise claims about both structure and function. Researchers have begun to use fMRI to discover the distributions of brain regions responsible for many of your most important cognitive abilities, such as attention, perception, language processing, and memory (Spiers & Maguire, 2007).

As you've just learned, cultural evolution has provided neuroscientists with the technology necessary to reveal some

functional MRI (fMRI) A brain-imaging technique that combines benefits of both MRI and PET scans by detecting magnetic changes in the flow of blood to cells in the brain.

central nervous system (CNS) The part of the nervous system consisting of the brain and spinal cord.

peripheral nervous system (PNS) The part of the nervous system composed of the spinal and cranial nerves that connect the body's sensory receptors to the CNS and the CNS to the muscles and glands.

somatic nervous system The subdivision of the peripheral nervous system that connects the central nervous system to the skeletal muscles and skin.

autonomic nervous system (ANS) The subdivision of the peripheral nervous system that controls the body's involuntary motor responses by connecting the sensory receptors to the central nervous system (CNS) and the CNS to the smooth muscle, cardiac muscle, and glands.

of your brain's most important secrets. The remainder of this chapter describes some of those secrets.

The Nervous System

The nervous system is composed of billions of highly specialized nerve cells, or *neurons,* that constitute the brain and the nerve fibers found throughout the body. The nervous system is subdivided into two major divisions: the **central nervous system (CNS)** and the **peripheral nervous system (PNS)**. The CNS is composed of all the neurons in the brain and spinal cord; the PNS is made up of all the neurons forming the nerve fibers that connect the CNS to the body. **Figures 3.11** (on page 66) and **3.12** (on page 67) show the relationship of the CNS to the PNS.

The job of the CNS is to integrate and coordinate all bodily functions, process all incoming neural messages, and send out commands to different parts of the body. The CNS sends and receives neural messages through the *spinal cord,* a trunk line of neurons that connects the brain to the PNS. The trunk line itself is housed in a hollow portion of the vertebral column called the spinal column. Spinal nerves branch out from the spinal cord between each pair of vertebrae in the spinal column, eventually connecting with sensory receptors throughout the body and with muscles and glands. The spinal cord coordinates the activity of the left and right sides of the body and is responsible for simple fast-action reflexes that do not involve the brain. For example, an organism whose spinal cord has been severed from its brain can still withdraw its limb from a painful stimulus. Although an intact brain would normally be notified of such action, the organism can complete the action without directions from above. Damage to the nerves of the spinal cord can result in paralysis of the legs or trunk, as seen in paraplegic individuals. The extent of paralysis depends on how high up on the spinal cord the damage occurred; higher damage produces greater paralysis.

Despite its commanding position, the CNS is isolated from any direct contact with the outside world. It is the role of the PNS to provide the CNS with information from sensory receptors, such as those found in the eyes and ears, and to relay commands from the brain to the body's organs and muscles. The PNS is actually composed of two sets of nerve fibers (see Figure 3.12). The **somatic nervous system** regulates the actions of the body's skeletal muscles. For example, imagine you are typing an e-mail. The movement of your fingers over the keyboard is managed by your somatic nervous system. As you decide what to say, your brain sends commands to your fingers to press certain keys. Simultaneously, the fingers send feedback about their position and movement to the brain. If you strike the wrong key (th**w**), the somatic nervous system informs the brain, which then issues the necessary correction, and, in a fraction of a second, you delete the mistake and hit the right key (th**e**).

The other branch of the PNS is the **autonomic nervous system (ANS)**, which sustains basic life processes. This system is on the job 24 hours a day, regulating bodily functions that you usually don't consciously control, such as respiration, digestion, and arousal. The ANS must work even when you are asleep, and it sustains life processes during anesthesia and prolonged coma states.

The autonomic nervous system deals with survival matters of two kinds: those involving threats to the organism and those involving bodily maintenance. To carry out these functions, the autonomic nervous system is further subdivided into

Central nervous system

Peripheral nervous system

FIGURE 3.11 Divisions of the Central and Peripheral Nervous Systems

The sensory and motor nerve fibers that constitute the peripheral nervous system are linked to the brain by the spinal cord.

Reprinted by permission of Richard McAnulty.

the sympathetic and parasympathetic nervous systems (see Figure 3.12). These divisions work in opposition to accomplish their tasks. The **sympathetic division** governs responses to emergency situations; the **parasympathetic division** monitors the routine operation of the body's internal functions. The sympathetic division can be regarded as a troubleshooter. In an emergency or stressful situation, it arouses the brain structures that prepare the organism either to fight the threat or flee from it—a pattern of activity called the *fight-or-flight response*. Digestion stops, blood flows away from internal organs to the muscles, oxygen transfer increases, and heart rate increases. After the danger is over, the parasympathetic division takes charge, and the individual begins to calm down. Digestion resumes, heartbeat slows, and breathing is relaxed. The parasympathetic division carries out the body's nonemergency housekeeping chores, such as elimination of bodily wastes, protection of the visual system (through tears and pupil constriction), and long-term conservation of body energy. The separate duties of the sympathetic and parasympathetic nervous systems are illustrated in **Figure 3.13** on page 66.

Brain Structures and Their Functions

The brain is the most important component of your central nervous system. The brains of human beings have three interconnected layers. In the deepest recesses of the brain, in a region called the *brain stem,* are structures involved primarily with autonomic processes such as heart rate, breathing, swallowing, and digestion. Enveloping this central core is the *limbic system,* which is involved with motivation, emotion, and memory processes. Wrapped around these two regions is the *cerebrum.* The universe of the human mind exists in this region. The cerebrum, and its surface layer, the *cerebral cortex,* integrates sensory information, coordinates your movements, and facilitates abstract thinking and reasoning (see **Figure 3.14** on page 67). Let's look

sympathetic division The subdivision of the autonomic nervous system that deals with emergency response and the mobilization of energy.

parasympathetic division The subdivision of the autonomic nervous system that monitors the routine operation of the body's internal functions and conserves and restores body energy.

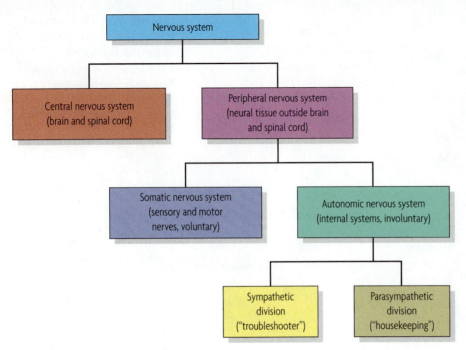

FIGURE 3.12 Hierarchical Organization of the Human Nervous System

The central nervous system is composed of the brain and the spinal cord. The peripheral nervous system is divided according to function: The somatic nervous system controls voluntary actions, and the autonomic nervous system regulates internal processes. The autonomic nervous system is subdivided into two systems: The sympathetic nervous system governs behavior in emergency situations, and the parasympathetic nervous system regulates behavior and internal processes in routine circumstances.

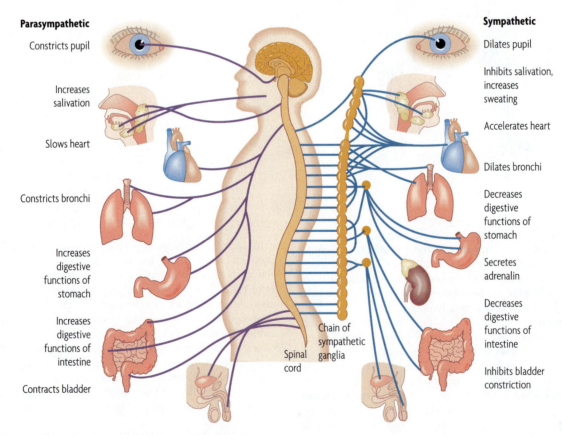

FIGURE 3.13 The Autonomic Nervous System

The parasympathetic nervous system, which regulates day-to-day internal processes and behavior, is shown on the left. The sympathetic nervous system, which regulates internal processes and behavior in stressful situations, is shown on the right. Note that on their way to and from the spinal cord, the nerve fibers of the sympathetic nervous system innervate, or make connections with, ganglia, which are specialized clusters of neuron chains.

Limbic system: regulates emotions and motivated behavior

Cerebral cortex: involved in complex mental processes

Limbic system

Hypothalamus: manages the body's internal state

Cerebellum: regulates coordinated movement

Brain stem: sets brain's general alertness level and warning system

Spinal cord: pathway for neural fibers traveling to and from brain

Thalamus: relays sensory information

Thalamus

Brain stem and cerebellum

FIGURE 3.14 Brain Structures

The brain contains several major components, including the brain stem, cerebellum, limbic system, and cerebral cortex, all of which fit together in an intricate design.

more closely at the functions of the three major brain regions, beginning with the brain stem, thalamus, and cerebellum. 👁

The Brain Stem, Thalamus, and Cerebellum   The **brain stem** is found in all vertebrate species. It contains structures that collectively regulate the internal state of the body (see **Figure 3.15**). The **medulla**, located at the very top of the spinal cord, is the center for breathing, blood pressure, and the beating of the heart. Because these processes are essential for life, damage to the medulla can be fatal. Nerve fibers ascending from the body and descending from the brain cross over at the medulla, which means that the left side of the body is linked to the right side of the brain and the right side of the body is connected to the left side of the brain.

Directly above the medulla is the **pons**, which provides inputs to other structures in the brain stem and to the cerebellum (*pons* is the Latin word for *bridge*). The **reticular formation** is a dense network of nerve cells that serves as the brain's sentinel. It arouses the cerebral cortex to attend to new stimulation and keeps the brain alert even during sleep. Massive damage to this area often results in a coma.

....

👁 **Watch** the **Video** *The Basics: How the Brain Works Part 2* on **MyPsychLab**

brain stem The brain structure that regulates the body's basic life processes.

medulla The region of the brain stem that regulates breathing, waking, and heartbeat.

pons The region of the brain stem that connects the spinal cord with the brain and links parts of the brain to one another.

reticular formation The region of the brain stem that alerts the cerebral cortex to incoming sensory signals and is responsible for maintaining consciousness and awakening from sleep.

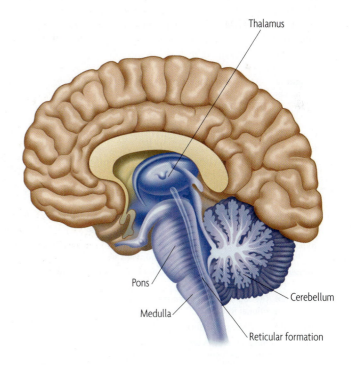

Thalamus

Pons

Medulla

Cerebellum

Reticular formation

FIGURE 3.15 The Brain Stem, Thalamus, and Cerebellum

These structures are primarily involved in basic life processes: breathing, pulse, arousal, movement, balance, and simple processing of sensory information.

The reticular formation has long tracts of fibers that run to the **thalamus**, which channels incoming sensory information to the appropriate area of the cerebral cortex, where that information is processed. For example, the thalamus relays information from the eyes to cortical areas for vision.

Neuroscientists have long known that the **cerebellum**, attached to the brain stem at the base of the skull, coordinates bodily movements, controls posture, and maintains equilibrium. Damage to the cerebellum interrupts the flow of otherwise smooth movement, causing it to appear uncoordinated and jerky. However, more recent research suggests a more diverse range of functions for the cerebellum. For example, the cerebellum plays an important role in the ability to learn and perform sequences of body movements (Bellebaum & Daum, 2011; Timmann et al., 2010). Evidence is also accumulating that the cerebellum is involved in some higher cognitive functions such as language processing and the experience of pain (Moulton et al., 2010; Murdoch, 2010).

The Limbic System The **limbic system** mediates motivated behaviors, emotional states, and memory processes. It also regulates body temperature, blood pressure, and blood-sugar level and performs other housekeeping activities. The limbic system comprises three structures: the hippocampus, amygdala, and hypothalamus (see **Figure 3.16**).

The **hippocampus**, which is the largest of the limbic system structures, plays an important role in the acquisition of memories (Wang & Morris, 2010). Considerable clinical evidence supports this conclusion, including the notable studies of a patient, H.M., perhaps psychology's most famous subject. When he was 27, H.M. underwent surgery in an attempt to reduce the frequency and severity of his epileptic seizures. During the operation, parts of his hippocampus were removed. As a result, H.M.'s memory performance was completely altered. H.M. served as a gracious participant for 50 years of

....

thalamus The brain structure that relays sensory impulses to the cerebral cortex.

cerebellum The region of the brain attached to the brain stem that controls motor coordination, posture, and balance as well as the ability to learn control of body movements.

limbic system The region of the brain that regulates emotional behavior, basic motivational urges, and memory, as well as major physiological functions.

hippocampus The part of the limbic system that is involved in the acquisition of explicit memory.

amygdala The part of the limbic system that controls emotion, aggression, and the formation of emotional memory.

hypothalamus The brain structure that regulates motivated behavior (such as eating and drinking) and homeostasis.

homeostasis Constancy or equilibrium of the internal conditions of the body.

cerebrum The region of the brain that regulates higher cognitive and emotional functions.

cerebral cortex The outer surface of the cerebrum.

cerebral hemispheres The two halves of the cerebrum, connected by the corpus callosum.

corpus callosum The mass of nerve fibers connecting the two hemispheres of the cerebrum.

frontal lobe Region of the brain located above the lateral fissure and in front of the central sulcus; involved in motor control and cognitive activities.

research. When he passed away in 2008, he left a remarkable legacy of critical information about brain function.

Let's consider aspects of H.M.'s experience. Long after his surgery, he continued to believe he was living in 1953, which was the year the operation was performed. If H.M. had encountered information frequently before the surgery, he was able to recall that information. However, after the surgery, he was able to acquire new information only if it was "massively repeated" (MacKay et al., 2007, p. 388). H.M. was able to acquire new skills (such as drawing figures from their mirror images) but he did not recall having participated in the training sessions. The damage to H.M.'s hippocampus also had consequences for his ability to produce and understand language (MacKay et al., 2011). Thus, research with H.M. provided extensive evidence about the broader function of the hippocampus beyond its role in the acquisition of particular types of memories. In Chapter 7, we will return to the functions of the hippocampus for memory acquisition.

The **amygdala** plays a role in emotional control. Because of this control function, damage to areas of the amygdala may have a calming effect on otherwise mean-spirited individuals. (Chapter 15 discusses *psychosurgery*.) However, damage to some areas of the amygdala also impairs the ability to recognize when facial expressions communicate negative emotions such as sadness and fear (Adolphs & Tranel, 2004). The amygdala also plays a critical role in the formation and retrieval of memories with emotional content (Murty et al. 2011). For that reason, people with amygdala damage often have difficulty making correct decisions in situations that have an emotional component—such as responses to winning or losing money (Gupta et al., 2011).

The **hypothalamus** is one of the smallest structures in the brain, yet it plays a vital role in many of your most important daily actions. It is actually composed of several nuclei, small bundles of neurons that regulate physiological processes involved in motivated behavior (including eating, drinking, temperature regulation, and sexual arousal). The hypothalamus maintains the body's internal equilibrium, or **homeostasis**. When the body's energy reserves are low, the hypothalamus is involved in stimulating the organism to find food and to eat. When body temperature drops, the hypothalamus causes blood vessel constriction, or minute involuntary movements you commonly refer to as "shivering." The hypothalamus also regulates the activities of the endocrine system.

The Cerebrum In humans, the **cerebrum** dwarfs the rest of the brain, occupying two thirds of its total mass. Its role is to regulate the brain's higher cognitive and emotional functions. The outer surface of the cerebrum, made up of billions of cells in a layer about a tenth of an inch thick, is called the **cerebral cortex**. The cerebrum is also divided into two almost symmetrical halves, the **cerebral hemispheres** (a later section of the chapter discusses the two hemispheres at length). The two hemispheres are connected by a thick mass of nerve fibers, collectively referred to as the **corpus callosum**. This pathway sends messages back and forth between the hemispheres.

Neuroscientists have mapped the brain to define four areas, or lobes, for each hemisphere (see **Figure 3.17**). The **frontal lobe**, involved in motor control and cognitive activities, such as planning, making decisions, and setting goals, is located above the lateral fissure and in front of the central sulcus.

FIGURE 3.16 The Limbic System

The structures of the limbic system, which are present only in mammals, are involved in motivated behavior, emotional states, and memory processes.

Hypothalamus
Amygdala
Hippocampus

Accidents that damage the frontal lobes can have devastating effects on human action and personality. This was the location of the injury that brought about such a dramatic change in Phineas Gage (Macmillan, 2008). The frontal lobe also includes *Broca's area,* the region of the brain that Paul Broca identified from his research on patients with language disorders.

The **parietal lobe,** responsible for sensations of touch, pain, and temperature, is located directly behind the central sulcus. The **occipital lobe,** the final destination for visual information, is located at the back of the head. The **temporal lobe,** responsible for the processes of hearing, is found below the lateral fissure, on the sides of each cerebral hemisphere. The temporal lobe includes a region called **Wernicke's area.** In 1874, **Carl Wernicke** (1848–1905) discovered that patients who had damage to this region produced speech that was fluent but meaningless and had disrupted language comprehension.

It would be misleading to say that any lobe alone controls any one specific function. The structures of the brain perform their duties in concert, working smoothly as an integrated unit, similar to a symphony orchestra. Whether you are doing the dishes, solving a calculus problem, or carrying on a conversation with a friend, your brain works as a unified whole, each lobe interacting and cooperating with the others. Nevertheless, neuroscientists can identify areas of the four lobes of the cerebrum that are necessary for specific functions, such as vision,

hearing, language, and memory. When they are damaged, their functions are disrupted or lost entirely.

The actions of the body's voluntary muscles, of which there are more than 600, are controlled by the **motor cortex,** located just in front of the central sulcus in the frontal lobes. Recall that commands from one side of the brain are directed to muscles

....

parietal lobe Region of the brain behind the frontal lobe and above the lateral fissure; contains somatosensory cortex.

occipital lobe Rearmost region of the brain; contains primary visual cortex.

temporal lobe Region of the brain found below the lateral fissure; contains auditory cortex.

Wernicke's area A region of the brain that allows fluent speech production and comprehension.

motor cortex The region of the cerebral cortex that controls the action of the body's voluntary muscles.

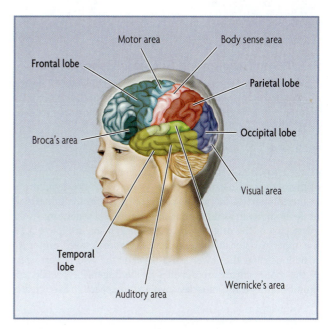

FIGURE 3.17 The Cerebral Cortex

Each of the two hemispheres of the cerebral cortex has four lobes. Different sensory and motor functions are associated with specific parts of each lobe

A. Primary motor

Primary
motor

Primary
somatosensory

Primary
auditory
and auditory
association areas

Primary visual
(buried deep in
rear of brain)

B. Primary somatosensory

FIGURE 3.18 Motor and Somatosensory Cortex

Different parts of the body are more or less sensitive to environmental stimulation and brain control. Sensitivity in a particular region of the body is related to the amount of space in the cerebral cortex devoted to that region. In this figure, the body is drawn so that the size of body parts is relative to the cortical space devoted to them. The larger the body part in the drawing, the greater its sensitivity to environmental stimulation and the greater the brain's control over its movement.

on the opposite side of the body. Also, muscles in the lower part of the body—for example, the toes—are controlled by neurons in the top part of the motor cortex. Muscles in the upper part of the body, such as the throat, are controlled by neurons in the lower part of the motor cortex. As you can see in **Figure 3.18**, the upper parts of the body receive far more detailed motor instructions than the lower parts. In fact, the two largest areas of the motor cortex are devoted to the fingers—especially the thumb—and to the muscles involved in speech. Their greater

....

◉ **Watch** the **Video** *The Big Picture: My Brain Made Me Do It* on **MyPsychLab**

somatosensory cortex The region of the parietal lobes that processes sensory input from various body areas.

auditory cortex The area of the temporal lobes that receives and processes auditory information.

visual cortex The region of the occipital lobes in which visual information is processed.

brain area reflects the importance in human activity of manipulating objects, using tools, eating, and talking. ◉

The **somatosensory cortex** is located just behind the central sulcus in the left and right parietal lobes. This part of the cortex processes information about temperature, touch, body position, and pain. Similar to the motor cortex, the upper part of the sensory cortex relates to the lower parts of the body, and the lower part to the upper parts of the body. Most of the area of the sensory cortex is devoted to the lips, tongue, thumb, and index fingers—the parts of the body that provide the most important sensory input (see Figure 3.18). And like the motor cortex, the right half of the somatosensory cortex communicates with the left side of the body, and the left half communicates with the right side of the body.

Auditory information is processed in the **auditory cortex**, which is in the two temporal lobes. The auditory cortex in each hemisphere receives information from *both* ears. Visual input is processed at the back of the brain in the **visual cortex**, located in the occipital lobes. Here the greatest area is devoted to input from the center part of the retina, at the back of the eye, the area that transmits the most detailed visual information.

Not all of the cerebral cortex is devoted to processing sensory information and commanding the muscles to action. In fact, the majority of it is involved in *interpreting* and *integrating* information. Processes such as planning and decision making are believed to occur in the **association cortex**. Association areas are distributed to several areas of the cortex—one region is labeled in Figure 3.18. The association cortex allows you to combine information from various sensory modalities to plan appropriate responses to stimuli in the environment.

We have now considered the many important structures in your nervous system. Recall that the discussion of the cerebrum noted that each cerebral structure is represented in both hemispheres of your brain. Let's turn now to differences between your brain's two hemispheres.

Hemispheric Lateralization

What types of information originally led researchers to suspect that the functions of the brain's two hemispheres differed? Recall that when Paul Broca carried out his autopsy on Tan, he discovered damage in the left hemisphere. As he followed up this original discovery, Broca found that other patients who showed similar disruption of their language abilities—a pattern now known as *Broca's aphasia*—also had damage on the *left* side of their brains. Damage to the same areas on the *right* side of the brain did not have the same effect. What should one conclude?

The chance to investigate hemispheric differences first arose in the context of a treatment for severe epilepsy in which

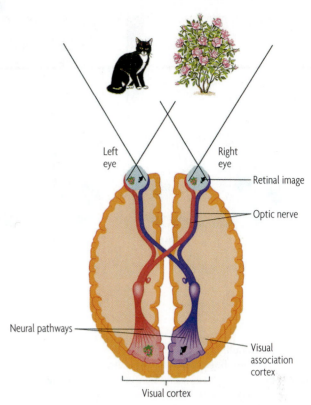

FIGURE 3.20 The Neural Pathways for Visual Information

The neural pathways for visual information coming from the inside portions of each eye cross from one side of the brain to the other at the corpus callosum. The pathways carrying information from the outside portions of each eye do not cross over. Severing the corpus callosum prevents information selectively displayed in the right visual field from entering the right hemisphere, and left visual field information cannot enter the left hemisphere.

surgeons sever the corpus callosum—the bundle of about 200 million nerve fibers that transfers information back and forth between the two hemispheres (see **Figure 3.19**). The goal of this surgery is to prevent the violent electrical activity that accompanies epileptic seizures from crossing between the hemispheres. The operation is usually successful, and a patient's subsequent behavior in most circumstances appears normal. Patients who undergo this type of surgery are often referred to as *split-brain* patients.

To test the capabilities of the separated hemispheres of epileptic patients, **Roger Sperry** (1968) and **Michael Gazzaniga** (1970) devised situations that could allow visual information to be presented separately to each hemisphere. Sperry and Gazzaniga's methodology relies on the anatomy of the visual system (see **Figure 3.20**). For each eye, information from the *right visual field* goes to the left hemisphere, and information from the *left visual field* goes to the right hemisphere. Ordinarily, information

FIGURE 3.19 The Corpus Callosum

The corpus callosum is a massive network of nerve fibers that channels information between the two hemispheres. Severing the corpus callosum impairs this communication process.

....

association cortex The parts of the cerebral cortex in which many high-level brain processes occur.

A   B

FIGURE 3.21 Testing a Split-Brain Patient

When the split-brain patient uses his left hand to find a match to an object flashed briefly in the left visual field, he is successful because both the visual and tactile (touch) information are registered in the right hemisphere, as shown in A. Nevertheless, the patient cannot name the object, because speech is mainly a left-hemisphere function. Now consider the same patient asked to perform the same task with the right hand, as shown in B. In this case, he is unsuccessful in picking out the object by touch, because the visual information and the tactile information are processed in different hemispheres. In this test, however, the patient is able to name the object in his hand!

Zimbardo, Philip G.; Johnson, Robert L.; McCann, Vivian, *Psychology: Core Concepts,* 6th Edition, © 2009. Printed and electronically reproduced by permission of Pearson Education Inc., Upper Saddle River, New Jersey.

arriving from both hemispheres is shared very quickly across the corpus callosum. But because these pathways have been severed in split-brain patients, information presented to the right or left visual field may remain only in the left or right hemisphere (see **Figure 3.21**).

Because for most people speech is controlled by the left hemisphere, the left hemisphere could "talk back" to the researchers, whereas the right hemisphere could not. Communication with the right hemisphere was achieved by confronting it with manual tasks involving identification, matching, or assembly of objects—tasks that did not require the use of words. Consider the following demonstration of a split-brain subject using his left half brain to account for the activity of his left hand, which was being guided by his right half brain.

A snow scene was presented to the right hemisphere and a picture of a chicken claw was simultaneously presented to the left hemisphere (Gazzaniga, 1985). The subject selected, from an array of objects, those that "went with" each of the two scenes. With his right hand, the patient pointed to a chicken head; with his left hand, he pointed to a shovel. The patient reported that the shovel was needed to clean out the chicken shed (rather than to shovel snow). Because the left brain was not privy to what the right brain "saw" due to the severed corpus callosum, it needed to explain why the left hand was pointing at a shovel when the only picture the left hemisphere was aware of seeing was a chicken claw. The left brain's cognitive system provided a theory to make sense of the behavior of different parts of its body.

Simulate the **Experiment** *Hemispheric Specialization* on **MyPsychLab**

From a variety of research methods in addition to split-brain studies, we now know that, for most people, many language-related functions are *lateralized* to the left hemisphere. A function is considered lateralized when one cerebral hemisphere plays the primary role in accomplishing that function. Speech—the ability to produce coherent spoken language—is perhaps the most highly lateralized of all functions. Neuroscientists have found that only about 5 percent of right-handers and 15 percent of left-handers have speech controlled by the right hemisphere; another 15 percent of left-handers have speech processes occurring in both sides of the brain (Rasmussen & Milner, 1977).

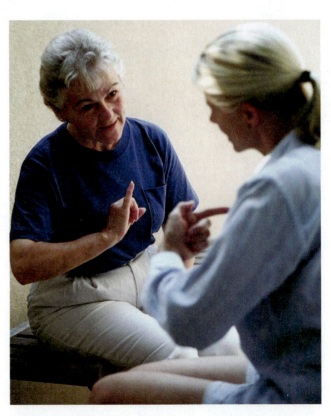

How have studies with individuals who use sign language influenced researchers' beliefs about the lateralization of brain function?

Thyroids and parathyroids

Thyroids and parathyroids

Adrenals
Pancreas

Adrenals
Pancreas

Ovaries

Testes

Pituitary

FIGURE 3.22 Endocrine Glands in Males and Females

The pituitary gland is shown at the far right; it is the master gland that regulates the glands shown at the left. The pituitary gland is under the control of the hypothalamus, an important structure in the limbic system.

For most people, therefore, speech is a left-hemisphere function. As a consequence, damage to the left side of most people's brains can cause speech disorders. What is interesting is that for users of languages like American Sign Language—which use systems of intricate hand positions and movements to convey meaning—left-brain damage is similarly disruptive (MacSweeney et al., 2008). What is lateralized, therefore, is not speech as such, but rather, the ability to produce the sequences of gestures—either vocal or manual—that encode communicative meaning.

You should not conclude that the left hemisphere is somehow better than the right hemisphere. Although the left hemisphere plays a dominant role for speech, the right hemisphere plays a dominant role for other tasks. For example, most people show greater right-hemisphere activity when they make judgments about spatial relationships and facial expressions (Badzakova-Trajkov et al., 2010). Still, it is the combined action of the right and left hemispheres that gives fullness to your experiences. For example, you might not be surprised to learn that the left hemisphere, with its greater endowment for language use, plays a key role in most forms of problem solving. However, the function of the right hemisphere becomes more apparent when problems require bursts of insight. Those individuals who show relatively greater activity in their right hemispheres are more likely to have those bursts of insight (Kounios et al., 2008).

This section reviewed the many important structures of your nervous system. Now we will consider the endocrine system, a bodily system that functions in close cooperation with the nervous system to regulate bodily functions.

The Endocrine System

The human genotype specifies a second highly complex regulatory system, the **endocrine system**, to supplement the work of the nervous system. The endocrine system is a network of glands that manufacture and secrete chemical messengers called **hormones** into the bloodstream (see **Figure 3.22**). Hormones are important in everyday functioning, although they are more vital at some stages of life and in some situations than others. Hormones influence body growth. They initiate, maintain, and stop development of primary and secondary sexual characteristics; influence levels of arousal and awareness; serve as the basis for mood changes; and regulate metabolism, the rate at which the body uses its energy stores. The endocrine system promotes the survival of an *organism* by helping fight infections and disease. It advances the survival of the *species* through regulation of sexual arousal, production of reproductive cells, and production of milk in nursing mothers. Thus you could not survive without an effective endocrine system.

Endocrine glands respond to the levels of chemicals in the bloodstream or are stimulated by other hormones or by nerve impulses from the brain. Hormones are then secreted into the blood and travel to distant target cells that have

endocrine system The network of glands that manufacture and secrete hormones into the bloodstream.

hormone One of the chemical messengers, manufactured and secreted by the endocrine glands, that regulate metabolism and influence body growth, mood, and sexual characteristics.

specific receptors; hormones exert their influence on the body's program of chemical regulation only at the places that are genetically predetermined to respond to them. In influencing diverse, but specific, target organs or tissue, hormones regulate an enormous range of biochemical processes. This multiple-action communication system allows for control of slow continuous processes such as maintenance of blood-sugar levels and calcium levels, metabolism of carbohydrates, and general body growth. But what happens during crises? The endocrine system also releases the hormone adrenaline into the bloodstream; adrenaline energizes your body so that you can respond quickly to challenges.

As you saw earlier, the brain structure known as the *hypothalamus* serves as a relay station between the endocrine system and the central nervous system. Specialized cells in the hypothalamus receive messages from other brain cells, commanding it to release a number of different hormones to the pituitary gland, where they either stimulate or inhibit the release of other hormones. Hormones are produced in several different regions of the body. These "factories" make a variety of hormones, each of which regulates different bodily processes, as outlined in **Table 3.1**. Let's examine the most significant of these processes.

The **pituitary gland** is often called the master gland, because it produces about 10 different kinds of hormones that influence the secretions of all the other endocrine glands, as

well as a hormone that influences growth. The absence of this growth hormone results in dwarfism; its excess results in gigantic growth. In males, pituitary secretions activate the testes to secrete **testosterone**, which stimulates production of sperm. The pituitary gland is also involved in the development of male secondary sexual characteristics, such as facial hair, voice change, and physical maturation. Testosterone may even increase aggression and sexual desire. In females, a pituitary hormone stimulates production of **estrogen**, which is essential to the hormonal chain reaction that triggers the release of ova from a woman's ovaries, making her fertile. Certain birth control pills work by blocking the mechanism in the pituitary gland that controls this hormone flow, thus preventing the ova from being released.

Plasticity and Neurogenesis: Our Changing Brains

You now have a good basic idea of your nervous system at work: At all times, millions of neurons are communicating to do the essential work of your body and mind. What makes the brain even more interesting, however, is one consequence of all that neural communication: The brain itself changes over time. Do you want to take a moment to change your brain? Go back a few pages and memorize the definition of *action potential*. If you are successful at learning that definition—or any other new information—you will have brought about a modification of your brain. Researchers refer to changes in the performance of the brain as **plasticity**. A good deal of research in neuroscience focuses on the physical bases for plasticity. For example, researchers examine how learning arises from the formation of new synapses or from changes in communication across existing synapses (Miyashita et al., 2008). 👁

Because brain plasticity depends on life experiences, you won't be surprised to learn that brains show the impact of different environments and activities. One line of research, pioneered by **Mark Rosenzweig,** demonstrated the consequences for rats of being raised in impoverished or enriched environments (for reviews, see Rosenzweig, 1996, 1999). Early research demonstrated an advantage for young animals: The average cortex of rats reared in the enriched environments was heavier and thicker—positive attributes—than that of their impoverished littermates. Researchers have now demonstrated that environmental enrichment continues to have an impact on the brains of adult animals.

Table 3.1 • Major Endocrine Glands and the Functions of the Hormones They Produce

These Glands:	Produce Hormones That Regulate:
Hypothalamus	Release of pituitary hormones
Anterior pituitary	Testes and ovaries
	Breast milk production
	Metabolism
	Reactions to stress
Posterior pituitary	Water conservation
	Breast milk excretion
	Uterus contraction
Thyroid	Metabolism
	Growth and development
Parathyroid	Calcium levels
Gut	Digestion
Pancreas	Glucose metabolism
Adrenals	Fight-or-flight responses
	Metabolism
	Sexual desire in women
Ovaries	Development of female sexual traits
	Ova production
Testes	Development of male sexual traits
	Sperm production
	Sexual desire in men

....

👁 **Watch** the **Video** *Brain* on **MyPsychLab**

pituitary gland Located in the brain, the gland that secretes growth hormone and influences the secretion of hormones by other endocrine glands.

testosterone The male sex hormone, secreted by the testes, that stimulates production of sperm and is also responsible for the development of male secondary sex characteristics.

estrogen The female sex hormone, produced by the ovaries, that is responsible for the release of eggs from the ovaries as well as for the development and maintenance of female reproductive structures and secondary sex characteristics.

plasticity Changes in the performance of the brain; may involve the creation of new synapses or changes in the function of existing synapses.

With brain-imaging techniques, it is possible to measure very specific brain differences related to individuals' life experiences. Consider those musicians who play the violin. They are required to control the fingers of their left hands with an extremely delicate touch. If you refer back to Figure 3.18, you'll see that a good deal of sensory cortex is devoted to the fingers. Brain scans reveal that the representation of fingers of the left hand is even more enhanced for violin players, as compared to nonplayers (Elbert et al., 1995). No such increase is found for fingers of the right hand, which do not have as great a sensory role in violin playing. The extra representation of the left fingers was greatest for violinists who took up the instrument before age 12. The *Critical Thinking in Your Life* box on page 76 explains how your cultural experience modifies your brain.

One important aspect of research on plasticity concerns circumstances in which humans or animals have sustained injuries to the brain or spinal cord, through strokes, degenerative diseases, or accidents. A good deal of clinical evidence confirms that the brain is sometimes able to heal itself. For example, patients who suffer from strokes that cause disruptions in language often recover over time. In some instances, the damaged brain areas themselves have enough lingering function that recovery is possible; in other cases other brain areas take over the functions of those that were damaged (Turkeltaub et al., 2011). Researchers have also begun to develop techniques to help the brain along in the healing process. In recent years, attention has focused on *stem cells*—unspecialized cells that, under appropriate conditions, can be prompted to function as new neurons (Li et al., 2008). Researchers hope that stem cells may ultimately provide a means to replace damaged tissue in the nervous system with new neural growth. Because the most flexible stem cells come from embryos and aborted fetuses, stem cell research

has been subject to political controversy. Still, researchers believe that stem cell research could lead to cures for paralysis and other serious malfunctions in the nervous system. For that reason, the scientific community is highly motivated to discover ways to continue research within accepted societal norms. ✳

Research on brain repair has accelerated in recent years in the face of important new data suggesting that **neurogenesis**—the production of new brain cells from naturally occurring stem cells—occurs in the brains of adult mammals, including humans (Leuner & Gould, 2010). For nearly 100 years, neuroscientists believed that the adult brains of mammals had their full supply of neurons—all that could happen over the adult years was that neurons could die out. However, the new data have challenged that view. Recall, for example, that the hippocampus is an important structure for the formation of certain types of memories. Now that researchers have documented neurogenesis in the adult hippocampus, they are trying to understand how newly born neurons provide a resource for the acquisition of new memories across the life span (Kempermann, 2008).

In this chapter, we have taken a brief peek at the marvelous 3-pound universe that is your brain. It is one thing to recognize that the brain controls behavior and your mental processes but quite another to understand how the brain serves all those functions. Neuroscientists are engaged in the fascinating quest to understand the interplay among brain, behavior, and environment. You now have the type of background that will allow you to appreciate new knowledge as it unfolds.

Stop *and* Review

① What are the advantages of fMRI over other brain-imaging techniques?
② What are the two major divisions of the autonomic nervous system?
③ What are some of the major functions of the amygdala?
④ For what activities do most people show more activity in the right hemisphere?
⑤ Why is the pituitary gland often called the master gland?
⑥ What is neurogenesis?

✓ **Study** and **Review** on **MyPsychLab**

✳ **Explore** the **Concept** *Virtual Brain: Brain Damage and Neuroplasticity* on **MyPsychLab**

neurogenesis The creation of new neurons.

Critical Thinking in Your Life

HOW DOES CULTURE BECOME "EMBRAINED"?

As *Psychology and Life* unfolds, you will have several opportunities to appreciate the impact of culture on people's behavior. Those cultural differences, of course, emerge from the activity of each individual's brain. In fact, researchers have suggested that, over the course of development, an individual's culture becomes "embrained" (Kitayama & Uskul, 2011). Let's explore that idea.

The process of embrainment begins as individuals are raised in an environment in which a particular set of values is transmitted. Those values have an impact on how people respond to a wide range of situations. For example, a good deal of cross-cultural research has demonstrated that people from Western cultures (such as the United States) most often conceptualize themselves as independent actors whereas people from Eastern cultures (such as Japan, China, and India) most often conceptualize themselves as being part of a larger group. (We'll explore this difference at greater length in Chapter 13.) This difference in conceptualization has a number of consequences for behavior.

Suppose, for example, you are given an ordinary coffee mug with your school logo. How painful would it be for you to part with it? Research suggests that the answer will depend on the culture in which you were nurtured (Maddux et al., 2010). For people from Western cultures, possessions become, in a sense, part of the self. Therefore, giving them up is like giving part of the self away. People from Eastern cultures don't have that relationship with their possessions. As such, they should experience less distress when they think about giving up a possession.

To obtain a measure of how much individuals valued a coffee mug, the researchers gave some experimental participants mugs as gifts and asked them how much someone would need to offer them before they would sell it. Other participants were shown the mugs and simply asked how much they would pay for them. Sellers from Western cultures wanted $3.24 more than what buyers thought the mug was worth. Sellers from Eastern cultures wanted just $1.60 more. This difference illustrates the way in which Western participants more highly value their possessions.

Think about all the moments in your life in which you came to acquire or give up possessions. In each case, cultural values prompt you to think about those possessions in a particular way. As those cases accumulate over time, your brain engages in repeated patterns of neural activity to execute your responses. When you read about brain plasticity, you probably weren't surprised that extensive experience with the violin changes players' brains (Elbert et al., 1995). The violinists' brains grow more efficient at carrying out the highly practiced activities. Violin playing becomes embrained. Similarly, as people repeat the behavioral responses that a culture makes available, the brain grows more efficient at producing those responses. Culture has become embrained.

- How might brain imaging techniques help you demonstrate that culture has become embrained?
- What might happen when someone grows up in a multicultural family?

Recapping Main Points

Heredity and Behavior

- Species originate and change over time because of natural selection.
- In the evolution of humans, bipedalism and encephalization were responsible for subsequent advances, including language and culture.
- The basic unit of heredity is the gene. Genes interact with environments to yield phenotypic traits.

The Nervous System in Action

- The neuron, the basic unit of the nervous system, receives, processes, and relays information to other cells, glands, and muscles.
- Neurons relay information from the dendrites through the cell body (soma) to the axon to the terminal buttons.

- Sensory neurons receive messages from specialized receptor cells and send them toward the CNS. Motor neurons direct messages from the CNS to muscles and glands. Interneurons relay information from sensory neurons to other interneurons or to motor neurons. Mirror neurons respond when an individual observes another individual performing a motor action.
- Once the summation of inputs to a neuron exceeds a specific threshold, an action potential is sent along the axon to the terminal buttons.
- All-or-none action potentials are created when the opening of ion channels allows an exchange of ions across the cell membrane.
- Neurotransmitters are released into the synaptic gap between neurons. Once they diffuse across the gap,

they lodge in the receptor molecules of the postsynaptic membrane.

- Whether these neurotransmitters excite or inhibit the membrane depends on the nature of the receptor molecule.

Biology and Behavior

- Neuroscientists use several methods to research the relation between brain and behavior: studying brain-damaged patients, producing lesions at specific brain sites, electrically stimulating the brain, recording brain activity, and imaging the brain with computerized devices.
- The brain and the spinal cord make up the central nervous system (CNS).
- The peripheral nervous system (PNS) is composed of all neurons connecting the CNS to the body. The PNS consists of the somatic nervous system, which regulates the body's skeletal muscles, and the autonomic nervous system (ANS), which regulates life-support processes.

- The brain consists of three integrated layers: the brain stem, limbic system, and cerebrum.
- The brain stem is responsible for breathing, digestion, and heart rate.
- The limbic system is involved in long-term memory, aggression, eating, drinking, and sexual behavior.
- The cerebrum controls higher mental functions.
- Some functions are lateralized to one hemisphere of the brain. For example, most individuals have speech localized in the left hemisphere.
- Although the two hemispheres of the brain work smoothly in concert, they play relatively greater roles for different tasks.
- The endocrine system produces and secretes hormones into the bloodstream.
- Hormones help regulate growth, primary and secondary sexual characteristics, metabolism, digestion, and arousal.
- New cell growth and life experiences reshape the brain after birth.

KEY TERMS

action potential (p. 56)
all-or-none law (p. 57)
amygdala (p. 68)
association cortex (p. 71)
auditory cortex (p. 70)
autonomic nervous system (ANS) (p. 64)
axon (p. 54)
brain stem (p. 67)
Broca's area (p. 62)
central nervous system (CNS) (p. 64)
cerebellum (p. 68)
cerebral cortex (p. 68)
cerebral hemispheres (p. 68)
cerebrum (p. 68)
computerized axial tomography (CT or CAT) (p. 63)
corpus callosum (p. 68)
dendrite (p. 54)
DNA (deoxyribonucleic acid) (p. 51)
electroencephalogram (EEG) (p. 63)
endocrine system (p. 73)
estrogen (p. 74)
evolutionary psychology (p. 51)
excitatory input (p. 56)
frontal lobe (p. 68)
functional MRI (fMRI) (p. 64)
gene (p. 51)
genetics (p. 51)
genome (p. 52)

genotype (p. 49)
glia (p. 56)
heredity (p. 51)
heritability (p. 52)
hippocampus (p. 68)
homeostasis (p. 68)
hormone (p. 73)
human behavior genetics (p. 51)
hypothalamus (p. 68)
inhibitory input (p. 56)
interneuron (p. 54)
ion channel (p. 57)
lesion (p. 62)
limbic system (p. 68)
magnetic resonance imaging (MRI) (p. 63)
medulla (p. 67)
mirror neuron (p. 56)
motor cortex (p. 69)
motor neuron (p. 54)
myelin sheath (p. 56)
natural selection (p. 48)
neurogenesis (p. 75)
neuromodulator (p. 60)
neuron (p. 54)
neuroscience (p. 54)
neurotransmitter (p. 59)
occipital lobe (p. 69)
parasympathetic division (p. 65)
parietal lobe (p. 69)

peripheral nervous system (PNS) (p. 64)
phenotype (p. 49)
pituitary gland (p. 74)
plasticity (p. 74)
polygenic trait (p. 52)
pons (p. 67)
positron emission tomography (PET) scan (p. 63)
refractory period (p. 58)
repetitive transcranial magnetic stimulation (rTMS) (p. 62)
resting potential (p. 57)
reticular formation (p. 67)
sensory neuron (p. 54)
sex chromosome (p. 51)
sociobiology (p. 51)
soma (p. 54)
somatic nervous system (p. 64)
somatosensory cortex (p. 70)
sympathetic division (p. 65)
synapse (p. 58)
synaptic transmission (p. 58)
temporal lobe (p. 69)
terminal button (p. 54)
testosterone (p. 74)
thalamus (p. 68)
visual cortex (p. 70)
Wernicke's area (p. 69)

1. When Peter and Rosemary Grant studied several species of Darwin's finches, they discovered that major climate changes affected which populations of finches survived. This is an example of
   a. heritability.
   c. natural selection.
   b. the all-or-none law.
   d. nature versus nurture.

2. Sharon is involved in a project in which she observes the behaviors of young children. She is most able to directly observe their
   a. genotypes.
   c. chromosomes.
   b. phenotypes.
   d. DNA.

3. Suppose you carried out a study to assess whether there is a genetic component to "sense of humor." To conclude that genetics plays a role, you would want to find that
   a. DZ twins are more similar in their sense of humor than MZ twins.
   b. DZ twins always have better senses of humor than MZ twins.
   c. MZ twins always have better senses of humor than DZ twins.
   d. MZ twins are more similar in their sense of humor than DZ twins.

4. One of the jobs of _____ is to receive stimulation from other neurons.
   a. axons
   c. synapses
   b. terminal buttons
   d. dendrites

5. After Jonas withdraws money from the bank, he has to wait two minutes before his card will work again. This sounds a lot like the _____ in neural transmission.
   a. all-or-none law
   c. refractory period
   b. action potential
   d. ion channels

6. Wilma is creating an illustration of neural transmission. She leaves a small gap between a terminal button on one neuron and the dendrite of the next. She should label that gap the
   a. ion channel.
   c. node of Ranvier.
   b. glia.
   d. synapse.

7. Bea has decided to undergo an acupuncture treatment to help her with her back pain. You explain that researchers believe that acupuncture leads to the release of _____ in the brain.
   a. GABA
   c. endorphins
   b. acetylcholine
   d. dopamine

8. Researchers suggest that culture becomes embrained because
   a. people in different cultures do not face the same problems.
   b. people's cultural values lead them to repeat the same patterns of neural responses.
   c. people from different cultures cannot produce the same neural responses.
   d. people's behavioral responses can only be predicted from cultural values.

9. Which technique allows researchers to create reversible "lesions"?
   a. fMRI
   c. PET scans
   b. rTMS
   d. EEG

10. The _____ nervous system processes incoming neural messages and sends commands to different parts of the body.
    a. central
    c. somatic
    b. autonomic
    d. peripheral

11. After he experienced damage to his _____, H.M. had difficulties acquiring new information.
    a. reticular formation
    c. hippocampus
    b. thalamus
    d. Broca's area

12. After Jeff inhales oxytocin through a nasal spray, you expect him to display _____ trust toward Mona due, in part, to _____ activity in his amygdala.
    a. more; reduced
    c. less; reduced
    b. more; increased
    d. less; increased

13. As you are chatting with Tejus, you noticed that she is right-handed. You think that it's most likely that her ability to produce speech is controlled by
    a. her left hemisphere.
    b. her right hemisphere.
    c. both the left and right hemispheres.
    d. neither the left nor the right hemisphere.

14. Which brain structure serves as a relay station between the brain and the endocrine system?
    a. the hippocampus
    c. the pons
    b. the hypothalamus
    d. the amygdala

15. Brain-imaging techniques reveal that the brain representation of the fingers of the left hand is enhanced for people who play the violin versus nonplayers. This result provides an example of
    a. neurogenesis.
    c. lateralization.
    b. heritability.
    d. brain plasticity.

ESSAY QUESTIONS

1. What important contrasts exist between research in human behavior genetics and research in evolutionary psychology?

2. Why does a neuron's behavior depend on the balance of excitatory and inhibitory inputs it receives?

3. What does research on enriched environments suggest about brain plasticity?

Sensation and Perception

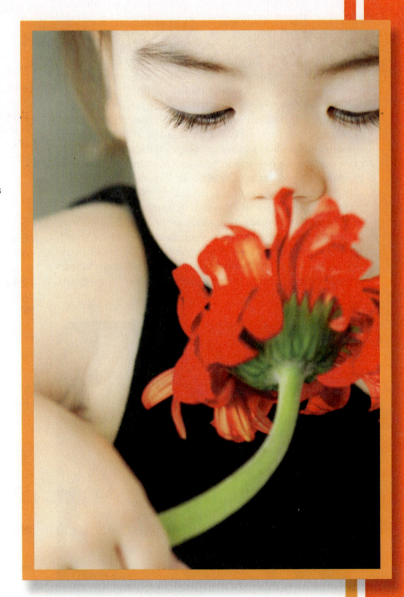

Have you ever wondered how your brain—locked in the dark, silent chamber of the skull—experiences the blaze of color in a van Gogh painting, the driving melodies and rhythms of rock 'n' roll, the refreshing taste of watermelon on a hot day, the soft touch of a child's kiss, or the fragrance of wildflowers in the springtime? The task for this chapter is to explain how your body and brain make sense of the buzz of stimulation—sights, sounds, and so on—constantly around you. You will see how evolution has equipped you with the capability to detect many different dimensions of experience.

In this chapter, you will learn how your experience of the world relies on processes of *perception*. The term **perception**, in its broad usage, refers to the overall process of apprehending objects and events in the environment—to sense them, understand them, recognize and label them, and prepare to react to them. A *percept* is what is perceived—the phenomenological, or experienced, outcome of the process of perception. Your perceptual processes serve the dual functions of *survival* and *sensuality*. These processes help you survive by sounding alarms of danger, priming you to take swift action to ward off hazards, and directing you toward agreeable experiences. These processes also provide you with sensuality. Sensuality is the quality of being devoted to the gratification of the senses; it entails enjoying the experiences that appeal to your various senses of sight, sound, touch, taste, and smell.

The process of perception is best understood divided into three stages: sensation, perceptual organization, and identification (or recognition) of objects. **Sensation** is the process by which stimulation of *sensory receptors*—the structures in your eyes, ears, and so on—produces neural impulses that represent experiences inside or outside the body. For example, sensation provides the basic facts of the visual field. Nerve cells in your eyes pass information along to cells in your brain.

Perceptual organization refers to the stage in which your brain integrates evidence from your senses with prior knowledge of the world to form an internal representation of an external stimulus. With respect to vision, organizational processes provide estimates of an object's likely size, shape, movement, distance, and orientation. These mental activities most often occur swiftly and efficiently, without conscious awareness.

The processes of **identification and recognition** assign meaning to percepts. With respect to vision, earlier stages of perception answer the question "What does the object look like?" At this stage, the questions become those of identification—"What is this object?"—and recognition—"What is the object's function?" You identify circular objects as baseballs, coins, clocks, oranges, and moons; you identify people as male or female, friend or foe, relative or rock star.

In everyday life, perception seems to be entirely effortless. You have very little awareness that you require these different stages of processing to arrive at a meaningful understanding of the world. This chapter should convince you that you actually do quite a bit of sophisticated processing, a lot of mental work, to arrive at this "illusion of ease." ✳

SENSORY KNOWLEDGE OF THE WORLD

Your experience of external reality must be relatively accurate and error free. If not, you couldn't survive. You need food to sustain you, shelter to protect you, interactions with other people to fulfill social needs, and awareness of danger to keep out of harm's way. To meet these needs, you must get reliable information about the world. This section provides an overview of how your sensory processes address these goals.

The Proximity and Distal Stimuli

Imagine you are the person in **Figure 4.1A**, surveying a room from an easy chair. Some of the light reflected from the objects in the room enters your eyes and forms images on your retinas. **Figure 4.1B** shows what would appear to your left eye as you sit in the room. (The bump on the right is your nose, and the hand and knee at the bottom are your own.) How does this retinal simage compare with the environment that produced it?

One very important difference is that the retinal image is *two dimensional,* whereas the environment is *three dimensional.* This difference has many consequences. For instance, compare the shapes of the physical objects in Figure 4.1A with the shapes of their corresponding retinal images (**Figure 4.1C**).

What senses are involved in the enjoyment of a slice of watermelon?

....

✳ **Explore** the **Concept** *Virtual Brain: Mechanisms of Perception* on **MyPsychLab**

perception The processes that organize information in the sensory image and interpret it as having been produced by properties of objects or events in the external, three-dimensional world.

sensation The process by which stimulation of a sensory receptor gives rise to neutral impulses that result in an experience, or awareness, of conditions inside or outside the body.

perceptual organization The processes that put sensory information together to give the perception of a coherent scene over the whole visual field.

identification and recognition Two ways of attaching meaning to percepts.

A.

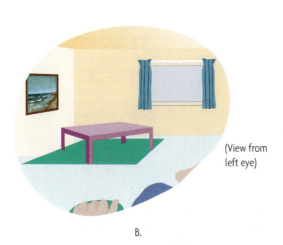

(View from left eye)

B.

(Picture)   (Window)

(Tabletop)

(Rug)

C.

FIGURE 4.1 Interpreting Retinal Images

Suppose you are sitting in an easy chair, looking around a room (A). The light reflected from objects in the room forms images on your retina. Consider the information that arrives at your left eye (B). When you see that information out of context (C), you can appreciate the task that faces your visual system: Your visual perception must interpret or identify distal stimulus, the actual object in the environment, using the information from the proximal stimulus, the retinal image produced by the object.

The table, rug, window, and picture in the real-world scene are all rectangular, but only the image of the window actually produces a rectangle in your retinal image. The image of the picture is a trapezoid, the image of the tabletop is an irregular four-sided figure, and the image of the rug is actually three separate regions with more than 20 different sides! Here's our first perceptual puzzle: How do you manage to perceive all of these objects as simple standard rectangles?

The situation, however, is even a bit more complicated. You can also notice that many parts of what you perceive in the room are not actually present in your retinal image. For instance, you perceive the vertical edge between the two walls as going all the way to the floor, but your retinal image of that edge stops at the tabletop. Similarly, in your retinal image parts of the rug are hidden behind the table; yet this does not keep you from correctly perceiving the rug as a single unbroken rectangle. In fact, when you consider all the differences between the environmental objects and the images of them on your retina, you may be surprised that you perceive the scene as well as you do.

The differences between a physical object in the world and its optical image on your retina are so profound and important that psychologists distinguish carefully between them as two different stimuli for perception. The physical object in the world is called the **distal stimulus** (distant from the observer) and the optical image on the retina is called the **proximal stimulus** (proximate, or near, to the observer).

The critical point of this discussion can now be restated more concisely: What you wish to *perceive* is the *distal stimulus*—the "real" object in the environment—whereas the stimulus from which you must derive your information is the *proximal stimulus*—the image on the retina. You can think of the major computational task of perception as the process of determining the distal stimulus from information contained in the proximal stimulus. This is true across perceptual domains. For hearing, touch, taste, and so on, perception involves processes that use information in the proximal stimulus to tell you about properties of the distal stimulus.

To show you how the distal stimulus and proximal stimulus fit with the three stages in perceiving, let's examine one of the objects in the scene from Figure 4.1: the picture hanging on the wall. In the sensory stage, this picture corresponds to a two-dimensional trapezoid in your retinal image; the top and bottom sides converge toward the right, and the left and right sides are different in length. This is the proximal stimulus. In the perceptual organization stage, you see this trapezoid as a rectangle turned away from you in three-dimensional space. You perceive the top and bottom sides as parallel but receding into the distance toward the right; you perceive the left and right sides as equal in length. Your perceptual processes have developed a strong *hypothesis* about the physical properties of the distal stimulus; now it needs an identity. In the recognition stage, you identify this rectangular object as a picture. **Figure 4.2** on page 82 is a flowchart illustrating this sequence

....

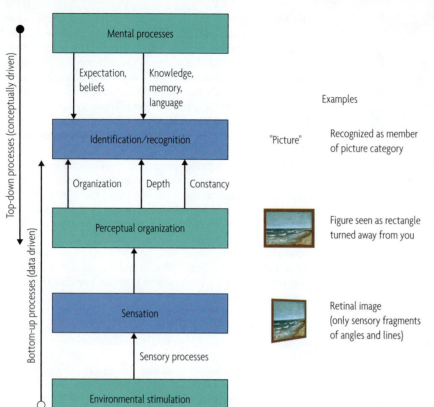

FIGURE 4.2 Sensation, Perceptual Organization, and Identification/Recognition Stages

The diagram outlines the processes that give rise to the transformation of incoming information at the stages of sensation, perceptual organization, and identification/recognition. Bottom-up processing occurs when the perceptual representation is derived from the information available in the sensory input. Top-down processing occurs when the perceptual representation is affected by an individual's prior knowledge, motivations, expectations, and other aspects of higher mental functioning.

of events. The processes that take information from one stage to the next are shown as arrows between the boxes. By the end of this chapter, you will learn about the interactions represented in this figure.

The task of perception is to identify the distal stimulus from the proximal stimulus. However, the earliest researchers on sensation recognized that people's experiences of the world have a psychological component. As you'll see next, those researchers examined the relationship between events in the environment and people's experience of those events.

Psychophysics

How loud must a fire alarm at a factory be for workers to hear it over the din of the machinery? How bright does a warning light on a pilot's control panel have to be to appear twice as bright as the other lights? How much sugar do you need to put in a cup of coffee before it begins to taste sweet? To answer these questions, we must be able to measure the intensity of sensory experiences. This is the central task of **psychophysics,** the study of the relationship between physical stimuli and the behavior or mental experiences the stimuli evoke.

The most significant figure in the history of psychophysics was the German physicist **Gustav Fechner** (1801–1887). Fechner coined the term *psychophysics* and provided a set of procedures to relate the intensity of a physical stimulus—measured in physical units—to the magnitude of the sensory experience—measured in psychological units (Fechner, 1860/1966). Fechner's techniques are the same whether the stimuli are for light,

sound, taste, odor, or touch: Researchers determine thresholds and construct psychophysical scales relating strength of sensation to strength of stimuli.

Absolute Thresholds and Sensory Adaptation   What is the smallest, weakest stimulus energy that an organism can detect? How soft can a tone be, for instance, and still be heard? These questions refer to the **absolute threshold** for stimulation—the minimum amount of physical energy needed to produce a sensory experience. Researchers measure absolute thresholds by asking vigilant observers to perform detection tasks, such as trying to see a dim light in a dark room or trying to hear a soft sound in a quiet room. During a series of many trials, the stimulus is presented at varying intensities, and on each trial the observers indicate whether they were aware of it. (If you've ever had your hearing evaluated, you participated in an absolute threshold test.)

The results of an absolute threshold study can be summarized in a **psychometric function:** a graph that shows the percentage of detections (plotted on the vertical axis) at each

psychophysics The study of the correspondence between physical simulation and psychological experience.

absolute threshold The minimum amount of physical energy needed to produce a reliable sensory experience; operationally defined as the stimulus level at which a sensory signal is detected half the time.

psychometric function A graph that plots the percentage of detections of a stimulus (on the vertical axis) for each stimulus intensity (on the horizon axis).

FIGURE 4.3 Calculation of Absolute Thresholds
Because a stimulus does not suddenly become detectable at a certain point, absolute threshold is defined as the intensity at which the stimulus is detected half of the time over many trials.

stimulus intensity (plotted on the horizontal axis). A typical psychometric function is shown in **Figure 4.3**. For very dim lights, detection is at 0 percent; for bright lights, detection is at 100 percent. If there were a single, true absolute threshold, you would expect the transition from 0 to 100 percent detection to be very sharp, occurring right at the point where the intensity reached the threshold. But this does not happen, for at least two reasons: Viewers themselves change slightly each time they try to detect a stimulus (because of changes in attention, fatigue, and so on), and viewers sometimes respond even in the absence of a stimulus (the type of false alarm we will consider shortly in the context of signal detection theory). Thus the psychometric curve is usually a smooth S-shaped curve, in which there is a region of transition from no detection to occasional detection to detection all the time.

Because a stimulus does not suddenly become clearly detectable at all times at a specific intensity, the operational definition of absolute threshold is *the stimulus level at which a sensory signal is detected half the time*. Thresholds for different senses can be measured using the same procedure, simply by changing the stimulus dimension. **Table 4.1** shows absolute threshold levels for several familiar natural stimuli.

Although it is possible to identify absolute thresholds for detection, it is also important to note that your sensory systems are more sensitive to *changes* in the sensory environment than to steady states. The systems have evolved so that they favor new environmental inputs over old through a process called adaptation. **Sensory adaptation** is the diminishing

responsiveness of sensory systems to prolonged stimulus input. You may have noticed, for example, that sunshine seems less blinding after a while outdoors. People often have their most fortunate experiences of adaptation in the domain of smell: You walk into a room, and something really has a foul odor; over time, however, as your smell system adapts, the odor fades out of awareness. Your environment is always full of a great diversity of sensory stimulation. The mechanism of adaptation allows you to notice and react quickly to the challenges of new sources of information.

Response Bias and Signal Detection Theory The discussion so far has assumed that all observers are created equal. However, threshold measurements can also be affected by **response bias,** the systematic tendency for an observer to favor responding in a particular way because of factors unrelated to the sensory features of the stimulus. Suppose, for example, you are in an experiment in which you must detect a weak light. In the first phase of the experiment, the researcher gives you $5 when you are correct in saying, "Yes, a light was there." In the second phase, the researcher gives you $5 when you are correct in saying, "No, there wasn't any light." In each phase, you are penalized $2 any time you are incorrect. Can you see how this reward structure would create a shift in response bias from phase 1 to phase 2? Wouldn't you say *yes* more often in the first phase—with the same amount of certainty that the stimulus was present?

Signal detection theory (SDT) is a systematic approach to the problem of response bias (Green & Swets, 1966). Instead of focusing strictly on sensory processes, SDT emphasizes the process of making a *judgment* about the presence or absence of stimulus events. Whereas classical psychophysics conceptualized a single absolute threshold, SDT identifies two distinct processes in sensory detection: (1) an initial *sensory process,* which reflects the observer's sensitivity to the strength of the stimulus; and (2) a subsequent separate *decision process,* which reflects the observer's response biases.

....

sensory adaptation A phenomenon in which receptor cells lose their power to respond after a period of unchanged stimulation; allows a more rapid reaction to new sources of information.

response bias The systematic tendency as a result of nonsensory factors for an observer to favor responding in a particular way.

signal detection theory A systematic approach to the problem of response bias that allows an experimenter to identify and separate the roles of sensory stimuli and the individual's criterion level in producing the final response.

Table 4.1 • Approximate Thresholds of Familiar Events

Sense Modality	Detection Threshold
Light	A candle flame seen at 30 miles on a dark clear night
Sound	The tick of a watch under quiet conditions at 20 feet
Taste	One teaspoon of sugar in 2 gallons of water
Smell	One drop of perfume diffused into the entire volume of a three-room apartment
Touch	The wing of a bee falling on your cheek from a distance of 1 centimeter

Response given

		Yes	No
Stimulus signal	On	Hit	Miss
	Off	False alarm	Correct rejection

FIGURE 4.4 The Theory of Signal Detection
The matrix shows the possible outcomes when a subject is asked if a target stimulus occurred on a given trial.

SDT offers a procedure for evaluating both the sensory process and the decision processes at once. The basic design is given in **Figure 4.4**. A weak stimulus is presented in half the trials; no stimulus is presented in the other half. In each trial, observers respond by saying *yes* if they think the signal was present and *no* if they think it wasn't. As shown in the figure, each response is scored in one of four ways:

- A response is a *hit* when the signal is present and the observer says "yes."
- A response is a *miss* when the signal is present and the observer says "no."
- A response is a *false alarm* when the signal is absent and the observer says "yes."
- A response is a *correct rejection* when the signal is absent and the observer says "no."

How can we see the impact of the perceivers' decision processes? If Carol is a yea-sayer (she chronically answers *yes*), she will almost inevitably say *yes* when the stimulus was present, so she'll have a large number of hits. However, she'll also have a high number of false alarms because she'll also say *yes* quite often when the stimulus was absent. If Bob is a naysayer (he chronically answers *no*), he will give a lower number of hits but also a lower number of false alarms.

Working with the percentages of hits and false alarms, researchers use mathematical procedures to calculate separate

If you decline a dinner invitation, will you be avoiding a dull evening (a correct rejection) or sacrificing the chance for a lifetime of love (a miss)?

measures of observers' sensitivity and response biases. This procedure makes it possible to find out whether two observers have the same sensitivity despite large differences in response criterion. By providing a way of separating sensory process from response bias, the theory of signal detection allows an experimenter to identify and separate the roles of the sensory stimulus and the individual's criterion level in producing the final response.

Difference Thresholds   Imagine you have been employed by a beverage company that wants to produce a cola product that tastes noticeably sweeter than existing colas, but (to save money) the firm wants to put as little extra sugar in the cola as possible. You are being asked to measure a **difference threshold,** the smallest physical difference between two stimuli that can still be recognized as a difference. To measure a difference threshold, you use pairs of stimuli and ask your observers whether they believe the two stimuli to be the same or different.

For the beverage problem, you would give your observers two colas on each trial, one of some standard recipe and one just a bit sweeter. For each pair, the individual would say *same* or *different*. After many such trials, you would plot a psychometric function by graphing the percent of *different* responses on the vertical axis as a function of the actual differences, plotted on the horizontal axis. The difference threshold is operationally defined as *the point at which the stimuli are recognized as different half of the time*. This difference threshold value is known as a **just noticeable difference,** or **JND**. The JND is a quantitative unit for measuring the magnitude of the psychological difference between any two sensations.

In 1834, **Ernst Weber** (1795–1878) pioneered the study of JNDs. He discovered the important relationship that is known as **Weber's law:** *The JND between stimuli is a constant fraction of the intensity of the standard stimulus.* Thus, the bigger or more intense the standard stimulus, the larger the increment needed to get a just noticeable difference. Suppose, for example, you were trying to lift a suitcase that weighed 25 pounds. Research on the psychophysics of "lifted weight" suggests that the suitcase would only feel heavier—you would notice a difference—if you added another half-pound of clothes. However, if the suitcase already weighed 50 pounds, you'd need to add a pound to feel the difference. Note that the fraction remains the same ($0.5/25 = 1/50 = 0.02$). Weber's constant has different values for different sensory dimensions. You can differentiate two sound frequencies more precisely than light intensities, which, in turn, are detectable with a smaller JND than odor or taste differences are. Your beverage company would need a relatively large amount of extra sugar to produce a noticeably sweeter cola! ⊙▶

· ·

⊙▶ **Simulate** the **Experiment** *Weber's Law* on **MyPsychLab**

difference threshold The smallest physical difference between two stimuli that can still be recognized as a difference; operationally defined as the point at which the stimuli are recognized as different half of the time.

just noticeable difference (JND) The smallest difference between two sensations that allows them to be discriminated.

Weber's law An assertion that the size of a difference threshold is proportional to the intensity of the standard stimulus.

From Physical Events to Mental Events

This review of psychophysics has made you aware of the central mystery of sensation: How do physical energies give rise to particular psychological experiences? How, for example, do the various physical wavelengths of light give rise to your experience of viewing a rainbow? Before we consider specific sensory domains, let's start with an overview of the flow of information from physical events—waves of light and sound, complex chemicals, and so on—to mental events—your experiences of sights, sounds, tastes, and smells.

The conversion of one form of physical energy, such as light, to another form, such as neural impulses, is called **transduction.** Because all sensory information is transduced, or converted, into identical types of neural impulses, your brain differentiates sensory experiences by devoting special areas of cortex to each sensory domain. For each domain, researchers try to discover how the transduction of physical energy into the electrochemical activity of the nervous system gives rise to sensations of different quality (red rather than green) and different quantity (loud rather than soft).

Sensory systems share the same basic flow of information. The trigger for any sensing system is the detection of an environmental event, or *stimulus*. Environmental stimuli are detected by specialized **sensory receptors.** Sensory receptors convert the physical form of the sensory signal into cellular signals that can be processed by the nervous system. These cellular signals contribute information to higher-level neurons that integrate information across different detector units. At this stage, neurons extract information about the basic qualities of the stimulus, such as its size, intensity, shape, and distance. Deeper into the sensory systems, information is combined into even more complex codes that are passed on to specific areas of the sensory and association cortex of the brain. ◉

Let's move now to specific sensory domains.

Stop *and* Review

① What is the proximal stimulus?
② What is the subject matter of psychophysics?
③ What is the operational definition of an absolute threshold?
④ In signal detection theory, what two processes contribute to observers' judgments?
⑤ What is a difference threshold?
⑥ What is transduction?

✓—**Study** and **Review** on **MyPsychLab**

....

◉ **Watch** the **Video** *The Big Picture: The Role of Sensation and Perception in Psychology* on **MyPsychLab**

transduction Transformation of one form of energy into another; for example, light is transformed into neutral impulses.

sensory receptor Specialized cell that converts physical signals into cellular signals that are processed by the nervous system.

THE VISUAL SYSTEM

Vision is the most complex, highly developed, and important sense for humans and most other mobile creatures. Animals with good vision have an enormous evolutionary advantage. Good vision helps animals detect their prey or predators from a distance. Vision enables humans to be aware of changing features in the physical environment and to adapt their behavior accordingly. Vision is also the most studied of all the senses.

The Human Eye

The eye is the camera for the brain's motion pictures of the world (see **Figure 4.5**). A camera views the world through a lens that gathers and focuses light. The eye also gathers and focuses light—light enters the *cornea*, a transparent bulge on the front of the eye. Next it passes through the *anterior chamber*, which is filled with a clear liquid called the *aqueous humor*. The light then passes through the *pupil*, an opening in the opaque *iris*. To focus a camera, you move its lens closer to or farther from the object viewed. To focus light in the eye, a bean-shaped crystalline *lens* changes its shape, thinning to focus on distant objects and thickening to focus on near ones. To control the amount of light coming into a camera, you vary the opening of the lens. In the eye, the muscular disk of the iris changes the size of the pupil, the opening through which light passes into the eyeball. At the back of a traditional camera body is the photosensitive film that records the variations in light that have come through the lens. Similarly, in the eye, light travels through the *vitreous humor*, finally striking the *retina*, a thin sheet that lines the rear wall of the eyeball.

As you can see, the features of a camera and the eye are very similar. Now let's examine the components of the vision process in more detail.

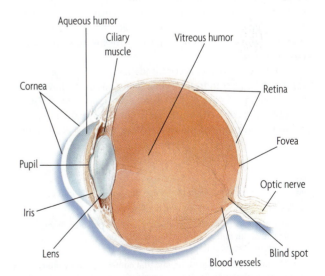

FIGURE 4.5 Structure of the Human Eye
The cornea, pupil, and lens focus light onto the retina. Nerve signals from the retina are carried to the brain by the optic nerve.

Nearsightedness

Farsightedness

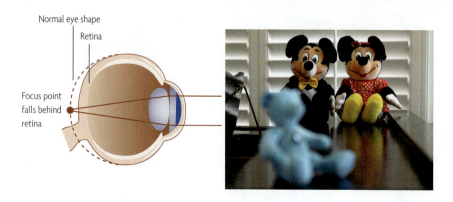

FIGURE 4.6 Nearsightedness and Farsightedness

People experience nearsightedness when light from distant objects focuses in front of the retina. They experience farsightedness when light from near objects focuses behind the retina. The photos suggest how the world might appear to nearsighted and farsighted people if their vision remained uncorrected by glasses or contact lenses.

The Pupil and The Lens

The **pupil** is the opening in the iris through which light passes. The iris makes the pupil dilate or constrict to control the amount of light entering the eyeball. Light passing through the pupil is focused by the **lens** on the retina; the lens reverses and inverts the light pattern as it does so. The lens is particularly important because of its variable focusing ability for near and far objects. The ciliary muscles can change the thickness of the lens and hence its optical properties in a process called **accommodation.**

People with normal accommodation have a range of focus from about 3 inches in front of their nose to as far as they can see. However, many people suffer from accommodation problems. For example, people who are nearsighted have their range of accommodation shifted closer to them with the consequence that they cannot focus well on distant objects; those who are farsighted have their range of accommodation shifted farther away from them so that they cannot focus normally on nearby objects (see **Figure 4.6**). Aging also leads to problems in accommodation. The lens starts off as clear, transparent, and convex. As people age, however, the lens becomes more amber tinted, opaque, and flattened, and it loses its elasticity. The effect of some of these changes is that the lens cannot become thick enough for close vision. When people age past the 45-year mark, the *near point*—the closest point at which they can focus clearly—gets progressively farther away.

The Retina

You look with your eyes but see with your brain. The eye gathers light, focuses it, and starts a neural signal on its way toward the brain. The eye's critical function, therefore, is to convert information about the world from light waves into neural signals. This happens in the **retina,** at the back of the eye. Under the microscope, you can see that the retina has several highly organized layers of different types of neurons.

The basic conversion from light energy to neural responses is performed in your retina by *rods* and *cones*—receptor cells sensitive to light. These **photoreceptors** are uniquely placed in the visual system between the outer world, ablaze with light, and the inner world of neural processing. Because you sometimes operate in near darkness and sometimes in bright light, nature has provided two ways of processing light, rods and cones (see **Figure 4.7**). The 120 million thin **rods** operate

pupil The opening at the front of the eye through which light passes.

lens The flexible tissue that focuses light on the retina.

accommodation The process by which the ciliary muscles change the thickness of the lens of the eye to permit variable focusing on near and distant objects.

retina The layer at the back of the eye that contains photoreceptors and converts light energy to neutral responses.

photoreceptor Receptor cell in the retina that is sensitive to light.

rod One of the photoreceptors concentrated in the periphery of the retina that are most active in dim illumination; rods do not produce sensation of color.

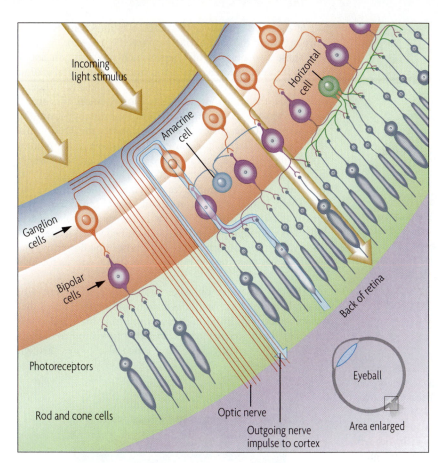

FIGURE 4.7 Retinal Pathways

This is a stylized and greatly simplified diagram showing the pathways that connect three of the layers of nerve cells in the retina. Incoming light passes through all these layers to reach the receptors, at the back of the eyeball, which are pointed away from the source of light. Note that the bipolar cells gather impulses from more than one receptor cell and send the results to ganglion cells. Nerve impulses (blue arrow) from the ganglion cells leave the eye via the optic nerve and travel to the next relay point.

best in near darkness. The 7 million fat **cones** are specialized for the bright, color-filled day.

You experience differences between the functions of your rods and cones each time you turn off the lights to go to sleep at night. You have noticed many times that at first it seems as though you can't see much of anything in the dim light that remains, but over time your visual sensitivity improves again. You are undergoing the process of **dark adaptation**—the gradual improvement of the eyes' sensitivity after a shift in illumination from light to near darkness. Dark adaptation occurs because, as time passes in the dark, your rods become more sensitive than your cones; over time, your rods are able to respond to less light from the environment than your cones are.

Near the center of the retina is a small region called the **fovea,** which contains nothing but densely packed cones—it is rod free. The fovea is the area of your sharpest vision—both color and spatial detail are most accurately detected there. Other cells in your retina are responsible for integrating information across regions of rods and cones. The **bipolar cells** are nerve cells that combine impulses from many receptors and send the results to ganglion cells. Each **ganglion cell** then integrates the impulses from one or more bipolar cells into a single firing rate. The cones in the central fovea send their impulses to the ganglion cells in that region while, farther out on the periphery of the retina, rods and cones converge on the same bipolar and ganglion cells. The axons of the ganglion cells make up the optic nerve, which carries this visual information out of the eye and back toward the brain.

Your **horizontal cells** and **amacrine cells** integrate information across the retina. Rather than send signals toward

the brain, horizontal cells connect receptors to each other, and amacrine cells link bipolar cells to other bipolar cells and ganglion cells to other ganglion cells.

An interesting curiosity in the anatomical design of the retina exists where the optic nerve leaves each eye. This region, called the optic disk, or **blind spot,** contains no receptor cells at all. You do not experience blindness there, except under very special circumstances, for two reasons: First, the blind spots of

cone One of the photoreceptors concentrated in the center of the retina that are responsible for visual experience under normal viewing conditions for all experiences of color.

dark adaptation The gradual improvement of the eyes' sensitivity after a shift in illumination from light to near darkness.

fovea Area of the retina that contains densely packed cones and forms the point of sharpest vision.

bipolar cell Nerve cell in the visual system that combines impulses from many receptors and transmits the results to ganglion cells.

ganglion cell Cell in the visual system that integrates impulses from many bipolar cells in a single firing rate.

horizontal cell One of the cells that integrates information across the retina; rather than sending signals toward the brain, horizontal cells connect receptors to each other.

amacrine cell One of the cells that integrates information across the retina; rather than sending signals toward the brain, amacrine cells link bipolar cells to other bipolar cells and ganglion cells to other ganglion cells.

blind spot The region of the retina where the optic nerve leaves the back of the eye; no receptor cells are present in this region.

FIGURE 4.8 Find Your Blind Spot

To find your blind spot, hold this book at arm's length, close your right eye, and fixate on the bank figure with your left eye as you bring the book slowly closer. When the dollar sign is in your blind spot, it will disappear, but you will experience no gaping hole in your visual field. Similarly, if you use the same procedure to focus on the plus sign, the line will appear whole when the gap is in your blind spot. In both cases, your visual system fills in the background whiteness of the surrounding area so you "see" the whiteness, which isn't there.

the two eyes are positioned so that receptors in each eye register what is missed in the other; second, the brain fills in this region with appropriate sensory information from the surrounding area.

To find your blind spot, you will have to look at **Figure 4.8** under special viewing conditions. Hold this book at arm's length, close your right eye, and fixate on the bank figure with your left eye as you bring the book slowly closer. When the dollar sign is in your blind spot, it will disappear, but you will experience no gaping hole in your visual field. Instead, your visual system fills in this area with the background whiteness of the surrounding area so you "see" the whiteness, which isn't there, while failing to see your money, which you should have put in the bank before you lost it!

For a second demonstration of your blind spot, use the same procedure to focus on the plus sign in Figure 4.8. As you pull the book closer to you, do you see the gap disappear and the line become whole? ❈

Processes in the Brain

The ultimate destination of much visual information is the part of the occipital lobe of the brain known as primary *visual cortex*. However, most information leaving the retinas passes through other brain regions before it arrives at the visual cortex. Let's trace the pathways visual information takes.

The million axons of the ganglion cells that form each **optic nerve** come together in the *optic chiasma*, which resembles the Greek letter χ (*chi*, pronounced *kye*). The axons in each optic nerve are divided into two bundles at the optic chiasma. Half of the fibers from each retina remain on the side of the body from which they originated. The axons from the inner

....

❈ **Explore** the **Concept** *Virtual Brain: The Visual System* on **MyPsychLab**

optic nerve The axons of the ganglion cells that carry information from the eye toward the brain.

half of each eye cross over the midline as they continue their journey toward the back of the brain (see **Figure 4.9**).

These two bundles of fibers, which now contain axons from both eyes, are renamed *optic tracts*. Visual information next flows through the lateral geniculate nucleus (a structure within the thalamus), which relays information to cortical areas for vision (see **Figure 4.10**). Once information from the eyes arrives at the cortex, research supports the theory that visual analysis is largely separated into pathways for *pattern recognition*—what things are—and *place recognition*—where things are (Konen & Kastner, 2008). The division into pattern and place recognition gives you an example of the way in which your visual system consists of several separate subsystems that analyze different aspects of the same retinal image. Although your final perception is of a unified visual scene, your vision of it is accomplished through a host of pathways in your visual system that, under normal conditions, are exquisitely coordinated.

(Before we move on, take another look at Figure 4.10 which shows the location of the thalamus. Chapter 3 noted that thalamus channels incoming sensory information to the appropriate area of the cerebral cortex. In fact, information for others senses such as hearing, taste, and touch also passes through

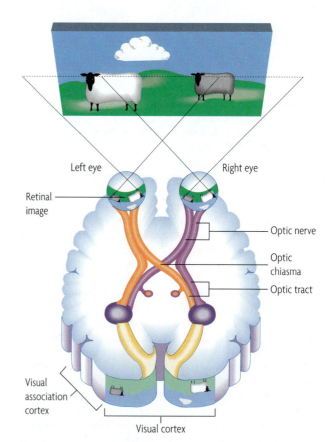

FIGURE 4.9 Pathways in the Human Visual System

The diagram shows the way light from the visual field projects onto the two retinas and the routes by which neural messages from the retina are sent to the two visual centers of each hemisphere.

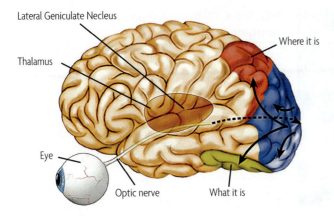

Lateral Geniculate Neucleus

Thalamus

Where it is

Eye

Optic nerve

What it is

FIGURE 4.10 Visual Pathways to the Cortex

Visual information collected by the eye passses through the lateral geniculate nucleus—a structure within the thalamus—on its way to the cortex. The signals arrive at different areas in the cortex that process the "what" and "where" of the visual world.

structures within the thalamus. Now that you have that extra appreciation for your thalamus, let's return to vision.)

Researchers obtain valuable information about visual processing when the exquisite coordination among different cortical areas breaks down. Brain damage can affect either the pattern or place pathways—or communication between the pathways—to yield several different disorders known as *agnosias*. People who experience an agnosia generally have difficulty recognizing or identifying objects or people. For example, a patient known as K.E. suffered a stroke that produced

the specific condition known as *simultanagnosia* (Coslett & Lie, 2008). People with this disorder have difficulty experiencing more than one feature of the visual world simultaneously. For example, K.E. was asked to view color words (e.g., the word *red*) written in different color inks (e.g., *red* would be printed in blue ink). When the researchers asked K.E. to name the color word, he was correct on 47 out of 48 trials. However, when they asked him to name the color of the ink, K.E. was always wrong. In fact, he "explicitly stated that he did not see a color" (p. 41). Note that K.E.'s color vision was perfectly normal. When he was asked to identify the color of color patches, he was 100 percent correct. What K.E., apparently, couldn't do was to experience two attributes of the same perceptual object (e.g., the meaning of a word and the color in which it was written) simultaneously in the same spatial location.

Sensory information from the visual world ultimately arrives at the brain's visual cortex. The sensory physiologists **David Hubel** and **Torsten Wiesel** won a Nobel Prize in 1981 for their pioneering studies of *receptive fields* of cells in the visual cortex. The **receptive field** of a cell is the area in the visual field from which it receives stimulation. As shown in **Figure 4.11**, Hubel and Wiesel discovered that cells at different levels of the visual system responded most strongly to different patterns of stimulation. For example, one type of cortical cell, *simple* cells, responded most strongly to bars of light in their "favorite" orientation (see Figure 4.11). *Complex* cells also each have a "favorite" orientation, but they require as well that the bar be moving. *Hypercomplex* cells require moving bars of a particular length or moving corners or angles. The cells

....

receptive field The area of the visual field to which a neuron in the visual system responds.

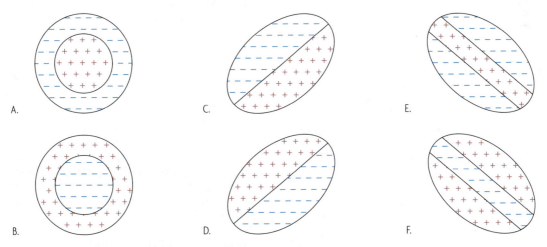

FIGURE 4.11 Receptive Fields of Ganglion and Cortical Cells

The receptive field of a cell in the visual pathway is the area in the visual field from which it receives stimulation. The receptive fields of the ganglion cells in the retina are circular (A, B); those of the simplest cells in the visual cortex are elongated in a particular orientation (C, D, E, F). In both cases, the cell responding to the receptive field is excited by light in the regions marked with plus signs and inhibited by light in the regions marked with minus signs. In addition, the stimulus that most excites the cell is the one in which areas where light is excitatory (marked with plus signs) are illuminated, but areas where light is inhibitory (marked by minus signs) are in darkness.

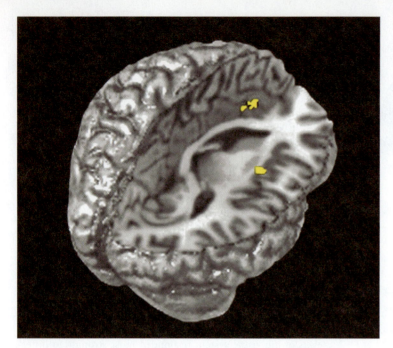

FIGURE 4.12 Brain Regions That Respond to Images of Bodies

The *extrastriate body area* (EBA) and the *fusiform body area* (FBA) in women's right hemispheres showed more activity when they were looking at photographs of their own bodies versus those of other women.

Source: Vocks, S., Busch, M., Gronemeyer, D., Schulte, D., Herpertz, S., & Suchan, B. (2010). Different neuronal responses to the self and others in the extrastriate body area (EBA) and the fusiform body area. *Cognitive, Affective, and Behavioral Neuroscience, 10*, 422-429.

provide types of information to higher visual centers in the brain that ultimately allow the brain to recognize objects in the visual world.

The advances in imaging techniques you saw in Chapter 3 have enabled researchers to discover regions of the cortex that are specially responsive to even more complex environmental images. These studies have identified cortical regions that "preferentially respond to images of faces, animals, tools, places, written words and body parts" (Mahon & Caramazza, 2011, p. 97). Let's consider one study that examined the brain's responses to images of bodies.

Featured Study

You have two brain regions that are particularly active when you view images of human bodies. These brain regions are known as the extrastriate body area *(EBA) and the* fusiform body area *(FBA). A team of researchers wondered whether these areas respond differently when people view their own bodies versus the bodies of others (Vocks et al., 2010). To answer that question, the researchers recruited 31 women, ages 18 to 50. The stimuli for the experiments were photographs of each woman dressed in a bikini, from the neck down (so just the body, and not the face, was visible). As shown in* **Figure 4.12**, *the EBA and FBA in the women's right hemispheres showed greater activity when the women were viewing photographs of their own bodies. The researchers suggested that this greater activity may arise, in part, from the women's different emotional responses to the photographs of their own bodies.*

Given that different brain areas have special responsibilities for particular environmental experiences, you might wonder whether these regions have special functions at birth or if those functions are the product of a lifetime of experience.

Researchers have begun to undertake projects to sort out the balance of nature and nurture that leads to these brain responses (Cantlon et al., 2011).

You have now learned the basics of how visual information is distributed from the eyes to various parts of the brain. Researchers still have more to learn: There are roughly 30 anatomical subdivisions of primate visual cortex, and theories vary about the pattern of communication among those areas (Orban et al., 2004). For now, let's turn to particular aspects of the visual world. One of the most remarkable features of the human visual system is that your experiences of form, color, position, and depth are based on processing the same sensory information in different ways. How do the transformations occur that enable you to see these different features of the visual world?

Seeing Color

Physical objects seem to have the marvelous property of being painted with color. You most often have the impression of brightly colored objects—red valentines, green fir trees, or blue robins' eggs—but your vivid experience of color relies on the rays of light these objects reflect onto your sensory receptors. Color is created when your brain processes the information coded in the light source.

Wavelengths and Hues The light you see is just a small portion of a physical dimension called the *electromagnetic spectrum* (see **Figure 4.13**). Your visual system is not equipped to detect other types of waves in this spectrum, such as X-rays, microwaves, and radio waves. The physical property that distinguishes types of electromagnetic energy, including light, is *wavelength,* the distance between the crests of two adjacent waves. Wavelengths of visible light are measured in *nanometers* (billionths of a meter). What you see as light is

THE ELECTROMAGNETIC SPECTRUM

Wavelength

3000 mi.   1 mi.   100 ft.   1 ft.   .01 ft.   .0001 ft.   10 nm.   1 nm.   .001 nm.   .00001 nm.

| Radio | TV | Microwaves | Infrared | | U-V | X-rays | Gamma rays | Cosmic rays |

Infrared   Visible spectrum   Ultraviolet

1500   1000   700   600   500   400   300

Wavelength in nanometers

FIGURE 4.13 The Electromagnetic Spectrum

Your visual system can sense only a small range of wavelengths in the electromagnetic spectrum. You experience that range of wavelengths, which is enlarged in the figure, as the colors violet through red.

From Wade, Carole; Tavris, Carol, *Psychology*, 10th Edition, © 2011. Reprinted and electronically reproduced by permission of Pearson Education, Inc., Upper Saddle River, New Jersey.

the range of wavelengths from 400 to about 700 nanometers. Light rays of particular physical wavelengths give rise to experiences of particular colors—for example, violet–blue at the lower end and red–orange at the higher end. Thus light is described physically in terms of wavelengths, not colors; colors exist only in your sensory system's interpretation of the wavelengths.

All experiences of color can be described in terms of three basic dimensions: hue, saturation, and brightness. **Hue** is the dimension that captures the color of a light: red, blue, green, and so on. Hue is largely determined by the wavelength of the light. As shown in **Figure 4.14**, hues can be arranged in a circle. The hues people perceive to be most similar are in adjacent positions. **Saturation** is the dimension that captures the purity of color sensations. Undiluted colors have the most saturation; muted, muddy, and pastel colors have intermediate amounts of saturation; and grays have zero saturation. **Brightness** is the dimension that captures the intensity of a color. White has the most brightness; black has the least. When colors are analyzed along these three dimensions, a remarkable finding emerges: Humans are capable of visually discriminating about 7 million different colors! However, most people can label only a small number of those colors.

Let's explain some facts about your everyday experience of color. At some point in your science education, you may

have repeated Sir Isaac Newton's discovery that sunlight combines all wavelengths of light: You repeated Newton's proof by using a prism to separate sunlight into the full rainbow of colors. The prism shows that the right combination of wavelengths yields white light. The combination of wavelengths is called *additive color mixture*. Take another look at Figure 4.14. Wavelengths of light that appear directly across from each other on the color circle—called **complementary colors**—will create the sensation of white light when mixed. Do you want to prove to yourself the existence of complementary colors?

----

hue The dimension of color space that captures the qualitative experience of the color of light.

saturation The dimension of color space that captures the purity and vividness of color sensations.

brightness The dimension of color space that captures the intensity of light.

complementary colors Colors opposite each other on the color circle; when additively mixed, they create the sensation of white light.

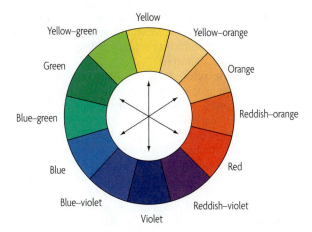

FIGURE 4.14 The Color Circle

Colors are arranged based on similarity. Complementary colors are placed directly opposite each other. Mixing complementary color lights yields a white light.

Reprinted from *Color workbook*, 3rd Edition by Becky Koenig. Prentice-Hall, 2003–2009. Reprinted by permission of the author.

FIGURE 4.15 Color Afterimages

Stare at the dot in the center of the green, black, and yellow flag for at least 30 seconds. Then fixate on the center of a sheet of white paper or a blank wall. Try this aftereffect illusion on your friends.

Consider **Figure 4.15**. The green–yellow–black flag should give you the experience of a *negative afterimage* (the afterimage is called "negative" because it is the opposite of the original color). For reasons that will become clear when we consider theories of color vision, when you stare at any color long enough to partially fatigue your photoreceptors, looking at a white surface will allow you to experience the complement of the original color.

You have probably noticed afterimages from time to time in your everyday exposure to colors. Most of your experience with colors, however, does not come from complementary lights. Instead, you have probably spent your time at play with colors by combining crayons or paints of different hues. The colors you see when you look at a crayon mark, or any other colored surface, are the wavelengths of light that are not absorbed by the surface. Although yellow crayon looks mostly yellow, it lets some wavelengths escape that give rise to the sensation of green. Similarly, blue crayon lets wavelengths escape that give rise to the sensations of blue and some green. When yellow and blue crayon are combined, yellow absorbs blue and blue absorbs yellow—the only wavelengths that are not absorbed look green! This phenomenon is called *subtractive color mixture*. The remaining wavelengths that are not absorbed—the wavelengths that are reflected—give the crayon mixture the color you perceive.

Some of these rules about the experience of color do not apply to those people born with a color deficiency. *Color blindness* is the partial or total inability to distinguish colors. The negative afterimage effect of viewing the green, yellow, and black flag will not work if you are color blind. Color blindness is usually a sex-linked hereditary defect associated with a gene on the X chromosome (Neitz & Neitz, 2011). Because males have a single X chromosome, they are more likely than females to show this recessive trait. Females would need to have a defective gene on both X chromosomes to be color blind. An estimate for color blindness among white males is about 8 percent, but less than 0.5 percent among females (Coren et al., 1999).

Most color blindness involves difficulty distinguishing red from green, especially at weak saturations. Color blindness of those who confuse yellows and blues is rarer. Rarest of all are those who see no color at all, only variations in brightness. **Figure 4.16** provides an example of the figures researchers use to test for color blindness. Individuals who have appropriate deficiencies in their red–green system will not see the number. Let's see next how scientists have explained facts about color vision such as complementary colors and color blindness.

Theories of Color Vision   The first scientific theory of color vision was proposed by **Sir Thomas Young** (1773–1829) around 1800. He suggested that there were three types of color receptors in the normal human eye that produced

FIGURE 4.16 A Color Blindness Test

Individuals who cannot see a number in this display are unable to discriminate red and green.

psychologically primary sensations: red, green, and blue. All other colors, he believed, were additive or subtractive combinations of these three primaries. Young's theory was later refined and extended by **Hermann von Helmholtz** (1821–1894) and came to be known as the Young-Helmholtz **trichromatic theory.**

The trichromatic theory provided a plausible explanation for people's color sensations and for color blindness (according to the theory, color-blind people had only one or two kinds of receptors). However, other facts and observations were not as well explained by the theory. Why did adaptation to one color produce color afterimages that had the complementary hue? Why did color-blind people always fail to distinguish pairs of colors: red and green or blue and yellow?

Answers to these questions became the cornerstones for a second theory of color vision proposed by **Ewald Hering** (1834–1918) in the late 1800s. According to his **opponent-process theory,** all color experiences arise from three underlying systems, each of which includes two opponent elements: red versus green, blue versus yellow, or black (no color) versus white (all colors). Hering theorized that colors produced complementary afterimages because one element of the system became fatigued (from overstimulation) and thus increased the relative contribution of its opponent element. Acccording to Hering's theory, types of color blindness came in pairs because the color system was actually built from pairs of opposites, not from single primary colors.

For many years, scientists debated the merits of the theories. Eventually, scientists recognized that the theories were not really in conflict; they simply described two different stages of processing that corresponded to successive physiological structures in the visual system (Hurvich & Jameson, 1974). We now know, for example, that there are, indeed, three types of cones. Although the three types each respond to a range of wavelengths, they are each *most* sensitive to light at a particular wavelength. The responses of these cone types confirm Young and Helmholtz's prediction that color vision relies on three types of color receptors. People who are color blind lack one or more of these types of receptor cones.

We also now know that the retinal ganglion cells combine the outputs of these three cone types in accordance with Hering's opponent-process theory (De Valois & Jacobs, 1968). According to the contemporary version of opponent-process theory the two members of each color pair work in opposition (are opponents) by means of neural inhibition (Conway et al., 2010; Shapley & Hawken, 2011). Some ganglion cells receive excitatory input from lights that appear red and inhibitory input from lights that appear green. Other cells in the system have the opposite arrangement of excitation and inhibition. Together, these two types of ganglion cells form the physiological basis of the red/green opponent-process system. Other

ganglion cells make up the blue/yellow opponent system. The black/white system contributes to your perception of color saturation and brightness.

We turn now from the world of sight to the world of sound.

Stop *and* Review

① In the visual system, what is meant by accommodation?
② What percentages of rods and cones are found in the fovea?
③ What patterns of stimulation cause complex cells to respond?
④ Which theory of color vision explains why you experience a blue afterimage after staring at a patch of yellow?

CRITICAL THINKING   Recall the study that contrasted women's brain responses to photographs of their own and other women's bodies. Why would the researchers have used photographs of the women in bikinis?

✓•—[**Study** and **Review** on **MyPsychLab**

HEARING

Hearing and vision play complementary functions in your experience of the world. You often hear stimuli before you see them, particularly if they take place behind you or on the other side of opaque objects such as walls. Although vision is better than hearing for identifying an object once it is in the field of view, you often see the object only because you have used your ears to point your eyes in the right direction. To begin this discussion of hearing, we consider the types of physical energy that arrive at your ears.

The Physics of Sound

Clap your hands. Whistle. Tap your pencil on the table. Why do these actions create sounds? The reason is that they cause objects to vibrate. The vibrational energy is transmitted to the surrounding medium—usually air—as the vibrating objects push molecules of the medium back and forth. The resulting slight changes in pressure spread outward from the vibrating objects in the form of a combination of *sine waves* traveling at a rate of about 1,100 feet per second (see **Figure 4.17** on page 94). Sound cannot be created in a true vacuum (such as outer space) because there are no air molecules in a vacuum for vibrating objects to move.

A sine wave has two basic physical properties that determine how it sounds to you: frequency and amplitude. *Frequency* measures the number of cycles the wave completes in a given amount of time. A cycle, as indicated in Figure 4.17, is the left-to-right distance from the peak in one wave to the peak in the next wave. Sound frequency is usually expressed in *hertz* (Hz), which measures cycles per second.

....

trichromatic theory The theory that there are three types of color receptors that produce the primary color sensations of red, green, and blue.

opponent-process theory The theory that all color experiences arise from three systems, each of which includes two "opponent" elements (red versus green, blue versus yellow, and black versus white).

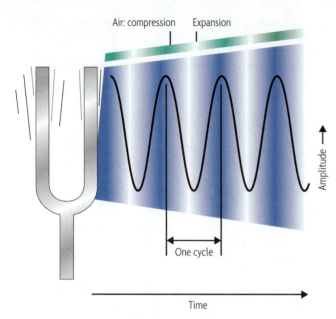

FIGURE 4.17 An Idealized Sine Wave
The two basic properties of sine waves are their frequency—the number of cycles in a fixed unit of time—and their amplitude—the vertical range of their cycles.

Amplitude measures the physical property of strength of the sound wave, as shown in its peak-to-valley height. Amplitude is defined in units of sound pressure or energy.

Psychological Dimensions of Sound

The physical properties of frequency and amplitude give rise to the three psychological dimensions of sound: pitch, loudness, and timbre. Let's see how these phenomena work.

Pitch **Pitch** is the highness or lowness of a sound determined by the sound's frequency; high frequencies produce high pitch, and low frequencies produce low pitch. The full range of human sensitivity to pure tones extends from frequencies as low as 20 Hz to frequencies as high as 20,000 Hz. (Frequencies

What physical properties of sounds allow you to pick out the timbres of individual instruments from a musical ensemble?

below 20 Hz may be experienced through touch as vibrations rather than as sound.) You can get a sense of how big this range is by noting that the 88 keys on a piano cover only the range from about 30 to 4,000 Hz.

As you might expect from the earlier discussion of psychophysics, the relationship between frequency (the physical reality) and pitch (the psychological effect) is not a linear one. At the low end of the frequency scale, increasing the frequency by just a few hertz raises the pitch quite noticeably. At the high end of frequency, you require a much bigger increase in order to hear the difference in pitch. For example, the two lowest notes on a piano differ by only 1.6 Hz, whereas the two highest ones differ by 235 Hz. This is another example of the psychophysics of just noticeable differences.

Loudness The **loudness,** or physical intensity, of a sound is determined by its amplitude; sound waves with large amplitudes are experienced as loud and those with small amplitudes as soft. The human auditory system is sensitive to an enormous range of physical intensities. At one limit, you can hear the tick of a wristwatch at 20 feet. This is the system's absolute threshold—if it were more sensitive, you would hear the blood flowing in your ears. At the other extreme, a jetliner taking off 100 yards away is so loud that the sound is painful. In terms of physical units of sound pressure, the jet produces a sound wave with more than a billion times the energy of the ticking watch.

Because the range of hearing is so great, physical intensities of sound are usually expressed in ratios rather than absolute amounts; sound pressure—the index of amplitude level that gives rise to the experience of loudness—is measured in units called decibels (dB). **Figure 4.18** shows the decibel measures of some representative natural sounds. It also shows the corresponding sound pressures for comparison. You can see that two sounds differing by 20 dB have sound pressures in a ratio of 10 to 1. Note that sounds louder than about 90 dB can produce hearing loss, depending on how long a person is exposed to them.

Timbre The **timbre** of a sound reflects the components of its complex sound wave. Timbre is what sets apart, for example, the sound of a piano from the sound of a flute. A small number of physical stimuli, such as a tuning fork, produce pure tones consisting of a single sine wave. A *pure tone* has only one frequency and one amplitude. Most sounds in the real world are not pure tones. They are complex waves, containing a combination of frequencies and amplitudes.

The sounds that you call *noise* do not have the clear simple structures of frequencies. Noise contains many frequencies that are not systematically related. For instance, the static noise you hear between radio stations contains energy at all audible

....

pitch Sound quality of highness or lowness; primarily dependent on the frequency of the sound wave.

loudness A perceptual dimension of sound influenced by the amplitude of a sound wave; sound waves in large amplitudes are generally experienced as loud and those with small amplitudes as soft.

timbre The dimension of auditory sensation that reflects the complexity of a sound wave.

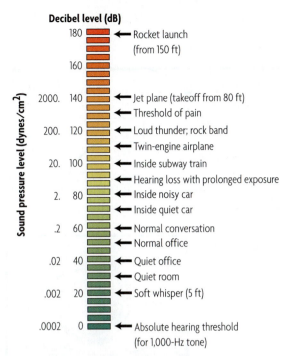

Decibel level (dB)

Sound pressure level (dynes/cm²)	Decibel level (dB)	
	180	← Rocket launch (from 150 ft)
	160	
2000.	140	← Jet plane (takeoff from 80 ft)
		← Threshold of pain
200.	120	← Loud thunder; rock band
		← Twin-engine airplane
20.	100	← Inside subway train
		← Hearing loss with prolonged exposure
2.	80	← Inside noisy car
		← Inside quiet car
.2	60	← Normal conversation
		← Normal office
.02	40	← Quiet office
		← Quiet room
.002	20	← Soft whisper (5 ft)
.0002	0	← Absolute hearing threshold (for 1,000-Hz tone)

FIGURE 4.18 Decibel Levels of Familiar Sounds
This figure shows the range in decibels of the sounds to which you respond from the absolute threshold for hearing to the noise of a rocket launch. Decibels are calculated from sound pressure, which is a measure of a sound wave's amplitude level and generally corresponds to what you experience as loudness.

frequencies; you perceive it as having no pitch because it has no fundamental frequency.

The Physiology of Hearing

Now that you know something about the physical bases of your psychological experiences of sound, let's see how those experiences arise from physiological activity in the auditory system. First, we look at the way the ear works. Then we consider some theories about how pitch experiences are coded in the auditory system and how sounds are localized.

The Auditory System You have already learned that sensory processes transform forms of external energy into forms of energy within your brain. For you to hear, as shown in **Figure 4.19** on page 96, four basic energy transformations must take place: (1) Airborne sound waves must get translated into *fluid* waves within the *cochlea* of the ear, (2) the fluid waves must then stimulate mechanical vibrations of the *basilar membrane,* (3) these vibrations must be converted into electrical impulses, and (4) the impulses must travel to the *auditory cortex*. Let's examine each of these transformations in detail.

In the first transformation, vibrating air molecules enter the ears (see Figure 4.19). Some sound enters the external canal of the ear directly, and some enters after having been reflected off the *external ear,* or *pinna*. The sound wave travels along the canal through the outer ear until it reaches the end of the canal. There it encounters a thin membrane called the eardrum, or *tympanic membrane*. The sound wave's pressure

variations set the eardrum into motion. The eardrum transmits the vibrations from the outer ear into the middle ear, a chamber that contains the three smallest bones in the human body: the *hammer,* the *anvil,* and the *stirrup*. These bones form a mechanical chain that transmits and concentrates the vibrations from the eardrum to the primary organ of hearing, the *cochlea,* which is located in the *inner ear*.

In the second transformation, which occurs in the cochlea, the airborne sound wave becomes "seaborne." The **cochlea** is a fluid-filled coiled tube that has a membrane, known as the **basilar membrane,** running down its middle along its length. When the stirrup vibrates against the oval window at the base of the cochlea, the fluid in the cochlea causes the basilar membrane to move in a wavelike motion (hence "seaborne"). Researchers speculate that the cochlea's distinctive spiral shape provides greater sensitivity to low-frequency sounds than would be possible without the spiral (Manoussaki et al., 2008).

In the third transformation, the wavelike motion of the basilar membrane bends the tiny hair cells connected to the membrane. The hair cells are the receptor cells for the auditory system. As the hair cells bend, they stimulate nerve endings, transforming the mechanical vibrations of the basilar membrane into neural activity.

Finally, in the fourth transformation, nerve impulses leave the cochlea in a bundle of fibers called the **auditory nerve.** These fibers meet in the *cochlear nucleus* of the brain stem. Similar to the crossing over of nerves in the visual system, stimulation from one ear goes to both sides of the brain. Auditory signals pass through a series of other nuclei on their way to the *auditory cortex,* in the temporal lobes of the cerebral hemispheres. Higher-order processing of these signals begins in the auditory cortex. (As you will learn shortly, other parts of the ear labeled in Figure 4.19 play roles in your other senses.)

The four transformations occur in fully functioning auditory systems. However, millions of people suffer from some form of hearing impairment. The two general types of hearing impairment are each caused by a defect in one or more of the components of the auditory system. The less serious type of impairment is *conduction deafness,* a problem in the conduction of the air vibrations to the cochlea. Often in this type of impairment, the bones in the middle ear are not functioning properly, a problem that may be corrected in microsurgery by insertion of an artificial anvil or stirrup. The more serious type of impairment is *nerve deafness,* a defect in the neural mechanisms that create nerve impulses in the ear or relay them to the auditory cortex. Damage to the auditory cortex can also create nerve deafness.

Theories of Pitch Perception To explain how the auditory system converts sound waves into sensations of pitch, researchers have outlined two distinct theories: place theory and frequency theory.

cochlea The primary organ of hearing; a fluid-filled coiled tube located in the inner ear.

basilar membrane A membrane in the cochlea that, when set into motion, stimulates hair cells that produce the neural effects of auditory stimulation.

auditory nerve The nerve that carries impulses form the cochlea to the cochlear nucleus of the brain.

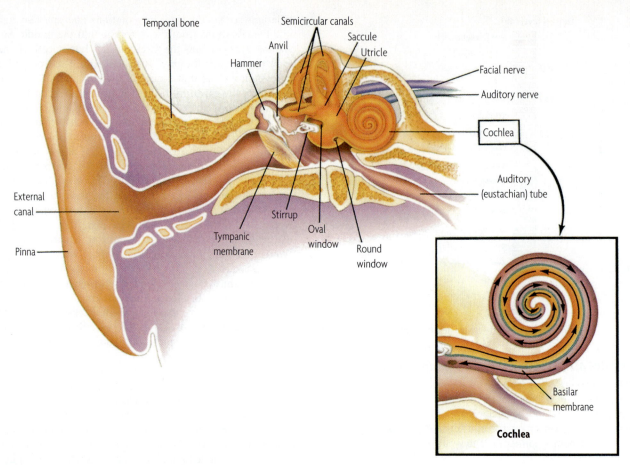

FIGURE 4.19 Structure of the Human Ear

Sound waves are channeled by the external ear, or pinna, through the external canal, causing the tympanic membrane to vibrate. This vibration activates the tiny bones of the inner ear—the hammer, anvil, and stirrup. Their mechanical vibrations are passed along from the oval window to the cochlea, where they set in motion the fluid in its canal. Tiny hair cells lining the coiled basilar membrane within the cochlea bend as the fluid moves, stimulating nerve endings attached to them. The mechanical energy is then transformed into neural energy and sent to the brain via the auditory nerve.

Place theory was initially proposed by Hermann von Helmholtz in the 1800s and was later modified, elaborated on, and tested by **Georg von Békésy** (1899–1972), who won a Nobel Prize for this work in 1961. Place theory is based on the fact that the basilar membrane moves when sound waves are conducted through the inner ear. Different frequencies produce their most movement at particular locations along the basilar membrane. For high-frequency tones, the wave motion is greatest at the base of the cochlea, where the oval and round windows are located. For low-frequency tones, the greatest wave motion of the basilar membrane is at the opposite end. So place theory suggests that perception of pitch depends on the specific location on the basilar membrane at which the greatest stimulation occurs.

The second theory, **frequency theory,** explains pitch by the rate of vibration of the basilar membrane. This theory predicts that a sound wave with a frequency of 100 Hz will set the basilar membrane vibrating 100 times per second. The frequency theory also predicts that the vibrations of the basilar membrane will cause neurons to fire at the same rate, so that rate of firing is the neural code for pitch. One problem with this theory is that individual neurons cannot fire rapidly enough to represent high-pitched sounds because none of them can fire more than 1,000 times per second. This limitation makes it impossible for

one neuron to distinguish sounds above 1,000 Hz—which, of course, your auditory system can do quite well. The limitation might be overcome by the **volley principle,** which explains what might happen at such high frequencies. This principle suggests that several neurons in a combined action, or volley, fire at the frequency that matches a stimulus tone of 2,000 Hz, 3,000 Hz, and so on (Wever, 1949).

As with the trichromatic and opponent-process theories of color vision, the place and frequency theories each successfully account for different aspects of your experience of pitch.

place theory The theory that different frequency tones produce maximum activation at different locations along the basilar membrane, with the result that pitch can be coded by the place at which activation occurs.

frequency theory The theory that a tone produces a rate of vibration in the basilar membrane equal to its frequency, with the result that pitch can be coded by the frequency of the neural response.

volley principle An extension of frequency theory, which proposes that when peaks in a sound wave come too frequently for a single neuron to fire at each peak, several neurons fire as a group at the frequency of the stimulus tone.

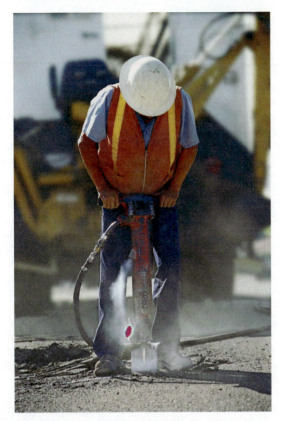

Sustained exposure to loud noise can lead to hearing loss. What can people do to avoid such losses?

Frequency theory accounts well for coding frequencies below about 5,000 Hz. At higher frequencies, neurons cannot fire quickly and precisely enough to code a signal adequately, even in volley. Place theory accounts well for perception of pitch at frequencies above 1,000 Hz. Below 1,000 Hz, the entire basilar membrane vibrates so broadly that it cannot provide a signal distinctive enough for the neural receptors to use as a means of distinguishing pitch. Between 1,000 and 5,000 Hz, both

mechanisms can operate. Thus a complex sensory task is divided between two systems that, together, offer greater sensory precision than either system alone could provide. We see next that you also possess two converging neural systems to help you localize sounds in the environment.

Sound Localization   Suppose you are walking across campus and you hear someone call your name. In most cases, you can readily locate the spatial location of the speaker. This example suggests how efficiently your auditory system carries out the task of **sound localization**—you are able to determine the spatial origins of auditory events. You do so through two mechanisms: assessments of the relative timing and relative intensity of the sounds that arrive at each ear (Recanzone & Sutter, 2008).

The first mechanism involves neurons that compare the relative times at which incoming sound reaches each ear. A sound occurring off to your right side, for example, reaches your right ear before your left (see point B in **Figure 4.20**). Neurons in your auditory system are specialized to fire most actively for specific time delays between the two ears. Your brain uses this information about disparities in arrival time to make precise estimates for the likely origins of a sound in space.

The second mechanism relies on the principle that a sound has a slightly greater intensity in the first ear at which it arrives—because your head itself casts a *sound shadow* that weakens the signal. These intensity differences depend on the relative size of the wavelength of a tone with respect to your head. Large-wavelength, low-frequency tones show virtually no intensity differences, whereas small-wavelength, high-frequency tones show measurable intensity differences. Your brain, once again, has specialized cells that detect intensity differences in the signals arriving at your two ears.

But what happens when a sound creates neither a timing nor an intensity difference? In Figure 4.20, a sound originating at point A would have this property. With your eyes closed, you cannot tell its exact location. So you must move your head—to

Why might bats have evolved the ability to use echolocation to navigate through their environment?

FIGURE 4.20 Time Disparity and Sound Localization

The brain uses differences in the time course with which sounds arrive at the two ears to localize the sounds in space.

sound localization The auditory processes that allow the spatial origins of environmental sounds.

reposition your ears—to break the symmetry and provide the necessary information for sound localization.

It's interesting to note that porpoises and bats use their auditory systems rather than their visual systems to locate objects in dark waters or dark caves. These species use *echolocation*—they emit high-pitched sounds that bounce off objects, giving them feedback about the objects' distances, locations, sizes, textures, and movements. In fact, one species of bat is able to use echolocation to differentiate between objects that are just 0.3 millimeters apart (Simmons et al., 1998).

Stop *and* Review

① What physical property of a sound produces the perception of pitch?
② What role do hair cells play in the auditory system?
③ Which theory suggests that the perception of pitch depends on the location on the basilar membrane at which the greatest stimulation occurs?
④ What timing difference would you expect if a sound originated off to your right side?

✓●━ **Study** and **Review** on **MyPsychLab**

YOUR OTHER SENSES

This chapter has devoted the most attention to vision and hearing because scientists have studied them most thoroughly. However, your ability both to survive in and to enjoy the external environment relies on your full repertory of senses. To close the discussion of sensation, let's briefly consider several of your other senses.

Smell

You can probably imagine circumstances in which you'd be just as happy to give up your sense of smell: Did you ever have a family dog that lost a battle with a skunk? But to avoid that skunk experience, you'd also have to give up the smells of fresh roses, hot buttered popcorn, and hot chocolate. Each of these substances releases odors into the air in the form of *odorant molecules*. The process of **olfaction**—the technical term for the sense of smell—begins when those molecules interact with receptor proteins on the membranes of *olfactory cilia* (see **Figure 4.21**). It takes only 8 molecules of a substance to initiate one of these nerve impulses, but at least 40 nerve endings must be stimulated before you can smell the substance. Once initiated, these nerve impulses convey odor information to the **olfactory bulb,** located just above the receptors and just below the frontal lobes of the cerebrum. Odor stimuli start the process of smell by stimulating an influx of chemical substances into ion channels in olfactory neurons, an event that, as you may recall from Chapter 3, triggers an action potential.

The anatomical location of the olfactory nerves and olfactory bulb leaves them vulnerable to damage. For example, when people suffer from blows to the head, the axons of the nerve cells that carry impulses to the olfactory bulb may be damaged. In one sample of 49 patients who had experienced a mild traumatic brain injury underwent tests of their olfactory ability (Fortin et al., 2010). On one smell test, 28 experienced *hyposmia* (a diminished sense of smell), and 11 experienced *anosmia* (a total loss of smell). However, there's some hope for recovery: The olfactory system generates new cells in both olfactory receptors and the olfactory bulb. For that reason,

··

olfaction The sense of smell.

olfactory bulb The center where odor-sensitive receptors send their signals, located just below the frontal lobes of the cortex.

A. View of skull

B. Enlarged aspect of olfactory receptors

FIGURE 4.21 Receptors for Smell
The olfactory receptor cells in your nasal cavities are stimulated by chemicals in the environment. They send information to the olfactory bulb in your brain.

some patients are able to regain some or all of their ability to smell as time passes after brain injury (London et al., 2008).

The significance of the sense of smell varies greatly across species. Smell presumably evolved as a system for detecting and locating food (Moncrieff, 1951). Humans seem to use the sense of smell primarily in conjunction with taste, to seek and sample food. However, for many species smell is also used to detect potential sources of danger. Dogs, rats, insects, and many other creatures for whom smell is central to survival have a far keener sense of smell than humans do. Relatively more of their brain is devoted to smell. Smell serves these species well because organisms do not have to come into direct contact with other organisms to smell them.

In addition, smell can be a powerful form of active communication. Members of many species communicate by secreting and detecting chemical signals called **pheromones,** chemical substances used within a given species to signal sexual receptivity, danger, territorial boundaries, and food sources (Thomas, 2011; Wolf, 2011). For example, females of various insect species produce sex pheromones to signal that they are available for mating (Herbst et al., 2011; Yang et al., 2011). We revisit the topic of pheromones when we consider both human and nonhuman sexual behaviors in Chapter 11. 👁

Taste

Although food and wine gourmets are capable of making remarkably subtle and complex taste distinctions, many of their sensations are really smells, not tastes. **Gustation**—the technical term for the sense of taste—and smell work together closely when you eat. In fact, when you have a cold, food seems tasteless because your nasal passages are blocked and you can't smell the food. Demonstrate this principle for yourself: Hold your nose and try to tell the difference between foods of similar texture but different tastes, such as pieces of apple and raw potato. Because the sense of smell has such a broad impact on how food tastes, people who suffer from olfactory disorders often experience a loss of appetite.

The surface of your tongue is covered with *papillae,* which give it a bumpy appearance. Many of these papillae contain clusters of taste receptor cells called the *taste buds* (see **Figure 4.22** on page 100). Single-cell recordings of taste receptors show that individual receptor cells respond best to one of the four primary taste qualities: sweet, sour, bitter, and saline (salty) (Frank & Nowlis, 1989). In recent years, researchers have found receptors for a fifth basic taste quality, *umami* (McCabe & Rolls, 2007). Umami is the flavor of monosodium glutamate (MSG), the chemical that is often added to Asian foods and occurs naturally in foods rich in protein, such as meat, seafood, and aged cheese. Although receptor cells for the five qualities may produce small responses to other tastes, the "best" response most directly encodes quality. There appear to

Why would a man with a cold be ill-advised to take up wine tasting?

be separate transduction systems for each of the basic classes of taste (Carleton et al., 2010).

Taste receptors can be damaged by many things you put in your mouth, such as alcohol, cigarette smoke, and acids. Fortunately, your taste receptors get replaced about every 10 days—even more frequently than smell receptors (Breslin & Spector, 2008). Indeed, the taste system is the most resistant to damage of all your sensory systems; it is extremely rare for anyone to suffer a total, permanent taste loss.

From all the meals you've shared with family and friends, you are probably aware that people have very different taste preferences. For example, some people love spicy food whereas others shudder at the thought of a hot pepper. Some preferences are explained by differences in the flavors people experience quite early in life. In fact, the foods mothers eat change the flavor of amniotic fluid, so some food preferences may be shaped in utero (Beauchamp & Mennella, 2011). However, people also show remarkable differences in the numbers of taste buds they possess. **Figure 4.23** on page 100 shows two tongues: The group of individuals who have considerably more than an average number of taste buds are called *supertasters* (Bartoshuk, 1993). As you can see in the figure, supertasters form a sharp contrast, in the extremes of their sensory experiences, to *nontasters*. The variations in the density of taste buds on different people's tongues appear to be genetic (Bartoshuk & Beauchamp, 1994). Women are much more likely than men to be supertasters. Supertasters generally have more sensitivity to bitter chemicals—a sensory quality shared

· ·

👁 **Watch** the **Video** *The Basics: In Full Appreciation of the Cookie* on **MyPsychLab**

pheromone Chemical signal released by an organism to communicate with other members of the species; pheromones often serve as long-distance sexual attractors.

gustation The sense of taste.

A. Top view of tongue   B. Enlarged side view of papilla   C. Enlarged view of taste bud

Gustatory cell

Taste bud

Papillae

FIGURE 4.22 Receptors for Taste

Part A shows the distribution of the papillae on the upper side of the tongue. Part B shows a single papilla enlarged so that the individual taste buds are visible. Part C shows one of the taste buds enlarged.

by most poisons. You can imagine that if women generally were responsible for nurturing and feeding offspring over the course of evolution, the children of women with greater taste sensitivity would be more likely to survive.

Touch and Skin Senses

The skin is a remarkably versatile organ. In addition to protecting you against surface injury, holding in body fluids, and helping regulate body temperature, it contains nerve endings that produce sensations of pressure, warmth, and cold. These sensations are called the **cutaneous senses** (skin senses).

Consider how you become aware that a stimulus is creating *pressure* on your skin. Because you receive so much sensory information through your skin, different types of receptor cells operate close to the surface of the body (McGlone & Reilly, 2010). Each type of receptor responds to somewhat different patterns of contact with the skin (Lumpkin & Caterina, 2007). As two examples, *Meissner corpuscles* respond best when

something rubs against the skin, and *Merkel disks* are most active when a small object exerts steady pressure against the skin.

The skin's sensitivity to pressure varies tremendously over the body. For example, you are 10 times more accurate in sensing the position of stimulation on your fingertips than on your back. The variation in sensitivity of different body regions is shown by the greater density of nerve endings in these regions and also by the greater amount of sensory cortex devoted to them. In Chapter 3, you learned that your sensitivity is greatest where you need it most—on your face, tongue, and hands. Precise sensory feedback from these parts of the body permits effective eating, speaking, and grasping.

Suppose someone rubs an ice cube along your arm. You now have some ideas about how you would feel the pressure of the ice cube. But how would you sense that the *temperature*

···

cutaneous senses The skin senses that register sensations of pressure, warmth, and cold.

FIGURE 4.23 The Tongues of a Supertaster (A) and a Nontaster (B)

Some taste preferences are explained by considerable differences in the number of tastebuds people possess.

is cold? You may be surprised to learn that you have separate receptors for warmth and coolness. Rather than having one type of receptor that works like a thermometer, your brain integrates separate signals from *cold fibers* and *warm fibers* to monitor changes in environmental temperature.

One aspect of cutaneous sensitivity plays a central role in human relationships: touch. Through touch, you communicate to others your desire to give or receive comfort, support, love, and passion (Gallace & Spence, 2010). However, where you get touched or touch someone else makes a difference; those areas of the skin surface that give rise to erotic, or sexual, sensations are called *erogenous zones*. Other touch-sensitive erotic areas vary in their arousal potential for different individuals, depending on learned associations and the concentration of sensory receptors in the areas.

The Vestibular and Kinesthetic Senses

The next pair of senses may be entirely new to you because they do not have receptors you can see directly, like eyes, ears, or noses. Your **vestibular sense** tells you how your body—especially your head—is oriented in the world with respect to gravity. The receptors for this information are tiny hairs in fluid-filled sacs and canals in the inner ear. The hairs bend when the fluid moves and presses on them, which is what happens when you turn your head quickly. The *saccule* and *utricle* (shown in Figure 4.19 on page 96) tell you about acceleration or deceleration in a straight line. The three canals, called the *semicircular canals,* are at right angles to each other and thus can tell you about motion in any direction. They inform you how your head is moving when you turn, nod, or tilt it.

People who lose their vestibular sense because of accidents or disease are initially quite disoriented and prone to falls and dizziness. However, most of these people eventually compensate by relying more heavily on visual information. *Motion sickness* can occur when the signals from the visual system conflict with those from the vestibular system. People feel nauseated when reading in a moving car because the visual signal is of a stationary object while the vestibular signal is of movement. Drivers rarely get motion sickness because they are both seeing and feeling motion.

Whether you are standing erect, drawing pictures, or making love, your brain needs to have accurate information about the current positions and movement of your body parts relative to one another. The **kinesthetic sense** (also called *kinesthesis*) provides constant sensory feedback about what the body is doing during motor activities. Without it, you would be unable to coordinate most voluntary movements.

You have two sources of kinesthetic information: receptors in the joints and receptors in the muscles and tendons. Receptors that lie in the joints respond to pressures that accompany different positions of the limbs and to pressure changes that accompany movements of the joints. Receptors in the

What role does the kinesthetic sense play in the performance of skilled athletes?

muscles and tendons respond to changes in tension that accompany muscle shortening and lengthening.

The brain often integrates information from your kinesthetic sense with information from touch senses. Your brain, for example, can't grasp the full meaning of the signals coming from each of your fingers if it doesn't know exactly where your fingers are in relation to one another. Imagine that you pick up an object with your eyes closed. Your sense of touch may allow you to guess that the object is a stone, but your kinesthetic sense will enable you to know how large it is.

Pain

Pain is the body's response to stimulation from harmful stimuli—those that are intense enough to cause tissue damage or threaten to do so. Are you entirely happy that you have such a well-developed pain sense? Your answer probably should be "yes and no." On the "yes" side, your pain sense is critical for survival. People born with congenital insensitivity to pain feel no hurt, but their bodies often become scarred and their limbs

Why would riding in the front seat of a roller coaster be less likely to make you nauseated than riding in the rear?

....

vestibular sense The sense that tells how one's own body is oriented in the world with respect to gravity.

kinesthetic sense The sense concerned with bodily position and movement of the body parts relative to one another.

pain The body's response to noxious stimuli that are intense enough to cause, or threaten to cause, tissue damage.

deformed from injuries that they could have avoided, had their brains been able to warn them of danger (Cox et al., 2006). Their experience shows that pain serves as an essential defense signal—it warns you of potential harm. On the "no" side, there are certainly times when you would be happy to be able to turn off your pain sense. In one survey of 4,090 adults, 26 percent reported that they suffered from chronic pain—"pain that occurs constantly or flares up frequently" (Toblin et al., 2011, p. 1250).

Scientists have begun to identify the specific sets of receptors that respond to pain-producing stimuli. They have learned that some receptors respond only to temperature, others to chemicals, others to mechanical stimuli, and still others to combinations of pain-producing stimuli. This network of pain fibers is a fine meshwork that covers your entire body. Peripheral nerve fibers send pain signals to the central nervous system by two pathways: a fast-conducting set of nerve fibers that are covered with myelin and slower, smaller nerve fibers without any myelin coating. Starting at the spinal cord, the impulses are relayed to the thalamus and then to the cerebral cortex, where the location and intensity of the pain are identified, the significance of the injury is evaluated, and action plans are formulated.

Within your brain, *endorphins* have an impact on your experience of pain. Recall from Chapter 3 that pain-killing drugs such as morphine bind to the same receptor sites in the brain—the term *endorphin* comes from *endogenous* (self-produced) *morphines*. The release of endorphins within the brain controls your experience of pain. Researchers believe that endorphins are at least partially responsible for the pain-reducing effects of acupuncture and placebos (Han, 2011; Pollo et al., 2011). 👁

Your emotional responses, context factors, and your interpretation of the situation can be as important as actual physical stimuli in determining how much pain you experience (Gatchel et al., 2007; Hollins, 2010). How are pain sensations affected by the psychological context? One theory about the way pain may be modulated is known as the **gate-control theory**, developed by **Ronald Melzack** (1973, 1980). This theory suggests that cells in the spinal cord act as neurological gates, interrupting and blocking some pain signals and letting others get through to the brain. Receptors in the skin and the brain send messages to the spinal cord to open or close those gates. Suppose, for example, you bump your shin on a table while running to answer the telephone. As you rub the skin around the bump, you send inhibitory messages to your spinal cord—closing the gates. Messages descending from the brain also can close the gates. If, for example, the phone call includes urgent news, your brain might close the gates to prevent you from experiencing the distraction of pain. Melzack (2005) has proposed an updated *neuromatrix theory* of pain that incorporates the reality that people often experience pain with little or no physical cause: In these cases, the experience of pain originates wholly in the brain.

We've just seen that the way you perceive pain may reveal more about your psychological state than about the intensity

....

👁 **Watch** the **Video** *In the Real World: Pain Management* on **MyPsychLab**

gate-control theory A theory about pain modulation that proposes that certain cells in the spinal cord act as gates to interrupt and block some pain signals while sending others to the brain.

Individuals taking part in religious rituals, such as walking on a bed of hot coals, are able to block out pain. What does that tell you about the relationship between the physiology and psychology of pain?

of the pain stimulus: What you perceive may be different from, and even independent of, what you sense. This discussion of pain prepares you for the rest of the chapter, which discusses the perceptual processes that allow you to organize and label your experiences of the world.

Stop *and* Review

① What is an important brain structure involved in the sense of smell?
② To what basic taste qualities do your taste buds respond?
③ How does your skin sense temperature?
④ What is the purpose of the vestibular sense?
⑤ What is the goal of gate-control theory?

✔●─ **Study** and **Review** on **MyPsychLab**

ORGANIZATIONAL PROCESSES IN PERCEPTION

Imagine how confusing the world would be if you were unable to put together and organize the information available from the output of your millions of retinal receptors. You would experience a kaleidoscope of disconnected bits of color moving and swirling before your eyes. The processes that put sensory information together to give you the perception of coherence are referred to collectively as processes of perceptual organization.

The discussion of perceptual organization begins with a description of the processes of *attention* that prompt you to focus on a subset of stimuli from your kaleidoscope of experience. We then consider the organizational processes first described by *Gestalt* theorists, who argued that what you perceive depends on laws of organization, or simple rules by which you perceive shapes and forms.

DOES A PAINFUL BREAK-UP *REALLY* HURT?

At some point in their life, almost everyone goes through a romantic break-up. If you are part of that large group, you might have told friends that the break-up was "painful" and that you were "hurt" by the rejection. We've seen in this chapter that the brain has characteristic responses to physical pain. But here's an interesting question: Does the brain respond in the same way to intense social pain as intense physical pain?

To address this question, a team of researchers recruited 40 participants, all of whom had weathered an unwanted break-up of a romantic relationship sometime in the six months before the study (Kross et al., 2011). The researchers made a distinction between the emotional response to pain and the actual physical experience. Physical pain causes emotional distress, as does social rejection. Earlier research confirmed that people's brains show similar patterns of emotional responses to both physical and social pain (MacDonald & Leary, 2005). However, the researchers wanted to demonstrate that intense social pain also brings about the same brain response as the actual sensory experience of pain. To provide this demonstration, the researchers asked participants to experience both physical and social pain while undergoing fMRI scans.

For physical pain, the participants experienced trials on which intense heat was applied to their left forearms. The level of heat was determined separately for each participant so that it was near the limit of what he or she could personally tolerate. In other trials, the participants experienced a warm stimulus that they had agreed was not painful. The contrast between the hot and warm trials allowed the researchers to see which brain regions were particularly active when the participants were experiencing physical pain.

The study provided a similar contrast for social pain. The participants arrived at the laboratory with two photographs: One of their ex-partners and another of a friend who was the same sex as their ex-. On some trials, participants viewed the headshots of their ex-partners while thinking about the rejection they had felt during the break-up. On other trials, participants viewed the headshots of their friends while thinking about a recent positive experience they had shared. Again, the researchers examined differences in brain response to the painful and nonpainful stimuli.

For each trial, the participants used a 5-point scale to rate the intensity of their distress. Lower numbers indicated greater distress. The researchers wished to equate the intensity of the physical and social pain. The participants' ratings suggested that this goal was met: The average reported intensity of physical pain was 1.88; the average reported intensity of social pain was 1.72.

So what did the fMRI scans show? As you'd expect, the physical pain produced activity in sensory areas of the brain that respond when the body is undergoing harmful stimulation. In addition, just as the researchers predicted, the same brain regions were active when participants ruminated on their break-ups! The conclusion here is, if you've ever claimed that a break-up "hurt," you were absolutely telling the truth.

Attentional Processes

Take a moment now to find 10 things in your environment that had not been, so far, in your immediate awareness. Had you noticed a spot on the wall? Had you noticed the ticking of a clock? If you start to examine your surroundings very carefully, you will discover that there are literally thousands of things on which you could focus. The processes of **attention** enable you to direct your awareness to a subset of all the information available to you. Generally, the more closely you attend to some object or event in the environment, the more you can perceive and learn about it.

What forces determine the objects that become the focus of your attention? The answer to this question has two components, which are called goal-directed attention and stimulus-driven attention (Chun et al., 2011). **Goal-directed attention** reflects the choices that you make about the objects to which you'd like to attend, as a function of your own goals. If, for example, you are contemplating a case full of pastries, you might direct your attention to only those desserts covered in chocolate. You are probably already comfortable with the idea that you can explicitly choose objects for particular scrutiny. **Stimulus-driven attention** occurs when features of the stimuli—objects in the environment—themselves automatically capture your attention, independent of your local goals as a perceiver. You've experienced stimulus-driven attention, for example, if you've ever been day-dreaming at a stoplight while out for a drive. The stoplight's abrupt change from red to green

attention A state of focused awareness on a subset of the available perceptual information.

goal-directed attention A determinant of why people select some parts of sensory input for further processing; it reflects the choices made as a function of one's own goals.

stimulus-driven attention A determinant of why people select some parts of sensory input for further processing; occurs when features of stimuli—objects in the environment—automatically capture attention, independent of the local goals of a perceiver.

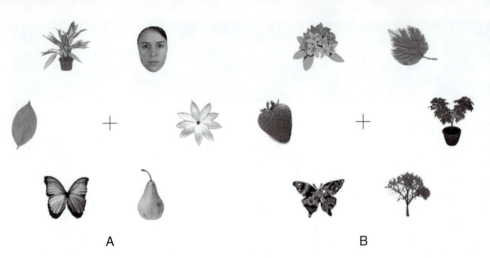

A   B

FIGURE 4.24 Processes That Select Attention

Participants viewed displays of six objects. They attempted to respond as quickly as possible whether each display included a butterfly. The objects were presented in grayscale so that participants couldn't use color to help them find the butterflies. When displays included a human face (Part A) participants' responses were slower than when no face was present (Part B).

will often capture your attention even if you were not particularly focused on it.

You might wonder what the relationship is between these two processes: Research suggests that, at least under some circumstances, stimulus-driven attention wins out over goal-directed attention.

*The researchers began with the hypothesis that "because of their biological and social significance," human faces are likely to capture attention (Langton et al., 2008, p. 331). To test that hypothesis, the researchers asked participants to view the types of displays shown in Parts A and B of **Figure 4.24**. The participants' task, in each case, was to answer as quickly as possible whether a butterfly was present in the display. For both parts of the figure, the answer is "yes." (There were, of course, other displays for which the answer was "no"!) Note that in Part A the the display also includes a human face. The researchers predicted that participants' attention would be captured by such faces. As a consequence, the researchers expected participants to take longer to find the butterflies than when no faces were present (as in Part B of the figure). That prediction was confirmed: The presence of the faces made it more difficult for participants to find the butterflies. To rule out the possibility that the faces were just more visually interesting, the researchers replicated the experiment except that they turned all the stimulus pictures upside down. Under those circumstances, the faces no longer looked facelike. As such, they no longer interfered with the participants' ability to find the butterflies.*

You can recognize this phenomenon as stimulus-driven attention because it works in the opposite direction of the perceiver's goals. If participants could ignore the faces, they would perform the task better. Because participants almost always prefer to perform as well as possible on experimental tasks, we can conclude that the faces captured their attention despite their goal-directed desire to attend to the butterflies as efficiently as possible.

Let's suppose that you have focused your attention on some stimulus in the environment. It's time for your processes of perceptual organization to go to work.

Principles of Perceptual Grouping

Consider the image on the left in **Figure 4.25**. If you're like most people, you'll see a vase as *figure* against a black *ground*. A figure is seen as an objectlike region in the forefront, and ground is seen as the backdrop against which the figures stand out. As you can see on the right of Figure 4.25, it's possible to change the relationship between figure and ground—to see two faces rather than one vase. One of the first tasks your perceptual processes carry out is to decide what in a scene counts as figure and what as ground.

How do your perceptual processes determine what should be gathered together into the figure? The principles of perceptual grouping were studied extensively by proponents of **Gestalt psychology,** such as **Kurt Koffka** (1935), **Wolfgang Köhler** (1947), and **Max Wertheimer** (1923). Members of this group maintained that psychological phenomena could be understood only when viewed as organized, structured *wholes*

FIGURE 4.25 Figure and Ground

An initial step in perceptual grouping is for your perceptual processes to interpret part of a scene as a figure standing out against a ground.

Gestalt psychology A school of psychology that maintains that psychological phenomena can be understood only when viewed as organized, structured wholes, not when broken down into primitive perceptual elements.

and not when broken down into primitive perceptual elements. The term *gestalt* roughly means "form," "whole," "configuration," or "essence." In their experiments, the Gestalt psychologists studied how perceptual arrays give rise to gestalts: They demonstrated that the whole is often quite different from the sum of its parts. By varying a single factor and observing how it affected the way people perceived the structure of the array, they were able to formulate a set of laws:

1. *The law of proximity.* People group together the nearest (most proximal) elements. That's why you see this display as five columns of objects instead of four rows.

2. *The law of similarity.* People group together the most similar elements. That's why you see a square of *Os* against a field of *Xs* rather than columns of mixed *Xs* and *Os*.

```
X  X  X  X  X
X  O  O  O  X
X  O  O  O  X
X  O  O  O  X
X  X  X  X  X
```

3. *The law of good continuation.* People experience lines as continuous even when they are interrupted. That's why you interpret this display as an arrow piercing the heart rather than as a design with three separate pieces.

4. *The law of closure.* People tend to fill in small gaps to experience objects as wholes. That's why you fill in the missing piece to perceive a whole circle.

5. *The law of common fate.* People tend to group together objects that appear to be moving in the same direction. That's why you experience this figure as alternating rows moving apart.

• • • • •

• • • • •

• • • • •

• • • • •

Spatial and Temporal Integration

All the gestalt laws you have seen so far should have convinced you that a lot of perception consists of putting the pieces of your world together in the "right way." Often, however, you can't perceive an entire scene in one glance, or *fixation* (recall the discussion of attention). What you perceive at a given time is often a restricted glimpse of a large visual world extending in all directions to unseen areas of the environment. To get a complete idea of what is around you, you must combine information from fixations of different spatial locations—*spatial integration*—at different moments in time—*temporal integration*.

What may surprise you is that your visual system does not work very hard to create a moment-by-moment, integrated picture of the environment. Research suggests that your visual memory for each fixation on the world does not preserve precise details.

Featured Study

Consider the two photos in **Figure 4.26** *on page 106: They show the same scene but one in close-up and the other in wide-angle. Suppose you viewed just one of these two photos and, after a brief delay, you had to say which one it had been. You might think you'd do quite well at this memory test. However, researchers have demonstrated that participants make systematic errors after a delay of less than 1/20th of a second (Dickinson & Intraub, 2008). In a series of studies, participants viewed three photographs—either close-up or wide-angle—in quick succession. Then, after brief delays, the participants saw either a close-up or wide-angle version of one of the three photos. The participants had to respond whether the view was the one they had seen before on a 5-point scale that ranged from –2 ("much closer up") to 0 ("the same") to +2 ("much farther away"). Participants made a very consistent error in their judgments: They rated identical views as being too close up. The researchers called this error boundary extension because participants regularly believed that the original photos included information beyond the boundaries of the original photo.*

Why might boundary extension happen and happen so quickly? Consider what it's like to look out a window. You don't believe that the world stops at the window's edges. Instead, you use your world knowledge to extend the view beyond what you can see. In many respects, looking at a photograph is the same as looking out a window. Because you complete the scene around the edges of the photo, you are quite likely to recall that the photo included more than was actually present. This explanation of boundary extension should suggest to you why this "error" makes sense: It's not a bad thing for you to complete the larger scene from the sample of a single glimpse.

Researchers have identified a number of instances in which people have difficulty noticing changes from one view of a scene to the next (Simons & Ambinder, 2005). Some instances of what is often called *change blindness* can be quite dramatic. For example, in one study, participants failed to notice that the person with whom they were having a conversation had changed (Simons & Levin, 1998)! The study unfolded somewhat like a magic trick—the two experimenters changed places as a door passed through the middle of the conversation. In fact, stage magicians have long taken advantage of change

(A)
Wide-Angle View

(B)
Close-Up View

FIGURE 4.26 Boundary Extension

When people view photographs they are quite likely to use memory processes to extend the boundaries of the scene. For that reason, they often recall seeing a wide-angle view when, in fact, they originally experienced a close-up.

blindness to accomplish a variety of their tricks. (For examples of the perceptual basis of several famous illusions, see Macknik et al., 2008.) How is it possible for people to be blind to such large changes in their visual world? Recall the earlier discussion of attention. To notice a change, it is important that you have attended to both the original and changed features of the world. Even then, you often need to expend mental resources to try to detect a change.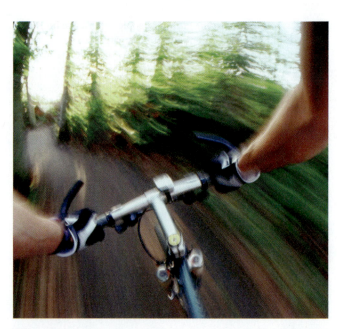

Motion Perception

One type of perception that does require you to make comparisons across different glimpses of the world is motion perception. Suppose you see a friend across a classroom. If he stands still, the size of his image on your retina will expand as you walk toward him. The rate at which this image has expanded gives you a sense of how quickly you have been approaching (Gibson, 1979).

You can appreciate the consequences of how your perceptual processes combine those glimpses of the world when you experience the **phi phenomenon.** This phenomenon occurs when two stationary spots of light in different positions in the visual field are turned on and off alternately at a rate of about four to five times per second. This effect occurs on outdoor advertising signs and in strobe light displays. Even at this relatively slow rate of alternation, it appears that a single light is moving back and forth between the two spots.

Motion perception also helps you piece together the elements of the visual world. Imagine that you are viewing a rabbit bounding through tall grass. You probably cannot see the whole of the rabbit at any one time. However, your brain finds the common motion among the different pieces to conclude that they all belong to one coherent object (Schwarzkopf et al., 2011).

Depth Perception

Until now, we have considered only two-dimensional patterns on flat surfaces. Everyday perceiving, however, involves objects in three-dimensional space. Perceiving all three spatial

dimensions is absolutely vital for you to approach what you want, such as interesting people and good food, and avoid what is dangerous, such as speeding cars and falling pianos. This perception requires accurate information about *depth* (the distance from you to an object) as well as about its *direction* from you. Your ears can help in determining direction, but they are not much help in determining depth. Your interpretation of

What makes you aware that the "protagonist" in this photo is moving—and in what direction is the motion?

....

👁 **Watch** the **Video** *What's In It For Me?: Perceptual Magic in Art and Movies* on **MyPsychLab**

phi phenomenon The simplest form of apparent motion, the movement illusion in which one or more stationary lights going on and off in succession are perceived as a single moving light.

Daffodil

Tulip

Observer

Left-eye view

Right-eye view

Daffodil

Tulip

Observer

Left-eye view

Right-eye view

FIGURE 4.27 Retinal Disparity

Retinal disparity increases with the distance in depth between two objects.

depth relies on many different information sources about distance (often called *depth cues*)—among them binocular cues, motion cues, and pictorial cues.

Binocular and Motion Cues Have you ever wondered why you have two eyes instead of just one? The second eye is more than just a spare. Your two eyes together provide you with compelling information about depth. Cues to depth that involve comparisons of the visual information that arrives at your two eyes are called **binocular depth cues.** The two sources of binocular depth information are *retinal disparity* and *convergence.*

Because the eyes are about 2 to 3 inches apart horizontally, they receive slightly different views of the world. To convince yourself of this, try the following experiment. First, close your left eye and use the right one to line up your two index fingers with some small object in the distance, holding one finger at arm's length and the other about a foot in front of your face. Now, keeping your fingers stationary, close your right eye and open the left one while continuing to fixate on the distant object. What happened to the position of your two fingers? The second eye does not see them lined up with the distant object because it gets a slightly different view.

This displacement between the horizontal positions of corresponding images in your two eyes is called **retinal disparity.** It provides depth information because the amount of disparity, or difference, depends on the relative distance of objects from you (see **Figure 4.27**). For instance, when you switched eyes, the closer finger was displaced farther to the side than was the distant finger.

When you look at the world with both eyes open, most objects that you see stimulate different positions on your two retinas. If the disparity between corresponding images in the two retinas is small enough, the visual system is able to fuse them into a perception of a single object in depth. (However, if the images are too far apart, you actually see the double images, as when you cross your eyes.) When you stop to think about it, what your visual system does is pretty amazing: It takes two different retinal images, compares them for horizontal displacement of corresponding parts, and produces a

unitary perception of a single object in depth. In effect, the visual system interprets horizontal displacement between the two images as depth in the three-dimensional world.

Other binocular information about depth comes from **convergence.** Your eyes turn inward to some extent whenever they are fixated on an object (see **Figure 4.28**). When the object

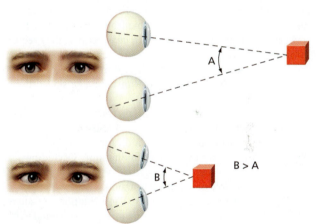

Convergence

FIGURE 4.28 Convergence Cues to Depth

When an object is close to you, your eyes must converge more than when an object is at a greater distance. Your brain uses information from your eye muscles to use convergence as a cue to depth.

From Ciccarelli, Saundra K; White, J. Noland, *Psychology*, 3rd Edition, © 2012. Reprinted and electronically reproduced by permission of Pearson Education, Inc., Upper Saddle River, New Jersey.

. . . .

binocular depth cue Depth cue that uses information from both eyes.

retinal disparity The displacement between the horizontal positions of corresponding images in the two eyes.

convergence The degree to which the eyes turn inward to fixate on an object.

is very close—a few inches in front of your face—the eyes must turn toward each other quite a bit for the same image to fall on both foveae. You can actually see the eyes converge if you watch a friend focus first on a distant object and then on one a foot or so away. Your brain uses information from your eye muscles to make judgments about depth. However, convergence information from the eye muscles is useful for depth perception only up to about 10 feet. At greater distances, the angular differences are too small to detect because the eyes are nearly parallel when you fixate on a distant object.

To see how *motion* is another source for depth information, try the following demonstration. As you did before, close one eye and line up your two index fingers with some distant object. Then move your head to the side while fixating on the distant object and keeping your fingers still. As you move your head, you see both your fingers move, but the close finger seems to move farther and faster than the more distant one. The fixated object does not move at all. This source of information about depth is called **motion parallax.** Motion parallax provides information about depth because, as you move, the relative distances of objects in the world determine the amount and direction of their relative motion in your retinal image of the scene. Next time you sit in the passenger seat of a car, keep a watch out the window for motion parallax at work. Objects at a distance from the moving car will appear much more stationary than those closer to you.

Monocular Cues   But suppose you had vision in only one eye. Would you not be able to perceive depth? In fact, further information about depth is available from just one eye. These sources are called **monocular depth cues** because they require information just from one or the other eye. Artists who create images in what appear to be three dimensions (on the two dimensions of a piece of paper or canvas) make skilled use of monocular depth cues.

Interposition, or *occlusion,* arises when an opaque object blocks out part of a second object (see **Figure 4.29**). Interposition gives you depth information indicating that the occluded object is farther away than the occluding one. Occluding surfaces also block out light, creating shadows that can be used as an additional source of depth information.

Three more sources of pictorial information are all related to the way light projects from a three-dimensional world onto a two-dimensional surface such as the retina: relative size, linear perspective, and texture gradients. *Relative size* involves a basic rule of light projection: Objects of the same size at different distances project images of different sizes on the retina. The closest one projects the largest image and the farthest one the smallest image. This rule is called the *size/distance relation.* As you can see in **Figure 4.30**, if you look at an array with identical objects, you interpret the smaller ones to be farther away.

Linear perspective is a depth cue that also depends on the size/distance relation. When parallel lines (by definition

FIGURE 4.29 Interposition Cues to Depth
What visual cues tell you whether this woman is behind the bars?

separated along their lengths by the same distance) recede into the distance, they converge toward a point on the horizon in your retinal image (see **Figure 4.31**). Your visual system's interpretation of converging lines gives rise to the Ponzo illusion. The upper line looks longer because you interpret

FIGURE 4.30 Relative Size as a Depth Cue
Objects that are closer project larger images on the retina. As a consequence, when you look at an array with identical objects, you interpret the smaller ones to be at a greater distance.

....

motion parallax A source of information about depth in which the relative distances of objects from a viewer determine the amount and direction of their relative motion in the retinal image.

monocular depth cue Depth cue that uses information from only one eye.

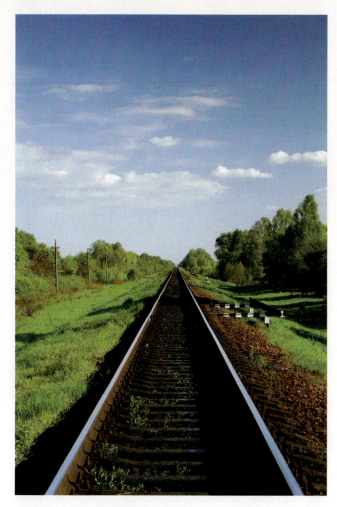

FIGURE 4.31 The Ponzo Illusion

The converging lines add a dimension of depth, and therefore the distance cue makes the top line appear larger than the bottom line, even though they are actually the same length.

the converging sides according to linear perspective as parallel lines receding into the distance. In this context, you interpret the upper line as though it were farther away, so you see it as longer—a farther object would have to be longer than a nearer one for both to produce retinal images of the same size.

Texture gradients provide depth cues because the density of a texture becomes greater as a surface recedes in depth. The wheat field in **Figure 4.32** is an example of the way texture is used as a depth cue. You can think of this as another consequence of the size/distance relation. In this case, the units that make up the texture become smaller as they recede into the distance, and your visual system interprets this diminishing grain as greater distance in three-dimensional space.

By now, it should be clear that there are many sources of depth information. Under normal viewing conditions, however, information from these sources comes together in a single, coherent three-dimensional interpretation of the environment. You experience depth, not the different cues to depth that existed in the proximal stimulus. In other words, your visual system uses cues such as differential motion, interposition, and

relative size automatically, without your conscious awareness, to make the complex computations that give you a perception of depth in the three-dimensional environment.

Perceptual Constancies

To help you discover another important property of visual perception, I'd like you to play a bit with your textbook. Put your book down on a table, then move your head closer to it so that it's just a few inches away. Then move your head back to a normal reading distance. Although the book stimulated a much larger part of your retina when it was up close than when it was far away, didn't you perceive the book's size to remain the same? Now set the book upright and try tilting your head clockwise. When you do this, the image of the book rotates counterclockwise on your retina, but didn't you still perceive the book to be upright?

In general, you see the world as *invariant, constant,* and *stable* despite changes in the stimulation of your sensory receptors. Psychologists refer to this phenomenon as **perceptual constancy.** Roughly speaking, it means that you perceive the properties of the distal stimuli, which are usually constant, rather than the properties of proximal stimuli, which change every time you move your eyes or head. For survival, it is critical that you perceive constant and stable properties of objects in the world despite the enormous variations in the properties of the light patterns that stimulate your eyes. The critical task of perception is to discover *invariant* properties of your environment despite the variations in your retinal impressions of them. We see next how this works for size, shape, and orientation.

Size and Shape Constancy What determines your perception of the size of an object? In part, you perceive an object's actual size on the basis of the size of its retinal image. However, the demonstration with your book shows that the size of the

FIGURE 4.32 Examples of Texture as a Depth Cue

The wheat field is a natural example of the way texture can be used as a depth cue. Notice the way the wheat slants.

....

perceptual constancy The ability to retain an unchanging percept of an object despite variations in the retinal image.

Ames Room

Viewer

FIGURE 4.33 The Ames Room

The Ames room is designed to be viewed through a peephole with one eye—that is the vantage point from which these photographs were taken. The Ames room is constructed from nonrectangular surfaces at odd angles in depth and height. However, with only the view from the peephole, your visual system interprets it as an ordinary room and makes some unusual guesses about the relative heights of the occupants.

retinal image depends on both the actual size of the book and its distance from the eye. As you now know, information about distance is available from a variety of depth cues. Your visual system combines that information with retinal information about image size to yield a perception of an object size that usually corresponds to the actual size of the distal stimulus. **Size constancy** refers to your ability to perceive the true size of an object despite variations in the size of its retinal image.

If the size of an object is perceived by taking distance cues into account, then you should be fooled about size whenever you are fooled about distance. One such illusion occurs in the Ames room shown in **Figure 4.33**. In comparison to the child, the adult looks quite short in the left corner of this room, but he looks enormous in the right corner. The reason for this illusion is that you perceive the room to be rectangular, with the two back corners equally distant from you. Thus you perceive the child's actual size as being consistent with the size of the images on your retina in both cases. In fact, the child is not at the same distance because the Ames room creates a clever illusion. While it appears to be a rectangular room, it is actually made from nonrectangular surfaces at odd angles in depth and height, as you can see in the drawings that accompany the photos. Any person on the right will make a larger retinal image, because he or she is twice as close to the observer. (By the way, to get the illusion you must view the display with a single eye through a peephole—that's the vantage point of the

photographs in Figure 4.33. If you could move around while viewing the room, your visual system would acquire information about the unusual structure of the room.)

Another way that the perceptual system can infer objective size is by using prior knowledge about the characteristic size of similarly shaped objects. For instance, once you recognize the shape of a house, a tree, or a dog, you have a good idea of how big each is, even without knowing its distance from you. When past experience does not give you knowledge of what familiar objects look like at extreme distances, size constancy may break down. You have experienced this problem if you have looked down at people from the top of a skyscraper and thought that they resembled ants.

Shape constancy is closely related to size constancy. You perceive an object's actual shape correctly even when the object is slanted away from you, making the shape of the retinal image substantially different from that of the object itself. For instance, a rectangle tipped away projects a trapezoidal image onto your retina; a circle tipped away from you projects an elliptical image (see **Figure 4.34**). Yet you usually perceive the shapes accurately as a circle and a rectangle slanted away in space. When there is good depth information available, your visual system can determine an object's true shape simply by taking into account your distance from its different parts.

Lightness Constancy Consider the photograph in **Figure 4.35**. When you look at the brick wall in this picture, you don't perceive some of the bricks to be light red and some of them to be dark red—instead, you perceive this as a wall in which all the bricks are equally light or dark but some of them are in shadow (Kingdom, 2011). This is an example of lightness constancy: **Lightness constancy** is your tendency to perceive the whiteness, grayness, or blackness of objects as constant across changing levels of illumination.

....

size constancy The ability to perceive the true size of an object despite variations in the size of its retinal image.

shape constancy The ability to perceive the true shape of an object despite variations in the shape of the retinal image.

lightness constancy The tendency to perceive the whiteness, grayness, or blackness of objects as constant across changing levels of illumination.

FIGURE 4.34 Shape Constancy

As a coin is rotated, its image becomes an ellipse that grows narrower and narrower until it becomes a thin rectangle, an ellipse again, and then a circle. At each orientation, however, it is still perceived as a circular coin.

As with the other constancies, you experience lightness constancy quite frequently in everyday life. Suppose, for example, you are wearing a white T-shirt and walk from a dimly lit room outside into a bright sunny day. In bright sunshine, the T-shirt reflects far more light into your eyes than it does in the dim room, yet it looks about equally light to you in both contexts. In fact, lightness constancy works because the *percentage* of light an object reflects remains about the same even as the *absolute* amount of light changes. Your bright white T-shirt is going to reflect 80 to 90 percent of whatever light is available; your black jeans are going to reflect only about 5 percent of the available light. That's why—when you see them in the same context—the T-shirt will always look lighter than the jeans.

In this section, you have encountered a number of organizational processes in perception. In the final section of the chapter, let's consider the identification and recognition processes that give meaning to objects and events in the environment.

Illusions

You have just reviewed a number of processes that your perceptual system uses to provide you with accurate perception of the world. Even so, occasions remain on which your perceptual systems deceive you: When you experience a stimulus pattern in a manner that is demonstrably incorrect, you are experiencing an **illusion.** The word *illusion* shares the same root as *ludicrous*—both stem from the Latin *illudere,* which means "to mock at." Illusions are shared by most people in the same perceptual situation because of shared physiology in sensory systems and overlapping experiences of the world. (As you will learn in Chapter 5, this sets illusions apart from hallucinations. Hallucinations are nonshared perceptual distortions that individuals experience as a result of unusual physical or mental states.) Examine the classic visual illusions in **Figure 4.36** on page 112. Although it is most convenient to present you with visual illusions, illusions also exist in other sensory modalities such as hearing (Deutsch et al., 2011; Zheng et al., 2011), taste (Todrank & Bartoshuk, 1991), and touch (Tsakiris et al., 2010).

Researchers often invent new illusions or reconceive old ones to investigate important features of perceptual processes. Consider the first example in Figure 4.36, the Müller-Lyer illusion, which was first given as an illustrating by Franz Müller-Lyer in an 1889 work on optical illusions. Figure 4.36 shows a prominent explanation for this illusion. **Richard Gregory** (1966) suggested that people experience the standard arrow as the exterior corner of a building bulging toward them; people experience the open arrow as an interior corner, farther away. Because of the relationship between size and distance, people experience the arrow that looks like an interior corner as farther away. On this explanation, the Müller-Lyer illusion provides an example of ordinary processes of depth perception leading to an incorrect percept. However, the matter is far from settled. Contemporary researchers continue to provide evidence that sometimes supports and sometimes contradicts this explanation (Howe & Purves, 2005; Weidner & Fink, 2007)! Fortunately, ongoing investigations of the classic

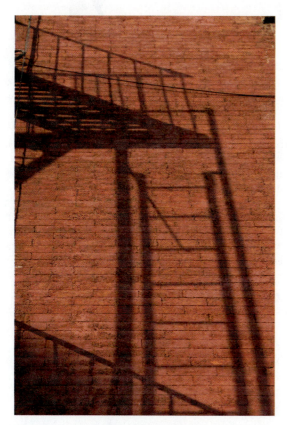

FIGURE 4.35 Lightness Constancy

Lightness constancy helps explain why you perceive all the bricks in the wall to be made of the same material.

illusion An experience of a stimulus pattern in a manner that is demonstrably incorrect but shared by others in the same perceptual environment.

Which vertical line is longer?

Müller-Lyer illusion

Is the diagonal line broken?

Poggendorf illusion

Are the vertical lines parallel?

Zöllner illusion

Which is larger: the brim or the top of the hat?

Top hat illusion

FIGURE 4.36 Four Illusions to Tease Your Brain
Each of these illusions represents circumstances in which perception is demonstrably incorrect. Researchers often use illusions to test their theories. These theories explain why perceptual systems that generally function quite accurately yield illusions in special circumstances.

illusions in Figure 4.36 continue to provide researchers with novel insights into perceptual processes.

Illusions are also a basic part of your everyday life. Consider your day-to-day experience of your home planet, Earth. You've seen the sun "rise" and "set" even though you know that the sun is sitting out there in the center of the solar system as decisively as ever. You can appreciate why it was such an extraordinary feat of courage for Christopher Columbus and other voyagers to deny the obvious illusion that Earth was flat and sail off toward one of its apparent edges. Similarly, when a full moon is overhead, it seems to follow you wherever you go even though you know the moon isn't chasing you. What you are experiencing is an illusion created by the great distance of the moon from your eye. When they reach Earth, the moon's light rays are essentially parallel and perpendicular to your direction of travel, no matter where you go.

People can control illusions to achieve desired effects. Architects and interior designers use principles of perception to create objects in space that seem larger or smaller than they really are. A small apartment becomes more spacious when it is painted with light colors and sparsely furnished with low small couches, chairs, and tables in the center of the room instead of against the walls. Psychologists working with NASA in the U.S. space program have researched the effects of environment on

perception in order to design space capsules that have pleasant sensory qualities. Set and lighting directors of movies and theatrical productions purposely create illusions on film and on stage.

Despite all of these illusions, you generally do pretty well getting around the environment. That is why researchers typically study illusions to help explain how perception ordinarily works so well. The study of illusions supplements other strands of research on organizational processes in perception.

Stop *and* **Review**

① What is meant by stimulus-driven attention?
② What is the law of closure?
③ What visual information allows you to understand that a man is walking toward you?
④ How does convergence provide cues to depth?
⑤ What is shape constancy?

CRITICAL THINKING   In the experiment on boundary extension, do you think the results would change if participants were warned about the error?

✓•—**Study** and **Review** on **MyPsychLab**

Critical Thinking in Your Life

ARE DRIVERS DISTRACTED WHEN THEY USE THEIR CELL PHONES?

Depending on where you live, it might already be illegal for you to use some types of cell phones while you drive. You probably also have strong opinions about whether such restrictions are necessary. Researchers have provided data to inform public policy debates on this issue. Much of that research has focused on drivers' ability to focus their attention both on their phone calls and on the driving environment (Strayer et al., 2011).

Consider a study in which participants drove through a suburban environment in a high-fidelity driving simulator (Strayer et al., 2003). The simulation required participants to display the full range of ordinary driving skills (including accelerating, maintaining speed, and braking). Each participant had two different driving experiences. Half the time, participants performed only the single task of navigating the route. At the other times, participants engaged in a second task: As they drove along, they had hands-free cell phone calls about a variety of ordinary topics. At all times, participants drove routes that included several billboards. At the end of the experiment, they were given a surprise memory test. Participants recognized 6.9 (out of 15) billboards from times when they were just driving; they recognized just 3.9 billboards from times when they were also having a cell phone conversation.

Let's try to establish the role that attention plays in this result. There are two reasonable explanations for why participants' memory would be less good when they were having their conversations: They might never have looked at the billboards at all or they might have *looked* at the billboards but not have *attended* to them. To understand this latter

hypothesis, look up from your textbook at the room around you. As you gaze in a particular direction, you can see many objects but to acquire detailed information you must focus your attention directly on an object.

In the driving experiment, the researchers obtained measures of participants' eye movements allowing for precise determination of where they looked. In fact, participants were equally likely to look at each billboard with and without the simultaneous conversation—and they even looked for the same amount of time. What seemed to impair participants' memory was that they looked at the billboards without actually focusing attention on them. Researchers have conducted similar experiments with participants driving real cars out on the road (Harbluk et al., 2007). This work has generated the same strong conclusion that cell phone conversations divert drivers' attention from the environment. In addition, this research documented the behavioral consequences of diversions of attention: The most distracted drivers also had to engage in the most "hard braking."

Do these studies convince you that people should be disallowed from using even hands-free cell phones while driving? What other data would you want to see?

- Why might the researchers have chosen research designs in which every participant carried out both the single and dual tasks?

- How do ethical considerations constrain the types of studies researchers can carry out on this issue?

IDENTIFICATION AND RECOGNITION PROCESSES

You can think of all the perceptual processes described so far as providing knowledge about physical properties of the distal stimulus—the position, size, shape, texture, and color of objects in a three-dimensional environment. However, you would not know what the objects were or whether you had seen them before. Your experience would resemble a visit to an alien planet where everything was new to you; you wouldn't know what to eat, what to put on your head, what to run away from, or what to date. Your environment appears nonalien because you are able to recognize and identify most objects as things you have seen before and as members of the meaningful categories that you know about from experience. Identification and recognition attach meaning to what you perceive.

Bottom-Up and Top-Down Processes

When you identify an object, you must match what you see to your stored knowledge. Taking sensory data in from the

environment and sending it toward the brain for extraction and analysis of relevant information is called bottom-up processing. **Bottom-up processing** is anchored in empirical reality and deals with bits of information and the transformation of concrete, physical features of stimuli into abstract representations (look back to Figure 4.2 on page 82). This type of processing is also called *data-driven processing* because your starting point for identification is the sensory evidence you obtain from the environment—the data.

In many cases, however, you can use information you already have about the environment to help you make a perceptual identification. If you visit a zoo, for example, you might be better prepared to recognize some types of animals than you otherwise would be. You are more likely to hypothesize that you are seeing a tiger there than you would be in your own backyard. When your expectations affect perception, the phenomenon is called top-down processing.

bottom-up processing Perceptual analyses based on the sensory data available in the environment; results of analysis are passed upward toward more abstract representations.

A

The soldier's thoughts of the dangerous

or $\Big\{$ bat **tle** ✦   (Noise added to signal; subject hears both "tle" and noise)

      bat ✦   (Noise replaces signal; subject hears only noise)

made him very nervous.

B

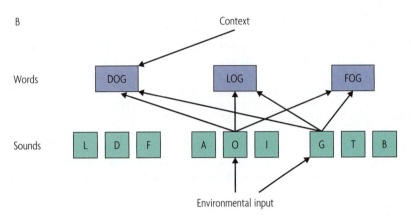

FIGURE 4.37 Phonemic Restoration

(A) Listeners are challenged to say whether noise has been added on top of a syllable or used to replace a syllable. Because of phonemic restoration, they often can't tell. They "hear" the missing information even when the sound is replaced by noise. (B) In this example, noise obscured the /d/ when your friend said "dog." Based only on the environmental input, your perceptual system can come up with several hypotheses: dog, log, fog, and so on. However, top-down information from the context—"I have to go home and walk my . . ."—supports the hypothesis that your friend said "dog."

Reprinted with permission from Irwin Rock, *The Logic of Perception*, Cambridge, MA: The MIT Press. Copyright © 1983.

Top-down processing involves your past experiences, knowledge, motivations, and cultural background in perceiving the world. With top-down processing, higher mental functioning influences how you understand objects and events. Top-down processing is also known as conceptually driven (or hypothesis-driven) processing because the concepts you have stored in memory affect interpretation of the sensory data.

For a more detailed example of top-down versus bottom-up processing, we turn to the domain of speech perception. You have undoubtedly had the experience of trying to carry on a conversation at a very loud party. Under those circumstances, it's probably true that not all of the physical signal you are producing arrives unambiguously at your acquaintance's ears: Some of what you had to say was almost certainly obscured by coughs, thumping music, or peals of laughter. Even so, people rarely realize that there are gaps in the physical signal they are experiencing. This phenomenon is known as *phonemic restoration* (Warren, 1970). As you'll see more fully in Chapter 10, *phonemes* are the minimal, meaningful units of sound in a language; phonemic restoration occurs when people use top-down processes to fill in missing phonemes. Listeners often find it difficult to tell whether they are hearing a word that has a noise replacing part of the original speech signal or whether they are hearing a word with a noise just superimposed on the intact signal (see part A of **Figure 4.37**) (Samuel, 2011).

Part B of Figure 4.37 shows how bottom-up and top-down processes could interact to produce phonemic

restoration. Suppose part of what your friend says at a noisy party is obscured so the signal that arrives at your ears is "I have to go home to walk my (noise)og." If noise covers the /d/, you are likely to think that you actually heard the full word *dog*. But why? In Figure 4.37, you see two of the types of information relevant to speech perception. We have the individual sounds that make up words and the words themselves. When the sounds /o/ and /g/ arrive in this system, they provide information—in a bottom-up fashion—to the word level (the figure gives only a subset of the words in English that end with /og/). This provides you with a range of candidates for what your friend might have said. Now top-down processes go to work—the context helps you select *dog* as the most likely word to appear in this utterance. When all of this happens swiftly enough—bottom-up identification of a set of candidate words and top-down selection of the likely correct candidate—you'll never know that the /d/ was missing. Your perceptual processes believe that the word was intact (Samuel, 1997). The next time you're in a noisy environment, you'll be glad your perceptual processes fill sounds in so efficiently!

The Influence of Contexts and Expectations

A primary goal of perception is to get an accurate "fix" on the world. Survival depends on accurate perceptions of objects and events in your environment: Is that motion in the bushes a tiger? However, there are many occasions on which bottom-up perceptual processes leave you with more than one hypothesis about the identity of the stimuli in the world—or in some cases, no particularly good hypotheses at all. In those cases, your top-down processes make use of contexts and expectations to help you get a clear sense of what's out in the world.

---

top-down processing Perceptual processes in which information from an individual's past experience, knowledge, expectations, motivations, and background influence the way a perceived object is interpreted and classified.

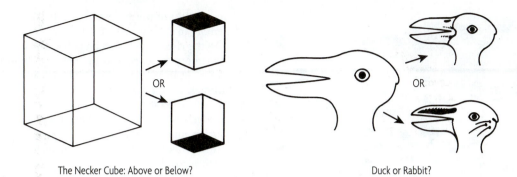

The Necker Cube: Above or Below?   Duck or Rabbit?

FIGURE 4.38 Perceptual Ambiguities

Each example allows two interpretations, but you cannot experience both at the same time. Do you notice your perception flipping back and forth between each pair of possibilities?

Consider **Figure 4.38**, which provides two examples in which the same sensory information permits two interpretations. The two examples are *ambiguous figures*. **Ambiguity** is an important concept in understanding perception because it shows that a single image can result in *multiple interpretations*. Look at each image until you can see the two alternative interpretations. Notice that once you have seen both of them, your perception flips back and forth between them as you look at the ambiguous figure. ⊙▸

Many prominent artists have used perceptual ambiguity as a central creative device in their works. **Figure 4.39** presents *Slave Market with the Disappearing Bust of Voltaire* by Salvador Dali. This work reveals a complex ambiguity in which a whole section of the picture must be radically reorganized and reinterpreted to allow perception of the "hidden" bust of the French philosopher-writer Voltaire. The white sky under the lower arch is Voltaire's forehead and hair; the white portions of the two ladies' dresses are his cheeks, nose, and chin. (If you have trouble seeing him, try blurring your vision or holding the book at arm's length.) Once you have seen the bust of Voltaire in this picture, however, you will never be able to look at it without knowing where this Frenchman is hiding.

When the environment provides ambiguous information, you use contextual information as well as prior expectations to help you settle on particular interpretations. Depending on what you already know, where you are, and what else you see around you, your identification may vary. Read the following words:

They say THE CAT, right? Now look again at the middle letter of each word. Physically, these two letters are exactly the same, yet you perceived the first as an *H* and the second as an *A*.

THE CAT

Why? Clearly, your perception was affected by what you know about words in English. The context provided by T_E makes an *H* highly likely and an *A* unlikely, whereas the reverse is true of the context of C_T (Selfridge, 1955).

In some cases, you need context to work even a bit harder. Consider **Figure 4.40** on page 116. What do you make of it? Suppose I tell you that it's a view into a neighbor's backyard, showing a tree around which his Dalmatian routinely sniffs? Now can you see a dog? (The dog's nose is roughly in the middle of the figure.) To perceive the Dalmatian requires the top-down use of information from memory. If you didn't have any prior experiences of sniffing dogs, you'd likely never be able to have an unambiguous percept of this scene.

Contexts and expectations play an important background role throughout your everyday life. Have you ever had the experience of seeing people you knew in places where you didn't expect to see them, such as in a different city or a different social group? It takes much longer to recognize them in such situations, and sometimes you aren't even sure that you really know them. The problem is not that they look any different but that the *context* is wrong; you didn't *expect* them to be there.

FIGURE 4.39 Ambiguity in Art

This painting by Salvador Dali is called *Slave Market with the Disappearing Bust of Voltaire. Can you find Voltaire?* Dali is one of a large number of modern and contemporary artists who have exploited ambiguity in their work.

....

⊙▸ **Simulate** the **Experiment** *Ambiguous Figures* on **MyPsychLab**

ambiguity Property of perceptual object that may have more than one interpretation.

FIGURE 4.40 An Ambiguous Picture

What do you see in this picture?

Reprinted by permission of Sylvia Rock.

The spatial and temporal context in which objects are recognized provides an important source of information because from the context you generate expectations about what objects you are and are not likely to see nearby.

Researchers have often documented the effects of context and expectation on perception (and response) by studying set. **Set** is a temporary readiness to perceive or react to a stimulus in a particular way. There are three types of set: motor, mental, and perceptual. A *motor set* is a readiness to make a quick, prepared response. A runner trains by perfecting a motor set to come out of the blocks as fast as possible at the sound of the starting gun. A mental set is a readiness to deal with a situation, such as a problem-solving task or a game, in a way determined by learned rules, instructions, expectations, or habitual tendencies. A *mental set* can actually prevent you from solving a problem when the old rules don't seem to fit the new situation, as we'll see when we study problem solving in Chapter 9. A *perceptual set* is a readiness to detect a particular stimulus in a given context. A new mother, for example, is perceptually set to hear the cries of her child.

Often a set leads you to change your interpretation of an ambiguous stimulus. Consider these two series of words:

FOX; OWL; SNAKE; TURKEY; SWAN; D?VE
BOB; RAY; TONY; BILL; HENRY; D?VE

Did you read through the lists? What word came to mind for D?VE in each case? If you thought DOVE and DAVE, it's

---

set A temporary readiness to perceive or react to a stimulus in a particular way.

because the list of words created a set that directed your search of memory in a particular way.

All the effects of context on perception clearly require that your memory be organized in such a fashion that information relevant to particular situations becomes available at the right times. In other words, to generate appropriate (or inappropriate) expectations, you must be able to make use of prior knowledge stored in memory. Sometimes you "see" with your memory as much as you see with your eyes. In Chapter 7, you'll meet the properties of memory that make context effects on perception possible.

Final Lessons

To solidify all that you have learned in this chapter, take a look back at Figure 4.2—you now have the knowledge necessary to understand the whole flowchart. Examination of Figure 4.2 will also confirm that the important lesson to be learned from the study of perception is that a perceptual experience in response to a stimulus event is a response of the whole person. In addition to the information provided when your sensory receptors are stimulated, your final perception depends on who you are, whom you are with, and what you expect, want, and value. A perceiver often plays two different roles that you might compare to gambling and interior design. As a gambler, a perceiver is willing to bet that the present input can be understood in terms of past knowledge and personal theories. As a compulsive interior decorator, a perceiver is constantly rearranging the stimuli so that they fit better and are more coherent. Incongruity and messy perceptions are rejected in favor of those with clear, clean, consistent lines.

If perceiving were completely bottom-up, you would be bound to the same mundane, concrete reality of the here and now. You could register experience but not profit from it on later occasions, nor would you see the world differently under different circumstances. If perceptual processing were completely top-down, however, you could become lost in your own fantasy world of what you expect and hope to perceive. A proper balance between the two extremes achieves the basic goal of perception: to experience what is out there in a way that optimally serves your needs as a biological and social being, moving about and adapting to your physical and social environment.

Stop *and* Review

① Why is phonemic restoration an example of top-down processing?
② What makes a stimulus ambiguous?
③ What is a set?

✓•⎯[**Study** and **Review** on **MyPsychLab**

Recapping Main Points

Sensory Knowledge of the World

- The task of perception is to determine what the distal (external) stimulus is from the information contained in the proximal (sensory) stimulus.
- Psychophysics investigates psychological responses to physical stimuli. Researchers measure absolute thresholds and just noticeable differences between stimuli.
- Signal detection allows researchers to separate sensory acuity from response biases.
- Researchers in psychophysics have captured the relationship between physical intensity and psychological effect.
- Sensation translates the physical energy of stimuli into neural codes via transduction.

The Visual System

- Photoreceptors in the retina, called rods and cones, convert light energy into neural impulses.
- Ganglion cells in the retina integrate input from receptors and bipolar cells. Their axons form the optic nerves that meet at the optic chiasma.
- Visual information is distributed to several different areas of the brain that process different aspects of the visual environment, such as how things look and where they are.
- The wavelength of light is the stimulus for color.
- Color sensations differ in hue, saturation, and brightness.
- Color vision theory combines the trichromatic theory of three color receptors with the opponent-process theory of color systems composed of opponent elements.

Hearing

- Hearing is produced by sound waves that vary in frequency, amplitude, and complexity.
- In the cochlea, sound waves are transformed into fluid waves that move the basilar membrane. Hairs on the basilar membrane stimulate neural impulses that are sent to the auditory cortex.
- Place theory best explains the coding of high frequencies, and frequency theory best explains the coding of low frequencies.
- To compute the direction from which the sound is arriving, two types of neural mechanisms compute the relative intensity and timing of sounds coming to each ear.

Your Other Senses

- Smell and taste respond to the chemical properties of substances and work together when people are seeking and sampling food.
- Olfaction is accomplished by odor-sensitive cells deep in the nasal passages.
- Taste receptors are taste buds embedded in papillae, mostly in the tongue.
- The cutaneous (skin) senses give sensations of pressure and temperature.
- The vestibular sense gives information about the direction and rate of body motion.
- The kinesthetic sense gives information about the position of body parts and helps coordinate motion.
- Pain is the body's response to potentially harmful stimuli.
- The physiological response to pain involves sensory response at the site of the pain stimulus and nerve impulses moving between the brain and the spinal cord.

Organizational Processes in Perception

- Perceptual processes organize sensations into coherent images and give you perception of objects and patterns.
- Both your personal goals and the properties of the objects in the world determine where you will focus your attention.
- The Gestalt psychologists provided several laws of perceptual grouping, including proximity, similarity, good continuation, closure, and common fate.
- Perceptual processes integrate over both time and space to provide an interpretation of the environment.
- Binocular, motion, and pictorial cues all contribute to the perception of depth.
- You tend to perceive objects as having stable size, shape, and lightness.
- Knowledge about perceptual illusions can provide constraints on ordinary perceptual processes.

Identification and Recognition Processes

- During the final stage of perceptual processing— identification and recognition of objects—percepts are given meaning through processes that combine bottom-up and top-down influences.
- Ambiguity may arise when the same sensory information can be organized into different percepts.
- Context, expectations, and perceptual sets may guide recognition of incomplete or ambiguous data in one direction rather than another equally possible one.

KEY TERMS

absolute threshold (p. 82)
accommodation (p. 86)
amacrine cell (p. 87)
ambiguity (p. 115)
attention (p. 103)
auditory nerve (p. 95)
basilar membrane (p. 95)

binocular depth cue (p. 107)
bipolar cell (p. 87)
blind spot (p. 87)
bottom-up processing (p. 113)
brightness (p. 91)
cochlea (p. 95)
complementary colors (p. 91)

cone (p. 87)
convergence (p. 107)
cutaneous sense (p. 100)
dark adaptation (p. 87)
difference threshold (p. 84)
distal stimulus (p. 81)
fovea (p. 87)

Chapter 4 • Practice Test

1. Suppose you are looking at a globe of the world. Although the _____ is a sphere, you'd expect the _____ to be a circle.
   a. distal; absolute
   b. distal; proximal
   c. threshold; distal
   d. proximal; distal

2. When you first walked into a room, you were overwhelmed by the smell of someone's perfume. Over time, you become less aware of the smell. This is an example of
   a. a psychometric function.
   b. sensory adaptation.
   c. an illusion.
   d. transduction.

3. You are carrying out an experiment in which you want to find a difference threshold for soft drinks that vary in their sugar concentration. You want to find the point at which the stimuli are recognized as different _____ percent of the time.
   a. 50
   b. 25
   c. 100
   d. 75

4. The conversion of one form of physical energy into another is called
   a. sensory adaptation.
   b. transduction.
   c. sensory reception.
   d. photoreception.

5. If you walk into a room that has very low illumination, your _____ are likely to contribute more than your _____ to your visual experience.
   a. rods; amacrine cells
   b. horizontal cells; rods
   c. cones; rods
   d. rods; cones

6. Which of these pairs does not play a role in opponent-process theory?
   a. red versus green
   b. white versus black
   c. yellow versus blue
   d. blue versus green

7. The airborne sound wave becomes "seaborne" when the auditory information reaches the
   a. auditory nerve.
   b. cochlea.
   c. tympanic membrane.
   d. fovea.

8. Which of these is *not* a primary taste quality?
   a. bitter
   b. sweet
   c. tangy
   d. sour

9. The purpose of _____ theory is to explain some aspects of the relationship between physical and psychological experiences of pain.
   a. gate-control
   b. volley
   c. frequency
   d. place

10. In a study of physical and social pain, researchers demonstrated that people's brains responded
    a. more strongly for physical pain.
    b. more strongly for social pain.
    c. in the same areas for both types of pain.
    d. in different areas for the two types of pain.

11. When Shirley walks into a party, she looks around the room to find her husband Paul. This is an example of
    a. goal-driven attention.
    b. stimulus-driven attention.
    c. temporal integration.
    d. sensory adaptation.

12. Tomas owns a ring with a very small gap in it. The law of _____ explains why most people perceive his ring to be intact.
    a. similarity
    b. common fate
    c. good continuation
    d. closure

13. While engaging in simulated driving, Michael had a conversation on a hands-free cell phone. Based on experimental evidence, you predict that Michael
    a. would behave differently if he were driving a real car out on the road.
    b. would pay more attention to the visual environment than to his conversation.
    c. failed to attend to objects in the visual environment.
    d. failed to look at objects in the visual environment.

14. Just as Chris says, "I love you," a truck sounds its horn. Although the horn covered the *l* sound in *love*, Pat still perceives *love* as intact. This is an example of
    a. bottom-up processing.
    b. perceptual constancy.
    c. top-down processing.
    d. good continuation.

15. For a short while after seeing a horror movie, Calvin perceives every shadow as a monster. It sounds as though he is experiencing
    a. a perceptual set.
    b. shape constancy.
    c. the phi phenomenon.
    d. the law of common fate.

ESSAY QUESTIONS

1. How does signal detection theory explain why people might make different judgments given the same sensory experiences?

2. How do trichromatic theory and opponent-process theory fit together to explain important aspects of color vision?

3. How do ambiguous stimuli demonstrate some of the challenges your sensory and perceptual processes face as they help you interpret the world?

5

Mind, Consciousness, and Alternate States

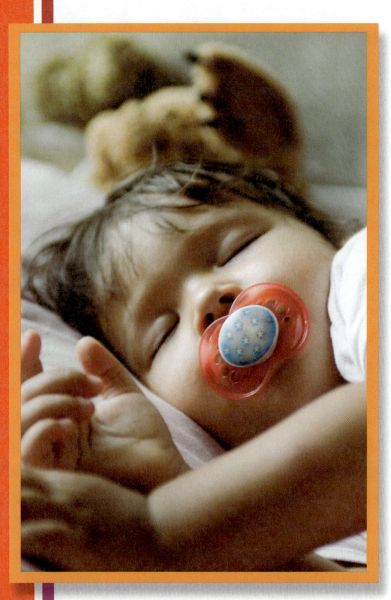

As you begin reading this chapter, take a moment to think about a favorite past event. Now think about what you'd like to have happen tomorrow or the next day. Where did these memories of the past and projections into the future *come* from and where did they *arrive*? Although you obviously have a vast body of information stored in your brain, it is very unlikely that these thoughts were "in mind" just as you were sitting down to read your psychology text. Therefore, you might feel comfortable saying that the thoughts arrived in your consciousness—and that they came from some part of your brain that was not then conscious. But how did these particular thoughts come to mind? Did you actually consider several different memories or options for the future? That is, were you consciously aware of making a choice? Or did thoughts somehow just emerge—by virtue of some set of unconscious operations—into your consciousness?

This series of questions provides a preview of the major topics of Chapter 5. We will begin by considering the contents and functions of your everyday consciousness. You will see that consciousness both aids survival and provides a sense of who you are and where you fit in the world. We then move to the changes in consciousness that accompany your daily cycles from waking to sleeping. We examine the approaches to dreams that have emerged in both Western and non-Western cultures. Finally, we will review the many instances in which people intentionally alter their states of consciousness by, for example, engaging in meditation and consuming mind-altering drugs. For all these topics, you will encounter the methods researchers use so that aspects of mind can be studied scientifically. You will learn how researchers have endeavored to externalize the internal, make public the private, and provide precise measures of subjective experiences.

the science of the mind. Wundt and Titchener used introspection to explore the contents of the conscious mind, and William James observed his own stream of consciousness. In fact, on the very first page of his classic 1892 text, *Psychology,* James endorsed as a definition of psychology "the description and explanation of states of consciousness as such."

Your ordinary waking consciousness includes your perceptions, thoughts, feelings, images, and desires at a given moment—all the mental activity on which you are focusing your attention. You are conscious of both what you are doing and also of the fact that you are doing it. At times, you are conscious of the realization that others are observing, evaluating, and reacting to what you are doing. A *sense of self* comes out of the experience of watching yourself from this privileged "insider" position. Taken together, these various mental activities form the contents of consciousness—all the experiences you are consciously aware of at a particular time (Legrand, 2007).

But what determines what is conscious right now? Were you, for example, aware of your breathing just now? Probably not; its control is part of *nonconscious processes.* Were you thinking about your last vacation or about the author of *Hamlet*? Again, probably not; control of such thoughts is part of *preconscious memories.* Were you aware of background noises, such as the ticking of a clock, the hum of traffic, or the buzzing of a fluorescent light? It would be difficult to be aware of all this and still pay full attention to the meaning of the material in this chapter; these stimuli are part of *unattended information.* Finally, there may be types of information that are *unconscious*—not readily accessible to conscious awareness—such as the set of grammatical rules that enable

THE CONTENTS
OF CONSCIOUSNESS

We must start by admitting that the term **consciousness** is ambiguous. We can use the term to refer to a general state of mind *or* to its specific contents: Sometimes you say you were "conscious" in contrast to being "unconscious" (for example, being under anesthesia or asleep); at other times, you say you were conscious—*aware*—of certain information or actions. There is, in fact, a certain consistency here—to be conscious of any particular information, you must be conscious. In this chapter, the *contents* of consciousness will mean the body of information of which you are aware. 👁

Awareness and Consciousness

As you saw in Chapter 1, some of the earliest research in psychology concerned the contents of consciousness. As psychology gradually diverged from philosophy in the 1800s, it became

Why is self-awareness considered such an important aspect of consciousness?

....

👁 **Watch** the **Video** *The Big Picture: The State of Our Consciousness* on **MyPsychLab**

consciousness A state of awareness of internal events and the external environment.

At any given time, thoughts about your job, your parents, or your hungry pet may flow below the level of consciousness until something occurs to focus your attention on one of these topics. Why are these memories considered preconscious, not unconscious?

you to understand this sentence. Let's examine each of these types of awareness. ⊙▸

Nonconscious Processes   There is a range of **nonconscious** bodily activities that rarely, if ever, impinge on consciousness. An example of nonconscious processes at work is the regulation of blood pressure. Your nervous system monitors physiological

information to detect and act on changes continually, without your awareness. At certain times, some ordinarily nonconscious activities can be made conscious: You can, for example, choose to exercise conscious control over your pattern of breathing. Even so, your nervous system takes care of many important functions without requiring conscious resources.

Preconscious Memories   Memories accessible to consciousness only after something calls your attention to them are known as **preconscious memories.** The storehouse of memory is filled with an incredible amount of information, such as your general knowledge of language, sports, or geography and recollections of your personally experienced events. Preconscious memories function silently in the background of your mind until a situation arises in which they are consciously necessary (as when I asked you to call to mind a favorite past event). You will learn much more about memory in Chapter 7.

Unattended Information   At any given time, you are surrounded by a vast amount of stimulation. As we saw in Chapter 4, you can focus your attention only on a small part of it. What you focus on, in combination with the memories it evokes, will determine, to a large extent, what is in your consciousness. In fact, people can remain unaware of pretty remarkable events when they fall outside their focus of attention. In one classic demonstration, research participants watched a video of two teams of students passing basketballs. The participants were instructed to count the number of times one team passed the ball. Meanwhile, as the video unfolded, someone dressed as a gorilla passed through the scene! Many of the participants remained completely unaware of the large intruder. Across the many variants of the experiment the researchers tried, about 50 percent of the participants never noticed the gorilla (Simons & Chabris, 1999). This phenomenon is called **inattentional blindness** because people fail to perceive objects when their attention is focused elsewhere. Given the results with the gorilla, it probably won't surprise you that real basketball players can suffer from inattentional blindness. They may, for example, fail to see that a teammate has become open because their attention is drawn to a nearby defensive player (Furley et al., 2010). ⊙▸

The Unconscious   You typically recognize the existence of *unconscious* information when you cannot explain some behavior by virtue of forces that were conscious at the time of the behavior. Sigmund Freud developed an initial theory of unconscious forces. As we will see in Chapter 13, Freud argued that people's psychological well-being is sufficiently threatened by certain life experiences that memories of those experiences are permanently banished from consciousness. Freud believed

⊙▸ **Simulate** the **Experiment** *Selective Attention* on **MyPsychLab**

⊙▸ **Simulate** the **Experiment** *Selective Attention* on **MyPsychLab**

nonconscious Not typically available to consciousness or memory.

preconscious memory Memory that is not currently conscious but that can easily be called into consciousness when necessary.

inattentional blindness People's failure to perceive objects when their attention is focused elsewhere.

that when the content of unacceptable ideas or motives is *repressed*—put out of consciousness—the strong feelings associated with the thoughts still remain and influence behavior. (We will revisit Freud's ideas when we consider the origin of your unique personality in Chapter 13.) 👁

Many psychologists now use the term *unconscious* to refer to information and processes that are more benign than the types of thoughts Freud suggested must be repressed (McGovern & Baars, 2007). For example, many types of ordinary language processing rely on unconscious processes. Consider this sentence (Vu et al., 2000):

She investigated the bark.

How did you interpret this sentence? Did you picture some woman looking after a dog or examining a tree? Because the word *bark* is ambiguous—and the sentence context provides little help—you can only guess at what the writer meant. Now consider the same sentence in a slightly larger context:

The botanist looked for a fungus. She investigated the bark.

Did you find the sentence easier to understand in this context? If you did, it's because your unconscious language processes used the extra context to make a very swift choice between the two meanings of *bark*.

This example demonstrates that processes that operate below the level of consciousness often affect your behavior—in this case, the ease with which you came to a clear understanding of the sentence. Thus, the discussion has shifted subtly from discussing the contents of consciousness to discussing the functions of consciousness. Before we take up that topic in detail, however, let's briefly describe two ways in which the contents of consciousness can be studied.

Studying the Contents of Consciousness

To study consciousness, researchers have had to devise methodologies to make deeply private experiences overtly measurable. One method asks experimental participants to speak aloud as they work through a variety of complex tasks. They report, in as much detail as possible, the sequence of thoughts they experience while they complete the tasks (Fox et al., 2011). The participants' reports, called *think-aloud protocols,* are used to document the mental strategies and representations of knowledge that the participants employ to do the task. For example, researchers collected think-aloud protocols to understand the different strategies experts and novices bring to their judgments about product designs (Locher et al., 2008).

In the *experience-sampling method,* participants provide information about their thoughts and feelings in the normal course of their daily lives (Hektner et al., 2007). Participants in experience-sampling research often carry devices that signal them when they should provide reports about the contents of their consciousness. For example, in one methodology, participants carry hand held electronic devices. The device produces a tone at random times each day (during waking hours) for a week or more. Whenever the tone sounds, participants may be asked to respond to statements such as "I am paying a lot of attention to how I feel right now" (Thompson et al., 2011, p. 1491). In this way, researchers can

Table 5.1 • Types of Comparisons in People's Thoughts

Type	Example
Social	"I'm a better basketball player than Tom."
Counterfactual	"If I'd left earlier, I could have gotten here on time."
Temporal–past	"I got more sleep when I was in high school."
Temporal–future	"My sister is going to start making new friends."

Based on A. Summerville & N. J. Roese, Dare to compare: Fact-based versus simulation-based comparison in daily life, *Journal of Experimental Social Psychology,* 44, pp. 664–671, Copyright 2008.

keep a running record of participants' thoughts, awareness, and focuses of attention as they go about their everyday lives. Consider an experiment that used handheld computers to obtain experience samples.

The researchers wished to determine how often people's thoughts focus on comparisons between their current reality and other possibilities (Summerville & Roese, 2008). At seven random times daily for two weeks, 34 participants were signaled by handheld computers to report what they were thinking in the moment. If the thoughts centered on comparisons, the participants placed them in the categories indicated in **Table 5.1***. The researchers found that 12 percent of the participants' thoughts were comparisons, which, as they noted, was "a remarkably large proportion given the sheer variety of mental experience" (p. 668). The comparisons were fairly evenly distributed across the four categories in Table 5.1. In addition, when participants' thoughts turned to changing the past (counterfactual comparisons) or contemplating the future (temporal–future comparisons), they were most often thoughts about how circumstances might have been or still could be better.*

Have you ever noticed how often these types of comparisons enter into your consciousness? The experience-sampling method allows researchers to provide a nuanced account of what and how people think about their lives.

If you take a quick look around the room in which you are reading, you can appreciate how many objects in your environment are readily available but are not (until you inspect the room) part of the contents of your consciousness. You can carry out the same quick review of your memory to demonstrate how much you have stored beyond the information that is the particular focus of your conscious attention. Techniques such as think-aloud protocols and experience sampling allow researchers to determine—for particular tasks and for particular times—which subset of all the information that individuals have available is present in consciousness.

....

👁 **Watch** the **Video** *Classic Footage of Carl Jung on Unconscious* on **MyPsychLab**

Stop *and* Review

① What is meant by a preconscious memory?
② How did Freud believe information became unconscious?
③ How do researchers obtain think-aloud protocols?

CRITICAL THINKING   Recall the experiment on comparisons. Why is it important that the experience samples be taken at random moments?

✓● Study and Review on MyPsychLab

THE FUNCTIONS OF CONSCIOUSNESS

When we address the question of the *functions* of consciousness, we are trying to understand why we *need* consciousness—what does it add to our human experience? In this section, we will consider the importance of consciousness to human survival and social function.

The Uses of Consciousness

Human consciousness was forged in the crucible of competition with the most hostile force in its evolutionary environment—other humans. The human mind may have evolved as a consequence of the extreme *sociability* of human ancestors, which was perhaps originally a group defense against predators and a means to exploit resources more efficiently. However, close group living then created new demands for cooperative as well as competitive abilities with other humans. Natural selection favored those who could think, plan, and imagine alternative realities that could promote both bonding with kin and victory over adversaries. Those who developed language and tools won the grand prize of survival of the fittest mind—and, fortunately, passed it on to us (Ramachandran, 2011).

Because consciousness evolved, you should not be surprised that it provides a range of functions that aid in the survival of the species (Bering & Bjorklund, 2007). Consciousness also plays an important role in allowing for the construction of both personal and culturally shared realities.

Aiding Survival   From a biological perspective, consciousness probably evolved because it helped individuals make sense of environmental information and use that information in planning the most appropriate and effective actions. Usually, you are faced with a sensory-information overload. William James described the massive amount of information that strikes the sensory receptors as a "blooming, buzzing confusion" assailing you from all sides. Consciousness helps you adapt to your environment by making sense of this profusion of confusion in three ways.

First, consciousness reduces the flow of stimulus input by restricting what you notice and what you focus on. You might recognize this *restrictive* function of consciousness from the discussion of *attention* in Chapter 4. Consciousness helps you tune out much of the information that is not relevant to your immediate goals and purposes. Suppose you decide to take a walk to enjoy a spring day. You notice trees blooming, birds singing, and children playing. If, all at once, a snarling dog appears on the scene, you use consciousness to restrict your attention to that dog and assess the level of danger. The restrictive function also applies to information you draw from your internal storehouse of information. At the outset of this chapter, I asked you to think about a favorite past event. When you did so, you were using your consciousness to restrict mental attention to a single past memory.

A second function of consciousness is *selective storage*. Even within the category of information to which you consciously attend, not all of it has continuing relevance to your ongoing concerns. After your encounter with the snarling dog, you might stop yourself and think, "I want to remember not to walk down this street." Consciousness allows you to selectively store—commit to memory—information that you want to analyze, interpret, and act on in the future; consciousness allows you to classify events and experiences as relevant or irrelevant to personal needs by selecting some and ignoring others. When we consider memory processes in Chapter 7, we will see that not all the information you add to memory requires conscious processing. Still, conscious memories have different properties—and involve different brain regions—than other types of memories.

A third function of consciousness is to make you stop, think, and consider alternatives based on past knowledge and imagine various consequences. This *planning* function enables you to suppress strong desires when they conflict with moral, ethical, or practical concerns. With this kind of consciousness you can plan a route for your next walk that avoids that snarling dog. Because consciousness gives you a broad time perspective in which to frame potential actions, you can call on knowledge of the past and expectations for the future to influence your current decisions. For all these reasons, consciousness gives you great potential for flexible, appropriate responses to the changing demands in your life.

Personal and Cultural Constructions of Reality   No two people interpret a situation in exactly the same way (Higgins & Pittman, 2008). Your *personal construction of reality* is your unique interpretation of a current situation based on your general knowledge, memories of past experiences, current needs, values, beliefs, and future goals. Each person attends more to certain features of the stimulus environment than to others precisely because his or her personal construction of reality has been formed from a selection of unique inputs. When your personal construction of reality remains relatively stable, your *sense of self* has continuity over time.

Individual differences in personal constructions of reality are even greater when people have grown up in different cultures, lived in different environments within a culture, or faced different survival tasks. The opposite is also true—because the people of a given culture share many of the same experiences, they often have similar constructions of reality. *Cultural constructions of reality* are ways of thinking about the world that are shared by most members of a particular group of people. When a member of a society develops a personal construction of reality that fits in with the cultural construction, it is affirmed by the culture and, at the same time, it affirms the cultural construction. In Chapter 13, we will consider more fully the relationship between the personal and the cultural sense of self.

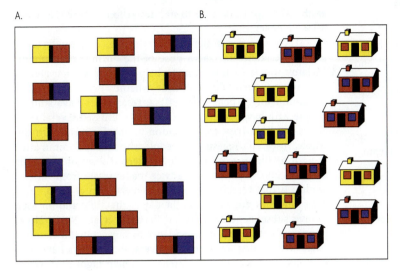

FIGURE 5.1 Search for the Conjunction of Two Colors

(A) Find the yellow and blue item. (B) Find the yellow house with blue windows. (A) Search is very inefficient when the conjunction is between the colors of two parts of a target. (B) However, search is much easier when the conjunction is between the color of the whole item and the color of one of its parts.

Data from Jeremy M. Wolfs, Parallel processing of part-whole information in visual search tasks, *Perception & Psychophysics*, 55 (1995), 537–550.

Studying the Functions of Consciousness

People's behavior is most often influenced by both conscious and unconscious processes. Many functions of consciousness include implicit comparisons with what remains unconscious. That is, conscious processes often affect or are affected by unconscious processes. To study the functions of consciousness, researchers often conduct research that demonstrates the different products of conscious and unconscious processes (McGovern & Baars, 2007).

For example, researchers have argued that people may bring either unconscious or conscious processes to bear on the many decisions they face in life (Kruglanski & Gigerenzer, 2011). Depending on which system of processes they use, people's responses can be quite different. Consider the domain of moral reasoning (to which we will return in Chapter 10). How would you respond to the classic "crying baby" dilemma in which you "must decide whether to smother one's own baby in order to prevent enemy soldiers from finding and killing oneself, one's baby, and several others" (Greene et al., 2008, p. 1147)? When people face this dilemma, their gut response—the product of unconscious processes—is that they could never smother their own child. However, when people face this problem with conscious deliberation, they often conclude that they must make the sacrifice to save the larger number of individuals.

To demonstrate that this shift reflects the use of conscious processes, researchers asked participants to consider dilemmas of this sort in two different circumstances (Greene et al., 2008). In one condition, participants read the dilemmas on a computer screen and indicated a "yes" or "no" judgment to a possible response (e.g., "Is it appropriate for you to smother your child in order to save yourself and the other townspeople?") as swiftly as possible. In the second condition, participants also read and responded to the dilemmas. However, they simultaneously had to monitor a stream of numbers scrolling across the computer screen and press a button every time they saw the number 5. The purpose of this second task is to overload participants' conscious processes. This simultaneous task should have made it much more difficult for them to use conscious processes to reason about the moral dilemmas. In fact, when participants had this extra load, it took them much longer to give the "yes" responses

to the moral dilemmas that represented the use of conscious reasoning. Thus, one way to study the function of consciousness is to demonstrate how people's responses change when conscious processes are not, in fact, allowed to function normally.

Another way to study the functions of consciousness is to determine which of the many tasks you carry out on a day-to-day basis require conscious intervention. To give you an example, I want you to put your book down for a moment and try to find an object in the room that is *red*. Let's assume that there is, in fact, a red object in your room. Under most circumstances, you should have felt as if your eyes were drawn to that object without any conscious effort. Research confirms that people can carry out a search for certain basic features of objects such as color, shape, and size, with little or no conscious attention (Wolfe, 2003). Suppose, now, that you try to find an object that is both *blue* and *red*. If you take a moment to carry out that task, you should have a very different sense of how much conscious effort is involved. Under most circumstances, you'll have to use conscious attention to find an object that has a combination of two features.

Figure 5.1 provides another example of the uses of conscious attention. In Part A, try to find the yellow and blue item. In Part B, try to find the yellow house with blue windows. Wasn't this second task much easier? Performance is much less affected by all the extra objects in the picture when the two colors are organized into *parts* and *wholes* (Wolfe et al., 1994). Could you feel your conscious attention being more engaged when you tried to find the yellow and blue item? From results of this sort, researchers are assembling a global view of the circumstances in which consciousness functions.

We have seen how the contents and functions of consciousness are defined and studied. We turn now to ordinary and then extraordinary alterations in consciousness.

Stop *and* Review

① What is the selective storage function of consciousness?

② What is a cultural construction of reality?

③ What role does consciousness play in visual search?

✓●─ **Study** and **Review** on **MyPsychLab**

SLEEP AND DREAMS

Almost every day of your life you experience a rather profound change in consciousness: When you decide it's time to end your day, you surrender yourself to sleep—and while you sleep you will undoubtedly dream. A third of your life is spent sleeping, with your muscles in a state of "benign paralysis" and your brain humming with activity. This section begins by considering the general biological rhythms of wakefulness and sleeping. We'll then focus more directly on the physiology of sleeping. Finally, we consider the major mental activity that accompanies sleep—dreaming—and explore the role dreams play in human psychology. ✳

Circadian Rhythms

All creatures are influenced by nature's rhythms of day and night. Your body is attuned to a time cycle known as a **circadian rhythm:** Your arousal levels, metabolism, heart rate, body temperature, and hormonal activity ebb and flow according to the ticking of your internal clock. For the most part, these activities reach their peak during the day and hit their low point at night while you sleep. The *Psychology in Your Life* box on page 133 discusses individual difference in circadian rhythms.

Research suggests that the clock your body uses is not exactly in synchrony with the clock on the wall: Without the corrective effects of external time cues, the human internal "pacemaker" establishes a 24.18-hour cycle (Czeisler et al., 1999). The exposure to sunlight that you get each day helps you make the small adjustment to a 24-hour cycle. Information about sunlight is gathered through your eyes, but receptors for regulation of circadian rhythms are not the same receptors that allow you to see the world (Guido et al., 2010). For example, animals without rods and cones (see Chapter 4) still sense light in a way that enables them to maintain their circadian rhythms.

Life circumstances that bring about a mismatch between your biological clock and your sleep cycle affect how you feel and act (Blatter & Cajochen, 2007; Kyriacou & Hastings, 2010). For example, individuals who work night shifts often experience both physical and cognitive difficulties because their circadian rhythms are disrupted (Arendt, 2010). Even after long periods on the night shift, most people are unable to adjust their circadian rhythms to overcome these negative effects (Folkard, 2008). People also experience disruptions when they engage in long-distance air travel. When people fly across time zones, they may experience *jet lag*, a condition whose symptoms include fatigue, irresistible sleepiness, and subsequent unusual sleep–wake schedules. Jet lag occurs because the internal circadian rhythm is out of phase with the normal temporal environment (Sack, 2010). For example, your body says it's 2 A.M.—and thus is at a low point on many physiological measures—when local time requires you to act as if it is noon.

What variables influence jet lag? The direction of travel and the number of time zones passed through are the most important variables. Traveling eastbound creates greater jet lag than traveling westbound because your biological clock can be more readily extended than shortened, as required on eastbound trips (it is easier to stay awake longer than it is to fall asleep sooner).

If you've ever suffered from jet lag, you might have gotten the advice to take a dose of the hormone *melatonin*. Melatonin acts in the brain to help regulate your cycles of waking and sleep. To determine whether external doses of melatonin might help with jet lag, researchers have studied people who have traveled on flights that crossed several time zones—such as trips from London to San Francisco. On the whole, research suggests that people who take melatonin after these long flights experience fewer sleep disruptions (Arendt & Skene, 2005). The general advice that emerges from various studies is that travelers should take melatonin at bedtime in their new time zone both on the day of the flight and for four or five subsequent days (Pandi-Perumal et al., 2007). Note, however, that there is little evidence to suggest that melatonin helps with jet lag for short stopovers. Researchers have also demonstrated melatonin's potential to help night shift workers adjust their cycles of sleeping and waking (Pandi-Perumal et al., 2007).

Circadian rhythms are also highly affected by exposure to light. For that reason, researchers have explored the possibilities of helping people adjust their circadian rhythms by exposing them to light (Sack, 2010). These interventions have often proved successful for night shift workers (Fahey & Zee, 2006). For example, night shift workers often suffer from difficulties in paying attention while on the job. In one study, participants experienced several hours of bright light to help them make the transition to a night shift (Santhi et al., 2008). The light treatment helped to reduce the negative impact on the participants' attentional performance.

The Sleep Cycle

About a third of your circadian rhythm is devoted to that period of behavioral quiescence called *sleep*. Most of what is known about sleep concerns the electrical activities of the brain. The methodological breakthrough for the study of sleep came in 1937 with the application of a technology that records brain wave activity of the sleeper in the form of an electroencephalogram (EEG). The EEG provided an objective, ongoing measure of the way brain activity varies when people are awake or asleep. With the EEG, researchers discovered that brain waves change in form at the onset of sleep and show further systematic, predictable changes during the entire sleep period (Loomis et al., 1937). The next significant discovery in sleep research was that bursts of **rapid eye movements (REM)** occur at periodic intervals during sleep (Aserinsky & Kleitman, 1953). The time when a sleeper is not showing REM is known as **non-REM (NREM) sleep.** You will see in a later section that

....

✳ **Explore** the **Concept** *Virtual Brain: Sleep and Dreaming* on **MyPsychLab**

circadian rhythm A consistent pattern of cyclical body activities, usually lasting 24 to 25 hours and determined by an internal biological clock.

rapid eye movements (REM) A behavioral sign of the phase of sleep during which the sleeper is likely to be experiencing dreamlike mental activity.

non-REM (NREM) sleep The period during which a sleeper does not show rapid eye movement; characterized by less dream activity than during REM sleep.

REM and NREM sleep have significance for one of the night's major activities—dreaming.

Let's track your brain waves through the night. As you prepare to go to bed, an EEG records that your brain waves are moving along at a rate of about 14 cycles per second (cps). Once you are comfortably in bed, you begin to relax, and your brain waves slow down to a rate of about 8 to 12 cps. When you fall asleep, you enter your *sleep cycle,* each of whose stages shows a distinct EEG pattern. In stage 1 sleep, the EEG shows brain waves of about 3 to 7 cps. During stage 2, the EEG is characterized by *sleep spindles,* minute bursts of electrical activity of 12 to 16 cps. In the next two stages (3 and 4) of sleep, you enter into a very deep state of relaxed sleep. Your brain waves slow to about 1 to 2 cps, and your breathing and heart rate decrease. In a final stage, the electrical activity of your brain increases; your EEG looks very similar to those recorded during stages 1 and 2. It is during this stage that you will experience REM sleep, and you will begin to dream (see **Figure 5.2**). (Because the EEG pattern during REM sleep resembles that of an awake person, REM sleep was originally termed *paradoxical sleep.*)

Cycling through the first four stages of sleep, which are NREM sleep, requires about 90 minutes. REM sleep lasts for about 10 minutes. Over the course of a night's sleep, you pass

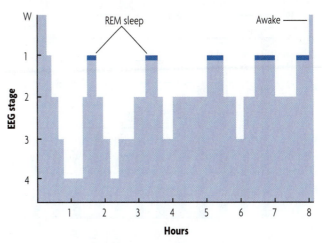

FIGURE 5.3 The Stages of Sleep

A typical pattern of the stages of sleep during a single night includes deeper sleep in the early cycles but more time in REM in the later cycles.

From Carlson, Neil R., *Physiology of Behavior,* 11th Ed., © 2013. Reprinted and Electronically reproduced by permission of Pearson Education, Inc., Upper Saddle River, New Jersey.

FIGURE 5.2 EEG Patterns Reflecting the Stages of a Regular Night's Sleep

Each sleep stage is defined by characteristic patterns of brain activity.

through this 100-minute cycle four to six times (see **Figure 5.3**). With each cycle, the amount of time you spend in deep sleep (stages 3 and 4) decreases, and the amount of time you spend in REM sleep increases. During the last cycle, you may spend as much time as an hour in REM sleep. NREM sleep accounts for 75 to 80 percent of total sleep time, and REM sleep makes up 20 to 25 percent of sleep time.

Not all individuals sleep for the same amount of time. Although a genetic sleep need is programmed into the human species, the actual amount of sleep each individual obtains is highly affected by conscious actions. People actively control sleep length in a number of ways, such as by staying up late or using alarm clocks. Sleep duration is also controlled by circadian rhythms; that is, the time one goes to sleep influences sleep duration. Getting adequate amounts of NREM and REM sleep is likely only when you standardize your bedtime and rising time across the entire week, including weekends. In that way, the time you spend in bed is likely to correspond closely to the sleepy phase of your circadian rhythm.

Of further interest is the dramatic change in patterns of sleep that occurs over an individual's lifetime (shown in **Figure 5.4** on page 128). You started out in this world sleeping for about 16 hours a day, with nearly half of that time spent in REM sleep. By age 50, you may sleep only 6 hours and spend only about 15 percent of the time in REM sleep. Young adults typically sleep 7 to 8 hours, with about 20 percent REM sleep.

The change in sleep patterns with age doesn't mean that sleep isn't as important as you grow older. One study followed healthy older adults—those in their 60s through 80s—to see if there was a relationship between their sleep behaviors and how long they lived (Dew et al., 2003). The researchers found that people who had higher sleep efficiency—a measure based on the amount of time they were asleep divided by the amount of time they spent in bed—were likely to live longer. This result leads directly to the next question: Why do people need sleep?

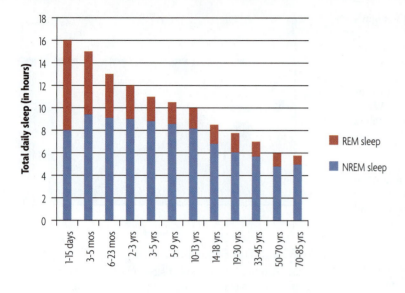

FIGURE 5.4 Patterns of Human Sleep over a Lifetime

The graph shows changes with age in total amounts of daily REM sleep and NREM sleep. Note that the amount of REM sleep decreases considerably over the years, and NREM diminishes less sharply.

Data from Roffwarg et al., Ontogenetic Development of the human sleep-dream cycle, *Science*, 152, 604–619. Reprinted with permission from AAAS.

Why Sleep?

The orderly progression of stages of sleep in humans and other animals suggests that there is an evolutionary basis and a biological need for sleep. People function quite well when they get the time-honored 7 to 8 hours of sleep a night (Foster & Wulff, 2005; Hublin et al., 2007). If you get too little sleep for a period of time, you typically will need to get extra sleep to compensate. People also show rebounds for particular types of sleep. For example, if you were to be deprived of REM sleep for a night, you would have more REM sleep than usual the next night. These patterns suggest that there's something critical about the amount and types of sleep that people get. In that context, let's consider the functions that sleep serves.

The most general function for sleep may be *conservation* (Siegel, 2009). Sleep may have evolved because it enabled animals to conserve energy at times when there was no need to forage for food, search for mates, or work. However, sleep also puts animals at risk for attacks from predators. Researchers speculate that cycles of brain activity across a period of sleep (see Figure 5.2) may have evolved to help animals minimize the risk of predation—some patterns of brain activity might allow animals to retain relatively greater awareness of activity in the environment even while they were asleep (Lesku et al., 2008).

Sleep might also play a critical role in learning and memory (Diekelmann & Born, 2010). In particular, researchers have suggested that sleep assists with the *consolidation* of new memories: Consolidation is the physical process through which new, fragile memories become more permanently encoded in the brain. (You'll see this concept again in Chapter 7, which reviews memory processes.) Let's consider an example of the role sleep plays in memory consolidation.

In an experiment, the participants' main task was to learn pairs of words (Wilhelm et al., 2011). For example, a participant might learn to produce girl *in response to the cue* boy. *After spending roughly an hour learning word pairs, some of the participants were told that they would be given another test of the words nine hours later. For this group, the memory test was* expected. *For the remaining participants, the memory test (when it happened) was* unexpected. *The reason the memory test was nine hours later was that some of the participants next went to sleep for the night. The rest of the participants stayed awake for nine hours. (The learning phase of the experiment sometimes started in the morning and sometimes at night.) The memory tests showed a clear pattern: Participants did best when they both expected a memory test and when they went to sleep right after they had learned the word pairs. Without the warning, performance was inferior and roughly the same for participants who slept and those who stayed awake. Without sleep, performance was inferior and roughly the same whether the test was expected or unexpected.*

The results of this experiments should suggest a plan of action as you prepare for future exams. Almost all the exams you take will be "expected." For that reason, you should seriously consider studying just before you go to bed. The sleep you get should help you consolidate what you have learned. Note that both REM and NREM both play roles in consolidation but that they affect different parts of the physical process by which memories become permanent (Diekelmann & Born, 2010).

After reading about all the important functions that sleep serves, it probably won't surprise you to learn that there are some serious consequences when people get too little sleep. Sleep deprivation has a range of negative effects on cognitive performance, including difficulties with attention and working memory (Banks & Dinges, 2007). Sleep deprivation also impairs people's ability to perform motor skills. For example, drivers who have been sleep deprived are more likely to have car accidents than their well-rested peers. This fact has led some commentators to suggest that engineers should invent a measurement device for excess sleepiness that would parallel the breathalyzer for excess alcohol (Yegneswaran & Shapiro, 2007).

What is the relationship between actual sleep patterns and people's perceptions of insomnia?

Sleep Disorders

It would be great if you could always take a good night's sleep for granted. Unfortunately, many people suffer from sleep disorders that pose a serious burden to their personal lives and careers. Their origins involve biological, environmental, and psychological forces. As you read, also remember that sleep disorders vary in severity. 👁

Insomnia When people are dissatisfied with their amount or quality of sleep, they are suffering from **insomnia.** This chronic failure to get adequate sleep is characterized by an inability to fall asleep quickly, frequent arousals during sleep, or early-morning awakening. In one sample of 3,643 adults in the United States, 52.5 percent of the participants reported that they had experienced insomnia at least once a month; 7 percent reported that they experienced insomnia almost every night (Hamilton et al., 2007). The study also demonstrated that insomnia had a consistent negative impact on people's sense of well-being.

Insomnia is a complex disorder caused by a variety of psychological, environmental, and biological factors (Bastien, 2011). Theories often focus on people's inability to disengage from waking life. People who experience insomnia may be less able to banish intrusive thoughts and feelings from consciousness while they are trying to sleep. Still, when insomniacs are studied in sleep laboratories, the objective quantity and quality of their actual sleep vary considerably, from disturbed sleep to normal sleep. Research has revealed that some insomniacs who complain of lack of sleep actually show completely normal physiological patterns of sleep—a condition described as *paradoxical insomnia.* For example, in one study 20 patients diagnosed with paradoxical insomnia and 20 control individuals (with no sleep disorders) spent a night a sleep lab (Parrino

et al., 2009). The actual sleep of the two groups was very similar: 447 minutes for the patients versus 464 minutes for the controls. However, the two groups' subjective estimates of their amounts of sleep were vastly different: 285 minutes for the patients versus 461 minutes for the controls. The researchers suggested that unusual patterns of sleep brain activity may help explain the discrepancy between reality and the patients' perceptions.

Narcolepsy **Narcolepsy** is a sleep disorder characterized by sudden and irresistible instances of sleepiness during the daytime. It is often combined with *cataplexy,* muscle weakness or a loss of muscle control brought on by emotional excitement (such as laughing, anger, fear, surprise, or hunger) that causes the afflicted person to fall down suddenly. When they fall asleep, narcoleptics enter REM sleep almost immediately. This rush to REM causes them to experience—and be consciously aware of—vivid dream images or sometimes terrifying hallucinations. Narcolepsy affects about 1 of every 2,000 individuals. The observation that narcolepsy runs in families has allowed scientists to uncover genes associated with the disorder (Raizen & Wu, 2011). Narcolepsy often has a negative social and psychological impact on sufferers because of their desire to avoid the embarrassment caused by sudden bouts of sleep (Jara et al., 2011).

....

👁 **Watch** the **Video** *Special Topics: Sleep Disorders* on **MyPsychLab**

insomnia The chronic inability to sleep normally; symptoms include difficulty in falling asleep, frequent waking, inability to return to sleep, and early-morning awakening.

narcolepsy A sleep disorder characterized by an irresistible compulsion to sleep during the daytime.

Sleep Apnea **Sleep apnea** is an upper-respiratory sleep disorder in which the person stops breathing while asleep. When this happens, the blood's oxygen level drops and emergency hormones are secreted, causing the sleeper to awaken and begin breathing again. Although most people have a few such apnea episodes a night, someone with sleep apnea disorder can have hundreds of such cycles every night. Sometimes apnea episodes frighten the sleeper, but often they are so brief that the sleeper fails to attribute accumulating sleepiness to them (Pagel, 2008). Among adults, sleep apnea affects roughly 2 percent of women and 4 percent of men (Kapur, 2010).

Sleep apnea also occurs frequently among premature infants, who sometimes need physical stimulation to start breathing again. Because of their underdeveloped respiratory system, these infants must remain attached to monitors in intensive care nurseries as long as the problem continues.

Somnambulism Individuals who suffer from **somnambulism,** or *sleepwalking,* leave their beds and wander while still remaining asleep. Sleepwalking is more frequent among children than among adults (Mason & Pack, 2007). For example, studies have found that about 7 percent of children sleepwalk (Nevéus et al., 2001) but only about 2 percent of adults do so (Bjorvatn et al., 2010). Sleepwalking is associated with NREM sleep. When monitored in a sleep laboratory, adult sleepwalkers demonstrated abrupt arousal—involving movement or speech—during stage 3 and stage 4 sleep (see Figure 5.2) in the first third of their night's sleep (Guilleminault et al., 2001). Contrary to popular conceptions, it is not particularly dangerous to wake sleepwalkers—they're just likely to be confused by the sudden awakening. Still, sleepwalking in itself can be dangerous because individuals are navigating in their environments without conscious awareness.

Nightmares and Sleep Terrors When a dream frightens you by making you feel helpless or out of control, you are having a **nightmare.** Most people report between 6 and 10 nightmares each year (Robert & Zadra, 2008). However, for the period between childhood and older adulthood, women experience somewhat more nightmares than do men (Schredl & Reinhard, 2011). This difference might be explained, in part, because women are more likely to recall their dreams. The peak time for nightmares is between ages 3 and 6, when a majority of children have them at least occasionally (Mason & Park, 2007). Also, people who have experienced traumatic events, such as rape or war, may have repetitive nightmares that force them to relive some aspects of their trauma (Davis et al., 2007). College students who experienced a major earthquake in the San Francisco Bay area were about twice as likely to experience nightmares as were a matched group of students who hadn't experienced an earthquake—and, as you might imagine, many

What is the difference between nightmares and sleep terrors?

of the nightmares were about the devastating effects of earthquakes (Wood et al., 1992).

Sleep terrors (or *night terrors*) are instances in which sleepers wake up suddenly in a state of extreme arousal, often marked by a panicky scream (*DSM-IV-TR,* 2000). These episodes typically occur during NREM sleep in the first third of a night's sleep. Most people who have sleep terrors have no memory of the episodes. Sleep terrors are most common during childhood, with the greatest number occurring between ages 5 and 7 (Mason & Pack, 2007). Between the ages of 4 and 12, about 3 percent of children experience sleep terrors. They occur in less than 1 percent of adults. Researchers have begun to document distinctive patterns of brain activity that identify children at particular risk for sleep terrors (Bruni et al., 2008).

Dreams: Theater of the Mind

During every ordinary night of your life, you enter into the complex world of dreams. Once the province only of prophets, psychics, and psychoanalysts, dreams have become a vital area of study for scientific researchers. Much dream research begins in sleep laboratories, where experimenters can monitor sleepers for REM and NREM sleep. Although individuals report more dreams when they are awakened from REM periods—on about 82 percent of their awakenings—dreaming also takes place during NREM periods—on about 54 percent of awakenings (Foulkes, 1962). Dreaming associated with NREM states is less likely to contain story content that is emotionally involving. It is more akin to daytime thought, with less sensory imagery.

Because dreams have such prominence in people's mental lives, virtually every culture has arrived at the same question: Do dreams have significance? The answer that has almost always emerged is *yes.* That is, most cultures encode the belief that, in one way or another, dreams have important personal and cultural meaning. Let's review some of the ways in which cultures attach meaning to dreams.

Freudian Dream Analysis The most prominent dream theory in modern Western culture was originated by Sigmund Freud. Freud called dreams "transient psychoses" and models of "everynight madness." He also called them "the royal

---

sleep apnea A sleep disorder of the upper respiratory system that causes the person to stop breathing while asleep.

somnambulism A disorder that causes sleepers to leave their beds and wander while still remaining asleep; also known as sleepwalking.

nightmare A frightening dream that usually wakes up the sleeper.

sleep terrors Episodes in which sleepers wake up suddenly in an extreme state of arousal and panic.

road to the unconscious." He made the analysis of dreams the cornerstone of psychoanalysis with his classic book, *The Interpretation of Dreams* (1900/1965). Freud suggested that all dreams are instances of *wish-fulfillment:* On his view, people's dreams allow them to express powerful unconscious wishes in disguised symbolic form. These wishes appear in disguised form because they harbor forbidden desires, such as sexual yearning for the parent of the opposite sex. The two dynamic forces operating in dreams are thus the *wish* and the *censorship,* a defense against the wish. The censor transforms the hidden meaning, or **latent content,** of the dream into **manifest content,** which appears to the dreamer after a distortion process that Freud referred to as **dream work.** The manifest content is the acceptable version of the story; the latent content represents the socially or personally unacceptable version but also the true, "uncut" one.

According to Freud, the interpretation of dreams requires working backward from the manifest content to the latent content. To the psychoanalyst who uses dream analysis to understand and treat a patient's problems, dreams reveal the patient's unconscious wishes, the fears attached to those wishes, and the characteristic defenses the patient employs to handle the resulting psychic conflict between the wishes and the fears. Freud believed in both idiosyncratic—special to particular individuals—and universal meanings—many of a sexual nature—for the symbols and metaphors in dreams:

> *Boxes, cases, chests, cupboards and ovens represent the uterus, and also hollow objects, ships, and vessels of all kinds. Rooms in dreams are usually women; if the various ways in and out of them are represented, this interpretation is scarcely open to doubt. . . . A dream of going through a suite of rooms is a brothel or harem dream. . . . It is highly probable that all complicated machinery and apparatus occurring in dreams stand for the genitals (and as a rule male ones). . . .*
> (Freud, 1900/1965, pp. 389–391)

Freud's theory of dream interpretation related dream symbols to his explicit theory of human psychology. Freud's emphasis on the psychological importance of dreams has pointed the way to contemporary examinations of dream content.

Non-Western Approaches to Dream Interpretation
Many people in Western societies may never think seriously about their dreams until they become students of psychology or enter therapy. By contrast, in many non-Western cultures, dream sharing and interpretation are part of the very fabric of the culture (Lohmann, 2010; Wax, 2004). Consider the daily practice of the Archur Indians of Ecuador (Schlitz, 1997, p. 2):

> *Like every other morning, the men [of the village] sit together in a small circle. . . . They share their dreams from the night before. This daily ritual of dream-sharing is vital to the life of the Archur. It is their belief that each individual dreams, not for themselves, but for the community as a whole. Individual experience serves collective action.*

During these morning gatherings, each dreamer tells his dream story and the others offer their interpretations, hoping to arrive at some consensus understanding of the meaning of the dream. Contrast the belief that individuals dream "for the community as a whole" with the view articulated by Freud, that dreams are the "royal road" to the individual unconscious.

In many cultures, specific groups of individuals are designated as possessing special powers to assist with dream interpretation. Consider the practices of Mayan Indians who live in various parts of Mexico, Guatemala, Belize, and Honduras. In the Mayan culture, *shamans* function as dream interpreters. In fact, among some subgroups of Mayans, the shamans are selected for these roles when they have dreams in which they are visited by deities who announce the shaman's calling. Formal instruction about religious rituals is also provided to these newly selected shamans by way of dream revelation. Although the shamans, and other religious figures, have special knowledge relevant to dream interpretation, ordinary individuals also recount and discuss dreams. Dreamers commonly wake their bed partners in the middle of the night to narrate dreams; mothers in some communities ask their children each morning to talk about their dreams. In contemporary times, the Mayan people have been the victims of civil war in their homelands; many people have been killed or forced to flee. One important response, according to anthropologist **Barbara Tedlock,** has been "an increased emphasis on dreams and visions that enable them to stay in touch with their ancestors and the sacred earth on which they live" (Tedlock, 1992, p. 471).

The cultural practices of many non-Western groups with respect to dreams also reflect a fundamentally different time perspective. Freud's theory had dream interpretation looking backward in time, toward childhood experiences and repressed wishes. In many other cultures, dreams are believed instead to present a vision of the future (Basso, 1987; Louw, 2010). For example, among the people of the Ingessana Hills, a region along the border of Ethiopia and the Sudan, the timing of festivals is determined by dream visions (Jedrej, 1995). The keepers of religious shrines are visited in their dreams by their fathers and other ancestors who instruct them to "announce the festival." Other groups have culturally given systems of relationships between dream symbols and meanings. Consider these interpretations from the Kalapalo Indians of central Brazil (Basso, 1987, p. 104):

> *When we dream we are burnt by fire, later we will be bitten by a wild thing, by a spider or a stinging ant, for example.*
> *When [we dream] we are making love to women, we will be very successful when we go fishing.*
> *When a boy is in seclusion and he dreams of climbing a tall tree, or another one sees a long path, they will live long. This would also be true if we dreamt of crossing a wide stream in a forest.*

Note how each interpretation looks to the future. The future orientation of dream interpretation is an important component of a rich cultural tradition.

....

latent content In Freudian dream analysis, the hidden meaning of a dream.

manifest content In Freudian dream analysis, the surface content of a dream, which is assumed to mask the dream's actual meaning.

dream work In Freudian dream analysis, the process by which the internal censor transforms the latent content of a dream into manifest content.

Contemporary Approaches to Dream Content The cornerstone of both Western and non-Western approaches to dream interpretation is that dreams provide information that is of genuine value to the person or community. When researchers first began to consider the biological underpinnings of dream they challenged this view. For example, the *activation-synthesis model* suggested that signals emerged from the brain stem that stimulated the forebrain and association areas of the cortex to produce random memories and connections with the dreamer's past experiences (Hobson, 1988; Hobson & McCarley, 1977). According to this view, there are no logical connections, no intrinsic meaning, and no coherent patterns to these random bursts of electrical "signals."

However, contemporary research on dreams contradicts the view that the content emerges from random signals (Nir & Tononi, 2010). In fact, neurological evidence suggests that dreams emerge from the same basic processes that are at work during waking experiences of daydreaming and mind wandering (Domhoff, 2011). Brain-imaging studies suggest that the hippocampus—the brain structure critical to the acquisition of certain types of memories (see Chapter 7)—is active during REM sleep (Nielsen & Stenstrom, 2005). Another brain structure that plays an important role for emotional memories—the amygdala—is also quite active during REM sleep. This deeper understanding of the physiological aspects of dreams supports the assertion that one of the functions of sleep is to draw together "an individual's recent experiences of the past few days along with their goals, desires, and problems" (Paller & Voss, 2004, p. 667). According to this view, the story of the dream reflects the brain's attempt to weave a narrative around the recent fragments of a person's life that become most prominent during REM sleep.

Studies confirm that the content of dreams shows a good deal of continuity with dreamers' waking concerns (Domhoff, 2005). However, dreams very rarely present exact replicas of events from waking life. Rather, dream content often emerges from more fragmented aspects of memories. For example, people who spent more waking time engaged in particular activities (such as sports or reading) reported a higher percentage of dreams that included those activities (Schredl & Erlacher, 2008). Dreams often display memory elements from the previous day. Dreams also show a *dream-lag* effect: They are more likely to include memory elements from the period five to seven days before the dream rather than two to four days before the dream (Blagrove et al., 2011). This dream-lag may be another consequence of the role that REM sleep plays in the consolidation of new memories.

You might consider keeping your own dream log—try to write your dreams as soon as you wake up each morning—to see both how your own dreams relate to daily concerns and how your dream content changes or remains stable over time. Still, be aware that some people have more difficulty recalling dreams than other people do (Wolcott & Strapp, 2002). For example, it's easier to recall dreams if you wake up during a REM period or close to one. If you want to recall your dreams, you might consider changing the time you set your alarm. Also, people who have more positive attitudes toward dreaming appear to find it easier to recall their dreams. In that sense, the interest you show in your dreams by undertaking a dream log might help increase your ability to recall them.

Before we leave the topic of dreaming, let's consider a final question: Is it possible to be aware that you are dreaming

Researcher Stephen LaBerge adjusts the special goggles that will alert the sleeping participant that REM sleep is occurring. The individual is trained to enter into a state of lucid dreaming, being aware of the process and content of dream activity. If you had the ability to experience lucid dreaming, in what ways would you shape your dreams?

while you are dreaming? The answer is yes! In fact, researchers who study **lucid dreaming** have demonstrated that being consciously aware that one is dreaming is a skill that can be perfected with regular practice (LaBerge, 2007). A variety of methods have been used to induce lucid dreaming. For example, in some lucid dreaming research, sleepers wear specially designed goggles that flash a red light when they detect REM sleep. The participants have learned previously that the red light is a cue for becoming consciously aware that they are dreaming (LaBerge & Levitan, 1995). Once aware of dreaming, yet still not awake, sleepers move into a state of lucid dreaming in which they can take control of their dreams, directing them according to their personal goals and making the dreams' outcomes fit their current needs. Even without special training, people sometimes become aware that they are dreaming. Researchers have begun to study the brain processes that make lucid dreaming possible (Neider et al., 2011; Voss et al., 2009).

....

lucid dreaming The theory that conscious awareness of dreaming is a learnable skill that enables dreamers to control the direction and content of their dreams.

ARE YOU A MORNING TYPE OR AN EVENING TYPE?

In the section on circadian rhythms, you learned that, across the day, people undergo changes in important biological functions such as arousal levels, metabolism, heart rate, and body temperature. However, the exact timing differs greatly from person to person. In fact, researchers have suggested that people can be sorted into *chronotypes* according to their preferred patterns of sleep and wakefulness.

Consider a study in which researchers asked thousands of European adults what sleep pattern they followed on days when they were not required to get up for work. The most frequent response had people going to sleep just after midnight and rising at about 8:20 A.M. (Roenneberg et al., 2007). How do your preferences compare to that norm? If you are in and out of bed earlier, you count as a *morning type*. If you habitually choose to go to bed after midnight, you count as an *evening type*. The further from the norm, the more morning or evening type you are. Across adulthood, people's preferences tend to switch toward morning: Grandparents generally prefer to rise much earlier than their teenage grandchildren. However, against this overall shift, individual differences seem to remain stable. Even as older adults, those individuals who were relatively more evening type as teenagers are likely to remain later risers than their peers.

Researchers have provided abundant demonstrations that circadian rhythms help determine the times of day at which people will experience peak performance (Blatter & Cajochen, 2007; Kyriacou & Hastings, 2010). Given this impact

of circadian rhythms, people with different chronotypes often peak at different times of day. Consider a study that involved 40 adolescents, ages 11 to 14, each of whom was explicitly morning type or evening type (Goldstein et al., 2007). The adolescents completed items from a standard intelligence test (the WISC; see Chapter 9) at either their optimal or nonoptimal time of day. For example, half the morning-type students took the test in the morning and half in the afternoon. Those participants who were tested at their preferred time of day scored, on average, 6 points higher on the intelligence measure. (If you turn to **Figure 9.2**, on page 245, you'll see how substantial a difference that is.)

The researchers also obtained information from the adolescents' parents and relatives about their day-to-day behavior. On these measures, morning-type students emerged as more socially competent—with fewer reports of attention problems and aggressive behaviors than their evening-type peers. Results of this sort support the idea that evening-type students suffer from a type of "social jet lag" (Wittmann et al., 2006, 2010). Because they are roused out of bed by their alarm clocks, they are routinely made to perform at times of day that are out of sync with their personal rhythms. That lack of synchrony has a negative impact on both achievement and behavior.

So, are you definitely a morning type or an evening type? If you are have a strong chronotype, think how you might arrange work and play to obtain your optimal performance.

We can consider dreams to be at the limit of ordinary consciousness. Let's turn now to circumstances in which individuals deliberately seek to go beyond those everyday experiences.

Stop *and* Review

① Why do you experience jet lag?
② How does the balance of NREM and REM sleep change over the course of a night?
③ What two functions might sleep serve?
④ What happens to a person who suffers from sleep apnea?
⑤ What did Freud mean by the latent content of a dream?

CRITICAL THINKING Recall the study that documented the impact of sleep on learning word pairs. Why was it important that some participants start the experiment in the morning and others in the late evening?

✔— **Study** and **Review** on **MyPsychLab**

ALTERED STATES OF CONSCIOUSNESS

In every culture, some people have been dissatisfied with ordinary transformations of their waking consciousness. They have developed practices that take them beyond familiar forms of consciousness to experiences of altered states of consciousness. Let's review hypnosis and meditation.

Hypnosis

As portrayed in popular culture, hypnotists wield vast power over their witting or unwitting participants. Is this view of hypnotists accurate? What is hypnosis, what are its important features, and what are some of its valid psychological uses? The term **hypnosis**

....

hypnosis An altered state of awareness characterized by deep relaxation, susceptibility to suggestions, and changes in perception, memory, motivation, and self-control.

is derived from Hypnos, the name of the Greek god of sleep. Sleep, however, plays no part in hypnosis, except that people may in some cases give the *appearance* of being in a deeply relaxed, sleeplike state. (If people were really asleep, they could not respond to hypnosis.) A broad definition of hypnosis is that it is an alternative state of awareness characterized by the special ability some people have of responding to suggestion with changes in perception, memory, motivation, and sense of self-control. In the hypnotic state, participants experience heightened responsiveness to the hypnotist's suggestions—they often feel that their behavior is performed without intention or any conscious effort.

Researchers have often disagreed about the psychological mechanisms involved in hypnosis (Lynn & Kirsch, 2006). Some early theorists suggested that hypnotized individuals enter into a *trance* state, far different from waking consciousness. Others argued that hypnosis was nothing more than heightened motivation. Still others believed it to be a type of social role playing, a kind of *placebo* response of trying to please the hypnotist (see Chapter 2). In fact, research has largely ruled out the idea that hypnosis involves a special trancelike change in consciousness. However, even though nonhypnotized individuals can produce some of the same patterns of behavior that hypnotized individuals can, there appears to be some added effects of hypnosis—beyond motivational or placebo processes. This section begins with a discussion of hypnotic induction and hypnotizability, and then turns to some effects of hypnosis.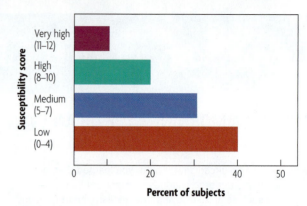

Hypnotic Induction and Hypnotizability Hypnosis begins with a *hypnotic induction,* a preliminary set of activities that minimizes external distractions and encourages participants to concentrate only on suggested stimuli and believe that they are about to enter a special state of consciousness. Induction activities involve suggestions to imagine certain experiences or to visualize events and reactions. When practiced repeatedly, the induction procedure functions as a learned signal so that participants can quickly enter the hypnotic state. The typical induction procedure uses suggestions for deep relaxation, but some people can become hypnotized with an active, alert induction—such as imagining that they are jogging or riding a bicycle (Banyai & Hilgard, 1976).

Hypnotizability represents the degree to which an individual is responsive to standardized suggestions to experience hypnotic reactions. There are wide individual differences in susceptibility, varying from a complete lack of responsiveness to total responsiveness. **Figure 5.5** shows the percentage of college-age individuals who presented various levels of hypnotizability the first time they were given a hypnotic induction test. What does it mean to have scored "high" or "very high" on this scale? When the test is administered, the hypnotist makes a series of posthypnotic suggestions, dictating the experiences each individual might have. When the hypnotist suggested that their extended arms had turned into bars of iron, highly hypnotizable individuals were likely to find themselves unable to bend those arms. With the appropriate suggestion,

---

Level of Hypnosis at First Induction

FIGURE 5.5 Level of Hypnosis at First Induction

The graph shows the results for 533 individuals hypnotized for the first time. Hypnotizability was measured on the Stanford Hypnotic Susceptibility Scale, which consists of 12 items.

they were likely to brush away a nonexistent fly. As a third example, highly hypnotizable individuals probably couldn't nod their heads "no" when the hypnotist suggested they had lost that ability. Students who scored "low" on the hypnotizability scale experienced few if any of these reactions.

Hypnotizability is a relatively stable attribute. When 50 men and women were retested 25 years after their college hypnotizability assessment, the results indicated a remarkably high correlation coefficient of 0.71 (Piccione et al., 1989). Children tend to be more suggestible than adults; hypnotic responsiveness peaks just before adolescence and declines thereafter. Researchers have identified relatively few personality traits that are correlated with hypnotizability (Kihlstrom, 2007). Highly hypnotizable people are not more likely to be gullible or conformist. In fact, the personality trait that has the highest positive correlation with hypnotizability is *absorption,* which is an individual's "predisposition to become highly involved in imaginative or sensory experiences" (Council & Green, 2004, p. 364). If, for example, you often find yourself losing track of the "real" world while you watch a movie, you might also be highly hypnotizable.

Some evidence indicates genetic determinants of hypnotizability. Early research demonstrated that hypnotizability scores of identical twins are more similar than are those of fraternal twins (Morgan et al., 1970). More recently, studies have begun to focus on the particular genes that underlie individual differences. For example, researchers have identified a gene known as *COMT* that influences the brain's use of the neurotransmitter dopamine. Variations in this gene are related to individual differences in hypnotizability (Szekely et al., 2010).

Effects of Hypnosis In describing the way in which hypnotizability is measured, I already mentioned some of the standard effects of hypnosis: While under hypnosis, individuals respond to suggestions about motor abilities (for example, their arms become unbendable) and perceptual experiences (for example, they hallucinate a fly). How can we be sure, however, that these behaviors arise from special properties of hypnosis and not just a strong willingness on participants' part to please the hypnotist? To address this important question, researchers have often conducted experiments that contrast the effectiveness of hypnosis versus relaxation training.

⦿ **Watch** the **Video** *What Altered States Have You Experienced?* on **MyPsychLab**

hypnotizability The degree to which an individual is responsive to standardized hypnotic suggestion.

For assessment of hypnosis, researchers recruited a group of women who were suffering from temporomandibular disorders, which produce "both acute and chronic pain in the jaws and surrounding tissues as well as limitation in jaw movements" (Abrahamsen et al., 2011, p. 345). Roughly half the women were randomly assigned to a hypnosis group. Those women experienced four one-hour hypnosis sessions in which they engaged in a series of activities including the post-hypnotic suggestion "to forget thinking about the pain [and] instead let the thoughts become occupied [with] good memories and favorite activities" (p. 348). The remaining participants were assigned to a control group. The women in that group also experienced four one-hour sessions but those sessions focused largely on relaxation techniques. However, women in the control group were also told that their treatment was a type of hypnotic intervention. All the participants provided self-reports of pain—three times a day for seven days before and seven days after the treatments. The hypnosis group reported consistent reduction in pain after the treatment; the control group showed no changes.

This experiment demonstrates the potential for hypnosis to bring about pain relief *(hypnotic analgesia)*. Your mind can amplify pain stimuli through anticipation and fear; you can diminish this psychological effect with hypnosis (Dillworth & Jensen, 2010). Pain control is accomplished through a variety of hypnotic suggestions: imagining the part of the body in pain as nonorganic (made of wood or plastic) or as separate from the rest of the body, thus taking one's mind on a vacation from the body and distorting time in various ways. People can control pain through hypnosis even when they banish all thoughts and images from consciousness.

Some evidence suggests that people who are high in hypnotizability are able to obtain greater pain relief through hypnosis (De Pascalis et al., 2008). Researchers are trying to understand the brain bases for this difference. For example, a brain-imaging study demonstrated that people who were higher in hypnotizability also had larger regions at the front of the corpus callosum (see Chapter 3) (Horton et al., 2004). This area of the corpus callosum plays a role in attention and the inhibition of unwanted stimuli, suggesting that people who are highly hypnotizable may have more brain tissue that allows them to use hypnosis to inhibit pain. Studies with EEG measures also demonstrate—in the context of hypnotic pain reduction—differences in the brain responses of low- and high-hypnotizable individuals (Ray et al., 2002).

One final note on hypnosis: The power of hypnosis does *not* reside in some special ability or skill of the hypnotist, but rather it resides in the relative hypnotizability of the person or persons being hypnotized. Being hypnotized does not involve giving up one's personal control; instead, the experience of being hypnotized allows an individual to learn new ways to exercise control that the hypnotist—as coach—can train the subject—as performer—to enact. Keep all of this in mind if you watch a stage show in which people perform outlandish acts under hypnosis: Stage hypnotists make a living entertaining audiences by getting highly exhibitionist people to do things in public that most others could never be made to do. As used by researchers and therapists, hypnosis is a technique with the potential to allow you to explore and modify your sense of consciousness.

Meditation

Many religions and traditional psychologies of the East work to direct consciousness away from immediate worldly concerns. They seek to achieve an inner focus on the mental and spiritual self.

Meditation is a form of consciousness change designed to enhance self-knowledge and well-being by achieving a deep state of tranquility. During *concentrative* meditation, a person may focus on and regulate breathing, assume certain body positions (yogic positions), minimize external stimulation, generate specific mental images, or free the mind of all thought. By contrast, during *mindfulness* meditation, a person learns to let thoughts and memories pass freely through the mind without reacting to them.

Research has often focused on the ability of meditation to relieve the anxiety of those who must function in stress-filled environments (Oman et al., 2006). For example, mindfulness meditation has served as the basis for mindfulness-based stress reduction (Kabat-Zinn, 1990). In one study, women suffering from heart disease were given eight weeks of training on mindfulness meditation; at the end of this intervention, the women reported consistently lower feelings of anxiety than they did before the study (Tacon et al., 2003). Women in the control group didn't experience improvement in their anxiety reports. Because feelings of anxiety play a role in the development of heart disease, this result provides evidence that the mind can help to heal the body. (The discussion of health psychology in Chapter 12 returns to this theme.)

Brain-imaging techniques have begun to reveal the ways in which meditation affects patterns of brain activity (Ives-Deliperi et al., 2011). In fact, recent evidence suggests that, over time, the practice of meditation might have a positive impact on the brain itself.

How does meditation create an altered state of consciousness?

meditation A form of consciousness alteration designed to enhance self-knowledge and well-being through reduced self-awareness.

The researchers reasoned that the activities associated with meditation—focused attention on internal and external sensations—would bring about changes in the strengths of the connections among brain regions associated with these activities (Kilpatrick et al., 2011). To test this hypothesis, the researchers provided eight weeks of Mindfulness-Based Stress Reduction (MBSR) training to 17 women. The connections among their brain regions were examined using a type of brain scan called functional connectivity MRI (fcMRI), which assesses networks of brain activity. The brains of the MBSR group were compared to those of 15 women who had not yet undergone the training (but received the training once the experiment was completed). The fcMRI scans revealed enhanced connectivity in the brains of the women who experienced the MBSR training. The researchers speculated that the short course of MBSR training produced "enhanced sensory processing, better attentional resource allocation and a more consistent attentional focus" (p. 297).

Other research suggests that meditation training might slow the loss of neurons that often accompanies aging. For example, one study compared 13 individuals with three or more years of experience at Zen meditation with 13 control participants who were matched for age, sex, and education level (Pagnoni & Cekic, 2007). Among the control participants, there was a negative correlation such that the older participants had the least brain volume. The participants who meditated regularly showed no such decline with age!

Practicers of meditation have suggested that, when practiced regularly, some forms of meditation can heighten your consciousness and help you achieve enlightenment by enabling you to see familiar things in new ways. This recent research suggests that meditation might also literally be good for your brain.

This section has reviewed several ways in which people achieve altered states of consciousness in their dreaming and waking lives. This chapter concludes with a discussion of what might be the most common means people use to affect their consciousness: mind-altering drugs. ◉

Stop and Review

① What does research suggest about the genetics of hypnotizability?
② What are two forms of meditation?

CRITICAL THINKING   Consider the study that found differences in pain reduction for a hypnosis group versus a control group. Why was it important that the women in the control group were led to believe that their training was also a hypnotic intervention?

✓—Study and Review on MyPsychLab

◉ Watch the Video What's In It For Me?: Self-Induced Altered States on MyPsychLab

psychoactive drug Chemical that affects mental processes and behavior by temporarily changing conscious awareness of reality.

tolerance A situation that occurs with continued use of a drug in which an individual requires greater dosages to achieve the same effect.

MIND-ALTERING DRUGS

Since ancient times, people have taken drugs to alter their perception of reality. Archaeological evidence indicates the uninterrupted use of sophora seed (mescal bean) for over 10,000 years in the southwestern United States and Mexico. The ancient Aztecs fermented mescal beans into a beer. From ancient times, individuals in North and South America also ingested teonanacatl, the Psilocybe mushroom also known as "the flesh of the gods," as parts of rituals. Small doses of these mushrooms produce vivid hallucinations.

In Western cultures, drugs are associated less with sacred communal rituals than with recreation. Individuals throughout the world take various drugs to relax, cope with stress, avoid facing the unpleasantness of current realities, feel comfortable in social situations, or experience an alternate state of consciousness. Over 100 years ago, William James—whom you have met several times as a founder of psychology in the United States—reported on his experiments with a mind-altering drug. After inhaling nitrous oxide, James explained that "the keynote of the experience is the tremendously exciting sense of intense metaphysical illumination. Truth lies open to the view in depth beneath depth of almost blinding evidence. The mind sees all the logical relations of being with an apparent subtlety and instantaneity to which its normal consciousness offer no parallel" (James, 1882, p. 186). Thus James's interest in the study of consciousness extended to the study of self-induced alternate states.

As you will see in Chapter 15, drugs that have an impact on an individual's psychological states are often a critical aspect of the treatment of psychological disorders. In fact, as Table 5.2 shows, many types of drugs have important medical uses. Still, many individuals use drugs that are not prescribed to enhance physical or psychological health. In a 2009 survey of U.S. citizens, with nearly 68,700 respondents age 12 and older, 8.7 percent reported using one or more illicit drugs during the past month (Substance Abuse and Mental Health Services Administration [SAMHSA], 2010). The rate was much higher for people in their late teen years—16.7 percent of 16- to 17-year-olds and 22.2 percent of 18- to 20-year-olds reported some type of illicit drug use. In addition, 51.9 percent of the individuals in the sample consumed alcohol sometime in the month before the survey, and 27.7 percent smoked cigarettes. These figures support the importance of understanding the physiological and psychological consequences of drug use.

Dependence and Addiction

Psychoactive drugs are chemicals that affect mental processes and behavior by temporarily changing conscious awareness. Once in the brain, they attach themselves to synaptic receptors, blocking or stimulating certain reactions. By doing so, they profoundly alter the brain's communication system, affecting perception, memory, mood, and behavior. However, continued use of a given drug creates tolerance—greater dosages are required to achieve the same effect. In Chapter 6, I will discuss learning processes that explain important aspects of the occurrence of drug tolerance (see page 154). You will learn how repeated episodes of drug use condition the brain to produce responses that push back against the drug's effects. Because the body pushes back, people require increasingly greater doses for the drug to have the same impact.

Table 5.2 • Medical Uses of Psychoactive Drugs

Drug	Medical Uses
Hallucinogens	
LSD	None
PCP (Phencyclidine)	Veterinary anesthetic
Cannabis (Marijuana)	Nausea associated with chemotherapy
Opiates (Narcotics)	
Morphine	Painkiller
Heroin	None
Depressants	
Barbiturates (e.g., Seconal)	Sedative, sleeping pill, anesthetic, anticonvulsant
Benzodiazepines (e.g., Valium)	Antianxiety, sedative, sleeping pill, anticonvulsant
Rohypnol	Sleeping pill
GHB	Treatment for narcolepsy
Alcohol	Antiseptic
Stimulants	
Amphetamines	Hyperkinesis, narcolepsy, weight control
Methamphetamines	None
MDMA (Ecstasy)	Potential aid to psychotherapy
Cocaine	Local anesthetic
Nicotine	Nicotine gum for cessation of smoking habit
Caffeine	Weight control, stimulant in acute respiratory failure, analgesic

Hand in hand with tolerance is **physiological dependence,** a process in which the body becomes adjusted to and dependent on the substance, in part because neurotransmitters are depleted by the frequent presence of the drug. The tragic outcome of tolerance and dependence is **addiction.** A person who is addicted requires the drug in his or her body and suffers painful withdrawal symptoms (shaking, sweating, nausea, and, in the case of alcohol withdrawal, even death) if the drug is not present.

When an individual finds the use of a drug so desirable or pleasurable that a *craving* develops, with or without addiction, the condition is known as **psychological dependence,** which can occur with any drug. The result of drug dependence is that a person's lifestyle comes to revolve around drug use so wholly that his or her capacity to function is limited or impaired. In addition, the expense involved in maintaining a drug habit of daily—and increasing—amounts often drives an addict to robbery, assault, prostitution, or drug peddling.

Varieties of Psychoactive Drugs

Table 5.2 lists common psychoactive drugs. (Chapter 15 will discuss other types of psychoactive drugs used to relieve mental illness.) Let's briefly consider how each class of drugs achieves its physiological and psychological impact. We will also consider the personal and societal consequences of drug use.

Hallucinogens   The most dramatic changes in consciousness are produced by drugs known as **hallucinogens** or *psychedelics;* these drugs alter both perceptions of the external environment and inner awareness. As the name implies, these drugs often create **hallucinations**—vivid perceptions that occur in the absence of objective stimulation. The hallucinations may lead to a loss of boundary between self and nonself. *LSD* and *PCP* are two common hallucinogens that are synthesized in laboratories. Hallucinogenic drugs typically act in the brain by affecting the use of the chemical neurotransmitter serotonin (Fantegrossi et al., 2008). For example, LSD binds very tightly to serotonin receptors so that neurons produce prolonged activation.

Cannabis is a plant with psychoactive effects. Its active ingredient is THC, found in both *hashish* (the solidified resin of the plant) and *marijuana* (the dried leaves and flowers of the plant). The experience derived from inhaling THC depends on its dose—small doses create mild, pleasurable highs, and large doses result in long hallucinogenic reactions. Regular users report euphoria, feelings of well-being, distortions of space and time, and, occasionally, out-of-body experiences. However, depending on the context, the effects may be negative—fear, anxiety, and confusion.

Researchers have known for several years that *cannabinoids,* the active chemicals in marijuana, bind to specific receptors in the brain—these cannabinoid receptors are particularly common in the hippocampus, a brain region involved in important memory processes (Goonawardena 2011). Researchers subsequently discovered substances internal to the brain that bind to the same receptors. The first *endocannabinoid* (from *endogenous cannabinoid*) to be discovered was *anandamide* (named for the Sanskrit word for bliss, *ananda*) (Di Marzo & Cristino, 2008). That discovery led to the insight that cannabinoids achieve their mind-altering effects by binding to brain sites sensitive to naturally occurring substances in the brain. These endocannabinoids function as neuromodulators. For example, they control the release of the neurotransmitter GABA in the hippocampus (Lee et al., 2010). The *Critical Thinking in Your Life* box discusses the important role these substances play in regulating appetite and feeding behaviors.

Opiates   *Opiates,* such as *heroin* and *morphine,* suppress physical sensation and response to stimulation. Pain killers such as *OxyContin* are also opiates and have the same effects. In the last few years, there has been a dramatic increase in the number of people who abuse OxyContin and other prescription opiates (Rawson et al., 2007). Chapter 3 noted that the

physiological dependence   The process by which the body becomes adjusted to or dependent on a drug.

addiction   A condition in which the body requires a drug in order to function without physical and psychological reactions to its absence; often the outcome of tolerance and dependence.

psychological dependence   The psychological need or craving for a drug.

hallucinogen   Drug that alters cognitions and perceptions and causes hallucinations.

Critical Thinking in Your Life

WHAT CAN WE LEARN FROM "THE MUNCHIES"?

Even if you've never smoked marijuana you probably know that marijuana gives people intense food cravings—cravings often called "the munchies." Observations about marijuana's effects on hunger go back at least to 300 A.D. when texts in India recommended that it be used to stimulate the appetite (Cota et al., 2003). Take a moment to consider how you might turn "the munchies" into a research agenda. What questions might you generate?

The first question you might wish to address could be "Why does marijuana affect people's appetite?" In the text, you've already learned important parts of that story: Researchers made the breakthrough discovery of the existence of endocannabinoids (endogenous cannabinoids) in the brain. With that discovery in hand, researchers confirmed the hypothesis that endocannabinoids play an ongoing role in regulating food consumption (Vemuri et al., 2008). That research also explained observations about the *types* of food people crave when they have the munchies. Besides their role in regulating appetite, endocannabinoids also play a role in reward systems in the brain (Cota et al., 2006). For that reason, endocannabinoids have the particular effect of making people seek foods that are tasty or sweet. Thus, it's no coincidence that the munchies are best satisfied with junk food.

So, you know that endocannabinoids increase appetite. Here's the next step your thinking might take: Can researchers devise drugs that will use this same system to *suppress* appetite? Over the last several years, researchers have begun to have great successes in this quest (Vemuri et al., 2008). One

drug that demonstrated early promise is called *rimonabant*. Rimonabant blocks the brain's cannabinoid receptors from carrying out their normal functions. In one double-blind study testing rimonabant, 1,036 overweight and obese individuals were given either a low or high dose of the drug or a placebo (i.e., an inert substance) (Després et al., 2005). Over the course of the year-long study, participants in the placebo group lost about 5 pounds. Participants who got the low dose of rimonabant lost about 9 pounds. Participants on the high dose lost about 19 pounds! Similarly, high-dose participants took considerably more inches off their waists (3.6 in.) than did low-dose (1.9 in.) or placebo (1.3 in.) participants. With results of this sort in hand, researchers have begun the quest for drugs that achieve the same effects as rimonabant with fewer side effects (such as depression, anxiety, nausea, or dizziness) (Christopoulou & Kiortsis, 2011).

From this example, you can see how research progresses from a real-world observation to a productive research agenda. In fact, the same course of research points to even greater promise for the future: Because the endocannabinoids have an important impact on the brain's reward circuits, researchers believe that drugs targeting the endocannabinoid system may provide successful treatments for both pain and addiction (Clapper et al., 2010; Fattore et al., 2007).

- What was it important for the study testing rimonabant to be double-blind?
- What might there be a link between the brain systems that regulate appetite and reward?

---

brain contains endorphins (short for *endogenous morphines*) that generate powerful effects on mood, pain, and pleasure. These endogenous opiates play a critical role in the brain's response to both physical and psychological stressors (Ribeiro et al., 2005). Drugs like opium and morphine bind to the same receptor sites in the brain as the endorphins (Trescot et al., 2008). Thus both opiates and, as the previous section noted, marijuana achieve their effects because they have active components that have similar chemical properties to substances that naturally occur in the brain.

The initial effect of an intravenous injection of heroin is a rush of pleasure. Feelings of euphoria supplant all worries and awareness of bodily needs. When the neural receptors in the endogenous opiate system are artificially stimulated, the brain loses its subtle balance. The brain pushes back so that the rush of pleasure recedes and is replaced by strong negative emotional states (Radke et al., 2011). Those negative emotions

motivate people to seek, once again, the initial rush of pleasure. This cycle of positive to negative is one of the reasons that heroin use often leads to addiction. People who try to withdraw from opiates often experience harsh physical symptoms (such as vomiting, pain, and insomnia) as well as intense craving for the drug.

Depressants The **depressants** include *barbiturates, benzodiazepines,* and *alcohol.* These substances tend to depress (slow down) the mental and physical activity of the body by inhibiting or decreasing the transmission of nerve impulses in the central nervous system. Depressants achieve this effect, in part, by facilitating neural communication at synapses that use

depressant Drug that depresses or slows down the activity of the central nervous system.

the neurotransmitter GABA (Licata & Rowlett, 2008). GABA often functions to inhibit neural transmission, which explains depressants' inhibiting outcomes. In the past, people were often prescribed barbiturates such as *Nembutol* and *Seconal* to act as sedatives or to treat insomnia. However, because of barbiturates' potential for addiction and overdose, people are now more likely to receive prescriptions for benzodiazepines such as *Valium* or *Xanax*. In Chapter 15, you will see that these drugs are also commonly used to counteract anxiety.

Two depressants, *Rohypnol* (more commonly known as *roofies*) and *GHB*, have achieved reputations as drugs used to carry out sexual assaults (Maxwell, 2005). These "date rape drugs" can be manufactured as colorless liquids so that they can be added to alcohol or other beverages without detection. In that way, victims can be unknowingly sedated and find themselves vulnerable to rape attacks. In addition, Rohypnol causes amnesia, so that victims may not remember events that occurred while they were under the drug's influence. Large-scale studies suggest that the threat of rape when women unknowingly ingest drugs is real. However, other drugs such as cannabinoids and stimulants (which we will consider shortly) are implicated more often than Rohypnol and GHB as the drugs used by rapists (DuMont et al., 2010). Moreover, women often put themselves at risk by voluntarily ingesting the next depressant we consider, alcohol (Lawyer et al., 2010).

Alcohol was apparently one of the first psychoactive substances used extensively by early humans. Under its influence, some people become silly, boisterous, friendly, and talkative; others become abusive and violent; still others become quietly depressed. Alcohol appears to stimulate the release of dopamine, which enhances feelings of pleasure. Also, as with other depressants, it appears to affect GABA activity (Lobo & Harris, 2008). At small dosages, alcohol can induce relaxation and slightly improve an adult's speed of reaction. However, the body can break down alcohol only at a slow rate, and large amounts consumed in a short time period overtax the central nervous system. As the concentration of alcohol increases to 0.05 to 0.10 percent, cognitive, perceptual, and motor processes begin rapidly to deteriorate. When the level of alcohol in the blood reaches 0.15 percent, there are gross negative effects on thinking, memory, and judgment, along with emotional instability and loss of motor coordination.

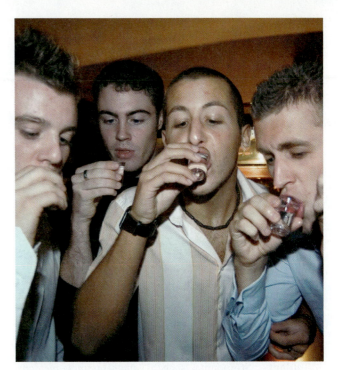

Why does alcohol remain the most popular way in which college students alter their consciousness?

Why does heroin use often lead to addiction?

Excess consumption of alcohol is a major social problem in the United States. When the amount and frequency of drinking interfere with job performance, impair social and family relationships, and create serious health problems, the diagnosis of *alcoholism* is appropriate. Physical dependence, tolerance, and addiction all develop with prolonged heavy drinking. For some individuals, alcoholism is associated with an inability to abstain from drinking. For others, alcoholism manifests itself as an inability to stop drinking once the person takes a few drinks. In a 2009 survey, 13.7 percent of 18- to 25-year-olds reported heavy drinking—defined as drinking five or more drinks on the same occasion on each of five or more days in a one month period (SAMHSA, 2010). Among 18- to 22-year-olds attending college, the rate of heavy drinking is 16.0 percent; for those 18- to 22-year-olds not attending college, the comparable rate is 11.7 percent.

Driving accidents and fatalities occur six times more often to individuals with 0.10 percent alcohol in their bloodstream than to those with half that amount. Alcohol-related automobile accidents are a leading cause of death among people between the ages of 15 and 25. Given these disturbing statistics, researchers have tried to understand the several ways in which alcohol has a negative impact on driving performance. Part of the answer lies in alcohol's effect on drinkers' ability to inhibit bad impulses.

Suppose you are driving to an important appointment for which you can't be late. As you drive, you might have an impulse to indulge in bad driving behaviors such as speeding or reckless lane changes. However, those negative impulses are offset by your knowledge that you might get a ticket, have an accident, and so on. A team of researchers tested the hypothesis that people under the influence of alcohol drive particularly badly when they are driving in those sorts of circumstances—in which there's a conflict between good and bad impulses (Fillmore et al., 2008). The participants in the study engaged in a simulated driving task after consuming either alcohol or a placebo. (You can understand why the researchers couldn't conduct the experiment on real roads.) Participants' driving was considerably worse after alcohol consumption on measures such as failures to stop at red lights and abrupt steering maneuvers. The impact of alcohol was even greater, however, when the researchers increased the participants' sense of response conflict. The researchers offered the participants cash rewards for reaching their destinations quickly, but they lost money if they drove poorly. When they were in this state of conflict, participants' performance was worst of all: Their bad impulses dramatically won out.

You are no doubt familiar with the claim that people will do things while they're drunk that they would never do if they were sober. In the realm of driving, the lack of impulse control can have deadly consequences.

Stimulants **Stimulants,** such as *amphetamines, methamphetamines,* and *cocaine,* keep the drug user aroused and induce states of euphoria. Stimulants achieve their effects by increasing the brain levels of neurotransmitters such as norepinephrine, serotonin, and dopamine. For example, stimulants act in the brain to prevent the action of molecules that ordinarily remove dopamine from synapses (Martin-Fardon et al., 2005). The serious addiction that often accompanies stimulant use may arise because of long-term changes in the neurotransmitter systems (Collins et al., 2011).

In recent years, research attention has focused on abuse of methamphetamine. Over a period of 10 years, from 1993 to 2003, admissions to facilities for the treatment of methamphetamine addiction increased by 400 percent (Homer et al., 2008). Poll data indicate that the rate of methamphetamine use has varied between 0.1 and 0.3 percent of the U.S. population, for the period from 2006 to 2009 (SAMHSA, 2010). As with other stimulants, methamphetamine has an impact on the brain's use of dopamine. People who take methamphetamine experience feelings of euphoria, decreased anxiety, and intense sexual craving. However, methamphetamine use very quickly has negative consequences: After only days or weeks of continuous use, people begin to experience frightening hallucinations and develop beliefs that others are out to harm them. These beliefs are known as *paranoid delusions.* Methamphetamine is highly addictive. Chronic use causes several types of damage in the brain, including the loss of nerve terminals in the dopamine system (Rose & Grant, 2008). Damage to brain regions involved in decision making and planning may explain why methamphetamine users become overly aggressive and suffer from social isolation (Homer et al., 2008).

MDMA—more commonly known as *ecstasy*—is a stimulant but also produces hallucinogen-like distortions of time and perception. The stimulant properties of the drug gives users feelings of boundless energy; the hallucinogenic properties make sounds, colors, and emotions more intense. Ecstasy brings about these effects by altering the functioning of neurotransmitters such as dopamine, serotonin, and norepinephrine. Because ecstasy has a broad impact on these neurotransmitter systems, considerable research has focused on the drug's long-term impact on the brain (Jager et al., 2008). Researchers have been particularly sensitive to ecstasy's status as a party drug. They have attempted to devise studies that accurately reflect human norms of drug use. Researchers recognize, for example,

stimulant Drug that causes arousal, increased activity, and euphoria.

Methamphetamine is so addictive that users will tolerate the physical deterioration that accompanies long-term use. The left photograph shows a 42-year-old woman before she became a methamphetamine addict. The right photo was taken 2 1/2 years later. Why is it so easy for people to become addicted to methamphetamine and other stimulants?

that users often ingest the drug at the same time that they have consumed alcohol. This leads to the question of how alcohol and ecstasy jointly affect the brain. Research suggests that the combination of ecstasy and alcohol produces negative effects in rats' brains that would not have occurred with ecstasy alone (Cassel et al., 2005).

Stimulants have three major effects that users seek: increased self-confidence, greater energy and hyperalertness, and mood alterations approaching euphoria. As you learned for metamphetamine, heavy users often experience hallucinations and paranoid delusions. A special danger with cocaine use is the contrast between euphoric highs and very depressive lows. This leads users to increase uncontrollably the frequency of drug use and the dosage. *Crack,* a crystallized form of cocaine, increases these dangers. Crack produces a swift high that wears off quickly; craving for the drug is intense.

Two stimulants that you may often overlook as psychoactive drugs are *caffeine* and *nicotine.* As you may know from experience, two cups of strong coffee or tea administer enough caffeine to have a profound effect on heart, blood, and circulatory functions and make it difficult for you to sleep. Nicotine, a chemical found in tobacco, is a sufficiently strong stimulant to have been used in high concentrations by Native American shamans to attain mystical states or trances. Unlike some modern users, however, the shamans knew that nicotine is addictive, and they carefully chose when to be under its influence. Like other addictive drugs, nicotine mimics natural chemicals released by the brain. In fact, research has uncovered common regions of brain activation for addiction to nicotine and cocaine (Vezina et al., 2007). Chemicals in nicotine have their effect on brain circuits that make you feel good whenever you have achieved a rewarding goal (De Biasi & Dani, 2011). Ordinarily these brain circuits help to aid survival. Unfortunately, nicotine teases those same brain receptors into responding as if it were good for you to be smoking. It's not. As you know, smoking is far from good for your health.

This chapter began by asking you to remember your past and plan for your future. These ordinary activities allowed us nonetheless to ponder some interesting questions about consciousness: Where did your thoughts come from? How did they emerge? When did they arrive? You've now learned some of the theories that apply to these questions and how it has been possible to test those theories. You've seen that consciousness ultimately allows you to have the full range of experiences that define you as human.

We have also considered some increasingly less ordinary uses of consciousness. Why, we asked, do people become dissatisfied with their everyday working minds and seek to alter their consciousness in so many ways? Ordinarily, your primary focus is on meeting the immediate demands of tasks and situations facing you. However, you are aware of these reality-based constraints on your consciousness. You realize they limit the range and depth of your experience and do not allow you to fulfill your potential. Perhaps, at times, you long to reach beyond the confines of ordinary reality. You may seek the uncertainty of freedom instead of settling for the security of the ordinary.

Stop *and* Review

① What is the definition of drug tolerance?
② How do drugs like heroin work in the brain?
③ To what category of drugs does nicotine belong?

✓ Study and Review on MyPsychLab

Recapping Main Points

The Contents of Consciousness

- Consciousness is an awareness of the mind's contents.
- The contents of waking consciousness contrast with nonconscious processes, preconscious memories, unattended information, the unconscious, and conscious awareness.
- Research techniques such as think-aloud protocols and experience sampling are used to study the contents of consciousness.

The Functions of Consciousness

- Consciousness aids your survival and enables you to construct both personal and culturally shared realities.
- Researchers have studied the relationship between conscious and unconscious processes.

Sleep and Dreams

- Circadian rhythms reflect the operation of a biological clock.
- Patters of brain activity change over the course of a night's sleep. REM sleep is signaled by rapid eye movements.
- The amount of sleep and relative proportion of REM to NREM sleep change with age.
- REM and NREM sleep serve different functions, including conservation and restoration.
- Sleep disorders such as insomnia, narcolepsy, and sleep apnea have a negative impact on people's ability to function during waking time.
- Freud proposed that the content of dreams is unconscious material slipped by a sleeping censor.
- In other cultures, dreams are interpreted regularly, often by people with special cultural roles.

- Some dream theories have focused on biological explanations for the origins of dreams.
- Lucid dreaming is an awareness that one is dreaming.

Altered States of Consciousness

- Hypnosis is an alternate state of consciousness characterized by the ability of hypnotizable people to change perception, motivation, memory, and self-control in response to suggestions.
- Meditation changes conscious functioning by ritual practices that focus attention away from external concerns to inner experience.

Mind-Altering Drugs

- Psychoactive drugs affect mental processes by temporarily changing consciousness as they modify nervous system activity.
- Among psychoactive drugs that alter consciousness are hallucinogens, opiates, depressants, and stimulants.

KEY TERMS

addiction (p. 137)
circadian rhythm (p. 126)
consciousness (p. 121)
depressant (p. 139)
dream work (p. 131)
hallucination (p. 137)
hallucinogen (p. 137)
hypnosis (p. 134)
hypnotizability (p. 134)
inattentional blindness (p. 122)

insomnia (p. 129)
latent content (p. 131)
lucid dreaming (p. 132)
manifest content (p. 131)
meditation (p. 135)
narcolepsy (p. 129)
nightmare (p. 130)
nonconscious (p. 122)
non-REM (NREM) sleep (p. 126)
physiological dependence (p. 137)

preconscious memory (p. 122)
psychoactive drug (p. 136)
psychological dependence (p. 137)
rapid eye movements (REM) (p. 126)
sleep apnea (p. 130)
sleep terrors (p. 130)
somnambulism (p. 130)
stimulant (p. 140)
tolerance (p. 137)

1. Freud suggested that some memories are sufficiently threatening that they are forced to reside in
   a. the unconscious.
   c. consciousness.
   b. the preconscious.
   d. manifest content.

2. You have a group of men and women watch the same TV commercial for a new car. If you want to determine what type of information the commercial brings to mind, you could use
   a. meditation.
   c. lucid dreaming.
   b. a visual search experiment.
   d. think-aloud protocols.

3. Which of these is an example of the selective storage function of consciousness?
   a. Rob kept his eye on the hoop while he shot the basketball.
   b. Laura decided to get chocolate ice cream instead of vanilla.
   c. Mel hit the gas pedal as soon as the light turned green.
   d. Salvatore committed to memory the address of his new girlfriend.

4. Because it requires more conscious attention, it is harder to find a _____ object than a _____ object.
   a. red; large and red
   b. green; green and yellow
   c. red and blue; green and yellow
   d. red and blue; red

5. To determine Garrick's chronotype, which question would you be mostly likely to ask him?
   a. How many times a month do you have nightmares?
   b. When do you usually go to bed?
   c. Do you have more NREM sleep or more REM sleep?
   d. Do you smoke marijuana or cigarettes?

6. Both NREM and REM sleep may be important for
   a. drug tolerance.
   b. unattended information.
   c. latent and manifest content.
   d. learning and memory.

7. Several times a night, Carolyn stops breathing and then she wakes up. It sounds as if Carolyn suffers from
   a. insomina.
   c. somnambulism.
   b. sleep apnea.
   d. narcolepsy.

8. The activation-synthesis model claimed that
   a. dreams arise from random brain activity.
   b. dream manifest content is synthesized from latent content.
   c. dream content reflects people's day-to-day concerns.
   d. girls and boys have different dream content.

9. To bring about a state of _____, researchers flash a red light when they detect REM sleep.
   a. lucid dreaming
   b. hypnosis
   c. meditation
   d. activation and synthesis

10. Which of these individuals would you expect to be most responsive to hypnosis?
    a. 19-year-old Paula
    c. 24-year-old Jeannine
    b. 11-year-old Ralph
    d. 46-year-old George

11. Research suggests that _____ can bring about greater connectivity between regions in people's brains.
    a. hypnosis
    c. somnambulism
    b. dreaming
    d. meditation

12. Craving for a drug in the absence of a physical need is the definition of
    a. addiction.
    b. drug tolerance.
    c. psychological dependence.
    d. physiological dependence.

13. Hallucinogens act in the brain by _____ the activation of _____ neurons.
    a. inhibiting; GABA
    c. prolonging; serotonin
    b. inhibiting; dopamine
    d. prolonging; dopamine

14. Heavy use of _____ may lead to paranoid delusions.
    a. stimulants
    c. opiates
    b. depressants
    d. hallucinogens

15. A team of researchers is developing a new drug treatment to help people control their weight. You suspect that the drug might target the brain's _____ system.
    a. barbiturate
    c. benzodiazepine
    b. opiate
    d. cannabinoid

ESSAY QUESTIONS

1. How has the concept of the unconscious been modified in the time since Freud's theory?

2. What practices of dream interpretation are carried out in non-Western cultures?

3. What physiological mechanisms explain why drug use often leads to addiction?

Learning and Behavior Analysis

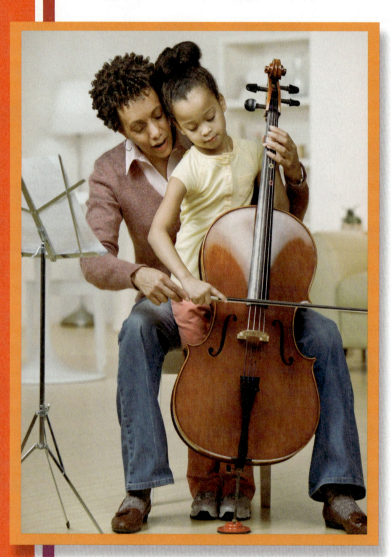

Imagine that you are in a movie theater, watching a horror film. As the hero approaches a closed door, the music on the movie's sound track grows dark and menacing. You suddenly feel the urge to yell, "Don't go through that door!" Meanwhile, you find that your heart is racing. But why? If you think about this question formally, you might come to the answer, "I have learned an association between movie music and movie events—and that's what's making me nervous!" But had you ever thought about this relationship before? Probably not. Somehow, by virtue of sitting in enough movie theaters, you have learned the association without any particular thought. The main topic of Chapter 6 is the types of associations that you acquire effortlessly in your day-to-day experience.

Psychologists have long been interested in *learning,* the ways in which organisms learn from experiences in the world. In just a moment, you will see a more precise definition of learning. We then consider particular types of learning: classical conditioning and operant conditioning. As you will see, each of these types of learning represents a different way in which organisms acquire and use information about the structure of their environments. For each of these types of learning, I describe both the basic mechanisms that govern its operation in the laboratory and applications to real-life situations.

This chapter also reflects on the way learning is similar and dissimilar across species. You will see that basic processes of conditioning are the same across a wide variety of species. However, you will also discover that some aspects of learning are constrained by species' particular genetic endowments. In particular, you will see how *cognition*—higher mental processes—affects learning processes in both humans and other species.

THE STUDY OF LEARNING

Our exploration of learning will begin with a definition of learning itself. We then consider two basic forms of learning. The section ends with a brief sketch of the history of psychological research on the topic.

What is Learning?

Learning is a process based on experience that results in a relatively consistent change in behavior or behavior potential. Let's look more closely at the three critical parts of this definition. 👁

A Process Based on Experience Learning can take place only through experience. Experience includes taking in information (and evaluating and transforming it) and making responses that affect the environment. Learning consists of a response influenced by the lessons of memory. Learned behavior does not include changes that come about because of physical maturation or brain development as the organism ages, nor those caused by illness or brain damage. Some lasting changes in behavior require experience following maturational readiness. For example, consider the timetable that determines when an infant is ready to crawl, stand, walk, run, and be toilet trained. No amount of training or practice will produce those behaviors before the child has matured sufficiently. Psychologists are especially interested in discovering what aspects of behavior can be changed through experience and how such changes come about.

A Change in Behavior or Behavior Potential It is obvious that learning has taken place when you are able to demonstrate the results, such as when you send a text message or drive a car. You can't directly observe learning itself—meaning, you can't ordinarily see the changes in your brain—but learning is apparent from improvements in your *performance.* Often, however, your performance doesn't show everything that you have learned. Sometimes, too, you have acquired general attitudes, such as an *appreciation* of modern art or an *understanding* of Eastern philosophy, that may not be apparent in your measurable actions. In such instances, you have achieved a potential for behavior change because you have learned attitudes and values that can influence the kinds of books you read or the way you spend your leisure time. This is an example of the **learning-performance distinction**—the difference between what has been learned and what is expressed, or performed, in overt behavior.

A Relatively Consistent Change To qualify as learned, a change in behavior or behavior potential must be relatively consistent over different occasions. Thus, once you learn to swim, you will probably always be able to do so. Note that consistent changes are not always permanent changes. You may, for example, have become quite a consistent dart thrower when you practiced every day. If you gave up the sport, however, your skills might have deteriorated toward their original level. But if you have learned once to be a championship dart thrower, it ought to be easier for you to learn a second time. Something has been "saved" from your prior experience. In that sense, the change may be permanent.

How does consistent form in ballet dancers fit the definition of learning?

👁 **Watch** the **Video** *The Big Picture: What Does It Mean to Learn?* on **MyPsychLab**

learning A process based on experience that results in a relatively permanent change in behavior or behavioral potential.

learning-performance distinction The difference between what has been learned and what is expressed in overt behavior.

Habituation and Sensitization To help you master the concept of learning, I will describe two of its most basic forms: *habituation* and *sensitization*. Imagine that you are examining a picture of a pleasant scene—an image, for example, of waterskiing or windsurfing. The first time you see it, you might have a fairly strong emotional response. However, if you view the same image repeatedly in short succession, your emotional response will become weaker over time (Leventhal et al., 2007). This is an example of **habituation:** You show a decrease in behavioral response when a stimulus is presented repeatedly. Habituation helps keep your focus on novel events in the environment—you don't expend behavioral effort to respond repeatedly to old stimuli.

Note how habituation fits the definition of learning. There's a change in behavior (your emotional response is weaker) that is based on experience (you've seen the image repeatedly), and that behavior change is consistent (you do not return to your original level of emotional response). However, the change in emotional response is unlikely to be permanent. If you see the same picture after sufficient time has passed, you might find it emotionally engaging once again.

When **sensitization** occurs, your response to a stimulus becomes stronger, rather than weaker, when it occurs repeatedly. Suppose, for example, you experience the same painful stimulus several times in short succession. Even if the intensity of the stimulus remained constant, you would report greater pain in response to the final stimulus in the series than you would in response to the first stimulus (Woolf, 2011). Once again, sensitization fits the definition of learning because experience in the world (repeated experiences of a painful stimulus) leads to a consistent change in behavioral response (reports that the pain is more intense). You might wonder what determines whether people will experience habituation or sensitization in response to different stimuli. In general, sensitization is more likely to occur when stimuli are intense or irritating.

Behaviorism and Behavior Analysis

Much of modern psychology's view of learning finds its roots in the work of **John Watson** (1878–1958). Watson founded the school of psychology known as *behaviorism*. For nearly 50 years, American psychology was dominated by the behaviorist tradition expressed in Watson's 1919 book, *Psychology from the Standpoint of a Behaviorist.* Watson argued that introspection—people's verbal reports of sensations, images, and feelings—was *not* an acceptable means of studying behavior because it was too subjective. How could scientists verify the accuracy of such private experiences? But once introspection has been rejected, what should the subject matter of psychology be? Watson's answer was *observable behavior.* In Watson's words, "States of consciousness, like the so-called phenomenon of spiritualism, are not objectively verifiable and for that reason can never become data for science" (Watson, 1919, p. 1). Watson also defined the chief goal of psychology as "the prediction and control of behavior" (Watson, 1913, p. 158).

B. F. Skinner (1904–1990) adopted Watson's cause and expanded his agenda. Skinner began the research that would lead him to formulate this position when, after reading Watson's 1924 book *Behaviorism,* he began his graduate study in psychology at Harvard. Over time, Skinner formulated a position known as *radical behaviorism.* Skinner embraced Watson's

B. F. Skinner expanded on Watson's ideas and applied them to a wide spectrum of behavior. Why did Skinner's psychology focus on environmental events rather than on internal states?

complaint against internal states and mental events. However, Skinner focused not so much on their legitimacy as data as on their legitimacy as *causes of behavior* (Skinner, 1990). In Skinner's view, mental events, such as thinking and imagining, do not cause behavior. Rather, they are examples of behavior that are caused by environmental stimuli.

Suppose that we deprive a pigeon of food for 24 hours, place it in an apparatus where it can obtain food by pecking a small disk, and find that it soon does so. Skinner would argue that the animal's behavior can be fully explained by environmental events—deprivation and the use of food as reinforcement. The subjective feeling of hunger, which cannot be directly observed or measured, is not a cause of the behavior but the result of deprivation. To explain what the bird does, you need not understand anything about its inner psychological states—you need only understand the principles of learning that allow the bird to acquire the association between behavior and reward. This is the essence of Skinner's brand of behaviorism.

This brand of behaviorism originated by Skinner served as the original philosophical cornerstone of **behavior analysis,** the area of psychology that focuses on discovering environmental determinants of learning and behavior (Cooper et al., 2007). In general, behavior analysts attempt to discover regularities in learning that are universal, occurring in all types of animal species, including humans, under comparable situations. That is why studies with nonhuman animals have been so critical to progress in this area. Complex forms of learning

....

habituation A decrease in a behavioral response when a stimulus is presented repeatedly.

sensitization An increase in behavioral response when a stimulus is presented repeatedly.

behavior analysis The area of psychology that focuses on the environmental determinants of learning and behavior.

represent combinations and elaborations of simpler processes and not qualitatively different phenomena. In the sections that follow, we consider classical conditioning and operant conditioning—two simple forms of learning that give rise to quite complex behaviors.

Stop *and* Review

① What is meant by the learning-performance distinction?
② What is the definition of habituation?
③ Why did Watson emphasize the study of observable behavior?
④ What is a major goal of behavior analysis?

✓● **Study** and **Review** on **MyPsychLab**

Physiologist Ivan Pavlov (shown here with his research team) observed classical conditioning while conducting research on digestion. What were some of Pavlov's major contributions to the study of this form of learning?

CLASSICAL CONDITIONING: LEARNING PREDICTABLE SIGNALS

Imagine once more that you are watching that horror movie. Why does your heart race when the sound track signals trouble for the hero? Somehow your body has learned to produce a physiological response (a racing heart) when one environmental event (for example, scary music) is associated with another (scary visual events). This type of learning is known as **classical conditioning,** a basic form of learning in which one stimulus or event predicts the occurrence of another stimulus or event. The organism learns a new *association* between two stimuli—a stimulus that did not previously elicit the response and one that naturally elicited the response. As you shall see, the innate capacity to quickly associate pairs of events in your environment has profound behavioral implications. ◉

Pavlov's Surprising Observation

The first rigorous study of classical conditioning was the result of what may well be psychology's most famous accident. The Russian physiologist **Ivan Pavlov** (1849–1936) did not set out to study classical conditioning or any other psychological phenomenon. He happened on classical conditioning while conducting research on digestion, for which he won a Nobel Prize in 1904.

Pavlov had devised a technique to study digestive processes in dogs by implanting tubes in their glands and digestive organs to divert bodily secretions to containers outside their bodies so that the secretions could be measured and analyzed.

◉ **Watch** the **Video** *The Basics 1: Classical Conditioning and Learning Predictable Signals* on **MyPsychLab**

classical conditioning A type of learning in which a behavior (conditioned response) comes to be elicited by a stimulus (conditioned stimulus) that has acquired its power through an association with a biologically significant stimulus (unconditioned stimulus).

To produce these secretions, Pavlov's assistants put meat powder into the dogs' mouths. After repeating this procedure a number of times, Pavlov observed an unexpected behavior in his dogs—they salivated *before* the powder was put in their mouths! They would start salivating at the mere sight of the food and, later, at the sight of the assistant who brought the food or even at the sound of the assistant's footsteps. Indeed, any stimulus that regularly preceded the presentation of food came to elicit salivation. Quite by accident, Pavlov had observed that learning may result from two stimuli becoming associated with each other.

Fortunately, Pavlov had the scientific skills and curiosity to begin a rigorous attack on this surprising phenomenon. He ignored the advice of the great physiologist of the time, Sir Charles Sherrington, suggesting he give up his foolish investigation of "psychic" secretions. Instead, Pavlov abandoned his work on digestion and, in so doing, changed the course of psychology forever (Pavlov, 1928). For the remainder of Pavlov's life, he continued to search for the variables that influence classically conditioned behavior. Classical conditioning is also called *Pavlovian conditioning* because of Pavlov's discovery of the major phenomena of conditioning and his dedication to tracking down the variables that influence it.

Pavlov's considerable research experience allowed him to follow a simple and elegant strategy to discover the conditions necessary for his dogs to be conditioned to salivate. As shown in **Figure 6.1** on page 148, dogs in his experiments were first placed in a restraining harness. At regular intervals, a stimulus such as a tone was presented, and a dog was given a bit of food. Importantly, the tone had no prior meaning for the dog with respect to food or salivation. As you might imagine, the dog's first reaction to the tone was only an *orienting response*—the dog pricked its ears and moved its head to locate the source of the sound. However, with repeated trials in which the tone preceded the food, the orienting response stopped and salivation began. What Pavlov had observed in his earlier research was no accident: The phenomenon could be replicated under controlled conditions. Pavlov demonstrated the generality of this effect by using a variety of other stimuli ordinarily neutral with respect to salivation, such as lights and ticking metronomes.

The main features of Pavlov's classical conditioning procedure are illustrated in **Figure 6.2** on page 148. At the core

FIGURE 6.1 Pavlov's Original Procedure

In his original experiments, Pavlov used a variety of stimuli such as tones, bells, lights, and metronomes to serve as neutral stimuli. The experimenter presented one of these neutral stimuli and then the food powder. The dog's saliva was collected through a tube.

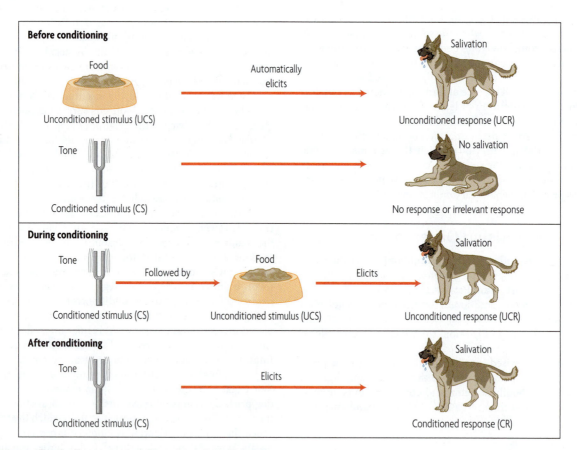

FIGURE 6.2 Basic Features of Classical Conditioning

Before conditioning, the unconditioned stimulus (UCS) naturally elicits the unconditioned response (UCR). A neutral stimulus, such as a tone, has no eliciting effect. During conditioning, the neutral stimulus is paired with the UCS. Through its association with the UCS, the neutral stimulus becomes a conditioned stimulus (CS) and elicits a conditioned response (CR) that is similar to the UCR.

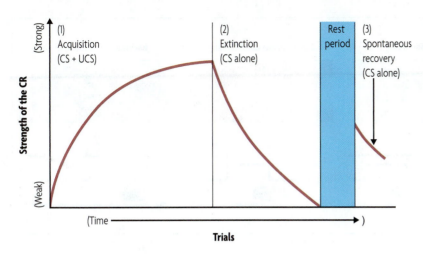

FIGURE 6.3 Acquisition, Extinction, and Spontaneous Recovery in Classical Conditioning

During acquisition (CS + UCS), the strength of the CR increases rapidly. During extinction, when the UCS no longer follows the CS, the strength of the CR drops to zero. The CR may reappear after a brief rest period, even when the UCS is still not presented. The reappearance of the CR is called spontaneous recovery.

of classical conditioning are *reflex* responses such as salivation, pupil contraction, knee jerks, or eye blinking. A **reflex** is a response that is naturally triggered—*elicited*—by specific stimuli that are biologically relevant for the organism. Any stimulus, such as the food powder used in Pavlov's experiments, that naturally elicits a reflexive behavior is called an **unconditioned stimulus (UCS)** because learning is not a necessary condition for the stimulus to control the behavior. The behavior elicited by the unconditioned stimulus is called the **unconditioned response (UCR).**

In Pavlov's experiments, the stimuli such as lights and tones did not originally trigger the reflex response of salivation. However, over time each neutral stimulus was repeatedly paired with the unconditioned stimulus. This neutral stimulus is called the **conditioned stimulus (CS):** Its power to elicit behavior is *conditioned* on its association with the UCS. After several trials, the CS will produce a response called the **conditioned response (CR).** The conditioned response is whatever response the conditioned stimulus elicits as a product of learning—you will see several examples as this section unfolds. Let's review. Nature provides the UCS–UCR connections, but the learning produced by classical conditioning creates the CS–CR connection. The conditioned stimulus acquires some of the power to influence behavior that was originally limited to the unconditioned stimulus. Let's now look in more detail at the basic processes of classical conditioning. 👁

....

👁 **Watch** the **Video** *Classic Footage of Pavlov* on **MyPsychLab**

reflex An unlearned response elicited by specific stimuli that have biological relevance for an organism.

unconditioned stimulus (UCS) In classical conditioning, the stimulus that elicits an unconditioned response.

unconditioned response (UCR) In classical conditioning, the response elicited by an unconditioned stimulus without prior training or learning.

conditioned stimulus (CS) In classical conditioning, a previously neutral stimulus that comes to elicit a conditioned response.

conditioned response (CR) In classical conditioning, a response elicited by some previously neutral stimulus that occurs as a result of pairing the neutral stimulus with an unconditioned stimulus.

acquisition The stage in a classical conditioning experiment during which the conditioned response is first elicited by the conditioned stimulus.

Processes of Conditioning

Pavlov's original experiments inspired extensive study of how classically conditioned responses appear and disappear. In this section, we consider several important conclusions researchers have reached about the basic processes of classical conditioning. These conclusions have emerged from hundreds of different studies across a wide range of animal species.

Acquisition and Extinction **Figure 6.3** displays a hypothetical classical conditioning experiment. The first panel displays **acquisition,** the process by which the CR is first elicited and gradually increases in frequency over repeated trials. In general, the CS and UCS must be paired several times before the CS reliably elicits a CR. With systematic CS–UCS pairings, the CR is elicited with increasing frequency, and the organism may be said to have acquired a conditioned response.

In classical conditioning, as in telling a good joke, *timing* is critical. The CS and UCS must be presented closely enough in time to be perceived by the organism as being related. (We will describe an exception to this rule in a later section on *taste-aversion learning*.) Researchers have studied four temporal patterns between the two stimuli, as shown in **Figure 6.4** on page 150 (Hearst, 1988). The most widely used type of conditioning is called *delay conditioning*, in which the CS comes on prior to and stays on at least until the UCS is presented. In *trace conditioning*, the CS is discontinued or turned off before the UCS is presented. *Trace* refers to the memory that the organism is assumed to have of the CS, which is no longer present when the UCS appears. In *simultaneous conditioning*, both the CS and UCS are presented at the same time. Finally, in the case of *backward conditioning*, the CS is presented after the UCS.

Conditioning is usually most effective in a delayed conditioning paradigm, with a short interval between the onsets of the CS and UCS. However, the exact time interval between the CS and the UCS that will produce optimal conditioning depends on several factors, including the intensity of the CS and the response being conditioned. Let's focus on the response being conditioned. For muscular responses, such as eye blinks, a short interval of a second or less is best. For visceral responses, such as heart rate and salivation, however, longer intervals of 5 to 15 seconds work best.

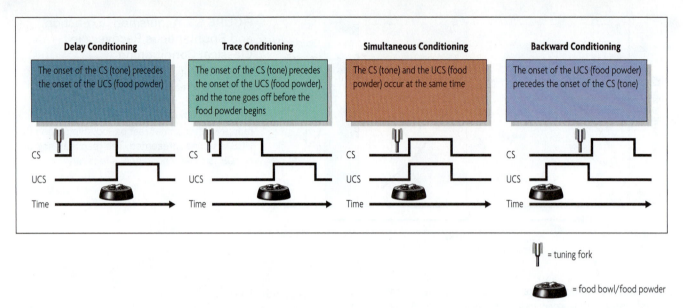

Delay Conditioning

The onset of the CS (tone) precedes the onset of the UCS (food powder)

CS

UCS

Time

Trace Conditioning

The onset of the CS (tone) precedes the onset of the UCS (food powder), and the tone goes off before the food powder begins

CS

UCS

Time

Simultaneous Conditioning

The CS (tone) and the UCS (food powder) occur at the same time

CS

UCS

Time

Backward Conditioning

The onset of the UCS (food powder) precedes the onset of the CS (tone)

CS

UCS

Time

= tuning fork

= food bowl/food powder

FIGURE 6.4 Four Variations of the CS–UCS Temporal Arrangement in Classical Conditioning

Researchers have explored the four possible timing arrangements between the CS and UCS. Conditioning is generally most effective in a delay conditioning paradigm with a short interval between the onsets of the CS and UCS.

From Baron, Robert A., *Psychology*, 5th Edition., © 2001. Printed and electronically reproduced by permission of Pearson Education Inc., Upper Saddle River, New Jersey.

Conditioning is generally poor with a simultaneous procedure and very poor with a backward procedure. Evidence of backward conditioning may appear after a few pairings of the UCS and CS but disappear with extended training as the animal learns that the CS is followed by a period free of the UCS. In both cases, conditioning is weak because the CS does not actually predict the onset of the UCS. (We will return to the importance of predictability, or *contingency,* in the next section.)

But what happens when the CS (for example, the tone) no longer predicts the UCS (the food powder)? Under those circumstances, the CR (salivation) becomes weaker over time and eventually stops occurring. When the CR no longer appears in the presence of the CS (and the absence of the UCS), the process of **extinction** is said to have occurred (see Figure 6.3, panel 2). Conditioned responses, then, are not necessarily a permanent aspect of the organism's behavioral repertoire. However, the CR will reappear in a weak form when the CS is presented alone again after extinction (see Figure 6.3, panel 3). Pavlov referred to this sudden reappearance of the CR after a rest period, or time-out, without further exposure to the UCS as **spontaneous recovery** after extinction.

When the original pairing is renewed, postextinction, the CR becomes rapidly stronger. This more rapid relearning is an instance of *savings:* Less time is necessary to reacquire the response than to acquire it originally. Thus some of the original conditioning must be retained by the organism even after experimental extinction appears to have eliminated the CR. In other words, extinction has only weakened performance, not wiped out the original learning. This is why the original definition of learning emphasized the distinction between learning and performance.

Stimulus Generalization Suppose we have taught a dog that presentation of a tone of a certain frequency predicts food powder. Is the dog's response specific to only that stimulus? If you think about this question for a moment, you will probably not be surprised that the answer is no. In general, once a CR has been conditioned to a particular CS, similar stimuli may also elicit the response. For example, if conditioning was to a high-frequency tone, a slightly lower tone could also elicit the response. A child bitten by a big dog is likely to respond with fear even to smaller dogs. This automatic extension of responding to stimuli that have never been paired with the original UCS is called **stimulus generalization.** The more similar the new stimulus is to the original CS, the stronger the response will be. When response strength is measured for each of a series of increasingly dissimilar stimuli along a given dimension, as shown in **Figure 6.5**, a *generalization gradient* is found.

The existence of generalization gradients should suggest to you the way classical conditioning serves its function in everyday experience. Because important stimuli rarely occur in exactly the same form every time in nature, stimulus generalization builds in a similarity safety factor by extending the range of learning beyond the original specific experience. With this feature, new but comparable events can be

extinction In conditioning, the weakening of a conditioned association in the absence of a reinforcer or unconditioned stimulus.

spontaneous recovery The reappearance of an extinguished conditioned response after a rest period.

stimulus generalization The automatic extension of conditioned responding to similar stimuli that have never been paired with the unconditioned stimulus.

FIGURE 6.5 Stimulus Generalization Gradients

Rabbits were trained so that they produced a conditioned response (they closed their outer eyelid) when they heard a 1000 hertz tone (Siegel et al., 1968). During an extinction phase, the rabbits were tested on the training tone as well as tones that varied in distance from that tone. Tones more similar to the training tone produced more conditioned responses than those further away.

Data from Siegel, S., Hearst, E., George, N., & O'Neal, E. (1968). Generalization gradients obtained from individual subjects following classical conditioning. *Journal of Experimental Psychology, 78,* 171–174.

recognized as having the same meaning, or behavioral significance, despite apparent differences. For example, even when a predator makes a slightly different sound or is seen from a different angle, its prey can still recognize and respond to it quickly.

Stimulus Discrimination In some circumstances, however, it is important that a response be made to only a very small range of stimuli. An organism should not, for example, exhaust itself by fleeing too often from animals that are only superficially similar to its natural predators. **Stimulus discrimination** is the process by which an organism learns to respond differently to stimuli that are distinct from the CS on some dimension (for example, differences in hue or in pitch). An organism's discrimination among similar stimuli (tones of 1,000, 1,200, and 1,500 Hz, for example) is sharpened with discrimination training in which only one of them (1,200 Hz, for example) predicts the UCS and in which the others are repeatedly presented without it. Early in conditioning, stimuli similar to the CS will elicit a similar response, although not quite as strong. As discrimination training proceeds, the responses to the other, dissimilar stimuli weaken: The organism gradually learns which event-signal predicts the onset of the UCS and which signals do not.

stimulus discrimination A conditioning process in which an organism learns to respond differently to stimuli that differ from the conditioned stimulus on some dimension.

For an organism to perform optimally in an environment, the processes of generalization and discrimination must strike a balance. You don't want to be overselective—it can be quite costly to miss the presence of a predator. You also don't want to be overresponsive—if you are fearful of every shadow, you will waste time and energy to dispel your worry. Classical conditioning provides a mechanism that allows creatures to react efficiently to the structure of their environments.

Focus on Acquisition

In this section, we will examine more closely the conditions that are necessary for classical conditioning to take place. So far, I have *described* the acquisition of classically conditioned responses, but I have not yet *explained* it. Pavlov believed that classical conditioning resulted from the mere pairing of the CS and the UCS. In his view, if a response is to be classically conditioned, the CS and the UCS must occur close together in time—that is, be *temporally contiguous*. But as you will see next, contemporary research has modified that view.

Pavlov's theory dominated classical conditioning until the mid-1960s, when **Robert Rescorla** (1966) conducted a very telling experiment using dogs as subjects. Rescorla designed an experiment using a tone (the CS) and a shock (the UCS). For one group of animals the CS and UCS were merely contiguous—which, if Pavlov were correct, would be sufficient to produce classical conditioning. For the other group of animals, the tone reliably predicted the presence of the shock.

In the first phase of the experiment, Rescorla trained dogs to jump a barrier from one side of a shuttlebox to the other to avoid an electric shock delivered through the grid floor (see **Figure 6.6** *on page 152). If the dogs did not jump, they received a shock; if they did jump, the shock was postponed. Rescorla used the frequency with which dogs jumped the barrier as a measure of fear conditioning.*

Featured Study

Why might a child who has been frightened by one dog develop a fear response to all dogs?

When the dogs were jumping across the barrier regularly, Rescorla divided his subjects into two groups and subjected them to another training procedure. To the random group, the UCS (the shock) was delivered randomly and independently of the CS (the tone) (see **Figure 6.7**). *Although the CS and the UCS often occurred close together in time—they were, by chance, temporally contiguous—the UCS was as likely to be delivered in the absence of the CS as it was in its presence. Thus the CS had no predictive value. For the contingency group, however, the UCS always followed the CS. Thus, for this group, the sounding of the tone was a reliable predictor of the delivery of the shock.*

Once this training was complete, the dogs were put back into the shuttlebox, but this time with a twist. Now the tone used in the second training procedure occasionally sounded, signaling shock. What happened? **Figure 6.8***, indicates that dogs exposed to the contingent (predictable) CS–UCS relation jumped more frequently in the presence of the tone than did dogs exposed only to the contiguous (associated) CS–UCS relation. Contingency was critical for the signal to serve the dogs as a successful cue for the shock.*

FIGURE 6.6 A Shuttlebox

Rescorla used the frequency with which dogs jumped over a barrier as a measure of fear conditioning.

Thus, in addition to the CS being contiguous—occurring close in time—with the UCS, the CS must also *reliably predict* the occurrence of the UCS in order for classical conditioning to occur (Rescorla, 1988). This finding makes considerable sense. After all, in natural situations, where learning enables organisms to adapt to changes in their environment, stimuli come in clusters and not in neat, simple units, as they do in laboratory experiments.

There's one last requirement for a stimulus to serve as a basis for classical conditioning: It must be *informative* in the environment. Consider an experimental situation in which rats have learned that a tone predicts a shock. Now, a light is added into the situation so that both the light and tone precede the

shock. However, when the light is subsequently presented alone, the rats do not appear to have learned that the light predicts the shock (Kamin, 1969). For these rats, the previous conditioning to the tone in the first phase of the experiment *blocked* any subsequent conditioning that could occur to the light. From the rat's point of view, the light may as well not have existed; it provided no additional information beyond that already given by the tone. The requirement of informativeness explains why conditioning occurs most rapidly when the CS stands out against the many other stimuli that may also be present in an environment. A stimulus is more readily noticed the more *intense* it is and the more it *contrasts* with other stimuli.

You can see that classical conditioning is more complex than even Pavlov originally realized. A neutral stimulus will become an effective CS only if it is both appropriately contingent and informative. But now let's shift your attention a bit. We want to identify real-life situations in which classical conditioning plays a role.

FIGURE 6.7 Rescorla's Procedure for Demonstrating the Importance of Contingency

For the random group, 5-second tones (the CS) and 5-second shocks (the UCS) were distributed randomly through the experimental period. For the contingency group, the dogs experienced only the subset of tones and shocks that occurred in a predictive relationship (the onset of the CS preceded the onset of the UCS by 30 seconds or less). Only the dogs in the contingency group learned to associate the CS with the UCS.

FIGURE 6.8 The Role of Contingency in Classical Conditioning

The arrow indicates the onset and offset of the 5-second CS tone. Rescorla demonstrated that dogs trained under the contingent CS–UCS relation showed more jumping (and thus conditioned fear) in the presence of the tone than did dogs trained under the contiguous but noncontingent CS–UCS relation.

Applications of Classical Conditioning

Your knowledge of classical conditioning can help you understand significant everyday behavior. In this section, we help you recognize some real-world instances of emotions and preferences as the products of this form of learning. We also explore the role classical conditioning plays in the unfolding of drug addiction.

Emotions and Preferences   Earlier we asked you to think about your experience at a horror movie. In that case, you (unconsciously) learned an association between scary music (the CS) and certain likely events (the UCS—the kinds of things that happen in horror movies that cause reflexive revulsion). If you pay careful attention to events in your life, you will discover that there are many circumstances in which you can't quite explain why you are having such a strong emotional reaction or why you have such a strong preference about something. You might take a step back and ask yourself, "Is this the product of classical conditioning?"

Consider these situations (Rozin & Fallon, 1987; Rozin et al., 1986):

- Do you think you'd be willing to eat fudge that had been formed into the shape of dog feces?
- Do you think you'd be willing to drink a sugar-water solution if the sugar was drawn from a container that you knew was incorrectly labeled poison?
- Do you think you would be willing to drink apple juice into which a sterilized cockroach had been dipped?

If each of these situations makes you say "No way!" you are not alone. The classically conditioned response—feelings of disgust

● **Watch** the **Video** *Classic Footage of Little Albert* on **MyPsychLab**

or danger—wins out over the knowledge that the stimulus is really OK. Because classically conditioned responses are not built up through conscious thought, they are also hard to eliminate through conscious reasoning!

One of the most extensively studied real-world products of classical conditioning is *fear conditioning* (Hartley et al., 2011; Linnman et al., 2011). In the earliest days of behaviorism, John Watson and his colleague Rosalie Rayner sought to prove that many fear responses could be understood as the pairing of a neutral stimulus with something naturally fear provoking. To test their idea, they experimented on an infant who came to be called Little Albert.

● *Watson and Rayner (1920) trained Albert to fear a white rat he had initially liked, by pairing its appearance with an aversive UCS—a loud noise just behind him created by striking a large steel bar with a hammer. The unconditioned startle response and the emotional distress to the noxious noise formed the basis of Albert's learning to react with fear to the appearance of the white rat. His fear was developed in just seven conditioning trials. The emotional conditioning was then extended to behavioral conditioning when Albert learned to escape from the feared stimulus. The infant's learned fear then generalized to other furry objects, such as a rabbit, a dog, and even a Santa Claus mask!*

Featured Study

Albert's mother, a wet nurse at the hospital where the study was conducted, took him away before the researchers could try to treat the experimentally conditioned fear. As you'll recall from Chapter 2, researchers in psychology are guided by important ethical principles. Those principles make them look back at Watson and Rayner's experiment with grave discomfort: No ethical researcher would ever replicate an experiment of this type.

Because Watson and Rayner never made Albert's true identity public, people have always wondered what happened to him in later life. One team of researchers carried out some detective work with archival materials (Beck et al., 2009). Based

How did John Watson and Rosalie Rayner condition Little Albert to fear small, furry objects?

on that work, they have argued that Albert was an infant whose actual name was Douglas Meritte who, quite unfortunately, died in 1925. However, other researchers remain unconvinced by that identification (Powell, 2011).

Fear conditioning has a powerful impact on people's lives. A single traumatic event can condition you to respond with strong physical, emotional, and cognitive reactions—perhaps for a lifetime. We will see in Chapter 15 that therapists have designed treatments for these types of fears that are intended to counter the effects of classical conditioning.

We don't want to leave you with the impression that only negative responses are classically conditioned. In fact, we suspect that you will also be able to interpret responses of happiness or excitement as instances of classical conditioning. Certainly toilers in the advertising industry hope that classical conditioning works as a positive force. They strive, for example, to create associations in your mind between their products (for example, jeans, sports cars, and soft drinks) and passion. They expect that elements of their advertisements—"sexy" individuals or situations—will serve as the UCS to bring about the UCR—feelings of sexual arousal. The hope then is that the product itself will be the CS, so that the feelings of arousal will become associated with it. To find more examples of the classical conditioning of positive emotions, you should monitor your life for circumstances in which you have a rush of good feelings when you return, for instance, to a familiar location.

Learning to be a Drug Addict   Consider this scenario. A man's body lies in a Manhattan alley, a half-empty syringe dangling from his arm. Cause of death? The coroner called it an overdose, but the man had ordinarily shot up far greater doses than the one that had supposedly killed him. This sort of incident baffled investigators. How could an addict with high drug tolerance die of an overdose when he didn't even get a full hit?

You now have the concepts to understand a complete version of the explanation we summarized in Chapter 5, on page 136. Some time ago, Pavlov (1927) and later his colleague Bykov (1957) pointed out that tolerance to opiates can develop when an individual anticipates the pharmacological action of a drug. Contemporary researcher **Shepard Siegel** refined these ideas. Siegel suggested that the setting in which drug use occurs acts as a conditioned stimulus for a situation in which the body learns to protect itself by preventing the drug from having its usual effect. When people take drugs, the drug (UCS) brings about certain physiological responses to which the body responds with countermeasures intended to reestablish homeostasis (see Chapter 3). The body's countermeasures to the drug are the unconditioned response (UCR). Over time, this *compensatory response* also becomes the conditioned response. That is, in settings ordinarily associated with drug use (the CS), the body physiologically prepares itself (the CR) for the drug's expected effects. Tolerance arises because, in that setting, the individual must consume an amount of the drug that overcomes the compensatory response before starting to get

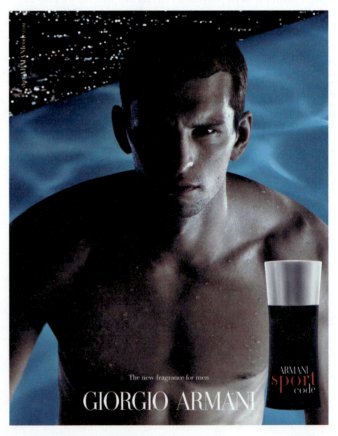

How do advertisers exploit classical conditioning to make you feel "passion" toward their products?

any "positive" effect. Increasingly larger doses are needed as the conditioned compensatory response itself grows.

Siegel tested these ideas in his laboratory by creating tolerance to heroin in laboratory rats.

Featured Study

In one study, Siegel and his colleagues classically conditioned rats to expect heroin injections (UCS) in one setting (CS_1) and dextrose (sweet sugar) solution injections in a different setting (CS_2) (Siegel et al., 1982). In the first phase of training, all rats developed heroin tolerance. On the test day, all animals received a larger-than-usual dose of heroin— nearly twice the previous amount. Half of them received it in the setting where heroin had previously been administered; the other half received it in the setting where dextrose solutions had been given during conditioning. Twice as many rats died in the dextrose-solution setting as in the usual heroin setting: 64 percent versus 32 percent!

Presumably, those receiving heroin in the usual setting were more prepared for this potentially dangerous situation because the context (CS_1) brought about a physiological response (CR) that countered the drug's typical effects.

To find out if a similar process might operate in humans, Siegel and a colleague interviewed heroin addicts who had come close to death from supposed overdoses. In 7 out of 10 cases, the addicts had been shooting up in a new and unfamiliar setting (Siegel, 1984). Although this natural experiment provides no conclusive data, it suggests that a dose for which an addict has developed tolerance in one setting may become an overdose in an unfamiliar setting. This analysis allows us to suggest that the addict we invoked at the beginning of this section might have died because he was shooting up in an unfamiliar setting.

Although we have mentioned research with heroin, classical conditioning is an important component to tolerance for a variety of drugs, including alcohol (S. Siegel, 2005). Thus the same principles Pavlov observed for dogs, bells, and salivation help explain some of the mechanisms underlying human drug addiction.

Biological Constraints

In the examples of classical conditioning you've seen so far, it seems that more or less any conditioned stimulus (such as a tuning fork) can work to signal more or less any unconditioned stimulus (such as food). However, some instances of conditioning depend not only on the relationship between stimuli and behavior but also on the way an organism is genetically predisposed toward stimuli in its environment. Animals appear to have encoded, within their genetic inheritance, the types of sensory cues—taste, smell, or appearance—that are most likely to signal dimensions of reward or danger. In those circumstances, researchers say that organisms have *biological preparedness:* A particular species has evolved so that the members require less learning experience than normal to acquire a conditioned response. Experimenters who try arbitrarily to break these genetic links will look forward to little success. In Chapter 14, we will see that researchers believe humans are biologically prepared to acquire intense fears—known as *phobias*—to stimuli

such as snakes and spiders that provided dangers over the course of human evolution. Here, we consider an important phenomenon called *taste-aversion learning* that provides an example of biological constraints on classical conditioning.

Imagine the strategy you might devise for tasting a variety of unfamiliar substances. If you had the genetic endowment of rats, you would be very cautious in doing so. When presented with a new food or flavor, rats take only a very small sample. Only if it fails to make them sick will they go back for more. To flip that around, suppose we include a substance with the new flavor that does make the rats ill—they'll never consume that flavor again. This phenomenon is known as **taste-aversion learning.** You can see why having this genetic capacity to sample and learn which foods are safe and which are toxic could have great survival value.

Taste-aversion learning is an enormously powerful mechanism. Unlike most other instances of classical conditioning, taste aversion is learned with only one pairing of a CS (the novel flavor) and its consequences (the result of the underlying UCS— the element that actually brings about the illness). This is true even with a long interval, 12 hours or more, between the time the rat consumes the substance and the time it becomes ill. Finally, unlike many classically conditioned associations that are quite fragile, this one is permanent after one experience. Again, to understand these violations of the norms of classical conditioning, consider how dramatically this mechanism aids survival.

John Garcia, the psychologist who first documented taste-aversion learning in the laboratory, and his colleague Robert Koelling used this phenomenon to demonstrate that, in general, animals are biologically prepared to learn certain associations. The researchers discovered that some CS–UCS combinations can be classically conditioned in particular species of animals, but others cannot.

Featured Study

In phase 1 of Garcia and Koelling's experiment, thirsty rats were first familiarized with the experimental situation in which licking a tube produced three CSs: saccharin-flavored water, noise, and bright light. In phase 2, when the rats licked the tube, half of them received only the sweet water and half received only the noise, light, and plain water. Each of these two groups was again divided: Half of each group was given electric shocks that produced pain, and half was given X-ray radiation that produced nausea and illness.

*The amount of water drunk by the rats in phase 1 was compared with the amount drunk in phase 2, when pain and illness were involved (see **Figure 6.9** on page 156). Big reductions in drinking occurred when flavor was associated with illness (taste aversion) and when noise and light were associated with pain. However, there was little change in behavior under the other two conditions—when flavor predicted pain or when the "bright-noisy water" predicted illness.*

The pattern of results suggests that rats have an inborn bias to associate particular stimuli with particular consequences (Garcia & Koelling, 1966).

....

taste-aversion learning A biological constraint on learning in which an organism learns in one trial to avoid a food whose ingestion is followed by illness.

Bright-noisy water
Saccharine water

FIGURE 6.9 Inborn Bias
Results from Garcia and Koelling's study (1966) showed that rats possess an inborn bias to associate certain cues with certain outcomes. Rats avoided saccharin-flavored water when it predicted illness but not when it predicted shock. Conversely, rats avoided the "bright-noisy water" when it predicted shock but not when it predicted illness.

Researchers have put knowledge of the mechanisms of taste-aversion learning to practical use. To stop coyotes from killing sheep (and sheep ranchers from shooting coyotes), John Garcia and colleagues have put toxic lamb burgers wrapped in sheep fur on the outskirts of fenced-in areas of sheep ranches. The coyotes that eat these lamb burgers get sick, vomit, and develop an instant distaste for lamb meat. Their subsequent disgust at the mere sight of sheep makes them back away from the animals instead of attacking.

In the classic research on taste-aversion learning, researchers paired novel flavors with substances that made the rats feel ill. However, other aspects of gustatory experience also yield conditioned aversions, including the temperature of the food.

In a preliminary experiment, 20 rats had the opportunity to drink from two bottles containing water at either 50° F or 104° F (Smith et al., 2010). The rats showed a consistent preference for the cold water over the warm water. In the next experiment, 16 rats were split into two groups. After drinking cold water, one group was injected with a substance that made the rats ill; the other group received a saline injection that had no negative effect. The rats that became ill now showed a conditioned aversion to the cold

Featured Study

water. Despite their initial dislike for warm water, they now mostly drank water at that temperature. In later experiments, the researchers introduced the novel flavor of saccharin. Rats that got sick after drinking water that was both cold and sweet acquired an aversion to both components of the novel stimulus: They subsequently avoided both cold water and warm saccharin.

You can see how these experiments extend the concept of biological preparedness. Food has both taste and temperature. When illness is associated with either dimension, rats swiftly acquire conditioned aversions.

Stop *and* Review

① What is the role of reflexive behaviors in classical conditioning?
② What is the difference between the UCS and the CS?
③ What is meant by stimulus discrimination?
④ Why is contingency so important in classical conditioning?
⑤ What is the conditioned response when classical conditioning plays a role in drug addiction?
⑥ What makes taste-aversion learning unusual as a conditioned response?

✓●―**Study** and **Review** on **MyPsychLab**

CRITICAL THINKING   Consider the experiment that demonstrated conditioned heroin tolerance in rats. Why were the rats given twice the normal dose of heroin on the test day?

OPERANT CONDITIONING: LEARNING ABOUT CONSEQUENCES

Let's return to the movie theater. The horror film is now over, and you peel yourself off your seat. Your companion asks you if you're hoping that a sequel will be made. You respond, "I've learned that I shouldn't go to horror films." You're probably right, but what kind of learning is this? Once again our answer begins around the turn of the 20th century.

How have researchers used taste-aversion conditioning to prevent coyotes from killing sheep?

Psychology in Your Life

HOW DOES CLASSICAL CONDITIONING AFFECT CANCER TREATMENT?

Medical researchers have made great strides in developing more effective treatments to combat cancers. Many of those treatments involve chemotherapy, drug treatments that kill or greatly weaken cancer cells. People who undergo chemotherapy often experience negative consequences such as fatigue and nausea. You might assume that those side effects would arise from the direct action of the chemotherapy drugs. Although that is partially the case, research suggests that processes of classical conditioning contribute greatly to the persistence of those side effects over time (Bovbjerg, 2006: Stockhorst et al., 2006).

Let's consider the concrete example of *anticipatory nausea*: Circumstances in which, over the course of cancer treatment, patients' nausea and vomiting begin even before they receive the chemotherapy drugs. Classical conditioning explains why this happens. The chemotherapy drugs serve as the unconditioned stimulus (UCS) producing posttreatment nausea as an unconditioned response (UCR). Distinctive features of the clinic environment serve as the conditioned stimulus (CS). Across visits to the clinic, the CS becomes paired with the UCS. The result is that patients experience anticipatory nausea as a conditioned response (CR) as soon as they arrived at the clinic. One study of 214 patients found that about 10 percent developed anticipatory nausea (Akechi et al., 2010). This situation had a measurable negative impact on their quality of life.

Classical conditioning might also explain why some of the aftereffects of chemotherapy endure well after the end of treatment. Researchers surveyed a group of 273 Hodgkin's disease survivors who ranged from 1 to 20 years beyond treatment (Cameron et al., 2001). The participants were asked to reflect over the past six months to indicate whether they "had noticed any smell or odor (anything [they had] seen / places [they had] gone to; any foods or drinks)" that had reminded them of treatment and made them "feel good or bad emotionally or physically" (p. 72). More than half of the participants—55 percent—reported lingering bad responses that were triggered by stimuli associated with their chemotherapy. The researchers suggest that these persistent responses were the result of classically conditioned associations between various aspects of the chemotherapy experience (the CS) and the drug infusions (the UCS).

As you've seen, research evidence strongly suggests that processes of classical conditioning amplify the negative effects of chemotherapy. The studies give researchers a context in which they can begin to design treatments. Some researchers have developed rat models of anticipatory nausea. Their goal is to develop drug treatments that will block the processes of classical conditioning, to prevent anticipatory nausea from developing (Chan et al., 2009; Ossenkopp et al., 2011). Other researchers have applied the types of behavioral therapies you will learn about in Chapter 15 (Roscoe et al., 2011). Those therapies use psychological interventions to counteract the initial classical conditioning. For example, patients might acquire techniques that enable them to experience deep relaxation—rather than nausea—in response to the conditioned stimulus. Interventions of this type couldn't eliminate the negative consequences of chemotherapy but they could help stop those negative consequences from enduring over time.

The Law of Effect

At about the same time that Pavlov was using classical conditioning to induce Russian dogs to salivate to the sound of a bell, **Edward L. Thorndike** (1874–1949) was watching American cats trying to escape from puzzle boxes (see **Figure 6.10** on page 158). Thorndike (1898) reported his observations and inferences about the kind of learning he believed was taking place in his subjects. The cats at first only struggled against their confinement, but once some "impulsive" action allowed them to open the door "all the other unsuccessful impulses [were] stamped out and the particular impulse leading to the successful act [was] stamped in by the resulting pleasure" (Thorndike, 1898, p. 13).

What had Thorndike's cats learned? According to Thorndike's analysis, learning was an association between stimuli in the situation and a response that an animal learned to make: a *stimulus–response (S–R) connection*. Thus the cats had learned to produce an appropriate response (for example, clawing at a button or loop) that in these stimulus circumstances (confinement in the puzzle box) led to a desired outcome (momentary freedom). Note that the learning of these S–R connections occurred gradually and automatically in a mechanistic way as the animal experienced the consequences of its actions through blind *trial and error*. Gradually, the behaviors that had satisfying consequences increased in frequency; they eventually became the dominant response when the animal was placed in the puzzle box. Thorndike referred to this relationship between behavior and its consequences as the **law of effect**: A response that is followed by satisfying consequences becomes more probable and a response that is followed by dissatisfying consequences becomes less probable.

law of effect A basic law of learning that states that the power of a stimulus to evoke a response is strengthened when the response is followed by a reward and weakened when it is not followed by a reward.

FIGURE 6.10 A Thorndike Puzzle Box

To get out of the puzzle box and obtain food, Thorndike's cat had to manipulate a mechanism to release a weight that would then pull the door open.

From Zimbardo/Johnson/McCann, *Psychology: Core Concepts,* © 2009. Reproduced by permission of Pearson Education, Inc.

Experimental Analysis of Behavior

B. F. Skinner embraced Thorndike's view that environmental consequences exert a powerful effect on behavior. Skinner outlined a program of research whose purpose was to discover, by systematic variation of stimulus conditions, the ways that various environmental conditions affect the likelihood that a given response will occur:

> *A natural datum in a science of behavior is the probability that a given bit of behavior will occur at a given time. An experimental analysis deals with that probability in terms of frequency or rate of responding. . . . The task of an experimental analysis is to discover all the variables of which probability of response is a function. (Skinner, 1966, pp. 213–214)*

Skinner's analysis was experimental rather than theoretical—theorists are guided by derivations and predictions about behavior from their theories, but empiricists, such as Skinner, advocate the bottom-up approach. They start with the collection and evaluation of data within the context of an experiment and are not theory driven.

To analyze behavior experimentally, Skinner developed **operant conditioning** procedures, in which he manipulated the *consequences* of an organism's behavior in order to see

....

◉ **Watch** the **Video** *The Basics 2: Operant Conditioning and Learning About Consequences* on **MyPsychLab**

◉ **Watch** the **Video** *Classic Footage of B.F. Skinner and the Skinner Box* on **MyPsychLab**

operant conditioning Learning in which the probability of a response is changed by a change in its consequences.

operant Behavior emitted by an organism that can be characterized in terms of the observable effects it has on the environment.

what effect they had on subsequent behavior. An **operant** is any behavior that is *emitted* by an organism and can be characterized in terms of the observable effects it has on the environment. Literally, *operant* means *affecting the environment,* or operating on it (Skinner, 1938). Operants are *not elicited* by specific stimuli as classically conditioned behaviors are. Pigeons peck, rats search for food, babies cry and coo, some people gesture while talking, and others stutter. The probability of these behaviors occurring in the future can be increased or decreased by manipulating the effects they have on the environment. If, for example, a baby's coo prompts desirable parental contact, the baby will coo more in the future. Operant conditioning, then, modifies the probability of different types of operant behavior as a function of the environmental consequences they produce. ◉

To carry out his new experimental analysis, Skinner invented an apparatus that allowed him to manipulate the consequences of behavior, the *operant chamber.* **Figure 6.11** shows how the operant chamber works. When, after having produced an appropriate behavior defined by the experimenter, a rat presses a lever, the mechanism delivers a food pellet. This device allows experimenters to study the variables that allow rats to learn—or not to learn—the behaviors they define. For example, if a lever press produces a food pellet only after a rat has turned a circle in the chamber, the rat will swiftly learn (through a process called *shaping* that we will consider shortly) to turn a circle before pressing the lever.

In many operant experiments, the measure of interest is how much of a particular behavior an animal carries out in a period of time. Researchers record the pattern and total amount of behavior emitted in the course of an experiment. This methodology allowed Skinner to study the effect of reinforcement contingencies on animals' behavior. ◉

FIGURE 6.11 Operant Chamber

In this specially designed apparatus, typical of those used with rats, a press on the lever may be followed by delivery of a food pellet.

Reinforcement Contingencies

A **reinforcement contingency** is a consistent relationship between a response and the changes in the environment that it produces. Imagine, for example, an experiment in which a pigeon's pecking a disk (the response) is generally followed by the presentation of grain (the corresponding change in the environment). This consistent relationship, or reinforcement contingency, will usually be accompanied by an increase in the rate of pecking. For delivery of grain to increase *only* the probability of pecking, it must be contingent *only* on the pecking response—the delivery must occur regularly after that response but not after other responses, such as turning or bowing. Based on Skinner's work, modern behavior analysts seek to understand behavior in terms of reinforcement contingencies. Let's take a closer look at what has been discovered about these contingencies.

Positive and Negative Reinforcers Suppose you are now captivated by the idea of getting your pet rat to turn a circle in its cage. To increase the probability of circle-turning behavior, you would want to use a **reinforcer,** any stimulus that—when made contingent on a behavior—increases the probability of that behavior over time. *Reinforcement* is the delivery of a reinforcer following a response.

Reinforcers are always defined empirically, in terms of their effects on changing the probability of a response. If you look out at the world, you can probably find three classes of stimuli: those toward which you are neutral, those that you find *appetitive* (you have an "appetite" for them), and those

that you find *aversive* (you seek to avoid them). The compositions of these classes of stimuli clearly are not the same for all individuals: What is appetitive or aversive is defined by the behavior of the individual organism. Consider the strawberry. Although many people find strawberries quite delicious, I find strawberries virtually inedible. If you intend to use strawberries to change my behavior, it's important to know that I find them aversive rather than appetitive.

When a behavior is followed by the delivery of an appetitive stimulus, the event is called **positive reinforcement.** Your pet rat will turn circles if a consequence of circle turning is the delivery of desirable food. Humans will tell jokes if a consequence of their joke telling is a type of laughter they find pleasurable.

When a behavior is followed by the removal of an aversive stimulus, the event is called **negative reinforcement.** For example, I would be more likely to perform a behavior if it would allow me to cease eating strawberries. There are two general types of learning circumstances in which negative reinforcement applies. In **escape conditioning,** animals learn that a response will allow them to escape from an aversive stimulus. Raising an umbrella during a downpour is a common example of escape conditioning. You learn to use an umbrella to escape the aversive stimulus of getting wet. In **avoidance conditioning,** animals learn responses that allow them to avoid aversive stimuli before they begin. Suppose your car has a buzzer that sounds when you fail to buckle your seat belt. You will learn to buckle up to avoid the aversive noise.

To distinguish clearly between positive and negative reinforcement, remember the following: Both positive reinforcement and negative reinforcement *increase* the probability of the response that precedes them. Positive reinforcement increases response probability by the presentation of an appetitive stimulus following a response; negative reinforcement does the same in reverse, through the removal, reduction, or prevention of an aversive stimulus following a response.

Recall that for classical conditioning, when the unconditioned stimulus is no longer delivered, the conditioned response suffers extinction. The same rule holds for operant conditioning—if reinforcement is withheld, **operant extinction** occurs. Thus, if a behavior no longer produces predictable consequences, it returns to the level it was at before operant conditioning—it is extinguished. You can probably catch your own behaviors being reinforced and then *extinguished.* Have you ever had the experience of dropping a few coins into a

What environmental contingencies might cause babies to smile more often?

....

reinforcement contingency A consistent relationship between a response and the changes in the environment that it produces.

reinforcer Any stimulus that, when made contingent on a response, increases the probability of that response.

positive reinforcement A behavior is followed by the presentation of an appetitive stimulus, increasing the probability of that behavior.

negative reinforcement A behavior is followed by the removal of an aversive stimulus, increasing the probability of that behavior.

escape conditioning A form of learning in which animals acquire a response that will allow them to escape from an aversive stimulus.

avoidance conditioning A form of learning in which animals acquire responses that allow them to avoid aversive stimuli before they begin.

operant extinction When a behavior no longer produces predictable consequences, its return to the level of occurrence it had before operant conditioning.

soda machine and getting nothing in return? If you kicked the machine one time and your soda came out, the act of kicking would be reinforced. However, if the next few times, your kicking produced no soda, kicking would quickly be extinguished.

As with classical conditioning, *spontaneous recovery* is also a feature of operant conditioning. Suppose you had reinforced a pigeon by providing food pellets when it pecked a key in the presence of a green light. If you discontinued the reinforcement, the pecking behavior would extinguish. However, the next time you put the pigeon back in the apparatus with the green light on, the pigeon would likely spontaneously peck again. This is called spontaneous recovery. In human terms, you might kick the soda machine again with a time lag after your initial extinction experiences.

Positive and Negative Punishment

You are probably familiar with another technique for decreasing the probability of a response—punishment. A **punisher** is any stimulus that—when it is made contingent on a response—decreases the probability of that response over time. *Punishment* is the delivery of a punisher following a response. Just as we could identify positive and negative reinforcement, we can identify positive punishment and negative punishment. When a behavior is followed by the delivery of an aversive stimulus, the event is called **positive punishment** (you can remember *positive* because something is added to the situation). Touching a hot stove, for example, produces pain that punishes the preceding response so that you are less likely next time to touch the stove. When a behavior is followed by the removal of an appetitive stimulus, the event is referred to as **negative punishment** (you can remember *negative* because something is subtracted from the situation). Thus when a parent withdraws a child's allowance after she hits her baby brother, the child learns not to hit her brother in the future. Which kind of punishment explains why you might stay away from horror movies?

Although punishment and reinforcement are closely related operations, they differ in important ways. A good way to differentiate them is to think of each in terms of its effects on behavior. Punishment, by definition, always *reduces* the probability of a response occurring again; reinforcement, by definition, always *increases* the probability of a response recurring. For example, some people get severe headaches after drinking caffeinated beverages. The headache is the stimulus that positively punishes and reduces the behavior of drinking coffee. However, once the headache is present, people often take aspirin or another pain reliever to eliminate the headache. The aspirin's analgesic effect is the stimulus that negatively reinforces the behavior of ingesting aspirin.

....

punisher Any stimulus that, when made contingent on a response, decreases the probability of that response.

positive punishment A behavior is followed by the presentation of an aversive stimulus, decreasing the probability of that behavior.

negative punishment A behavior is followed by the removal of an appetitive stimulus, decreasing the probability of that behavior.

discriminative stimulus Stimulus that acts as a predictor of reinforcement, signaling when particular behaviors will result in positive reinforcement.

three-term contingency The means by which organisms learn that, in the presence of some stimuli but not others, their behavior is likely to have a particular effect on the environment.

Discriminative Stimuli and Generalization

You are unlikely to want to change the probability of a certain behavior at all times. Rather, you may want to change the probability of the behavior in a particular context. For example, you often want to increase the probability that a child will sit quietly in class without changing the probability that he or she will be noisy and active during recess. Through their associations with reinforcement or punishment, certain stimuli that precede a particular response—**discriminative stimuli**—come to set the context for that behavior. Organisms learn that, in the presence of some stimuli but not of others, their behavior is likely to have a particular effect on the environment. For example, in the presence of a green street light, the act of crossing an intersection in a motor vehicle is reinforced. When the light is red, however, such behavior may be punished—it may result in a traffic ticket or an accident. Skinner referred to the sequence of discriminative stimulus–behavior–consequence as the **three-term contingency** and believed that it could explain most human action (Skinner, 1953). **Table 6.1** describes how the three-term contingency might explain several different kinds of human behavior.

Under laboratory conditions, manipulating the consequences of behavior in the presence of discriminative stimuli can exert powerful control over that behavior. For example, a pigeon might be given grain after pecking a disk in the presence of a green light but not a red light. The green light is a discriminative stimulus that sets the occasion for pecking; the red is a discriminative stimulus that sets the occasion for not pecking. Organisms learn quickly to discriminate between these conditions, responding regularly in the presence of one stimulus and not responding in the presence of the other. By manipulating the components of the three-term contingency, you can constrain a behavior to a particular context.

Organisms also generalize responses to other stimuli that resemble the discriminative stimulus. Once a response has been reinforced in the presence of one discriminative stimulus, a similar stimulus can become a discriminative stimulus for that same response. For example, pigeons trained to peck a disk in the presence of a green light will also peck the disk in the presence of lights that are lighter or darker shades of green than the original discriminative stimulus. Similarly, you generalize to different shades of green on stop lights as a discriminative stimulus for your "resume driving" behavior.

Using Reinforcement Contingencies

Are you ready to put your new knowledge of reinforcement contingencies to work? Here are some considerations you might have:

- *How can you define the behavior that you would like to reinforce or eliminate?* You must always carefully target the specific behavior whose probability you would like to change. Reinforcement should be contingent on exactly that behavior. When reinforcers are presented so that they are not contingent, their presence has little effect on behavior. For example, if a parent praises poor work as well as good efforts, a child will not learn to work harder in school—but because of the positive reinforcement, other behaviors are likely to increase. (What might those be?)
- *How can you define the contexts in which a behavior is appropriate or inappropriate?* Remember that you rarely want to allow or disallow every instance of a behavior.

Table 6.1 • The Three-Term Contingency: Relationships among Discriminative Stimuli, Behavior, and Consequences

	Discriminative Stimulus	Emitted Response	Stimulus Consequence
1. Positive reinforcement: A response in the presence of an effective signal produces the desired consequence. This response increases.	Soft-drink machine	Put coin in slot	Get drink
2. Negative reinforcement (escape): An aversive situation is escaped from by an operant response. This escape response increases.	Heat	Fan oneself	Escape from heat
3. Positive punishment: A response is followed by an aversive stimulus. The response is eliminated or suppressed.	Attractive matchbox	Play with matches	Get burned or get caught and spanked
4. Negative punishment: A response is followed by the removal of an appetitive stimulus. The response is eliminated or suppressed.	Brussels sprouts	Refusal to eat them	No dessert

We suggested earlier, for example, that you might want to increase the probability that a child will sit quietly in class without changing the probability that he or she will be noisy and active during recess. You must define the discriminative stimuli and investigate how broadly the desired response will be generalized to similar stimuli. If, for example, the child learned to sit quietly in class, would that behavior generalize to other "serious" settings?

• *Have you unknowingly been reinforcing some behaviors?* Suppose you want to eliminate a behavior. Try to determine whether you can identify reinforcers for that behavior. If so, you can try to extinguish the behavior by eliminating those reinforcers. Imagine, for example, that a young boy throws a large number of tantrums. You might ask yourself, "Have I been reinforcing those tantrums by paying the boy extra attention when he screams?" That extra attention would count as a *secondary gain* from the bad behavior (that is, the boy might have learned that when he throws the tantrum, he'll gain the extra attention). If this is the case, you can try to eliminate the tantrums by eliminating the reinforcement. Even better, you can combine extinction with positive reinforcement of more socially approved behaviors.

It's important to be aware that the reinforcers parents produce can make children's conduct problems, such as tantrums, more likely. In fact, parenting research has identified unknowing reinforcement as one cause of serious behavior problems in children. For example, Gerald Patterson and his colleagues

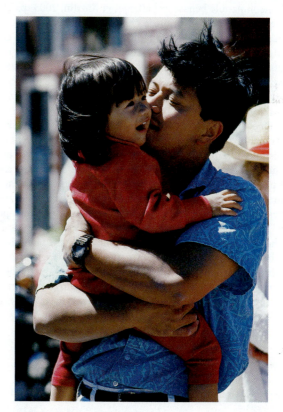

How can parents use reinforcement contingencies to affect their children's behavior?

(Granic & Patterson, 2006) have outlined a *coercion model* for antisocial behavior. Family observations suggest that children are put at risk when their parents issue threats in response to small misbehaviors (such as whining, teasing, or yelling) without following through. At some moments, however, these parents would issue harsh or explosive discipline toward the same behaviors. The children appear to learn the lesson that relatively large acts of aggressive and coercive behavior are appropriate and necessary for achieving goals—leading to a cycle of increase in the severity of the children's antisocial behavior.

The coercion model suggests that parents' attempts to use punishment to affect children's behavior are often ineffective. There are other reasons that psychologists recommend against punishment. For example, an abundance of data suggests that physical punishment leads to negative child outcomes (Gershoff & Bitensky, 2007). For example, one study involving over 1,000 children examined the relationship between the amount of physical punishment the children received as 15-month-olds and the behavior problems they displayed as 36-month-olds and as first graders (Mulvaney & Mebert, 2007). To account for the fact that some children are more difficult than others—and, therefore, might be more likely to elicit punishment—the analyses focused on changes in each child's behavior. The study demonstrated that, for both "easy" and "difficult" children (as reported by their parents), the more the children had been spanked early in life the more likely they were to show increases in, for example, aggressive behaviors at both 36 months and in first grade. These types of data explain why experts advise that parents first try positive reinforcement rather than punishment: "Many undesirable behaviors can be completely suppressed by positive reinforcement of alternative and incompatible behaviors" (Benjet & Kazdin, 2003, p. 215). For example, you can praise a child for sitting quietly rather than spanking him for running around. Thus reinforcing children for behaving well is often a better long-term strategy than punishing them for behaving poorly. The *Critical Thinking in Your Life* box, on page 163, discusses "time outs" as another strategy to change children's behavior without using physical punishment.

One final thought. It's often the case that real-life situations will involve intricate combinations of reinforcement and punishment. Suppose, for example, parents use negative punishment by grounding a teenager for two weeks when he stays out past curfew. To soften up his parents, the teen helps more than usual around the house. Assuming his helping behavior appeals to the parents, the teen is trying to reinforce his parents' "reducing the sentence" behavior. If this strategy succeeds in changing the punishment to only one week, the teen's helping behavior will have been negatively reinforced—because helping led to the removal of the aversive stimulus of being grounded. Whenever the teen is grounded again (a discriminative stimulus), his helping behavior should be more likely. Do you see how all the contingencies fit together to change both the teen's and the parents' behaviors? ◉

Let's now take a look at the ways in which various objects and activities may come to function as reinforcers.

Properties of Reinforcers

Reinforcers are the power brokers of operant conditioning: They change or maintain behavior. Reinforcers have a number of interesting and complex properties. They can be learned through experience rather than be biologically determined and can be activities rather than objects. In some situations, even ordinarily powerful reinforcers may not be enough to change a dominant behavior pattern (in this case, we would say that the consequences were not actually reinforcers).

Conditioned Reinforcers When you came into the world, there were a handful of **primary reinforcers,** such as food and water, whose reinforcing properties were biologically determined. Over time, however, otherwise neutral stimuli have become associated with primary reinforcers and now function as **conditioned reinforcers** for operant responses. Conditioned reinforcers can come to serve as ends in themselves. In fact, a great deal of human behavior is influenced less by biologically significant primary reinforcers than by a wide variety of conditioned reinforcers. Money, grades, smiles of approval, gold stars, and various kinds of status symbols are among the many potent conditioned reinforcers that influence much of your behavior.

Virtually any stimulus can become a conditioned reinforcer by being paired with a primary reinforcer. In one experiment, simple tokens were used with animal learners.

With raisins as primary reinforcers, chimps were trained to solve problems (Cowles, 1937). Then tokens were delivered along with the raisins. When only the tokens were presented, the chimps continued working for their "money" because they could later deposit the hard-earned tokens in a "chimp-o-mat" designed to exchange tokens for the raisins.

Featured Study

Teachers and experimenters often find conditioned reinforcers more effective and easier to use than primary reinforcers because (1) few primary reinforcers are available in the classroom, whereas almost any stimulus event that is under control of a teacher can be used as a conditioned reinforcer; (2) they can be dispensed rapidly; (3) they are portable; and (4) their reinforcing effect may be more immediate because it depends only on the perception of receiving them and not on biological processing, as in the case of primary reinforcers.

In some institutions, such as psychiatric hospitals or drug treatment programs, *token economies* are set up based on these principles. Desired behaviors (grooming or taking medication, for example) are explicitly defined, and token payoffs are given by the staff when the behaviors are performed. These tokens can later be exchanged by the patients for a wide array of rewards and privileges (Dickerson et al., 2005; Matson & Boisjoli, 2009). These systems of reinforcement are especially effective in modifying patients' behaviors regarding self-care, upkeep of their environment, and, most important, frequency of their positive social interactions.

····································

◉ **Watch** the **Video** *Thinking Like a Psychologist: Physical Punishment– You Decide!* on **MyPsychLab**

primary reinforcer Biologically determined reinforcer, such as food and water.

conditioned reinforcer In classical conditioning, a formerly neutral stimulus that has become a reinforcer.

Critical Thinking in Your Life

WHEN DO "TIME OUTS" CHANGE CHILDREN'S BEHAVIOR?

One of the classic threats that children receive is that if they don't "start behaving," they will be made to "go stand in a corner." This threat is one version of a strategy that experts call a *time out*. Here's an official definition: A time out is "the contingent withholding of the opportunity to earn reinforcement . . . from rewarding stimuli including attention from the parent, as a consequence of some form of misbehavior" (Morawska & Sanders, 2011, p. 2). You now know enough about operant conditioning to understand that definition! The important idea is that children learn that if they misbehave, they will lose access to rewarding stimuli. For that reason, time outs are a form of punishment.

Let's focus our attention on an imaginary boy named Timothy. To implement a time out, Timothy's parents make him sit on a kitchen chair. Will that work? Researchers have explored a number of variables that affect the likelihood that time outs will function effectively to change children's behavior (Everett et al., 2010). To begin, the contrast between "time in" and "time out" is very important (Morawska & Sanders, 2011). If Timothy doesn't actually find interactions with his parents rewarding, then a time out that suspends those interactions will not reduce his misbehavior (in fact, it's likely the time out will cause him to misbehave more).

Research also suggests that we should consider Timothy's age. Time outs are probably most effective for children ages 3 to 7 (Everett et al., 2010). Timothy's parents should choose a duration of one to five minutes. That should

be sufficient to create behavior change (Morawska & Sanders, 2011). Timothy's parents may want to explain to him why he is getting the time out. However, it's more important that they be the ones who decide when the time out is over. In that way, Timothy's parents can ensure that he has met the requirements for the time out (for example, three minutes without talking).

It's also very important that Timothy not learn that time outs allow him to escape from tasks he'd rather not perform (Everett et al., 2007). Suppose that Timothy's parents ask him to clean up his room. When he refuses to comply, they give him a time out. In that case, Timothy might very well prefer the time out to completing the chore—he will learn, more generally, that he can escape from aversive tasks if he is willing to weather a time out. Timothy's parents must ensure that they reaffirm their request once the time out period has passed.

As the text has noted, experts generally recommend that parents first try positive reinforcement when they ponder changing their children's behavior. However, when children behave in ways that make other strategies necessary, time outs provide a reliable alternative to reduce children's misbehavior.

- Why must parents understand what their children find rewarding before they implement a time out?
- How might parents detect when their children are accepting time outs to escape aversive tasks?

Response Deprivation and Positive Reinforcers   Suppose you need to get a child to do something. You don't want to pay her or give her a gold star, so instead you strike this bargain: "When you finish your homework, you can play with your video game." Why might this tactic work? According to *response deprivation theory*, behaviors become preferred and, therefore, reinforcing when an animal is prevented from engaging in them (Klatt & Morris, 2001). For example, water-deprived rats learned to increase their running in an exercise wheel when their running was followed by an opportunity to drink. Conversely, exercise-deprived rats learned to increase their drinking when that response was followed by a chance to run (Premack, 1965). Can you see how the promise of video games after homework follows this same pattern? For a period of time, the child is video game–deprived—the rate at which the child would ordinarily play the video game is restricted below normal. To overcome that deprivation, she will learn to work on her homework.

This analysis suggests two important lessons. First, these examples remind you why you shouldn't assume that the same activity will function as a reinforcer for an animal at all

times. You need to know, for example, whether the animal is food-deprived before you attempt to use food as a reinforcer. Second, these examples suggest why virtually any activity can come to serve as a reinforcer. You can experience deprivation along any number of dimensions. In fact, if you didn't allow a child to do homework for a period of time, she would learn other behaviors to overcome homework-doing deprivation.

Schedules of Reinforcement

What happens when you cannot, or do not want to, reinforce your pet on every occasion when it performs a special behavior? Consider a story about the young B. F. Skinner. It seems that one weekend he was secluded in his laboratory with not enough of a food-reward supply for his hardworking rats. He economized by giving the rats pellets only after a certain interval of time—no matter how many times they pressed in between, they couldn't get any more pellets. Even so, the rats responded as much with this *partial reinforcement schedule* as they had with continuous reinforcement. And what do you

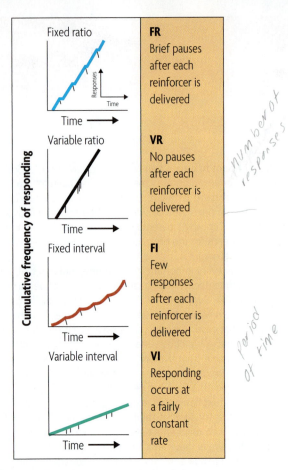

Fixed ratio

FR
Brief pauses after each reinforcer is delivered

Variable ratio

VR
No pauses after each reinforcer is delivered

Fixed interval

FI
Few responses after each reinforcer is delivered

Variable interval

VI
Responding occurs at a fairly constant rate

number of responses

period of time

FIGURE 6.12 Reinforcement Schedules

These different patterns of behavior are produced by four simple schedules of reinforcement. The hash marks indicate when reinforcement is delivered.

predict happened when these animals underwent extinction training and their responses were followed by no pellets at all? The rats whose lever pressing had been partially reinforced continued to respond longer and more vigorously than did the rats who had gotten payoffs after every response. Skinner was on to something important!

The discovery of the effectiveness of partial reinforcement led to extensive study of the effects of different **schedules of reinforcement** on behavior (see **Figure 6.12**). You have experienced different schedules of reinforcement in your daily life. When you raise your hand in class, the teacher sometimes calls on you and sometimes does not; some slot machine players continue to put coins in the one-armed bandits even though the reinforcers are delivered only rarely. In real life or in the laboratory, reinforcers can be delivered according to either a *ratio schedule,* after a certain number of responses, or an *interval schedule,* after the first response following a specified interval of time. In each case, there can be either a constant, or *fixed,* pattern of reinforcement or an irregular, or *variable,* pattern of reinforcement, making four major types of schedules in all. So far you've learned about the **partial reinforcement effect:** Responses acquired under schedules of partial reinforcement are more resistant to extinction than those acquired with

continuous reinforcement. Let's see what else researchers have discovered about different schedules of reinforcement.

Fixed-Ratio Schedules In **fixed-ratio (FR) schedules,** the reinforcer comes after the organism has emitted a fixed number of responses. When reinforcement follows only one response, the schedule is called an FR-1 schedule (this is the original continuous reinforcement schedule). When reinforcement follows only every 25th response, the schedule is an FR-25 schedule. FR schedules generate high rates of responding because there is a direct correlation between responding and reinforcement. A pigeon can get as much food as it wants in a period of time if it pecks often enough. Figure 6.12 shows that FR schedules produce a pause after each reinforcer. The higher the ratio, the longer the pause after each reinforcement. Stretching the ratio too thin by requiring a great many responses for reinforcement without first training the animal to emit that many responses may lead to extinction. Many salespeople are on FR schedules: They must sell a certain number of units before they can get paid.

Variable-Ratio Schedules In a **variable-ratio (VR) schedule,** the average number of responses between reinforcers is predetermined. A VR-10 schedule means that, on average, reinforcement follows every 10th response, but it might come after only 1 response or after 20 responses. Variable-ratio schedules generate the highest rate of responding and the greatest resistance to extinction, especially when the VR value is large. Suppose you start a pigeon with a low VR value (for example, VR-5) and then move it toward a higher value. A pigeon on a VR-110 schedule will respond with up to 12,000 pecks per hour and will continue responding for hours even with no reinforcement. Gambling would seem to be under the control of VR schedules. The response of dropping coins in slot machines is maintained at a high, steady level by the payoff, which is delivered only after an unknown, variable number of coins has been deposited. VR schedules leave you guessing when the reward will come—you gamble that it will be after the next response, not many responses later.

Fixed-Interval Schedules On a **fixed-interval (FI) schedule,** a reinforcer is delivered for the first response made after a fixed period of time. On an FI-10 schedule, the subject, after receiving reinforcement, has to wait 10 seconds before another response can be reinforced irrespective of the number of responses. Response rates under FI schedules show a scalloped pattern. Immediately after each reinforced response, the animal

....

schedule of reinforcement In operant conditioning, a pattern of delivering and withholding reinforcement.

partial reinforcement effect The behavioral principle that states that responses acquired under intermittent reinforcement are more difficult to extinguish than those acquired with continuous reinforcement.

fixed-ratio (FR) schedule A schedule of reinforcement in which a reinforcer is delivered for the first response made after a fixed number of responses.

variable-ratio (VR) schedule A schedule of reinforcement in which a reinforcer is delivered for the first response made after a variable number of responses whose average is predetermined.

fixed-interval (FI) schedule A schedule of reinforcement in which a reinforcer is delivered for the first response made after a fixed period of time.

makes few if any responses. As the payoff time approaches, the animal responds more and more. You experience an FI schedule when you reheat a slice of pizza. Suppose you set the oven's timer for 2 minutes. You probably won't check very much for the first 90 seconds, but in the last 30 seconds, you'll peek in more often.

Variable-Interval Schedules For **variable-interval (VI) schedules,** the average interval is predetermined. For example, on a VI-20 schedule, reinforcers are delivered at an average rate of 1 every 20 seconds. This schedule generates a moderate but very stable response rate. Extinction under VI schedules is gradual and much slower than under fixed-interval schedules. In one case, a pigeon pecked 18,000 times during the first 4 hours after reinforcement stopped and required 168 hours before its responding extinguished completely (Ferster & Skinner, 1957). You have experienced a VI schedule if you've taken a course with a professor who gave occasional, irregularly scheduled pop quizzes. Did you study your notes each day before class?

Shaping

As parts of experiments, we have spoken of rats pressing levers to get food. However, even lever pressing is a learned behavior. When a rat is introduced to an operant chamber, it is quite unlikely it will ever press the lever spontaneously; the rat has learned to use its paws in many ways, but it probably has never pressed a lever before. How should you go about training the rat to perform a behavior that it would rarely, if ever, produce on its own? You've settled on a reinforcer, food, and a schedule of reinforcement, FR-1—now what? To train new or complex behaviors, you will want to use a method called **shaping by successive approximations**—in which you reinforce any responses that successively approximate and ultimately match the desired response.

Here's how you'd do it. First, you deprive the rat of food for a day. (Without deprivation, food is not likely to serve as a reinforcer.) Then you systematically make food pellets available in the food hopper in an operant chamber so that the rat learns to look there for food. Now you can begin the actual shaping process by making delivery of food contingent on specific aspects of the rat's behavior, such as orienting itself toward the lever. Next, food is delivered only as the rat moves closer and closer to the lever. Soon the requirement for reinforcement is actually to touch the lever. Finally, the rat must depress the lever for food to be delivered. In small increments, the rat has learned that a lever press will produce food. Thus, for *shaping* to work, you must define what constitutes progress toward the target behavior and use *differential reinforcement* to refine each step along the way.

Let's look at another example, in which shaping was used to improve the performance of a Canadian pole vaulter who was an international competitor.

....

variable-interval (VI) schedule A schedule of reinforcement in which a reinforcer is delivered for the first response made after a variable period of time whose average is predetermined.

shaping by successive approximations A behavioral method that reinforces responses that successively approximate and ultimately match the desired response.

This woman is assisted by a monkey who has been operantly shaped to perform tasks such as getting food or drink, retrieving dropped or out-of-reach items, and turning lights on or off. For each of these behaviors, can you think through the successive approximations you would reinforce to arrive at the end point?

Featured Study

A 21-year-old university pole vaulter sought a research team's assistance to help him correct a technical problem with his vaulting technique (Scott et al., 1997). The vaulter's particular problem was that he didn't sufficiently extend his arms (holding the pole) above his head before he planted the pole to lift himself off. At the beginning of the intervention, the vaulter's average hand-height at takeoff was calculated as 2.25 meters. The goal was set to use a shaping procedure to help him achieve his physical potential of 2.54 meters. A photoelectric beam was set up so that, when the vaulter achieved a desired extension, the beam was broken and equipment produced a beep. The beep served as a conditioned positive reinforcer. At first, the beam was set at 2.30 meters, but once the vaulter was able to reach that height with 90 percent success, the beam was moved to 2.35 meters. Further success brought further increments of 2.40, 2.45, 2.50, and 2.52 meters. In that way, the vaulter's behavior was successfully shaped toward the desired goal.

You can imagine how difficult it would have been for the vaulter to show spontaneous improvement of 0.27 meters. (That's about 10½ inches.) The shaping procedure allowed him to achieve that gain through successive approximations to the desired behavior.

Let's return to your rat. Recall that we suggested you might wish to teach it to turn circles in its cage. Can you devise a plan, using shaping, to bring about this behavior? Think about what each successive approximation would be. At the beginning, for example, you might reinforce the rat if it just turned its head in a particular direction. Next, you would let the rat obtain a food pellet only if it turned its whole body in the right direction. What might you do after that?

Operant conditioning has most often been studied with the assumption that processes of learning are consistent across all animals. In fact, we have cited examples from different species to show exactly such consistency. However, researchers have come to understand that learning may be modified by the particular biological capabilities of individual species. Next, let's examine that phenomenon.

Biological Constraints

You have no doubt seen animals performing tricks on television or in the circus. Some animals play baseball or Ping-Pong, and others drive tiny race cars. For years, **Keller Breland** and **Marion Breland** used operant conditioning techniques to train thousands of animals to perform a remarkable array of behaviors. The Brelands had believed that general principles derived from laboratory research using virtually any type of response could be directly applied to the control of animal behavior outside the laboratory.

At some point after training, though, some of the animals began to "misbehave." For example, a raccoon was trained pick up a coin, put it into a toy bank, and collect an edible reinforcer. However, when there were two coins to be deposited, conditioning broke down—the raccoon would not give up the coins. Instead, it would rub the coins together, dip them into the bank, and then pull them back out. But is this really so strange? Raccoons often engage in rubbing and washing behaviors as they remove the outer shells of a favorite food, crayfish. Similarly, when pigs were given the task of putting their hard-earned tokens into a large piggy bank, they instead would drop the coins onto the floor, root (poke at) them with their snouts, and toss them into the air. Again, should you consider this strange? Pigs root and shake their food as a natural part of their inherited food-gathering repertory.

These experiences convinced the Brelands that even when animals have learned to make operant responses perfectly, the "learned behavior drifts toward instinctual behavior" over time. They called this tendency **instinctual drift** (Breland & Breland, 1951, 1961). The behavior of their animals is not explainable by ordinary operant principles, but it is understandable if you consider biological constraints: The species-specific tendencies imposed by an inherited genotype. These tendencies override the changes in behavior brought about by operant conditioning.

....

instinctual drift The tendency for learned behavior to drift toward instinctual behavior over time.

How does instinctual drift affect the behaviors raccoons can learn to perform?

The bulk of traditional research on animal learning focused on arbitrarily chosen responses to conveniently available stimuli. The Brelands' theory and demonstration of instinctual drift make it evident that not all aspects of learning are under the control of the experimenters' reinforcers. Behaviors will be more or less easy to change as a function of an animal's normal, genetically programmed responses in its environment. Conditioning will be particularly efficient when you can frame a target response as biologically relevant. For example, what change might you make to get the pigs to place their tokens in a bank? You might consider pairing the token with a water reward for a thirsty pig. It would then not be rooted as food but would be deposited in the bank as a valuable commodity

You have now seen why modern behavior analysts must be attentive to the types of responses each species is best suited to learn. If you want to teach an old dog new tricks, you're best off adapting the tricks to the dog's genetic behavioral repertory! Our survey of learning is not complete, however, because we have not yet dealt with types of learning that might require more complex cognitive processes. We turn now to those types of learning.

Stop *and* Review

① What is the law of effect?
② How do reinforcement and punishment affect the probability of behaviors?
③ What is the role of discriminative stimuli in operant conditioning?
④ What is the difference between fixed-ratio and fixed-interval schedules of reinforcement?
⑤ What is meant by shaping?
⑥ What is instinctual drift?

CRITICAL THINKING   In the experiment with chimps, why did the researcher start the training with raisins before moving to tokens?

✓●—**Study** and **Review** on **MyPsychLab**

COGNITIVE INFLUENCES ON LEARNING

The reviews of classical and operant conditioning have demonstrated that a wide variety of behaviors can be understood as the products of simple learning processes. You might wonder, however, if certain classes of learning require more complex, more cognitive types of processes. *Cognition* is any mental activity involved in the representation and processing of knowledge, such as thinking, remembering, perceiving, and language use. This section looks at forms of learning in animals and humans that cannot be explained only by principles of classical or operant conditioning. These phenomena suggest, therefore, that the behaviors are partially the product of cognitive processes.

Comparative Cognition

This chapter has emphasized that, species-specific constraints aside, rules of learning acquired from research on rats and pigeons apply as well to dogs, monkeys, and humans. Researchers who study **comparative cognition** consider even broader ranges of behavior to trace the development of cognitive abilities across species and the continuity of abilities from nonhuman to human animals (Wasserman & Zentall, 2006). This field is called *comparative cognition* because researchers often compare abilities across different species; because of the focus on nonhuman species, the field is also called *animal cognition*. In his original formulation of the theory of evolution, Charles Darwin suggested that cognitive abilities evolved along with the physical forms of animals. In this section, we will describe two impressive types of animal performance that indicate further continuity in the cognitive capabilities of nonhuman and human animals.

Cognitive Maps Edward C. Tolman (1886–1959) pioneered the study of cognitive processes in learning by inventing experimental circumstances in which mechanical one-to-one associations between specific stimuli and responses could not explain animals' observed behavior. Consider the maze shown in **Figure 6.13**. Tolman and his students demonstrated that, when an original goal path is blocked in a maze, a rat with prior experience in the maze will take the shortest detour around the barrier, even though that particular response was never previously reinforced (Tolman & Honzik, 1930). The rats, therefore, behaved as if they were responding to an internal **cognitive map**—a representation of the overall layout of the maze—rather than blindly exploring different parts of the maze through trial and error (Tolman, 1948). Tolman's results showed that conditioning involves more than the simple formation of associations between sets of stimuli or between responses and reinforcers. It includes learning and representing other facets of the total behavioral context (Lew, 2011).

....

comparative cognition The study of the development of cognitive abilities across species and the continuity of abilities from nonhuman to human animals.

cognitive map A mental representation of physical space.

FIGURE 6.13 Use of Cognitive Maps in Maze Learning

Subjects preferred the direct path (Path 1) when it was open. With a block at A, they preferred Path 2. When a block was placed at B, the rats usually chose Path 3. Their behavior seemed to indicate that they had a cognitive map of the best way to get the food.

Research in Tolman's tradition has consistently demonstrated an impressive capacity for spatial memory in birds, bees, rats, humans, and other animals (for examples, see Joly & Zimmermann, 2011; Menzel et al., 2011). To understand the efficiency of spatial cognitive maps, consider the functions they serve (Poucet, 1993):

- Animals use spatial memory to recognize and identify features of their environments.
- Animals use spatial memory to find important goal objects in their environments.
- Animals use spatial memory to plan their route through an environment.

You can see these different functions of cognitive maps at work in the many species of birds that store food over a dispersed area but are able to recover that food with great accuracy when they need it. For example, pinyon jays bury thousands of pine seeds each fall and retrieve them four to seven months later to survive through the winter into the early spring (Stafford et al., 2006). By the time they are 8 months old, these birds appear to have the spatial memory they require to find their way back to their seeds. Other species use their spatial abilities to disperse seeds in ways that protect them against theft by other animals. Coal tits, for example, use their memories for the positions of their old seed caches to make decisions about proper locations for new caches (Male & Smulders, 2007). These seed-caching birds do not just roam their environments and come upon the seeds through good fortune. Only if their cognitive maps remain accurate can they later recover the seeds and survive to reproduce.

Conceptual Behavior We have seen that cognitive maps, in part, help animals preserve details of the spatial locations of objects in their environments. But what other cognitive processes can animals use to find structure in the diverse stimuli they encounter in their environments? Let's consider judgments

From left to right: Adult models aggression; boy imitates aggression; girl imitates aggression. What does this experiment demonstrate about the role models play in learning?

of *same* versus *different*. Take a moment to contemplate all the moments in a day in which you make these judgments: Does the milk you poured on your cereal taste funny? Will your friends realize you wore the same clothes two days in a row? Did you already watch this YouTube video? Researchers have begun to demonstrate that humans are not the only species that can make some judgments of same versus different (Wasserman & Young, 2010). Let's consider a study that documents pigeon's ability to detect changes in colored displays.

Featured Study

Pigeons viewed arrays that contained two colored circles (Wright et al., 2010). The arrays remained on view for five seconds. After a brief memory delay, a second array appeared in which one of the colors had changed (for example, from purple to orange). To get a reward, the pigeons needed to peck on the circle with the changed color. Pigeons were able to learn this response with trials using a set of colors on which they'd specifically been trained. Importantly, this pecking behavior also transferred to a new set of colors, for which they hadn't received explicit training. These results suggest that the pigeons had acquired the concept of same versus different colors.

Recall that a cornerstone of operant conditioning is that animals will repeat behaviors for which they have been reinforced. What makes these results particularly interesting is that pigeons learned to peck the new colors: the color that explicitly had not previously yielded reinforcement. Instead of responding to each individual color, the pigeons had acquired the higher-order concept of color change. We will devote Chapters 7 and 8 to an analysis of cognitive processes in humans. However, this experiment that demonstrates concept acquisition in pigeons should convince you that humans are not the only species with impressive and useful cognitive capabilities.

Before we conclude this chapter, let's move to another type of learning that requires cognitive processes.

Observational Learning

To introduce this further type of learning, we'd like you to return for a moment to the comparison of rats' and humans' approaches to sampling new foods. The rats are almost certainly more cautious than you are, but that's largely because they are missing an invaluable source of information—input from other rats. When you try a new food, it's almost always in

a context in which you have good reason to believe that other people have eaten and enjoyed the food. The probability of your "food-eating behavior" is thus influenced by your knowledge of patterns of reinforcement for other individuals. This example illustrates your capacity to learn via *vicarious reinforcement* and *vicarious punishment*. You can use your cognitive capacities for memory and reasoning to change your own behaviors in light of the experience of others. ◉

In fact, much *social learning* occurs in situations where learning would not be predicted by traditional conditioning theory because a learner has made no active response and has received no tangible reinforcer. The individual, after simply watching another person exhibiting behavior that was reinforced or punished, later behaves in much the same way, or refrains from doing so. This is known as **observational learning.** Cognition often enters into observational learning in the form of expectations. In essence, after observing a model, you may think, "If I do exactly what she does, I will get the same reinforcer or avoid the same punisher." A younger child may be better behaved than his older sister because he has learned from the sister's mistakes.

This capacity to learn from watching as well as from doing is extremely useful. It enables you to acquire large integrated patterns of behavior without going through the tedious trial-and-error process of gradually eliminating wrong responses and acquiring the right ones. You can profit immediately from the mistakes and successes of others. Researchers have demonstrated that observational learning is not special to humans. Among other species, lemurs (Carlier & Jamon, 2006), ravens (Schwab et al., 2008), and chorus frog tadpoles (Ferrari & Chivers, 2008) are capable of changing their behavior after observing the performance of another member of their species.

A classic demonstration of human observational learning occurred in the laboratory of **Albert Bandura.** After watching adult models punching, hitting, and kicking a large plastic BoBo doll, the children in the experiment later showed a greater frequency of the same behaviors than did children in control conditions who had not observed the aggressive models (Bandura et al., 1963). Subsequent studies showed that children imitated such behaviors just from watching filmed

⸱⸱

◉ **Watch** the **Video** *What's In It For Me?: Personal Behavior Modification* on **MyPsychLab**

observational learning The process of learning new responses by watching the behavior of another.

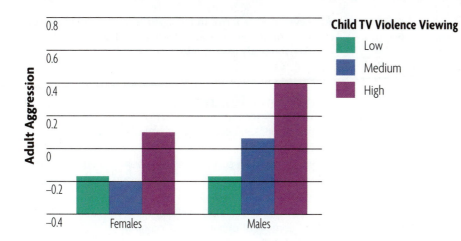

FIGURE 6.14 TV Violence and Aggression

For both men and women, those individuals who had viewed the most violent TV as children also displayed the most aggression as adults. The measure of aggression is a composite score that reflects the individuals' self-ratings and ratings of them by others. Higher scores indicate higher levels of aggression.

sequences of models, even when the models were cartoon characters.

There is little question now that we learn much—both prosocial (helping) and antisocial (hurting) behaviors—through observation of models, but there are many possible models in the world. What variables are important in determining which models will be most likely to influence you? Research suggests that there are four processes that determine when a model's observed behavior will be most influential (Bandura, 1977):

- *Attention.* The observer must pay attention to the model's behavior and its consequences. This is more likely when there are perceived similarities between features and traits of the model and the observer.
- *Retention.* The observer must store a representation of the model's behavior in memory.
- *Reproduction.* The observer must have the physical or mental ability to reproduce the model's behavior.
- *Motivation.* The observer must have a reason to reproduce the model's behavior. For example, the model's behavior could be seen as having reinforcing consequences.

Imagine yourself in modeling situations and see how each process on the list would apply. Suppose, for example, you were learning to perform surgery by observing an experienced doctor. How would each process affect your ability to learn?

Because people learn so efficiently from models, you can understand why a good deal of psychological research has been directed at the behavioral impact of television: Are viewers affected by what they see being rewarded and punished on TV? Attention has focused on the link between televised acts of violence—murder, rape, assault, robbery, terrorism, and suicide—and children's and adolescents' subsequent behavior. Does exposure to acts of violence foster imitation? Let's see what research has revealed.

Featured Study

The project began in 1977 when a team of researchers measured two years of television viewing for 557 children starting in either first or third grade. In particular, the researchers obtained measures of the extent to which the children watched TV shows with violent content. Fifteen years later, the researchers were able to conduct interviews with 329 of those children, who were now 20 to 22 years old (Huesmann et al., 2003). The researchers sought to determine whether there would be a relationship between the amount of television violence the individuals viewed in childhood and their level of aggression as young adults. Their adult level of aggression was measured both through their own self-reports and through the reports of others, such as spouses. As shown in **Figure 6.14***, the men and women who had watched the most violent TV as children also displayed the highest adult levels of aggression. These data suggest that early TV viewing of violence causes later aggression. You might wonder, however, if the causality works in the opposite direction: Could it be that the children destined to be aggressive were already more interested in violent content as children? Fortunately, the researchers collected data that allowed them to argue against this possibility. For example, the data found only a small relationship between childhood aggression and the individuals' viewing of TV violence as adults.*

This study argues strongly that children who watch violent TV are at risk to become overly aggressive as adults. ◉

Several decades of research have demonstrated three ways in which television violence has a negative impact on viewers' lives. First, as we have just seen, the viewing of television violence brings about, through the mechanisms of observational learning, increases in aggressive behavior. This causal association has particularly important implications for children: Aggressive habits borne of heavy television viewing early in life may serve as the basis for antisocial behavior later in life. Second, the viewing of television violence leads viewers to overestimate the occurrences of violence in the everyday world. Television viewers may be unduly afraid of becoming victims of real-world violence. Third, the viewing of television violence may bring about *desensitization,* a reduction in both emotional arousal and distress at viewing violent behavior.

Note that research has also shown that children can learn prosocial, helping behaviors when they watch television programs that provide prosocial behavioral models (Mares & Woodard, 2005). You should take seriously the idea that

◉ **Watch** the **Video** *In the Real World: Learned Aggression* on **MyPsychLab** children learn from the television they watch. As a parent or caretaker, you may want to help children select appropriate televised models.

An analysis of observational learning acknowledges both that principles of reinforcement influence behavior and that humans have the capacity to use their cognitive processes to change behaviors with vicarious rewards and punishment. This approach to the understanding of human behavior has proven very powerful. In Chapter 15, we will look at successful programs of therapy that have emerged from the cognitive modification of maladaptive patterns of behavior.

Let's close this chapter by calling back to mind a visit to a horror movie. How can behavior analysis explain your experiences? Suppose you went to the movie because of a friend's recommendation. You succumbed to vicarious reinforcement. Suppose you made it to the theater, despite having to forgo your normal route. That shows evidence of a cognitive map. Suppose the sound of scary music made you feel increasingly anxious. If the music was repeated over a short period of time, you felt the effects of sensitization. If the music was spread across the movie, that's more likely to be an effect of classical conditioning. Suppose your failure to enjoy the film made you vow never to see a horror movie again. You have discovered the effect a punisher has on your subsequent behavior!

Are you ready to return to the theater?

Stop *and* Review

① What conclusions did Tolman draw from his pioneering work?
② What evidence suggests that pigeons are able to learn the concepts of same versus different?
③ What is meant by vicarious reinforcement?
④ Why is it important to evaluate children's TV viewing in the context of observational learning?

CRITICAL THINKING Consider the TV viewing study. What steps did the researchers take to assert that they had given the right causal explanation for the correlation revealed in their data?

✔•⌐Study and Review on MyPsychLab

Recapping Main Points

The Study of Learning

- Learning entails a relatively consistent change in behavior or behavior potential based on experience.
- Behaviorists believe that much behavior can be explained by simple learning processes.
- They also believe that many of the same principles of learning apply to all organisms.

Classical Conditioning: Learning Predictable Signals

- In classical conditioning, first investigated by Pavlov, an unconditioned stimulus (UCS) elicits an unconditioned response (UCR). A neutral stimulus paired with the UCS becomes a conditioned stimulus (CS), which elicits a response, called the conditioned response (CR).
- Extinction occurs when the UCS no longer follows the CS.
- Stimulus generalization is the phenomenon whereby stimuli similar to the CS elicit the CR.
- Discrimination learning narrows the range of CSs to which an organism responds.
- For classical conditioning to occur, a contingent and informative relationship must exist between the CS and UCS.
- Classical conditioning explains many emotional responses and drug tolerance.
- Taste-aversion learning suggests that species are genetically prepared for some forms of associations.

Operant Conditioning: Learning about Consequences

- Thorndike demonstrated that behaviors that bring about satisfying outcomes tend to be repeated.

- Skinner's behavior analytic approach centers on manipulating contingencies of reinforcement and observing the effects on behavior.
- Behaviors are made more likely by positive and negative reinforcement. They are made less likely by positive and negative punishment.
- Contextually appropriate behavior is explained by the three-term contingency of discriminative stimulus–behavior–consequence.
- Primary reinforcers are stimuli that function as reinforcers even when an organism has not had previous experience with them. Conditioned reinforcers are acquired by association with primary reinforcers.
- Probable activities function as positive reinforcers.
- Behavior is affected by schedules of reinforcement that may be varied or fixed and delivered in intervals or in ratios.
- Complex responses may be learned through shaping.
- Instinctual drift may overwhelm some response–reinforcement learning.

Cognitive Influences on Learning

- Some forms of learning reflect more complex processes than those of classical or operant conditioning.
- Animals develop cognitive maps to enable them to function in a complex environment.
- Other species may be able to encode concepts such as same versus different.
- Behaviors can be vicariously reinforced or punished. Humans and other animals can learn through observation.

KEY TERMS

acquisition (p. 149)
avoidance conditioning (p. 159)
behavior analysis (p. 146)
classical conditioning (p. 147)
cognitive map (p. 167)
comparative cognition (p. 167)
conditioned reinforcers (p. 162)
conditioned response (CR) (p. 149)
conditioned stimulus (CS) (p. 149)
discriminative stimulus (p. 160)
escape conditioning (p. 159)
extinction (p. 150)
fixed-interval (FI) schedule (p. 164)
fixed-ratio (FR) schedule (p. 164)
habituation (p. 146)
instinctual drift (p. 166)

law of effect (p. 157)
learning (p. 145)
learning-performance distinction (p. 145)
negative punishment (p. 160)
negative reinforcement (p. 159)
observational learning (p. 168)
operant (p. 158)
operant conditioning (p. 158)
operant extinction (p. 159)
partial reinforcement effect (p. 164)
positive punishment (p. 160)
positive reinforcement (p. 159)
primary reinforcer (p. 162)
punisher (p. 160)
reflex (p. 149)
reinforcement contingency (p. 159)

reinforcer (p. 159)
schedule of reinforcement (p. 164)
sensitization (p. 146)
shaping by successive approximations (p. 165)
spontaneous recovery (p. 150)
stimulus discrimination (p. 151)
stimulus generalization (p. 150)
taste-aversion learning (p. 155)
three-term contingency (p. 160)
unconditioned response (UCR) (p. 149)
unconditioned stimulus (UCS) (p. 149)
variable-interval (VI) schedule (p. 165)
variable-ratio (VR) schedule (p. 164)

1. When Joan first moved to the city, she couldn't sleep because of the traffic noise. Now she hardly hears the traffic at all. This is an example of
   a. sensitization.
   c. consistency.
   b. habituation.
   d. classical conditioning.

2. You would *not* expect a close adherent to Skinner's ideas to focus on
   a. internal states as causes of behavior.
   b. forms of learning conserved across species.
   c. association between behaviors and rewards.
   d. the environmental stimuli that cause behaviors.

3. In Pavlov's experiments, _____ served as the unconditioned stimulus.
   a. salivation
   c. the sight of the assistant
   b. food powder
   d. tones

4. Six-year-old Pavel has a neighbor with a small dog who barks at him every day. Over time, Pavel has become frightened of all dogs. This is an example of
   a. stimulus discrimination.
   c. spontaneous recovery.
   b. backward conditioning.
   d. stimulus generalization.

5. Peter wishes to use classical conditioning in which a light will be the CS and an electric shock will be the UCS. You tell him that the light must _____ the shock.
   a. be temporally contiguous with
   b. reliably predict
   c. be in a blocking relationship with
   d. occur after

6. When classical conditioning contributes to drug tolerance, the conditioned stimulus is the
   a. setting in which individuals take the drugs.
   b. body's compensatory reaction to the drug.
   c. high the drugs give when individuals take them.
   d. individual's fear of an overdose.

7. One night after eating a hot dog you get very sick; now you shudder at the idea of eating a hot dog. A friend suggests that extinction trials will allow you to overcome this aversion. This means that you should
   a. associate hot dogs with foods you like.
   b. make yourself sick eating something else.
   c. eat some more hot dogs.
   d. use hot dogs as a reward.

8. For people undergoing chemotherapy, an unconditioned response would be
   a. anticipatory fatigue.
   b. the setting in which the individual receives the treatment.
   c. the infusion of drugs into their bodies.
   d. their bodies' reaction to the drugs.

9. In an operant conditioning experiment, you offer people expensive chocolate each time they perform a desired behavior. You think it's likely that the chocolate will be a _____ of the people.
   a. reinforcer for all
   c. punisher for all
   b. reinforcer for none
   d. reinforcer for some

10. Carlotta's parents haven't allowed her to watch television for three days. If she eats her brussels sprouts, she'll be allowed to watch TV that night. It sounds as if Carlotta's parents might be familiar with
    a. operant extinction.
    b. conditioned reinforcement.
    c. response deprivation theory.
    d. token economies.

11. In one study, the children who had received the most physical punishment as 15-month-olds showed _____ behavior problems at 36 months and _____ behavior problems in first grade then their less-punished peers.
    a. fewer; fewer.
    c. more; fewer
    b. fewer; more
    d. more; more

12. A time out may work best to change a child's behavior if the child is _____ years old and the time out lasts for _____ minutes.
    a. 10; 2
    c. 10; 12
    b. 4; 4
    d. 2; 3

13. In your new job, you get paid $2 every time you finish polishing 20 apples. This situation puts you on a _____ schedule.
    a. variable-interval
    c. fixed-ratio
    b. variable-ratio
    d. fixed-interval

14. Birds like Clark's nutcrackers are very successful at finding the seeds they have buried. This provides evidence for species-specific
    a. spatial memory.
    b. conditioning processes.
    c. applications of classical conditioning.
    d. shaping processes.

15. Zoe watches her older sister slip on ice and bruise her arm. After that, Zoe is very careful when she walks on ice. This is an example of
    a. observational learning.
    c. operant extinction.
    b. classical conditioning.
    d. sensitization.

ESSAY QUESTIONS

1. What information about classical conditioning might you share with someone who is about to undergo chemotherapy?

2. Why might you choose one schedule of reinforcement (that is, fixed interval versus variable interval) over another?

3. What mechanisms explain why viewing of TV violence might cause aggressive behavior?

Memory

As you begin this chapter on memory processes, please take a moment to call to mind your own earliest memory. How long ago did the memory originate? How vivid a scene do you recall? Has your memory been influenced by other people's recollections of the same event?

Now, a slightly different exercise. Please imagine what it would be like if you suddenly had no memory of your past—of the people you have known or of events that have happened to you. You wouldn't remember your best friend's face, or your 10th birthday, or your senior prom. Without such time anchors, how would you maintain a sense of who you are—of your self-identity? Or suppose you lost the ability to form any new memories. What would happen to your most recent experiences? Could you follow a conversation or untangle the plot of a TV show? Everything would vanish, as if events had never existed, as if you had never had any thoughts in mind. 👁

If you have never given much thought to your memory, it's probably because it tends to do its job reasonably well—you take it for granted, alongside other bodily processes, like digestion or breathing. But as with stomachaches or allergies, the times you notice your memory are likely to be the times when something goes wrong: You forget your car keys, an important date, lines in a play, or the answer to an examination question that you know you "really know." There's no reason you shouldn't find these occasions irritating, but you should also reflect for a moment on the estimate that the average human brain can store 100 trillion bits of information. The task of managing such a vast array of information is a formidable one. Perhaps you shouldn't be too surprised when an answer is sometimes not available when you need it!

The goal for this chapter is to explain how you usually remember so much and why you forget some of what you have known. We will explore how you get your everyday experiences into and out of memory. You will learn what psychology has discovered about different types of memories and about how those memories work. In the course of learning the many facts of memory, you're likely to gain an appreciation for how wonderful memory is.

One last thing: Because this is a chapter on memory, let's put your memory immediately to work. Please try to remember the number 51. Do whatever you need to do to remember 51. And yes, there will be a test!

WHAT IS MEMORY?

Memory is the capacity to encode, store, and retrieve information. In this chapter, we will consider memory to be a type of *information processing*. The bulk of our attention, therefore, will be trained on the flow of information in and out of your memory systems. Our examination of the processes that guide the acquisition and retrieval of information will enable you to refine your sense of what *memory* means.

Functions of Memory

When you think about memory, what is most likely to come to mind at first are situations in which you use your memory to recall (or try to recall) specific events or information: your favorite movie, the dates of World War II, or your student ID number.

How are actors and actresses able to remember all the different aspects—movements, expressions, and words—of their performances?

In fact, one of the important functions of memory is to allow you to have conscious access to the personal and collective past. But memory does much more for you than that. It also enables you to have effortless continuity of experience from one day to the next. When you walk through your neighborhood, for example, it is this second function of memory that makes the buildings along the way seem familiar. In defining types of memories, I will make plain to you how hard your memory works to fulfill these functions, often outside of conscious awareness.

Implicit and Explicit Memory   Consider **Figure 7.1**. What's wrong with this picture? It probably strikes you as unusual that there's a rabbit in the kitchen. But where does this feeling come from? You probably didn't go through the objects in the picture one by one and ask yourself, "Does the toaster belong?" "Do the cabinets belong?" Rather, the image of the rabbit jumps out at you as being out of place.

This simple example allows you to understand the difference between explicit and implicit uses of memory. For circumstances in which you engage conscious effort to encode or retrieve information, those are **explicit uses of memory**. When you encode or retrieve information without conscious effort, those are **implicit uses of memory.** Your discovery of

👁 **Watch** the **Video** *The Big Picture: The Woman Who Cannot Forget* on **MyPsychLab**

memory The mental capacity to encode, store, and retrieve information.

explicit use of memory Conscious effort to encode or recover information through memory processes.

implicit uses of memory Availability of information through memory processes without conscious effort to encode or recover information.

FIGURE 7.1 What's Wrong with This Picture?

Did you think right away, "What's a rabbit doing in the kitchen?" If the image of the rabbit immediately jumped out at you, it is because your memory processes performed an analysis of the scene outside of consciousness and delivered the rabbit as the odd element.

the rabbit is implicit because your memory processes brought past knowledge of kitchens to bear on your interpretation of the picture without any particular effort on your part. Suppose now I asked you, "What's missing from the picture?" To answer this second question, you probably have to put explicit memory to work. What appears in the typical kitchen? What's missing? (Did you think of the sink or the stove?) Thus, when it comes to using knowledge stored in memory, sometimes the use will be implicit—the information becomes available without any conscious effort—and sometimes it will be explicit—you make a conscious effort to recover the information.

The same distinction applies when it comes to the initial acquisition of memories. How do you know what should appear in a kitchen? Did you ever memorize a list of what appears there and what the appropriate configuration should be? Probably not. Rather, it's likely that you acquired most of this knowledge without conscious effort. By contrast, you probably learned the names of many of the objects in the room explicitly. As you'll see in Chapter 10, to learn the association between words and experiences, your younger self needed to engage in explicit memory processes. You learned the word *refrigerator* because someone called your explicit attention to the name of that object.

The distinction between implicit and explicit memory greatly expands the range of questions researchers must address about memory processes (Roediger, 2008). Most early memory research focused on the explicit acquisition of information. Experimenters most frequently provided participants with new information to retain, and theories of memory were directed to explaining what participants could and could not remember under those circumstances. However, as you will see in this chapter, researchers have now devised methods for studying implicit memory as well. Thus you can obtain a more complete account of the variety of uses to which you put your memory. In fact, most circumstances in which you encode or retrieve information represent a mix of implicit and explicit uses of memory. Let's turn now to a second dimension along which memories are distributed.

Declarative and Procedural Memory Can you whistle? Go ahead and try. Or if you can't whistle, try snapping your fingers. What kind of memory allows you to do these sorts of things? You probably remember having to learn these skills, but now they seem effortless. The earlier examples of implicit and explicit memories all involved the recollection of *facts* and *events*, which is called **declarative memory.** Now we see that you also have memories for *how to do things,* which is called **procedural memory.** Because the bulk of this chapter will be focused on how you acquire and use facts, let's take a moment now to consider how you acquire the ability to do things.

Procedural memory refers to the way you remember how things get done. With enough practice, you are able to acquire, retain, and employ procedural memories for perceptual, cognitive, and motor skills. Theories of procedural memory often concern themselves with how much practice you need and over what period of time: How do you go from a conscious list of declarative facts about some activity to unconscious, automatic performance of that same activity (Taatgen et al., 2008)? And why is it that after learning a skill, you often find it difficult to go back and talk about the component declarative facts?

We can see these phenomena at work in even the very simple activity of punching in a phone number that, over time, has become highly familiar. At first, you probably had to think

....

declarative memory Memory for information such as facts and events.

procedural memory Memory for how things get done; the way perceptual, cognitive, and motor skills are acquired, retained, and used.

Why does pretending to punch in a number help you to remember it?

your way through each digit, one at a time. You had to work through a list of declarative facts:

> First, I must punch 2,
> Next, I must punch 0,
> Then I punch 7,
> and so on.

However, when you began to punch in the number often enough, you could start to produce it as one unit—a swift sequence of actions on the touch-tone pad. The process at work is called *production compilation*: The mental commands that *produce* separate actions get *compiled* together (Taatgen & Lee, 2003). As a consequence of practice, you are able to carry out longer sequences of the activity without conscious intervention and mental effort (Stocco et al., 2010). But you also don't have conscious access to the content of these compiled units: Back at the telephone, it's not uncommon to find someone who can't actually remember the phone number without pretending to punch it in. In general, production compilation makes it hard to share your procedural knowledge with others. You may have noticed this if your parents tried to teach you to drive. Although they may be good drivers themselves, they may not have been very good at communicating the content of compiled good-driving procedures.

....

👁 **Watch** the **Video** *The Basics: Do You Remember When . . .?* on **MyPsychLab**

encoding The process by which a mental representation is formed in memory.

storage The retention of encoded material over time.

retrieval The recovery of stored information from memory.

You may also have noticed that production compilation can lead to errors. If you are a skilled typist, you've probably suffered from the *the* problem: As soon as you hit the *t* and the *h* keys, your finger may fly to the *e*, even if you're really trying to type *throne* or *thistle*. Once you have sufficiently committed the execution of *the* to procedural memory, you can do little else but finish the sequence. Without procedural memory, life would be extremely laborious—you would be doomed to go step by step through every activity. However, each time you mistakenly type *the,* you can reflect on the trade-off between efficiency and potential error. Let's continue now to an overview of the basic processes that apply to all these different types of memory.

An Overview of Memory Processes

No matter what the category of memory, being able to use knowledge at some later time requires the operation of three mental processes: encoding, storage, and retrieval. **Encoding** is the initial processing of information that leads to a representation in memory. **Storage** is the retention over time of encoded material. **Retrieval** is the recovery at a later time of the stored information. Simply put, encoding gets information in, storage holds it until you need it, and retrieval gets it out. Let's now expand on these ideas. 👁

Encoding requires that you form *mental representations* of information from the external world. You can understand the idea of mental representations by analogy to representations outside your head. Imagine I wanted to know something about the best gift you got at your last birthday party. (Let's suppose it's not something you have with you.) What could you do to inform me about the gift? You might describe the properties of the object. Or you might draw a picture. Or you might pretend that you're using the object. In each case, these are representations of the original object. Although none of the representations is likely to be quite as good as having the real thing present, they should allow me to acquire knowledge of the most important aspects of the gift. Mental representations work much the same way. They preserve important features of past experiences in a way that enables you to *re-present* those experiences to yourself.

If information is properly encoded, it will be retained in *storage* over some period of time. Storage requires both short- and long-term changes in the structures of your brain. At the end of the chapter, we will see how researchers are attempting to locate the brain structures that are responsible for storing new and old memories. We will also see what happens in cases of extreme amnesia, where individuals become incapable of storing new memories.

Retrieval is the payoff for all your earlier effort. When it works, it enables you to gain access—often in a split second—to information you stored earlier. Can you remember what comes before storage: decoding or encoding? The answer is simple to retrieve now, but will you still be able to retrieve the answer as swiftly and confidently when you are tested on this chapter's contents days or weeks from now? Discovering how you are able to retrieve one specific bit of information from the vast quantity of information in your memory storehouse is a challenge facing psychologists who want to know how memory works.

Although it is easy to define encoding, storage, and retrieval as separate memory processes, the interaction among

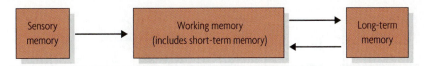

FIGURE 7.2 The Flow of Information In and Out of Long-Term Memory
Memory theories describe the flow of information to and from long-term memory. The theories address initial encodings of information in sensory and working memory, the transfer of information into long-term memory for storage, and the transfer of information from long-term memory to working memory for retrieval.

the three processes is quite complex. For example, to be able to encode the information that you have seen a tiger, you must first retrieve from memory information about the concept *tiger*. Similarly, to commit to memory the meaning of a sentence such as "He's as honest as Benedict Arnold," you must retrieve the meanings of each individual word, retrieve the rules of grammar that specify how word meanings should be combined in English, and retrieve cultural information that specifies exactly how honest Benedict Arnold (a famous Revolutionary War traitor) was.

We are now ready to look in more detail at the encoding, storage, and retrieval of information. The discussion will start with memory processes that preserve information for the short term such as sensory memory and working memory. We then move to the more permanent forms of long-term memory (see **Figure 7.2**). You will learn about how you remember and why you forget. The plan is to make you forever self-conscious about all the ways in which you use your capacity for memory. The hope is that your new knowledge will even allow you to improve some aspects of your memory skills.

Stop *and* Review

① What is the difference between explicit and implicit uses of memory?
② Suppose you are a skilled juggler. Does your skill rely more on declarative or procedural memory?
③ You suddenly can't remember the password for your e-mail account. Which memory process is most likely to be causing the difficulty?

✔–[**Study** and **Review** on **MyPsychLab**

MEMORY USE FOR THE SHORT TERM

Let's begin with a demonstration of the impermanence of some memories. **Figure 7.3**, on page 178, provides you with a reasonably busy visual scene. Please take a quick look at it—about 10 seconds—and then cover it up. Consider these questions about the scene:

1. What tool is the little boy at the bottom holding?
2. What is the middle man at the top doing?
3. In the lower right-hand corner, does the woman's umbrella handle hook to the left or to the right?

To answer these questions, wouldn't you be more comfortable if you could go back and have an extra peek at the picture?

This quick demonstration reminds you that much of the information you experience never lodges itself securely in your memory. Instead, you possess and use the information only for the short term. This section examines properties of three less permanent uses of memory: *iconic memory*, *short-term memory*, and *working memory*.

Iconic Memory

When you first covered up Figure 7.3, did you have the impression that you could briefly still "see" the whole picture? This extra peek at the picture is provided by your **iconic memory**—a memory system in the visual domain that allows large amounts of information to be stored for very brief durations (Neisser, 1967). Iconic memory is an example of a *sensory memory*: Researchers have speculated that each sensory system has a memory store that preserves representations of physical features of environmental stimuli for, at most, a few seconds (Radvansky, 2006). For example, people retain brief sensory representations of stimuli that have touched their fingertips (Auvray et al., 2011). We focus on iconic memory because it has received the most research attention.

A visual memory, or icon, lasts about half a second. Iconic memory was first revealed in experiments that required participants to retrieve information from visual displays that were exposed for only one-twentieth of a second.

George Sperling (1960, 1963) presented participants with arrays of three rows of letters and numbers.

Featured Study

7	1	V	F
X	L	5	3
B	4	W	7

Participants were asked to perform two different tasks. In a whole-report procedure, they tried to recall as many of the items in the display as possible. Typically, they could report only about four items. Other participants underwent a partial-report procedure, which required them to report only one row rather than the whole pattern. A signal of a high, medium, or low tone was sounded immediately after the presentation to indicate which row the participants were to report. Sperling found that regardless of which row he asked for, the participants' recall was quite high.

iconic memory Memory system in the visual domain that allows large amounts of information to be stored for very brief durations.

FIGURE 7.3 How Much Can You Remember from This Scene?

After viewing this scene for about 10 seconds, cover it up and try to answer the questions in the text. Under ordinary circumstances, iconic memory preserves a glimpse of the visual world for a brief time after the scene has been removed.

Because participants could accurately report any of the three rows in response to a tone, Sperling concluded that all of the information in the display must have gotten into iconic memory. That is evidence for its large capacity. At the same time, the difference between the whole- and partial-report procedures suggests that the information fades rapidly: The participants in the whole-report procedure were unable to recall all the information present in the icon. This second point was reinforced by experiments in which the identification signal was slightly delayed. **Figure 7.4** shows that as the delay interval increases from 0 seconds to 1 second, the number of items accurately reported declines steadily. Researchers have measured quite accurately the time course with which information must be transferred from the fading icon (Graziano & Sigman, 2008). To take advantage of the "extra peek" at the visual world, your memory processes must very quickly transfer information to more durable stores.

Note that iconic memory is not the same as the "photographic memory" that some people claim to have. The technical term for "photographic memory" is *eidetic imagery*: People who experience eidetic imagery are able to recall the details of a picture, for periods of time considerably longer than iconic memory, as if they were still looking at a photograph. "People" in this case really means children: Researchers have estimated that roughly 8 percent of preadolescent children are eidetickers, but virtually no adults (Neath & Surprenant, 2003). No satisfactory theory has been proposed for why eidetic imagery fades over time. However, if you are reading this book as a high school or college student, you almost certainly have iconic memory but not eidetic images.

Short-Term Memory

Before you began to read this chapter, you may not have been aware that you had iconic memory. It is very likely, however, that you were aware that there are some memories that you possess only for the short term. Consider the common occurrence of consulting a Web page to find the start time for a movie. If you don't get to act on the information immediately, you often have to go right back to the Web. When you consider this experience, it's easy to understand why researchers

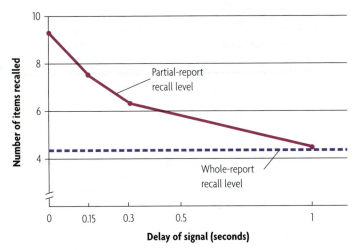

FIGURE 7.4 Recall by the Partial-Report Method
The solid line shows the average number of items recalled using the partial-report method, both immediately after presentation and at four later times. For comparison, the dotted line shows the number of items recalled by the whole-report method.
Adapted from Sperling, 1960.

have hypothesized a special type of memory called **short-term memory (STM).**

You shouldn't think of short-term memory as a particular place that memories go to, but rather as a built-in mechanism for focusing cognitive resources on some small set of mental representations (Shiffrin, 2003). But the resources of STM are fickle. As even your experience with phone numbers shows, you have to take some special care to ensure that memories become encoded into more permanent forms.

The Capacity Limitations of STM In Chapter 4, you learned how your attentional resources are devoted to selecting the objects and events in the external world on which you will expend your mental resources. Just as there are limits on your capacity to attend to more than a small sample of the available information, there are limits on your ability to keep more than a small sample of information active in STM. The limited capacity of STM enforces a sharp focus of mental attention.

To estimate the capacity of STM, researchers at first turned to tests of *memory span*. At some point in your life, you have probably been asked to carry out a task like this one:

Read the following list of random numbers once, cover them, and write down as many as you can in the order they appear:

8 1 7 3 4 9 4 2 8 5

How many did you get correct?

Now read the next list of random letters and perform the same memory test:

J M R S O F L P T Z B

How many did you get correct?

If you are like most individuals, you probably could recall somewhere in the range of five to nine items. **George Miller** (1956) suggested that seven (plus or minus two) was the "magic number" that characterized people's memory performance on random lists of letters, words, numbers, or almost any kind of meaningful, familiar item. ⊙▶

Tests of memory span, however, overestimate the true capacity of STM because participants are able to use other sources of information to carry out the task. When other sources of memory are factored out, researchers have estimated

the pure contribution of STM to your seven (or so) item memory span to be only between three and five items (Cowan, 2001). But if that's all the capacity you have to commence the acquisition of new memories, why don't you notice your limitations more often? Despite the capacity limitations of STM, you function efficiently for at least two reasons. As you will see

What role does short-term memory play when you punch in your ATM password?

⊙▶ **Simulate** the **Experiment** *Digit Span* on **MyPsychLab**

short-term memory (STM) Memory processes associated with preservation of recent experiences and with retrieval of information from long-term memory; short-term memory is of limited capacity and stores information for only a short length of time without rehearsal.

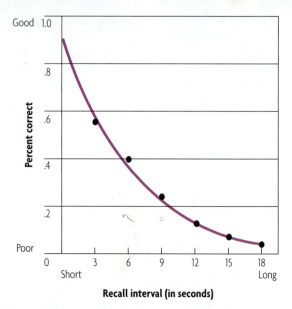

FIGURE 7.5 Short-Term Memory Recall without Rehearsal

When the interval between stimulus presentation and recall was filled with a distracting task, recall became poorer as the interval grew longer.

in the next two sections, the encoding of information in STM can be enhanced through rehearsal and chunking.

Rehearsal   You probably know that a good way to keep your movie time in mind is to keep repeating the digits in a cycle in your head. This memorization technique is called *maintenance rehearsal*. The fate of unrehearsed information was demonstrated in an ingenious experiment.

Participants heard three consonants, such as F, C, and V. After a delay of 3 to 18 seconds, the participants heard a signal that instructed them to recall the consonants (Peterson & Peterson, 1959). To prevent rehearsal, a distractor task was put between the stimulus input and the recall signal— the participants were given a three-digit number and told to count backward from it by 3s until the recall signal was presented. Many different consonant sets were given, and several short delays were used over a series of trials with a number of participants.

*As shown in **Figure 7.5**, recall became increasingly poorer as the time required to retain the information became longer. After even 3 seconds, there was considerable memory loss, and by 18 seconds, loss was nearly total. In the absence of an opportunity to rehearse the information, short-term recall was impaired with the passage of time.*

Performance suffered because information could not be rehearsed. It also suffered because of interference from the competing information of the distractor task. (We will consider interference as a cause of forgetting later in this chapter.) You may have noticed how often a new acquaintance says his or her name—and then you immediately forget it. One of the

most common reasons for this is that you are distracted from performing the type of rehearsal necessary to acquire a new memory. As a remedy, try to encode and rehearse a new name carefully before you continue with a conversation.

Our conclusion so far is that rehearsal will help you to keep information from fading out of STM. But suppose the information you wish to acquire is, at least at first, too cumbersome to be rehearsed? You might turn to the strategy of chunking.

Chunking   A *chunk* is a meaningful unit of information. A chunk can be a single letter or number, a group of letters or other items, or even a group of words or an entire sentence. For example, the sequence 1–9–8–4 consists of four digits that could exhaust your STM capacity. However, if you see the digits as a year or the title of George Orwell's book *1984*, they constitute only one chunk, leaving you much more capacity for other chunks of information. **Chunking** is the process of reconfiguring items by grouping them on the basis of similarity or some other organizing principle, or by combining them into larger patterns (Cowan et al., 2010).

See how many chunks you find in this sequence of 20 numbers: 19411917186118121776. You can answer "20" if you see the sequence as a list of unrelated digits, or "5" if you break down the sequence into the dates of major wars in U.S. history. If you do the latter, it's easy for you to recall all the digits in proper sequence after one quick glance. It would be impossible for you to remember them all from a short exposure if you saw them as 20 unrelated items.

Your memory span can always be greatly increased if you can discover ways to organize an available body of information into smaller chunks. One famous subject, S.F., was an avid runner. He was able to memorize 84 random digits by using his knowledge of race results to find chunks in the strings of digits (Chase & Ericsson, 1981; Ericsson & Chase, 1982). Like S.F., you can structure incoming information according to its personal meaning to you (linking it to the ages of friends and relatives, for example); or you can match new stimuli with various codes that have been stored in your long-term memory. Even if you can't link new stimuli to rules, meanings, or codes in your long-term memory, you can still use chunking. You can simply group the items in a rhythmical pattern or temporal group (181379256460 could become 181, pause, 379, pause, 256, pause, 460). You know from everyday experience that this grouping principle works well for remembering telephone numbers.

Working Memory

Our focus so far has been on short-term memory, and specifically the role that STM plays in the explicit acquisition of new memories. However, you need more memory resources on a moment-by-moment basis than those that allow you to acquire facts. For example, you also need to be able to retrieve preexisting memories. At the start of this chapter, I asked you to commit a number to memory. Can you remember now what it was? If you can remember (if not, peek), you have made your

chunking The process of taking single items of information and recoding them on the basis of similarity or some other organizing principle.

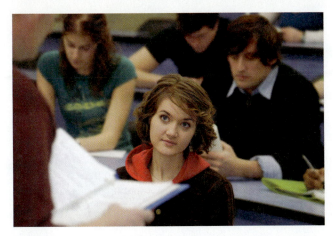

How can you put chunking to good use while listening to a lecture?

mental representation of that memory active once more—that's another memory function. If you do something more complicated—suppose you try to count backward by 3s from 132 while you toss a ball from hand to hand—you'll put even more demands on your memory resources.

Based on an analysis of the memory functions you require to navigate through life, researchers have articulated theories of **working memory**—the memory resource that you use to accomplish tasks such as reasoning and language comprehension. Suppose you are trying to remember a movie time while you search for a pencil and pad to write it down. Whereas your short-term memory processes allow you to keep the number in mind, your more general working memory resource allows you to execute the mental operations to accomplish an efficient search. Working memory provides a foundation for the moment-by-moment fluidity of thought and action.

Alan Baddeley (2002, 2003) has provided evidence for four components of working memory:

- *A phonological loop.* This resource holds and manipulates speech-based information. The phonological loop overlaps most with short-term memory. When you rehearse a telephone number by "listening" to it as you run it through your head, you are making use of the phonological loop.
- *A visuospatial sketchpad.* This resource performs the same types of functions as the phonological loop for visual and spatial information. If, for example, someone asked you how many desks there are in your psychology classroom, you might use the resources of the visuospatial sketchpad to form a mental picture of the classroom and then estimate the number of desks from that picture.
- *The central executive.* This resource is responsible for controlling attention and coordinating information from the phonological loop and the visuospatial sketchpad. Any time you carry out a task that requires a combination of mental processes—imagine, for example, you are asked to describe a picture from memory—you rely on the central executive function to apportion your mental resources to different aspects of the task (we return to this idea in Chapter 8).

- *The episodic buffer* is a storage system with limited capacity that is controlled by the central executive. The episodic buffer allows you to retrieve information from long-term memory and combine it with information from the current situation. Most life events include a complex array of sights, sounds, and so on. The episodic buffer provides a resource to integrate those different types of perceptual stimulation with past experiences to provide a unified interpretation of each situation.

The incorporation of short-term memory into the broader context of working memory should help reinforce the idea that STM is not a place but a process. To do the work of cognition—to carry out cognitive activities like language processing or problem solving—you must bring a lot of different elements together in quick succession. You can think of working memory as short-term special focus on the necessary elements. If you wish to get a better look at a physical object, you can shine a brighter light on it; working memory shines a brighter mental light on your mental objects—your memory representations. Working memory also coordinates the activities required to take action with respect to those objects.

In everyday life, you often run up against the capacity limitations of working memory. Let's apply that insight in the academic domain.

Featured Study

What happens when you sit down to begin an exam? Often, thoughts rush in about how prepared you are for the exam, how hard it's likely to be, and so on. A pair of researchers wished to test the hypothesis that these anxious thoughts often exhaust students' working memory capacity—and, by doing so, make it difficult for the students to perform well on their exam (Ramirez & Beilock, 2011). To test that hypothesis, the researchers created a testing situation that put particular pressure on students (by promising them a monetary reward if they did well). The researchers assigned a subset of the students to a control group. Those students sat quietly for 10 minutes waiting for the exam to start. The other students experienced an intervention: They spent the same 10 minutes "writing about their thoughts and feelings regarding the math problems they were about to perform" (p. 212). The researchers argued that the thoughts and feelings, once expressed, would no longer compete for the students' working memory capacity once the exam began. In fact, students in the expressive writing group performed about 20 percent better than the control group on a series of math problems!

Next time you experience anxiety before an exam, consider spending a few minutes writing about your thoughts and feelings. By doing so, you could free up working memory capacity you need to excel on the exam.

Researchers have demonstrated that working memory capacity differs among individuals. They have devised several

working memory A memory resource that is used to accomplish tasks such as reasoning and language comprehension; consists of the phonological loop, visuospatial sketchpad, and central executive.

Table 7.1 • Sample Items for a Test of Operation Span

Try to answer "yes" or "no" to each math problem and then memorize the words at the end of each problem. Once you're done with all four problems, cover them up and try to recall the four words.
IS (6 ÷ 2) − 2 = 2? SNOW
IS (8 × 1) − 5 = 3? TASTE
IS (9 × 2) − 6 = 12? KNIFE
IS (8 ÷ 4) + 3 = 6? CLOWN

procedures to measure those differences (Conway et al., 2005). Let's consider an example of one of those measures, which is called *operation span* (Turner & Engle, 1989). Take a look at **Table 7.1**. To determine operation span, researchers ask participants to read each math problem aloud and then answer "yes" or "no" to indicate whether the equation was correct. After solving each problem, participants try to memorize the word that comes after it. (In the real version of the test, participants get the words only after they've solved the problems, and they get the problems one at a time.) After completing a whole group of problems, participants try to recall all the words in the correct order. Try to get a feel for the task by working through Table 7.1. Operation span requires people to carry out one task (such as solving math problems) while maintaining a second task (such as remembering words). For that reason, it provides an index of individual differences in the efficiency of the central executive to apportion mental resources to different tasks.

Researchers use measures of working memory capacity (WMC) to predict performance on a variety of tasks. For example, in one study people tried to comprehend brief texts while irrelevant speech was played over headphones (Sörqvist et al., 2010). Because people with higher WMC are better able to focus their attention, their reading comprehension was less disrupted. Another project examined the impact of WMC on police officers' performance (Kleider et al., 2010). Police officers viewed a series of slides of armed and unarmed men. When the officers were experiencing negative emotions (after watching a disturbing video), those with lower WMC were more likely to shoot unarmed targets and less likely to shoot armed targets. The researchers suggested that negative emotions tax working memory resources. For officers with lower WMC, negative emotions leave them with insufficient resources to make accurate decisions.

A final note on working memory: Working memory helps maintain your psychological present. It is what sets a context for new events and links separate episodes together into a continuing story. It enables you to maintain and continually update your representation of a changing situation and to keep track of topics during a conversation. All of this is true because working memory serves as a conduit for information coming and going to long-term memory. Let's turn our attention now to the types of memories that can last a lifetime.

....

long-term memory (LTM) Memory processes associated with the preservation of information for retrieval at any later time.

retrieval cue Internally or externally generated stimulus available to help with the retrieval of a memory.

Stop *and* Review

① Why do researchers believe that the capacity of iconic memory is large?
② What is the contemporary estimate of the capacity of short-term memory?
③ What does it mean to *chunk* some group of items?
④ What are the components of working memory?

CRITICAL THINKING   Recall the study that demonstrated the importance of rehearsal to maintain information in short-term memory. In that study, why were participants asked to count backward by 3s (for example, 167, 164, 161 . . .) rather than by 1s (167, 166, 165 . . .)?

✔ **Study** and **Review** on **MyPsychLab**

LONG-TERM MEMORY: ENCODING AND RETRIEVAL

How long can memories last? At the chapter's outset, I asked you to recall your own earliest memory. How old is that memory? Fifteen years? Twenty years? Longer? When psychologists speak of *long-term memory*, it is with the knowledge that memories often last a lifetime. Therefore, whatever theory explains how memories are acquired for the long term must also explain how they can remain accessible over the life course. **Long-term memory (LTM)** is the storehouse of all the experiences, events, information, emotions, skills, words, categories, rules, and judgments that have been acquired from sensory and short-term memories. LTM constitutes each person's total knowledge of the world and of the self.

Psychologists know that it is often easier to acquire new long-term information when an important conclusion is stated in advance. With that conclusion in place, you have a framework for understanding the incoming information. For memory, here is the appropriate conclusion: Your ability to remember will be greatest when there is a good match between the circumstances in which you encoded information and the circumstances in which you attempt to retrieve it. You will see over the next several sections what it means to have a "good match."

Retrieval Cues

To begin the exploration of the match between encoding and retrieval, let's consider this general question: How do you "find" a memory? The basic answer is that you use retrieval cues. **Retrieval cues** are the stimuli available as you search for a particular memory. These cues may be provided externally, such as questions on a quiz ("What memory concepts do you associate with the research of Baddeley and Sperling?"), or generated internally ("Where have I met her before?"). Each time you attempt to retrieve an explicit memory, you do so for some purpose, and that purpose often supplies the retrieval cue. It won't surprise you that memories can be easier or harder to retrieve depending on the quality of the retrieval cue. If a friend asks you, "Who's the one Roman emperor I can't remember?"

In what ways is retrieval from long-term memory analogous to retrieval from a vast research library?

you're likely to be involved in a guessing game. If she asks instead, "Who was the emperor after Claudius?" you can immediately respond "Nero."

A good way for you to appreciate the importance of retrieval cues is by attempting to learn some word pairs. This procedure replicates classic memory experiments. Keep working at it until you can go through the six pairs three times in a row without an error.

    Apple–Boat
    Hat–Bone
    Bicycle–Clock
    Mouse–Tree
    Ball–House
    Ear–Blanket

Now that you've committed the pairs to memory, it's time to make the test more interesting. You need to have a *retention interval*—a period of time over which you must keep the information in memory. Let's spend a moment, therefore, discussing some of the procedures researchers might use to test your memory. You might assume that you either know something or you don't and that any method of testing what you know will give the same results. Not so. Let's consider two tests for explicit memory, recall and recognition. 👁

Recall and Recognition When you **recall,** you reproduce the information to which you were previously exposed. "What are the components of working memory?" is a recall question. **Recognition** refers to the realization that a certain stimulus event is one you have seen or heard before. Here's a recognition question: "Which is the term for a visual sensory memory: (1) echo; (2) chunk; (3) icon; or (4) abstract code?" You can relate recall

....

👁 **Watch** the **Video** *Classic Footage of Assessment of Memory with the Stanford-Binet Intelligence Scale* on **MyPsychLab**

recall A method of retrieval in which an individual is required to reproduce the information previously presented.

recognition A method of retrieval in which an individual is required to identify stimuli as having been experienced before.

episodic memory Long-term memory for an autobiographical event and the context in which it occurred.

and recognition to your day-to-day experiences of explicit memory. When trying to identify a criminal, the police would be using a recall method if they asked the victim to describe, from memory, some of the perpetrator's distinguishing features: "Did you notice anything unusual about the attacker?" They would be using the recognition method if they showed the victim photos, one at a time, from a file of criminal suspects or if they asked the victim to identify the perpetrator in a police lineup.

Let's now use these two procedures to test you on the word pairs you learned a few moments ago. What words finished the pairs?

    Hat–?   Bicycle–?   Ear–?

Can you select the correct pair from these possibilities?

Apple–Baby	Mouse–Tree	Ball–House
Apple–Boat	Mouse–Tongue	Ball–Hill
Apple–Bottle	Mouse–Tent	Ball–Horn

Was the recognition test easier than the recall test? It should be. Let's try to explain this result with respect to retrieval cues.

Both recall and recognition require a search using cues. The cues for recognition, however, are much more useful. For recall, you have to hope that the cue alone will help you locate the information. For recognition, part of the work has been done for you. When you look at the pair *Mouse–Tree,* you only have to answer *yes* or *no* to "Did I have this experience?" By contrast, for *Mouse–?* You need to answer, "What was the experience I had?" In this light, you can see that I made the recognition test reasonably easy for you. Suppose you had viewed, instead, recombinations of the original pairs. Which of these are correct?

    Hat–Clock   Ear–Boat
    Hat–Bone   Ear–Blanket

Now you must recognize not just that you saw the word before, but that you saw it in a particular context. (We will return to the idea of context shortly.) If you are a veteran of difficult multiple-choice exams, you have come to learn how tough even recognition situations can be. However, in most cases, your recognition performance will be better than your recall because retrieval cues are more straightforward for recognition. Let's look at some other aspects of retrieval cues.

Episodic and Semantic Memories The earlier discussion of the functions of memories made a distinction between declarative and procedural memories. Declarative memories themselves differ along another dimension with respect to the cues that are necessary to retrieve them from memory. Canadian psychologist **Endel Tulving** (1972) first proposed the distinction between *episodic* and *semantic* types of declarative memories (see **Figure 7.6** on page 184).

Episodic memories preserve, individually, the specific events that you have personally experienced. For example, memories of your happiest birthday or of your first kiss are stored in episodic memory. To recover such memories, you need retrieval cues that specify something about the time at which the event occurred and something about the content of the events. Depending on how the information has been encoded, you may or may not be able to produce a specific memory representation for an event. For example, do you have any specific memories to differentiate the 10th time ago you brushed your teeth from the 11th time ago?

FIGURE 7.6 Dimensions of Long-Term Memory

Researchers have suggested that people store different types of memories.

Everything you know, you began to acquire in some particular context. However, there are large classes of information that, over time, you encounter in many different contexts. These classes of information come to be available for retrieval without reference to their multiple times and places of experience. These **semantic memories** are generic, categorical memories, such as the meanings of words and concepts. For most people, facts like the formula $E = MC2$ and the capital of France don't require retrieval cues that make reference to the episodes, the original learning contexts, in which the memory was acquired.

Of course, this doesn't mean that your recall of semantic memories is foolproof. You know perfectly well that you can forget many facts that have become dissociated from the contexts in which you learned them. A good strategy when you can't recover a semantic memory is to treat it like an episodic memory again. By thinking to yourself, "I know I learned the names of the Roman emperors in my Western civilization course," you may be able to provide the extra retrieval cues that will shake loose a memory.

Context and Encoding

To continue our exploration of encoding and retrieval, let's now consider a phenomenon that you might call "context shock." You see someone across a crowded room, and you know that you know the person but you just can't place her. Finally, after staring for longer than is absolutely polite, you remember who it is—and you realize you were having difficulty identifying her because you have never seen her in this particular context. What is the woman who delivers your mail doing at your best friend's party? Whenever you have this type of experience, you have rediscovered the principle of **encoding specificity**: Memories emerge most efficiently when the context of retrieval matches the context of encoding. Let's see how researchers have demonstrated that principle.

Encoding Specificity What are the consequences of learning information in a particular context? Endel Tulving and Donald Thomson (1973) first demonstrated the power of encoding specificity by reversing the usual performance relationship between recall and recognition.

Featured Study

Participants were asked to learn pairs of words like train–black, but they were told that they would be responsible for remembering only the second word of the pair. In a subsequent phase of the experiment, participants were asked to generate four free associates to words like white. *Those words were chosen so that it was likely that the original to-be-remembered words (like* black) *would be among the associates. The participants were then asked to check off any words on their associates lists that they recognized as to-be-remembered words from the first phase of the experiment.*

Events of personal importance, like seeing a good friend for the first time after a year's separation, are retained in *episodic* memory. What types of information from *semantic* memory might contribute to a reunion?

----

semantic memory Generic, categorical memory, such as the meaning of words and concepts.

encoding specificity The principle that subsequent retrieval of information is enhanced if cues received at the time of recall are consistent with those present at the time of encoding.

They were able to do so 54 percent of the time. However, when the participants were later given the first words of the pair, like train, and asked to recall the associate, they were 61 percent accurate.

Why was recall better than recognition? Tulving and Thomson suggested that what mattered was the change in context. After the participants had studied the word *black* in the context of *train,* it was hard to recover the memory representation when the context was changed to *white.* Given the significant effect of even these minimal contexts, you can anticipate that richly organized real-life contexts would have an even greater effect on your memory.

Researchers have provided several remarkable demonstrations of *context-dependent* memory. In one experiment, scuba divers learned lists of words either on a beach or under water. They were then tested for retention of those words, again in one of those two contexts. Performance was nearly 50 percent better when the context at encoding and recall matched—even though the material had nothing at all to do with water or diving (Godden & Baddeley, 1975). Researchers have demonstrated similar context-dependent memory effects for word lists when encoding and retrieval varied between the third and fifth floors of a psychology building (Unsworth et al., 2012). But it's not just word lists: Piano students performed a brief composition more accurately when they played it on the same piano on which they had first learned it (Mishra & Backlin, 2007).

In each of the examples so far, memories are encoded with respect to a context in the external environment—for example, the test room or the type of piano. However, encoding specificity also occurs based on people's internal states. For example, in one study participants drank either alcohol or a placebo before the study and test sessions for a free recall task

After receiving a traffic warning from this man, why might you not recognize him if you ran into him at a party?

(Weissenborn & Duka, 2000). In general, alcohol impaired memory performance. However, participants who drank alcohol at both study and test were able to retrieve information that eluded participants who drank alcohol at only study or test alone. When internal states provide the basis for encoding specificity, those effects are called *state-dependent memory.* Researchers have demonstrated that state-dependent memory occurs for other drugs such as marijuana and amphetamine. Also, if you take antihistamines for allergies, you might be interested to learn that they lead to state-dependent memory (Carter & Cassaday, 1998). How might you use that information when allergy season rolls around?

These various examples of encoding specificity point to the same conclusion. It's easiest to find your way back to information when you can reinstate the original context in which you encoded it.

The Serial Position Effect   Changes in context also explain one of the classic effects in memory research: the **serial position effect.** Suppose a professor required you to learn a list of unrelated words. If you tried to recall those words in order, your data would almost certainly conform to the pattern shown in **Figure 7.7** on page 186: You would do very well on the first few words (the **primacy effect**) and very well on the last few words (the **recency effect**) but rather poorly on the middle part of the list. Figure 7.7 shows the generality of this pattern when students are asked to try to remember word lists of varying lengths (6, 10, and 15 words) using either *serial recall* ("Recite the words in the order you heard them") or *free recall* ("Recite as many words as you can") (Jahnke, 1965). Researchers have found primacy and recency in a wide variety of test situations (Neath & Surprenant, 2003). What day is it today? Do you believe that you would be almost a second faster to answer this question at the beginning or end of the week than in the middle (Koriat & Fischoff, 1974)?

The role context plays in producing the shape of the serial position curve has to do with the **temporal distinctiveness** of different items on a list, different experiences in your life, and so on (Guérard et al., 2010; Neath et al., 2006). Temporal distinctiveness refers to the extent to which a particular item stands out from or is distinct from other items in time. It's easiest to understand the concept of temporal distinctiveness by analogy to distinctiveness in space. **Figure 7.8** on page 186 provides that spatial analogy. Imagine, in Part A, that you are looking at train tracks. What you can see is that they look as if they clump together at the horizon—even though they are equally spaced apart. The early tracks are not distinctive; they blur together. By contrast, the nearest tracks stand out most; they are most distinctive.

Imagine now that you are trying to remember the last 10 movies you've seen. The movies are like the train tracks. Under most circumstances, you should remember the last movie best—giving you a recency effect—because it stands out most clearly in time. Meanwhile, this logic suggests that "middle" information will become more memorable if each item is

serial position effect A characteristic of memory retrieval in which the recall of beginning and end items on a list is often better than recall of items appearing in the middle.

primacy effect Improved memory for items at the start of a list.

recency effect Improved memory for items at the end of a list.

temporal distinctiveness The extent to which a particular item stands out from or is distinct from other items in time.

FIGURE 7.7 The Serial Position Effect

This figure shows the generality of the serial position effect. Students were asked to try to remember word lists of varying lengths (6, 10, and 15 words) using either *serial recall* ("Recite the words in the order you heard them") or *free recall* ("Recite as many words as you can"). Each curve shows better memory for both the beginning (the *primacy* effect) and end (the *recency* effect) of the list. ⊙

made more distinctive. The idea with respect to the analogy, as shown in Part B of Figure 7.8, is to make the train tracks seem equally far apart.

To make the train tracks seem evenly spaced, engineers would have to make the more distant ones actually be farther apart. Researchers have used the same logic for a memory test, by exploiting the analogy between space and time (Neath & Crowder, 1990). They had participants try to learn lists of letters, but they manipulated how far apart in time the letters were made to seem. This manipulation was accomplished by asking participants to read out

some number of random digits that appeared on a computer screen between the letters. In the conventional condition (like Part A of Figure 7.8), each pair of letters was separated by two digits. In the proportional condition (like Part B), the first pair had four digits and the last pair had zero digits; this should have the effect of making the early digits more distinctive, just like moving distant train tracks farther apart. Participants, in fact, showed better memory for early items on the list when those items had been made more separate.

⊙▸ **Simulate** the **Experiment** *Serial Position Effect* on **MyPsychLab**

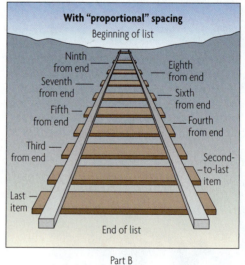

FIGURE 7.8 Temporal Distinctiveness

You can think of items you put into memory as train tracks. In Part A, you can imagine that memories farther back in time become blurred together, just like train tracks in the distance. In Part B, you see that one way to combat this effect is to make the earlier tracks physically farther apart, so the distances look proportional. Similarly, you can make early memories more distinctive by moving them apart psychologically.

This experiment suggests that the standard recency effect arises because the last few items are almost automatically distinctive. The same principle may explain primacy—each time you begin something new, your activity establishes a new temporal context. In that new context, the first few experiences are particularly distinctive. Thus you can think of primacy and recency as two views of the same set of train tracks—one from each end!

The Processes of Encoding and Retrieval

You have seen so far that a match between the context of encoding and of retrieval is beneficial to good memory performance. To refine that conclusion, we must consider the actual processes that are used to get information to and from long-term memory. This section will adopt a perspective called **transfer-appropriate processing:** The perspective suggests that memory is best when the type of processing carried out at encoding *transfers* to the processes required at retrieval (Roediger, 2008). Let's review research that illustrates this perspective.

Levels of Processing

We'll begin with the idea that the type of processing you perform on information—the type of attention you pay to information at time of encoding—will have an influence on your memory for the information. **Levels-of-processing theory** suggests that the deeper the level at which information was processed, the more likely it is to be committed to memory (Craik & Lockhart, 1972; Lockhart & Craik, 1990). If processing involves more analysis, interpretation, comparison, and elaboration, it should result in better memory. ◉►

The depth of processing is often defined by the types of judgments participants are required to make with respect to experimental materials. Consider the word *GRAPE*. You could make a physical judgment about this item—is the word in capital letters? Or a rhyme judgment—does the word rhyme with *tape*? Or a meaning judgment—does the word represent a type of fruit? Do you see how each of these questions requires you to think a little bit more deeply about *GRAPE*? In fact, the deeper the original processing participants carry out, the more words they remember (Lockhart & Craik, 1990).

Why does the depth of processing have an impact? One explanation is that the type of processing people do at "deeper" levels provides a better match to the processes that are required at retrieval (Roediger et al., 2002). When you use explicit memory processes to remember a word, you typically use information about its meaning (rather than, for example, its physical appearance). In that way, the meaning judgment at encoding provides a better match to processes of retrieval. This explanation makes the levels-of-processing effect a type of transfer-appropriate processing.

....

◉► **Simulate** the **Experiment** *Depth of Processing* on **MyPsychLab**

transfer-appropriate processing The perspective that suggests that memory is best when the type of processing carried out at encoding matches the processes carried out at retrieval.

levels-of-processing theory A theory that suggests that the deeper the level at which information was processed, the more likely it is to be retained in memory.

priming In the assessment of implicit memory, the advantage conferred by prior exposure to a word or situation.

Memory performance based on levels of processing confirms that the way in which information is committed to memory—the mental processes that you use to encode information—has an effect on whether you can retrieve that information later. However, so far we have looked at only explicit memory. We will now see that the match between processes at encoding and retrieval is particularly critical for implicit memory.

Processes and Implicit Memory Recall that the explicit versus implicit dimension applies both at encoding and at retrieval (Bowers & Marsolek, 2003). Under many circumstances, for example, you will retrieve implicitly memories that you originally encoded explicitly. This is true when you greet your best friend by name without having to expend any particular mental effort. Even so, implicit memories reveal the importance of the match between the processes at implicit encoding and the processes at implicit retrieval.

To explore the properties of implicit memory, researchers have often demonstrated that the same circumstances of encoding have quite a different impact on people's performance on explicit and implicit memory tasks. Consider a study that measured the memory performance of marathon runners (Eich & Metcalfe, 2009). Members of the *marathon* group had just completed the New York City marathon. Members of the *control* group were also marathoners, but they completed the memory tests one to three days before the marathon. Each group began the experiment by rating the pleasantness of a list of 26 words. The pleasantness ratings allowed participants to think about the meaning of a word without purposefully committing it to memory. Next, the participants completed a test of implicit memory known as *word stem completion*. In this task, participants see a stem, like *uni_____*, and write the first word that comes to mind. Suppose *unicorn* was on the original word list. People might write *unicorn* down in response to *uni_____* without being aware that they are experiencing the influence of the original list. Finally, the participants completed an explicit memory task in which they explicitly tried to recall the words they had rated earlier.

What affect should running a marathon have on memory performance? The researchers suggested that the stress of the run would make it more difficult for people to encode explicit information. For that reason, explicit memory should suffer post-marathon. However, the implicit memory task only relies on a *physical* match between the original stimulus and the information given at test. Whatever *perceptual* processes allowed people to encode *unicorn* as a physical stimulus should also make that physical reality available when they complete the stem *uni_____*. On this analysis, implicit memory should be unaffected by post-marathon stress. In fact, the researchers proposed that the marathoners' implicit memory might be even better than the control group's memory: The marathoners' post-run stress might have prompted them to focus more attention on the physical properties of the words than on the words' meaning.

Figure 7.9 on page 188 presents the experiments' results. As you can see, the marathoners did, in fact, have worse explicit memory but better implicit memory. You are probably familiar with "proportion recalled" as a measure of explicit memory. The measure for implicit memory will be less familiar. It is known as **priming** because the first experience of the word *primes* memory for later experiences. This measure indicates

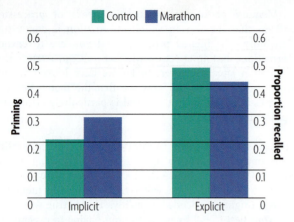

FIGURE 7.9 Comparison of Implicit and Explicit Memory Performance

People's explicit memory performance was worse after running a marathon. However, their implicit memory performance was better than that of members of the control group.

how much more likely participants were to provide *unicorn* in response to *uni*_____ if the word had appeared on the initial list. (For some participants, *unicorn* would not have been on the list.) Figure 7.9 shows priming for both the marathon and the control group, but more for the marathon group.

This experiment demonstrates priming based on perceptual processes that encode physical aspects of words. People also experience priming when conceptual processes function at encoding and retrieval.

A group of researchers wished to demonstrate that priming of conceptual information could last over a period of four to eight weeks (Thomson et al., 2010). Because they taught at a Canadian university, they used the names of U.S. states as their stimuli. Early in the semester, in several classes over a period of 10 years, the researchers introduced one U.S. state (which varied across years). They introduced the target state in the context of a lecture on memory retrieval. They suggested, one year, that a good strategy for remembering the states was to go through the alphabet. They noted, "when you come to the letter 'D,' you'll have a good chance of remembering Delaware" (p. 43). Each semester, a month or two later, the researchers asked students to write down all 50 states. By comparing across years, the researchers demonstrated that students were much more likely to remember a state when it had been mentioned in the earlier lecture.

You might think that participants were just able to remember the target state because they recalled their professors mentioning it in class. However, the researchers asked their students about their prior memories. Very few could recall what had happened earlier in the semester. Based on these responses, the researchers concluded that the conceptual priming of the particular state endured over the whole period of one to two months!

Are you impressed by the longevity of implicit memory? You should keep these results in mind as we turn to circumstances in which your memory processes fall short.

Why We Forget

Much of the time, your memory works just fine. You see a new acquaintance walking toward you, and you retrieve his name from memory without hesitation. Unfortunately, every once in a while, you end up greeting him in awkward silence—with that awful realization that you can't remember his name. How does that happen? Sometimes the answer will reside with the forces you've already learned. It could be the case, for example, that you're trying to recall the name in a context that's very different from the one in which you learned it. However, researchers have studied other explanations for forgetting. In fact, the earliest formal body of research on memory, published in 1885, focused directly on that topic. Let's begin with that work.

Ebbinghaus Quantifies Forgetting The study of forgetting was pioneered by by the German psychologist **Hermann Ebbinghaus** (1850–1909). Ebbinghaus served as his own subject. He began each study by reading through a list of nonsense syllables (e.g., *CEG* or *DAX*) one at a time. Then he read through the list again in the same order, and again, until he could recite all the items in the correct order. Next he distracted himself from rehearsing the original list by forcing himself to learn other lists. After this interval, Ebbinghaus measured his memory by seeing how many trials it took him to *relearn* the original list. If he needed fewer trials to relearn it than he had needed to learn it initially, information had been *saved* from his original study. (This concept should be familiar from Chapter 6. Recall that there is often a savings when animals relearn a conditioned response.)

For example, if Ebbinghaus took 12 trials to learn a list and 9 trials to relearn it several days later, his savings score for that elapsed time would be 25 percent (12 trials − 9 trials = 3 trials; 3 trials ÷ 12 trials = 0.25, or 25 percent). Using savings as his measure, Ebbinghaus recorded the memory retained after different time intervals. The curve he obtained is shown in **Figure 7.10**. As you can see, he found a rapid initial loss of memory. In fact, after one hour Ebbinghaus already had to spend half the original time to relearn the list. This initial period of rapid loss was followed by a gradually declining rate (Ebbinghaus, 1885/1964).

You have experienced the pattern revealed in Ebbinghaus's forgetting curve countless times in your life. Consider, for example, how reluctant you'd be to take an exam a week after

FIGURE 7.10 Ebbinghaus's Forgetting Curve

Ebbinghaus calculated his retention of nonsense syllables over a 30-day period using the savings method. The curve shows rapid forgetting and then reaches a plateau of little change.

Bread

Orange juice

Ice cream

Bananas

FIGURE 7.12 The Method of Loci

In the method of loci, you associate the items you wish to remember (such as the items on a grocery list) with locations along a familiar path (such as your route to and from school).

If you made an accurate feeling-of-knowing judgment, you should have been less likely to get the correct answer, d, if you gave a 1 rating than if you gave a 6. (Of course, to have a fair test you'd need to answer a long series of questions.) Hart found that when participants gave 1 ratings, they answered the questions correctly only 30 percent of the time, whereas 6 ratings predicted 75 percent success. That's pretty impressive evidence that feelings-of-knowing can be accurate.

You probably make another type of metamemory judgment, called a *judgment-of-learning* (JOL), each time you prepare for an exam. JOLs are your estimates of how well you have learned something. Research suggests that students use their JOLs to decide how to apportion their study time (Metcalfe, 2009). They spend more time reviewing material they believe they haven't already mastered. This real-world practice leads to an important question: Do JOLs allow people to predict their future performance on exams? You should want the answer to be "yes." If you *believe* that you've learned some information, you should want that to mean that you have, in fact, learned that material. However, as you might anticipate, the real answer to whether JOLs predict performance is "sometimes." Researchers have devoted a good deal of effort to try to understand when JOLs do and do not predict future performance

(Rhodes & Tauber, 2011; Undorf & Erdfelder, 2011). Much of that research focuses on how activities at encoding influence JOLs. For that reason, the most important question you can ask yourself is, "*Why*: Why do I believe I know (or don't know) this material?"

You have now learned quite a bit about how you get information in and out of memory. You know what is meant by a "good match" between the circumstances of encoding and of retrieval. The next section shifts focus from your memory processes to the content of your memories.

Stop *and* Review

① Do circumstances of recall or recognition generally provide more retrieval cues?

② At a party, why might you have the best recall of the first person to whom you spoke?

③ What does the perspective known as transfer-appropriate processing suggest?

④ For your English class, you memorize "The Raven." When you're done, you can no longer recite last

Critical Thinking in Your Life

HOW CAN MEMORY RESEARCH HELP YOU PREPARE FOR EXAMS?

One important use of critical thinking is to apply new knowledge to your life's important tasks. As you read about memory, you might ask yourself, "How will this research help me prepare for my next exam?" Let's see what advice can be generated from this type of critical thinking:

- *Encoding specificity.* As you'll recall, the principle of encoding specificity suggests that the context of retrieval should match the context of encoding. In school settings, "context" often will mean "the context of other information." If you always study material in the same context, you may find it difficult to retrieve it in a different context. As a remedy, change contexts even while you study. Ask yourself questions that mix different topics together. If you get stuck while you're taking an exam, try to generate as many retrieval cues as you can that reinstate the original context: "Let's see. We heard about this in the same lecture we learned about short-term memory...."

- *Serial position.* The serial position curve suggests that, under very broad circumstances, information presented in the "middle" is least well remembered. In fact, college students fail more exam items on material from the middle of a lecture than on material from the start or end of the lecture (Holen & Oaster, 1976; Jensen, 1962). When you're listening to a lecture, remind yourself to pay special attention in the middle of the session. When it comes time to study, devote some extra time and effort to that material—and make sure not to study the material in the same order each time.

- *Elaborative rehearsal and mnemonics.* Sometimes when you study for exams, you will feel as if you are trying to acquire "unstructured information." You might, for example, be asked to memorize the dimensions of the five-factor model of personality (see Chapter 13). This feels just like a list with five items, so you need to find ways to provide structure yourself. Try to form visual images or make up sentences or stories that use the concepts in creative ways. For the five-factor model, I use the mnemonic OCEAN. See if that helps when you reach Chapter 13.

- *Metamemory.* Research on metamemory suggests that people generally have good intuitions about what they know and what they don't know. If you are in an exam situation in which there is time pressure, you should allow those intuitions to guide how you allocate your time. You might, for example, read the whole test over quickly and see which questions give you the strongest feelings-of-knowing.

As you read the basic facts from memory research, you might not have immediately seen how to put the information to use. Can you now see how critical thinking will allow you to apply psychological knowledge directly to your life?

- Why might it be a good idea to shuffle your notes before you study for an exam?
- What could a professor do to help students overcome the impact of serial position on lecture material?

---

week's assignment. Is this an example of proactive or retroactive interference?

⑤ How could you use the method of loci to remember the order of elements in the periodic table?

⑥ What is a judgment of learning?

CRITICAL THINKING Recall the experiment that tested implicit memory for U.S. states. Why did the researchers use a different state each time they replicated the experiment?

✔—Study and Review on MyPsychLab

STRUCTURES IN LONG-TERM MEMORY

Our focus so far has been on how you encode and later retrieve information from memory. This next section focuses on an important aspect of memory storage: the way in which the

information you acquire over time becomes represented in large bodies of *organized knowledge*. Recall, for example, that I asked you to consider whether *grape* is a fruit. You could say *yes* very quickly. How about *porcupine*? Is it a fruit? How about *tomato*? In this section, we will consider how the difficulty of these types of judgments relates to the way information is structured in memory. You will also learn how memory organization allows you to make a best guess at the content of experiences you can't remember exactly.

Memory Structures

An essential function of memory is to draw together similar experiences, to enable you to discover patterns in your interactions with the environment. You live in a world filled with countless individual events, from which you must continually extract information to combine them into a smaller, simpler set that you can manage mentally. But apparently you don't need to expend any particular conscious effort to find structure in the world. It's unlikely that you ever formally thought to yourself something like, "Here's what belongs in a kitchen." It is through ordinary experience in the world that you have acquired mental structures to mirror environmental structures. Let's look at the types of memory structures you have formed in your moment-by-moment experience of the world.

Categories and Concepts   Let's begin by previewing one of the topics you will see in Chapter 10—the mental effort a child must go through to acquire the meaning of a word, such as *doggie*. For this word to have meaning, the child must be able to store each instance in which the word *doggie* is used, as well as information about the context. In this way, the child finds out what common core experience—a furry creature with four legs—is meant by *doggie*. The child must acquire the knowledge that *doggie* applies not just to one particular animal, but to a *whole category* of creatures. This ability to categorize individual experiences—to take the same action toward them or give them the same label—is one of the most basic abilities of thinking organisms (Murphy, 2002).

The mental representations of the categories you form are called **concepts.** The concept *doggie*, for example, names the set of mental representations of experiences of dogs that a young child has gathered together in memory. (As you will see in Chapter 10, if the child hasn't yet refined his or her meaning for *doggie*, the concept might also include features that adults wouldn't consider to be appropriate.) You have acquired a vast array of concepts. You have categories for *objects* and *activities*, such as *barns* and *baseball*. Concepts may also represent *properties*, such as *red* or *large*; *abstract ideas*, such as *truth* or *love*; and *relations*, such as *smarter than* or *sister of*. Each concept represents a summary unit for your experience of the world.

As you consider the many categories you experience in the world, you will recognize that some category members are more or less typical. You can develop this intuition if you think about a category like *bird*. You would probably agree that a robin is a typical bird, whereas an ostrich or a penguin is atypical. The degree of typicality of a category member has real-life consequences. Classic research has shown, for example, that people respond more quickly to typical members of a category than to its more unusual ones. Your reaction time

How does the formation of categories—such as what constitutes a healthy head of lettuce, a sweet melon, or a flavorful tomato—help you make daily decisions like what to buy for dinner?

to determine that a robin is a bird would be quicker than your reaction time to determine that an ostrich is a bird (Rosch et al., 1976). But what makes people consider a robin to be a typical bird, rather than an ostrich? Answers to this question have often focused on *family resemblance*—typical category members have attributes that overlap with many other members of the category (Rosch & Mervis, 1975). Robins have most of the attributes you associate with birds—they are about the right size, they fly, and so on. Ostriches, by contrast, are unusually large, and they do not fly. These examples suggest that family resemblance plays a role in judgments of typicality. However, recent research suggests that the most typical category members are also the *ideal* category members.

A team of researchers recruited individuals from two communities who had several decades of fishing experience: One group was Native American Menominee Indians from northern central Wisconsin; the second group was European Americans from roughly the same geographical location (Burnett et al., 2005). The experiment used these two groups because they differ with respect to the species of fish they consider to be most desirable or ideal. For example, the Menominee people consider sturgeon to be sacred. The researchers presented the participants with a group of 44 cards printed with the names of local fish. Participants sorted these cards into groups—the researchers used the participants' verbal justifications (for example, "good eating") for which fish they grouped together as an index of desirability. Also, the participants rated the extent to which each species was a good example of the "fish" category. The researchers found a 0.80 correlation between desirability and typicality. (Recall from Chapter 2 that correlations range from −1.0 to +1.0.) That's impressive evidence that the participants' notions of the "ideal" fish played a role in their judgments of typicality. In addition, the ratings were influenced by cultural differences in desirability. For example, the Menominee group rated sturgeon as even more typical than did the European American group.

If you don't have a lot of fishing experience, you might have less of a sense than these participants did about which fish are desirable. However, you can think about categories with which you have a lot of experience to see how your notions of what is ideal inform your judgments about what is typical.

Hierarchies and Basic Levels   Concepts do not exist in isolation. As shown in **Figure 7.13** on page 194, concepts can often be arranged into meaningful organizations. A broad category like *animal* has several subcategories, such as *bird* and *fish*, which in turn contain exemplars such as *canary, ostrich, shark,* and *salmon*. The animal category is itself a subcategory of the still larger category of *living beings*. Concepts are also linked to other types of information: You store the knowledge that some birds are *edible*, some are *endangered*, some are *national symbols*.

There seems to be a level in such hierarchies at which people best categorize and think about objects. This has been called

....

concepts   Mental representation of a kind or category of items and ideas.

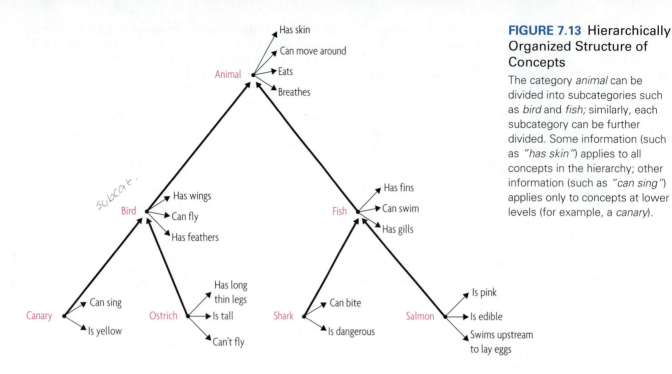

FIGURE 7.13 Hierarchically Organized Structure of Concepts
The category *animal* can be divided into subcategories such as *bird* and *fish;* similarly, each subcategory can be further divided. Some information (such as *"has skin"*) applies to all concepts in the hierarchy; other information (such as *"can sing"*) applies only to concepts at lower levels (for example, a *canary*).

the **basic level** (Rosch, 1973, 1978). For example, when you buy an apple at the grocery store, you could think of it as a *piece of fruit*—but that seems imprecise—or a *Golden Delicious*—but that seems too specific or narrow. The basic level is just *apple.* If you were shown a picture of such an object, that's what you'd be likely to call it. You would also be faster to say that it was an apple than that it was a piece of fruit (Rosch, 1978). The basic level emerges through your experience of the world. You are more likely to encounter the term *apple* than its more or less specific alternatives. If you became an apple grower, however, you might find yourself having daily conversations about *Cortlands* or *Granny Smiths.* With those experiences, your basic level would probably shift lower in the hierarchy.

Schemas We have seen that concepts are the building blocks of memory hierarchies. They also serve as building blocks for more complex mental structures. Recall Figure 7.1 on page 175. Why did you instantly know that the rabbit didn't belong in the kitchen? I suggested earlier that this judgment relied on implicit memory—but I didn't say what type of memory structure you were using. Clearly, what you need is some representation in memory that combines the individual concepts of a kitchen—your knowledge about ovens, sinks, and refrigerators—into a larger unit. We call that larger unit a schema. **Schemas** are conceptual frameworks, or clusters of knowledge, regarding objects, people, and situations. Schemas are "knowledge packages" that encode complex generalizations about your experience of the structure of the environment. You have schemas for kitchens and bedrooms, race car drivers and professors, surprise parties and graduations. A *script* is a

....

basic level The level of categorization that can be retrieved from memory most quickly and used most efficiently.

schema General conceptual framework, or cluster of knowledge, regarding objects, people, and situations; knowledge package that encodes generalizations about the structure of the environment.

more specific type of memory representation that specifies how events unfold in time (Schank & Abelson, 1977). For example, you have likely encoded scripts that specify what happens when you go to a restaurant or visit a doctor's office.

Later chapters will provide more illustrations of the types of schemas that shape your day-to-day experiences. For example, in Chapter 10, we'll see that the attachment relationships children form with their parents provide schemas for later social interactions. In Chapter 13, we'll see that you possess a *self-schema*—a memory structure that allows you to organize information about yourself.

One thing you may have guessed is that your schemas do not include all the individual details of all your varied experiences. A schema represents your average experience of situations in the environment. Thus your schemas are not permanent but shift with your changing life events. Your schemas also include only those details in the world to which you have devoted sufficient attention. For example, when asked to draw the information on the head sides of U.S. coins, college students virtually never filled in the word *Liberty,* although it appears on every coin (Rubin & Kontis, 1983). Check a coin! Thus your schemas provide an accurate reflection of what you've *noticed* about the world. Let's now look at all the ways in which you use your concepts and schemas.

Using Memory Representations Let's consider some instances of memory structures in action. To begin, consider the picture in Part A of **Figure 7.14.** What is it? Although this is certainly an unusual member of the category, you probably reached the conclusion "It's a chair" with reasonable ease. However, to do so, you needed to draw on your memory representations of members of that category. You can say "It's a chair" because the object in the figure calls to mind your past experiences of chairs.

Researchers have provided two theories of how people use concepts in memory to categorize the objects they encounter in the world. One theory suggests that, for each concept

FIGURE 7.14 Theories of Categorization

A. What is this unusual object? B. One theory suggests that you categorize this object as a chair by comparing it to a single prototype stored in memory. C. An alternative theory suggests that you categorize this object by comparing it to the many exemplars you have in memory.

in memory, you encode a **prototype**—a representation of the most central or average member of a category (Rosch, 1978). On this view, you recognize objects by comparing them to prototypes in memory. Because the picture in Part A of Figure 7.14 matches many of the important attributes of the prototype in Part B, you can recognize the picture as a chair.

An alternative theory suggests that people retain memories of the many different **exemplars** they experience for each category. Part C of Figure 7.14 gives you a subset of the exemplars of chairs you might have seen. On the exemplar view, you recognize an object by comparing it to the exemplars you have stored in memory. You recognize the picture as a chair because it is similar to several of those exemplars. Researchers have conducted a large number of studies to contrast prototype and exemplar accounts of categorization. The data largely support the exemplar view: People appear to categorize the objects they encounter by comparing them to multiple representations in memory (Nosofsky, 2011; Voorspoels et al., 2008).

The picture in Figure 7.14 was meant to be an unusual chair but clearly a chair nonetheless. However, as you saw in

Chapter 4, sometimes the world provides ambiguous stimuli—and you use prior knowledge to help interpret those stimuli. Do you remember **Figure 7.15** on page 196? Do you see a duck or a rabbit? Let's suppose you have the expectation that you're going to see a duck. If you match the features of the picture against the features of a duck present in exemplars in memory, you're likely to be reasonably content. The same thing would happen if you were expecting a rabbit. You use information from memory to generate—and confirm—expectations.

As previously noted, memory representations also allow you to understand when something is unusual in the world. That's why you could quickly notice the anomalous rabbit in the center of Figure 7.1. Because the rabbit is inconsistent with your kitchen schema, you'd also be particularly likely to remember seeing it in the picture. That claim is supported by a study in which researchers filled a graduate student office with both typical objects (such as notebook, pencil) and atypical objects (such as harmonica, toothbrush) (Lampinen et al., 2001). Participants spent one minute in the room. Later in the experiment, the participants indicated which items on a list had been present in the room. Their memory was consistently more accurate for the atypical items than for the typical items. This study illustrates how memory structures direct your attention to unusual aspects of a scene.

prototype The most representative example of a category.

exemplar Member of a category that people have encountered.

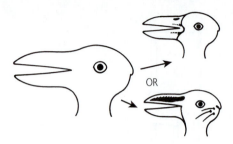

FIGURE 7.15 Recognition Illusion
Duck or rabbit?

Taken together, these examples demonstrate that the availability of memory representations influences the way you think about the world. Your past experiences color your present experiences and provide expectations for the future. You will see shortly that, for much the same reasons, concepts and schemas can sometimes work against accurate memory.

Remembering as a Reconstructive Process

Let's turn now to another important way in which you use memory structures. In many cases, when you are asked to remember a piece of information, you can't remember the information directly. Instead, you *reconstruct* the information based on more general types of stored knowledge. To experience **reconstructive memory,** consider this trio of questions:

- Did Chapter 3 have the word *the* in it?
- Did 1991 contain the day July 7?
- Did you breathe yesterday between 2:05 and 2:10 P.M.?

You probably were willing to answer "Yes!" to each of these questions without much hesitation, but you almost certainly don't have specific, episodic memories to help you (unless, of course, something happened to fix these events in memory—perhaps July 7 is your birthday or you crossed out all the *the*'s in Chapter 3 to curb your boredom). To answer these questions, you must use more general memories to reconstruct what is likely to have happened. Let's examine this process of reconstruction in a bit more detail.

The Accuracy of Reconstructive Memory If people reconstruct some memories, rather than recovering a specific memory representation for what happened, then you might expect that you could find occasions on which the reconstructed memory differed from the real occurrence—distortions. One of the most impressive demonstrations of memory distortions is also the oldest. In his classic book *Remembering: A Study in Experimental and Social Psychology* (1932), **Sir Frederic Bartlett** (1886–1969) undertook a program of research to demonstrate how individuals' prior knowledge influenced the way they remembered new information. Bartlett studied the way British undergraduates

....

reconstructive memory The process of putting information together based on general types of stored knowledge in the absence of a specific memory representation.

remembered stories whose themes and wording were taken from another culture. His most famous story was "The War of the Ghosts," an American Indian tale.

Bartlett found that his readers' reproductions of the story were often greatly altered from the original. The distortions Bartlett found involved three kinds of reconstructive processes:

- *Leveling*—simplifying the story.
- *Sharpening*—highlighting and overemphasizing certain details.
- *Assimilating*—changing the details to better fit the participant's own background or knowledge.

Thus readers reproduced the story with words familiar in their culture taking the place of those unfamiliar: *Boat* might replace *canoe* and *go fishing* might replace *hunt seals*. Bartlett's participants also often changed the story's plot to eliminate references to supernatural forces that were unfamiliar in their culture.

Following Bartlett's lead, contemporary researchers have demonstrated a variety of memory distortions that occur when people use constructive processes to reproduce memories. How, for example, do you remember what you did as a child? Participants in one experiment were asked to indicate whether, before the age of 10, they had "Met and shook hands with a favorite TV character at a theme resort" (Braun et al., 2002, p. 7). After answering that question—as part of a larger life-experiences inventory—some of the participants read an advertisement for Disneyland that evoked the idea of a family visit: "Go back to your childhood . . . and remember the characters of your youth, Mickey, Goofy, and Daffy Duck." Later the ad described circumstances in which the visitor was able to shake hands with a childhood hero: "Bugs Bunny, the character you've idolized on TV, is only several feet away. . . . You [reach up] to grab his hand" (p. 6). After reading this type of ad, participants were now more likely to indicate—though they hadn't before—that they shook a character's hand. Moreover, they were more likely to report a specific memory that they had shaken Bugs Bunny's hand at Disneyland: 16 percent of the participants in this advertisement group remembered having done so versus 7 percent of the participants in a group that hadn't read the autobiographical ad. Of course, none of these memories can be accurate: Bugs Bunny isn't a Disney character!

This study suggests how even memories for your own life events are reconstructed from various sources. The study also illustrates the fact that people are not always accurate at recalling the original sources for various components of their memories (Mitchell & Johnson, 2009). In fact, researchers have demonstrated that individuals will sometimes come to believe that they actually carried out actions that they, in fact, only accomplished in their imaginations.

A group of 40 college students participated in an experiment that had three sessions (Seamon et al., 2006). In session 1, the students joined an experimenter for a one-hour walk around campus. The pair stopped 48 times during the walk. At each stop, the experimenter read an action statement such as "Check the Pepsi machine for change." After hearing each statement, the students did one of four things: They performed the actions themselves, they watched the experimenter perform the actions, they imagined that they were performing the actions, or they imagined that the experimenter was

Suppose, while you were at a party, someone told you the man you had just met was a millionaire. How would this affect your memories for his actions at the party? What if you had been told he only had delusions of being a millionaire?

performing them. In addition, half the actions were bizarre. For example, rather than "Check the Pepsi machine for change," half the students got "Get down on one knee and propose marriage to the machine." The experimenter and the participants took a second walk during session 2, which took place 24 hours later. On the second walk, the students imagined themselves or the experimenter performing some new and some old actions (both ordinary and bizarre) at locations that were also divided between new and old. In session 3, which took place two weeks after session 2, the students were asked to think back to the first session. They tried to recall whether each action had been performed or imagined. For both ordinary and bizarre actions, the same finding held true: Students often recalled that the actions they had only been asked to imagine had actually been performed by them or the experimenter. Thus, some participants agreed that they had actually proposed marriage to a Pepsi machine or patted a dictionary to ask how it was doing when they had only imagined doing so.

Can you find applications of this result in your own life? Suppose you keep reminding yourself to set your alarm clock before you go to bed. Each time you remind yourself, you form a picture in your head of the steps you must go through. If you imagine setting the clock often enough, you might mistakenly come to believe that you actually did so!

It is important to keep in mind, however, that just as in Chapter 4's discussion of perceptual illusions, psychologists often infer the normal operation of processes by demonstrating circumstances in which the processes lead to errors. You can think of these memory distortions as the consequences of processes that usually work pretty well. In fact, a lot of the time, you don't need to remember the exact details of a particular episode. Reconstructing the gist of events will serve just fine.

Flashbulb Memories   For most of your past life experiences, you would probably agree that you need to reconstruct the memories. For example, if someone asked you how you celebrated your birthday three years ago, you'd likely count backwards and try to reconstruct the context. However, there are some circumstances in which people believe that their memories remain completely faithful to the original events. These types of memories—which are called **flashbulb memories**—arise when people experience emotionally charged events: People's memories are so vivid that they seem almost to be photographs of the original incident. The first research on flashbulb memories focused on people's recollections of public events (Brown & Kulik, 1977). For example, the researchers asked participants if they had specific memories of how they first learned about the assassination of President John F. Kennedy. All but one of the 80 participants reported vivid recollections.

The concept of flashbulb memory applies to both private and public events. People might have vivid memories, for example, of an accident they experienced or how they learned about the September 11 attacks. However, research on flashbulb memories has largely focused on public events. To conduct these studies, researchers recruit participants and ask them to share their memories of emotionally resonant events. For different age groups, such events might be the *Challenger* explosion, the death of Princess Diana, or the attack on Pearl Harbor. The content of flashbulb memories reflects how people learned about the events. For example, people who acquired their information from the media tend to include more event facts in their memory reports than do people who acquired information from another individual (Bohannon et al., 2007). U.S. citizens had more specific recollections of the September 11 attacks than did citizens of other countries such as Italy, the Netherlands, and Japan (Curci & Luminet, 2006).

Research on these public events confirms that people acquire flashbulb memories. The question remains, however, whether these memories are as accurate as people believe them to be. To address the question of accuracy, researchers recruit participants directly after the events and then assess their memories at one or more points later in time. One such study began on September 12, 2001.

The day after the September 11 attacks, students provided answers to a series of questions, including "Where were you when you first heard the news?" and "Were there others with you and, if so, who?" (Talarico & Rubin, 2003). For purposes of comparison, the students also reported memories

flashbulb memories People's vivid and richly detailed memory in response to personal or public events that have great emotional significance.

for an everyday event (such as a party or sporting event) that occurred in the few days before the attack. The students answered the same types of questions for those everyday memories (for example, "Where were you physically?" and "Were there others present and, if so, who?"). The researchers called the students back to the laboratory 1, 6, or 32 weeks after the initial memory test. At each delay, the students answered the same series of memory questions they had answered on September 12. The researchers determined which details were consistent with the original reports and which were inconsistent. As you can see in Figure 7.16, there were no differences between September 11 memories and everyday memories. The students recalled consistent details and introduced inconsistent details at nearly the same rate for both types of memories.

The researchers extended their project by inviting the original participants for another memory test after a full year had passed (Talarico & Rubin, 2007). The conclusions remained the same: In a pattern that was quite similar for both types of memories, the participants' ability to provide correct details decreased, whereas their tendency to introduce incorrect details increased. There was, however, one feature that set flashbulb memories apart from everyday memories: For their flashbulb memories, participants were considerably more confident that they were providing accurate memories.

That final result indicates why it is often difficult for people to accept the results of research on flashbulb memories. How could memories that feel so vivid and true actually be inaccurate (or, at least, be no more accurate than other less

FIGURE 7.16 Students' Recall of Flashbulb and Everyday Memories

On September 12, 2001, students reported details of their memories of the September 11 attack as well as an everyday memory that occurred in the few days preceding that event. When they were tested for the memories 1, 6, or 32 weeks later, the students' performance was highly similar for both types of memories. Over time, they reported fewer details consistent with their first reports and more details that were inconsistent.

From Jennifer M. Talarico and David C. Rubin, "Confidence, not consistency, characterizes flashbulb memories" *Psychological Science 14*, pages 445–461, copyright © 2003 the Association for Psychological Science. Reprinted by permission of Sage Publications.

Why might the different words eyewitnesses use to describe an accident affect their later recall?

vivid memories)? The same processes of reconstruction we saw earlier apply to flashbulb memories. However, people's desire to hold tight to their memories for particularly emotional events makes it quite difficult for them to consider the possibility that those memories might not be accurate. In Chapter 12, where you'll learn more about emotions themselves, you'll have another opportunity to consider the impact of moods and emotions on memory.

Let's turn now to a domain in which people's overconfidence in their memories can have negative real-world consequences. In the domain of eyewitness testimony, people are always held responsible for reporting *exactly* what happened. ◉

Eyewitness Memory A witness in a courtroom swears "to tell the truth and nothing but the truth." Throughout this chapter, however, you have seen that whether a memory is accurate or inaccurate depends on the care with which it was encoded and the match of the circumstances of encoding and retrieval. Consider the cartoon of a crowd scene you examined earlier in the chapter, in Figure 7.3. Without looking back, try to write down or think through as much as you can about the scene. Now turn back to page 178. How did you do? Was everything you recalled accurate? Because researchers understand that people may not be able to report "the truth," even when they genuinely wish to do so, they have focused a good deal of attention on the topic of *eyewitness memory*. The goal is to help the legal system discover the best methods for ensuring the accuracy of witnesses' memories.

Influential studies on eyewitness memory were carried out by **Elizabeth Loftus** (1979; Wells & Loftus, 2003) and her colleagues. The general conclusion from their research was that eyewitnesses' memories for what they had seen were quite vulnerable to distortion from *postevent information*. For example, participants in one study were shown a film of an automobile accident and were asked to estimate the speeds of the cars involved (Loftus & Palmer, 1974). However, some participants were asked, "How fast were the cars going when they smashed into each other?" while others were asked, "How fast were the cars going when they contacted each other?" *Smash* participants estimated the cars' speed to have been over 40 miles per hour; *contact* participants estimated the speed at 30 miles per hour. About a week later, all the eyewitnesses were

◉ **Watch** the **Video** *Thinking Like a Psychologist: Eyewitness Testimony* on **MyPsychLab**

Psychology in Your Life

HOW CAN YOU BENEFIT FROM THE "TESTING EFFECT"?

What strategies do you use when you want to learn important information? If you're like many students, your impulse might be to study the material as often as you can. However, a large body of research supports the existence of the *testing effect:* Students have better long-term retention of information when they take a test on the material rather than engaging in repeated study (Roediger & Butler, 2011).

Consider a project in which students read two brief science passages (Roediger & Karpicke, 2006). In the project's first phase, participants read one of the passages twice. That's the *Study, Study* condition. The participants read the second passage once and then immediately tried to recall its contents. That's the *Study, Test* condition. In the project's second phase, participants tried to recall both passages either five minutes, two days, or one week later. The figure presents the results. As you can see, when participants were tested after just five minutes, there was an advantage for repeated study. However, after either two days or one week, participants were much better off when they had engaged in study followed by a test.

Another project demonstrated the testing effect in the context of more elaborate study procedures. College undergraduates studied material from a science text (Karpicke & Blunt, 2011). In one condition, participants learned to create *concept maps* for the texts: "In concept mapping, students construct a diagram in which nodes are used to represent concepts, and links connecting the nodes represent relations among the concepts" (p. 772). You can imagine carrying out that exercise as a way to commit science concepts to memory. In another condition, participants obtained *retrieval practice:* They studied the text and then attempted to recall the information; they studied the text a second time and once again recalled it. One week later, the students returned to the laboratory to complete a short-answer test. Students who had engaged in concept mapping answered 45 percent of the questions correctly. Students who engaged in retrieval practice got 67 percent correct. That's quite a difference! (And

consider all the extra work the students carried out to create the concept maps.)

Do these studies suggest a plan of action? After you have studied material, you should give yourself a test! For *Psychology and Life*, read each chapter, take the practice exam, consult the answer key, and then ensure you know why the right answer is, in fact, the right answer. You might also ask your professor to give you more exams. Researchers carried out a project in a middle-school science classroom in which students took a series of multiple-choice quizzes across a semester (McDaniel et al., 2011). The multiple-choice questions covered a subset of the material the teacher taught. On the end-of-semester exam, students got 79 percent of the questions right for material on which they had been quizzed. They got 72 percent correct on the material for which they hadn't previously been quizzed. Just taking the quizzes (which didn't count toward their grades) gave the students a 7 percent boost on the material those quizzes covered!

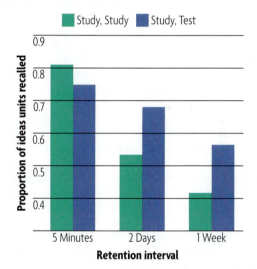

---

asked, "Did you see any broken glass?" In fact, no broken glass had appeared in the film. However, about a third of the *smash* participants reported that there had been glass, whereas only 14 percent of the *contact* eyewitnesses did so. Thus postevent information had a substantial effect on what eyewitnesses reported they had experienced.

This experiment represents what is probably the real-life experience of most eyewitnesses: After the events, they have a lot of opportunities to acquire new information that can interact with their original memories. In fact, Loftus and her colleagues demonstrated that participants often succumb to a *misinformation effect* (Frenda et al., 2011). For example, in

one study participants watched a slide show of a traffic accident. They were then asked a series of questions. For half of the participants, one question was, "Did another car pass the red Datsun while it was stopped at the stop sign?" For the other half, the question read, "Did another car pass the red Datsun while it was stopped at the yield sign?" The original slide show displayed a stop sign. Still, when participants were asked to recognize the original slide between options with a stop sign or a yield sign, those who had been asked about the stop sign were 75 percent correct, whereas those who had been asked about a yield sign were only 41 percent correct (Loftus et al., 1978). That's a large impact of misinformation.

Research on eyewitness memory has evolved to capture a broader range of the experiences of real eyewitnesses. For example, researchers have turned their attention to circumstances in which witnesses discuss events with other people who saw the same events, co-witnesses, before they provide testimony. Survey data confirm the importance of this question: In one sample, 86 percent of the individuals who had witnessed serious events such as physical assault and property vandalism had discussed the events with a co-witness (Paterson & Kemp, 2006). When people spoke to the police about the events, they were discouraged only 14 percent of the time from having such conversations. This is problematic because co-witnesses may serve as a source of information that taints the witnesses' own memories.

A team of researchers sought to demonstrate that people's memory performance can be harmed if they discuss events with co-witnesses (Paterson et al., 2011). Each participant watched one of two versions of a robbery video. The two versions differed in several details (for example, the thief called himself Joe versus James in the two versions). After watching a video, the participants were paired up to discuss what they'd seen. In some pairs, both participants had watched the same video. In other pairs, the participants had watched contrasting videos. That different-video condition should increase the probability that participants will acquire misinformation from their co-witness. One week later, the participants were interviewed to elicit their memories for the robbery. At the end of the interview, the participants signed transcripts of their statements to indicate that they were "accurate and complete" (p. 46). The researchers compared the participants' statements to the original videos they had watched. Of the participants in the different-video condition, 42 percent reported misinformation compared to only 19 percent in the same-video condition.

The interviewer actually warned some participants that their co-witness might have seen a slightly different video. However, that warning had almost no impact on the participants' ability to exclude misinformation from their statements. This experiment suggests that, after discussing events with co-witnesses, people may find it difficult to isolate their own eyewitness memories from what they have learned from others. Such results are important because when people testify in court, they swear to report just information they obtained from their own experience of the events.

We have now considered several important features of the encoding, storage, and retrieval of information. The final section of the chapter discusses the brain bases of these memory functions.

Stop *and* Review

① What is the relationship between categories and concepts?
② What claim is made by the exemplar theory of categorization?
③ On Frederic Bartlett's account, what three processes create distortions in reconstructive memory?

④ How did Elizabeth Loftus and her colleagues demonstrate misinformation effects?

CRITICAL THINKING Recall the study that investigated the typicality of fish. Why might the researchers have used two groups from the same geographical region?

✓— **Study** and **Review** on **MyPsychLab**

BIOLOGICAL ASPECTS OF MEMORY

The time has come, once again, for you to recall the number you committed to memory at the beginning of the chapter. Can you still remember it? What was the point of this exercise? Think for a minute about biological aspects of your ability to look at an arbitrary piece of information and commit it instantly to memory. How can you do that? To encode a memory requires that you instantly change something inside your brain. If you wish to retain that memory for at least the length of a chapter, the change must have the potential to become permanent. Have you ever wondered how memory storage is possible? My excuse for having you recall an arbitrary number was so that I could ask you to reflect on how remarkable the biology of memory really is. Let's take a closer look inside the brain.

Searching for the Engram

Let's consider your memory for the number 51 or, more specifically, your memory that the number 51 was the number you tried to remember. How could we determine where in your brain that memory resides? **Karl Lashley** (1929, 1950), who performed pioneering work on the anatomy of memory, referred to this question as the search for the **engram,** the physical memory representation. Lashley trained rats to learn mazes, removed varying-size portions of their cortexes, and then retested their memories for the mazes. Lashley found that memory impairment from brain lesioning was proportional to the amount of tissue removed. The impairment grew worse as more of the cortex was damaged. However, memory was not affected by *where* in the cortex the tissue was removed. Lashley concluded that the elusive engram did not exist in any localized regions but was widely distributed throughout the entire cortex.

Perhaps Lashley could not localize the engram partly because of the variety of types of memories that are called into play even in an apparently simple situation. Maze learning, in fact, involves complex interactions of spatial, visual, and olfactory signals. Neuroscientists now believe that memory for complex sets of information is distributed across many neural systems, even though discrete types of knowledge are separately processed and localized in limited regions of the brain (Nadel & Hardt, 2011).

Five major brain structures are involved in memory:

- The *cerebellum,* essential for procedural memory, memories acquired by repetition, and classically conditioned responses

....

engram The physical memory trace for information in the brain.

FIGURE 7.17 Brain Structures Involved in Memory

This simplified diagram shows some of the main structures of the brain that are involved in the formation, storage, and retrieval of memories.

Thalamus

Striatum

Prefrontal cortex

Amygdala

Cerebellum

Brain stem

Hippocampus

- The *striatum,* a complex of structures in the forebrain; the likely basis for habit formation and for stimulus response connections
- The *cerebral cortex,* responsible for sensory memories and associations between sensations
- The *hippocampus,* largely responsible for declarative memory of facts, dates, and names, and the consolidation of spatial memories
- The *amygdala,* which plays a critical role in the formation and retrieval of memories with emotional significance

Other parts of the brain, such as the thalamus, the basal forebrain, and the prefrontal cortex, are involved also as way stations for the formation of particular types of memories (see **Figure 7.17**).

Chapter 3 focused directly on brain anatomy. Here, let's take a look at the methods that neuroscientists use to draw conclusions about the role of specific brain structures for memory. This section examines two types of research. First, we consider the insights generated by "experiments of nature"—circumstances in which individuals who have suffered brain damage volunteer to further memory research. Second, we reflect on the ways in which researchers are applying new brain-imaging techniques to improve their understanding of memory processes in the brain.

Memory Disorders

In 1960, Nick A., a young Air Force radar technician, experienced a freak injury that permanently changed his life. Nick had been sitting at his desk while his roommate played with a miniature fencing foil. Then, suddenly, Nick stood up and turned around—just as his buddy happened to lunge with the sword. The foil pierced Nick's right nostril and continued to cut into the left side of his brain. The accident left Nick seriously disoriented. His worst problem was **amnesia,** the failure of memory over a prolonged period. Because of Nick's amnesia, he forgets many events immediately after they happen. After he reads a few paragraphs of writing, the first sentences slip

from his memory. He cannot remember the plot of a television show unless, during commercials, he actively thinks about and rehearses what he was just watching.

The particular type of amnesia from which Nick suffers is called **anterograde amnesia.** This means that Nick can no longer form explicit memories for events that occur after the time at which he suffered physical damage. One consequence of chronic alcoholism is *Korsakoff's syndrome,* for which anterograde amnesia is a prominent symptom. Other patients suffer from **retrograde amnesia.** In those cases, brain damage prevents access to memories that preceded the moment of injury. If you've ever had the misfortune of receiving a sharp blow to the head (during, for example, a car crash), you're likely to have experienced retrograde amnesia for the events leading up to the accident. ◉

Researchers are grateful to patients like Nick for allowing themselves to be studied as "experiments of nature." By relating the locus of brain injuries like Nick's to patterns of performance deficit, researchers have begun to understand the mapping between the types of memories reviewed in this chapter and regions of the brain (Squire & Wixted, 2011). Nick still remembers how to do things—his procedural knowledge appears to be intact even in the absence of declarative knowledge. So, for example, he remembers how to mix, stir, and bake the ingredients in a recipe, but he forgets what the ingredients are.

The selective impairment of explicit memory of the sort demonstrated by Nick is one of the major facts of the biology of memory: There is abundant evidence to support the conclusion

....

◉ **Watch** the **Video** *Special Topics: When Memory Fails* on **MyPsychLab**

amnesia A failure of memory caused by physical injury, disease, drug use, or psychological trauma.

anterograde amnesia An inability to form explicit memories for events that occur after the time of physical damage to the brain.

retrograde amnesia An inability to retrieve memories from the time before physical damage to the brain.

that different brain regions underlie explicit and implicit uses of memory (Voss & Paller, 2008). However, researchers continue to explore which exact functions are subsumed by each brain area.

A team of researchers tested people who had experienced damage to the hippocampus (Aly et al., 2010). The participants studied colored drawings of faces and lists of words. Then, they completed recognition memory tests for each type of stimulus. The participants indicated their recognition on a scale ranging from 1 (certain it is new) to 6 (certain it is old). The participants' recognition performance was much more impaired for words than for faces. The researchers wanted to understand that result, so that they could further pinpoint the hippocampus's role in recognition memory. Their analysis focused on the distinction between recollection and familiarity. Suppose you recognize a woman walking by you. If you have a concrete sense of how you know the woman, that's recollection. If you know that you know the woman, but you can't recall how or why, that's familiarity. The researchers suggested that faces are more likely to create experiences of familiarity than are words. On that view, the reason that the participants with hippocampal damage had greater recognition memory for faces than for words is because the hippocampus is necessary for recollection but not for familiarity. The data supported that hypothesis for the hippocampus's particular function.

This experiment demonstrates how research on people who have amnesia can provide a deeper understanding of the way that precise memory functions are distributed to particular brain structures.

The cases in which people lose the ability to recall past information or acquire new information are the most dramatic forms of memory disorders. However, people experience less extensive memory disruptions as a result of injury or disease. *Alzheimer's disease* is the most common disease that affects memory function. The disease affects about 13 percent of Americans ages 65 and older; it affects 43 percent of Americans 85 and older (Alzheimer's Association, 2011). In the earliest stages of Alzheimer's disease, people often have difficulty retaining new information. As the disease progresses, the memory loss becomes much more extensive. In Chapter 10, we will see that human aging is accompanied by some ordinary changes in memory function. To make a timely diagnosis of Alzheimer's disease, doctors must determine whether older adults' memory impairments are something more than ordinary change. The symptoms of Alzheimer's disease were first described in 1906 by the German psychiatrist Alois Alzheimer. In those earliest investigations, Alzheimer noted that the brains of individuals who had died from the disease contained unusual tangles of neural tissue and sticky deposits called plaques. Still, Alzheimer could not determine whether those brain changes were the cause of the disease or its products. Contemporary researchers have provided evidence that plaques themselves cause the brain to deteriorate (Hardy & Selkoe, 2002). Researchers study individuals who are at high risk for Alzheimer's disease to understand the biological basis for successive changes in memory function (Murphy et al., 2008). ◉

Researchers often seek out people who have damage in particular brain regions to test specific theories about the biology

◉ **Watch** the **Video** *Memory Hazards and What Happens with Alzheimer's* on **MyPsychLab**

of memory processes. Recall, for example, the discussion of metamemory which revealed that people's feeling-of-knowing judgments are often reasonably accurate. Researchers suggested that regions of the prefrontal cortex (PFC) (see Figure 7.17) provide the brain basis for those judgments (Modirrousta & Fellows, 2008). To test that claim, the researchers identified five individuals who had damage in those PFC regions. These individuals with PFC damage and matched controls all tried to learn new associations between faces and names. Even when the two participant groups performed equally well on a recognition test, the individuals with PFC damage were consistently less accurate on their feeling-of-knowing judgments. This experiment supports the claim that the prefrontal cortex plays a role in metamemory. It also provides an example of the value of research that examines more subtle forms of memory disorder.

Brain Imaging

Psychologists have gained a great deal of knowledge about the relationship between anatomy and memory from the amnesic patients who generously serve as participants in these experiments. However, the advent of brain-imaging techniques has enabled researchers to study memory processes in individuals without brain damage. (You may want to review the section on imaging techniques in Chapter 3.) For example, using positron emission tomography (PET), Endel Tulving and his colleagues (Habib et al., 2003) have identified a difference in activation between the two brain hemispheres in the encoding and retrieval of episodic information. Their studies parallel standard memory studies, except that the participants' cerebral blood flow is monitored through PET scans during encoding or retrieval. As you can see in **Figure 7.18** these researchers discovered

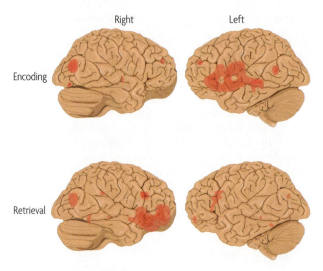

FIGURE 7.18 Brain Activity for Encoding and Retrieval

When this set of brain regions was particularly active at time of encoding, people were more likely to remember details from their viewing of a sitcom. The areas are the right temporal pole (TP), superior temporal gyrus (STG), anterior parahippocampal cortex (aPHG), posterior parahippocampal gyrus (pPHG), and temporal parietal junction (TPJ). RH and LH refer to the right and left hemispheres.

Reprinted from *Trends in Cognitive Sciences* 7(6), Reza Habib, Lars Nyberg, Endel Tulving, "Hemispheric asymmetries of memory: The HERA model revisited," pp 241–245, © 2003, with permission from Elsevier.

FIGURE 7.19 Brain Regions That Predict Successful Memory

When this set of brain regions was particularly active at time of encoding, people were more likely to remember details from their viewing of a sitcom. The areas are the right temporal pole (TP), superior temporal gyrus (STG), anterior parahippocampal cortex (aPHG), posterior parahippocampal gyrus (pPHG), and temporal parietal junction (TPJ). RH and LH refer to the right and left hemispheres.

disproportionately high brain activity in the left prefrontal cortex for encoding of episodic information and in the right prefrontal cortex for retrieval of episodic information. Thus the processes show some anatomical distinctions in addition to the conceptual distinctions made by cognitive psychologists.

Research with functional magnetic resonance imaging (fMRI) has also provided remarkable detail about the way that memory operations are distributed in the brain. For example, studies with fMRI have begun to identify the specific brain regions that are activated when new memories are formed. Consider a study in which participants underwent fMRI scans while watching an episode of the sitcom "Curb Your Enthusiasm" that was new to them (Hasson et al., 2008). Over the course of 27 minutes, the main character engaged in a series of events such as attending a dinner party and arguing with friends. Three weeks later, the participants returned to the laboratory to take a 77-question memory test on the episode. Each participant remembered some details but not others. The researchers analyzed the fMRI data to identify those brain regions that were particularly active when information was successfully encoded. As shown in **Figure 7.19**, several brain regions emerged from that analysis. Unless you pursue studies in cognitive neuroscience, you needn't worry why it is activity in exactly this set of structures that predicts later recall. Figure 7.19 should suggest to you that researchers are making progress toward the goal of witnessing the birth and consolidation of new memories.

Brain scans also provide information about how memory processes unfold in time. If you try to recall the capital of France, the answer might present itself to you (or not) rather quickly. However, if you try to recall what happened the first time you met someone from France, you'll likely need more time to retrieve and elaborate that memory. For those sorts of rich autobiographical memories, the role of different regions of the brain changes over time.

A team of researchers asked participants to retrieve autobiographical memories while undergoing fMRI scans (Daselaar et al., 2008). Participants heard a cue word, such as tree, and attempted to bring a specific event to mind that was associated with the word. Participants pushed a button on a response box to indicate when they had retrieved a memory. Because this process unfolded over several seconds,

the researchers were able to determine how different brain areas became involved in different aspects of autobiographical memory. For example, early on, structures like the hippocampus were active as participants searched their episodic memories. As participants elaborated their memories, activity in other areas became more prominent. For example, participants' visual cortex became more active as they enriched their memories with visual images. When the visual cortex was particularly active, participants reported the strongest sense that they were actually reliving the memory.

Take a moment to retrieve your own memory in response to *tree*. Do you feel your recollection of the event become more elaborate over time? The fMRI scans provide a moment-by-moment account of where and how that elaboration occurs in your brain.

The results from imaging studies illustrate why researchers draw from different disciplines in the quest for a full understanding of memory processes. Classic memory research provides the fuel for neuropsychologists' detection of specialized brain structures. At the same time, the realities of physiology constrain psychologists' theories of the mechanisms of encoding, storage, and retrieval. Through shared effort, scientists in several fields of research provide great insight into the operation of memory processes.

Stop *and* Review

① What did Karl Lashley conclude about the location of the engram?

② What has been learned about the impairment of implicit memory for individuals with amnesia?

③ What have PET studies indicated about the brain bases of encoding and retrieval of episodic information?

CRITICAL THINKING Recall the study that looked at memory for sitcom details. Why was it important that participants hadn't seen the episode before?

✓•—**Study** and **Review** on **MyPsychLab**

Recapping Main Points

What Is Memory?

- Cognitive psychologists study memory as a type of information processing.
- Memories involving conscious effort are explicit. Unconscious memories are implicit.
- Declarative memory is memory for facts; procedural memory is memory for how to perform skills.
- Memory is often viewed as a three-stage process of encoding, storage, and retrieval.

Memory Use for the Short Term

- Iconic memory has large capacity but very short duration.
- Short-term memory (STM) has a limited capacity and lasts only briefly without rehearsal.
- Maintenance rehearsal can extend the presence of material in STM indefinitely.
- STM capacity can be increased by chunking unrelated items into meaningful groups.
- The broader concept of working memory includes STM.
- The four components of working memory provide the resources for moment-by-moment experiences of the world.

Long-Term Memory: Encoding and Retrieval

- Long-term memory (LTM) constitutes your total knowledge of the world and of yourself. It is nearly unlimited in capacity.
- Your ability to remember information relies on the match between circumstances of encoding and retrieval.
- Retrieval cues allow you to access information in LTM.
- Episodic memory is concerned with memory for events that have been personally experienced. Semantic memory is memory for the basic meaning of words and concepts.
- Similarity in context between learning and retrieval aids retrieval.
- The serial position curve is explained by distinctiveness in context.
- Information processed more deeply is typically remembered better.

- For implicit memories, it is important that the processes of encoding and retrieval be similar.
- Ebbinghaus studied the time course of forgetting.
- Interference occurs when retrieval cues do not lead uniquely to specific memories.
- Memory performance can be improved through elaborative rehearsal and mnemonics.
- In general, feelings-of-knowing accurately predict the availability of information in memory.

Structures in Long-Term Memory

- Concepts are the memory building blocks of thinking. They are formed when memory processes gather together classes of objects or ideas with common properties.
- Concepts are often organized in hierarchies, ranging from general, to basic level, to specific.
- Schemas are more complex cognitive clusters.
- All these memory structures are used to provide expectations and a context for interpreting new information.
- Remembering is not simply recording but is a constructive process.
- People encode flashbulb memories in response to events with great emotional significance, but those memories may not be more accurate than everyday memories.
- New information can bias recall, making eyewitness memory unreliable when contaminated by postevent input.

Biological Aspects of Memory

- Difference brain structures (including the hippocampus, the amygdala, the cerebellum, the striatum, and the cerebral cortex) have been shown to be involved in different types of memories.
- Experiments with individuals with memory disorders have helped investigators understand how different types of memories are acquired and represented in the brain.
- Brain-imaging techniques have extended knowledge about the brain bases of memory encoding and retrieval.

KEY TERMS

amnesia (p. 201)
anterograde amnesia (p. 201)
basic level (p. 194)
chunking (p. 180)
concept (p. 193)
declarative memory (p. 175)
elaborative rehearsal (p. 190)
encoding (p. 176)
encoding specificity (p. 184)
engram (p. 200)
episodic memory (p. 183)
exemplar (p. 195)
explicit use of memory (p. 174)
flashbulb memory (p. 197)

iconic memory (p. 177)
implicit use of memory (p. 174)
levels-of-processing theory (p. 187)
long-term memory (LTM) (p. 182)
memory (p. 174)
metamemory (p. 190)
mnemonic (p. 190)
primacy effect (p. 185)
priming (p. 187)
proactive interference (p. 189)
procedural memory (p. 175)
prototype (p. 195)
recall (p. 183)
recency effect (p. 185)

recognition (p. 183)
reconstructive memory (p. 196)
retrieval (p. 176)
retrieval cue (p. 182)
retroactive interference (p. 189)
retrograde amnesia (p. 201)
schema (p. 194)
semantic memory (p. 184)
serial position effect (p. 185)
short-term memory (STM) (p. 179)
storage (p. 176)
temporal distinctiveness (p. 185)
transfer-appropriate processing (p. 187)
working memory (p. 181)

1. At her school's talent show, Noa answers questions about politics while spinning basketballs on her fingers. The question and answering mostly require _____ memory, whereas the ball spinning mostly requires _____ memory.
   a. implicit; procedural
   b. declarative; procedural
   c. procedural; declarative
   d. implicit; declarative

2. To demonstrate the capacity of iconic memory, George Sperling showed that participants performed better with the _____ procedure.
   a. whole-report
   b. procedural memory
   c. partial-report
   d. implicit memory

3. Mark looks a number up in a phone book, but he forgets it before he has a chance to make the call. It sounds like Mark should have spent more effort on
   a. rehearsal.
   b. chunking.
   c. memory span.
   d. iconic memory.

4. Which of these is *not* a component of working memory?
   a. the iconic memory buffer
   b. the phonological loop
   c. the central executive
   d. the visuospatial sketchpad

5. Because of the usefulness of the retrieval cues, _____ is usually easier than _____.
   a. recall; episodic memory
   b. recognition; recall
   c. semantic memory; recognition
   d. recall; recognition

6. After Meghan meets a group of people, she can remember the name of only the last person she met. This is an example of a(n) _____ effect.
   a. primacy
   b. temporal distinctiveness
   c. encoding specificity
   d. recency

7. Consider the word *Mississippi*. Which of these questions asks you to process that word at the deepest level of processing?
   a. How many times does the letter *s* appear in the word?
   b. Is this word the name of a river?
   c. How many syllables does the word have?
   d. What is the word's first letter?

8. You've just memorized a list of nonsense words. You are going to try to recall the words every day for the next 30 days (without looking back at the list). You would expect to show the most forgetting between
   a. day 1 and day 2.
   b. day 3 and day 5.
   c. day 5 and day 10.
   d. day 10 and day 30.

9. Pavel needs to learn the order of the planets with respect to their distance from the sun. To begin, he imagines Mercury as a giant bun and Venus shaped like a shoe. It sounds like Pavel is using
   a. the method of loci.
   b. the peg-word method.
   c. metamemory.
   d. iconic memory.

10. At the start of each exam, Sarah reads over the full set of questions to determine which ones she feels pretty sure she'll get right. To make these judgments, Sarah is using
    a. encoding specificity.
    b. mnemonics.
    c. elaborative rehearsal.
    d. metamemory.

11. When you enter a restaurant to enjoy a meal, you'll probably put a memory structure known as a(n)_____ to good use.
    a. script
    b. exemplar
    c. prototype
    d. chunk

12. Your professor wants to give you advice based on the "testing effect." What is he likely to say?
    a. Quiz yourself after you finish reading each chapter!
    b. Study material from the middle of the chapter most carefully!
    c. Use your judgments-of-learning to decide what to study more!
    d. Try to study in the same room in which you're going to take the test!

13. Karl Lashley carried out his search for the engram by training rats on mazes and then removing different amounts of the
    a. cerebellum.
    b. cortex.
    c. striatum.
    d. amygdala.

14. Alois Alzheimer was able to demonstrate that
    a. plaques in the brain caused Alzheimer's disease.
    b. amyloid β-peptide caused Alzheimer's disease.
    c. people who died of Alzheimer's disease had plaques in their brains.
    d. plaques in the brain could be used to prevent Alzheimer's disease.

15. If you were asked to identify the brain bases of the encoding and retrieval of episodic memories, you should point to the
    a. striatum.
    b. cerebellum.
    c. amygdala.
    d. prefrontal cortex.

ESSAY QUESTIONS

1. What are the relationships among encoding, storage, and retrieval?

2. What are the primary functions of working memory?

3. In what ways have brain-imaging techniques helped confirm some of the theoretical distinctions made by memory researchers?

8

Cognitive Processes

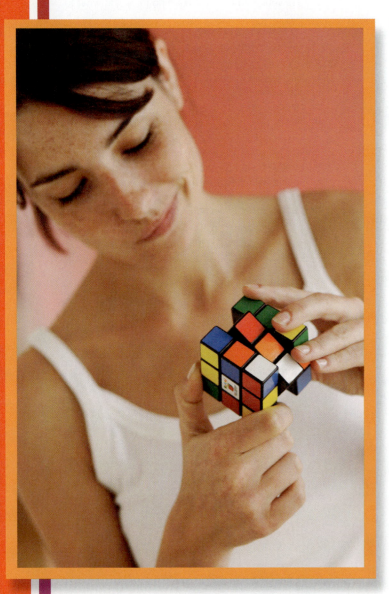

It is midnight. There's a knock on your door. When you answer, no one is there, but you see an envelope on the floor. Inside the envelope is a single sheet of paper with a handwritten message: "The cat is on the mat." What do you make of this?

You must now begin to engage a variety of cognitive processes. You will need language processes to put together some basic meanings for the words, but what then? Can you find any episode in memory to which these words are relevant? (Recall that Chapter 7 discussed memory as a type of cognitive processing.) If you can't, you'll have to give other types of thought to the matter. Is the message a code? What kind of code? Whom do you know who might encode a message? Does the fate of civilization rest in your hands?

Perhaps this is getting a bit carried away, but I want to make plain to you what kinds of activities count as **cognitive processes** and why they might interest you. The capacity to use language and to think in abstract ways has often been cited as the essence of the human experience. You tend to take cognition for granted because it's an activity you do continually during your waking hours. Even so, when a carefully crafted speech wins your vote or when you read a detective story in which the sleuth combines a few scraps of apparently trivial clues into a brilliant solution to a crime, you are forced to acknowledge the intellectual triumph of cognitive processes. 👁

Cognition is a general term for all forms of knowing: As shown in **Figure 8.1**, the study of cognition is the study of your mental life. (Note that Chapters 4 and 7 already discussed some of the topics shown in Figure 8.1.) Cognition includes both contents and processes. The *contents* of cognition are *what* you know—concepts, facts, propositions, rules, and memories: "A dog is a mammal." "A red light means stop." "I first left home at age 18." Cognitive *processes* are *how* you manipulate

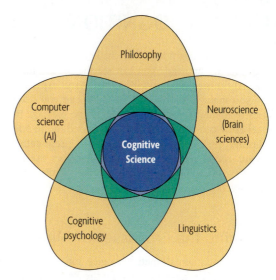

FIGURE 8.2 The Domain of Cognitive Science
The domain of cognitive science occupies the intersection of philosophy, neuroscience, linguistics, cognitive psychology, and computer science (artificial intelligence[AI]).

these mental contents—in ways that enable you to interpret the world around you and to find creative solutions to your life's dilemmas.

Within psychology, the study of cognition is carried out by researchers in the field of **cognitive psychology.** Over the past three decades, the field of cognitive psychology has been supplemented by the interdisciplinary field of **cognitive science** (see **Figure 8.2**). Cognitive science focuses the collected knowledge of several academic specialties on the same theoretical issues. It benefits the practitioners of each of these fields to share their data and insights. You saw this cognitive science philosophy at work when Chapter 7 described how studies of the biology of memory can be used to limit and refine theories of memory processes. Many of the theories we consider in this chapter have similarly been shaped through the interactions of researchers from a number of disciplinary perspectives.

This study of cognition will begin with a brief description of the ways in which researchers try to measure the inner, private processes involved in cognitive functioning. Then we'll turn to topics in cognitive psychology that generate much basic research and practical application: language use, visual cognition, problem solving, reasoning, judging, and decision making.

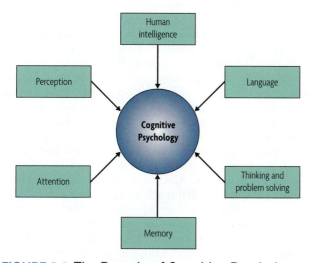

FIGURE 8.1 The Domain of Cognitive Psychology
Cognitive psychologists study higher mental functions, with particular emphasis on the ways in which people acquire knowledge and use it to shape and understand their experiences in the world.

From Solso, Robert L., *Cognitive Psychology*, 3rd Edition, © 1991. Printed and electronically reproduced by permission of Pearson Education Inc., Upper Saddle River, New Jersey.

....

👁 **Watch** the **Video** *The Big Picture: I Am, Therefore I Think* on **MyPsychLab**

cognitive process One of the higher mental processes, such as perception, memory, language, problem solving, and abstract thinking.

cognition Processes of knowing, including attending, remembering, and reasoning; also the content of the processes, such as concepts and memories.

cognitive psychology The study of higher mental processes such as attention, language use, memory, perception, problem solving, and thinking.

cognitive science The interdisciplinary field of study of systems and processes that manipulate information.

STUDYING COGNITION

How can you study cognition? The challenge, of course, is that it goes on inside the head. You can see the input—for example, in a text message that says "Call me"—and experience the output—you make a phone call—but how can you determine the series of mental steps that connected the message to your response? How can you reveal what happened in the middle—the cognitive processes and the mental representations on which your action relies? This section describes the types of logical analyses that have made possible the scientific study of cognitive psychology.

Discovering the Processes of Mind

One of the fundamental methodologies for studying mental processes was devised, in 1868, by the Dutch physiologist **F. C. Donders** (1818–1889). To study the "speed of mental processes," Donders invented a series of experimental tasks that he believed were differentiated by the mental steps involved for successful performance (Brysbaert & Rastle, 2009). **Table 8.1** provides a paper-and-pencil experiment that follows Donders's logic. Before reading on, please take a moment to complete each task.

How long did you take to do task 1? Suppose you wanted to give a list of the steps you carried out to perform the task. It might look something like this:

a. Determine whether a character is a capital letter or a lowercase letter.
b. If it is a capital letter, draw a *C* on top.

How long did you take for task 2? Students often take an additional half minute or more beyond their time for task 1.

Table 8.1 • Donders's Analysis of Mental Processes

Note how long (in seconds) it takes you to complete each of these three tasks. Try to complete each task accurately, but as quickly as possible.

Task 1: Draw a *C* on top of all the capitalized letters:
TO Be, oR noT To BE: tHAT Is thE qUestioN:
WhETher 'Tis noBlEr In tHE MINd tO SuFfER
tHe SLings AnD ARroWS Of OUtrAgeOUs forTUNe,
or To TAke ARmS agaINST a sEa Of tROUBleS,
AnD by oPPOsinG END theM. TIME: _____

Task 2: Draw a *V* on top of the capitalized vowels and a *C* on top of the capitalized consonants:
TO Be, oR noT To BE: tHAT Is thE qUestioN:
WhETher 'Tis noBlEr In tHE MINd tO SuFfER
tHe SLings AnD ARroWS Of OUtrAgeOUs forTUNe,
or To TAke ARmS agaINST a sEa Of tROUBleS,
AnD by oPPOsinG END theM. TIME: _____

Task 3: Draw a *V* on top of all the capitalized letters:
TO Be, oR noT To BE: tHAT Is thE qUestioN:
WhETher 'Tis noBlEr In tHE MINd tO SuFfER
tHe SLings AnD ARroWS Of OUtrAgeOUs forTUNe,
or To TAke ARmS agaINST a sEa Of tROUBleS,
AnD by oPPOsinG END theM. TIME: _____

You can understand why, once you appreciate the necessary steps:

a. Determine whether a character is a capital letter or a lowercase letter.
b. Determine whether each capital letter is a vowel or a consonant.
c. If it is a consonant, draw a *C* on top. If it is a vowel, draw a *V*.

Thus, going from task 1 to task 2, you add the two mental steps of *stimulus categorization* (vowel or consonant?) and *response selection* (draw a *C* or draw a *V*). Task 1 requires one stimulus categorization step. Task 2 requires two such categorizations. Task 2 also requires selecting between two responses. Because task 2 requires you to do everything you did for task 1 and more, it takes you more time. That was Donders's fundamental insight: Extra mental steps will often result in more time to perform a task.

You may be wondering why task 3 is there. This is a necessary procedural control for the experiment. It's important to ensure that the time difference between tasks 1 and 2 does not stem from the fact that it takes much longer to draw *V*s than to draw *C*s. Task 3 should still be much swifter than task 2. Was it?

Researchers still follow Donders's basic logic. They frequently use *reaction time*—the amount of time it takes experimental participants to perform particular tasks—as a way of testing specific accounts of how some cognitive process is carried out. Donders's basic premise that extra mental steps will result in extra time is still fundamental to a great deal of cognitive psychological research. Let's see how this successful idea has been developed over the past 140 years.

Mental Processes and Mental Resources

When cognitive psychologists break down high-level activities, like language use or problem solving, into their component processes, they often act as if they are playing a game with blocks. Each block represents a different component that must be carried out. The goal is to determine the shape and size of each block and to see how the blocks fit together to form the whole activity. For the Donders tasks, you saw that the blocks can be laid out in a row (see **Figure 8.3**, part A). Each step comes directly after another. The block metaphor allows you to see that we could also stack the blocks so more than one process occurs simultaneously (part B). These two pictures illustrate the distinction between **serial** and **parallel processes.** Processes are *serial* when they take place one after the other. Suppose you're in a restaurant and you need to decide what to order. You focus on entries one at a time and then judge whether they qualify as "yes," "no," or "maybe." For each entry, your judgment processes follow your reading processes. Processes are *parallel* when they overlap in time. When it comes time to place your order, the language processes that enable you to understand the waiter's question ("What can I get for you?") are likely to operate at the same time as the processes that allow you to formulate your reply ("I'd like the osso buco"). That's why you're ready to respond as soon as the waiter finishes his question. ●

....

● **Watch** the **Video** *The Basics: The Mind is What the Brain Does* on **MyPsychLab**

serial processes Two or more mental processes that are carried out in order, one after the other.

parallel processes Two or more mental processes that are carried out simultaneously.

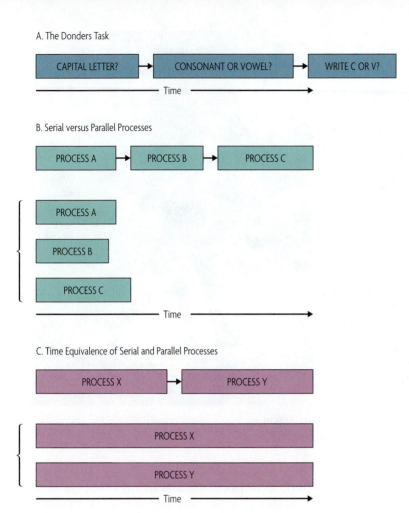

A. The Donders Task

| CAPITAL LETTER? | → | CONSONANT OR VOWEL? | → | WRITE C OR V? |

————— Time —————

B. Serial versus Parallel Processes

| PROCESS A | → | PROCESS B | → | PROCESS C |

| PROCESS A |

| PROCESS B |

| PROCESS C |

————— Time —————

C. Time Equivalence of Serial and Parallel Processes

| PROCESS X | → | PROCESS Y |

| PROCESS X |

| PROCESS Y |

————— Time —————

FIGURE 8.3 Breaking Down High-Level Cognitive Activities

Cognitive psychologists attempt to determine the identity and organization of the mental processes that are the building blocks of high-level cognitive activities.

(A) This version of the Donders task requires that at least three processes be carried out one after the other.

(B) Some processes are carried out serially, in sequence; others are carried out in parallel, all at the same time.

(C) The time taken to perform a task does not always allow researchers to conclude whether serial or parallel processes were used.

Cognitive psychologists often use reaction times to determine whether processes are carried out in parallel or serially. However, the examples in part C of Figure 8.3 should convince you that this is a tricky business. Imagine that we have a task that we believe can be broken down into two processes, *X* and *Y*. If the only information we have is the total time needed to complete the process, we can never be sure if processes *X* and *Y* happen side by side or one after the other. Much of the challenge of research in cognitive psychology is to invent task circumstances that allow the experimenter to determine which of many possible configurations of blocks is correct. In task 2 of the exercise you just did, we could be reasonably certain that the processes were serial because some activities logically required others. For example, you couldn't execute your response (prepare to draw a *C* or a *V*) until you had determined what the response might be.

In many cases, theorists try to determine if processes are serial or parallel by assessing the extent to which the processes place demands on *mental resources*. Suppose, for example, you are walking to class with a friend. Ordinarily, it should be easy for you to walk a straight path at the same time you carry on a conversation—your navigation processes and your language processes can go on in parallel. But what would happen if you suddenly get to a patch of sidewalk that's dotted with puddles? As you pick your way among the puddles, you may have to stop talking. Now your navigation processes require extra resources for planning, and your language processes are momentarily squeezed out.

A key assumption in this example is that you have *limited* processing resources that must be spread over different mental tasks (Daffner et al., 2011; Wyble et al., 2011). Your *attentional processes* are responsible for distributing these resources. Chapter 4 discussed attention as the set of processes that allow you to select, for particular scrutiny, some small subset of available perceptual information. The use of *attention* here preserves the idea of selectivity. The decision now, however, concerns which mental processes will be selected as the recipients of processing resources. ◉►

There's one more complication to add: Not all processes put the same demands on resources. Researchers define a dimension that goes from processes that are *controlled* to those that are *automatic* (Shiffrin & Schneider, 1977). **Controlled processes** require attention; **automatic processes** generally do not. It is often difficult to carry out more than one controlled process at a time because they require more resources; automatic processes can often be performed alongside other tasks without interference.

Let's consider an example of an automatic process. To get started, take a moment to carry out the task in **Table 8.2** on page 210. Make

··

◉► **Simulate** the **Experiment** *Selective Attention* on **MyPsychLab**

controlled process Process that requires attention; it is often difficult to carry out more than one controlled process at a time.

automatic process Process that does not require attention; it can often be performed along with other tasks without interference.

Table 8.2 • Size Judgments

Your task is to circle the number that is *physically* larger in each pair. Try to judge which list is harder.

List A			
61—67	22—28	25—29	47—41
68—64	27—23	43—49	44—48
List B			
47—41	61—67	27—23	25—29
22—28	68—64	43—49	44—48

sure you circle the number that is *physically* larger. Did you find one list to be somewhat harder?

Featured Study

Experimental participants were asked to make the types of judgments illustrated in Table 8.2. If you look closely at the table, you'll see that the items on List A present a mismatch between physical size and the magnitude of each number (i.e., 61 is physically larger but it's a number of smaller magnitude than 67). On List B, there is a match between the physical size and the magnitude of the numbers. If you worked your way through Table 8.2, you won't be surprised to learn that participants took longer to make size judgments when there was a mismatch (List A) than when there was a match (List B) (Ganor-Stern et al., 2007). But why should the magnitude of the numbers matter for a judgment of physical size? The researchers suggested that when you look at 61 or 67 you can't help but think of the quantity it represents—even when the quantity, in this case, impairs performance on the task you've been asked to carry out. That is, you automatically access the meaning of a number, even when you don't need (or want) to do so.

This number task illustrates that automatic processes rely heavily on the efficient use of memory (Barrett et al., 2004). When you see 61, 67, and so on, your memory processes swiftly provide information about quantity. The number task also illustrates the way in which tasks that first involved controlled processes can become automatic with sufficient practice. You probably remember, as a small child, having to learn how numbers work. Now, the association between numbers and the quantities they represent has become so automatic, you can't shut off the association.

Let's apply this knowledge of controlled and automatic processes back to the situation of walking and talking. When you are walking a straight route, you feel little interference between the two activities, suggesting that maintaining your path and planning your utterances are each relatively automatic activities. The situation changes, however, when the puddles force you to choose between a greater number of options for your path. Now you must select where to go and what to say. Because you can't make both choices simultaneously, you have come up against the limits of your processing resources (Chun et al., 2011).

Why is it difficult to carry on a conversation while you are trying to avoid puddles?

You now know a lot about the logic of mental processes. To explain how complex mental tasks are carried out, theorists propose models that combine serial and parallel and controlled and automatic processes. The goal of much cognitive psychological research is to invent experiments that confirm each of the components of such models. Now that you understand some of the logic behind cognitive psychological research into mental processes, it is time to move to more specific domains in which you put cognitive processes to work. Let's begin with language use.

Stop *and* Review

① What was Donders's goal when he had participants carry out different experimental tasks?
② What is the distinction between serial and parallel processes?
③ What types of processes do not generally require attentional resources?

✓●—**Study** and **Review** on **MyPsychLab**

LANGUAGE USE

Let's return to the message you received at midnight, "The cat is on the mat." What in this situation could change so that this message immediately made sense to you? The easiest step would be to introduce appropriate background knowledge. Suppose you are a secret agent who always gets instructions in this curious fashion. You might know that "the cat" is your contact and that "on the mat" means in the wrestling arena. Off you go.

But you don't have to be a spy for "The cat is on the mat" to take on a variety of meanings:

- Suppose your cat waits on a mat by the door when she wants to be let out. When you say to your roommate, "The cat is on the mat," you use those words to communicate, "Could you get up and let the cat out?"
- Suppose your friend is worried about pulling the car out of the driveway because she's uncertain where the cat is. When you say, "The cat is on the mat," you use those words to communicate, "It's safe to pull out of the driveway."
- Suppose you are trying to have a race between your cat and your friend's dog. When you say, "The cat is on the mat," you use those words to communicate, "My cat won't race!"

These examples illustrate the difference between *sentence meaning*—the generally simple meaning of the combined words of a sentence—and *speaker's meaning*—the unlimited number of meanings a speaker can communicate by putting a sentence to good use (Grice, 1968). When psychologists study language use, they want to comprehend both the *production* and the *understanding* of speakers' meaning:

- How do speakers produce the right words to communicate the meaning they intend?
- How do listeners recover the messages the speakers wished to communicate?

This section will examine each of these questions in turn. We will also consider the evolutionary and cultural context of language use.

Language Production

Look at **Figure 8.4**. Try to formulate a few sentences about this picture. What did you think to say? Suppose now you needed to describe the person for someone who was blind. How would your description change? Does this second description seem to require more mental effort? The study of **language production** concerns both what people say—what they choose to say at a given time—and the processes they go through to produce the message. Note that language users need not produce language out loud. Language production also includes both signing and writing. For convenience, however, I will call language producers *speakers* and language understanders *listeners*. 👁

Audience Design   I asked you to imagine the different descriptions you'd give of Figure 8.4 to a sighted and a blind person as a way of getting you to think about **audience design** in language production. Each time you produce an utterance, you must have in mind the audience to whom the utterance will be directed, and what knowledge you share with members of that audience (Brennan & Hanna, 2009). For example, it won't do you the least bit of good to say, "The cat is on the mat" if your listener does not know that the cat sits on the mat only when she wishes to be let out. An overarching rule of audience design, the *cooperative principle,* was first proposed by the philosopher **H. Paul Grice** (1975). Grice phrased the cooperative principle as an instruction to speakers that they should produce utterances appropriate to the setting and meaning of the ongoing conversation. To expand on this instruction, Grice defined four maxims that cooperative speakers live by.

FIGURE 8.4 Language Production
How would you describe this person to a friend? How might your description change if your friend were blind?

Table 8.3 on page 212 presents each of those maxims, as well as an invented conversation that illustrates the effect the maxims have on moment-by-moment choices in language production. The illustrations should feel quite familiar from your own experiences in conversation. For example, when Chris says, "I loved all the bed bugs," he is expressing sarcasm. Think about your own uses of sarcasm. In almost every instance, you are violating Grice's maxim of quality (because you are saying something that you believe to be false). When you do so, you are trusting that your listener will recognize the violation. In Table 8.3, Chris assumes that Pat will recover what he means ("Yuck!") from what he said.

As you can see from Table 8.3, being a cooperative speaker depends, in large part, on having accurate expectations about what your listener is likely to know and understand. Thus you certainly wouldn't tell a friend "I'm having lunch with Alex" if you didn't have good reason to believe that your friend knew who Alex was. You also must assure yourself that, of all the Alexes your friend might know and that she knows that you know, only one would come to mind as the specific Alex you would mention in these circumstances. More formally, we can say that there must be some Alex who is prominent in the *common ground*—common knowledge—you share with your friend.

....

👁 **Watch** the **Video** *Thinking Like a Psychologist: Speaking One's Mind* on **MyPsychLab**

language production   What people say, sign, and write, as well as the processes they go through to produce these messages.

audience design   The process of shaping a message depending on the audience for which it is intended.

Table 8.3 • Grice's Maxims in Language Production

1. **Quantity:** Make your contribution as informative as is required (for the current purposes of the exchange). Do not make your contribution more informative than is required.
   The consequence for the speaker: You must try to judge how much information your audience really needs. Often this judgment will require you to assess what your listener is likely to know already.

2. **Quality:** Try to make your contribution one that is true. Do not say what you believe to be false. Do not say that for which you lack adequate evidence.
   The consequence for the speaker: When you speak, listeners will assume that you can back up your assertions with appropriate evidence. As you plan each utterance, you must have in mind the evidence on which it is based.

3. **Relation:** Be relevant.
   The consequence for the speaker: You must make sure that your listeners will see how what you are saying is relevant to what has come before. If you wish to shift the topic of conversation—so that your utterance is not directly relevant—you must make that clear.

4. **Manner:** Be perspicacious. Avoid obscurity of expression. Avoid ambiguity. Be brief. Be orderly.
   The consequence for the speaker: It is your responsibility to speak in as clear a manner as possible. Although you will inevitably make errors, as a cooperative speaker you must ensure that your listeners can understand your message.

In this conversation, can you see how Chris follows (or violates) Grice's maxims?

What Is Said	What Chris Might Be Thinking
Pat: *Have you ever been to New York City?* Chris: *I was there once in 2009.*	I don't know why Pat is asking me this question, so I probably should say a little more than just "yes."
Pat: *I'm supposed to visit, but I'm worried about being mugged.* Chris: *I think a lot of areas are safe.*	I can't say that he shouldn't worry because he won't believe me. What can I say that will sound true but make him feel OK?
Pat: *How was your hotel?* Chris: *I loved all the bed bugs.*	I'm counting on Pat to conclude that I didn't really love sharing the room with bed bugs.
Pat: *Would you like to go to New York with me?* Chris: *I'd have to find a way to see if it would be possible for me to leave without it being too impossible.*	I don't want to go, but I don't want to seem rude. Will Pat notice that I'm being evasive in my response?
Pat: *Huh?* Chris: *Well. . . .*	Trapped.

Herbert Clark (1996) suggested that language users have different bases for their judgments of common ground:

- *Community membership.* Language producers often make strong assumptions about what is likely to be mutually known based on shared membership in communities of various sizes.
- *Copresence for actions.* Language producers often assume that the actions and events they have shared with other conversationalists become part of common ground. This includes information discussed in earlier parts of a conversation (or in past conversations).
- *Perceptual copresence.* Perceptual copresence exists when a speaker and a listener share the same perceptual events (sights, sounds, and so on).

Thus your use of Alex in "I'm having lunch with Alex" might succeed because your friend and you are part of a small community (for example, roommates) that includes only one Alex (community membership). Or it might succeed because you've introduced the existence of Alex earlier in the conversation (copresence for actions). Or Alex might be standing right there in the room (perceptual copresence). You can see from this example why judgments of common ground often rely on the ability of your memory processes to provide information about individuals and communities (Horton, 2007; Horton & Gerrig, 2005).

The discussion so far has focused on language production at the level of the message: How you shape what you wish to say will depend on the audience to whom you are speaking. Let's turn now to a discussion of the mental processes that allow you to produce these messages.

Speech Execution and Speech Errors Would you like to be famous for tripping over your tongue? Consider the Reverend W. A. Spooner of Oxford University, who lent his name to the term *spoonerism:* an exchange of the initial sounds of two or more words in a phrase or sentence. Reverend Spooner came by this honor honestly. When, for example, he was tongue-lashing a lazy student for wasting the term, Reverend Spooner said, "You have tasted the whole worm!" A spoonerism is one of the limited types of speech errors that language producers make. These errors

Table 8.4 • Errors in Planning Speech Production

Types of Planning:

- Speakers must choose the content words that best fit their ideas.

  If the speaker has two words in mind, such as *grizzly* and *ghastly*, a blend like *grastly* might result.

- Speakers must put the chosen words in the right places in the utterance.

  Because speakers plan whole units of their utterances while they produce them, content words will sometimes become misplaced.

  a tank of gas → a gas of tank

  wine is being served at dinner → dinner is being served at wine

- Speakers must fill in the sounds that make up the words they wish to utter.

  Once again, because speakers plan ahead, sounds will sometimes get misplaced.

  left hemisphere → heft lemisphere

  pass out → pat ous

FIGURE 8.5 Selecting a Sentence Structure
How would you describe this scene?

give researchers insight into the planning that goes on as speakers produce utterances. As you can see in **Table 8.4**, you need to engage in several types of planning, and speech errors give evidence for each type (Dell, 2004). What should impress you about all these examples of errors is that they are not just random—they make sense given the structure of spoken English. Thus a speaker might exchange initial consonants—"tips of the slung" for "slips of the tongue"—but would never say "tlips of the sung," which would violate the rule of English that "tl" does not occur as an initial sound (Fromkin, 1980).

Given the importance of speech errors to developing theoretical models of speech production, researchers have not always been content just to wait around for errors to happen naturally. Instead, researchers have explored a number of ways to produce artificial errors in controlled experimental settings (for example, Corley et al., 2011; Humphreys et al., 2010). One classic technique is called SLIP (for "spoonerisms of laboratory-induced predisposition"; Baars, 1992). In this procedure, participants are asked to read silently lists of word pairs that provide models for the sound structure of a target spoonerism: *ball doze, bash door, bean deck, bell dark*. They then are required to pronounce out loud a word pair like *darn bore*, but under the influence of the earlier pairs it will sometimes come out *barn door*.

With this technique, researchers can study the factors that affect the likelihood that speakers will produce errors. For example, a spoonerism is more likely when the error will still result in real words (Baars et al., 1975). Thus an error on *darn bore* (to produce *barn door*) is more likely than an error on *dart board* (to produce *bart doard*). Findings like this one suggest that while you are producing utterances, some of your cognitive processes are devoted to detecting and editing potential errors (Nooteboom & Quené, 2008). Those processes are reluctant to let you pronounce sounds like *doard*, which are not real English words.

Contemporary theories of speech production attempt to predict how people's utterances unfold in time for sounds,

words, and structures. For example, researchers might study why speakers find it easier to produce some sounds than others in ongoing speech (Goldrick & Larson, 2008). The analyses focus on such factors as the relative frequency of certain sounds in particular positions (for example, an *s* sound is more likely than a *z* sound to occur at the beginning of an English word). Other projects examine the time course with which people produce the particular words of an utterance. Researchers have demonstrated, for example, that people find it harder to produce a word (such as *cow*) when they have recently spoken another word with which it is associated (such as *milk*). Such results are explained as a consequence of different memory representations competing to be included in an utterance (Rahman & Melinger, 2007).

For structures, researchers often examine the factors that lead speakers to choose one or another way of expressing the same idea. Consider **Figure 8.5**. If you described this scene, you might either say "The mailman was chased by the dog" or "The dog chased the mailman." To understand why speakers choose a particular structure, researchers point to such factors as the recent language that the speaker has heard and understood (Bock et al., 2007). If, for example, you have recently heard a sentence such as "The embassy staff isn't being evacuated by the government," you would be more likely to produce an utterance that has the same global structure (such as "The mailman was chased by the dog").

Speech execution is also affected by speakers' assessments of common ground. For example, the way in which people pronounce words is affected by the experiences they have shared with their listeners.

In the first phase of an experiment, students watched a cartoon in which Wile E. Coyote made repeated (unsuccessful) attempts to capture the Road Runner (Galati & Brennan, 2010). In the next phase of the experiment, the students (the Speakers) narrated the cartoon's events to another student who had not seen the cartoon. In the experiment's final phase, the Speakers narrated the events two more times, once to the same peer (Listener A) and once to a new

Featured Study

one (Listener B). Note that for this second narration, each Speaker already had common ground with his or her Listener A (because of the first narration) but not with Listener B. The researchers reasoned that common ground would allow the speakers to be more casual in the way they executed their speech. To test this hypothesis, the researchers found words that the Speakers had repeated across narrations (such as "parachute" and "dynamite"). They edited these words from the sound recordings of the narratives and asked a new group of participants to judge the relative clarity of the different versions. These judges consistently rated the words as less clear when they were addressed to those listeners (Listeners A) with whom the speakers shared the prior narration.

As you have conversations with friends and strangers, think about this result. Do you, in fact, find yourself speaking less carefully when you address yourself to someone with whom you share relatively more common ground?

We have now looked at some of the forces that lead speakers to produce particular utterances and at some of the processes that allow them to do so. We turn next to the listeners, who are responsible for understanding what speakers intend to communicate. ✴

....

✴ **Explore** the **Concept** *Virtual Brain: Lateralization and Language* on **MyPsychLab**

Language Understanding

Suppose a speaker has produced the utterance "The cat is on the mat." You already know that, depending on the context, this utterance can be used to communicate any number of different meanings. How, as a listener, do you settle on just one meaning? To begin this discussion of language understanding, we will consider more fully the problem of ambiguity.

Resolving ambiguity What does the word *bank* mean? You can probably think of at least two meanings, one having to do with rivers and the other having to do with money. Suppose you hear the utterance "He came from the bank." How do you know which meaning is intended? You need to be able to resolve the *lexical ambiguity* between the two meanings. (*Lexical* is related to *lexicon,* a synonym for *dictionary.*) If you think about this problem, you'll realize that you have some cognitive processes that allow you to use surrounding context to eliminate the ambiguity—to *disambiguate*—the word. Have you been talking about rivers or about money? That broader context should enable you to choose between the two meanings. But how?

Before we get to an answer for that question, let's meet another type of ambiguity. What does this sentence mean: "The mother of the boy and the girl will arrive soon"? You may detect only one meaning right off, but there is a *structural ambiguity* here (Akmajian et al., 1990). Take a look at **Figure 8.6**. Linguists often represent the structure of sentences with tree diagrams to show how the various words are gathered together

Structure A

Structure B

Structure C

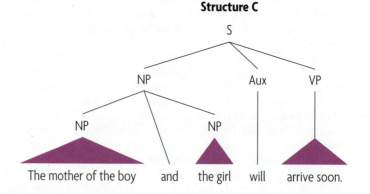

Art = article
Aux = auxiliary
NP = noun phrase
PP = prepositional phrase
S = sentence
VP = verb phrase

FIGURE 8.6 Sentence Structures

Linguists use tree diagrams to display the grammatical structure of sentences. Part A shows the structure of "The cat is on the mat." Parts B and C show that the sentence "The mother of the boy and the girl will arrive soon" can be represented by two different structural analyses. Who will arrive soon, one person (structure B) or two (structure C)?

into grammatical units. In part A, you can see an analysis of "The cat is on the mat." The structure is pretty simple: a noun phrase made up of an article and a noun, plus a verb phrase made up of a verb and a prepositional phrase. In the other two parts, you see the more complex structures for the two different meanings of "The mother . . . ." In part B, the analysis shows that the whole phrase "of the boy and the girl" applies to the mother. One person—the mother of two children—will arrive soon. In part C, the analysis shows that there are two noun phrases, "the mother of the boy" and "the girl." There are two people, both of whom will arrive soon. Which understanding of the sentence did you come to when you first read it? Now that you can see that two meanings are possible, we arrive at the same question we did for lexical ambiguity: How does prior context enable you to settle on one meaning when more than one is possible?

Let's return to lexical ambiguity (an ambiguity of word meaning). Consider this sentence (from Mason & Just, 2007):

> To their surprise, the bark was unusual because it sounded high-pitched and hoarse.

When you read this sentence, how do you interpret the word *bark*? If you imagine that you have a dictionary in your head, your entry for bark might look something like this:

Definition 1. The exterior covering of a tree.
Definition 2. The sound a dog makes.

Research suggests that both definitions become accessible in memory when you first encounter such an ambiguous word, but you swiftly use contextual information to determine which definition is appropriate. The word *bark* is called a *balanced*

ambiguity because people use its two meanings with roughly equal frequency. Now consider this sentence:

> Last year the pen was abandoned because it was too dirty for the animals to live in.

Did that sentence give you any trouble? *Pen* also has two definitions:

Definition 1. An implement for writing with ink.
Definition 2. An enclosure for animals.

Pen is called a *biased ambiguity* because people use one meaning (that is, Definition 1) much more often than the other. You may have experienced some momentary trouble understanding this sentence because your initial bias toward understanding *pen* to mean "an implement for writing with ink" was proved wrong by the context that followed its use. Research suggests that your brain responds differently to these two types of ambiguity.

Twelve participants read sentences while undergoing fMRI scans. The sentences included balanced or biased ambiguities or were matched control sentences (Mason & Just, 2007). For example, in the sentence "To their surprise, the bark was unusual because it sounded high-pitched and hoarse," howl replaced bark (that is, "the howl was unusual . . .) to provide an unambiguous sentence. The researchers predicted that, because participants need to select between meanings, ambiguous sentences would produce different patterns of brain activity than control sentences. As seen in **Figure 8.7**, that prediction was confirmed. The reseachers also predicted that, because participants need to

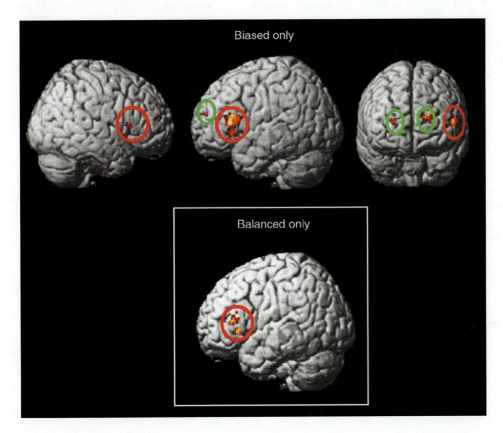

FIGURE 8.7 The Brain Bases of Ambiguity Resolution

Participants underwent fMRI scans while reading sentences with balanced or biased ambiguities or matched control sentences. The brain region circled in red showed greater activity for both types of ambiguity (with respect to the control sentences). The brain region circled in green only showed more activity for the sentences with biased ambiguities.

Now that you are looking at a picture of an animal pen, what comes to mind when you think of the word *pen?*

recover from their biased interpretations, the biased ambiguities would produce different brain activity than balanced ambiguities. Again, the brain scans shown in Figure 8.7 confirm that prediction.

This experiment identifies brain regions that help you understand an ambiguous word: You put contextual information to swift and efficient use to arrive at a single meaning. Context wields a similar influence on structural ambiguities (Farmer et al., 2007; Patson & Warren, 2011). Contextual information speeds decisions when you must choose among different possible grammatical structures. In fact, some of the same brain structures are active when people hear sentences with either lexial or syntactic ambiguities (Rodd et al., 2010).

The overall conclusion you can draw is that your language processes use context powerfully and efficiently to resolve ambiguities. In a way, this shows that there is a good match between production and understanding. The discussion of language production emphasized audience design—the processes by which speakers try to make their utterances appropriate in the current context. This analysis of understanding suggests that listeners expect speakers to have done their jobs well. Under those circumstances, it makes sense for listeners to let context guide their expectations about what speakers will have meant.

The Products of Understanding   The discussion of ambiguity resolution focused on the *processes* of understanding. In this section, we shift attention to the *products* of understanding. The question now is: What *representations* result in memory when listeners understand utterances or texts? What, for example, would be stored in memory when you hear the old standby "The cat is on the mat"? Research has suggested that meaning representation begins with basic units called *propositions* (Clark & Clark, 1977; Kintsch, 1974). Propositions are the main ideas of utterances. For "The cat is on the mat," the main idea is that something is on something else. When you read the utterance, you will extract the proposition *on* and understand the relationship that it expresses between *the cat* and *the mat.* Often propositions are written like this: *ON (cat, mat).* Many utterances contain more than one proposition. Consider "The cat watched the mouse run under the sofa." We have as the first component proposition *UNDER (mouse,*

sofa). From that, we build up *RUN (mouse, UNDER [mouse, sofa]).* Finally, we get to *WATCH (cat, RUN [mouse, UNDER (mouse, sofa)]).*

How can we test whether your mental representations of meaning really work this way? Some of the earliest experiments in the psychology of language were devoted to showing the importance of propositional representations in understanding (Kintsch, 1974). Research has shown that if two words in an utterance belong to the same proposition, they will be represented together in memory even if they are not close together in the actual sentence.

Consider the sentence "The mausoleum that enshrined the tzar overlooked the square." Although mausoleum *and* square *are far apart in the sentence, a propositional analysis suggests that they should be gathered together in memory in the proposition OVERLOOKED* (mausoleum, square)*. To test this analysis, researchers asked participants to read lists of words and say whether each had appeared in the sentence (Ratcliff & McKoon, 1978). Some participants saw* mausoleum *directly after* square *on the list. Other participants saw* mausoleum *after a word from another proposition. The response "Yes, I saw* mausoleum*" was swifter when* mausoleum *came directly after* square *than when its predecessor came from another proposition. This finding suggests that the concepts "mausoleum" and "square" had been represented together in memory.*

Featured Study

Have you ever noticed how hard it is to remember *exactly* what someone said? You might, for example, have tried to remember a line from a movie word-for-word—but you realized when you got home that you could only remember the general sense of what was said. This experiment indicates why word-for-word memory isn't so good: Because one of the main operations your language processes carry out is the extraction of propositions, the exact form with which those propositions were rendered gets lost pretty quickly (for example, "The cat chased the mouse" versus "The mouse was chased by the cat").

Not all the propositions listeners store in memory are made up of information directly stated by the speaker. Often listeners fill gaps with **inferences**—logical assumptions made possible by information in memory. Consider this pair of utterances:

I'm heading to the deli to meet Donna.
She promised to buy me a sandwich for lunch.

To understand how these sentences go together, you must draw at least two important inferences. You must figure out both who *she* is in the second sentence and how going to a deli is related to a promise to buy a sandwich. Note that a friend who actually uttered this pair of sentences would be confident you could figure these things out. You'd never expect to hear this:

I'm heading to the deli to meet Donna. She—and by she I mean Donna—promised to buy me a sandwich—and a deli is a place where you can buy a sandwich—for lunch.

inference Missing information filled in on the basis of a sample of evidence or on the basis of prior beliefs and theories.

Speakers count on listeners to draw inferences of this sort.

A great deal of research has been directed toward determining what types of inferences listeners draw on a regular basis (McNamara & Magliano, 2009). The number of potential inferences after any utterance is unlimited. For example, because you know that Donna is likely to be a human, you could infer that she has a heart, a liver, a pair of lungs, and so on (and on), but it's unlikely that you would feel compelled to call any of those (perfectly valid) inferences to mind when you heard "I'm heading to the deli to meet Donna."

Research suggests, in fact, that the models readers develop for the whole situation of a text affect which inferences they encode. For example, read the text numbered 1 in **Table 8.5**. At the end of this text, did you encode the inference that Carol is likely to dump the spaghetti on the customer? Research suggests that readers consistently draw that inference (Guéraud et al., 2008). Now read the text numbered 2. In this latter case, readers now infer that Carol will experience pain.

This discussion of language use has demonstrated how much work a speaker does to produce the right sentence at the right time and how much work a listener does to figure out exactly what the speaker meant. You usually aren't aware of all this work! Does this give you a greater appreciation for the elegant efficiency of your cognitive processes?

Language and Evolution

We have just seen that you have a range of processes that are working diligently in the background to help you produce and understand language. A question that has long fascinated researchers is whether any other species possesses the same range of processes. We know of no other species that uses a language as complex as any human language. That observation raises an interesting question: What processes did humans evolve that make human language possible? To answer

that question, researchers have largely turned to research with other species: They attempt to define what makes humans and human languages special. An important focus is on *language structure*.

One property that makes human language special is that people can produce an unlimited number of messages with a limited number of words: You follow the grammatical rules of your language—of the types represented by the structures in **Figure 8.6**—to produce as many sentences as you'll ever need from the set of words you know. Meanwhile, there is considerable diversity among the rules that apply within different languages. Humans appear to be the only species that are biologically prepared to learn rules of the complexity found across human languages (Fitch, 2011).

But how do we know that other species cannot learn communication systems with the complexity of human languages? Beginning as early as the 1920s, psychologists tried to address this question by attempting to teach language to chimpanzees. Chimps don't have the appropriate vocal apparatus to produce spoken language, so researchers had to devise other methods of communication. For example, a chimp named Washoe was taught a highly simplified version of American Sign Language (Gardner & Gardner, 1969); a chimp named Sarah was taught to manipulate plastic symbols (which stood for concepts like *apple* and *give*) on a magnetic board (Premack, 1971). The results of these experiments inspired great controversy (Seidenberg & Petitto, 1979). Skeptics asked whether the chimps' occasional combinations of gestures or symbols (for example, *Washoe sorry. You more drink*) constituted any meaningful kind of language use. They also wondered whether most of the meaning attributed to the chimps' utterances wasn't arising in the heads of the humans rather than in the heads of the chimps. 👁

Sue Savage-Rumbaugh and her colleagues (Savage-Rumbaugh et al., 1998) have conducted research that has provided more solid insights into the language capabilities of chimps. Savage-Rumbaugh works primarily with *bonobos,* a species of great ape that is evolutionarily more similar to humans even than common chimpanzees. Rather remarkably, two of the bonobos in her studies, Kanzi and Mulika, acquired the meanings of plastic symbols (similar to the ones the chimp Sarah had used) with no explicit training: They acquired the symbols *spontaneously* by observing others (humans and bonobos) using them to communicate. Moreover, Kanzi and Mulika were able to understand some *spoken* English. For example, when Kanzi heard a spoken word, he was able to locate either the symbol for the word or a photograph of the object. Kanzi was also able to follow simple commands such as "Take off Sue's shoe." Kanzi's performance strongly suggests that some aspects of human language performance can be found in other species. However, Kanzi still falls short of human abilities: He wasn't able to acquire the type of rule system that would allow him to produce an unlimited number of utterances.

Contemporary researchers have shifted their focus away from these attempts to teach primates approximations of human languages. Instead, researchers now fous on particular

Table 8.5 • Text Situations and Inferences

1. Carol was a single mother with two young children. She had to work two jobs to make ends meet. She worked full-time as a teacher and part-time as a waitress. She hated not having much free time. Carol was known for her short temper and her tendency to act without thinking. She never thought about the consequences of her actions, so she often suffered negative repercussions. She refused to let people walk all over her. In fact, she had just gotten a ticket for road rage. She decided she would never put up with anyone that was not nice to her. One particular night, Carol had an extremely rude customer. He complained about the spaghetti, and he yelled at Carol as if it were her fault. Carol lifted the spaghetti above his head.

2. Carol was a single mother with two young children. She had to work two jobs to make ends meet. She worked full-time as a teacher and part-time as a waitress. She hated not having much free time. Carol had just come back to work after having had shoulder surgery. She needed to be careful whenever raising anything from a customer's table. Every time she did, it would hurt so much that she thought she might faint. If she raised something too high, she was extremely uncomfortable all night. But, usually, she asked for help when she needed to clear a table. One particular night, Carol had an extremely rude customer. He complained about the spaghetti, and he yelled at Carol as if it were her fault. Carol lifted the spaghetti above his head.

👁 **Watch** the **Video** *Classic Footage of Chimpanzees and Sign Language* on **MyPsychLab**

Some bonobos have learned the meanings of words without explicit training. What other abilities must these animals demonstrate before it can be said that they have genuinely acquired a human language?

aspects of human languages that may or may not be within the competence of other species (Endress et al., 2009; Saffran et al., 2008). The results of these studies help to define what exactly is special about human languages and our species's ability to acquire those languages.

An evolutionary perspective on language examines the critical processes humans evolved to make language possible. However, that general set of processes allows a wide variety of languages to emerge. The next section discusses some potential consequences of the differences among languages.

Language, Thought, and Culture

Have you had the opportunity to learn more than one language? If so, do you believe that you *think* differently in those languages? Does language affect thought? Scholarly work on this question was originated by **Edward Sapir** (1941/1964) and his student **Benjamin Lee Whorf** (1956), whose cross-linguistic explorations led them to the somewhat radical conclusion that differences in language would create differences in thought. Here's how Sapir put it:

> We see and hear and otherwise experience very largely as we do because the language habits of our community predispose certain choices of interpretation.
> (Sapir, 1941/1964, p. 69)

For Sapir and Whorf, this conclusion emerged directly from relationships they believed to exist in their own data. From the hypotheses that Sapir and Whorf proposed, the one that has received the most attention is called **linguistic relativity** (Brown, 1976). According to this hypothesis, the structure of the language an individual speaks has an impact on the way in which that individual thinks about the world. Contemporary researchers in psychology, linguistics, and anthropology have

attempted to create rigorous tests of these ideas. Let's look at some of that research.

You may be surprised to learn that languages of the world differ with respect to the number of basic color terms they use. As determined by linguistic analysis, English has 11 *(black, white, red, yellow, green, blue, brown, purple, pink, orange, and gray)*; some languages of the world, such as the language spoken by the Dani people of Papua New Guinea, have only two, a simple distinction between *black* and *white* (or *light* and *dark*) (Berlin & Kay, 1969). Researchers have speculated that the category structure implied by color terms might influence the ways in which speakers of different languages think about colors. For example, one study asked speakers of Himba from northern Namibia to examine triads of color chips all taken from the blue–green continuum. The participants' task was to indicate "which of these three colors look most like each other, in the way that brothers look like each other?" (Roberson et al., 2005, p. 395). Unlike English, the Himba language doesn't make a lexical distinction between *blue* and *green*. Instead, Himba speakers use the term *borou* that covers most green and blue hues. The researchers looked for evidence of *categorical perception:* They assessed the extent to which Himba speakers perceived hues to be more similar within the categories marked by the language than between categories. Indeed, the Himba participants' similarity judgments showed a clear impact of the categorical structure of their language.

Number terms have provided a second context for research on language and thought. Consider the Pirahã people, who live in the Amazon rainforest in Brazil. The Pirahã people have only three number terms, *hói*, *hoí*, and *baágiso*. The nearest translation of those terms into English appears to be "small size or amount," "somewhat larger size or amount," and "cause to come together/many" (Everett, 2005). The question, from the perspective of linguistic relativity, is whether the language's lack of a precise number system has an impact on the Pirahã people's ability to carry out tasks involving number (Gordon, 2004). In fact, members of the tribe are not very good at remembering quantities over a brief delay (Frank et al., 2008). When, for example, spools of thread are laid out and then

The Dani people of Papua New Guinea speak a language with only two basic color terms—they make a distinction between black and white (or light and dark). English, by comparison, has 11 basic color terms. Could this language difference affect the way people experience the world?

WHY AND HOW DO PEOPLE LIE?

You saw earlier that one principle for cooperative conversation is, "Try to make your contribution one that is true." However, you surely know that not all utterances are truthful. When people keep diaries of the lies they tell, most report one or two a day (DePaulo et al., 2003). But why do people lie? A study with 286 college students identified two major motives (Phillips et al., 2011). First, students lied to manipulate others' impressions of them (with the expectation that they would gain from the deception). Second, students lied to avoid unpleasantness or to protect against harm to themselves or to other people.

These data suggest that you are frequently challenged to decide whether people are deceiving you. Unfortunately, people don't seem to be very successful at catching lies (Hartwig & Bond, 2011). We actually have a pretty good sense of how the behavior of liars differs from that of truth-tellers. For example, we are correct to believe that liars provide fewer details in their accounts than do people who are telling the truth. However, when we hear one particular statement, how can we confidently assess whether it had fewer details than it ought to have had? The problem with catching liars is not that they don't behave differently—it's that the differences in behavior usually aren't dramatic enough!

So, people's behavior may not always give a clear indication of their truthfulness. However, there's substantial evidence that different brain activity underlies truth-telling and lying. In one study, participants were asked to lie or tell the truth about their participation in an incident in which a gun was fired (Mohamed et al., 2006). To make the experience of lying as real as possible, participants in the *guilty* condition actually fired a starter pistol (loaded with blanks) in the testing room. Participants in both the *guilty* and *not-guilty* conditions answered a series of questions while undergoing fMRI scans. Participants in the guilty condition received instructions to lie about their role in the incident. The fMRI scans revealed that several areas of the brain were more active for lying than for truth-telling. For example, brain regions responsible for planning and emotion were harder at work when participants prepared their lies.

Research of this sort led people to wonder whether fMRI might be used as a high-tech form of lie detection. Although researchers were initially enthusiastic about that possibility, it seems that it's not so difficult to disrupt the process of detection. Lie detection using fMRI relies on clear contrasts between true and false responses. However, people are able to learn countermeasures (as simple as a subtle curling of the left toe while being scanned) that make it difficult to detect clear differences (Ganis et al., 2011). Alas, even in the 21st century, liars retain their edge!

- How might people's motives for lying affect the validity of research on lying?
- What does the study with the starter pistol suggest about ethical constraints for studying lying in laboratory settings?

---

hidden by a folder, Pirahã individuals' memory for the number of spools is relatively poor. Can you understand why a lack of precise numbers would make that task difficult?

As a final example of research on linguistic relativity, let's turn to a contrast between English and Spanish. Suppose an English speaker and Spanish speaker both witness an accident. How might language affect what they remember?

Featured Study

In an initial experiment, researchers asked English and Spanish speakers to watch short videos of accidents and described what happened (Fausey & Boroditsky, 2011). The English speakers produced sentences that included the person who caused the accident (for example, "She broke the vase") 75 percent of the time. By contrast, Spanish speakers were about 15 percent more likely to produce sentences that omitted that information (for example, "Se rompió el florere," which translates to "The vase broke itself"). In a second experiment, new groups of English and Spanish speakers watched the videos. Ten minutes later, they engaged in a memory task in which they were challenged to recognize the individual who had been involved in the accident. The English speakers were correct 79 percent of the time versus 74 percent for the Spanish speakers.

The researchers suggested that the somewhat more common English practice of explicitly mentioning the person who caused the accident explains the English speakers' better memory performance. The memory difference is small, but consistent across speakers. In fact, the size of the memory difference should remind you that language only *influences* thought; you are not completely constrained by the language you speak.

There are thousands of languages in the world, which provide many interesting distinctions. As researchers have examined a broader range of those distinctions, they find the hypothesis of linguistic relativity is better supported in some domains than in others (see January & Kako, 2007; Papafragou et al., 2007). Still, interesting hypotheses about the link between language and thought have yet to be tested. As *Psychology and Life* visits a range of cultural differences, it is worth keeping an open mind about linguistic relativity. Given the many situations in which members of different cultures speak very different languages, we can wonder to what extent language plays a causal role in bringing about cultural differences.

Let's turn now from circumstances in which meaning is communicated through words to those in which meaning relies also on visual information.

Stop *and* Review

① What is the relationship between the cooperative principle and audience design?

② Suppose you are trying to pronounce "big pet" and "bird pen." Why would you be more likely to commit the speech error "pig bet" than "pird ben"?

③ How would you detect inferences in people's representations?

④ What language ability have researchers suggested sets humans apart from other species?

⑤ What does the linguistic relativity hypothesis suggest?

✓•─ **Study** and **Review** on **MyPsychLab**

CRITICAL THINKING   Recall the study on speech execution. How might the clarity of the Speakers' words change if the listeners had also watched the cartoon?

VISUAL COGNITION

In **Figure 8.8**, you have two choices for visual representations of the sentence "The cat is on the mat." Which one seems right? If you think in terms of language-based propositions, each alternative captures the right meaning—the cat *is* on the mat. Even so, you're probably happy only with option A because it matches the scene you likely called to mind when you first read the sentence (Searle, 1979). How about option B? It probably makes you somewhat nervous because it seems as if the cat is going to tip right over. This anxious feeling must arise because you can think with pictures. In a sense, you can *see* exactly what's going to happen. This section explores some of the ways in which visual images and visual processes contribute to the way you think.

History is full of examples of famous discoveries apparently made on the basis of mental imagery (Shepard, 1978). Frederich Kekulé, the discoverer of the chemical structure of benzene, often conjured up mental images of dancing atoms that fastened themselves into chains of molecules. His discovery of the benzene ring occurred in a dream in which a snakelike molecule chain suddenly grabbed its own tail, thus forming a ring. Michael Faraday, who discovered many properties of magnetism, knew little about mathematics, but he had vivid mental images of the properties of magnetic fields. Albert Einstein claimed to have thought entirely in terms of visual images, translating his findings into mathematical symbols and words only after the work of visually based discovery was finished.

These examples should encourage you to try to indulge in visual thinking. But even without trying, you regularly use your

FIGURE 8.8 Visual Representations
Are both of these cats on the mat?

capabilities for manipulating visual images. Consider a classic experiment in which participants were asked to transform images in their heads.

*Researchers presented students with examples of the letter R and its mirror image that had been rotated various amounts, from 0 to 180 degrees (see **Figure 8.9**) (Shepard & Cooper, 1982). As the letter appeared, the student had to identify it as either the normal R or its mirror image. The reaction time taken to make that decision was longer in direct proportion to the amount the figure had been rotated. This finding indicated that a subject was imagining the figure in his or her "mind's eye" and rotating the image into an upright position at some fixed rate before deciding whether the figure was an R or a mirror image. The consistency of the rate of rotation suggested that the process of mental rotation was very similar to the process of physical rotation.*

▸ **Simulate** the **Experiment** *Mental Rotation* on **MyPsychLab**

People's ability to engage in efficient mental rotation depends, in part, on their visual experiences. For that reason, some researchers recommend that people play complex video games as a way to improve performance on mental rotation (Spence & Feng, 2010)!

FIGURE 8.9 Rotated *R* Used to Assess Mental Imagery

Participants presented with these figures in random order were asked to say, as quickly as possible, whether each figure was a normal *R* or a mirror image. The more the figure was rotated from upright, the longer the reaction time was.

You can also use visual images to answer certain types of questions about the world. Suppose, for example, I asked you whether a golf ball is bigger than a Ping-Pong ball. If you can't retrieve that fact directly from memory, you might find it convenient to form a visual image of them side by side. Your mental images also allow you to recover visual properties of objects that might have escaped your attention when you first saw them (Thompson et al., 2008). For example, try to create a mental image of the first letter of the English alphabet as a capital letter. Does your image include a diagonal line? Does your image have an enclosed space? Did you get the sense of zooming in on the image to answer these different questions? Once again, this use of an image has much in common with the properties of real visual perception. When an object is physically present, you can refocus your attention to acquire more information. The same is true for visual images.

There are, of course, limits to the use of your visual imagination. Consider this problem:

> *Imagine that you have a large piece of blank paper. In your mind, fold it in half (making two layers), fold it in half again (four layers), and continue folding it over 50 times. About how thick is the paper when you are done?* (Adams, 1986)

The actual answer is about 50 million miles (250 • 0.028 inches, the thickness of a piece of paper), approximately half the distance between Earth and the sun. Your estimate was probably considerably lower. Your mind's eye was overwhelmed by the information you asked it to represent.

Please try one last exercise using visual imagery. Find any object in your environment and examine it for a few seconds. Now, close your eyes and try to create a visual image of the same object. Consider this question: How much overlap was there in the brain regions that were active when you engaged in visual perception versus visual imagery? To answer this question, researchers had participants learn a series of line drawings of common objects such as a tree (Ganis et al., 2004).

In the next phase of the experiment, participants underwent fMRI scans while they either inspected the same drawings on a computer screen or generated visual images of the drawings. For each drawing, they answered a simple question such as whether the object contained circular parts. **Figure 8.10** on page 222 presents the results of the fMRI scans from different regions of the brain. The left and middle columns show the regions of the brain that differed for each task from the baseline condition (that is, when participants were not engaged in a task). The right column shows the brain regions that were particular to the perception task. These data support two important conclusions. First, there was substantial overlap between brain processes for perception and imagery. Second, brain regions for imagery were a subset of those for perception—participants didn't use any special regions to create a visual image. With respect to brain activity, you use much the same resources to encode the visual world as to re-create a visual representation.

This discussion so far has largely focused on the types of visual representations that you form by committing to memory—or in the case of imagery, retrieving from memory—visual stimuli from the environment. However, you often form visual images based on verbal descriptions. When you read, you can form a *spatial mental model* to keep track of the whereabouts of characters (Rinck, 2008). Researchers have often focused on the ways in which spatial mental models capture properties of real spatial experiences. Suppose, for example, you read a passage of a text that places you in the middle of an interesting environment.

> *You are hob-nobbing at the opera. You came tonight to meet and chat with interesting members of the upper class. At the moment, you are standing next to the railing of a wide, elegant balcony overlooking the first floor. Directly behind you, at your eye level, is an ornate lamp attached to the balcony wall. The base of the lamp, which is attached to the wall, is gilded in gold.* (Franklin & Tversky, 1990, p. 65)

In a series of experiments, readers studied descriptions of this sort that vividly described the layout of objects around the viewer (Franklin & Tversky, 1990). The researchers wished to show that readers were faster or slower to access information about the scene, depending on where the objects were in the

● **Watch** the **Video** *Special Topics: Mental Imagery: In the Mind's Eye* on **MyPsychLab**

Perception   Imagery   Perception-Imagery

Frontal
Cortex

Temporal
Cortex

Pariental
Cortex

Occipital
Cortex

FIGURE 8.10 The Brain Bases
of Visual Imagery

The figure shows the results of fMRI scans
when participants were engaged in either a
perception task or an imagery task. The left and
middle columns show brain activity for each task:
Regions marked with red, orange, and yellow
were more active with respect to a no-task
baseline; regions marked in shades of blue were
less active. The right column shows the brain
regions that were affected by the perception
task but not the imagery task. These fMRI scans
demonstrate that much the same brain regions
are used for perception and imagery.

Reprinted from *Cognitive Brain Research, 20,*
G. Ganis et al., "Brain areas underlying visual mental
imagery and visual perception: An fMRI study," pp. 226–241,
copyright © 2004, with permission from Elsevier.

FIGURE 8.11 Spatial Mental Models
You can use imagination to project yourself into the middle
of a scene. Just as if you were really standing in the room, you
would take less time to say what is in front of you (the lamp)
than what is behind you (the bust).

mental space around them. Readers, for example, were quicker
to say what object was in front of them in the scene than what
object was behind them, even though all objects were introduced
equally carefully in the stories (see **Figure 8.11**). It's easiest to
understand this result if you believe that the representation you
form while reading actually places you, in some sense, in the
scene. You are able to transform a verbal experience into a visual, spatial experience.

In this section, we have seen that you have visual processes
and representations to complement your verbal abilities. These
two types of access to information give you extra help in dealing with the demands and tasks of your life. We turn now to domains in which you put both visual and verbal representations
to use in coping with your life's complexities: *problem solving*
and *reasoning*.

Stop *and* Review

① How similar are the processes of physical rotation and
mental rotation?

② What has research shown about the brain bases of
visual images?

③ If you're imagining yourself in a scene, does it matter
how you place yourself in the room?

✓● **Study** and **Review** on **MyPsychLab**

PROBLEM SOLVING AND REASONING

Let's return for a minute to your mysterious message, "The cat is on the mat." If you've come to understand the message, what do you do next? For those of you whose lives are less filled with mystery, consider a more common situation: You've accidentally locked yourself out of your home, room, or car. Again, what do you do next? For both situations, reflect on the types of mental steps you might take to overcome your difficulty. Those mental steps will almost certainly include the cognitive processes that make up **problem solving** and **reasoning.** Both of these activities require you to combine current information with information stored in memory to work toward some particular goal: a conclusion or a solution. We will look at aspects of problem solving and at two types of reasoning, deductive and inductive.

Problem Solving

What goes on four legs in the morning, on two legs at noon, and on three legs in the twilight? According to Greek mythology, this was the riddle posed by the Sphinx, an evil creature who threatened to hold the people of Thebes in tyranny until someone could solve the riddle. To break the code, Oedipus had to recognize elements of the riddle as metaphors. Morning, noon, and twilight represented different periods in a human life. A baby crawls and so (effectively) has four legs, an adult walks on two legs, and an older person walks on two legs but uses a cane, making a total of three legs. Oedipus's solution to the riddle was *humans.*

Although your daily problems may not seem as monumental as the one faced by young Oedipus, problem-solving activity is a basic part of your everyday existence. You continually come up against problems that require solutions: how to manage work and tasks within a limited time frame, how to succeed at a job interview, how to break off a relationship, and so on. Many problems involve discrepancies between what you know and what you need to know. When you solve a problem, you reduce that discrepancy by finding a way to get the missing information. To get into the spirit of problem solving, try the problems in **Figure 8.12**. After you're done,

problem solving Thinking that is directed toward solving specific problems and that moves from an initial state to a goal state by means of a set of mental operations.

reasoning The process of thinking in which conclusions are drawn from a set of facts; thinking directed toward a given goal or objective.

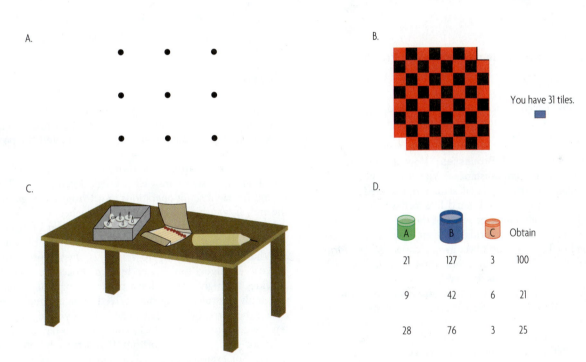

FIGURE 8.12 Try to Solve These Classic Problems

Can you solve each of these problems? (The answers are given in **Figure 8.13** on page 224, but don't look until you try to solve them all.)

(A) Try to connect all nine dots using four straight lines without lifting your pen from the paper or retracing the same line.

(B) Two corners have been cut out of this checkerboard. You have 31 tiles. Each tile covers two of the squares on the checkerboard. Try to cover every square on the checkerboard with the 31 tiles.

(C) You are given a candle, a box of tacks, and a book of matches. Try to attach the candle to the wall above the table so that no wax will drip on the table.

(D) You are given three water jugs each of which holds a different amount of water. For example, in the first problem the jugs hold 21 quarts, 127 quarts, and 3 quarts respectively. For each problem, you need to pour water among the three jugs to obtain the desired quantity of water. Try to solve each of the three problems.

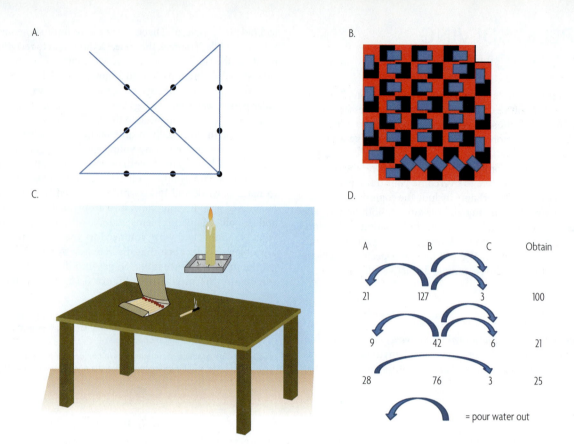

FIGURE 8.13 Solutions to the Classic Problems

How did you do? We will revisit these problems as you learn more about the processes of problem solving.

we'll see how psychological research can shed light on your performance—and, perhaps, provide some suggestions about how to improve it. 👁

Problem Spaces and Processes How do you define a problem in real-life circumstances? You usually perceive the difference between your current state and a desired goal: For example, you are broke, and you'd like to have some money. You are also usually aware of some of the steps you would be able (or willing) to take to bridge the gap: You will try to get a part-time job, but you won't become a pickpocket. The formal definition of a *problem* captures these three elements (Newell & Simon, 1972). A problem is defined by (1) an *initial state*—the incomplete information or unsatisfactory conditions you start with; (2) a *goal state*—the information or state of the world you hope to obtain; and (3) a *set of operations*—the steps you may take to move from an initial state to a goal state. Together, these three parts define the **problem space.** You can think of solving a problem as walking through a maze (the problem space) from where you are (the initial state) to where you want to be (the goal state), making a series of turns (the allowable operations).

Much of the initial difficulty in solving a problem will arise if any of these elements are not well defined (Simon, 1973). A *well-defined problem* is similar to a textbook problem in which the initial state, the goal state, and the operations are all clearly specified. Your task is to discover how to use allowable, known operations to get the answer. By contrast, an *ill-defined problem* is similar to designing a home, writing a novel, or finding a cure for AIDS. The initial state, the goal state, and/or the operations may be unclear and vaguely

specified. In such cases, the problem solver's first task is to work out, as much as possible, exactly what the problem is—to make explicit a beginning, an ideal solution, and the possible means to achieve it.

As you know from your own experience, even when the initial and goal states are well defined, it can still be difficult to find the right set of operations to get from the beginning to the end. If you think back to your experience in math classes, you know that this is true. Your teacher gave you a formula like $x2 + x - 12 = 0$ and asked you to solve for possible values of x. What do you do next? To solve this algebra problem, you can use an **algorithm:** a step-by-step procedure that always provides the right answer for a particular type of problem. If you apply the rules of algebra correctly, you are guaranteed to obtain the correct values of x (3 and –4). If you've ever forgotten the combination to a lock, you may also have engaged in behavior guided by an algorithm. If you try solutions systematically (for example, 1, 2, 3; 1, 2, 4) you will definitely arrive at the right combination—though you may be at it for a good

· ·

👁 **Watch** the **Video** *In the Real World: A Crash Course In Problem Solving* on **MyPsychLab**

problem space The elements that make up a problem: the initial state, the incomplete information or unsatisfactory conditions the person starts with; the goal state, the set of information or state the person wishes to achieve; and the set of operations, the steps the person takes to move from the initial state to the goal state.

algorithm A step-by-step procedure that always provides the right answer for a particular type of problem.

long while! Because well-defined problems have clear initial states and goal states, algorithms are more likely to be available for them than for ill-defined problems. When algorithms are unavailable, problem solvers often rely on **heuristics,** which are strategies or "rules of thumb." Suppose, for example, you are reading a mystery and you'd like to solve the problem of who murdered an e-commerce tycoon. You might rule out the possibility that "the butler did it" because you use the heuristic that authors wouldn't use such a trite plot line. As we shall see shortly, heuristics are also a critical aspect of *judgment* and *decision making.*

Researchers have been interested in understanding the way people apply both algorithms and heuristics as they make their way through a problem space. To study the steps problem solvers take, researchers have often turned to **think-aloud protocols.** In this procedure, participants are asked to verbalize their ongoing thoughts (Fox et al., 2011). For example, a pair of researchers were interested in capturing the mental processes that enable participants to solve the mutilated checkerboard problem that is part B of Figure 8.12 (Kaplan & Simon, 1990). Here is one of their participants having the crucial breakthrough that the problem cannot be solved with only horizontal and vertical placement of pieces (the checkerboard was pink and black):

> *So you're leaving . . . it's short—how many, you're leaving uhhhh . . . there's more pinks than black, and in order to complete it you'd have to connect two pinks but you can't because they are diagonally . . . is that getting close?* (Kaplan & Simon, 1990, p. 388)

The solver has just realized that the goal cannot be accomplished if the dominoes can just be placed horizontally or vertically. Researchers have often used participants' own accounts of their thinking as the starting point for more formal models of problem solving.

Improving your Problem Solving

What makes problem solving hard? If you reflect on your day-to-day experience, you might come up with the answer, "There are too many things to consider all at once." Research on problem solving has led to much the same conclusion. What often makes a problem difficult to solve is that the mental requirements for solving a particular problem overwhelm processing resources (Cho et al., 2007; Kirschner et al., 2011). To solve a problem, you need to plan the series of operations you will take. If that series becomes too complex, or if each operation itself is too complex, you may be unable to see your way through from the initial state to the goal state. How might you overcome this potential limitation?

An important step in improving problem solving is to find a way to represent a problem so that each operation is possible, given your processing resources. If you must habitually solve similar problems, a useful procedure is to practice each of the components of the solution so that, over time, those components require fewer resources (Kotovsky et al., 1985). Suppose, for example, you were a cab driver in New York City and were faced with daily traffic jams. You might mentally practice your responses to jams at various points in the city, so that you'd have ready solutions to components of the overall problem of getting your fare from a pickup spot to a destination. By practicing these component solutions, you could keep more of your attention on the road!

Sometimes, finding a useful representation means finding a whole new way to think about the problem (Novick & Bassok,

Table 8.6 • The Hiker Puzzle

> For his summer vacation, a skilled hiker decided to climb to the top of Mt. Clark and camp out over night. First thing Monday morning, he set out along the narrow winding trail that led to the summit. Because it was such a beautiful day, the hiker maintained a leisurely pace. From time to time, he stopped to photograph the scenery and to text several friends, "Wish you were here." When the hiker arrived at the top of Mt. Clark, he rolled out his sleeping bag and settled in for a good night's sleep. The hiker started his descent early the next morning. Because there were threatening clouds in the sky, he hurried down the trail to get back to his car.
>
> How could you prove that there was one spot along the trail the hiker crossed at exactly the same time on both days?
> See a "proof" for the Hiker Puzzle in Figure 8.14 on page 226.

2005). Read the puzzle given in **Table 8.6** (based on Duncker, 1945). How would you go about offering this proof? Think about it for a few minutes before you read on. How well did you do? If the word *proof* suggested to you something mathematical, you probably didn't make much progress. A better way to think about the problem is to imagine two hikers, one starting at the top and another starting at the bottom (Adams, 1986). As one climbs and one descends, it's clear that they will pass at some point along the mountain, right (see **Figure 8.14** on page 226)? Now replace the pair of hikers with just the one—conceptually it's the same—and there's your proof. What makes this problem suddenly very easy is using the right sort of representation: visual rather than verbal or mathematical.

If you go back to the problems in Figure 8.12 you'll have another good example of the importance of an appropriate representation of the problem space. To mount the candle on the wall, you had to alter your usual perspective and perceive the tack box as a platform instead of as a container. This problem shows a phenomenon called functional fixedness (Duncker, 1945; Maier, 1931). **Functional fixedness** is a mental block that adversely affects problem solving by inhibiting the perception of a new function for an object that was previously associated with some other purpose. Whenever you are stuck on a problem, you should ask yourself, "How am I representing the problem? Are there different or better ways that I can think about the problem or components of its solution?" If words don't work, try drawing a picture. Or try examining your assumptions and see what "rules" you can break by making novel combinations.

Let's turn now to another concept that likely comes to mind when you consider improving problem solving—creativity.

Creativity

You have almost certainly experienced many moments in which people have encouraged you to be more creative. **Creativity** is an individual's ability to generate ideas or products that are both *novel* and *appropriate* to the circumstances in which they were generated (Hennessey & Amabile, 2010). Consider the

....

heuristic Cognitive strategies, or "rules of thumb," often used as shortcuts in solving a complex inferential task.

think-aloud protocol Report made by an experimental participant of the mental processes and strategies he or she uses while working on a task.

functional fixedness An inability to perceive a new use for an object previously associated with some other purpose; adversely affects problem solving and creativity.

creativity The ability to generate ideas or products that are both novel and appropriate to the circumstances.

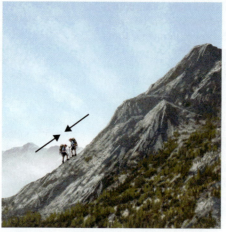

A   B

FIGURE 8.14 A "Proof" for the Hiker Puzzle

Panel A shows two hikers, one who starts at the bottom of the mountain and one who starts at the top. Panel B shows that they must meet at some time during the day. Replace the two hikers with a single hiker, and you have your proof!

invention of the wheel. The device was novel because no one before its unknown inventor had seen the application of rolling objects. It was appropriate because the use to which the novel object could be put was very clear. Without appropriateness, new ideas or objects are often considered strange or irrelevant. 👁

How might you go about rating individuals as (relatively) creative or uncreative? Researchers have used tasks that measure both *divergent* and *convergent thinking* (Nielsen et al., 2008; Runco, 2007). Many approaches focus on **divergent thinking,** which is defined as the ability to generate a variety of unusual solutions to a problem. Questions that test divergent thinking give the test taker the opportunity to demonstrate *fluid* (swift) and *flexible* thinking (Torrance, 1974; Wallach & Kogan, 1965):

- Name all the things you can think of that are square.
- List as many white edible things as you can in three minutes.
- List all the uses that you can think of for a *brick.*

Responses are scored along such dimensions as *fluency,* the overall number of distinct ideas; *uniqueness,* the number of ideas that were given by no other person in an appropriate sample; and *unusualness,* the number of ideas that were given by, for example, less than 5 percent of a sample (Runco, 1991).

Convergent thinking is defined as the ability to gather together different sources of information to solve a problem. We would credit people as being creative if they can put information together in a way that produces novel solutions. One test researchers use to study convergent thinking is called the *remote associates test.* Test takers are challenged to find the term that provides a link for other words (Bowden & Beeman, 2003):

- What word are all three of these words related to? *Cottage, Swiss, cake*
- What word are all three of these words related to? *Fish, mine, rush*
- What word are all three of these words related to? *Flower, friend, scout*

(Look for the answers at the end of this section.) Other measures of convergent thinking focus on **insight,** which is defined as circumstances in which solutions suddenly come to mind. Take another look back at Figure 8.12. In Part A, the problem challenged you to connect nine dots with four continuous lines. That problem requires insight. You must realize that the lines

need to extend beyond the boundaries of the square created by the nine dots. To solve the problem, you must literally think outside the box! We would credit people whose bursts of insight give rise to novel solutions as being creative.

A different approach to judging some individuals as creative or uncreative is to ask them specifically to generate a creative product—a drawing, a poem, or a short story. Judges then rate the creativity of each of the products. Consider the two photographs shown in **Figure 8.15**. Which do you think is more creative? Could you explain why you think so? Do you think your friends would agree? Research has shown that agreement is quite high when judges rank products for creativity (Hennessy & Amabile, 2010). People can be reliably identified across judges as being high or low in creativity. In fact, people are also pretty accurate at judging whether their own efforts are creative.

In one study, 226 students completed a test of divergent thinking (Slivia, 2008). For example, the students tried to generate unusual uses for a knife. After completing each task, the participants read their responses and chose the two they thought showed the most creativity. The participants' responses were also evaluated by a group of three judges. On the whole, the participants and the judges showed good agreement about which responses counted as the most creative. Still, some students were better than others at judging their own products. In particular, those students who judged themselves as being particularly creative and open to new experiences were also best at identifying their most creative responses. The researcher concluded that "creative people are doubly skilled: they are better at generating creative ideas and at discerning which ones are the best" (p. 145).

Featured Study

👁 **Watch** the **Video** *What is Creativity?* on **MyPsychLab**

divergent thinking An aspect of creativity characterized by an ability to produce unusual but appropriate responses to problems.

convergent thinking An aspect of creativity characterized by the ability to gather together different sources of information to solve a problem.

insight Circumstances of problem solving in which solutions suddenly come to mind.

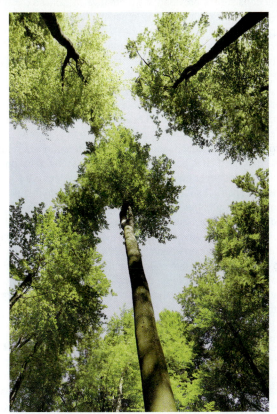

FIGURE 8.15 Making Judgments about Creativity
Hypothetical photography class assignment: Take the best picture you can of a tree. (A) a noncreative response; (B) a creative response.

You might be happy to know that others are likely to agree with your judgments when you believe you have been creative. In fact, highly creative individuals pursue their tasks because of the enjoyment and satisfaction they take in the products they generate; this pattern is known as *intrinsic motivation* (Hennessey & Amabile, 2010). The *Psychology in Your Life* box on page 228 reviews research on how you might increase your creativity.

....

deductive reasoning A form of thinking in which one draws a conclusion that is intended to follow logically from two or more statements or premises.

Meanwhile, how did you do on the convergent thinking problems? The answers were *cheese, gold,* and *girl.*

Often, when you try to solve problems, you engage in special forms of thinking that are called reasoning. Let's turn now to a first type of reasoning you use to solve problems, deductive reasoning.

Deductive Reasoning

Suppose you are on your way to a restaurant and you want to pay for your meal with your only credit card, American Express. You call the restaurant and ask, "Do you accept American Express?" The restaurant's hostess replies, "We accept all major credit cards." You can now safely conclude that they accept American Express. To see why, we can reformulate your interchange to fit the structure of the *syllogism*, introduced by the Greek philosopher Aristotle over 2,000 years ago:

Premise 1. The restaurant accepts all major credit cards.
Premise 2. American Express is a major credit card.
Conclusion. The restaurant accepts American Express.

Aristotle was concerned with defining the logical relationships between statements that would lead to *valid* conclusions. **Deductive reasoning** involves the correct application of such logical rules. The credit-card example shows that you are quite capable of drawing conclusions that have the form of logical, deductive proofs. However, your real-world deductive reasoning is affected both by the specific knowledge you possess about the world and the representational resources you can bring to bear on a particular reasoning problem. Let's expand on these conclusions.

Psychology in Your Life

HOW CAN YOU BECOME MORE CREATIVE?

Do you believe that creativity is something that some people have and others do not? If so, you might be surprised to learn how consistently contexts influence the quality of people's creative products. Let's consider three examples.

The first example focuses on students' multicultural experiences (Leung & Chiu, 2010). The researchers reasoned that exposure to another culture gives people experience in recruiting "ideas from unfamiliar sources and places" and synthesizing "seemingly incompatible ideas from diverse cultures" (p. 173). To test those ideas, the researchers had participants watch different versions of a 45-minute slide show. One version focused only on Chinese culture (which was unfamiliar to the participants). The other version juxtaposed Chinese and American cultures. After each slideshow, the participants attempted to write a creative version of the Cinderella story. Those participants who watched the slideshow juxtaposing the two cultures were consistently more creative. The key to increased creativity was that the students experienced the two cultures side-by-side.

A second method to increase creativity contrasts people's thoughts about the near and distant future (Förster et al., 2004). Suppose I asked you how you might plan a party either for tomorrow or for next year. When you consider the near future, you're likely to focus on concrete details; when you consider the far future, you're thoughts are likely to be more abstract. The researchers predicted that they could increase creativity by getting participants to think in that more abstract fashion. To test that prediction, the researchers asked participants to spend two minutes imagining their lives either

"tomorrow" or "one year from now." After a brief interval, participants responded to this scenario: "Ms. Miller likes her plants. Please help her to find as many creative ways as you can regarding how she can further improve her room" (p. 184). Participants who had imagined what their lives would be like in a year consistently provided more creative responses.

A third method to increase creativity focuses on how people ponder what might have been (Markman et al., 2007). When people think back on their lives, they often contemplate counterfactual thoughts (for example, "If I hadn't eaten that omelette, I wouldn't have gotten sick."). Some of those counterfactuals are *additive* because they encode a broader range of possible actions (such as, "If I had done . . . , the outcome would have been better"). Some of the counterfactuals are *subtractive* because they encode a narrower range of actions (such as, "If I had *not* done . . . , the outcome would have been better"). The researchers asked some participants to construct additive counterfactuals and some to construct subtractive counterfactuals with respect to a negative outcome. The researchers reasoned that "additive counterfactuals—those that add new . . . elements to reconstruct reality—evoke an expansive processing style that facilitates creative generation" (p. 322). In fact, participants who constructed additive counterfactuals produced more short-term creative behavior (e.g., they were able to generate more creative novel uses for a brick) than participants who generated subtractive counterfactuals.

Can you see how you might apply each of these projects to improve your everyday creativity?

How does knowledge influence deductive reasoning? Consider this syllogism:

Premise 1. All things that have a motor need oil.
Premise 2. Automobiles need oil.
Conclusion. Automobiles have motors.

Is this a valid conclusion? According to the rules of logic, it is *not* because Premise 1 leaves open the possibility that some things that don't have motors will also need oil. The difficulty is that what is invalid in a logic problem is not necessarily untrue in real life. That is, if you take Premises 1 and 2 to be all the information in your possession—as you should if you accept this simply as an exercise in formal logic—the conclusion is not valid.

This example illustrates the **belief-bias effect:** People tend to judge as valid those conclusions that they find believable

and judge as invalid those conclusions they find unbelievable (Janis & Frick, 1943). One explanation for belief bias emerges from signal detection theory, which you learned about in Chapter 4 (see pages 83–84). Recall that the mathematics of signal detection theory enables researchers to determine the extent to which people's judgments are subject to responses biases. In the case of deductive reasoning, people must judge a conclusion as "valid" or "invalid." These responses are parallel to the "yes" and "no" judgments from the example in Chapter 4. In the face of uncertainty, a deductive conclusion that is consistent with prior knowledge creates a response bias toward a "valid" judgment; a conclusion that is inconsistent with prior knowledge creates a bias toward an "invalid" judgment (Dube et al., 2010).

In some cases, your ability to apply past experience helps you to perform better on reasoning tasks. Imagine that you are given the array of four cards pictured in **Figure 8.16**, which have printed on them *A, D, 4,* and *7.* Your task is to determine which cards you must turn over to test the rule "If a card has a vowel on one side, then it has an even number on

---

belief-bias effect A situation that occurs when a person's prior knowledge, attitudes, or values distort the reasoning process by influencing the person to accept invalid arguments.

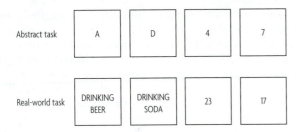

FIGURE 8.16 Abstract versus Real-World Reasoning

In the top row, you are required to say which cards you must turn over to test the rule "If a card has a vowel on one side, then it has an even number on the other side." In the bottom row, you must say which cards you need to turn over to test the rule "If a customer is to drink an alcoholic beverage, then she *must* be at least 18." People typically do better on the second task, which allows them to use real-world strategies.

the other side" (Johnson-Laird & Wason, 1977). What would you do? Most people say that they would turn over the *A*, which is correct, and the *4*—which is incorrect. No matter what character appears on the flip side of the *4*, the rule will not be falsified. Suppose there's an E on the flip side. The rule would be confirmed. Suppose there's a T. The rule doesn't say anything about consonants, so you gather no information with respect to it. Do you now see why you can't test the rule by turning the 4 over? Instead, you must flip the 7. If you were to find a vowel there, you would have invalidated the rule.

The original research on this task, which is often called the *Wason selection task,* prompted doubts about people's ability to reason effectively. However, deductive reasoning is improved when participants are able to apply their real-world knowledge to the Wason task. Suppose you were asked to perform what is a logically comparable task, on the lower set of cards in Figure 8.16. In this case, however, you are asked to evaluate the rule "If a customer is to drink an alcoholic beverage, then she *must* be at least 18" (Cheng & Holyoak, 1985). Now you can probably see immediately which are the correct cards to turn over: *17* and *drinking beer*. If you look at Figure 8.16, you'll see that *7* and *17* have the same logical function. You need to turn *17* over for the same reasons of logic you need to turn *7* over. However, your real-world experience helps you appreciate why turning *17* over is logically necessary.

This example of age and alcohol comes from the more general category of permission situations. You probably have a good deal of experience with these sorts of situations—recall all the times you were given conditions like, "You can't watch television unless you do your homework." You most likely never recognized that deductive inference was involved in such circumstances! However, the experience you've accumulated with these situations now allows you to make correct judgments without much difficulty.

This section began by describing a situation in which you drew a valid deductive inference about your ability to use your American Express card to buy a meal. Unfortunately, life provides many occasions on which you cannot be so certain that you have drawn valid inferences from valid premises. We turn now to a version of the restaurant scenario that requires you to use a different form of reasoning.

Inductive Reasoning

Let's suppose that you have arrived outside the restaurant and only then think to check to see if you have enough cash. Once again you find that you'll want to use your American Express card, but there's no helpful sign on the outside. You peek through the restaurant's windows and see well-dressed clientele. You look at the expensive prices on the menu. You consider the upscale quality of the neighborhood. All these observations lead you to believe that the restaurant is likely to take your credit card. This is not deductive reasoning because your conclusion is based on probabilities rather than logical certainties. Instead, this is **inductive reasoning**—a form of reasoning that uses available evidence to generate likely, but not certain, conclusions.

Although the name might be new, you have already encountered several examples of inductive reasoning. You saw in both Chapters 4 and 7 that people use past information to generate expectations about the present and future. You are using inductive reasoning, for example, if you decide that a certain odor in the air indicates that someone is making popcorn; you are using inductive reasoning if you agree that the words on this page are unlikely to suddenly become invisible (and that, if you study, your knowledge of this material won't become invisible on test day). Finally, the language understanding section of this chapter discussed the types of inferences people draw when they use language. Your belief that *she* must be *Donna* in the sequence of utterances you read earlier relies on inductive inference.

In real-life circumstances, much of your problem-solving ability relies on inductive reasoning. Return to the opening example: You have accidentally locked yourself out of your home, room, or car. What should you do? A good first step is to call up from memory solutions that worked in the past. This process is called *analogical problem solving*: You establish an analogy between the features of the current situation and the features of previous situations (Christensen & Schunn, 2007; Lee & Holyoak, 2008). In this case, your past experiences of "being locked out" may have allowed you to form the *generalization* "find other people with keys." With that generalization in hand, you can start to figure out who those individuals might be and how to find them. This task might require you to retrieve the method you developed for tracking down your roommates at their afternoon classes. If this problem seems easy to you, it's because you have grown accustomed to letting your past inform your present: Inductive reasoning allows you to access tried-and-true methods that speed current problem solving.

There's one caution to add about inductive reasoning. Often a solution that has worked in the past can be reused for a successful solution. But sometimes you must recognize that reliance on the past can hamper your problem-solving ability when there is a critical difference between the old and current situations. The water-jar problem given in Figure 8.12 is a classic example of circumstances in which reliance on the past may cause you to miss a solution to a problem (Luchins, 1942). If you had discovered, in the first two problems in part D, the conceptual rule that $B - A - 2(C) = answer,$ you probably tried the same formula for the third problem and found it didn't work. Actually, simply filling jar *A* and pouring off enough to fill jar

....

inductive reasoning A form of reasoning in which a conclusion is made about the probability of some state of affairs, based on the available evidence and past experience.

C would have left you with the right amount. If you were using your initial formula, you probably did not notice this simpler possibility—your previous success with the other rule would have given you a mental set. A **mental set** is a preexisting state of mind, habit, or attitude that can enhance the quality and speed of perceiving and problem solving under some conditions. However, the same set may inhibit or distort the quality of your mental activities at times when old ways of thinking and acting are nonproductive in new situations. When you find yourself frustrated in a problem-solving situation, you might take a step back and ask yourself, "Am I allowing past successes to narrow my focus too much?" Try to make your problem solving more creative by considering a broader spectrum of past situations and past solutions.

This section has examined a range of types of problem solving and reasoning—with suggestions, in each case, for concrete steps you can take to improve your performance in real-world circumstances. The final section of the chapter follows the same strategy. I describe some major research findings on the processes of *judgment* and *decision making* and then suggest how you can apply those findings to important situations in your life.

Stop *and* Review

① With respect to problem solving, what is an algorithm?
② What does it mean to overcome functional fixedness?
③ What are two important criteria for judging ideas or products as creative?
④ What happens when people succumb to the belief-bias effect?
⑤ What role does memory play in inductive reasoning?

✓— **Study** and **Review** on **MyPsychLab**

CRITICAL THINKING   Recall the experiment on judgments of creativity. Why would the researchers have used multiple judges to assess the responses?

JUDGMENT AND DECISION MAKING

For a final time, we're back to "The cat is on the mat." Let's engage the processes of *judgment* and *decision making*. How likely is it that the message was just a prank? How likely is it that the message has some real importance that has eluded you? Should you just give up and go to sleep?

....

◉ **Watch** the **Video** *What's In It For Me?: Making Choices* on **MyPsychLab**

mental set   The tendency to respond to a new problem in the manner used to respond to a previous problem.

judgment   The process by which people form opinions, reach conclusions, and make critical evaluations of events and people based on available material; also, the product of the mental activity.

decision making   The process of choosing between alternatives; selecting or rejecting available options.

This series of questions illustrates one of the great truths of your day-to-day experience: You live in a world filled with *uncertainty*. Here are some more questions, of a sort that will be entirely familiar. Should you spend $10 on a movie you may or may not enjoy? Before an exam, would you be better off studying your notes or rereading the chapter? Are you ready to commit yourself to a long-term relationship? Because you can only guess at the future, and because you almost never have full knowledge of the past, very rarely can you be completely certain that you have made a correct judgment or decision. Thus the processes of judgment and decision making must operate in a way that allows you to deal efficiently with uncertainty (Gigerenzer & Gaissmaier, 2011).

Before we move on, let's quickly distinguish between the two processes of judgment and decision making. **Judgment** is the process by which you form opinions, reach conclusions, and make critical evaluations of events and people. You often make judgments spontaneously, without prompting. **Decision making** is the process of choosing between alternatives, selecting and rejecting available options. Judgment and decision making are interrelated processes. For example, you might meet someone at a party and, after a brief discussion and a dance together, *judge* the person to be intelligent, interesting, honest, and sincere. You might then *decide* to spend most of your party time with that person and to arrange a date for the next weekend; decision making is more closely linked to behavioral actions. Let's turn now to research on these two types of thinking. ◉

Heuristics and Judgment

What's the best way to make a judgment? Suppose, for example, you are asked whether you enjoyed a movie. To answer this question, you could fill out a chart with two columns, "What I liked about the movie" and "What I didn't like about the movie," and see which column came out longer. To be a bit more accurate, perhaps you'd weight the entries in each list according to their importance (thus you might weight "the actors' performances" as more important on the plus side than "the blaring sound track" on the minus side). If you went through

What processes influence your decision that you are ready to commit to a long-term relationship?

this whole procedure, you'd probably be pretty confident of your judgment—but you know already that this is an exercise you rarely undertake. In real-life circumstances, you have to make judgments frequently and rapidly. You don't have the time—and often you don't have sufficient information—to use such a formal procedure.

What do you do instead? An answer to this question was pioneered by **Amos Tversky** and **Daniel Kahneman,** who argued that people's judgments often rely on heuristics rather than on formal methods of analysis. As the discussion of problem solving noted, heuristics are informal rules of thumb that provide shortcuts, reducing the complexity of making judgments. Following the lead of Tversky and Kahneman, researchers have suggested that humans evolved an *adaptive toolbox:* a repertoire of "fast and frugal" heuristics that yield judgments that are most often likely to be correct (Gigerenzer & Gaissmaier, 2011). The important claim is that the ability to make correct judgments quickly (fast) and with limited resources (frugal) is adaptive—the ability has survival value. Researchers have defined a number of fast and frugal heuristics and demonstrated that they often lead to correct judgments (Hertwig et al., 2008).

Even so, research on heuristics has often focused on circumstances in which they lead to *incorrect* judgments. There are two explanations for this focus. To begin, the research follows a logic that might sound familiar from earlier chapters: Just as you can understand perception by studying perceptual illusion and memory by studying memory failures, you can understand judgment processes by studying judgment errors. In addition, there's value in being able to recognize circumstances in which heuristics might lead to errors. That gives people the opportunity to engage other mental properties to make better judgments.

Still, as you read this section, keep in mind that "fast and frugal" heuristics mostly yield correct judgments. Keep that conclusion in mind as you read about three heuristics—availability, representativeness, and anchoring—try to get some concrete ideas about circumstances in which conscious intervention may be necessary.

Availability Heuristic   Let's begin by considering a rather trivial judgment. Suppose you were to read a few pages from a novel. Do you believe more words in the excerpt would begin with the letter *k* (for example, *kangaroo*) or have *k* in third position (for example, *duke*)? If you are like the participants in a study by Tversky and Kahneman (1973), then you probably judged that *k* is found more often at the beginning of words. In fact, *k* appears about twice as often in the third position.

Why do most people believe that *k* is more likely to appear in first position? The answer has to do with the *availability* of information from memory. It's much easier to think of words that begin with *k* than to think of those in which *k* comes third. Your judgment, thus, arises from use of the **availability heuristic:** You base your judgment on information that is readily available in memory. This heuristic has two components. The first component is the relative ease or *fluency* with which you can retrieve information. Suppose you try to

judge which sport is more dangerous, bowling or hang gliding. You'll probably find it easier to retrieve memories of hang gliding accidents than memories of bowling accidents. If you based your judgment on the ease of retrieval, you'd be likely to conclude that hang gliding is more dangerous. The second component of availability is the content of the memories you find easy to retrieve. Suppose you described the first five memories that come to mind about bowling. If all those memories were unhappy memories, you'd likely conclude that bowling might not be your best choice for a leisure time activity. Let's see how each of these components of availability can lead to potential problems.

Recall from Chapter 7 the discussion of how retrieval cues function to give you access to memories. You learned that the same retrieval cues will be more or less effective, depending on the context in which you put them to use. Suppose, before I asked you the *k* question, I started you out with some examples of *k* in the third position (such as *bike, cake, poke,* and *take*). That change in the context of retrieval could possibly change your judgment. In that way, the fluency of information—the ease with which you can retrieve information from memory—will vary from context to context. Consider a study in which participants provided typicality ratings for exemplars from categories (Oppenheimer & Frank, 2008). In some cases, the exemplars appeared in easy-to-read fonts:

hummingbird

In other cases, the exemplars were hard to read:

hummingbird

Participants gave higher typicality ratings to the same exemplars when they appeared in the easy-to-read fonts! An explanation for this result is that participants' assessments of fluency—the difficulty they experienced making their way from the printed word to their representations in memory— contributed to their judgments of typicality. This study illustrates how judgments you make based on fluency may depend on context. Different contexts may yield different judgments (as with the change in font). When you are making important judgments, ask yourself, "How might this context affect the ease with which I can retrieve particular information?"

You may also experience difficulties with availability when the information you have stored in memory has a bias to it. Consider what happens when you take a a multiple-choice exam. You answer a question, but then, after giving it some additional thought, you decide to change your answer. Are you more likely to change from wrong to right or right to wrong? If you are like most students, you probably believe that you should stick with your first answer—it probably makes you nervous to change your answer. But should it? In fact, many students show a bias in the way they commit information to memory that has a negative impact on test performance.

Researchers inspected the multiple-choice exams of a group of 1,561 students to determine the consequences of answer changes (Kruger et al., 2005). Of the 3,291 answers those students changed, 23 percent were from one wrong answer to another wrong answer. Of the remaining changes, 51 percent made a wrong answer right; 25 percent made a right answer wrong. This pattern suggests that you shouldn't be reluctant to consider changing an answer. However, when

Featured Study

---

availability heuristic A judgment based on the information readily available in memory.

a subset of this group were asked about the wisdom of changing answers, 75 percent indicated that it's a better idea to stick with one's original answer. The researchers argued that students' prejudice against changing answers comes from a memory bias: They suggested that students find more memorable instances in which changed answers led to negative outcomes than when they led to positive outcomes. How many times have you complained to yourself, "I had that one right!" Now, how many times have you complained, "I had that one wrong!" To test the hypothesis that students are more likely to commit negative outcomes to memory, the researchers carried out a second experiment. In this case, the researchers gave students feedback on correct and incorrect answers shortly after they completed a multiple-choice exam. Four to six weeks later, the researchers asked the participants to try to recall the instances in which they had considered changing their answers, what they had decided, and the consequences of those decisions. A student might, for example, have reported that she had deliberated on three problems and always stuck with her original answer. The memory data showed a consistent bias: Participants overestimated how often they switched an answer and then got the question wrong; they underestimated how often they switched an answer and then got the question right.

Put yourself in a classroom while you are taking a test. You get to a moment at which you're trying to decide whether to change an answer. These data suggest that you make this judgment with respect to a biased database: You have committed more negative outcomes to memory than positive outcomes—those are the outcomes that are available. This analysis certainly doesn't mean that you should *always* change your answers. However, you should be aware now of why your feelings of distress arise when you contemplate a change.

Representativeness Heuristic When you make judgments based on the **representativeness heuristic,** you assume that if something has the characteristics considered typical of members of a category, it is, in fact, a member of that category. This heuristic will seem familiar to you because it captures the idea that people use past information to make judgments about similar circumstances in the present. That is the essence of inductive reasoning. Under most circumstances—as long as you have unbiased ideas about the features and categories that go together—making judgments along the lines of similarity will be quite reasonable. Thus, if you are deciding whether to begin a new activity like hang gliding, it makes sense to determine how representative that sport is of the category of activities you have previously enjoyed.

Representativeness will lead you astray, however, when it causes you to ignore other types of relevant information (Kahneman & Frederick, 2002; Kahneman & Tversky, 1973). Consider the description of a successful attorney given in **Figure 8.17** (Bar-Hillel & Neter, 1993). Which option seems

....

representativeness heuristic A cognitive strategy that assigns an object to a category on the basis of a few characteristics regarded as representative of that category.

A successful Jerusalem attorney. Colleagues say his whims prevent him from being a team worker, attributing his success to competitiveness and drive. Slim and not tall, he watches his body and is vain. Spends several hours a week on his favorite sport. What sport is that?

a. Fast walking
b. A ball game
c. Tennis
d. A track and field sport

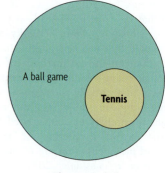

The more inclusive category <u>must</u> be more probable.

FIGURE 8.17 Using the Representativeness Heuristic

When asked to choose the attorney's favorite sport, the representativeness heuristic leads most people to choose "tennis." However, as shown in the bottom part of the figure, the more probable answer is "a ball game," because that includes within it "tennis."

correct to you? Most people who address this problem choose *tennis* rather than *a ball game*. The lower part of Figure 8.17 shows why *tennis* shouldn't be the first choice: Tennis is included within the category *a ball game*. Participants judge *tennis* to be a better answer because it seems to have all the features of the sport the attorney is likely to play. However, this judgment by representativeness causes participants to neglect another sort of information—category structure. The implication for your day-to-day life is that you should not be fooled into grabbing at a representative alternative before you consider the structure of all the alternatives.

Let's look at another use of representativeness. Consider the last time you went to hear live music. Suppose a friend asked you, "How much did you enjoy the concert?" How do you answer such a question? Most live performances unfold over a period of time; they have some good moments and some not-so-good moments. To answer the global question (that is, "How much . . . ?"), you need to provide a value that is representative of all those various moments. Research suggests that representative values often reflect an average of an event's moment of *peak* intensity and the intensity at the event's *end* (Kahneman & Frederick, 2002). Let's look at a study that tested this hypothesis in an academic context.

....

Featured Study

Participants in the study tried to learn the English translations for Spanish words (Finn, 2010). In the short trial, they studied 30 Spanish-English translations that other students had found extremely difficult. In the extended trial, participants also studied 30 extremely difficult translations followed by 15 translations that were only moderately difficult. All the participants completed both trials, but some did the short trial first whereas the others did the extended trial first. After the two study trials, participants answered this question: "Suppose we paid you to come back tomorrow to complete one more study list. Would you rather study a list (of new words) that was more like List 1 or like List 2?" (p. 1550). In response, 73 percent of the participants chose the list that had been their extended trial. That is, they expressed a preference for learning 45 words rather than 30!

Do you see why the average of the peak and the end would be the lower for the extended trial? For the short trial, the peak equals the end so the average would be "extremely difficult." For the extended trial, the peak is "extremely difficult," but that would be combined with the end point of "moderately difficult" to 'yield a lower average. That pattern explains the preference for the extended trial. The same peak-end rule applies to positive experiences (Do et al., 2008). In one study, people were happier when they received *less* candy if the single piece of "peak" candy was better than the average of the "peak" candy and the "end" candy.

Can you see how you might apply this peak-end rule to your own life? To influence people's evaluation of an event, you should think about how to arrange the components of the event so that people encode the desired representative value.

Anchoring Heuristic   To introduce you to a third heuristic, you need you to try a thought experiment. First take five seconds to estimate the following mathematical product and write down your answer:

$$1 \times 2 \times 3 \times 4 \times 5 \times 6 \times 7 \times 8 = \underline{\hspace{2cm}}$$

In five seconds, you can probably make only a couple of calculations. You get a partial answer, perhaps 24, and then adjust up from there. Now try this series of numbers:

$$8 \times 7 \times 6 \times 5 \times 4 \times 3 \times 2 \times 1 = \underline{\hspace{2cm}}$$

Even if you notice that this is the same list in reverse, you can see how the experience of carrying out the multiplication would feel quite different. You'd start with 8×7, which is 56, and then attempt 56×6, which already feels quite large. Once again, you can only make a partial guess and then adjust upward. When Tversky and Kahneman (1974) gave these two arrangements of the identical problem to experimental participants, the 1 to 8 order produced median estimates of 512, and the 8 to 1 group produced estimates of 2,250 *(the real answer is 40,320)*. Apparently, when participants adjusted up from their five-second estimates, the higher partial solutions led to higher estimates.

Performance on this simple multiplication task provides evidence for the **anchoring heuristic:** People's judgments of the probable value of some event or outcome represent

How might retailers use "original prices" as anchors to get you to pay more for an item?

insufficient adjustments—either up or down—from an original starting value. In other words, your judgment is "anchored" too firmly to an original guess. Consider a study in which business students were asked to say how much they would pay for a "35 mm–75 mm with a flash" (Adaval & Wyer, 2011). Some participants provided their estimate in the context of a high anchor: They first said whether they thought the camera would cost greater or less than $419; then they indicated what they would pay. Other participants provided their estimates in the context of a low anchor: They made the "greater or less" judgment with respect to $49 before indicating their own price. The anchor had a $238 effect: Participants who started with the high anchor, on average, said that they'd be willing to pay $317; those who started with the low anchor said they'd be willing to pay $78.

Why do people make insufficient adjustments from anchors? Researchers have begun to address this question in real-life circumstances—in which people produce their own anchors before beginning the adjustment process. Consider this question: What is the duration of Mars's orbit around the sun? How might you answer that question? Research suggests that you start with the duration of Earth's orbit of 365 days as an anchor. What next? You might use the knowledge that Mars is farther from the sun than Earth is to adjust away from the 365-day anchor toward a larger value. In fact, participants in an experiment estimated Mars's orbit to be about 492 days (Epley & Gilovich, 2006). This estimate is still short of the actual value, which is 869 days. What people appeared to do in the experiment was to start with a reasonable anchor (365 days) and keep adjusting until they reached a value that seemed *plausible*. When you find yourself in situations of anchoring and adjustment, put this result to use: You should expend some extra effort to confirm that a plausible value is, in fact, the right answer.

You employ judgmental heuristics like availability, representativeness, and anchoring because, in most situations, they allow you to make efficient, acceptable judgments. Given the uncertainties of situations and constraints on your processing resources, you are doing quite well! However, you have also seen that heuristics can lead to errors. Try to use this knowledge when the time comes to make important judgments. Be

---

anchoring heuristic An insufficient adjustment up or down from an original starting value when judging the probable value of some event or outcome.

Table 8.7 • The Effect of Framing

Survival Frame

Surgery. Of 100 people having surgery, 90 live through the postoperative period, 68 are alive at the end of the first year, and 34 are alive at the end of five years.

Radiation therapy. Of 100 people having radiation therapy, all live through the treatment, 77 are alive at the end of one year, and 22 are alive at the end of five years.

What do you choose: surgery or radiation?

Mortality Frame

Surgery. Of 100 people having surgery, 10 die during surgery or the postoperative period, 32 die by the end of one year, and 66 die by the end of five years.

Radiation therapy. Of 100 people having radiation therapy, none dies during treatment, 23 die by the end of one year, and 78 die by the end of five years.

What do you choose: surgery or radiation?

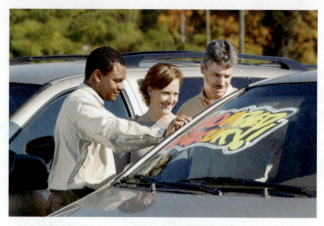

In what ways can salespeople frame their products to get prospective customers to consider them in a positive light?

especially critical when you feel others might be trying to bias your judgments. Let's move now to the decisions you make, often on the basis of those judgments.

The Psychology of Decision Making

Your life is filled with decisions both great ("With whom should I share my life?") and small ("What pen should I bring to my exam?"). This section will explore important psychological aspects of decision making. You will see that the way in which a question is phrased can have great consequences for the decision you will make. You'll learn, in addition, how your decisions are affected both by the consequences you anticipate and those you experience.

The Framing of Decisions One of the most natural ways to make a decision is to judge which option will bring about the biggest gain or which option will bring about the smallest loss. Thus, if someone offers you either $5 or $10, you will feel very little uncertainty that the better option is $10. What makes the situation a bit more complicated, however, is that the perception of a gain or a loss often depends on the way in which a decision is *framed*. A **frame** is a particular description of a choice. Suppose, for example, you were asked how happy you would be to get a $1,000 raise in your job. If you were expecting no raise at all, this would seem like a great gain, and you'd probably be quite happy. But suppose you'd been told several times to expect a raise of $10,000. Now how do you feel? Suddenly, you may feel as if you've lost money because the $1,000 is less than what you had expected. You're not happy at all! In either case, you'd be getting $1,000 more a

year—objectively, you'd be in exactly the same position—but the psychological effect is very different. That's why *reference points* are important in decision making (Kahneman, 1992). What seems like a gain or a loss will be determined in part by the expectations—a $0 raise or a $10,000 raise—to which a decision maker refers. (The decision, in this case, might be whether to stay in the job.)

Let's now take a look at a slightly more complex example in which framing has a sizable impact on the decisions people make. In **Table 8.7**, you are asked to imagine making a choice between surgery and radiation for treatment of lung cancer. First, read the *survival* frame for the problem and choose your preferred treatment; then read the *mortality* frame and see if you feel like changing your preference. Note that the data are objectively the same in the two frames. The only difference is whether statistical information about the consequences of each treatment is presented in terms of survival rates or of mortality rates. When this decision was presented to participants, the focus on relative gains and losses had a marked effect on choice of treatment. Radiation therapy was chosen by only 18 percent of the participants who were given the survival frame but by 44 percent of those given the mortality frame. This framing effect held equally for a group of clinic patients, statistically sophisticated business students, and experienced physicians (McNeil et al., 1982).

Now that you know about frames, you should start to look for them in your everyday life. You're especially likely to find them when people are trying to get you to buy their products. Consider a study that looked at people's judgments about the choices they would make between two butchers.

The participants in an experiment read a brief scenario that described two neighborhood butchers (Keren, 2007). Butcher A advertised his meat as 25 percent fat; Butcher B advertised his meat as 75 percent lean. Participants imagined that they were preparing for a large dinner party and had to buy their meat from one of the two butchers. Which would they choose? The majority of the participants (82 percent) went with Butcher B. You can probably see why: The meat that's 75 percent lean sounds much healthier. Of course, the two butchers are actually offering

Featured Study

---

frame A particular description of a choice; the perspective from which a choice is described or framed affects how a decision is made and which option is ultimately exercised.

the same product (because meat that is 75 percent lean would have 25 percent fat). Despite that math, the frame has a large impact. Now consider a judgment made by a second group of participants: They indicated which of the two butchers they would trust more. For trust judgments, participants' preferences were reversed: A majority (73 percent) said they trusted more the butcher who told them how much fat the meat had!

This experiment illustrates that the same frame can have an opposite impact on different judgments. Do you suppose the butchers would be happier to be trusted by their customers or to sell their products? As you think about frames in the real world, you should consider what judgments people are trying to affect.

These results should encourage you to think about important decisions from the perspective of different frames. Suppose, for example, you are going to buy a new car. The salesperson will be inclined to frame everything as a gain: "Seventy-eight percent of the Xenons require no repairs in the first year!" You can reframe that to "Twenty-two percent require some repairs in the first year!" Would the new frame change how you feel about the situation? It's an exercise worth trying in real life.

The car salesperson is a good example of a situation in which someone is trying to frame information in a fashion that will have a desired effect on your decision. This, of course, is a regular part of your life. For example, as each election approaches, the opposing candidates compete to have their framings of themselves and of the issues prevail among the voters. One candidate might say, "I believe in sticking with policies that have been successful." His opponent might counter, "He is afraid of new ideas." One candidate might say, "That policy will bring about economic growth." Her opponent might counter, "That policy will bring about environmental destruction." Often both claims are true—the same policy often will bring about both economic good and environmental harm. In this light, whichever frame seems more compelling may be largely a matter of personal history. Thus your knowledge of framing effects can help you understand how people can come to such radically different decisions when they are faced with exactly the same evidence. If you want to understand other people's actions, try to think about how those individuals have framed a decision.

Consequences of Decision Making What happens when you make a decision? In the best of all possible worlds, everything goes well—and you never look back. However, as you likely know, not all decisions yield the best of all possible worlds. When decisions turn out badly, you will likely experience *regret*. Studies suggest that the categories in which people express the greatest regret is their decisions with respect to their education and careers (Roese & Summerville, 2005). To explain this finding, researchers point to the fact that these two domains provide a particularly wide range of opportunities: There are many ways to pursue an education and many careers to which someone might aspire. That range of opportunities makes it quite easy for people to wonder, "Did I make the right decision?"

People also experience more regret when they are clear on the costs associated with particular decisions (van Dijk &

Zeelenberg, 2005). Consider a moment on a game show when a contestant must choose between *Box A* and *Box B*. If the contestant chooses the box with $10 instead of $10,000, it's easy to understand why he would experience regret. Some decisions in life are like the game show. You have the apple pie. Your friend has the pecan pie. After you each take one bite, you know that you made the wrong decision. You experience regret because you have a clear grasp on what you gave up. In other cases, you have a much vaguer grasp on the consequences of your decision. If you choose a poodle as a pet, you'll never know exactly how different your life would have been had you gone for a bulldog. In that type of situation, it's less likely that you will experience regret.

Let's take a moment to consider the brain bases of regret. The examples we've considered so far have largely focused on people's regret over missed opportunities. In what way does the brain respond to those circumstances?

*In one study, participants looked at a computer display that showed a row of eight closed boxes (Büchel et al., 2011). The participants had the option of opening as many boxes as they wished, left to right. Seven of the boxes contained "gold" and one contained "a devil." On each of about 70 rounds, the participants could open as many boxes as they wished. They kept all the gold they found—unless they opened the box with the devil, at which point they lost their gold. Thus, after each box participants had to decide whether to keep their winnings or go on. If they chose to stop without finding the devil, the position of the devil was revealed to them. **Figure 8.18** on page 236 displays fMRI data from a structure in the brain called the putamen. The figure's top portion shows the location of this structure in your brain. The bottom portion shows that the change in the putamen's activity depended on the size of the missed opportunity. When the devil was in the very next box (marked as 1 at the bottom of the figure), the participants had stopped at exactly the right box. The putamen activity changed very little. When the devil was several boxes in the future (5 in the figure), the putamen showed considerably greater change.*

When participants experienced larger missed opportunities they subsequently took greater risks (that is, they often opened more boxes on the next round). The activity in the putamen appeared to provide information to other brain structures that ultimately produced that pattern of risk taking.

One final observation: Not all decision makers are created equal. Suppose you go to the Web to choose a movie to download for a Saturday night viewing. If you are a *satisficer*, you would likely to consider options until you got to one that struck you as interesting enough. If you are a *maximizer*, you would likely browse through a long list until you had convinced yourself that you'd found exactly the best one. Researchers have demonstrated that there are both satisficers and maximizers in the world—and that the style of decision making has important consequences (Parker et al., 2007; Schwartz et al., 2002).

For example, one study followed a group of 548 students from 11 colleges and universities as they went onto the job market (Iyengar et al., 2006). The students completed a questionnaire that revealed the extent to which they were

Featured Study

A

Y = 8mm   R

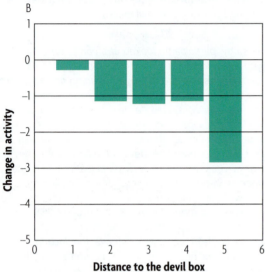

B

FIGURE 8.18 The Brain's Response to Missed Opportunities

Participants engaged in a task that allowed for missed opportunities that were relatively small or large. Activity in the putamen changed the most in response to the largest missed opportunity.

satisficers or maximizers: They indicated their agreement with statements such as "When shopping, I have a hard time finding clothes that I really love." The researchers contacted the students three months and six months after they completed the initial questionnaire—at those points in time, the

students were interviewing and then accepting jobs. The researchers collected a variety of data to determine how the students experienced the process. Those data showed a clear pattern: The maximizers had accepted jobs that, on average, provided 20 percent higher salaries—yet they were miserable. As the researchers put it, "Despite their relative success, maximizers [were] less satisfied with the outcomes of the job search, and more pessimistic, stressed, tired, anxious, worried, overwhelmed, and depressed throughout the process" (Iyengar et al., 2006, p. 147). Apparently, the quest for an elusive "best" outcome provided the maximizers with a substantial psychological burden. Most people would probably like to have a good job without making themselves miserable. As you undertake your own job searches, you might think back to this distinction between maximizers and satisficers—to consider how you might achieve a decision that affords your life a sense of balance.

Throughout this chapter, you've had several opportunities to contemplate the mysterious midnight message, "The cat is on the mat." The goal has been to get you to consider your many types of cognitive processing—language use, visual cognition, problem solving, reasoning, judging, and deciding. Now that this chapter has come to an end, I hope that the example will stick with you—so that you'll never take your cognitive processes for granted. Every chance you get, give some thought to your thought! You will be reflecting on the essence of the human experience.

Stop and Review

① Why do people rely on heuristics when they are making judgments?

② What heuristic might you use to answer the question, "What is the age of the oldest living human being?"

③ Why do frames play such a large role in the psychology of decision making?

④ What is the distinction between satisficers and maximizers?

✓ **Study** and **Review** on **MyPsychLab**

CRITICAL THINKING Recall the study on the length of Spanish-English word lists. Why was it important that some participants had the extended lists first and some had them second?

Recapping Main Points

Studying Cognition

- Cognitive psychologists study the mental processes and structures that enable you to perceive, use language, reason, solve problems, and make judgments and decisions.
- Researchers use reaction time measures to break up complex tasks into underlying mental processes.

Language Use

- Language users both produce and understand language.
- Speakers design their utterances to suit particular audiences.
- Speech errors reveal many of the processes that go into speech planning.

- Language understanding often requires the use of context to resolve ambiguities.
- Memory representations of meaning begin with propositions supplemented with inferences.
- Studies of language evolution have focused on grammatical structure.
- The language individuals speak may play a role in determining how they think.

Visual Cognition

- Visual representations can be used to supplement propositional representations.
- Visual representations allow you to think about visual aspects of your environment.
- People form visual representations that combine verbal and visual information.

Problem Solving and Reasoning

- Problem solvers must define initial state, goal state, and the operations that get them from the initial to the goal state.

- Creativity is often assessed using tests of divergent and convergent thinking.
- Deductive reasoning involves drawing conclusions from premises based on rules of logic.
- Inductive reasoning involves inferring a conclusion from evidence based on its likelihood or probability.

Judgment and Decision Making

- Much of judgment and decision making is guided by heuristics—mental shortcuts that can help individuals reach solutions quickly.
- Availability, representativeness, and anchoring all allow for efficient judgments under uncertainty.
- Decision making is affected by the way in which different options are framed.
- The possibility of regret makes some decisions hard, particularly for individuals who are maximizers rather than satisficers.

KEY TERMS

algorithm (p. 224)
anchoring heuristic (p. 233)
audience design (p. 211)
automatic process (p. 209)
availability heuristic (p. 231)
belief-bias effect (p. 228)
cognition (p. 207)
cognitive process (p. 207)
cognitive psychology (p. 207)
cognitive science (p. 207)
controlled process (p. 209)

convergent thinking (p. 226)
creativity (p. 225)
decision making (p. 230)
deductive reasoning (p. 227)
divergent thinking (p. 226)
frame (p. 234)
functional fixedness (p. 225)
heuristic (p. 225)
inductive reasoning (p. 229)
inference (p. 216)
insight (p. 226)

judgment (p. 230)
language production (p. 211)
linguistic relativity (p. 218)
mental set (p. 230)
parallel processes (p. 208)
problem solving (p. 223)
problem space (p. 224)
reasoning (p. 223)
representativeness heuristic (p. 232)
serial processes (p. 208)
think-aloud protocol (p. 225)

1. According to the logic of Donders's analysis,
   a. categorization is among the hardest mental processes.
   b. it should always take longer to draw a capital *C* than a capital *V*.
   c. extra mental steps often result in more time to complete a task.
   d. reaction time is useful for understanding the order of mental processes.

2. When Jerry goes with friends to a fast-food restaurant, they each wait in a different line to see who gets to the counter first. That's a good example of _____ processing.
   a. serial
   b. automatic
   c. parallel
   d. ambiguity

3. Lauren can juggle and talk at the same time. Warren cannot. It sounds as if juggling is more of a(n) _____ process for Lauren than for Warren.
   a. controlled
   b. automatic
   c. parallel
   d. serial

4. A friend walks up to you and says, "Remember what I said yesterday? Well, forget about it." If you understand all of this, it's because your friend has made an appropriate assessment of common ground based on
   a. copresence for actions.
   b. perceptual copresence.
   c. community membership.
   d. linguistic membership.

5. Research has demonstrated that _____ can learn the meanings of plastic symbols without any explicit training.
   a. vervet monkeys
   b. orangutans
   c. chimpanzees
   d. bonobos

6. The hypothesis of linguistic relativity suggests that
   a. languages can carve up the color spectrum in any way they choose.
   b. the languages individuals speak affect the way they think about the world.
   c. people have evolved to use languages with greater complexity than other species.
   d. some languages do not allow people to engage in audience design.

7. Research using fMRI scans suggests that lying draws heavily on brain areas responsible for _____ and _____.
   a. aggression; planning
   b. emotion; pattern recognition
   c. planning; emotion
   d. ambiguity resolution; aggression

8. You are lying on your side when a friend walks up to say hello. To recognize your friend, you might have to use
   a. mental rotation.
   b. mental scanning.
   c. a spatial mental model.
   d. a problem space.

9. Suppose you study a text that inserts you into the middle of a room with objects around you. It should take you the least time to verify that object that is
   a. in front of you.
   b. behind you.
   c. on your left side.
   d. on your right side.

10. A(n) _____ is *not* one component of the definition of a problem space.
    a. algorithm
    b. set of operations
    c. goal state
    d. initial state

11. An explanation based on signal detection theory suggests that the belief-bias effect happens because of
    a. inductive reasoning.
    b. the representativeness heuristic.
    c. response bias.
    d. the influence of framing.

12. When you are engaging in _____ reasoning, you should be wary of a(n) _____.
    a. inductive; algorithm
    b. inductive; mental set
    c. deductive; premise
    d. deductive; think-aloud protocol

13. Suppose you are asked to estimate whether Hollywood releases more comedies or horror flicks each year. To answer this question, you are most likely to use the _____ heuristic.
    a. anchoring
    b. adjustment
    c. representativeness
    d. availability

14. Because Paul is a satisficer, you would expect him to
    a. watch the first TV channel that catches his interest.
    b. be unhappy even though he recently obtained a high-paying job.
    c. test drive dozens of new cars before making a purchase.
    d. try every flavor of coffee at the new corner market.

15. Suppose you wanted to provide a short-term boost to the creativity of your friend Constance. You ask her to think about a negative event in her life and construct _____ counterfactuals about it.
    a. additive
    b. near
    c. distant
    d. subtractive

ESSAY QUESTIONS

1. Why is ambiguity an important problem for language comprehension?

2. What factors affect your ability to engage in accurate deductive reasoning?

3. Under what circumstances are decisions more likely to cause people regret?

9

Intelligence and Intelligence Assessment

Suppose you were asked to define the word *intelligence*. What types of behaviors would you include in your definition? Think back on your own experiences. What was it like when you first started school? What was it like when you labored at your first job? It's very likely that you heard your behaviors labeled as intelligent or unintelligent—smart or not so smart—in those and other situations. When those labels are applied in casual conversation, they have relatively few consequences. However, there are many settings in which it matters whether your behaviors are considered intelligent or not. For example, if you grew up in the United States, it is likely that your "potential" was measured at an early age. In most school districts, teachers and administrators attempt, very early in your life, to measure your *intelligence*. The goal, most often, is to match students with classroom work that makes appropriate demands. However, as you've almost certainly observed, people's lives often seem to be affected by intelligence testing in areas well outside the classroom.

This chapter examines the foundations and uses of intelligence assessment. It will review the contributions psychologists have made to the understanding of individual differences in the areas of intelligence. We will also consider the types of controversies that almost inevitably arise when people begin to interpret these differences. The focus will be on how intelligence tests work, what makes any test useful, and why they do not always do the job they were intended to do. The chapter will conclude by considering the role of psychological assessment in society.

Let's begin with a brief overview of the general practice of psychological assessment.

WHAT IS ASSESSMENT?

Psychological assessment is the use of specified testing procedures to evaluate the abilities, behaviors, and personal qualities of people. Psychological assessment is often referred to as the measurement of *individual differences* because the majority of assessments specify how an individual is different from or similar to other people on a given dimension. Let's begin with a brief history of assessment. This historical overview will help you to understand both the uses and limitations of assessment, as well as prepare you to appreciate some current controversies.

History of Assessment

The development of formal tests and procedures for assessment is a relatively new enterprise in Western psychology, coming into wide use only in the early 1900s. However, long before Western psychology began to devise tests to evaluate people, assessment techniques were commonplace in ancient China. In fact, China employed a sophisticated program of civil service testing over 4,000 years ago—officials were required to demonstrate their competence every third year at an oral examination. Two thousand years later, during the Han Dynasty, written civil service tests were used to measure competence in

the areas of law, the military, agriculture, and geography. During the Ming Dynasty (A.D. 1368–1644), public officials were chosen on the basis of their performance at three stages of an objective selection procedure. During the first stage, examinations were given at the local level. The 4 percent who passed these tests had to endure the second stage: 9 days and nights of essay examinations on the classics. The 5 percent who passed the essay exams were allowed to complete a final stage of tests conducted at the nation's capital.

China's selection procedures were observed and described by British diplomats and missionaries in the early 1800s. Modified versions of China's system were soon adopted by the British and later by the Americans for the selection of civil service personnel (Wiggins, 1973).

The key figure in the development of Western intelligence testing was an upper-class Englishman, **Sir Francis Galton** (1822–1911). His book *Hereditary Genius,* published in 1869, greatly influenced subsequent thinking on the methods, theories, and practices of testing. Galton, a half cousin to Charles Darwin, attempted to apply Darwinian evolutionary theory to the study of human abilities. He was interested in how and why people differ in their abilities. He wondered why some people were gifted and successful—like him—while many others were not.

Galton was the first to postulate four important ideas about the assessment of intelligence. First, differences in intelligence were *quantifiable* in terms of degrees of intelligence. In other words, numerical values could be assigned to distinguish among different people's levels of intelligence. Second, differences among people formed a *bell-shaped curve*, or *normal distribution*. On a bell-shaped curve, most people's scores cluster in the middle, and fewer are found toward the two extremes of genius and mental deficiency (we'll return to the bell-shaped curve later in the chapter). Third, intelligence, or mental ability, could be measured by objective tests, tests on which each question had only one "right" answer. And fourth, the precise extent to which two sets of test scores were related could be determined by a statistical procedure he called *co-relations*, now known as *correlations*. These ideas proved to be of lasting value.

What important ideas about the assessment of intelligence are credited to Sir Francis Galton (1822–1911)?

....

psychological assessment The use of specified procedures to evaluate the abilities, behaviors, and personal qualities of people.

Unfortunately, Galton postulated a number of ideas that proved considerably more controversial. He believed, for example, that genius was inherited. In his view, talent, or eminence, ran in families; nurture had only a minimal effect on intelligence. In his view, intelligence was related to Darwinian species' fitness and, somehow, ultimately to one's moral worth. Galton attempted to base public policy on the concept of genetically superior and inferior people. He started the *eugenics* movement, which advocated improving the human species by applying evolutionary theory to encouraging biologically superior people to interbreed while discouraging biologically inferior people from having offspring. Galton wrote, "There exists a sentiment, for the most part quite unreasonable, against the gradual extinction of an inferior race" (Galton, 1883/1907, p. 200). You'll see later in the chapter that remnants of these elitist ideas are still being proposed today.

Sir Francis Galton's work created a context for contemporary intelligence assessment. Let's now see what features define circumstances of formal assessment.

Basic Features of Formal Assessment

To be useful for classifying individuals or for selecting those with particular qualities, a **formal assessment** procedure should meet three requirements. The assessment instrument should be (1) reliable, (2) valid, and (3) standardized. If it fails to meet these requirements, we cannot be sure whether the conclusions of the assessment can be trusted. Although this chapter focuses on intelligence assessment, formal assessment procedures apply to all types of psychological testing. To ensure that you'll understand the broad application of these principles, I will draw on examples both from intelligence testing and other domains of psychological assessment.

Reliability As you'll recall from Chapter 2, *reliability* is the extent to which an assessment instrument can be trusted to give consistent scores. If you stepped on your bathroom scale three times in the same morning and it gave you a different reading each time, the scale would not be doing its job. You would call it *unreliable* because you could not count on it to give consistent results. Of course, if you ate a big meal in between two weighings, you wouldn't expect the scale to produce the same result. That is, a measurement device can be considered reliable or

How would you feel if someone used your adult height to assess intelligence? The measure would be reliable, but would it be valid?

unreliable only to the extent that the underlying concept it is measuring should remain unchanged.

One straightforward way to find out if a test is reliable is to calculate its **test–retest reliability**—a measure of the correlation between the scores of the same people, on the same test, given on two different occasions. A perfectly reliable test will yield a correlation coefficient of $+1.00$. This means that the identical pattern of scores emerges both times. The same people who got the highest and lowest scores the first time do so again. A totally unreliable test results in a 0.00 correlation coefficient. That means there is no relationship between the first set of scores and the second set. Someone who initially got the top score gets a completely different score the second time. As the correlation coefficient moves higher (toward the ideal of $+1.00$), the test is increasingly reliable. Another measure of reliability is the **internal consistency** of responses on a single test. For example, we can compare a person's score on the odd-numbered items of a test with the score on the even-numbered items. A reliable test yields the same score for each of its halves.

The researchers who develop and administer assessment devices work hard to ensure reliability. Did you take the SAT I exam for college admissions? You may not know this, but one section of the exam you took did not have an impact on your score. The questions on this unscored section were most likely being considered for future exams. The researchers who develop the exam can compare performance on the scored questions to performance on the unscored questions to ensure that people's scores on future exams are comparable to the scores on the exam that you took. For that reason, if you took the SAT I, you provided some of the information that helps to make the test reliable.

Validity Recall from Chapter 2 that the *validity* of a test is the degree to which it measures what an assessor intends it to measure. A valid test of intelligence measures that trait and predicts performance in situations where intelligence is important. Scores on a valid measure of creativity reflect actual creativity, not drawing ability or moods. In general, then, validity reflects a test's ability to make accurate predictions about behaviors or outcomes related to the purpose or design of the test. The conditions under which a test is valid may be very specific, so it is always important to ask about a test, "For what purpose is it valid?" Three important types of validity are *content validity, criterion-related validity,* and *construct validity.*

A test has **content validity** if it measures the full range of the domain of interest. Suppose you wanted to assess people's satisfaction with their lives. It wouldn't be enough to focus, for example, on success in school. To develop a measure that had content validity, you'd want to sample broadly from the different domains of people's lives. You would ask people if they were satisfied with their jobs, their relationships, and so on.

To assess **criterion-related validity,** psychologists compare a person's score on the test with his or her score on some other standard, or *criterion,* associated with what the test measures. For example, if a test is designed to predict success in college, then college grades would be an appropriate criterion. If the test scores correlate highly with college grades, then the test has criterion-related validity. A major task of test developers is to find appropriate, measurable criteria. Let's see how researchers demonstrated the criterion-related validity of a measure of juror bias.

Featured Study

When people become members of juries they are supposed to consider the evidence without any biases. A pair of researchers sought to demonstrate the validity of a measurement device—the Pretrial Juror Attitude Questionnaire (PJAQ)—that would enable them to identify potential jurors who could not meet that unbiased standard (Lecci & Myers, 2008). The PJAQ consists of a series of 29 statements (for example, "If a suspect runs from police, then he probably committed the crime," "Many accident claims filed against insurance companies are phony"). People who take the PJAQ indicate their agreement to each statement on a 5-point scale ranging from strongly disagree to strongly agree. To assess the criterion-related validity of the PJAQ, the researchers asked 617 participants to complete the measure. Next, they had the same group of participants read summaries of trials for murder, rape, and armed robbery cases. The participants indicated what verdict they thought was appropriate for each case. When participants arrive at more guilty verdicts than the majority of their peers, that pattern suggests that some prior bias may be at work. The PJAQ successfully predicted which participants were likely to provide a high number of guilty verdicts.

Once criterion-related validity has been demonstrated for an assessment device, researchers feel confident using the device to make future predictions.

For many personal qualities of interest to psychologists, no ideal criterion exists. No single behavior or objective measure of performance can indicate, for example, how anxious,

How would you test the validity of a measure of juror attitudes?

depressed, or aggressive a person is overall. Psychologists have theories, or *constructs,* about these abstract qualities—what causes them, how they affect behavior, and how they relate to other variables. The **construct validity** of a test is the degree to which it adequately measures the underlying construct. For example, a new measure of depression has construct validity if the scores it produces correlate highly with valid measures of the features that define the construct of depression. In addition, the new measure should not show relationships with features that fall outside the construct of depression.

Consider for a moment the relationship between validity and reliability. Whereas reliability is measured by the degree to which a test correlates with itself (administered at different times or using different items), validity is measured by the degree to which the test correlates with something external to it (another test, a behavioral criterion, or judges' ratings). Usually, a test that is not reliable is also not valid because a test that cannot predict itself will be unable to predict anything else. For example, if your class took a test of aggressiveness today and scores were uncorrelated with scores from a parallel form of the test tomorrow (demonstrating unreliability), it is unlikely that the scores from either day would predict which students had fought or argued most frequently over a week's time: After all, the two sets of test scores would not even make the same prediction! Conversely, it is quite possible for a test to be highly reliable without being valid. Suppose, for example, we decided to use your current height as a measure of intelligence. Do you see why that would be reliable but not valid?

Norms and Standardization So we have a reliable and valid test, but we still need *norms* to provide a context for interpreting different test scores. Suppose, for example, you get a score of 18 on a test designed to reveal how depressed you are. What does that mean? Are you a little depressed, not at all depressed, or about averagely depressed? To find out what your score means, you would want to compare your individual score with typical scores, or statistical **norms,** of other students. You would check the test norms to see what the usual range of scores is and what the average is for students of your age and sex. That would provide you with a context for interpreting your depression score.

You probably encountered test norms when you received your scores on aptitude tests, such as the SAT I. The norms told you how your scores compared with those of other students and helped you interpret how well you had done relative to that *normative population.* Group norms are most useful for interpreting individual scores when the comparison group shares important qualities with the individuals tested, such as age, social class, culture, and experience.

For norms to be meaningful, everyone must take the same test under standardized circumstances. **Standardization** is the administration of a testing device to all persons, in the same way,

....

criterion-related validity The degree to which test scores indicate a result on a specific measure that is consistent with some other criterion of the characteristic being assessed.

construct validity The degree to which a test adequately measures an underlying construct.

norm Standard based on measurement of a large group of people; used for comparing the scores of an individual with those of others within a well-defined group.

standardization A set of uniform procedures for treating each participant in a test, interview, or experiment, or for recording data.

under the same conditions. The need for standardization sounds obvious, but it does not always occur in practice. Some people may be allowed more time than others, be given clearer or more detailed instructions, be permitted to ask questions, or be motivated by a tester to perform better. When procedures do not include explicit instructions about the way to administer a test or the way to score the results, it is difficult to interpret what a given test score means or how it relates to any comparison group.

You have now seen some of the concerns researchers have when they construct a test and find out whether it is indeed testing what they wish to test. They must assure themselves that the test is reliable and valid. They must also specify the standard conditions under which it should be administered, so that resulting norms have meaning. Therefore, you should evaluate any test score you get in terms of the test's reliability and validity, the norms of performance, and the degree of standardization of the circumstances in which you took the test.

We are now ready to turn to the measurement of intelligence.

Stop *and* Review

① What overarching ideas did Sir Francis Galton contribute to the study of intelligence?

② How would a researcher determine whether a measure has criterion-related validity?

③ Why is it important to have norms for measures?

CRITICAL THINKING   Recall the study that assessed the criterion-related validity of the Pretrial Juror Attitude Questionnaire. How might you assess the PJAQ's validity in the context of real-world trials?

✔—[Study and Review on MyPsychLab

INTELLIGENCE ASSESSMENT

How intelligent are you or your friends? To answer this question, you must begin by defining **intelligence.** Doing so is not an easy task, but a group of 52 intelligence researchers concurred on this general definition: "Intelligence is a very general mental capability that, among other things, involves the ability to reason, plan, solve problems, think abstractly, comprehend complex ideas, learn quickly and learn from experience" (Gottfredson, 1997, p. 13). Given this range of capabilities, it should be clear immediately why controversy has almost always surrounded how intelligence is measured. The way in which theorists conceptualize intelligence and higher mental functioning greatly influences the way they try to assess it.

....

◉ **Watch** the **Video** *The Big Picture: What is Intelligence?* on **MyPsychLab**

intelligence The global capacity to profit from experience and to go beyond given information about the environment.

mental age In Binet's measure of intelligence, the age at which a child is performing intellectually, expressed in terms of the average age at which normal children achieve a particular score.

chronological age The number of months or years since an individual's birth.

Some psychologists believe that human intelligence can be quantified and reduced to a single score. Others argue that intelligence has many components that should be separately assessed. Still others say that there are actually several distinct kinds of intelligence, across different domains of experience. ◉

In this section, you'll learn how tests of intelligence mesh with these different conceptions of intelligence. Let's begin by considering the historical context in which interest in intelligence and intelligence testing first arose.

The Origins of Intelligence Testing

The year 1905 marked the first published account of a workable intelligence test. **Alfred Binet** (1857–1911) had responded to the call of the French minister of public instruction for the creation of more effective teaching methods for developmentally disabled children. Binet and his colleague **Theodore Simon** (1873–1961) believed that measuring a child's intellectual ability was necessary for planning an instructional program. Binet attempted to devise an objective test of intellectual performance that could be used to classify and separate developmentally disabled from normal schoolchildren. He hoped that such a test would reduce the school's reliance on the more subjective, and perhaps biased, evaluations of teachers.

To *quantify*—measure—intellectual performance, Binet designed age-appropriate problems or test items on which many children's responses could be compared. The problems on the test were chosen so that they could be scored objectively as correct or incorrect, could vary in content, were not heavily influenced by differences in children's environments, and assessed judgment and reasoning rather than rote memory (Binet, 1911).

Children of various ages were tested, and the average score for normal children at each age was computed. Each individual child's performance was then compared with the average for other children of his or her age. Test results were expressed in terms of the average age at which normal children achieved a particular score. This measure was called the **mental age.** For instance, when a child's score equaled the average score of a group of 5-year-olds, the child was said to have a *mental age* of 5, regardless of his or her actual **chronological age,** the number of years since birth.

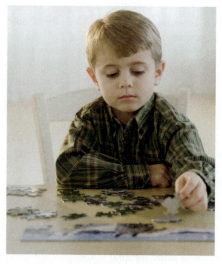

Why did Binet's measure of intelligence compare chronological age and mental age?

Binet's successful development of an intelligence test had great impact in the United States. A unique combination of historical events and social-political forces had prepared the United States for an explosion of interest in assessing mental ability. At the beginning of the 20th century, the United States was a nation in turmoil. As a result of global economic, social, and political conditions, millions of immigrants entered the country. New universal education laws flooded schools with students. Some form of assessment was needed to identify, document, and classify immigrant adults and schoolchildren (Brysbaert & Rastle, 2009). When World War I began, millions of volunteers marched into recruiting stations. Recruiters needed to determine who of these many people had the ability to learn quickly and benefit from special leadership training. New nonverbal, group-administered tests of mental ability were used to evaluate over 1.7 million recruits. A group of prominent psychologists, including Lewis Terman, Henry Goddard, and Robert Yerkes, responded to the wartime emergency and designed these tests in only one month's time (Thorne & Henley, 2005).

One consequence of this large-scale testing program was that the American public came to accept the idea that intelligence tests could differentiate people in terms of leadership ability and other socially important characteristics. This acceptance led to the widespread use of tests in schools and industry. Assessment was seen as a way to inject order into a chaotic society and as an inexpensive, democratic way to separate those who could benefit from education or military leadership training from those who could not. To facilitate the wide-scale use of intelligence testing, researchers strove for more broadly applicable testing procedures. ◉

IQ Tests

Although Binet began the standardized assessment of intellectual ability in France, U.S. psychologists soon took the lead. They also developed the IQ, or intelligence quotient. The IQ was a numerical, standardized measure of intelligence. Two families of individually administered IQ tests are used widely today: the Stanford–Binet scales and the Wechsler scales.

The Stanford–Binet Intelligence Scale   Stanford University's **Lewis Terman,** a former public school administrator, appreciated the importance of Binet's method for assessing intelligence. He adapted Binet's test questions for U.S. schoolchildren, he standardized the administration of the test, and he developed age-level norms by giving the test to thousands of children. In 1916, he published the Stanford Revision of the Binet Tests, commonly referred to as the *Stanford–Binet Intelligence Scale* (Terman, 1916).

With his new test, Terman provided a base for the concept of the **intelligence quotient, or IQ** (a term coined by William Stern, 1914). The IQ was the ratio of mental age to chronological age multiplied by 100 to eliminate decimals:

$$\text{IQ} = \text{mental age} \div \text{chronological age} \times 100$$

A child with a chronological age of 8 whose test scores revealed a mental age of 10 had an IQ of 125 ($10 \div 8 \times 100 = 125$), whereas a child of that same chronological age who performed at the level of a 6-year-old had an IQ of 75 ($6 \div 8 \times 100 = 75$). Individuals who performed at the mental age

equivalent to their chronological age had IQs of 100. Thus the score of 100 was considered to be the average IQ.

The new Stanford–Binet test soon became a standard instrument in clinical psychology, psychiatry, and educational counseling. The Stanford–Binet contains a series of subtests, each tailored for a particular mental age. Since it was first introduced, the Stanford–Binet has undergone a series of revisions (Terman & Merrill, 1937, 1960, 1972; Thorndike et al., 1986). Through those revisions, the range of the test has been extended to measure the IQ of very young children and very intelligent adults. In addition, the revisions have provided updated norms for age-appropriate average scores. The most recent, fifth edition of the Stanford–Binet test provides IQ estimates for individuals in the normal range of performance as well as for those individuals who are either mentally impaired or mentally gifted (Roid, 2003). ◉

The Wechsler Intelligence Scales   David **Wechsler** of Bellevue Hospital in New York set out to correct the dependence on verbal items in the assessment of adult intelligence. In 1939, he published the Wechsler–Bellevue Intelligence Scale, which combined verbal subtests with nonverbal, or performance, subtests. Thus, in addition to an overall IQ score, people were given separate estimates of verbal IQ and nonverbal IQ. After a few changes, the test was retitled the *Wechsler Adult Intelligence Scale*—the WAIS—in 1955. Today, you would take the WAIS-IV (Wechsler, 2008).

The WAIS-IV has 10 core subtests and five supplemental subtests that span several aspects of IQ. **Table 9.1,** provides examples of the types of questions you would find on the test. As you can see in the table, the WAIS-IV organizes the subtests into four scales that measure verbal comprehension, perceptual reasoning, working memory, and processing speed. If you were to take the WAIS-IV, you could receive an overall, or Full Scale, IQ as well as separate measures for each of the four scales.

The WAIS-IV is designed for people age 16 years and older, but similar tests have been developed for children (see Figure 9.1). *The Wechsler Intelligence Scale for Children— Fourth Edition* (WISC-IV; Wechsler, 2003) is suited for children ages 6 to 16, and the *Wechsler Preschool and Primary Scale of Intelligence—Third Edition* (WPPSI-III; Wechsler, 2002) for children ages 2½ to 7¼ years. The revisions of both tests have made the materials more colorful, more contemporary, and more enjoyable for children. However researchers continue to strive for improvements: Testing for a new WPPSI-IV began in 2011.

The WAIS-IV, the WISC-IV, and the WPPSI-III form a family of intelligence tests that yield Full Scale IQ scores at all age levels. In addition, they provide comparable subtest scores that allow researchers to track the development over time of more specific intellectual abilities. For this reason, the Wechsler scales are particularly valuable when the same individual is to be tested at different ages—for example, when a child's progress in response to different educational programs is monitored.

....

◉ **Watch** the **Video** *Special Topics: Intelligence Testing, Then and Now* on **MyPsychLab**

◉ **Watch** the **Video** *Classic Footage of Assessment of Memory with the Stanford-Binet Intelligence Scale* on **MyPsychLab**

intelligence quotient (IQ)   An index derived from standardized tests of intelligence; originally obtained by dividing an individual's mental age by chronological age and then multiplying by 100; now directly computed as an IQ test score.

Table 9.1 • Questions and Problems Similar to Those on the WAIS-IV

Verbal Comprehension Scale	
Similarities	In what ways are airplanes and submarines alike?
Vocabulary	What does *emulate* mean?
Perceptual Reasoning Scale	
Block Design	The test taker uses patterned blocks to reproduce designs provided by the examiner.
Picture Completion	The test taker examines a picture and says what is missing (for example, a horse without a mane).
Working Memory Scale	
Digit Span	Repeat the following numbers: 3 2 7 5 9.
Arithmetic	If you paid $8.50 for a movie ticket and $2.75 for popcorn, how much change would you have left from a $20 bill?
Processing Speed Scale	
Symbol Search	The test taker tries to determine whether one of two abstract symbols (such as Θ, A) appears on a longer list of symbols.
Cancellation	The test taker looks at visual displays and carries out the examiner's instructions (for example, "Draw a line through each blue square and green triangle").

Extremes of Intelligence

IQ scores are no longer derived by dividing mental age by chronological age. If you took the test today, your score would be added up and directly compared with the scores of other people your age. An IQ of 100 is "average" and would indicate that 50 percent of those your age had earned lower scores. **Figure 9.2** shows the distribution of IQ scores as measured by the WAIS. In this section, we consider the individuals whose IQ scores are below 70 and above 130. As you can see in Figure 9.2, those scores are quite rare.

Intellectual Disability and Learning Disorders   When individuals below the age of 18 obtain valid IQ scores that are

approximately two standard deviations below the mean on an intelligence test, they meet one criterion for a classification of **intellectual disability.** For the WAIS, that criterion would represent an IQ score of 70. However, as shown in **Table 9.2,** on page 246,

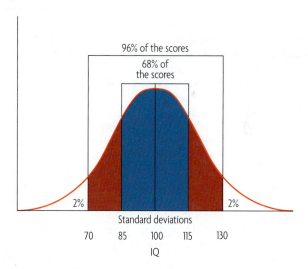

FIGURE 9.2 Distribution of IQ Scores in the General Population

IQ scores are normed so that a score of 100 is the population average (as many people score below 100 as score above 100). Scores between 85 and 115 are labeled average. Scores above 130 may indicate that an individual is gifted; scores below 70 contribute to a diagnosis of intellectual disability.

From Craig, Grace J.; Dunn, Wendy L., *Understanding Human Development*, 2nd Edition, © 2010. Printed and electronically reproduced by permission of Pearson Education Inc., Upper Saddle River, New Jersey.

FIGURE 9.1 Intelligence Testing

A psychologist administers an intelligence test to a 4-year-old child. The performance part of the test includes sorting an array of colored candy. Why is performance an important component of an IQ assessment?

intellectual disability Condition in which individuals have IQ scores of 70 to 75 or below and also demonstrate limitations in the ability to bring adaptive skills to bear on life tasks.

Table 9.2 • Diagnosis of Intellectual Disability

Intellectual disability is diagnosed if:
• The individual's IQ is approximately two standard deviations below the mean on an intelligence test.
• The individual demonstrates limitations in adaptive behavior, such as
Conceptual skills
Language use
Reading and writing
Money concepts
Social skills
Follow rules/obey laws
Social responsibility
Avoid victimization
Practical skills
Personal care
Health care
Occupational skills
• The age of onset is below 18.

Source: Excerpted from American Association on Mental Retardation, 2010, p. 44.

to be considered intellectually disabled, individuals must also demonstrate limitations in adaptive behavior, which is defined as "the collection of conceptual, social, and practical skills that have been learned are performed by people in their everyday lives" (American Association on Intellectual and Developmental Disabilities, 2010, p. 15). In earlier times, the term *mental retardation* was used to refer to people with IQs of 70 to 75 and below. However, because of the expanded definition that includes consideration of adaptive behavior, intellectual disability has become the more appropriate term (Schalock et al., 2007). When clinicians diagnose individuals with intellectual disability, they attempt to understand as much as possible what limitations each individual has with adaptive skills. Rather than categorizing people just on IQ, the contemporary goal is to provide environmental and social supports that are closely matched to each individual's needs.

Intellectual disability can be brought about by a number of genetic and environmental factors. For example, individuals with *Down syndrome*—a disorder caused by extra genetic material on the 21st chromosome—often have low IQs. Another genetic disorder, known as *phenylketonuria* (PKU), also has a potential negative impact on IQ (Brumm & Grant, 2010). However, through strict adherence to a special diet, people can control the negative effects of PKU if it is diagnosed in infancy. Family studies suggest that genetic inheritance likely plays a role for intellectual disability only in the IQ range of 55 to 70 (Plomin & Spinath, 2004). The more severe forms of disability appear to be caused by the occurrence of spontaneous genetic abnormalities in an individual's development that are not heritable. The environment that is most often critical for intellectual disability is the prenatal environment. Pregnant women who suffer diseases such as rubella and syphilis are at risk for

having children with intellectual disabilities. In addition, pregnant women who consume alcohol or other drugs, particularly during the early weeks of pregnancy, also increase the likelihood of having children with cognitive deficits (Bennett et al., 2008; Huizink & Mulder, 2006).

Historically, individuals with intellectual disabilities were educated—to the extent that they were educated—almost entirely in separate facilities. However, evidence accumulated that these separate programs were not effective. In 1975, the U.S. government passed legislation requiring that students with disabilities be educated to the greatest extent possible in general classrooms (McLeskey et al., 2011). The law recognizes that some levels of impairment still require students to receive separate instruction. However, educational practice has changed over the decades so that increasing numbers of students diagnosed with an intellectual disability spend some or much of each school day in classrooms with their peers.

IQ scores give general information about how well people are able to perform—with respect to age-appropriate norms—on a variety of verbal and nonverbal tasks. In some instances, there is cause for concern when IQ scores and performance fail to match up. People who present a sufficiently large discrepancy between their achievement and their measured IQ might be diagnosed with a learning disorder. Before clinicians diagnose a **learning disorder,** they need to rule out other factors that can lead to poor performance, such as low motivation, mediocre teaching, or physical problems (such as visual deficits). Many schools provide special assistance to students who have been diagnosed with learning disorders.

Giftedness Individuals are most likely to be labeled as *gifted* if they have an IQ score above 130. However, as with the definition of intellectual disability, researchers have suggested that the conception of giftedness is not adequately captured just by IQ. For example, **Joseph Renzulli** (2005) has argued in favor of a "three-ring" conception of giftedness that characterizes giftedness along the dimensions of ability, creativity, and task commitment (see **Figure 9.3**). On this view, individuals can be considered gifted with IQs that are

FIGURE 9.3 The Three-Ring Conception of Giftedness

According to the three-ring conception, gifted individuals are found at the intersection of above-average ability, high levels of creativity, and high levels of task commitment.

Reprinted by permission of the author.

learning disorder A disorder defined by a large discrepancy between individuals' measured IQ and their actual performance.

Critical Thinking in Your Life

WHY DO INTELLIGENT PEOPLE HAVE LONGER LIVES?

Let's begin with a fact: People with higher IQs tend to live longer lives (Deary et al., 2010b). Consider a study that examined the mortality of 1,181 people born in Scotland in 1936 (Deary et al., 2008). Their intelligence was measured as children, in 1947, using a standard IQ test. The researchers determined who had died in the period from 1968 to 2003. When the researchers related IQ to mortality, they discovered a strong pattern: For each standard deviation increase in IQ score (see Figure 9.2), there was "a 30% reduced hazard of dying" (p. 876). This pattern of greater longevity for people with higher IQs has been replicated across several national samples (Deary et al., 2010b).

This fact about IQ and mortality has given rise to four explanations (Deary, 2008):

- Lower IQ scores in childhood might arise, in part, from circumstances in the pre- of postnatal environment that caused an individual's brain not to function at full potential. The same brain deficiencies that lead to lower IQ might also hasten death.

- Some people might possess not just more efficient brains but a whole "well-put-together system" (Deary, 2008, p. 176) that extends to the whole body. That well-put-together system might yield both higher IQ and greater physical health.

- People with higher IQs typically obtain more education and, as a consequence, pursue more professional careers. Higher IQs might, therefore, ultimately allow people to lead lives in environments that provide fewer potential dangers to their health.

- People with higher IQs might engage in fewer behaviors that are dangerous to their health. In fact, evidence suggests that "people with higher intelligence in early life are more likely to have better diets, take more exercise, avoid accidents, give up smoking, engage in less binge drinking and put on less weight in adulthood" (Deary, 2008, p. 176).

Note that these explanations are not mutually exclusive. That is, each of them could contribute to the correlation between IQ and longevity.

Let's focus on the idea that people with higher IQs engage in fewer unhealthy behaviors. Two researchers examined data from over 10,000 Wisconsin high school students (Hauser & Palloni, 2011). They found a strong relationship between IQ and survival. However, they found an even stronger relationship between class rank and survival. Students who had ranked at the top of their class greatly outlived their peers at the bottom. Based on these results, the researchers called attention to the students' attitudes and behaviors: They suggested that the same qualities that led the students to excel in high school helped assure them longer lives. This conclusion is important because people don't need high IQs to make intelligent decisions about school, work, and healthful lifestyles.

- The relationship between IQ and longevity provides a strong example of correlation not being causation. How does each explanation attempt to identify the factors that contribute to the correlation?

- Which explanations give people the opportunity to change the relationship between their own IQ and their potential longevity?

---

above average but not necessarily superior. In addition, they need to show high levels of creativity and exert high levels of commitment to particular problems or domains of performance. This expanded definition of giftedness explains why people often are not gifted across the academic spectrum (Sternberg, 2010). Abilities, creativity, and task commitment may all differ, for example, between verbal and mathematical domains.

What qualities do gifted children generally possess? The formal study of gifted children began in 1921 when Lewis Terman (1925) began a long-term study of a group of over 1,500 boys and girls who tested in the top 1 percent of their school populations. This group of individuals was followed all the way into their 80s (Holahan & Sears, 1995). Terman and his successors wanted to see how these children fared as they made their way through life. The questions Terman asked continue to shape the research agenda. For example, Terman explored the myth that gifted children have problems with social and emotional adjustment. Terman concluded just the opposite: He found his sample to be better adjusted than their less gifted peers. Contemporary research comparing the personality attributes of gifted and non-gifted students continues to contradict the stereotype that gifted students are less well-adjusted than their peers (Martin et al., 2010; Zeidner & Shani-Zinovich, 2011). In fact, gifted students may have some advantages, such as lower levels of anxiety.

Terman also documented that the gifted children were largely successful in life. This is not surprising because IQ is a good predictor of occupational status and income. Thus the concern about gifted individuals is not that they aren't doing well. The concern, instead, is that they don't receive sufficient educational support to allow them to develop their gifts fully (Reis & Renzulli, 2010). When giftedness is recognized as a multidimensional construct, gifted education must also have the flexibility to address individual students' particular talents.

Stop *and* Review

① What measures were originally used to compute the intelligence quotient?
② What type of subtests did David Wechsler introduce to the measurement of IQ?
③ What factors contribute to the diagnosis of intellectual disability?
④ What dimensions define giftedness in the "three-ring" conception?

✓ **Study** and **Review** on **MyPsychLab**

THEORIES OF INTELLIGENCE

So far, we have seen some of the ways in which intelligence has been measured. You are now in a position to ask yourself: Do these tests capture everything that is meant by the word *intelligence*? Do these tests capture all abilities you believe constitute your own intelligence? To help you to think about those questions, I now review theories of intelligence. As you read about each theory, ask yourself whether its proponents would be comfortable using IQ as a measure of intelligence. 👁

Psychometric Theories of Intelligence

Psychometric theories of intelligence originated in much the same philosophical atmosphere that gave rise to IQ tests. **Psychometrics** is the field of psychology that specializes in mental testing in any of its facets, including personality assessment, intelligence evaluation, and aptitude measurement. Thus psychometric approaches are intimately related to methods of testing. These theories examine the *statistical relationships* between different measures of ability, such as the 14 subtests of the WAIS-III, and then make inferences about the nature of human intelligence on the basis of those relationships. The technique used most frequently is called *factor analysis,* a statistical procedure that detects a smaller number of dimensions, clusters, or factors within a larger set of independent variables. The goal of factor analysis is to identify the basic psychological dimensions of the concept being investigated. Of course, a statistical procedure only identifies statistical regularities; it is up to psychologists to suggest and defend interpretations of those regularities.

Charles Spearman carried out an early and influential application of factor analysis in the domain of intelligence. Spearman discovered that the performance of individuals on each of a variety of intelligence tests was highly correlated. From this pattern he concluded that there is a factor of *general*

....

👁 **Watch** the **Video** *The Basics: Theories of Intelligence* on **MyPsychLab**

psychometrics The field of psychology that specializes in mental testing.

g According to Spearman, the factor of general intelligence underlying all intelligent performance.

crystallized intelligence The facet of intelligence involving the knowledge a person has already acquired and the ability to access that knowledge; measures by vocabulary, arithmetic, and general information tests.

fluid intelligence The aspect of intelligence that involves the ability to see complex relationships and solve problems.

intelligence, or ***g***, underlying all intelligent performance (Spearman, 1927). Each individual domain also has associated with it specific skills that Spearman called *s*. For example, a person's performance on tests of vocabulary or arithmetic depends both on his or her general intelligence and on domain-specific abilities.

Raymond Cattell (1963), using more advanced factor analytic techniques, determined that general intelligence can be broken down into two relatively independent components, which he called crystallized and fluid intelligence. **Crystallized intelligence** involves the knowledge a person has already acquired and the ability to access that knowledge; it is measured by tests of vocabulary, arithmetic, and general information. **Fluid intelligence** is the ability to see complex relationships and solve problems; it is measured by tests of block designs and spatial visualization in which the background information needed to solve a problem is included or readily apparent. Crystallized intelligence allows you to cope well with your life's recurring, concrete challenges; fluid intelligence helps you attack novel, abstract problems.

Since Cattell, many psychologists have broadened their conceptions of intelligence to include much more than performance on traditional IQ tests. Let's now examine two types of theories that go beyond IQ.

Sternberg's Triarchic Theory of Intelligence

Robert Sternberg (1999) also stresses the importance of cognitive processes in problem solving as part of his more general theory of intelligence. Sternberg outlines a triarchic—three-part—theory. His three types of intelligence, analytical, creative, and practical, all represent different ways of characterizing effective performance. Sternberg suggests that *successful intelligence* reflects performance in all three domains.

Analytical intelligence provides the basic information-processing skills that people apply to life's many familiar tasks. This type of intelligence is defined by the components, or mental processes, that underlie thinking and problem solving. Sternberg identifies three types of components that are central to information processing: (1) knowledge acquisition components, for learning new facts; (2) performance components, for problem-solving strategies and techniques; and (3) metacognitive components, for selecting strategies and monitoring progress toward success. To put some of your analytical intelligence to work, you can try the exercise in **Table 9.3**.

How did you do on the anagrams? To solve these anagrams, you mostly needed to use performance components and metacognitive components. The performance components are what allowed you to manipulate the letters in your head; the metacognitive components are what allowed you to have strategies for finding solutions. Consider T-R-H-O-S. How did you mentally transform that into SHORT? A good strategy to get started is to try consonant clusters that are probable in English—such as S-H and T-H. Selecting strategies requires metacognitive components; carrying them out requires performance components. Note that a good strategy will sometimes fail. Consider T-N-K-H-G-I. What makes this anagram hard for many people is that K-N is not a very likely combination to start a word, whereas T-H is. Did you stare at this anagram for a while, trying to turn it into a word beginning with T-H?

Table 9.3 • Using Analytical Intelligence

The following is a list of *anagrams*—scrambled words. As quickly as possible, try to find a solution for each anagram

1. H-U-L-A-G	_____
2. P-T-T-M-E	_____
3. T-R-H-O-S	_____
4. T-N-K-H-G-I	_____
5. T-E-W-I-R	_____
6. L-L-A-O-W	_____
7. R-I-D-E-V	_____
8. O-C-C-H-U	_____
9. T-E-N-R-E	_____
10. C-I-B-A-S	_____

Turn to page 258 for the solutions.

From Sternberg, R. J. 1986. *Intelligence applied.* San Diego: Harcourt Brace Jovanovich. Reprinted by permission of the author.

By breaking down various tasks into their components, researchers can pinpoint the processes that differentiate the performance outcomes of individuals with different IQs. For example, researchers might discover that the metacognitive components of high-IQ students prompt them to select different strategies to solve a particular type of problem than do their lower-IQ peers. The difference in strategy selection accounts for the high-IQ students' greater problem-solving success.

Creative intelligence captures people's ability to deal with novel problems. Sternberg (2006) suggests that "creative intelligence involves skills used to create, invent, discover, imagine, suppose, or hypothesize" (p. 325). Suppose, for example, a group of individuals found themselves stranded after an accident. You would credit with intelligence the person in the group who could most quickly help the group find its way home.

Practical intelligence is reflected in the management of day-to-day affairs. It involves your ability to *adapt* to new and different environments, *select* appropriate environments, and effectively *shape* your environment to suit your needs. Practical intelligence is bound to particular contexts. To measure practical intelligence, researchers must immerse themselves in those contexts to develop appropriate measures.

Featured Study

A team of researchers wanted to assess the importance of practical intelligence for executives in the printing and graphics industry (Baum et al., 2011). They developed a measure of practical intelligence that comprised scenarios relevant to the industry (for example, company sales have fallen). The participants who completed the measure—all of whom were leaders of companies in the industry—then read a list of 10 possible actions to address the situation. Their task was to put the actions in sequence from "most important to do first" to "least important to do first" (p. 413). To calculate practical intelligence, the researchers compared each leader's responses to the rankings of 50 industry experts. The researchers assessed the relationship between practical intelligence and the growth of each business in the four years after the assessment took place. Among leaders who indicated that they wished their companies to grow,

greater practical intelligence was associated with higher growth.

You can see from this example why practical intelligence requires different measures for different contexts. However, the general idea remains the same: People can bring more or less practical intelligence to bear on their day-to-day tasks.

Critics of Sternberg's theory have typically wondered whether measures of creative and practical intelligence can be meaningfully separated from more classic concepts like *g* (Brody, 2003; Gottfredson, 2003). The underlying question is whether Sternberg's anlaysis of successful intelligence actually predicts success better than classic IQ measures. To counter these criticisms, Sternberg has created real-world applications of his theory. For example, he and his collaborators have measured the theory's broader range of intellectual skills with the goal of improving the college admissions process (Sternberg, 2010). Sternberg asserts that the combined measures of successful intelligence allow for better predictions of students' academic performance in their first year of college.

Gardner's Multiple Intelligences and Emotional Intelligence

Howard Gardner (1999, 2006) has also proposed a theory that expands the definition of intelligence beyond those skills covered on an IQ test. Gardner identifies numerous intelligences that cover a range of human experience. The value of any of the abilities differs across human societies, according to what is needed by, useful to, and prized by a given society. As shown in **Table 9.4** on page 250, Gardner identified eight intelligences. ✳

Gardner argues that Western society values logical–mathematical and linguistic intelligence, whereas non-Western societies often value other types of intelligence. For example, in the Caroline Island of Micronesia, sailors must be able to navigate long distances without maps, using only their spatial intelligence and bodily kinesthetic intelligence. Such abilities count more in that society than the ability to write a term paper. In Bali, where artistic performance is part of everyday life, musical intelligence and talents involved in coordinating intricate dance steps are highly valued. Interpersonal intelligence is more central to collectivist societies such as Japan, where cooperative action and communal life are emphasized, than it is in individualistic societies such as the United States (Triandis, 1990).

Many people have embraced Gardner's theory because it suggests that people can excel in domains that are not recognized by traditional conceptions of intelligence. However, Gardner's theory has not been without critics. To begin, research suggests that there is overlap among people's functioning on what Gardner argues are separate types of intelligence (Almeida et al., 2010; Visser et al., 2006). For example, measures of Linguistic, Logial/Mathematical, Spatial, Naturalistic, and Interpersonal intelligence all show strong correlations with *g*. These correlations suggest that Gardner might just be relabeling different aspects of traditional conceptions of intelligence. Other critiques have focused on particular intelligences. For example, research evidence argues against the idea that language learning ability reflects an innate talent (Mercer, 2012).

✳ **Explore** the **Concept** *Gardner's Multiple Intelligences* on **MyPsychLab**

Table 9.4 • Gardner's Multiple Intelligences

Form of Intelligence	Definition	Examples of Professions in Which the Form Is Important
Logical-mathematical	The ability to manipulate abstract symbols	Science, computer programming
Linguistic	The ability to use language well	Journalism, law
Naturalist	The ability to observe aspects of the natural environment carefully	Forest conservation
Musical	The ability to compose and understand music	Audio engineering, music
Spatial	The ability to reason well about spatial relations	Architecture, surgery
Bodily-kinesthetic	The ability to plan and understand sequences of movements	Dance, athletics
Interpersonal	The ability to understand other people and social interactions	Politics, teaching
Intrapersonal	The ability to understand yourself	Ministry
Existential (tentative; Gardner, 1999)	The ability to address "the big questions" about existence	Philosophy professor

From Kosslyn, Stephen M.; Rosenberg, Robin S., *Introducing psychology: Brain, Person, Group*, 4th Edition, © 2011. Reprinted and Electronically reproduced by permission of Pearson Education, Inc., Upper Saddle River, New Jersey.

In recent years, researchers have begun to explore a type of intelligence—*emotional intelligence*—that is related to Gardner's concepts of *interpersonal* and *intrapersonal* intelligence (see Table 9.4). On one prominent view, **emotional intelligence** has four major components (Mayer et al., 2008a, 2008b):

- The ability to perceive, appraise, and express emotions accurately and appropriately
- The ability to use emotions to facilitate thinking
- The ability to understand and analyze emotions and to use emotional knowledge effectively
- The ability to regulate one's emotions to promote both emotional and intellectual growth

This definition reflects a view of the positive role of emotion as it relates to intellectual functioning—emotions can make thinking more intelligent, and people can think intelligently about their emotions and those of others.

Researchers have begun to demonstrate that emotional intelligence has important consequences for everyday life. Consider the emotional experiences of athletes as they anticipate and participate in sports events. Greater emotional intelligence may help athletes cope with stressors.

A team of researchers hypothesized that athletes who were high in emotional intelligence (EI) would be better able to control their emotions in response to stressful competition-related stimuli (Laborde et al., 2011). The researchers recruited 30 male handball players and measured their EI. To provide the players with a stressful experience, the researchers had them listen to a 20-minute audio tape that featured negative statements (for example, "Your motivation is leaving you," p. 24) as well as the sound of a hissing crowd. The researchers assessed the impact of this stressful experience by measuring the players' heart rates before and after they heard the tape. Players with low EI showed changes in their heart rate that indicated that the tape caused them to experience stress. By contrast, players with high EI showed very little impact of the stressful experience on their heart rates.

This study illustrates how players high in emotional intelligence are able to use their ability to understand and regulate emotions to cope with stressors. You can imagine how that ability might be useful in the heat of competition!

This review of intelligence testing and theories of intelligence sets the stage for a discussion of the societal circumstances that make the topic of intelligence so controversial.

Stop *and* Review

① Why did Spearman come to believe in *g*, general intelligence?
② What are the three types of intelligence in Sternberg's triarchic theory?
③ In Gardner's theory, what kind of intelligence might determine whether someone could be a successful sculptor?

emotional intelligence Type of intelligence defined as the abilities to perceive, appraise, and express emotions accurately and appropriately, to use emotions to facilitate thinking, to understand and analyze emotions, to use emotional knowledge effectively, and to regulate one's emotions to promote both emotional and intellectual growth.

CRITICAL THINKING Consider the study relating practical intelligence to business growth. Why was it useful to to assess the impact of practical intelligence over a period of four years?

✔─▯**Study** and **Review** on **MyPsychLab**

THE POLITICS OF INTELLIGENCE

We have seen that contemporary conceptions of intelligence reject the narrow linking of a score on an IQ test with a person's intelligence. Even so, IQ tests remain the most frequent measure of "intelligence" in Western society. Because of the prevalence of IQ testing and the availability of IQ scores, it becomes easy to compare different groups according to their "average" IQ. In the United States, such ethnic and racial group comparisons have often been used as evidence for the innate genetic inferiority of members of minority groups. This section will briefly examine the history of this practice of using IQ test scores to index the alleged mental inferiority of certain groups. Then we will look at current evidence on the nature and nurture of intelligence and IQ test performance. You will see that this is one of the most politically volatile issues in psychology because public policies about immigration quotas, educational resources, and more may be based on how group IQ data are interpreted. ◉

The History of Group Comparisons

In the early 1900s, psychologist **Henry Goddard** (1866–1957) advocated mental testing of all immigrants and the *selective exclusion* of those who were found to be "mentally defective." Such views may have contributed to a hostile national climate against admission of certain immigrant groups (Zenderland, 1998). Indeed, Congress passed the 1924 Immigration Restriction Act, which made it national policy to administer intelligence tests to immigrants as they arrived at Ellis Island in New York Harbor. Vast numbers of Jewish, Italian, Russian, and immigrants of other nationalities were classified as "morons" on the basis of IQ tests. Some psychologists interpreted these statistical findings as evidence that immigrants from Southern and Eastern Europe were genetically inferior to those from the hardy Northern and Western European stock (see Ruch, 1937). However, these "inferior" groups were also least familiar with the dominant language and culture, embedded in the IQ tests, because they had immigrated most recently. (Within a few decades, these group differences completely disappeared from IQ tests, but the theory of racially inherited differences in intelligence persisted.)

The argument for genetic inferiority advanced by Goddard (1917) and others was reinforced by World War I Army Intelligence tests on which African Americans and other racial minorities scored lower than the White majority. Louis Terman, whom as we saw promoted IQ testing in the United States, commented in this unscientific manner on the data he had helped collect on U.S. racial minorities:

> *Their dullness seems to be racial. . . . There seems no possibility at present of convincing society that they should not be allowed to reproduce, although from a eugenics point of view, they constitute a grave problem because of their unusually prolific breeding.* (Terman, 1916, pp. 91–92)

The names have changed, but the problem remains the same. In the United States today, African Americans and Latinos score, on average, lower than Asian Americans and Whites on standardized intelligence tests. Of course, there are individuals in all groups who score at the highest (and the lowest) extremes of the IQ scale. How should these group differences in IQ scores be interpreted? One tradition has been to attribute these differences to genetic inferiority (nature). After this section discusses the evidence for genetic differences in IQ, we will consider a second possibility, that differences in environments (nurture) exert a significant impact on IQ. The validity of either explanation, or some combination of them, has important social, economic, and political consequences.

Heredity and IQ

How can researchers assess the extent to which intelligence is genetically determined? Any answer to this question requires that the researcher choose some measure as an index of intelligence. Thus the question becomes not whether "intelligence," in the abstract, is influenced by heredity but, in most cases, whether IQs are similar within family trees. To answer this more limited question, researchers need to tease apart the effects of shared genes and shared environment. One method

Why were IQ tests given to immigrants as they arrived at Ellis Island? How were these tests used to draw conclusions about genetic inferiority?

◉ **Watch** the **Video** *In the Real World: Intelligence Tests and Stereotypes* on **MyPsychLab**

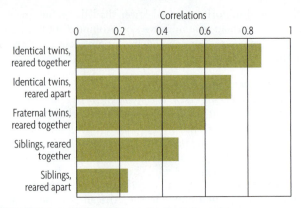

Correlations

| | 0 | 0.2 | 0.4 | 0.6 | 0.8 | 1 |

Identical twins, reared together

Identical twins, reared apart

Fraternal twins, reared together

Siblings, reared together

Siblings, reared apart

FIGURE 9.4 IQ and Genetic Relationship

This figure presents the correlations between the IQ scores of identical (monozygotic), fraternal (dizygotic) twins, and other sibling pairs. The data demonstrate the importance of both genetic factors and environmental factors. For example, identical twins show higher correlations between their IQs than do fraternal twins or other sibling pairs—a genetic influence. However, the correlations are also higher when the twins and other sibling pairs were raised together—an environmental influence.

Data from Bouchard, T. J., & McGue, M. (1981). Familial studies of intelligence: A review. *Science, 212,* 1055–1059.

is to compare functioning in identical twins (monozygotic), fraternal twins (dizygotic), and relatives with other degrees of genetic overlap. **Figure 9.4** presents correlations between IQ scores of individuals on the basis of their degree of genetic relationship (Bouchard & McGue, 1981). As you can see, the greater the genetic similarity, the greater the IQ similarity. (Note in these data that the impact of environment is also revealed in the greater IQ similarities among those who have been reared together.) ✳

Researchers use results of this sort to try to estimate the *heritability* of IQ. A **heritability estimate** of a particular trait, such as intelligence, is based on the proportion of the variability in test scores on that trait that can be traced to genetic factors. The estimate is found by computing the variation in all the test scores for a given population (college students or psychiatric patients, for example) and then identifying what portion of the total variance is due to genetic or inherited factors. This is done by comparing individuals who have different degrees of genetic overlap. Researchers who have reviewed the variety of studies on heritability of IQ conclude that about 30 to 80 percent of the variance in IQ scores is due to genetic makeup (Deary et al., 2010a).

That range in heritability estimates arises, in part, because heritability *increases* across the life span: To document this increase, researchers have often assessed twins' IQ repeatedly over several years (van Soelen et al., 2011). Let's consider a study that took 13 years to complete.

·······

✳ **Explore** the **Concept** *Correlations Between IQ Scores of Persons of Varying Relationships* on **MyPsychLab**

heritability estimate A statistical estimate of the degree of inheritance of a given trait or behavior, assessed by the degree of similarity between individuals who vary in their extent of genetic similarity.

A team of researchers began their study by recruiting 209 pairs of 5-year-old twins (Hoekstra et al., 2007). At age 5, the children completed an IQ test that provided estimates for both verbal and nonverbal IQ. The researchers measured the twins' IQs again at ages 7, 10, 12, and 18 years. Given the duration of the study, you won't be surprised that some twins dropped out over time. However, the researchers were able to obtain IQs for 115 pairs at all five ages. The data analyses showed that the twins' IQs were reasonably stable over time. Across all the twin pairs, the correlations between scores at age 5 and scores at age 18 were 0.51 for verbal IQ and 0.47 for nonverbal IQ. To estimate heritability, the researchers compared the correlations between MZ and DZ twins at each age. For verbal IQ, the heritability estimate was 46 percent at age 5 and increased to 84 percent at age 18. For nonverbal IQ, the heritability estimate was 64 percent at age 5 and increased to 74 percent at age 18.

Many people are surprised by a result of this sort, because it seems that environments should have more, not less, of an effect as people get older. Here's how researchers explain such counterintuitive findings: "It is possible that genetic dispositions nudge us toward environments that accentuate our genetic propensities, thus leading to increased heritability throughout the life span" (Plomin & Petrill, 1997, p. 61).

Let's return now to the point at which genetic analysis becomes controversial: test score differences between African Americans and White Americans. Several decades ago, the gap between the scores of Whites and Blacks was roughly 15 IQ points. However, researchers estimated that the gap closed by 4 to 7 points in the 30 years from 1972 to 2002 (Dickens &

This photo shows Nobel Prize–winning chemist Marie Curie with her daughters Irene (on the left) and Eve (on the right). Irene also won a Nobel Prize in chemistry, and Eve became a famous author. Why do families like this one encourage researchers to attempt to understand the impact of heredity and environment on IQ?

Flynn, 2006). Although the close in the gap suggests environmental influences, the lingering difference has prompted many people to suggest that there are unbridgeable genetic differences between the races (Hernnstein & Murray, 1994). However, even if IQ is highly heritable, does this difference reflect genetic inferiority of individuals in the lower-scoring group? The answer is no. Heritability is based on an estimate *within* one given group. It cannot be used to interpret differences *between* groups, no matter how large those differences are on an objective test.

Heritability estimates pertain only to the average in a given population of individuals. We know, for instance, that the heritability estimate for height is quite high—in the range of 0.93 to 0.96 (Silventoinen et al., 2006). Still, you cannot determine how much of your height is due to genetic influences. The same argument is true for IQ; despite high heritability estimates, we cannot determine the specific genetic contribution to any individual's IQ or to mean IQ scores among groups. The fact that on an IQ test one racial or ethnic group scores lower than another group does not mean that the difference between these groups is genetic in origin, even if the heritability estimate for IQ scores is high as assessed within a group (Hunt & Carlson, 2007).

Another point of controversy is the concept of race itself. When people assert that an IQ gap is caused by genetics, they make the strong assumption that genetic analysis permits clear distinctions among races. Researchers on IQ generally acknowledge that race is both a *biological* and a *social* construct. For example, the social convention in the United States is typically to call people who have any African ancestry Black. Consider the remarkable golfer Tiger Woods, who has often been labeled— and discriminated against—as African American even though his actual heritage is much more complex (his ancestors were White, Black, Thai, Chinese, and Native American). Woods provides an excellent example of circumstances in which social judgments do not follow biological reality. Even so, some intelligence researchers argue that there are sufficient differences among races that meaningful comparisons can be made (Daley & Onwuegbuzie, 2011; Hunt & Carlson, 2007). Other researchers argue just as strenuously that the concept of race is so driven by social circumstances that group comparisons are useless (Sternberg & Grigorenko, 2007; Sternberg et al., 2005).

Surely genetics plays a sizable role in influencing individuals' scores on IQ tests, as it does on many other traits and abilities. We have seen, however, that heredity does not constitute an adequate explanation for IQ differences between racial and ethnic groups. It has a necessary, but not sufficient, role in our understanding of such performance effects. Let's turn now to the role the environment may play in creating the IQ gap.

Environments and IQ

Because heritability estimates are less than 1.0, we know that genetic inheritance is not solely responsible for anyone's IQ. Environments must also affect IQ. But how can we assess what aspects of the environment are important influences on IQ? What features of your environment affect your potential to score well on an IQ test (Kristensen & Bjerkedal, 2007; van der Sluis et al., 2008)? Environments are complex stimulus packages that vary on many dimensions, both physical and social, and may be experienced in different ways by those within them. Even children in the same family setting do not necessarily share the same critical, psychological environment. Think back to growing up in your family. If you had siblings, did they

Tiger Woods has ancestors who were White, African American, Thai, Chinese, and Native American. What does that suggest about the construct of race in the United States?

all get the same attention from your parents? Did conditions of stress change over the course of time? Did your family's financial resources change? Did your parents' marital status change? It is obvious that environments are made up of many components that are in a dynamic relationship and that change over time. So it becomes difficult for psychologists to say what kinds of environmental conditions—attention, stress, poverty, health, war, and so on—actually have an impact on IQ.

Researchers have most often focused on more global measures of environment, like the socioeconomic status (SES) of the family. Children who come from more privileged, high-SES backgrounds are likely to have higher IQs than their less privileged, low-SES peers (Daley & Onwuegbuzie, 2011; Hackman et al., 2010). Why does SES affect IQ? Wealth versus poverty can affect intellectual functioning in many ways, health and educational resources being two of the most obvious. Poor health during pregnancy and low birth weight are solid predictors of a child's lowered mental ability. Furthermore, impoverished homes may suffer from a lack of books, written media, computers, and other materials that add to one's mental stimulation. The "survival orientation" of poor parents, especially in single-parent families, that leaves parents little time or energy to play with and intellectually stimulate their children is detrimental to performance on tasks such as those on standard IQ tests.

We have seen that both nature and nurture have an impact on people's intellectual functioning. However, recall from Chapter 3 that researchers increasingly focus their attention on interactions of genes and environments. To demonstrate such an interaction for intelligence, a team of researchers followed

The personal attention children receive can affect their intelligence. In the "separate but equal" schoolroom of 1940s, African American children received little attention. In contrast, the parent shown below is deeply involved in her child's education. How do these types of environmental differences affect IQ?

750 twin pairs from ages 10 months to 2 years (Tucker-Drob et al., 2011). The children performed tests of mental abilities at both those ages. We know from research on the heritibility of intelligence that the children will have inherited genes that would predict a range of intellectual performance. However, at 10 months the children's mental ability showed very little impact of genes. This was true for children from both high- and low-SES homes. By 2 years, a different pattern emerged. Now, the children raised in high-SES homes showed levels of mental ability that were greatly influenced by their genes. By contrast, the mental ability of children from low-SES homes still failed to show an impact of genes. This pattern suggests that the environments in which low-SES children were reared did not allow them to experience their full genetic potential.

Researchers have spent the past 40 years developing programs intended to counteract the effects of impoverished environments. The Head Start program was first funded by the federal government in 1965 to address the "physical health, developmental, social, educational, and emotional needs of low-income children and to increase the capacity of the families to care for their children, through empowerment and supportive services" (Kassebaum, 1994, p. 123). The idea of Head Start and similar programs was not to move children to privileged environments but to improve the environments into which they were born. Children are exposed to special preschool education, they receive decent daily meals, and their parents are given advice on health and other aspects of child rearing.

Consider a program started in 1962 at the High/Scope Perry preschool in Ypsilanti, Michigan (Schweinhart, 2004). The program focused on a group of 3- and 4-year-old low-income African American children who had been evaluated as being at risk for school failure. The High/Scope Perry program provided the children with a classroom environment that focused on *participatory education*—children were encouraged to initiate and plan their own activities and activities for the classroom group. In addition, the program involved parents in the children's educations through home visits and parent group meetings. The researchers followed the students who participated in the program for the next 40 years. **Figure 9.5** compares the outcomes of participants to a group of students from the same population who did not participate. As you can see, High/Scope Perry students had higher IQs at age 5 than their peers outside the program. They were also considerably more likely to graduate from a regular high school and have higher-paying jobs at age 40.

Assessments of early intervention programs often provide encouraging results. A project that reviewed the impact of Head Start on 2,803 children from 18 U.S. cities found consistent improvements in the childrens' cognitive development and social competence (Zhai et al., 2011). Another project evaluated the experiences of a different sample of 1,260 children (Lee, 2011). Some of the children were classified as "high risk" because their family environments included factors such as parents who were unemployed, prone to violence, or substance abusers. Children with more family risk factors benefited the most from the Head Start program. In addition, when children started at age 3, and therefore were able to spend two years in the program, they demonstrated more improvements in academic outcomes than children who started at age 4. These studies provide strong evidence for the importance of

FIGURE 9.5 The Impact of a Preschool Intervention

Students who participated in the High/Scope Perry preschool program had better outcomes than students who were not participants.

From *Lifetime Effects: The High/Scope Perry Preschool Study Through Age 40* (p. 196) by Lawrence J. Schweinhart, JU. Montie, Z. Xiang, W.S. Barnett, C.R. Belfield & M. Nores, Ypsilanti, MI: HighScope Press. © 2005 HighScope Educational Research Foundation. Used with permission.

the environment for intellectual development. They also provide concrete models for programs that can change the lives of children who are at risk.

Culture and the Validity of IQ Tests

People would probably care much less about IQ scores if they didn't allow for such useful predictions: Extensive research shows that IQ scores are valid predictors of school grades from elementary school through college, of occupational status, and of performance in many jobs (Gottfredson, 2002; Nettelbeck & Wilson, 2005). These patterns of results suggest that IQ tests validly measure intellectual abilities that are very basic and important toward the types of success that are valued in Western cultures—intelligence, as measured by IQ, directly affects success. IQ distinctions can also affect academic and job performance indirectly by changing one's motives and beliefs. Those with higher IQ scores are likely to have had more success experiences in school, become more motivated to study, develop an achievement orientation, and become optimistic about their chances of doing well. Also, children scoring low on IQ tests may get "tracked" into schools, classes, or programs that are inferior and may even be stigmatizing to the students' sense of self-competence. In this way, IQ can be affected by environment and, in turn, can create new environments for the child—some better, some worse. IQ assessment may thus become destiny—whatever the child's underlying genetic endowment for intelligence. ◉

Even though IQ tests have proven to be valid for mainstream uses, many observers still question their validity for comparisons among different cultural and racial groups (Greenfield, 1997; Serpell, 2000). To make meaningful comparisons, researchers must use tests that have been validated for each separate group (Hunt & Carlson, 2007). However, critics have often argued that there are systematic biases in IQ tests that make them invalid across cultures. For example, questions on IQ tests that assess verbal comprehension presuppose that certain types of knowledge will have been accessible to all test takers (see Table 9.2). In reality, people from different cultures often have quite different background knowledge that affects the difficulty of those questions (Fagan & Holland, 2007). In addition, forms of tests and testing may not match cultural notions of intelligence or appropriate behavior (Sternberg, 2007). Consider one case of negative evaluations in the classroom:

> When children of Latino immigrant parents go to school, the emphasis on understanding rather than speaking, on respecting the teacher's authority rather than expressing one's own opinions leads to negative academic assessment. . . . Hence, a valued mode of communication in one culture—respectful listening—becomes the basis for a rather sweeping negative evaluation in the school setting where self-assertive speaking is the valued mode of communication. (Greenfield, 1997, p. 1120)

These immigrant children must learn how they must behave in U.S. classrooms to make their teachers understand the extent of their intelligence. ◉

Although concerns about cross-cultural comparisons often focus on the *content* of tests, major problems also lie in the *context* of intelligence testing. **Claude Steele** (1997; Steele & Aronson, 1995, 1998) has argued that people's performance on ability tests is influenced by **stereotype threat**—the threat of being at risk for confirming a negative stereotype of one's group. Research suggests that a person's belief that a negative stereotype is relevant in a situation can function to bring about the poor performance encoded in the stereotype. Let's consider an example of stereotype threat at work.

*The study focused on first- and second-generation immigrants from the West Indies (Deaux et al., 2007). The researchers hypothesized that first-generation immigrants, who were born in the West Indies, would not generally have had enough U.S. cultural experience to acquire the negative stereotypes about their intellectual abilities. By contrast, the researchers expected that second-generation immigrants, who had been born in the United States, would possess these stereotypes. That prediction was upheld when groups of students who were first- and second-generation immigrants completed scales that assessed their knowledge of the stereotypes. To demonstrate the consequences of this distribution of knowledge, the researchers had both types of immigrants complete a series of questions from the verbal portion of a GRE practice test. The researchers led half the students to believe that their performance was diagnostic of their verbal abilities. The researchers told the other half that they were only answering the questions to assist with test development. As you can see in **Figure 9.6**, on page 256, for the second-generation immigrants who possessed the negative stereotype, performance was impaired in the diagnostic condition: When the situation made the stereotype relevant, stereotype threat had a negative impact. However, because the first-generation immigrants didn't possess the stereotype, they didn't suffer the effects of stereotype threat.*

Let me emphasize again that what affected the performance of the second-generation immigrants was how they defined the situation. Only when people believe the situation is relevant to the stereotype—because, for example, they believe that the test measures their intelligence—does knowledge of the stereotype impair performance. Given results of this type, do you think it would be possible to measure IQ without invoking stereotype threat?

Why does stereotype threat have a negative impact? Researchers have identified three mechanisms that disrupt performance (Schmader et al., 2008). First, stereotype threat produces a physiological stress response (of the type Chapter 12 will describe) that has a negative impact on people's ability to focus their attention. Second, stereotype threat leads people to monitor their performance more closely in ways that can lead, for example, to more cautious and less creative responses. Third, when people experience stereotype threat they have to expend mental resources to suppress negative thoughts and feelings. Recall the discussion

◉ **Watch** the **Video** *Thinking Like a Psychologist: Intelligence Tests and Success* on **MyPsychLab**

◉ **Watch** the **Video** *Cultural Influences on Intelligence: Robert Sternberg* on **MyPsychLab**

stereotype threat The threat associated with being at risk for confirming a negative stereotype of one's group.

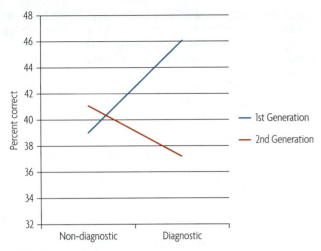

FIGURE 9.6 Stereotype Threat

The study contrasted second-generation immigrants—who possessed a negative stereotype about their group's intellectual ability—with first-generation immigrants—who did not possess that stereotype. Because the second-generation immigrants possessed the stereotype, their performance was impaired when they believed a test was diagnostic of their intellectual ability.

Based on Kay Deaux, Nida Bikmen, Alwyn Gilkes, Ana Ventuneac, Yvanne Joseph, Yasser A. Payne and Claude M. Steele, Becoming American: Stereotype threat effects in Afro-Caribbean immigrant groups, *Social Psychological Quarterly*, 70, pages 384-404, copyright © 2007 by the American Sociological Association.

of working memory in Chapter 7. The net effect of stereotype threat is to overwhelm test takers' working memory resources—leaving them less able to succeed on the problems at hand.

You have now learned some of the ways in which psychologists assess and interpret individual differences in intelligence. You have a good understanding of how researchers have tried to measure and understand this difficult concept. In this chapter's final section, we will consider why psychological assessment can sometimes generate controversy.

Stop *and* Review

① Under what circumstances did Goddard and others begin to make IQ comparisons among groups?

② Why is it inappropriate to use heritability estimates to make claims about racial differences in IQ?

③ What aspects of people's lives are affected by preschool interventions?

CRITICAL THINKING Consider the study on stereotype threat. In what ways do real-life test-givers create the belief that tests are diagnostic?

✓●─ **Study** and **Review** on **MyPsychLab**

....

◉ **Watch** the **Video** *Are Intelligence Tests Valid: Robert Guthrie* on **MyPsychLab**

ASSESSMENT AND SOCIETY

The primary goal of psychological assessment is to make accurate assessments of people that are as free as possible of errors of assessors' judgments. This goal is achieved by replacing subjective judgments of teachers, employers, and other evaluators with more objective measures that have been carefully constructed and are open to critical evaluation. This is the goal that motivated Alfred Binet in his pioneering work. Binet and others hoped that testing would help democratize society and minimize decisions based on arbitrary criteria of sex, race, nationality, privilege, or physical appearance. However, despite these lofty goals, there is no area of psychology more controversial than assessment. Three ethical concerns that are central to the controversy are the fairness of test-based decisions, the utility of tests for evaluating education, and the implications of using test scores as labels to categorize individuals.

Critics concerned with the fairness of testing practices argue that the costs or negative consequences may be higher for some test takers than for others (Helms, 2006; Hosp et al., 2011). The costs are quite high, for example, when tests on which minority groups receive low scores are used to keep them out of certain jobs. Sometimes, minority group members test poorly because their scores are evaluated relative to inappropriate norms. To address these issues, researchers have studied methods of personnel selection that combine assessments of an array of cognitive and noncognitive skills (Newman & Lyon, 2009). The goal is to predict job success with composite measures that recognize group differences in test scores.

A second ethical concern is that testing not only helps evaluate students; it may also play a role in the shaping of education. The quality of school systems and the effectiveness of teachers are frequently judged on the basis of how well their students score on standardized achievement tests (Crocco & Costigan, 2007). Local support of the schools through tax levies, and even individual teacher salaries, may ride on test scores. The high stakes associated with test scores may lead to cheating. For example, one study analyzed standardized test scores for public elementary schools in Chicago. The researchers estimated that serious cases of administrator or teacher

When schools are rewarded for high scores on standardized tests, are teachers likely to place more emphasis on test-taking skills than on broader learning goals?

Psychology in Your Life

WHAT BRAIN DIFFERENCES ACCOMPANY HIGHER INTELLIGENCE?

As you've learned in this chapter, psychometricians have been measuring differences in intelligence for about 150 years. Contemporary imaging techniques have allowed researchers to examine the brain bases of these differences. Those analyses have led to conclusions both about the structure and function of different brains.

Let's begin with structural differences. Research points to the conclusion that "bigger is better" (Deary et al., 2010a). Consider a study in which individuals completed the WAIS and then underwent MRI scans to identify the brain basis for *g*. The brain scans identified several regions in which people who were relatively high on general intelligence had more brain tissue than people who were lower (Haier et al., 2004). Note, however, that this conclusion that "bigger is better" is the product of brain development. One study assessed the relationship between IQ and thickness of cortex (assessed with MRI scans) for children who ranged in age from 7 to 19 (Shaw et al., 2006). For the youngest children, there was a negative correlation between IQ and cortical thickness (that is, the children with the highest IQs were likely to have the lowest thickness). However, over the period of adolescence, the correlation reversed so that children with higher IQs ended up with thicker cortexes. Thus, what made the brains of high-IQ children special was the extremely rapid rate at which their brains grew over time. This pattern led the researchers to conclude that "intelligence is related to dynamic properties of cortical maturation" (p. 678).

Let's turn to brain function. The basic conclusion is that more intelligent people use their brain resources more efficiently when they perform cognitive tasks. In particular, they are likely to demonstrate better performance with less overall activity in the frontal cortex (Neubauer & Fink, 2009). Recall from earlier chapters that the frontal cortex plays a critical role in many higher cognitive activities. For example, one study demonstrated the importance of the frontal cortex when people solve spatial analogies (Preusse et al., 2011). (Participants had to discover the relationship between two geometrical figures and determine whether a second pair preserved the same relationship.) The researchers divided their participants into a group that was high in fluid intelligence and a group that was average in fluid intelligence. Participants with average fluid intelligence were less accurate on the task. In addition, as shown by fMRI scans, people with average fluid intelligence showed increases in frontal activity as the problems grew harder; people with high fluid intelligence did not show similar increases. This pattern supports the conclusion that those with high fluid intelligence were making more efficient use of the frontal cortex: They were getting better results with less activity. Note that an exception to the rule of greater efficiency occurs when tasks are particularly difficult. Under those circumstances, more intelligent people tend to expand more brain resources whereas less intelligent people tend to give up on the task.

You can see how contemporary research has begun to explain the brain underpinnings of differences in intelligence.

---

cheating occur in at least 4 to 5 percent of the classrooms (Jacob & Levitt, 2003). In 2011, the state of Georgia released a report documenting extensive cheating in Atlanta's school system (Severson, 2011). The state's investigation found cheating at 44 schools involving 178 teachers and principals. The district first came under scrutiny because it had reported improvements in test scores that were statistically improbable. Many teachers confessed that they had felt pressure to cheat. These circumstances illustrate how damaging it can be when test scores are taken to matter more than education.

A third ethical concern is that test outcomes can take on the status of unchangeable labels. People too often think of themselves as being an IQ of 110 or a B student, as if the scores were labels stamped on their foreheads. Such labels may become barriers to advancement as people come to believe that their mental and personal qualities are fixed and unchangeable—that they cannot improve their lot in life. For those who are negatively assessed, the scores can become self-imposed motivational limits that lower their sense of self-efficacy and restrict the challenges they are willing to tackle. That is another dangerous consequence of pronouncements about group deficiencies in IQ.

Those stigmatized publicly in this way come to believe what the "experts" are saying about them, and so disidentify with schools and education as means to improve their lives.

This chapter has reviewed important aspects of intelligence. You've learned how researchers have defined and redefined intelligence to recognize important aspects of human performance. You've also seen why the measure of IQ remains controversial. People must give careful consideration of the broader context in which people take tests before they make claims about the abilities of particular individuals and groups.

Stop *and* Review

① Why might assessment have negative consequences for particular groups of individuals?

② Why might assessment play a role in shaping education?

③ Why might test scores become labels that have broad consequences?

✔●─[**Study** and **Review** on **MyPsychLab**

Recapping Main Points

What Is Assessment?

- Psychological assessment has a long history, beginning in ancient China. Many important contributions were made by Sir Francis Galton.
- A useful assessment tool must be reliable, valid, and standardized. A reliable measure gives consistent results. A valid measure assesses the attributes for which the test was designed.
- A standardized test is always administered and scored in the same way; norms allow a person's score to be compared with the averages of others of the same age, sex, and culture.

Intelligence Assessment

- Binet began the tradition of objective intelligence testing in France in the early 1900s. Scores were given in terms of mental ages and were meant to represent children's current level of functioning.
- In the United States, Terman created the Stanford–Binet Intelligence Scale and popularized the concept of IQ.
- Wechsler designed intelligence tests for adults, children, and preschoolers.
- The definitions of both intellectual disability and giftedness focus both on IQ scores and day-to-day performance.

Theories of Intelligence

- Psychometric analyses of IQ suggest that several basic abilities, such as fluid and crystallized aspects of intelligence, contribute to IQ scores.
- Contemporary theories conceive of and measure intelligence very broadly by considering the skills and insights people use to solve the types of problems they encounter.

- Sternberg differentiates analytical, creative, and practical aspects of intelligence.
- Gardner identifies eight types of intelligence that both include and go beyond the types of intelligence assessed by standard IQ measures. Recent research has focused on emotional intelligence.

The Politics of Intelligence

- Almost from the outset, intelligence tests have been used to make negative claims about ethnic and racial groups.
- Because of the reasonably high heritability of IQ, some researchers have attributed the lower scores of some racial and cultural groups to innate inferiority.
- Environmental disadvantages and stereotype threat appear to explain the lower scores of certain groups. Research shows that group differences can be affected through environmental interventions.

Assessment and Society

- Though often useful for prediction and as an indication of current performance, test results should not be used to limit an individual's opportunities for development and change.
- When the results of an assessment will affect an individual's life, the techniques used must be reliable and valid for that individual and for the purpose in question.

Solutions to the anagrams in Table 9.3:

1. laugh
2. tempt
3. short
4. knight
5. write
6. allow
7. drive
8. couch
9. enter
10. basic

KEY TERMS

chronological age (p. 243)
construct validity (p. 242)
content validity (p. 241)
criterion-related validity (p. 242)
crystallized intelligence (p. 248)
emotional intelligence (p. 250)
fluid intelligence (p. 248)
formal assessment (p. 241)

g (p. 248)
heritability estimate (p. 252)
intellectual disability (p. 245)
intelligence (p. 243)
intelligence quotient (IQ) (p. 244)
internal consistency (p. 241)
learning disorder (p. 246)
mental age (p. 243)

norm (p. 242)
psychological
   assessment (p. 240)
psychometrics (p. 248)
standardization (p. 242)
stereotype threat (p. 255)
test–retest reliability (p. 241)

1. Which of these was *not* one of the ideas Sir Francis Galton formulated about intelligence assessment?
   a. Differences in intelligence are quantifiable.
   b. Intelligence can be measured by objective tests.
   c. Intelligence scores follow a bell-shaped curve.
   d. Intelligence scores change over the life span.

2. When Poindexter took IQ tests on the Internet, he took four tests at the same site and obtained scores of 116, 117, 129, and 130. Given these scores, you conclude that the IQ tests are
   a. neither reliable nor valid.
   b. both reliable and valid.
   c. reliable but not valid.
   d. valid but not reliable.

3. Martin filled out a test to measure his happiness. He got a score of 72. To interpret that score, Martin needs to consult the _____ the test.
   a. test–retest reliability
   b. norms for
   c. standardization of
   d. criterion-related validity of

4. Deborah is 10 years old, but she has a mental age of 12. Using the original method for calculating IQ, you conclude that Deborah has an IQ of
   a. 90.
   b. 100.
   c. 150.
   d. 120.

5. Which cause of intellectual disability is easiest to treat?
   a. Down syndrome
   b. PKU
   c. The mother's prenatal consumption of alcohol
   d. The mother's prenatal consumption of cocaine

6. Which of these qualities is *not* part of the "three-ring" conception of giftedness?
   a. creativity
   b. mathematical genius
   c. task commitment
   d. high ability

7. At age 9, Don and Betty both had their IQs tested. Don scored 103 and Betty scored 118. Based on just that information you predict that
   a. Betty will live 15 years longer than Don.
   b. Don is likely to live longer than Betty.
   c. Betty is likely to live longer than Don.
   d. Don and Betty are likely to live roughly the same number of years.

8. _____ intelligence is defined as the knowledge a person has already acquired.
   a. Crystallized
   b. Analytical
   c. Fluid
   d. Creative

9. Felix is applying for chef school. He takes an entrance exam that poses a series of questions on food preparation. This sounds most like a test of _____ intelligence.
   a. fluid
   b. analytic
   c. practical
   d. creative

10. Julian is rarely aware when the people around him are upset. You suspect that Julian is not very high on _____ intelligence.
    a. naturalist
    b. emotional
    c. spatial
    d. bodily kinesthetic

11. Goneril and Regan are sisters. You would expect them to have the most similar IQs if they
    a. are identical twins.
    b. are fraternal twins.
    c. grew up in the same home.
    d. were adopted before age 2.

12. Studies of the impact of socioeconomic status (SES) on mental ability suggest that
    a. SES only has an impact on IQ scores for particular racial groups.
    b. SES has no overall impact on mental ability.
    c. individuals with lower SES do not benefit from preschool programs.
    d. individuals with higher SES generally demonstrate more mental ability.

13. Stereotype threat has an impact on people's test performance when they believe that
    a. the stereotype is widespread in a culture.
    b. the testing situation is unfair to certain ethnic groups.
    c. the testing situation is relevant to the stereotype.
    d. stereotypes change over time.

14. Brain research on intelligence differences suggests that, by comparison to people with lower IQs, people with higher IQs
    a. acquire greater cortical thickness across adolescence.
    b. always have greater cortical thickness.
    c. never have greater cortical thickness.
    d. have greater cortical thickness as young children.

15. When Cyrus was 12, he was told he was a genius. As an adult, he never feels as if he is living up to his potential. This is a good example of circumstances in which assessment has
    a. generated an incorrect outcome.
    b. yielded a label that has personal implications.
    c. shaped the educational experiences of an individual.
    d. had negative consequences for Cyrus's group.

ESSAY QUESTIONS

1. Why can a test be reliable but not valid?

2. What is the goal of Howard Gardner's theory of multiple intelligences?

3. How have Head Start and other early intervention programs demonstrated the impact of environments on IQ?

10

Human Development across the Life Span

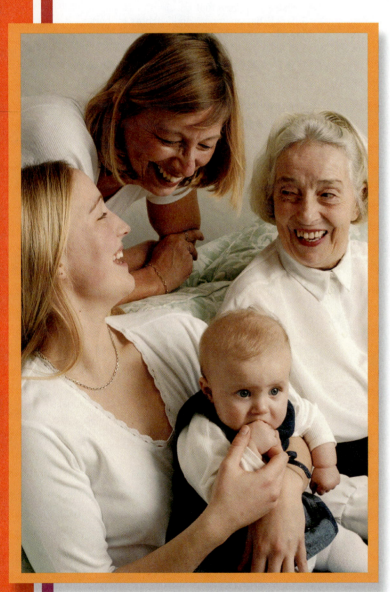

Imagine you are holding a newborn baby. How might you predict what this child will be like as a 1-year-old? At 5 years? At 15? At 50? At 70? At 90? In this chapter, we consider theories that enable us to think systematically about the types of predictions we can make for the life course of a newborn child. **Developmental psychology** is the area of psychology that is concerned with changes in physical and psychological functioning that occur from conception across the entire life span. The task of developmental psychologists is to document and explain how mental functioning, social relationships, and other vital aspects of human nature develop and change throughout the entire life cycle. **Table 10.1** presents a rough guide to the major periods of the life span.

This chapter provides a general account of how researchers document development and the theories they use to explain patterns of change over time. The chapter divides your life experiences into different domains such as physical, cognitive, language, and social development and traces each domain across the life span. Let's begin with the question of what it means to study development.

STUDYING DEVELOPMENT

Suppose you try to make a list of all the ways in which you believe you have changed in the last year. What sorts of things would you put on the list? Have you undertaken a new physical fitness program? Or have you let an injury heal? Have you developed a range of new hobbies? Or have you decided to focus on just one interest? Have you developed a new circle of friends? Or have you become particularly close to one individual? This chapter will conceptualize development in terms of *change*. I've asked you to perform this exercise of thinking about your own changes to make the point that change almost always involves trade-offs.

Often people conceptualize the life span as mostly *gains*—changes for the better—in childhood and mostly *losses*—changes for the worse—over the course of adulthood. However, the perspective on development you'll see here emphasizes that *options*, and therefore gains and losses, are features of all development (Dixon, 2003; Lachman, 2004). When, for example, people choose a lifetime companion,

they give up variety but gain security. When people retire, they give up status but gain leisure time. It is also important that you not think of development as a *passive* process. You will see that many developmental changes require an individual's *active* engagement with his or her environment (Bronfenbrenner, 2004).

Recall that Chapter 2 reviewed important aspects of research methods in psychology. Here, we consider methods that are particularly relevant to developmental research. Chapter 2 also discussed the ethics of psychological research. Recall that adults must give *informed consent* to indicate that they understand the procedures, risks, and benefits of their research participation. In most cases, parents or guardians must give permission for children under the age of 18 to participate in research. In addition, children over the age of 7 typically give *assent* to research participation. Researchers are required to write materials that describe procedures, risks, and benefits at age-appropriate levels. Children also retain all the rights of adult participants. They can, for example, withdraw from a study at any time. Because it is not always clear that young participants understand those rights, developmental researchers must be particularly careful to monitor for signs of particpants' discomfort or distress.

To document developmental change, a good first step is to determine what an average person is like—in physical appearance, cognitive abilities, and so on—at a particular age. **Normative investigations** seek to describe a characteristic of a specific age or developmental stage. By systematically testing individuals of different ages, researchers can determine developmental landmarks. These data provide *norms,* standard patterns of development or achievement, based on observation of many people.

Normative standards allow psychologists to make a distinction between chronological age—the number of months or years since a person's birth—and **developmental age**—the chronological age at which most people show the particular level of physical or mental development demonstrated by that child. A 3-year-old child who has verbal skills typical of most 5-year-olds is said to have a developmental age of 5 for verbal skills. Norms provide a standard basis for comparison both between individuals and between groups.

Developmental psychologists use several types of research designs to understand possible mechanisms of change. In a **longitudinal design,** the same individuals are repeatedly observed and tested over time, often for many years (see **Figure 10.1** on page 262). For example, one group of researchers tested children at ages 15, 25, 37, and 63 months to document the impact of children's home environment on the growth of their vocabulary (Rodriguez & Tamis-LeMonda, 2011). Longitudinal data collection allowed the researchers to draw

(see **Figure 10.1** on page 262)

Table 10.1 • Stages in Life Span Development

Stage	Age Period
Prenatal	Conception to birth
Infancy	Birth at full term to about 18 months
Early childhood	About 18 months to about 6 years
Middle childhood	About 6 years to about 11 years
Adolescence	About 11 years to about 20 years
Early adulthood	About 20 years to about 40 years
Middle adulthood	About 40 years to about 65 years
Late adulthood	About 65 years and older

developmental psychology The branch of psychology concerned with interaction between physical and psychological processes and with stages of growth from conception throughout the entire life span.

normative investigation Research effort designed to describe what is characteristic of a specific age or developmental stage.

developmental age The chronological age at which most children show a particular level of physical or mental development.

longitudinal design A research design in which the same participants are observed repeatedly, sometimes over many years.

In a longitudinal design, observations are made of the same individual at different ages, often for many years. This well-known woman might be part of a longitudinal study of British children born in 1926. How might she be similar to and different from other children in that cohort?

strong conclusions about the long-term impact of features of the children's early environments. Researchers also often use longitudinal designs to study *individual differences.* To understand the life outcomes of different people, researchers may assess a range of potential causal factors early in life and see how those factors influence each individual's life course.

A general advantage of longitudinal research is that because the participants have lived through the same socioeconomic period, age-related changes cannot be confused with variations in differing societal circumstances. A disadvantage, however, is that some types of generalizations can be made only to the same

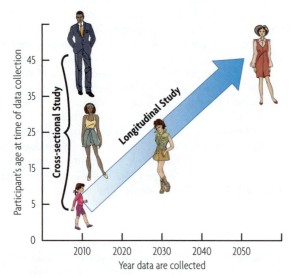

FIGURE 10.1 Longitudinal and Cross-Sectional Research

In longitudinal studies, researchers follow the same group of individuals over days, months, or years. In cross-sectional studies, researchers test individuals of different ages at the same moment in time.

cohort, the group of individuals born in the same time period as the research participants. Suppose, for example, we discovered that current 50-year-olds showed a gain in happiness in the years after their children left home. That result might not apply to a future cohort of 50-year-olds who grew up with different expectations about how long children would remain in their parents' homes. Also, longitudinal studies are costly because it is difficult to keep track of the participants over extended time, and data are easily lost because participants quit or disappear.

Much research on development uses a **cross-sectional design,** in which groups of participants, of different chronological ages, are observed and compared at one and the same time. A researcher can then draw conclusions about behavioral differences that may be related to age changes. For example, researchers who wanted to determine how people's ability to lie changes as they age tested samples of 8- through 16-year-old children (Evans & Lee, 2011). A disadvantage of cross-sectional designs comes from comparing individuals who differ by year of birth as well as by chronological age. Age-related changes are confounded by differences in the social or political conditions experienced by different birth cohorts. Thus a study comparing samples of 10- and 18-year-olds now might find that the participants differ from 10- and 18-year-olds who grew up in the 1970s, in ways related to their different eras as well as to their developmental stages.

Each methodology gives researchers the opportunity to document change from one age to another. Researchers use these methodologies to study development in each of several domains. As we now consider some of those domains—physical, cognitive, and social development—you'll come to appreciate and understand some of the vast changes you've already experienced.

....

cross-sectional design A research method in which groups of participants of different chronological ages are observed and compared at a given time.

A drawback of cross-sectional research is the cohort effect. What differences might exist between these two groups of women as a result of the eras in which they lived?

Stop *and* Review

① What is developmental age?

② Why are longitudinal designs often used to study individual differences?

③ What is the relevance of birth cohorts to cross-sectional designs?

✓ **Study** and **Review** on **MyPsychLab**

PHYSICAL DEVELOPMENT ACROSS THE LIFE SPAN

Many of the types of development we consider in this chapter require some special knowledge to detect. For example, you might not notice landmarks in social development until you read about them here. We will begin, however, with a realm of development in which changes are often plainly visible to the untrained eye: **physical development.** There is no doubt that you have undergone enormous physical change since you were born. Such changes will continue until the end of your life. Because physical changes are so numerous, the section will focus on the types that have an impact on psychological development.

Prenatal and Childhood Development

You began life with unique genetic potential: At the moment of conception a male's sperm cell fertilized a female's egg cell to form the single-cell **zygote;** you received half of the 46 chromosomes found in all normal human body cells from your mother and half from your father. This section begins with physical development in the *prenatal period,* from the moment of conception until the moment of birth. Next, we consider some of the sensory abilities children have obtained even before birth. Finally, we turn to important physical changes that you experienced during childhood.

Physical Development in the Womb   The first two weeks after formation of the zygote are known as the **germinal stage** of prenatal development. During this stage, cells begin to divide rapidly; after about one week a mass of microscopic cells attaches itself to the mother's uterine wall. The third through eighth week of prenatal development is called the **embryonic stage.** During this stage, rapid cell division continues, but the cells begin to become specialized to form different organs. As these organs develop, the first heartbeat occurs. Responses to stimulation have been observed as early as the sixth week, when the *embryo* is not yet an inch long. Spontaneous movements are observed by the seventh or eighth week (Stanojevic et al., 2011).

The **fetal stage** lasts from the end of the eighth week through the birth of the child. The mother will feel the *fetus* move in about the sixteenth week after conception. At this point, the fetus is about 7 inches long (the average length at birth is 20 inches). Most of the 100 billion neurons in the mature human brain are generated in utero (Stiles & Jernigan, 2010). In humans and many other mammals, most of this cell proliferation and migration of neurons to their correct locations take place before birth; the development of the branching processes of axons and dendrites largely occurs after birth. The sequence of brain development, from 30 days to 9 months, is shown in **Figure 10.2** on page 264. ✺

Over the course of pregnancy, environmental factors such as infection, radiation, or drugs can prevent the normal

....

✺ **Explore** the **Concept** *Virtual Brain: Development of the Brain* on **MyPsychLab**

physical development The bodily changes, maturation, and growth that occur in an organism starting with conception and continuing across the life span.

zygote The single cell that results when a sperm fertilizes an egg.

germinal stage The first two weeks of prenatal development following conception.

embryonic stage The second stage of prenatal development, lasting from the third through eighth weeks after conception.

fetal stage The third stage of prenatal development, lasting from the ninth week through birth of the child.

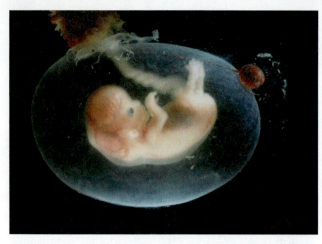

The brain grows rapidly in the developing fetus, accumulating billions of neurons by birth. What must the brain be prepared to do, as soon as the child enters the world?

formation of organs and body structures. Any environmental factor that causes structural abnormalities in the fetus is called a **teratogen.** For example, when mothers are infected with rubella (German measles), their children often suffer negative consequences such as mental retardation, eye damage, deafness, or heart defects. When the infection occurs

| 25 days | 35 days | 40 days | 50 days |

| 100 days | 5 months | 6 months |

| 7 months | 8 months | 9 months |

FIGURE 10.2 The Development of the Human Brain
During the nine months before birth, the brain reaches its complement of about 100 billion neurons.

Adapted from *The Brain* by R. Restak. Copyright © 1984. Bantam Books.

....

teratogen Environmental factors such as diseases and drugs that cause structural abnormalities in a developing fetus.

in the first six weeks after conception, the probability of birth defects may be 100 percent (De Santis et al., 2006). If exposure occurs later in the pregnancy, the probability of adverse effects becomes lower (for example, 50 percent in the fourth month; 6 percent in the fifth month). Mothers who consume alcohol during sensitive periods put their unborn children at risk for brain damage and other impairments (Bailey & Sokol, 2008). *Fetal alcohol syndrome* is the most serious consequence of a mother's alcohol consumption during pregnancy. Children with fetal alcohol syndrome often have small heads and bodies and facial abnormalities. Disruptions of the central nervous system cause cognitive and behavioral problems (Niccols, 2007).

Pregnant women who smoke also put their children at risk. Smoking during pregnancy increases the risk of miscarriage, premature births, and low-birth-weight babies (Salihu & Wilson, 2007). In fact, women who are exposed to secondhand smoke during pregnancy are also more likely to have babies with low birth weights (Crane et al., 2011). Finally, almost all illicit drugs cause damage to the fetus. Cocaine, for example, travels through the placenta and can affect fetal development directly. In adults, cocaine causes blood vessels to constrict; in pregnant women, cocaine restricts placental blood flow and oxygen supply to the fetus. If severe oxygen deprivation results, blood vessels in the fetus's brain may burst. Such prenatal strokes can lead to lifelong mental handicaps (Bennett et al., 2008; Singer et al., 2002). Research suggests that the brain systems most damaged by cocaine are those responsible for controlling attention: Children exposed to cocaine in the womb may spend their lives overcome by the distractions of irrelevant sights and sounds.

Babies Prewired for Survival   What capabilities were programmed into your body and brain at birth? We are accustomed to thinking about newborns as entirely helpless. John Watson, the founder of behaviorism, described the human infant as "a lively, squirming bit of flesh, capable of making a few simple responses." If that sounds right, you might be surprised to learn that, moments out of the womb, infants reveal remarkable abilities. They might be thought of as *prewired for survival,* well suited to respond to adult caregivers and to influence their social environments.

To begin, infants are born with a repertory of reflexes that provide many of their earliest behavioral responses to the environment. Recall from Chapter 6 that a *reflex* is a response that is naturally triggered by specific stimuli that are biologically relevant for the organism. Consider two reflexes that quite literally prewire infants for survival. When something brushes against infants' cheeks, they turn their heads in that direction. This *rooting reflex* allows newborns to find their mothers' nipples. When an object is placed in their mouths, infants begin to suck. This *sucking reflex* allows infants to begin feeding. Reflexes of this sort keep infants alive in the early months of their lives.

For example, infants can hear even before birth. Researchers have demonstrated that what infants hear while in the womb has consequences. Newborns prefer to listen to their mothers' voices rather than the voices of other women (Spence & DeCasper, 1987; Spence & Freeman, 1996). In fact, research suggests that children recognize their mothers' voices even before they are born: In one study, the heart rate of fetuses increased

When something touches a newborn's cheek, the rooting reflex prompts the baby to seek something to suck. In what other ways are children prewired for survival?

in response to recordings of their mothers' voices and remained unchanged in response to strangers' voices (Kisilevsky et al., 2009). Newborns may find it relatively easy to learn to recognize their mothers' faces because they are associated with voices with which they are already familiar (Sai, 2005). Given these important results for mothers' voices, you might wonder whether children also respond more to their fathers' voices. Unfortunately, fetal heart rates do not change in a comparable pattern in response to fathers' voices, suggesting that fathers' voices do not become sufficiently familiar when children are in utero. In fact, newborns still show no preference for their fathers' voices (DeCasper & Prescott, 1984).

Most children begin to obtain visual experience during their last two months in utero (Del Giudice, 2011). They are able to perceive their own movements. Given this head start, it's not surprising that newborns put their visual systems to work almost immediately: A few minutes after birth, a newborn's eyes are alert, turning in the direction of a voice and searching inquisitively for the source of certain sounds. Even so, vision is less well developed than the other senses at birth. The visual acuity of adults is roughly 40 times better than the visual acuity of newborns (Sireteanu, 1999). However, visual acuity improves rapidly over the first six months of a baby's life. Newborns also are ill equipped to experience the world in three dimensions. Recall from Chapter 4 that you use a great variety of cues to experience depth. Researchers have begun to document the time course with which infants are able to interpret each type of cue. For example, at 4 months, infants start being able to use cues such as relative motion and interposition to infer three-dimensional structures from two-dimensional images of objects (Shuwairi et al., 2007; Soska & Johnson, 2008).

Even without perfect vision, however, children have visual preferences. Pioneering researcher **Robert Fantz** (1963) observed that babies as young as 4 months old preferred looking at objects with contours rather than those that were plain, complex ones rather than simple ones, and whole faces rather than faces with features in disarray. More recent research suggests that—by the age of 3 days—infants have a preference for *top-heavy patterns* (Macchi Cassia et al., 2004). To experience a top-heavy pattern, take a look at your face in a mirror—notice that your eyes,

eyebrows, and so on, take up much more space than your lips. The fact that faces are top-heavy might explain why infants prefer to look at human faces versus other types of visual displays.

Once children start to move around in their environment, they quickly acquire other perceptual capabilities. For example, classic research by **Eleanor Gibson** and **Richard Walk** (1960) examined how children respond to depth information. This research used an apparatus called a *visual cliff*. The visual cliff had a board running across the middle of a solid glass surface. As shown in **Figure 10.3** on page 266, checkerboard cloth was used to create a deep end and a shallow end. In their original research, Gibson and Walk demonstrated that children would readily leave the center board to crawl across the shallow end, but they were reluctant to crawl across the deep end. Subsequent research has demonstrated that fear of the deep end depends on crawling experience: Children who have begun to crawl experience fear of the deep end, whereas their noncrawling same-age peers do not (Campos et al., 1992; Witherington et al., 2005). Thus wariness of heights is not quite "prewired," but it develops quickly as children begin to explore the world under their own power. ◉

Growth and Maturation in Childhood Newborn infants change at an astonishing rate but, as shown in **Figure 10.4** on page 266, physical growth is not equal across all physical structures. You've probably noticed that babies seem to be all head. At birth, a baby's head is already about 60 percent of its adult size and measures a quarter of the whole body length (Bayley, 1956). An infant's body weight doubles in the first six months and triples by the first birthday; by the age of 2, a child's trunk is about half of its adult length. Genital tissue shows little change until the teenage years and then develops rapidly to adult proportions.

....

◉ **Watch** the **Video** *Classic Footage of Eleanor Gibson, Richard Walk, and the Visual Cliff* on **MyPsychLab**

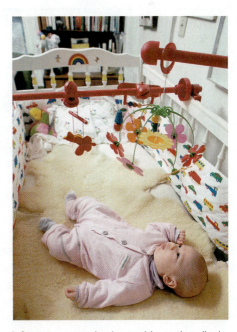

Early on, infants can perceive large objects that display a great deal of contrast. What visual experiences do newborns find particularly appealing?

FIGURE 10.3 The Visual Cliff

Once children have gained experience crawling around their environment, they show fear of the deep side of the visual cliff.

For most children, physical growth is accompanied by the maturation of motor ability. **Maturation** refers to the process of growth typical of all members of a species who are reared in the species's usual habitat. The characteristic maturational sequences newborns experience are determined by the interaction of inherited biological boundaries and environmental inputs. To understand the impact of environmental inputs, developmental researchers make a distinction between *sensitive periods* and *critical periods*. A sensitive period is an optimal age range for children to have appropriate environmental experiences relevant to normal development. Development will proceed most smoothly if children have those experiences during the sensitive period. However, if they have those experiences later in life, they will still be able to experience development—just with more difficulty. Critical periods impose stronger constraints on development: A critical period is an age range in which children must obtain appropriate environmental experiences. Without appropriate experiences during a crtical period, a child may not be able to develop a particular function.

Let's consider a particular example of motor development. In the sequence for locomotion, as shown in **Figure 10.5**, a child learns to walk without special training. Note that Figure 10.5 captures a sequence for an "average" child. Individual children often reach these motor milestones in their own particular orders (Adolph et al., 2010). In fact, some children skip stages like crawling altogether. Research on the development of walking also allows for an understanding of the importance of environmental inputs. Children who experience extra motor practice may reach motor milestones more quickly, whereas children whose motor experiences are restricted may develop more slowly. Still, within this individual variation, you can think of all unimpaired newborn children as possessing the same potential for physical maturation.

Children's physical development follows two general principles. The *cephalocaudal principle* states that development proceeds in a direction from head to foot. For example, children typically develop control of their arms before they develop control of their legs. The *proximodistal principle* states that parts of the body near the center develop before the extremities. For example, children's arms develop before their hands and their hands develop before their fingers. Finally, development typically proceeds from *gross* to *fine* motor skills. Gross motor skils involve larger muscles as when infants kick their legs or roll over. Fine motor skills require more presice coordination of smaller muscles. As they develop fine motor skills, infants become able to hold objects or put them in their mouths.

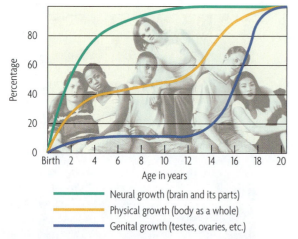

FIGURE 10.4 Growth Patterns across the First Two Decades of Life

Neural growth occurs very rapidly in the first year of life. It is much faster than overall physical growth. By contrast, genital maturation does not occur until adolescence.

maturation The continuing influence of heredity throughout development, the age-related physical and behavioral changes characteristic of a species.

Physical Development in Adolescence

The first concrete indicator of the end of childhood is the *pubescent growth spurt.* At around age 10 for girls and age 12

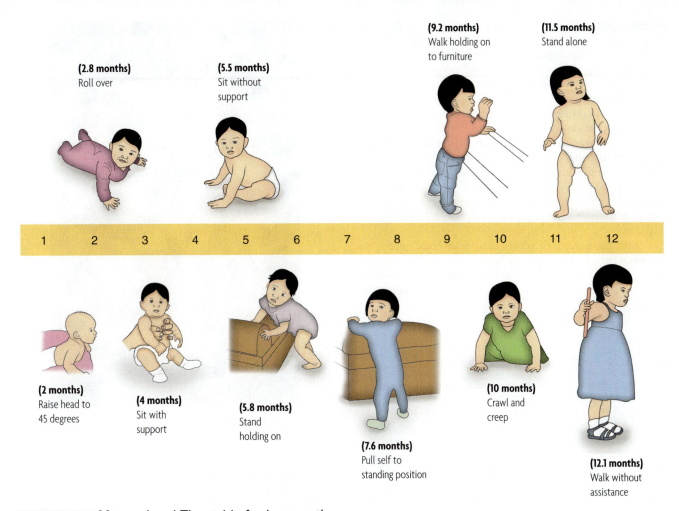

FIGURE 10.5 Maturational Timetable for Locomotion

The development of walking requires no special teaching. Physically capable members of our species pass through many of the same stages over the first year of life.

for boys, growth hormones flow into the bloodstream. For several years, the adolescent may grow 3 to 6 inches a year and gain weight rapidly as well. The adolescent's body does not reach adult proportions all at once. Hands and feet grow to full adult size first. The arms and legs come next, with the torso developing most slowly. Thus an individual's overall shape changes several times over the teenage years.

Another important process that occurs during adolescence is **puberty,** which brings about sexual maturity. (The Latin word *pubertas* means "covered with hair" and signifies the growth of hair on the arms and legs, under the arms, and in the genital area.) Puberty for males brings about the production of live sperm; for girls it leads to **menarche,** the onset of menstruation. In the United States, the average time for menarche is between the ages of 12 and 13, although the normal range extends from 11 to 15. For boys, the production of live sperm first occurs, on average, between the ages of 12 and 14,

but again there is considerable variation in this timing. These physical changes often bring about an awareness of sexual feelings. Chapter 11 will discuss the onset of sexual motivation.

Some other important physical changes happen inside adolescents' brains. Researchers once thought that most brain growth was over within the first few years of life. However, recent studies using brain-imaging techniques have demonstrated continuing development within the adolescent brain (Paus, 2005). Researchers have documented particularly important changes in the *limbic system*—which regulates emotional processes—and the *frontal lobes*—the areas responsible for planning and control of emotions (see Chapter 3). However, maturation of the limbic system precedes maturation of the frontal lobes. The relative timing of changes within those regions may explain one of most salient aspects of social development in adolescence: Adolescents tend to engage in risky behavior (Andrews-Hanna et al., 2011). 👁

We'll return to social aspects of risky behavior in the review of social development across the life span. For now, our focus is on physical development. Researchers speculate that maturation of the limbic system readies adolescents to go out into the world: "Evolutionarily speaking, adolescence is the period in which independence skills are acquired to increase

··

👁 **Watch** the **Video** *Special Topics: Risky Behavior and Brain Development* on **MyPsychLab**

puberty The process through which sexual maturity is attained.

menarche The onset of menstruation.

success upon separation from the protection of the family" (Casey et al., 2008, p. 70). In that evolutionary context, it makes sense that regions of the frontal cortex that inhibit and control the emotional drive toward independence would mature somewhat later in life. To survive apart from their families, adolescents would have to take some initial risks. The difficulty is that in contemporary times people no longer typically leave their families during adolescence. Thus, the evolutionary impulse toward novelty seeking and risk taking no longer has an adaptive function. Fortunately, as people develop from adolescence into adulthood, the frontal lobes achieve maturity (Steinberg, 2008). New connections form between the frontal lobes and limbic system. Those new connections enable individuals to exercise more cognitive control over their emotional impulses.

With the passing of adolescence, your body once again reaches a period of the life span in which biological change is comparatively minimal. You may affect your body in a variety of ways—by diet and exercise, for example—but the next striking set of changes that are consistent consequences of aging occurs in middle and late adulthood.

Physical Changes in Adulthood

Some of the most obvious changes that occur with age concern your physical appearance and abilities. As you grow older, you can expect your skin to wrinkle, your hair to thin and gray, and your height to decrease an inch or two. You can also expect some of your senses to become less acute. These changes do not appear suddenly at age 65. They occur gradually, beginning as soon as early adulthood. However, before we consider some common age-related changes, here's a more general point: Many physical changes arise not from aging but from *disuse;* research supports a general belief in the maxim "Use it or lose it." Older adults who maintain (or renew) a program of physical fitness may experience fewer of the difficulties that are often thought to be inevitable consequences of aging. Let's now look, however, at some changes that are largely unavoidable and frequently have an impact on the way adults think about their lives.

Vision Beginning at ages 40 to 50, most people begin experiencing changes in the function of their visual system: The lenses of their eyes become less flexible and the muscles that change the thickness of the lens become less effective. These changes can make seeing objects at close range difficult. Lens rigidity also affects dark adaptation, making night vision a problem for older people. Many of these normal visual changes can be aided with corrective lenses. With age, the lenses of people's eyes also become yellowed. The yellowing of the lens is thought to be responsible for diminished color vision experienced by some older people. Colors of lower wavelengths—violets, blues, and greens—are particularly hard for some older adults to discriminate. In one sample of 1,219 adults in the United States, 17 percent of adults reported visual impairments at age 45. This figure increased to 26 percent in adults 75 and older (Horowitz et al., 2005).

Hearing Hearing loss is common among those 60 and older. The average older adult has difficulty hearing high-frequency

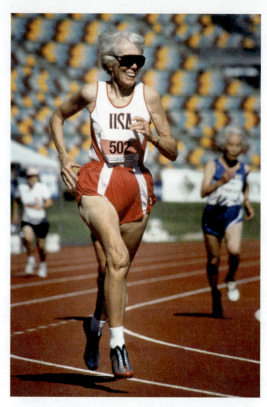

Why do researchers give the advice "Use it or lose it"?

sounds (Mendelson & Rajan, 2011). Older adults can have a hard time understanding speech—particularly that spoken by high-pitched voices. (Oddly enough, with age, people's speaking voices increase in pitch due to stiffening of the vocal cords.) Deficits in hearing can be gradual and hard for an individual to notice until they are extreme. In addition, even when individuals become aware of hearing loss, they may deny it because it is perceived as an undesirable sign of aging. Some of the physiological aspects of hearing loss can be overcome with the help of hearing aids. You should also be aware, as you grow older or interact with older adults, that it helps to speak in low tones, enunciate clearly, and reduce background noise.

Reproductive and Sexual Functioning We saw that puberty marks the onset of reproductive functioning. In middle and late adulthood, reproductive capacity diminishes. Around age 50, most women experience *menopause,* the cessation of menstruation and ovulation. For men, changes are less abrupt, but the quantity of viable sperm falls off after age 40, and the volume of seminal fluid declines after age 60. Of course, these changes are relevant primarily to reproduction. Increasing age and physical change do not necessarily impair other aspects of sexual experience (DeLamater & Sill, 2005; Lindau et al., 2007). Indeed, sex is one of life's healthy pleasures that can enhance successful aging because it is arousing, provides aerobic exercise, stimulates fantasy, and is a vital form of social interaction.

You have had a brief review of the landmarks of physical development. Against that background, let's turn now to the ways in which you developed an understanding of the world around you.

Stop *and* Review

① How does experience with crawling influence children's performance on the visual cliff?

② What have recent studies demonstrated with respect to brain development in adolescence?

③ Why does increasing age often have an effect on color vision?

✔●─│Study│ *and* **Review** on **MyPsychLab**

COGNITIVE DEVELOPMENT ACROSS THE LIFE SPAN

How does an individual's understanding of physical and social reality change across the life span? **Cognitive development** is the study of the processes and products of the mind as they emerge and change over time. Because researchers have been particularly fascinated by the earliest emergence of cognitive capabilities, this section will largely focus on on the earliest stages of cognitive development. However, we will also consider some of the discoveries researchers have made about cognitive development across the adult years.

The discussion of cognitive development begins with the pioneering work of the late Swiss psychologist Jean Piaget.

Piaget's Insights into Mental Development

For nearly 50 years, **Jean Piaget** (1929, 1954, 1977) developed theories about the ways that children think, reason, and solve problems. Perhaps Piaget's interest in cognitive development grew out of his own intellectually active youth: Piaget published his first article at age 10 and was offered a post as a museum curator at age 14 (Brainerd, 1996). Piaget used simple demonstrations and sensitive interviews with his own children and with other children to generate complex theories about early mental development. His interest was not in the amount of information children possessed but in the ways their thinking and inner representations of physical reality changed at different stages in their development.

Building Blocks of Developmental Change Piaget gave the name **schemes** to the mental structures that enable individuals to interpret the world. Schemes are the building blocks of developmental change. Piaget characterized the infant's initial schemes as *sensorimotor intelligence*—mental structures or programs that guide sensorimotor sequences, such as sucking, looking, grasping, and pushing. With practice, elementary schemes are combined, integrated, and differentiated into ever-more-complex, diverse action patterns, as when a child pushes away undesired objects to seize a desired one behind him or her. According to Piaget, two basic processes work in tandem to achieve cognitive growth—assimilation and accommodation. **Assimilation** modifies new environmental information to fit into what is already known; the child accesses existing schemes to structure incoming sensory data. **Accommodation** restructures or modifies the child's existing schemes so that new information is accounted for more completely.

Consider the transitions a baby must make from sucking at a mother's breast, to sucking the nipple of a bottle, to sipping through a straw, and then to drinking from a cup. The initial sucking response is a reflex action present at birth, but it must be modified somewhat so that the child's mouth fits the shape and size of the mother's nipple. In adapting to a bottle, an infant still uses many parts of the sequence unchanged (assimilation) but must grasp and draw on the rubber nipple somewhat differently from before and learn to hold the bottle at an appropriate angle (accommodation). The steps from bottle to straw to cup require more accommodation but continue to rely on earlier skills. Piaget saw cognitive development as the result of exactly this sort of interweaving of assimilation and accommodation. The balanced application of assimilation and accommodation permits children's behavior and knowledge to become less dependent on concrete external reality, relying more on abstract thought.

Stages in Cognitive Development Piaget believed that children's cognitive development could be divided into a series of four ordered, discontinuous stages (see **Table 10.2** on page 270). All children are assumed to progress through these stages in the same sequence, although one child may take longer to pass through a given stage than does another.

Sensorimotor Stage The sensorimotor stage extends roughly from birth to age 2. In the early months, much of an infant's behavior is based on a limited array of inborn schemes, like sucking, looking, grasping, and pushing. During the first year, sensorimotor sequences are improved, combined, coordinated, and integrated (sucking and grasping, looking and manipulating, for example). They become more varied as infants discover that their actions have an effect on external events. ●

The most important cognitive acquisition of the infancy period is the ability to form mental representations of absent objects—those with which the child is not in direct sensorimotor contact. **Object permanence** refers to children's understanding that objects exist and behave independently of their actions or awareness. In the first months of life, children follow objects with their eyes, but, when the objects disappear from view, they turn away as if the objects had also disappeared from their minds. At around 3 months of age, however, they keep looking at the place where the objects had disappeared.

....

● **Watch** the **Video** *Sensorimotor Development* on **MyPsychLab**

cognitive development The development of processes of knowing, including imagining, perceiving, reasoning, and problem solving.

scheme Piaget's term for a cognitive structure that develops as infants and young children learn to interpret the world and adapt to their environment.

assimilation According to Piaget, the process whereby new cognitive elements are fitted in with old elements or modified to fit more easily; this process works in tandem with accommodation.

accommodation According to Piaget, the process of restructuring or modifying cognitive structures so that new information can fit into them more easily; this process works in tandem with assimilation.

object permanence The recognition that objects exist independently of an individual's action or awareness; an important cognitive acquisition of infancy.

Table 10.2 • Piaget's Stages of Cognitive Development

Stage/Ages	Characteristics and Major Accomplishments
Sensorimotor (0–2)	Child begins life with small number of sensorimotor sequences.
	Child develops object permanence and the beginnings of symbolic thought.
Preoperational (2–7)	Child's thought is marked by egocentrism and centration.
	Child has improved ability to use symbolic thought.
Concrete operations (7–11)	Child achieves understanding of conservation.
	Child can reason with respect to concrete, physical objects.
Formal operations (11→)	Child develops capacity for abstract reasoning and hypothetical thinking.

according to what the child *cannot* do. For example, Piaget believed that young children's preoperational thought is marked by **egocentrism,** the child's inability to take the perspective of another person. You have probably noticed egocentrism if you've heard a 2-year-old's conversations with other children. Children at this age often seem to be talking to themselves rather than interacting.

Preoperational children also experience **centration**—they tend to focus (center) their attention on only one aspect of a situation and disregard other relevant aspects. Centration is illustrated by Piaget's classic demonstration of a child's inability to understand that the amount of a liquid does not change as a function of the size or shape of its container.

When an equal amount of lemonade is poured into two identical glasses, children of ages 5 and 7 report that the glasses contain the same amount. When, however, the lemonade from one glass is poured into a tall, thin glass, their opinions diverge. The 5-year-olds know that the lemonade in the tall glass is the same lemonade, but they report that it now is more. The 7-year-olds correctly assert that there is no difference between the amounts.

Featured Study

In Piaget's demonstration, the younger children center on a single, perceptually noticeable dimension—the height of the lemonade in the glass. The older children take into account both height and width and correctly infer that appearance is not reality.

Between 8 and 12 months, children begin to search for those disappearing objects. By age 2 years, children have no remaining uncertainty that "out of sight" objects continue to exist (Flavell, 1985).

Preoperational Stage

The preoperational stage extends roughly from 2 to 7 years of age. The big cognitive advance in this developmental stage is an improved ability to represent mentally objects that are not physically present. Except for this development, Piaget characterizes the preoperational stage

egocentrism In cognitive development, the inability of a young child at the preoperational stage to take the perspective of another person.

centration Preoperational children's tendency to focus their attention on only one aspect of a situation and disregard other relevant aspects.

Concrete Operations Stage

The concrete operations stage goes roughly from 7 to 11 years of age. At this stage, the child has become capable of mental operations, actions performed in the mind that give rise to logical thinking. The preoperational and concrete operations stages are often put in contrast because children in the concrete operation stage are now capable of what they failed earlier on. Concrete operations allow children to replace physical action with mental action. For example, if a child sees that Adam is taller than Zara and, later, that Zara is taller than Tanya, the child can reason that Adam is the tallest of the three—without physically manipulating the three individuals. However, the child still cannot draw the

Piaget observed that the typical 6-month-old will attend to an attractive toy (left) but will quickly lose interest if a screen blocks the toy from view (right). What understanding about objects will the child achieve by age 2?

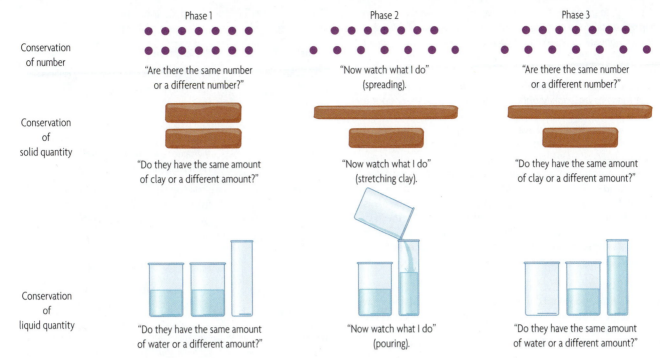

	Phase 1	Phase 2	Phase 3

Conservation of number

Phase 1: "Are there the same number or a different number?"

Phase 2: "Now watch what I do" (spreading).

Phase 3: "Are there the same number or a different number?"

Conservation of solid quantity

Phase 1: "Do they have the same amount of clay or a different amount?"

Phase 2: "Now watch what I do" (stretching clay).

Phase 3: "Do they have the same amount of clay or a different amount?"

Conservation of liquid quantity

Phase 1: "Do they have the same amount of water or a different amount?"

Phase 2: "Now watch what I do" (pouring).

Phase 3: "Do they have the same amount of water or a different amount?"

FIGURE 10.6 Tests of Conservation

appropriate inference ("Adam is tallest") if the problem is just stated with a verbal description. Children only become able to solve problems of this sort with abstract thought when they arrive at the stage of concrete operations.

The lemonade study illustrates another hallmark of the concrete operations period. The 7-year-olds have mastered what Piaget called **conservation:** They know that the physical properties of objects do not change when nothing is added or taken away, even though the objects' appearances change. **Figure 10.6** presents examples of Piaget's tests of conservation for different dimensions. One of the newly acquired operations children can bring to bear on conservation tasks is reversibility. *Reversibility* is the child's understanding that both physical actions and mental operations can be reversed: The child can reason that the amount of lemonade *couldn't* have changed because when the physical action is reversed—when the lemonade is poured back into the original glass—the two volumes will once again look identical. 👁

Formal Operations Stage The formal operations stage covers a span roughly from age 11 on. In this final stage of cognitive growth, thinking becomes abstract. Adolescents can see how their particular reality is only one of several imaginable realities, and they begin to ponder deep questions of truth, justice, and existence. They seek answers to problems in a systematic fashion: Once they achieve formal operations, children can start to play the role of scientist, trying each of a series of

possibilities in careful order. Adolescents also begin to be able to use the types of advanced deductive logic that Chapter 8 described. Unlike their younger siblings, adolescents have the ability to reason from abstract premises ("If *A*, then *B*" and "not *B*") to their logical conclusions ("not *A*").

Contemporary Perspectives on Early Cognitive Development

Piaget's theory remains the classic reference point for the understanding of cognitive development (Feldman, 2004; Flavell, 1996). However, contemporary researchers have come up with more flexible ways of studying the development of the child's cognitive abilities.

Infant Cognition You've already met some of the tasks Piaget used to draw conclusions about cognitive development. However, contemporary researchers have developed innovative techniques that have allowed them to reevaluate some of Piaget's conclusions. Consider object permanence, which Piaget suggested was the major accomplishment of the 2-year-old child. Contemporary research techniques suggest that infants as young as 3 months old have already developed aspects of this concept. This important finding has been shown with different tasks devised by researcher **Renée Baillargeon** and her colleagues.

👁 **Watch** the **Video** *Conservation Tasks* on **MyPsychLab**

conservation According to Piaget, the understanding that physical properties do not change when nothing is added or taken away, even though appearances may change.

In one study, 4-month-old infants watched while an experimenter lowered a wide rectangular object (Wang et al., 2004). In one condition, the path of the object would put it behind a wide occluder—a barrier wide enough to hide the rectangular object completely. In the other condition, the object was

destined to pass behind a narrow occluder—a barrier too narrow to occlude the object fully. As this event unfolded, a screen appeared that hid the final moment in which the object was lowered. When the screen disappeared, the object was fully hidden. How did the infants respond in the two conditions? If they didn't have object permanence, we would expect them to be equally unbothered in both cases—once the rectangular object was gone, we would expect them to have no recollection that it had ever existed. Suppose they did have some recollection of the object. In that case, we would expect that they—like adults who watched the events—would be rather surprised that a wide object could be hidden by a narrow occluder. To assess the infants' degree of surprise, the researchers recorded how long infants looked at the displays after the screen disappeared. The infants who saw the narrow occluder event looked at the display for about 16 seconds longer than their peers who saw the wide occluder event. The rectangular object was out of sight but not out of mind.

We can't take the infants' surprise as evidence that they have acquired the full concept of object permanence—they may only know that something is wrong without knowing exactly what that something is. Even so, the research by Baillargeon and her colleagues suggests that event very young children have acquired important knowledge of the physical world.

The innovative methods researchers have developed to penetrate infants' minds continue to transform our understanding of what infants know and how they know it. Consider the development of perceptual processes. We saw earlier that children come into the world "prewired for survival." Still, experience in the world expands their perceptual and conceptual abilities. For example, as an adult you are easily able to recognize that a two-dimensional drawing provides a representation of a three-dimensional object. When did this ability first emerge? Using a measure of looking time (similar to the methods used by Baillargeon and her colleagues), researchers demonstrated that 9-month-olds could recognize that, for example, a line drawing of a sheep corresponded to a three-dimensional stuffed animal (Jowkar-Baniani & Schmuckler, 2011). Let's consider a second example that shows how infants piece together the workings of the world. Suppose you watched a video clip in which either a living creature or a moving ball caused a jumble of blocks to become neatly ordered. As an adult you know that non-living objects don't typically make the world more orderly. For that reason, you'd likely be more surprised by the clip with the ball. As measured by looking times, 12-month-old infants showed the same type of surprise (Newman et al., 2010). However, 7-month-olds looked equally as long at the clips that used living agents and balls. Thus, an understanding of the causal properties of living and non-living entities develops past the middle of the first year of life.

Theory of Mind Even as children's own cognitive abilities develop, they also come to understand that other people have cognitive experiences of the world—and that those cognitive experiences may not be exactly the same. Over time, children develop a **theory of mind,** which is the ability to explain and predict other people's behavior based on an understanding of their mental states. **Table 10.3** provides examples of the tasks researchers use to assess the development of theory of mind (Wellman et al.,

Table 10.3 • Tasks Used to Assess the Development of Theory of Mind

Task	Description
Diverse desires	Child judges that two persons (the child vs. someone else) have different desires about the same object
Diverse beliefs	Child judges that two persons (the child vs. someone else) have different beliefs about the same object, when the child does not know which belief is true or false
Knowledge access	Child sees what is in a box and judges (yes–no) the knowledge of another person who does not sees what is in the box
Contents false belief	Child judges another person's false belief about what is in a distinctive container when child knows what is in the container
Hidden emotion	Child judges that a person can feel one thing but display a different emotion

From Sequential progressions in a theory -of-mind scale: Longitudinal perspectives by Henry M. Wellman, Fuxi Fang, and Candida C. Peterson, *Child Development*, 82, pages 780–79, copyright © 2011 Society for Research in Child Development. Reprinted by permission of John Wiley and Sons.

2011). Each task explores the extent to which children understand that what they desire, believe, know, or feel about the world might be different from what other people desire, believe, know, or feel. Children acquire different aspects of theory of mind at different times: For most children in the United States, the sequence follows the top-to-bottom order of Table 10.3 and acquisition occurs over several years from ages 2 to 6.

Still, researchers have documented how some aspects of theory of mind emerge even in infancy. Consider the relationship between actions and goals (people's intentions). As an adult, you are accustomed to inferring people's goals when you watch them perform actions. For example, if you see someone pull out a set of keys, you easily infer that he or she needs to unlock something. When did you start to understand how actions relate to goals? Research suggests that 7-month-olds have begun to divide the world up into actions that are goal-directed and those that are not (Hamlin et al., 2008). As a second example, consider how you respond when a friend points at an object. As an adult, you infer your friend's behavior is guided by an intention: You are meant to shift your attention in the direction of the gesture. Similarly, 12-month-old infants are able to use pointing gestures produced by adults to find a hidden toy (Behne et al., 2012). These studies illustrate how carefully infants attend to the world around them to develop an understanding of the mental states that underlie other people's behaviors.

Social and Cultural Influences on Cognitive Development
Another focus of contemporary research is on the role of social interactions in cognitive development. Much of this research has its origins in the theories of Russian psychologist

··

 Watch the **Video** *False Belief Task* on **MyPsychLab**

theory of mind The ability to explain and predict other people's behavior based on an understanding of their mental states.

Lev Vygotsky. Vygotsky argued that children develop through a process of **internalization:** They absorb knowledge from their social context that has a major impact on how cognition unfolds over time.

The social theory that Vygotsky pioneered has found support in cross-cultural studies of development (Gauvain et al., 2011). As Piaget's theory initially seized the attention of developmental researchers, many of them sought to use his tasks to study the cognitive achievements of children in diverse cultures (Maynard, 2008). These studies began to call into question the universality of Piaget's claims because, for example, people in many cultures failed to show evidence that they had acquired formal operations. Late in his life, Piaget himself began to speculate that the specific achievements he characterized as formal operations may rely more on the particular type of science education children obtain rather than on an unfolding of biologically predetermined stages of cognitive development (Lourenço & Machado, 1996).

Vygotsky's concept of internalization helps explain the effect culture has on cognitive development. Children's cognition develops to perform culturally valued functions (Fleer & Hedegaard, 2010; Serpell, 2000). Piaget, for example, invented tasks that reflected his own preconceptions about appropriate and valuable cognitive activities. Other cultures prefer their children to excel in other ways. If Piaget's children had been evaluated with respect to their understanding of the cognitive complexities of weaving, they probably would have appeared to be retarded in their development relative to Mayan children in Guatemala (Rogoff, 1990). Cross-cultural studies of cognitive development have quite often demonstrated that type of schooling plays a large role in determining children's achievement on Piagetian tasks (Rogoff & Chavajay, 1995). Psychologists must use these types of findings to sort out the nature and nurture of cognitive development.

The developmental changes we've considered so far are very dramatic. It's easy to tell that a 12-year-old has all sorts of cognitive capabilities unknown to a 1-year-old. We now shift to the more subtle changes that take place throughout adulthood.

Cognitive Development in Adulthood

As we have traced cognitive development across childhood into adolescence, "change" has usually meant "change for the better." When we arrive at the period of late adulthood, though, cultural stereotypes suggest that "change" means "change for the worse" (Parr & Siegert, 1993). However, even when people believe that the course of adulthood brings with it general decline, they still anticipate certain types of gains very late into life (Dixon & de Frias, 2004). We will consider intelligence and memory to see the interplay of losses and gains.

Intelligence There is little evidence to support the notion that general cognitive abilities decline among the healthy elderly. Only about 5 percent of the population experiences

major losses in cognitive functioning. When age-related decline in cognitive functioning occurs, it is usually limited to only some abilities. When intelligence is separated into the components that make up your verbal abilities (*crystallized intelligence*) and those that are part of your ability to learn quickly and thoroughly (*fluid intelligence*), fluid intelligence shows the greater decline with age (Hertzog, 2011). Much of the decrease in fluidity has been attributed to a general slowing down of processing speed: Older adults' performance on intellectual tasks that require many mental processes to occur in small amounts of time is greatly impaired (Sheppard & Vernon, 2008).

Researchers who study cognitive performance have been quite interested in determining what older adults might do to minimize declines with age. Much research attention has considered the maxim "Use it or lose it." One study, for example, focused on a group of older adults whose average age was 69 (Bielak et al., 2007). The adults whose everyday lives had the highest levels of social, physical, and intellectual activities also showed the fastest processing speed on cognitive tasks. These results appear to support "use it or lose it." However, interpretation of results of this sort is muddied by a concern you encournted in Chapter 2: Correlation is not causation (Salthouse, 2006). The result *could* indicate that a high level of activity causes processing speed to remain relatively high. However, we must also consider the possibility that a smaller decline in processing speed allows some older adults to remain more active.

Even if it proves difficult to demonstrate that "using it" prevents "losing it," researchers have provided evidence that "using it more" can bring about better intellectual functioning (Hertzog et al., 2008). Let's consider evidence that frequent computer use works against intellectual decline.

Participants whose ages ranged from 32 to 84 provided information about the frequency of their computer use (Tun & Lachman, 2010). In addition, the 2,671 participants completed a battery of cognitive tests. The data showed positive correlations between computer use and cognitive ability: More computer use was associated with greater ability. For example, one cognitive task assessed participants' ability to respond to stimuli by switching quickly between two different rules. Participants who used computers more performed better on this task. The benefit of this particular task was especially large for participants who otherwise showed lower intellectual ability.

Featured Study

The researchers acknowledged that these results are correlational: They raise the possibility that people with more cognitive ability may choose to use computers more. However, they argue that the particular pattern of benefits favors the explanation that computer use prevents people from "losing it." To understand this claim, try to contemplate the multiple cognitive activities in which you engage the next time you navigate through cyberspace.

It's important to note that there's one intelligence measure on which people show improvement over the life span. Psychologists have demonstrated age-related gains in **wisdom**—expertise in the fundamental practices of life (Staudinger & Glück, 2011). **Table 10.4** on page 274 presents some of the types of knowledge

---

internalization According to Vygotsky, the process through which children absorb knowledge from the social context.

Many prominent figures, such as Nelson Mandela, continue to make important professional contributions through their 70s and beyond. How can some aspects of intellectual performance be kept from decline through late adulthood?

that define wisdom (Smith & Baltes, 1990). You can see that each type of knowledge is best acquired over a long and thoughtful life.

Memory   A common complaint among the elderly is the feeling that their ability to remember things is not as good as it used to be. On a number of tests of memory, adults over 60 *do* perform worse than young adults in their 20s (Hess, 2005). Aging does *not* seem to diminish elderly individuals' ability to access their general knowledge store and personal information about events that occurred long ago. In a study of name and face recognition, middle-aged adults could identify 90 percent of their high school classmates in yearbooks 35 years after graduation; older adults were still able to recognize 70 to 80 percent of their

Table 10.4 • Features of Wisdom

- *Rich factual knowledge.* General and specific knowledge about the conditions of life and its variations
- *Rich procedural knowledge.* General and specific knowledge about strategies of judgment and advice concerning life matters
- *Life span contextualism.* Knowledge about the contexts of life and their temporal (developmental) relationships
- *Uncertainty.* Knowledge about the relative indeterminacy and unpredictability of life and ways to manage it

....

wisdom Expertise in the fundamental pragmatics of life.

classmates some 50 years later (Bahrick et al., 1975). However, aging affects the processes that allow new information to be effectively organized, stored, and retrieved (Buchler & Reder, 2007).

As yet, researchers have been unable to develop a wholly adequate description of the mechanisms that underlie memory impairment in older adults—perhaps because the impairment has multiple sources (Hess, 2005). Some theories focus on differences between older and younger people in their efforts to organize and process information. Other theories point to elderly people's reduced ability to pay attention to information. Another type of theory looks to neurobiological changes in the brain systems that produce the physical memory traces (Charlton et al., 2010). Note that these brain changes are not the same as the abnormal tangles of neural tissue and plaques that cause the memory loss of Alzheimer's disease (see Chapter 7). Researchers also believe that older adults' performance may be impaired by their very belief that their memory will be poor (Hess & Hinson, 2006). Researchers continue to evaluate the relative contributions of each of these factors.

Let's now narrow our focus from general cognitive development to the more specific topic of the acquisition of language.

Stop *and* Review

① In Piaget's theory, what is the relationship between assimilation and accommodation?
② What does it mean when a child is able to overcome centration?
③ How has contemporary research modified conclusions about object permanence?
④ What was the major emphasis of Lev Vygotsky's theory?
⑤ What happens to processing speed across the life span?

CRITICAL THINKING   Recall the experiment that looked at object permanence in 4-month-olds. Why was looking time an appropriate measure to test the researchers' hypothesis?

✓—[**Study** and **Review** on **MyPsychLab**

ACQUIRING LANGUAGE

Here's a remarkable fact: By the time they are 6 years old, children can analyze language into its units of sound and meaning, use the rules they have discovered to combine sounds into words and words into meaningful sentences, and take an active part in coherent conversations. Children's remarkable language accomplishments have prompted most researchers to agree that the ability to learn language is biologically based—that you are born with an innate language capacity (Tomasello, 2008). Even so, depending on where a child happens to be born, he or she may end up as a native speaker of any one of the world's

4,000 different languages. In addition, children are prepared to learn both spoken languages and gestural languages, like American Sign Language. This means that the innate predisposition to learn language must be both quite strong and quite flexible (Schick et al., 2006). 👁

To explain how it is that infants are such expert language learners, we will consider evidence that supports the claim of an innate language capacity. But we will also acknowledge the role that the environment plays—after all, children learn the particular languages that are being used in the world around them. **Table 10.5** outlines the various types of knowledge children must acquire for their particular signed or spoken language. You might review the language use section of Chapter 8 (pages 210–220) to remind yourself how adults put all these types of knowledge to use in fluent conversation.

Perceiving Speech and Perceiving Words

Imagine you are a newborn child, hearing a buzz of noise all around you. How do you start to understand that some of those sounds are relevant to communicating with other people? A child's first step in acquiring a particular language is to take note of the sound contrasts that are used meaningfully in that language. (For signed languages, the child must attend to contrasts in hand positions, for example.) Each spoken language samples from the set of possible distinctions that can be produced by the human vocal tract; no language uses all of the speech–sound contrasts that can be made. The minimal meaningful units of speech that allow people to distinguish one word from another are called **phonemes.** There are about

Table 10.5 • The Structure of Language

Grammar is the field of study that seeks to describe the way language is structured and used. It includes several domains:

Phonology—the study of the sounds that are put together to form words.

A **phoneme** is the smallest unit of speech that distinguishes between any two utterances. For example, *b* and *p* distinguish *bin* from *pin*.

Phonetics is the study and classification of speech sounds.

Syntax—the way in which words are strung together to form sentences. For example, subject *(I)* + verb *(like)* + object *(you)* is standard English word order.

A **morpheme** is the minimum distinctive unit of grammar that cannot be divided without losing its meaning. The word *bins* has two morphemes, *bin* and *s,* indicating the plural.

Semantics—the study of the meanings of words and their changes over time.

Lexical meaning is the dictionary meaning of a word. Meaning is sometimes conveyed by the *context* of a word in a sentence ("Run *fast*" versus "Make the knot *fast*") or the *inflection* with which it is spoken (try emphasizing different words in *white house cat*).

Pragmatics—rules for participation in conversations; social conventions for communicating, sequencing sentences, and responding appropriately to others.

45 distinct phonemes in English. Imagine you heard someone speak the words *right* and *light*. If you are a native speaker of English, you would have no trouble hearing the difference—/r/ and /l/ are different phonemes in English. If your only language experience was with Japanese, however, you would not be able to hear the difference between these two words because /r/ and /l/ are not distinct phonemes in Japanese. Do English speakers acquire the ability to make this distinction, or do Japanese speakers lose it?

To answer this type of question, researchers needed to develop methods to obtain linguistic information from prelinguistic children.

Using principles of operant conditioning you saw in Chapter 5, researchers condition infants to turn their heads toward a sound source when they detect a change from one speech sound to another. The reward that reinforces this behavior is an illuminated box that contains a clapping and drumming toy animal. The procedure ensures that, if the children detect changes, they are very likely to turn toward the sound source. To measure the children's ability to perceive a distinction, researchers monitor how frequently the children turn their heads when a change is present.

Janet Werker *and her colleagues (Werker, 1991; Werker & Lalond, 1988) have used this technique to examine the innate basis of speech perception abilities, a version of the /r/–/l/ question I posed earlier. Werker studied sound distinctions that are used in Hindi, but not in English—distinctions that make it difficult for adult English speakers to learn Hindi. Werker and her colleagues measured the ability of infants learning English or Hindi, as well as adults who spoke English or Hindi, to hear the differences between the Hindi phonemes. She found that all the infants, regardless of which language they were learning, could hear the differences until the age of 8 months. However, of the infants older than 8 months and of the adults, only the Hindi speakers or speakers-to-be could hear the Hindi contrasts.*

Research of this type strongly suggests that you started out with an innate ability to perceive sound contrasts that are important for spoken languages. However, you swiftly lose the ability to perceive some of the contrasts that are not present in the language you begin to acquire (Werker & Tees, 1999).

Along with this biological head start for speech perception, many children also get an environmental head start. When adults in many cultures speak to infants and young children, they use a special form of language that differs from language addressed to adults. For example, when talking to infants and children, adults tend to slow down their rate of speech and use an exaggerated, high-pitched intonation; they tend to produce utterances that are shorter and have simpler structures (Soderstrom, 2007). Depending on the age of the child,

👁 **Watch** the **Video** *Language Development* on **MyPsychLab**

phoneme Minimal unit of speech in any given language that makes a meaningful difference in speech and production and reception; *r* and *l* are two distinct phonemes in English but variations of one in Japanese.

researchers call the forms of speech either **infant-directed speech** or **child-directed speech.** The features that define infant- and child-directed speech appear in many but not all cultures (Kitamura et al., 2002; Lee & Davis, 2010). Researchers suggest that these special forms of speech provide infants and children with information that makes them better able to acquire phonemes and words from the language being used around them (Song et al., 2010; Thiessen et al., 2005).

At what age are children able to perceive the repetition of patterns of sounds—words—within the stream of speech directed to them? This is the first big step toward acquiring language: You can't learn that *doggie* has something to do with the shaggy thing in the corner until you recognize that the sound pattern *doggie* seems to recur in that shaggy thing's presence. Infants, on average, appear to gain the insight that repeated sounds have significance somewhere between ages 6 and 7 months (Jusczyk, 2003; Jusczyk & Aslin, 1995). For one special word, however, the breakthrough comes a couple of months early: Children at age 4 months already show a recognition preference for their own names (Mandel et al., 1995)!

Learning Word Meanings

Once you could detect the co-occurrence of sounds and experiences, you were prepared to start learning word meanings. There's no denying that children are excellent word learners. At around 18 months, children's word learning often takes off at an amazing rate. Researchers have called this phase the *naming explosion* because children begin to acquire new words, especially names for objects, at a rapidly increasing rate (see **Figure 10.7**). By the age of 6, the average child is estimated to understand 14,000 words (Templin, 1957). Assuming that most of these words are learned between the ages of 18 months and 6 years, this works out to about nine new words a day or almost one word per waking hour (Carey, 1978). Children have an ability that researchers call *fast mapping:* They are able to learn the meanings of new words with minimal experience—sometimes with only a single exposure to a word and its referent (Gershkoff-Stowe & Hahn, 2007). How is this possible?

Imagine a straightforward situation in which a child and her father are walking through a park and the father points and says, "That's a doggie." The child must decide to which piece of the world *doggie* applies. This is no easy feat (Quine, 1960). Perhaps *doggie* means "any creature with four legs" or "the animal's fur" or "the animal's bark" or any of the other large set of meanings that will be true each time someone points toward a dog. Given all the possibilities, how are children able to fix the meanings of individual words?

Researchers suggest that children act like scientists—developing *hypotheses* about what each new word might mean. You can, for example, see children's scientific minds actively at

work when they *overextend* words, using them incorrectly to cover a wide range of objects. They may use the word *doggie* to refer to all animals or the word *moon* to refer to all round objects, including clocks and coins. Other times, children might *underextend* a word—believing, for example, that *doggie* refers only to their own family dog.

The view that children form hypotheses, however, does not explain how children acquire particular meanings in particular contexts. Researchers have suggested that children's hypotheses are guided by expectations such as the *principle of contrast.* This principle suggests that differences in *forms* signal differences in *meaning*: When children hear new words, they should look for meanings that contrast with those for the words they already know (Clark, 2003). Suppose, for example, a father and daughter are watching a TV scene in which a kangaroo is jumping. The child knows the word *jump* but not the word *kangaroo.* Suppose the parent says, "Kangaroo!" What might happen next? Because the child knows *jump*, she supposes that her parent would just say *jump* if *kangaroo* just meant "jump"—different forms should signal contrasts in meaning. The child can now hypothesize that *kangaroo* must label the object rather than the action. She is on her way to acquiring a meaning for *kangaroo.* If you've spent time around small children, you've probably noticed the principle of contrast at work. For example, a child will often become upset if his mother calls his fire *engine* a fire *truck*!

Acquiring Grammar

To explain how children acquire meanings, I characterized children as scientists whose hypotheses are constrained by innate principles. The same analogy describes how children acquire the rules by which units of meaning are combined into larger units—in other words, grammar. The challenge

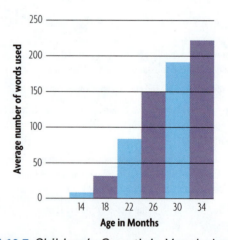

FIGURE 10.7 Children's Growth in Vocabulary

Soon after their first words occur, children's vocabulary increases rapidly. These longitudinal data show the number of different words that children used while engaged in 90 minutes of ordinary activities with their caregivers.

Source: Data from Huttenlocher, J., Waterfall, H., Vasilyeva, M., Vevea, J., & Hedges, L. V. (2010). Sources of variability in children's language growth. *Cognitive Psychology, 61,* 343–365.

Children develop linguistic fluency by listening to the speech patterns of those around them. What evidence suggests that they have a biological head start on acquiring grammar?

for the child is that different languages follow different rules. For example, in English the typical ordering of units in a sentence is subject-verb-object, but in Japanese the ordering is subject-object-verb. Children must discover what order is present in the language being used around them. How do they do that?

Most researchers now believe that a large part of the answer resides in the human genome. Linguist **Noam Chomsky** (1965, 1975), for example, argued that children are born with mental structures that facilitate the comprehension and production of language. Some of the best evidence for such a biological basis for grammar comes from children who acquire complete grammatical structure in the absence of well-formed input. For example, researchers have studied deaf children whose hearing loss was sufficiently severe that they could not acquire spoken language but whose parents did not expose them to full-fledged signed languages such as American Sign Language (Franklin et al., 2011; Goldin-Meadow, 2003). These children began to invent signing systems of their own and—despite the lack of environmental support for these invented languages—the gestural systems came to have regular, grammatical structure: "With or without an established language as a guide, children appear to be 'ready' to seek structure at least at word and sentence levels when developing systems for communication" (Goldin-Meadow & Mylander, 1990, p. 351).

But how can researchers go about specifying exactly what knowledge is innately given? The most productive approach to this question is to study language acquisition across many languages—*cross-linguistically.* By examining what is hard and what is easy for children to acquire across the world's many languages, researchers can determine what aspects of grammar are most likely to be supported by innate predispositions.

Here we arrive back at the child as scientist. Children bring innate constraints to the task of learning a particular language. **Dan Slobin** has defined these guidelines as a set of *operating principles* that together constitute the child's

language-making capacity. According to Slobin's (1985) theory, the operating principles take the form of directives to the child. Here, for example, is an operating principle that helps children discover the words that go together to form a grammatical unit: "store together ordered sequences of word classes and functor classes that co-occur in the expression of a particular proposition type, along with a designation of the proposition type" (p. 1252). In simpler language, this operating principle suggests that children must keep track of the relationship between the order in which words appear and the meanings they express. Slobin derived the operating principles by summarizing across the data provided by a large number of other researchers, who examined a variety of different languages. I will use English examples to demonstrate the principles at work.

Consider what English-speaking children can do when they begin, at about age 2, to use combinations of words—the *two-word stage.* Children's speech at this point has been characterized as *telegraphic* because it is filled with short, simple sequences using mostly nouns and verbs. Telegraphic speech lacks function words, such as *the, and,* and *of,* which help express the relationships between words and ideas. For example, "Allgone milk" is a telegraphic message.

For adults to understand two-word utterances, they must know the context in which the words are spoken. "Tanya ball," for example, could mean, among other things, "Tanya wants the ball" or "Tanya throws the ball." Even so, children at the two-word stage show evidence that they have already acquired some knowledge of the grammar of English. Operating principles allow them to discover that word order is important in English and that the three critical elements are actor-action-object (subject-verb-object), arranged in that order. Evidence for this "discovery" comes when children misinterpret a sentence such as "Mary was followed by her little lamb to school" as *Mary* (actor) *followed* (action) *her lamb* (object) (see **Figure 10.8** on page 278). Over time, children must apply other operating principles to discover that there are exceptions to the actor-action-object rule.

Consider now an operating principle, which Slobin calls *extension,* that requires children to try to use the same unit of meaning, or *morpheme,* to mark the same concept. Examples of such concepts are possession, past tense, and continuing action. In English, each of these concepts is expressed by adding a grammatical morpheme to a content word, such as *-'s* (as in Maria's), *-ed* (as in called), and *-ing* (as in laughing). Note how the addition of each of these sounds to a noun or verb changes its meaning.

Children use operating principles like extension to form hypotheses about how these morphemes work. Because this principle requires that the child try to mark all cases in the same way, however, the error of **overregularization** often results. For example, once children learn the past-tense rule (adding *-ed* to the verb), they add *-ed* to all verbs, forming words such as *doed* and *breaked.* As children learn the rule for plurals (adding the sound *-s* or *-z* to the end of a word), they

language-making capacity The innate guidelines or operating principles that children bring to the task of learning a language.

overregularization A grammatical error, usually appearing during early language development, in which rules of the language are applied too widely, resulting in incorrect linguistic forms.

FIGURE 10.8 Acquiring Grammar

Many toddlers would interpret "Mary was followed by the lamb" and "Mary followed the lamb" to have identical meanings.

again overextend the rule, creating words such as *foots* and *mouses*. Overregularization is an especially interesting error because it usually appears *after* children have learned and used the correct forms of verbs and nouns. The children first use the correct verb forms (for example, *came* and *went*), apparently because they learned them as separate vocabulary items; but when they learn the general rule for the past tense, they extend it even to verbs that are exceptions to the rule—words that they previously used correctly. Over time, children use other operating principles to overcome this temporary overapplication.

Children's acquisition of language has a major impact on their ability to participate in social interactions. Keep them in mind as we shift our focus now to social development across the life span.

Stop *and* Review

① What are some ways in which infant- and child-directed speech differ from adult-directed speech?
② Why do children overextend word meanings?
③ How does research with deaf children support the idea that aspects of grammar are innate?
④ How would you notice when a child is overregularizing English past-tense constructions?

CRITICAL THINKING Consider the study on children's ability to perceive sound distinctions. Why was it important to compare English-speaking adults with infants who are English-speakers-to-be?

✔●⎡**Study** and **Review** on **MyPsychLab**

SOCIAL DEVELOPMENT ACROSS THE LIFE SPAN

We have seen so far how radically you change as a physical and cognitive being from birth to older adulthood. This section of the chapter explores **social development:** how individuals' social interactions and expectations change across the life span. You will see that the social and cultural environment interacts with biological aging to provide each period of the life span with its own special challenges and rewards.

As you ponder social development, it is particularly important for you to consider the way in which culture and environment affect certain aspects of our lives. For example, people who live in circumstances of economic hardship undergo types of stresses that are absent from the "normal" course of development (Conger et al., 2010; Edin & Kissane, 2010). Current trends in the United States and in other countries throughout the world make it imperative for developmental psychologists to consider the difficult circumstances in which many children, adolescents, and adults are forced to live—circumstances that continually put their sanity, safety, and survival at risk. U.S. culture also enforces different outcomes for men and for women and for individuals who belong to minority groups. For example, in 2007 12 percent of women over 65 were living in poverty compared to 7 percent of men in this age range; 27 percent of African American women over 65 were living in poverty compared to 9 percent of White women over 65 (Federal Interagency Forum on Aging-Related Statistics, 2010). These differences are direct products of structural inequities in contemporary U.S. society.

When I draw conclusions about the "average" life course, keep in mind that culture dictates that some individuals will depart from this average; as I describe the psychological challenges facing the "ordinary" individual, bear in mind that many individuals face extraordinary challenges. It is the role of researchers to document the impact of contemporary problems—and to design interventions to alleviate their harshest consequences.

As you read the remainder of this chapter, keep in mind how the tasks of life are jointly determined by a biological accumulation of years and a social accumulation of cultural experiences. This discussion of social development begins with Erik Erikson's life span theory, which makes explicit the challenges and rewards in each of life's major periods.

Erikson's Psychosocial Stages

Erik Erikson (1902–1994), who was trained by Sigmund Freud's daughter, Anna Freud, proposed that every individual must successfully navigate a series of **psychosocial stages,** each of which presented a particular conflict or crisis. Erikson (1963)

social development The ways in which individuals' social interactions and expectations change across the life span.

psychosocial stage Proposed by Erik Erikson, one of the successive developmental stages that focus on an individual's orientation toward the self and others; these stages incorporate both the sexual and social aspects of a person's development and the social conflicts that arise from the interaction between the individual and the social environment.

Psychology in Your Life

WHAT HAPPENS WHEN CHILDREN BECOME BILINGUAL?

The section on language acquisition focused on the processes that allow children to learn a single language. However, across the globe many children become *bilingual* at an early age—they learn more than one language at the same time. You might wonder how that works. For example, how do children cope when their environment provides two words that have the same meaning, such as *dog* in English and *perro* in Spanish? One possibility might be that children unite both languages into one big mental dictionary. However, that does not seem to be the case. Remarkably, from the earliest moments of bilingual acquisition, children seem to keep two or more vocabularies separate (Montanari, 2010). They quickly become able to produce the appropriate word in the appropriate language context.

Still, there are potential costs for bilingual children. Essentially, they need to spread the same time for language-learning across two different languages. One consequence is that bilingual children tend to know less vocabulary in each language than their monolingual peers. For example, one study looked at the ability of 1,738 children between ages 3 and 10 to understand words in either one or two languages (Bialystok et al., 2010). Although some bilingual children had larger vocabularies than their monolingual peers, the average was lower for bilingual children all the way across the 7-year age range.

Before you decide never to let a child become an early bilingual, here's an important clarification: This difference in vocabulary size and skill is the only consistent negative consequence of bilingualism (Bialystok & Craik, 2010). In fact, researchers have demonstrated that bilingualism has a number of positive consequences. Consider a study in which 6-year-old monolingual and bilingual children viewed four ambiguous figures (Bialystok & Shapero, 2005). One of the stimuli was the duck-rabbit that appears on p. 196. The researchers assessed the ease with which the children were able to perceive the two different interpretations of each figure. The bilingual children consistently outperformed the monolingual children. But why? The researchers suggested that the "processing advantage most likely stems from the constant need [for bilingual children] to manage two active language systems in order to use one of them fluently" (p. 596).

The more general claim is that bilingual children are better able to control their cognitive resources in tasks that require selective attention and cognitive flexibility. This ability is known as *executive control*. Bilinguals as young as 24 months demonstrate better executive control than their monolingual age-mates (Poulin-Dubois et al., 2011). In addition, because of the benefit for executive control, lifelong bilingualism may protect people from some forms of the cognitive decline that accompany aging (Bialystok & Craik, 2010).

You can see that bilingualism presents interesting circumstances. People who become early bilinguals may have lifelong reductions in their vocabularies in each language. At the same time, they are likely to maintain better performance in the very wide range of tasks that require executive control. Does that sound like an acceptable trade-off?

---

identified eight stages in the life cycle. At each stage, a particular crisis comes into focus, as shown in **Table 10.6** on page 280. Although each conflict never completely disappears, it needs to be sufficiently resolved at a given stage if an individual is to cope successfully with the conflicts of later stages.

Trust vs. Mistrust   In Erikson's first stage, an infant needs to develop a basic sense of *trust* in the environment through interaction with caregivers. Trust is a natural accompaniment to a strong attachment relationship with a parent who provides food, warmth, and the comfort of physical closeness. But a child whose basic needs are not met, who experiences inconsistent handling, lack of physical closeness and warmth, and the frequent absence of a caring adult, may develop a pervasive sense of mistrust, insecurity, and anxiety.

Autonomy vs. Self-Doubt   With the development of walking and the beginnings of language, there is an expansion of a child's exploration and manipulation of objects (and sometimes people). With these activities should come a comfortable sense of *autonomy,* or independence, and of being a capable and worthy person. Excessive restriction or criticism at this second stage may lead instead to self-doubts, whereas demands beyond the child's ability, as in too-early or too-severe toilet training, can discourage the child's efforts to persevere in mastering new tasks.

Initiative vs. Guilt   Toward the end of the preschool period, a child who has developed a basic sense of trust, first in the immediate environment and then in himself or herself, can now *initiate* both intellectual and motor activities. The ways that parents respond to the child's self-initiated activities either encourage the sense of freedom and self-confidence needed for the next stage or produce guilt and feelings of being an inept intruder in an adult world.

Competence vs. Inferiority   During the elementary school years, the child who has successfully resolved the crises of the earlier stages is ready to go beyond random exploring and testing to the systematic development of *competencies.* School and

Table 10.6 • Erikson's Psychosocial Stages

Crisis	Age	Challenge
Trust vs. mistrust	Birth to 1 year	Developing a sense that the world is safe and good
Autonomy vs. self-doubt	1 to 3 years	Realizing that one is an independent person with the ability to make decisions
Initiative vs. guilt	3 to 6 years	Developing a willingness to try new things and to handle failure
Competence vs. inferiority	6 years to adolescence	Learning competence in basic skills and to cooperate with others
Identity vs. role confusion	Adolescence	Developing a coherent, integarted sense of inner self
Intimacy vs. isolation	Young adulthood	Establishing ties to another in a trusting, loving relationship
Generativity vs. stagnation	Middle adulthood	Finding meaning in career, family, and community via productive work
Ego integrity vs. despair	Late life	Viewing one's life as satisfactory and worth living

From Morris, Charles G.; Maisto, Albert A., *Understanding Psychology*, 9th Ed., © 2010. Reprinted the Electronically reproduced by permission of Pearson Education, Inc., Upper Saddle River, New Jersey.

sports offer arenas for learning intellectual and motor skills, and interaction with peers offers an arena for developing social skills. Successful efforts in these pursuits lead to feelings of competence. Some youngsters, however, become spectators rather than performers or experience enough failure to give them a sense of inferiority, leaving them unable to meet the demands of the next life stages.

Identity vs. Role Confusion   Erikson believed that the essential crisis of adolescence is discovering one's true *identity* amid the confusion created by playing many different roles for the different audiences in an expanding social world. Resolving

Erik Erikson's psychosocial stage model is a widely used tool for understanding human development over the life span. What crisis did Erikson suggest dominates individuals of your age?

this crisis helps the individual develop a sense of a coherent self; failing to do so adequately may result in a self-image that lacks a central, stable core.

Intimacy vs. Isolation   The essential crisis for the young adult is to resolve the conflict between *intimacy* and *isolation*—to develop the capacity to make full emotional, moral, and sexual commitments to other people. Making that kind of commitment requires that the individual compromise some personal preferences, accept some responsibilities, and yield some degree of privacy and independence. Failure to resolve this crisis adequately leads to isolation and the inability to connect to others in psychologically meaningful ways. ◉

Generativity vs. Stagnation   The next major opportunity for growth, which occurs during adult midlife, is known as *generativity*. People in their 30s and 40s move beyond a focus on self and partner to broaden their commitments to family, work, society, and future generations. Those people who haven't resolved earlier developmental tasks are still self-indulgent, question past decisions and goals, and pursue freedom at the expense of security.

Ego integrity vs. Despair   The crisis in later adulthood is the conflict between *ego integrity* and *despair*. Resolving the crises at each of the earlier stages prepares the older adult to look back without regrets and to enjoy a sense of wholeness. When previous crises are left unresolved, aspirations remain unfulfilled, and the individual experiences futility, despair, and self-depreciation.

You will see that Erikson's framework is very useful for tracking individuals' progress across the life span. Let's begin with childhood.

Social Development in Childhood

Children's basic survival depends on forming meaningful, effective relationships with other people. **Socialization** is

◉ Watch the **Video** *Classic Footage of Erik Erikson* on **MyPsychLab**

socialization The lifelong process whereby an individual's behavioral patterns, values, standards, skills, attitudes, and motives are shaped to conform to those regarded as desirable in a particular society.

the lifelong process through which an individual's behavior patterns, values, standards, skills, attitudes, and motives are shaped to conform to those regarded as desirable in a particular society. This process involves many people—relatives, friends, teachers—and institutions—schools, houses of worship—that exert pressure on the individual to adopt socially approved values and standards of conduct. The family, however, is the most influential shaper and regulator of socialization. The concept of family itself is being transformed to recognize that many children grow up in circumstances that include either less (a single parent) or more (an extended household) than a mother, father, and siblings. Whatever the configuration, though, the family helps the individual form basic patterns of responsiveness to others—and these patterns, in turn, become the basis of the individual's lifelong style of relating to other people. ◉

Temperament Even as infants begin the process of socialization, they do not all start at the same place. Children begin life with differences in **temperament**—biologically based levels of emotional and behavioral response to the environment (Thomas & Chess, 1977). Researcher **Jerome Kagan** and his colleagues have demonstrated that some infants are "born shy" and others are "born bold" (Kagan & Snidman, 2004). These groups of children differ in sensitivity to physical and social stimulation: The shy or *inhibited* babies are consistently "cautious and emotionally reserved when they confront unfamiliar persons or contexts"; the bold or *uninhibited* babies are consistently "sociable, affectively spontaneous, and minimally fearful in the same unfamiliar situations" (Kagan & Snidman, 1991, p. 40). In one sample, about 10 percent of the infants were inhibited and about 25 percent were uninhibited; the rest of the infants fell in between those end points (Kagan & Snidman, 1991). Researchers have begun to explore the genetic and brain bases of differences in temperament (LoBue et al., 2011; Rothbart, 2007).

Longitudinal studies have demonstrated the long-term impact of early temperament. For example, one study followed a group of children from ages 4 months to 5 years (Degnan et al., 2011). The researchers measured the extent to which the children, as 4-month-olds, showed a pattern of sociability and positive emotional reactions toward new experiences—a pattern the researchers called *exuberance*. The children's levels of low or high exuberance were quite stable when they were measured at 9, 24, and 36 months. At 5 years of age, the more exuberant children displayed greater competence when they interacted with unfamiliar peers. At the same time, when they became frustrated, the more exuberant children were likely to engage in disruptive behaviors.

Infant temperament sets the stage for later aspects of social development. Next, we consider the *attachment* bonds children form as their first social relationships.

Attachment Social development begins with the establishment of a close emotional relationship between a child and a mother, father, or other regular caregiver. This intense, enduring, social–emotional relationship is called **attachment**. Because children are incapable of feeding or protecting themselves, the earliest function of attachment is to ensure survival. In some species, the infant automatically becomes

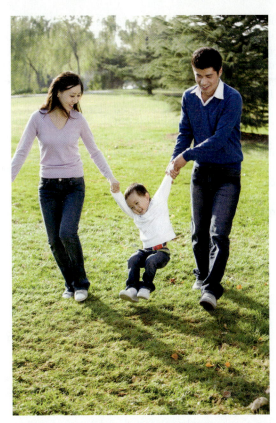

Why is it important for a child to develop a secure attachment to a parent or other caregiver?

imprinted on the first moving object it sees or hears (Bolhuis & Honey, 1998). **Imprinting** occurs rapidly during a critical period of development and cannot easily be modified. The automaticity of imprinting can sometimes be problematic. Ethologist **Konrad Lorenz** demonstrated that young geese raised by a human imprint on the human instead of on one of their own kind. In nature, fortunately, young geese mostly see other geese first.

You won't find human infants imprinting on their parents. Even so, **John Bowlby** (1973), an influential theorist on human attachment, suggested that infants and adults are biologically predisposed to form attachments. That attachment relationship has broad consequences. Beginning with Bowlby (1973), theorists have suggested that the experiences that give rise to an attachment relationship provide individuals with a lifelong schema for social relationships called an *internal working model* (Dykas & Cassidy, 2011). An internal

....

◉ Watch the **Video** *In the Real World: Socialization* on **MyPsychLab**

temperament A child's biologically based level of emotional and behavioral response to environmental events.

attachment Emotional relationship between a child and the regular caregiver.

imprinting A primitive form of learning in which some infant animals physically follow and form an attachment to the first moving object they see and/or hear.

working model is a memory structure that gathers together a child's history of interactions with his or her caretakers, the interactions that yielded a particular pattern of attachment. The internal working model provides a template that an individual uses to generate expectations about future social interactions.

One of the most widely used research procedures for assessing attachment is the *Strange Situation Test,* developed by **Mary Ainsworth** and her colleagues (Ainsworth et al., 1978). In the first of several standard episodes, the child is brought into an unfamiliar room filled with toys. With the mother present, the child is encouraged to explore the room and to play. After several minutes, a stranger comes in, talks to the mother, and approaches the child. Next, the mother exits the room. After this brief separation, the mother returns, there is a reunion with her child, and the stranger leaves. The researchers record the child's behaviors at separation and reunion. Researchers have found that children's responses on this test fall into three general categories (Ainsworth et al., 1978):

- *Securely attached* children show some distress when the parent leaves the room; seek proximity, comfort, and contact upon reunion; and then gradually return to play.
- *Insecurely attached–avoidant* children seem aloof and may actively avoid and ignore the parent upon her return.
- *Insecurely attached–anxious/ambivalent* children become quite upset and anxious when the parent leaves; at reunion, they cannot be comforted, and they show anger and resistance to the parent but, at the same time, express a desire for contact.

In samples from several different countries, about 65 percent of babies are classified as securely attached; among the insecurely attached children, about 20 percent are classified as avoidant and 15 percent as anxious (Ein-Dor et al., 2010). ◉

Categorizations based on the Strange Situation Test have proven to be highly predictive of a child's later behavior in a wider variety of settings, particularly the overall division between children who are securely and insecurely attached. For example, children who were securely attached at 12 months played more comfortably with their mothers at 24 months than did their insecurely attached peers (Donovan et al., 2007). Similarly, research has revealed that children who showed secure or insecure behavior in the Strange Situation at 15 months differed widely in their school behavior at age 8 to 9 years (Bohlin et al., 2000). Those children who had been securely attached at 15 months were more popular and less socially anxious than their peers who had been insecurely attached. Similar continuity from the quality of attachment to later years has been demonstrated in 10-year-olds (Urban et al., 1991) and adolescents (Weinfield et al., 1997). Researchers have also developed measures that assess attachment beyond infancy. Those measures also predict an individual's social functioning (Shmueli-Goetz et al., 2008). In Chapter 16, you will see that researchers also use attachment measures to predict the quality of adults' loving relationships.

Attachment relationships are quite important in young lives. Secure attachment to adults who offer dependable social support enables the child to learn a variety of prosocial behaviors, to take risks, to venture into novel situations, and to seek and accept intimacy in personal relationships.

Parenting Styles As you saw earlier, children bring individual temperaments to their interactions with their parents. Children's temperaments may make parents' best (or worst) efforts at parenting have unexpected consequences. Researchers recognize that children's temperaments and parents' behaviors each influence the other to yield developmental outcomes such as the quality of attachment relationships: As much as parents change their children, children change their parents (Collins et al., 2000).

Even so, researchers have located a **parenting style** that is generally most beneficial. This style resides at the intersection of the two dimensions of *demandingness* and *responsiveness* (Maccoby & Martin, 1983): "Demandingness refers to the parent's willingness to act as a socializing agent, whereas responsiveness refers to the parent's recognition of the child's individuality" (Darling & Steinberg, 1993, p. 492). As shown in **Figure 10.9**, *authoritative* parents make appropriate demands on their children—they demand that their children conform to appropriate rules of behavior—but are also responsive to their children. They keep channels of communication open to foster their children's ability to regulate themselves (Gray & Steinberg, 1999). This authoritative style is most likely to produce an effective parent–child bond. The contrast, as seen in Figure 10.9, is to parenting styles that are *authoritarian*—parents apply discipline with little attention to the child's autonomy—or *indulgent*—parents are responsive, but they fail to help children learn about the structure of social rules in which they must live—or *neglecting*—parents neither apply discipline nor are they responsive to their children's individuality.

Konrad Lorenz, the researcher who pioneered the study of imprinting, graphically demonstrates what can happen when young animals become imprinted on someone other than their mother. Why is imprinting important for many animal species?

◉ **Watch** the **Video** *Separation Anxiety* on **MyPsychLab**

parenting style The manner in which parents rear their children; an authoritative parenting style, which balances demandingness and responsiveness, is seen as the most effective.

Parent's Responsiveness

	Accepting Responsive Child-centered	Rejecting Unresponsive Parent-centered
Demanding, controlling	Authoritative- reciprocal High in bidirectional communication	Authoritarian Power assertive
Undemanding, low in control attempts	Indulgent	Neglecting, ignoring, indifferent, uninvolved

Parent's Demandingness

FIGURE 10.9 A Classification of Parenting Styles

Parenting styles can be classified with respect to the two dimensions of demandingness—the parent's willingness to act as a socializing agent—and responsiveness—the parent's recognition of the child's individuality. The authoritative style is most likely to produce an effective parent–child bond.

As you might expect, parenting styles have an impact on children's attachment relationships. Children whose parents use an authoritative style are more likely to be securely attached through childhood into adolescence (Karavasilis et al., 2003). Still, the impact of parenting may depend, in part, on a child's particular genetic make-up.

Featured Study

A team of researchers assessed 601 children to determine which versions of the mineralocorticoid receptor (MR) gene they had inherited (Luijk et al., 2011). When the children were, on average, 14.7 months old, their attachment security was evaluated using the Strange Situation Test. During the same visit to the laboratory, observers watched the mothers' behavior toward their children. The observations yielded two measures of the mothers' behavior: maternal sensitive responsiveness *reflected a mother's sensitivity toward and cooperation with her child;* maternal extreme insensitivity *reflected a mother's harsh behaviors, including withdrawal from and neglect of the child. The data indicated that both genes and environment mattered. For children who inherited at least one copy of the "minor" version of the MR gene, sensitive responsiveness led to greater attachment security and extreme insensitivity led to lower attachment security. Attachment security was unaffected by maternal behaviors for children who did not inherit a "minor" version of the gene.*

Other research suggests that children's outcomes can improve when parenting improves. For example, one study followed over 1,000 children and their mothers from when the children were 15 months old until they began first grade (NICHD Early Child Care Research Network, 2006). The researchers assessed the children's attachment relationships at 15 months in the Strange Situation. Evaluations of the mothers' parenting styles were based on videotapes of their interactions with their children. The researchers analyzed the videotapes to see whether the mothers' parenting styles changed over the course of the three-year project. Changes in mothers' parenting style had an impact on the fates of the insecurely attached children: When parenting quality improved, children's outcomes were consistently better than when parenting quality decreased. Results of this sort encourage researchers to design interventions to improve parenting practices (Van Zeijl et al., 2006). As we have seen, those interventions should also be responsive to children's particular genetic inheritance.

A close interactive relationship with loving adults is a child's first step toward healthy physical growth and normal socialization. As the original attachment to the primary caregiver extends to other family members, they too become models for new ways of thinking and behaving. From these early attachments, children develop the ability to respond to their own needs and to the needs of others.

Contact Comfort and Social Experience What do children obtain from the attachment bond? Sigmund Freud and other psychologists argued that babies become attached to their parents because the parents provide them with food—their most basic physical need. This view is called the *cupboard theory* of attachment. If the cupboard theory were correct, children should thrive as long as they are adequately fed. Does this seem right?

Harry Harlow (1958) did not believe that the cupboard theory explained the importance of attachment. He set out to test the cupboard theory against his own hypothesis that infants might also attach to those who provide **contact comfort** (Harlow & Zimmerman, 1958). Harlow separated macaque monkeys from their mothers at birth and placed them in cages, where they had access to two artificial "mothers": a wire one and a terry cloth one. Harlow found that the baby monkeys nestled close to the terry cloth mother and spent little time on the wire one. They did this even when only the wire mother gave milk! The baby monkeys also used the cloth mother as a source of comfort when frightened and as a base of operations when exploring new stimuli. When a fear stimulus (for example, a toy bear beating a drum) was introduced, the baby monkeys would run to the cloth mother. When novel and intriguing stimuli were introduced, the baby monkeys would

contact comfort Comfort derived from an infant's physical contact with the mother or caregiver.

gradually venture out to explore and then return to the terry cloth mother before exploring further. ◉

Further studies by Harlow and his colleagues found that the monkeys' formation of a strong attachment to the mother substitute was not sufficient for healthy social development. At first, the experimenters thought the young monkeys with terry cloth mothers were developing normally, but a very different picture emerged when it was time for the female monkeys who had been raised in this way to become mothers. Monkeys who had been deprived of chances to interact with other responsive monkeys in their early lives had trouble forming normal social and sexual relationships in adulthood.

Let's see now what lessons research with monkeys holds for human deprivation.

Human Deprivation Tragically, human societies have sometimes created circumstances in which children are deprived of contact comfort. Many studies have shown that a lack of close, loving relationships in infancy affects physical growth and even survival. In 1915, a doctor at Johns Hopkins Hospital reported that, despite adequate physical care, 90 percent of the infants admitted to orphanages in Baltimore

How did Harlow demonstrate the importance of contact comfort for normal social development?

....

◉ **Watch** the **Video** *Classic Footage of Harlow's Monkeys: Contact Comfort* on **MyPsychLab**

died within the first year. Studies of hospitalized infants over the next 30 years found that, despite adequate nutrition, the children often developed respiratory infections and fevers of unknown origin, failed to gain weight, and showed general signs of physiological deterioration (Bowlby, 1969; Spitz & Wolf, 1946).

Contemporary studies continue to demonstrate patterns of disruption. For example, one study compared attachment outcomes for children raised at home to those for children largely (90 percent of their lives) raised in institutions (Zeanah et al., 2005). The researchers found that 74 percent of the home-reared children had secure attachments; for institution-reared children, only 20 percent had secure attachments. Moreover, a lack of normal social contact may have a long-lasting effect on children's brain development. One study measured children's brain responses to pictures of faces displaying happy, angry, fearful, and sad expressions (Moulson et al., 2009). By comparison to children being reared by their families, children who were living in institutions showed disruptions in their brain responses to emotional expressions.

Unfortunately, no matter what the setting in which children live, there is a potential for abuse. In a recent analysis, the U.S. government found that about 125,000 children experienced physical abuse in a single year, and roughly 66,700 experienced sexual abuse (U.S. Department of Health and Human Services, 2010). One study looked at the psychological well-being of 2,759 adults who had been sexually abused as children (Cutajar et al., 2010). Of that group, 23 percent had sought mental health services compared to 8 percent of a control sample that was matched for sex and age. Instances of child abuse provide psychologists with a very important agenda: to determine what types of interventions are in the best interest of the child. In the United States, roughly 424,000 children and youths were living in some type of foster care (such as a foster home or group residence) (Child Welfare Information Gateway, 2011. Are these children always happy to be removed from their abusive homes? The answer is complex because even abused children have often formed an attachment to their caretakers: The children may remain loyal to their natural family and hope that everything could be put right if they were allowed to return. This is one reason that much research attention is focused on designing intervention programs to reunite families (Miller et al., 2006).

In this section, you have seen how experiences during childhood have an impact on later social development. Let's now shift our focus to later periods of life, beginning with adolescence.

Social Development in Adolescence

Earlier in the chapter, adolescence was defined by physical changes. In this section, those changes will serve as background to social experiences. Because the individual has reached a certain level of physical and mental maturity, new social and personal challenges present themselves. We will first consider the general experience of adolescence and then turn to the individual's changing social world.

The Experience of Adolescence The traditional view of adolescence predicts a uniquely tumultuous period of life, characterized by extreme mood swings and unpredictable, difficult behavior: "storm and stress." This view can be traced back to romantic writers of the late 18th and early 19th centuries, such as Goethe. The storm-and-stress conception of adolescence was strongly propounded by **G. Stanley Hall,** the first psychologist of the modern era to write at length about adolescent development (1904). Following Hall, the major proponents of this view have been psychoanalytic theorists working within the Freudian tradition (for example, Blos, 1965; Freud, 1946, 1958). Some of them have argued that not only is extreme turmoil a normal part of adolescence but that failure to exhibit such turmoil is a sign of arrested development. **Anna Freud** wrote that "to be normal during the adolescent period is by itself abnormal" (1958, p. 275).

Two early pioneers in cultural anthropology, **Margaret Mead** (1928) and **Ruth Benedict** (1938), argued that the storm-and-stress theory is not applicable to many non-Western cultures. They described cultures in which children gradually take on more and more adult responsibilities without any sudden stressful transition or period of indecision and turmoil. Contemporary research has confirmed that the experience of adolescence differs across cultures (Arnett, 1999). Those cross-cultural differences argue against strictly biological theories of adolescent experience. Instead, researchers focus on the transitions children are expected to make in different cultures.

Most researchers reject "storm and stress" as a biologically programmed aspect of development. Nonetheless, people typically do experience more extreme emotions and more conflict as they pass from childhood into adolescence. The discussion of physical development noted that brain areas that control emotional responses show growth during adolescence. That brain maturation may explain why adolescents experience both extreme positive and extreme negative emotions (Casey et al., 2008; Steinberg, 2008).

Identity Formation   Recall Erikson's claim that the essential task of adolescence is to weather a crisis to discover one's true identity. **James Marcia** (1966, 1980) expanded on Erikson's analysis to claim that each adolescent can be classified according to an *identity status*:

- *Identity diffusion:* An individual has not yet gone through an identity crisis or made commitments to goals and values.
- *Foreclosure:* An individual has never gone through an identity crisis because he or she committed, for example, to parental values.
- *Moratorium:* An individual is actively involved in exploring different identities but has not yet made a commitment.
- *Identity achievement:* An individual has explored different identities and made a tentative commitment to one.

Longitudinal analyses of adolescents' experiences suggest that indivudals often follow a progression that starts with identity diffusion and ends with identity achievement (Meeus, 2011). In addition, adolescents who have achieved more mature identities tend to experience greater well-being. 👁

Adolescents' quest to achieve identity helps explain the conflicts they have with their parents. For cultures like the

....

👁 **Watch** the **Video** *What's In It For Me?: Identity* on **MyPsychLab**

majority culture in the United States, one consequence is that children attempt to achieve *independence* from their parents. Parents and their adolescent children must weather a transition in their relationship from one in which a parent has unquestioned authority to one in which the adolescent seeks reasonable autonomy to make important decisions (Daddis, 2011). Consider the results of a study that followed 1,330 adolescents from age 11 to age 14 (McGue et al., 2005). As 14-year-olds, these adolescents reported greater conflict with their parents than they had at age 11. At age 14, the adolescents' parents were less involved in their lives; the adolescents had less positive regard for their parents and they believed that their parents had less positive regard for them. These data illustrate some of the relationship costs that arise when children strive for independence.

Still, adolescents' conflicts with their parents often do not lead to harmful outcomes. Most adolescents at most times are able to use their parents as ready sources of practical and emotional support (Smetana et al., 2006). For that reason, many adolescents have conflicts with their parents that leave their basic relationship unharmed. When conflict occurs in the context of otherwise positive relationships, there may be few negative consequences. However, in the context of negative relationships, adolescent conflict can lead to other problems such as social withdrawal and delinquency (Adams & Laursen, 2007). Thus, family contexts may explain why some adolescents experience unusual levels of "storm and stress."

Peer Relationships   Much of the study of social development in adolescence focuses on the changing roles of family (or adult caretakers) and friends (Smetana et al., 2006). We have already seen that attachments to adults form soon after birth. Children also begin to have friends at very young ages. Adolescence, however, marks the first period in which peers appear to compete with parents to shape a person's attitudes and behaviors. Adolescents participate in peer relations at the three levels of friendships, cliques, and crowds (Brown & Klute, 2003). Over the course of these years, adolescents come to count increasingly on their one-on-one *friendships* to provide them with help and support (Bauminger et al., 2008; Branje et al., 2007). *Cliques* are groups that most often consist of 6 to 12 individuals. Membership in these groups may change over time, but they tend to be drawn along lines of, for example, age and race (Smetana et al., 2006). Finally, *crowds* are the larger groups such as "jocks" or "nerds" that exist more loosely among individuals of this age. Through interaction with peers at these three levels, adolescents gradually define the social component of their developing identities, determining the kinds of people they chose to be and the kinds of relationships they choose to pursue.

The peer relationships that adolescents form are quite important to social development. They give individuals opportunities to learn how to function in what can often be demanding social circumstances. In that sense, peer relationships play a positive role in preparing adolescents for their futures. At the same time, parents often worry—with reasonable cause—about negative aspects of peer influence (Brechwald & Prinstein, 2011; Dishion & Tipsord, 2011). In fact, adolescents are more likely to engage in risky behavior when they are under the influence of their peers.

Critical Thinking in Your Life

HOW DOES DAY CARE AFFECT CHILDREN'S DEVELOPMENT?

If you plan to have both children and a career, you're likely to face a difficult question: Is it wise to put your children in day care? Fortunately, psychological research can be brought to bear on this important question.

A team of researchers has been studying a group of 1,364 children since they were 1 month old; the children are now in their late teens (Vandell et al., 2010). Some children in the sample were tended by their mothers for the whole period before they started school; many others experienced various types of day care for small or large parts of each day. The research team's earliest publications focused on day care's impact on children's attachment security. The data indicated that children who attended day care were at risk for insecure attachments but only if it was also true that their mothers were insensitive to their needs (NICHD Early Child Care Research Network, 1997). Otherwise, children who attended day care had equally secure attachments as their peers who remained at home.

As the children have gotten older, the research team has measured their intellectual and social development. Those studies have confirmed both positive and negative consequences of time spent in day care. On the positive side, the children who experienced day care have often performed better on standardized tests of, for example, memory and vocabulary (Belsky et al., 2007). On the negative side, the children who experienced day care have often had more social and behavior problems in their classrooms. However, the likelihood of social problems depends on the exact type of day care. Children's outcomes were better when they experienced quality day care (Belsky et al., 2010). But what does "quality" mean?

Alison Clarke-Stewart (1993; Clarke-Stewart & Alhusen, 2005), an expert on day care, has summarized the research literature to provide guidelines for quality day care. Some recommendations relate to the physical comfort of the children:

- The day care center should be physically comfortable and safe.
- There should be at least one caretaker for every six or seven children (more for children under age 3).

Other recommendations cover educational and psychological aspects of the day care curriculum:

- Children should have a free choice of activities intermixed with explicit lessons.
- Children should be taught social problem-solving skills.

Clarke-Stewart has also suggested that day care providers should share the qualities of good parents:

- Caregivers should be responsive to the children's needs and actively involved in their activities.
- Caregivers should not put undue restrictions on the children.
- Caregivers should have sufficient flexibility to recognize differences among the needs of individual children.

If these guidelines are followed, quality day care can be provided to all children whose parents work outside the home.

- If you are trying to compare outcomes for children who do and do not participate in day care, on what dimensions should you try to match the children?
- How might you assess whether day care providers interact with children in appropriate ways?

Featured Study

A team of researchers wished to examine the impact of adults and peers on teenagers' driving (Simons-Morton et al., 2011). To do so, the researchers outfitted the cars of newly licensed drivers (with a mean age of 16.4 years) with equipment that recorded the details of the teens' driving. The equipment allowed the researchers to determine when the teens' driving had resulted in crashes or near crashes. The cars also had video cameras that enabled the researchers to determine whether the teens' passengers were adults or friends. The teens provided ratings to indicate which of them had risk-taking friends. In the 18-month period of the study, the teens had 37 crashes and 242 near crashes. When the teens had an adult passenger, their crash/near crash rates were 75 percent lower than when they did not. Meanwhile, among teens with risk-taking friends, the crash/near crash rate was 96 percent higher!

This study confirms a general tendency for peer influence to shift adolescents toward riskier behaviors. However, some adolescents are more susceptible to peer influence than others—and that susceptibility has consequences. In a longitudinal study, students who were more susceptible to their close friends' influence at the study's outset were more likely to have problems with drugs and alcohol one year later (Allen et al., 2006). Note, once again, that adolescence need not be a time of storm and stress. However, research of this type indicates the patterns of behavior that put some adolescents at risk.

Social Development in Adulthood

Erikson defined two tasks of adulthood as intimacy and generativity. Freud identified the needs of adulthood as *Lieben und Arbeiten,* or love and work. Abraham Maslow (1968, 1970) described the needs of this period of life as love and belonging,

What might happen when an adolescent driver has risk-taking friends as his passengers?

which, when satisfied, develop into the needs for success and esteem. Other theorists label these needs as affiliation or social acceptance and achievement or competence needs. The shared core of these theories is that adulthood is a time in which both social relationships and personal accomplishments take on special priority. This section will track these themes across the breadth of adulthood.

Intimacy Erikson described **intimacy** as the capacity to make a full commitment to another person. Intimacy, which can occur in both friendships and romantic relationships, requires openness, courage, ethical strength, and usually some compromise of one's personal preferences. Research has consistently confirmed Erikson's supposition that social intimacy is a prerequisite for a sense of psychological well-being across the adult life stages (Kesebir & Diener, 2008). Chapters 11 and 16 discuss the forces that affect people's particular choices for friends, romantic partners, and sexual partners. Here, the focus is on the role intimate relationships play in social development.

Young adulthood is the period in which many people enter into marriages or other stable relationships. In 2010, 13.6 percent of 20- to 24-year-olds were married; among 25- to 29-year-olds that figure increased to 38.2 percent (U.S. Census Bureau, 2011). In addition, many other individuals live with partners to whom they are not married. In 2007, 4.9 percent of U.S. households had opposite-sex partners, and 0.7 percent of households had same-sex partners (U.S. Census Bureau, 2008). In recent years, some states have allowed same-sex couples to enter into civil commitments or legal marriages. Researchers try to understand the consequences of all these types of relationships for social development in adulthood. For example, research attention has focused on differences and similarities between heterosexual and homosexual couples (Balsam et al., 2008; Roisman et al., 2008). Studies suggest that the strategies heterosexuals and homosexuals use to maintain relationships over time have much in common: Both types of couples try to remain close by, for example, sharing tasks and activities together (Haas & Stafford, 2005).

....

intimacy The capacity to make a full commitment—sexual, emotional, and moral—to another person.

However, heterosexual couples obtain more societal support for their relationships (Herek, 2006). To combat a lack of social acceptance, homosexual couples often take special measures to maintain relationships, such as being publicly "out" as a couple.

Each of these types of relationships increases the role of family in adults' social lives. Families also grow when individuals decide to include children in their lives. What may surprise you, however, is that the birth of children can often pose a threat to the overall happiness of a couple (Lawrence et al., 2007; Twenge et al., 2003). Why might that be? Researchers have focused on differences in the way that men and women make the transition to parenthood in heterosexual relationships (Cowan & Cowan, 2000; Dew & Wilcox, 2011). In contemporary Western society, marriages are more often founded on notions of equality between men and women than was true in the past. However, children's births can have the effect of pushing husbands and wives in the direction of more traditional gender roles. The wife may feel too much of the burden of child care; the husband may feel too much pressure to support a family. The net effect may be that, following the birth of a child, the marriage changes in ways that both spouses find to be negative. In recent years, researchers have begun to study gay male and lesbian couples raising children. As you might expect, homosexual relationships are less troubled by concerns about gender roles in the context of parenting (Goldberg & Perry-Jenkins, 2007; Patterson, 2002). Even so, in parallel to results for heterosexual couples, a study of lesbian couples found decreasing love and increasing conflict across the transition to parenthood (Goldberg & Sayer, 2006).

For many couples, satisfaction with the marriage continues to decline because of conflicts as the child or children

What factors have an impact on marital happiness and the likelihood that couples will stay together?

pass through their adolescent years. Contrary to the cultural stereotype, many parents look forward to the time when their youngest child leaves home and leaves them with an "empty nest" (Gorchoff et al., 2008). Parents may enjoy their children most when they are no longer under the same roof. Are you discouraged from having children? I certainly hope not! The goal, as always, is to make you aware of research that can help you anticipate and interpret the patterns in your own life.

You've now learned that marriages are happier, on the whole, when the spouses reach late adulthood. However, you're certainly aware that many marriages end in divorce long before late adulthood arrives. Researchers would like to be able to determine which couples are fundamentally mismatched and which couples could avoid divorce (Amato, 2010). Studies that follow couples over time have identified a number of factors that put marriages at risk, including frequent conflict, infidelity, and low levels of love and trust.

Let's conclude this section where we began, with the idea that social intimacy is a prerequisite for psychological well-being. What matters most is not the quantity of social interaction but the quality. As you grow into older adulthood, you will begin to protect your need for intimacy by selecting those individuals who provide the most direct emotional support.

Let's turn now to a second aspect of adult development, generativity.

Generativity   Those people who have established an appropriate foundation of intimate relationships are most often able to turn their focus to issues of **generativity.** This is a commitment beyond oneself to family, work, society, or future generations—typically a crucial step in development in one's 30s and 40s (Whitbourne et al., 2009). An orientation toward the greater good allows adults to establish a sense of psychological well-being that offsets any longing for youth. Let's consider an example of how generativity functions in an academic setting.

Many professors play an important role as mentors for younger colleagues. A team of researchers wished to demonstrate that professors' individual levels of generativity would help predict how successful they would be in their mentorship roles (Zacher et al., 2011). A research assistant to each of 128 professors provided information about each professor's level of generativity by responding to questions like, "My supervisor devotes more energy to building up the next generation of scientists than to getting ahead him-/herself" (p. 244). The research assistants also evaluated the professors' success as mentors. The data suggested that professors higher in generativity were able to remain successful as mentors later in life than professors with lower generativity.

This study illustrates how people with greater generativity continue to pass along their wisdom to future generations.

generativity A commitment beyond one's self and one's partner to family, work, society, and future generations; typically, a crucial state in development in one's 30s and 40s.

sex difference One of the biologically based characteristics that distinguish males from females.

Note also that in a sample of 2,507 adults between the ages of 35 and 74, higher generativity was associated with greater reports of well-being along dimensions such as self-acceptance and personal growth (Rothrauff & Cooney, 2008).

Late adulthood is a time when goals are shifted; priorities change when the future does not apparently flow as freely. Across that change in priorities, however, older adults preserve their sense of the value of their lives. Erikson defined the last crisis of adulthood to be the conflict between ego integrity and despair. The data suggest that few adults look back over their lives with despair. In fact, people report more emotional well-being as they age (Carstensen et al., 2011). Most older adults review their lives—and look to the future—with a sense of wholeness and satisfaction.

We have worked our way through the life span by considering social and personal aspects of childhood, adolescence, and adulthood. To close out the chapter, let's consider two particular domains in which experience changes over time, the domains of sex and gender differences and moral development.

Stop *and* Review

① At what life stage did Erik Erikson suggest people navigate the crisis of intimacy versus isolation?
② What long-term consequences have been demonstrated for children's early attachment quality?
③ What dimensions define parenting styles?
④ In what levels of peer relationships do adolescents engage?
⑤ What impact does the birth of a child often have on marital satisfaction?

CRITICAL THINKING   Recall the study that examined risk taking by teenage drivers. Why might the researchers focused on newly licensed drivers?

✓•⎡**Study** and **Review** on **MyPsychLab**

SEX AND GENDER DIFFERENCES

One type of information most children begin to acquire in the first few months in life is that there are two categories of people in their social world: males and females. Over time, children learn that there are many respects in which the psychological experiences of males and females are quite similar. However, when differences do occur, children acquire an understanding that some of those differences arise from biology and others arise from cultural expectations. Biologically based characteristics that distinguish males and females are referred to as **sex differences.** These characteristics include different reproductive functions and differences in hormones and anatomy. However, the first differences children perceive are entirely social: They begin to sense differences between males and females well before they understand anything about anatomy. In contrast to biological sex, **gender** is a psychological phenomenon referring to learned sex-related behaviors and attitudes. Cultures vary in how strongly gender is linked to daily activities and in the amount of tolerance for what is perceived as cross-gender behavior. In this section, we consider both sex differences and gender development: the nature and nurture of children's sense of maleness or femaleness.

Sex Differences

Starting at about six weeks after conception, male fetuses begin to diverge from female fetuses when the male testes develop and begin to produce the hormone *testosterone*. The presence or absence of testosterone plays a critical role in determining whether a child will be born with male or female anatomy. Prenatal exposure to testerone also plays an important role in establishing sex-typical behaviors and characteristics (Hines, 2011). Reserachers have carried out studies in which they determine the level of testosterone in the amniotic fluid of each individual participant. The researchers have correlated those fetal testosterone levels with, for example, the quality of each boy's or girl's social relationships when they were 4 years old (Knickmeyer et al., 2005). In general, boys had higher levels of fetal testosterone than girls. Against that background, individuals' higher levels of fetal testosterone were associated with poorer social relationships for both boys and girls. These results suggest that the extent to which individuals conform to expectations for male and female behavior may depend, in part, on their prenatal hormonal environment (Morris et al., 2004).

Brain scans have revealed consistent structural differences between men's and women's brains. Men typically have bigger brains than women (Lenroot & Giedd, 2010). Appropriate comparisons across the sexes adjust for that overall variation. The differences that remain after those adjustments are intriguing with respect to behavioral dissimilarities between men and women. For example, MRI scans reveal that the regions of the frontal lobe that play an important role in regulating social behavior and emotional functioning are relatively bigger in women than in men (Welborn et al., 2009). To confirm that sex differences of this type are biological—rather than the product of a lifetime of experience as men or women in particular cultural roles—researchers have undertaken similar studies with children and adolescents (Lenroot et al., 2007). Those studies confirm that sex differences emerge in the brain as a part of ordinary biological development.

Other analyses of sex differences focus on the distinct ways in which men's and women's brains accomplish cognitive and emotional tasks (Canli et al., 2002). Consider the brain processes engaged when the two sexes view humorous pictures.

Featured Study

Fifteen men and 14 women underwent fMRI scans while viewing 80 funny and 80 neutral pictures (Kohn et al., 2011). After viewing each image for 7 seconds, the participants answered "How funny was this picture?" on a scale of 1 to 5. Overall, women found more humor in the funny pictures than did the men (with average ratings of 3.79 versus 3.48). The women's and men's patterns of brain activities

suggested an origin for the difference in these judgments: Women showed relatively more activity in regions of the brain, such as the amygdala (see Chapter 3), that play a role in emotional responses. The relatively lower activity of men's emotion areas may have resulted in less appreciation of the humor.

Further studies of the brain at work confirm sex differences in the encoding and recognition of emotionally laden stimuli (Cahill et al., 2004; Derntl et al., 2010). These studies suggest that some of the behavioral differences that set men and women apart can be traced to biological differences rather than to cultural roles.

Gender Identity and Gender Stereotypes

You have just seen that important aspects of men's and women's behavior are shaped by biological differences. However, cultural expectations also have an important impact on **gender identity**—an individual's sense of maleness or femaleness. Very early in life, children start to understand that the world is divided into two genders (Martin & Ruble, 2010). For example, 10- to 14-month-old children already demonstrate a preference for a video showing the abstract movements of a child of the same sex (Kujawski & Bower, 1993). In their earliest years, children begin to understand that they are either boys or girls—they settle into their gender identity. At the same time, they acquire knowledge of **gender stereotypes,** which are beliefs about attributes and behaviors regarded as appropriate for males and females in a particular culture.

Researchers have documented the time course with which most children acquire those gender stereotypes (Martin & Ruble, 2010). Through the preschool years, children's experience in the world provides them with knowledge about cultural expectations for men and women. Between ages 5 and 7, children consolidate that knowledge into gender stereotypes. In fact, those are the years of the children's greatest rigidity with respect to those stereotypes. For example, one study assessed children's gender stereotypes by asking them to indicate which children "like to play toy shop" or "are cruel and hurt others on purpose" (Trautner et al., 2005). For each statement, children dropped cards into different boxes that represented *only males, more males than females, equal numbers of males and females, more females than males,* or *only females.* Children of ages 5 to 7 gave the most "only" responses, indicating the strongest gender stereotypes. Older children showed more flexibility in their thinking about gender and behavior. That is, they were more likely to indicate that both males and females engage in a variety of behaviors. Thus, by around age 8, children have begun to understand that there are also similarities between boys and girls.

gender A psychological phenomenon that refers to learned sex-related behaviors and attitudes of males and females.

gender identity One's sense of maleness or femaleness; usually includes awareness and acceptance of one's biological sex.

gender stereotype Belief about attributes and behaviors regarded as appropriate for males and females in a particular culture.

How do children acquire the information that leads to gender identity and gender stereotypes? Parents provide one ready source. Parents dress their sons and daughters differently, give them different kinds of toys to play with, and communicate with them differently. When parents play with their children, they consider some toys to be "masculine" and some to be "feminine." When they play with their children, they are more likely to choose gender-appropriate toys—though that preference may be stronger for play with boys than for play with girls (Wood et al., 2002). In general, children receive encouragement from their parents to engage in sex-typed activities (McHale et al., 2003).

Peers provide another important sources of gender socialization. **Eleanor Maccoby** (2002) argues, for example, that young children are segregationists—they seek out peers of the same sex even when adults are not supervising them or in spite of adult encouragement for mixed-group play. Maccoby believes that many of the differences in gender behavior among children are the results of peer relationships. In fact, boys and girls show consistent differences in their patterns of social interaction. For example, at least by the age of 6, boys prefer to interact in groups, whereas girls prefer one-on-one interactions (Benenson et al., 1997; Benenson & Heath, 2006). Girls are more likely to engage in social conversations and disclose information about themselves; boys are more likely to engage in rough-and-tumble play (Rose & Rudolph, 2006). These differences continue as children grow older. The friendships of adolescent girls are likely to display greater intimacy and more self-disclosure; the friendships of adolescent boys are likley to display more competition and excitement (Perry & Pauletti, 2011).

We have been considering factors that affect gender development across all children. However, as with other domains of development, it's important to acknowledge individual differences among children. Consider a study that examined children's gender-typed behaviors over a six-year period.

The mothers of 5,501 children provided information about their gender-typed behaviors when the children were age 2 (Golombok et al., 2008). The mothers completed the Preschool Activities Inventory *(PSAI), which asked them to indicate, for example, how often their children had played with jewelry or engaged in fighting in the last month. The mothers provided PSAI ratings again when their children were 3 and 5 years old. When the children were 8, they reported their own behavior by completing the* Children's Activities Inventory *(CAI). For this inventory, children listened to pairs of statements that described different types of children: "Some children play with jewelry. . . . but other children don't play with jewelry" (p. 1586). The children indicated how similar they felt to the two types of children. Based on these longitudinal assessments, the researchers concluded that the likelihood that individual children will engage in gender-typed behavior remains very stable over time. For example,* Figure 10.10 *plots children's PSAI scores at age 3 against their CAI scores at age 8. You can see a strong match between children's scores at the two ages.*

Why is the children's behavior so stable? The researchers pointed to both nature and nurture. With respect to nature, the researchers suggested that children may experience prenatal environments that cause their brains to be relatively more

How do parents and peers influence children's acquisition of gender roles?

masculine or feminine. With respect to nurture, the researchers considered differences among the behaviors of both parents and peers. Parents who have less flexible gender stereotypes may also have children who produce more gender-typed behavior. In addition, children may seek friends who are similar to them with respect to their levels of gender-typed behavior—creating a context for those behaviors to be stable over time.

We have briefly considered how and why it is that boys and girls experience social development in different fashions. Let's now consider moral development.

Stop *and* Review

① What is the distinction between sex differences and gender differences?
② What does research suggest about differences in brain activity between men and women for the processing of humorous pictures?
③ In what ways are young children "segregationists"?

CRITICAL THINKING   Recall the study on the stability of gender-typed behaviors. Why might the researchers have switched to self-reports from the children at age 8?

✓—**Study** and **Review** on **MyPsychLab**

MORAL DEVELOPMENT

So far we have seen, across the life span, how important it is to develop close social relationships. Let's now consider another aspect of what it means to live as part of a social group: On many occasions you must judge your behavior according to the needs of society, rather than just according to your own needs. This is the basis of *moral behavior*. **Morality** is a system of

morality A system of beliefs and values that ensures that individuals will keep their obligations to others in society and will behave in ways that do not interfere with the rights and interests of others.

Boys

Girls

FIGURE 10.10 The Stability of Gender-Typed Behavior over Time

Mothers indicated children's gender-typed behavior on the PSAI at age 3, and children indicated their own behaviors at age 8. For each group of children who scored in a particular PSAI range at age 3 (with lower scores indicating more stereotypically feminine behavior), the researchers calculated their mean CAI value at age 8. The plot shows that children's levels of gender-typed behavior were quite similar at the two points in time.

From "Longitudinal general population study of sex-typed behavior in boys and girls: A longitudinal general population study of children aged 2.5–8 years" by Susan Golombok, John Rust, Karyofyllis Zervoulis, Tim Croudace, Jean Golding and Melissa Hines, *Child Development*, September 1, 2008, pages 1583–1593, copyright © 2008 by the Society for Research in Child Development. Reprinted by permission of John Wiley and Sons.

beliefs, values, and underlying judgments about the rightness or wrongness of human acts.

Before we consider how moral development unfolds for each individual, we want to consider the question for the whole human species: How did morality evolve? To answer that question, contemporary researchers have built on Charles Darwin's foundational observations about how humans function as a social species (Krebs, 2008). From an evolutionary perspective, moral behaviors are consequences of adaptive solutions to situations that have recurred across human history. For example, many early human endeavors (such as killing large game or defending territory) required cooperation among large groups of people. Thus, it was adaptive for humans to evolve a disposition "to resolve fundamental social dilemmas in cooperative ways" (Krebs, p. 154). In contemporary times, moral questions often have a dimension of self-interested versus cooperative behavior: Should a person drive his or her car less so that everyone can breathe cleaner air? The evolutionary perspective suggests that our reflexive responses to such questions is part of our genetic inheritance (Haidt, 2007).

However, even if people share some evolved moral responses, what constitutes moral and immoral behavior in particular situations can become a matter of heated public debate. Perhaps it is no coincidence, therefore, that the study of moral development has also proved to be controversial. The controversy begins with the foundational research of Lawrence Kohlberg.

Kohlberg's Stages of Moral Reasoning

Lawrence Kohlberg (1964, 1981) founded his theory of moral development by studying *moral reasoning*—the judgments people make about what courses of action are correct or incorrect in particular situations. Kohlberg's theory was shaped by the earlier insights of Jean Piaget (1965), who sought to tie the development of moral judgment to a child's general cognitive development. In Piaget's view, as the child progresses through the stages of cognitive growth, he or she assigns differing relative weights to the *consequences* of an act and to the actor's *intentions*. For example, to the preoperational child, someone who breaks 10 cups accidentally is "naughtier" than someone who breaks one cup intentionally. As the child gets older, the actor's intentions weigh more heavily in the judgment of morality.

Kohlberg expanded Piaget's view to define stages of moral development. Each stage is characterized by a different basis for making moral judgments (see **Table 10.7** on page 292). The lowest level of moral reasoning is based on self-interest; higher levels center on social good, regardless of personal gain. To document these stages, Kohlberg used a series of dilemmas that pit different moral principles against one another:

In one dilemma, a man named Heinz is trying to help his wife obtain a certain drug needed to treat

Table 10.7 • Kohlberg's Stages of Moral Reasoning

Levels and Stages	Reasons for Moral Behavior
I Preconventional morality	
Stage 1 Pleasure/pain orientation	To avoid pain or not to get caught
Stage 2 Cost–benefit orientation; reciprocity—an eye for an eye	To get rewards
II Conventional morality	
Stage 3 Good-child orientation	To gain acceptance and avoid disapproval
Stage 4 Law and order orientation	To follow rules, avoid censure by authorities
III Principled morality	
Stage 5 Social contract orientation	To promote the society's welfare
Stage 6 Ethical principle orientation	To achieve justice and avoid self-condemnation
Stage 7 Cosmic orientation	To be true to universal principles and feel oneself part of a cosmic direction that transcends social norms

her cancer. An unscrupulous druggist will only sell it to Heinz for ten times more than what the druggist paid. This is much more money than Heinz has and more than he can raise. Heinz becomes desperate, breaks into the druggist's store, and steals the drug for his wife. Should Heinz have done that? Why? An interviewer probes the participant for the reasons for the decision and then scores the answers.

The scoring is based on the *reasons* the person gives for the decision, not on the decision itself. For example, someone who says that the man should steal the drug because of his obligation to his dying wife or that he should not steal the drug because of his obligation to uphold the law (despite his personal feelings) is expressing concern about meeting established obligations and is scored at Stage 4.

Four principles govern Kohlberg's stage model: (1) An individual can be at only one stage at a given time; (2) everyone goes through the stages in a fixed order; (3) each stage is more comprehensive and complex than the preceding; and (4) the same stages occur in every culture. Kohlberg inherited much of this stage philosophy from Piaget, and, in fact, the progression from Stages 1 to 3 appears to match the course of normal cognitive development. The stages proceed in order, and each can be seen to be more cognitively sophisticated than the preceding. Almost all children reach Stage 3 by the age of 13.

Much of the controversy with Kohlberg's theory occurs beyond Stage 3. In Kohlberg's original view, people would continue their moral development in a steady progression beyond level 3. However, not all people attain Stages 4 to 7. In fact, many adults never reach Stage 5, and only a few go beyond it. The content of Kohlberg's later stages appears to be subjective, and it is hard to understand each successive stage as more comprehensive and sophisticated than the preceding. For example, "avoiding self-condemnation," the basis for moral judgments at Stage 6, does not seem obviously more sophisticated than "promoting society's welfare," the basis for Stage 5. Furthermore, Kohlberg's own research ultimately demonstrated that the higher stages are not

found in all cultures (Gibbs et al., 2007). Let's turn now to contemporary research that enlarges Kohlberg's theory to include considerations of gender and culture.

Gender and Cultural Perspectives on Moral Reasoning

Most critiques of Kohlberg's theory take issue with his claims of universality: Kohlberg's later stages have been criticized because they fail to recognize that adult moral judgments may reflect different, but equally moral, principles. In a well-known critique, **Carol Gilligan** (1982) argued that Kohlberg overlooked potential differences between the habitual moral judgments of men and women. Gilligan proposed that women's moral development is based on a standard of *caring for others* and progresses to a stage of self-realization, whereas men base their reasoning on a standard of *justice*. Research has confirmed that concerns about caring and justice are relevant to moral reasoning—but not that these concerns are found especially in women or in men (Jaffee & Hyde, 2000). Although Gilligan's specific proposals have received limited support, men and women do appear to differ in some aspects of moral reasoning. For example, women tend to display more awareness of how their actions affect other people, an ability that is called *moral sensitivity* (You et al., 2011). In addition, men and women show differences in brain activity when they view images (for example, an injured child) that cause an emotional response of compassion (Mercadillo et al., 2011). These brain differences likely relate to the more general sex differences in emotional processing you encountered earlier in the chapter.

Cross-cultural research has also expanded researchers' understanding about the range of concerns that contribute to moral reasoning (Gibbs et al., 2007; Sachdeva et al., 2011). One analysis has identified three types of concern (Jensen, 2008). The first set of concerns relates to *autonomy:* "A focus on people who have needs, desires, and preferences"; "the moral goal is to recognize" people's right "to the fulfillment of these needs and desires" (Jensen, 2008, p. 296). The second set of concerns relates to *community*: A focus on people "as members of social groups such as family, school, and nation"; the moral goal is "the fulfillment of role-based duties to others, and the protections and positive functioning of social groups." The third set of concerns relates to *divinity*: A focus "on people as spiritual or religious entities"; "the moral goal is for the self to become increasingly connected to . . . [the] pure or divine."

If you think through these three types of concerns you can see how their importance might vary cross-culturally. Consider this situation: You see a stranger at the side of the road with a flat tire. Should you stop to help? Suppose you say no. Is that immoral? If you have grown up in the United States, you probably think helping, under these circumstances, is a matter of personal choice, so it isn't immoral. But if you had grown up in India, in a culture that puts considerably more emphasis on interdependence and mutual assistance, you probably *would* view a failure to help as immoral (Miller et al., 1990).

It's also important to recognize that people's life experiences will have an impact on their judgments. Consider individuals who have grown up in circumstances of great violence.

Featured Study

The researchers recruited a group of children and adolescents from a highly impoverished area in Bogotá, Columbia (Posada & Wainryb, 2008). A large majority of the participants (88 percent) had witnessed or experienced some severe type of violence: They had, for example, seen people shot at, shot, or killed. The researchers first asked the participants to share their moral judgments in the abstract. The participants answered questions like, "Is it okay or not okay to take other people's things?" On such abstract questions, all the participants presented responses based on norms of justice. They indicated, for example, that it would not be okay to steal. However, the pattern changed when the participants made similar judgments in concrete contexts. For example, the participants read a scenario in which 15-year-old Julio had the opportunity to steal a bicycle from one of "the people who hurt his father and his brother and forced his family to move" (p. 886). After hearing that scenario, participants often indicated their belief that Julio would steal the bicycle. In addition, despite their general aversion to stealing, many participants approved of that behavior in this concrete instance.

The researchers note that the participants' violent life experiences have not completely overwhelmed ordinary moral development: "Even the impoverished environments of war and displacement present youths with opportunities for reflecting on the intrinsic features of actions that harm others" (p. 896). Still, the researchers speculate that, because of their impact on moral judgments, "contexts underscoring revenge might give rise to cycles of violence" (p. 896). The same behavior that seems very wrong framed against one set of moral concerns may look very right framed against another.

We have now visited several domains in which people undergo developmental change. The final section of the chapter offers some thoughts for your future.

Stop *and* Review

① What are the three major levels of moral reasoning in Kohlberg's theory?
② What distinction did Carol Gilligan believe separates the moral reasoning of men and women?
③ What are three types of concerns people may bring to circumstances of moral reasoning?

CRITICAL THINKING Consider the study that looked at moral judgments by children and adolescents in Columbia. Why might the researchers have chosen scenarios that involved revenge?

✔●[**Study** and **Review** on **MyPsychLab**

LEARNING TO AGE SUCCESSFULLY

Let's now review some of the themes of this chapter, to form a prescription for successful aging. Early in the chapter, I encouraged you to think of development as a type of change that always brings with it gains and losses. In this light, the trick to prospering across the life span is to solidify one's gains and minimize one's losses. Many of the changes that are stereotypically associated with aging are functions of disuse rather than decay. The fundamental advice is straightforward: Keep at it!

How can older adults cope successfully with whatever changes inevitably accompany increasing age? Successful aging might consist of making the most of gains while minimizing the impact of the normal losses that accompany aging. This strategy for successful aging, proposed by psychologists **Paul Baltes** and **Margaret Baltes,** is called **selective optimization with compensation** (Baltes et al., 1992; Freund & Baltes, 1998). *Selective* means that people scale down the number and extent of their goals for themselves. *Optimization* refers to people exercising or training themselves in areas that are of highest priority to them. *Compensation* means that people use alternative ways to deal with losses—for example, choosing age-friendly environments. Let's consider an example:

> *When the concert pianist [Arthur] Rubinstein was asked, in a television interview, how he managed to remain such a successful pianist in his old age, he mentioned three strategies: (1) In old age he performed fewer pieces, (2) he now practiced each piece more frequently, and (3) he produced more ritardandos [slowings of the tempo] in his playing before fast segments, so that the playing speed sounded faster*

selective optimization with compensation A strategy for successful aging in which one makes the most gains while minimizing the impact of losses that accompany normal aging.

than it was in reality. These are examples of selection (fewer pieces), optimization (more practice), and compensation (increased use of contrast in speed). (Baltes, 1993, p. 590)

This example provides a template for how you might think about your own life. Although the selective optimization perspective originated in research on the aging process, it is a good way to characterize the choices you must make throughout your life span. You should always try to select the goals most important to you, optimize your performance with respect to those goals, and compensate when progress toward those goals is blocked. That's the final bit of advice about life span development. I hope you will age wisely and well!

Recapping Main Points

Studying Development

- Researchers collect normative, longitudinal, and cross-sectional data to document change.

Physical Development across the Life Span

- Environmental factors can affect physical development while a child is still in the womb.
- Newborns and infants possess a remarkable range of capabilities: They are prewired for survival.
- Through puberty, adolescents achieve sexual maturity.
- Some physical changes in late adulthood are consequences of disuse, not inevitable deterioration.

Cognitive Development across the Life Span

- Piaget's key ideas about cognitive development include development of schemes, assimilation, accommodation, and the four-stage theory of discontinuous development. The four stages are sensorimotor, preoperational, concrete operational, and formal operational.
- Many of Piaget's theories are now being altered by ingenious research paradigms that reveal infants and young children to be more competent than Piaget had thought.
- Children develop a theory of mind, which is the ability to explain and predict other people's behavior based on an understanding of their mental states.
- Cross-cultural research has questioned the universality of cognitive developmental theories.
- Age-related declines in cognitive functioning are typically evident in only some abilities.

Acquiring Language

- Many researchers believe that humans have an inborn language-making capacity. Even so, interactions with adult speakers is an essential part of the language acquisition process.
- Like scientists, children develop hypotheses about the meanings and grammar of their language. These hypotheses are often constrained by innate principles.

Social Development across the Life Span

- Social development takes place in a particular cultural context.
- Erik Erikson conceptualized the life span as a series of crises with which individuals must cope.
- Children begin the process of social development with different temperaments.
- Socialization begins with an infant's attachment to a caregiver.
- Failure to make this attachment leads to numerous physical and psychological problems.
- Adolescents must develop a personal identity by forming comfortable social relationships with parents and peers.
- The central concerns of adulthood are organized around the needs of intimacy and generativity.
- People become less socially active as they grow older because they selectively maintain only those relationships that matter most to them emotionally.
- People assess their lives, in part, by their ability to contribute positively to the lives of others.

Sex and Gender Differences

- Research has revealed biologically based sex differences between the brains of men and women.
- Children's gender stereotypes are most rigid between ages 5 and 7.
- Beginning at birth, parents and peers help bring about the socialization of gender roles.

Moral Development

- Kohlberg defined stages of moral development.
- Subsequent research has evaluated gender and cultural differences in moral reasoning.

Learning to Age Successfully

- Successful cognitive aging can be defined as people optimizing their functioning in select domains that are of highest priority to them and compensating for losses by using substitute behaviors.

KEY TERMS

accommodation (p. 269)
assimilation (p. 269)
attachment (p. 281)
centration (p. 270)
child-directed speech (p. 276)
cognitive development (p. 269)
conservation (p. 271)
contact comfort (p. 283)
cross-sectional design (p. 262)
developmental age (p. 261)
developmental psychology (p. 261)
egocentrism (p. 270)
embryonic stage (p. 263)
fetal stage (p. 263)
gender (p. 289)
gender identity (p. 289)

gender stereotype (p. 289)
generativity (p. 288)
germinal stage (p. 263)
imprinting (p. 281)
infant-directed speech (p. 276)
internalization (p. 273)
intimacy (p. 287)
language-making capacity (p. 277)
longitudinal design (p. 261)
maturation (p. 266)
menarche (p. 267)
morality (p. 290)
normative investigation (p. 261)
object permanence (p. 269)
overregularization (p. 277)
parenting style (p. 282)

phoneme (p. 275)
physical development (p. 263)
psychosocial stage (p. 278)
puberty (p. 267)
scheme (p. 269)
selective optimization
   with compensation (p. 293)
sex difference (p. 288)
social development (p. 278)
socialization (p. 280)
temperament (p. 281)
teratogen (p. 264)
theory of mind (p. 272)
wisdom (p. 273)
zygote (p. 263)

1. Rachel just turned 4, but she has the language ability of a 6-year-old. For language ability, Rachel's _____ age is greater than her _____ age.
   a. chronological; normative
   b. developmental; cross-sectional
   c. developmental; chronological
   d. chronological; developmental

2. Your friend Pat says, "I'm sure Caroline recognized my voice as soon as she was born." If Pat is Caroline's _____, Pat's claim is probably correct.
   a. mother
   b. father
   c. mother or father
   d. sister

3. Jack and Jill are twins. Under most circumstances, you would expect that Jack would begin his pubescent growth spurt _____ Jill.
   a. at the same time as
   b. earlier than
   c. a year before
   d. later than

4. Tamara is a child whose thought is marked by egocentrism and centration. With respect to Piaget's theory, you infer that Tamara is in the _____ stage.
   a. sensorimotor
   b. preoperational
   c. concrete operations
   d. formal operations

5. You are testing 20-year-old Keith and his 45-year-old father, Matthew. If they are both average members of their age groups, you'd expect Keith to show more _____ and Matthew to show more _____.
   a. crystallized intelligence; fluid intelligence
   b. wisdom; crystallized intelligence
   c. wisdom; fluid intelligence
   d. fluid intelligence; wisdom

6. You are examining data from an experiment on speech perception. Participant 27 was able to hear a sound distinction that is used in Hindi but not in English. You conclude the Participant 27 is least likely to be an
   a. adult who is an English speaker.
   b. infant in a Hindi-language environment.
   c. adult who is a Hindi speaker.
   d. infant in an English-language environment.

7. If Siyun believes that "mommy" applies to all women, that is an _____. If she believes that "mommy" applies only to her own mother, that is an _____.
   a. contrast; overextension
   b. underextension; hypothesis
   c. hypothesis; contrast
   d. overextension; underextension

8. Mona and Bianca are both 6-year-olds. Mona speaks English. Bianca speaks both English and Turkish. You expect that _____ will have a bigger vocabulary in English and that _____ will show better executive control.
   a. Mona; Mona
   b. Bianca; Mona
   c. Mona; Bianca
   d. Bianca; Bianca

9. According to Erik Erikson, the major crisis of age 6 to puberty is
   a. autonomy versus self-doubt.
   b. identity versus role confusion.
   c. generativity versus stagnation.
   d. competence versus inferiority.

10. As a mother, Lisbeth is high on the dimension of demandingness and low on the dimension of responsiveness. This combination would be described as a(n) _____ style of parenting.
    a. indulgent
    b. authoritative
    c. neglecting
    d. authoritarian

11. Which of these statements was not mentioned as a recommendation for quality day care?
    a. Children should be taught social problem-solving skills.
    b. Children should have similar levels of intellectual development.
    c. Caregivers should not put undue restrictions on the children.
    d. Children should have a free choice of activities intermixed with explicit lessons.

12. Whereas _____ differences are affected by culture, _____ differences are affected by biology.
    a. gender; sex
    b. generativity; gender
    c. sex; identity
    d. sex; gender

13. You are asked to guess whether 6-year-old Chris is a girl or boy. Which observation would most lead you to believe that Chris is a girl?
    a. Chris enjoys rough-and-tumble play.
    b. Chris doesn't like to engage in social conversations.
    c. Chris most enjoys one-on-one relationships.
    d. Chris prefers to have social interactions in groups.

14. For moral behavior, Gracie is most concerned about following rules and avoiding the censure of authorities. She is at the stage of _____ morality.
    a. principled
    b. cultural
    c. preconventional
    d. conventional

15. Carol Gilligan criticized Kohlberg's theory by arguing that women are more focused on the standard of _____, whereas men are more focused on the standard of _____.
    a. caring for others; avoiding pain
    b. caring for others; justice
    c. justice; caring for others
    d. avoiding self-condemnation; justice

ESSAY QUESTIONS

1. What types of abilities signal that children are acquiring a theory of mind?

2. Why do deprivation and abuse have consequences for social development?

3. Why is it sometimes difficult to discriminate between sex differences and gender differences?

11

Motivation

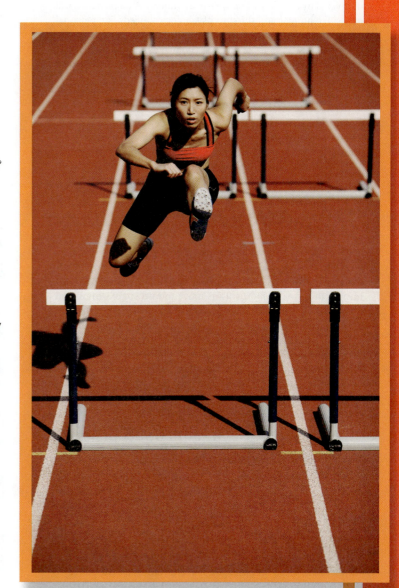

Your alarm clock went off this morning. You would have loved to hit the snooze button to get a few extra minutes of sleep, but you dragged yourself right out of bed. Why? Were you desperately hungry? Did you have to complete some important assignment? Had you made a date with someone who has captured your heart? When you consider the question "Why did I get out of bed this morning?" you have arrived directly at the core question of *motivation:* What makes you act as you do? What makes you persistently try to attain some goals despite the high effort, pain, and financial costs involved? Why, conversely, do you sometimes procrastinate too long before attempting to achieve other goals or give in and quit too soon? 👁

It is the task of psychological researchers to bring theoretical rigor to such questions of motivation. How might motivational states affect the outcome of a sports competition or an exam? Why do some people become overweight and others starve themselves to death? Are our sexual behaviors determined by our genetic heritage? In this chapter, you will learn that human actions are motivated by a variety of needs—from fundamental physiological needs like hunger and thirst to psychological needs like personal achievement. But you will see that physiology and psychology are often not easy to separate. Even a seemingly biological drive such as hunger competes with an individual's need for personal control and social acceptance to determine patterns of eating.

This chapter begins by providing you with a framework to understand general issues about the nature and study of motivation. The bulk of the chapter looks in depth at three types of motivation, each important in a different way and each varying in the extent to which biological and psychological factors operate. These three are hunger, sex, and personal achievement.

your bodily functioning and help you survive. Why did you get out of bed this morning? You may have been hungry, thirsty, or cold. In each case, internal states of deprivation trigger bodily responses that motivate you to take action to restore your body's balance.

- *To account for behavioral variability.* Why might you do well on a task one day and poorly on the same task another day? Why does one child do much better at a competitive task than another child with roughly the same ability and knowledge? Psychologists use motivational explanations when the variations in people's performance in a constant situation cannot be traced to differences in ability, skill, practice, or chance. If you were willing to get up early this morning to get in some extra studying but your friend was not, we would be comfortable describing you as being in a different motivational state than your friend.

- *To infer private states from public acts.* You see someone sitting on a park bench, chuckling. How can you explain this behavior? Psychologists and laypersons are alike in typically moving from observing some behavior to inferring some internal cause for it. People are continually interpreting behavior in terms of likely reasons for why it occurred as it did. The same rule applies to your own behaviors. You often seek to discover whether your own actions are best understood as internally or externally motivated.

- *To assign responsibility for actions.* The concept of personal responsibility is basic in law, religion, and ethics. Personal responsibility presupposes inner motivation and the ability to control your actions. People are judged less responsible for their actions when (1) they did not intend negative consequences to occur, (2) external forces were

UNDERSTANDING MOTIVATION

Motivation is the general term for all the processes involved in starting, directing, and maintaining physical and psychological activities. The word *motivation* comes from the Latin *movere,* which means "to move." All organisms move toward some stimuli and activities and away from others, as dictated by their appetites and aversions. Theories of motivation explain both the general patterns of "movement" of each animal species, including humans, and the personal preferences and performances of the individual members of each species. Let's begin our analysis of motivation by considering the different ways in which motivation has been used to explain and predict species and individual behavior. 👁

Functions of Motivational Concepts

Psychologists have used the concept of motivation for five basic purposes:

- *To relate biology to behavior.* As a biological organism, you have complex internal mechanisms that regulate

What different motivational questions might be asked of this individual's behavior?

....

👁 Watch the **Video** *The Big Picture: What Drives Us?* on **MyPsychLab**

👁 Watch the **Video** *The Basics: Theories of Emotion and Motivation* on **MyPsychLab**

motivation The process of starting, directing, and maintaining physical and psychological activities; includes mechanisms involved in preferences for one activity over another and the vigor and persistence of responses.

powerful enough to provoke the behaviors, or (3) the actions were influenced by drugs, alcohol, or intense emotion. Thus a theory of motivation must be able to discriminate among the different potential causes of behavior.

- *To explain perseverance despite adversity.* A final reason psychologists study motivation is to explain why organisms perform behaviors when it might be easier not to perform them. Motivation gets you to work or class on time even when you're exhausted. Motivation helps you persist in playing the game to the best of your ability even when you are losing and realize that you can't possibly win.

You now have a general sense of the circumstances in which psychologists might invoke the concept of motivation to explain and predict behavior. Before we turn to specific domains of experience, let's consider general sources of motivation.

Sources of Motivation

In 1999, cyclist Lance Armstrong won the Tour de France—completing one of the most remarkable comebacks in sports history. In 1996, Armstrong had been diagnosed with testicular cancer that had spread to his lungs and brain. After enduring aggressive chemotherapy, Armstrong chose to go back into training. Within three years, he was victorious in his sport's most prestigious event. In 2005, Armstrong won the Tour de France for the seventh time in a row. Detractors had claimed that the field he beat in 1999 was weak; his six additional victories proved that he could repeatedly beat the world's best cyclists.

Could you do what Lance Armstrong did? Could you come back from a serious illness to challenge your body again? Do you think that whatever motivated his behavior was something *internal* to him? Would it take a special set of life experiences for someone to persevere in this manner? Or was it something *external,* something about the situation? Would many or most people behave in this way if they were put in the same situation? Or does his behavior represent an *interaction* of aspects of the person and features of the situation? To help you think about the sources of motivation, I will explore this distinction between internal and external forces. Let's begin with theories that explain certain types of behavior as arising from internal biological drives.

Drives and Incentives Some forms of motivation seem very basic: If you feel hungry, you eat; if you feel thirsty, you drink. The theory that much important behavior is motivated by internal drives was most fully developed by theorist **Clark Hull** (1884–1952). In Hull's (1943, 1952) view, **drives** are internal states that arise in response to an animal's physiological needs. Organisms seek to maintain a state of equilibrium, or **homeostasis,** with respect to biological conditions (see Chapter 3, p. 68). Consider how your body responds to keep your temperature close to 98.6 °F: If you get too hot, you begin to sweat; if you get too cold, you start to shiver. These mechanisms

What combination of internal and external motivational forces may have helped cyclist Lance Armstrong to overcome cancer and win the Tour de France?

serve to restore equilibrium. Now consider what happens when an animal has been deprived of food for several hours. On Hull's view, such deprivation creates disequilibrium, or *tension,* which arouses a drive. This drive activates the organism toward *tension reduction;* when the drive is satisfied or reduced—when homeostasis is restored—the organism ceases to act. Thus, according to Hull, the food-deprived animal experiences a drive that motivates food-seeking and eating behaviors. The animal's responses that have led to the food goal will be reinforced because they are associated with the tension reduction that eating produces. 👁

Can tension reduction explain all motivated behavior? Apparently not. Let's consider an experiment that demonstrated that hunger and thirst are not always rats' most important motivation.

Featured Study

Groups of either food- or water-deprived rats were placed in a square maze that consisted of nine equally sized units with doorways that allowed passage between the units (Zimbardo & Montgomery, 1957). Each unit of the maze had a sunken bowl that could contain either water or food. Drive theory would predict that the rats experiencing deprivation would eat or drink at their first opportunity. However, rather than immediately reducing that tension, the rats often chose to explore the maze instead. For example, rats that had been deprived of food for 48 or 72 hours spent 80 percent of their first two minutes in the maze exploring the maze; they spent only 20 percent of their time eating.

👁 **Watch** the **Video** *Classic Footage of Carl Rogers on Drive Theory* on **MyPsychLab**

drive Internal state that arises in response to a disequilibrium in an animal's physiological needs.

homeostasis Constancy or equilibrium of the internal conditions of the body.

In this experiment, it appeared that the rats began to satisfy their hunger or thirst only once they had first satisfied their curiosity. Researchers have provided several similar examples of instances in which other motivational forces prevail over drive reduction (Berlyne, 1960; Fowler, 1965).

These results illustrate why theorists came to believe that internal drives are not the only source of motivation.

We know now that behavior is also motivated by **incentives**—external stimuli or rewards that do not relate directly to biological needs. When the rats were attuned to objects in the environment rather than to their own internal states, they demonstrated that their behavior was controlled by incentives. Human behavior is also controlled by a variety of incentives. Why do you stay up late watching YouTube videos instead of getting a good night's sleep? Why do you watch a movie that you know will make you feel anxious or frightened? Why do you eat junk food at a party even when you're already feeling full? In each case, elements of the environment serve as incentives to motivate your behavior.

You can see already that behaviors find their origins in a mixture of internal and external sources of motivation. Even though rats might feel biological pressure to eat or drink, they also indulge an impulse to explore a new environment. We turn now to a different tradition of research on motivation, one that focuses on species-specific *instinctual* behaviors.

Instinctual Behaviors and Learning Why do organisms behave the way they do? Part of the answer is that some aspects of a species's behavior are governed by **instincts,** preprogrammed tendencies that are essential for the survival of their species. Instincts provide repertoires of behavior that are part of each animal's genetic inheritance. Salmon swim thousands of miles back to the exact stream where they were spawned, leaping up waterfalls until they come to the right spot, where the surviving males and females engage in ritualized courtship and mating. Fertilized eggs are deposited, the parents die, and, in time, their young swim downstream to live in the ocean until, a few years later, it is time for them to return to complete their part in this continuing drama. Similarly remarkable activities can be reported for most species of animals. Bees communicate the location of food to other bees, army ants go on highly synchronized hunting expeditions, birds build nests, and spiders spin complex webs—exactly as their parents and ancestors did.

Early theories of human function tended to overestimate the importance of instincts for humans. William James, writing in 1890, stated his belief that humans rely even more on instinctual behaviors than other animals (although human instincts were generally not carried out with fixed-action patterns). He argued, for example, that humans have a host of social instincts for sympathy, modesty, sociability, and love. By the 1920s, psychologists had compiled lists of over 10,000 human instincts (Bernard, 1924). At this same time, however, the notion of instincts as universal explanations for human behavior was beginning to stagger under the weight of critical attacks. Cross-cultural anthropologists, such as Ruth Benedict (1959) and Margaret Mead (1939), found enormous behavioral

....

incentive External stimulus or reward that motivates behavior although it does not relate directly to biological needs.

instinct Preprogrammed tendency that is essential to a species' survival.

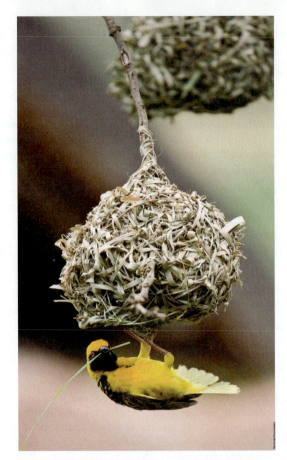

Instinctive behaviors, like the nest-building practices of the golden weaver, are motivated by genetic inheritance. What instincts have theorists attributed to human practice?

variation between cultures. Their observations contradicted theories that considered only the universals of inborn instincts.

Within psychology, behaviorists objected to the circular reasoning that often gave rise to claims about human instincts: People are sympathetic because they have an instinct to be sympathetic; sympathetic behavior confirms the existence of the instinct. In addition, as we saw in Chapter 6, behaviorists provided empirical demonstrations that important behaviors and emotions are learned rather than inborn. Human and nonhuman animals alike are highly sensitive to the ways in which stimuli and responses are associated in the environment. If you want to explain why one animal performs a behavior and another does not, you may need to know only that one animal's behavior was reinforced and the other's was not. Under those circumstances, you don't need a separate account of motivation at all (that is, it would be a mistake to say that one animal is "motivated" and the other is not). Thus, if we wish to explain why particular organisms behave in the way they do, it's important to separate out instinctual behaviors from the products of learning.

Expectations and Cognitive Approaches to Motivation
One final look back to Chapter 6: We saw there that cognitively oriented researchers have challenged the belief that instincts and reinforcement history are sufficient to explain all the details of an animal's behavior. Cognitive analyses of motivation suggest that significant human motivation comes not from objective realities in the external world but from subjective

interpretations of reality. The reinforcing effect of a reward is lost if you don't perceive that your actions obtained it. What you do now is often controlled both by what you think was responsible for your past outcomes and by what you believe is possible for you to do. In addition, cognitive analyses suggest that humans are often motivated by *expectations* of future events—what they anticipate the outcomes of actions will be.

The importance of expectations in motivating behavior was developed by **Julian Rotter** (1954) in his **social learning theory** (Chapter 6 touched on social learning in the discussion of observational learning). For Rotter, the probability that you will engage in a given behavior (studying for an exam instead of partying) is determined by your *expectation* of attaining a goal (getting a good grade) that follows the activity and by the *personal value* of that goal. A *discrepancy* between expectations and reality can motivate an individual to perform corrective behaviors (Festinger, 1957; Lewin, 1936). Suppose you find that your own behaviors do not match the standards or values of a group to which you belong—you might be motivated to change your behaviors to achieve a better fit with the group. You might, for example, be motivated to change your style of dress or the music to which you listen to reduce the discrepancy between expectations and reality.

Fritz Heider (1896–1988) outlined how expectations relate to internal and external forces of motivation. Heider (1958) postulated that the outcome of your behavior (a poor grade, for example) can be attributed to *dispositional forces,* such as lack of effort or insufficient intelligence, or to *situational forces,* such as an unfair test or a biased teacher. These attributions influence the way you will behave. You are likely to try harder next time if you see your poor grade as a result of your lack of effort, but you may give up if you see it as resulting from injustice or lack of ability (Dweck, 1975). Thus the identification of a source of motivation as internal or external may depend, in part, on your own subjective interpretation of reality.

Let's review the various sources of motivation. We began with the observation that researchers can differentiate internal and external factors that bring about behaviors. Drives, instincts, and histories of learning are all internal sources of motivation that affect behaviors in the presence of appropriate external stimuli. Once organisms begin to think about their behaviors— something humans are particularly prone to do—expectations about what should or should not happen also begin to provide motivation. Thinking animals can choose to attribute some motivations to themselves and others to the outside world.

A Hierarchy of Needs

We have now reviewed several sources of motivation. As a preview for the rest of the chapter, we return to a more global account of the domains in which motivational concepts apply. The intent is to give you a general sense of the forces that could guide your life.

Humanist psychologist **Abraham Maslow** (1908–1970) formulated the theory that basic motives form a **hierarchy of needs,** as illustrated in **Figure 11.1** on page 302. In Maslow's (1970) view, the needs at each level of the hierarchy must be satisfied—the needs are arranged in a sequence from primitive to advanced—before the next level can be achieved. At the bottom of this hierarchy are the basic *biological needs,* such as hunger and thirst. They must be met before any other needs

can begin to operate. When biological needs are pressing, other needs are put on hold and are unlikely to influence your actions. When they are reasonably well satisfied, the needs at the next level—*safety needs*—motivate you. When you are no longer concerned about danger, you become motivated by *attachment needs*—needs to belong, to affiliate with others, to love, and to be loved. If you are well fed and safe and if you feel a sense of social belonging, you move up to *esteem needs*—to like oneself, to see oneself as competent and effective, and to do what is necessary to earn the esteem of others.

At the top of the hierarchy are people who are nourished, safe, loved and loving, secure, thinking, and creating. These people have moved beyond basic human needs in the quest for the fullest development of their potentials, or *self-actualization.* A self-actualizing person is self-aware, self-accepting, socially responsive, creative, spontaneous, and open to novelty and challenge, among other positive attributes. 👁

Maslow's theory is a particularly upbeat view of human motivation. At the core of the theory is the need for each individual to grow and actualize his or her highest potential. However, you know from your own experience that Maslow's strict hierarchy breaks down. You may, for example, have skipped a meal so that you could help out a friend. You may have endured the danger of a wilderness trek to boost your self-esteem. Even so, I hope Maslow's scheme will enable you to bring some order to different aspects of your motivational experiences.

You now have a general framework for understanding motivation. The remainder of the chapter will take a closer look

Where does the need to belong, to form attachments and experience love, fit in Maslow's hierarchy?

👁 **Watch** the **Video** *What's In It For Me?: Meeting Our Needs* on **MyPsychLab**

social learning theory The learning theory that stresses the role of observation and the imitation of behaviors observed in others.

hierarchy of needs Maslow's view that basic human motives form a hierarchy and that the needs at each level of the hierarchy must be satisfied before the next level can be achieved; these needs progress from basic biological needs to the need for self-actualization. Where does the need to belong, to form attachments and experience love, fit in Maslow's hierarchy?

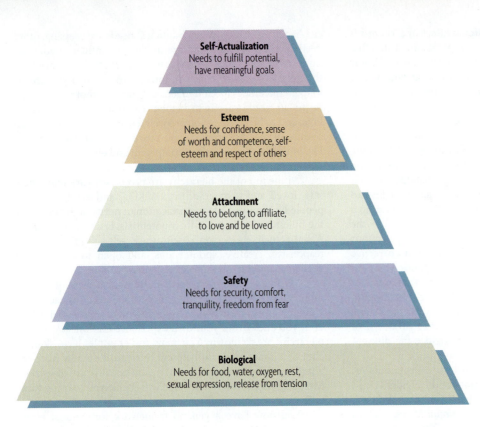

FIGURE 11.1 Maslow's Hierarchy of Needs
According to Maslow, needs at the lower level of the hierarchy dominate an individual's motivation as long as they are unsatisfied. Once these needs are adequately met, the higher needs occupy the individual's attention.

at three different types of behaviors that are influenced by interactions of motives: eating, sexual performance, and personal achievement.

Stop *and* Review

① As you're sitting on a bench, you see another student go running by. Which function of motivational concepts applies to how you interpret the situation?

② What does it mean for an organism to achieve homeostasis?

③ Why did cross-cultural research cast doubt on claims about human instincts?

④ What distinction did Fritz Heider make with respect to explanations for outcomes?

⑤ What did Abraham Maslow mean by attachment needs?

CRITICAL THINKING   Recall the experiment on food- or water-deprived rats. Why was it important that each unit of the maze could contain food or water?

✔•—Study and Review on MyPsychLab

EATING

I am about to offer a slice of pizza to a student enrolled in my introductory psychology course. How likely do you think it is that the student will eat the slice of pizza? What information

should you have before you make your prediction? The last section gave you a way of organizing the extra information you need to acquire. You would want to know about *internal* information. How much has the student eaten already? Is the student trying to diet? You would also want to know about *external* information. Is the pizza tasty? Are friends there to share the pizza and conversation? You can see already that many motivational forces can influence even a simple outcome, such as whether someone is going to eat a slice of pizza. Let's begin with some of the physiological processes that evolution has provided to regulate eating.

The Physiology of Eating

When does your body tell you it's time to eat? You have been provided with a variety of mechanisms that contribute to your physical sense of hunger or satiety. To regulate food intake effectively, organisms must be equipped with mechanisms that accomplish four tasks: (1) detect internal food need, (2) initiate and organize eating behavior, (3) monitor the quantity and quality of the food eaten, and (4) detect when enough food has been consumed and stop eating. Researchers have tried to understand these processes by relating them either to *peripheral* mechanisms in different parts of the body, such as stomach contractions, or to *central* brain mechanisms, such as the functioning of the hypothalamus. Let's look at these processes in more detail.

Peripheral Responses   Where do sensations of hunger come from? Does your stomach send out distress signals to indicate that it is empty? A pioneering physiologist, **Walter Cannon** (1871–1945), believed that gastric activity in an empty stomach was the sole basis for hunger. To test this hypothesis, Cannon's intrepid student A. L. Washburn trained himself to swallow an uninflated balloon attached to a rubber tube. The other end of the tube was attached to a device that recorded changes in air pressure. Cannon then inflated the balloon in Washburn's stomach. As the student's stomach contracted, air was expelled from the balloon and activated the recording device. Reports of Washburn's hunger pangs were correlated with periods when the record showed his stomach was severely contracted. Cannon thought he had proved that stomach cramps were responsible for hunger (Cannon, 1934; Cannon & Washburn, 1912).

Although Cannon and Washburn's procedure was ingenious, later research showed that stomach contractions are not even a necessary condition for hunger. Injections of sugar into the bloodstream will stop the stomach contractions but not the hunger of an animal with an empty stomach. Human patients who have had their stomachs entirely removed still experience hunger pangs (Janowitz & Grossman, 1950), and rats without stomachs still learn mazes when rewarded with food (Penick et al., 1963). So, although sensations originating in the stomach may play a role in the way people usually experience hunger, they do not fully explain how the body detects its need for food and is motivated to eat.

Your empty stomach may not be necessary to feel hungry, but does a "full" stomach terminate eating? Research has shown that gastric pressure caused by food—but not by an inflated balloon—will cause an individual to end a meal (Logue, 1991). Thus the body is sensitive to the source of pressure in the stomach. The oral experience of food also provides a peripheral source of *satiety* cues—cues relevant to feelings of satiation or fullness. You may have noticed that you become less enthusiastic about the tastes of even your favorite foods over the course of a meal, a phenomenon called *sensory-specific satiety* (Remick et al., 2009). This reduction in interest for foods as you eat them may be one way in which your body regulates intake. However, the "specific" in sensory-specific satiety means that the satiety applies to specific flavors and not to the food itself. In one experiment, participants had reached satiety for particular foods, such as pineapple or cucumber. However, when the flavors of the food were slightly altered—by the addition of vanilla-flavored whipped cream or salt and pepper—people showed renewed interest in the foods (Romer et al., 2006). This body of research suggests that variety in food tastes—as is common in many multicourse meals—might counteract other bodily indications that you've already had enough to eat.

Let's turn now to the brain mechanisms involved in eating behaviors, where information from peripheral sources is gathered together. ✳

Central Responses As is often the case, simple theories about the brain centers for the initiation and cessation of eating have given way to more complex theories. The earliest theories of the brain control of eating were built around observations of the *lateral hypothalamus (LH)* and the *ventromedial hypothalamus (VMH)*. (The location of the hypothalamus is shown in Figure 3.16 on page 69.) Research showed that if the VMH was lesioned (or the LH stimulated), the animal consumed more food. If the procedure was reversed, so that the LH was lesioned (or the VMH stimulated), the animal consumed less food. These observations gave rise to the *dual-center model,* in which the LH was thought to be the "hunger center" and the VMH the "satiety center."

Over time, however, researchers provided additional data to suggest that this simple theory was incomplete

Why do people tend to eat more food when a variety of tastes are available?

(Gao & Horvath, 2007). For example, rats with VMH lesions only overeat foods they find palatable; they strongly avoid foods that don't taste good. Thus the VMH could not just be a simple center for signaling "eat more" or "don't eat more"—the signal depends on the type of food. In fact, destruction of the VMH may, in part, have the effect of exaggerating ordinary reflex responses to food (Powley, 1977). If the rat's reflex response to good-tasting food is to eat it, its exaggerated response will be to overeat. If the rat reflexively avoids bad-tasting food by gagging or vomiting, its exaggerated response could keep the rat from eating altogether. Researchers have also discovered that two other regions of the hypothalamus, known as the *arcuate nucleus* (ARC) and the *paraventicular nucleus* (PVN), supplement the roles of the VMH and LH to regulate eating.

Some of the most important information these hypothalamic regions use to regulate eating comes from your bloodstream (Gao & Horvath, 2007). For example, receptors monitor blood levels of sugar (in the form of glucose). The hormone *insulin* helps to regulate the level of glucose in the bloodstream. Glucose is one of the energy sources for metabolism. When stored glucose is low or unavailable for metabolism, signals from liver cell receptors are sent to the LH, where neurons acting as glucose detectors change their activity to initiate eating behavior. Other hypothalamic neurons respond to hormones that play contrasting roles in regulating appetite (Schloeg et al., 2011). For example, a hormone called *leptin* acts to inhibit eating. Recall from Chapter 5 that brain cannabinoids play a role in stimulating appetite. Leptin works in opposition to those cannabinoids to keep appetite under control (Jo et al., 2005). The hormone *ghrelin* is secreted by an empty stomach and promotes an awareness of hunger. By contrast, the hormone *cholecystokinin* (CCK) is secreted by your small intestine while you eat. CCK provides information to your brain that you are becoming full.

We have seen so far that you have body systems that are dedicated to getting you to start and to stop eating. You almost certainly know, however, from an enormous amount of personal experience, that your need for food depends on more than just the cues generated by your body. Let's look now at psychological factors that motivate you to eat more food or less food.

✳ **Explore** the **Concept** *Virtual Brain: Hunger and Eating* on **MyPsychLab**

The Psychology of Eating

You know now that your body is equipped with a variety of mechanisms that regulate the amount of food you eat. But do you eat only in response to hunger? You are likely to respond, "Of course not!" If you think back over the last couple of days, you can probably recall several occasions on which when and what you ate had little to do with hunger. This section on the psychology of eating will begin by reviewing the impact of culture on what and how much you eat. Next it will focus on some of the roots and consequences of obesity and dieting. We will then consider how eating disorders may arise as an extreme response to concerns about body image and weight.

Cultural Impact on Eating How do you decide when and what you should eat? To answer this question, first think about the impact of culture. For example, people in the United States typically eat three daily meals at set times; the timing of those meals relies more on social norms than on body cues. Moreover, people often choose what to eat based on social or cultural norms. Would you say yes if you were offered a free lobster dinner? Your answer might depend on whether, for example, you are an observant Jew (in which case you would say no) or a vegetarian (in which case your answer would still depend on whether you are the type of vegetarian who eats seafood). These examples suggest immediately why culture can trump your body's cues.

Let's look more closely at the culture of eating in the United States. One important source of information is the U.S. government, which serves a number of functions. First, the government regulates what counts as a "serving size" and what types of nutritional information food manufacturers must provide to their customers. Second, the government provides periodic advice on the components of a healthy diet. For example, the U.S. Department of Agriculture (2010) issues publications such as *Dietary Guidelines for Americans*. This publication provides general advice about weight management and physical exercise as well as specific recommendations about how individuals can maintain a healthy diet. The government's publications reflect the current state of scientific knowledge: Recommendations change over time as research advances. You can be quite certain that the dietary guidelines will change again in your lifetime. As with any other type of research-based advice, it's important for you to understand how data support the recommendations as they evolve.

Unfortunately, other aspects of U.S. culture work against recommendations for healthy eating. For example, unhealthy food is relatively inexpensive compared to healthy food. People with limited amounts of money might find a healthy diet relatively unaffordable. This observation has led to the suggestion that people's nutrition would improve if the price differential between healthy and unhealthy food changed (Andreyeva et al., 2010). Consider a study in which researchers worked with an Alabama deli to decrease prices on healthy foods (Horgen & Brownell, 2002). When the healthy food cost less, people ate more of it. This type of research supports the conclusion that some barriers to healthy eating are the product of economic constraints.

Obesity and Dieting Psychologists have spent a good deal of time considering circumstances that have given rise to what has often been labeled an "epidemic" of obesity. To determine who is overweight and who is obese, researchers often turn to a measure called *body mass index (BMI)*. To calculate BMI, one divides an individual's weight in kilograms by the square of height in meters. For example, someone who weighed 154 lb and was 5'7" would have a BMI of 24.2. (154 lb = 69.8 kilograms. 5'7" = 1.70 meters. 69.8/(1.70)2 = 24.2). (You can also use Google to find a BMI calculator on the Web.) In most instances, individuals who have BMIs between 25 and 29.9 are considered overweight. Those individuals with BMIs 30 and above are considered obese. By those standards, roughly 34.2 percent of U.S. adults are overweight and 39.5 percent are obese (Ogden & Carroll, 2010). Among children and adolescents, 31.6 percent are overweight and 16.4 percent are obese (Singh et al., 2010).

These figures suggest why there's a certain urgency to answer the question, Why do people become overweight? It probably will not surprise you that, as you have seen throughout *Psychology and Life*, the answer lies partly in nature: Some people have a genetic predisposition toward obesity. Researchers have provided ample evidence that people are born with innate tendencies to be lighter or heavier. For example, studies of monozygotic (identical) twins reveal higher correlations for BMI and other measures of body size than those for dizygotic (fraternal) twins (Schousboe et al., 2004; Silventoinen et al., 2007). That consistent pattern provides strong evidence for a genetic influence on people's weight.

Researchers have begun to discover some of the genetic mechanisms that may predispose some individuals to obesity (Ramachandrappa & Farooqi, 2011). For example, a gene has been isolated that influences the production of the hormone leptin, which, as you will recall from the earlier section, plays a role in appetite control. If leptin fails to play its critical role, people may overeat. Thus the gene that controls leptin appears to have a critical influence on weight regulation and the potential for obesity (Gautron & Elmquist, 2011). Evidence is also accumulating that genes and environments interact to define the risk of obesity. For example, on average people are about 3.3 pounds heavier for each "minor" version of the *FTO* gene they inherit. However, researchers have demonstrated that adolescents who engage in more than 60 minutes of moderate to vigorous physical activity a day experience less of the negative impact of that risky version of the gene (Ruiz et al., 2010). Among students with relatively lower physical activity, those who inherited two copies of the risky version of the gene had substantially higher BMIs. However, the students who had the same genetic inheritance—but who were more physically active—didn't differ in BMI from their peers.

How do interactions of genes and physical activity affect the risk of obesity?

This result reminds you again why we must always monitor the mutual impact of nature and nurture.

Genetic approaches to obesity largely focus on the regulation of internal hunger cues. However, as we've already seen, people's choices are not just dictated by hunger. What matters, in addition, is the way in which an individual *thinks* about food and eating behaviors. Early research on psychological aspects of eating focused on the extent to which overweight individuals are attentive to their bodies' internal hunger cues versus food in the external environment (Schachter, 1971b). The suggestion was that, when food is available and prominent, overweight individuals ignore the cues their bodies give them. This theory proved to be insufficient, however, because weight itself does not always predict eating patterns. That is, not all people who are overweight have the same psychological makeup with respect to eating behaviors. Let's see why.

Janet Polivy and **Peter Herman** have proposed that the critical dimension that underlies the psychology of eating behaviors is *restrained* versus *unrestrained* eating (Polivy & Herman, 1999). *Restrained* eaters put constant limits on the amount of food they will let themselves eat: They are chronically on diets; they constantly worry about food. Although obese people may be more likely to report these kinds of thoughts and behaviors, individuals can be restrained eaters whatever their body size. How do people gain weight if they are constantly on a diet? Research suggests that when restrained eaters become *disinhibited*—when life circumstances cause them to let down their restraints—they tend to indulge in high-calorie binges. Unfortunately, many types of life circumstances appear to lead restrained eaters to become disinhibited. Disinhibition will occur, for example, when restrained eaters are made to feel stress about their capabilities and self-esteem (Tanofsky-Kraff et al., 2000; Wallis & Hetherington, 2004). Let's see what happens when restrained eaters believe they've already overeaten.

*Based on self-evaluations of their behaviors and thoughts with respect to food and dieting, female college students were classified as either restrained or unrestrained eaters. The students believed they were taking part in market research. At the study's outset, the researchers asked each participant to eat a slice of pizza. They explained that the pizza was intended "to ensure that [all participants] had the same taste experience and same level of fullness before completing taste ratings" (Polivy et al., 2010, p. 427). The researchers gave each participant exactly the same size slice of pizza. However, some participants believed that their slice was larger than those others would get (because it was on a tray with a smaller slice); other participants believed that their slice was smaller than those others would get (because it was on a tray with a larger slice). Next, all the participants had the opportunity to taste chocolate chip cookies. **Figure 11.2** shows how much participants ate. As you can see, when restrained eaters believed that they had already overeaten—by having an extra-large slice of pizza—they lost restraint and consumed a considerably greater amount of the cookies.*

This result suggests how easily restrained eaters can become disinhibited. Recall that the actual slice of pizza was the same in all cases. It was the restrained eaters' perception of what they had eaten (as being larger than the slices others would get) that made them feel that they had already blown their diets.

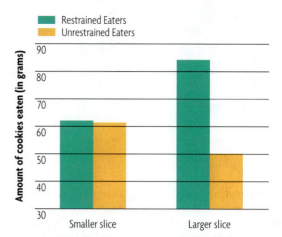

FIGURE 11.2 The Effects of Perceptions on Food Consumption

Restrained and unrestrained eaters were led to believe that they had consumed a slice of pizza that was smaller or larger than the slices offered to other participants. In fact, all the slices they ate were exactly the same size. Next, the participants tasted chocolate chip cookies. The restrained eaters who believed they had eaten a larger slice ate the greatest amount of cookies.

You see now why it might be difficult for people to lose weight once they have become overweight. Many overweight people report themselves as constantly on diets—they are often restrained eaters. If stressful life events occur that cause these eaters to become disinhibited, binge eating can easily lead to weight gain. Thus the psychological consequences of being constantly on a diet can, paradoxically, create circumstances that are more likely to lead to weight gain than to weight loss. In the next section, we will see how these same psychological forces can lead to health- and life-threatening eating disorders.

Eating Disorders We have already seen that people's internal cues—the hunger they experience—only partially determine how much they eat. For people with *eating disorders*, the mismatch between the body's internal signals and their eating behavior becomes particularly dramatic. **Anorexia nervosa** is diagnosed when an individual weighs less than 85 percent of her or his expected weight but still expresses an intense fear of becoming fat (*DSM-IV-TR*, 2000). The behavior of people diagnosed with **bulimia nervosa** is characterized by binges—periods of intense, out-of-control eating—followed by measures to purge the body of the excess calories—self-induced vomiting, misuse of laxatives, fasting, and so on (*DS-IV-TR*, 2000). Sufferers of anorexia nervosa may also binge and then purge as a way of minimizing calories absorbed. Both of these syndromes can have serious medical consequences. In the worst cases, sufferers may starve to death.

....

● **Watch** the **Video** *In the Real World: Eating Disorders* on **MyPsychLab**

anorexia nervosa An eating disorder in which an individual weighs less than 85 percent of her or his expected weight but still expresses intense fear of becoming fat.

bulimia nervosa An eating disorder characterized by binge eating followed by measures to purge the body of excess calories.

Table 11.1 • Prevalence of Eating Disorders

	Women	Men
Anorexia nervosa	0.9%	0.3%
Bulimia nervosa	1.5	0.5
Binge eating disorder	3.5	2.0

Note: Each figure is the percent of the sample of 9,282 U.S. adults who had experienced the disorder in his or her lifetime.

Binge eating disorder is diagnosed when people engage in regular episodes of binge eating without the purges that accompany bulimia nervosa. People who suffer from this disorder feel, during their binges, that they have lost control; the binges cause them great distress. Compared to anorexia and bulimia, binge eating disorder is a relatively new diagnostic category. Chapter 14 presents a *Critical Thinking in Your Life* box that discusses its emergence. The focus here will be on anorexia and bulimia because larger bodies of research have examined their causes.

Table 11.1 presents the prevalence for each eating disorder. These data are drawn from face-to-face interviews of 9,282 men and women in the United States, ages 18 and over (Hudson et al., 2007). Table 11.1 shows that women suffer from these disorders more than men. However, the difference in prevalence has become smaller in the last few years. Earlier estimates suggested that women suffered from anorexia and bulimia at approximately 10 times the rate of men (*DSM-IV-TR*, 2000). However, the data in Table 11.1 show only a three-to-one ratio between women and men. As you read about the causes of eating disorders, you will learn why the gap might be closing.

Research on the causes of eating disorders has confirmed the importance of genetic factors. There is evidence that a predilection toward eating disorders may be genetically transmitted (Calati et al., 2011; Campbell et al. 2011). One study followed pairs of female twins longitudinally from ages 11 to 18 (Klump et al., 2007). The researchers made comparisons between monozygotic (MZ) and dizygotic (DZ) twins of the sort you have encountered before. The data revealed that genetics played a larger role as the twins got older: Over the seven-year period, MZ twins tended to remain similar, whereas, by mid to late adolescence, greater differences emerged within the pairs of the DZ twins. This pattern suggests that genetic risk mattered more as the young girls passed through puberty. Researchers have also conducted twin studies to explore personality variables that may put people at risk for eating disorders. For example, female twins who had high levels of perfectionism (such as concerns over mistakes or doubts about actions) were also more likely to be diagnosed with anorexia (Wade et al., 2008). If this general drive for perfection leads people to seek a "perfect" body, eating disorders may be a consequence.

In fact, high levels of *body dissatisfaction*—discomfort with weight, body shape, and appearance—put people at risk for eating disorders (Lynch et al., 2008). For many people with eating disorders, body dissatisfaction is not related to their actual bodies but to their own inaccurate perceptions of their bodies.

....

binge eating disorder An eating disorder characterized by out-of-control binge eating without subsequent purges.

People with anorexia who are perceived by others as dangerously thin often look in the mirror and still perceive themselves as overweight. Consider a study that looks at the brain bases of these misperceptions.

Ten women with anorexia and 10 control women (without the disorder) underwent fMRI scans while they viewed a series of digital images (Sachdev et al., 2008). Each participant had a personalized set of images: Half of the images showed each woman herself; the other half were images of another woman matched for age and body mass index. The women were all photographed wearing the same outfit that made the body's contour easy to detect. Finally, so that participants would pay most attention to the bodies, the faces in the images were obscured. As they viewed each image, participants were told whether it was a self-image or an other-image. For women in the control group, the fMRI scans revealed the same patterns of brain activity when they studied both types of images. However, for the women with anorexia the patterns for self-images and other-images were quite distinct. For example, when viewing self-images, women with anorexia showed less activity in brain regions that allow people to obtain accurate information from the external world.

Featured Study

An important aspect of this result is that the women with anorexia showed entirely normal patterns of brain activity when looking at the bodies of other women. Only the self-images yielded unusual patterns of brain activity.

Research on body dissatisfaction has yielded consistent group differences in judgments about body size (Roberts et al., 2006). For example, in one study of women ages 25–45, White women revealed themselves to be less satisfied with their bodies than did their Black peers. In addition, when asked to choose a drawing to represent their preferred size, White women chose smaller figures than Black women (Kronenfeld et al., 2010). To explain these differences between Black and White women, researchers often call attention to the role cultural norms and media plays in shaping White women's expectations for their ideal weight and ideal bodies (Durkin & Paxton, 2002; Striegel-Moore & Bulik, 2007). In one study, Black and White college women rated their body dissatisfaction before viewing a PowerPoint presentation of women who represented the "mass media ideal" (DeBraganza & Hausenblas, 2010, p. 706). After watching the presentation, the students rated their body dissatisfaction a second time. The Black students' scores remained unchanged. However, the White women's ratings of their body dissatisfaction went up after being reminded of the media ideal.

Against this background, you will probably not be surprised to learn that White females are also more likely to suffer from eating disorders than are Black females. One study involved 985 White women and 1,061 Black women who were all about 21 years of age (Striegel-Moore et al., 2003). In those groups, 1.5 percent of the White women had suffered from anorexia nervosa at some point in their lives; no Black women had experienced that disorder. Bulimia nervosa had affected 2.3 percent of the White women but only 0.4 percent of the Black women. Fewer studies have examined other racial and ethnic groups, but evidence to date suggests that eating disturbances are also less frequent in Asian Americans than Whites but equally as common among Hispanic females as among

What do these photographs of Nicole Richie and Marilyn Monroe suggest about changes over time in how thin women must be for the media to promote them as sexy?

whites. For each of these findings, researchers try to draw a link between cultural values about body size and dieting behaviors.

To close out this section, let's return to the decreasing gap in the prevalence of eating disorders for women and for men. Researchers have begun to study the impact of media images on men's body dissatisfaction. That research interest has emerged because, in the last decade, the number of media images of thin, muscular men has grown considerably. In general, men who view images of ideal male bodies experience increases in body dissatisfaction (Blond, 2008). One study, for example, measured the extent to which Euro-American and Hispanic men in the United States agreed with statements such as "I believe that clothes look better on men that are in good physical shape" and "I wish I looked like men pictured in magazines who model underwear" (Warren, 2008, p. 260). The men from both groups who most agreed with media norms for male appearance also reported the most body dissatisfaction. Other research suggests that men who are dissatisfied, in particular, with their amount of body fat are likely to have disordered eating (Smith et al., 2011). Although a causal link must still be demonstrated, these studies support the speculation that changes in media representations of men's bodies have led to the increasing prevalence of male eating disorders.

Stop *and* Review

① What is sensory-specific satiety?
② What evidence suggests that the VMH plays a different role in eating from that suggested by the dual-center model?
③ What pattern of eating do restrained eaters generally follow?
④ What are the symptoms of bulimia nervosa?

CRITICAL THINKING Recall the study that demonstrated differences in brain responses for women with anorexia. Why were the photographs matched for age and body mass index?

✓●⊣ **Study** and **Review** on **MyPsychLab**

SEXUAL BEHAVIORS

Your body physiology makes it essential that you think about food every day. Eating is essential to individual survival. But what about sex? Sexual behaviors are biologically necessary only for reproduction. Sex is not necessary for your survival as an individual. Some animals and humans remain celibate for a lifetime without apparent detriment to their daily functioning. But reproduction is crucial to the survival of the species as a whole. To ensure that effort will be expended toward reproduction, nature has made sexual stimulation intensely pleasurable. An orgasm serves as the ultimate reinforcer for the energy expended in mating.

This potential for pleasure gives to sexual behaviors motivating power well beyond the need for reproduction. Individuals will perform a great variety of behaviors to achieve sexual gratification. But some sources of sexual motivation are external. Cultures establish norms or standards for what is acceptable or expected sexual behavior. Whereas most people may be motivated to perform behaviors that accord with those norms, some people achieve their sexual satisfaction primarily by violating them.

This section will first consider some of what is known about the sex drive and mating behavior in nonhuman animals. Then we shift our attention to selected issues in human sexuality.

Nonhuman Sexual Behaviors

The primary motivation for sexual behaviors in nonhuman animals is reproduction. For species that use sex as a means of reproduction, evolution has generally provided two sexual

Psychology in Your Life

HOW DOES THE PRESENCE OF OTHERS INFLUENCE YOUR EATING?

Think back to the last meal you shared with other people. Do you think you ate more, less, or about the same amount you would have eaten if you'd been eating alone? Research suggests that the social context—the presence of others—is an important external cue that affects people's eating. In fact, when you eat with others your most important motive may be to produce a positive impression (Herman et al., 2003). Let's see what impact that motive has.

Consider a study in which college students had 10-minute conversations with their romantic partners, friends, or strangers (Salvy et al., 2007). To make the conversations more "convivial," the researchers provided bowls of cookies and crackers. At the end of each conversation, the researchers determined how much food each participant had consumed. The amounts differed substantially across the different pairings: Males chatting with male friends ate the most; females chatting with male strangers ate the least. Can you see how those results might emerge if the participants were motivated to make a positive impression?

A similar study examined the impact of social context on food consumption for overweight and normal-weight children (Salvy et al., 2008). The 10- to 12-year-old participants visited the laboratory for two sessions. In one session, the children played and ate snacks on their own. In the other session, the children played and ate snacks in a peer's company. The normal-weight children ate about the same amount of food in both sessions. However, the overweight children consistently

ate *less* while they were with a peer. These results suggest that the overweight children controlled their eating to make a positive impression.

The researchers discussed their results in the context of changes that have taken place in family's eating patterns over the last decades—the "trend away from family meals towards grazing and eating alone" (p. 195). They suggested that, historically, children may have learned to limit food consumption in the context of meals with parents and siblings. The absence of that social context could explain some aspects of the increase in childhood obesity. The researchers suggest that social interventions—returning to circumstances in which children eat in the presence of others—could help overweight children eat less.

A final thought on the social context of eating: People tend to underestimate greatly its influence. In one study, pairs of students were able to eat pizza while watching a video together. Within the pairs, the correlation for pizza consumption was 0.64. Even so, when asked why they had eaten the amount they had, only 3 out of 122 participants mentioned being influenced by their companion's consumption (Vartanian et al., 2008). The participants were much more likely to mention other factors such as how hungry they felt, the time since the last meal, or how good the food tasted.

The next time you eat with other people, try to think about how your consumption might reflect your desire to provide a particular impression.

---

types, males and females. The female produces relatively large eggs (which contain the energy store for the embryo to begin its growth), and the male produces sperm that are specialized for motility (to move into the eggs). The two sexes must synchronize their activity so that sperm and egg meet under the appropriate conditions, resulting in conception.

Sexual arousal is determined primarily by physiological processes. Animals become receptive to mating largely in response to the flow of hormones controlled by the pituitary gland and secreted from the *gonads,* the sex organs. In males, these hormones are known as *androgens,* and they are continuously present in sufficient supply so that males are hormonally ready for mating at almost any time. In the females of many species, however, the sex hormone *estrogen* is released according to regular time cycles of days or months, or according to seasonal changes. Therefore, the female is not always hormonally receptive to mating.

These hormones act on both the brain and genital tissue and often lead to a pattern of predictable *stereotyped sexual behavior* for all members of a species. If, for example, you've seen one pair of rats in their mating sequence, you've seen them

all. Much of the sequence is taken up by the male chasing the female. Every so often the female makes herself available, and the pair copulates briefly. Apes also copulate only briefly (for about 15 seconds). For sables, copulation is slow and long, lasting for as long as 8 hours. Predators, such as lions, can afford to indulge in long, slow copulatory rituals—as much as every 30 minutes over 4 consecutive days. Their prey, however, such as antelope, copulate for only a few seconds, often on the run (Ford & Beach, 1951).

Sexual arousal is often initiated by stimuli in the external environment. In many species, the sight and sound of ritualized display patterns by potential partners is a necessary condition for sexual response. Furthermore, in species as diverse as sheep, bulls, and rats, the novelty of the female partner affects a male animal's behavior. A male that has reached sexual satiation with one female partner may renew sexual activity when a new female is introduced (Dewsbury, 1981). Touch, taste, and smell can also serve as external stimulants for sexual arousal. As you learned in Chapter 4, some species secrete chemical signals, called *pheromones,* that attract suitors, sometimes from great distances (Herbst et al., 2011; Yang et al., 2011). In many

What factors determine the sexual behaviors of most species?

species, the female emits pheromones when her fertility is optimal (and hormone level and sexual interest are peaking). These secretions are unconditioned stimuli for arousal and attraction in the males of the species, who have inherited the tendency to be aroused by the stimuli.

Although sexual response in nonhuman animals is largely determined by innate biological forces, this still leaves room for "cultural" aspects to affect choices of mate. Consider the Atlantic molly, a particular species of fish.

Under most circumstances, male Atlantic mollies show a mating preference for larger females. However, what happens when a male molly observes another male showing a preference for a smaller female? To answer this question, researchers arranged a set of tanks so that male mollies swam in a large tank that had smaller tanks at each end (Bierbach et al., 2011). In the initial phase of the experiment, a large and a small female fish were put into small tanks at either end. The males spent considerably more time swimming in proximity to the larger female. In the second phase of the experiment, a second male was placed in another small tank so that he appeared to be swimming near the smaller of the two females. The original males had 20 minutes to observe the second male fraternizing with the smaller female. In the final phase of the experiment, the researchers removed the second male and again observed the original males' preferences. In the second preference test, the males' behavior had shifted so that they now spent considerably more time swimming near the smaller females. Their preferences had shifted to copy those of the other male!

Are you surprised to learn that innocent fish swimming in aquariums are paying attention to which fish have been judged desirable and undesirable? This experiment sets the stage for the discussion of human sexuality. We will soon see that researchers believe that human sexual response is also shaped both by our evolutionary history and the preferences of those around us.

Human Sexual Arousal and Response

Hormonal activity, so important in regulating sexual behavior among other animal species, has relatively little effect on sexual receptiveness or gratification in the majority of men

and women. Individual differences in hormone levels, within normal limits, are not predictive of the frequency or quality of sexual activity. However, when hormone levels fall below normal levels because of illness or aging, there is often a negative impact on sexual desire. This is particularly true for the hormone *testosterone*. Both men and women experience restored sexual desire when they undergo treatments that supplement low testosterone levels (Davison & Davis, 2011; Allan et al., 2008). Still, men who have undergone surgical castration (and, therefore, no longer produce testosterone) often continue to experience some level of sexual desire, illustrating that human sexuality is motivated by more than hormones (Weinberger et al., 2005).

Sexual arousal in humans is the motivational state of excitement and tension brought about by physiological and cognitive reactions to erotic stimuli. *Erotic stimuli*, which may be physical or psychological, give rise to sexual excitement or feelings of passion. Sexual arousal induced by erotic stimuli is reduced by sexual activities that are perceived by the individual as satisfying, especially by achieving orgasm.

Researchers have studied sexual practices and sexual responses in nonhuman animals for several decades, but for many years studies of similar behaviors in humans were off limits. **William Masters** and **Virginia Johnson** (1966, 1970, 1979) broke down this traditional taboo. They legitimized the study of human sexuality by directly observing and recording, under laboratory conditions, the physiological patterns involved in ongoing human sexual performance. By doing so, they explored not what people said about sex but how individuals actually reacted or performed sexually.

For their direct investigation of the human response to sexual stimulation, Masters and Johnson conducted controlled laboratory observations of thousands of volunteer males and females during tens of thousands of sexual response cycles of intercourse and masturbation. Four of the most significant conclusions drawn from this research are that (1) men and women have similar patterns of sexual response; (2) although the sequence of phases of the sexual response cycle is similar

How did William Masters and Virginia Johnson legitimize the study of human sexuality?

sexual arousal The motivational state of excitement and tension brought about by physiological and cognitive reactions to erotic stimuli.

FIGURE 11.3 Phases of Human Sexual Response
The phases of human sexual response in males and females have similar patterns. The primary differences are in the time it takes for males and females to reach each phase and in the greater likelihood that females will achieve multiple orgasms.

in the two sexes, women are more variable, tending to respond more slowly but often remaining aroused longer; (3) many women can have multiple orgasms, whereas men rarely do in a comparable time period; and (4) penis size is generally unrelated to any aspect of sexual performance (except in the male's attitude toward having a large penis).

Four phases were found in the human sexual response cycle: excitement, plateau, orgasm, and resolution (see **Figure 11.3**).

- In the excitement phase (lasting from a few minutes to more than an hour), there are vascular (blood vessel) changes in the pelvic region. The penis becomes erect and the clitoris swells; blood and other fluids become congested in the testicles and vagina; a reddening of the body, or sex flush, occurs.
- During the plateau phase, a maximum (though varying) level of arousal is reached. There are rapidly increased heartbeat, respiration, and blood pressure, increased glandular secretions, and both voluntary and involuntary muscle tension throughout the body. Vaginal lubrication increases, and the breasts swell.
- During the orgasm phase, males and females experience a very intense, pleasurable sense of release from the sexual tension that has been building. Orgasm is characterized by rhythmic contractions that occur approximately every eight-tenths of a second in the genital areas. Respiration and blood pressure reach very high levels in both men and women, and heart rate may double. In men, throbbing contractions lead to ejaculation.
- During the resolution phase, the body gradually returns to its normal preexcitement state, with both blood pressure and heartbeat slowing down. After one orgasm, most men enter a refractory period, lasting anywhere from a few minutes to several hours, during which no further orgasm is possible. With sustained arousal, some women are capable of multiple orgasms in fairly rapid succession.

Although Masters and Johnson's research focused on the physiology of sexual response, perhaps their most important discovery was the central significance of *psychological* processes in both arousal and satisfaction. They demonstrated that problems in sexual response often have psychological, rather than physiological, origins and can be modified or overcome through therapy. Of particular concern is the inability to

complete the response cycle and achieve gratification. Often the source of the inability is a preoccupation with personal problems, fear of the consequences of sexual activity, anxiety about a partner's evaluation of one's sexual performance, or unconscious guilt or negative thoughts. However, poor nutrition, fatigue, stress, and excessive use of alcohol or drugs can also diminish sexual drive and performance.

We have now reviewed some physiological aspects of human sexuality and sexual arousal. But we have not yet considered the forces that give rise to *differences* in sexual expression. We begin with the idea that the goal of reproduction ensures different patterns of sexual behavior for men and for women.

The Evolution of Sexual Behaviors

For nonhuman animals, we have already seen that the pattern of sexual behaviors was largely fixed by evolution. The main goal is reproduction—preservation of the species—and sexual behaviors are highly ritualized and stereotyped. Can the same claim be made for general patterns of human sexual behaviors?

Evolutionary psychologists have explored the idea that men and women have evolved to have different *strategies* that underlie sexual behavior (Buss, 2008). To describe these strategies, I have to remind you of some of the realities of human reproduction. Human males could reproduce hundreds of times a year if they could find enough willing mates. To produce a child, all they need to invest is a few minutes of intercourse. Women can reproduce at most about once a year, and each child then requires a huge investment of time and energy. (Incidentally, the world record for the number of times a woman has given birth falls short of 50, but men have fathered many more children. A Moroccan despot, King Ismail the Blood-Thirsty, fathered over 700 children, and the first emperor of China is said to have fathered over 3,000; both had large harems.) 👁

Thus, when reproduction is an objective, eggs are the limited resource and males compete for opportunities to fertilize them. The basic goal for a male animal is to maximize the number of offspring he produces, by mating with the largest number of females possible. But the basic goal for a female animal is to find a high-quality male to ensure the best, healthiest offspring from her limited store of eggs. Furthermore, human offspring take so long to mature and are so helpless while growing that substantial **parental investment** is required (Bell, 2001; Sear & Mace, 2008). Mothers and fathers must spend time and energy raising the children—unlike fish or spiders, which simply lay eggs and depart. Females thus have the problem of selecting not just the biggest, strongest, smartest, highest-status, most thrilling mate but also the most loyal, committed partner to help raise their children.

One evolutionary psychologist, **David Buss** (2008), has suggested that men and women evolved different strategies, emotions, and motivations for short-term mating versus long-term mating. The male strategy of seducing and abandoning as many women as possible—showing signs of loyalty and commitment and then leaving—is a short-term strategy. The male strategy of staying committed to the female and investing in

....

👁 **Watch** the **Video** *The Big Picture: The Power of Sex* on **MyPsychLab**

parental investment The time and energy parents must spend raising their offspring.

the offspring is a long-term strategy. The female strategy of attracting a loyal male who will stay to help raise her children is a long-term strategy. The female strategy of acquiring resources or obtaining men of high status is a short-term strategy. Because these claims about men's and women's differing strategies are based on evolutionary analyses, researchers have sought cross-cultural data to support them. For example, one study involved over 16,000 participants from 52 nations (Schmitt, 2003). The men and women in the study provided information about their interest in short-term sexual relationships. Across the whole sample, men consistently reported greater desire for sexual variety than did women. This result supports the evolutionary claim that men's and women's different reproductive roles have an impact on sexual behavior.

Researchers have provided a variety of types of evidence to support the evolutionary perspective on human sexual response. In recent years, particular attention has focused on the way in which men's and women's behavior changes when women are in the fertile period of their menstrual cycle, in the time around ovulation. Let's consider an experiment that required women to judge men as straight or gay. (Note that the chapter's next section provides a discussion of homosexuality.)

A team of researchers suggested that "a disposition toward mating increases heterosexual women's accuracy in detecting the sexual orientation of members of the opposite sex" (Rule et al., 2011, p. 824). To test that hypothesis, the researchers had 40 heterosexual women view a series of 80 photographs of men. Forty of the men in the photographs self-identified as straight and 40 self-identified as gay. The women's task was to guess at each man's sexual orientation. After completing judgments of the photographs, each woman provided information that allowed the researchers to estimate where she was in her menstrual cycle. **Figure 11.4** *shows that the women's accuracy was best when they were closest to the time of ovulation.*

Featured Study

These data support the idea that, when women are most likely to get pregnant, they are also more careful about judging the qualities of the men (which is important toward women's long-term

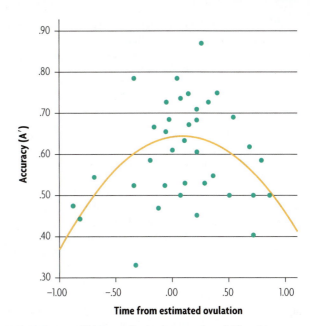

FIGURE 11.4 Women's Judgments of Men's Sexual Orientation

Women were more accurate at correctly judging men as gay or straight when they were closest to the time of ovulation. Note that A′ is a measure of accuracy where 0.50 means participants were guessing. Each point represents an individual woman's performance. The curved line indicates the general trend across the group of women.

From Nicholas O. Rule, Katherine S. Rosen, Michael L. Slepian, Nalini Ambady, "Mating interest improves women's accuracy in judging male sexual orientation," Psychological Science, 22, pages 881-886, copyright © 2011 the Association for Psychological Science. Reprinted by permission of Sage Publications.

mating strategy). Other research supports the hypothesis that men can detect when women are ovulating and that they change their behavior in response (Haselton & Gildersleeve, 2011). For example, men made more risky decisions in a laboratory version of blackjack when they played in the company of a woman who was in the fertile phase of her menstrual cycle (Miller & Maner, 2011). Risk taking signals personality characteristics such as confidence and ambition that, according to the evolutionary perspective, women find attractive when making mate selections. Thus, these results suggest that men shift their behavior to appear more attractive when women are ovulating. Bear in mind that the men are not aware that the women are in a fertile phase. These behavioral changes are unconscious responses!

Although research supports many of the predictions of the evolutionary account of human sexual behaviors, other theorists believe that the account greatly underestimates the role of culture (Eastwick et al., 2006; Perrin et al., 2011). Consider circumstances in which people cheat on their partners by having sexual relationships with other individuals. An evolutionary analysis suggests that men should be more likely to cheat than women—because they are motivated to seek multiple partners. However, research suggests that cheating is more a function of the amount of power people have, for example, in their occupations (Lammers et al., 2011). As both men and women accrue power, they are more likely to cheat on their partners. The appearance that men are more likely to be cheaters arises from the cultural reality that men are more likely to have power.

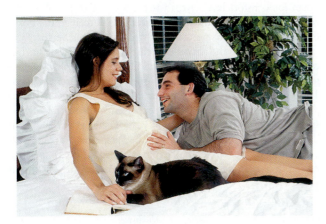

Although sex fulfills the biological function of reproduction, most humans engage in sex many more times than they reproduce. Even so, how does the evolutionary perspective explain contemporary sexual strategies?

Although the evolutionary approach explains some aspects of human sexual behavior, the critique calls attention to variability imposed by culture. Norms of sexual behavior are highly sensitive to time and place. We turn now to sexual norms.

Sexual Norms

What is an average sex life like? Scientific investigation of human sexual behavior was given the first important impetus by the work of **Alfred Kinsey** and his colleagues beginning in the 1940s (1948, 1953). They interviewed some 17,000 Americans about their sexual behavior and revealed—to a generally shocked public—that certain behaviors, previously considered rare and even abnormal, were actually quite widespread—or at least were reported to be. The norms for sexual behavior have changed over the years, in part because of scientific advances. For example, the availability of birth control pills in the early 1960s allowed women more sexual freedom because it reduced the likelihood of pregnancy. The arrival of Viagra in 1998 allowed men to prolong their years of sexual activity. Alongside the impact of science, there has been a general trend in many cultures toward more open discourse about sexual issues. **Table 11.2** indicates the percent of large representative samples of high school students in the United States who have engaged in sexual activities (U.S. Department of Health and Human Services, 2010). As you can see, the rate of sexual intercourse over the last 20 years has decreased while the rate of condom use has increased.

These sexual norms are part of what people acquire as a member of a culture. You already saw that some general "male" and "female" aspects of sexual behavior may be products of the evolution of the human species. Even so, different cultures define ranges of behavior that are considered to be appropriate for expressing sexual impulses. **Sexual scripts** are socially learned programs of sexual responsiveness that include prescriptions, usually unspoken, of what to do; when, where, and how to do it; with whom, or with what, to do it; and why it should be done (Krahé et al., 2007; Seal et al., 2008). Different aspects of these scripts are assembled through social interaction over your lifetime. The attitudes and values embodied in your sexual script are an external source of sexual motivation: The script suggests the types of behaviors you might or should undertake. 👁

Let's focus more specifically on the sexual practices of college students. Researchers have often been interested in understanding the decisions students make about their sexual activities—and how students feel about those decisions. For example, in one sample of 152 sexually active college women,

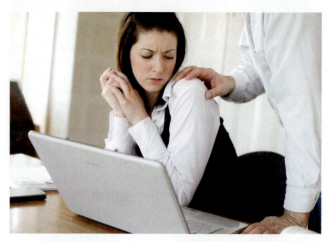

How might instances of sexual harassment arise from conflicting sexual scripts?

77 percent expressed at least "a few" regrets about their sexual decisions (Eshbaugh & Gute, 2008). Two particular behaviors prompted the most intense regret. First, "engaging in intercourse with someone once and only once" (p. 83), something 36 percent of the women reported having done. Second, "engaging in intercourse with someone known for less than 24 [hours]" (p. 83), something 29 percent of the women said they had done. You may recognize those behaviors as part of the definition of "hooking up" (Bogle, 2008). Another study of 327 college undergraduates defined "hooking up" as "a sexual encounter between two people who may or may not know each other well, but who usually are *not* seriously dating" (Lambert et al., 2003, p. 131). Given that definition, 78 percent of the women and 84 percent of the men reported that they had hooked up. The researchers also asked the students who had hooked up to make two judgments: The students rated how comfortable they personally were with the amount of hooking up that went on at their school; they also rated how comfortable the *average* student was with the amount of hooking up. As you can see in **Figure 11.5**, men reported themselves more comfortable with hooking up than did women. However, what you also see is that people's self-ratings were consistently lower than their guesses about others' comfort levels. Thus, the true norm for comfort level (which is the average of people's self-reports) was lower than what the students perceived the norm to be! How might this perception affect people's behaviors?

Research into the sexual experience of college students has revealed an area in which male and female sexual scripts come into devastating conflict: *rape*. In one study, researchers asked 4,446 women at two- or four-year colleges and universities to provide information about their experiences of sexual aggression in seven months of a school year (Fisher et al., 2000). In that reference period, 1.7 percent had experienced rape and 1.1 percent of the women had experienced attempted rape. The researchers extended those numbers to estimate the likelihood

---

Table 11.2 • Sexual Behaviors among Students in 9th through 12th Grade

	1991	2001	2009
Ever had sexual intercourse	54.1	45.6	46.0
Had sexual intercourse with four or more persons	18.7	14.2	13.8
Used a condom during last sexual intercourse	46.2	57.9	61.1

U.S. Department of Health and Human Services. (2010). *Trends in the prevalence of sexual behaviors.* Retrieved from www.cdc.gov/HealthyYouth/yrbs/pdf/us_sexual_trend_yrbs.pdf.

....

👁 **Watch** the **Video** *Special Topics: Cultural Norms and Sexual Behavior* on **MyPsychLab**

sexual script Socially learned program of sexual responsiveness.

date rape Unwanted sexual violation by social acquaintance in the context of a consensual dating situation.

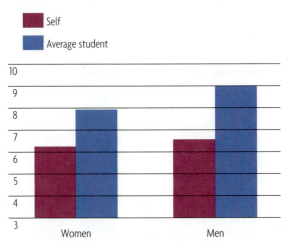

Self

Average student

FIGURE 11.5 Judgments about Hooking Up

College students provided ratings on a scale of 1 (not at all comfortable) to 11 (very comfortable) to two questions about "hooking up." For the self ratings, they indicated how comfortable they personally were with the amount of hooking up that went on at their school. For the average student ratings, they indicated how comfortable they believed the average student was with the amount of hooking up.

Data from "Pluralistic ignorance and hooking up" by Tracy A. Lambert, Arnold S. Kahn and Kevin J. Apple, *Journal of Sex Research 40*(2), 2003, pages 129–133. Reprinted by permission of Taylor & Francis Group, http://www.informaworld.com

that a woman would experience rape or attempted rape during her college career: They concluded that the number of victimized women might climb to 20 to 25 percent. The researchers also examined a particular type of rape: **date rape.** Date rape applies to circumstances in which someone is coerced into sexual activity by a social acquaintance. For this sample of women, 12.8 percent of rapes and 35.0 percent of attempted rapes occurred on dates. Researchers have documented that men and women have different *date rate scripts*. In one study, college men and women read the same account of a scenario in which a woman had resisted having sex (Clark & Carroll, 2008). Male participants were less likely than female participants to label the incident as a rape. Male participants were also more likely to place responsibility on the victim.

Most of this discussion of sexual motivation has ignored a major category of sexual experience: homosexuality. This section concludes with a discussion of lesbians and gay men. This discussion will give us another opportunity to see how sexual behaviors are controlled by the interplay of internal and external motivational forces.

Homosexuality

The discussion so far has focused on the motivations that cause people to perform a certain range of sexual behaviors. In this same context we can consider the existence of homosexuality. That is, rather than presenting homosexuality as a set of behaviors that is "caused" by a deviation from heterosexuality, the discussion of sexual motivation should allow you to see that all

⊙ **Watch** the **Video** *Thinking Like a Psychologist: The Origins of Sexual Orientation* on **MyPsychLab**

sexual behavior is "caused." In this view, homosexuality and heterosexuality result from similar motivational forces. Neither of them represents a motivated departure from the other. ⊙

Most surveys of sexual behavior have tried to obtain an accurate estimate of the incidence of homosexuality. In his early research, Alfred Kinsey found that 37 percent of men in his sample had had at least some homosexual experience and that about 4 percent were exclusively homosexual (percentages for women were somewhat smaller). In a more recent survey of over 2,000 adults in the United States, 3.2 percent of the men and 2.5 percent of the women reported same-sex activity in the previous year (Turner et al., 2005). Are these figures correct? As long as there is societal hostility directed toward acting on homosexual desires, it may be impossible to get entirely accurate estimates of the incidence of homosexuality because of people's reluctance to confide in researchers.

This section reviews the origins of homosexuality and heterosexuality. We also consider research on societal and personal attitudes toward homosexual behavior.

The Nature and Nurture of Homosexuality   After the discussion of evolution and sexual behaviors, it should not surprise you to learn that research evidence suggests that sexual preference has a genetic component (Långström et al., 2010). As is often the case, researchers have made this assertion based on studies that compare concordance rates of *monozygotic*

What evidence suggests that sexual orientation has a genetic component?

Sexual Behaviors   **313**

(MZ) twins (those who are genetically identical) and *dizygotic* (DZ) twins (those who, like siblings, share only half their genes). When both members of a pair of twins have the same orientation—homosexual or heterosexual—they are concordant. If one twin is homosexual and the other is heterosexual, they are discordant. Studies of both gay men and lesbians have demonstrated considerably higher concordance rates for MZ than for DZ twins (Rahman & Wilson, 2003). For example, in one sample of roughly 750 pairs of twins, 32 percent of the MZ twins were concordant for nonheterosexual orientations versus 8 percent of DZ twins (Kendler et al., 2000). Although MZ twins may also be reared in more similar environments than DZ twins—they may be treated more similarly by their parents—this pattern strongly suggests that sexuality is, in part, genetically determined.

Researchers have also begun to document brain differences between homosexuals and heterosexuals. For example, one study used MRI and PET scans to compare brain shape and volumes (Savic & Lindström, 2008). The brain images revealed that heterosexual men had asymmetric brains, with slightly larger right cerebral hemispheres—as did homosexual women. Both the heterosexual women and the homosexual men had symmetrical cerebral hemispheres. The study also identified patterns of connections between the amygdala (which, as you might recall, plays an important role in emotional control and memories) and other brain regions. Once again, the patterns of connections in the homosexual participants' brains were more similar to those in the opposite-sex heterosexual participants. Further research may strengthen or weaken the case for such broad brain differences. Still, it seems clear that some aspects of homosexuality and heterosexuality emerge in response to purely biological forces.

Social psychologist **Daryl Bem** (1996, 2000) has suggested that biology does not affect sexual preference directly but rather has an indirect impact by influencing the temperaments and activities of young children. Recall from Chapter 10 that researchers have suggested that boys and girls engage in different activities—boys' play, for example, tends to be more rough-and-tumble. According to Bem's theory, depending on whether they engage in sex-typical or sex-atypical play, children come to feel dissimilar to either their same-sex or opposite-sex peers. In Bem's theory, "exotic becomes erotic": Feelings of dissimilarity lead to emotional arousal; over time this arousal is transformed into erotic attraction. For example, if a young girl feels dissimilar from other girls because she does not wish to engage in girl-typical activities, over time her emotional arousal will be transformed into homosexual feelings. Note that Bem's theory supports the assertion that homosexuality and heterosexuality arise from the same causal forces: In both cases, the gender the child perceives as dissimilar becomes, over time, eroticized.

Society and Homosexuality Suppose Bem is correct to argue that childhood experiences matter enormously. Does everyone act on the urgings set down in childhood? What, perhaps, most sets homosexuality apart from heterosexuality is the continuing hostility toward homosexual behaviors in many corners of society. In one survey, a sample of 1,335 heterosexual men and women were asked how uncomfortable they would feel being around "a man who is homosexual" or "a woman who is a lesbian" (Herek, 2002). **Figure 11.6** presents the percentage who responded that they would be "somewhat" or "very" uncomfortable. You can see that both men and

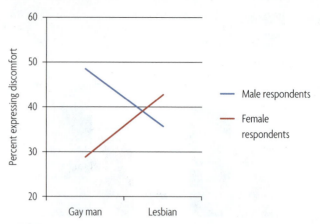

FIGURE 11.6 Attitudes toward Homosexuality

Participants were asked how uncomfortable they would feel being around "a man who is homosexual" or "a woman who is a lesbian." The figure indicates the percentage of men and women who responded that they would be "somewhat" or "very" uncomfortable.

Data from Gregory M. Herek, "Gender Gaps in Public Opinion about Lesbians and Gay Men," *Public Opinion Quarterly, 66,* 40–66.

women anticipate more discomfort being around homosexuals who match their own sex. Researchers have labeled highly negative attitudes toward gay people *homophobia*.

Most homosexuals come to the realization that they are motivated toward same-sex relationships in the hostile context of societal homophobia. Even so, research suggests that many individuals begin to recognize those feelings at quite young ages. For example, researchers asked students from the southeastern United States attending a conference for gay, lesbian, bisexual, and transgendered youth to indicate the age at which they became aware of their sexual orientation (Maguen et al., 2002). Among the gay men, the mean age was 9.6 years; among the lesbians the mean age was 10.9 years. The men reported having same-sex sexual contact at 14.9 years, and the women reported same-sex contact at 16.7 years. These data suggest that many people become aware of their homosexual orientation at a time when they must still function in school environments that are often quite hostile to homosexuality (Espelage et al., 2008). In addition, homosexual youths must often make the difficult decision of whether to disclose their sexual orientation to their parents (Heatherington & Lavner, 2008). Most adolescents rely on their parents for both emotional and financial support; to disclose their homosexuality puts them at risk to lose both types of sustenance. In fact, parental rejection is related to increases in suicide attempts (Bouris et al., 2010).

These findings for adolescents reinforce the point that most gay and lesbian individuals find homophobia more psychologically burdensome than homosexuality itself. In 1973, the American Psychiatric Association voted to remove homosexuality from the list of psychological disorders; the American Psychological Association followed in 1975 (Morin & Rothblum, 1991). Spurring this action were research reports suggesting that, in fact, most gay men and lesbians are happy and productive. Contemporary research suggests that much of the stress associated with homosexuality arises not from the sexual motivation itself—gay people are happy with their orientations—but from the way in which people respond to the revelation of that sexual motivation. Much of lesbians' and gay men's anxiety about homosexuality arises not from being homosexual, but from an ongoing need either to reveal ("come out") to or conceal ("stay in the closet") their sexual identity from family, friends, and coworkers (Legate et al., 2012). More generally, homosexuals experience distress because they can't speak openly about their lives (Lewis et al., 2006). As you might expect, gay men and lesbians also spend time worrying about establishing and maintaining loving relationships, just as heterosexuals do.

The willingness of lesbians and gay men to "come out" may serve as a first step toward decreasing societal hostility. Research has shown that people's attitudes toward gay men and lesbians are much less negative when they actually *know* individuals in these groups; in fact, on average the more gay men and lesbians a person knows, the more favorable is his or her attitude (Smith et al., 2009). (When we turn to the topic of prejudice in Chapter 16, we will see there again how experiences with members of minority groups can lead to more positive attitudes.)

This brief review of homosexuality reinforces the main conclusions about human sexual motivation. Some of the impetus for sexual behaviors is internal—genetic endowment and species evolution provide internal models for both heterosexual and homosexual behaviors. But the external environment also gives rise to sexual motivation. You learn to find some stimuli particularly alluring and some behaviors culturally acceptable. In the case of homosexuality, external societal norms may work against the internal dictates of nature.

Let's move now to a third example of important motivation: the forces that set an individual's course for relative success or failure.

Stop *and* Review

① What is meant by stereotyped sexual behavior?
② What four phases did Masters and Johnson identify for human sexual response?
③ According to evolutionary theories, why do men desire more sexual variety than do women?
④ What are sexual scripts?
⑤ What does twin research suggest about the genetics of homosexuality?

CRITICAL THINKING   Recall the study that looked at male mollies' preferences for female fish. Why was it important to test the preferences of the male fish both before and after they saw the females in the company of other males?

✓●—|Study and Review on MyPsychLab

MOTIVATION FOR PERSONAL ACHIEVEMENT

Why do some people succeed, whereas other people, relatively speaking, fail? Why, for example, are some people able to swim the English Channel, whereas other people just wave woefully from the shore? You are likely to attribute some of the

How can motivation explain variability among individuals—the fact, for example, that some people take on dangerous challenges?

difference to genetic factors like body type, and you're correct to do so. But you also know that some people are simply much more interested in swimming the English Channel than are others. So we are back at one of the core reasons for studying motivation. We want, in this case, to understand the motivational forces that lead different people to seek different levels of personal achievement. Let's begin with a construct that's actually called the *need for achievement*.

Need for Achievement

As early as 1938, **Henry Murray** had postulated a need to achieve that varied in strength in different people and influenced their tendency to approach success and evaluate their own performances. **David McClelland** and his colleagues (1953) devised a way to measure the strength by using his participants' fantasies. On what is called the **Thematic Apperception Test (TAT)**, participants were asked to generate stories in response to a series of ambiguous drawings. Participants shown TAT pictures were asked to make up stories about them—to say what was happening in the picture and describe probable outcomes. According to McClelland, "If you want to find out what's on a person's mind, don't ask him, because he can't always tell you accurately. Study his fantasies and dreams. If you do this over a period of time, you will discover the themes to which his mind returns again and again. And these themes can be used to explain his actions" (McClelland, 1971, p. 5).

....

Thematic Apperception Test (TAT) A projective test in which pictures of ambiguous scenes are presented to an individual, who is encouraged to generate stories about them.

FIGURE 11.7 Alternative Interpretations of a TAT Picture

Story Showing High n Ach

This boy has just finished his violin lesson. He's happy at the progress he is making and is beginning to believe that all his progress is making the sacrifices worthwhile. To become a concert violinist, he will have to give up much of his social life to practice for many hours each day. Although he knows he could make more money by going into his father's business, he is more interested in being a great violinist and giving people joy with his music. He renews his personal commitment to whatever it takes to make it.

Story Showing Low n Ach

This boy is holding his brother's violin and wishes he could play it. But he knows it is not worth the time, energy, and money for lessons. He feels sorry for his brother; he has given up all the enjoyable things in life to practice, practice, practice. It would be great to wake up one day and be a top-notch musician, but it doesn't work that way. The reality is boring practice, no fun, and the strong possibility of becoming just another guy playing a musical instrument in a small-town band.

From participant responses to a series of TAT pictures, McClelland worked out measures of several human needs, including needs for power, affiliation, and achievement. The **need for achievement** was designated as *n Ach*. It reflected individual differences in the importance of planning and working toward attaining one's goals. The caption for **Figure 11.7** shows an example of how a high *n Ach* individual and a low *n Ach* individual might interpret a TAT picture. Studies in both laboratory and real-life settings have validated the usefulness of this measure.

For example, high-scoring *n Ach* people were found to be more upwardly mobile than those with low scores; sons who had high *n Ach* scores were more likely than sons with low *n Ach* measures to advance above their fathers' occupational status (McClelland et al., 1976). Men and women who measured high on *n Ach* at age 31 tended to have higher salaries than their low *n Ach* peers by age 41 (McClelland & Franz, 1992). Do these findings indicate that high *n Ach* individuals are always willing to work harder? Not really. In the face of a task that they are led to believe will be difficult, high *n Ach* individuals quit early on (Feather, 1961). What, in fact, seems to typify high *n Ach* individuals is a need for *efficiency*—a need to get the

same result for less effort. If they earn more than their peers, it might be because they also value concrete feedback on how well they are doing. As a measure of progress, salary is very concrete (McClelland, 1961; McClelland & Franz, 1992).

Need for achievement also predicts success in particular types of careers. Consider *entrepreneurs*—individuals who originate new business ventures. People higher in need for achievement are more likely to choose a career as entrepreneurs; entrepreneurs with higher need for achievement are more likely to succeed (Collins et al., 2004; Stewart & Roth, 2007). Note, however, that need for achievement does not always guarantee success. For example, people with high need for achievement may fail as politicians because complex real-world problems leave them unable to exercise personal control (Winter, 2010).

Attributions for Success and Failure

Need for achievement is not the only variable that affects motivation toward personal success. To see why, let's begin with a hypothetical example. Suppose you have two friends who are taking the same class. On the first midterm, each gets a C. Do you think they would be equally motivated to study hard for the second midterm? Part of the answer will depend on the *attributions* they each made to explain the C to themselves. **Attributions** are judgments about the causes of outcomes. (Chapter 16 will develop attribution theory at greater length.) Attributions can have an important impact on motivation. Let's see why.

Suppose that one friend attributed her performance to construction noise during the exam, whereas the other attributed his performance to poor memory. These attributions provide an answer to the question, "To what extent does a causal factor reside within an individual, or is it a general factor in the environment?" In this example, one friend made an external attribution (construction noise) whereas the other made an internal attribution (poor memory). These attributions would often have an effect on motivation. If your friend attributes her performance to construction noise, she is likely to study hard for the next midterm. If your other friend thinks the fault lies in his poor memory, he's more likely to give up.

The internal–external dimension is one of three dimensions along which attributions can vary. We can also ask: "To what extent is a causal factor likely to be stable and consistent over time, or unstable and varying?" The answer gives us the dimension of *stability* versus *instability*. Or we can ask: "To what extent is a causal factor highly specific, limited to a particular task or situation, or global, applying widely across a variety of settings?" This gives us the dimension of *global* versus *specific*.

An example of how two of these dimensions can interact is given in **Figure 11.8**. Let's stay with the example of attributions about exam grades. Students can interpret their grades as the result of internal factors, such as ability (a stable personality characteristic) or effort (a varying personal quality). Or they may view the grades as caused primarily by external

....

need for achievement (*n Ach*) An assumed basic human need to strive for achievement of goals that motivates a wide range of behavior and thinking.

attribution Judgment about the causes of outcomes.

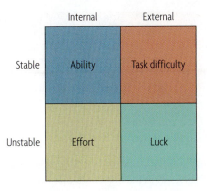

	Internal	External
Stable	Ability	Task difficulty
Unstable	Effort	Luck

FIGURE 11.8 Attributions Regarding Causes for Behavioral Outcomes

Four possible outcomes are generated with just two sources of attributions about behavior. Ability attributions are made for the internal–stable combination, effort for the internal but unstable combination, a difficult task (test) when external–stable forces are assumed to be operating, and luck for the unstable–external combination.

factors such as the difficulty of the task, the actions of others (a stable situational problem), or luck (an unstable external feature). The type of interpretation will influence subsequent motivation—to study harder or blow off work—regardless of the true reason for the success or failure.

Let's return to your two friends. We concluded that one friend made an external attribution (construction noise) whereas the other made an internal attribution (poor memory). Researchers have shown that the way people explain events in their lives—from winning at cards to being turned down for a date—can become lifelong, habitual *attributional styles* (Cole et al., 2008). In Chapter 14, we will see that an internal–global–stable attributional style ("I never do anything right") puts individuals at risk for depression (and one of the symptoms of depression is impaired motivation). For now, however, let's focus on the way in which attributional style might lead one of your friends to have an *A* and the other an *F* by the end of the semester. The key ingredient to their success and failure might turn out to be familiar and seemingly simple: *optimism* versus *pessimism* (Carver et al., 2010). These two divergent ways of looking at the world influence motivation and behavior.

The *optimistic attributional style* sees failure as the result of external causes—"The test was unfair"—and of events that are unstable or modifiable and specific—"If I put in more effort next time, I'll do better, and this one setback won't affect how I perform any other task that is important to me." The *pessimistic attributional style* focuses on the causes of failure as internally generated. Furthermore, the bad situation and the individual's role in causing it are seen as stable and global—"It won't ever change, and it will affect everything." Because they believe themselves to be doomed to fail, pessimists perform worse than others would expect, given objective measures of their talent. In academic settings, students who are more optimistic report higher levels of motivation. They are also more likely to stay in school. In one sample of 2,189 students entering college, 85 percent of optimistic students returned for a second year versus 68 percent of pessimistic students (Solberg Nes et al., 2009).

To close this section, let's look at a research example of the powerful impact of causal attributions in an academic setting.

When minority group students attend college, they often report that they do not feel socially comfortable in their new environment. Those feelings of social displacement can undermine students' achievement motivation. A pair of researchers predicted that they could improve Black students' academic performance if they changed the students' attributions about their lack of social belonging (Walton & Cohen, 2007). Participants in the study read survey material about college experiences. For the experimental group, some of that material provided a new way to make attributions about difficulties with social belonging: The survey asserted, for example, that "quantitative statistics indicated that most upperclassmen had 'worried [as 1st-year students] whether other students would accept them,' but that now most are sure 'that other students accept them'" (p. 88). The control group did not read this type of information. To test the impact of this brief intervention, the researchers obtained participants' grades for the following semester. They calculated whether each student's grades were higher or lower than would be expected based on earlier semesters. Participants in the experimental group obtained grades that were better than expected; participants in the control group did worse than expected.

The researchers subsequently followed students who had received this intervention for three full years: The students achieved higher GPAs and even had better health by comparison to students in the control group (Walton & Cohen, 2011). Because of the way in which attributions affect motivation, a small amount of information about feelings of social belonging had a lasting effect on students' performance.

There is much value to you in this line of psychological research. You can work at developing an optimistic explanatory style for your successes and failures. You can avoid making negative, stable, dispositional attributions for your failures by examining possible causal forces in the situation. Finally, don't let your motivation be undermined by momentary setbacks. You can apply this research-based advice to better your life—a recurring theme of *Psychology and Life*.

Work and Organizational Psychology

Now suppose your positive philosophy has helped you to get a job in a big corporation. Can we predict exactly how motivated you'll be just by knowing about you, as an individual—your *n Ach* score or your explanatory style? Your individual level of motivation will depend, in part, on the overall context of people and rules in which you work. Recognizing that work settings are complex social systems, **organizational psychologists** study various aspects of human relations, such as communication among employees, socialization or enculturation of workers, leadership, attitudes and commitment toward a job

organizational psychologist Psychologist who studies various aspects of the human work environment, such as communication among employees, socialization or enculturation of workers, leadership, job satisfaction, stress and burnout, and overall quality of life.

HOW DOES MOTIVATION AFFECT ACADEMIC ACHIEVEMENT?

Suppose you've signed up for your introductory psychology course with two friends, Angela and Blake. On the first day of class, Angela says, "I want to get the top grade in the class." Blake replies, "I'll be happy if I just don't get an *F*." Can you see how Angela's and Blake's goals would motivate them to engage in very different behaviors? The purpose of this review is to allow you to think critically about the relationship between goals, motivation, and academic outcomes.

Analyses of students' performance have identified four general types of achievement goals that represent the combination of two dimensions (Elliot & McGregor, 2001; Murayama et al., 2011). The first dimension contrasts *performance* and *mastery*. Performance refers to students' sense of their achievement relative to other students; mastery refers to students' sense of their own personal competence. The second dimension is *approach* versus *avoidance*. This dimension captures whether a student is motivated to achieve success or avoid failure. Along these dimensions, Angela is representative of a student who has *performance-approach goals*. She focuses on appearing more competent than others. Blake is representative of a student who has *performance-avoidance goals*. He focuses on avoiding being judged as less competent than others. If Connie focuses on improving her own level of understanding, she is displaying *mastery-approach goals*; if Dirk is largely concerned with preventing himself from doing worse than he's done in the past, he is exhibiting *mastery-avoidance goals*. Researchers measure students' goal orientation by asking them to agree with statements such as "I desire to completely master the material presented in this class" and "I just want to avoid doing poorly in this class" (McGregor & Elliot, 2002, p. 381).

In general, students with approach goals are more highly motivated to engage in the behaviors that help ensure academic achievement. One study assessed students' behaviors two weeks before an introductory psychology exam and then immediately before the exam (McGregor & Elliot, 2002). Those students with performance-avoidance goals avoided studying: Two weeks before the exam, they admitted that they hadn't yet done much to prepare; immediately before the exam they admitted that they didn't feel ready. Students with mastery-approach goals and performance-approach goals all started preparing for the exam well in advance. (The study did not examine mastery-avoidance goals.)

Given the effects of students' goals on their study behaviors, you won't be surprised to learn that students with approach goals most often outperform their peers with avoidance goals. For example, one study demonstrated an advantage on an oral examination for students with performance-approach goals (Darnon et al., 2009). By comparison to their performance-avoidance classmates, the performance-approach students were not overwhelmed by the difficulty of the class material.

In light of this research, you might take a moment to consider your own goals and how they affect your study practices and coursework.

- Why might students with performance-avoidance goals delay their studying?

- What could students do to change from avoidance to approach goals?

---

and/or an organization, job satisfaction, stress and burnout, and overall quality of life at work (Blustein, 2008; Hodgkinson & Healey, 2008). As consultants to businesses, organizational psychologists may assist in recruitment, selection, and training of employees. They also make recommendations about job redesign—tailoring a job to fit the person. Organizational psychologists apply theories of management, decision making, and development to improve work settings.

Let's look at a pair of theories organizational psychologists have developed to understand motivation in the workplace. *Equity theory* and *expectancy theory* attempt to explain and predict how people will respond under different working conditions. These theories assume that workers engage in certain cognitive activities, such as assessing fairness through processes of social comparison with other workers or estimating expected rewards associated with their performance. Although both equity theory and expectancy theory originated over

45 years ago, researchers continue to use these perspectives to understand workplace motivation (for example, Bolino & Turnley, 2008; Liao et al., 2011; Siegel et al., 2008).

Equity theory proposes that workers are motivated to maintain fair or equitable relationships with other relevant persons (Adams, 1965). Workers take note of their inputs (investments or contributions they make to their jobs) and their outcomes (what they receive from their jobs), and then they compare these with the inputs and outcomes of other workers. When the ratio of outcomes to inputs for Worker *A* is equal to the ratio for

....

equity theory A cognitive theory of work motivation that proposes that workers are motivated to maintain fair and equitable relationships with other relevant persons; also, a model that postulates that equitable relationships are those in which the participants' outcomes are proportional to their inputs.

Worker *B* (outcome *A* ÷ input *A* = outcome *B* ÷ input *B*), then Worker *A* will feel satisfied. Dissatisfaction will result when these ratios are not equal. Because feeling this inequity is aversive, workers will be motivated to restore equity by changing the relevant inputs and outcomes. These changes could be behavioral (for example, reducing input by working less, increasing outcome by asking for a raise). Or they could be psychological (for example, reinterpreting the value of the inputs—"My work isn't really that good"—or the value of the outcome—"I'm lucky to have a weekly paycheck I can count on").

If you end up in a management position, you should try to address the psychological needs of your employees with respect to equity. Employees are often able to obtain information about how much people are paid both within a particular organization and in similar positions within other organizations. Equity theory suggests that employees will change their behavior in response to that type of information. Keep in mind the benefit of adequate explanations for changes in the relationship of inputs to outcomes.

Expectancy theory proposes that workers are motivated when they expect that their effort and performance on the job will result in desired outcomes (Harder, 1991; Porter & Lawler, 1968; Vroom, 1964). In other words, people will engage in work they find attractive (leading to favorable consequences) and achievable. Expectancy theory emphasizes three components: expectancy, instrumentality, and valence. *Expectancy* refers to the perceived likelihood that a worker's efforts will result in a certain level of performance. *Instrumentality* refers to the perception that performance will lead to certain outcomes, such as rewards. *Valence* refers to the perceived attractiveness of particular outcomes. With respect to a particular work situation, you can imagine different probabilities for these three components. You might, for example, have a job in which there is a high likelihood of reward if performance is successful (high instrumentality) but a low likelihood that performance will be successful (low expectancy) or a low likelihood that the reward will be worthwhile (low valence). According to expectancy theory, workers assess the probabilities of these three components and combine them by multiplying their individual values. The highest levels of motivation, therefore, result when all three components have high probabilities, whereas the lowest levels result when any single component is zero.

Can you see how an expectancy theory analysis might help you if you were in a management position? You should be able to think more clearly about expectancy, instrumentality, and valence. You should be able to determine if one piece of the picture is out of kilter. Suppose, for example, your employees came to believe that there wasn't enough of a relationship between their efforts and how much they are rewarded. What

How does expectancy theory explain some players' choice to favor hitting home runs over achieving a higher batting average?

could you do to change the workplace to restore high values for instrumentality?

We have come a long way since I asked you to consider why you got out of bed this morning. We have considered the biology and psychology of hunger and eating, and the evolutionary and social dimensions of human sexuality. We have explored individual differences in people's need to achieve and explain personal success. Throughout this discussion, you have seen the intricate interplay of nature and nurture, at the level of both the species and the individual. So, with all this information in hand, why *did* you get out of bed this morning?

Stop *and* Review

① What is need for achievement?
② Along what dimensions do people make attributions?
③ How does expectancy theory explain motivation in the workplace?

CRITICAL THINKING   Consider the study that demonstrated the impact of attributions on academic performance. How might your own college or university apply the study's findings?

✔●—**Study** and **Review** on **MyPsychLab**

---

expectancy theory A cognitive theory of work motivation that proposes that workers are motivated when they expect their efforts and job performance to result in desired outcomes.

Recapping Main Points

Understanding Motivation

- Motivation is a dynamic concept used to describe the processes directing behavior.
- Motivational analysis helps explain how biological and behavioral processes are related and why people pursue goals despite obstacles and adversity.
- Drive theory conceptualizes motivation as tension reduction.
- People are also motivated by incentives, external stimuli that are not related to physiological needs.
- Instinct theory suggests that motivation often relies on innate stereotypical responses.
- Social and cognitive psychologists emphasize the individual's perception of, interpretation of, and reaction to a situation.
- Abraham Maslow suggested that human needs can be organized hierarchically.
- Although real human motivation is more complex, Maslow's theory provides a useful framework for summarizing motivational forces.

Eating

- The body has a number of mechanisms to regulate the initiation and cessation of eating.
- Cultural norms have an impact on what and how much people eat.
- Genes play an important role in obesity but the impact of genes is affected by environmental factors.
- If individuals become restrained eaters, their diets may result in weight gain rather than weight loss.
- Eating disorders are life-threatening illnesses that may arise from genetic factors, misperceptions of body image, and cultural pressures.

Sexual Behaviors

- From an evolutionary perspective, sex is the mechanism for producing offspring.
- In animals, the sex drive is largely controlled by hormones.
- The work of Masters and Johnson provided the first hard data on the sexual response cycles of men and women.
- Evolutionary psychologists suggest that much of human sexual behavior reflects different mating strategies for men and women.
- Sexual scripts define culturally appropriate forms of sexual behavior.
- Homosexuality and heterosexuality are determined both by genetics and personal and social environments.

Motivation for Personal Achievement

- People have varying needs for achievement. Motivation for achievement is influenced by how people interpret success and failure.
- Two attributional styles, optimism and pessimism, lead to different attitudes toward achievement and influence motivation.
- Organizational psychologists study human motivation in work settings.

KEY TERMS

anorexia nervosa (p. 305)
attribution (p. 316)
binge eating disorder (p. 306)
bulimia nervosa (p. 305)
date rape (p. 312)
drive (p. 299)
equity theory (p. 318)

expectancy theory (p. 319)
hierarchy of needs (p. 301)
homeostasis (p. 299)
incentive (p. 300)
instinct (p. 300)
motivation (p. 298)
need for achievement (n Ach) (p. 316)

organizational psychologist (p. 317)
parental investment (p. 310)
sexual arousal (p. 309)
sexual script (p. 312)
social learning theory (p. 301)
Thematic Apperception
    Test (TAT) (p. 315)

Chapter 11 • Practice Test

1. You are watching your friend Carlos play tennis with little success. At the end of the match, he comes over and says, "I just couldn't get motivated today." How is Carlos using the concept of motivation?
   a. to infer private states from public acts
   b. to relate biology to behavior
   c. to account for behavioral variability
   d. to explain perseverance despite adversity

2. A(n) _____ is a preprogrammed tendency that is essential for the survival of a species.
   a. incentive
   b. drive
   c. metamotivational state
   d. instinct

3. According to Maslow, you should always try to satisfy your _____ needs before you satisfy your _____ needs.
   a. attachment; biological
   b. esteem; attachment
   c. safety; esteem
   d. self-actualization; esteem

4. At every meal, Jonah eats food with only one flavor. Because of _____, this should generally _____ the amount of food Jonah eats.
   a. stomach contractions; increase
   b. lateral hypothalamus stimulation; decrease
   c. sensory-specific satiety; increase
   d. sensory-specific satiety; decrease

5. When restrained eaters become disinhibited, they tend to
   a. engage in high-calorie binges.
   b. reduce their food consumption further.
   c. go off their diets permanently.
   d. behave more like unrestrained eaters.

6. Which of these statements is not true?
   a. Anorexia is diagnosed when people weigh less than 85 percent of their expected body weight.
   b. Men and women suffer from anorexia at the same rate.
   c. Bulimia is characterized by binging and purging.
   d. Bulimia occurs more often than anorexia.

7. Barney and Wilma have just watched a movie together while eating popcorn. Suppose you asked Barney why he ate the amount of popcorn he ate. It's least likely that he would mention
   a. how hungry he had been.
   b. being influenced by the amount that Wilma ate.
   c. how long it had been since he had eaten a meal.
   d. the taste of the popcorn.

8. Because of the action of _____, you would expect _____ of many species not always to be receptive to mating.
   a. androgens; females
   b. estrogen; males
   c. androgens; males
   d. estrogen; females

9. According to Masters and Johnson's research on human sexual arousal, the _____ phase precedes the _____ phase.
   a. resolution; plateau
   b. plateau; excitement
   c. plateau; orgasm
   d. resolution; orgasm

10. You have a friend who focuses a lot of energy on having brief sexual relationships. This sounds like a _____ mating strategy for a _____.
    a. long-term; female
    b. short-term; male
    c. long-term; male
    d. short-term; female

11. According to research, which pair of siblings should be most likely to share the same sexual orientation?
    a. Larry and John, DZ twins
    b. Deborah and Patty, MZ twins
    c. Rose and Leo, DZ twins
    d. Anne and Charlotte, DZ twins

12. Which of these statements is not true for individuals high in need for achievement?
    a. They always complete their tasks.
    b. They like work to go efficiently.
    c. They like to attain their goals.
    d. They spend time on planning.

13. Every day, Victor gets a perfect score on his local newspaper's trivia quiz. Victor thinks this is possible because the trivia questions are really easy. This is an _____ attribution for his performance.
    a. internal-stable
    b. external-unstable
    c. external-stable
    d. internal-unstable

14. During a lecture, your professor talks a lot about "valence" and "instrumentality." The lecture most likely concerns
    a. attributions.
    b. equity theory.
    c. need for achievement.
    d. expectancy theory.

15. On the way into an exam, you overhear Trudy say, "I'm going to get the best score on this exam." You suspect that Trudy is motivated by _____ goals.
    a. performance-approach
    b. mastery-avoidance
    c. performance-avoidance
    d. equity

ESSAY QUESTIONS

1. How does culture affect the development of eating disorders?

2. What is the origin of sexual scripts?

3. What impact do optimistic versus pessimistic attributional styles have on people's lives?

12

Emotion, Stress, and Health

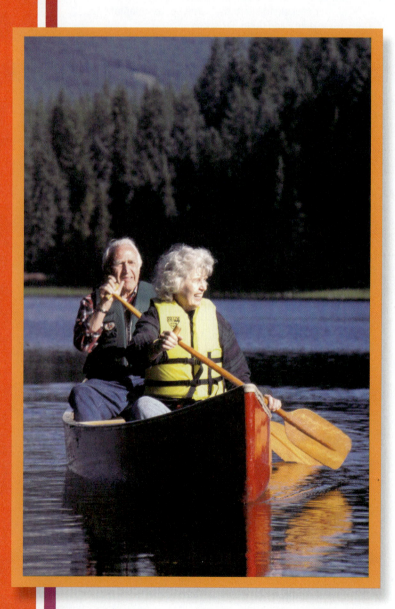

Suppose you walk into class and a friend asks, "How are you feeling?" How would you answer that question? There are at least three different types of information you might provide. First, you might reveal the mood you are in—the *emotions* you are feeling. Are you happy because you know you can finish reading this chapter in time to go to a party? Are you angry because your boss just yelled at you over the telephone? Second, you might say something more general about the amount of *stress* you are experiencing. Do you feel as if you can cope with all the tasks you have to get done? Or are you feeling a bit overwhelmed? Third, you might report on your psychological or physical *health*. Do you feel some illness coming on? Or do you feel an overall sense of wellness?

This chapter will explore interactions among these three ways in which you might answer the question "How are you feeling?"—in relation to your emotions, stress, and health. *Emotions* are the touchstones of human experience. They give richness to your interactions with people and nature, and significance to your memories. This chapter will discuss the experience and functions of emotions. But what happens if the emotional demands on your biological and psychological functioning are too great? You may become overwhelmed and unable to deal with the stressors of your life. This chapter will also examine how *stress* affects you and how you can combat it. Finally, the focus will broaden to consider psychology's contributions to the study of health and illness. *Health psychologists* investigate the ways in which environmental, social, and psychological processes contribute to the development of disease. Health psychologists also use psychological processes and principles to help treat and prevent illness while also developing strategies to enhance personal wellness.

We begin now by looking at the content and meaning of emotions.

EMOTIONS

Just imagine what your life would be like if you could think and act but not feel. Would you be willing to give up the capacity to experience fear if you would also lose the passion of a lover's kiss? Would you give up sadness at the expense of joy? Surely these would be bad bargains, promptly regretted. We will soon see that emotions serve a number of important functions. Let's begin, however, by offering a definition of emotion and by describing the roots of your emotional experiences.

Although you might be tempted to think of emotion as only a feeling—"I feel happy" or "I feel angry"—we need a more inclusive definition of this important concept that involves both the body and the mind. Contemporary psychologists define **emotion** as a complex pattern of bodily and mental changes that includes physiological arousal, feelings, cognitive processes, visible expressions (including face and posture), and specific behavioral reactions made in response to a situation perceived as personally significant. To see why

....

◉ **Watch** the **Video** *Thinking Like a Psychologist: Affective Forecasting* on **MyPsychLab**

emotion A complex pattern of changes, including physiological arousal, feelings, cognitive processes, and behavioral reactions, made in response to a situation perceived to be personally significant.

all of these components are necessary, you should imagine a situation in which you would feel a surge of happiness. Your physiological arousal might include a gently beating heart. Your feeling would be positive. The associated cognitive processes include interpretations, memories, and expectations that allow you to label the situation as happy. Your overt behavioral reactions might be expressive (smiling) and/or action-oriented (embracing a loved one).

Before I provide an account that unites arousal, feelings, thoughts, and actions, you need to learn the distinction between emotions and moods. As you've just seen, emotions are specific responses to specific events—in that sense, emotions are typically relatively short lived and relatively intense. By contrast, *moods* are often less intense and may last several days. There's often a weaker connection between moods and triggering events. You might be in a good or bad mood without knowing exactly why. Keep this distinction between emotions and moods in mind as you meet the theories that explain them.

Basic Emotions and Culture

Suppose you could gather together in one room representatives from a great diversity of human cultures. What would be common in their experiences of emotion? For an initial answer, you might look to Charles Darwin's book *The Expression of Emotions in Man and Animals* (1872/1965). Darwin believed that emotions evolve alongside other important aspects of human and nonhuman structures and functions. He was interested in the *adaptive* functions of emotions, which he thought of not as vague, unpredictable, personal states but as highly specific, coordinated modes of operation of the human brain. Darwin viewed emotions as inherited, specialized mental states designed to deal with a certain class of *recurring situations* in the world (Hess & Thibault, 2009). Suppose, for example, you find yourself in a situation in which another individual is making it impossible for you to achieve your goals. Our evolutionary ancestors might have undertaken combat to resolve the situation. Now, a facial expression of anger communicates your mental state and signals your readiness to take action. Communication through emotions may avert direct conflict.

Over the history of our species, humans have been attacked by predators, fallen in love, given birth to children, fought each other, confronted their mates' sexual infidelity, and witnessed the death of loved ones—innumerable times. We might expect, therefore, that certain types of emotional responses would emerge in all members of the human species. Researchers have tested this claim of the *universality of emotions* by looking at the emotional responses of newborn children as well as the consistency of facial expressions across cultures.

Are Some Emotional Responses Innate? If the evolutionary perspective is correct, we would expect to find much the same patterns of emotional responses in children all over the world. **Silvan Tomkins** (1911–1991) was one of the first psychologists to emphasize the pervasive role of immediate, unlearned affective (emotional) reactions. Tomkins (1962, 1981) pointed out that, without prior learning, infants respond to loud sounds with fear or with difficulties in breathing. They seem "prewired" to respond to certain stimuli with an emotional response general enough to fit a wide range of circumstances. ◉

Charles Darwin was one of the first to use photographs in the study of emotion. These plates are from *The Expression of Emotions in Man and Animals* (1872/1965). Why did Darwin believe that emotions were the product of evolution?

Early accounts of emotional development focused on their facial expressions and suggested that infants produce facial expressions to convey specific emotions (Izard, 1994). However, contemporary research suggests that infants start life with facial expressions that are just broadly positive and negative (Camras & Shutter, 2010). For example, 11-month-old infants from the United States, Japan, and China produce the same facial expression when they are experiencing fear and anger (Camras et al., 2007). Apparently, children's ability to display distinct facial expressions for negative emotions emerges after the first year of life. Note, however, that infants' emotional responses are not restricted to facial expressions; they can indicate emotions through other types of motor activity. For example, 11-month-olds are more likely to increase their breathing rate as an indication of fear versus anger (Camras et al., 2007). That behavioral response was similar for infants from the United States, Japan, and China. These results suggest that infants may begin to differentiate emotions through other behavioral means, before they mark the emotions clearly with facial expressions.

Infants may nonetheless have an innate ability to interpret the facial expressions of others. In one experiment, 5-month-old infants habituated—they showed decreasing interest—to repeated presentations of an adult face showing smiles of different intensities (Bornstein & Arterberry, 2003). The infants were subsequently shown two new photographs: One photograph showed the same adult with a novel smile (that is, a smile with a different intensity); the second photograph showed the same adult with a fearful expression. The infants consistently spent more time looking at the fearful expression—suggesting both that they experienced the fearful expression as something new and also that they sorted the different smiles into the same category. Other research has demonstrated that patterns of brain activity for 7-month-old infants are different in response to angry and fearful expressions (Kobiella et al., 2008). Thus, infants have distinctive responses to facial expressions that, as we just saw for 11-month-olds, they are not yet able to produce.

Are Facial Expressions Universal? We have seen that infants are able to interpret standard emotional expressions. If that is so, we might also expect to find adult members of even vastly different cultures showing reasonable agreement in the way they believe emotion is communicated by facial expressions.

According to **Paul Ekman,** the leading researcher on the nature of facial expressions, all people share an overlap in "facial language" (Ekman, 1984, 1994). Ekman and his associates have demonstrated what Darwin first proposed—that a set of emotional expressions is universal to the human species, presumably because they are innate components of our evolutionary heritage. Before you read on, take a look at **Figure 12.1** to see how well you can identify these seven universally recognized expressions of emotion (Ekman & Friesen, 1986).

There is considerable evidence that these seven expressions are recognized and produced worldwide in response to the emotions of happiness, surprise, anger, disgust, fear, sadness, and contempt. Cross-cultural researchers have asked people from a variety of cultures to identify the emotions associated with expressions in standardized photographs. Individuals are generally able to identify the expressions associated with the seven emotions.

In one study, members of a preliterate culture in New Guinea (the Fore culture), who had had almost no exposure to Westerners or to Western culture prior to this experiment, accurately identified the emotions expressed in the White faces shown in Figure 12.1. They did so by referring to situations in which they had experienced the same emotion.

Why do researchers believe that some emotional responses are innate?

FIGURE 12.1 Judgments of Emotional Expressions

Match these seven emotion terms with the faces shown at left: fear, disgust, happiness, surprise, contempt, anger, and sadness. The answers are given at the end of the chapter (see p. 354).

For example, photo 5 (fear) suggested being chased by a wild boar when you didn't have your spear, and photo 6 (sadness) suggested your child had died. Their only confusion came in distinguishing surprise, photo 2, from fear, perhaps because these people are most fearful when taken by surprise.

Next, researchers asked other members of the culture (who had not participated in the first study) to model the expressions that they used to communicate six of the emotions (excluding contempt). When U.S. college students viewed videotapes of the facial expressions of the Fore people, they were able to identify their emotions accurately— with one exception. Not surprisingly, the Americans had difficulty distinguishing between the Fore poses of fear and surprise, the same emotions that the Fore had confused in the Western poses (Ekman & Friesen, 1971).

Other research has compared judgments of facial expressions across individuals in Hungary, Japan, Poland, Sumatra, the United States, and Vietnam—high agreement was found across these diverse populations (Biehl et al., 1997). Still, Japanese adults were worse at identifying anger than were U.S., Hungarian, Polish, and Vietnamese adults. Vietnamese adults were worse at identifying disgust than the participants from all the other countries.

These cross-cultural differences support the hypothesis that cultures have different *dialects* for facial expressions (Dailey et al., 2010; Elfenbein et al., 2007). For languages, dialects are regional or social variation in, for example, pronunciation and word use. Within the domain of emotions, proponents of a dialect theory argue for similar cultural variation in the production of facial expressions. In fact, there are consistent cross-cultural differences in the specific movements of facial muscles people perform to create different facial expressions. Furthermore, people find it easier to recognize facial expressions when they are produced by members of their own culture (Dailey et al., 2010; Elfenbein et al., 2007). Culture also has an impact on the way in which people gather information when they view a face: People from Eastern cultures are more likely to focus attention on the eyes whereas people from Western cultures spread their attention across the whole face (Jack et al., 2009). These habitual differences in examining faces may lead people from different cultures to have different expectations for how faces will look when they are conveying particular emotional expressions (Jack et al., 2012).

How Does Culture Constrain Emotional Expression?

We've just seen that some aspects of emotional expression may remain constant across cultures. Even so, different cultures have different standards for how emotion should be managed. Some forms of emotional response, even facial expressions, are unique to each culture. Cultures establish social rules for when people may show certain emotions and for the social appropriateness of certain types of emotional displays by given types of people in particular settings (Mesquita & Leu, 2007). Let's look at three examples of cultures that express emotions in manners different from the Western norm.

The Wolof people of Senegal live in a society where status and power differences among people are rigidly defined. High-caste members of this culture are expected to show great restraint in their expressions of emotionality; low-caste individuals are expected to be more volatile, particularly a caste called the *griots*. The griots, in fact, are often called upon to express the "undignified" emotions of the nobility:

> *One afternoon, a group of women (some five nobles and two griots) were gathered near a well on the edge of town when another woman strode over to the well and threw herself down it. All the women were shocked at the apparent suicide attempt, but the noblewomen were shocked in silence. Only the griot women screamed, on behalf of all. (Irvine, 1990, p. 146)*

Can you imagine how you would respond in this situation? It might be easier to put yourself in the place of the griots rather than in the place of the noblewomen: How could you help but

In what ways do cultures constrain emotional expressions in situations like funerals?

scream? The answer, of course, is that the noblewomen have acquired cultural norms for emotional expression that require them not to show any overt response.

As a second example, consider the practice of Mẽbengokre women in Central Brazil (Lea, 2004). When the women experience loss they engage in ceremonial wailing. The wailing uses a particular high-pitched tone but also special words that are not used in other circumstances. As you might imagine, the women wail in response to family deaths. However, wailing occurs in other circumstances as well: "The theme uniting all situations that give rise to wailing is the feeling of separation and loss that is canonically associated with death" (p. 114). So, for example, Mẽbengokre women wail when a close relative is leaving on an extended trip.

For a third example, let's turn to a cross-cultural difference in norms for emotional displays related to pain. Recall from Chapter 4 that psychological context has a major impact on the extent to which people experience pain. Similarly, the cultural context has an impact on the extent to which it is considered appropriate for people to perform behaviors that reveal they are experiencing pain. For example, one study demonstrated a contrast between what people in the United States and Japan consider proper behavioral displays for pain (Hobara, 2005). Participants in both cultures completed the Appropriate Pain Behavior Questionnaire (APBQ) that includes such items as "Women should be able to tolerate pain in most circumstances" and "It is acceptable for men to cry when in pain." In general, Japanese participants provided lower scores on the APBQ: They indicated less approval for open emotional expressions of pain. In addition, both cultural groups suggested more approval for women's emotional displays than men's displays. The researcher attributed the cultural difference to the "traditional stoicism . . . of many Asian cultures" (Hobara, 2005, p. 392).

When you think about the types of emotional patterns that may have evolved over the course of human experience, always bear in mind that culture may have the last word. Western notions of what is necessary or inevitable in emotional expression are as bound to U.S. culture as those of any other societies. Can you see how different standards for emotional expression could cause misunderstandings between people of different cultural origins?

Let's turn now to theories that explore the link between different aspects of emotions.

Theories of Emotion

Theories of emotion generally attempt to explain the relationship between physiological and psychological aspects of the experience of emotion. This section begins by discussing the responses your body gives in emotionally relevant situations. It then reviews theories that explore the way these physiological responses contribute to your psychological experience of emotion.

Physiology of Emotion What happens when you experience a strong emotion? Your heart races, your respiration goes up, your mouth dries, your muscles tense, and maybe you even shake. In addition to these noticeable changes, many others occur beneath the surface. All these responses are designed to mobilize your body for action to deal with the source of the emotion. Let's look at their origins.

The *autonomic nervous system* (ANS) prepares the body for emotional responses through the action of both its sympathetic and parasympathetic divisions (see Chapter 3). The balance between the divisions depends on the quality and intensity of the arousing stimulation. With mild, *unpleasant* stimulation, the *sympathetic* division is more active; with mild, *pleasant* stimulation, the *parasympathetic* division is more active. With more intense stimulation of either kind, both divisions are increasingly involved. Physiologically, strong emotions such as fear or anger activate the body's *emergency reaction system,* which swiftly and silently prepares the body for potential danger. The sympathetic nervous system takes charge by directing the release of hormones (epinephrine and norepinephrine) from the adrenal glands, which in turn leads the internal organs to release blood sugar, raise blood pressure, and increase sweating and salivation. To calm you after the emergency has passed, the parasympathetic nervous system inhibits the release of the activating hormones. You may remain aroused for a while after an experience of strong emotional activation because some of the hormones continue to circulate in your bloodstream.

Particular emotional experiences give rise to distinct patterns of activity in the autonomic nervous system (Friedman, 2010). Consider a cross-cultural study in which a team of researchers measured autonomic responses such as heart rate and skin temperature while men and women from the United States and Minangkabau men from West Sumatra generated

How does the brain respond differently to experiences of puppies and spiders?

emotions and emotional expressions. Members of the Minang-kabau culture are socialized not to display negative emotions. Would they, even so, show the same underlying autonomic patterns for negative emotions as did the U.S. participants? The data revealed a high level of similarity across the two cultures, leading the researchers to suggest that patterns of autonomic activity are "an important part of our common evolved biological heritage" (Levenson et al., 1992, p. 986).

Let's move now from the autonomic nervous system to the central nervous system. Integration of both the hormonal and the neural aspects of arousal is controlled by the *hypothalamus* and the *limbic system,* control systems for emotions and for patterns of attack, defense, and flight. Neuroanatomy research has particularly focused on the *amygdala* as a part of the limbic system that acts as a gateway for emotion and as a filter for memory. The amygdala does this by attaching significance to the information it receives from the senses. It plays an especially strong role in attaching meaning to negative experiences—the amygdala serves as a "threat detector" to make us aware of dangers in our environment (Kim et al., 2011).

The *cortex* is involved in emotional experiences through its internal neural networks and its connections with other parts of the body. The cortex provides the associations, memories, and meanings that integrate psychological experience and biological responses. Research using brain-scanning techniques has begun to map particular responses for different emotions. For example, positive and negative emotions are not just opposite responses in the same portions of the cortex. Rather, opposite emotions lead to greatest activity in quite different parts of the brain. Consider a study in which participants underwent fMRI scans while viewing positive pictures (such as puppies, brownies, and sunsets) and negative pictures (angry people, spiders, and guns). The scans showed greater activity in the brain's left hemisphere for positive pictures and in the right hemisphere for negative pictures (Canli et al., 1998). In fact, researchers have suggested that there are two distinct systems in the brain that handle

approach-related and *withdrawal-related* emotional responses (Davidson et al., 2000; Maxwell & Davidson, 2007). Consider puppies and spiders. It is likely that most people would want to approach the puppies but withdraw from the spiders. Research suggests that different brain circuits—apportioned to the different hemispheres of the brain—underlie those responses.

We have seen so far that your body provides many responses to situations in which emotions are relevant. But how do you know which feeling goes with which physiological response? Let's now consider three theories that attempt an answer to this question.

James–Lange Theory of Body Reaction   You might think, at first, that everyone would agree that emotions precede responses: For example, you yell at someone (response) because you feel angry (emotion). However, over 100 years ago, William James argued, as Aristotle had much earlier, that the sequence was reversed—you feel *after* your body reacts. As James put it, "We feel sorry because we cry, angry because we strike, afraid because we tremble" (James, 1890/1950, p. 450). This view that emotion stems from *bodily feedback* became known as the **James–Lange theory of emotion** (Carl Lange was a Danish scientist who presented similar ideas the same year as James). According to this theory, perceiving a stimulus causes autonomic arousal and other bodily actions that lead to the experience of a specific emotion (see **Figure 12.2** on page 328). The James–Lange theory is considered a *peripheralist* theory because it assigns the most prominent role in the emotion chain to visceral reactions, the actions of the autonomic nervous system that are peripheral to the central nervous system.

....

James–Lange theory of emotion   A peripheral-feedback theory of emotion stating that an eliciting stimulus triggers a behavioral response that sends different sensory and motor feedback to the brain and creates the feeling of a specific emotion.

FIGURE 12.2 The James–Lange Theory of Emotion

In the James–Lange theory, events trigger both autonomic arousal and behavioral action, which are perceived and then result in a specific emotional experience.

From Ciccarelli, Saundra; White, J. Noland, Psychology, 3rd Edition, © 2012. Printed and electronically reproduced by permission of Pearson Education Inc., Upper Saddle River, New Jersey.

Cannon–Bard Theory of Central Neural Processes Physiologist Walter Cannon (1927, 1929) rejected the peripheralist theory in favor of a *centralist* focus on the action of the central nervous system. Cannon (and other critics) raised a number of objections to the James–Lange theory (Leventhal, 1980). They noted, for example, that visceral activity is irrelevant for emotional experience—experimental animals continue to respond emotionally even after their viscera are separated surgically from the CNS. They also argued that ANS responses are typically too slow to be the source of split-second elicited emotions. According to Cannon, emotion requires that the brain intercede between the input stimulation and the output response.

Another physiologist, Philip Bard, also concluded that visceral reactions were not primary in the emotion sequence. Instead, an emotion-arousing stimulus has two simultaneous effects, causing both bodily arousal via the sympathetic nervous system and the subjective experience of emotion via the cortex. The views of these physiologists were combined in the **Cannon–Bard theory of emotion.** This theory states that an emotion stimulus produces two concurrent reactions, arousal and experience of emotion, that do not cause each other (see **Figure 12.3**). If something makes you angry, your heartbeat increases at the same time as you think "I'm ticked off!"—but neither your body nor your mind dictates the way the other responds.

The Cannon–Bard theory predicts independence between bodily and psychological responses. We will see next that contemporary theories of emotion reject the claim that these responses are necessarily independent.

Cognitive Appraisal Theories of Emotion Because arousal symptoms and internal states are similar for many different emotions, it is possible to confuse them at times when they are experienced in ambiguous or novel situations. **Stanley Schachter** (1922–1997) originated the **two-factor theory of emotion** to explain how people deal with such uncertainty. According to Schachter (1971a), the experience of emotion is the joint effect of the two factors of physiological arousal and cognitive appraisal. Both parts are necessary for an emotion to occur. In this view, all arousal is assumed to be general and undifferentiated, and arousal is the first step in the emotion sequence. You appraise your physiological arousal in an effort to discover what you are feeling, what emotional label best fits,

....

Cannon–Bard theory of emotion A theory stating that an emotional stimulus produces two co-occurring reactions—arousal and experience of emotion—that do not cause each other.

two-factor theory of emotion The theory that emotional experiences arise from autonomic arousal and cognitive appraisal.

FIGURE 12.3 The Cannon–Bard Theory of Emotion

In the Cannon–Bard theory, events are first processed at various centers in the brain, which then direct the simultaneous reactions of arousal, behavioral action, and emotional experience.

From Ciccarelli, Saundra; White, J. Noland, Psychology, 3rd Edition, © 2012. Printed and electronically reproduced by permission of Pearson Education Inc., Upper Saddle River, New Jersey.

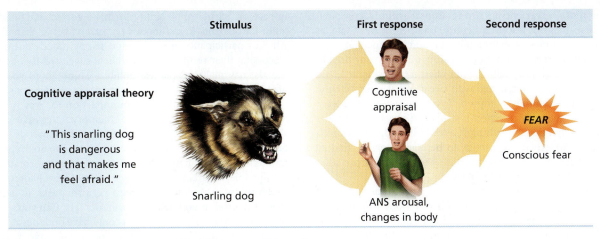

Stimulus	First response	Second response

Cognitive appraisal theory

"This snarling dog is dangerous and that makes me feel afraid."

Snarling dog

Cognitive appraisal

ANS arousal, changes in body

FEAR

Conscious fear

FIGURE 12.4 The Cognitive Appraisal Theory of Emotion

In the cognitive appraisal theory, both stimulus events and physiological arousal are cognitively appraised at the same time using situational cues and contextual factors. The emotional experience results from the appraisal of the arousal.

From Ciccarelli, Saundra; White, J. Noland, Psychology, 3rd Edition, (c) 2012. Printed and electronically reproduced by permission of Pearson Education Inc., Upper Saddle River, New Jersey.

and what your reaction means in the particular setting in which it is being experienced.

Richard Lazarus (1922–2002) was another leading proponent of the importance of cognitive appraisal. Lazarus (1991, 1995; Lazarus & Lazarus, 1994) maintained that "emotional experience cannot be understood solely in terms of what happens in the person or in the brain, but grows out of ongoing transactions with the environment that are evaluated" (Lazarus, 1984a, p. 124). Lazarus also emphasized that appraisal often occurs without conscious thought. When you have past experiences that link emotions to situations—here comes that bully I've clashed with before!—you need not explicitly search the environment for an interpretation of your arousal. This position has become known as the **cognitive appraisal theory of emotion** (see **Figure 12.4**).

To test this theory, experimenters have sometimes created situations in which environmental cues were available to provide a label for an individual's arousal.

An attractive female researcher interviewed male participants who had just crossed one of two bridges in Vancouver, Canada (Dutton & Aron, 1974). One bridge was a safe, sturdy bridge; the other was a wobbly, precarious bridge. The researcher pretended to be interested in the effects of scenery on creativity and asked the men to write brief stories about an ambiguous picture that included a woman. She also invited them to call her if they wanted more information about the research. Those men who had just crossed the dangerous bridge wrote stories with more sexual imagery, and four times as many of those men called the female researcher than did those who had crossed the safe bridge. To show that arousal was the independent variable influencing the emotional misinterpretation, the research team also arranged for another group of men to be interviewed 10 minutes or more after crossing the dangerous bridge, enough time for their physical arousal symptoms to be reduced. These nonaroused men did not show the signs of sexual response that the aroused men did.

In this situation, we can see that the main source of arousal is the danger the men feel from the wobbly bridge. However, when the men themselves appraised the situation to assess the source of their arousal, they made a *misattribution*: They believed it was caused by the attractive woman. Based on this appraisal, the men made an emotional judgment ("I am interested in this woman"). This study supports the idea that people appraise environmental cues to interpret their physiological arousal.

However, some of the specific aspects of the cognitive appraisal theory have been challenged. For example, you learned earlier that arousal states—the activity of the autonomic nervous system—accompanying different emotions are not identical (Friedman, 2010). Therefore, interpretations of at least some emotional experiences may not require appraisal.

What emotions would you be likely to feel if people all around you were wildly cheering your favorite team?

cognitive appraisal theory of emotion A theory stating that the experience of emotion is the joint effect of physiological arousal and cognitive appraisal, which serves to determine how an ambiguous inner state of arousal will be labeled.

Furthermore, experiencing strong arousal without any obvious cause does not lead to a neutral, undifferentiated state, as the theory assumes. Stop for a moment and imagine that, right now, your heart suddenly starts beating quickly, your breathing becomes fast and shallow, your chest muscles tighten, and your palms become drenched with sweat. What interpretation would you put on these symptoms? Are you surprised to learn that people generally interpret *unexplained* physical arousal as *negative,* a sign that something is wrong? In addition, people's search for an explanation tends to be biased toward finding stimuli that will explain or justify this negative interpretation (Marshall & Zimbardo, 1979; Maslach, 1979).

Another critique of the cognitive appraisal theory of emotion comes from researcher **Robert Zajonc** (pronounced *Zy-Onts*). Zajonc demonstrated conditions under which people have preferences—emotional responses to stimuli—without knowing why (Zajonc, 2000, 2001). In an extensive series of experiments on the *mere exposure effect,* participants were presented with a variety of stimuli, such as foreign words, Chinese characters, sets of numbers, and strange faces. These stimuli were flashed so briefly that participants could not consciously recognize the items. Later on, participants were asked how much they liked particular stimuli, some of which were old (that is, those stimuli previously had been flashed below the threshold of consciousness) whereas some were new. The participants tended to give higher ratings to the old items. Because participants experienced these positive emotions without conscious awareness of their origins, the emotional response could not emerge from an appraisal process.

It is probably safest to conclude that cognitive appraisal is an important process of emotional experience but not the only one (Izard, 1993). Under some circumstances, you will, in fact, look to the environment (at least unconsciously) to try to interpret why you feel the way you do. Under other circumstances, however, your emotional experiences may be under the control of the innate links provided by evolution. The physiological response will not require any interpretation. These different routes to emotional experiences suggest that emotions may have a variety of impacts on your day-to-day experiences. We will now consider some of those consequences of moods and emotions.

The Impact of Mood and Emotions

Let's begin with the impact of moods. The moods you experience have a strong effect on how you process information (Clore & Huntsinger, 2007; Forgas, 2008). In particular, people in negative moods tend to process information in a more detailed and effortful fashion than their peers in positive moods. This difference in processing style has a number of consequences. Consider judgment and decision making. You would probably agree that you will often make different judgments and decisions depending on the amount of effort you expend. In that light, think about the consequences of people's moods on the ways they made judgments of guilt or innocence. In one study, participants watched short films that put them in happy, neutral, or sad moods (Forgas & East, 2008). Once the mood was established, participants watched four videotapes of people denying that they had stolen a movie ticket; some of the people were lying. After watching each videotape, the participants judged the person's guilt or innocence. Mood had a major

impact on participants' ability to make correct judgments of guilt: Participants in sad moods performed better than chance whereas participants in neutral and happy moods did not. In discussing their results, the researchers suggested that negative moods may make people less gullible. Think about your own life: Are you more skeptical when you are in a sad mood?

Your mood will also have an impact on the way in which information gets committed to memory. Negative moods sharpen the focus of attention whereas positive moods tend to broaden that focus. For that reason, people who are in positive moods may find it harder to ignore irrelevant information. In fact, people have better implicit memory (see Chapter 7) for irrelevant information when they perform tasks in positive (versus neutral) moods (Biss & Hasher, 2011). Can you see how this mood-driven change in focus could have both negative and positive consequences? When you are in a positive mood it's hard for you to concentrate on just critical information. If you need to keep your focus tight, you might want to keep yourself in a slightly negative mood. However, because positive moods produce a broader and more flexible processing style, people in positive moods produce more creative thinking and problem solving than people in neutral moods (Baas et al., 2008). Thus, if you need to be creative, you should try to maintain a positive mood!

Let's turn from long-lasting moods to more acute emotions. Suppose you view a crime in which the perpetrator wields

Why might you worry that a positive mood could make you more gullible?

a gun. You are likely to have negative emotional arousal! That negative emotional arousal will often cause you to fall prey to an effect known as *weapon focus* (Fawcett et al., 2012). Let's see what that means.

Students in a study watched a video of a crime unfolding (Pickel, 2009). In one version of the video, the perpetrator was holding a 9-mm handgun; in the other version, the perpetrator held a music CD in a plastic case. After watching the video, the students completed a questionnaire that tested their ability to recall the perpetrator's appearance. Participants' recall was much lower when the perpetrator was holding the handgun. In different versions of the video, the perpetrator was male or female. Participants performed worst when a female was holding the gun.

Why might the female perpetrator have increased weapon focus? To answer that question, we need to take a step back to consider the more general impact of emotional arousal. Any time you look at the world, some aspects of it are more prominent (because of perceptual properties you learned about in Chapter 4) or more important to you (because of your goals in the moment). Let's call those types of stimuli *high priority*. Emotional arousal causes people to focus more mental resources on high-priority stimuli (Mather & Sutherland, 2011). That will generally make memory for those stimuli better and memory for other stimuli worse, explaining why the presence of a weapon impairs memory for other details. So, why does a female perpetrator increase weapon focus? A woman holding a gun may be a higher-priority stimulus, a more arousing stimulus, or both. In any case, when you have a strong emotional response to a particular situation, you should expect your perception of and memory for the situation to be quite different than when you have no strong arousal.

Still, it's important to acknowledge that you have some control over the impact your emotions will have on you and on others. You have the capacity for **emotion regulation**, which are processes through which people change the intensity and duration of the emotions they experience (Gyurak et al., 2011). Consider what it's like to be frightened while watching a horror movie. You may remind yourself, "This is only a movie! This is only a movie!" This strategy has two effects. First, you are distracting yourself from the events on screen that are making you anxious. Second, you are engaging in a reappraisal of the source of the arousal. Both distraction and reappraisal are successful strategies for emotion regulation (McCrae et al., 2010). Meanwhile, by making yourself seem less frightened, your successful emotion regulation will change how other people perceive your reaction to the movie.

To complete this exploration of emotions, let's turn to research that addresses individual differences in people's long-term feelings of happiness.

Subjective Well-Being

At the outset of the chapter, you addressed the question, "How are you feeling?" So far, the focus has been on the present moment: What mood or emotion are you experiencing *now*? However, the question can also apply over time, to ask "How are you feeling about your life in general?" This question addresses **subjective well-being**—individuals' overall evaluation of life satisfaction and happiness. In recent years, psychologists have paid considerable research attention to the factors that contribute to people's judgments about their own subjective well-being (Kesebir & Diener, 2008; Tay & Diener, 2011). This research focus reflects, in part, the emergence of **positive psychology** as an important movement within the profession of psychology. The goal of positive psychology is to provide people with the knowledge and skills that allow them to experience fulfilling lives. Positive psychology asks this question: "Can psychologists take what they have learned about the science and practice of treating mental illness and use it to create a practice of making people lastingly happier?" (Seligman et al., 2005, p. 410). Much of the research on subjective well-being focuses on trying to determine why some people are happier than others. As is true in most psychological domains, researchers have tried to assess the impact of genetics and environment.

To understand the impact of genetics, researchers have conducted studies using the classic methodology of behavior genetics: They have examined the extent to which monozygotic (MZ) twins and dizygotic (DZ) twins show similar reports of subjective well-being. For example, in one study, researchers obtained measures of subjective well-being from 4,322 Norwegian twins (Nes et al., 2006). Comparisons between MZ and DZ twins revealed that genetic factors accounted for 51 percent of the variance in subjective well-being for men and 49 percent of the variance for women. The researchers also gathered subjective well-being judgments at two points in time, six years apart. Genetic factors accounted for 85 percent of the correlation across time for men and 78 percent of that correlation for women. Research with a sample of 973 U.S. twin pairs also indicated a large impact of genetics on subjective well-being (Weiss et al., 2008). However, those data also suggested that personality plays an important role in these genetic effects. Chapter 13 will discuss the evidence that personality traits are highly heritable. Results from the U.S. twin sample suggest that differences in subjective well-being are consequences of the personality traits people inherit at birth. For example, people who are high in emotional stability and social engagement are also more likely to report high subjective-well being.

We have just seen that genetics has an important impact on individual differences in subjective well-being. Still, life experiences also matter. An important component of people's judgments of subjective well-being is the balance of positive and negative emotions in their lives.

A team of researchers obtained data from 8,557 participants across 46 countries (Kuppens et al., 2008). Participants provided ratings of their life satisfaction by responding to statements such as "In most ways, my life is close to my

emotion regulation The processes through which people change the intensity and duration of the emotions they experience.

subjective well-being Individuals' overall evaluation of life satisfaction and happiness.

positive psychology A movement within psychology that applies research to provide people with the knowledge and skills that allow them to experience fulfilling lives.

ideal" (p. 71) on a 7-point scale that ranged from "strongly disagree" to "strongly agree." They used a 9-point scale—ranging from "not at all" to "all the time"—to indicate how often they had felt positive emotions (such as pride, gratitude, and love) and negative emotions (such as guilt, shame, and jealousy) in the last week. The researchers' analyses disclosed consistent relationships among these measures. In general, participants reported higher levels of life satisfaction when they had more positive emotional experiences and fewer negative emotional experiences. However, positive emotions had about twice as much impact on life satisfaction judgments as did negative emotions. The analyses also revealed somewhat different patterns across cultures. For example, cultures differ with respect to the amount of effort people need to expend to ensure their day-to-day survival. For cultures in which survival is an issue, judgments of life satisfaction depended less on positive emotional experiences.

You can probably relate these results to your own feelings of subjective well-being: As you cast your thoughts over the last week, what types of emotional experiences come readily to mind?

You might also think about the features of your life that gave rise to that particular assortment of emotional experiences. Researchers have tested a variety of hypotheses about life events that may affect subjective well-being. For example, major negative life events, such as the loss of a job or the death of a spouse, often have a damaging impact on subjective well-being (Lucas, 2007). Researchers have also looked at ongoing differences in the circumstances of people's lives. For example, researchers have suggested that "the single most important source of happiness" is good social relationships (Kesebir & Diener, 2008, p. 122). That conclusion should be familiar from earlier sections of *Psychology and Life*; later in this chapter you'll see that social support is an important resource for coping with stress. Researchers have also tried to understand the relationship between wealth and subjective well-being. When people struggle to meet their basic needs, they often report low levels of life satisfaction and happiness (Diener et al., 2010; Howell & Howell, 2008). However, once people pass the threshold at which those basic needs are secure, the correlation between wealth and subjective well-being is quite modest. If you must make a choice between more money and more friends, the results of positive psychology suggest that you should most often opt for more friends.

We have now explored important short- and long-term consequences of moods and emotions. The next section turns to the topic of stress and how to cope with it. You will learn how to take cognitive control over how you are "feeling."

Stop *and* Review

① What has cross-cultural research revealed about the recognition of facial expressions?

② What role does the autonomous nervous system play in experience of emotions?

③ What is the main claim of the Cannon–Bard theory of emotion?

④ What is the general impact of mood on information processing?

⑤ What might be the single most important source of happiness?

CRITICAL THINKING   Recall the study that examined weapon focus. Why might the researcher have chosen to test memory for the perpetrator's appearance?

✓— **Study** and **Review** on **MyPsychLab**

STRESS OF LIVING

Suppose I asked you to keep track of how you are "feeling" over the course of a day. You might report that for brief periods, you felt happiness, sadness, anger, astonishment, and so on. There is one feeling, however, that people often report as a kind of background noise for much of their day-to-day experience, and that is stress. Modern industrialized society sets a rapid, hectic pace for living. People often have too many demands placed on their time, are worried about uncertain futures, and have little time for family and fun. But would you be better off without stress? A stress-free life would offer no challenge—no difficulties to surmount, no new fields to conquer, and no reasons to sharpen your wits or improve your abilities. Every organism faces challenges from its external environment and from its personal needs. The organism must solve these problems to survive and thrive. ◉

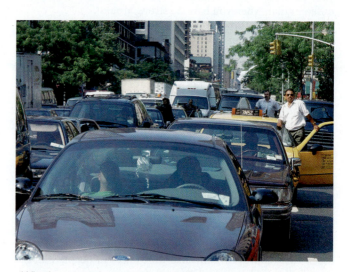

Whether at work or play, individuals in contemporary society are likely to encounter a stressful environment. What situations in your life do you find most stressful?

◉ **Watch** the **Video** *The Basics: Stress and Your Health* on **MyPsychLab**

Psychology in Your Life

CAN YOU ACCURATELY PREDICT YOUR FUTURE EMOTIONS?

Suppose you're about to submit an assignment. A researcher stops you and asks you to look into the future. First, he asks you to predict what grade you think you'll get. Next, he asks you to predict how you imagine you will feel—on the dimensions of rejoicing and regret—if your actual grade were higher or lower than that prediction or pretty much accurate. How might you respond?

When researchers conducted this experiment, their goal was to compare students' predictions about their emotional responses to their actual responses (Sevdalis & Harvey, 2007). After the students received their grades, the researchers found them again to ask them how the outcomes made them feel. On average, the students did somewhat better on their assignments than they had predicted. However, those better-than-expected outcomes didn't make them nearly as happy as they thought they would: The students experienced much less rejoicing than they anticipated.

Let's consider a second example of people's predictions about future emotions. Suppose, as a city dweller, you dash down a stairway just in time to watch the doors close on your subway car. How would you feel? Suppose instead you missed the train by a wider margin of time. Now how would you feel?

A team of researchers conducted exactly that study (Gilbert et al., 2004). They approached people on a subway platform and offered them $1 to fill out a brief questionnaire. One group of participants were *Experiencers*. Those people

had actually missed a train by either a narrow margin (one minute) or a wide margin (five minutes). They indicated how regretful they felt by providing a rating on a scale ranging from "not at all" to "extremely." Participants cast in the role of *Forecasters* used the same scale to predict how regretful they imagined they would feel had they missed the train by a narrow or wide margin. (Each Forecaster answered the question for just one margin.)

Forecasters predicted that people would experience more regret for the narrow margin than for the wide margin. However, the Experiencers actually reported nearly the same regret for the narrow margin and the wide margin. Once again, we see that people's predictions about their future feelings aren't very accurate.

Why do people have difficulty predicting how they might respond to particular outcomes? In large part, it seems that people are better than they anticipate at putting outcomes into a broader perspective (Kermer et al., 2006). When people actually miss a subway train, they are able to take that outcome in stride by putting it in the larger context of their unfolding day. They don't dwell on the isolated event in a way that makes them continue to feel negative emotions. By contrast, when people predict how they're going to feel, they aren't able to interpret the outcome in the fuller context. The same is true for positive emotions. You might not rejoice as much as you predict to a better-than-expected grade because that outcome occurs as part of your whole ongoing life.

Stress is the pattern of responses an organism makes to stimulus events that disturb its equilibrium and tax or exceed its ability to cope. The stimulus events include a large variety of external and internal conditions that collectively are called stressors. A **stressor** is a stimulus event that places a demand on an organism for some kind of adaptive response: a bicyclist swerves in front of your car, your professor moves up the due date of your term paper, you're asked to run for class president. An individual's response to the need for change is made up of a diverse combination of reactions taking place on several levels, including physiological, behavioral, emotional, and cognitive. People typically associate stress with *distress*—and assume that all stress is bad. However, you also experience *eustress*. (*Eu* is an ancient Greek suffix meaning "good.") As you'll see by the end of this section, in many circumstances stress can bring about positive changes in your life. ⊙➤

Figure 12.5 on page 334 diagrams the elements of the stress process. The goal for this section is to give you a clear understanding of all the features represented in this figure. The

section begins by considering general physiological responses to stressors.

Physiological Stress Reactions

How would you respond if you arrived at a class and discovered that you were about to have a pop quiz? You would probably agree that this would cause you some stress, but what does that mean for your body's reactions? Many of the physiological responses that occur for emotional situations are also relevant to

---

⊙➤ **Simulate** the **Experiment** *How Stressed Are You?* on **MyPsychLab**

stress The pattern of specific and nonspecific responses an organism makes to stimulus events that disturb its equilibrium and tax or exceed its ability to cope.

stressor An internal or external event or stimulus that induces stress.

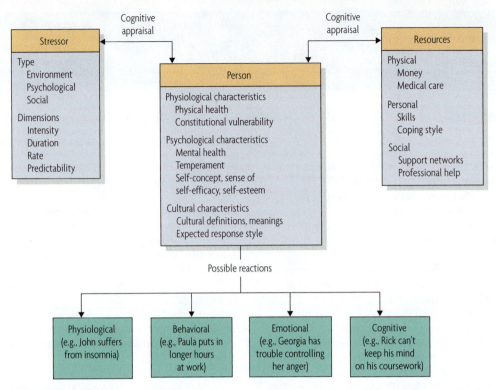

FIGURE 12.5 A Model of Stress

Cognitive appraisal of the stress situation interacts with the stressor and the physical, social, and personal resources available for dealing with the stressor. Individuals respond to threats on various levels: physiological, behavioral, emotional, and cognitive. Some responses are adaptive, and others are maladaptive or even lethal.

day-to-day instances of stress. Such transient states of arousal, with typically clear onset and offset patterns, are examples of **acute stress**. **Chronic stress,** in contrast, is a state of enduring arousal, continuing over time, in which demands are perceived as greater than the inner and outer resources available for dealing with them. An example of chronic stress might be a continuous frustration with your inability to find time to do all the things you want to do. Let's see how your body responds to these different types of stresses.

Emergency Reactions to Acute Threats In the 1920s, Walter Cannon outlined the first scientific description of the way animals and humans respond to danger. He found that a sequence of activity is triggered in the nerves and glands to prepare the body either to defend itself and struggle or to run away to safety. Cannon called this dual stress response the **fight-or-flight response.** At the center of this stress response is the *hypothalamus,* which is involved in a variety of emotional responses. The hypothalamus has sometimes been referred to as the stress center because of its twin functions in emergencies: (1) It controls the autonomic nervous system (ANS) and (2) it activates the pituitary gland. ✳

The ANS regulates the activities of the body's organs. In stressful conditions, breathing becomes faster and deeper, heart rate increases, blood vessels constrict, and blood pressure rises. In addition to these internal changes, muscles open the passages of the throat and nose to allow more air into the lungs while also producing facial expressions of strong emotion. Messages go to smooth muscles to stop certain bodily functions, such as digestion, that are irrelevant to preparing for the emergency at hand.

Another function of the ANS during stress is to get adrenaline flowing. It signals the inner part of the adrenal glands, the *adrenal medulla,* to release two hormones, *epinephrine* and *norepinephrine,* which, in turn, signal a number of other organs to perform their specialized functions. The spleen releases more red blood corpuscles (to aid in clotting if there is an injury), and the bone marrow is stimulated to make more white corpuscles (to combat possible infection). The liver is stimulated to produce more sugar, building up body energy.

The *pituitary gland* responds to signals from the hypothalamus by secreting two hormones vital to the stress reaction.

....

✳ **Explore** the **Concept** *Virtual Brain: Emotion, Stress, and Health* on **MyPsychLab**

acute stress A transient state of arousal with typically clear onset and offset patterns.

chronic stress A continuous state of arousal in which an individual perceives demands as greater than the inner and outer resources available for dealing with them.

fight-or-flight response A sequence of internal activities triggered when an organism is faced with a threat; prepares the body for combat and struggle or for running away to safety; recent evidence suggests that the response is characteristic only of males.

FIGURE 12.6 The Body's Reaction to Stress

Stress produces a wide range of physiological changes in your body.

Blood vessels in skin, skeletal muscles, brain, and viscera constrict.

Sweating increases.

Skin and body hair produce "goose bumps."

Adrenal glands stimulate adrenaline secretion, increasing blood sugar, blood pressure, and heart rate.

Anal sphincter closes.
Urinary sphincter closes.

Pupil dilates and ciliary muscle relaxes for far vision.

Bronchi dilate.

Heart accelerates; rate of beating increases strength of contraction.

Digestive tract decreases peristalsis.

Liver releases sugar into the bloodstream.
Secretions of the pancreas decrease.
Secretions of digestive fluids decrease.
Blood vessels in external genitalia dilate.
Urinary bladder relaxes.

The *thyrotropic hormone* (TTH) stimulates the *thyroid gland,* which makes more energy available to the body. The *adreno-corticotropic hormone* (ACTH), known as the "stress hormone," stimulates the outer part of the adrenal glands, the *adrenal cortex,* resulting in the release of hormones that control metabolic processes and the release of sugar from the liver into the blood. ACTH also signals various organs to release about 30 other hormones, each of which plays a role in the body's adjustment to this call to arms. A summary of this physiological stress response is shown in **Figure 12.6**.

An analysis by health psychologist **Shelley Taylor** and her colleagues (2000; Taylor, 2006) suggests that these physiological responses to stress may have different consequences for females than for males. Taylor and her colleagues suggest that females do not experience *fight-or-flight*. Rather, these researchers argue that stressors lead females to experience a **tend-and-befriend response:** In times of stress, females ensure the safety of their offspring by tending to their needs; females befriend other members of their social group with the same goal of reducing the vulnerability of their offspring. You can see how this analysis of sex differences in stress responses fits with the earlier discussions of evolutionary perspectives on human behavior. For example, the discussion in Chapter 11 of human sexual behaviors noted that men and women's *mating strategies* differ, in part, because of the relative roles men and women have played—over the course of evolution—in child rearing. The idea here is very much the same: Because of men and women's different evolutionary niches with respect to nurturing offspring, the same initial physiological responses to stress ultimately produce quite different behaviors.

Unfortunately, neither the fight-or-flight nor the tend-and-befriend response is entirely useful for contemporary lives. Many of the stressors both men and women experience on a day-to-day basis make the physiological stress responses fairly maladaptive. Suppose, for example, you are taking a difficult exam and the clock is swiftly ticking away. Although you might value the heightened attentiveness brought about by your stress response, the rest of the physiological changes do you no good: There's no one to fight or to tend, and so on. The responses that developed in the species as adaptive preparations for dealing with external dangers are counterproductive for dealing with many contemporary types of psychological stressors. This is particularly true because, as you will see next, many people live their lives under circumstances of chronic stress.

The General Adaptation Syndrome (GAS) and Chronic Stress The first modern researcher to investigate the effects of continued severe stress on the body was **Hans Selye** (1907–1982), a Canadian endocrinologist. Beginning in the late 1930s, Selye reported on the complex response of laboratory animals to damaging agents such as bacterial infections, toxins, trauma, forced restraint, heat, cold, and so on. According to Selye's theory of stress, many kinds of stressors can trigger the same reaction or general bodily response. All stressors call for *adaptation:* An organism must maintain or regain its integrity

....

tend-and-befriend response A response to stressors that is hypothesized to be typical for females; stressors prompt females to protect their offspring and join social groups to reduce vulnerability.

Stage I: Alarm reaction (continuously repeated throughout life)	Stage II: Resistance (continuously repeated throughout life)	Stage III: Exhaustion
• Enlargement of adrenal cortex • Enlargement of lymphatic system • Increase in hormone levels • Response to specific stressor • Epinephrine release associated with high levels of physiological arousal and negative affect • Greater susceptibility to increased intensity of stressor • Heightened susceptibility to illness (If prolonged, the slower components of the GAS are set into motion, beginning with Stage II.)	• Shrinkage of adrenal cortex • Return of lymph nodes to normal size • Sustaining of hormone levels • High physiological arousal • Counteraction of parasympathetic branch of ANS • Enduring of stressor; resistance to further debilitating effects • Heightened sensitivity to stress (If stress continues at intense levels, hormonal reserves are depleted, fatigue sets in, and individual enters Stage III.)	• Enlargement/dysfunction of lymphatic structures • Increase in hormone levels • Depletion of adaptive hormones • Decreased ability to resist either original or extraneous stressors • Affective experience—often depression • Illness • Death

FIGURE 12.7 The General Adaptation Syndrome (GAS)

Following exposure to a stressor, the body's resistance is diminished until the physiological changes of the corresponding alarm reaction bring it back up to the normal level. If the stressor continues, the bodily signs characteristic of the alarm reaction virtually disappear; resistance to the particular stressor rises above normal but drops for other stressors. This adaptive resistance returns the body to its normal level of functioning. Following prolonged exposure to the stressor, adaptation breaks down; signs of alarm reaction reappear, the stressor effects are irreversible, and the individual becomes ill and may die.

and well-being by restoring equilibrium, or homeostasis. The response to stressors was described by Selye as the **general adaptation syndrome (GAS).** It includes three stages: an alarm reaction, a stage of resistance, and a stage of exhaustion (Selye, 1976a, 1976b). *Alarm reactions* are brief periods of bodily arousal that prepare the body for vigorous activity. If a stressor is prolonged, the body enters a stage of *resistance*—a state of moderate arousal. During the stage of resistance, the organism can endure and *resist* further debilitating effects of prolonged stressors. However, if the stressor is sufficiently long lasting or intense, the body's resources become depleted and the organism enters the stage of *exhaustion.* The three stages are diagrammed and explained in **Figure 12.7**

Selye identified some of the dangers associated with the stage of exhaustion. Recall, for example, that ACTH plays a role in the short-term response to stress. In the long term, however, its action reduces the ability of natural killer cells to destroy cancer cells and other life-threatening infections. When the body is stressed chronically, the increased

production of "stress hormones" compromises the integrity of the immune system. This application of the general adaptation syndrome has proven valuable to explain **psychosomatic disorders**—illnesses that could not be wholly explained by physical causes—that had baffled physicians who had never considered stress as a cause for illness and disease. What serves the body well in adapting to acute stress impairs the body's response to chronic stress.

Selye's research makes disease seem an inevitable response to stress. We will see, however, that your psychological interpretation of what is stressful and what is not stressful—the way in which you appraise potentially stressful events—has an impact on your body's physiological response. To give a full account of the effect of stress on your body, we will have to combine Selye's foundational physiological theory with later research on psychological factors.

Psychological Stress Reactions

Your physiological stress reactions are automatic, predictable, built-in responses over which you normally have no conscious control. However, many psychological reactions are learned. They depend on perceptions and interpretations of the world. This section will discuss psychological responses to different categories of stressors, such as major life events and traumatic experiences.

general adaptation syndrome (GAS) The pattern of nonspecific adaptational physiological mechanisms that occurs in response to continuing threat by almost any serious stressor.

psychosomatic disorder Physical disorder aggravated by or primarily attributable to prolonged emotional stress or other psychological causes.

What are the physiological consequences of chronic stress?

Major Life Events The influence of life events on subsequent mental and physical health has been a target of considerable research. It started in the 1960s with the development of the Social Readjustment Rating Scale (SRRS), a simple measure for rating the degree of adjustment required by the various life changes, both pleasant and unpleasant, that many people experience. The scale was developed from the responses of adults, from all walks of life, who were asked to identify from a list those life events that applied to them. These adults rated the amount of readjustment required for each change by comparing each to marriage, which was arbitrarily assigned a value of 50 life-change units. Researchers then calculated the total number of **life-change units (LCUs)** an individual had undergone, using the units as a measure of the amount of stress the individual had experienced (Holmes & Rahe, 1967).

The SRRS was updated in the 1990s (see **Figure 12.8**). The researchers used the same procedure of asking participants to rate the stress of life events as compared to marriage (Miller & Rahe, 1997). In this update, the LCU estimates went up 45 percent over the original values—that is, participants in the 1990s reported that they were experiencing overall much higher levels of stress than their peers had in the 1960s. Women in the 1990s also reported experiencing more stress in their lives than did men. Researchers continue to relate reports on the SRRS to mental and physical health outcomes. Consider a study in which 268 people completed the scale (Lynch et al., 2005). There was a positive correlation between SRRS scores and participants' total number of medical visits in the following six months: In general, the participants who had the highest SRRS scores also visited their doctors most often.

Researchers have found a variety of ways to examine the relationship between life events and health outcomes. For example, one study followed 16,881 adults for two years (Lietzén et al., 2011). At the beginning of the study, none of the participants had been diagnosed with asthma. Two years later, participants who had experienced high numbers of stressful life events (such as the illness of a family member or marital problems) were considerably more likely to have developed asthma. Consider another study that should have immediate relevance to the choices you make about how to organize your schoolwork.

When a professor gives you an assignment—a stressful life event in every student's life—do you try to take care of it as soon as possible, or do you put it off to the very last minute? Psychologists have developed a measurement

Featured Study

life-change unit (LCU) In stress research, the measure of the stress levels of different types of change experienced during a given period.

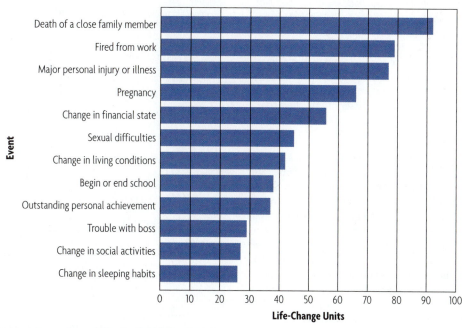

FIGURE 12.8 Life-Change Units for Some Major Life Events
Students may have to adapt to a number of important changes during their school years. Researchers have calculated the number of life-change units associated with such major life events.

Data from M. A. Miller and R. H. Rahe. Life changes scaling for the 1990s. *Journal of Psychosomatic Research, 43*(3): 279–292, Copyright (1997), with permission from Elsevier.

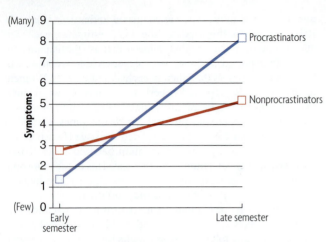

FIGURE 12.9 The Health Costs of Procrastination

Researchers identified students who were, generally, procrastinators and nonprocrastinators. The students were asked to report, early and late in the semester, how many symptoms of physical illness they had experienced. By late in the semester all students showed increases in symptoms. However—as all their work came due—procrastinators were reporting even more symptoms than their nonprocrastinating peers.

device called the General Procrastination Scale (Lay, 1986) to differentiate those individuals who habitually put things off—procrastinators—from those who don't—nonprocrastinators. A pair of researchers administered this scale to students in a health psychology course who had a paper due late in the semester. The students were also asked to report, early and late in the semester, how many symptoms of physical illness they had experienced. Not surprisingly, procrastinators, on average, turned their papers in later than did nonprocrastinators; procrastinators also, on average, obtained lower grades on those papers. **Figure 12.9** *displays the effect of procrastination on physical health. As you can see, early in the semester, procrastinators reported fewer symptoms, but by late in the semester, they were reporting more symptoms than their nonprocrastinating peers (Tice & Baumeister, 1997).*

You see in this study why not all life events have the same impact on all people. The nonprocrastinators got to work right away and so experienced stress and symptoms early in the semester. However, the consequence for the procrastinators of avoiding the early semester stress was a great increase in physical illness toward the end of the semester. Therefore, they were likely to be feeling ill just at the point in the semester when they needed to be in good health to complete all the work they had put off! Think about these results as you develop your own plan for navigating each semester. If you believe that you habitually procrastinate, consider consulting with a psychologist or school counselor to modify your behavior. Your grades and health are at stake!

Traumatic Events   An event that is negative but also uncontrollable, unpredictable, or ambiguous is particularly stressful.

These conditions hold especially true in the case of *traumatic events.* Some traumatic events, such as rape and automobile crashes, affect individuals. Others, such as earthquakes, tornadoes, and terrorist attacks, have a broader impact. On September 11, 2001, attacks on the World Trade Center and the Pentagon with commercial aircraft led to the deaths of almost 3,000 people. With the goal of providing appropriate mental health care, researchers moved swiftly to assess the psychological aftermath of the attacks.

One particular focus was on the prevalence of **posttraumatic stress disorder (PTSD).** PTSD is a stress reaction in which individuals suffer from persistent reexperiences of the traumatic event in the form, for example, of flashbacks or nightmares (*DSM-IV*, 1994). Sufferers experience an emotional numbing in relation to everyday events and feelings of alienation from other people. Finally, the emotional pain of this reaction can result in an increase in various symptoms, such as sleep problems, guilt about surviving, difficulty in concentrating, and an exaggerated startle response.

A team of researchers wished to assess the long-term impact of the events of 9/11/01 (DiGrande et al., 2011). The study focused on 3,271 civilians who had actually been evacuated from the World Trade Center that morning. The data were collected between September 2003 and November of 2004, two to three years after the attack. As seen in **Table 12.1**, only 4.4 percent of the participants had no symptoms associated with PTSD. Of the people who had been in the Twin Towers

Table 12.1 • The Psychological Impact of Exposure to the Events of September 11, 2001

Symptoms of Posttraumatic Stress Disorder	Percent of participants
No symptoms reported	4.4
Reported re-experiences of the events	
Intrusive memories	33.4
Dreams or nightmares	13.5
Reported avoidance of stimuli associated with the event	
Avoidance of thoughts and feelings	31.5
Avoidance of reminders	25.9
Reported increased arousal	
Insomnia	31.6
Irritability or anger	25.4
Probable diagnosis of PTSD	15.0

Data from DiGrande, L., Neria, Y., Brackbill, R. M., Pulliam, P., & Galea, S. (2011). Long-term posttraumatic stress symptoms among 3,271 civilian survivors of the September 11, 2001, terrorist attacks on the World Trade Center. *American Journal of Epidemiology*, 173, 271–281.

posttraumatic stress disorder (PTSD) An anxiety disorder characterized by the persistent re-experience of traumatic events through distressing recollections, dreams, hallucinations, or dissociative flashbacks; develops in response to rapes, life-threatening events, severe injury, and natural disasters.

What factors changed the likelihood that an individual would develop PTSD after the events of September 11, 2001?

the morning of the attack, the vast majority reported some symptoms: re-experiences of the events, avoidance of stimuli associated with the event, and/or increased arousal that stemmed from the event. Despite the passage of two to three years, 15 percent of the sample met the diagnostic criteria for full PTSD. The study revealed several factors that made PTSD more likely. For example, people who were evacuated from higher floors, people who personally witnessed horrors, and people who were themselves injured had higher rates of PTSD.

As noted earlier, people also suffer from individual traumatic events with a negative impact on their psychological health. For example, rape victims often show many of the signs of posttraumatic stress (Ullman et al., 2007). In assessments two weeks after being assaulted, 94 percent of rape victims were diagnosed with PTSD; 12 weeks after the assault, 51 percent of the victims still met diagnostic criteria (Foa & Riggs, 1995). These data illustrate that the emotional responses of posttraumatic stress can occur in an acute form immediately following a trauma and can subside over a period of several months. Chapter 14 will return to the topic of PTSD in the discussion of anxiety disorders.

Chronic Stressors The discussion of physiological responses to stress made a distinction between stressors that are acute, with clear onsets and offsets, versus those that are chronic—that is, endure over time. With psychological stressors, it's not always easy to draw a sharp distinction. Suppose, for example, your bicycle is stolen. Originally, this is an acute source of stress. However, if you begin to worry constantly that your new bike will also be stolen, the stress associated with this

event can become chronic. Researchers have found this pattern in people who suffer from serious illnesses like cancer, HIV infection, and diabetes (de Ridder et al., 2008; Morris et al., 2011). The chronic stress of coping with the anxiety of a diagnosis and treatment may impair health more rapidly than the disease alone would.

For many people, chronic stress arises from conditions in society and the environment. What cumulative effects do crime, economic conditions, pollution, and the threat of terrorism have on you? How do these and other environmental stressors affect your mental well-being? Some groups of people suffer chronic stress by virtue of their socioeconomic status or racial identity, with stark consequences for overall well-being (Santiago et al., 2011; Sternthal et al., 2011). Consider a longitudinal study of 1,037 New Zealanders that investigated the relationship between socioeconomic disadvantage in childhood and health outcomes when the participants were 32 years old (Danese et al., 2009). Early economic hardship predicted higher levels of adult health risks such as excess weight, high blood pressure, and high cholesterol. Childhood maltreatment by parents and social isolation also had negative consequences for the participants' psychological and physical health as adults. In fact, the more chronic stressors participants had endured as children, the greater the disease risks as adults.

Daily Hassles You may agree that the end of a relationship, an earthquake, or prejudice might cause stress, but what about the smaller stressors you experience on a day-to-day basis? What happened to you yesterday? You probably didn't get a divorce or survive a plane crash. You're more likely to have lost your notes or textbook. Perhaps you were late for an important appointment, or you got a parking ticket, or a noisy neighbor ruined your sleep. These are the types of recurring day-to-day stressors that confront most people, most of the time.

This trader on the floor of the New York Stock Exchange has likely experienced chronic stress as a result of the uncertain economy. What are some possible consequences for his physical and mental health?

In a diary study, a group of White middle-class middle-aged men and women kept track of their daily hassles over a one-year period (along with a record of major life changes and physical symptoms). A clear relationship emerged between hassles and health problems: The more frequent and intense the hassles people reported, the poorer was their health, both physical and mental (Lazarus, 1981, 1984b). Consider a study that demonstrated the impact of daily hassles on adolescents.

Featured Study

A group of 236 adolescents (with an average age of 16.1 years) completed a daily hassles scale. The scale asked the adolescents to indicate how frequently they had experiences such as "Being 'put down' by a family member," "Having to lie to my parents," and "Being bullied or teased" (Wright et al., 2010, p. 222). The adolescents indicated the frequency of such experiences on a 5-point scale that ranged from "never" to "daily." They also completed measures of anxiety, depression, and life satisfaction. In general, the adolescents who reported the highest levels of daily hassles also reported the most negative states of mental health (that is, they reported more anxiety and more depression). In addition, adolescents with more daily hassles reported lower levels of life satisfaction.

This study confirms that daily hassles have a considerable impact on people's sense of well-being.

Although this section has focused on day-to-day hassles, it's worth noting that, for many people, daily hassles may be balanced out by daily positive experiences (Lazarus & Lazarus, 1994). For example, one study asked 132 men and women to report the frequency and intensity of the hassles (that is, irritating events) and uplifts (that is, happy events) in their lives (Jain et al., 2007). The researchers also measured the participants' blood levels of substances (such as inflammatory factors) that are indicators of risk for cardiovascular disease. Higher levels of reported hassles were associated with higher levels of these risk indicators; higher levels of reported uplifts were associated with lower levels. Therefore, if we want to predict your life course based on daily hassles, we also need to know something about the daily uplifts your life provides (Lyubomirsky et al., 2005).

You have just learned about many sources of stress in people's lives. Psychologists have recognized for quite a long time that the impact of these different types of stressors depends in large part on how effectively people can cope with them. Let's now consider how people cope successfully and unsuccessfully with stress.

Coping with Stress

If living is inevitably stressful, and if chronic stress can disrupt your life and even kill you, you need to learn how to manage stress. **Coping** refers to the process of dealing with internal or external demands that are perceived as straining or exceeding an individual's resources (Lazarus & Folkman, 1984). Coping

....

◉ **Watch** the **Video** *In the Real World: Reducing Stress, Improving Health* on **MyPsychLab**

✳ **Explore** the **Concept** *The Effect of Cognitive Appraisal on Responses to Stressors* on **MyPsychLab**

coping The process of dealing with internal or external demands that are perceived to be threatening or overwhelming.

may consist of behavioral, emotional, or motivational responses and thoughts. This section begins by describing how cognitive appraisal affects what you experience as stressful. We then consider types of coping responses, including both general principles of coping and specific interventions. Finally, we consider some individual differences in individuals' ability to cope with stress. ◉

Appraisal of Stress   When you cope with stressful situations, your first step is to define in what ways they are, in fact, stressful. Cognitive appraisal is the cognitive interpretation and evaluation of a stressor. Cognitive appraisal plays a central role in defining the situation—what the demand is, how big a threat it is, and what resources you have for meeting it (Lazarus, 1993; Lazarus & Lazarus, 1994). Some stressors, such as undergoing bodily injury or finding one's house on fire, are experienced as threats by almost everyone. However, many other stressors can be defined in various ways, depending on your personal life situation, the relation of a particular demand to your central goals, your competence in dealing with the demand, and your self-assessment of that competence. The situation that causes acute distress for another person may be all in a day's work for you. Try to notice, and understand, the life events that are different for you and your friends and family: Some situations cause you stress but not your friends and family; other events cause them stress but not you. Why? ✳

Richard Lazarus, whose general theory of appraisal was addressed in the discussion of emotions, distinguished two stages in the cognitive appraisal of demands. *Primary appraisal* describes the initial evaluation of the seriousness of a demand. This evaluation starts with the questions "What's happening?" and "Is this thing good for me, stressful, or irrelevant?" If the answer to the second question is "stressful," you appraise the potential impact of the stressor by determining whether harm has occurred or is likely to and whether action is required (see **Table 12.2**). Once you decide something must be done, *secondary appraisal* begins. You evaluate the personal and social resources that are available to deal with the stressful

Table 12.2 • Stages in Stable Decision Making/Cognitive Appraisal

Stage	Key Questions
1. Appraising the challenge	Are the risks serious if I don't change?
2. Surveying alternatives	Is this alternative an acceptable means for dealing with the challenge? Have I sufficiently surveyed the available alternatives?
3. Weighing alternatives	Which alternative is best? Could the best alternative meet the essential requirements?
4. Deliberating about commitment	Will I implement the best alternative and allow others to know?
5. Adhering despite negative feedback	Are the risks serious if I *don't* change? Are the risks serious if I *do* change?

circumstance and consider the action options that are needed. Appraisal continues as coping responses are tried; if the first ones don't work and the stress persists, new responses are initiated, and their effectiveness is evaluated.

Cognitive appraisal is an example of a stress moderator variable. **Stress moderator variables** are those variables that change the impact of a stressor on a given type of stress reaction. Moderator variables filter or modify the usual effects of stressors on the individual's reactions. For example, your level of fatigue and general health status are moderator variables influencing your reaction to a given psychological or physical stressor. When you are in good shape, you can deal with a stressor better than when you aren't. You can see how cognitive appraisal also fits the definition of a moderator variable. The way in which you appraise a stressor will determine the types of coping responses you need to bring to it. Let's now consider general types of coping responses.

Types of Coping Responses   Suppose you have a big exam coming up. You've thought about it—you've appraised the situation—and you're quite sure that this is a stressful situation. What can you do? It's important to note that coping can precede a potentially stressful event in the form of **anticipatory coping** (Folkman, 1984). How do you deal with the stress of the upcoming exam? How do you tell your parents that you are dropping out of school or your lover that you are no longer in love? Anticipating a stressful situation leads to many thoughts and feelings that themselves may be stress inducing, as in the cases of interviews, speeches, or blind dates. You need to know how to cope.

The two main ways of coping are defined by whether the goal is to confront the problem directly—*problem-directed coping*—or to lessen the discomfort associated with the stress—*emotion-focused coping* (Billings & Moos, 1982; Lazarus & Folkman, 1984). Several subcategories of these two basic approaches are shown in **Table 12.3**. ✳

Let's begin with problem-directed coping. "Taking the bull by the horns" is how we usually characterize the strategy of facing up to a problem situation. This approach includes all strategies designed to deal *directly* with the stressor, whether through overt action or through realistic problem-solving activities. You face up to a bully or run away; you try to win him or her over with bribes or other incentives. Your focus is on the problem to be dealt with and on the agent that has induced the stress. You acknowledge the call to action, you appraise the situation and your resources for dealing with it, and

you undertake a response that is appropriate for removing or lessening the threat. Such problem-solving efforts are useful for managing *controllable stressors*—those stressors that you can change or eliminate through your actions, such as overbearing bosses or underwhelming grades.

The emotion-focused approach is useful for managing the impact of more *uncontrollable stressors*. Suppose you are responsible for the care of a parent with Alzheimer's. In that situation, there is no "bully" you can eliminate from the environment; you cannot make the disease go away. Even in this situation, some forms of problem-directed coping would be useful. For example, you could modify your work schedule to make it easier to provide care. However, because you cannot eliminate the source of stress, you also can try to change your feelings and thoughts about the disease. For example, you might take part in a support group for Alzheimer's caregivers or learn relaxation techniques. These approaches still constitute a coping strategy because you are acknowledging that there is a threat to your well-being and you are taking steps to modify that threat.

You will be better off if you have multiple strategies to help you cope in stressful situations (Bonanno et al., 2011). For coping to be successful, your resources need to match the perceived demand. Thus the availability of multiple coping strategies is adaptive because you are more likely to achieve a match and manage the stressful event. Consider a study that examined the ways in which women cope with the stress of undergoing surgery for breast cancer (Roussi et al., 2007). The women reported their distress levels and coping strategies (such as problem-directed and/or emotion-focused strategies) a day before the surgeries, three days after the procedure, and again three months later. The women who reported that they were using multiple coping strategies in the days after their surgeries reported less distress three months later.

Researchers who study coping have discovered that some individuals meet stressors with a particular degree of

....

✳ **Explore** the **Concept** *Coping Strategies and Their Effects* on **MyPsychLab**

stress moderator variable Variable that changes the impact of a stressor on a given type of stress reaction.

anticipatory coping Efforts made in advance of a potentially stressful event to overcome, reduce, or tolerate the imbalance between perceived demands and available resources.

Table 12.3 • Taxonomy of Coping Strategies

Type of Coping Strategy	Example
PROBLEM-DIRECTED COPING	
Change stressor or one's relationship to it through direct actions and/or problem-solving strategies	Fight (destroy, remove, or weaken the threat)
	Flight (distance oneself from the threat)
	Seek options to fight-or-flight (negotiating, bargaining, compromising)
	Prevent future stress (act to increase one's resistance or decrease strength of anticipated stress)
EMOTION-FOCUSED COPING	
Change self through activities that make one feel better but do not chnage the stressor	Somatically focused activities (use of antianxiety medication, relaxation, biofeedback)
	Cognitively focused activities (planned distractions, fantasies, thoughts about oneself)
	Therapy to adjust conscious or unconscious processes that lead to additional anxiety

Why are multiple coping strategies beneficial for individuals such as Alzheimer's caregivers?

critics sitting there in the nude—this surely takes away a great deal of their fearsome power. Anxious about being shy at a party you must attend? Think about finding someone who is more shy than you and reducing his or her social anxiety by initiating a conversation.

You can also manage stress by changing what you tell yourself about it and by changing your handling of it. Cognitive-behavior therapist **Donald Meichenbaum** (1977, 1985, 1993) has proposed a three-phase process that allows for such *stress inoculation*. In Phase 1, people work to develop a greater awareness of their actual behavior, what instigates it, and what its results are. One of the best ways of doing this is to keep daily logs. By helping people redefine their problems in terms of their causes and results, these records can increase their feelings of control. You may discover, for example, that your grades are low (a stressor) because you always leave too little time to do a good job on your class assignments. In Phase 2, people begin to identify new behaviors that negate the maladaptive, self-defeating behaviors. Perhaps you might create a fixed "study time" or limit your phone calls to 10 minutes each night. In Phase 3, after adaptive behaviors are being emitted, individuals appraise the consequences of their new behaviors, avoiding the former internal dialogue of put-downs. Instead of telling themselves, "I was lucky the professor called on me when I happened to have read the text," they say, "I'm glad I was prepared for the professor's question. It feels great to be able to respond intelligently in that class."

This three-phase approach means initiating responses and self-statements that are incompatible with previous defeatist cognitions. Once started on this path, people realize that they are changing—and can take full credit for the change, which promotes further successes. **Table 12.4** gives examples of the new kinds of self-statements that help in dealing with stressful situations. *Stress inoculation training* has been used successfully in a wide variety of domains. Many children live in situations in which, tragically, they are very likely to be exposed to stressful circumstances. Let's consider successful stress inoculation for children.

resilience—they are able to achieve positive outcomes despite serious threats to their well-being (Stewart & Yuen, 2011). Research has focused on the types of coping skills that resilient individuals have acquired and how they have acquired them. An important part of the answer is that children who become resilient have been raised by parents with good parenting skills (Masten, 2011). For example, research with homeless families suggests that higher-quality parenting helps children to acquire the cognitive skills necessary to control their attention and behavior (Herbers et al., 2011). These control skills have positive consequences for the children's performance in school.

Up to now, we have been considering general approaches to coping with stressors. Let's now turn to specific cognitive and social approaches to successful coping.

Modifying Cognitive Strategies A powerful way to adapt to stress is to change your evaluations of stressors and your self-defeating cognitions about the way you are dealing with them. You need to find a different way to think about a given situation, your role in it, and the causal attributions you make to explain the undesirable outcome. Two ways of mentally coping with stress are *reappraising* the nature of the stressors themselves and *restructuring* your cognitions about your stress reactions.

You have already seen the idea that people control the experience of stress in their lives in part by the way they appraise life events (Lazarus & Lazarus, 1994). Learning to think differently about certain stressors, to relabel them, or to imagine them in a less-threatening (perhaps even funny) context is a form of cognitive reappraisal that can reduce stress. Worried about giving a speech to a large, forbidding audience? One stressor reappraisal technique is to imagine your potential

The teachers of 748 fourth- and fifth-grade students in southern Israel provided a program of stress inoculation in their classrooms (Wolmer et al., 2011). Over the course of 14 weeks, the children received a series of lessons that taught them coping skills and gave them opportunities to rehearse those skills. The lessons also helped students recognize their strong emotions and, again, taught them skills for regulating those emotions. A control group of 740 children did not receive this training. After the training period, a conflict began in the Gaza Strip. All 1,488 of the children experienced three weeks of rocket and mortar attacks. Three months after the conflict ended, the children completed measures to assess the presence of posttraumatic stress disorder. Among the students in the control group, 11.3 percent met criteria for PTSD; among the students who had received the stress inoculation training, 7.2 percent met criteria for PTSD. Thus, stress inoculation training reduced the number of children experiencing PTSD by about one-third.

This study suggests how classroom-based stress inoculation training could help children cope with stressors that,

Table 12.4 • Examples of Coping Self-Statements

Preparation

I can develop a plan to deal with it.

Just think about what I can do about it. That's better than getting anxious.

No negative self-statements, just think rationally.

Confrontation

One step at a time; I can handle this situation.

This anxiety is what the doctor said I would feel; it's a reminder to use my coping exercises.

Relax; I'm in control. Take a slow, deep breath.

Coping

When fear comes, just pause.

Keep focused on the present; what is it I have to do?

Don't try to eliminate fear totally; just keep it manageable.

It's not the worst thing that can happen.

Just think about something else.

Self-Reinforcement

It worked; I was able to do it.

It wasn't as bad as I expected.

I'm really pleased with the progress I'm making.

---

quite unfortunately, may be regularly anticipated in some young lives.

Another main component of successful coping is for you to establish **perceived control** over the stressor, a belief that you can make a difference in the course or the consequences of some event or experience (Endler et al., 2000; Roussi, 2002). If you believe that you can affect the course of an illness or the daily symptoms of a disease, you are probably adjusting well to the disorder. However, if you believe that the source of the stress is another person whose behavior you cannot influence or a situation that you cannot change, chances increase for a poor psychological adjustment to your chronic condition. Consider a study of women who had undergone surgery for breast cancer (Bárez et al., 2007). The women who reported higher levels of perceived control experienced the least physical and psychological distress over the whole year following surgery.

While you file away these control strategies for future use, we will turn to a final aspect of coping with stress—the social dimension.

Social Support as a Coping Resource **Social support** refers to the resources others provide, giving the message that one is loved, cared for, esteemed, and connected to other people in a network of communication and mutual obligation. In addition to these forms of *emotional support,* other people may provide *tangible support* (money, transportation, housing) and *informational support* (advice, personal feedback, information). Anyone with whom you have a significant social relationship—such as family members, friends, coworkers, and

neighbors—can be part of your social support network in time of need.

Much research points to the power of social support in moderating the vulnerability to stress (Kim et al., 2008). When people have other people to whom they can turn, they are better able to handle job stressors, unemployment, marital disruption, and serious illness, as well as their everyday problems of living. Consider individuals who serve as peacekeepers in the world's many troubled regions. The traumas associated with life in battle zones often leads to posttraumatic stress disorder. However, a study of Dutch peacekeepers who served in Lebanon demonstrated that those individuals who experienced higher levels of positive social interactions had fewer symptoms of PTSD (Dirkzwager et al., 2003).

Researchers are trying to identify which types of social supports provide the most benefit for specific life events. One study examined the impact of informational support and emotional support for men and women who were undergoing facial surgery (Krohne & Slangen, 2005). Overall, people who had more social support anticipated their surgery with less anxiety, required less anesthesia during surgery, and had briefer hospital stays. However, the more specific results differed for men and women. Although patients of both sexes obtained an advantage from greater informational support, only women were much affected by the level of emotional support. More generally, what appears to matter is the match between the type of support an individual needs and what that individual gets. As shown in **Figure 12.10**, there are four different possibilities for how desires and reality can be related (Reynolds & Perrin, 2004). People are best off when there's a match between what they want and what they get. For a sample of women with breast cancer, they had the worst psychological outcomes when they received support they did not want ("support commission") (Reynolds & Perrin, 2004). This pattern might have emerged because the unwanted assistance made it difficult for women to obtain the emotional support they really needed.

Support is	wanted	not wanted
received	positive congruent support	support commission
not received	support omission	null support

FIGURE 12.10 Matches and Mismatches for Social Support

When people need to cope with difficult situations, there can be matches or mismatches between the social support they want and the social support they receive.

From Julie S. Reynolds and Nancy Perrin, "Matches and Mismatches for Social Support and Psychosocial Adjustment to Breast Cancer," *Health Psychology, 23*(4), 425–430. Copyright © 2004 by the American Psychological Association. Reprinted with permission.

....

perceived control The belief that one has the ability to make a difference in the course of the consequences of some event or experience; often helpful in dealing with stressors.

social support Resources, including material aid, socioemotional support, and informational aid, provided by others to help a person cope with stress.

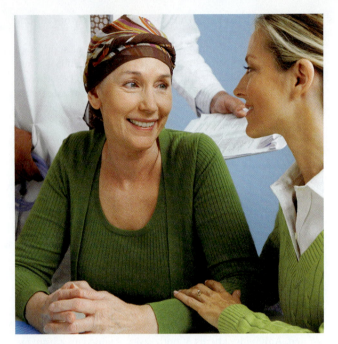

Why are some forms of social support more welcome than others?

Researchers are also trying to determine how different coping resources interact to affect responses to stressors. Let's consider a study that examined both perceived control and social support.

The 70 participants in the study all had been diagnosed with colorectal cancer (Dagan et al., 2011). Three months after their diagnosis, the participants completed a scale to indicate their perceptions of personal control over the events in their lives. The participants also completed a scale on which they reported the extent to which their spouses engaged in supportive behaviors (such as providing a context to share feelings) and unsupportive behaviors (such as making disapproving remarks). Six months later, the participants specified the extent of their psychological distress. The researchers looked for relationships between personal control, social support, and participants' distress. Participants who were low on personal control reported less distress if they had good social support and more distress if they had poor social support. However, participants who were relatively high on personal control reported low levels of distress irrespective of the behavior of their spouses.

These results suggest that people who believe they can control their own lives are less likely to look toward others as a coping resource. For that reason, they are less affected by the quality of the available social support.

However, even people with high personal control are likely to discover circumstances in which social support proves valuable. Being part of an effective social support network means that you believe others will be there for you if you need them—even if you don't actually ask for their help when you experience stress. One of the most important take-home messages from *Psychology and Life* is that you should always work at being part of a social support network and never let yourself become socially isolated.

Positive Effects of Stress

This section has focused largely on the potential for stress to bring about negative life outcomes. This focus reflects the great effort researchers have expended to help people prevent and overcome those negative outcomes. However, in recent years, psychologists have turned more attention to the potential for stress to have positive effects in people's lives. This new focus is another outcome of the positive psychology movement that you encountered as part of the discussion of subjective well-being. Let's consider stress and coping from a positive psychology perspective.

The initial definition of stress made a distinction between distress and eustress. It's probably easy for you to generate circumstances in which you experienced distress—but what about eustress? Consider the last time you watched any kind of running race. Did you enjoy the experience of seeing who would win? Did you feel your heart race as the runners approached the finish line? Researchers have demonstrated that eustress—the experience of excitement and anxiety—is often an important motivation for people to watch, for example, sporting events (Cohen & Avrahami, 2005; Hu & Tang, 2010). If a team or competitor you favor ultimately- loses, you may experience some distress. However, along the way, you probably have a more positive emotional experience when competitions stimulate eustress. Search your life for other circumstances in which the experience of stressful events gives you pleasure. Here's one more example: Why do you feel happy while you're riding a roller coaster?

For some types of stressful events, it might be hard to anticipate how any positive effects could emerge. However, research has demonstrated that people can experience positive outcomes and personal growth from deeply negative events. One type of research focuses on *benefit finding*—people's ability to identify positive aspects of negative life events (Helgeson et al., 2006; Littlewood et al., 2008). Consider a study of adolescents diagnosed with diabetes.

A team of researchers recruited 252 adolescents (ages 10 to 14) who had been diagnosed with Type 1 diabetes. The adolescents completed a measure of benefit finding that allowed them to list personally relevant benefits. The adolescents provided a number of benefits: They suggested, for example, that diabetes had made them "feel more independent," had "brought [their] family a lot closer," and had made them "able to accept change easily" (Tran et al., 2011, p. 214). The adolescents also provided information about other aspects of their experience of diabetes, including how effectively they believed they were able to cope with stressful disease-related events and how closely they were able to adhere to their treatment regimens. The researchers found that adolescents who were able to find more benefits were also better able to cope with stressful events and keep up with their treatments.

The researchers suggested that benefit finding has the potential to act as a stress buffer: By engaging in benefit finding, people are able to keep negative emotions from overwhelming their coping responses to a disease.

People also may experience *posttraumatic growth*— positive psychological change—in response to serious illnesses, accidents, natural disasters, and other traumatic events. Post-traumatic growth occurs in five domains (Cryder et al., 2006; Tedeschi & Calhoun, 2004):

- New possibilities: "I have new things that I like to do."
- Relating to others: "I feel closer to other people than I did before."
- Personal strength: "I learned I can count on myself."
- Appreciation of life: "I learned that life is important."
- Spiritual change: "I understand religious ideas more."

Not everyone who experiences trauma will experience post-traumatic growth. For example, one study focused on a group of 7- to 10-year-old children affected by Hurricane Katrina in New Orleans (Kilmer & Gil-Rivas, 2010). The children who experienced the most posttraumatic growth were the ones whose thoughts turned frequently back to the original traumatic events. This was true even when the thoughts were distressing. Children focused on the events to try to understand what had happened and make sense of those events.

At many points in this discussion of stress, I have noted the effect of stress on physical or psychological well-being. Let's now turn directly to the ways in which psychologists apply their research knowledge to issues of illness and health.

Stop *and* Review

① What are the three stages of the general adaptation syndrome?
② How did life-change unit estimates change from the 1960s to the 1990s?
③ How do daily hassles and daily pleasures affect well-being?
④ What does it mean to engage in emotion-focused coping?
⑤ Why is perceived control important in the context of coping?
⑥ What is meant by benefit finding?

CRITICAL THINKING Recall the study that demon-strated the value of stress inoculation training. Why might the training have been effective as part of the school curriculum?

✓●─**Study** and **Review** on **MyPsychLab**

HEALTH PSYCHOLOGY

How much do your psychological processes contribute to your experiences of illness and wellness? You have already seen ex-amples that suggest that the right answer may be "quite a bit."

This acknowledgment of the importance of psychological and social factors in health has spurred the growth of a new field, health psychology. **Health psychology** is the branch of psy-chology devoted to understanding the way people stay healthy, the reasons they become ill, and the way they respond when they do get ill. **Health** refers to the general condition of the body and mind in terms of soundness and vigor. It is not sim-ply the absence of illness or injury, but is more a matter of how well all the body's component parts are working together. The discussion of health psychology will begin with a discussion of how the field's underlying philosophy departs from a tradi-tional Western medical model of illness. We then consider the contributions of health psychology to the prevention and treat-ment of illness and dysfunction. ◉

The Biopsychosocial Model of Health

Health psychology is guided by a *biopsychosocial model* of health. We can find the roots of this perspective in many non-Western cultures. To arrive at a definition of the biopsycho-social model, this section starts with a description of some of these non-Western traditions.

Traditional Health Practices Psychological principles have been applied in the treatment of illness and the pursuit of health for all of recorded time. Many cultures understand the importance of communal health and relaxation rituals in the enhancement of the quality of life. Among the Navajo, for example, disease, illness, and well-being have been attributed to social harmony and mind–body interactions. The Navajo concept of **hozho** (pronounced *whoa-zo*) means harmony, peace of mind, goodness, ideal family relationships, beauty in arts and crafts, and health of body and spirit. Illness is seen as the outcome of any *disharmony,* caused by evil introduced through violation of taboos, witchcraft, overindulgence, or bad dreams. Traditional healing ceremonies seek to banish illness and restore health, not only through the medicine of the sha-man but also through the combined efforts of all family mem-bers, who work together with the ill person to reachieve a state of hozho. The illness of any member of a tribe is seen not as his or her individual responsibility (and fault) but rather as a sign of broader disharmony that must be repaired by communal healing ceremonies. This cultural orientation guarantees that a powerful social support network will automatically come to the aid of the sufferer.

Toward a Biopsychosocial Model You have just seen that healing practices in non-Western cultures often assumed a link between the body and the mind. By contrast, modern

....

◉ **Watch** the **Video** *The Big Picture: Health Psychology* on **MyPsychLab**

health psychology The field of psychology devoted to understanding the ways people stay healthy, the reasons they become ill, and the ways they respond when they become ill.

health A general condition of soundness and vigor of body and mind; not simply the absence of illness or injury.

hozho A Navajo concept referring to harmony, peace of mind, goodness, ideal family relationships, beauty in arts and crafts, and health of body and spirit.

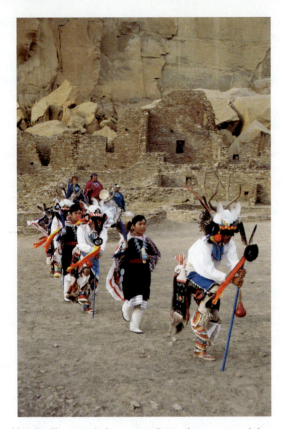

The Navajo, like people in many other cultures around the world, place a high value on aesthetics, family harmony, and physical health. What do the Navajo people consider to be the origins of illness?

Western scientific thinking has relied almost exclusively on a *biomedical model* that has a dualistic conception of body and mind. According to this model, medicine treats the physical body as separate from the psyche; the mind is important only for emotions and beliefs and has little to do with the reality of the body. Over time, however, researchers have begun to document types of interactions that make the strict biomedical model unworkable. You have already seen some of the evidence: Good and bad life events can affect immune function; people are more or less resilient with respect to the negative consequences of stress; adequate social support can change the length of hospital stays. These realizations yield the three components of the **biopsychosocial model.** The *bio* acknowledges the reality of biological illness. The *psycho* and the *social* acknowledge the psychological and social components of health.

The biopsychosocial model links your physical health to your state of mind and the world around you. Health psychologists view health as a dynamic, multidimensional experience. Optimal health, or **wellness,** incorporates physical, intellectual, emotional, spiritual, social, and environmental aspects of your life. When you undertake an activity for the purpose of preventing disease or detecting it in the asymptomatic stage, you are exhibiting health behavior. The general goal of health psychology is to use psychological knowledge to promote wellness and positive health behaviors. Let's now consider theory and research relevant to this goal.

Health Promotion

Health promotion means developing general strategies and specific tactics to eliminate or reduce the risk that people will get sick. The prevention of illness in the 21st century poses a much different challenge than it did at the beginning of the 20th century. In 1900, the primary cause of death was infectious disease. Health practitioners at that time launched the first revolution in American public health. Over time, through the use of research, public education, the development of vaccines, and changes in public health standards (such as waste control and sewage), they were able to reduce substantially the deaths associated with such diseases as influenza, tuberculosis, polio, measles, and smallpox.

If researchers wish to contribute to the trend toward improved quality of life, they must attempt to decrease those deaths associated with lifestyle factors. Smoking, being overweight, eating foods high in fat and cholesterol, drinking too much alcohol, driving without seat belts, and leading stressful lives all play a role in heart disease, cancer, strokes, accidents, and suicide. Changing behaviors will prevent much illness and premature death. To show you how that works, we now consider a pair of concrete domains: smoking and AIDS. ◉

Smoking It would be impossible to imagine that anyone reading this book wouldn't know that smoking is extremely dangerous. In the United States, roughly 443,000 people die each year from smoking-related illnesses and 49,400 people die from exposure to secondhand smoke (Centers for Disease Control and Prevention, 2011). Even so, 58.7 million people in the United States still smoke cigarettes (Substance Abuse and Mental Health Services Administration, 2010). Health psychologists would like to understand both why people begin to smoke—so that the psychologists can help prevent it—and how to assist people in quitting—so they can reap the substantial benefits of becoming ex-smokers.

Analyses of why some people start smoking have focused on interactions of nature and nurture. Studies comparing monozygotic and dizygotic twins for the similarity of their tobacco use consistently find heritability estimates of 0.50 or higher (Munafò & Johnstone, 2008). Consider one study that examined the smoking behavior of 1,198 pairs of adolescent siblings (that is, identical twins, fraternal twins, and nontwin pairs) (Boardman et al., 2008). The researchers reported heritability estimates of 0.51 for whether individuals began to smoke and 0.58 for how much they smoked each day. The study also documented an impact of the environment. For example, when the adolescents attended schools in which

....

◉ **Watch** the **Video** *What's In It For Me?: The Challenge Of Quitting Bad Habits* on **MyPsychLab**

biopsychosocial model A model of health and illness that suggests links among the nervous system, the immune system, behavioral styles, cognitive processing, and environmental domains of health.

wellness Optimal health, incorporating the ability to function fully and actively over the physical, intellectual, emotional, spiritual, social, and environmental domains of health.

health promotion The development and implementation of general strategies and specific tactics to eliminate or reduce the risk that people will become ill.

the popular students were also smokers, genes mattered more: Apparently, in that social context, students could realize their "genetic potential."

To understand the link between genes and smoking, researchers have often focused on personality differences that predict which people will start smoking. One personality type that has been associated with the initiation of smoking is called *sensation seeking* (Zuckerman, 2007). Individuals characterized as sensation seeking are more likely to engage in risky activities. One study measured sensation seeking in several thousand U.S. adolescents, ages 10 to 14 (Sargent et al., 2010). To determine which of the adolescents had become smokers, the researchers contacted them 8, 16, and 24 months after sensation seeking was originally measured. High levels of sensation seeking were a strong predictor of which adolescents would begin smoking in that two-year follow-up period.

The best approach to smoking is never to start at all. But for those of you who have begun to smoke, what has research revealed about quitting? Although many people who try to quit have relapses, an estimated 35 million Americans have quit. Ninety percent have done so on their own, without professional treatment programs. Researchers have identified stages people pass through that represent increasing readiness to quit (Norman et al., 1998, 2000):

- *Precontemplation.* The smoker is not yet thinking about quitting.
- *Contemplation.* The smoker is thinking about quitting but has not yet undertaken any behavioral changes.
- *Preparation.* The smoker is getting ready to quit.
- *Action.* The smoker takes action toward quitting by setting behavioral goals.
- *Maintenance.* The smoker is now a nonsmoker and is trying to stay that way.

This analysis suggests that not all smokers are psychologically equivalent in terms of readiness to quit. Interventions can

Why should interventions recognize that not all smokers are the same with respect to their readiness to quit?

be designed that nudge smokers up the scale of readiness, until, finally, they are psychologically prepared to take healthy action (Velicer et al., 2007).

Successful smoking-cessation treatment requires that both smokers' physiological and psychological needs be met (Fiore et al., 2008). On the physiological side, smokers are best off learning an effective form of *nicotine replacement therapy,* such as nicotine patches or nicotine gum. On the psychological side, smokers must understand that there are huge numbers of ex-smokers and realize that it is possible to quit. Furthermore, smokers must learn strategies to cope with the strong temptations that accompany efforts to quit. Treatments often incorporate the types of cognitive coping techniques described earlier, which allow people to alleviate the effects of a wide range of stressors. For smoking, people are encouraged to find ways to avoid or escape from situations that may bring on a renewed urge to smoke.

AIDS AIDS is an acronym for *acquired immune deficiency syndrome.* Although hundreds of thousands are dying from this virulent disease, many more are now living with HIV infection. **HIV** *(human immunodeficiency virus)* is a virus that attacks the white blood cells (T lymphocytes) in human blood, thus damaging the immune system and weakening the body's ability to fight other diseases. The individual then becomes vulnerable to infection by a host of other viruses and bacteria that can cause such life-threatening illnesses as cancer, meningitis, and pneumonia. The period of time from initial infection with the virus until symptoms occur (incubation period) can be five years or longer. Although most of the estimated millions of those infected with the HIV virus do not have AIDS (a medical diagnosis), they must live with the continual stress that this life-threatening disease might suddenly emerge. At the present time, there are treatments that delay the onset of full-blown AIDS, but there is neither a cure for AIDS nor a vaccine to prevent its spread.

The HIV virus is not airborne; it requires direct access to the bloodstream to produce an infection. The HIV virus is generally passed from one person to another in one of two ways: (1) the exchange of semen or blood during sexual contact and (2) the sharing of intravenous needles and syringes used for injecting drugs. The virus has also been passed through blood transfusions and medical procedures in which infected blood or organs are unwittingly given to healthy people. Many people suffering from hemophilia have gotten AIDS in this way. However, everyone is at risk for AIDS.

The only way to protect oneself from being infected with the AIDS virus is to change those lifestyle habits that put one at risk. This means making permanent changes in patterns of sexual behavior and use of drug paraphernalia. Health psychologist **Thomas Coates** is part of a multidisciplinary research team that is using an array of psychological principles in a concerted effort to prevent the further spread of AIDS (Coates & Szekeres, 2004). The team is involved in many aspects of applied psychology, such as assessing psychosocial

---

AIDS Acronym for *acquired immune deficiency syndrome*, a syndrome caused by a virus that damages the immune system and weakens the body's ability to fight infection.

HIV Human immunodeficiency virus, a virus that attacks white blood cells (T lymphocytes) in human blood, thereby weakening the functioning of the immune system; HIV causes AIDS.

Critical Thinking in Your Life

CAN HEALTH PSYCHOLOGY HELP YOU GET MORE EXERCISE?

An important goal of health psychology is to increase the likelihood that people will engage in behaviors that are good for their health. High on that list is exercise: People who get enough exercise generally experience better health. The U.S. government makes these recommendations (U.S. Department of Health and Human Services, 2008, p. vii):

- "For substantial health benefits, adults should do at least 150 minutes (2 hours and 30 minutes) a week of moderate-intensity, or 75 minutes (1 hour and 15 minutes) a week of vigorous-intensity aerobic physical activity, or an equivalent combination of moderate- and vigorous-intensity aerobic activity. Aerobic activity should be performed in episodes of at least 10 minutes, and preferably, it should be spread throughout the week."

- "Adults should also do muscle-strengthening activities that are moderate or high intensity and involve all major muscle groups on 2 or more days a week, as these activities provide additional health benefits."

The activities in these recommendations lead to increased fitness of the heart and respiratory systems, improvement of muscle tone and strength, and many other health benefits. So, how can research in health psychology help people reap these benefits?

Researchers have tried to determine what programs or strategies are most effective in getting people to start and continue exercising (Nigg et al., 2008). In fact, much the same model that describes people's readiness to *quit* smoking applies to people's readiness to *begin* exercising (Buckworth et al., 2007). In the *precontemplation* stage, an individual is still more focused on the barriers to exercise (for example, too little time) rather than the benefits (for example, improves appearance). As the individual moves through the *contemplation* and *preparation* stages, the emphasis shifts from barriers to benefits. People who have been exercising for less than six months are in the *action* stage; those who have exercised regularly for over six months are in the *maintenance* stage.

If you do not exercise regularly now, how can you get beyond precontemplation? Research suggests that individuals can learn strategies that allow them to overcome obstacles to exercise (Scholz et al., 2008). One strategy is to formulate *action plans:* You should create specific plans about when, where, and how you foresee becoming physically active. Another strategy is to formulate *coping plans:* You should anticipate what obstacles might arise to interfere with your action plans and determine how best to cope with those obstacles. In one study, researchers taught patients with coronary heart disease how to formulate these types of plans (Sniehotta et al., 2006). Two months later, patients who combined both types of planning had engaged in considerably more physical activity than patients in the control group (who did not receive the training).

Studies of this sort indicate why you can treat exercise like any other situation in which you can use cognitive appraisal to work toward goals for healthy living.

- Why might the same stages apply to undertaking healthy behaviors and overcoming unhealthy behaviors?
- Why is it stressful to contemplate healthy behaviors such as regular exercise?

---

risk factors, developing behavioral interventions, training community leaders to be effective in educating people toward healthier patterns of sexual and drug behavior, assisting with the design of media advertisements and community information campaigns, and systematically evaluating changes in relevant attitudes, values, and behaviors (Fernández-Dávila et al., 2008; Hendriksen et al., 2007). Successful AIDS interventions require three components (Starace et al., 2006):

- *Information.* People must be provided with knowledge about how AIDS is transmitted and how its transmission may be prevented; they should be counseled to practice safer sex (for example, use condoms during sexual contact) and use sterile needles.
- *Motivation.* People must be motivated to practice AIDS prevention.
- *Behavioral skills.* People must be taught how to put the knowledge to use.

Why are all three of these components necessary? People might be highly motivated but uninformed, or vice versa. They may have both sufficient knowledge and sufficient motivation but lack requisite skills. In addition, information must be delivered in a fashion that does not undermine people's motivation. For example, people were more likely to participate in HIV-prevention counseling when information was framed so that the participants felt in control of their own behavior (Albarracín et al., 2008).

Treatment

Treatment focuses on helping people adjust to their illnesses and recover from them. This section will look at three aspects of treatment. First, we consider the role of psychologists in encouraging patients to adhere to the regimens prescribed by health-care practitioners. Next, we look at techniques that allow people to explicitly use psychological techniques to take control over the body's responses. Finally, we examine instances in which the mind can contribute to the body's cure.

Patient Adherence

Patients are often given a *treatment regimen*. This might include medications, dietary changes, prescribed periods of bed rest and exercise, and follow-up procedures such as return checkups, rehabilitation training, and chemotherapy. Failing to adhere to treatment regimens is one of the most serious problems in health care (Christensen & Johnson, 2002; Quittner et al., 2008). The rate of patient nonadherence is estimated to be as high as 50 percent for some treatment regimens.

What factors affect the likelihood that patients will adhere to prescribed treatments? One type of research has focused on the relationship between patients' perceptions of the severity of their disease. As you might expect, people who perceive greater threat from a disease also show greater likelihood to adhere to treatments (DiMatteo et al., 2007). However, the relationship becomes more complicated when researchers consider patients' objective health (rather, that is, than patients' subjective perceptions). Patients who face serious diseases that leave them in poor physical health show lower levels of adherence than patients who are less debilitated by the same diseases. This lack of adherence may reflect growing pessimism about the likelihood that the treatment will succeed. A second type of research has demonstrated the importance of social support for patient adherence (DiMatteo, 2004). Patients obtain the greatest benefits when they receive practical support that allows them to accomplish their regimens correctly.

Research has shown that health-care professionals can take steps to improve patient adherence. Consider a study that demonstrated the importance of a match between patients' and physicians' attitudes.

Featured Study

A team of researchers recruited 224 patients and the 18 physicians who had provided them with medical care (Christensen et al., 2010). Both the patients and the physicians completed a questionnaire that assessed their attitudes about the role patients play in their own health outcomes. Patients responded to statements such as "I am in control of my own health" and "When I get sick it is my own behavior which determines how soon I get well again." The physicians responded to a version of the questionnaire that focused on the patients (for example, "Patients are in control of their own health."). To assess the patients' adherence with their treatment regimens, the researchers obtained medication refill information from pharmacy records. The results indicated that patients were more likely to adhere when their attitudes matched their physicians' attitudes.

To understand this result, imagine what might happen when, for example, a patient who believes she is in control of her own health faces a physician who believes otherwise. That mismatch is likely to undermine the patient's trust in her physician. The researchers suggest that physicians should try to understand their patients' attitudes—and modify their behaviors to match those attitudes.

Harnessing the Mind to Heal the Body More and more often, the treatments to which patients must adhere involve a psychological component. Many investigators now believe that psychological strategies can improve well-being. For example, many people react to stress with tension, resulting in tight muscles and high blood pressure. Fortunately, many tension responses can be controlled by psychological techniques, such as *relaxation* and *biofeedback*.

Relaxation through meditation has ancient roots in many parts of the world. In Eastern cultures, ways to calm the mind and still the body's tensions have been practiced for centuries. Today, Zen discipline and yoga exercises from Japan and India are part of daily life for many people both there and, increasingly, in the West. Growing evidence suggests that complete relaxation is a potent antistress response (Samuelson et al., 2010). The **relaxation response** is a condition in which muscle tension, cortical activity, heart rate, and blood pressure all decrease and breathing slows (Benson, 2000). There is reduced electrical activity in the brain, and input to the central nervous system from the outside environment is lowered. In this low level of arousal, recuperation from stress can take place. Four conditions are regarded as necessary to produce the relaxation response: (1) a quiet environment, (2) closed eyes, (3) a comfortable position, and (4) a repetitive mental device such as the chanting of a brief phrase over and over again. The first three conditions lower input to the nervous system, and the fourth lowers its internal stimulation. ⊙▸

Biofeedback is a self-regulatory technique used for a variety of special applications, such as control of blood pressure, relaxation of forehead muscles (involved in tension headaches), and even diminishment of extreme blushing. As pioneered by psychologist **Neal Miller** (1978), biofeedback is a procedure that makes an individual aware of ordinarily weak or internal responses by providing clear external signals. The patient is allowed to "see" his or her own bodily reactions, which are monitored and amplified by equipment that transforms them into lights and sound cues of varying intensity. The patient's task is then to control the level of these external cues.

Let's consider one application of biofeedback. Participants who suffered from either high or low blood pressure were brought into a laboratory (Rau et al., 2003). Feedback from equipment measuring an index of the participants' blood pressure on each heart cycle was delivered to a computer screen so that growing green bars indicated changes in the right direction and growing red bars indicated changes in the wrong direction. In addition, the researchers provided verbal reinforcement: "You did it the right way!" After three training sessions, the participants were able to raise or lower their blood pressure, as

⊙▸ **Simulate** the **Experiment** *Stress and Health* on **MyPsychLab**

relaxation response A condition in which muscle tension, cortical activity, heart rate, and blood pressure decrease and breathing slows.

biofeedback A self-regulatory technique by which an individual acquires voluntary control over nonconscious biological processes.

Why does relaxation through meditation have health benefits?

flu, you'd like your body to produce abundant antibodies. Those antibodies will lower the probability that you'll get sick. However, people who report more stress in their lives have less antibody response (Pedersen et al., 2009). Thus, for people who experience high levels of stress, vaccinations may be less likely to protect them from illness.

Let's consider another basic function of your immune system, to heal small wounds in your skin. In one study, a research team led by **Janet Kiecolt-Glaser** gave 13 caretakers for relatives with Alzheimer's disease (see Chapter 7) and 13 control participants standardized small wounds to their skin. On average, the Alzheimer's caretakers, who experience chronic stress, took nine days longer for their wounds to heal (Kiecolt-Glaser et al., 1995)! People can also experience chronic stress as a consequence of their own personalities—with similar implications for immune function. For example, individuals who reported having difficulty controlling their anger generally took more days to heal the same type of standardized wounds than individuals with better anger control (Gouin et al., 2008). You can see from these data how small differences in stress level may affect the speed with which a person's body can heal even the smallest scratch or scrape. From that basic insight, you can understand why research suggests that stress responses play an even more profound role with respect to the progression of serious medical conditions such as infectious diseases and cancer. Researchers wish to understand how the mind affects immune function so they can harness that power to slow these serious illnesses.

Psychological Impact on Health Outcomes One last note on treatment. Have you ever had a secret too shameful to tell anyone? If so, talking about the secret could very well improve your health. That is the conclusion from a large body of research by health psychologist **James Pennebaker** (1990, 1997; Petrie et al., 1998), who has shown that suppressing thoughts and feelings associated with personal traumas, failures, and guilty or shameful experiences takes a devastating toll on mental and physical health. Such inhibition is psychologically hard work and, over time, it undermines the body's defenses against illness. The experience of letting go often is followed by improved physical and psychological health weeks and months later. Consider the effects of emotional disclosure on health outcomes for people with HIV infection.

desired. If you ever become concerned about your blood pressure or other physical disorders, results of this sort might encourage you to seek a course of biofeedback to complement a drug regimen.

Psychoneuroimmunology In the early 1980s, researchers made a series of discoveries that confirmed another way in which the mind affects the body: Psychological states can have an impact on immune function. Historically, scientists had assumed that immunological reactions—rapid production of antibodies to counterattack substances that invade and damage the organism—were automatic biological processes that occurred without any involvement of the central nervous system. However, using the types of conditioning experiments described in Chapter 6, **Robert Ader** and **Nicholas Cohen** (1981) demonstrated that immune function can be modified by psychological states. Their research gave rise to a new field of study, **psychoneuroimmunology,** which explores interactions of psychological states, the nervous system, and the immune system (Ader & Cohen, 1993; Coe, 1999).

Research over the past 40 years has confirmed that stressors—and how people cope with them—have a consistent impact on the ability of the immune system to function effectively. For example, when you get a vaccination for the

....

psychoneuroimmunology The research area that investigates interactions between psychological processes, such as responses to stress, and the functions of the immune system.

Featured Study

Thirty-seven adults with HIV infection participated in this study. Roughly half of the patients were assigned to an emotional writing group. In four 30-minute sessions on consecutive days, participants wrote about "the most traumatic and emotional experiences of their lives" (Petrie et al., 2004, p. 273). The control group spent the same amount of time on a neutral task, writing accounts, for example, about what they had done in the previous day. To assess the impact of emotional writing, the researchers measured HIV viral load—the number of HIV copies in a milliliter of blood. **Figure 12.11** *displays the dramatic impact of emotional writing. Those participants who had engaged in emotional writing had consistently lower viral loads two weeks, three months, and six months after the writing sessions.*

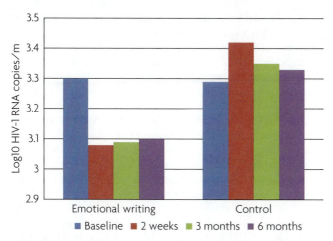

FIGURE 12.11 The Impact of Emotional Writing on HIV Infection

Participants engaged in four sessions of either emotional or neutral writing. Their HIV viral load was assessed two weeks, three months, and six months after the writing sessions. Participants who had engaged in emotional writing had consistently lower viral loads.

Data from figure "Viral Load" in "Effect of written emotional expression on immune function in patients with human immunodeficiency virus infection: A randomized trial" by Keith J. Petrie, Iris Fontanilla, Mark G. Thomas, Roger J. Booth, and James W. Pennebaker, *Psychosomatic Medicine 66*(2), March 2004.

This result is consistent with other data indicating that an individual's stress level has an impact on the course of HIV infection. Emotional writing helped participants cope with some negative psychological consequences of the infection.

Personality and Health

Do you know a person like this: someone who is driven to succeed, no matter what obstacles; someone whose high school class voted him or her "most likely to have a heart attack before age 20"? Are you that person? As you've observed the way in which some people charge through life while others take a more relaxed pace, you may have wondered whether these different personalities affect health. Research in health psychology strongly suggests that the answer is yes (Deary et al., 2010b). ◉

In the 1950s, Meyer Friedman and Ray Rosenman reported what had been suspected since ancient times: There was a relationship between a constellation of personality traits and the probability of illness, specifically coronary heart disease (Friedman & Rosenman, 1974). These researchers identified two behavior patterns that they labeled Type A and Type B. The **Type A behavior pattern** is a complex pattern of behavior and emotions that includes being excessively competitive, aggressive, impatient, time urgent, and hostile. Type A people are often dissatisfied with some central aspect of their lives and have an intense drive for achievement. The **Type B behavior pattern** is everything Type A is not—individuals are less competitive, less hostile, and so on. Importantly, these behavior patterns have an impact on health. In their original discussion, Friedman and Rosenman reported that people who showed

Type A behavior patterns were stricken with coronary heart disease considerably more often than individuals in the general population.

Because the Type A behavior pattern has many components, researchers have focused their attention on identifying the specific Type A elements that most often put people at risk. A personality trait that has emerged most forcefully as "toxic" is hostility (Chida & Steptoe, 2009).

A longitudinal study began in 1986, with 774 men in the sample who were free of any evidence of cardiovascular disease (Niaura et al., 2002). In 1986, each participant's level of hostility was measured (using a set of questions from the Minnesota Multiphasic Personality Inventory, a device you'll encounter in Chapter 13). Hostility is defined as the consistency with which individuals look at the world and other people in a cynical and negative manner. To display the relationship between hostility and coronary heart disease, the researchers divided the hostility scores into percentile groups. As shown in Figure 12.12, those individuals whose hostility scores were in the upper 20 percent had a dramatically larger number of episodes of incident coronary heart disease in the subsequent years. In this sample of men, hostility was a better predictor of future illness than several behavioral risk factors, such as smoking and drinking.

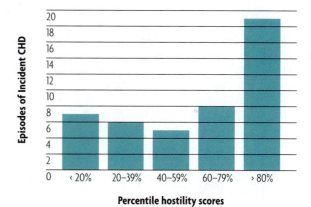

FIGURE 12.12 Hostility Predicts Coronary Heart Disease

Study participants were divided into percentile groups based on their self-reports of hostility. Men whose scores placed them in the top 20 percent on the measure (that is, the group greater than 80 percent) had the highest levels of coronary heart disease.

◉ **Watch** the **Video** *Thinking Like a Psychologist: Personality and Health* on **MyPsychLab**

Type A behavior pattern A complex pattern of behaviors and emotions that includes excessive emphasis on competition, aggression, impatience, and hostility; hostility increases the risk of coronary heart disease.

Type B behavior pattern As compared to Type A behavior pattern, a less competitive, less aggressive, less hostile pattern of behavior and emotion.

Hostility may affect health for both physiological reasons—by leading to chronic overarousal of the body's stress responses—and psychological reasons—by leading hostile people to practice poor health habits and avoid social support (Smith & Ruiz, 2002).

The good news is that researchers have begun to implement behavioral treatments to reduce hostility and other aspects of the Type A behavior pattern (Pischke et al., 2008). For example, one intervention focused on African American students in ninth grade (Wright et al., 2011). African Americans are at greater risk than other ethnic groups for heart disease; differences in blood pressure begin to emerge in childhood. These facts provided the motivation for a team of researchers to design an intervention using mindfulness-based stress reduction (see Chapter 5). The students learned to pay attention to their breathing and to passively observe their thoughts. After three months of training, the students who self-reported lower levels of hostility also had lower blood pressure than at the study's outset. Do you recognize yourself in the definition of hostility? If you do, protect your health by seeking out this type of intervention.

To round out this section on personality and health let's revisit the concept of *optimism* you met in Chapter 11. We saw there that optimistic individuals attribute failures to external causes and to events that were unstable or modifiable. This style of coping has a strong impact on the optimist's well-being (Carver et al., 2010). The particular impact depends on the difficulty of the stressor (Segerstrom, 2005). Because optimists believe they can prevail over stressors, they tend to engage them head on. When the stressor is difficult, this strategy of continued engagement may have negative physiological consequences. Consider a study that assessed the health impact of optimism for students making the transition to law school (Segerstrom, 2006, 2007). For some students this transition was relatively more stressful—because they had social and family demands on top of their academic demands. Each student completed a test that measured optimism. Each student also underwent a procedure to assess immune response. They received an injection of a preparation that tests susceptibility to mumps. In response to the injection, the skin swells. The measure of immune response is the amount of swelling, or *induration*. As shown in **Figure 12.13**, those students with the highest optimism showed better immune response in the face of lower demands; they showed worse immune response in the face of higher demands. These data suggest that optimists must recognize that there are some stressors for which the best style of coping is not to engage them directly.

Job Burnout and the Health-Care System

One final focus of health psychology is to make recommendations about the design of the health-care system. Researchers, for example, have examined the stress associated with being a health-care provider. Even the most enthusiastic health-care providers run up against the emotional stresses of working intensely with large numbers of people suffering from a variety of personal, physical, and social problems.

The special type of emotional stress experienced by these professional health and welfare practitioners has been termed *burnout* by **Christina Maslach,** a leading researcher on this widespread problem. **Job burnout** is a syndrome of emotional exhaustion, depersonalization, and reduced personal accomplishment that is often experienced by workers in professions that demand high-intensity interpersonal contact with patients, clients, or the public. Health practitioners begin to lose their caring and concern for patients and may come to treat them in detached and even dehumanized ways. They feel bad about themselves and worry that they are failures. Burnout is correlated with greater absenteeism and turnover, impaired job performance, poor relations with coworkers, family problems, and poor personal health (Maslach & Leiter, 2008).

Job burnout in today's workforce is reaching ever higher levels because of the effects of organizational downsizing, job restructuring, and greater concerns for profits than for employee morale and loyalty. Burnout, then, is not merely a concern of workers and health caregivers, but it also reveals organizational dysfunction that needs to be corrected by reexamining goals, values, workloads, and reward structures (Leiter & Maslach, 2005).

What recommendations can be made? Several social and situational factors affect the occurrence and level of burnout and, by implication, suggest ways of preventing or minimizing it (Leiter & Maslach, 2005; Prosser et al., 1997). For example, the quality of the patient–practitioner interaction is greatly influenced by the number of patients for whom a practitioner is providing care—the greater the number, the greater the cognitive, sensory, and emotional overload. Another factor in the quality of that interaction is the amount of direct contact with patients. Longer work hours in continuous direct contact with patients are correlated with greater burnout. This is especially

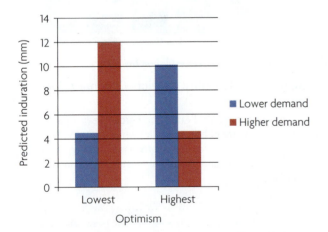

FIGURE 12.13 Optimism and Immune Function

Students with the highest levels of optimism showed better immune response in the face of lower demands. However, they showed worse immune response in the face of higher demands.

Data from Suzanne C. Segerstrom, "Stress, energy and immunity: An Ecological view," *Current directions in Psychological Science,* December 1, 2007, © 2007 by the Association for Psychological Science.

job burnout The syndrome of emotional exhaustion, depersonalization, and reduced personal accomplishment, often experienced by workers in high-stress jobs.

Why are health-care providers particularly prone to job burnout?

true when the nature of the contact is difficult and upsetting, such as contact with patients who are dying (Jackson et al., 2008). The emotional strain of such prolonged contact can be eased by a number of means. For example, practitioners can modify their work schedules to withdraw temporarily from such high-stress situations. They can use teams rather than only individual contact. They can arrange opportunities to get positive feedback for their efforts.

A Toast to Your Health

It's time for some final advice. Instead of waiting for stress or illness to come and then reacting to it, set goals and structure your life in ways that are most likely to forge a healthy foundation. The following nine steps to greater happiness and better mental health are presented as guidelines to encourage you to take a more active role in your own life and to create a more positive psychological environment for yourself and others. Think of the steps as *year-round resolutions*.

1. Never say bad things about yourself. Look for sources of your unhappiness in elements that can be modified by future actions. Give yourself and others only *constructive criticism*—what can be done differently next time to get what you want?

2. Compare your reactions, thoughts, and feelings with those of friends, coworkers, family members, and others so that you can gauge the appropriateness and relevance of your responses against a suitable social norm.

3. Have several close friends with whom you can share feelings, joys, and worries. Work at developing, maintaining, and expanding your social support networks.

4. Develop a sense of *balanced time perspective* in which you can flexibly focus on the demands of the task, the situation, and your needs; be future-oriented when there is work to be done, present-oriented when the goal is achieved and pleasure is at hand, and past-oriented to keep you in touch with your roots.

5. Always take full credit for your successes and happiness (and share your positive feelings with other people). Keep an inventory of all the qualities that make you special and unique—those qualities you can offer others. For example,

a shy person can provide a talkative person with the gift of attentive listening. Know your sources of personal strength and available coping resources.

6. When you feel you are losing control over your emotions, distance yourself from the situation by physically leaving it, role-playing the position of another person in the situation or conflict, projecting your imagination into the future to gain perspective on what seems an overwhelming problem now, or talking to a sympathetic listener. Allow yourself to feel and express your emotions.

7. Remember that failure and disappointment are sometimes blessings in disguise. They may tell you that your goals are not right for you or may save you from bigger letdowns later on. Learn from every failure. Acknowledge setbacks by saying, "I made a mistake," and move on. Every accident, misfortune, or violation of your expectations is potentially a wonderful opportunity in disguise.

8. If you discover you cannot help yourself or another person in distress, seek the counsel of a trained specialist in your student health department or community. In some cases, a problem that appears to be psychological may really be physical, and vice versa. Check out your student mental health services before you need them and use them without concern about being stigmatized.

9. Cultivate healthy pleasures. Take time out to relax, to meditate, to get a massage, to fly a kite, and to enjoy hobbies and activities you can do alone and that help you get in touch with and better appreciate yourself.

So how are you feeling? If the stressors in your life have the potential to put you in a bad mood, try to use cognitive reappraisal to minimize their impact. If you are feeling ill, try to use your mind's healing capacity to speed your way back toward health. Never underestimate the power of these different types of "feelings" to exercise control over your life. Harness that power!

Stop *and* Review

① What has research revealed about the genetics of smoking?
② What are the three components of successful AIDS interventions?
③ What conditions are necessary to produce the relaxation response?
④ What is the central goal for researchers who study psychoneuroimmunology?
⑤ What is the "toxic" aspect of Type A personalities?
⑥ How is job burnout defined?

CRITICAL THINKING Consider the study that examined the health impact of emotional disclosure. Why did the researchers ask participants in the control group to write texts?

✓—**Study** and **Review** on **MyPsychLab**

Recapping Main Points

Emotions

- Emotions are complex patterns of changes made up of physiological arousal, cognitive appraisal, and behavioral and expressive reactions.
- As a product of evolution, all humans may share a basic set of emotional responses.
- Cultures, however, vary in their rules of appropriateness for displaying emotions.
- Classic theories emphasize different parts of emotional response, such as peripheral bodily reactions or central neural processes.
- More contemporary theories emphasize the appraisal of arousal.
- Moods and emotions affect information processing and memory.
- Subjective well-being is influenced by both genetics and life experiences.

Stress of Living

- Stress can arise from negative or positive events. At the root of most stress are change and the need to adapt to environmental, biological, physical, and social demands.
- Physiological stress reactions are regulated by the hypothalamus and a complex interaction of the hormonal and nervous systems.
- Depending on the type of stressor and its effect over time, stress can be a mild disruption or lead to health-threatening reactions.
- Cognitive appraisal is a primary moderator variable of stress.
- Coping strategies either focus on problems (taking direct actions) or attempt to regulate emotions (indirect or avoidant).

- Cognitive reappraisal and restructuring can be used to cope with stress.
- Social support is also a significant stress moderator, as long as it is appropriate to the circumstances.
- Stress can lead to positive changes such as posttraumatic growth.

Health Psychology

- Health psychology is devoted to treatment and prevention of illness.
- The biopsychosocial model of health and illness looks at the connections among physical, emotional, and environmental factors in illness.
- Illness prevention focuses on lifestyle factors such as smoking and AIDS-risk behaviors.
- Psychological factors influence immune function.
- Psychosocial treatment of illness adds another dimension to patient treatment.
- Individuals who are characterized by Type A (especially hostile), Type B, and optimistic behavior patterns will experience different likelihoods of illness.
- Health-care providers are at risk for burnout, which can be minimized by appropriate situational changes in their helping environment.

Answers for Figure 12.1 (p. 325)

1. happiness
2. surprise
3. anger
4. disgust
5. fear
6. sadness
7. contempt

KEY TERMS

acute stress (p. 334)
AIDS (p. 347)
anticipatory coping (p. 341)
biofeedback (p. 349)
biopsychosocial model (p. 346)
Cannon–Bard theory of emotion (p. 328)
chronic stress (p. 334)
cognitive appraisal theory of emotion
  (p. 329)
coping (p. 340)
emotion (p. 323)
emotion regulation (p. 331)
fight-or-flight response (p. 334)
general adaptation syndrome (GAS)
  (p. 336)

health (p. 345)
health promotion (p. 346)
health psychology (p. 345)
HIV (p. 347)
hozho (p. 345)
James–Lange theory of emotion (p. 327)
job burnout (p. 352)
life-change unit (LCU) (p. 337)
perceived control (p. 343)
positive psychology (p. 331)
posttraumatic stress disorder (PTSD)
  (p. 338)
psychoneuroimmunology (p. 350)
psychosomatic disorder (p. 336)
relaxation response (p. 349)

social support (p. 343)
stress (p. 333)
stress moderator variable (p. 341)
stressor (p. 333)
subjective well-being (p. 331)
tend-and-befriend response (p. 335)
two-factor theory of emotion (p. 328)
Type A behavior pattern (p. 351)
Type B behavior pattern (p. 351)
wellness (p. 346)

1. Which statement is true of moods, but not emotions?
   a. They may last several days.
   b. They can be either positive or negative.
   c. They may arise from specific events.
   d. They are relatively intense.

2. Which of these facial expressions is *not* among the seven universally recognized expressions of emotion?
   a. concern   c. disgust
   b. contempt   d. happiness

3. The _____ prepares the body for physiological aspects of emotional responses.
   a. hypothalamus
   b. amygdala
   c. autonomous nervous system
   d. hippocampus

4. According to the _____ theory of emotion, you feel after your body reacts.
   a. Cannon–Bard   c. James–Lange
   b. cognitive appraisal d. approach-related

5. Your friend Yasumasa just found out he did better than expected on a calculus exam. An experimenter asks you to predict how happy Yasumasa is feeling. The experimenter also asks Yasumasa the same question. It would probably be the case that your rating would be _____ Yasumas's rating.
   a. equal to   c. higher than
   b. lower than   d. much lower than

6. The brain structure that plays an important role in the fight-or-flight response is the
   a. pituitary gland.   c. hypothalamus.
   b. amygdala.   d. thyroid gland.

7. If you are faced by _____ stressors, the type of coping that is likely to be most useful is _____ coping.
   a. uncontrollable; problem-directed
   b. controllable; emotion-focused
   c. controllable; delay-based
   d. uncontrollable; emotion-focused

8. When May was diagnosed with skin cancer, Al searched the Web to help her learn more about treatment options. This type of social support is _____ support.
   a. tangible   c. emotional
   b. informational   d. inoculation

9. A few months after surviving a tornado, Judy says, "I am grateful for every new day." It sounds like Judy experienced posttraumatic growth in which domain?
   a. spiritual change   c. appreciation of life
   b. relating to others d. personal strength

10. Consider the stages people pass through as they attempt to quit smoking. Which of these pairs is in the wrong order?
    a. preparation; contemplation
    b. contemplation; action
    c. action; maintenance
    d. preparation; maintenance

11. Marsea is participating in a laboratory study. Every time her blood pressure goes up, she sees a "sad face" on a computer display. It seems that Marsea is learning how to use
    a. the relaxation response.   c. anticipatory coping.
    b. biofeedback.   d. stress inoculation.

12. Researchers gave caretakers of Alzheimer's patients and control individuals standardized wounds. What was the result of the study?
    a. The wounds of the Alzheimer's caretakers took longer to heal.
    b. The wounds of the control individuals took longer to heal.
    c. There was no difference in the time it took the wounds to heal.
    d. The wounds of the control individuals were larger.

13. The aspect of the _____ behavior pattern that has the greatest impact on health is _____.
    a. Type B; hostility   c. Type B; pessimism
    b. Type A; optimism   d. Type A; hostility

14. Which of these features is *not* part of the definition of job burnout?
    a. depersonalization
    b. disharmony
    c. emotional exhaustion
    d. reduced personal accomplishment

15. Evanthia is using coping strategies to increase her level of physical activities. Which of these sounds most like a coping plan?
    a. "I will do sit-ups every day before I eat breakfast."
    b. "I will learn how to use an elliptical trainer."
    c. "I will join a gym."
    d. "I will read my textbook while I'm on the treadmill."

ESSAY QUESTIONS

1. What evidence suggests that some emotional responses are innate while others are not?

2. Why does perceived control have an impact on people's ability to cope with stress?

3. What factors affect the likelihood that patients will adhere to treatment regimens?

13

Understanding Human Personality

Please take a moment to compare and contrast your two closest friends. In what ways are they similar? In what ways are they different? It seems likely that your analysis would very quickly come to focus on your friends' *personalities*. You might, for example, assert that one is friendlier than the other or that one has more self-confidence. Assertions of this sort would suggest that you've brought your own personality theory to bear on your relationships—you have your own system for appraising personality.

Psychologists define **personality** as the complex set of psychological qualities that influence an individual's characteristic patterns of behavior across different situations and over time. In this chapter, you'll encounter several theories of personality. Theories of personality are hypothetical statements about the structure and functioning of individual personalities. Each theory has two major goals. First, the theories try to understand the *uniqueness* of each individual with respect to the structure, origins, and correlates of personality. Second, they attempt to understand how each unique personality yields *characteristic patterns of behavior*. Different theories make different predictions about the way people will respond and adapt to life events.

Before we meet some of the major theoretical approaches, we should ask why there are so many different (often competing) theories. Theorists differ in their approaches to personality by varying their starting points and sources of data and by trying to explain different types of phenomena. Some are interested in the structure of individual personality and others in how that personality developed and will continue to grow. Some are interested in what people do, either in terms of specific behaviors or important life events; others study how people feel about their lives. Finally, some theories try to explain the personalities of people with psychological problems, whereas others focus on healthy individuals. Thus each theory can teach something about personality, and together they can teach much about human nature.

The goal for this chapter is to provide you with a framework for understanding your everyday experience of personality. As we begin, consider this series of questions: If psychologists studied *you*, what portrait of your personality would they draw? What early experiences might they identify

as contributing to the way you now act and think? What conditions in your current life exert strong influences on your thoughts and behaviors? What makes you different from other individuals who are functioning in many of the same situations as you? This chapter should help you formulate specific answers to these questions.

TRAIT PERSONALITY THEORIES

One of the oldest approaches to personality involves scaling the degree to which people can be described by *different traits*. There seems to be a natural tendency for people to classify their own and others' behavior along different dimensions. Let's examine the formal theories psychologists have developed to capture these intuitions.

Describing with Traits

Traits are enduring qualities or attributes that predispose individuals to behave consistently across situations. For example, you may demonstrate honesty on one day by returning a lost wallet and on another day by not cheating on a test. Some trait theorists think of traits as *predispositions* that cause behavior, but more conservative theorists use traits only as *descriptive dimensions* that simply summarize patterns of observed behavior. Let's examine prominent trait theories.

Allport's Trait Approach Gordon Allport (1897–1967) viewed traits as the building blocks of personality and the source of individuality. According to Allport (1937, 1961, 1966), traits produce coherence in behavior because they connect and unify a person's reactions to a variety of stimuli. Traits may act as *intervening variables*, relating sets of stimuli and responses that might seem, at first glance, to have little to do with each other (see **Figure 13.1**).

Allport identified three kinds of traits: cardinal traits, central traits, and secondary traits. *Cardinal traits* are traits around which a person organizes his or her life. For Mother Teresa, a cardinal trait might have been self-sacrifice for the good of others. However, not all people develop such overarching cardinal traits. Instead, *central traits* are traits that represent major characteristics of a person, such as honesty or optimism. *Secondary traits* are specific personal features that help predict an individual's behavior but are less useful for understanding an individual's personality. Food or dress preferences are examples of secondary traits. Allport was interested in discovering the

....

👁 **Watch** the **Video** *The Big Picture: What is Personality?* on **MyPsychLab**

👁 **Watch** the **Video** *The Basics: Personality Theories* on **MyPsychLab**

personality The psychological qualities of an individual that influence a variety of characteristic behavior patterns across different situations and over time.

trait Enduring personal quality or attribute that influences behavior across situations.

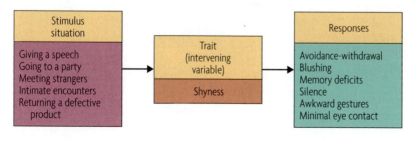

FIGURE 13.1 Shyness as a Trait

Traits may act as intervening variables, relating sets of stimuli and responses that might seem, at first glance, to have little to do with each other.

In the absence of personality test results, traits can be inferred from observed behavior. For example, Martin Luther King Jr. (left) would be thought to have the cardinal trait of peacefully resisting injustice; honesty would be one of Abraham Lincoln's (center) central traits; and Lady Gaga's (right) predilection for changeable styles would be a secondary trait. What do you think may be your cardinal, central, and secondary traits?

unique combination of these three types of traits that make each person a singular entity and championed the use of case studies to examine these unique traits. 👁

Allport saw *personality structures*, rather than *environmental conditions*, as the critical determiners of individual behavior. "The same fire that melts the butter hardens the egg" was a phrase he used to show that the same stimuli can have different effects on different individuals. Many contemporary trait theories have followed in Allport's tradition.

Identifying Universal Trait Dimensions In 1936, a dictionary search by Gordon Allport and his colleague H. S. Odbert found 17,953 adjectives in the English language to describe individual differences. Researchers since that time have attempted to identify the fundamental dimensions that underlie that enormous trait vocabulary. They have tried to determine how many dimensions exist and which ones will allow psychologists to give a useful, universal characterization of all individuals.

Raymond Cattell (1979) used Allport and Odbert's list of adjectives as a starting point in his quest to uncover the appropriate small set of basic trait dimensions. His research led him to propose that 16 factors underlie human personality. Cattell called these 16 factors *source traits* because he believed they provide the underlying source for the surface behaviors we think of as personality. Cattell's 16 factors included important behavioral oppositions such as *reserved* versus *outgoing*, *trusting* versus *suspicious*, and *relaxed* versus *tense*. Even so, contemporary trait theorists argue that even fewer dimensions than 16 capture the most important distinctions among people's personalities.

Hans Eysenck (1973, 1990) derived just three broad dimensions from personality test data: *extraversion* (internally versus externally oriented), *neuroticism* (emotionally stable versus emotionally unstable), and *psychoticism* (kind and considerate

versus aggressive and antisocial). As shown in **Figure 13.2**, Eysenck plotted the two dimensions of extraversion and neuroticism to form a circular display. Individuals can fall anywhere around the circle, ranging from very introverted to very extraverted and from very unstable (neurotic) to very stable. The traits listed around the circle describe people with combinations of these two dimensions. For example, a person who is very extraverted and somewhat unstable is likely to be impulsive.

FIGURE 13.2 The Four Quadrants of Eysenck's Personality Circle
The two dimensions of extraversion and neuroticism yield a circular display.

👁 **Watch** the **Video** *Classic Footage of Gordon Allport on Personality Traits* on **MyPsychLab**

Table 13.1 • The Five-Factor Model

Factor	End Points of the Dimension
Extraversion	Talkative, energetic, and assertive versus quiet, reserved, and shy
Agreeableness	Sympathetic, kind, and affectionate versus cold, quarrelsome, and cruel
Conscientiousness	Organized, responsible, and cautious versus careless, frivolous, and irresponsible
Neuroticism	Stable, calm, and contented versus anxious, unstable, and temperamental
Openness to experience	Creative, intellectual, and open-minded versus simple, shallow, and unintelligent

Five-factor Model Research evidence supports many aspects of Eysenck's theory. However, in recent years, a consensus has emerged that five factors, which overlap imperfectly with Eysenck's three dimensions, best characterize personality structure. The five dimensions are very broad because each brings into one large category many traits that have unique connotations but a common theme. These five dimensions of personality are now called the **five-factor model,** or, more informally, the *Big Five* (McCrae & Costa, 2008). The five factors are summarized in **Table 13.1**. You'll notice again that each dimension has two poles—terms that are similar in meaning to the name of the dimension describe the high pole, and terms that are opposite in meaning describe the low pole. ✳

The movement toward the five-factor model represented attempts to find structure among the large list of traits that Allport and Odbert (1936) had extracted from the dictionary. The traits were boiled down into about 200 synonym clusters that were used to form trait dimensions that have a high pole and a low pole, such as *responsible* versus *irresponsible*. Next, people were asked to rate themselves and others on the bipolar dimensions, and the ratings were subjected to statistical procedures to determine how the synonym clusters were interrelated. Using this method, several independent research teams came to the same conclusion: that there are only *five basic dimensions* underlying the traits people use to describe themselves and others (Norman, 1963, 1967; Tupes & Christal, 1961).

To demonstrate the universality of the five-factor model, researchers have broadened their studies beyond the English language: The five-factor structure has been replicated in 56 different nations (Schmitt et al., 2007). The five factors are not meant to replace the many specific trait terms that carry their own nuances and shades of meaning. Rather, they outline a taxonomy—a classification system—that allows you to give a description of all the people you know in ways that capture the important dimensions on which they differ.

As you've seen, the five-factor model originally emerged from statistical analyses of clusters of trait terms rather than from a theory that said, "These are the factors that must exist" (Ozer & Reise, 1994). However, researchers have started

✳ **Explore** the **Concept** *The Five Factor Mode* on **MyPsychLab**

five-factor model A comprehensive descriptive personality system that maps out the relationships among common traits, theoretical concepts, and personality scales; informally called the Big Five.

to demonstrate that there are differences in the ways that individuals' brains function that correspond to trait differences in the five-factor model.

Featured Study

Recall from Chapter 12 that a brain structure called the amygdala plays an important role in the processing of emotional stimuli. However, researchers had begun to suspect that not all amygdalas—and, therefore, not all people—responded to stimuli in the same way. To test this idea, a team of researchers recruited 15 participants who differed in their level of extraversion (Canli et al., 2002b). The researchers predicted that extraversion would have an impact on emotional processing because that trait captures important aspects of people's emotional lives. To look for individual differences, the researchers had the participants view fearful, happy, and neutral faces while they underwent fMRI scans. **Figure 13.3** *displays the correlation between participants' self-reports of extraversion and activity in the left and right amygdalas: The areas in red are those areas for which high levels of extraversion were associated with high levels of brain activity. As you can see, extraversion was not correlated with the brains' responses to fearful faces (that is, there are no areas in red). In fact, fearful faces activated both the left and right amygdalas, but more or less equally across all levels of extraversion. By contrast, for happy faces the highly extraverted individuals showed abundant activity in the left amygdala.*

Fearful

Happy

FIGURE 13.3 Extraversion Affects the Function of the Left Amygdala

Participants viewed fearful and happy faces. The figure displays in red those areas of the brain for which there was a positive correlation between extraversion and amygdala activity. For the fearful faces, there was no correlation. However, for happy faces, the most extraverted participants also showed the highest levels of activity in their left amygdalas.

From "Amygdala response to happy faces as a function of extraversion" by Turhan Canli, Heidi Sivers, Susan L. Whitfield, Ian H. Gotlib, and John D. E. Gabrieli, *Science*, June 1, 2002. Reprinted with permission from AAAS.

You might recall from Chapter 12 that researchers have characterized emotions as either *approach-related* or *withdrawal-related*. This study suggests that people who are most content to approach other people—that's what makes them extraverted—have more activation in brain regions that support approach-related emotions.

Evolutionary Perspectives on Trait Dimensions   Supporters of the five-factor model have tried to explain why exactly these five dimensions emerge by looking to evolution: They try to relate the five dimensions to consistent types of interactions that people had with each other and with the external world over the course of human evolution (Buss, 2009; Michalski & Shackelford, 2010). Because, for example, humans are essentially a social species, we can view variation on the five dimensions as answers to fundamental social questions: "who is good company (Extraversion), who is kind and supportive (Agreeableness), who puts in sustained effort (Conscientiousness), who is emotionally undependable (Neuroticism), and who has ideas that pan out (Openness [to experience])" (Bouchard & Loehlin, 2001, p. 250). This evolutionary analysis would help explain the universality of the five factors across diverse cultures (Yamagata et al., 2006).

Researchers who take this evolutionary approach have also considered why there is such great variation along these dimensions (Penke et al., 2007). Consider extraversion. As I just noted, humans are a highly social species. For that reason, it might seem maladaptive for an individual to be unsociable and reserved rather than sociable and active. However, we need to factor in differences among environments. People who are highly extraverted are more likely to engage in risky behaviors than those who are not (Nettle, 2006). In particularly dangerous environments, people who were relatively more cautious about social interactions would be more likely to survive. The diversity of environments over human evolution explains why people embody both low and high values on each of the five dimensions. If this explanation is correct, we might also expect that, like other aspects of human experience that have been shaped by evolution, traits can be passed from one generation to the next. We turn now to that claim.

Traits and Heritability

You've probably heard people say things such as "Jim's artistic, like his mother" or "Mary's as stubborn as her grandfather." Or maybe you've felt frustrated because the characteristics that you find irritating in your siblings are those you would like to change in yourself. Let's look at the evidence that supports the heritability of personality traits.

Recall that *behavioral genetics* is the study of the degree to which personality traits and behavior patterns are inherited. To determine the effect of genetics on personality, researchers study the personality traits of family members who share different proportions of genes and who have grown up in the same or different households. For example, if a personality characteristic such as *sociability* is passed on genetically, then sociability should correlate more highly between identical, *monozygotic* (MZ) twins (who share close to 100 percent of their genes) than between fraternal, *dizygotic* (DZ) twins or other siblings (who share, on average, 50 percent of their genes). ◉

Heritability studies show that almost all personality traits are influenced by genetic factors (McCrae et al., 2010; Munafò &

Research with identical twins demonstrates the heritability of personality traits. Are there personality traits you believe run in your family?

Flint, 2011). The findings are the same with many different measurement techniques, whether they measure broad traits, such as extraversion and neuroticism, or specific traits, such as self-control or sociability. Let's consider one sample study.

To study the importance of heritability for personality, a team of researchers followed samples of 696 monozygotic twin pairs and 387 dizygotic twin pairs for a period of 13 years (Kandler et al., 2010). Across those years, the researchers obtained the twins' self-reports of personality as well as personality evaluations by the twins' peers. Comparisons of the MZ and DZ twins suggested that personality stability over time relied on genetic factors, whereas change over time was produced by environmental factors. However, on the whole, genetic factors were more powerful. The researchers suggested that their data were consistent with a set-model *of personality, in which "environmental fluctuations are assumed to affect short-term changes (a few days, weeks, or even several months) in personality, whereas genetic factors determine individual set-points to which individuals will regress on a long-term basis" (p. 995).*

Featured Study

These data illustrate the general conclusion that genetics have a strong impact on personality. Look back to Table 13.1. Which poles of the five factors seem to apply best to you? Can you find similarities between you and your parents?

Do Traits Predict Behaviors?

Suppose a professor asks you to choose some trait terms that you believe apply particularly well to yourself. You might say, for example, that you are *very friendly*. What does your professor now know? If personality theories allow for predictions about behaviors, what can your professor predict from knowing that you rate yourself as being very friendly? How can he or she determine the validity of your belief? Let's explore this question.

◉ **Watch** the **Video** *Special Topics: Twins and Personality* on **MyPsychLab**

One idea you might have is that knowing that a person can be characterized by a particular trait would enable you to predict his or her behavior across different *situations*. Thus, we would expect you to produce friendly behaviors in all situations. However, in the 1920s, several researchers who set out to observe trait-related behaviors in different situations were surprised to find little evidence that behavior was consistent across situations. For example, two behaviors presumably related to the trait of honesty—lying and cheating on a test—were only weakly correlated among schoolchildren (Hartshorne & May, 1928). Similar results were found by other researchers who examined the *cross-situational consistency* for other traits such as introversion or punctuality (Dudycha, 1936; Newcomb, 1929).

If trait-related behaviors are not cross-situationally consistent—that is, if people's behavior changes in different situations—why do you perceive your own and others' personalities to be relatively stable? Even more puzzling, the personality ratings of observers who know an individual from one situation correlate with the ratings of observers who know the individual from another situation. The observation that personality ratings across time and among different observers *are consistent,* whereas behavior ratings of a person across situations *are not consistent,* came to be called the **consistency paradox** (Mischel, 1968).

The identification of the consistency paradox led to a great deal of research (Mischel, 2004). Over time, the consensus emerged that the appearance of behavioral inconsistency arose, in large part, because situations had been categorized in the wrong way: The paradox fades away once theorists can provide an appropriate account of the *psychological features* of situations (Mischel & Shoda, 1995, 1999). Suppose, for example, you

want to try to assess behavioral consistency by determining if a friend acts in much the same way at every party she attends. You're likely to discover that her behavior varies widely if your level of analysis is just "parties." What you need to determine is what psychologically relevant features separate parties into different categories. Perhaps your friend feels uncomfortable in situations in which she is expected to disclose personal information to strangers. As a consequence, she might seem very unfriendly at some parties (where she is expected to disclose personal information) but quite friendly at others (where she is not). Meanwhile, other situations that require her to be disclosing—such as job interviews—might also bring out negative behaviors. Thus we find consistency in the way that features of situations elicit people's distinctive responses.

Researchers have described the knowledge people have of the relationships between dispositions and situations as *if . . . then . . . personality signatures:* If an individual brings a particular disposition to a specific situation *then* he or she will behave in a particular way (Mischel, 2004). This perspective suggests that we understand other people, in part, by acquiring knowledge of their particular if-then patterns. Consider a study that demonstrated the consequences of if-then knowledge for close relationships.

The researchers hypothesized that people who have a better understanding of how their friends will respond in different situations would have less conflict with those friends (Friesen & Kammrath, 2011). To test this hypothesis, the researchers asked pairs of friends to complete the if-then trigger profile questionnaire. The questionnaire presents participants with types of behaviors. They were asked to imagine, for example, that they were responding to someone who was being "overly skeptical of information that he/she receives" (p. 568). For each behavior, the participants indicated to what extent the behavior was likely to serve as a "trigger" for strong negative emotions. Participants

consistency paradox The observation that personality ratings across time and among different observers are consistent while behavior ratings across situations are not consistent.

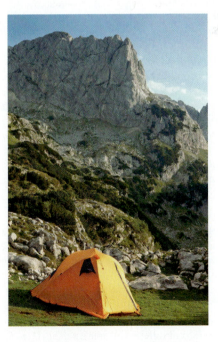

Assuming you could afford either one, which of these vacations would you prefer? What might that tell us about the ways in which personality traits interact with features of situations?

Psychology in Your Life

DO YOU BELIEVE THAT PERSONALITY CAN CHANGE?

In this chapter, you will encounter a diverse set of theories psychologists have originated to explore human personality. However, it's likely that there's one aspect of personality about which you already have a theory of your own—the extent to which personality can change. Take a moment to contemplate these two statements: "Everyone is a certain kind of person, and there is not much that can be done to really change that"; "Everyone can change even their most basic qualities" (Plaks et al., 2009, p. 1070). Do you agree more strongly with one of those two sentiments?

The statements capture two different theories that ordinary people have about personality change (Dweck, 1999). The first theory is an *entity theory,* which suggests that personality traits are essentially fixed; people change little over time. The second theory is an *incremental theory,* which suggests that personality traits are malleable; people are capable of change over time. In samples of college and elementary schoolchildren, about 80 percent of people can be firmly categorized as holding an entity theory or an incremental theory (Plaks et al., 2009). Let's look at some consequences of people's theories.

Consider what it means to be shy, from the perspective of the two theories. Shy people who are entity theorists believe that there's not much they can do to overcome their shyness; shy people who are incremental theorists are more likely to think that they can change, so they view social situations as learning opportunities (Beer, 2002). In one study, both types

of shy people experienced three five-minute interactions with strangers. As you would guess, early in the sessions all the shy participants expressed discomfort in these social interactions. However, as the sessions unfolded, the entity theorists continued to experience high levels of anxiety, whereas the incremental theorists grew less uncomfortable (Beer, 2002). Each individual's theory about the potential for change had a major impact on his or her behavior.

As a second example, think about times in which someone has done something to upset you. How did you respond to the events? People with entity theories tend to believe that wrong-doers cannot change and, therefore, they must be punished; people with incremental theories are more likely to believe that people are not inescapably bad and, therefore, punishment is not always required (Yeager et al., 2011). In one study, adolescents recalled recent events in which acquaintances had upset them. They then indicated the extent to which they were interested in revenge by responding how much they felt like "hurting this person" and "finding a way to punish this person" (Yeager et al., p. 1094). The adolescents who qualified as entity theorists were much more interested in revenge than their incremental theorist peers.

So, let's return to the question posed in this box's title: Do you believe that personality can change? These research examples should convince you that holding an entity theory or an incremental theory can have a broad impact on how people get through their lives.

---

completed the measure both for themselves ("How much does this behavior trigger you?") and their friends ("How much does this behavior trigger your friend?"). Based on these two sets of scores, the researchers were able to derive a measure of accuracy indicating how much the pairs knew about each others' if-then behaviors. The participants also completed a measure of the amount of conflict in the relationship. The researchers found that pairs with the highest if-then accuracy were likely to have the least conflict in their relationships.

Take a moment to consider the if-then knowledge for your friends. Do you see why it would be helpful to understand "*if* this situation occurs, *then* they are likely to respond negatively"?

Evaluation of Trait Theories

We have seen that trait theories allow researchers to give concise descriptions of different people's personalities. These theories have been criticized, however, because they do not generally explain how behavior is generated or how personality develops;

they identify and describe only characteristics that are correlated with behavior. Although contemporary trait theorists have begun to address these concerns, trait theories typically portray a *static,* or at least stabilized, view of *personality structure* as it currently exists. By contrast, psychodynamic theories of personality, to which we next turn, emphasize conflicting forces within the individual that lead to change and development.

Stop *and* Review

① What are the end points of the trait dimension of neuroticism?
② How have researchers assessed the heritability of traits?
③ What is the consistency paradox?

CRITICAL THINKING Recall the study that looked at personality stability over time. Why might the researchers have used both self- and peer-ratings to assess personality?

✓●[Study and Review on MyPsychLab

PSYCHODYNAMIC THEORIES

Common to all **psychodynamic personality theories** is the assumption that powerful inner forces shape personality and motivate behavior. Sigmund Freud, the originator of psychodynamic theories, was characterized by his biographer Ernest Jones as "the Darwin of the mind" (1953). Freud's theory of personality boldly attempts to explain the origins and course of personality development, the nature of mind, aspects of abnormal personality, and the way personality can be changed by therapy. The focus here will only be on normal personality; Chapters 14 and 15 will treat Freud's views on psychopathology. After we explore Freud, we will consider some criticisms and reworkings of his theories.

Freudian Psychoanalysis

According to psychoanalytic theory, at the core of personality are events within a person's mind *(intrapsychic events)* that motivate behavior. Often, people are aware of these motivations; however, some motivation also operates at an unconscious level. The *psychodynamic* nature of this approach comes from its emphasis on these inner wellsprings of behavior, as well as the clashes among these internal forces. For Freud, *all behavior was motivated*. No chance or accidental happenings cause behavior; all acts are determined by motives. Every human action has a cause and a purpose that can be discovered through analysis of thought associations, dreams, errors, and other behavioral clues to inner passions. The primary data for Freud's hypotheses about personality came from clinical observations and in-depth case studies of individual patients in therapy. He developed a theory of normal personality from his intense study of those with mental disorders. Let's look at some of the most important aspects of Freud's theory.

Drives and Psychosexual Development Freud's medical training as a neurologist led him to postulate a common biological basis for the behavioral patterns he observed in his patients. He ascribed the source of motivation for human actions to *psychic energy* found within each individual. Each person was assumed to have inborn instincts or drives that were *tension*

systems created by the organs of the body. These energy sources, when activated, could be expressed in many different ways.

Freud postulated two basic drives. One he saw as involved with *self-preservation* (meeting such needs as hunger and thirst). The other he called *Eros*, the driving force related to sexual urges and preservation of the species. Freud greatly expanded the notion of human sexual desires to include not only the urge for sexual union but all other attempts to seek pleasure or to make physical contact with others. He used the term **libido** to identify the source of energy for sexual urges—a psychic energy that drives us toward sensual pleasures of all types. Sexual urges demand immediate satisfaction, whether through direct actions or through indirect means such as fantasies and dreams.

According to Freud, Eros, as a broadly defined sexual drive, does not suddenly appear at puberty but operates from birth. Eros is evident, he argued, in the pleasure infants derive from physical stimulation of the genitals and other sensitive areas, or *erogenous zones*. Freud's five stages of *psychosexual development* are shown in **Table 13.2**. Freud believed that the physical source of sexual pleasure changed in this orderly progression. One of the major obstacles of psychosexual development, at least for boys, occurs in the phallic stage. Here, the 4- or 5-year-old child must overcome the *Oedipus complex*. Freud named this complex after the mythical figure Oedipus, who unwittingly killed his father and married his mother. Freud believed that every young boy has an innate impulse to view his father as a sexual rival for his mother's attentions. Because the young boy cannot displace his father, the Oedipus complex is generally resolved when the boy comes to *identify* with his father's power. (Freud was inconsistent with respect to his theoretical account of the experiences of young girls.) ✷

According to Freud, either too much gratification or too much frustration at one of the early stages of psychosexual

....

✷ **Explore** the **Concept** *Freud's Five Psychosexual Stages of Personality Development* on **MyPsychLab**

psychodynamic personality theory Theory of personality that shares the assumption that personality is shaped by and behavior is motivated by inner forces.

libido The psychic energy that drives individuals toward sensual pleasures of all types, especially sexual ones.

Table 13.2 • Freud's Stages of Psychosexual Development

Stage	Age	Erogenous Zones	Major Developmental Task (Potential Source of Conflict)	Some Adult Characteristics of Children Who Have Been Fixated at This Stage
Oral	0–1	Mouth, lips, tongue	Weaning	Oral behavior, such as smoking, overeating; passivity and gullibility
Anal	2–3	Anus	Toilet training	Ordeliness, parsimoniousness, obstinacy, or the opposite
Phallic	4–5	Genitals	Oedipus complex	Vanity, recklessness, or the opposite
Latency	6–12	No specific area	Development of defense mechanisms	None: Fixation does not normally occur at this stage
Genitals	13–18	Mature sexual intimacy		Adults who have successfully integrated earlier stages should emerge with a sincere interest in others and a mature sexuality

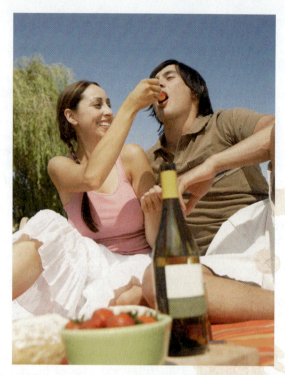

Why did Freud believe that eating is motivated not only by the self-preservation drive to satisfy hunger but also by the "erotic" drive to seek oral gratification?

is not aware. You may act without knowing why or without direct access to the true cause of your actions. There is a *manifest* content to your behavior—what you say, do, and perceive—of which you are fully aware, but there is also a concealed, *latent* content. The meaning of neurotic (anxiety-based) symptoms, dreams, and slips of the pen and tongue is found at the unconscious level of thinking and information processing. Many psychologists today consider this concept of the unconscious to be Freud's most important contribution to the science of psychology. Much modern literature and drama, as well, explores the implications of unconscious processes for human behavior.

According to Freud, impulses within you that you find unacceptable still strive for expression. A *Freudian slip* occurs when an unconscious desire is betrayed by your speech or behavior. For example, I once felt obligated to write a thank-you note although I hadn't much enjoyed a weekend I'd spent at a friend's home. I intended to write, "I'm glad we got to spend a chunk of time together." However, in a somewhat testy phone call, the friend informed me that I'd actually written "I'm glad we got to spend a *junk* of time together." Do you see how the substitution of *junk* for *chunk* could be the expression of an unconscious desire? The concept of unconscious motivation adds a new dimension to personality by allowing for greater complexity of mental functioning.

You've now learned some basic aspects of Freud's theory. Let's see how they contribute to the structure of personality.

development leads to **fixation,** an inability to progress normally to the next stage of development. As shown in Table 13.2, fixation at different stages can produce a variety of adult characteristics. The concept of fixation explains why Freud put such emphasis on early experiences in the continuity of personality. He believed that experiences in the early stages of psychosexual development had a profound impact on personality formation and adult behavior patterns.

Psychic Determinism   The concept of fixation gives us a first look at Freud's belief that early conflicts help *determine* later behaviors. **Psychic determinism** is the assumption that all mental and behavioral reactions (symptoms) are determined by earlier experiences. Freud believed that symptoms were not arbitrary. Rather, symptoms were related in a meaningful way to significant life events.

Freud's belief in psychic determinism led him to emphasize the **unconscious**—the repository of information that is unavailable to conscious awareness (see **Figure 13.4**). Other writers had discussed this construct, but Freud put the concept of the unconscious determinants of human thought, feeling, and action at center stage in the human drama. According to Freud, behavior can be motivated by drives of which a person

FIGURE 13.4 Freud's Conception of the Human Mind

Freudian theory likens the human mind to an iceberg. The tip of the iceberg, which you can see, represents consciousness. The unconscious is the vast bulk of the iceberg, which remains hidden beneath the water.

fixation A state in which a person remains attached to objects or activities more appropriate for an earlier stage of psychosexual development.

psychic determinism The assumption that mental and behavioral reactions are determined by previous experiences.

unconscious The domain of the psyche that stores repressed urges and primitive impulses.

The Structure of Personality In Freud's theory, personality differences arise from the different ways in which people deal with their fundamental drives. To explain these differences, Freud pictured a continuing battle between two antagonistic parts of the personality—the *id* and the *superego*—moderated by a third aspect of the self, the *ego*. Although it might sound almost as if these aspects of self are separate creatures, keep in mind that Freud believed them all to be just different mental *processes*. He did not, for example, identify specific brain locations for the id, ego, and superego. ✳

The **id** is the storehouse of the fundamental drives. It operates irrationally, acting on impulse and pushing for expression and immediate gratification without considering whether what is desired is realistically possible, socially desirable, or morally acceptable. The id is governed by the *pleasure principle*, the unregulated search for gratification—especially sexual, physical, and emotional pleasures—to be experienced here and now without concern for consequences.

The **superego** is the storehouse of an individual's values, including moral attitudes learned from society. The superego corresponds roughly to the common notion of *conscience*. It develops as a child comes to accept as his or her own values the prohibitions of parents and other adults against socially undesirable actions. It is the inner voice of *oughts* and *should nots*. The superego also includes the *ego ideal*, an individual's view of the kind of person he or she should strive to become. Thus the superego is often in conflict with the id. The id wants to do what feels good, whereas the superego insists on doing what is right.

The **ego** is the reality-based aspect of the self that arbitrates the conflict between id impulses and superego demands. The ego represents an individual's personal view of physical and social reality—his or her conscious beliefs about the causes and consequences of behavior. Part of the ego's job is to choose actions that will gratify id impulses without undesirable consequences. The ego is governed by the *reality principle*, which puts reasonable choices before pleasurable demands. Thus the ego would block an impulse to cheat on an exam because of concerns about the consequences of getting caught, and it would substitute the resolution to study harder the next time or solicit the teacher's sympathy. When the id and the superego are in conflict, the ego arranges a compromise that at least partially satisfies both. However, as id and superego pressures intensify, it becomes more difficult for the ego to work out optimal compromises.

Repression and Ego Defense Sometimes this compromise between id and superego involves "putting a lid on the id." Extreme desires are pushed out of conscious awareness into the privacy of the unconscious. **Repression** is the psychological process that protects an individual from experiencing extreme anxiety or guilt about impulses, ideas, or memories that are unacceptable and/or dangerous to express. The ego remains unaware of both the mental content that is censored and the process by which repression keeps information out of consciousness. Repression is considered to be the most basic of the various ways in which the ego defends against being overwhelmed by threatening impulses and ideas.

Ego defense mechanisms are mental strategies the ego uses to defend itself in the daily conflict between id impulses that seek expression and the superego's demand to deny them (see **Table 13.3**). In psychoanalytic theory, these mechanisms are considered vital to an individual's psychological coping

Table 13.3 • Major Ego Defense Mechanisms

Denial of reality	Protecting self from unpleasant reality by refusing to perceive it
Displacement	Discharging pent-up feelings, usually of hostility, on objects less dangerous than those that initially aroused the emotion
Fantasy	Gratifying frustrated desires in imaginary achievements ("daydreaming" is a common form)
Identification	Increasing feelings of worth by identifying self with another person or institution, often of illustrious standing
Isolation	Cutting off emotional charge from hurtful situations or separating incompatible attitudes into logic-tight compartments (holding conflicting attitudes that are never thought of simultaneously or in relation to each other); also called compartmentalization
Projection	Placing blame for one's difficulties on others or attributing one's own "forbidden" desires to others
Rationalization	Attempting to prove that one's behavior is "rational" and justifiable and thus worthy of the approval of self and others
Reaction formation	Preventing dangerous desires from being expressed by endorsing opposing attitudes and types of behavior and using them as "barriers"
Regression	Retreating to earlier developmental levels involving more childish responses and usually a lower level of aspiration
Repression	Pushing painful or dangerous thoughts out of consciousness, keeping them unconscious; this is considered to be the most basic of the defense mechanisms
Sublimation	Gratifying or working off frustrated sexual desires in substitutive nonsexual activities socially accepted by one's culture

with powerful inner conflicts. By using them, a person is able to maintain a favorable self-image and to sustain an acceptable social image. For example, if a child has strong feelings of hatred toward his father—which, if acted out, would be

✳ **Explore** the **Concept** *The Id, Ego, and Superego* on **MyPsychLab**

id The primitive, unconscious part of the personality that represents the internalization of society's values, standards, and morals.

superego The aspect of personality that represents the internalization of society's values, standards, and morals.

ego The aspect of personality involved in self-preservation activities and in directing instinctual drives and urges into appropriate channels.

repression The basic defense mechanism by which painful or guilt-producing thoughts, feelings, or memories are excluded from conscious awareness.

ego defense mechanism Mental strategy (conscious or unconscious) used by the ego to defend itself against conflicts experienced in the normal course of life.

dangerous—repression may take over. The hostile impulse is then no longer consciously pressing for satisfaction or even recognized as existing. However, although the impulse is not seen or heard, it is not gone; these feelings continue to play a role in personality functioning. For example, by developing a strong *identification* with his father, the child may increase his sense of self-worth and reduce his unconscious fear of being discovered as a hostile agent. ✻

In Freudian theory, **anxiety** is an intense emotional response triggered when a repressed conflict is about to emerge into consciousness. Anxiety is a danger signal: Repression is not working! Red alert! More defenses needed! This is the time for a second line of defense, one or more additional ego defense mechanisms that will relieve the anxiety and send the distressing impulses back down into the unconscious. For example, a mother who does not like her son and does not want to care for him might use *reaction formation,* which transforms her unacceptable impulse into its opposite: "I hate my child" becomes "I love my child. See how I smother the dear little thing with love?" Such defenses serve the critical coping function of alleviating anxiety.

If defense mechanisms defend you against anxiety, why might they still have negative consequences for you? Useful as they are, ego mechanisms of defense are ultimately self-deceptive. When overused, they create more problems than they solve. It is psychologically unhealthy to spend a great deal of time and psychic energy deflecting, disguising, and rechanneling unacceptable urges in order to reduce anxiety. Doing so leaves little energy for productive living or satisfying human relationships. Freud argued that some forms of mental illness result from excessive reliance on defense mechanisms to cope with anxiety, as you will see in a later chapter on mental disorders.

Evaluation of Freudian Theory

This chapter has devoted a great deal of space to outlining the essentials of psychoanalytic theory because Freud's ideas have had an enormous impact on the way many psychologists think about normal and abnormal aspects of personality. However, there probably are more psychologists who criticize Freudian concepts than who support them. What is the basis of some of their criticisms?

First, psychoanalytic concepts are vague and not operationally defined; thus much of the theory is difficult to evaluate scientifically. Because some of its central hypotheses cannot be disproved, even in principle, Freud's theory remains questionable. How can the concepts of libido, the structure of personality, and repression of infantile sexual impulses be studied in any direct fashion?

A second, related criticism is that Freudian theory is good history but bad science. It does not reliably *predict* what will occur; it is applied *retrospectively*—after events have occurred. Using psychoanalytic theory to understand personality typically involves historical reconstruction, not scientific

. . . .

✻ **Explore** the **Concept** *Defense Mechanisms* on **MyPsychLab**

anxiety An intense emotional response caused by the preconscious recognition that a repressed conflict is about to emerge into consciousness.

construction of probable actions and predictable outcomes. In addition, by overemphasizing historical origins of current behavior, the theory directs attention away from the current stimuli that may be inducing and maintaining the behavior.

There are three other major criticisms of Freudian theory. First, it is a developmental theory, but it never included observations or studies of children. Second, it minimizes traumatic experiences (such as child abuse) by reinterpreting memories of them as fantasies (based on a child's desire for sexual contact with a parent). Third, it has an *androcentric* (male-centered) bias because it uses a male model as the norm without trying to determine how females might be different.

Some aspects of Freud's theory, however, continue to gain acceptance as they are modified and improved through empirical scrutiny. For example, in Chapter 5, we saw that the concept of the unconscious is being systematically explored by contemporary researchers (McGovern & Baars, 2007). This research reveals that much of your day-to-day experience is shaped by processes outside of your awareness. These results support Freud's general concept but weaken the link between unconscious processes and psychopathology: Little of your unconscious knowledge will cause you anxiety or distress.

Researchers have also found evidence for some of the habits of mind Freud characterized as defense mechanisms. We saw earlier that individuals are most likely to use defense mechanisms when they are experiencing anxiety. Researchers have tested this hypothesis in a variety of ways.

Featured Study

One study focused on a group of 9- to 11-year-old girls (Sandstrom & Cramer, 2003). The researchers carried out interviews with their peers to determine who among the group of 50 girls was relatively popular and who was relatively unpopular. Each of the 50 girls underwent a laboratory experience in which they were rejected by another young girl. The researchers reasoned that—because of their history of negative social interactions—the unpopular girls would experience more anxiety than the popular girls in the face of this rejection. The researchers suggested that, to cope with that anxiety, the unpopular girls would show evidence for more frequent use of defense mechanisms. To test this hypothesis, the researcher asked the girls to tell stories based on cards from the Thematic Apperception Test *(see p. 435). The stories were analyzed for evidence of the defense mechanisms denial and projection (see Table 13.3). These analyses supported the hypothesis: The unpopular girls used more defense mechanisms than the popular girls after the episode of peer rejection.*

Some of the styles for coping with stress that Chapter 12 described fall within the general category of defense mechanisms. You might recall, for example, that inhibiting the thoughts and feelings associated with personal traumas or guilty or shameful experiences can take a devastating toll on mental and physical health (Pennebaker, 1997; Petrie et al., 2004). These findings echo Freud's beliefs that repressed psychic material can lead to psychological distress.

Freud's theory is the most complex, comprehensive, and compelling view of normal and abnormal personality functioning—even when its predictions prove wrong. However, like any other theory, Freud's is best treated as one that must be confirmed or disconfirmed element by element. Freud retains his influence on contemporary psychology because some of his ideas have been widely accepted. Others have been abandoned. Some of the earliest revisions of Freud's theory arose from within his own original circle of students. Let's see how they sought to amend Freud's views.

Extending Psychodynamic Theories

Some of those who came after Freud retained his basic representation of personality as a battleground on which unconscious primal urges conflict with social values. However, many of Freud's intellectual descendants made major adjustments in the psychoanalytic view of personality. In general, these post-Freudians have made the following changes:

- They put greater emphasis on ego functions, including ego defenses, development of the self, conscious thought processes, and personal mastery.
- They view social variables (culture, family, and peers) as playing a greater role in shaping personality.
- They put less emphasis on the importance of general sexual urges, or libidinal energy.
- They extended personality development beyond childhood to include the entire life span.

We will now see how these themes emerged in the theories of Alfred Adler, Karen Horney, and Carl Jung.

Alfred Adler (1870–1937) rejected the significance of Eros and the pleasure principle. Adler (1929) believed that as helpless, dependent, small children, people all experience feelings of *inferiority*. He argued that all lives are dominated by the search for ways to overcome those feelings. People compensate to achieve feelings of adequacy or, more often, overcompensate in an attempt to become *superior*. Personality is structured around this underlying striving; people develop lifestyles based on particular ways of overcoming their basic, pervasive feelings of inferiority. Personality conflict arises from incompatibility between external environmental pressures and internal strivings for adequacy, rather than from competing urges within the person.

Karen Horney (1885–1952) was trained in the psychoanalytic school but broke from orthodox Freudian theory in

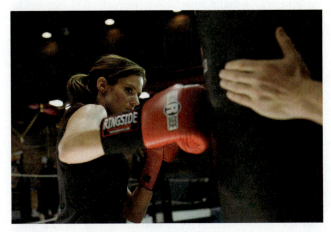

Why might a person's enthusiasm for boxing suggest the use of displacement as an ego defense mechanism?

Jung recognized creativity as a means to release images from both the personal and collective unconscious. Why did Jung believe in the two types of unconscious?

several ways. She challenged Freud's phallocentric emphasis on the importance of the penis, hypothesizing that male envy of pregnancy, motherhood, breasts, and suckling is a dynamic force in the unconscious of boys and men. This "womb envy" leads men to devalue women and to overcompensate by unconscious impulses toward creative work. Horney also placed greater emphasis than did Freud on cultural factors and focused on present character structure rather than on infantile sexuality (Horney, 1937, 1939). Because Horney also had influence on the development of humanistic theories, we will return to her ideas in the next section.

Carl Jung (1875–1961) greatly expanded the conception of the unconscious. For Jung (1959), the unconscious was not limited to an individual's unique life experiences but was filled with fundamental psychological truths shared by the whole human race, a **collective unconscious.** The collective unconscious explains your intuitive understanding of primitive myths, art forms, and symbols, which are the universal archetypes of existence. An **archetype** is a primitive symbolic representation of a particular experience or object. Each archetype is associated with an instinctive tendency to feel and think about it or experience it in a special way. Jung postulated many archetypes that give rise to myths and symbols: the sun god, the hero, the earth mother. *Animus* was the male archetype, *anima* was the female archetype, and all men and women experienced both archetypes in varying degrees. The archetype of the self is the *mandala,* or magic circle; it symbolizes striving for unity and wholeness (Jung, 1973).

Jung saw the healthy, integrated personality as balancing opposing forces, such as masculine aggressiveness and feminine sensitivity. This view of personality as a constellation of compensating internal forces in dynamic balance was called **analytic psychology.** In addition, Jung rejected the primary importance of libido so central to Freud's own theory. Jung

....

collective unconscious The part of an individual's unconscious that is inherited, evolutionarily developed, and common to all members of the species.

archetype A universal, inherited, primitive, and symbolic representation of a particular experience or object.

analytic psychology A branch of psychology that views the person as a constellation of compensatory internal forces in a dynamic balance.

added two equally powerful unconscious instincts: the need to create and the need to become a coherent, whole individual. In the next section on humanist theories, we will see this second need paralleled in the concept of *self-actualization*.

Stop *and* Review

① According to Freud's theory, what behaviors might arise if an individual became fixated at the oral stage of development?

② How is the ego guided by the reality principle?

③ Although Leon is highly aggressive, he always blames others for starting fights. What defensive mechanism might be at work here?

④ According to Alfred Adler's view, what drive motivates much of people's behavior?

CRITICAL THINKING   Recall the study on the use of defense mechanisms. Why might the researchers have specifically used a rejection episode to produce anxiety?

✓●⌐**Study** and **Review** on **MyPsychLab**

HUMANISTIC THEORIES

Humanistic approaches to understanding personality are characterized by a concern for the integrity of an individual's personal and conscious experience and growth potential. In this section, you will see how humanistic theorists have developed concepts related to the self. You will learn, in addition, what additional features set humanistic theories apart from other types of personality theories.

Features of Humanistic Theories

For **Carl Rogers** (1902–1987), the *self* is a central concept for personality. Rogers suggested that we develop a **self-concept,** a mental model of our typical behaviors and unique qualities. Rogers believed that, as we go through life, we strive to experience congruence between our self-concept and our actual life experiences. Rogers's emphasis on the self signals a key feature of all humanistic theories, which is an emphasis on the drive toward self-actualization. **Self-actualization** is a constant striving to realize one's inherent potential. Recall from Chapter 11 that **Abraham Maslow** placed self-actualization at the pinnacle of his hierarchy of needs. The striving toward self-fulfillment

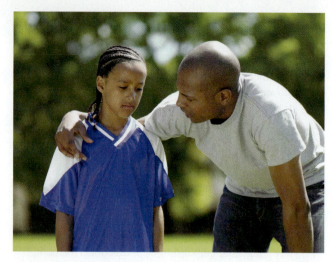

Why did Carl Rogers emphasize parents' unconditional positive regard for their children?

is a constructive, guiding force that moves each person toward generally positive behaviors and enhancement of the self.

The drive for self-actualization at times comes into conflict with the need for approval from the self and others, especially when the person feels that certain obligations or conditions must be met in order to gain approval. For example, Rogers (1947, 1951, 1977) stressed the importance of **unconditional positive regard** in raising children. By this, he meant that children should feel they will always be loved and approved of, in spite of their mistakes and misbehavior—that they do not have to earn their parents' love. He recommended that, when a child misbehaves, parents should emphasize that it is the behavior they disapprove of, not the child. Unconditional positive regard is important in adulthood, too, because worrying about seeking approval interferes with self-actualization. As an adult, you need to give to and receive unconditional positive regard from those to whom you are close. Most important, you need to feel unconditional positive *self-regard,* or acceptance of yourself, in spite of the weaknesses you might be trying to change.

Although not often given due credit, Karen Horney was another major theorist whose ideas created the foundation of humanistic psychology (Frager & Fadiman, 1998). Horney came to believe that people have a "real self" that requires favorable environmental circumstances to be actualized, such as an atmosphere of warmth, the goodwill of others, and parental love of the child as a "particular individual" (Horney, 1945, 1950). In the absence of those favorable nurturing conditions, the child develops a basic anxiety that stifles spontaneity of expression of real feelings and prevents effective relations with others. To cope with their basic anxiety, individuals resort to interpersonal or intrapsychic defenses. Interpersonal defenses produce movement toward others (through excessive compliance and self-effacing actions), against others (by aggressive, arrogant, or narcissistic solutions), and away from others (through detachment). Intrapsychic defenses operate to develop for some people an unrealistic idealized self-image that generates a "search for glory" to justify it and a pride system that operates on rigid rules of conduct to live up to a grandiose self-concept. Such people often live by the "tyranny of shoulds," self-imposed obligations, such as "I should be perfect,

self-concept A person's mental model of his or her typical behaviors and unique qualities.

self-actualization A concept in personality psychology referring to a person's constant striving to realize his or her potential and to develop inherent talents and capabilities.

unconditional positive regard Complete love and acceptance of an individual by another person, such as a parent for a child, with no conditions attached.

generous, attractive, brave," and so forth. Horney believed that the goal of a humanistic therapy was to help the individual achieve the joy of self-realization and promote the inherent constructive forces in human nature that support a striving for self-fulfillment.

As you have seen, humanistic theories emphasize self-actualization or progress toward the real self. In addition, humanistic theories have been described as being holistic, dispositional, and phenomenological. Let's see why.

Humanistic theories are *holistic* because they explain people's separate acts in terms of their entire personalities; people are not seen as the sum of discrete traits that each influence behavior in different ways. Maslow believed that people are intrinsically motivated toward the upper levels of the hierarchy of needs (discussed in Chapter 11), unless deficiencies at the lower levels weigh them down.

Humanistic theories are *dispositional* because they focus on the innate qualities within a person that exert a major influence over the direction behavior will take. Situational factors are seen as constraints and barriers (like the strings that tie down balloons). Once freed from negative situational conditions, the actualizing tendency should actively guide people to choose life-enhancing situations. However, humanistic theories are not dispositional in the same sense as trait theories or psychodynamic theories. In those views, personal dispositions are recurrent themes played out in behavior again and again. Humanistic dispositions are oriented specifically toward creativity and growth. Each time a humanistic disposition is exercised, the person changes a little, so that the disposition is never expressed in the same way twice. Over time, humanistic dispositions guide the individual toward self-actualization, the purest expression of these motives.

Humanistic theories are *phenomenological* because they emphasize an individual's frame of reference and subjective view of reality—not the objective perspective of an observer or of a therapist. Thus a humanistic psychologist always strives to see each person's unique point of view. This view is also a present-oriented view; past influences are important only to the extent that they have brought the person to the present situation, and the future represents goals to achieve. Thus, unlike psychodynamic theories, humanistic theories do not see people's present behaviors as unconsciously guided by past experiences.

The upbeat humanist view of personality was a welcome treat for many psychologists who had been brought up on a diet of bitter-tasting Freudian medicine. Humanistic approaches focus directly on improvement—on making life more palatable—rather than dredging up painful memories that are sometimes better left repressed. The humanist perspective emphasizes each person's ability to realize his or her fullest potential.

Evaluation of Humanistic Theories

Freud's theory was often criticized for providing the too-pessimistic view that human nature develops out of conflicts, traumas, and anxieties. Humanistic theories arose to celebrate the healthy personality that strives for happiness and self-actualization. It is difficult to criticize theories that encourage and appreciate people, even for their faults. Even so, critics have complained that humanistic concepts are fuzzy and

difficult to explore in research. They ask, "What exactly is self-actualization? Is it an inborn tendency, or is it created by the cultural context?" Humanistic theories also do not traditionally focus on the particular characteristics of individuals. They are more theories about human nature and about qualities all people share than about the individual personality or the basis of differences among people. Other psychologists note that, by emphasizing the role of the self as a source of experience and action, humanistic psychologists neglect the important environmental variables that also influence behavior.

Despite these limitations, a type of contemporary research can be traced in part to the humanist tradition that focuses directly on individual *narrative identities* or *life stories* (McAdams & Olson, 2010). The tradition of using psychological theory to understand the details of an individual's life—to produce a *psychobiography*—can be traced back to Freud's analysis of Leonardo da Vinci (Freud, 1910/1957; see Elms, 1988, for a critique of Freud's work). **Psychobiography** is defined as "the systematic use of psychological (especially personality) theory to transform a life into a coherent and illuminating story" (McAdams, 1988, p. 2). Consider the great artist Pablo Picasso. Picasso suffered a series of traumas as a young child, including a serious earthquake and the death of a young sister. A psychobiography might attempt to explain some of Picasso's vast artistic creativity as the lifelong residue of his responses to these early traumas (Gardner, 1993). When a well-known or historical figure is the subject of a psychobiography, a researcher may turn to published work, diaries, and letters as sources of relevant data. For more ordinary individuals, researchers may directly elicit narratives of life experiences. The request might be, for example, for participants to reflect on key events in their lives: "Why do you think that this [was] an important event in your life story? What does this event say about who you are, who you were, who you might be, or how you have developed over time?" (McAdams et al., 2006, p. 1379). The characteristic themes that emerge over a series of narrative accounts support the holistic and phenomenological version of personality that was put forth by the early humanists: People construct their identities by weaving life stories out of the strands of narrative. Personal accounts provide a window on people's views of themselves and interpersonal relationships.

Humanistic theorists emphasized each individual's drive toward self-actualization. This group recognized, however, that people's progress toward this goal is determined, in part, by realities of their environments. We turn now to theories that directly examine how individuals' behaviors are shaped by their environments.

Stop *and* Review

① What is self-actualization?
② In what ways are humanistic theories dispositional?
③ What is a psychobiography?

✓•⎼ **Study** and **Review** on **MyPsychLab**

....

psychobiography The use of psychological (especially personality) theory to describe and explain an individual's course through life.

SOCIAL-LEARNING AND COGNITIVE THEORIES

Common to all the theories you've seen so far is an emphasis on hypothesized inner mechanisms—traits, instincts, impulses, tendencies toward self-actualization—that propel behavior and form the basis of a functioning personality. What most of these theories lacked, however, was a solid link between personality and particular behaviors. Psychodynamic and humanistic theories, for example, provide accounts of the total personality but do not predict specific actions. Another tradition of personality theory emerged from a more direct focus on individual differences in behavior. Recall from Chapter 6 that much of a person's behavior can be predicted from contingencies in the environment. Psychologists with a *learning theory* orientation look to the environmental circumstances that control behavior. Personality is seen as the sum of the overt and covert responses that are reliably elicited by an individual's *reinforcement history*. Learning theory approaches suggest that people are different because they have had different histories of reinforcement.

This next set of theories has as a shared starting point that behavior is influenced by environmental contingencies. However, these contemporary social-learning and cognitive theories go one step further to emphasize the importance of cognitive processes as well as behavioral ones. Those researchers who have proposed cognitive theories of personality point out that there are important individual differences in the way people think about and define any external situation. Like humanistic theories, cognitive theories emphasize that you participate in creating your own personality. For example, you actively *choose* your own environments to a great extent; you do not just react passively. You weigh alternatives and select the settings in which you act and are acted upon—you choose to enter situations that you expect to be reinforcing and to avoid those that are unsatisfying and uncertain.

Let's look now at more concrete embodiments of these ideas. We visit the theories of Julian Rotter, Walter Mischel, and Albert Bandura.

Rotter's Expectancy Theory

Julian Rotter (1954) focused his theory on **expectancy,** which is the extent to which people believe that their behaviors in particular situations will bring about rewards. Suppose, for example, that you need to decide how much to practice before a presentation in class. You'd like to get at least a *B*. Having a high expectancy means that you think it's very likely that extra practice will lead to a *B* or better; having a low expectancy means that you're not at all confident that extra practice will help with your grade. Your expectancies arise, in part, because of your own history of reinforcement: If practice has led to rewards in the past, you'll have a stronger expectancy that it will lead to a reward again. Rotter also emphasized *reward*

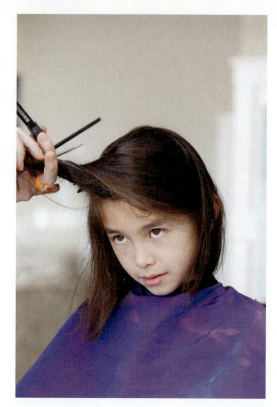

If your parents complimented you every time you got a new haircut, how might that affect your confidence about your appearance and grooming as an adult? Suppose they were regularly critical. What effect could that have?

value—the value that an individual assigns to a particular reward. If you've had a tough semester, a *B* might have more value to you than it would in a different context. On Rotter's view, you can only begin to predict people's behavior if you can assess both their expectancy with respect to a reward and the extent to which they value a reward.

Rotter emphasized that people bring specific expectancies to the many situations they face in life. However, Rotter also believed that people develop a more general expectancy about the extent to which they can control the rewards they obtain. Rotter (1966) defined a dimension of **locus of control:** Some people—known as *internals*—believe more strongly that the outcomes of their actions are contingent on what they do; other people—known as *externals*—believe that the outcomes of their actions are contingent on environmental factors. In **Table 13.4**, you'll see sample items from Rotter's *Internal-External Scale*. To complete the scale, you choose (a) or (b) from each item as the statement you believe to be more accurate. These examples should give you a sense of some differences in the ways that internals and externals generate expectancies about life outcomes. Researchers have consistently demonstrated the importance of people's locus of control orientations. For example, one study examined the relationship between people's locus of control orientation at age 10 and their mental and physical health at age 30 (Gale et al., 2008). The 30-year-olds who had been more internally oriented as children were, on the whole, in better health. They were, for example, at lower risk for obesity, high blood pressure, and psychological distress. The

---

expectancy The extent to which people believe that their behaviors in particular situations will bring about rewards.

locus of control People's general expectancy about the extent to which the rewards they obtain are contingent on their own actions or on environmental factors.

Table 13.4 • Sample Items from the Internal–External Scale

1. a. In the long run people get the respect they deserve in the world.
   b. Unfortunately, an individual's worth often passes unrecognized no matter how hard he tries.

2. a. Without the right breaks, one cannot be an effective leader.
   b. Capable people who fail to become leaders have not taken advantage of their opportunities.

3. a. Most people don't realize the extent to which their lives are controlled by accidental happenings.
   b. There really is no such thing as "luck."

4. a. What happens to me is my own doing.
   b. Sometimes I feel that I don't have enough control over the direction my life is taking.

Note: 1a, 2b, 3b, and 4a indicate a more internal locus of control orientation.

From J. B. Rotter, Generalized expectancies for internal versus external locus of control of reinforcement, Table 1. *Psychological Monographs, 80* (1):11–12. Copyright © 1966 by the American Psychological Association. Adapted with permission.

researchers suggested that people with external orientations might be in poorer shape because they believe that their health is outside their control—and therefore they take few actions to better their health.

Mischel's Cognitive–affective Personality Theory

Walter Mischel developed an influential theory of the cognitive basis of personality. Mischel emphasizes that people actively participate in the cognitive organization of their interactions with the environment. His approach emphasizes the importance of understanding how behavior arises as a function of interactions between persons and situations (Mischel, 2004). Consider this example:

> John's unique personality may be seen most clearly in that he is always very friendly when meeting someone for the first time, but that he also predictably becomes

rather abrupt and unfriendly as he begins to spend more time with that person. Jim, on the other hand, is unique in that he is typically shy and quiet with people who he does not know well but becomes very gregarious once he begins to know someone well. (Shoda et al., 1993a, p. 1023)

If we were to average John's and Jim's overall friendliness, we would probably get about the same value on this trait—but that would fail to capture important differences in their behavior. According to Mischel (1973, 2004), how you respond to a specific environmental input depends on the variables defined in **Table 13.5**. Do you see how each variable listed would affect the way in which a person would behave in particular situations? Try to invent a situation in which you would produce behavior different from the characters listed in the table because you contrast on the particular variable. You may wonder what determines the nature of these variables for a specific individual. Mischel believes that they result from his or her history of observations and interactions with other people and with inanimate aspects of the physical environment (Mischel, 1973).

I want to provide you with a concrete example of how the variables in Mischel's theory explain differences with respect to the particular behaviors people produce in the same situations. Let's consider a study that documented how interactions of competencies and self-regulatory plans (see Table 13.5) interact to predict aggressive behavior among 10-year-old boys.

Featured Study

The study focused on 59 boys who were attending a summer camp (Ayduk et al., 2007). To measure their competencies, the researchers gave each boy a test of verbal intelligence. To measure their self-regulatory abilities, the researchers had each boy engage in a task that measured his capacity to delay his gratification. The boys were brought into a room with a small and large pile of food of a type they particularly enjoyed (for example, M&M candies). To obtain the larger pile, the boys had to wait 25 minutes without ringing a bell to call a researcher back—if they used the bell, they got only the small pile. To endure the 25-minute wait, the boys needed to be able to regulate their own behavior. In particular, to make the time pass more easily,

Table 13.5 • Person Variables in Mischel's Cognitive–Affective Personality Theory

Variable		
Encodings	The way you categorize information about yourself, other people, events, and situations	As soon as Bob meets someone, he tries to figure out how wealthy he or she is.
Expectancies and beliefs	Your beliefs about the social world and likely outcomes for given actions in particular situations; your beliefs about your ability to bring outcomes about	Greg invites friends to the movies, but he never expects them to say "yes."
Affects	Your feelings and emotions, including physiological responses	Cindy blushes very easily.
Goals and values	The outcomes and affective states you do and do not value; your goals and life projects	Peter wants to be president of his college class.
Competencies and self-regulatory plans	The behaviors you can accomplish and plans for generating cognitive and behavioral outcomes	Jan can speak English, French, Russian, and Japanese and expects to work for the United Nations.

they needed to be able to divert their attention from the candy and the bell. For that reason, the researchers used the boys' ability to control their attention as a measure of self-regulatory ability. Finally, to measure aggression, the researchers obtained multiple assessments from the camp counselors about the boys' verbal and physical aggression during group activities. As you can see in **Figure 13.5**, *to predict the boys' levels of aggression it's important to know both about competencies and self-regulatory abilities. In particular, boys with high verbal intelligence but low ability to control their attention were substantially more aggressive than their peers who had both high intelligence and high ability to control their attention.*

You might expect that more intelligent boys would have knowledge that would allow them to function in social environments without resorting to aggression. This study demonstrates that knowledge alone is not sufficient—the boys also need to have the ability and motivation to perform alternative behaviors. The results allow you to understand why Mischel's personality theory focuses on the interactions among several different types of variables.

As you can see in Table 13.5, Mischel's theory also considers the role that people's goals have in defining their responses to particular situations. Research suggests that people differ both in their choice of life goals and the strategies they use to implement those goals (Cantor & Kihlstrom, 1987; Kihlstrom & Cantor, 2000). Can you see how choices and skills with respect to goals could produce the different patterns of behavior you would recognize as personality? For example, some people have *intimacy* as an important goal—they strongly seek to foster

Would you feel comfortable making personality judgments about these boys from this one snapshot? Why might you want to know their patterns of behavior across different types of situations?

interdependence and engage in self-disclosure—whereas other people don't bring those needs to friendships. These goals influence behavior: People with strong intimacy goals work harder in relationships to minimize conflicts (Sanderson et al., 2005). In this case, you recognize personality in the consistent way in which people's goals lead them to behave.

Bandura's Cognitive Social-learning Theory

Through his theoretical writing and extensive research with children and adults, Albert Bandura (1986, 1999) has been an eloquent champion of a social-learning approach to understanding personality (recall from Chapter 6 his studies of aggressive behavior in children). This approach combines principles of learning with an emphasis on human interactions in social settings. From a social-learning perspective, human beings are not driven by inner forces, nor are they helpless pawns of environmental influence. The social-learning approach stresses the cognitive processes that are involved in acquiring and maintaining patterns of behavior and, thus, personality.

Bandura's theory points to a complex interaction of individual factors, behavior, and environmental stimuli. Each can influence or change the others, and the direction of change is rarely one way—it is *reciprocal*. Your behavior can

FIGURE 13.5 Boys' Levels of Aggressive Behavior

Boys' levels of aggressive behavior at a summer camp reflected an interaction between their verbal intelligence and their ability to control their attention to delay gratification.

Data from O. Ayduk, M. L. Rodriguez, W. Mischel, Y. Shoda, & J. Wright. Verbal intelligence and self-regulatory competencies, *Journal of Research in Personality (41)*: 374–388, Copyright © 2007.

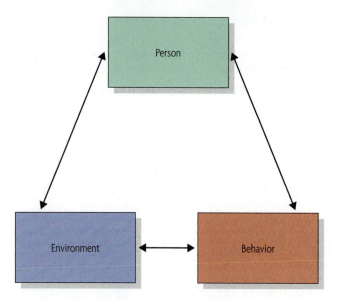

FIGURE 13.6 Reciprocal Determinism

In reciprocal determinism, the individual, the individual's behavior, and the environment all interact to influence and modify the other components.

be influenced by your attitudes, beliefs, or prior history of reinforcement as well as by stimuli available in the environment. What you do can have an effect on the environment, and important aspects of your personality can be affected by the environment or by feedback from your behavior. This important concept, **reciprocal determinism,** implies that you must examine all components if you want to completely understand human behavior, personality, and social ecology (Bandura, 1999; see **Figure 13.6**). So, for example, if you don't generally think of yourself as an athlete, you may not choose to be active in track-and-field events, but if you live near a pool, you may nonetheless spend time swimming. If you are outgoing, you'll talk to others sitting around the pool and thereby create a more sociable atmosphere, which, in turn, makes it a more enjoyable environment. This is one instance of reciprocal determinism among person, place, and behavior.

You may recall from Chapter 6 that Bandura's social-learning theory emphasizes observational learning as the process by which a person changes his or her behavior based on observations of another person's behavior. Through observational learning, children and adults acquire an enormous range of information about their social environment. Through observation, you learn what is appropriate and gets rewarded and what gets punished or ignored. Because you can use memory and think about external events, you can foresee the possible consequences of your actions without having to actually experience them. You may acquire skills, attitudes, and beliefs simply by watching what others do and the consequences that follow.

As his theory developed, Bandura (1997) elaborated self-efficacy as a central construct. **Self-efficacy** is the belief that one can perform adequately in a particular situation. Your sense of self-efficacy influences your perceptions, motivation, and performance in many ways. You don't even try to do things or take

chances when you expect to be ineffectual. You avoid situations when you don't feel adequate. Even when you do, in fact, have the ability—and the desire—you may not take the required action or persist to complete the task successfully, if you think you lack what it takes.

Beyond actual accomplishments, there are three other sources of information for *self-efficacy judgments*:

- vicarious experience—your observations of the performance of others
- persuasion—others may convince you that you can do something, or you may convince yourself
- monitoring of your emotional arousal as you think about or approach a task—for example, anxiety suggests low expectations of efficacy; excitement suggests expectations of success

Self-efficacy judgments influence how much effort you expend and how long you persist when faced with difficulty in a wide range of life situations (Bandura, 1997, 2006).

Let's consider the impact of self-efficacy in academic settings. Research suggests, for example, that how vigorously and persistently you study this chapter may depend more on your sense of self-efficacy than on actual ability.

A group of 1,291 sophomores from five California State University campuses participated in a study that examined the impact of self-efficacy beliefs on college performance (Vuong et al., 2010). Each student completed measures of self-efficacy that related to his or her college experience: self-efficacy in academic coursework and self-efficacy for social interactions with faculty, counselor, and peers. They used a 10-point scale ranging from "Not confident" to "Extremely confident" to indicate how they felt about completing various tasks such as "Asking questions in class" and "Making friends at school" (Zajacova et al., 2005, p. 700). The sophomores also reported their GPAs and how likely they were to persist with their education. Self-efficacy for academic coursework predicted both the students' GPAs and persistence (Vuong et al., 2010). However, self-efficacy for social interactions was unrelated to the measures of academic performance.

This study illustrates how people have self-efficacy for different domains of life experience. In fact, we'd expect that people would often have different amounts of self-efficacy in different domains. What might the researchers have measured to assess the importance of self-efficacy for social interactions in the sophomores' college experiences?

Bandura's theory of self-efficacy also acknowledges the importance of the environment. Expectations of failure or

reciprocal determinism A concept of Albert Bandura's social-learning theory that refers to the notion that a complex reciprocal interaction exists among the individual, his or her behavior, and environmental stimuli and that each of these components affects the others.

self-efficacy A belief that one can perform adequately in a particular situation.

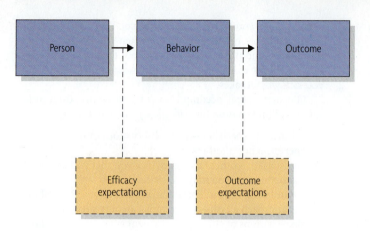

FIGURE 13.7 Bandura's Self-Efficacy Model

This model positions efficacy expectations between the person and his or her behavior; outcome expectations are positioned between behavior and its anticipated outcomes.

success—and corresponding decisions to stop trying or to persevere—may be based on perceptions of the supportiveness or unsupportiveness of the environment, in addition to perceptions of one's own adequacy or inadequacy. Such expectations are called *outcome-based expectancies.* **Figure 13.7** displays how the parts of Bandura's theory fit together. Behavioral outcomes depend both on people's perceptions of their own abilities and their perceptions of the environment.

Evaluation of Social-Learning and Cognitive Theories

One set of criticisms leveled against social-learning and cognitive theories is that they often overlook emotion as an important component of personality. In psychodynamic theories, emotions like anxiety play a central role. In social-learning and cognitive theories, emotions are perceived merely as by-products of thoughts and behavior or are just included with other types of thoughts rather than being assigned independent importance. For those who feel that emotions are central to the functioning of human personality, this is a serious flaw. Cognitive theories are also attacked for not fully recognizing the impact of unconscious motivation on behavior and affect.

A second set of criticisms focuses on the vagueness of explanations about the way personal constructs and competencies are created. Cognitive theorists have often had little to say about the developmental origins of adult personality; their focus on the individual's perception of the current behavior setting obscures the individual's history.

Despite these criticisms, cognitive personality theories have made major contributions to current thinking. Mischel's awareness of the situation has brought about a better understanding of the interaction between what a person brings to a behavior setting and what that setting brings out of the person. Bandura's ideas have led to improvements in the way teachers educate children and help them achieve as well as new treatments in the areas of health, business, and sports performance.

Do these cognitive personality theories provide you with insights about your own personality and behaviors? You can start to see how you define yourself in part through interactions with the environment. Let's turn now to theories that can add even further to your definition of self.

Stop *and* Review

① In Julian Rotter's theory, what does it mean to have an external locus of control orientation?

② In Walter Mischel's theory, what five types of variables explain individual differences?

③ What three components are involved in Albert Bandura's theory of reciprocal determinism?

CRITICAL THINKING   Recall the study that examined boys' aggression in summer camp. Why was it important that the researchers obtained multiple assessments of the boys' levels of aggression?

✓—[**Study** and **Review** on **MyPsychLab**

SELF THEORIES

We have arrived now at theories of personality that are most immediately personal: They deal directly with how each individual manages his or her sense of *self.* What is your conception of your *self?* Do you think of your *self* reacting consistently to the world? Do you try to present a consistent *self* to your friends and family? What impact do positive and negative experiences have on the way you think about your *self?* Let's begin our consideration of these questions with a brief historical review.

The concern for analysis of the self found its strongest early advocate in William James (1892). James identified three components of self-experience: the *material me* (the bodily self, along with surrounding physical objects), the *social me* (your awareness of how others view you), and the *spiritual me* (the self that monitors private thoughts and feelings). James believed that everything that you associate with your identity becomes, in some sense, a part of the self. This explains why people may react defensively when their friends or family members—a part of the self—have been attacked. The concept of self was also central to psychodynamic theories. Self-insight was an important part of the psychoanalytic cure in Freud's theory, and Jung stressed that to fully develop the self, one must integrate and accept all aspects of one's conscious and unconscious life. Finally for this historical review, you already learned that Carl Rogers had the self as the cornerstone of his humanistic theory of personality development.

How has the self been treated in contemporary theory? We will first consider cognitive aspects of self-concepts. We then visit the concept of self-esteem and the steps people take to preserve self esteem. Finally, we'll look at the important topic of how views of the self differ across cultures.

Self-Concepts and Self-Esteem

The self-concept is a dynamic mental structure that motivates, interprets, organizes, mediates, and regulates intrapersonal and interpersonal behaviors and processes. The self-concept includes many components. Among them are your memories about yourself; beliefs about your traits, motives, values, and abilities; the ideal self that you would most like to become; the possible selves that you contemplate enacting; positive or negative evaluations of yourself (self-esteem); and beliefs about what others think of you (Chen et al., 2006). Chapter 7 discussed *schemas* as "knowledge packages" that embody complex generalizations about the structure of the environment. Your self-concept contains schemas about the self—*self-schemas*—that allow you to organize information about yourself, just as other schemas allow you to manage other aspects of your experience. However, self-schemas influence more than just the way you process information about yourself. Research indicates that these schemas, which you frequently use to interpret your own behavior, influence the way you process information about other people as well (Krueger & Stanke, 2001; Mussweiler & Bodenhausen, 2002). Thus you interpret other people's actions in terms of what you know and believe about yourself.

A person's **self-esteem** is a *generalized* evaluation of the self. People differ in their levels of self-esteem. Because I have described the importance of genetics for other aspects of personality, you may not be surprised to learn that individual differences in self-esteem have a genetic component: People inherit a tendency toward high or low self-esteem (Neiss et al., 2006). However, environmental factors also have important effects. For example, people's satisfaction or dissatisfaction with their physical appearance has a major impact on their reports of self-esteem (Donnellan et al., 2007). Self-esteem also varies with respect to people's perceptions of their ability to navigate in the social world. People who are high in self-esteem typically feel that they will function well in social relationships; people with low self-esteem have doubts about their social value (Anthony et al., 2007).

Self-esteem can strongly influence people's thoughts, moods, and behavior (Swann et al., 2007). In fact, researchers have linked a number of negative outcomes to low levels of self-esteem. For example, among adolescents and college students, low self-esteem was related to aggression and antisocial behavior (Donnellan et al., 2005). Similarly, people who reported low self-esteem as adolescents had poorer mental and physical health as well as more financial problems as adults (Orth et al., 2008; Trzeniewski et al., 2006). These results suggest that having low self-esteem can undermine people's ability to set goals for positive outcomes and cope with negative life events.

Some people clearly experience low self-esteem. However, evidence suggests that most people go out of their way to maintain self-esteem and to sustain the integrity of their self-concept

(Vignoles et al., 2006). To preserve their self-image, people engage in a variety of forms of *self-enhancement*: People take steps to view their own actions and behaviors as consistently positive (Sedikides & Gregg, 2008). For example, when people doubt their ability to perform a task, they may engage in **self-handicapping** behavior. They deliberately sabotage their performance! The purpose of this strategy is to have a ready-made excuse for failure that does not imply *lack of ability* (McCrae & Hirt, 2001). Thus, a student might party with friends instead of studying for an important exam. That way, if he doesn't succeed, he can blame his failure on low effort rather than low aptitude. Note that my use of "he" in this example is deliberate. Research suggests that men consistently engage in more self-handicapping than do women.

Before taking an intelligence test, male and female psychology students were given the opportunity to work through 18 practice items (McCrae et al., 2008). The researchers gave half the students practice matters *instructions: Those students were told that without appropriate practice their intelligence tests scores would not be valid. The other students received* practice does not matter *instructions: Those students were told that practice would likely have no effect on their test scores. Suppose you were in the* practice matters *condition. If you wanted to have a ready excuse for your (potentially) low intelligence score, you might choose not to practice very much. As you can see in* **Figure 13.8** *on page 376, that's, on average, what the men chose to do. Women who were told that practiced mattered, practiced quite a bit. Men who had the same instructions practiced least of all. To understand this difference, the researchers asked the participants to complete a scale that had items such as "I try to devote my full effort to every class I take" and "I pride myself in being a hard worker" (p. 309). The women consistently agreed more with such statements than did their male peers.*

Featured Study

These results support the researchers' claim that women put too much value on effort to engage in self-handicapping. The effort women expend is an important contributor to their self-esteem.

In recent years, researchers have provided support for a theory that places self-esteem in a broader perspective. **Terror management theory** proposes that self-esteem helps people cope with the inevitability of death (Greenberg, 2008). Terror management theory suggests that people wish to achieve *symbolic immortality* which "is conferred by cultural institutions that enable people to feel part of something larger, more significant, and more eternal than their own individual lives through connections and contributions to their families, nations, professions, and ideologies" (Pyszczynski et al., 2004, p. 436).

....

self-esteem A generalized evaluative attitude toward the self that influences both moods and behavior and that exerts a powerful effect on a range of personal and social behaviors.

self-handicapping The process of developing, in anticipation of failure, behavioral reactions and explanations that minimize ability deficits as possible attributions for the failure.

terror management theory A theory proposing that self-esteem helps people cope with the inevitability of death.

FIGURE 13.8 Men's and Women's Self-Handicapping

The *practice index* combined the number of practice items a student completed and the amount of time he or she spent practicing into a single measure. Positive scores indicate more than average practice; negative scores indicate less than average practice. When instructions suggested that practice didn't matter, the difference between men's and women's practice was small. However, when students believed their practice did matter, women practiced considerably more than the men.

Data from S. M. McCrae, E. R. Hirt, & B. J. Milner, She works hard for the money, *Journal of Experimental Social Psychology (44)*: 292–311, © 2008.

People attain self-esteem when they believe that they have made valuable contributions that provide a route to symbolic immortality. To support terror management theory, researchers have demonstrated many ways in which people's behavior changes when their attention is called to the inevitability of death. For example, one project instilled *mortality salience* in a subset of participants by asking them to "Jot down, as specifically as you can, what you think will happen to you as you physically die and once you are physically dead" (Greenberg et al., 2010, p. 5). Members of the control group did not complete this exercise. Later in the experimental session, the participants answered questions like "How much would you like to become famous?" and "How famous do you think you will become in the future?" Participants for whom mortality was made salient reported themselves to be more interested in pursuing and achieving fame than their peers who had not contemplated death. Can you see how expectations of fame relate to self-esteem and symbolic immortality?

This section has emphasized that people engage in behaviors such as self-handicapping to maintain a high sense of self-esteem. For that reason, you might not be surprised to learn that people's global ratings of self-esteem are often not a good predictor of their performance across domains (Baumeister et al.,

....

independent construal of self Conceptualization of the self as an individual whose behavior is organized primarily by reference to one's own thoughts, feelings, and actions, rather than by reference to the thoughts, feelings, and actions of others.

2003). Instead, people's self-views with respect to more specific domains of performance (such as particular academic subjects) provide better predictive information about their likely performance (Swann et al., 2007). Similarly, programs to boost self-esteem are best targeted toward particular domains in which people can learn strategies that actually change performance.

The Cultural Construction of Self

The discussion so far has focused on constructs relevant to the self, such as self-esteem and self-handicapping, that apply quite widely across individuals. However, researchers on the self have also begun to study the way in which self-concepts and self-development are affected by differing cultural constraints. If you have grown up in a Western culture, you are likely to be pretty comfortable with the research reviewed so far: The theories and constructs match the ways that Western cultures conceptualize the *self*. However, the type of culture from which the Western self emerges—an *individualistic* culture—is in the minority with respect to the world's population, which includes about 70 percent *collectivist* cultures. Individualistic cultures emphasize individuals' needs, whereas collectivist cultures emphasize the needs of the group (Triandis, 1994, 1995). This overarching emphasis has important implications for how each member of these cultures conceptualizes his or her *self*: Hazel Markus and Shinobu Kitayama (1991; Kitayama et al., 1995; Markus et al., 1997) have argued that each culture gives rise to different interpretations of the meaning of self—or different *construals* of self:

- Individualistic cultures encourage **independent construals of self**—"Achieving the cultural goal of independence requires construing oneself as an individual whose behavior is organized and made meaningful primarily by reference to one's own internal repertoire of thoughts, feelings, and action, rather than by reference to the thoughts, feelings, and actions of others" (Markus & Kitayama, 1991, p. 226).

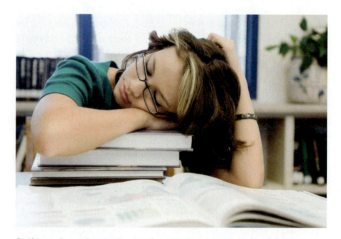

Self-handicapping behavior in action: Instead of studying for tomorrow's exam, you fall asleep in the library, thereby enabling yourself to say, "Well, I didn't really study" if you don't ace the test. Are there situations in which you resort to self-handicapping?

- Collectivist cultures encourage **interdependent construals of self**—"Experiencing interdependence entails seeing oneself as part of an encompassing social relationship and recognizing that one's behavior is determined, contingent on, and, to a large extent organized by what the actor perceives to be the thoughts, feelings, and actions of *others* in the relationship" (Markus & Kitayama, 1991, p. 227).

Researchers have documented the reality and implications of these distinctions in a number of ways (Cross et al., 2011).

One type of cross-cultural research on the self has used a measurement device called the *Twenty Statements Test* (TST) (Kuhn & McPartland, 1954). When they take this test, participants are asked to give 20 different answers to the question "Who am I?" Take a moment to reflect on that question. As shown in **Table 13.6**, responses typically fall into six different categories. Culture has an impact on the categories that are most likely for people's responses. For example, one study had roughly 300 students from the United States and India perform the TST procedure (Dhawan et al., 1995). In keeping with their independent sense of self, about 65 percent of the responses of U.S. women and 64 percent of the responses of U.S. men fell into the category of *self-evaluations*. For the Indian students, 33 percent of women's responses and 35 percent of men's responses fell into this category. Thus the Indian students were about half as likely to produce self-evaluations. Note that differences between men and women overall were rather small—culture mattered more.

You might wonder how the export of Western culture affects the self-concepts of members of collectivist cultures. One study compared the TST responses of Kenyans who had virtually no exposure to Western culture—members of pastoral Samburu and Maasai tribes—to those who had moved to the Westernized capital city of Nairobi. Roughly 82 percent of the tribe members' responses on the TST were social responses; workers in Nairobi gave only 58 percent social responses, and students at the University of Nairobi gave only 17 percent social responses (Ma & Schoeneman, 1997). This pattern

In what ways is an individual's sense of self different when he or she is a member of a culture with an interdependent construal of self rather than an independent construal of self?

Table 13.6 • Categories of Twenty Statements Test Responses

Category	Examples
Social identity	I'm a student. I'm a daughter.
Ideological beliefs	I believe that all human beings are good. I believe in God.
Interests	I like playing the piano. I enjoy visiting new places.
Ambitions	I want to become a doctor. I want to learn more psychology.
Self-evaluations	I am honest and hardworking. I am a tall person. I worry about the future.
Other	I have noisy friends. I own a dog.

suggests that when a nation imports Western products, it may also import a Western sense of self.

These studies illustrate that the cultures to which people belong have a strong impact on the way they construe their selves. You will encounter this distinction again in Chapter 16 when we consider, for example, how people from different cultures assess causal forces in the world. For now, let's consider a study that relates back to terror management theory and mortality salience. Recall that mortality salience generally makes people wish to bolster their self. However, that impulse has different outcomes for people with different construals of self.

At the start of a study, European American and Asian American students were randomly assigned to a mortality salience group or a control group (Ma-Kellams & Blascovich, 2011). Students in the mortality salience group wrote down thoughts about their death whereas students in the control group wrote about dental pain. Next, the students read a scenario that described a serious car accident in which a university employee named Steve had been the victim. After reading the scenario, participants completed an Assignment of Blame Scale (ABS) to indicate how much they held Steve responsible. As you can see in **Figure 13.9** *on page 378, mortality salience pushed European American and Asian American responses in different directions. Perhaps to protect their independent construals of self from the fear of being accident victims, European Americans blamed Steve more when they were experiencing mortality salience. By contrast, Asian Americans who were experiencing mortality salience appeared to include Steve within their interdependent construals of self and, as a consequence, blamed him less.*

Featured Study

interdependent construal of self Conceptualization of the self as part of an encompassing social relationship; recognizing that one's behavior is determined, contingent on, and, to a large extent, organized by what the actor perceived to be the thoughts, feelings, and actions of others.

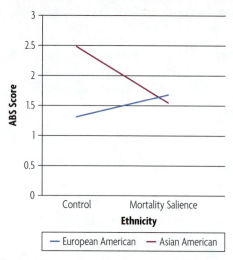

FIGURE 13.9 Culture and Mortality Salience
European American and Asian American students assigned blame (on the Assignment of Blame Scale, ABS) to Steve, who had been the victim of a serious car accident. Mortality salience affected the students' ratings quite differently, as a product of their cultural construal of self.

Data from Christine Ma-Kellams and Jim Blascovich, "Culturally divergent responses to mortality salience," *Psychological Science*, August 1, 2011, copyright © 2011 Association for Psychological Science.

Over the next few days, you might try to experience both construals of self by trying to attend to how the events that happen around you have an impact both on your self as an individual and your self as a member of a larger social structure.

Evaluation of Self Theories

Self theories succeed at capturing people's own concepts of their personalities and the way they wish to be perceived by others. Furthermore, examinations of cross-cultural construals of the self have had great influence on the way psychologists assess the universality of their theories. However, critics of self theory approaches to personality argue against their limitless boundaries. Because so many things are relevant to the self and to the self-concept, it is not always clear which factors are most important for predicting behavior. In addition, the emphasis on the self as a social construct is not entirely consistent with evidence that some facets of personality may be inherited. As with other theories, self theories capture some but not all of what you think of as personality.

Stop *and* Review

① What is self-esteem?
② What is self-handicapping?
③ What does it mean to have an interdependent construal of self?

CRITICAL THINKING Recall the study that demonstrated gender differences in self-handicapping. Why was it important that participants completed the worker scale before they had the opportunity to practice?

✓•⬛Study and Review on MyPsychLab

COMPARING PERSONALITY THEORIES

There is no unified theory of personality that a majority of psychologists can endorse. Several differences in basic assumptions have come up repeatedly in this survey of the various theories. It may be helpful to recap five of the most important differences in assumptions about personality and the approaches that advance each assumption: ✳

1. *Heredity versus environment.* As you have learned throughout *Psychology and Life,* this difference is also referred to as *nature versus nurture.* What is more important to personality development: genetic and biological factors or environmental influences? Trait theories have been split on this issue; Freudian theory depends heavily on heredity; humanistic, social-learning, cognitive, and self theories all emphasize either environment as a determinant of behavior or interaction with the environment as a source of personality development and differences.

2. *Learning processes versus innate laws of behavior.* Should emphasis be placed on the view that personalities are modified through learning or on the view that personality development follows an internal timetable? Again, trait theories have been divided. Freudian theory has favored the inner determinant view, whereas humanists postulate an optimistic view that experience changes people. Social-learning, cognitive, and self theories clearly support the idea that behavior and personality change as a result of learned experiences.

3. *Emphasis on past, present, or future.* Trait theories emphasize past causes, whether innate or learned; Freudian theory stresses past events in early childhood; social-learning theories focus on past reinforcements and present contingencies; humanistic theories emphasize present reality or future goals; and cognitive and self theories emphasize past and present (and the future if goal setting is involved).

4. *Consciousness versus unconsciousness.* Freudian theory emphasizes unconscious processes; humanistic, social-learning, and cognitive theories emphasize conscious processes. Trait theories pay little attention to this distinction; self theories are unclear on this score.

5. *Inner disposition versus outer situation.* Social-learning theories emphasize situational factors; traits play up dispositional factors; and the others allow for an interaction between person-based and situation-based variables.

Each type of theory makes different contributions to the understanding of human personality. Trait theories provide a catalog that describes parts and structures. Psychodynamic theories add a powerful engine and the fuel to get the vehicle moving. Humanistic theories put a person in the driver's seat. Social-learning theories supply the steering wheel, directional signals, and other regulation equipment. Cognitive theories add reminders that the way the trip is planned, organized,

✳**Explore** the **Concept** *Psychodynamic, Behavioral, Trait and Type, Humanistic and Cognitive Approaches to Personality* on **MyPsychLab**

HOW IS PERSONALITY CONVEYED IN CYBERSPACE?

Let's start with a straightforward question: Does your e-mail address allow people to make accurate guesses about your personality? To address that question, a team of researchers used a web-based survey to obtain e-mail addresses and self-reports of personality from 599 individuals (Back et al., 2008). Next, the researchers asked a different group of 100 students to make personality judgments based only on the e-mail addresses. Consider the researchers' example, honey. bunny77@hotmail.de. How aggreeable and conscientious would you imagine the person with that e-mail address to be?

The researchers found that personality ratings based on just the e-mail addresses were quite consistent among the group of 100 raters. The researchers also found positive correlations between the raters' assessments and the e-mail users' self-reports on most of the personality dimensions. The raters were able to make reasonably valid personality judgments based on just the e-mail addresses! The raters appeared to be responding to a number of features of the addresses. For example, the raters gave higher conscientiousness ratings to addresses with a larger number of characters; they gave lower conscientiousness ratings to addresses with a larger number of digits.

Of course, if you are like many students, your e-mail address is only one of a very large number of decisions you need to make to determine your exact presence in cyberspace. Suppose you have a page on Facebook. To manage the impression you make, you need to make decisions about any number of variables, including how many friends you allow, how much personal detail you provide, and what types of photos you upload (Krämer & Winter, 2008). These variables contribute to visitors' perceptions. For example, one study varied the number of friends (102, 302, 502, 702, or 902) on a mock Facebook page (Tong et al., 2008). Participants rated the *social attractiveness* of the page's owner. Those ratings were highest for 302 friends: Too few and too many friends counted against the owner. Why 302? The participants reported that they had a median number of 300 friends. Perhaps participants gave the highest ratings when they thought the page owner was similar to them.

Another study examined how Facebook photographs contributed to judgments on the particular personality trait of *narcissism* (Buffardi & Campbell, 2008). People who are narcissistic have an overly positive self-image. How might that trait be expressed through Facebook photos? The researchers found that participants rated page owners as being particularly narcissistic when the main photo on their Facebook pages was attractive and self-promoting (that is, the photo seemed dedicated to "persuading others about [the page owner's] own positive qualities," p. 1307). In addition, there was a positive correlation between raters' judgments and the page owner's self-reports of narcissism: The Facebook pages communicated valid information on this trait!

Do these results make you rethink how you present yourself in cyberspace?

- Why might people be comfortable making personality judgments based on Facebook content?
- How might you determine other circumstances in which similarity has an impact on people's judgments of Facebook pages?

---

and remembered will be affected by the mental map the driver chooses for the journey. Finally, self theories remind the driver to consider the image his or her driving ability is projecting to backseat drivers and pedestrians.

To complete this review of personality, we will now consider personality assessment. You will see some of the ways in which psychologists obtain information about the range of personality attributes that make each individual unique.

Stop *and* Review

① In what ways do personality theories differ on the dimension of heredity versus environment?
② Does Freud's theory of personality focus most directly on the past, present, or future?
③ Which dimension of personality theories refers to people's awareness of the forces that shape their behaviors?

✓ Study and **Review** on **MyPsychLab**

ASSESSING PERSONALITY

Think of all the ways in which you differ from your best friend. Psychologists wonder about the diverse attributes that characterize an individual, set one person apart from others, or distinguish people in one group from those in another (for example, shy people from outgoing or depressed individuals from happy). Two assumptions are basic to these attempts to understand and describe human personality: first, that there are personal characteristics of individuals that give coherence to their behavior and, second, that those characteristics can be assessed or measured. Personality tests must meet the standards of reliability and validity (see Chapter 9). In addition, clinicians and researchers receive thorough training to administer and interpret the tests. We will consider *objective* and *projective* personality tests. Psychologists often combine different measures to obtain a full understanding of an individual's personality. 👁

Objective Tests

Objective tests of personality are those in which scoring and administration are relatively simple and follow well-defined rules. Some objective tests are scored by computer programs. The final score is usually a single number, scaled along a single dimension (such as *adjustment* versus *maladjustment*), or a set of scores on different traits (such as impulsiveness, dependency, or extraversion) reported in comparison with the scores of a normative sample.

A *self-report inventory* is an objective test in which individuals answer a series of questions about their thoughts, feelings, and actions. One of the first self-report inventories, the *Woodworth Personal Data Sheet* (written in 1917) asked questions such as "Are you often frightened in the middle of the night?" (see DuBois, 1970). Today, a person taking a **personality inventory** reads a series of statements and indicates whether each one is true or typical for him- or herself. Let's consider two prominent personality inventories, the *Minnesota Multiphasic Personality Inventory,* or MMPI, and the *NEO Personality Inventory* (NEO-PI).

The MMPI   The MMPI was developed at the University of Minnesota during the 1930s by psychologist Starke Hathaway and psychiatrist J. R. McKinley (Hathaway & McKinley, 1940, 1943). Its basic purpose is to diagnose individuals according to a set of psychiatric labels. The first test consisted of 550 items, which individuals determined to be either true or false for themselves or to which they responded, "Cannot say." From that item pool, scales were developed that were relevant to the kinds of problems patients showed in psychiatric settings.

The MMPI scales were unlike other existing personality tests because they were developed using an *empirical* strategy rather than the intuitive, theoretical approach that dominated at the time. Items were included on a scale only if they clearly distinguished between two groups—for example, patients with schizoprehnia and a normal comparison group. Each item had to demonstrate its validity by being answered similarly by members within each group but differently between the two groups. Thus the items were not selected on a theoretical basis (what the content seemed to mean to experts) but on an empirical basis (did they distinguish between the two groups?).

The MMPI has 10 *clinical scales,* each constructed to differentiate a special clinical group (such as individuals with schizophrenia) from a normal comparison group. The test also includes *validity scales* that detect suspicious response patterns, such as blatant dishonesty, carelessness, defensiveness,

···

👁 **Watch** the **Video** *In the Real World: Putting Popular Personality Assessments to the Test* on **MyPsychLab**

personality inventory A self-report questionnaire used for personality assessment that includes a series of items about personal thoughts, feelings, and behaviors.

Table 13.7 • MMPI-2 Clinical Scales

Hypochondriasis (Hs): Abnormal concern with bodily functions

Depression (D): Pessimism; hopelessness; slowing of action and thought

Conversion hysteria (Hy): Unconscious use of mental problems to avoid conflicts or responsibility

Psychopathic deviate (Pd): Disregard for social custom; shallow emotions; inability to profit from experience

Masculinity–femininity (Mf): Differences between men and women

Paranoia (Pa): Suspiciousness; delusions of grandeur or persecution

Psychasthenia (Pt): Obsessions; compulsions; fears; guilt; indecisiveness

Schizophrenia (Sc): Bizarre, unusual thoughts or behavior; withdrawal; hallucinations; delusions

Hypomania (Ma): Emotional excitement; flight of ideas; overactivity

Social introversion (Si): Shyness; disinterest in others; insecurity

Excerpted from the MMPI(R)-2 (Minnesota Mulitphasic Personality Inventory(R)-2) Manual for Administration, Scoring and Interpretation, Revised Edition. Copyright © 2001 by the Regents of the University of Minnesota. All rights reserved. Used by permission of the University of Minnesota Press. "MMPI" and "Minnesota Multiphasic Personality Inventory" are trademarks owned by the Regents of the University of Minnesota.

or evasiveness. When an MMPI is interpreted, the tester first checks the validity scales to be sure the test is valid and then looks at the rest of the scores. The pattern of the scores—which are highest, how they differ—forms the "MMPI profile." Individual profiles are compared with those common for particular groups, such as felons and gamblers.

In the mid-1980s, the MMPI underwent a major revision, and it is now called the *MMPI-2* (Butcher et al., 2001). The MMPI-2 has updated language and content to better reflect contemporary concerns, and new populations provided data for norms. The MMPI-2 also adds 15 new *content scales* that were derived using, in part, a theoretical method. For each of 15 clinically relevant topics (such as anxiety or family problems), items were selected on two bases: if they seemed theoretically related to the topic area and if they statistically formed a *homogeneous scale,* meaning that each scale

Table 13.8 • MMPI-2 Content Scales

Anxiety Practices	
Fears	Type A (workaholic)
Obsessiveness	Low self-esteem
Depression	Social discomfort
Health concerns	Family problems
Bizarre mentation (thoughts)	Work interference
Anger and cynicism	Negative treatment indicators (negative attitudes about doctors and treatment)

Excerpted from the MMPI(R)-2 (Minnesota Mulitphasic Personality Inventory(R)-2) Manual for Administration, Scoring and Interpretation, Revised Edition. Copyright © 2001 by the Regents of the University of Minnesota. All rights reserved. Used by permission of the University of Minnesota Press. "MMPI" and "Minnesota Multiphasic Personality Inventory" are trademarks owned by the Regents of the University of Minnesota.

measures a single, unified concept. The clinical and content scales of the MMPI-2 are given in **Table 13.7** and **Table 13.8**. You'll notice that most of the clinical scales measure several related concepts and that the names of the content scales are simple and self-explanatory.

Because the MMPI-2 plays such a critical role in clinical research and practice, researchers continue to assess the test's reliability and validity to make appropriate clinical judgments. Important aspects of that research were incorporated into the MMPI-2-RF (for "revised form"), which appeared in 2008 (Tellegen & Ben-Porath, 2008). The MMPI-2-RF features revised clinical scales that supplement the MMPI-2 clinical scales. The goal of these revised scales is to allow better discrimination among people with different types of psychological disorders. The revised clinical scales have begun to undergo tests of reliability and validity that will allow psychologists to put the MMPI-2-RF to appropriate uses (Forbey et al., 2010; Rouse et al., 2008).

The NEO-PI   Recall that the MMPI was designed to assess individuals with clinical problems. By contrast, the NEO Personality Inventory (NEO-PI) was designed to assess personality characteristics in nonclinical adult populations. It measures the five-factor model of personality you met earlier. If you took the NEO-PI, you would receive a profile sheet that showed your standardized scores relative to a large normative sample on each of the five major dimensions: Neuroticism, Extraversion, Openness, Agreeableness, and Conscientiousness (Costa & McCrae, 1985). The recent NEO-PI-3 assesses 30 separate traits organized within the five major factors (McCrae et al., 2005). For example, the Neuroticism dimension is broken down into six facet scales: Anxiety, Angry hostility, Depression, Self-consciousness, Impulsiveness, and Vulnerability. Much research has demonstrated that the NEO-PI dimensions show good reliability and validity (McCrae et al., 2004, 2011). The NEO-PI is being used to study personality stability and change across the life span as well as the relationship of personality characteristics to physical health and various life events, such as career success or early retirement.

Projective Tests

As you just saw, objective tests take one of two forms: Either they provide test takers with a series of statements and ask them to give a simple response (such as "true," "false," or "cannot say") or they ask test takers to rate themselves with respect to some dimension (such as "anxious" versus "nonanxious"). Thus the respondent is constrained to choose one of the predetermined responses. *Projective tests,* by contrast, have no predetermined range of responses. In a **projective test,** a person is given a series of stimuli that are purposely ambiguous, such as abstract patterns, incomplete pictures, or drawings that can be interpreted in many ways. The person may be asked to describe the patterns, finish the pictures, or tell stories about the drawings. Projective tests were first used by psychoanalysts, who hoped that such tests would reveal their patients' unconscious personality dynamics. Because the stimuli are ambiguous, responses to them are determined partly by what the person brings to the situation—namely, inner feelings, personal motives, and conflicts from prior life experiences. These personal, idiosyncratic aspects, which are *projected* onto the stimuli, permit the personality assessor to make various interpretations.

Projective tests are among the assessment devices most commonly used by psychological practitioners (Butcher, 2010; Musewicz et al., 2009). However, because projective tests are so widespread, critics have often worried that they are used in ways that are not valid. The next sections review two of the most common projective tests, the Rorschach test and the Thematic Apperception Test, and includes discussion of those issues of validity.

The Rorschach   In the Rorschach test, developed by Swiss psychiatrist **Hermann Rorschach** in 1921, the ambiguous stimuli are symmetrical inkblots (Rorschach, 1942). Some are black and white, and some are colored (see **Figure 13.10**). During the test, a respondent is shown an inkblot and asked, "What might this be?" Respondents are assured that there are no right or wrong answers (Exner, 1974). Testers record verbatim what people say, how much time they take to respond, the total time they take per inkblot, and the way they handle the inkblot card. Then, in a second phase called an *inquiry,* the respondent is reminded of the previous responses and asked to elaborate on them.

The responses are scored on three major features: (1) the *location,* or part of the card mentioned in the response—whether the respondent refers to the whole stimulus or to part of it and the size of the details mentioned; (2) the *content* of the response—the nature of the object and activities seen; and (3) the *determinants*—which aspects of the card (such as its color or shading) prompted the response. Scorers may also note whether responses are original and unique or popular and conforming.

You might think that ambiguous inkblots would give rise to an uninterpretable diversity of responses. In fact, researchers have devised a comprehensive scoring system for Rorschach responses that allows for meaningful comparisons among different test takers (Exner, 2003; Exner & Weiner, 1994). For example, the scoring system specifies content categories that frequently appear in people's responses. Those categories include *whole human* (the response mentions or implies a whole human form) and *blood* (the response mentions blood, either human or animal). Researchers have developed training

FIGURE 13.10 An Inkblot Similar to Those Used in the Rorschach Test

What do you see? Does your interpretation of this inkblot reveal anything about your personality?

....

projective test   A method of personality assessment in which an individual is presented with a standardized set of ambiguous, abstract stimuli and asked to interpret their meanings; the individual's responses are assumed to reveal inner feelings, motives, and conflicts.

FIGURE 13.11 The Type of Image Used on the TAT Test

What story do you want to tell? What does your story reveal about your personality?

procedures to ensure that clinicians can learn to use the comprehensive scoring system reliably (Hilsenroth et al., 2007). In addition, researerchers have undertaken formal studies to determine whether the results from the scoring system make it possible to diagnose specific psychological disorders such as posttraumatic stress disorder (Arnon et al., 2011). However, practitioners also make diagnoses based on people's Rorschach responses without any formal evidence that supports the validity of the practitioners' inferences. For that reason, the Rorschach test remains controversial (Garb et al., 2005).

The TAT In the Thematic Apperception Test (TAT), developed by **Henry Murray** in 1938, respondents are shown pictures of ambiguous scenes and asked to generate stories about them, describing what the people in the scenes are doing and thinking, what led up to each event, and how each situation will end (see **Figure 13.11**). The person administering the TAT evaluates the structure and content of the stories as well as the behavior

• **Watch** the **Video** *Thinking Like a Psychologist: Testing Personality* on **MyPsychLab**

of the individual telling them, in an attempt to discover some of the respondent's major concerns, motivations, and personality characteristics. For example, an examiner might evaluate a person as conscientious if his or her stories concerned people who lived up to their obligations and if the stories were told in a serious, orderly way. As with the Rorschach test, critics have suggested that the TAT is often used for purposes for which its validity remains uncertain (Lilienfeld et al., 2001). Chapter 11 noted one use of the TAT that has received research support: The TAT has often been used to reveal individual differences in dominant needs, such as needs for power, affiliation, and achievement (McClelland, 1961). Reserachers have also used the TAT to investigate group differences, such as changes across generations in the dominant needs of students entering medical school (Borges et al., 2010).

As you learned about these personality assessment devices, did you see the relationship between them and the theories of personality you encountered earlier? Earlier, you saw that each of the types of theories illuminated test different aspects of human experience. Here, the same conclusion applies for personality tests: Each has the potential to provide unique insights into an individual's personality. Clinicians most often use a combination of tests when they carry out a personality assessment. •

To close the chapter, please consider a series of questions in light of what you have just learned: If psychologists studied you, what portrait of your personality would they draw? Which early experiences might they identify as contributing to how you now act and think? What conditions in your current life exert strong influences on your thoughts and behaviors? What makes you different from other individuals who are functioning in many of the same situations as you? You now can see that each type of personality theory provides a framework against which you can begin to form your answers to these questions. Suppose the time has really come to paint your psychological portrait. Where would you begin?

Stop *and* Review

① What is the purpose of the MMPI's 10 clinical scales?
② What is the purpose of the NEO Personality Inventory (NEO-PI)?
③ What three major features do clinicians use to interpret Rorschach responses?

✓ **Study** and **Review** on **MyPsychLab**

Recapping Main Points

Trait Personality Theories

- Some theorists view traits—attributes along continuous dimensions—as the building blocks of personality.
- The five-factor model is a personality system that maps out the relationships among common trait words, theoretical concepts, and personality scales.
- Twin and adoption studies reveal that personality traits are partially inherited.
- People display behavioral consistency when situations are defined with respect to relevant psychological features.

Psychodynamic Theories

- Freud's psychodynamic theory emphasizes instinctive biological energies as sources of human motivation.
- Basic concepts of Freudian theory include psychic energy as powering and directing behavior, early experiences as key determinants of lifelong personality, psychic determinism, and powerful unconscious processes.
- Personality structure consists of the id, the superego, and the reconciling ego.

- Unacceptable impulses are repressed and ego defense mechanisms are developed to lessen anxiety and bolster self-esteem.
- Post-Freudians like Adler, Horney, and Jung put greater emphasis on ego functioning and social variables and less on sexual urges. They saw personality development as a lifelong process.

Humanistic Theories

- Humanistic theories focus on self-actualization—the growth potential of the individual.
- These theories are holistic, dispositional, and phenomenological.
- Contemporary theories in the humanist tradition focus on individuals' life stories.

Social-Learning and Cognitive Theories

- Social-learning theorists focus on understanding individual differences in behavior and personality as a consequence of different histories of reinforcement.
- Cognitive theorists emphasize individual differences in perception and subjective interpretation of the environment.
- Julian Rotter emphasized people's expectancies about rewards, including general internal or external locus of control orientations.
- Walter Mischel explored the origins of behaviors as interactions of persons and situations.
- Albert Bandura described the reciprocal determinism among people, environments, and behaviors.

Self Theories

- Self theories focus on the importance of the self-concept for a full understanding of human personality.
- People engage in behaviors such as self-handicapping to maintain self-esteem.
- Terror management theory suggests that self-esteem helps people cope with thoughts about death.
- Cross-cultural research suggests that individualistic cultures give rise to independent construals of self, whereas collectivist cultures give rise to interdependent construals of self.

Comparing Personality Theories

- Personality theories can be contrasted with respect to the emphasis they put on heredity versus environment; learning processes versus innate laws of behavior; the past, present, or future; consciousness versus unconsciousness; and inner dispositions versus outer situations.
- Each theory makes different contributions to the understanding of human personality.

Assessing Personality

- Personality characteristics are assessed by both objective and projective tests.
- The most common objective test, the MMPI-2, is used to diagnose clinical problems.
- The NEO-PI is an objective test that measures five major dimensions of personality.
- Projective tests of personality ask people to respond to ambiguous stimuli.
- Two important projective tests are the Rorschach test and the TAT.

KEY TERMS

analytic psychology (p. 367)
anxiety (p. 366)
archetype (p. 367)
collective unconscious (p. 367)
consistency paradox (p. 361)
ego (p. 365)
ego defense mechanism (p. 365)
expectancy (p. 370)
five-factor model (p. 359)
fixation (p. 364)
id (p. 365)

independent construal of self (p. 376)
interdependent construal of self (p. 377)
libido (p. 363)
locus of control (p. 370)
personality (p. 357)
personality inventory (p. 380)
projective test (p. 381)
psychic determinism (p. 364)
psychobiography (p. 369)
psychodynamic personality theory (p. 363)
reciprocal determinism (p. 373)

repression (p. 365)
self-actualization (p. 368)
self-concept (p. 368)
self-efficacy (p. 373)
self-esteem (p. 375)
self-handicapping (p. 375)
superego (p. 365)
terror management theory (p. 375)
trait (p. 357)
unconditional positive regard (p. 368)
unconscious (p. 364)

1. Sheldon doesn't like movies that make him cry. This is an example of a(n)_____ trait.
   a. cardinal
   b. secondary
   c. central
   d. peripheral

2. Which of these factors is *not* a trait dimension in the five-factor model?
   a. creativeness
   b. neuroticism
   c. agreeableness
   d. extraversion

3. You overhear Rick say, "Bad people must be punished!" Based just on that evidence, you begin to suspect that Rick may believe in a(n) _____ theory of personality.
   a. incremental
   b. humanistic
   c. entity
   d. collectivist

4. According to Freud, at ages 4 to 5 children are in the _____ stage of development.
   a. genital
   b. oral
   c. phallic
   d. anal

5. You attend a lecture that is focusing on archetypes in the collective unconscious. The lecture seems to be about the ideas of
   a. Carl Jung.
   b. Sigmund Freud.
   c. Karen Horney.
   d. Alfred Adler.

6. One of the most important claims of humanistic theories of personality is that people strive for
   a. superiority.
   b. zones.
   c. self-preservation.
   d. self-actualization.

7. Humanistic theories are _____ because they emphasize an individual's subjective view of reality.
   a. holistic
   b. deterministic
   c. phenomenological
   d. dispositional

8. With respect to Walter Mischel's personality theory, which of these statements relates to the variable of goals and values?
   a. Bart wants to graduate from college before he turns 30.
   b. Reese thinks she can persuade her brother to lend her his car.
   c. Piper sweats a lot before she takes an exam.
   d. Vito can do multiplication without a calculator.

9. Jason's best friend Buffy is trying to convince him that he can get a new job. If Buffy is successful, that could have an impact on Jason's sense of
   a. self-efficacy.
   b. self-regulation.
   c. reciprocal determinism.
   d. libido.

10. Brian spends the whole night before he is going to compete in a triathalon reviewing the notes for his philosophy class. This might be an example of
    a. self-efficacy.
    b. psychic determinism.
    c. self-handicapping.
    d. neuroticism.

11. Because Miriam lives in a _____ culture she is likely to have a(n) _____ construal of self.
    a. collectivist; dependent
    b. collectivist; interdependent
    c. individualistic; interdependent
    d. collectivist; independent

12. Which features of Facebook pages were *not* related to judgments of narcissism?
    a. The number of funny quotations.
    b. The attractiveness of the main photograph.
    c. The self-promotion of the main photograph.
    d. The owner's amount of social interaction.

13. Chad and Jeremy are both personality theorists. Chad believes that personalities are largely determined before birth. Jeremy believes that personalities arise from life experiences. The dimension on which they disagree is
    a. learning processes versus innate laws of behavior.
    b. consciousness versus unconsciousness.
    c. inner disposition versus outer situation.
    d. heredity versus environment.

14. The personality test that most directly assesses the dimensions of the five-factor model is the
    a. Rorschach.
    b. NEO-PI.
    c. TAT.
    d. MMPI-2.

15. If you wanted to measure need for achievement, your first choice might be the
    a. Rorschach.
    b. TAT.
    c. MMPI-2.
    d. NEO-PI.

ESSAY QUESTIONS

1. How do traits and situations interact to affect predictions of behaviors?

2. How do humanistic theories give rise to a focus on life stories and psychobiography?

3. What theoretical ideas led to the development of projective personality tests?

Psychological Disorders

Consider these words, written by a 30-year-old woman who was receiving treatment for schizophrenia:

I want to let you know what it is like to be a functional person with schizophrenia in these days and times and what someone with my mental illness faces . . . . I live pretty normal and no one can tell [I'm] mentally ill unless I tell them . . . . The delusions before I got my medicine picked any story line it chose, and changed it at will. As time went by before help, I felt it was taking over my whole brain, and I'd cry wanting my mind and life back.

What are your reactions as you read this young woman's words?

If your reactions are similar to those of other students, you feel a mixture of sadness at her plight, of delight in her willingness to do all she can to cope with the many problems her mental illness creates, of anger toward those who stigmatize her because she may act differently at times, and of hope that, with medication and therapy, her condition may improve. These are but a few of the emotions that clinical and research psychologists and psychiatrists feel as they try to understand and treat mental disorders.

This chapter focuses on the nature and causes of psychological disorders: what they are, why they develop, and how we can explain their causes. The next chapter builds on this knowledge to describe the strategies used to treat, and to prevent, mental illness. Research indicates that 46.4 percent of individuals over age 18 in the United States have suffered from a psychological disorder at some point in their lives (Kessler et al., 2005a). Thus many of you who read this text are likely to benefit directly from knowledge about psychopathology. Facts alone, however, will not convey the serious impact psychological disorders have on the everyday lives of individuals and families. As this chapter discusses categories of psychological disorders, try to envision the real people who live with such a disorder every day. I will share with you their words and lives, as I did at the start of the chapter. Let's begin now with a discussion of the concept of abnormality.

THE NATURE OF PSYCHOLOGICAL DISORDERS

Have you ever worried excessively? Felt depressed or anxious without really knowing why? Been fearful of something you rationally knew could not harm you? Had thoughts about suicide? Used alcohol or drugs to escape a problem? Almost everyone will answer yes to at least one of these questions, which

....

👁 **Watch** the **Video** *The Big Picture: What is Abnormal, Anyway?* on **MyPsychLab**

psychopathological functioning Disruptions in emotional, behavioral, or thought processes that lead to personal distress or block one's ability to achieve important goals.

abnormal psychology The area of psychological investigation concerned with understanding the nature of individual pathologies of mind, mood, and behavior.

What do you imagine the lives of people with mental illnesses are like?

means that almost everyone has experienced the symptoms of a psychological disorder. This chapter looks at the range of psychological functioning that is considered unhealthy or abnormal, often referred to as *psychopathology* or *psychological disorder*. **Psychopathological functioning** involves disruptions in emotional, behavioral, or thought processes that lead to personal distress or that block one's ability to achieve important goals. The field of **abnormal psychology** is the area of psychological investigation most directly concerned with understanding the nature of individual pathologies of mind, mood, and behavior.

This section begins by exploring a more precise definition of abnormality and then looks at problems of objectivity. We then consider how this definition evolved over hundreds of years of human history.

Deciding What is Abnormal

What does it mean to say someone is *abnormal* or *suffering from a psychological disorder*? How do psychologists and other clinical practitioners decide what is abnormal? Is it always clear when behavior moves from the normal to the abnormal category? The judgment that someone has a mental disorder is typically based on the evaluation of the individual's *behavioral functioning* by people with some special authority or power. The terms used to describe these phenomena—*mental disorder, mental illness,* or *abnormality*—depend on the particular perspective, training, and cultural background of the evaluator, the situation, and the status of the person being judged. 👁

Let's consider seven criteria you might use to label behavior as "abnormal" (Butcher et al., 2008):

1. *Distress or disability.* An individual experiences personal distress or disabled functioning, which produces a risk of physical or psychological deterioration or loss of freedom of action. For example, a man who cannot leave his home without weeping would be unable to pursue ordinary life goals.
2. *Maladaptiveness.* An individual acts in ways that hinder goals, do not contribute to personal well-being, or interfere strongly with the goals of others and the needs

of society. Someone who is drinking so heavily that she cannot hold down a job or who is endangering others through her intoxication is displaying maladaptive behavior.

3. *Irrationality.* An individual acts or talks in ways that are irrational or incomprehensible to others. A man who responds to voices that do not exist in objective reality is behaving irrationally.

4. *Unpredictability.* An individual behaves unpredictably or erratically from situation to situation, as if experiencing a loss of control. A child who smashes his fist through a window for no apparent reason displays unpredictability.

5. *Unconventionality and statistical rarity.* An individual behaves in ways that are statistically rare and that violate social standards of what is acceptable or desirable. Just being statistically unusual, however, does not lead to a psychological judgment of abnormality. For example, possessing genius-level intelligence is extremely rare, but it is also considered desirable. Conversely, having extremely low intelligence is also rare but is considered undesirable; thus it has often been labeled abnormal.

6. *Observer discomfort.* An individual creates discomfort in others by making them feel threatened or distressed in some way. A woman walking down the middle of the sidewalk, having a loud conversation with herself, creates observer discomfort in other pedestrians trying to avoid her.

7. *Violation of moral and ideal standards.* An individual violates expectations for how one ought to behave with respect to societal norms. Thus, if people generally think it is important to provide care to one's offspring, parents who abandoned their children might be considered abnormal.

Can you see why most of these indicators of abnormality may not be immediately apparent to all observers? Consider just the last criterion. Are you mentally ill if you don't wish to work, even if that is abnormal with respect to the norms of society? Or consider a more serious symptom. It is "bad" to have hallucinations in our culture because they are taken as signs of mental disturbance, but it is "good" in cultures in which hallucinations are interpreted as mystical visions from spirit forces. Whose judgment is correct? At the end of this chapter, we will consider some negative consequences and dangers associated with such socially regulated judgments and the decisions based on them.

We are more confident in labeling behavior as "abnormal" when more than just one of the indicators is present and valid. The more extreme and prevalent the indicators are, the more confident we can be that they point to an abnormal condition. None of these criteria is a *necessary* condition shared by all cases of abnormality: For example, during his murder trial, a Stanford University graduate student who had killed his math professor with a hammer, and then taped to his office door a note that read "No office hours today," reported feeling neither guilt nor remorse. Despite the absence of personal suffering, we would not hesitate to label his overall behavior as abnormal. It is also true that no single criterion, by itself, is a *sufficient* condition that distinguishes all cases of abnormal behavior from normal variations in behavior. The distinction between normal and abnormal is not so much a difference between two

independent types of behaviors as it is a matter of the degree to which a person's actions resemble a set of agreed-upon criteria of abnormality. Mental disorder is best thought of as a *continuum* that varies between *mental health* and *mental illness*.

How comfortable do you feel with these ideas about abnormality? Although the criteria seem fairly clear-cut, psychologists still worry about the problem of objectivity.

The Problem of Objectivity

The decision to declare someone psychologically disordered or abnormal is always a *judgment* about behavior: The goal for many researchers is to make these judgments *objectively,* without any type of bias. For some psychological disorders, like depression or schizophrenia, diagnosis often easily meets the standards of objectivity. Other cases are more problematic. As you have seen throughout your study of psychology, the meaning of behavior is jointly determined by its *content* and by its *context.* The same act in different settings conveys very different meanings. A man kisses another man; it may signify a gay relationship in the United States, a ritual greeting in France, or a Mafia "kiss of death" in Sicily. The meaning of a behavior always depends on context.

Let's see why objectivity is such an important issue. History is full of examples of situations in which judgments of abnormality were made by individuals to preserve their moral or political power. Consider an 1851 report, entitled "The Diseases and Physical Peculiarities of the Negro Race," published in a medical journal. Its author, Dr. Samuel Cartwright, had been appointed by the Louisiana Medical Association to chair a committee to investigate the "strange" practices of African American slaves. "Incontrovertible scientific evidence" was amassed to justify the practice of slavery. Several "diseases" previously unknown to the White race were discovered. One finding was that Blacks allegedly suffered from a sensory disease that made them insensitive "to pain when being punished" (thus no need to spare the whip). The committee also invented the disease *drapetomania,* a mania to seek freedom—a mental disorder that caused certain slaves to run away from their masters. Runaway slaves needed to be caught so that their illness could be properly treated (Chorover, 1981)!

Once an individual has obtained an "abnormal" label, people are inclined to interpret later behavior to confirm that judgment. **David Rosenhan** (1973, 1975) and his colleagues demonstrated that it may be impossible to be judged "sane" in an "insane place."

Rosenhan and seven other sane people gained admission to different psychiatric hospitals by pretending to have a single symptom: hallucinations. All eight of these pseudopatients were diagnosed on admission as having either paranoid schizophrenia or bipolar disorder. Once admitted, they behaved normally in every way. Rosenhan observed, however, that when a sane person is in an insane place, he or she is likely to be judged insane, and any behavior is likely to be re-interpreted to fit the context. If the pseudopatients discussed their situation in a rational way with the staff, they were reported to be using "intellectualization" defenses, while their taking notes of their observations were evidence of "writing behavior." The pseudopatients remained on the wards for almost three weeks, on average, and not one was identified by

Featured Study

the staff as sane. When they were finally released—only with the help of spouses or colleagues—their discharge diagnosis was still "schizophrenia" but "in remission." That is, their symptoms were no longer active.

Rosenhan's research demonstrates how judgments of abnormality rely on factors beyond behavior itself.

In the view of psychiatrist **Thomas Szasz,** mental illness does not even exist—it is a "myth" (1974, 2004). Szasz argues that the symptoms used as evidence of mental illness are merely medical labels that sanction professional intervention into what are social problems—deviant people violating social norms. Once labeled, these people can be treated either benignly or harshly for their problem "of being different," with no threat of disturbing the existing status quo.

Few clinicians would go this far, in large part because the focus of much research and treatment is on understanding and alleviating personal distress. For most of the disorders this chapter describes, individuals experience their own behavior as abnormal, or poorly adapted to the environment. Even so, this discussion suggests that there can be no altogether objective assessments of abnormality. As you learn about each type of psychological disorder, try to understand why clinicians believe the cluster of symptoms represents behavior patterns that are more serious for the individual than mere violations of social norms.

Classifying Psychological Disorders

Why is it helpful to have a classification system for psychological disorders? What advantages are gained by moving beyond a global assessment that abnormality exists to distinguish among different types of abnormalities? A **psychological diagnosis** is the label given to an abnormality by classifying and categorizing the observed behavior pattern into an approved diagnostic system. Such a diagnosis is in many ways more difficult to make than a medical diagnosis. In the medical context, a doctor can rely on physical evidence, such as X-rays, blood tests, and biopsies, to inform a diagnostic decision. In the case of psychological disorders, the evidence for diagnosis comes from interpretations of a person's actions. To create greater consistency among clinicians and coherence in their diagnostic evaluations, psychologists have helped to develop a system of diagnosis and classification that provides precise descriptions of symptoms, as well as other criteria to help practitioners decide whether a person's behavior is evidence of a particular disorder.

To be most useful, a diagnostic system should provide the following three benefits:

- *Common shorthand language.* To facilitate a quick and clear understanding among clinicians or researchers working in the field of psychopathology, practitioners seek a common set of terms with agreed-upon meanings. A diagnostic category, such as *depression,* summarizes a large and complex collection of information, including characteristic symptoms and the typical course of the

The Salem witchcraft trials were an outgrowth of a desperate attempt to affix blame for frighteningly bizarre behavior among the Puritan colonists. The colonists theorized that the symptoms were the work of the devil, who, through the efforts of earthbound witches, had taken over the minds and bodies of young women.

disorder. In clinical settings, such as clinics and hospitals, a diagnostic system allows mental health professionals to communicate more effectively about the people they are helping. Researchers studying different aspects of psychopathology or evaluating treatment programs must agree on the disorder they are observing.

- *Understanding of causality.* Ideally, a diagnosis of a specific disorder should make clear the causes of the symptoms. As is the case for physical illness, the same symptoms may arise for more than one disorder. A goal of a classification system is to indicate why practitioners should interpret particular patterns of symptoms as evidence for specific underlying disorders.
- *Treatment plan.* A diagnosis should also suggest what types of treatments to consider for particular disorders. Researchers and clinicians have found that certain treatments or therapies work most effectively for specific kinds of psychological disorders. For example, drugs that are quite effective in treating schizophrenia do not help and may even hurt people with depression. Further advances in knowledge about the effectiveness and specificity of treatments will make fast and reliable diagnosis even more important.

In 1896, **Emil Kraepelin** (1855–1926), a German psychiatrist, was responsible for creating the first truly comprehensive *classification system* of psychological disorders. Strongly motivated by a belief that there was a physical basis to psychological problems, he gave the process of psychological diagnosis and classification the flavor of medical diagnosis. That flavor remains today in the diagnostic system I now review.

DSM-IV-TR   In the United States, the most widely accepted classification scheme is one developed by the American Psychiatric Association. It is called the *Diagnostic and Statistical Manual of Mental Disorders.* The most recent version, published in 2000 as a revision of the fourth edition, is known by

psychological diagnosis The label given to psychological abnormality by classifying and categorizing the observed behavior pattern into an approved diagnostic system.

clinicians and researchers as **DSM-IV-TR**. It classifies, defines, and describes over 200 mental disorders. ◉

To reduce the diagnostic difficulties caused by variability in approaches to psychological disorders, *DSM-IV-TR* emphasizes the *description* of patterns of symptoms and courses of disorders rather than etiological theories or treatment strategies. The purely descriptive terms allow clinicians and researchers to use a common language to describe problems while leaving room for disagreement and continued research about which theoretical models best *explain* the problems.

The first version of *DSM*, which appeared in 1952 *(DSM-I)*, listed several dozen mental illnesses. *DSM-II*, introduced in 1968, revised the diagnostic system to make it more compatible with another popular system, the World Health Organization's *International Classification of Diseases (ICD)*. The fourth edition of the *DSM (DSM-IV*, 1994) emerged after several years of intense work by committees of scholars. To make their changes (from the *DSM-III-Revised*, which appeared in 1987), these committees carefully scrutinized large bodies of research on psychopathology and also tested proposed changes for workability in actual clinical settings. *DSM-IV* is also fully compatible with the 10th edition of the *ICD*. *DSM-IV-TR* (2000) incorporated a review of the research literature that had accumulated since *DSM-IV*. Because the changes largely affected the supporting text, rather than the system of classification, the revision was termed a "text revision," which yielded the name *DSM-IV-TR*. After this brief history of the *DSM*, you probably won't be surprised to learn that committees are meeting to bring the newest research to bear on *DSM-5*, which is scheduled to appear in 2013. In the *Critical Thinking in Your Life* box on page 393, you'll get a sense of the process that could lead to the inclusion of new disorders in *DSM-5*.

To encourage clinicians to consider the psychological, social, and physical factors that may be associated with a psychological disorder, *DSM-IV-TR* uses dimensions, or *axes,* that portray information about all these factors (see **Table 14.1**). Most of the principal clinical disorders are contained on Axis I. Included here are all disorders that emerge in childhood, except for mental retardation. Axis II lists mental retardation as well as personality disorders. These problems may accompany Axis I disorders. Axis III incorporates information about general medical conditions, such as diabetes, that may be relevant to understanding or treating an Axis I or II disorder. Axes IV and V provide supplemental information that can be useful when planning an individual's treatment or assessing the *prognosis* (predictions of future change). Axis IV assesses psychosocial and environmental problems that may explain patients' stress responses or their resources for coping with stress. On Axis V, a clinician evaluates the global level of an individual's functioning. A full diagnosis in the *DSM-IV-TR* system would involve consideration of each of the axes. ✳

This chapter will provide estimates of the frequency with which individuals experience particular psychological disorders. These estimates arise from research projects in which mental health histories are obtained from large samples of the population. Figures are available for the prevalence of different disorders over one-year and lifetime periods (Kessler et al., 2005a, 2005b). This chapter will generally cite figures from the *National Comorbidity Study (NCS),* which sampled 9,282 U.S. adults ages 18 and older (Kessler et al., 2005a). It is important to emphasize that often the same individuals have experienced more than one disorder simultaneously at some point in their life span, a phenomenon known as **comorbidity.** (*Morbidity* refers to the occurrence of disease. *Comorbidity* refers to the co-occurrence of diseases.) The NCS found that 45 percent of the people who had experienced one disorder in a 12-month period had actually experienced two or more. Researchers have begun to study intensively the patterns of comorbidity of different psychological disorders (Kessler et al., 2005b).

Evolution of Diagnostic Categories The diagnostic categories and the methods used to organize and present them have shifted with each revision of the *DSM*. These shifts reflect changes in the opinions of a majority of mental health experts about exactly what constitutes a psychological disorder and where the lines between different types of disorders should be

....

◉ **Watch** the **Video** *Special Topics: DSM-IV* on **MyPsychLab**

✳ **Explore** the **Concept** *The Axes of the DSM* on **MyPsychLab**

DSM-IV-TR The current diagnostic and statistical manual of the American Psychological Association that classifies, defines, and describes mental disorders.

comorbidity The experience of more than one disorder at the same time.

Table 14.1 • The Five Axes of *DSM-IV-TR*

Axis	Classes of Information	Description
Axis I	Clinical disorders	These mental disorders present symptoms or patterns of behavioral or psychological problems that typically are painful or impair an area of functioning. Included are disorders that emerge in infancy, childhood, or adolescence.
Axis II	(a) Personality disorders (b) Mental retardation	These are dysfunctional patterns of perceiving and responding to the world.
Axis III	General medical conditions	This axis codes physical problems relevant to understanding or treating an individual's psychological disorders on Axes I and II.
Axis IV	Psychosocial and environmental problems	This axis codes psychosocial and environmental stressors that may affect the diagnosis and treatment of an individual's disorder and the likelihood of recovery.
Axis V	Global assessment of functioning	This axis codes the individual's overall level of current functioning in the psychological, social, and occupational domains.

drawn. They also reflect changing perspectives among the public about what constitutes *abnormality*.

In the revision process of each *DSM,* some diagnostic categories were dropped, and others were added. For example, with the introduction of *DSM-III,* in 1980, the traditional distinction between *neurotic* and *psychotic* disorders was eliminated. **Neurotic disorders,** or *neuroses,* were originally conceived of as relatively common psychological problems in which a person did not have signs of brain abnormalities, did not display grossly irrational thinking, and did not violate basic norms; but he or she did experience subjective distress or a pattern of self-defeating or inadequate coping strategies. **Psychotic disorders,** or *psychoses,* were thought to differ in both quality and severity from neurotic problems. It was believed that psychotic behavior deviated significantly from social norms and was accompanied by a profound disturbance in rational thinking and general emotional and thought processes. The *DSM-III* advisory committees felt that the terms *neurotic disorders* and *psychotic disorders* had become too general in their meaning to have much usefulness as diagnostic categories (however, they continue to be used by many psychiatrists and psychologists to characterize the general level of disturbance in a person).

Let's note one final aspect of classification that has evolved over time. Historically, people with mental illnesses were often labeled with the name of their disorder. For example, clinicians referred to people as "schizophrenics" or "phobics." That didn't happen for physical illnesses—people with cancer were never known as "cancerics." Clinicians and researchers now take care to separate the person from the diagnosis. People have schizophrenic disorders or phobias, just as they have cancer or the flu. The hope is that appropriate treatments can alleviate each condition so they no longer apply to the person.

The Concept of Insanity Before we consider the causes of mental illness, let's turn our attention briefly to the concept of insanity. **Insanity** is not defined in *DSM-IV-TR;* there is no accepted clinical definition of insanity. Rather, insanity is a concept that belongs to popular culture and to the legal system. The treatment of insanity in the law dates back to England in 1843, when Daniel McNaughton was found not guilty of murder by reason of insanity. McNaughton's intended victim was the British prime minister—McNaughton believed that God had instructed him to commit the murder. (He accidentally killed the prime minister's secretary instead.) Because of McNaughton's delusions, he was sent to a mental hospital rather than to prison.

In an attempt to murder Representative Gabrielle Giffords, Jared Loughner killed six people. Commentators debated whether he qualified as insane. Why has the legal definition of "insanity" changed over time?

The anger surrounding this verdict—even Queen Victoria was infuriated—prompted the House of Lords to articulate a guideline, known as the *McNaughton rule,* to limit claims of insanity. This rule specifies that a criminal must not "know the nature and quality of the act he was doing; or, if he did know it, that he did not know he was doing what was wrong." Does the McNaughton rule seem like a fair test of guilt or innocence? With advances in the understanding of mental illness, researchers became more aware of circumstances in which a criminal might know right from wrong—a criminal might understand that what he or she was doing was illegal or immoral—but still might not be able to suppress the actions.

Despite the great attention that insanity pleas receive in the media—and, thus, the public's great awareness of them—such pleas are quite rare (Kirschner & Galperin, 2001). For example, one study found that in 60,432 indictments in Baltimore, Maryland, only 190 defendants (0.31 percent) entered insanity pleas; of the 190 pleas, only 8 (4.2 percent) were successful (Janofsky et al., 1996). Thus the likelihood that you will ever be asked to sit on a jury and judge another person as sane or insane is quite low.

The Etiology of Psychopathology

Etiology refers to the factors that cause or contribute to the development of psychological and medical problems. Knowing why the disorder occurs, what its origins are, and how it affects thought and emotional and behavioral processes may lead to new ways of treating and, ideally, preventing it. An analysis of causality will be an important part of the discussion of each individual disorder. This section introduces two general categories of causal factors: biological and psychological. 👁

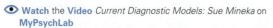

👁 **Watch** the **Video** *Current Diagnostic Models: Sue Mineka* on **MyPsychLab**

neurotic disorder Mental disorder in which a person does not have signs of brain abnormalities and does not display grossly irrational thinking or violate basic norms but does experience subjective distress; a category dropped from *DSM-III.*

psychotic disorder Severe mental disorder in which a person experiences impairments in reality testing manifested through thought, emotional, or perceptual difficulties; no longer used as diagnostic category after *DSM-III.*

insanity The legal (not clinical) designation for the state of an individual judged to be legally irresponsible or incompetent.

etiology The causes of, or factors related to, the development of a disorder.

Biological Approaches Building on the heritage of the medical model, modern biological approaches assume that psychological disturbances are directly attributable to underlying biological factors. Biological researchers and clinicians most often investigate structural abnormalities in the brain, biochemical processes, and genetic influences.

The brain is a complex organ whose interrelated elements are held in delicate balance. Subtle alterations in its chemical messengers—the neurotransmitters—or in its tissue can have significant effects. Genetic factors, brain injury, and infection are a few of the causes of these alterations. You have seen in earlier chapters that technological advances in brain-imaging techniques allow mental health professionals to view the structure of the brain and specific biochemical processes. Using these techniques, biologically oriented researchers are discovering new links between psychological disorders and specific abnormalities in the brain. In addition, continuing advances in the field of behavioral genetics have improved researchers' abilities to identify the links between specific genes and the presence of psychological disorders. We will look to these different types of biological explanations throughout the chapter as we try to understand the nature of various forms of abnormality.

Psychological Approaches Psychological approaches focus on the causal role of psychological or social factors in the development of psychopathology. These approaches perceive personal experiences, traumas, conflicts, and environmental factors as the roots of psychological disorders. There are four dominant psychological models of abnormality: the psychodynamic, the behavioral, the cognitive, and the sociocultural.

Psychodynamic Like the biological approach, the psychodynamic model holds that the causes of psychopathology are located inside the person. However, according to Sigmund Freud, who developed this model, the internal causal factors are psychological rather than biological. As earlier chapters noted, Freud believed that many psychological disorders were simply an extension of "normal" processes of psychic conflict and ego defense that all people experience. In the psychodynamic model, early childhood experiences shape both normal and abnormal behavior.

In psychodynamic theory, behavior is motivated by drives and wishes of which people are often unaware. Symptoms of psychopathology have their roots in *unconscious conflict* and thoughts. If the unconscious is conflicted and tension filled, a person will be plagued by anxiety and other disorders. Much of this psychic conflict arises from struggles between the irrational, pleasure-seeking impulses of the *id* and the internalized social constraints imposed by the *superego*. The *ego* is normally the arbiter of this struggle; however, its ability to perform its function can be weakened by abnormal development in childhood. Individuals attempt to avoid the pain caused by conflicting motives and anxiety with *defense mechanisms,* such as repression or denial. Defenses can become overused, distorting reality or leading to self-defeating behaviors. The individual may then expend so much psychic energy in defenses against anxiety and conflict that there is little energy left to provide a productive and satisfying life.

Behavioral Because of their emphasis on observable responses, behavioral theorists have little use for hypothetical psychodynamic processes. These theorists argue that abnormal behaviors are acquired in the same fashion as healthy behaviors—through learning and reinforcement. They do not focus on internal psychological phenomena or early childhood experiences. Instead, they focus on the *current* behavior and the *current* conditions or reinforcements that sustain the behavior. The symptoms of psychological disorders arise because an individual has learned self-defeating or ineffective ways of behaving. By discovering the environmental contingencies that maintain any undesirable, abnormal behavior, an investigator or clinician can then recommend treatment to change those contingencies and extinguish the unwanted behavior. Behaviorists rely on both classical and operant conditioning models (recall Chapter 6) to understand the processes that can result in maladaptive behavior.

Cognitive Cognitive perspectives on psychopathology are often used to supplement behavioral views. The cognitive perspective suggests that the origins of psychological disorders cannot always be found in the objective reality of stimulus environments, reinforcers, and overt responses. What matters as well is the way people perceive or think about themselves and about their relations with other people and the environment. Among the cognitive variables that can guide—or misguide—adaptive responses are a person's perceived degree of control over important reinforcers, a person's beliefs in his or her ability to cope with threatening events, and interpretations of events in terms of situational or personal factors. The cognitive approach suggests that psychological problems are the result of distortions in perceptions of the reality of a situation, faulty reasoning, or poor problem solving.

Sociocultural The sociocultural perspective on psychopathology emphasizes the role culture plays in both the diagnosis and etiology of abnormal behavior. You already got a taste of the impact of culture on diagnosis when we considered the problem of objectivity. You saw that behaviors are interpreted in different ways in different cultures: the threshold at which a certain type of behavior will cause an individual problems in adjustment will depend, in part, on how that behavior is viewed in its cultural context. With respect to etiology, the particular cultural circumstances in which people live may define an environment that helps bring about distinctive types or subtypes of psychopathology.

You now have a general sense of the types of explanations researchers give for the emergence of mental illness. It is worth noting that contemporary researchers increasingly take an *interactionist* perspective on psychopathology, seeing it as the product of a complex interaction between a number of biological and psychological factors. For example, genetic predispositions may make a person vulnerable to a psychological disorder by affecting neurotransmitter levels or hormone levels, but psychological or social stresses or certain learned behaviors may be required for the disorder to develop fully.

Now that you have a basic framework for thinking about abnormality, we turn to the core information that you will want to know—the causes and consequences of major psychological disorders, such as anxiety, depression, and schizophrenia. The description of each disorder will begin with an account of what sufferers experience and how they appear to observers. Then we will consider how each of the major biological and psychological approaches to etiology explains the development of these disorders.

There are many other categories of psychopathology that we will not have time to examine. However, what follows is a capsule summary of some of the most important omitted here:

- *Substance-use disorders* include both dependence on and abuse of alcohol and drugs. You learned about issues of substance abuse in the broader context of states of consciousness (see Chapter 5, pages 136 to 141).
- *Sexual disorders* involve problems with sexual inhibition or dysfunction and deviant sexual practices.
- *Eating disorders,* such as anorexia and bulimia, were discussed in Chapter 11 (see pages 302 to 307).

As you read about the symptoms and experiences that are typical of the various psychological disturbances, you may begin to feel that some of the characteristics seem to apply to you—at least part of the time—or to someone you know. Beginning students of psychology sometimes fall prey to a version of what has been called *medical students' disease*—the tendency for medical students to diagnose themselves or their acquaintances with each disease about which they are learning. You should try to avoid that tendency with respect to your new knowledge of psychological disorders. Some of the disorders we'll consider are not uncommon, so it would be surprising if they sounded completely alien. Many people have human frailties that appear on the list of criteria for a particular psychological disorder. Recognition of this familiarity can further your understanding of abnormal psychology, but remember that a diagnosis for any disorder depends on a number of criteria and requires the judgment of a trained mental health professional. Please resist the temptation to use this new knowledge to diagnose friends and family members as pathological. However, if the chapter leaves you uneasy about mental health issues, please note that most colleges and universities have counseling centers for students with such concerns.

Stop *and* Review

① Jerry has such an overwhelming fear of spiders that he will not enter a room until someone he trusts assures him the room has no spiders in it. By what criteria might we decide that Jerry's behavior is abnormal?

② What are three important benefits provided by the classification of mental disorders?

③ Why does culture play a role in the diagnosis of psychopathology?

CRITICAL THINKING Consider the study in which David Rosenhan and seven other people were admitted

....

anxiety disorder Mental disorder marked by psychological arousal, feeling of tension, and intense apprehension without apparent reason.

generalized anxiety disorder An anxiety disorder in which an individual feels anxious and worried most of the time for at least six months when not threatened by any specific danger or object.

panic disorder An anxiety disorder in which sufferers experience unexpected, severe panic attacks that begin with a feeling of intense apprehension, fear, or terror.

to psychiatric hospitals. Why might they have chosen "hallucinations" as their pretend symptom?

✓● **Study** and **Review** on **MyPsychLab**

ANXIETY DISORDERS

Everyone experiences anxiety or fear in certain life situations. For some people, however, anxiety becomes problematic enough to interfere with their ability to function effectively or enjoy everyday life. It has been estimated that 28.8 percent of the adult population has, at some time, experienced symptoms characteristic of the various **anxiety disorders** (Kessler et al., 2005a). Although anxiety plays a key role in each of these disorders, they differ in the extent to which anxiety is experienced, the severity of the anxiety, and the situations that trigger the anxiety. This section reviews five major categories: generalized anxiety disorder, panic disorder, phobic disorder, obsessive-compulsive disorder, and posttraumatic stress disorder. We then consider the causes of these disorders.

Generalized Anxiety Disorder

When a person feels anxious or worried most of the time for at least six months, when not threatened by any specific danger, clinicians diagnose **generalized anxiety disorder.** The anxiety is often focused on specific life circumstances, such as unrealistic concerns about finances or the well-being of a loved one. The way the anxiety is expressed—the specific symptoms—varies from person to person, but for a diagnosis of generalized anxiety disorder to be made, the patient must also suffer from at least three other symptoms, such as muscle tension, fatigue, restlessness, poor concentration, irritability, or sleep difficulties. Among U.S. adults, 5.7 percent have experienced generalized anxiety disorder (Kessler et al., 2005a).

Generalized anxiety disorder leads to impaired functioning because the person's worries cannot be controlled or put aside. With the focus of attention on the sources of anxiety, the individual cannot attend sufficiently to social or job obligations. These difficulties are compounded by the physical symptoms associated with the disorder.

Panic Disorder

In contrast to the chronic presence of anxiety in generalized anxiety disorder, sufferers of **panic disorder** experience unexpected, severe *panic attacks* that may last only minutes. These attacks begin with a feeling of intense apprehension, fear, or terror. Accompanying these feelings are physical symptoms of anxiety, including autonomic hyperactivity (such as rapid heart rate), dizziness, faintness, or sensations of choking or smothering. The attacks are unexpected in the sense that they are not brought about by something concrete in the situation. A panic disorder is diagnosed when an individual has recurrent unexpected panic attacks and also begins to have persistent concerns about the possibility of having more attacks. Research suggests that 4.7 percent of U.S. adults have experienced panic disorder (Kessler et al., 2006b).

Critical Thinking in Your Life

HOW DO DISORDERS ENTER THE *DSM*?

This chapter will present several descriptions of psychological disorders that are outlined in *DSM-IV-TR* (2000). Before you consider these disorders, it's valuable for you to reflect on the process through which clinicians achieve consensus that a particular disorder belongs in the *DSM*. Although *DSM-IV-TR* is a formidable volume, clinical observation continues to lead to proposals for new disorders: Therapists and researchers pay careful attention to people's symptoms and how those symptoms cluster together. To provide a concrete example of how researchers build the case for a new disorder, we will consider *binge eating disorder*.

You already had a brief encounter with binge eating disorder (BED) in Chapter 11. Recall that BED is diagnosed when people engage in regular episodes of binge eating without the purges that accompany bulimia nervosa. In addition, people who suffer from BED experience a loss of control during these binges and the binges cause them great distress.

Note two important features of this definition (Striegel-Moore & Franko, 2008). First, the definition suggests how BED is different from other eating disorders, despite the overlap in some symptoms (that is, binge eating). When clinicians propose a new diagnostic category, they must firmly establish that the new disorder is distinct from well-established disorders. Second, the definition mentions a cluster of symptoms. When clinicians propose a new diagnostic category, they are making a strong assertion that a particular set of experiences regularly co-occurs.

The definition of a disorder serves, in a sense, as a hypothesis: The clinicians who propose the disorder are predicting that data will confirm that people experience this distinctive constellation of symptoms. For BED, this has proven to be the case. In one study, researchers engaged in face-to-face interviews with 9,282 adults in the United States (Hudson et al., 2007). To determine whether people suffered from BED, they used criteria from *DSM-IV*. In their sample, 3.5 percent of the women and 2.0 percent of the men met those criteria. These data support the hypothesis that BED exists as a disorder with a unique set of symptoms and consequences.

Still, some data on BED has encouraged researchers to reexamine features of the diagnosis (Striegel-Moore & Franko, 2008). For example, the definitions of other eating disorders include the diagnostic feature "undue influence of body weight or shape on self-evaluation" (*DSM-IV*, 1994, p. 545). Researchers have begun to consider whether this feature should also be included for BED (Grilo et al., 2008). Studies suggest that people who meet the criteria for BED and who also show "undue influence" experience greater distress than people who do not show this influence. However, researchers have yet to reach consensus on how the inclusion of this feature would affect diagnoses of BED.

The goal of research on BED—as well as on other disorders, old and new—is to provide valid diagnoses. Valid diagnoses allow for the provision of appropriate treatments—and, ultimately, for a minimization of people's distress.

- Why do the definitions of disorders include clusters of symptoms?
- Why does improved diagnosis often allow improved treatment?

In *DSM-IV-TR*, panic disorder must be diagnosed as occurring with or without the simultaneous presence of agoraphobia. **Agoraphobia** is an extreme fear of being in public places or open spaces from which escape may be difficult or embarrassing. Individuals with agoraphobia usually fear such places as crowded rooms, malls, and buses. They are often afraid that, if they experience some kind of difficulty outside the home, such as a loss of bladder control or panic attack symptoms, help might not be available or the situation will be embarrassing to them. These fears deprive individuals of their freedom, and, in extreme cases, they become prisoners in their own homes. ◉

Can you see why agoraphobia is related to panic disorder? For some (but not all) people who suffer from panic attacks, the dread of the next attack—the helpless feelings it engenders—can be enough to imprison them. The person suffering from agoraphobia may leave the safety of home but almost always with extreme anxiety.

Phobias

Fear is a rational reaction to an objectively identified external danger (such as a fire in one's home or a mugging attack) that may induce a person to flee or to attack in self-defense. In contrast, a person with a **phobia** suffers from a persistent and irrational fear of a specific object, activity, or situation that is excessive and unreasonable given the reality of the threat.

◉ **Watch** the **Video** *Phobias* on **MyPsychLab**

agoraphobia An extreme fear of being in public places or open spaces from which escape may be difficult or embarrassing.

fear A rational reaction to an objectively identified external danger that may induce a person to flee or attack in self-defense.

phobia A persistent and irrational fear of a specific object, activity, or situation that is excessive and unreasonable, given the reality of the threat.

Table 14.2 • Common Phobias

Social phobias (fear of being observed doing something humiliating)
Specific phobias

Animal type
    Cats (ailurophobia)
    Dogs (cynophobia)
    Insects (insectophobia)
    Spiders (arachnophobia)
    Snakes (ophidiophobia)
    Rodents (rodentophobia)

Natural environment type
    Storms (brontophobia)
    Heights (acrophobia)

Blood–injection–injury type
    Blood (hemophobia)
    Needles (belonephobia)

Situational type
    Closed spaces (claustrophobia)
    Railways (siderodromophobia)

Many people feel uneasy about spiders or snakes (or even multiple-choice tests). These mild fears do not prevent people from carrying out their everyday activities. Phobias, however, interfere with adjustment, cause significant distress, and inhibit necessary action toward goals. Even a very specific, apparently limited phobia can have a great impact on one's whole life. *DSM-IV-TR* defines two categories of phobias: *social phobias* and *specific phobias* (see **Table 14.2**).

Social phobia is a persistent, irrational fear that arises in anticipation of a public situation in which an individual can be observed by others. A person with a social phobia fears that he or she will act in ways that could be embarrassing. The person recognizes that the fear is excessive and unreasonable yet feels compelled by the fear to avoid situations in which public scrutiny is possible. Social phobia often involves a self-fulfilling prophecy. A person may be so fearful of the scrutiny and rejection of others that enough anxiety is created to actually impair performance. Even positive social exchanges cause anxiety for people with social phobia: They worry that they have set standards that they will not be able to meet in the future (Weeks et al., 2008). Among U.S. adults, 12.1 percent have experienced a social phobia (Ruscio et al., 2008).

Specific phobias occur in response to several different types of objects or situations. As shown in **Table 14.2**, specific phobias are further categorized into several subtypes. For example, an individual suffering from an *animal-type specific phobia* might have a phobic response to spiders. In each case,

....

social phobia A persistent, irrational fear that arises in anticipation of a public situation in which an individual can be observed by others.

specific phobia Phobia that occurs in response to a specific type of object or situation.

obsessive-compulsive disorder (OCD) A mental disorder characterized by obsessions—recurrent thoughts, images, or impulses that recur or persist despite efforts to suppress them—and compulsions—repetitive, purposeful acts performed according to certain rules or in a ritualized manner.

the phobic response is produced either in the presence of or in anticipation of the feared specific object or situation. Research suggests that 12.5 percent of adults in the United States have experienced a specific phobia (Kessler et al., 2005a).

Obsessive-Compulsive Disorder

Some people with anxiety disorders get locked into specific patterns of thought and behavior. Consider the following case:

> Only a year or so ago, 17-year-old Jim seemed to be a normal adolescent with many talents and interests. Then, almost overnight, he was transformed into a lonely outsider, excluded from social life by his psychological disabilities. Specifically, he developed an obsession with washing. Haunted by the notion that he was dirty—in spite of what his senses told him—he began to spend more of his time cleansing himself of imaginary dirt. At first, his ritual washings were confined to weekends and evenings, but soon they began to consume all his time, forcing him to drop out of school. (Rapoport, 1989)

Jim is suffering from a condition known as **obsessive-compulsive disorder (OCD),** which has been estimated to affect 1.6 percent of U.S. adults at some point during their lives (Kessler et al., 2005a). *Obsessions* are thoughts, images, or impulses (such as Jim's belief that he is unclean) that recur or persist despite a person's efforts to suppress them. Obsessions are experienced as an unwanted invasion of consciousness, they seem to be senseless or repugnant, and they are unacceptable to the person experiencing them. You probably have had some sort of mild obsessional experience, such as the intrusion of petty worries—"Did I really lock the door?" or "Did I turn off the oven?" The obsessive thoughts of people

Why might agoraphobia cause people to become "prisoners" in their own homes?

Why do people with obsessive-compulsive disorder engage in behaviors such as repetitive hand-washing?

with obsessive-compulsive disorder are much more compelling, cause much more distress, and may interfere with their social or occupational functioning. ☛

Compulsions are repetitive, purposeful *acts* (such as Jim's washing) performed according to certain rules or in a ritualized manner in response to an obsession. Compulsive behavior is performed to reduce or prevent the discomfort associated with some dreaded situation, but it is either unreasonable or clearly excessive. Typical compulsions include irresistible urges to clean, to check that lights or appliances have been turned off, and to count objects or possessions.

At least initially, people with obsessive-compulsive disorder resist carrying out their compulsions. When they are calm, they view their compulsion as senseless. When anxiety rises, however, the power of the ritual compulsive behavior to relieve tension seems irresistible. Part of the pain experienced by people with this mental problem is created by their frustration at recognizing the irrationality or excessive nature of their obsessions without being able to eliminate them.

Posttraumatic Stress Disorder

Chapter 12 described one psychological consequence of traumatic events: People experience posttraumatic stress disorder (PTSD), an anxiety disorder that is characterized by the persistent reexperience of those traumatic events through distressing recollections, dreams, hallucinations, or flashbacks. Individuals may develop PTSD in response to rape, life-threatening events or severe injury, and natural disasters. People develop PTSD both when they themselves have been the victim of the trauma and when they have witnessed others being victimized. People who suffer from PTSD are also likely to suffer simultaneously from other psychopathologies, such as major depression, substance-abuse problems, and suicide attempts (Pietrzak et al., 2011).

Research suggests that about 6.4 percent of adults in the United States will experience PTSD at some point during their lifetime (Pietrzak et al., 2011). Studies consistently reveal that most adults have experienced an event that could be defined as traumatic, such as a serious accident, a tragic death, or physical

or sexual abuse (Widom et al., 2005). One study with 1,824 Swedish adults found that 80.8 percent had experienced at least one traumatic event (Frans et al., 2005). In this sample, men had experienced more traumatic events than women, but women were twice as likely to develop PTSD. The researchers suggested that women's greater distress in response to traumatic events helped explain this difference.

Much attention has focused on the prevalence of PTSD in the wake of traumas with widespread impact. Recall, from Chapter 12, the study that found that about 15 percent of individuals who were evacuated from the World Trade Center on September 11, 2001, met diagnostic criteria for PTSD two to three years after the terrorist attack (DiGrande et al., 2011). Similar data emerge from other tragedies. For example, in 2008 the Wenchuan earthquake in China killed almost 70,000 people. In a sample of roughly 2,100 adolescents assessed six months after the earthquake, 15.8 percent met criteria for a diagnosis of PTSD (Fan et al., 2011).

Posttraumatic stress disorder severely disrupts sufferers' lives. How do researchers go about the complex task of exploring the origins of PTSD and other anxiety disorders? Understanding the origins gives hope to eliminating the psychological distress.

Causes of Anxiety Disorders

How do psychologists explain the development of anxiety disorders? Each of the four etiological approaches outlined earlier (biological, psychodynamic, behavioral, and cognitive) emphasizes different factors. Let's analyze how each adds something unique to the understanding of anxiety disorders. ◉

Biological Various investigators have suggested that anxiety disorders have biological origins. One theory attempts to explain why certain phobias, such as those for spiders or heights, are more common than fears of other dangers, such as electricity. Because many fears are shared across cultures, it has been proposed that, at one time in the evolutionary past, certain fears enhanced our ancestors' chances of survival. Perhaps humans are born with a predisposition to fear whatever is related to sources of serious danger in the evolutionary past. This *preparedness hypothesis* suggests that we carry around an evolutionary tendency to respond quickly and "thoughtlessly" to once-feared stimuli (LoBue & DeLoache, 2008; Öhman & Mineka, 2001). However, this hypothesis does not explain types of phobias that develop in response to objects or situations that would not have had survival meaning over evolutionary history, like fear of needles or driving or elevators.

The ability of certain drugs to relieve and of others to produce symptoms of anxiety offers evidence of a biological role in anxiety disorders (Croarkin et al., 2011; Hoffman & Mathew, 2008). For example, recall from Chapter 3 that when the level of the neurotransmitter GABA in the brain becomes low, people often experience feelings of anxiety. Disorders in the brain's

☛ **Simulate** the **Experiment** *The Obsessive Compulsive Test* on **MyPsychLab**

◉ **Watch** the **Video** *When Does a Fear Become a Phobia: Sue Mineka* on **MyPsychLab** use of the neurotransmitter serotonin are also associated with some anxiety disorders. As we'll see in Chapter 15, drugs that affect GABA or serotonin levels are used as successful treatments for some types of anxiety disorders.

Researchers are also using imaging techniques to examine the brain bases of these disorders (Radua et al., 2010; van Tol et al., 2010). For example, PET scans have revealed a difference in the function of serotonin receptors between the brains of individuals who suffer from panic disorder and those of control individuals (Nash et al., 2008). These differences may help explain the onset of panic disorder. As another example, MRI techniques have revealed very widespread abnormalities in OCD patients' brains. For example, patients with OCD have greater cortical thickness in areas of the brain that normally allow people to inhibit behaviors (Narayan et al., 2008). This brain abnormality that potentially hinders communication among neurons may partially explain why people with OCD have difficulty controlling their behavioral compulsions.

Finally, family and twin studies suggest that there is a genetic basis for the predisposition to experience anxiety disorders (Hettema et al., 2005; Li et al., 2011). For example, the probability that a pair of male identical twins both suffered from a social or specific phobia was consistently greater than the probability that both male fraternal twins were sufferers (Kendler et al., 2001). Still, it's important to remember that nature and nurture always interact. For example, recall from Chapter 13 that many aspects of personality are heritable. Research suggests that part of the influence of genes on PTSD arises because people with different personality traits make life choices that decrease or increase the probability that they will experience traumas (Stein et al., 2002).

Psychodynamic The psychodynamic model begins with the assumption that the symptoms of anxiety disorders come from underlying psychic conflicts or fears. The symptoms are attempts to protect the individual from psychological pain. Thus panic attacks are the result of unconscious conflicts bursting into consciousness. Suppose, for example, a child represses conflicting thoughts about his or her wish to escape a difficult home environment. In later life, a phobia may be activated by an object or situation that symbolizes the conflict. A bridge, for example, might come to symbolize the path that the person must traverse from the world of home and family to the outside world. The sight of a bridge would then force the unconscious conflict into awareness, bringing with it the fear and anxiety common to phobias. Avoiding bridges would be a symbolic attempt to stay clear of anxiety about the childhood experiences at home.

In obsessive-compulsive disorders, the obsessive behavior is seen as an attempt to displace anxiety created by a related but far more feared desire or conflict. By substituting an obsession that symbolically captures the forbidden impulse, a person gains some relief. For example, the obsessive fears of dirt experienced by Jim, the adolescent described earlier, may have their roots in the conflict between his desire to become sexually active and his fear of "dirtying" his reputation. Compulsive preoccupation with carrying out a minor ritualistic task also allows the individual to avoid the original issue that is creating unconscious conflict.

Behavioral Behavioral explanations of anxiety focus on the way symptoms of anxiety disorders are reinforced or conditioned. Investigators do not search for underlying unconscious conflicts or early childhood experiences because these phenomena can't be observed directly. As we saw in Chapter 6, behavioral theories are often used to explain the development of phobias, which are seen as classically conditioned fears: Recall Little Albert, in whom John Watson and Rosalie Rayner instilled a fear of a white rat (see page 153). The behavioral account suggests that a previously neutral object or situation becomes a stimulus for a phobia by being paired with a frightening experience. For example, a child whose mother yells a warning when he or she approaches a snake may develop a phobia about snakes. After this experience, even thinking about snakes may produce a wave of fear. Phobias continue to be maintained by the reduction in anxiety that occurs when a person withdraws from the feared situation.

A behavioral analysis of obsessive-compulsive disorders suggests that compulsive behaviors tend to reduce the anxiety associated with obsessive thoughts—thus reinforcing the compulsive behavior. For example, if a woman fears contamination by touching garbage, then washing her hands reduces the anxiety and is therefore reinforcing. In parallel to phobias, obsessive-compulsive disorders continue to be maintained by the reduction in anxiety that follows from the compulsive behaviors.

Cognitive Cognitive perspectives on anxiety concentrate on the perceptual processes or attitudes that may distort a person's estimate of the danger that he or she is facing. A person may either overestimate the nature or reality of a threat or underestimate his or her ability to cope with the threat effectively. For example, before delivering a speech to a large group, a person with a social phobia may feed his or her anxiety:

> What if I forget what I was going to say? I'll look foolish in front of all these people. Then I'll get even more nervous and start to perspire, and my voice will shake, and I'll look even sillier. Whenever people see me from now on, they'll remember me as the foolish person who tried to give a speech.

People who suffer from anxiety disorders may often interpret their own distress as a sign of impending disaster. Their reaction may set off a vicious cycle in which the person fears disaster, which leads to an increase in anxiety, which in turn worsens the anxiety sensations and confirms the person's fears (Beck & Emery, 1985).

Psychologists have tested this cognitive account by measuring *anxiety sensitivity*: individuals' beliefs that bodily symptoms—such as shortness of breath or heart palpitations—may have harmful consequences. People high in anxiety sensitivity are likely to agree with statements such as "When I notice that my heart is beating rapidly, I worry that I might have a heart attack." Let's consider a study that demonstrated the role of anxiety sensitivity in phobia for flying.

Participants with flight phobia as well as control participants provided information about their flight anxiety, their bodily symptoms related to flight, and their anxiety sensitivity (Vanden Bogaerde & De Raedt, 2011). The participants provided final data while they were on an actual flight, waiting for the plane to take off. The participants with flight phobia had higher average scores on all measures: They reported *more flight anxiety, more bodily symptoms, and more anxiety sensitivity. However, the relationship among these measures also proved to be important. Consider two participants who experienced the same level of bodily symptoms to the impending flight. In response to those bodily symptoms, a participant with high levels of anxiety sensitivity was likely to experience a great deal of flight anxiety whereas a participant with low levels of anxiety sensitivity was not. The researchers concluded that when participants "experience aversive bodily sensations due to the flying environment," those "with higher levels of [anxiety sensitivity] are prone to interpret these in a threatening way which leads to higher levels of anxiety" (p. 425).*

Another study demonstrated the importance of anxiety sensitivity for posttraumatic stress disorder. Researchers assessed the anxiety sensitivity of a group of 68 children, ages 10 to 17, all of whom had been exposed to traumatic events (for example, they had witnessed people being killed) (Leen-Feldner et al., 2008). The researchers found a positive correlation between anxiety sensitivity and the children's symptoms of PTSD: The children who reported the highest levels of anxiety sensitivity were also most likely to report PTSD symptoms. The researchers suggested that high levels of anxiety sensitivity would make reexperiences of traumatic events (such as flashbacks) even more frightening.

Research has also found that anxious patients contribute to the *maintenance* of their anxiety by employing cognitive biases that highlight the threatening stimuli. For example, patients whose symptoms of obsessive-compulsive disorder focused on issues of cleanliness watched a researcher touch a series of objects with a "clean and unused" tissue or a "dirty and already used" tissue. In a later memory test, these OCD patients showed greater ability to recall which objects were "dirty" than which were "clean" (Ceschi et al., 2003). Similarly, people with social anxiety are *more* likely to attend to threatening social information and *less* likely to attend to positive social information. In one study, participants with social anxiety had to give an impromptu five-minute speech—a serious social stressor (Taylor et al., 2010). The participants also completed a task that measured bias against attending to positive social information. The participants who showed the greatest tendency to avoid positive social information also experienced the most distress

giving their five-minute talk. Studies of this type confirm that people suffering from anxiety disorders focus their attention in ways that serve to sustain their anxiety.

Each of the major approaches to anxiety disorders may explain part of the etiological puzzle. Continued research of each approach will clarify causes and, therefore, potential avenues for treatment. Let's turn now to another major category of abnormality—*mood disorders*.

Stop *and* Review

① What is the relationship between fear and phobias?
② What is the difference between an obsession and a compulsion?
③ With respect to phobias, what is the preparedness hypothesis?
④ What is the impact of anxiety sensitivity?

CRITICAL THINKING Recall the study that focused on the role of anxiety sensitivity for flight phobia. Why was it important for the researchers to collect their data on actual flights?

✓● **Study** and **Review** on **MyPsychLab**

MOOD DISORDERS

There have almost certainly been times in your life when you would have described yourself as terribly depressed or incredibly happy. For some people, however, extremes in mood come to disrupt normal life experiences. A **mood disorder** is an emotional disturbance, such as severe depression or depression alternating with mania. Researchers estimate that 20.8 percent of adults have suffered from mood disorders (Kessler et al., 2005a). We will consider two major categories: major depressive disorder and bipolar disorder.

Major Depressive Disorder

Depression has been characterized as the "common cold of psychopathology," both because it occurs so frequently and because almost everyone has experienced elements of the full-scale disorder at some time in his or her life. Everyone has, at one time or another, experienced grief after the loss of a loved one or felt sad or upset when failing to achieve a desired goal. These sad feelings are only one symptom experienced by people suffering from a **major depressive disorder** (see **Table 14.3** on page 398). Consider one individual's description

How does anxiety sensitivity affect people's fear of flying?

mood disorder A mood disturbance such as severe depression or depression alternating with mania.

major depressive disorder A mood disorder characterized by intense feelings of depression over an extended time, without the manic high phase of bipolar depression.

Table 14.3 • Characteristics of Major Depressive Disorder

Characteristics	Example
Dysphoric mood	Sad, blue, hopeless; loss of interest or pleasure in almost all usual activities
Appetite	Significant weight loss (while not dieting) or weight gain
Sleep	Insomnia or hypersomnia (sleeping too much)
Motor activity	Markedly slowed down (motor retardation) or agitated
Guilt	Feelings of worthlessness; self-reproach
Concentration	Diminished ability to think or concentrate; forgetfulness
Suicide	Recurrent thoughts of death; suicidal ideas or attempts

of his struggle to carry out normal daily tasks while in the depths of depression:

> *It seemed to take the most colossal effort to do simple things. I remember bursting into tears because I had used up the cake of soap that was in the shower. I cried because one of the keys stuck for a second on my computer. I found everything excruciatingly difficult, and so, for example, the prospect of lifting the telephone receiver seemed to me like bench-pressing four hundred pounds. The reality that I had to put on not just one but two socks and then two shoes so overwhelmed me that I wanted to go back to bed.* (Solomon, 2001, pp. 85–86)

This excerpt illustrates some vivid consequences of major depressive disorder.

People diagnosed with depression differ in terms of the severity and duration of their symptoms. Many individuals struggle with clinical depression for only several weeks at one point in their lives, whereas others experience depression episodically or chronically for many years. Estimates of the prevalence of mood disorders reveal that about 16.6 percent of adults suffer from major depression at some time in their lives (Kessler et al., 2005a).

Depression takes an enormous toll on those afflicted, on their families, and on society. A study undertaken on behalf of the World Health Organization estimated the loss of healthy life years that could be attributed to physical and mental illnesses (World Health Organization, 2008). In this analysis, major depressive disorder ranked third (behind lower respiratory infections and diarrheal diseases) in terms of the burden it places on people's lives around the world. For middle- and high-income countries, major depressive disorder ranked first. In the United States, depression accounts for the majority of all mental hospital admissions, but it is still believed to be underdiagnosed and undertreated. The National Comorbidity Study found that only 37.4 percent of individuals sought treatment in the first year after a major depressive episode (Wang et al., 2005). In fact, the median period people waited between experiencing a major depressive episode and seeking treatment was eight years.

Bipolar Disorder

Bipolar disorder is characterized by periods of severe depression alternating with manic episodes. A person experiencing a **manic episode** generally acts and feels unusually elated and expansive. However, sometimes the individual's predominant mood is irritability rather than elation, especially if the person feels thwarted in some way. During a manic episode, a person often experiences an inflated sense of self-esteem or an unrealistic belief that he or she possesses special abilities or powers. The person may feel a dramatically decreased need to sleep and may engage excessively in work or in social or other pleasurable activities.

Caught up in a manic mood, the person shows unwarranted optimism, takes unnecessary risks, promises anything, and may give everything away.

When the mania begins to diminish, people are left trying to deal with the damage and predicaments they created during their period of frenzy. Manic episodes almost always give way to periods of severe depression.

The duration and frequency of the mood disturbances in bipolar disorder vary from person to person. Some people experience long periods of normal functioning punctuated by occasional short manic or depressive episodes. A small

What are some differences between the occasional feelings of unhappiness that most people feel and the symptoms of major depressive disorder?

bipolar disorder A mood disorder characterized by alternating periods of depression and mania.

manic episode A component of bipolar disorder characterized by periods of extreme elation, unbounded euphoria without sufficient reason, and grandiose thoughts or feelings about personal abilities.

percentage of unfortunate individuals go right from manic episodes to clinical depression and back again in continuous, unending cycles that are devastating to them, their families, their friends, and their coworkers. While manic, they may gamble away life savings or give lavish gifts to strangers, acts that later add to guilt feelings when they are in the depressed phase. Bipolar disorder is rarer than major depressive disorder, occurring in about 3.9 percent of adults (Kessler et al., 2005a). ◉

Causes of Mood Disorders

What factors are involved in the development of mood disorders? To address this question, we'll once again visit the biological, psychodynamic, behavioral, and cognitive perspectives. Note that, because of its prevalence, major depressive disorder has been studied more extensively than bipolar disorder. This review will reflect that distribution of research.

Biological   Several types of research provide clues to the contribution of biology to mood disorders. For example, the ability of different drugs to relieve manic and depressive symptoms provides evidence that different brain states underlie the two extremes of bipolar disorder (Thase & Denko, 2008). Reduced levels of two chemical messengers in the brain, serotonin and norepinephrine, have been linked to depression; increased levels of these neurotransmitters are associated with mania.

Researchers are using brain-imaging techniques to understand the causes and consequences of mood disorders (Gotlib & Hamilton, 2008). For example, researchers have used fMRI to demonstrate that the brains of people who suffer from bipolar disorder respond differently when they are in depressed versus manic states. One study focused on 36 individuals with bipolar disorder (Blumberg et al., 2003). At the time of the study, 11 were in elevated moods, 10 were in depressed moods, and 15 were in *euthymic* (or balanced) emotional states. All of the individuals performed the same cognitive task—naming the colors in which words were printed—while undergoing fMRI scans. The scans indicated that particular regions of the cortex were more active or less active depending on each individual's particular phase of bipolar disorder.

The contribution of biology to the etiology of mood disorders is also confirmed by evidence that the incidence of mood disorder is influenced by genetic factors (Edvardsen et al., 2008; Kendler et al., 2006). For example, one twin study assessed the likelihood that both twins were diagnosed with bipolar disorder. The correlation was 0.82 for monozygotic (MZ) twins but only 0.07 for dizygotic (DZ) twins. These data led to a heritably estimate of 0.77 (Edvarsen et al., 2008). You will see in the *Psychology in Your Life* box on page 403 that researchers have begun to make progress identifying the way that genes interact with environments to influence individuals' likelihoods of experiencing mood disorders.

Let's see now what the three major psychological approaches can add to your understanding of the onset of mood disorders.

Psychodynamic   In the psychodynamic approach, unconscious conflicts and hostile feelings that originate in early childhood are seen to play key roles in the development of depression. Freud was struck by the degree of self-criticism and guilt that depressed people displayed. He believed that the source of this self-reproach was anger, originally directed at someone else, that had been turned inward against the self. The anger was believed to be tied to an especially intense and dependent childhood relationship, such as a parent–child relationship, in which the person's needs or expectations were not met. Losses, real or symbolic, in adulthood reactivate hostile feelings, now directed toward the person's own ego, creating the self-reproach that is characteristic of depression.

Behavioral   Rather than searching for the roots of depression in the unconscious, the behavioral approach focuses on the effects of the amount of positive reinforcement and punishments a person receives (Dimidjian et al., 2011). In this view, depressed feelings result when an individual receives insufficient positive reinforcements and experiences many punishments in the environment following a loss or other major life changes. As people begin to experience depression, they will often withdraw from situations they perceive as stressful. This strategy of avoidance often also reduces the opportunities people have to obtain positive reinforcement (Carvalho & Hopko, 2011). Thus, as depression leads to avoidance, the depression will often become more entrenched. In addition, depressed people tend to underestimate positive feedback and overestimate negative feedback (Kennedy & Craighead, 1988).

Cognitive   At the center of the cognitive approach to depression are two theories. One theory suggests that negative *cognitive sets*—"set" patterns of perceiving the world—lead people to take a negative view of events in their lives for which they feel responsible. The second theory, the *explanatory style* model, proposes that depression arises from the belief that one has little or no personal control over significant life events. Each of these models explains some aspects of the experience of depression. Let's see how.

Aaron Beck (1967; Disner et al., 2011), a leading researcher on depression, has developed the theory of cognitive sets. Beck has argued that depressed people have three types of negative cognitions, which he calls the *cognitive triad* of depression: negative views of themselves, negative views of ongoing experiences, and negative views of the future. Depressed people tend to view themselves as inadequate or defective in some way, to interpret ongoing experiences in a negative way, and to believe that the future will continue to bring suffering and difficulties. This pattern of negative thinking clouds all experiences and produces the other characteristic signs of depression. An individual who always anticipates a negative outcome is not likely to be motivated to pursue any goal, leading to the *paralysis of will* that is prominent in depression.

In the explanatory style view, pioneered by **Martin Seligman,** individuals believe, correctly or not, that they cannot control future outcomes that are important to them. Seligman's theory evolved from research that demonstrated depressionlike symptoms in dogs (and later in other species). Seligman and Maier (1967) subjected dogs to painful, unavoidable shocks: No matter what the dogs did, there was no way to escape the

◉ **Watch** the **Video** *DSM in Context: Speaking Out: Feliziano: Bipolar Disorder* on **MyPsychLab** shocks. The dogs developed what Seligman and Maier called **learned helplessness.** Learned helplessness is marked by three types of deficits: *motivational deficits*—the dogs were slow to initiate known actions; *emotional deficits*—they appeared rigid, listless, frightened, and distressed; and *cognitive deficits*—they demonstrated poor learning in new situations. Even when put in a situation in which they could, in fact, avoid shock, they did not learn to do so (Maier & Seligman, 1976).

Seligman believed that depressed people are also in a state of learned helplessness: They have an expectancy that nothing they can do matters (Abramson et al., 1978; Peterson & Seligman, 1984; Seligman, 1975). However, the emergence of this state depends, to a large extent, on how individuals explain their life events. As Chapter 11 discussed (see p. 316), there are three dimensions of explanatory style: *internal–external, global–specific,* and *stable–unstable.* Suppose that you have just received a poor grade on a psychology exam. You attribute the negative outcome on the exam to an internal factor ("I'm stupid"), which makes you feel sad, rather than to an external one ("The exam was really hard"), which would have made you angry. You could have chosen a less stable internal quality than intelligence to explain your performance ("I was tired that day"). Rather than attributing your performance to an internal, stable factor that has global or far-reaching influence (stupidity), you could even have limited your explanation to the psychology exam or course ("I'm not good at psychology courses"). Explanatory style theory suggests that individuals who attribute failure to internal, stable, and global causes are vulnerable to depression. This prediction has been confirmed repeatedly (Lau & Eley, 2008; Peterson & Vaidya, 2001).

Once people begin to experience the negative moods associated with major depressive disorder, ordinary cognitive processes make it more difficult for them to escape those moods. Consider a study that demonstrated that depression changes the way in which people attend to information in the world.

Featured Study

Researchers recruited a group of 15 depressed participants and 45 control participants (who had never experienced depression) (Kellough et al., 2008). The participants wore a device that allowed the researchers to monitor eye movements while they viewed visual displays. Each display had four photographs that represented the emotion categories sad, threat, positive, and neutral. For example, one display had photographs of a boy crying, a pointing gun, a couple embracing, and a fire hydrant. The participants were told that they were wearing the eye-tracking device so that the researchers could determine the relationship between pupil dilation and emotional images. In fact, the researchers wished to test the hypothesis that depressed individuals would spend more time than control individuals (who had never been depressed) looking at the sad photos and less time looking at the positive photos. The data supported that prediction. As you can see in **Figure 14.1***, individuals with depression spent more time looking at sad photos whereas individuals who had never experienced depression spent more time looking at positive photos.*

learned helplessness A general pattern of nonresponding in the presence of noxious stimuli that often follows after an organism has previously experienced noncontingent, inescapable aversive stimuli.

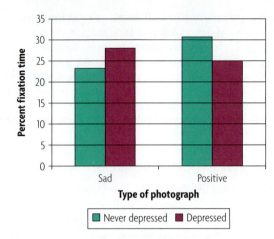

FIGURE 14.1 Attentional Biases in Major Depressive Disorder

Depressed participants and control participants (who had never been depressed) viewed displays with sad, threat, positive, and neutral photographs. Compared to never-depressed participants, depressed participants spent more time looking at sad photographs and less time looking at positive photographs.

Data from *Behaviour Research and Therapy 46*(11), Kellough, J. L., Beevers, C. G., Ellis, A. J., & Wells, T. T. "Time course of selective attention in clinically depressed young adults," pp 1238–1243, 2008.

This research supports the more general conclusion that people with major depressive disorder find their attention drawn to negative information in the world (Peckham et al., 2010). You can understand how this attentional bias could help make depression feel inescapable.

In Chapter 15, you will see that insights generated from cognitive theories of depression have given rise to successful forms of therapy. For now, there are two other important aspects of the study of depression that we will consider: the large differences between the prevalence of depression in men and women, and the link between depression and suicide.

Gender Differences in Depression

One of the central questions of research on depression is why women are afflicted almost twice as often as men (Hyde et al., 2008). Estimates of the prevalence of mood disorders reveal that about 21 percent of females and 13 percent of males suffer a major depression at some time in their lives (Kessler et al., 1994). This gender difference emerges in adolescence, by about ages 13 to 15. One factor that contributes to this difference is, unfortunately, quite straightforward: On average, women experience more negative events and life stressors than men do (Kendler et al., 2004; Shih et al., 2006). For example, women have a greater likelihood of experiencing physical or sexual abuse, and they are more likely to live in poverty while being the primary caregiver for children and elderly parents. Thus women's lives provide more of the types of experiences that lay the groundwork for serious depression.

Research on gender differences has focused on a number of factors that might make women more vulnerable to depression (Hyde et al., 2008). Some of those factors are biological: There might, for example, be hormonal differences that start

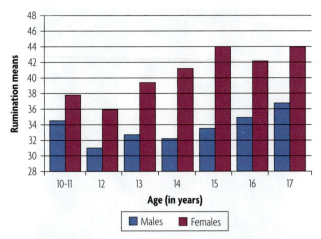

FIGURE 14.2 Gender Differences in Rumination

Across the adolescent years, the gap grows between girls' and boys' reports of rumination.

Data from Jose, P. E. & Grown, I. "When does the gender difference in rumination begin?" *Journal of Youth and Adolescence 37*(2), 2008, 180–192.

at puberty that put adolescent girls more at risk for depression than their male peers. Researchers have also looked intensively at cognitive factors that set men and women apart. For example, research by **Susan Nolen-Hoeksema** (Nolen-Hoeksema & Hilt, 2009) contrasts the response styles of men and women once they begin to experience negative moods. On this view, when women experience sadness, they tend to think about the possible causes and implications of their feelings. In contrast, men attempt actively to distract themselves from depressed feelings, either by focusing on something else or by engaging in a physical activity that will take their minds off their current mood state.

This model suggests that the more thoughtful, *ruminative* response style of women—the tendency to focus obsessively on their problems—increases women's vulnerability to depression. Consider a study that examined rumination among a large sample of adolescents.

Featured Study

A group of 1,218 students between the ages of 10 and 17 completed a questionnaire that assessed their responses to life events (Jose & Brown, 2008). The questionnaire included statements like "I sit at home and think about how I feel" and "I think no one will want to be around me if I don't snap out of this mood." The students responded to each statement on a 5-point scale that ranged from "never" to "always." As you can see in **Figure 14.2,** *at the youngest ages there was a modest difference between males and females. However, over the adolescent years the gap grows, with girls engaging in considerably more rumination. The students in the study also completed a measure of depression. For both boys and girls, the students who ruminated the most were also most likely to report the most symptoms of depression. However, the relationship between rumination and depression was even stronger for the girls.*

This study supports the hypothesis that rumination is a risk factor for depression: Paying attention to negative moods can increase thoughts of negative events, which eventually increases the quantity and/or the intensity of negative feelings. The study also confirms that men who ruminate are also at risk for depression. The gender difference for depression emerges, in part, because more women ruminate.

Suicide

"The will to survive and succeed had been crushed and defeated. . . . There comes a time when all things cease to shine, when the rays of hope are lost" (Shneidman, 1987, p. 57). This sad statement by a suicidal young man reflects the most extreme consequence of any psychological disorder—*suicide*. Although most depressed people do not commit suicide, analyses suggest that many suicides are attempted by those who are suffering from depression (Bolton et al., 2008). In the general U.S. population, the number of deaths officially designated as suicide is around 30,000 each year (Nock et al., 2008). Because many suicides are attributed to accidents or other causes, the actual rate is probably much higher. Because depression occurs more frequently in women, it is not surprising that women *attempt* suicide more often than men do; attempts by men, however, are more often successful (Nock et al., 2008). This difference occurs largely because men use guns more often, and women tend to use less lethal means, such as sleeping pills.

One of the most alarming social problems in recent decades is the rise of *youth suicide*. Although suicide is the eleventh leading cause of death in the United States for all ages, it is third for people ages 15 to 24 (Miniño et al., 2010). For every completed suicide, there may be as many as 8 to

What factors help explain why more women than men experience depression?

20 suicide attempts. To assess the risk of youth suicide, a team of researchers reviewed 128 studies that involved about 500,000 individuals between the ages of 12 and 20 (Evans et al., 2005). Across that broad sample, 29.9 percent of the adolescents had thought about suicide at some point in their lives, and 9.7 percent had actually attempted suicide. Adolescent girls were roughly twice as likely as adolescent boys to have made a suicide attempt.

Youth suicide is not a spur-of-the-moment, impulsive act, but, typically, it occurs as the final stage of a period of inner turmoil and outer distress. The majority of young suicide victims have talked to others about their intentions or have written about them. Thus talk of suicide should always be taken seriously (Rudd et al., 2006). As is the case for adults, adolescents are more likely to attempt suicide when they are experiencing depression (Gutierrez et al., 2004; Nrugham et al., 2008). Feelings of hopelessness and isolation, as well as negative self-concepts, are also associated with suicide risk (Rutter & Behrendt, 2004). Furthermore, gay and lesbian youths are at even higher risk for suicide than are other adolescents. A team of researchers reviewed several studies comparing the suicide rates of heterosexual and "sexual minority youth" (adolescents who reported same-sex attraction and/or behavior). The average rates of suicidal thoughts and behaviors were 28 percent for sexual minority youth and 12 percent for heterosexuals (Marshal et al., 2011). These higher suicide rates undoubtedly reflect the relative lack of social support for homosexual orientation. Suicide is an extreme reaction that occurs especially when adolescents feel unable to cry out to others for help. Being sensitive to signs of suicidal intentions and caring enough to intervene are essential for saving the lives of both youthful and mature people who have come to see no exit for their troubles except total self-destruction.

Stop and Review

① What experiences characterize bipolar disorder?
② In Aaron Beck's theory, what types of negative cognitions make up the cognitive triad?
③ How does the ruminative response style help explain gender differences in depression?
④ What are some suicide risk factors for adolescents?

CRITICAL THINKING   Recall the study that demonstrated attentional biases in major depressive disorder. Why might participants have been led to believe the study was about pupil dilation?

✓●─Study and Review on MyPsychLab

SOMATOFORM AND DISSOCIATIVE DISORDERS

As this chapter has reviewed various types of psychological disorders, you have seen how certain everyday experiences can, pushed to the limit, lead to disability or maladaptive behavior.

Even highly successful individuals, like actor Owen Wilson, are not immune to the feelings of despair that can trigger suicidal thoughts. What has research revealed about the relationship between depression and suicide?

For example, everyone experiences anxiety, but for some people those experiences become so severe that they develop an anxiety disorder. Similarly, many people experience symptoms for physical illnesses that don't have any obvious causes; many people have days when they just "don't feel like themselves." However, when those types of experiences impair individuals' day-to-day life, they may indicate *somatoform disorders* or *dissociative disorders*. Let's review the symptoms and etiology of each type of disorder.

Somatoform Disorders

A person suffering from a **somatoform disorder** has physical illnesses or complaints that cannot be fully explained by actual medical conditions. To be diagnosed with one of these disorders, people must experience the illnesses or complaints to an extent that they cause sufficient distress to interfere with their everyday functioning. Let's review *hypochondriasis, somatization disorder*, and *conversion disorder*.

Individuals with **hypochondriasis** believe they have physical illnesses despite assurance from medical practitioners that they do not. Even when they are currently healthy, they may be constantly fearful that they will contact physical illnesses.

....

somatoform disorder A disorder in which people have physical illnesses or complaints that cannot be fully explained by actual medical conditions.

hypochondriasis A disorder in which individuals are preoccupied with having or getting physical ailments despite reassurances that they are healthy.

Psychology in Your Life

HOW CAN WE PINPOINT INTERACTIONS OF NATURE AND NURTURE?

Throughout *Psychology and Life* you have seen instances in which people's life outcomes—for example, their attachment to their mothers and their intellectual performance—reflects an interaction of nature and nurture: Environments change the impact of genes. These types of interactions are particularly important in the study of psychopathology. Causal models for many types of mental illness assert that particular genes put people at risk, but features of the environment play an important role to determine whether the risk brings about illness. Let's explore an interaction of nature and nurture for major depressive disorder.

The discussion of mood disorders noted that disruptions in the function of the neurotransmitter serotonin play a role in depression. For that reason, researchers have focused attention on a gene, known as 5-HTTLPR, that has an impact on the serotonin system (Caspi et al., 2010; Karg et al., 2011). The gene comes in short (S) and long (L) forms. In one study with 144 college undergraduates, 19 percent had two short versions of the gene (SS), 53 percent had one short and one long (SL), and 28 percent had two long versions (LL) (Carver et al., 2011). The students themselves provided information about the family circumstances in which they had been raised. They used 5-point scales (1 = not at all; 5 = very often) to provide information about factors such as how often they felt loved and cared for, how often they were insulted, and how often they were abused. Based on those responses, the researchers calculated the extent to which each student had been raised in a "risky family." Each student also underwent a clinical evaluation to determine whether he or she had ever met the diagnostic criteria for major depressive disorder.

In the figure, positive numbers for "Risky families" indicate that the family had more risk factors (so that the student's childhood experience was more stressful). Positive numbers for "Depression diagnosis" indicate a higher probability of a diagnosis. As you can see, the interaction of genes and environments was quite dramatic: For students with two long versions of the gene (LL), a family environment

that was highly risky actually yielded fewer diagnoses of major depressive disorder.

Another study followed people over several decades to evaluate environmental interactions with this same gene (Uher et al., 2011). Participants entered the study when they were small children (some as 3-year-olds and some as 5-year-olds) and maltreatment was assessed during their childhood. They were followed through young adulthood (through ages 32 or 40) to determine which individuals experienced persistent depression. Once again, the impact of childhood maltreatment—with respect to the likelihood of persistent depression—depended on which versions of the 5-HTTLPR gene each participant had inherited.

These studies make plain the importance of both nature and nurture. A known genetic difference in combination with negative life events greatly changes the likelihood that people will experience depression. Breakthroughs in the understanding of the human genome allow researchers to determine exactly how nature and nurture interact.

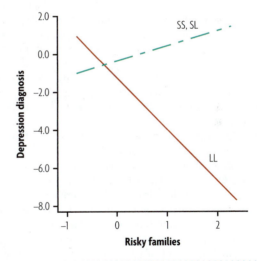

In addition, this preoccupation with being or getting ill causes such sufficient distress that individuals are impaired in their day-to-day lives. To assess the prevalence of hypochondriasis and other somatoform disorders, researchers often focus on people who present themselves for medical treatment. In that context, the question becomes what proportion of people have physical complaints that don't allow medical explanations. Research suggests that 4.7 percent of adults 18 and older who seek medical treatment meet *DSM-IV-TR* criteria for hypochondriasis (Fink et al., 2004).

Individuals with **somatization disorder** present a long history of physical complaints over many years. Those complaints—which remain medically unexplained—must span several medical categories. To meet *DSM-IV-TR* criteria for the diagnosis, individuals must have experienced four pain symptoms (such as headaches or stomachaches), two gastrointestinal

somatization disorder A disorder characterized by unexplained physical complaints in several categories over many years.

What role do attentional biases play in the development of somatoform disorders?

Featured Study

The study focused on a 36-year-old woman who had partial paralysis of her upper arm that could not be explained by any physical disorder (Cojan et al., 2009). The patient completed a motor task in which she attempted to use her hands to execute or inhibit responses to visual stimuli on a computer screen. The researchers used fMRI scans to contrast her patterns of brain activity with that of a group of healthy controls who attempted to simulate a left-hand paralysis (in parallel to the patient's symptoms). The patterns of brain activity for the patient and controls showed intriguing differences. For example, the fMRI scans for the simulating controls suggested that they were engaging in conscious effort when they tried not to move their hand. The patient's fMRI scans showed activity in different brain regions—the pattern suggested that her inability to move her hand was not voluntary.

symptoms (such as nausea or diarrhea), one sexual symptom (such as erectile dysfunction or excessive menstrual bleeding), and one neurological symptom (such as paralysis or double vision). Among adults seeking medical treatment, 1.5 percent meet criteria for somatization disorder (Fink et al., 2004).

Both hypochondriasis and somatization disorder are defined by people's complaints about physical symptoms. However, people with hypochondriasis worry about having a specific underlying disease whereas those with somatization disorder focus more on the symptoms themselves. In addition, as you've just seen, to be diagnosed with somatization disorder people must have reported a wide variety of unexplained physical complaints.

Conversion disorder is characterized by a loss of motor or sensory function that cannot be explained by damage to the nervous system or other physical damage. For example, individuals may experience paralysis or blindness without a medical cause. In addition, the onset of the physical symptoms must be preceded by psychological factors such as interpersonal conflict or emotional stressors. Historically, conversion disorder was called *hysteria*—and was believed to represent, in some eras, possession by the devil. Sigmund Freud helped bring about the contemporary understanding of conversion disorder. One of his most enduring insights was that psychological trauma could yield physical symptoms. Conversion disorder is present in 1.5 percent of adults seeking medical treatment (Fink et al., 2004).

Causes of Somatoform Disorders The defining characteristic of somatoform disorders is that individuals experience physical ailments that have no adequate medical explanation. Researchers have attempted to understand how that could be possible: How, for example, could individuals whose motor systems are intact experience paralysis? Studies have used neuroimaging techniques to discover the brain bases of conversion disorder (Mailis-Gagnon & Nicholson, 2011; Ellenstein et al., 2011). Consider a study that demonstrated that an individual with conversion symptoms showed different patterns of brain activity than individuals who were only simulating the same symptoms.

To understand these results, you might take a moment to see what it feels like to simulate paralysis in your left hand. It takes some mental effort not to let the hand move. The study suggests that people with conversion symptoms are not expending any such effort; their symptoms are not just pretense.

Researchers have also examined cognitive processes that contribute to somatoform disorders (Brown, 2004; Rief & Broadbent, 2007). For example, an important aspect of hypochondriasis is an attentional bias in the way that individuals respond to bodily sensations. Suppose you wake up one morning with a scratchy throat. If you have an attentional bias that makes it difficult to divert your thoughts from that scratchy throat, you might come to believe that you are seriously ill. In fact, one study demonstrated that the attention of people who experience a high level of anxiety about their health is drawn to pictures that show health threats (such as a man with a rash on his arms) (Jasper & Witthöft, 2011). The tight focus on symptoms and illness contributes to a vicious cycle: Stress and anxiety have physical consequences (for example, increased sweating and elevated heart rate) that can feel like the symptoms of illness—providing further proof that health-focused anxiety is appropriate. Someone who attributes all physical symptoms to illness may perceive a perilous pattern in the co-occurrence of a scratchy throat, excessive sweating, and a swiftly beating heart. Thus the cognitive biases associated with somatoform disorders serve to exaggerate minor bodily sensations.

Dissociative Disorders

A **dissociative disorder** is a disturbance in the integration of identity, memory, or consciousness. It is important for people to see themselves as being in control of their behavior, including emotions, thoughts, and actions. Essential to this perception of self-control is the sense of selfhood—the consistency of different aspects of the self and the continuity of identity over time and place. Psychologists believe that, in dissociated states, individuals escape from their conflicts by giving up this precious consistency and continuity—in a sense, disowning part of

conversion disorder A disorder in which psychological conflict or stress brings about loss of motor or sensory function.

dissociative disorder A personality disorder marked by a disturbance in the integration of identity, memory, or consciousness.

themselves. The forgetting of important personal experiences, a process caused by psychological factors in the absence of any organic dysfunction, called **dissociative amnesia,** is one example of dissociation. For some people, the loss of ability to recall their past is accompanied by an actual flight from their home or place of work. This disorder is called **dissociative fugue.** People may remain in a fugue state for hours, days, or months; they may live with a new identity in a new location.

Dissociative identity disorder (DID), formerly known as *multiple personality disorder,* is a dissociative mental disorder in which two or more distinct personalities exist within the same individual. At any particular time, one of these personalities is dominant in directing the individual's behavior. Dissociative identity disorder is popularly known as *split personality* and sometimes mistakenly called *schizophrenia,* a disorder, as you will see in the next section, in which personality often is impaired but is not split into multiple versions. In DID, each of the emerging personalities contrasts in some significant way with the original self—it might be outgoing if the person is shy, tough if the original personality is weak, and sexually assertive if the other is fearful and sexually naive. Each personality has a unique identity, name, and behavior pattern. In some cases, dozens of different characters emerge to help the person deal with a difficult life situation. Here is an excerpt from a first-person account of a woman who experiences DID (Mason, 1997, p. 44):

Just as waves turn the ocean inside out and rearrange the water, different ones of us cycle in and out in an ebb and flow that is sometimes gentle, sometimes turbulent. A child colors with Crayola markers. She moves aside to make way for the administrator, who reconciles the bank statement. A moment later, the dead baby takes over and lies paralyzed on the floor. She remains that way for a while, but no one gets upset—it's her turn. The live baby stops in her crawl, engrossed by a speck of dust. The cooker prepares meals for three days and packages each separately—we all have different likes and dislikes. A terrified one screams aloud, a wounded one moans, a grieving one wails.

From Vivian Ann Conan, "Divided She Stands." Originally appeared in New York Magazine August 4, 1997 under the pseudonym Laura Emily Mason. Reprinted by permission of the author.

Can you put yourself in this woman's place, and imagine what it would be like to have this range of "individuals"—the child, the dead baby, the live baby, the cooker, and so on—inside your one head?

Causes of Dissociative Disorders Psychologists who take a psychodynamic perspective have suggested that dissociation serves a vital survival function. They suggest that people who have experienced traumatic stress will sometimes use defense mechanisms to push the traumatic events out of conscious awareness. Consider a study that focused on the life experiences of 891 11- to 17-year-old adolescents in Puerto Rico (Martínez-Taboas et al., 2006). The children completed questionnaires that assessed the presence of victimization experiences and dissociative symptoms in their lives. As you can see in **Figure 14.3** on page 406, relatively few of the children in the sample had experienced high levels of victimization. For example, 74 percent of the adolescents had not experienced any emotional abuse. However, Figure 14.3 also reveals that increasing levels of emotional, physical, and sexual abuse were accompanied by higher levels of dissociative symptoms.

Although these data—and personal accounts of the type quoted earlier—seem compelling, many psychologists remain skeptical about the link between trauma and dissociation (Giesbrecht et al., 2008). This skepticism has been particularly focused on dissociative identity disorder. No solid data exist about the prevalence of this disorder (*DSM-IV-TR*, 2000). In fact, some critics have suggested that diagnoses of DID have increased because of the media attention paid to individuals who claim to have large numbers of distinct personalities (Lilienfeld & Lynn, 2003). Skeptics have often suggested that therapists who "believe" in DID may create DID—these therapists question their patients, often under hypnosis, in a way that encourages multiple personalities to "emerge." Researchers have tried to find rigorous methods to test the claims people with DID make about the separation between different identities. For example, studies have examined *interidentity amnesia* by assessing the extent to which information acquired by one identity is known to another. Research results fail to support the claim that amnesia occurs between identities (Kong et al., 2008).

Researchers on DID generally acknowledge that not all diagnoses are appropriate. However, many psychologists believe that sufficient evidence has accumulated in favor of the DID diagnosis to indicate that it is not always the product of zealous therapists (Gleaves et al., 2001: Ross, 2009). The safest conclusion may be that, of the group of people diagnosed with DID, some cases are genuine, whereas other cases emerge in response to therapists' demands.

Stop *and* Review

① Howard believes that his headaches prove he has a brain tumor, despite his doctor's assurances that he is fine. From which somatoform disorder might Howard suffer?

② How is dissociative amnesia defined?

③ What does research suggest about the life experiences that play a role in the etiology of dissociative identity disorder?

✓▪──[**Study** and **Review** on **MyPsychLab**

SCHIZOPHRENIC DISORDERS

Everyone knows what it is like to feel depressed or anxious, even though most of us never experience these feelings to the degree of severity that constitutes a disorder. Schizophrenia, however, is a disorder that represents a qualitatively different

....

dissociative amnesia The inability to remember important personal experiences, caused by psychological factors in the absence of any organic dysfunction.

dissociative fugue A disorder characterized by a flight from home or work accompanied by a loss of ability to recall the personal past.

dissociative identity disorder (DID) A dissociative mental disorder in which two or more distinct personalities exist within the same individual; formerly known as multiple personality disorder.

Type of abuse	Percent	Dissociative experiences

Emotional abuse

No emotional abuse	74%	
Low	15%	
High	11%	

(scale: 0, 0.5, 1, 1.5, 2, 2.5)

Physical abuse

No physical abuse	72%	
Low abuse	12%	
Moderate abuse	6%	
High abuse	11%	

(scale: 0, 0.5, 1, 1.5, 2, 2.5)

Sexual abuse

| No abuse | 93% | |
| Some abuse | 7% | |

(scale: 0, 0.5, 1, 1.5, 2, 2.5)

FIGURE 14.3 Victimization and Dissociative Symptoms

Adolescents provided information about their experiences of victimization and their dissociative symptoms. As indicated by the percent figures, the majority of the children had not experienced any abuse. The children who had been abused reported more dissociative symptoms.

Data from Martínez-Taboas, A. et al. (2006). Prevalence of victimization correlates of pathological dissociation in a community sample of youths, *Journal of Traumatic Stress, 19*, 439–448.

experience from normal functioning. A **schizophrenic disorder** is a severe form of psychopathology in which personality seems to disintegrate, thought and perception are distorted, and emotions are blunted. The person with a schizophrenic disorder is the one you most often conjure up when you think about madness or insanity. Although schizophrenia is relatively rare—approximately 0.7 percent of U.S. adults have suffered from schizophrenia at some point in their lives (Tandon et al., 2008)—this figure translates to around 2 million people affected by this most mysterious and tragic mental disorder.

Mark Vonnegut, son of novelist Kurt Vonnegut, was in his early 20s when he began to experience symptoms of schizophrenia. In *The Eden Express* (1975), he tells the story of his break with reality and his eventual recovery. Once, while pruning some fruit trees, his reality became distorted:

I began to wonder if I was hurting the trees and found myself apologizing. Each tree began to take on personality. I began to wonder if any of them liked me. I became completely absorbed in looking at each tree and began to notice that they were ever so slightly luminescent, shining with a soft inner light that played around the branches. And from out of nowhere came an incredibly wrinkled, iridescent face. Starting as a small point infinitely distant, it rushed forward, becoming infinitely huge. I could see nothing else. My heart had stopped. The moment stretched forever. I tried to make the face go away but it mocked me. . . . I tried to look the face in the eyes and realized I had left all familiar ground. (1975, p. 96)

Vonnegut's description gives you a glimpse at the symptoms of schizophrenia.

In the world of schizophrenia, *thinking* becomes illogical; associations among ideas are remote or without apparent pattern. *Hallucinations* often occur, involving imagined sensory perception—sights, smells, or, most commonly, sounds (usually voices)—that patients assume to be real. A person may hear a voice that provides a running commentary on his or her behavior or may hear several voices in conversation. **Delusions** are also common; these are false or irrational beliefs maintained in spite of clear contrary evidence. *Language* may become incoherent—a "word salad" of unrelated or made-up words—or an individual may become mute. *Emotions* may be flat, with no visible expression, or they may be inappropriate to the situation. *Psychomotor behavior* may be disorganized (grimaces, strange mannerisms), or posture may become rigid. Even when only some of these symptoms are present, deteriorated functioning in work and interpersonal relationships is likely as the patient withdraws socially or becomes emotionally detached.

Psychologists divide the symptoms between a positive category and a negative category. During *acute* or *active phases* of schizophrenia, the positive symptoms—hallucinations, delusions, incoherence, and disorganized behavior—are prominent.

....

schizophrenic disorder Severe form of psychopathology characterized by the breakdown of integrated personality functioning, withdrawal from reality, emotional distortions, and disturbed thought processes.

At other times, the negative symptoms—social withdrawal and flattened emotions—become more apparent. Some individuals, such as Mark Vonnegut, experience only one or a couple of acute phases of schizophrenia and recover to live normal lives. Others, often described as chronic sufferers, experience either repeated acute phases with short periods of negative symptoms or occasional acute phases with extended periods of negative symptoms. Even the most seriously disturbed are not acutely delusional all the time.

Major Types of Schizophrenia

Because of the wide variety of symptoms that can characterize schizophrenia, investigators consider it not a single disorder but rather a constellation of separate types. The five most commonly recognized subtypes are outlined in **Table 14.4**. ☀

Disorganized Type   In this subtype of schizophrenia, a person displays incoherent patterns of thinking and grossly bizarre and disorganized behavior. Emotions are flattened or inappropriate to the situation. Often, a person acts in a silly or childish manner, such as giggling for no apparent reason. Language can become so incoherent, full of unusual words and incomplete sentences, that communication with others breaks down. If delusions or hallucinations occur, they are not organized around a coherent theme.

Catatonic Type   The major feature of the catatonic type of schizophrenia is a disruption in motor activity. Sometimes people with this disorder seem frozen in a stupor. For long periods of time, the individual can remain motionless, often in a bizarre position, showing little or no reaction to anything in the environment. At other times, these patients show excessive motor activity, apparently without purpose and not influenced by external stimuli. The catatonic type is also characterized by extreme *negativism*, an apparently unmotivated resistance to all instructions.

Paranoid Type   Individuals suffering from this form of schizophrenia experience complex and systematized delusions focused around specific themes:

- *Delusions of persecution.* Individuals feel that they are being constantly spied on and plotted against and that they are in mortal danger.

What patterns of thoughts may indicate that a person is experiencing schizophrenia?

- *Delusions of grandeur.* Individuals believe that they are important or exalted beings—millionaires, great inventors, or religious figures such as Jesus Christ. Delusions of persecution may accompany delusions of grandeur—an individual is a great person but is continually opposed by evil forces.
- *Delusional jealousy.* Individuals become convinced—without due cause—that their mates are unfaithful. They contrive data to fit the theory and "prove" the truth of the delusion.

Individuals with paranoid schizophrenia rarely display obviously disorganized behavior. Instead, their behavior is likely to be intense and quite formal.

Undifferentiated Type   This is the grab-bag category of schizophrenia, describing a person who exhibits prominent delusions, hallucinations, incoherent speech, or grossly disorganized behavior that fits the criteria of more than one type or of no clear type. The hodgepodge of symptoms experienced by these individuals does not clearly differentiate among various schizophrenic reactions.

Residual Type   Individuals diagnosed as residual type have usually suffered from a major past episode of schizophrenia but are currently free of major positive symptoms such as hallucinations or delusions. The ongoing presence of the disorder is signaled by minor positive symptoms or negative symptoms like flat emotion. A diagnosis of residual type may indicate that the person's disease is entering *remission*, or becoming dormant.

Causes of Schizophrenia

Different etiological models point to very different initial causes of schizophrenia, different pathways along which it develops,

Table 14.4 • Types of Schizophrenic Disorders

Types of Schizophrenia	Major Symptoms
Disorganized	Inappropriate behavior and emotions; incoherent language
Catatonic	Frozen, rigid, or excitable motor behavior
Paranoid	Delusions of persecution or grandeur
Undifferentiated	Mixed set of symptoms with thought disorders and features from other types
Residual	Free from major symptoms but evidence from minor symptoms of continuation of the disorder

☀ **Explore** the **Concept** *Types and Symptoms of Schizophrenia* on **MyPsychLab**

delusion False or irrational belief maintained despite clear evidence to the contrary.

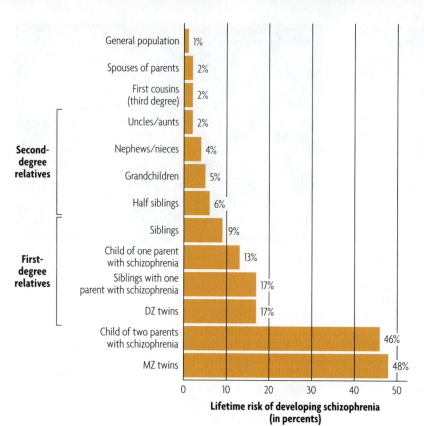

FIGURE 14.4 Genetic Risk of Developing Schizophrenia

The graph shows average risks for developing schizophrenia. Data were compiled from family and twin studies conducted in European populations between 1920 and 1987; the degree of risk correlates highly with the degree of genetic relatedness. Except when the label indicates otherwise, the data reflect the relationship between an individual and someone who has been diagnosed with schizophrenia. For example, the DZ twin of someone diagnosed with schizophrenia has a 17 percent chance of sharing the diagnosis.

and different avenues for treatment. Let's look at the contributions several of these models can make to an understanding of the way a person may develop a schizophrenic disorder.

Genetic Approaches   It has long been known that schizophrenia tends to run in families (Bleuler, 1978; Kallmann, 1946). Three independent lines of research—family studies, twin studies, and adoption studies—point to a common conclusion: Persons related genetically to someone who has had schizophrenia are more likely to become affected than those who are not (Riley, 2011). A summary of the risks of being affected with schizophrenia through various kinds of relatives is shown in **Figure 14.4**. Schizophrenia researcher **Irving Gottesman** (1991) pooled these data from about 40 reliable studies conducted in Western Europe between 1920 and 1987; he dropped the poorest data sets. As you can see, the data are arranged according to degree of genetic relatedness, which correlates highly with the degree of risk. For example, when both parents have suffered from schizophrenia, the risk for their offspring is 46 percent, as compared with 1 percent in the general population. When only one parent has had schizophrenia, the risk for the offspring drops sharply, to 13 percent. Note also that the probability that identical twins will both have schizophrenia is roughly three times greater than the probability for fraternal twins.

Because the heritability of schizophrenia is so firmly established, researchers have turned their attention toward discovering the specific genes that may put people at risk for the disorder. As you've seen, there are several major types of schizophrenia with a variety of different symptoms. For that reason, researchers believe that a number of genes will have

an impact on when and how people will be affected: Research evidence has emerged that associates several candidate genes with the disorder (Shi et al., 2008). Different people's experience of schizophrenia—with respect, for example, to the severity of their symptoms—may depend on exactly the combination of genes they inherit. ◉

Brain Function   Another biological approach to the study of schizophrenia is to look for abnormalities in the brains of individuals suffering from the disorder. Much of this research now relies on brain-imaging techniques that allow direct comparisons to be made between the structure and functioning of the brains of individuals with schizophrenia and normal control individuals (Keshavan et al., 2008). For example, as shown in **Figure 14.5**, magnetic resonance imaging has shown that the *ventricles*—the brain structures through which cerebrospinal fluid flows—are often enlarged in individuals with schizophrenia (Barkataki et al., 2006). MRI studies also demonstrate that individuals with schizophrenia have measurably thinner regions in frontal and temporal lobes of cerebral cortex; the loss of neural tissue presumably relates to the disorder's behavioral abnormalities (Bakken et al., 2011).

Researchers have also begun to document that some brain abnormalities are related to the progress of the disease (Brans et al., 2008). For example, **Figure 14.6** presents the data from a longitudinal study of 12 individuals who began to experience symptoms of schizophrenia by age 12 (Thompson et al., 2001).

....

◉ **Watch** the **Video** *Genetics Research in Schizophrenia* on **MyPsychLab**

FIGURE 14.5 Schizophrenia and Ventricle Size

Male identical twins underwent MRI scans. The scan of the twin with schizophrenia (on the right) reveals enlarged ventricles compared to the scan of the twin without the disorder (on the left).

Photo courtesy of Drs. E. Fuller Torrey and Daniel Weinberger.

The study focused on changes in gray matter (largely the cell bodies and dendrites of nerve cells in the cortex) over a five-year period. The 12 patients underwent repeated MRI scans, as did an age-matched group of healthy control participants. You may recall from Chapter 10 that adolescent brains are still undergoing processes of change. That's why even the normal adolescents experience some loss of gray matter. However, as you can see in **Figure 14.6**, the loss of gray matter for the adolescents with schizophrenia was quite dramatic. By monitoring for such changes in people at genetic risk for schizophrenia, clinicians may be able to offer diagnosis and treatment earlier in the disorder (Wood et al., 2008).

Given the wide range of symptoms of schizophrenia, you are probably not surprised by the comparably wide range of biological abnormalities that may be either causes or consequences of the disorder. What are the ways in which features of the environment may prompt people who are at risk to develop the disease?

Environmental Stressors We have been focusing on genetic and biological aspects of schizophrenia. However, as you can see in **Figure 14.5**, even in the groups with the greatest genetic similarity, the risk factor is less than 50 percent. This indicates that, although genes play a role, environmental

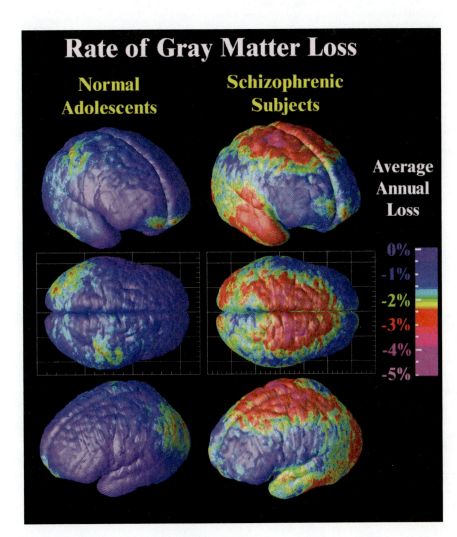

FIGURE 14.6 Gray Matter Loss in Adolescents with Schizophrenia

Researchers carried out MRI scans on 12 adolescents with schizophrenia and 12 age-matched healthy controls. Over a five-year period, the adolescents with schizophrenia showed substantial loss of gray matter in several areas of their brains.

From Thompson, P. M., Vidal, C., Giedd, J. N., Gochman, P., Blumenthal, J., Nicolson, R., Toga, A. W., & Rapoport, J. L. (2001). Mapping adolescent brain change reveals dynamic wave of accelerated gray matter loss in very early-onset schizophrenia. *PNAS, 98*, 11650–11655.

conditions may also be necessary to give rise to the disorder. A widely accepted hypothesis for the cause of schizophrenia is the *diathesis-stress hypothesis*. According to the **diathesis-stress hypothesis,** genetic factors place the individual at risk, but environmental stress factors must impinge for the potential risk to be manifested as a schizophrenic disorder. Let's consider some of those factors.

For example, research has demonstrated that people who live in urban settings, people who experience greater economic difficulties, and people who have migrated from one country to another all experience higher rates of schizophrenia (Bourque et al., 2011; Tandon et al., 2008). Explanations for these relationships often focus on social stressors and social adversity. Research also suggests that people who experience traumatic life events are at higher risk for schizophrenia. One study examined large samples of individuals in both the United States and Great Britain: The more people had experienced traumas such as physical or sexual abuse, the more likely they were to suffer from a schizophrenic disorder (Shevlin et al., 2008).

Researchers have also examined how life events affect changes in people's symptoms once they have been diagnosed with a schizophrenic disorder. Consider a study that demonstrated a relationship between patients' responses to life events and changes in their symptoms.

Featured Study

Researchers assessed the symptoms of patients with a schizophrenic disorder at the beginning and end of a nine-month period (Docherty et al., 2009). At the study's outset, the researchers also measured each patient's emotional reactivity—the intensity of an individual's emotional responses to life events. The patients, for example, responded to statements such as "I have big ups and downs in mood" and "I experience very intense emotions" on a scale ranging from "never, or almost never" to "always, or almost always." Nine months later, the patients gave an account of life events from the preceding month. Based on their reports, the researchers sorted them into categories of people who had experienced moderate or severe life events in the past month and those who hadn't. The researchers predicted that negative life events would lead to greater symptoms of schizophrenia—but only for patients who regularly had intense emotional responses to those events. As you can see in **Figure 14.7,** *the data supported the prediction. Only patients who both had negative life events and high emotional reactivity showed increases in symptoms (that is, delusions and hallucinations).*

We saw earlier that differences in people's responses to life events affect the likelihood that they will experience, for example, major depressive disorder. This study demonstrated a similar pattern for symptoms of schizophrenia.

Research has also looked at family stressors that may affect both the likelihood that people develop schizophrenic disorders and the likelihood that they will relapse if the symptoms go into remission (Miklowitz & Tompson, 2003; Schlosser et al., 2010). For example, several studies have focused on the concept of *expressed emotion*. Families are high on expressed emotion if they make a lot of critical comments about the patient, if they are emotionally overinvolved with the patient (that is, if they are

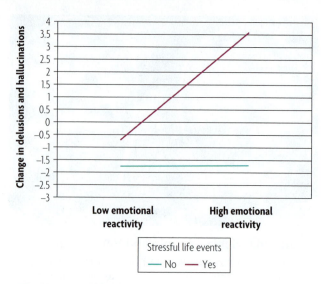

FIGURE 14.7 Changes in Symptoms of Schizophrenic Disorders

Researchers measured patients' emotional reactivity and symptom change over a nine-month-period. Only patients who both had negative life events and high emotional reactivity showed increases in symptoms (that is, delusions and hallucinations).

Data from Docherty, N. M. et al. (2008). Life events and high-trait reactivity together predict psychotic symptom increases in schizophrenia. *Schizophrenia Bulletin, 35*(3). Reprinted by permission of Oxford University Press.

overprotective and intrusive), and if they have a generally hostile attitude toward the patient. When patients in remission leave hospitals and return to high-expressed-emotion homes, the risk of relapse is more than twice as high as when they return to low-expressed-emotion homes (Hooley, 2007). The implication is that treatment should be for the entire family as a *system*, to change the operating style toward the disturbed child (Kuipers et al., 2010).

The number of explanations of schizophrenia this section has reviewed—and the questions that remain despite significant research—suggests how much there is to learn about this powerful psychological disorder. Complicating understanding is the likelihood that the phenomenon called schizophrenia is probably better thought of as a group of disorders, each with potentially distinct causes. Genetic predispositions, brain processes, and family interactions have all been identified as participants in at least some cases. Researchers must still determine the exact ways in which these elements may combine to bring about schizophrenia.

Stop *and* Review

① Are social withdrawal and flattened emotions positive or negative symptoms of schizophrenia?

....

diathesis-stress hypothesis A hypothesis about the cause of certain disorders, such as schizophrenia, that suggests that genetic factors predispose an individual to a certain disorder but that environmental stress factors must impinge in order for the potential risk to manifest itself.

② For what type of schizophrenic disorder would delusions of persecution or grandeur be symptoms?

③ What impact does family expressed emotion have on relapse for schizophrenic disorders?

CRITICAL THINKING Recall the study that looked at the impact of life events on symptoms of schizophrenia. Why was emotional reactivity measured at the beginning of the nine-month period?

✓●─ **Study** and **Review** on **MyPsychLab**

PERSONALITY DISORDERS

A **personality disorder** is a long-standing (chronic), inflexible, maladaptive pattern of perceiving, thinking, or behaving. These patterns can seriously impair an individual's ability to function in social or work settings and can cause significant distress. They are usually recognizable by the time a person reaches adolescence or early adulthood. Personality disorders are coded on Axis II of *DSM-IV-TR*. As shown in **Table 14.5**, *DSM-IV-TR* organizes 10 types of personality disorders into three clusters.

Diagnoses of personality disorders have sometimes been controversial because of the overlap among the disorders: Some of the same behaviors contribute to diagnoses of different disorders. In addition, researchers have tried to understand the relationship between normal and abnormal personalities. They ask, at what point does an extreme on a particular dimension of personality indicate a disorder (Livesley & Lang, 2005)? For example, most people are somewhat dependent on other people. When does dependence become sufficiently extreme to signal dependent personality disorder? As with other types of psychological disorders, clinicians must understand when and how personality traits become maladaptive—when and how those traits cause either the person or society to suffer. To illustrate that conclusion, this section will focus on *borderline personality disorder* and *antisocial personality disorder*.

Borderline Personality Disorder

Individuals with **borderline personality disorder** experience great instability and intensity in personal relationships. These difficulties arise in part from difficulties controlling anger. The disorder leads people to have frequent fights and temper tantrums. In addition, people with this disorder display great impulsivity in their behaviors—particularly with respect to behaviors that can relate to self-harm, such as substance abuse or suicide attempts. Among adults in the United States, the prevalence of borderline personality disorder is about 1.6 percent (Lenzenweger et al., 2007).

One important component of borderline personality disorder is an intense fear of abandonment (Bornstein et al., 2010). People with this disorder engage in frantic behaviors to prevent abandonment such as frequent phone calls and physical

Table 14.5 • Personality Disorders

Disorder	Characteristics
Cluster A: People's behavior appears odd or eccentric	
Paranoid	Distrust and suspiciousness about the motives of the individuals with whom they interact
Schizoid	Lack of desire to have social relationships; lack of emotionality in social situations
Schizotypal	Cognitive or perceptual distortions as well as discomfort in social relationships
Cluster B: People's behavior appears dramatic or erratic	
Antisocial	Inability to respect the rights of others; irresponsible or unlawful behavior that violates social norms
Borderline	Instability and intensity in personal relationships; impulsivity, particularly with respect to behaviors that include self-harm
Histrionic	Excessive emotionality and attention seeking; inappropriate sexual or seductive behavior
Narcissistic	Grandiose sense of self-importance and a need for constant admiration; lack of empathy for others
Cluster C: People's behavior appears anxious or fearful	
Avoidant	Avoid interpersonal contact because of risk of rejection; fear criticism and feel inadequate in social situations
Dependent	Need others to take responsibility for major areas of life; feel uncomfortable or helpless without support from other people
Obsessive-Compulsive	Preoccupied with rules and lists; perfectionism interferes with being able to complete tasks

clinging. Let's consider a study that demonstrated a relationship between rejection and rage for individuals with borderline personality disorder.

Featured Study

Researchers recruited 45 individuals who met diagnostic criteria for borderline personality disorder (BPD) and 40 healthy controls (Berenson et al., 2011). The participants carried handheld computers that prompted them for responses at 105 randomly selected times over the course of 21 days. Each time the computer beeped, participants indicated how much rejection they were experiencing at that moment by responding to statements such as "I am abandoned."

personality disorder A chronic, inflexible, maladaptive pattern of perceiving, thinking, and behaving that seriously impairs an individual's ability to function in social or other settings.

borderline personality disorder A disorder defined by instability and intensity in personal relationships as well as turbulent emotions and impulsive behaviors.

Participants also reported their feelings of rage at that moment by answering questions such as "Right now to what extent do you feel like lashing out?" Individuals in the BPD group reported both more rejection and more rage over the three-week period. In addition, for the BPD group, small momentary increases in rejection led to relatively large increments in rage. Members of the control group did not react to momentary feelings of rejection with that same pattern of rage.

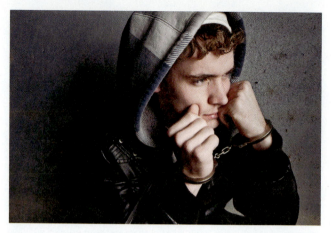

Why do people with antisocial personality disorder often have legal difficulties?

This study illustrates the difficulties with emotional control that make it quite difficult to maintain relationships with people with borderline personality disorder. One study that followed people with this disorder over the course of 10 years found impaired social functioning across the whole period (Choi-Kain et al., 2010). This research suggests that borderline personality disorder remains stable over time.

Causes of Borderline Personality Disorder As with other disorders, researchers have focused on both the nature and nurture of borderline personality disorder. Twin studies provide strong evidence in favor of a genetic contribution (Distel et al., 2008). For example, one study compared the rate of concordance for monozygotic versus dizygotic twins (Torgersen et al., 2000). When MZ twins had borderline personality disorder, 35.3 percent of their siblings also had the disorder; for DZ twins, only 6.7 percent of their siblings also had the disorder. If you recall the discussion in Chapter 13 about the strong heritability of personality traits, you might not be surprised that disorders of those traits are also heritable.

Still, research suggests that environmental factors make a strong contribution in the etiology of borderline personality disorder (Cohen et al., 2008; Lieb et al., 2004). One study compared the incidence of early traumatic events for 66 patients with the disorder to 109 healthy controls (Bandelow et al., 2005). The patients had considerably different lives. For example, 73.9 percent of the patients with borderline personality disorder reported childhood sexual abuse; only 5.5 percent of the controls did so. The patients reported, on average, that the abuse started at age 6 and lasted for 3½ years. That early trauma likely contributed to the incidence of the disorder. However, not all people who endure childhood sexual abuse develop borderline personality disorder—witness the 5.5 percent of control participants in this study who survived childhood sexual abuse but did not develop the disorder. It is likely that a combination of genetic risk and traumatic events explains the etiology of the disorder.

Antisocial Personality Disorder

Antisocial personality disorder is marked by a long-standing pattern of irresponsible or unlawful behavior that violates social norms. Lying, stealing, and fighting are common behaviors. People with antisocial personality disorder often do not experience shame or remorse for their hurtful actions. Violations of

---

antisocial personality disorder A disorder characterized by stable patterns of irresponsible or unlawful behavior that violates social norms.

---

social norms begin early in their lives—disrupting class, getting into fights, and running away from home. Their actions are marked by indifference to the rights of others. Among adults in the United States, the prevalence of antisocial personality disorder is about 1.0 percent (Lenzenweger et al., 2007).

Antisocial personality disorder is often comorbid with other pathologies. For example, in one study of adults with histories of alcohol or drug abuse the prevalence of antisocial personality disorder was 18.3 percent for men and 14.1 percent for women—considerably higher than the 1.0 percent prevalence for the general population (Goldstein et al., 2007). In addition, antisocial personality disorder also puts people at risk for suicide, even in the absence of major depressive disorder (Javdani et al., 2011; Swogger et al., 2009). This suicide risk is likely to be a product of the impulsivity and disregard for safety that characterizes the disorder.

Causes of Antisocial Personality Disorder Researchers have used twin studies to examine genetic components of specific behaviors associated with antisocial personality disorder. For example, one study examined the concordance in behaviors for 3,687 pairs of twins (Viding et al., 2005). Teachers responded to statements about each twin to indicate the presence of callous-unemotional traits (such as "Does not show feelings or emotions") and antisocial behavior (such as "Often fights with other children or bullies them"). The comparisons of MZ and DZ twins suggested that the tendency to display callous-unemotional traits had a strong genetic component. In addition, for twins who displayed high levels of those callous-emotional traits, genetics also made a strong contribution to antisocial behavior.

Research has also focused on the environmental circumstances that give rise to antisocial personality disorder (Paris, 2003). As was the case for borderline personality disorder, people with antisocial personality disorder are more likely than healthy individuals to have experienced childhood abuse. To verify this relationship, one team of researchers searched court records (from around 1970) to compile a sample of 641 individuals whose abuse and neglect as children was officially documented (Horwitz et al., 2001). Those individuals were interviewed 20 years later to assess the prevalence of psychological disorders. Compared to a control group of 510 individuals with no history of abuse, the maltreated individuals were considerably more likely to meet the criteria for antisocial personality disorder. What mattered, in addition, was that the people who had been mistreated as children had often experienced a higher level of stressors throughout their lives. Further research suggests that physical abuse, in particular, puts individuals at risk for antisocial personality disorder (Lobbestael et al., 2010).

Stop *and* Review

① What intense fear do people with borderline personality disorder have with respect to interpersonal relationships?

② How do the early lives of people with borderline personality disorder compare to those of healthy controls?

③ Why are people with antisocial personality disorder at risk for suicide?

CRITICAL THINKING Consider the study that assessed the relationship between rejection and rage for borderline personality disorder. Why was it important that the sampling was done at randomly selected times?

✓•—[**Study** and **Review** on **MyPsychLab**

PSYCHOLOGICAL DISORDERS OF CHILDHOOD

The discussion so far has largely focused on adults who suffer from psychopathology. It is important to note, however, that many individuals begin to experience symptoms of mental illness in childhood and adolescence. Researchers have recently intensified their study of the time course with which psychopathology emerges in young lives (Zahn-Waxler et al., 2008). Researchers often try to identify behavior patterns that allow for early diagnosis and treatment. For example, problems with social functioning may provide clues that children and adolescents are at risk for schizophrenia (Tarbox & Pogue-Geile, 2008).

DSM-IV-TR also identifies a range of disorders that are "usually first diagnosed in infancy, childhood, or adolescence." Chapter 9 discussed one of these disorders, *mental retardation*. Here, the focus will be on *attention-deficit hyperactivity disorder* and *autistic disorder*.

Attention-Deficit Hyperactivity Disorder

The definition of **attention-deficit hyperactivity disorder** (ADHD) refers to two clusters of symptoms (*DSM-IV-TR*, 2000). First, children must show a degree of *inattention* that is not consistent with their level of development. They might, for example, have difficulty paying attention in school or often lose items such as toys or school assignments. Second, children must show signs of *hyperactivity-impulsivity* that, once again, is not consistent with their developmental level. Hyperactive behaviors include squirming, fidgeting, and excessive talking; impulsive behaviors include blurting out answers

and interrupting. A diagnosis of ADHD requires that children have shown these patterns of behavior for at least six months before age 7.

Researchers estimate the prevalence of ADHD to be 9 percent among children ages 5 to 17 in the United States (Akinbami et al., 2011). The rate is 12.3 percent for boys and 5.5 percent for girls. Note, however, that research suggests that cultural biases (for example, expectations of gender differences) lead to fewer diagnoses of ADHD among girls than are justified—making it difficult to provide an exact estimate of the gender difference. However, in one large-scale study of adults, 3.2 percent of women and 5.4 percent of men met diagnostic criteria for ADHD (Kessler et al., 2006a). These figures may accurately reflect gender differences across the life span. When they are diagnosed with ADHD, boys and girls show much the same patterns of problematic behavior (Rucklidge, 2010). However, girls may experience more social isolation as a consequence of ADHD than do boys (Elkins et al., 2011).

The diagnosis of ADHD is complicated by the fact that many children are prone to episodes of inattention, hyperactivity, or impulsiveness. For that reason, the diagnosis has sometimes been controversial: People have worried that children's normal disorderliness was being labeled as abnormal. However, there is now a large consensus among clinicians that some children's behavior reaches a level at which it is maladaptive—the children are unable to control their behavior or complete tasks. Although there has often been a popular perception that ADHD is overdiagnosed, research evidence contradicts that perception (Sciutto & Eisenberg, 2007). In fact, as noted earlier, ADHD might actually be underdiagnosed for girls.

As with the other disorders, researchers have considered both the nature and nurture of ADHD. Twin and adoption studies have provided strong evidence for the heritability of the disorder (Greven et al., 2011). Researchers have started to document relationships between specific genes that affect the brain's development and neurotransmitter functions (Poelmans et al., 2011; Smoller et al., 2006). There are also important environmental variables associated with ADHD. For example, children who come from families with economic disadvantages or families with high levels of conflict are more likely to experience the disorder (Akinbami et al., 2011; Biederman et al., 2002). Some environmental variables have greater impact on children in different birth positions. For example, the eldest children in families that lack cohesion—families in which members are not committed to providing support to each other—are more at risk for ADHD than are younger siblings in such families (Pressman et al., 2006). Results of this sort suggest that parenting experience has an impact on the incidence of ADHD.

Autistic Disorder

Children with **autistic disorder** present severe disruption in their ability to form social bonds. They are likely to have greatly delayed and very limited development of spoken language as

....

attention-deficit hyperactivity disorder (ADHD) A disorder of childhood characterized by inattention and hyperactivity-impulsivity.

autistic disorder A developmental disorder characterized by severe disruption of children's ability to form social bonds and use language.

What psychological disorders of childhood might lead to classroom disruptions?

As you saw in Chapter 10, under ordinary circumstances, children develop a theory of mind. At first, they interpret the world only from their own perspective. However, with rapid progress between ages 3 and 4, children develop an understanding that other people have different knowledge, beliefs, and intentions than they do. Research suggests that individuals with autistic disorder lack the ability to develop this understanding. Without a theory of mind, it is quite difficult for people to establish social relationships. Individuals with autistic disorder find it virtually impossible to understand and predict other people's behavior, making everyday life seem mysterious and hostile.

Stop and Review

① What types of behaviors characterize ADHD?
② Why has it been difficult to diagnose autistic disorder before age 2 or 3?
③ Why is theory of mind relevant to autistic disorder?

✔●─|**Study** and **Review** on **MyPsychLab**

well as very narrow interests in the world. Consider a report on a child who was diagnosed with this disorder:

> [Audrey] seemed frightened by nearly any changes in her customary routine, including the presence of strange people. She either shrank from contact with other children or avoided them altogether, seemingly content to engage in nonfunctional play by herself for hours at a time. When she was with other children, she seldom engaged in reciprocal play or even copied any of their motor movements. (Meyer, 2003, p. 244)

Many children with autistic disorder also engage in repetitive and ritualistic behaviors: They might, for example, place objects in lines or symmetrical patterns (Greaves et al., 2006; Leekam et al., 2011).

Research suggests that the prevalence of autistic disorder (and related disorders) is about one out of 110 children (Centers for Disease Control and Prevention, 2009). Because many of the symptoms of autistic disorder relate to language and social interaction, it has often been difficult to diagnose the disorder until parents notice that their children are failing to use language or interact. However, recent research has begun to document behaviors in the first year of life that predict later diagnoses of autistic disorder (Zwaigenbaum et al., 2005). For example, children at risk for autistic disorder are less likely to smile in response to social smiles and respond to their names than are other children.

Causes of Autistic Disorder As with ADHD, autistic disorder has a large genetic component. In fact, researchers have begun to identify the variations in the human genome that may predispose individuals to experience the disorder (Vieland et al., 2011). Researchers have also discovered brain markers of the disorder. For example, individuals with autistic disorder experience more rapid brain growth than do their peers (Amaral et al., 2008). The ongoing question is how such brain abnormalities bring about the symptoms of the disorder.

Researchers have suggested that individuals who suffer from autistic disorder have an inability to develop an understanding of other people's mental states (Baron-Cohen, 2008).

THE STIGMA OF MENTAL ILLNESS

One of the most important goals for this chapter has been to demystify mental illness—to help you understand how, in some ways, abnormal behavior is really ordinary. People with psychological disorders are often labeled as *deviant*. However, the deviant label is not true to prevailing realities: When 46.4 percent of adults in the United States report having experienced some psychiatric disorder in their lifetime (Kessler et al., 2005a), psychopathology is, at least statistically, relatively normal.

Even given the frequency with which psychopathology touches "normal lives," people who are psychologically disordered are often stigmatized in ways that most physically ill people are not. A **stigma** is a mark or brand of disgrace; in the psychological context, it is a set of negative attitudes about a person that places him or her apart as unacceptable (Hinshaw & Stier, 2008). The woman with schizophrenia quoted at the beginning of the chapter had this to say: "The patient and public, in my [opinion] needs to be educated about mental illness because people ridicule and mistreat, even misunderstand us at crucial times." Negative attitudes toward the psychologically disturbed come from many sources: The mass media portray psychiatric patients as prone to violent crime; jokes about the mentally ill are acceptable; families deny the mental distress of one of their members; legal terminology stresses mental incompetence. People also stigmatize themselves by hiding current psychological distress or a history of mental health care.

Researchers have documented a number of ways in which the stigma of mental illness has a negative impact on people's

....

stigma The negative reaction of people to an individual or group because of some assumed inferiority or source of difference that is degraded.

lives (Hinshaw & Stier, 2008). In one sample of 84 men who had been hospitalized for mental illness, 6 percent reported having lost a job because of their hospitalization; 10 percent reported having been denied an apartment or room; 37 percent reported being avoided by others; and 45 percent reported that others had used their history of mental illness to hurt their feelings. Only 6 percent of the men reported no incidents of rejection (Link et al., 1997). This group of men went through a yearlong course of treatment that resulted in considerable improvement in their mental health. Even so, at the end of that year, there were no changes in their perception of stigma: Despite their improvements in functioning, the patients did not expect to be treated any more kindly by the world. This type of research shows the great duality of many people's experience with mental disorders: Seeking help—allowing one's problems to be labeled—generally brings both relief *and* stigma.

Unfortunately, many people who suffer from mental illnesses internalize negative stereotypes and stigmatize themselves. In one study, 144 people with serious mental illnesses completed a questionnaire that evaluated internalized stigma (West et al., 2011). The questionnaire assessed, for example, the extent to which participants agreed with negative stereotypes of people with mental illness. In the sample, 41 percent of the women and 35 percent of the men indicated substantial internalized stigma. Such internalized stigma has serious consequences: People with high levels of internalized stigma tend to experience more hopelessness, lower self-esteem, and decreased quality of life (Livingston & Boyd, 2010).

A final note on stigma: Research suggests that people who have had prior contact with individuals with mental illnesses hold attitudes that are less affected by stigma (Couture & Penn, 2003). Let's look at one study that supports this conclusion.

Featured Study

A team of researchers surveyed 911 participants about their personal contact with mental illness (Boyd et al., 2010). Some participants had no contact whereas others had themselves been hospitalized for mental illness or had family members or friends who had been hospitalized. The participants were given vignettes that described an individual who had been diagnosed with either schizophrenia or major depressive disorder. Participants answered a number of questions to indicate how they might respond to the individual. For example, participants indicated how much social distance they would maintain by responding to statements such as, "How willing would you be to make friends with [the patient]?" (p. 1066). Participants with more personal contact indicated that they would establish less personal distance. In addition, people with more personal contact expressed less anger and blame toward the patient.

I hope that one consequence of reading this chapter will be to help modify your beliefs about what it means to be mentally ill—and to increase your tolerance and compassion for mentally ill individuals.

In making sense of psychopathology, you are forced to come to grips with basic conceptions of normality, reality, and social values. In discovering how to understand, treat, and, ideally, prevent psychological disorders, researchers not only help those who are suffering and losing out on the joys of living, they also expand the basic understanding of human nature. How do psychologists and psychiatrists intervene to right minds gone wrong and to modify behavior that doesn't work? The next chapter addresses that important question.

Stop *and* Review

1. In the context of mental illness, how does stigma function?
2. Why does treatment for mental illness often bring about both relief and stigma?
3. What types of experience reduce stigma?

CRITICAL THINKING Consider the study on personal contact and responses to mental illness. Why is social distance an important measure?

✓ **Study** and **Review** on **MyPsychLab**

Recapping Main Points

The Nature of Psychological Disorders

- Abnormality is judged by the degree to which a person's actions resemble a set of indicators that include distress, maladaptiveness, irrationality, unpredictability, unconventionality, observer discomfort, and violation of standards or societal norms.
- Objectivity is an important problem for discussions of mental illness.
- Classification systems for psychological disorders should provide a common shorthand for communicating about general types of psychopathologies and specific cases.
- The most widely accepted diagnostic and classification system is *DSM-IV-TR*.

- The biological approach to the etiology of mental illness concentrates on abnormalities in the brain, biochemical processes, and genetic influences.
- Psychological approaches include psychodynamic, behavioral, cognitive, and sociocultural models.

Anxiety Disorders

- The five major types of anxiety disorders are generalized, panic, phobic, obsessive-compulsive, and posttraumatic stress.
- Research has confirmed genetic and brain bases for anxiety disorders as well as behavioral and cognitive components of causality.

Mood Disorders

- Major depressive disorder is the most common mood disorder; bipolar disorder is much rarer.
- People have genetic predispositions toward mood disorders.
- Mood disorders change the way people respond to life experiences.
- Women's higher levels of major depressive disorder may reflect differences in negative life experiences as well as cognitive responses to those experiences.
- Suicides are most frequent among people suffering from depression.

Somatoform and Dissociative Disorders

- Somatoform disorders such as hypochondriasis, somatization disorder, and conversion disorder are characterized by circumstances in which physical illnesses or complaints cannot be fully explained by actual medical conditions.
- Dissociative disorders involve a disruption of the integrated functioning of memory, consciousness, or personal identity.

Schizophrenic Disorders

- Schizophrenia is a severe form of psychopathology characterized by extreme distortions in perception, thinking, emotion, behavior, and language.

- The five subtypes of schizophrenia are disorganized, catatonic, paranoid, undifferentiated, and residual.
- Evidence for the causes of schizophrenia has been found in a variety of factors, including genetics, brain abnormalities, and environmental stressors.

Personality Disorders

- Personality disorders are patterns of perception, thought, or behavior that are long-standing and inflexible and impair an individual's functioning.
- Both borderline personality disorder and antisocial personality disorder arise because of genetic and environmental factors.

Psychological Disorders of Childhood

- Children with ADHD display inattention and hyperactivity-impulsivity.
- Autistic disorder is characterized by severe disruption of children's ability to form social bonds and use language.

The Stigma of Mental Illness

- Those with psychological disorders are often stigmatized in ways that most physically ill people are not.
- Although treatment for psychological disorders brings about positive changes, the stigma associated with mental illness has a negative impact on quality of life.

KEY TERMS

abnormal psychology (p. 386)
agoraphobia (p. 393)
antisocial personality disorder (p. 412)
anxiety disorder (p. 392)
attention-deficit hyperactivity disorder (ADHD) (p. 413)
autistic disorder (p. 413)
bipolar disorder (p. 398)
borderline personality disorder (p. 411)
comorbidity (p. 389)
conversion disorder (p. 404)
delusion (p. 407)
diathesis-stress hypothesis (p. 410)
dissociative amnesia (p. 405)
dissociative disorder (p. 404)

dissociative fugue (p. 405)
dissociative identity disorder (DID) (p. 405)
DSM-IV-TR (p. 389)
etiology (p. 390)
fear (p. 393)
generalized anxiety disorder (p. 392)
hypochondriasis (p. 402)
insanity (p. 390)
learned helplessness (p. 400)
major depressive disorder (p. 397)
manic episode (p. 398)
mood disorder (p. 397)
neurotic disorder (p. 390)

obsessive-compulsive disorder (OCD) (p. 394)
panic disorder (p. 392)
personality disorder (p. 411)
phobia (p. 393)
psychological diagnosis (p. 388)
psychopathological functioning (p. 386)
psychotic disorder (p. 390)
schizophrenic disorder (p. 406)
social phobia (p. 394)
somatization disorder (p. 403)
somatoform disorder (p. 402)
specific phobia (p. 394)
stigma (p. 414)

1. *Comorbidity* refers to circumstances in which an individual
   a. cannot be accurately diagnosed using *DSM-IV-TR*.
   b. has a neurotic disorder that cannot be easily cured.
   c. has a psychotic disorder that includes a fear of death.
   d. experiences more than one psychological disorder at the same time.

2. Professor Hexter believes that unconscious conflicts often cause psychological disorders. Which approach to psychopathology does Professor Hexter use?
   a. psychodynamic   c. cognitive
   b. sociocultural   d. behavioral

3. Analyses of legal records suggest that the use of the insanity defense is quite _____ and the probability of it succeeding is quite _____.
   a. rare; low   c. common; low
   b. rare; high   d. common; high

4. For binge eating disorder, which criterion is still being researched as a potential part of the diagnosis?
   a. regular episodes of binge eating without purges
   b. a loss of control during binges
   c. binges causing great distress
   d. undue influence of body weight or shape on self-evaluation

5. For over a year, Jane has felt anxious or worried throughout the day. It sounds as though Jane is suffering from
   a. panic disorder.
   b. generalized anxiety disorder.
   c. obsessive-compulsive disorder.
   d. agoraphobia.

6. What attribution style puts people at risk for depression?
   a. internal–specific–stable
   b. external–specific–unstable
   c. internal–global–stable
   d. external–global–unstable

7. When something bad happens, Chris spends a lot of time ruminating about the problem. Based on this behavior, you think it is
   a. more likely that Chris is a man.
   b. equally likely that Chris is a man or a woman.
   c. likely that Chris will develop a specific phobia.
   d. more likely that Chris is a woman.

8. You are trying to assess the probability that Paula will develop major depressive disorder. You would be least concerned if she inherited _____ of the 5-HTTLPR serotonin gene.
   a. two short versions
   b. two long versions
   c. one short and one long version
   d. one or more short versions

9. Nadine alternates between yelling at Tricia and begging her to remain friends. Tricia is convinced that Nadine suffers from _____ personality disorder.
   a. schizotypal   c. borderline
   b. narcissistic   d. obsessive-compulsive

10. To diagnose conversion disorder, you'd try to find _____ that preceded the appearance of symptoms.
    a. a serious physical illness
    b. psychological conflict or stress
    c. a visit to a medical doctor
    d. both pain and gastrointestinal complaints

11. Although Eve doesn't have any organic dysfunction, she often forgets important personal experiences. This could be an instance of
    a. dissociative amnesia.
    b. hypochondriasis.
    c. somatization disorder.
    d. dependent personality disorder.

12. Which of these is a negative symptom of schizophrenia?
    a. hallucinations   c. delusions
    b. incoherent language   d. social withdrawal

13. Which of these behaviors would *not* generally support a diagnosis of attention-deficit hyperactivity disorder?
    a. Manfred blurts out answers during class activities.
    b. Manfred loses his toys and school assignments.
    c. Manfred squirms and fidgets in the classroom.
    d. Manfred cries when other children tease him.

14. Professor Wyatt believes that 1-year-old Brian is at risk for autistic disorder. The professor might observe Brian to determine whether he
    a. fails to respond to his name.
    b. can walk without assistance.
    c. responds appropriately to loud noises.
    d. shows smooth pursuit with his eyes.

15. As part of an introductory psychology class, a professor has her students interview people who have recovered from psychological disorders. This exercise should
    a. prompt the students to be more affected by the stigma of mental illness.
    b. have no impact on the students' experience of stigma.
    c. prompt the students to be less affected by the stigma of mental illness.
    d. decrease the probability that students would seek treatment for mental illness.

ESSAY QUESTIONS

1. Why is it not always possible to be objective about diagnoses of mental illness?

2. What are some benefits of a useful classification system for psychological disorders?

3. What life circumstances lead some people to contemplate suicide?

15

Therapies for Psychological Disorders

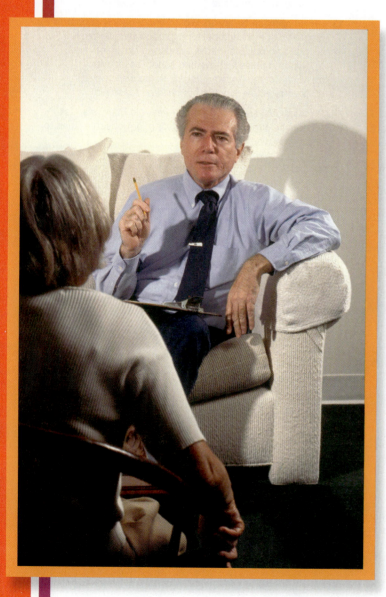

While you were reading Chapter 14, you might at some points have felt overwhelmed by all the ways in which individuals can experience mental illness. Fortunately, psychologists and other providers of mental health care have worked intently to create therapies that address the full range of psychopathology. You will see in this chapter that researchers continue to generate innovations in therapeutic techniques. The more researchers learn about the causes and consequences of psychopathology—the research Chapter 14 described—the better they are able to fine-tune their repertory of therapies.

This chapter examines the types of therapies that can help restore personal control to individuals with a range of disorders. It surveys the major types of treatments currently used by health-care providers: psychoanalysis, behavior modification, cognitive alteration, humanistic therapies, and drug therapies. We will consider the way these treatments work and assess claims about the likelihood of their success. 👁

As you read this chapter, bear in mind that many people who seek help from therapists haven't been diagnosed with a psychological disorder. There may be times in your life when you can use some help dealing with a variety of psychological stressors. Recall that Chapter 12 emphasized the importance of having a flexible repertory of coping skills. Therapists can help you develop strategies for coping with life circumstances that are causing you distress.

THE THERAPEUTIC CONTEXT

There are different types of therapies for mental disorders, and there are many reasons some people seek help (and others who need it do not). The purposes or goals of therapy, the settings in which therapy occurs, and the kinds of therapeutic helpers also vary. Despite any differences between therapies, however, all are *interventions* into a person's life, designed to change the person's functioning in some way.

Goals and Major Therapies

The therapeutic process can involve four primary tasks or goals:

1. Reaching a *diagnosis* about what is wrong, possibly determining an appropriate psychiatric *(DSM-IV-TR)* label for the presenting problem, and classifying the disorder.
2. Proposing a probable *etiology* (cause of the problem)— that is, identifying the probable origins of the disorder and the functions being served by the symptoms.
3. Making a *prognosis,* or estimate, of the course the problem will take with and without any treatment.
4. Prescribing and carrying out some form of *treatment,* a therapy designed to minimize or eliminate the troublesome symptoms and, perhaps, their sources.

Biomedical therapies focus on changing the mechanisms that run the central nervous system. Practiced largely by psychiatrists and physicians, these therapies try to alter brain functioning with chemical or physical interventions, including surgery, electric shock, and drugs that act directly on the brain–body connection.

Psychological therapies, which are collectively called **psychotherapy,** focus on changing the faulty behaviors people have learned: the words, thoughts, interpretations, and feedback that direct daily strategies for living. These therapies are practiced by clinical psychologists as well as by psychiatrists. There are four major types of psychotherapies: psychodynamic, behavioral, cognitive, and existential-humanistic.

The *psychodynamic* approach views suffering as the outer symptom of inner, unresolved traumas and conflicts. Psychodynamic therapists treat mental disorder with a "talking cure," in which a therapist helps a person develop insights about the relation between the overt symptoms and the unresolved hidden conflicts that presumably caused them.

Behavior therapy treats the behaviors themselves as disturbances that must be modified. Disorders are viewed as learned behavior patterns rather than as the symptoms of mental disease. Behaviors are transformed in many ways, including changing reinforcement contingencies for desirable and undesirable responding, extinguishing conditioned responses, and providing models of effective problem solving.

Cognitive therapy tries to restructure the way a person thinks by altering the often distorted self-statements a person makes about the causes of a problem. Restructuring cognitions changes the way a person defines and explains difficulties, often enabling the person to cope with the problems.

Therapies that have emerged from the *humanistic tradition* emphasize the patients' values. They are directed toward self-actualization, psychological growth, the development of more meaningful interpersonal relationships, and the enhancement of freedom of choice. They tend to focus more on improving the functioning of essentially healthy people than on correcting the symptoms of seriously disturbed individuals.

Although I have introduced each type of psychotherapy separately, it is important to note that many psychotherapists take an *integrative* approach to practice: They integrate different theoretical approaches to provide maximum benefit to their patients or clients. In many cases, psychotherapists begin their careers adhering to a particular theoretical orientation. However, as their careers unfold, they begin to mix together the most effective elements of different therapies (Norcross et al., 2005; Thoma & Cecero, 2009). Psychotherapists integrate across virtually every pair of orientations (for example, cognitive and humanistic; behavioral and psychodynamic). However, the most prominent integrative therapies combine aspects of the cognitive and behavioral approaches (Goldfried, 2003; Norcross et al., 2005). Later, the chapter describes integrative cognitive behavioral therapies. 👁

Therapists and Therapeutic Settings

When psychological problems arise, most people initially seek out informal counselors who operate in familiar settings. Many

....

👁 **Watch** the **Video** *The Basics, Part 1: Living With Disorder* on **MyPsychLab**

👁 **Watch** the **Video** *The Basics, Part 2: Therapies in Action* on **MyPsychLab**

biomedical therapy Treatment for a psychological disorder that alters brain functioning with chemical or physical interventions such as drug therapy, surgery, or electroconvulsive therapy.

psychotherapy Any of a group of therapies, used to treat psychological disorders, that focus on changing faulty behaviors, thoughts, perceptions, and emotions that may be associated with specific disorders.

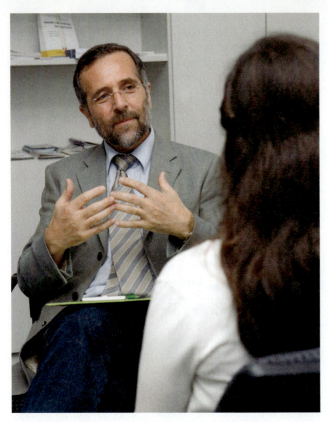

Why do many psychotherapists integrate different theoretical approaches in their clinical practices?

people turn to family members, close friends, personal physicians, lawyers, or favorite teachers for support, guidance, and counsel. Those with religious affiliations may seek help from a clergy member. Others get advice and a chance to talk by opening up to bartenders, salesclerks, cabdrivers, or other people willing to listen. In our society, these informal therapists carry the bulk of the daily burden of relieving frustration and conflict. When problems are limited in scope, informal therapists can often help.

Although more people seek out therapy now than in the past, people usually turn to trained mental health professionals only when their psychological problems become severe or persist for extended periods of time. When they do, they can turn to several types of therapists. ◉

A **clinical social worker** is a mental health professional whose specialized training in a school of social work prepares him or her to work in collaboration with psychiatrists and clinical psychologists. Unlike many psychiatrists and psychologists, these counselors are trained to consider the social contexts of people's problems, so these practitioners may also involve other family members in the therapy or at least become acquainted with clients' homes or work settings.

A **pastoral counselor** is a member of a religious group who specializes in the treatment of psychological disorders. Often, these counselors combine spirituality with practical problem solving.

A **clinical psychologist** is required to have concentrated his or her graduate school training in the assessment and treatment of psychological problems, completed a supervised internship in a clinical setting, and earned a PhD or PsyD.

These psychologists tend to have a broader background in psychology, assessment, and research than do psychiatrists.

A **counseling psychologist** also typically has obtained a PhD or PsyD. He or she usually provides guidance in areas such as vocation selection, school problems, drug abuse, and marital conflict. Often, these counselors work in community settings related to the problem areas—within a business, a school, a prison, the military service, or a neighborhood clinic—and use interviews, tests, guidance, and advising to help individuals solve specific problems and make decisions about future options.

A **psychiatrist** must have completed all medical school training for an MD degree and also have undergone some postdoctoral specialty training in mental and emotional disorders. Psychiatrists are largely trained in the biomedical basis of psychological problems.

A **psychoanalyst** is a therapist with either an MD or a PhD degree who has completed specialized postgraduate training in the Freudian approach to understanding and treating mental disorders.

These different types of therapists practice in many settings: hospitals, clinics, schools, and private offices. Some humanistic therapists prefer to conduct group sessions in their homes to work in a more natural environment. Community-based therapies, which take the treatment to the client, may operate out of local storefronts or houses of worship. Finally, some therapists work with clients in the life setting that is associated with their problem. For example, they work in airplanes with clients who suffer from flying phobias or in shopping malls with people who have social phobias. In recent years, psychotherapists have also begun to provide mental health care using the Internet. The *Critical Thinking in Your Life* box on page 442 explores that topic.

People who enter therapy are usually referred to as either patients or clients. The term **patient** is used by professionals who take a biomedical approach to the treatment of psychological problems. The term **client** is used by professionals who

⊙ **Watch** the **Video** *Classic Footage of Carl Rogers on Role of a Therapist* on **MyPsychLab**

clinical social worker A mental health professional whose specialized training prepares him or her to consider the social context of people's problems.

pastoral counselor A member of a religious order who specializes in the treatment of psychological disorders, often combining spirituality with practical problem solving.

clinical psychologist An individual who has earned a doctorate in psychology and whose training is in the assessment and treatment of psychological problems.

counseling psychologist Psychologist who specializes in providing guidance in areas such as vocational selections, school problems, drug abuse, and marital conflict.

psychiatrist An individual who has obtained an MD degree and also has completed postdoctoral specialty training in mental and emotional disorders; a psychiatrist may prescribe medications for the treatment of psychological disorders.

psychoanalyst An individual who has earned either a PhD or an MD degree and has completed postgraduate training in the Freudian approach to understanding and treating mental disorders.

patient The term used by those who take a biomedical approach to the treatment of psychological problems to describe the person being treated.

client The term used by clinicians who think of psychological disorders as problems in living, and not as mental illnesses, to describe those being treated.

think of psychological disorders as "problems in living" and not as mental illnesses. I will use the preferred term for each approach: *patient* for biomedical and psychoanalytic therapies and *client* for other therapies.

Diversity Issues in Psychotherapy

An important goal for clinicians is to provide relief to all people who suffer from psychological disorders. However, that goal is complicated by cultural and gender diversity. To begin, not all cultural groups are equally likely to undergo treatment (Wang et al., 2005; Youman et al., 2010). For example, Caucasians in the United States are more likely to seek treatment than are members of minority groups. An important part of that difference is unequal access to both physical and mental health care. However, cultural norms also affect the extent to which people seek psychological care (Snowden & Yamada, 2005). For example, research suggests that African Americans are more likely to interpret mental illness as physical illness. They are, therefore, less likely to obtain psychotherapy when it would be appropriate (Bolden & Wickes, 2005).

Another diversity issue arises once people actually seek therapy: The important question becomes whether particular therapies are equally effective across all cultural groups. In fact, researchers have begun to demonstrate the importance of *culturally adapted psychotherapy,* which is defined as "the systematic modification of a [treatment] . . . to consider language, culture, and context in such a way that it is compatible with the client's cultural patterns, meanings, and values" (Bernal et al., 2009, p. 362). Recall from Chapter 13 that cultures differ with respect to their sense of self. One cultural adaptation would be to modify forms of psychotherapy to recognize when people come from individualistic or collectivist cultures (Smith et al., 2011). Recent research suggests that culturally adapted psychotherapy have more therapeutic value than standard therapies for members of racial and ethnic minority groups (Benish et al., 2011; Smith et al., 2011). More research is required to confirm these early results.

Similarly, more research is needed to assess the extent to which men and women benefit from the same therapies (Sigmon et al., 2007). Earlier chapters reviewed gender differences in the prevalence of psychological disorders. Recall, for example, that women experience more eating disorders than men do. For that reason, most psychotherapies for eating disorders have been developed for girls and young women (Greenberg & Schoen, 2008). Researchers must determine to what extent the same approaches are effective for men. Similarly, researchers must determine whether therapies that clinicians originated to treat men must be modified to bring relief to women.

A final diversity issue arises with respect to the training of psychotherapists: Therapists must be prepared to provide treatments that are sensitive to cultural differences. Researchers have suggested, in particular, that therapists must have *cultural competence* (Imel et al., 2011). Cultural competence has been defined as having three components (Sue, 2006, p. 238):

- "Cultural awareness and beliefs: Provider's sensitivity to her or his personal values and biases and how these may influence perceptions of the client, client's problem, and the counseling relationship."
- "Cultural knowledge: Counselor's knowledge of the client's culture, worldview, and expectations for the counseling relationship."

Treatment of mental disorders in the 18th century focused on banishing "ill humors" from the body. Shown here is the "tranquilizing chair" advocated by Philadelphia physician Benjamin Rush. Why did attitudes toward the treatment of people with mental illness change?

- "Cultural skills: Counselor's ability to intervene in a manner that is culturally sensitive and relevant."

Research suggests that therapists with greater cultural competence also have better therapeutic outcomes with patients and clients from diverse groups (Worthington et al., 2008).

Before we turn to contemporary therapies and therapists in more detail, let's first consider the historical contexts in which treatment of the mentally ill was developed.

Historical Perspectives on Institutional Treatment

What kind of treatment might you have received in past centuries if you were suffering from psychological problems? For much of history, chances are the treatment would not have helped and could even have been harmful. This review will trace the institutional treatment of psychological disorders to the 21st century, in which **deinstitutionalization**—the practice of moving people from psychiatric hospitals to other venues for treatment—has become an important issue.

History of Treatment Population increases and migration to big cities in 14th-century Western Europe created unemployment and social alienation. These conditions led to poverty, crime, and psychological problems. Special institutions were

....

deinstitutionalization The movement to treat people with psychological disorders in the community rather than in psychiatric hospitals.

soon created to warehouse society's three emerging categories of so-called misfits: the poor, criminals, and the mentally disturbed.

In 1403, a London hospital—St. Mary of Bethlehem—admitted its first patient with psychological problems. For the next 300 years, mental patients of the hospital were chained, tortured, and exhibited to an admission-paying public. Over time, a mispronunciation of Bethlehem—*bedlam*—came to mean chaos because of the horrible confusion reigning in the hospital and the dehumanized treatment of patients there (Foucault, 1975).

It wasn't until the late 18th century that the perception of psychological problems as mental illness emerged in Europe. In 1792, the French physician Philippe Pinel received permission from the government installed after the French Revolution to remove the chains from some of the inmates in mental hospitals. In the United States, psychologically disturbed individuals were confined for their own protection and for the safety of the community, but they were given no treatment. However, by the mid-1800s, when psychology as a field of study was gaining some credibility and respectability, "a cult of curability" emerged throughout the country. Spurred on by her firsthand experience working in prison settings, **Dorothea Dix** (1802–1887) labored continuously between 1841 and 1881 to improve the physical treatment of the mentally ill.

In the late 19th and early 20th centuries, many people argued that mental illness arose from the environmental stresses brought on by the turmoil of newly developing cities. To ease those stresses, the disturbed were confined to asylums in rural areas, far from the stress of the city, not only for protection but also for treatment (Rothman, 1971). Unfortunately, many of the asylums that were built became overcrowded. The humane goal of alleviating mental illness was replaced with the pragmatic goal of containing strange people in remote places. These large understaffed state mental hospitals became little more than human warehouses for disturbed individuals (Scull, 1993). Beginning in the 1960s, reformers began to agitate against these warehouses, in favor of the deinstitutionalization of at least those mental patients who could thrive with outpatient treatment and appropriate community supports. Unfortunately, as we'll see next, many deinstitutionalized patients do not obtain adequate assistance in their communities.

Deinstitutionalization and Homelessness In 1986, 41 percent of the money spent for mental health treatment in the United States was spent on inpatient care; in recent years that figure has fallen to 24 percent (Mark et al., 2007). This change reflects the process of deinstitutionalization: Many people with disorders are now treated outside of hospital settings. Deinstitutionalization arose from both social forces (that is, the movement against the warehousing of people with mental illness) and genuine advances in treatment. For example, this chapter later describes drug treatments that allowed people with schizophrenia to live outside of institutions.

Many people have been deinstitutionalized with the assumption that they will receive mental health care in some other setting. Unfortunately, that hasn't always proven to be the case. In fact, many people who leave psychiatric hospitals are not able to cope with their psychological disorders once they are in the community. This reality has led to circumstances that have sometimes been called the "revolving door": People leave institutions for only brief periods of time before needing help once again. For example, one large-scale study looked

at 29,373 patients with schizophrenia who had been released from hospitals. The researchers found that 42.5 percent of the patients were readmitted within 30 days of their initial release (Lin et al., 2006). More generally, approximately 40 to 50 percent of psychiatric patients are readmitted within one year after their initial discharge (Bridge & Barbe, 2004). In many of these cases, individuals left institutional care with the symptoms of their psychological disorders at a level that could have allowed them to function in the outside world. Unfortunately, people often do not have appropriate community or personal resources to adhere to treatment outside the structure provided by an institution. In that sense, the problem is not so much with deinstitutionalization as it is with the lack of community resources outside the institutions.

When people cannot get adequate mental health care, they are often unable to maintain jobs or provide for their daily needs. For that reason, a large number of people with mental illnesses like schizophrenia or major depressive disorder become homeless. For example, in one sample of 1,562 chronically homeless people in Philadelphia, 53 percent had been diagnosed with serious mental illnesses (Poulin et al., 2010). The association of homelessness and mental illness also holds outside the United States. In a sample of 32,711 homeless people in Denmark, 62 percent of the men and 58 percent of the women had received diagnoses of psychiatric disorders (Nielsen et al., 2011). Even when people with serious mental illness are not homeless, ongoing mental health issues can cause substantial problems. For example, researchers examined the rate at which people with severe mental illness are the victims of violent crime such as robbery or assault (Teplin et al., 2005). In a sample of 936 men and women, 25.3 percent had experienced a violent crime—a rate 11 times higher than for individuals in the general population. The researchers suggested that the individuals' mental illnesses may prevent them from recognizing risk or appropriately protecting themselves.

As the chapter reviews the range of therapies clinicians have devised to alleviate distress, it's important for you to recognize that many people do not have adequate access to mental health care.

Stop *and* Review

① What are the primary goals of the therapeutic process?
② What special training does a psychoanalyst have?
③ Why is cultural competence important for therapists?
④ With respect to deinstitutionalization, what is meant by the "revolving door"?

✓ **Study** and **Review** on **MyPsychLab**

PSYCHODYNAMIC THERAPIES

Psychodynamic therapies assume that a patient's problems have been caused by the psychological tension between unconscious impulses and the constraints of his or her life situation. These therapies locate the core of the disorder inside the disturbed person. This section reviews the origins of this approach in the work of Sigmund Freud and his followers. We will then consider how contemporary clinicians use psychodynamic therapies.

Freudian Psychoanalysis

Psychoanalysis, as developed by Sigmund Freud, is an intensive and prolonged technique for exploring unconscious motivations and conflicts in neurotic, anxiety-ridden individuals. As you saw in earlier chapters, Freudian theory views anxiety disorders as inabilities to resolve adequately the inner conflicts between the unconscious, irrational impulses of the *id* and the internalized social constraints imposed by the *superego*. The goal of psychoanalysis is to establish intrapsychic harmony that expands awareness of the forces of the *id*, reduces overcompliance with the demands of the *superego*, and strengthens the role of the *ego*.

Of central importance to a therapist is to understand the way a patient uses the process of *repression* to handle conflicts. Symptoms are considered to be messages from the unconscious that something is wrong. A psychoanalyst's task is to help a patient bring repressed thoughts to consciousness and to gain *insight* into the relationship between the current symptoms and the repressed conflicts. In this psychodynamic view, therapy succeeds and patients recover when they are "released from repression" established in early childhood. Because a central goal of a therapist is to guide a patient toward discovering insights into the relationships between present symptoms and past origins, psychodynamic therapy is often called **insight therapy.**

Traditional psychoanalysis is an attempt to reconstruct long-standing repressed memories and then work through painful feelings to an effective resolution. The psychodynamic approach includes several techniques to bring repressed conflicts to consciousness and to help a patient resolve them (Luborsky & Barrett, 2006). These techniques include free association, analysis of resistance, dream analysis, and analysis of transference and countertransference.

Free Association and Catharsis The principal procedure used in psychoanalysis to probe the unconscious and release repressed material is called **free association.** A patient, sitting comfortably in a chair or lying in a relaxed position on a couch, lets his or her mind wander freely and gives a running account of thoughts, wishes, physical sensations, and mental images. The patient is encouraged to reveal every thought or feeling, no matter how unimportant it may seem.

Freud maintained that free associations are *predetermined*, not random. The task of an analyst is to track the associations to their source and identify the significant patterns that lie beneath the surface of what are apparently just words. The patient is encouraged to express strong feelings, usually toward authority figures, that have been repressed for fear of punishment or retaliation. Any such emotional release, by this or other processes within the therapeutic context, is called **catharsis.**

Resistance A psychoanalyst attaches particular importance to subjects that a patient does *not* wish to discuss. At some time during the process of free association, a patient will show **resistance**—an inability or unwillingness to discuss certain ideas, desires, or experiences. Such resistances are conceived of as *barriers* between the unconscious and the conscious. This material is often related to an individual's sexual life (which includes all things pleasurable) or to hostile, resentful feelings toward parents.

Why is psychoanalytic therapy, originally practiced in Freud's study, often called the "talking cure"?

When the repressed material is finally brought into the open, a patient generally claims that it is unimportant, absurd, irrelevant, or too unpleasant to discuss. The therapist believes the opposite. Psychoanalysis aims to break down resistances and enable the patient to face these painful ideas, desires, and experiences.

Dream Analysis Psychoanalysts believe that dreams are an important source of information about a patient's unconscious motivations. When a person is asleep, the superego is presumably less on guard against the unacceptable impulses originating in the id, so a motive that cannot be expressed in waking life may find expression in a dream. In analysis, dreams are assumed to have two kinds of content: *manifest* (openly visible) content that people remember upon awakening and *latent* (hidden) content—the actual motives that are seeking expression but are so painful or unacceptable that they are expressed in disguised or symbolic form. Therapists attempt to uncover these hidden motives by using **dream analysis,** a therapeutic technique that examines the content of a person's dreams to discover the underlying or disguised motivations and symbolic meanings of significant life experiences and desires.

Transference and Countertransference During the course of the intensive therapy of psychoanalysis, a patient usually develops an emotional reaction toward the therapist. Often, the therapist is identified with a person who has been at the center of an emotional conflict in the past—most often a parent or a lover.

....

psychoanalysis The form of psychodynamic therapy developed by Freud; an intensive prolonged technique for exploring unconscious motivations and conflicts in neurotic, anxiety-ridden individuals.

insight therapy A technique by which the therapist guides a patient toward discovering insights between present symptoms and past origins.

free association The therapeutic method in which a patient gives a running account of thoughts, wishes, physical sensations, and mental images as they occur.

catharsis The process of expressing strongly felt but usually repressed emotions.

resistance The inability or unwillingness of a patient in psychoanalysis to discuss certain ideas, desires, or experiences.

dream analysis The psychoanalytic interpretation of dreams used to gain insight into a person's unconscious motives or conflicts.

Table 15.1 • Excerpt from a Session with a Psychodynamic Therapist

Sara [angrily]: I can't connect with you anymore [after two years of twice-a-week treatment]—you don't seem to listen and, anyway, I have nothing to say. I think that after all this time I should have changed, but I'm still distant from my daughter, she still has problems, and she's still in therapy. I want to end this therapy. . . .

Therapist: What's happening now has so much to do with your fantasies about the adoption and your feelings about how your mother could have let you be adopted. Right now, I seem to be standing in for her.

Sara: I do hate you. How can you take a week off? You are leaving me—just like she did. How do I know you'll come back? She never came back—how could she have left me? And here I am, a crying, clinging baby and you'll leave me.

From Hall, J. S. (2004). Roadblocks on the journey of psychotherapy. Lanham, MD: Jason Aronson, pp. 73–74. Reprinted by permission.

This emotional reaction is called **transference.** Transference is called *positive transference* when the feelings attached to the therapist are those of love or admiration and *negative transference* when the feelings consist of hostility or envy. Often, a patient's attitude is ambivalent, including a mixture of positive and negative feelings. An analyst's task in handling transference is a difficult one because of the patient's emotional vulnerability; however, it is a crucial part of treatment. A therapist helps a patient to interpret the present transferred feelings by understanding their original source in earlier experiences and attitudes. Please take a moment to read **Table 15.1**, which provides an excerpt from a therapy session (Hall, 2004, pp. 73–74). The patient was adopted as a child. You can see how Sara's feelings of abandonment have been transferred from her birth mother to her therapist.

Personal feelings are also at work in a therapist's reactions to a patient. **Countertransference** refers to what happens when a therapist comes to like or dislike a patient because the patient is perceived as similar to significant people in the therapist's life. In working through countertransference, a therapist may discover some unconscious dynamics of his or her own. The therapist becomes a "living mirror" for the patient and the patient, in turn, for the therapist. If the therapist fails to recognize the operation of countertransference, the therapy may not be as effective (Hayes et al., 2011). Because of the emotional intensity of this type of therapeutic relationship and the vulnerability of the patient, therapists must be on guard about crossing the boundary between professional caring and personal involvement with their patients. The therapy setting is obviously one with an enormous power imbalance that must be recognized, and honored, by the therapist.

Later Psychodynamic Therapies

Freud's followers retained many of his basic ideas but modified certain of his principles and practices. In general, these therapists place more emphasis than Freud did on: (1) a patient's *current* social environment (less focus on the past); (2) the continuing influence of life experiences (not just childhood conflicts); (3) the role of social motivation and interpersonal relations of love (rather than of biological instincts and selfish concerns); (4) the significance of ego functioning and development of the self-concept (less on the conflict between id and superego).

In Chapter 13 we noted two other prominent theorists, Carl Jung and Alfred Adler. To get a flavor of more contemporary psychodynamic approaches, here we consider the work of Harry Stack Sullivan and of Melanie Klein (see Ruitenbeek, 1973, for a look at other members of the Freudian circle).

Harry Stack Sullivan (1953) felt that Freudian theory and therapy did not recognize the importance of social relationships and a patient's needs for acceptance, respect, and love. Mental disorders, he insisted, involve not only traumatic intrapsychic processes but also troubled interpersonal relationships and even strong societal pressures. Anxiety and other mental ills arise out of insecurities in relations with parents and significant others. Therapy based on this interpersonal view involves observing a *patient's feelings* about the *therapist's attitudes.* The therapeutic interview is seen as a social setting in which each party's feelings and attitudes are influenced by the other's.

Melanie Klein (1975) defected from Freud's emphasis on the Oedipus conflict as the major source of psychopathology. Instead of oedipal sexual conflicts as the most important organizing factors of the psyche, Klein argued that a *death instinct* preceded sexual awareness and led to an innate aggressive impulse that was equally important in organizing the psyche. She contended that the two fundamental organizing forces in the psyche are aggression and love, where love *unites* and aggression *splits* the psyche. On Klein's view, conscious love is connected to remorse over destructive hate and potential violence toward those we love. Thus Klein explained, "one of

In what ways did the theories of Melanie Klein and Sigmund Freud differ?

---

transference The process by which a person in psychoanalysis attaches to a therapist feelings formerly held toward some significant person who figured into past emotional conflict.

countertransference Circumstances in which a psychoanalyst develops personal feelings about a client because of perceived similarity of the client to significant people in the therapist's life.

Psychology in Your Life

ARE LIVES HAUNTED BY REPRESSED MEMORIES?

In December 1969, a patrolman found the lifeless body of 8-year-old Susan Nason. For 20 years, no one knew who had murdered her. Then, in 1989, Susan's friend Eileen Franklin-Lipsker contacted county investigators. Eileen reported that, with the help of psychotherapy, she had recalled a long-repressed memory of witnessing her father, George Franklin, sexually assault Susan and then bludgeon her to death with a rock (Marcus, 1990; Workman, 1990). This testimony was sufficient to have George Franklin convicted of first-degree murder. Over time, Franklin was released as strong doubts accumulated about the validity of his daughter's memories. Still, a jury had initially found the dramatic recovery of 20-year-old memories quite credible.

How, in theory, had these memories remained hidden for 20 years? The answer to this mystery finds its roots in Sigmund Freud's concept of repressed memories. As you'll recall, Freud (1923) theorized that some people's memories of life experiences become sufficiently threatening to their psychological well-being that the individuals banish the memories from consciousness—they repress them. Clinical psychologists are often able to help clients take control of their lives by interpreting disruptive life patterns as the consequences of repressed memories. But not all experiences of repressed memories remain in the therapist's office. After long intervals of time, individuals will sometimes make accusations about horrifying events, such as murders or childhood sexual abuse. Could these claims be real?

Clinicians worry that therapists who believe in repressed memories may, through the mechanisms of psychotherapy,

implant those beliefs in their patients (Lynn et al., 2003). Therapists who believe in repressed memories may instigate patients' efforts to find these memories—and verbally reward them when the "memories" come to light (de Rivera, 1997). In one study, researchers recruited 128 participants who all claimed that they had experienced childhood sexual abuse (Geraerts et al., 2007). A majority of the participants (71 of the 128) had continuous memories of the abuse. That is, there were no life periods in which they didn't recall the abuse. The other 57 participants had *discontinuous* memories; they believed that they had forgotten the abuse for some period of time. Of that group, 16 had recovered memories of abuse in therapy, whereas the other 41 had recovered the memories without any special prompting. The researchers sent interviewers into the field to try to find evidence to corroborate the participants' memories of abuse. This was possible for 45 percent of the participants with continuous memories and 37 percent of the participants who had recovered memories on their own. However, for participants who recovered memories during therapy the interviewers found 0 percent corroborating evidence.

This study confirms that some reports of recovered memories are based on real occurrences. However, the study also demonstrates the potential for processes of psychotherapy to lead people to create false memories. Belief in the recovery of repressed memories may provide a measurable benefit for patients in psychotherapy. Even so, patients must ensure that they are not passively accepting someone else's version of their life.

---

the great mysteries that all people face [is] that love and hate—our personal heaven and hell—cannot be separated from one another" (Frager & Fadiman, 1998, p. 135). Klein pioneered the use of forceful therapeutic interpretations of both aggressive and sexual drives in analytic patients.

In contemporary practice, psychodynamic therapists continue to draw upon the foundational concepts of Freud and his followers. Contemporary psychodynamic therapies have several distinctive features (Shedler, 2010). They emphasize patients' emotions and their moments of resistance; they emphasize the importance of past experiences on current reality. They also focus on interpersonal conflict. Against that background, individual therapists may put more or less emphasis on particular processes such as the interpretation of transference (Gibbons et al., 2008). Therapists also differ with respect to how active a role the therapist plays in interpreting the patient's life experiences. Finally, traditional psychoanalysis often takes a long time (several years at least, with as many as five sessions a week). It also requires introspective patients who are verbally fluent,

highly motivated to remain in therapy, and willing and able to undergo considerable expense. Newer forms of psychodynamic therapy are making therapy briefer in total duration.

An important goal of psychodynamic therapy is to provide patients with insights into the interpersonal conflicts that lie at the roots of their psychological disorders. Behavioral therapies, to which we now turn, focus their attention more directly on the maladaptive behaviors that define the disorders.

Stop *and* Review

① Why is psychodynamic therapy also known as insight therapy?
② What is transference?
③ What role did the death instinct play in Melanie Klein's theory?

✓ **Study** and **Review** on **MyPsychLab**

BEHAVIOR THERAPIES

Whereas psychodynamic therapies focus on presumed inner causes, behavior therapies focus on observable outer behaviors. Behavior therapists argue that abnormal behaviors are acquired in the same way as normal behaviors—through a learning process that follows the basic principles of conditioning and learning. Behavior therapies apply the principles of conditioning and reinforcement to modify undesirable behavior patterns associated with mental disorders.

The terms **behavior therapy** and **behavior modification** are often used interchangeably. Both refer to the systematic use of principles of learning to increase the frequency of desired behaviors and/or decrease that of problem behaviors. The range of deviant behaviors and personal problems that typically are treated by behavior therapy is extensive and includes fears, compulsions, depression, addictions, aggression, and delinquent behaviors. In general, behavior therapy works best with specific rather than general types of personal problems: It is better for a phobia than for unfocused anxiety.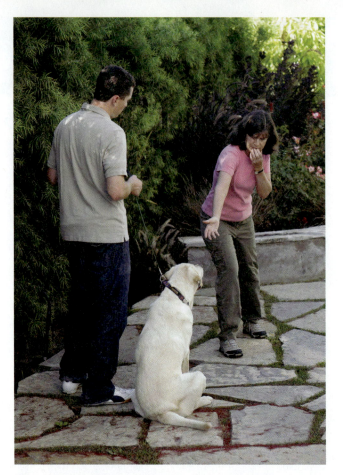

The therapies that have emerged from the theories of conditioning and learning are grounded in a pragmatic, empirical research tradition. The central task of all living organisms is to learn how to adapt to the demands of the current social and physical environment. When organisms do not learn how to cope effectively, their maladaptive reactions can be overcome by therapy based on principles of learning. The target behavior is not assumed to be a symptom of any underlying process. The symptom itself is the problem. Psychodynamic therapists predicted that treating only the outer behavior without confronting the true, inner problem would result in *symptom substitution,* the appearance of a new physical or psychological problem. However, no evidence has emerged to support the claim that when pathological behaviors are eliminated by behavior therapy, new symptoms are substituted (Tryon, 2008). "On the contrary, patients whose target symptoms improved often reported improvement in other, less important symptoms as well" (Sloane et al., 1975, p. 219).

Let's look at the different forms of behavior therapies that have brought relief to distressed individuals.

Counterconditioning

Why does someone become anxious when faced with a harmless stimulus, such as a spider, a nonpoisonous snake, or social contact? The behavioral explanation is that the anxiety arises due to the simple conditioning principles reviewed in

Why are many therapies for anxiety disorders known as exposure therapies?

Chapters 6 and 14: Strong emotional reactions that disrupt a person's life "for no good reason" are often conditioned responses that the person does not recognize as having been learned previously. In **counterconditioning,** a new response is conditioned to replace, or "counter," a maladaptive response. The earliest recorded use of behavior therapy followed this logic. **Mary Cover Jones** (1924) showed that a fear could be *unlearned* through conditioning. (Compare with the case of Little Albert in Chapter 6.)

> Her patient was Peter, a 3-year-old boy who, for some unknown reason, was afraid of rabbits. The therapy involved feeding Peter at one end of a room while the rabbit was brought in at the other end. Over a series of sessions, the rabbit was gradually brought closer until, finally, all fear disappeared and Peter played freely with the rabbit.

Following in Cover Jones's footsteps, behavior therapists now use several counterconditioning techniques, including systematic desensitization, implosion, flooding, and aversion therapy.

Exposure therapies The central component of **exposure therapy** is that individuals are made to confront the object or situation that causes anxiety. The therapeutic principle is that exposure permits counterconditioning—people learn to

----

Watch the **Video** *Overcoming Fears and Anxieties: Sue Mineka* on **MyPsychLab**

behavior therapy See behavior modification.

behavior modification The systematic use of principles of learning to increase the frequency of desired behaviors and/or decrease the frequency of problem behaviors.

counterconditioning A technique used in therapy to substitute a new response for a maladaptive one by means of conditioning procedures.

exposure therapy A behavioral technique in which clients are exposed to the objects or situations that cause them anxiety.

Table 15.2 • Hierarchy of Anxiety-Producing Stimuli for a Test-Anxious College Student (in order of increasing anxiety)

1. A month before an examination.
2. Two weeks before an examination.
3. A week before an examination.
4. Five days before an examination.
5. Four days before an examination.
6. Three days before an examination.
7. Two days before an examination.
8. One day before an examination.
9. The night before an examination.
10. The examination paper face down.
11. Awaiting the distribution of examination papers.
12. Before the unopened doors of the examination room.
13. In the process of answering an examination paper.
14. On the way to the university on the day of an examination.

remain relaxed in circumstances that once would have made them highly anxious. Individual exposure therapies differ with respect to the time course and circumstances in which people are exposed to their sources of anxiety.

For example, **Joseph Wolpe** (1958, 1973) observed that the nervous system cannot be relaxed and agitated at the same time because incompatible processes cannot be activated simultaneously. This insight was central to the *theory of reciprocal inhibition* that Wolpe applied to the treatment of fears and phobias. Wolpe taught his patients to *relax* their muscles and then to *imagine* visually their feared situation. They did so in gradual steps that moved from initially remote associations to direct images. Psychologically confronting the feared stimulus while being relaxed and doing so in a *graduated* sequence is the therapeutic technique known as **systematic desensitization.**

Desensitization therapy involves three major steps. First, the client identifies the stimuli that provoke anxiety and arranges them in a hierarchy ranked from weakest to strongest. For example, a student suffering from severe test anxiety constructed the hierarchy in **Table 15.2.** Note that she rated immediate anticipation of an examination (No. 14) as more stressful than taking the exam itself (No. 13). Second, the client is trained in a system of progressive deep-muscle relaxation. Relaxation training requires several sessions in which the client learns to distinguish between sensations of tension and relaxation and to let go of tension to achieve a state of physical and mental relaxation. Finally, the actual process of desensitization begins: The relaxed client vividly imagines the weakest anxiety stimulus on the list. If it can be visualized without discomfort, the client goes on to the next stronger one. After a number of sessions, the most distressing situations on the list can be imagined without anxiety.

Systematic desensitization represents a gradual course of exposure to stimuli that provoke anxiety. Therapists have explored a variety of other techniques, some of which bring about exposure with less delay. For example, in a technique known as *flooding*, clients agree to be put directly into the phobic situation. A person with claustrophobia is made to sit in a dark closet, and a child with a fear of water is put into a pool. Researchers successfully treated a 21-year-old student's

phobia of balloon pops by having him experience three sessions in which he endured hundreds of balloons being popped (Houlihan et al., 1993). In the third session, the student was able to pop the last 115 balloons himself. Another form of flooding therapy begins with the use of imagination. In this procedure, the client may listen to a tape that describes the most terrifying version of the phobic fear in great detail for an hour or two. Once the terror subsides, the client is then taken to the feared situation.

When exposure techniques were first created, therapists brought about exposure through mental imagery or actual contact. In recent years, clinicians have turned to virtual reality to provide exposure therapy (Powers & Emmelkamp, 2008). For example, people have been able to overcome a fear of flying through virtual experiences of flight (for example, sitting in an airplane, taking off, and landing) rather than venturing out to a physical airport (Rothbaum et al., 2006). As a second example, consider a study that used virtual reality therapy to treat a group of women with a phobia of cockroaches.

A team of researchers developed a virtual reality system that provided patients with the illusion that they were seeing cockroaches in their surrounding physical environment (Botella et al., 2010). For example, the system made it possible for patients to see cockroaches crawling on their hands. The system also allowed the therapists to manipulate features such as the number, size, and movement of the insects. Thus, it provided the flexibility the therapists needed to adapt the exposure therapy to suit the needs of each individual patient. The six patients in the study were systematically exposed to the virtual cockroaches in a single session that lasted, on average, just under two hours. After that single session of therapy, the patients showed considerable improvement in their ability, for example, to approach cockroaches. In follow-up assessments 3, 6, and 12 months after the original treatment, the patients continued to show substantial relief from their phobia.

Exposure therapies have proved to be highly effective for treating anxiety disorders. Virtual reality techniques hold the promise of providing powerful exposure experiences without the time and expense of venturing out into the real world.

Exposure therapy has also been used to combat obsessive-compulsive disorders. However, the therapy adds another component: *response prevention.* Not only are clients exposed to what they fear, but they are also prevented from performing the compulsive behaviors that ordinarily reduce their anxiety. Consider a study of 20 children and adolescents with OCD (Bolton & Perrin, 2008). Because each participant had different obsessions and compulsions, the treatment needed to be tailored to each individual. However, the core components remained the same: Each participant was exposed to the objects of his or her obsession while engaging in exercises to prevent the compulsive behaviors. This program of therapy brought about substantial relief.

systematic desensitization A behavioral therapy technique in which a client is taught to prevent the arousal of anxiety by confronting the feared stimulus while relaxed.

How might a behavior therapist use virtual reality exposure therapy to help a client overcome a fear of flying?

Imitation of models Another form of exposure therapy takes its inspiration from social-learning theory. Recall from Chapter 6 that social-learning theory predicts that individuals acquire responses through observation. Thus it should be the case that people with phobias should be able to unlearn fear reactions through imitation of models. For example, in treating a phobia of snakes, a therapist will first demonstrate fearless approach behavior at a relatively minor level, perhaps approaching a snake's cage or touching a snake. The client is aided, through demonstration and encouragement, to imitate the modeled behavior. Gradually, the approach behaviors are shaped so that the client can pick up the snake and let it crawl freely over him or her. At no time is the client forced to perform any behavior. Resistance at any level is overcome by having the client return to a previously successful, less threatening level of approach behavior.

The power of this form of **participant modeling** can be seen in research comparing this technique with symbolic modeling, desensitization, and a control condition. In *symbolic modeling therapy*, individuals who had been trained in relaxation techniques watched a film in which several models fearlessly handled snakes; they could stop the film and try to relax whenever a scene made them feel anxious. In the control condition, no therapeutic intervention was used. As you can see in **Figure 15.1**, participant modeling was clearly the most successful of these techniques. Snake phobia was eliminated in 11 of the 12 individuals in the participant modeling group (Bandura, 1970).

....

participant modeling A therapeutic technique in which a therapist demonstrates the desired behavior and a client is aided, through supportive encouragement, to imitate the modeled behavior.

aversion therapy A type of behavioral therapy used to treat individuals attracted to harmful stimuli; an attractive stimulus is paired with a noxious stimulus in order to elicit a negative reaction to the target stimulus.

contingency management A general treatment strategy involving changing behavior by modifying its consequences.

Aversion therapy The forms of exposure therapy we've considered so far help clients deal directly with stimuli that are not really harmful. What can be done to help those who are *attracted* to stimuli that *are* harmful? Drug addiction, sexual perversions, and uncontrollable violence are human problems in which deviant behavior is elicited by tempting stimuli. **Aversion therapy** uses counterconditioning procedures to pair these stimuli with strong noxious stimuli such as electric shocks or nausea-producing drugs. In time, the same negative reactions are elicited by the tempting stimuli, and the person develops an aversion that replaces his or her former desire.

For example, aversion therapy has been used with individuals who engage in *self-injurious behaviors,* such as hitting their heads or banging their heads against other objects. When an individual performs such a behavior, he or she is given a mild electric shock. This treatment effectively eliminates self-injurious behaviors in some, but not all, patients (van Oorsouw et al., 2008). Because aversion therapies may cause physical harm, ethical considerations require that therapists use them only when other therapies have failed (Prangnell, 2010).

Contingency Management

Counterconditioning procedures are appropriate when one response can be replaced with another. Other behavior modification procedures rely on the principles of operant conditioning that arose in the research tradition pioneered by B. F. Skinner. **Contingency management** refers to the general treatment strategy of changing behavior by modifying its consequences. The two major techniques of contingency management in behavior therapy are *positive reinforcement strategies* and *extinction strategies.*

Positive Reinforcement Strategies When a response is followed immediately by a reward, the response tends to be repeated and to increase in frequency over time. This central principle of operant learning becomes a therapeutic strategy when it is used to modify the frequency of a desirable response

FIGURE 15.1 Participant Modeling Therapy

The subject shown in the photo first watched a model make a graduated series of snake-approach responses and then repeated them herself. She eventually was able to pick up the snake and let it crawl about on her. The graph compares the number of approach responses subjects made before and after receiving participant modeling therapy (most effective) with the behavior of those exposed to two other therapeutic techniques and a control group.

Albert Bandura, from "Modeling Therapy." Reprinted by permission of Albert Bandura.

as it replaces an undesirable one. Dramatic success has been obtained from the application of positive reinforcement procedures to behavior problems.

You might recall from Chapter 6 a technique called *shaping* in which researchers reinforce successive approximations to a desired behavior. Consider how shaping was used to help smokers reduce the number of cigarettes they smoked (Lamb et al., 2007). The researchers measured the participants' breath carbon monoxide (BCO) to determine initial smoking habits. As the study unfolded, the participants received cash incentives if they were able to get their BCO below particular goal levels (which were set for each smoker). Those goals became more demanding over time—shaping participants toward the desired behavior of abstinence from smoking. Chapter 6 described *token economies,* in which desired behaviors (such as practicing personal care or taking medication) are explicitly defined, and token payoffs are given by institutional staff when the behaviors are performed. These tokens can later be exchanged for an array of rewards and privileges (Dickerson et al., 2005; Matson & Boisjoli, 2009). These systems of reinforcement are especially effective in modifying patients' behaviors regarding self-care, upkeep of their environment, and frequency of their positive social interactions.

In another approach, therapists differentially reinforce behaviors that are incompatible with the maladaptive behavior. This technique has been used successfully with individuals in treatment for drug addiction.

Researchers recruited 87 individuals who were seeking treatment for cocaine dependence into a 12-week study (Petry & Roll, 2011). All the participants received standard treatment of a series of counseling sessions that imparted strategies and skills for overcoming dependence. In addition to this standard treatment, the participants were given the opportunity to win prizes, contingent on negative urine specimens. To win the prizes, participants pulled slips of paper from a bowl. Half of the slips (50 percent) read "good job, try again." However, 44 percent of the slips provided $1 prizes and 6 percent provided $20 prizes. The bowl also had a single slip that resulted in a $100 prize. For the first negative specimen, participants got to pull one slip. For each subsequent negative specimen, they earned an extra one pull. A positive specimen reduced participants back to a single pull. Three months after completing this procedure, 26.9 percent of the participants were still abstinent from cocaine. Note that the actual amount each participant won was determined by the luck they had pulling slips from the bowl. The researchers found that the more prize money a participant had won, the more likely he or she was to be cocaine-free.

This study verifies that contingency management can be used successfully to treat drug dependence. Just for the chance to win prizes, drug users were able to get clean—and stay clean three months later. You might recognize the same philosophy at work here as the one that motivated the counterconditioning procedures described earlier: Basic principles of learning are used to increase the probability of adaptive behaviors.

Extinction Strategies Why do people continue to do something that causes pain and distress when they are capable of doing otherwise? The answer is that many forms of behavior have multiple consequences—some are negative, and some are positive. Often, subtle positive reinforcements keep a behavior going despite its obvious negative consequences. For example, children who are punished for misbehaving may continue to misbehave if punishment is the only form of attention they seem to be able to earn.

Extinction strategies are useful in therapy when dysfunctional behaviors have been maintained by unrecognized reinforcing circumstances. Those reinforcers can be identified through a careful situational analysis, and then a program can be arranged to withhold them in the presence of the undesirable response. When this approach is possible, and everyone in the situation who might inadvertently reinforce the person's behavior cooperates, extinction procedures work to diminish the frequency of the behavior and eventually to eliminate the behavior completely. Consider a classroom example. A boy with attention-deficit/hyperactivity disorder was causing problems for his teachers because he frequently engaged in disruptive off-task behaviors. Researchers discovered that the attention the teachers gave to the student when he engaged in off-task behaviors was positively reinforcing those behaviors (Stahr et al., 2006). When the teachers no longer paid attention to him when he behaved inappropriately, the student's behavior improved.

Generalization Techniques

An ongoing issue of concern for behavior therapists is whether new behavior patterns generated in a therapeutic setting will actually be used in the everyday situations faced by their clients (Kazdin, 1994). This question is important for all therapies, because any measure of treatment effectiveness must include maintenance of long-term changes that go beyond a therapist's couch, clinic, or laboratory.

When essential aspects of a client's real-life setting are absent from the therapy program, behavioral changes accomplished through therapy may be lost over time after therapy terminates. To prevent this gradual loss, it has become common practice to build generalization techniques into the therapeutic procedure itself. These techniques attempt to *increase* the similarity of target behaviors, reinforcers, models, and stimulus demands between therapy and real-life settings. For example, behaviors are taught that are likely to be reinforced naturally in a person's environment, such as showing courtesy or consideration. Rewards are given on a partial reinforcement schedule to ensure that their effect will be maintained in the real world, where rewards are not always forthcoming. Expectation of tangible extrinsic rewards is gradually *faded out* while social approval and more naturally occurring consequences, including reinforcing self-statements, are incorporated.

Behavior therapists, for example, used a fading procedure with a boy (aged 4 years, 10 months) who refused to drink milk (Tiger & Hanley, 2006). To get the boy to drink his milk, the therapists had his teacher mix a small amount of chocolate syrup into a glass of milk. With the chocolate syrup mixed in, the boy drank the milk. Over the next 48 meals, the teacher slowly decreased the amount of chocolate until the boy was offered only plain milk. At the end of this intervention, the boy consistently drank plain milk. This was also true at home, demonstrating generalization from the classroom to an additional setting.

Let's move now to cognitive therapies.

Stop *and* Review

① What is the basic principle of counterconditioning?
② What learning principle is at work when clinicians allow patients to earn prizes?
③ What is the goal of generalization techniques?

CRITICAL THINKING   Recall the study that used prizes to treat drug dependence. Why did the number of pulls from the prize bowl get set back to one when participants produced positive specimens?

✓•─[**Study** and **Review** on **MyPsychLab**

COGNITIVE THERAPIES

Cognitive therapy attempts to change problem feelings and behaviors by changing the way a client thinks about significant life experiences. The underlying assumption of such therapy is that abnormal behavior patterns and emotional distress start with problems in *what* people think (cognitive content) and *how* they think (cognitive process). Cognitive therapies focus on changing different types of cognitive processes and providing different methods of cognitive restructuring. Chapter 12 discussed some of these approaches as ways to cope with stress and improve health. This section describes two major forms of cognitive therapy: alteration of false belief systems and cognitive behavioral therapy.

Changing False Beliefs

Some cognitive behavior therapists have, as their primary targets for change, beliefs, attitudes, and habitual thought patterns. These cognitive therapists argue that many psychological problems arise because of the way people think about themselves in relation to other people and the events they face. Faulty thinking can be based on (1) unreasonable attitudes ("Being perfect is the most important trait for a student to have"), (2) false premises ("If I do everything they want me to, then I'll be popular"), and (3) rigid rules that put behavior on automatic pilot so that prior patterns are repeated even when they have not worked ("I must obey authorities"). Emotional distress is caused by cognitive misunderstandings and by failure to distinguish between current reality and one's imagination (or expectations).

Cognitive Therapy for Depression   A cognitive therapist helps a client to correct faulty patterns of thinking by substituting more effective problem-solving techniques. Aaron Beck (1976) has successfully pioneered cognitive therapy for the problem of depression. He states the formula for treatment in simple form: "The therapist helps the patient to identify his warped thinking and to learn more realistic ways to formulate his experiences" (p. 20). For example, depressed individuals may be instructed to write down negative thoughts about themselves, figure out why these self-criticisms are unjustified, and come up with more realistic (and less destructive) self-cognitions.

Beck believes that depression is maintained because depressed patients are unaware of the negative automatic thoughts that they habitually formulate, such as "I will never be as good as my brother"; "Nobody would like me if they really knew me"; and "I'm not smart enough to make it in this

....

cognitive therapy   A type of psychotherapeutic treatment that attempts to change feelings and behaviors by changing the way a client thinks about or perceives significant life experiences.

competitive school." A therapist then uses four tactics to change the cognitive foundation that supports the depression (Beck & Rush, 1989; Beck et al., 1979):

- Challenging the client's basic assumptions about his or her functioning.
- Evaluating the evidence the client has for and against the accuracy of automatic thoughts.
- Reattributing blame to situational factors rather than to the patient's incompetence.
- Discussing alternative solutions to complex tasks that could lead to failure experiences.

This therapy is similar to behavior therapies in that it centers on the present state of the client.

One of the worst side effects of being depressed is having to live with all the negative feelings and lethargy associated with depression. Becoming obsessed with thoughts about one's negative mood brings up memories of all the bad times in life, which worsens the depressive feelings. By filtering all input through a darkly colored lens of depression, depressed people see criticism where there is none and hear sarcasm when they listen to praise—further "reasons" for being depressed. Cognitive therapy has proved successful at arresting depression's downward spiral (Hollon et al., 2006).

Rational-Emotive Therapy One of the earliest forms of cognitive therapy was the **rational-emotive therapy (RET)** developed by **Albert Ellis** (1913–2007). RET is a comprehensive system of personality change based on the transformation of irrational beliefs that cause undesirable, highly charged emotional reactions, such as severe anxiety (Ellis, 1962, 1995; Windy & Ellis, 1997). Clients may have core values *demanding* that they succeed and be approved, *insisting* that they be treated fairly, and *dictating* that the universe be more pleasant.

Rational-emotive therapists teach clients how to recognize the "shoulds," "oughts," and "musts" that are controlling their actions and preventing them from choosing the lives they want. They attempt to break through a client's closed-mindedness by showing that an emotional reaction that follows some event is really the effect of unrecognized beliefs about the event. For example, failure to achieve orgasm during intercourse (event) is followed by an emotional reaction of depression and self-derogation. The belief that is causing the emotional reaction is likely to be "I am sexually inadequate and may be impotent because I failed to perform as expected." In therapy, this belief (and others) is openly disputed through rational confrontation and examination of alternative reasons for the event, such as fatigue, alcohol, false notions of sexual performance, or reluctance to engage in intercourse at that time or with that particular partner. This confrontation technique is followed by other interventions that replace dogmatic, irrational thinking with rational, situationally appropriate ideas.

Rational-emotive therapy aims to increase an individual's sense of self-worth and the potential to be self-actualized by getting rid of the system of faulty beliefs that block personal growth. As such, it shares much with humanistic therapies, which we consider later in the chapter.

Cognitive Behavioral Therapy

You are what you tell yourself you can be, and you are guided by what you believe you ought to do. This is a starting assumption

Suppose you were learning to knit. Assuming you wanted to get better at it over time, what would be the best internal message to give yourself about the activity?

of **cognitive behavioral therapy.** This therapeutic approach combines the cognitive emphasis on changing false beliefs with the behavioral focus on reinforcement contingencies in the modification of performance (Goldfried, 2003). Unacceptable behavior patterns are modified by *cognitive restructuring*—changing a person's negative self-statements into constructive coping statements.

A critical part of this therapeutic approach is the discovery by therapist and client of the way the client thinks about and expresses the problem for which therapy is sought. Once both therapist and client understand the kind of thinking that is leading to unproductive or dysfunctional behaviors, they develop new self-statements that are constructive and minimize the use of self-defeating ones that elicit anxiety or reduce self-esteem (Meichenbaum, 1977, 1985, 1993). **Table 15.3** on page 432 provides an example of how a session with a cognitive behavioral therapist might unfold. As you can see, the therapist helps the patient to reconsider the evidence that supports her belief that her best friend wants to end their relationship. In addition, as a homework assignment, the patient agrees to gather more evidence to explore other possibilities for her friend's behavior. ◉

Cognitive behavioral therapy has been used as a successful treatment for a variety of disorders. Let's see how it was used to treat clients with *compulsive buying disorder,* which is defined as "excessive and mostly senseless spending or excessive shopping impulses that cause marked distress, interfere with social or occupational functioning, and often result in financial problems" (Mueller et al., 2008, p. 1131).

....

◉ **Watch** the **Video** *Cognitive Behavioral Therapy for Schizophrenia* on **MyPsychLab**

rational-emotive therapy (RET) A comprehensive system of personality change based on changing irrational beliefs that cause undesirable, highly charged emotional reactions such as severe anxiety.

cognitive behavioral therapy A therapeutic approach that combines the cognitive emphasis on thoughts and attitudes with the behavioral emphasis on changing performance.

Table 15.3 • A Possible Session with a Cognitive Behavioral Therapist

Patient: I feel like my best friend, Marjorie, is rejecting me.

Therapist: I'm sure that's an unpleasant feeling. What makes you think she's rejecting you?

Patient: When we ran into each other at the mall yesterday, Marjorie barely said hello. She said, "How are you," and then raced off as fast as possible. It really didn't seem like she had any interest in talking to me.

Therapist: Hmm…, you've told me that you've been friends for a long time, right?

Patient: Yeah, but then why was she so rude to me yesterday? She made me feel awful.

Therapist: I can see why you'd feel upset. Can you think of other explanations for her behavior? Let's give that some thought.

Patient: Well, her mother has been sick, and she's moved back home to take care of her. Maybe she was feeling bad about shopping while her mother was home alone. That could be another reason.

Therapist: That could make sense. How could you find out if you're right?

Patient: I suppose I could call her to ask if she's doing okay? I could say that she looked stressed at the mall last night, and see if there's anything I could do to help her out.

Therapist: That sounds like a great way to get some information about your assumptions. Why don't you try that before our next session and then we can talk about what you learned?

Featured Study

Researchers randomly assigned 60 people with compulsive buying disorder to cognitive behavioral therapy or to a control group (Mueller et al., 2008). Participants in the treatment group had one therapy session a week over the course of 12 weeks. The therapy had several components (Burgard & Mitchell, 2000). One component of the therapy was for participants to identify the cues (such as social or psychological situations) in their lives that triggered buying behavior. Once participants identified these cues, the therapists worked with them to develop cognitive strategies to disrupt or avoid the cues' impact. Another component of the therapy was for participants to gain confidence that they could control their behavior. The researchers encouraged participants to undermine negative self-statements (for example, "I cannot control my urge to shop") by gathering evidence against such statements and by generating plans to achieve greater control. This program of therapy led to improvement both at the end of treatment and in follow-up assessment six months after treatment ended.

Note that the researchers needed the control group to demonstrate the effectiveness of the treatment (that is, members of the treatment group showed greater improvement than members of the control group). However, members of the control group were also offered treatment once the study came to an end.

As you can see from this example, cognitive behavioral therapy builds expectations of being effective. Therapists know that building these expectations increases the likelihood that people will behave effectively. Through setting attainable goals, developing realistic strategies for attaining them, and evaluating feedback realistically, you develop a sense of mastery and *self-efficacy* (Bandura, 1992, 1997). As you saw in Chapter 13, your sense of self-efficacy influences your perceptions, motivation, and performance in many ways. Self-efficacy judgments influence how much effort you expend and how long you persist in the face of difficult life situations (Bandura, 2006). Researchers have demonstrated the importance of self-efficacy in recovery from psychological disorders (Benight et al., 2008; Kadden & Litt, 2011). Consider a study of 108 women with binge eating disorder (Cassin et al., 2008). Women in the control group received a handbook that provided information about the disorder. Women in the treatment group received the handbook but also participated in a therapy session designed to raise self-efficacy. For example, each woman was encouraged to "recall past experiences in which she [had] shown mastery in the face of difficulties and challenges" (p. 421). Sixteen weeks after the treatment, 28 percent of women in the treatment group had refrained from binge eating versus only 11 percent in the control group. Within the treatment group, the women who abstained from binge eating had reported higher levels of self-efficacy. This study provides further evidence that cognitive behavioral approaches to therapy can bring relief.

Stop *and* Review

① What is the underlying assumption of cognitive therapy?

② With respect to rational-emotive therapy, what is the origin of highly charged emotional reactions?

③ Why is increased self-efficacy a goal for cognitive behavioral therapy?

CRITICAL THINKING Recall the study that assessed cognitive behavioral therapy for compulsive buying disorder. Why was it important to identify the cues that triggered buying behavior?

✓ **Study** and **Review** on **MyPsychLab**

HUMANISTIC THERAPIES

Humanistic therapies have at their core the concept of a whole person in the continual process of changing and of becoming. Although environment and heredity place certain restrictions, people always remain free to choose what they will become by creating their own values and committing to them through their own decisions. Along with this *freedom to choose*, however, comes the burden of responsibility. Because you are never fully aware of all the implications of your actions, you experience anxiety and despair. You also suffer from guilt over lost opportunities to achieve your full

How might volunteer work help people to maximize their human potential?

people with psychological disorders was extended to mentally healthy people who wanted to be more effective, more productive, and happier human beings.

Let's examine two types of therapies in the humanistic tradition: client-centered therapy and Gestalt therapy.

Client-Centered Therapy

As developed by Carl Rogers (1902–1987), *client-centered therapy* has had a significant impact on the way many different kinds of therapists define their relationships to their clients (Rogers, 1951, 1977). The primary goal of **client-centered therapy** is to promote the healthy psychological growth of the individual.

The approach begins with the assumption that all people share the basic tendency to self-actualize—that is, to realize their potential. Rogers believed that "it is the inherent tendency of the organism to develop all its capacities in ways which seem to maintain or enhance the organism" (1959, p. 196). Healthy development is hindered by faulty learning patterns in which a person accepts the evaluation of others in place of those provided by his or her own mind and body. A conflict between the naturally positive self-image and negative external criticisms creates anxiety and unhappiness. This conflict, or *incongruence,* may function outside of awareness, so that a person experiences feelings of unhappiness and low self-worth without knowing why.

The task of Rogerian therapy is to create a therapeutic environment that allows a client to learn how to behave to achieve self-enhancement and self-actualization. Because people are assumed to be basically good, the therapist's task is mainly to help remove barriers that limit the expression of this natural positive tendency. The basic therapeutic strategy is to recognize, accept, and clarify a client's feelings. This is accomplished within an atmosphere of *unconditional positive regard*—nonjudgmental acceptance and respect for the client. The therapist allows his or her own feelings and thoughts to be transparent to the client. In addition to maintaining this genuineness, the therapist tries to experience the client's feelings. Such total empathy requires that the therapist care for the client as a worthy, competent individual—not to be judged or evaluated but to be assisted in discovering his or her individuality (Meador & Rogers, 1979).

The emotional style and attitude of the therapist are instrumental in *empowering* the client to attend once again to the true sources of personal conflict and to remove the distracting influences that suppress self-actualization. Unlike practitioners of other therapies, who interpret, give answers, or instruct, the client-centered therapist is a supportive listener who reflects and, at times, restates the client's evaluative statements and feelings. Client-centered therapy strives to be *nondirective* by having the therapist merely facilitate the client's search for self-awareness and self-acceptance. **Table 15.4** on page 434 provides an excerpt from a session of client-centered therapy that captures these features (Rogers, 1951, p. 152).

Rogers believed that, once people are freed to relate to others openly and to accept themselves, individuals have the potential to lead themselves back to psychological health. This optimistic view and the humane relationship between

potential. Psychotherapies that apply the principles of this general theory of human nature attempt to help clients define their own freedom, value their experiencing selves and the richness of the present moment, cultivate their individuality, and discover ways of realizing their fullest potential (self-actualization).

In some cases, humanistic therapies also absorbed the lessons of *existentialist* approaches to human experience (May, 1975). This approach emphasizes people's ability to meet or be overwhelmed by the everyday challenges of existence. Existential theorists suggest that individuals suffer from *existential crises:* problems in everyday living, a lack of meaningful human relationships, and an absence of significant goals. A clinical version of existential theory, which integrates its various themes and approaches, assumes that the bewildering realities of modern life give rise to two basic kinds of human maladies. Depressive and obsessive syndromes reflect a retreat from these realities; sociopathic and narcissistic syndromes reflect an exploitation of these realities (Schneider & May, 1995).

The humanistic philosophy also gave rise to the **human-potential movement,** which emerged in the United States in the late 1960s. This movement encompassed methods to enhance the potential of the average human being toward greater levels of performance and greater richness of experience. Through this movement, therapy originally intended for

human-potential movement The therapy movement that encompasses all those practices and methods that release the potential of the average human being for greater levels of performance and greater richness of experience.

client-centered therapy A humanistic approach to treatment that emphasizes the healthy psychological growth of the individual based on the assumption that all people share the basic tendency of human nature toward self-actualization.

Table 15.4 • Excerpt from a Session with a Client-Centered Therapist

Alice: It seems—I don't know—It probably goes all the way back into my childhood. I've—for some reason I've—my mother told me that I was the pet of my father. Although I never realized it—I mean they never treated me as a pet at all. And other people always seemed to think I was sort of a privileged one in the family. But I never had any reason to think so. And as far I can see looking back on it now, it's just that the family let the other kids get away with more than they usually did me. And it seems for some reason to have held me to a more rigid standard than they did the other children.

Therapist: You're not so sure you were a pet in any sense, but more that the family situation seemed to hold you to pretty high standards. . . .

Alice: That's really the idea I've had. I think the whole business of my standards, or my values is one that I need to think about rather carefully, since I've been doubting for a long time whether I even have sincere ones.

Therapist: M-hm. Not sure whether you really have any deep values which you are sure of.

Reprinted by permission of Natalie Rogers, executor of the Estate of Carl Rogers.

therapist-as-caring-expert and client-as-person have influenced many practitioners.

Gestalt Therapy

Gestalt therapy focuses on ways to unite mind and body to make a person whole (recall the Gestalt school of perception, described in Chapter 4). Its goal of self-awareness is reached by helping clients express pent-up feelings and recognize unfinished business from past conflicts that is carried into new relationships and must be completed for growth to proceed. **Fritz Perls** (1893–1970), the originator of Gestalt therapy, asked clients to act out fantasies concerning conflicts and strong feelings and also to recreate their dreams, which he saw as repressed parts of personality. Perls said, "We have to *re-own* these projected, fragmented parts of our personality, and re-own the hidden potential that appears in the dream" (1969, p. 67).

In Gestalt therapy workshops, therapists encourage participants to regain contact with their "authentic inner voices" (Hatcher & Himelstein, 1996). Among the best known methods of Gestalt therapy is the *empty chair technique.* To carry out this technique, the therapist puts an empty chair near the client. The client is asked to imagine that a feeling, a person, an object, or a situation is occupying the chair. The client then "talks" to the chair's occupant. For example, clients would be encouraged to imagine their mother or father in the chair and reveal feelings they might otherwise be unwilling to reveal. The clients can then imagine those feelings in the chair to "talk" to the feelings about the impact they have on the clients' lives. This technique allows clients to confront and explore strong unexpressed feelings that may interfere with psychological well-being.

....

gestalt therapy Therapy that focuses on ways to unite mind and body to make a person whole.

Stop *and* Review

① What is the goal of the human-potential movement?
② In client-centered therapy, what is meant by unconditional positive regard?
③ In Gestalt therapy, what is the purpose of the empty chair technique?

✓—[**Study** and **Review** on **MyPsychLab**

GROUP THERAPIES

All the treatment approaches outlined thus far are primarily designed as one-to-one relationships between a patient or client and a therapist. Many people, however, now experience therapy as part of a group. There are several reasons why group therapy has flourished. Some advantages are practical. Group therapy is less expensive to participants and allows small numbers of mental health personnel to help more clients. Other advantages relate to the power of the group setting. The group (1) is a less threatening situation for people who have problems dealing on their own with authority; (2) allows group processes to be used to influence individual maladaptive behavior; (3) provides people with opportunities to observe and practice interpersonal skills within the therapy session; and (4) provides an analogue of the primary family group, which enables corrective emotional experiences to take place.

Group therapy also poses some special problems (Motherwell & Shay, 2005). For example, some groups establish a culture in which little progress can be made—members create a norm of passivity and limited self-disclosure. In addition, the effectiveness of groups can change dramatically when members leave or join the groups. Both arrivals and departures can change the delicate balance that allows groups to function well as a unit. Therapists who specialize in group therapy must take care to address these group dynamics.

Some of the basic premises of group therapies differ from those of individual therapy. The social setting of group therapies provides an opportunity to learn how one comes across to others, how the self-image that is projected differs from the one that is intended or personally experienced. In addition, the

What are some strengths of group therapies?

group provides confirmation that one's symptoms, problems, and "deviant" reactions are not unique but often are quite common. Because people tend to conceal from others negative information about themselves, it is possible for many people with the same problem to believe "It's only me." The shared group experience can help to dispel this pluralistic ignorance in which many share the same false belief about their unique failings. In addition, the group of peers can provide social support outside the therapy setting.

Couple and Family Therapy

Much group therapy consists of strangers coming together periodically to form temporary associations from which they may benefit. Couple and family therapy brings meaningful, existing units into a therapy setting.

Couple therapy for marital problems seeks to clarify the typical communication patterns of the partners and then to improve the quality of their interaction (Snyder & Balderrama-Durbin, 2012). By seeing a couple together, and often by videotaping and replaying their interactions, a therapist can help them appreciate the verbal and nonverbal styles they use to dominate, control, or confuse each other. Each party is taught how to reinforce desirable responding in the other and withdraw reinforcement for undesirable reactions. They are also taught nondirective listening skills to help the other person clarify and express feelings and ideas. Couple therapy has been shown to reduce marital crises and keep marriages intact (Christensen et al., 2006).

In *family therapy*, the client is a whole nuclear family, and each family member is treated as a member of a *system* of relationships (Nutt & Stanton, 2011). A family therapist works with troubled family members to help them perceive what is creating problems for one or more of them. Consider circumstances in which a child has been diagnosed with an anxiety disorder. Research suggests that certain parenting practices may, unfortunately, maintain the child's anxiety (McLeod et al., 2011). For example, if parents do not allow their children sufficient autonomy, the children may never gain enough self-efficacy to cope successfully with novel tasks. Under those circumstances, novel tasks will continue to provoke anxiety. Family therapy can focus on both the child's anxiety and the parent's behaviors that may maintain that anxiety.

> **Featured Study**
>
> *Researchers recruited 45 children, ages 9 to 13, to participate in a treatment study (Podell & Kendall, 2011). All the children had been diagnosed with an anxiety disorder (such as generalized anxiety disorder or social phobia). The children received a program of cognitive behavioral therapy that helped them recognize situations that provoked anxiety and develop skills to cope with the anxiety in those situations. The children's mothers and fathers also participated in the therapy sessions. The parents learned coping strategies alongside their children. In addition, the therapy attempted to modify parents' maladaptive behaviors with respect to the children's experience of anxiety and replace those behaviors with constructive responses. The researchers' analyses suggested that children whose parents were more engaged in the therapy sessions showed greater improvement.*

This study illustrates the importance of the family therapy approach. By engaging the whole family, the therapeutic intervention changed environmental factors that may have helped maintain the children's levels of anxiety.

Family therapy can reduce tensions within a family and improve the functioning of individual members by helping clients recognize the positive as well as the negative aspects in their relationships. **Virginia Satir** (1916–1988), a developer of family therapy approaches, noted that the family therapist plays many roles, acting as an interpreter and clarifier of the interactions that are taking place in the therapy session and as influence agent, mediator, and referee (Satir, 1967). Most family therapists assume that the problems brought into therapy represent *situational* difficulties between people or problems of social interaction, rather than *dispositional* aspects of individuals. These difficulties may develop over time as members are forced into or accept unsatisfying roles. Nonproductive communication patterns may be set up in response to natural transitions in a family situation—loss of a job, a child going to school, dating, getting married, or having a baby. The job of the family therapist is to understand the structure of the family and the many forces acting on it. Then he or she works with the family members to dissolve "dysfunctional" structural elements while creating and maintaining new, more effective structures (Fishman & Fishman, 2003).

Community Support Groups

A dramatic development in therapy has been the surge of interest and participation in *mutual support groups* and *self-help groups*. There are over 6,000 of these groups in the United States that focus on mental health issues; self-help groups report over 1 million members (Goldstrom et al., 2006). Also, 5 million people over the age of 12 attend self-help groups for alcohol and illicit drugs each year in the United States (Substance Abuse and Mental Health Services Administration, 2008a). These support group sessions are typically free, especially when they are not directed by a health-care professional, and they give people a chance to meet others with the same problems who are surviving and sometimes thriving. The self-help concept applied to community group settings was pioneered by Alcoholics Anonymous (AA), which was founded in 1935. However, it was the women's consciousness-raising movement of the 1960s that helped extend self-help beyond the arena of alcoholism. Now support groups deal with four basic categories of problems: addictive behavior, physical and mental disorders, life transition or other crises, and the traumas experienced by friends or relatives of those with serious problems. In recent years, people have begun to turn to the Internet as another venue for self-help groups (Barak et al., 2008; Finn & Steele, 2010). In general, Internet self-help groups engage the same range of issues as their physical counterparts (Goldstrom et al., 2006). However, the Internet provides a particularly important meeting place for people who suffer from conditions that limit mobility, such as chronic fatigue syndrome and multiple sclerosis: An inability to attend meetings physically no longer denies people the benefits of self-help.

Self-help groups appear to serve a number of functions for their members: For example, they provide people with a sense of hope and control over their problems, they engage social support for people's suffering, and they provide a forum for dispensing and acquiring information about disorders and treatments (Groh et al., 2008). Researchers have begun to demonstrate that self-help groups may help bring relief alongside other forms of therapy. For example, participation in self-help groups has the potential to reduce symptoms of depression (Pfeiffer et al., 2011). 👁

A valuable development in self-help is the application of group therapy techniques to the situations of terminally ill patients. The goals of such therapy are to help patients and their families live lives as fulfilling as possible during their illnesses, to cope realistically with impending death, and to adjust to the terminal illness (Kissane et al., 2004). One general focus of such support groups for the terminally ill is to help patients learn how to live fully until they "say goodbye."

Group therapies are the final examples of types of therapies that are based purely on psychological interventions. Let's now analyze how biomedical therapies work to alter the brain in order to affect the mind.

Stop *and* Review

① How does group therapy help inform participants about the uniqueness of their problems?
② What is a common goal for couple therapy?
③ Under what circumstances are Internet self-help groups particularly valuable?

CRITICAL THINKING   Recall the study that used family therapy to treat children's anxiety disorders. Why was it important to include both parents in the treatment?

✓—Study and Review on MyPsychLab

BIOMEDICAL THERAPIES

The ecology of the mind is held in delicate balance. When something goes wrong with the brain, we see the consequences in abnormal patterns of behavior and peculiar cognitive and emotional reactions. Similarly, environmental, social, or behavioral disturbances, such as drugs and violence, can alter brain chemistry and function. Biomedical therapies most often treat mental disorders as problems in the brain. This section describes four biomedical approaches: drug therapies, psychosurgery, electroconvulsive therapy (ECT), and repetitive transcranial magnetic stimulation (rTMS).

Drug Therapy

In the history of the treatment of mental disorders, nothing has rivaled the revolution created by the discovery of drugs that can calm anxious patients, restore contact with reality in withdrawn patients, and suppress hallucinations in psychotic

....

👁 **Watch** the **Video** *In the Real World: Self-Therapy* on **MyPsychLab**

👁 **Watch** the **Video** *Drugs Commonly Used to Treat Psychiatric Disorders* on **MyPsychLab**

psychopharmacology The branch of psychology that investigates the effects of drugs on behavior.

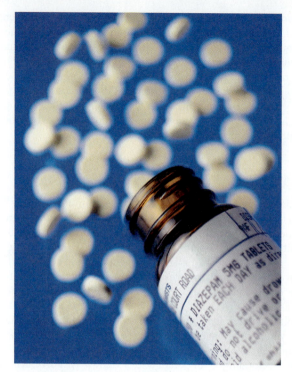

Why should people be cautious when they undertake drug therapies?

patients. This new therapeutic era began in 1953 with the introduction of tranquilizing drugs, notably *chlorpromazine*, into hospital treatment programs. Emerging drug therapies gained almost instant recognition and status as an effective way to transform patient behavior. **Psychopharmacology** is the branch of psychology that investigates the effects of drugs on behavior. Researchers in psychopharmacology work to understand the effect drugs have on some biological systems and the consequent changes in responding. 👁

The discovery of *drug therapies* had profound effects on the treatment of severely disordered patients. No longer did mental hospital staff have to act as guards, putting patients in seclusion or straitjackets; staff morale improved as rehabilitation replaced mere custodial care of the mentally ill (Swazey, 1974). Moreover, the drug therapy revolution had a great impact on the U.S. mental hospital population. Over half a million people were living in mental institutions in 1955, staying an average of several years. The introduction of chlorpromazine and other drugs reversed the steadily increasing numbers of patients. By the early 1970s, it was estimated that fewer than half the country's mental patients actually resided in mental hospitals; those who did were institutionalized for an average of only a few months.

The drugs that alleviate symptoms of various mental disorders are widely prescribed. As mental health care comes increasingly under the direction of health maintenance organizations (HMOs), cost-cutting practices are limiting the number of patients' visits to therapists for psychological therapies while substituting cheaper drug therapies. Researchers have documented great increases in prescriptions for drug therapies (Stagnitti, 2007). For that reason, it is important to understand the positive and negative features of drug therapies.

Three major categories of drugs are used today in therapy programs: *antipsychotic, antidepressant,* and *antianxiety* medications

Table 15.5 • Drug Therapies for Mental Illness

Disorder	Type of Therapy	Examples
Schizophrenia	Antipsychotic drug	chlorpromazine (Thorazine)
		haloperidol (Haldol)
		clozapine (Clozaril)
Depression	Tricyclic antidepressant	imipramine (Tofranil)
		amitriptyline (Elavil)
	Selective serotonin reuptake inhibitor	fluoxetine (Prozac)
		paroxetine (Paxil)
		sertraline (Zoloft)
	Serotonin and norepinephrine reuptake inhibitor	milnacipran (Dalcipran)
		venlafaxine (Effexor)
		phenelzine (Nardil)
	MAO inhibitor	isocarboxazid (Marplan)
Bipolar disorder	Mood stabilizer	lithium (Eshalith)
Anxiety disorders	Benzodiazepines	diazepam (Valium)
	Antidepressant drug	alprazolam (Xanax)
		fluoxetine (Prozac)

(see **Table 15.5**). As their names suggest, these drugs chemically alter specific brain functions that are responsible for psychotic symptoms, depression, and extreme anxiety.

Antipsychotic Drugs

Antipsychotic drugs alter symptoms of schizophrenia such as delusions, hallucinations, social withdrawal, and occasional agitation. Antipsychotic drugs work by reducing the activity of the neurotransmitter dopamine in the brain (Keshavan et al., 2011). The earliest drugs researchers developed, like *chlorpromazine* (marketed under the U.S. brand name *Thorazine*) and *haloperidol* (marketed as *Haldol*) blocked or reduced the sensitivity of dopamine receptors. Although those drugs functioned by decreasing the overall level of brain activity, they were not just tranquilizers. For many patients, they did much more than merely eliminate agitation. They also relieved or reduced the positive symptoms of schizophrenia, including delusions and hallucinations.

There were, unfortunately, negative side effects of these early antipsychotic drugs. Because dopamine plays a role in motor control, muscle disturbances frequently accompany a course of drug treatment. *Tardive dyskinesia* is a particular disturbance of motor control, especially of the facial muscles, caused by antipsychotic drugs. Patients who develop this side effect experience involuntary jaw, lip, and tongue movements.

Over time, researchers created a new category of drugs, which are called *atypical* antipsychotic drugs, that create fewer motor side effects. The first member of this category, *clozapine* (marketed as *Clozaril*), was approved in the United States in 1989. Clozapine both directly decreases dopamine activity and increases the level of serotonin activity, which inhibits the dopamine system. This pattern of activity blocks dopamine receptors more selectively, resulting in a lower probability of motor disturbance. Unfortunately, *agranulocytosis*, a rare disease in which the bone marrow stops making white blood cells, develops in 1 to 2 percent of patients treated with clozapine.

Researchers have created a range of atypical antipsychotic drugs that act in the brain in a fashion similar to clozapine. Large-scale studies suggest that each of these drugs is effective in relieving the symptoms of schizophrenia—but each also has the potential for side effects. For example, people who take these drugs are at risk for weight gain and diabetes (Rummel-Kluge et al., 2010; Smith et al., 2008). Unfortunately, the side effects often prompt patients to discontinue the drug therapy. The rate of relapse when patients go off the drugs is quite high—even by taking lower than recommended doses of the drugs, patients substantially increase the risk of increased symptoms (Subotnik et al., 2011). Patients who remain on the newer drugs such as clozapine still have about a 15 to 20 percent chance of relapse (Leucht et al., 2003). Thus antipsychotic drugs do not cure schizophrenia—they do not eliminate the underlying psychopathology. Fortunately, they are reasonably effective at controlling the disorder's most disruptive symptoms.

Antidepressant Drugs

Antidepressant drugs work by increasing the activity of the neurotransmitters norepinephrine and serotonin (Thase & Denko, 2008). Recall from Chapter 3 that nerve cells communicate by releasing neurotransmitters into synaptic clefts (the small gaps between neurons). *Tricyclics,* such as *Tofranil* and *Elavil,* reduce the reuptake (removal) of the neurotransmitters from the synaptic cleft (see **Figure 15.2**). Drugs such as *Prozac* are known as *selective serotonin reuptake inhibitors* (SSRIs) because they specifically reduce the reuptake of serotonin. The *monoamine oxidase* (MAO) *inhibitors* limit the action of the enzyme monoamine oxidase, which is responsible for breaking down (metabolizing) norepinephrine. When MAO is inhibited, more of the neurotransmitter is left available. Thus each type of drug leaves more neurotransmitters available to bring about neural signals.

Antidepressant drugs can be successful at relieving the symptoms of depression, although as many as 50 percent of patients will not show improvement (Hollon et al., 2002). In fact, for people with mild or moderate symptoms of depression, antidepressant drugs show little impact beyond placebos (pills containing no active medication); they provide more substantial benefits for people with severe depression (Fournier et al., 2010). Because antidepressant drugs affect important neurotransmitter systems in the brain, they have the potential

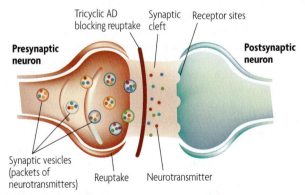

FIGURE 15.2 The Brain Mechanisms of Tricyclic Antidepressants

Tricyclic antidepressants block the reuptake of norepinephrine and serotonin so that the neurotransmitters remain in the synaptic cleft.

From Butcher, James N.; Mineka, Susan; Hooley, Jill M., *Abnormal Psychology,* 13th Ed., © 2007. Reprinted and electronically reproduced by permission of Pearson Education, Inc., Upper Saddle River, New Jersey.

for serious side effects. For example, people taking SSRIs such as Prozac may experience symptoms such as nausea, insomnia, nervousness, and sexual dysfunction. Tricyclics and MAO inhibitors may cause dry mouth, difficulty sleeping, and memory impairment. Research suggests that most of the major antidepressant drugs are roughly equal, across individuals, in their ability to bring relief (Hollon et al., 2002). For that reason, it is important for each individual to find the drug that yields the fewest side effects for him or her personally.

Researchers also continue to search for drugs that will help alleviate the symptoms of depression with fewer side effects. The newest class of drugs is called *serotonin and norepinephrine reuptake inhibitors,* or *SNRIs.* As that name suggests, these drugs, such as *Effexor* and *Dalcipran,* block the reuptake of both serotonin and norepinephrine. Clinical trials using these drugs have not found major differences in effectiveness with respect to SSRIs (Machado & Einarson, 2010). However, researchers still must determine which SNRIs function without serious side effects (Perahia et al., 2008).

In recent years, researchers have examined the important question of whether individuals—and, in particular, children and adolescents—who take antidepressant drugs are at greater risk for suicide. Although conclusions remain controversial, the majority of evidence supports the claim that drug treatment for depression does, in fact, yield a small increase in suicide risk (Möller et al., 2008). The important question is why this is the case. Some researchers believe that the drugs—in particular SSRIs—act in the brain to increase suicidal thoughts. Other researchers suggest that the small increase in suicide risk is an unfortunate consequence of the relief the drugs bring: Because major depressive order impairs motivation, people may be able to carry out suicidal behaviors only once their mental health starts to improve. For that reason, people who start drug treatment for major depressive disorder should receive consistent clinical attention to monitor for possible suicidal thoughts or intentions. Note also that many researchers have argued that, because antidepressant drugs bring relief from depression, they prevent many more suicides than they cause; their benefits outweigh their risks (Bridge et al., 2007).

Lithium salts have proven effective in the treatment of bipolar disorders (Thase & Denko, 2008). People who experience uncontrollable periods of hyperexcitement, when their energy seems limitless and their behavior extravagant and flamboyant, are brought down from their state of manic excess by doses of lithium. In addition, if people continue to take lithium when their symptoms are in remission, they are less likely to have recurrences of the disorder (Biel et al., 2007). However, for those people suffering from bipolar disorders who cycle frequently between manic episodes and depression, lithium appears to be less effective than other treatments such as the drug *valproate,* which was originally developed as a drug to prevent seizures (Cousins & Young, 2007).

Antianxiety Drugs Like antipsychotic and antidepressant drugs, antianxiety drugs generally have their effect by adjusting the levels of neurotransmitter activity in the brain. Different drugs are most effective at relieving different types of anxiety disorders (Hoffman & Mathew, 2008). Generalized anxiety disorder is best treated with a *benzodiazepine,* such as *Valium* or *Xanax,* which increases the activity of the neurotransmitter GABA. Because GABA regulates inhibitory neurons, increases in GABA activity decrease brain activity in areas of the brain

relevant to generalized anxiety responses. Panic disorders, as well as agoraphobia and other phobias, can be treated with antidepressant drugs, although researchers do not yet understand the biological mechanism involved. Obsessive-compulsive disorder, which may arise from low levels of serotonin, responds particularly well to drugs, like Prozac, that specifically affect serotonin function.

As with drugs that treat schizophrenia and mood disorders, benzodiazepines affect a major neurotransmitter system and therefore have a range of potential side effects (Macaluso et al., 2010). People who begin a course of therapy may experience daytime drowsiness, slurred speech, and problems with coordination. The drugs may also impair cognitive processes such as attention and memory (Stewart, 2005). Furthermore, people who begin treatment with benzodiazepines often experience drug tolerance—they must increase their dosage to maintain a stable effect (see Chapter 5). Discontinuation of treatment might also lead to withdrawal symptoms (Tan et al., 2011). Because of the potential for psychological and physical dependence, people should undertake treatment with antianxiety drugs in careful consultation with a health-care provider.

Psychosurgery

When other therapies have failed to bring about relief, doctors have sometimes considered direct interventions in the brain. **Psychosurgery** is the general term for surgical procedures performed on brain tissue to alleviate psychological disorders. Such intervention involves lesioning (severing) connections between parts of the brain or removing small sections of the brain. The best known form of psychosurgery is the **prefrontal lobotomy,** an operation that severs the nerve fibers connecting the frontal lobes of the brain with the diencephalon, especially those fibers of the thalamic and hypothalamic areas. The procedure was developed by neurologist **Egas Moniz** (1874–1955), who, in 1949, won a Nobel Prize for this treatment.

The original candidates for lobotomy were agitated patients with schizophrenia and patients who were compulsive and anxiety ridden. The effects of this psychosurgery were dramatic: A new personality emerged without intense emotional arousal and, thus, without overwhelming anxiety, guilt, or anger. However, the operation permanently destroyed basic aspects of human nature. The lobotomy resulted in inability to plan ahead, indifference to the opinions of others, childlike actions, and the intellectual and emotional flatness of a person without a coherent sense of self. (One of Moniz's own patients was so distressed by these unexpected consequences that she shot Moniz, partially paralyzing him.)

Because the effects of psychosurgery are permanent, its continued use is very limited. Clinicians consider psychosurgery only when other treatments have repeatedly failed. For example, one study evaluated the effectiveness of a procedure called a *cingulotomy,* in which surgeons create lesions in the

....

psychosurgery A surgical procedure performed on brain tissue to alleviate a psychological disorder.

prefrontal lobotomy An operation that severs the nerve fibers connecting the frontal lobes of the brain with the diencephalon, especially those fibers in the thalamic and hypothalamic areas; best known form of psychosurgery.

Electroconvulsive therapy has been very effective in cases of severe depression. Why does it remain controversial as a treatment?

limbic system structure called the cingulate gyrus (Shields et al., 2008). The 33 patients in the study had intractable major depression—they had failed to respond to four or more courses of drug treatment as well as other standard treatments. After the surgeries, 75 percent of the patients showed some relief from their symptoms. The cingulotomy procedure has also relieved the symptoms of patients with obsessive-compulsive disorder who were similarly unresponsive to drug treatments (Kim et al., 2003).

ECT and rTMS

Electroconvulsive therapy (ECT) is the use of electric shock applied to the brain to treat psychiatric disorders such as schizophrenia, mania, and, most often, depression. The technique consists of applying weak electric current to a patient's scalp until a seizure occurs. The strength of the current is adjusted to reflect seizure thresholds for particular patients (Kellner et al., 2010). The convulsion usually runs its course in 45 to 60 seconds. Patients are prepared for this traumatic intervention by sedation with a short-acting barbiturate and muscle relaxant, which renders the patient unconscious and minimizes the violent physical reactions.

Electroconvulsive therapy has proven quite successful at alleviating the symptoms of serious depression (Lisanby, 2007). ECT is particularly important because it works quickly. Typically, the symptoms of depression are alleviated in a three- or four-day course of treatment, as compared with the one- to two-week time window for drug therapies. Even so, most therapists hold ECT as a treatment of last resort. ECT is often reserved for emergency treatment for suicidal or severely malnourished, depressed patients and for patients who do not respond to antidepressant drugs or can't tolerate their side effects.

Although ECT is effective, it still remains controversial as a treatment. Scientific unease with ECT centers largely on the lack of understanding of how it works. Researchers have speculated that the treatment might rebalance neurotransmitters or hormones; they have also suggested that the repeated seizures might actually strengthen the brain (Keltner & Boschini, 2009). Much of the uncertainty remains because researchers cannot

ethically conduct experiments on human participants to provide definitive answers.

Critics have also worried about potential side effects of ECT. ECT produces temporary disorientation and a variety of cognitive deficits. For example, patients often suffer amnesia for events in the period of time preceding the treatment as well as difficulty forming new memories (Ingram et al., 2008). However, most patients recover from these deficits in the first few weeks after treatment. As a way of minimizing even short-term deficits, ECT is now often administered to only one side of the brain so as to reduce the possibility of speech impairment. Such unilateral ECT alleviates some of the cognitive consequences of the treatment and also remains an effective antidepressant (Fraser et al., 2008).

In recent years, researchers have explored an alternative to ECT called *repetitive transcranial magnetic stimulation (rTMS)*. As you might recall from Chapter 3, people who undergo rTMS receive repeated pulses of magnetic stimulation to the brain. As with ECT, researchers have not yet determined why rTMS can bring relief for major depressive disorder and other forms of psychopathology. However, evidence is mounting that rTMS can be just as effective as some antidepressant drugs (Schutter, 2008). Researchers are working to determine how variables such as the intensity of the magnetic stimulation affect rTMS's ability to bring relief (Daskalakis et al., 2008).

Stop *and* Review

① What advantages do atypical antipsychotic drugs have over early drug therapies for schizophrenia?
② What do SNRIs do in the brain?
③ What are some effects of prefrontal lobotomies?
④ What is the rTMS procedure?

✓— **Study** and **Review** on **MyPsychLab**

....

electroconvulsive therapy (ECT) The use of electroconvulsive shock as an effective treatment for severe depression.

TREATMENT EVALUATION AND PREVENTION STRATEGIES

Suppose you have come to perceive a problem in your life that you believe could be alleviated by interaction with a trained clinician. This chapter has mentioned a great variety of types of therapies. How can you know which one of them will work best to relieve your distress? How can you be sure that *any* of them will work? This section examines the projects researchers undertake to test the effectiveness of particular therapies and make comparisons between different therapies. The general goal is to discover the most efficient way to help people overcome distress. As you will see, this research has also identified some factors that are common to all successful therapy. We also consider briefly the topic of *prevention*: How can psychologists intervene in people's lives to prevent mental illness before it occurs?

Evaluating Therapeutic Effectiveness

British psychologist Hans Eysenck (1952) created a furor some years ago by declaring that psychotherapy does not work at all! He reviewed available publications that reported the effects of various therapies and found that patients who received no therapy had just as high a recovery rate as those who received psychoanalysis or other forms of insight therapy. He claimed that roughly two-thirds of all people with neurotic problems would recover spontaneously within two years of the onset of the problem.

Researchers met Eysenck's challenge by devising more accurate methodologies to evaluate the effectiveness of therapy. What Eysenck's criticism made clear was that researchers needed to have appropriate control groups. For a variety of reasons, *some* percentage of individuals in psychotherapy *does* improve without any professional intervention. This **spontaneous-remission effect** is one *baseline* criterion against which the effectiveness of therapies must be assessed. Simply put, doing something must be shown to lead to a greater percentage of improved cases than doing nothing.

Similarly, researchers generally try to demonstrate that their treatment does more than just take advantage of clients' own expectations of healing. You may recall the earlier discussions of *placebo* effects: In many cases, people's mental or physical health will improve because they expect that it will improve. The therapeutic situation helps bolster this belief by putting the therapist in the specific social role of *healer* (Frank & Frank, 1991). Although the placebo effects of therapy are an important

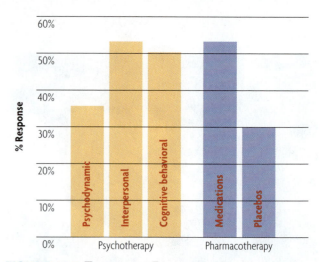

FIGURE 15.3 Treatment Evaluation for Depression

The figure displays the results from meta-analyses of treatments for depression. For each treatment, the figure presents the percentage of patients who typically respond to each category of treatment. For example, about 50 percent of patients taking antidepressant medication experience recognizable symptom relief, whereas 50 percent do not.

part of the therapeutic intervention, researchers typically wish to demonstrate that their specific form of therapy is more effective than a **placebo therapy** (a neutral therapy that just creates expectations of healing) (Hyland et al., 2007).

In recent years, researchers have evaluated therapeutic effectiveness using a statistical technique called meta-analysis. **Meta-analysis** provides a formal mechanism for detecting the general conclusions to be found in data from many different experiments. In many psychological experiments, the researcher asks, "Did most of my participants show the effect I predicted?" Meta-analysis treats experiments like participants. With respect to the effectiveness of therapy, the researcher asks, "Did most of the outcome studies show positive changes?" 👁

Consider **Figure 15.3**, which presents the results of meta-analyses of the research literature on treatments for depression (Hollon et al., 2002). The figure compares results for three types of psychotherapies and medications (averaged across different types of antidepressant drugs) to placebo treatments. The chapter earlier described psychodynamic and cognitive behavioral therapies. Interpersonal therapy focuses on a patient's current life and interpersonal relationships. As you can see, across all the studies reviewed in the meta-analyses that contributed to this figure, interpersonal therapy, cognitive behavioral therapy, and drug therapies had a consistently larger impact than did placebos. At least for treatment of depression, classic psychodynamic therapy did not fare well.

Note that these data reflect the impact of each type of treatment alone. Researchers have assessed the effectiveness of psychotherapy alone versus psychotherapy combined with drug therapy. One study found that combination therapy was most able to bring about full remission from chronic depression (Manber et al., 2008). Of participants who completed a course of treatment, 14 percent of the participants who received only drug therapy met the study's criterion for full remission, as did 14 percent of the participants who received only psychotherapy.

....

👁 **Watch** the **Video** *Thinking Like a Psychologist: Assessing the Effectiveness of Treatments* on **MyPsychLab**

spontaneous-remission effect The improvement of some mental patients and clients in psychotherapy without any professional intervention; a baseline criterion against which the effectiveness of therapies must be assessed.

placebo therapy A therapy interdependent of any specific clinical procedures that results in client improvement.

meta-analysis A statistical technique for evaluating hypotheses by providing a formal mechanism for detecting the general conclusions found in data from many different experiments.

For participants who received both drug therapy and psychotherapy, 29 percent showed the same level of improvement.

Because of such findings, contemporary researchers are less concerned about asking *whether* psychotherapy works and more concerned about asking why it works and whether any one treatment is most effective for any particular problem and for certain types of patients (Goodheart et al., 2006). For example, much treatment evaluation has been carried out in research settings that afford reasonable control over patients (often, the studies exclude individuals who have more than one disorder) and procedures (therapists are rigorously trained to minimize differences in treatment). Researchers need to ensure that therapies that work in research settings also work in community settings in which patients and therapists have more diversity of symptoms and experience (Kazdin, 2008). Another important issue for evaluation research is to assess the likelihood that individuals will complete a course of treatment. In almost all circumstances, some people choose to discontinue treatments (Barrett et al., 2008). Researchers seek to understand who leaves treatment and why—with the ultimate hope of creating treatments to which most everyone can adhere.

Let's turn now from comparisons of individual therapies to an analysis of the common factors that underlie successful therapies.

Common Factors

The last section described how researchers evaluate the effectiveness of specific therapies for particular disorders. However, other researchers have looked across the range of psychotherapies with the goal of identifying **common factors**—shared components that contribute to therapeutic effectiveness (Wampold, 2001). For successful therapies, these factors are most often present:

- The client has positive expectations and hope for improvement.
- The therapist is able to reinforce those expectations and cultivate hope.
- The therapy provides an explanation for how the client will change and allows the client to practice behaviors that will achieve that change.
- The therapy provides a clear plan for treatment.
- The client and therapist form a relationship that is characterized by trust, warmth, and acceptance.

As you consider this list of common factors, take a moment to see how they apply to each of the types of psychotherapy the chapter has reviewed.

Among these common factors, researchers have focused particular attention on the relationship between the therapist and the client. Whatever the form of the treatment, it's important that the individual seeking help enter into an effective therapeutic alliance. A *therapeutic alliance* is a mutual relationship that a client establishes with a therapist: The individual and the therapist collaborate to bring about relief. Research suggests that the quality of the therapeutic alliance has an impact on psychotherapy's ability to bring about improved mental health (Goldfried & Davila, 2005). In general, the more positive the therapeutic alliance, the more relief the client obtains (Horvath et al., 2011). The concept of the therapeutic alliance has several components, each of which also contributes to positive

How can prevention strategies encourage people to build habits to minimize the need for treatment?

outcomes. For example, clients experience more improvement from psychotherapy when they and the therapist share the same perspective on the goals for the therapy and agree on the processes that will achieve those goals (Tryon & Winograd, 2011). If you enter into therapy, you should believe that you can establish a strong therapeutic alliance with the therapist. ◉

The final section of this chapter reflects on an important principle of life: Whatever the effectiveness of treatment, it is often better to prevent a disorder than to heal it once it arises.

Prevention Strategies

The traditional therapies this chapter has examined share the focus of changing a person who is already distressed or disabled. This focus is necessary because, much of the time, people are unaware that they are at risk for psychological disorders. They present themselves for treatment only once they have begun to experience symptoms. However, as we saw in Chapter 14, researchers have identified a number of biological and psychological factors that put people at risk. The goal of *prevention* is to apply knowledge of those risk factors to reduce the likelihood and severity of distress.

Prevention can be realized at several different levels. *Primary* prevention seeks to prevent a condition before it begins. Steps might be taken, for example, to provide individuals with coping skills so they can be more resilient or to change negative aspects of an environment that might lead to anxiety or depression (Boyd et al., 2006; Hudson et al., 2004). *Secondary* prevention attempts to limit the duration and severity of a disorder once it has begun. This goal is realized by means of programs that allow for early identification and prompt treatment. For example, based on assessments of therapeutic effectiveness, a mental health practitioner might recommend a combination of psychotherapy and drug therapy to optimize secondary prevention (Manber et al., 2008). *Tertiary* prevention limits the long-term impact of a

....

◉▸ **Simulate** the **Experiment** *Ineffective Therapies* on **MyPsychLab**

◉ **Watch** the **Video** *What's In It For Me?: Finding a Therapist if You Need One* on **MyPsychLab**

common factors The components that psychotherapies share that contribute to therapeutic effectiveness.

CAN INTERNET-BASED THERAPY BE EFFECTIVE?

The therapies described in this chapter all share the common assumption that the therapist and client will meet face-to-face. However, as the Internet has become a standard element of most people's lives, psychotherapists have begun to explore possibilities of providing mental health care without traditional personal contact.

Let's consider an example of a successful program of Internet-based treatment for social phobia. Recall that people with social phobia experience anxiety when they anticipate public interactions. For that reason, the Internet holds the promise of providing treatment without requiring people with the disorder to enter the social sphere. In one study, people with social phobia completed a 10-week program of Internet modules that guided them through a course of cognitive behavioral therapy (Berger et al., 2009). Therapists were involved in the process via e-mail. They addressed the patients' questions and delivered motivating messages. At the end of the treatment, the patients' level of distress was compared to that of a control group of individuals who also had been diagnosed with social phobia. The patients who had completed the Internet-based treatment showed considerable improvement with respect to that control group.

Successes of this sort encourage therapists to pioneer innovative therapies delivered via the Internet. However, therapists have also taken a step back to consider some of the particular ethical issues that may arise when therapists and clients remain at a distance (Fitzgerald et al., 2010; Ross, 2011). For example, therapists worry that patients may be misdiagnosed if they present limited or distorted information without the extra scrutiny that is possible face-to-face Furthermore, consumers are rarely able to verify the credentials of online therapists; in cyberspace anyone can claim to be an expert. Finally, therapists who use the Internet are unable to assure their clients of confidentiality. There's a real danger that private information could be "hacked" and dragged into the public domain.

This concern about confidentiality may be particularly urgent because research evidence suggests that online therapy leads to disinhibition: The relative anonymity of this form of therapy allows clients to reveal their most pressing problems and concerns more quickly and with less embarrassment (Richards, 2009). Individuals may be more honest when they don't have to worry about their therapist's overt reactions to their difficult confessions.

But consider that rush of information in the context of the therapeutic alliance. Recall that the quality of the therapeutic alliance has a strong impact on psychotherapy's ability to bring about improved mental health (Goldfried & Davila, 2005; Horvath et al., 2011). Some therapists worry that the therapeutic alliance will necessarily be impaired if they are never face-to-face with their clients (Ross, 2011). Still, other therapists have suggested that Internet-based therapy has the capacity to bring relief because it activates the common factors that underlie the effectiveness of traditional therapies (Peck, 2010).

- In addition to social phobia, for what other psychological disorders might Internet-based therapy be particularly appropriate?
- What might therapists do to cope with confidentiality issues on the Internet?

---

psychological disorder by seeking to prevent a relapse. For example, this chapter noted earlier that individuals with schizophrenia who discontinue drug therapy have a very high rate of relapse (Fournier et al., 2010). To engage in tertiary prevention, mental health practitioners would recommend that their patients with schizophrenia continue their courses of antipsychotic drugs.

Within psychology, the field of *community psychology* plays a particular role in efforts to prevent psychological illness and promote wellness (Schueller, 2009). Community psychologists often design interventions that address the features of communities that put people at risk. For example, researchers have developed community-wide strategies to reduce substance abuse among urban adolescents (Diamond et al., 2009). These programs attempt to change community values with respect to drugs and alcohol and they also provide adolescents with drug-and-alcohol–free social activities.

Preventing mental disorders is a complex and difficult task. It involves not only understanding the relevant causal factors, but overcoming individual, institutional, and governmental resistance to change. A major research effort will be needed to demonstrate the long-range utility of prevention and the public health approach to psychopathology. The ultimate goal of prevention programs is to safeguard the mental health of all members of our society.

Stop and Review

① What conclusions can be drawn from meta-analyses of treatments for depression?
② What has research demonstrated about the importance of the therapeutic alliance?
③ What is the goal of primary prevention?

✓—[Study and **Review** on **MyPsychLab**

Recapping Main Points

The Therapeutic Context

- Therapy requires that a diagnosis be made and a course of treatment be established.
- Therapy may be medically or psychologically oriented.
- The four major types of psychotherapies are psychodynamic, behavior, cognitive, and humanistic.
- A variety of professionals practice therapy.
- Researchers must assess the effectiveness of psychotherapies across diverse groups.
- Harsh early treatment of those with mental illnesses led to a modern movement for deinstitutionalization.
- Unfortunately, many people do not have adequate resources outside the institution, so they may become homeless or quickly are readmitted to institutions.

Psychodynamic Therapies

- Psychodynamic therapies grew out of Sigmund Freud's psychoanalytic theory.
- Freud emphasized the role of unconscious conflicts in the etiology of psychopathology.
- Psychodynamic therapy seeks to reconcile these conflicts.
- Free association, attention to resistance, dream analysis, transference, and countertransference are all important components of this therapy.
- Other psychodynamic theorists place more emphasis on the patient's current social situation and interpersonal relationships.

Behavior Therapies

- Behavior therapies use the principles of learning and reinforcement to modify or eliminate problem behaviors.
- Counterconditioning techniques replace negative behaviors, like phobic responses, with more adaptive behaviors.
- Exposure is the common element in phobia-modification therapies.
- Contingency management uses operant conditioning to modify behavior, primarily through positive reinforcement and extinction.

Cognitive Therapies

- Cognitive therapy concentrates on changing negative or irrational thought patterns about the self and social relationships.
- Cognitive therapy has been used successfully to treat depression.
- Rational-emotive therapy helps clients recognize that their irrational beliefs about themselves interfere with successful life outcomes.

- Cognitive behavioral therapy calls for the client to learn more constructive thought patterns in reference to a problem and to apply the new technique to other situations.

Humanistic Therapies

- Humanistic therapies work to help individuals become more fully self-actualized.
- Therapists strive to be nondirective in helping their clients establish a positive self-image that can deal with external criticisms.
- Gestalt therapy focuses on the whole person—body, mind, and life setting.

Group Therapies

- Group therapy allows people to observe and engage in social interactions as a means to reduce psychological distress.
- Family and marital therapy concentrates on situational difficulties and interpersonal dynamics of the couple or family group as a system in need of improvement.
- Community and Internet self-help groups allow individuals to obtain information and feelings of control in circumstances of social support.

Biomedical Therapies

- Biomedical therapies concentrate on changing physiological aspects of mental illness.
- Drug therapies include antipsychotic medications for treating schizophrenia as well as antidepressants and antianxiety drugs.
- Psychosurgery is rarely used because of its radical, irreversible effects.
- Electroconvulsive therapy and repetitive transcranial magnetic stimulation (rTMS) can be effective with depressed patients.

Treatment Evaluation and Prevention Strategies

- Research shows that many therapies work better than the mere passage of time or nonspecific placebo treatment.
- Evaluation projects are helping to answer the question of what makes therapy effective.
- Common factors, including the quality of the therapeutic alliance, underlie the effectiveness of therapies.
- Prevention strategies are necessary to stop psychological disorders from occurring and minimize their effects once they have occurred.

KEY TERMS

aversion therapy (p. 428)
behavior modification (p. 426)
behavior therapy (p. 426)
biomedical therapy (p. 419)
catharsis (p. 423)
client (p. 420)
client-centered therapy (p. 433)
clinical psychologist (p. 420)
clinical social worker (p. 420)
cognitive behavioral therapy (p. 431)
cognitive therapy (p. 430)
common factors (p. 441)
contingency management (p. 428)
counseling psychologist (p. 420)

counterconditioning (p. 426)
countertransference (p. 424)
deinstitutionalization (p. 421)
dream analysis (p. 423)
electroconvulsive therapy (ECT) (p. 439)
exposure therapy (p. 426)
free association (p. 423)
Gestalt therapy (p. 434)
human-potential movement (p. 433)
insight therapy (p. 423)
meta-analysis (p. 440)
participant modeling (p. 428)
pastoral counselor (p. 420)
patient (p. 420)

placebo therapy (p. 440)
prefrontal lobotomy (p. 438)
psychiatrist (p. 420)
psychoanalysis (p. 423)
psychoanalyst (p. 420)
psychopharmacology (p. 436)
psychosurgery (p. 438)
psychotherapy (p. 419)
rational-emotive therapy (RET) (p. 431)
resistance (p. 423)
spontaneous-remission effect (p. 440)
systematic desensitization (p. 427)
transference (p. 424)

I magine circumstances in which you've done everything to get to a job interview on time, but nothing has gone your way. The electricity went off during the night, so your alarm didn't wake you. The friend who was supposed to give you a ride had a flat tire. You tried to get money for a taxi, but the ATM ate your card. When you finally get to the office, you can guess what the manager is thinking: "Why would I give a job to someone this unreliable?" You want to protest, "It's not me, it's the circumstances!" As you have contemplated this scenario, you have begun to enter the world of *social psychology*—that area of psychology that investigates the ways in which individuals create and interpret social situations.

Social psychology is the study of the ways in which thoughts, feelings, perceptions, motives, and behavior are influenced by interactions and transactions between people. Social psychologists try to understand behavior within its social context. This social context is the vibrant canvas on which are painted the movements, strengths, and vulnerabilities of the social animal. Defined broadly, the social context includes the real, imagined, or symbolic presence of other people; the activities and interactions that take place between people; the features of the settings in which behavior occurs; and the expectations and norms that govern behavior in a given setting (Sherif, 1981).

This chapter explores several major themes of social psychological research. The first part focuses on **social cognition**, which is the processes by which people select, interpret, and remember social information. We then consider the ways in which situations affect people's behavior and the processes by which attitudes and prejudices are formed and changed. We then turn to the social relationships you form with other people. Finally, the chapter examines aggression and prosocial behaviors. This chapter will also illustrate how research in social psychology has immediate applications to your life and the society you live in.

CONSTRUCTING SOCIAL REALITY

To open the chapter, I asked you to imagine everything that could go wrong in advance of a job interview. When you finally arrive at the manager's office, you and the manager have very different interpretations of the same event. You know you've been a victim of circumstances. However, at least in the short run, the manager judges you only by what is readily apparent: You are late, and you are disheveled. That's what is meant by *constructing social reality*. The manager considers the evidence you present and makes an interpretation of the situation. If you still wish to get the job, you'll have to get the manager to construct a new interpretation.

Social psychologists have provided abundant examples of circumstances in which people's beliefs lead them to view the same situation from different vantage points and make contrary conclusions about what "really happened." One classic study from the 1950s focused on distinctly different perceptions of a highly contentious football game (Hastorf & Cantril, 1954). Students from each school judged the other team to have been responsible for most of the bad behavior that occurred in

Why are fans who watch their favorite team play likely to perceive more instances of unfair play on the part of the opposing team?

a particularly rough game. You won't be surprised that sporting events continue to provide circumstances for the construction of different social realities.

Featured Study

This study makes clear that a complex social occurrence, such as a skating competition, cannot be observed in an objective, unbiased fashion. Social situations obtain significance when observers *selectively encode* what is happening in terms of what they expect to see and want to see. In the case of the skating performances, people *looked* at the same activity, but they *saw* different performances.

To explain how the American and Russian newspapers came to such different interpretations of the pairs' competition returns us to the realm of *perception*. Recall from Chapter 4 that you often must put prior knowledge to work to interpret

social psychology The branch of psychology that studies the effect of social variables on individual behavior, attitudes, perceptions, and motives; also studies group and intergroup phenomena.

social cognition The process by which people select, interpret, and remember social information.

ambiguous perceptual objects. The principle is the same for the competition—people bring past knowledge to bear on the interpretation of current events—but the objects for perceptual processing are people and situations. **Social perception** is the process by which people come to understand and categorize the behaviors of others. This section focuses largely on two issues of social perception. First, we consider how people make judgments about the forces that influence other people's behavior, their *causal attributions*. Next, we see how processes of social perception can sometimes bring the world in line with expectations.

The Origins of Attribution Theory

One of the most important inferential tasks facing all social perceivers is to determine the causes of events. You want to know the whys of life. Why did my girlfriend break off the relationship? Why did he, and not I, get the job? Why did my parents divorce after so many years of marriage? All such whys lead to an analysis of possible causal determinants for some action, event, or outcome. **Attribution theory** is a general approach to describing the ways the social perceiver uses information to generate causal explanations.

Attribution theory originated in the writings of Fritz Heider (1958). Heider argued that people continually make causal analyses as part of their attempts at general comprehension of the social world. People, he suggested, are all *intuitive psychologists* who try to figure out what people are like and what causes their behavior, just as professional psychologists do. Heider believed that the questions that dominate most attributional analyses are whether the cause of a behavior is found in the person (internal or *dispositional* causality) or in the situation (external or *situational* causality) and who is responsible for the outcomes. How do people make those judgments?

Harold Kelley (1967) formalized Heider's line of thinking by specifying the variables that people use to make their attributions. Kelly's **covariation model** suggested that people attribute a behavior to a causal factor if that factor was present whenever the behavior occurred but was absent whenever it didn't occur. Suppose, for example, you are walking down a street and you see a friend pointing at a horse and screaming. What evidence would you gather to decide whether your friend is crazy (a dispositional attribution) or danger is afoot (a situational attribution)? ✳

Kelley suggested that people make this judgment by assessing covariation with respect to three dimensions of information relevant to the person whose acts they are trying to explain: distinctiveness, consistency, and consensus:

- *Distinctiveness* refers to whether the behavior is specific to a particular situation—does your friend scream in response to all horses?
- *Consistency* refers to whether the behavior occurs repeatedly in response to this situation—has this horse made your friend scream in the past?
- *Consensus* refers to whether other people also produce the same behavior in the same situation—is everyone pointing and screaming?

Each of these three dimensions plays a role in the conclusions you draw. Suppose, for example, that your friend was the only one screaming. Would that make you more likely to make a dispositional or a situational attribution?

Thousands of studies have been conducted to refine and extend attribution theory beyond the solid foundation provided by Heider and Kelley (Försterling, 2001; Moskowitz, 2004). Many of those studies have concerned themselves with conditions in which attributions depart from a systematic search of available information. Let's consider circumstances in which bias may creep into your attributions.

The Fundamental Attribution Error

Suppose you have made an arrangement to meet a friend at 7 o'clock. It's now 7:30, and the friend still hasn't arrived. How might you be explaining this event to yourself?

- I'm sure something really important happened that made it impossible for her to be here on time.
- What a jerk! Couldn't she try a little harder?

Again, your choice here is between a situational and a dispositional attribution. Research has shown that people are more likely, on average, to choose the second type, the dispositional explanation (Ross & Nisbett, 1991). This tendency is so strong, in fact, that social psychologist **Lee Ross** (1977) labeled it the fundamental attribution error. The **fundamental attribution error (FAE)** represents the dual tendency for people to overestimate dispositional factors (blame or credit people) and to underestimate situational factors (blame or credit the environment) when searching for the cause of some behavior or outcome. ✳

Let's look at a laboratory example of the FAE. Ross and his colleagues (1977) created an experimental version of a "College Bowl" type of quiz game in which participants became questioners or contestants by the flip of a coin. After the coin flip, both the questioners- and contestants-to-be listened to the instructions: The experimenters asked the questioners to invent challenging questions based on their own personal knowledge. When the questioners were done, they posed those questions to the contestants. The contestant tried, often in vain, to answer the questions. At the end of the session, the questioner, the contestant, and observers (other participants who had watched the game) rated the general knowledge of both questioner and contestant. The results are shown in **Figure 16.1**. As you can see, questioners seem to believe that both they and the contestants are average. Both contestants and observers, however, rate the questioner as much more knowledgeable than the contestant—and contestants even rate themselves to be a bit below average! Is this fair? It should be clear

....

✳ **Explore** the **Concept** *Internal and External Attributions* on **MyPsychLab**

✳ **Explore** the **Concept** *Fundamental Attribution Error* on **MyPsychLab**

social perception The process by which a person comes to know or perceive the personal attributes.

attribution theory A social–cognitive approach to describing the ways the social perceiver uses information to generate causal explanations.

covariation model A theory that suggests that people attribute a behavior to a causal factor if that factor was present whenever the behavior occurred but was absent whenever it didn't occur.

fundamental attribution error (FAE) The dual tendency of observers to underestimate the impact of situational factors and to overestimate the influence of dispositional factors on a person's behavior.

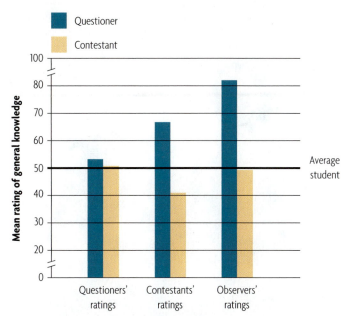

FIGURE 16.1 Ratings of Questioners' and Contestants' General Knowledge

After the quiz game, questioners, contestants, and observers rated each of the participant's general knowledge with respect to a rating of 50 for the average student. Questioners believed that both they and the contestants were average. However, both contestants and observers rated the questioner as much more knowledgeable than the contestant. Furthermore, contestants rated themselves to be a bit below average.

that the situation confers a great advantage on the questioner. (Wouldn't you prefer to be the one who gets to ask the questions?) The contestants' and observers' ratings ignore the way in which the situation allowed one person to look bright and the other to look dull. That's the fundamental attribution error.

You should be on a constant lookout for instances of the FAE. However, this may not always be easy: It often takes a bit of "research" to discover the situational roots of behavior. Situational forces are generally invisible. You can't, for example, *see* the biased perspectives that drive the construction of social reality; you can see only the behaviors they give rise to. What can you do to avoid the FAE? Particularly in circumstances in which you are making a dispositional attribution that is negative ("What a jerk!"), you should take a step back and ask yourself, "Could it be something about the situation that is bringing about this behavior?" You might think of such an exercise as "attributional charity." Do you see why?

This advice may be particularly important to those of us who live in Western society because evidence suggests that the FAE is due, in part, to cultural sources (Miller, 1984). Recall the discussion in Chapter 13 of cultural differences in construals of the self. As that chapter explained, most Western cultures embody *independent construals of self*, whereas most Eastern cultures embody *interdependent construals of self* (Markus & Kitayama, 1991). Research demonstrates that, as a function of the culture of interdependence, members of non-Western cultures are less likely to focus on individual actors in situations. We can see this cultural difference in another analysis of media coverage of Olympic athletes.

The researchers compiled television and newspaper reports from the United States and Japan that focused on athletes at the 2000 Summer Olympics and the 2002 Winter Olympics (Markus et al., 2006). Research assistants who were blind to the study's purpose analyzed each media report to determine what categories of explanations were used to discuss athletes' performance: For example, did the articles mention the athletes' strengths or weaknesses, their level of motivation, or the quality of the other competitors? The results showed that U.S. media coverage focused rather tightly on the personal characteristics of the athletes. The Japanese media considered a broader range of factors. The reports didn't ignore the athletes' characteristics, but they also discussed other background factors, including the extent to which the athletes met others' expectations. In addition, U.S. media reports focused almost entirely on athletes' positive characteristics whereas Japanese reports mentioned both positive and negative.

An impressive feature of this study is that it captures cultural attributional styles as they are represented on TV and in newspapers. The study makes clear one way in which a cultural style of attribution is transmitted and maintained for all those who are exposed to the media in a particular culture (Morling & Lamoreaux, 2008).

Self-Serving Biases

One of the most startling findings in the College Bowl study was the contestants' negative evaluation of their own abilities. This suggests that people will make the FAE even at their own expense. (In fact, you should recall from Chapter 14 that one theory of the origins of depression suggests that depressed people make too many negative attributions to themselves rather than to situational causes.) In many circumstances, however, people do just the opposite—their attributions err in the direction of being self-serving. A **self-serving bias** leads people to take credit for their successes while denying or explaining away responsibility for their failures. In many situations, people tend to make dispositional attributions for success and situational attributions for failure (Gilovich, 1991): "I got the prize because of my ability"; "I lost the competition because it was rigged."

These patterns of attribution may be good for short-term self-esteem. However, it may often be more important to have an accurate sense of what causal forces are at work in your life outcomes. Consider how you do in your classes. If you get an *A*, what attributions do you make? How about if you get a *C*? Research has demonstrated that students tend to attribute high grades to their own efforts and low grades to factors external to themselves (McAllister, 1996). In fact, professors show the same pattern—they make attributions to themselves for students' successes but not their failures. Once again, can you see what impact this pattern of attributions might have on your GPA? If you don't think about the external causes for your successes (for example, "That first exam was easy"), you might fail to study enough the next time; if you don't think about the

self-serving bias An attributional bias in which people tend to take credit for their successes and deny responsibility for their failures.

dispositional causes for failures (for example, "I shouldn't have stayed so long at that party"), you also might never get around to studying hard enough.

The last section suggested that people from cultures that have interdependent senses of self are less likely to succumb to the fundamental attribution error. Because they think more about the situation than individuals (even when they are the individuals), members of Eastern cultures are also less likely to demonstrate self-serving biases. Consider a study in which students from the United States and Japan recalled instances of successes and failures, such as a time when they received a grade that was better than usual (Imada & Ellsworth, 2011). The researchers asked the students to make attributions about the causes of the events they had recalled. U.S. students showed a self-serving bias by, for example, focusing more on self attributions for successes and situation attributions for failures. Japanese students did not show that same strong pattern. The students also reported the emotions they had experienced. For circumstances in which U.S. students recalled feelings proud, Japanese students recalled feeling lucky.

Why does it matter so much what attributions you make? Recall the example of your tardy friend. Suppose that, because you don't seek information about the situation, you decide that she isn't actually interested in being your friend. Can that incorrect belief actually cause the person to be unfriendly toward you in the future? To address that question, we turn now to the power of beliefs and expectations in constructing social reality.

How do self-fulfilling prophecies affect the likelihood that children will engage in underage drinking?

Expectations and Self-Fulfilling Prophecies

Can beliefs and expectations go beyond coloring the way you interpret experiences to actually shape social reality? Much research suggests that the very nature of some situations can be modified significantly by the beliefs and expectations people have about them. **Self-fulfilling prophecies** (Merton, 1957) are predictions made about some future behavior or event that modify behavioral interactions so as to produce what is expected. Suppose, for example, you go to a party expecting to have a great time. Suppose a friend goes expecting it to be boring. Can you imagine the different ways in which the two of you might behave, given these expectations? These alternative ways of behaving may, in turn, alter how others at the party behave toward you. In that case, which of you is actually more likely to have a good time at the party?

One of the most powerful demonstrations of social expectancy unfolded in elementary school classrooms in Boston. Researchers informed elementary school teachers that testing had revealed that some of their students were "intellectual bloomers who will show unusual gains during the academic year." In fact, the names of these bloomers were chosen randomly. However, by the end of that school year, 30 percent of the children arbitrarily named as bloomers had gained an average of 22 IQ points! Their gain in intellectual performance, as measured by a standard test of intelligence, was significantly

greater than that of their control-group classmates who had started out with the same average IQ (Rosenthal & Jacobson, 1968). The teachers' false expectations prompted them to behave quite differently toward the "bloomers" (Rosenthal, 1974). For example, the teachers created more opportunities for the special students to respond in class and be reinforced, thus giving them hard evidence that they were indeed as good as the teachers believed they were.

What is unusual, of course, about the situation in the Boston classrooms is that the teachers were purposefully given false expectations. In most real-world situations, however, expectations are based on fairly accurate social perceptions (Jussim & Harber, 2005). Teachers, for example, expect certain students to do well because those students arrive in the classroom with better qualifications; and those students, typically, do show the best performance. However, research suggests that some of the most potent self-fulfilling prophecies come from parents.

A team of researchers followed the academic performance of 332 adolescents for six years, starting when they were 12 years old. At the start of the study, their mothers indicated their expectations about their children's academic performance by responding to statements such as "How far do you expect this child to go in school?" (Scherr et al., 2011, p. 591). The researchers also obtained a range of background indicators (for example, standardized test scores) that were related to the children's likely academic performance. At age 18, the children's academic outcomes demonstrated the impact of their mother's beliefs: They performed better or worse than expected (with predictions based on the background indicators) as a function of how their mothers

Featured Study

- -

self-fulfilling prophecy A prediction made about some future behavior or event that modifies interactions so as to produce what is expected.

thought they would do. The data suggested that the adolescents constructed a self-image based on their mothers' expectations and matched their school performance to that self-image.

Much research on self-fulfilling prophecies has focused on school success. However, researchers have found evidence in other domains that people's mistaken beliefs and expectations can have an influence on what actually happens. For example, research suggests that when mothers overestimate the amount of alcohol their adolescents will consume, those expectations can become self-fulfilling prophecies (Madon et al., 2008).

The research described in this section focused on how people explain behaviors with respect to dispositions and situations. The next section provides evidence that people often underestimate the extent to which situations constrain people's actions.

Stop *and* Review

① What three dimensions did Harold Kelley suggest affect the attribution process?
② Why might self-serving biases have a negative impact on a student's GPA?
③ What limits do ordinary classroom practices place on self-fulfilling prophecies?

CRITICAL THINKING   Recall the study that examined cross-cultural differences in media reports. Why might the researchers have focused on Olympic athletes?

✔●─|**Study** and **Review** on **MyPsychLab**

THE POWER OF THE SITUATION

Throughout *Psychology and Life,* you have seen that psychologists who strive to understand the causes of behavior look in many different places for their answers. Some look to genetic factors and others to biochemical and brain processes; still others focus on the causal influence of the environment. Social psychologists believe that the primary determinant of behavior is the nature of the social situation in which that behavior occurs. They argue that social situations exert significant control over individual behavior, often dominating personality and a person's past history of learning, values, and beliefs. This section reviews both classic research and recent experiments that together explore the effect of subtle but powerful situational variables on people's behavior. 👁

Roles and Rules

What *social roles* are available to you? A **social role** is a socially defined pattern of behavior that is expected of a person when functioning in a given setting or group. Different

To open or not to open? How do people learn the etiquette for giving and receiving gifts in different cultures?

social situations make different roles available. When you are at home, you may accept the role of "child" or "sibling." When you are in the classroom, you accept the role of "student." At other times still, you are a "best friend" or "lover." Can you see how these different roles immediately make different types of behaviors more or less appropriate and also available to you?

Situations are also characterized by the operation of **rules**, behavioral guidelines for specific settings. Some rules are *explicitly* stated in signs (DON'T SMOKE; NO EATING IN CLASS) or are explicitly taught to children (Respect the elderly; Never take candy from a stranger). Other rules are *implicit*—they are learned through transactions with others in particular settings. How loud you can play your music, how close you can stand to another person, when you can call your teacher or boss by a first name, and what is the suitable way to react to a compliment or a gift—all of these actions depend on the situation. For example, the Japanese do not open a gift in the presence of the giver, for fear of not showing sufficient appreciation; foreigners not aware of this unwritten rule will misinterpret the behavior as rude instead of sensitive. Next time you get in an elevator, try to determine what rules you have learned about that situation. Why do people usually speak in hushed tones or not at all?

Ordinarily, you might not be particularly aware of the effects of roles and rules, but one classic social psychological experiment, the *Stanford Prison Experiment,* put these forces

....

👁 **Watch** the **Video** *The Power of the Situation: Phil Zimbardo* on **MyPsychLab**

social role A socially defined pattern of behavior that is expected of a person who is functioning in a given setting or group.

rule Behavioral guideline for acting in a certain way in a certain situation.

a–d The Stanford Prison Experiment created a new "social reality" in which the norms of good behavior were overwhelmed by the dynamics of the situation. Why did the student guards and inmates adopt their roles so powerfully?

to work with startling results (Zimbardo, 2007; replicated in Australia by Lovibond et al., 1979). 👁

On a summer Sunday in California, a siren shattered the serenity of college student Tommy Whitlow's morning. A police car screeched to a halt in front of his home. Within minutes, Tommy was charged with a felony, informed of his constitutional rights, frisked, and handcuffed. After he was booked and fingerprinted, Tommy was blindfolded and transported to the Stanford County Prison, where he was stripped, sprayed with disinfectant, and issued a smock-type uniform with an ID number on the front and back. Tommy became prisoner 647. Eight other college students were also arrested and assigned numbers.

Tommy and his cellmates were all volunteers who had answered a newspaper ad and agreed to be participants in a two-week experiment on prison life. By random flips of a coin, some of the volunteers had been assigned to the role of prisoners; the rest became guards. All had been selected from a large pool of student volunteers who, on the basis of extensive psychological tests and interviews, had been judged as law-abiding, emotionally stable, physically healthy, and "normal-average." The prisoners lived in the jail around the clock; the guards worked standard eight-hour shifts.

What happened once these students had assumed their randomly assigned roles? In guard roles, college students who had been pacifists and "nice guys" behaved aggressively—sometimes even sadistically. The guards insisted that prisoners obey all rules without question or hesitation. Failure to do so led to the loss of a privilege. At first, privileges included opportunities to read, write, or talk to other inmates. Later on, the slightest protest resulted in

···

👁 **Watch** the **Video** *Nature vs. Nurture and the Stanford Prison Experiment: Phil Zimbardo* on **MyPsychLab**

the loss of the "privileges" of eating, sleeping, and washing. Failure to obey rules also resulted in menial, mindless work such as cleaning toilets with bare hands, doing push-ups while a guard stepped on the prisoner's back, and spending hours in solitary confinement. The guards were always devising new strategies to make the prisoners feel worthless.

As prisoners, psychologically stable students soon behaved pathologically, passively resigning themselves to their unexpected fate. Less than 36 hours after the mass arrest, Prisoner 8412, one of the ringleaders of an aborted prisoner rebellion that morning, began to cry uncontrollably. He experienced fits of rage, disorganized thinking, and severe depression. On successive days, three more prisoners developed similar stress-related symptoms. A fifth prisoner developed a psychosomatic rash all over his body when the Parole Board rejected his appeal.

By the conclusion of the Stanford Prison Experiment, guards' and prisoners' behavior differed from each other in virtually every observable way (see **Figure 16.2**). However, the figure doesn't completely reveal the extremes of the guards' behavior. On many occasions, the guards stripped their prisoners naked. The guards hooded and chained their prisoners. They denied them food and bedding. Does this list of behaviors sound familiar? They are among the abuses the guards committed in 2003 at the Abu Ghraib prison in Iraq. The Stanford Prison Experiment helps shed light on this scandal: Situational forces can lead ordinary people to exhibit horrendous behaviors (Fiske et al., 2004; Zimbardo, 2007).

Before the Stanford Prison Experiment began, it underwent a thorough human subjects review of the type described in Chapter 2. No one anticipated the risks that lay ahead. Even though the researchers believed in the power of the situation, they were nonetheless caught by surprise by the extreme intensity of the situation and the rapidity of the negative psychological processes that emerged. They terminated their two-week study after only six days. They acknowledge, in retrospect, that they should have ended the experiment even sooner: Ethical concerns should have outweighed their scientific agenda. The researchers provided extensive debriefing for the participants. There was a three-hour session directly after the experiment was halted. Data collected after those debriefing sessions suggested that both prisoners and guards were in an emotional state comparable to the positive ones in which they had begun the study. Most participants returned for additional debriefing weeks later, to review and discuss videotapes from the study. Follow-ups over many years revealed no lasting negative effects. Fortunately, the students were basically healthy, and they readily bounced back from this highly charged situation.

As we evaluate the ethical balance of the costs to the participants versus the gains to science and society, we must also consider gains to the participants. Several of the participants have reflected on the long-term consequences of their participation. For example, the student-prisoner who was first to be released with extreme emotional distress became a forensic clinical psychologist and has worked in the San Francisco correctional system. His explicit goal has been to use his experience in the Stanford Prison Experiment to improve prisoner–guard relationships. Similalry, Tommy Whitlow has said that, although he wouldn't want to go through the experiment again, he valued the personal experience because he

How does social psychological research explain some aspects of the guards' behaviors at Abu Ghraib?

learned so much about himself and about human nature. (For an extended discussion of the ethical issues raised by this and related research, I recommend reviewing the material in Zimbardo, 2007.)

A critical feature of the Stanford Prison Experiment is that only chance, in the form of random assignment, decided the participants' roles as guards or prisoners. Those roles created status and power differences that were validated in the prison situation. No one taught the participants to play their roles. The student participants had already experienced such power differences in many of their previous social interactions: parent–child, teacher–student, doctor–patient, boss–worker, male–female. They merely refined and intensified their prior patterns of behavior for this particular setting. Each student could have played either role. Many students in the guard role reported being surprised at how easily they enjoyed controlling other people. Just putting on the uniform was enough to transform them from passive college students into aggressive prison guards. What sort of person do *you* become when you slip in and out of different roles? Where does your sense of personal self end and your social identity begin?

Social Norms

In addition to the expectations regarding role behaviors, groups develop many expectations for the ways their members *should* act. The specific expectations for socially appropriate attitudes and behaviors that are embodied in the stated or implicit rules of a group are called **social norms.** Social norms can be broad guidelines; if you are a member of Democrats for Social Action, you may be expected to hold liberal political beliefs, whereas members of the Young Republicans will advocate more conservative views. Social norms can also embody specific standards of conduct. For example, if you are employed as a server in a restaurant, you will be expected to treat

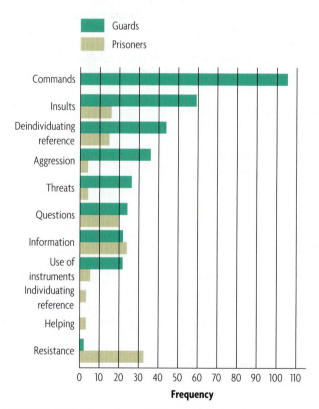

FIGURE 16.2 Guard and Prisoner Behavior

During the Stanford Prison Experiment, the randomly assigned roles of prisoners and guards drastically affected participants' behavior. The observations recorded in the six-day interaction profile show that across 25 observation periods, the prisoners engaged in more passive resistance, while the guards became more dominating, controlling, and hostile.

social norm The expectation a group has for its members regarding acceptable and appropriate attitudes and behaviors.

What impact does normative influence have on people's everyday behaviors?

your customers courteously no matter how unpleasant and demanding they are to you.

Belonging to a group typically involves discovering the set of social norms that regulates desired behavior in the group setting. This adjustment occurs in two ways: You notice the *uniformities* in certain behaviors of all or most members, and you observe the *negative consequences* when someone violates a social norm.

Norms serve several important functions. Awareness of the norms operating in a given group situation helps orient members and regulate their social interaction. Each participant can anticipate how others will enter the situation, how they will dress, and what they are likely to say and do, as well as what type of behavior will be expected of them to gain approval. You often feel awkward in new situations precisely because you may be unaware of the norms that govern the way you ought to act. Some tolerance for deviating from the standard is also part of the norm—wide in some cases, narrow in others. For example, shorts and a T-shirt might be marginally acceptable attire for a religious ceremony; a bathing suit would almost certainly deviate too far from the norm. Group members are usually able to estimate how far they can go before experiencing the coercive power of the group in the form of ridicule, reeducation, and rejection.

....

👁 **Watch** the **Video** *Conformity and Influence in Groups* on **MyPsychLab**

conformity The tendency for people to adopt the behaviors, attitudes, and values of other members of a reference group.

informational influence Group effects that arise from individuals' desire to be correct and right and to understand how best to act in a given situation.

normative influence Group effects that arise from individuals' desire to be liked, accepted, and approved of by others.

norm crystallization The convergence of the expectations of a group of individuals into a common perspective as they talk and carry out activities together.

Conformity

When you adopt a social role or bend to a social norm, you are, to some extent, *conforming* to social expectations. **Conformity** is the tendency for people to adopt the behavior and opinions presented by other group members. Why do you conform? Are there circumstances under which you ignore social constraints and act independently? Social psychologists have studied two types of forces that may lead to conformity:

- **Informational influence** processes—wanting to be *correct* correct and to understand the right way to act in a given situation.
- **Normative influence** processes—wanting to be liked, *liked* accepted, and approved of by others.

Let's consider classic experiments that illustrate each type of influence. 👁

Informational Influence: Sherif's Autokinetic Effect Many life situations in which you must make decisions about behaviors are quite ambiguous. Suppose, for example, you are dining at an elegant restaurant with a large group of people. Each place at the table is set with a dazzling array of silverware. How do you know which fork to use when the first course arrives? Typically, you would look to other members of the party to help you make an appropriate choice. This is *informational influence*.

A classic experiment, conducted by Muzafer Sherif (1935), demonstrated how informational influence can lead to **norm crystallization**—norm formation and solidification.

Featured Study

Participants were asked to judge the amount of movement of a spot of light, which was actually stationary but that appeared to move when viewed in total darkness with no reference points. This is a perceptual illusion known as the autokinetic effect. *Originally, individual judgments varied widely. However, when the participants were brought together in a group consisting of strangers and stated their*

Standard line   Standard line

FIGURE 16.3 Conformity in the Asch Experiments

In this photo from Asch's study, it is evident that the naive participant, Number 6, is distressed by the unanimous majority's erroneous judgment. The typical stimulus array is shown at the top left. At top right, the graph illustrates conformity across 12 critical trials when solitary participants were grouped with a unanimous majority, as well as their greater independence when paired with a dissenting partner. A lower percentage of correct estimates indicates the greater degree of an individual's conformity to the group's false estimate.

judgments aloud, their estimates began to converge. They began to see the light move in the same direction and in similar amounts. Even more interesting was the final part of Sherif's study—when alone in the same darkened room after the group viewing, these participants continued to follow the group norm that had emerged when they were together.

Once norms are established in a group, they tend to perpetuate themselves. In later research, these autokinetic group norms persisted even when tested a year later and without former group members witnessing the judgments (Rohrer et al., 1954). Norms can be transmitted from one generation of group members to the next and can continue to influence people's behavior long after the original group that created the norm no longer exists (Insko et al., 1980). How do we know that norms can have transgenerational influence? In autokinetic effect studies, researchers replaced one group member with a new one after each set of autokinetic trials until all the members of the group were new to the situation. The group's autokinetic norm

remained true to the one handed down to them across several successive generations (Jacobs & Campbell, 1961). Do you see how this experiment captures the processes that allow real-life norms to be passed down across generations?

Normative Influence: the Asch Effect What is the best way to demonstrate that people will sometimes conform because of *normative influence*—their desire to be liked, accepted, and approved of by others? One of the most important early social psychologists, **Solomon Asch** (1940, 1956), created circumstances in which participants made judgments under conditions in which the physical reality was absolutely clear—but the rest of a group reported that they saw that reality differently. Male college students were led to believe they were in a study of simple visual perception. They were shown cards with three lines of differing lengths and asked to indicate which of the three lines was the same length as the standard line (see **Figure 16.3**). The lines were different enough so that mistakes were rare, and their relative sizes changed on each series of trials.

The participants were seated next to last in semicircles of six to eight other students. Unknown to the participants, the others were all experimental confederates—accomplices of the experimenter—who were following a prearranged script. On the first three trials, everyone agreed on the correct comparison. However, the first confederate to respond on the fourth trial matched two lines that were obviously different. So did all members of the group up to the participant. That student had to decide if he should go along with everyone else's view of the situation and conform or remain independent, standing by what he clearly saw. That dilemma was repeated for the naive participant on 12 of the 18 trials. The participants showed signs of disbelief and obvious discomfort when faced with a majority who saw the world so differently. What did they do?

Roughly one-fourth of the participants remained completely independent—they never conformed. However, between 50 and 80 percent of the participants (in different studies in the research program) conformed with the false majority estimate at least once, and a third of the participants yielded to the majority's wrong judgments on half or more of the critical trials.

Asch describes some participants who yielded to the majority most of the time as "disoriented" and "doubt-ridden"; he states that they "experienced a powerful impulse not to appear different from the majority" (1952, p. 396). Those who yielded underestimated the influence of the social pressure and the frequency of their conformity; some even claimed that they really had seen the lines as the same length, despite their obvious discrepancy.

In other studies, Asch varied three factors: the size of the unanimous majority, the presence of a partner who dissented from the majority, and the size of the discrepancy between the correct physical stimulus comparison and the majority's position. He found that strong conformity effects were elicited with a unanimous majority of only three or four people. However, giving the naive participant a single ally who dissented from the majority opinion had the effect of sharply reducing conformity, as can be seen in Figure 16.3. With a partner, the participant was usually able to resist the pressures to conform to the majority (Asch, 1955, 1956).

How should we interpret these results? Asch himself was struck by the rate at which participants did *not* conform (Friend et al., 1990). He reported this research as studies in "independence." In fact, two-thirds of the time, participants gave the correct, nonconforming answer. However, most descriptions of Asch's experiment have emphasized the one-third conformity rate. Accounts of this experiment also often fail to note that not all participants were alike: The number of individuals who never conformed, about 25 percent, was roughly equal to the number who always or almost always conformed. Thus Asch's experiment teaches two complementary lessons. On the one hand, we find that people are not entirely swayed by normative influence—they assert their independence on a majority of occasions (and some people always do). On the other hand, we find that people will sometimes conform, even in the most unambiguous situations. That potential to conform is an important element of human nature.

Conformity in Everyday Life Although you've almost certainly never faced the exact circumstances of the Asch experiment, you can no doubt recognize conformity situations in your everyday life. Many of these situations are easy to spot. You might notice, for example, that you are wearing clothes that you find rather silly because someone has declared them to be fashionable. (Certainly that's true of *other* people.) Also, as you saw in Chapter 10, adolescents often conform with their peer groups with respect to risky behaviors such as drug use.

When people learn about the Asch experiment, they often wonder to what extent the results apply to the behavior of jurors: The study's procedure calls to mind a picture of jurors around a table, asserting "guilty" or "not guilty" at the start of deliberations. To examine conformity in jury descions, researchers compiled data from nearly 3,500 jurors who had participated in felony trials (Waters & Hans, 2009). The jurors indicated the verdicts at which they would have arrived had they been a "one-person jury." The researchers looked at cases in which juries were able to reach a majority decision (which indicated that all jurors had ultimately voted for the same verdict). They found that 38 percent of the juries included people whose private verdict was different from the one with which they publicly agreed! Note that real-life trials often have considerable ambiguity. For that reason, we cannot attribute the private dissenters' public conformity only to normative influence. Some of the conformity no doubt arises from informational influence. For example, the dissenters may have looked to their peers to clarify ambiguity in the evidence.

This study of juror behavior suggests why you need to be alert for conformity in everyday behavior. In fact, the strong tendency to succumb to normative influence holds out the possibility of considerably more negative consequences. For example, history has provided several instances of *suicide cults*—circumstances in which people have internalized group norms that have led them to take their own lives. Consider events that took place in San Diego, California, in March 1997. The members of a group called "Heaven's Gate" committed mass suicide: The police found 39 bodies wearing identical black uniforms and accompanied by travel bags packed for a journey (Balch & Taylor, 2002). Before their suicides, the cult members had accepted a belief system that required them to shed their earthly bodies so they could board a UFO that would take them to the Kingdom of Heaven. The group had posted much of its belief system to its official website. Researchers worry that the Internet will provide a particularly effective means to recruit people into cults and other alternative belief systems (Dawson & Hennebry, 2003). Does this strike you as a legitimate concern? You should consider that question in the context of the Asch experiment and other demonstrations of the ease with which conformity arises.

Minority Influence and Nonconformity Given the power of the majority to control resources and information, it is not surprising that people regularly conform to groups. Yet you know that sometimes individuals persevere in their personal views. How can this happen? How do people escape group domination, and how can anything new (counternormative) ever come about? Are there any conditions under which a small minority can turn the majority around and create new norms?

To address such questions, **Serge Moscovici** and his colleagues conducted a series of studies on minority influence. In one study where participants were given color-naming tasks,

When individuals become dependent on a group—such as a religious cult—for basic feelings of self-worth, they are prone to extremes of conformity. Twenty thousand identically dressed couples were married in this service conducted by the Reverend Sun Myung Moon. More recently, in August 1995, Moon simultaneously married 360,000 "Moonie" couples who were linked by satellite in 500 worldwide locations. Why do people find comfort in such large-scale conformity?

the majority correctly identified the color patches, but two of the experimenter's confederates consistently identified a green color as blue. Their consistent minority opposition had no immediate effect on the majority, but, when later tested alone, some of the participants shifted their judgments by moving the boundary between blue and green toward the blue side of the color continuum (Moscovici, 1976; Moscovici & Faucheux, 1972). Eventually, the power of the many may be undercut by the conviction of the dedicated few (Moscovici, 1980, 1985).

You can conceptualize these effects with respect to the distinction introduced earlier between normative influence and informational influence (Crano & Prislin, 2006; Wood et al., 1994). Minority groups have relatively little normative influence: Members of the majority are typically not particularly concerned about being liked or accepted by the minority. Conversely, minority groups do have informational influence: Minorities can encourage group members to understand issues from multiple perspectives (Sinaceur et al., 2010). Unfortunately, this potential for informational influence may only infrequently allow minorities to overcome majority members' normative desire to distance themselves from deviant or low-consensus views (Wood, 2000).

Decision Making in Groups

If you've ever tried to make a decision as part of a group, you know that it can be quite torturous. Imagine, for example, that you have just seen a movie with a bunch of friends. Although you thought the movie was "OK," by the end of a postmovie discussion you find yourself agreeing that it was "an incredible piece of trash." Is this change after group discussion typical? Are the judgments groups make consistently different from individuals' judgments? Researchers in social psychology have documented specific forces that operate when groups make decisions (Kerr & Tindale, 2004). This section will focus on *group polarization* and *groupthink*.

Your postmovie experience is an example of **group polarization:** Groups show a tendency to make decisions that are more extreme than the decisions that would be made by the members acting alone. Suppose, for example, you asked each member of the movie group to provide an attitude rating toward the movie; subsequently, as a group you agree on a single value to reflect your group attitude. If the group's rating is more extreme than the average of the individuals' ratings, that would be an instance of polarization. Depending on the initial group tendency—toward caution or risk—group polarization will tend to make a group more cautious or more risky.

Researchers have suggested that two types of processes underlie group polarization: the *information-influence* model and the *social comparison* model (Liu & Latané, 1998). The information-influence model suggests that group members contribute different information to a decision. If you and your friends each have a different reason for disliking a movie a little bit, all that information taken together would provide the evidence that you should actually dislike the movie a lot. The social comparison model suggests that group members strive to capture their peers' regard by representing a group ideal that is a bit more extreme than the group's true norm. Thus, if you come to decide that everyone was unhappy with a movie, you could try to present yourself as particularly astute by stating a more extreme opinion. If everyone in a group tries to capture the group's esteem in that same fashion, polarization will result.

Group polarization is one consequence of a general pattern of thought called *groupthink*. **Irving Janis** (1982) coined the term **groupthink** for the tendency of a decision-making group to filter out undesirable input so that a consensus may be reached, especially if it is in line with the leader's viewpoint. Janis's theory of groupthink emerged from his historical analysis of the Bay of Pigs invasion of Cuba in 1960. This disastrous

....

group polarization The tendency for groups to make decisions that are more extreme than the decisions that would be made by the members acting alone.

groupthink The tendency of a decision-making group to filter out undesirable input so that a consensus may be reached, especially if it is in line with the leader's viewpoint.

invasion was approved by President Kennedy after cabinet meetings in which contrary information was minimized or suppressed by those advisers to the president who were eager to undertake the invasion. From his analysis of this event, Janis outlined a series of features that he believed would predispose groups to fall prey to groupthink: He suggested, for example, that groups that were highly cohesive and insulated from experts and that operated under directed leadership would make groupthink decisions.

To test Janis's ideas, researchers have turned both to further historical analyses and laboratory experiments (Henningsen et al., 2006). This body of research suggests that groups are particularly vulnerable to groupthink when they embody a collective desire to maintain a shared positive view of a group (Turner & Pratkanis, 1998). Group members must understand that dissent often improves the quality of a group decision even if it may detract, on the surface, from the group's positive feel.

You've just seen some of the situational forces that have an impact on the decisions that groups make. We next consider one of the most important decisions people make as individuals: When should they obey authority?

Obedience to Authority

What made thousands of Nazis willing to follow Hitler's orders and send millions of Jews to the gas chambers? Why did U.S. soldiers follow the orders of their superiors and massacre hundreds of innocent citizens of the Vietnamese village of My Lai (Hersh, 1971; Opton, 1970, 1973)? Did character defects lead people to carry out orders blindly? Did they have no moral values? Stanley Milgram (1965, 1974), a student of Solomon Asch, conducted a series of studies that showed that blind obedience is less a product of dispositional characteristics than the outcome of situational forces that could engulf anyone. Milgram's program of obedience research is one of the most controversial because of its significant implications for real-world phenomena and the ethical issues it raises.

The Obedience Paradigm To separate the variables of personality and situation, Milgram used a series of 19 separate controlled laboratory experiments involving more than 1,000 participants. Milgram's first experiments were conducted at Yale University, with male residents of New Haven and surrounding communities who received payment for their

participation. In later variations, Milgram took his obedience laboratory away from the university. He set up a storefront research unit in Bridgeport, Connecticut, recruiting through newspaper ads a broad cross-section of the population, varying widely in age, occupation, and education and including members of both sexes.

Milgram's basic experimental paradigm involved individual participants delivering a series of what they thought were extremely painful electric shocks to another person. These volunteers thought they were participating in a scientific study of memory and learning. They were led to believe that the educational purpose of the study was to discover how punishment affects memory, so that learning could be improved through the proper balance of reward and punishment. In their *social roles* as *teachers*, the participants were to punish each error made by someone playing the role of *learner*. The major rule they were told to follow was to increase the level of shock each time the learner made an error until the learning was errorless. The white-coated experimenter acted as the *legitimate authority* figure—he presented the rules, arranged for the assignment of roles (by a rigged drawing of lots), and ordered the teachers to do their jobs whenever they hesitated or dissented. The dependent variable was the final level of shock—on a shock machine that went up to 450 volts in small, 15-volt steps—that a teacher gave before refusing to continue to obey the authority.

The Test Situation The study was staged to make a participant think that, by following orders, he or she was causing pain and suffering and perhaps even killing an innocent person. Each teacher had been given a sample shock of 45 volts to feel the amount of pain it caused. The learner was a pleasant, mild-mannered man, about 50 years old, who mentioned something about a heart condition but was willing to go along with the procedure. He was strapped into an "electric chair" in the next room and communicated with the teacher via an intercom. His task was to memorize pairs of words, giving the second word in a pair when he heard the first one. The learner soon began making errors—according to a prearranged schedule—and the teacher began shocking the learner. The protests of the victim rose with the shock level. At 75 volts, he began to moan and grunt; at 150 volts, he demanded to be released from the experiment; at 180 volts, he cried out that he could not stand the pain any longer. At 300 volts, he insisted that he would no longer take part in the experiment and must be freed. He yelled out about his heart condition and screamed. If a teacher hesitated

a–c Milgram's obedience experiment: the "teacher" (participant) with experimenter (authority figure), the shock generator, and the "learner" (the experimenter's confederate). What aspects of the situation affected the likelihood that the teachers would continue to the maximum shock level?

or protested delivering the next shock, the experimenter said, "The experiment requires that you continue" or "You have no other choice, you *must* go on."

As you might imagine, the situation was stressful for the participants. Most participants complained and protested, repeatedly insisting they could not continue. However, even in the face of their visible conflict, many of the participants continued to shock the learner up to the button that was marked "Danger: Severe Shock XXX (450 volts)." To achieve obedience, the experimenter only needed to remind the participants that the experiment required them to continue.

Why Do People Obey Authority? When 40 psychiatrists were asked by Milgram to predict the performance of participants in this experiment, they estimated that most would not go beyond 150 volts (based on a description of the experiment). In their professional opinions, fewer than 4 percent of the participants would still be obedient at 300 volts, and only about 0.1 percent would continue all the way to 450 volts. The psychiatrists presumed that only those few individuals who were *abnormal* in some way, sadists who enjoyed inflicting pain on others, would blindly obey orders to continue up to the maximum shock.

The psychiatrists based their evaluations on presumed *dispositional* qualities of people who would engage in such abnormal behavior; they were, however, overlooking the power of this special situation to influence the thinking and actions of most people caught up in its social context. The remarkable and disturbing conclusion is just how wrong these experts were: *The majority of participants obeyed the authority fully.* No participant quit below 300 volts. Sixty-five percent delivered the maximum 450 volts to the learner. Note that most people *dissented* verbally, but the majority did not *disobey* behaviorally. From the point of view of the victim, that's a critical difference. If you were the victim, would it matter much that the participants said they didn't want to continue hurting you (they dissented) if they then shocked you repeatedly (they obeyed)?

Milgram's research suggests that, to understand why people obey authority, you need to look closely at the psychological forces at work in the situation. We saw earlier how often situational factors constrain behaviors; in Milgram's research, we see an especially vivid instance of that general principle. Milgram and other researchers manipulated a number of aspects of the experimental circumstances to demonstrate that the obedience effect is overwhelmingly due to situational variables and not personality variables. For example, **Figure 16.4** shows how the proximity of the learner changed the probability that the participant would administer shocks all the way to the 450-volt limit. As the distance was reduced, obedience was also reduced. These findings all point to the idea that the *situation,* and not differences among individual participants, largely controlled behavior.

When contemporary students learn about Milgram's research, they often express the strong conviction that, because of cultural changes since the early 1960s, people would no longer obey. To answer this claim, social psychologist **Jerry Burger** (2009) completed a partial replication of one of Milgram's experiments. Burger modified the experiment to address ethical concerns present in Milgram's original procedure. Specifically, Burger halted participants if they continued to obey after they believed they had delivered a 150-volt shock. As noted earlier, 150 volts was the point at which the learner demanded to be

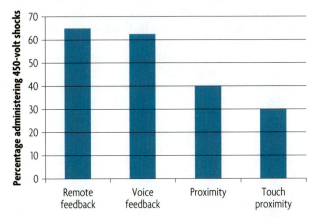

FIGURE 16.4 Obedience in Milgram's Experiments
The graph shows the impact of the situational variable of *proximity* on participants' obedience to authority. In the remote feedback condition, participants only heard the learner's pounding on the wall from the next room. In the voice feedback condition, the participants also heard the learner's verbal protests through the wall. In the proximity condition, the learner was in the same room as the participants. In the touch proximity condition, participants had to hold the learner's hand on the shock plate.

Data from *Obedience to Authority* by S. Milgram, copyright © 1974 Harper & Row.

released from the experiment. Based on Milgram's original data, Burger reasoned that participants who continued after 150 volts would have been quite likely to continue beyond that point. In Milgram's original experiment, 82.5 percent of the participants continued beyond 150 volts; in Burger's replication, 70.0 percent did so. Thus, in the replication, a large majority of participants continued to obey the experimenter. Burger concluded that "the same situational factors that affected obedience in Milgram's participants still operate today" (p. 9).

Two reasons people obey authority in these situations can be traced to the effects of *normative* and *informational* sources of influence: People want to be liked (normative influence), and they want to be right (informational influence). They tend to do what others are doing or requesting to be socially acceptable and approved. In addition, when in an ambiguous, novel situation—like the experimental situation—people rely on others for cues as to what is the appropriate and correct way to behave. They are more likely to do so when experts or credible communicators tell them what to do. A third factor in the Milgram paradigm is that participants were probably confused about *how* to *disobey;* nothing they said in dissent satisfied the authority. If they had a simple, direct way out of the situation—for example, by pressing a "quit" button—it is likely more would have disobeyed (Ross, 1988). Finally, obedience to authority in this experimental situation is part of an *ingrained habit* that is learned by children in many different settings—obey authority without question (Brown, 1986). This heuristic usually serves society well when authorities are legitimate and deserving of obedience. The problem is that the rule gets overapplied. Blind obedience to authority means obeying any and all authority figures simply because of their ascribed status, regardless of whether they are unjust or just in their requests and commands.

What is the personal significance to you of this obedience research? What choices will you make when faced with moral dilemmas throughout your life? Take a moment to reflect on the types of obedience to authority situations that might arise in your day-to-day experience. Suppose you were a salesclerk. Would you cheat customers if your boss encouraged such behavior? Suppose you were a member of Congress. Would you vote along party lines, rather than vote your conscience?

Milgram's obedience research challenges the myth that evil lurks in the minds of evil people—the bad "they" who are different from the good "us" or "you," who would never do such things. The purpose in recounting these findings is not to debase human nature but to make clear that even normal, well-meaning individuals are subject to the potential for frailty in the face of strong situational and social forces.

This section has argued that people are interconnected by the rules, norms, and situations they share. We next consider how people gather and apply information from their day-to-day experiences. We examine the question of how attitudes are formed and changed—and we explore the links among beliefs, attitudes, and actions.

Stop *and* Review

① What did the Stanford Prison Experiment demonstrate about social roles?
② Why are groups able to have normative influence?
③ What type of influence are minorities able to exert in a group?
④ How can you recognize circumstances of group polarization?
⑤ How did psychiatrists' predictions compare to participants' actual behavior in Milgram's experiments?

CRITICAL THINKING   Consider the study that looked at conformity in line-length judgments. Why was it important that the group members all gave the correct answer on the first few trials?

✔—[**Study** and **Review** on **MyPsychLab**

ATTITUDES, ATTITUDE CHANGE, AND ACTION

Have you already had a chance today to express an *attitude*? Has someone asked you, "What do you think of my shirt?" or "Was the chicken any good?" An **attitude** is a positive or negative evaluation of people, objects, and ideas. This definition of attitude allows for the fact that many of the attitudes you hold are not overt; you may not be consciously aware that you harbor certain attitudes. Attitudes are important because they influence your behavior and how you construct social reality.

....

attitude The learned, relatively stable tendency to respond to people, concepts, and events in an evaluative way.

How does your attitude toward Angelina Jolie affect your willingness to watch her movies?

Recall the Olympic skating completion. Those people who favored one pair "saw" a different performance than those people who favored the other; attributions about events were made in line with their attitudes. What are the sources of your attitudes, and how do they affect your behaviors?

Attitudes and Behaviors

You already saw that attitudes are positive or negative evaluations. As you start this section, take a moment to make an evaluation. To what extent do you agree with this statement? (Circle a number.)

I enjoy movies that star Angelina Jolie.

1 —— 2 —— 3 —— 4 —— 5 —— 6 —— 7 —— 8 —— 9
Strongly   Neutral   Strongly
disagree   agree

Let's say that you gave a rating of 3—you disagree somewhat. What is the origin of that judgment? There are three types of information that give rise to your attitude:

- *Cognitive.* What thoughts do you have in response to "Angelina Jolie"?
- *Affective.* What feelings does the mention of "Angelina Jolie" evoke?
- *Behavioral.* How do you behave when, for example, you have the opportunity to see one of Angelina Jolie's movies?

Some combination of these types of information most likely guided your hand when you circled "3" (or some other number). Your attitudes also generate responses in the same three categories. If you believe yourself to have a somewhat negative attitude toward Angelina Jolie, you might say, "She isn't a serious actor" (cognitive), "She looked better when she first started out" (affective), or "After *The Tourist*, I'm going to wait to read her reviews" (behavioral).

It isn't too hard to measure an attitude, but is that attitude always an accurate indication of how people will actually behave? You know from your own life experiences that the answer is "no": People will say they dislike Angelina Jolie but spend good money to see her anyway. At the same time, sometimes people's behaviors *do* follow their attitudes: They say they won't pay to see Angelina Jolie, and they don't. How can you determine when attitudes will or will not predict behavior? Researchers have worked hard to answer that question—to identify the circumstances in which the link is strongest between people's attitudes and how they act (Bohner & Dickel, 2011; Glasman & Albarracín, 2006).

One property of attitudes that predicts behavior is *accessibility*—the strength of the association between an attitude object and a person's evaluation of that object (Fazio & Roskos-Ewoldsen, 2005). When I asked you about Angelina Jolie, did an answer rush to mind or did you have to consider the question for a while? The more quickly an answer rushed in, the more likely it is that your behavior will be consistent with that attitude. But how do attitudes become more accessible? Research suggests that attitudes are more accessible when they are based on *direct experience*: You will have a more accessible attitude about Angelina Jolie movies if you've experienced several of them yourself rather than hearing or reading about them indirectly.

Attitudes are also more accessible when they have been rehearsed more often: Just as you might expect, the more often you've formulated an attitude about something (consider "chocolate" versus "kiwi"), the more accessible is the attitude. Let's consider a study that illustrates the behavioral consequences of attitude rehearsal.

The researchers were interested in understanding the factors that lead people to make repeated blood donations (Godin et al., 2008). The study focused on 4,672 people who had previously donated blood. Prior donors are quite likely to have positive attitudes about the importance of donating blood. The researchers reasoned that they could increase the likelihood that people would donate again if they made those attitudes more accessible. To increase attitude accessibility, the researchers randomly selected 2,900 people for the experimental group and mailed a questionnaire that asked them to report their attitudes toward blood donations. Of this group, 2,389 people completed the questionnaire. The 1,772 people randomly assigned to the control group did not receive the questionnaire. Six months and 12 months after the time the questionnaires went out, the researchers checked to see how many people had made blood donations. The impact of the questionnaire was clear: Members of the experimental group donated more blood. For example, after six months, 8.6 percent more people in the experimental group had registered to give blood.

There is a whole variety of reasons people might or might not donate blood in six months or a year. However, the very act of rehearsing and reporting their attitudes on a simple questionnaire had a major impact on people's subsequent behavior.

Attitudes also are better predictors of behavior when the attitudes remain stable over time. Suppose, for example, you had to agree or disagree with the statement "I trust politicians." Your judgment would depend on which politician or politicians came to mind: Was it George Washington, Winston Churchill, George W. Bush, or Barack Obama? Now, suppose you addressed the same question a week from now. If you called different politicians to mind, your overall attitude toward politicians would likely change (Lord et al., 2004; Sia et al., 1997). Only when the "evidence" for your attitude remains stable over time can we expect to find a strong relationship between your evaluation (thoughts) and what you do (actions).

Another way to improve the match between attitudes and behaviors would be to improve attitude measures. In recent years, researchers have created a number of new attitude measures that attempt to capture people's *automatic* or *implicit* attitudes—the attitudes they hold toward people, objects, or ideas that often remain outside conscious awareness (Bohner & Dickel, 2011; Stanley et al., 2008). The claim is that these implicit attitudes may sometimes allow for better predictions of behavior. Much research on implicit attitudes has focused on circumstances in which people are not consciously aware that they harbor prejudice. When we arrive at the topic of implicit prejudice, you will see that implicit attitudes often predict people's behavior.

Processes of Persuasion

You've just seen that, under appropriate circumstances, attitudes can predict behavior. That's good news for all the people who spend time and money to affect your attitudes. But quite often others *can't* affect your attitudes when they want to do so. You don't change brands of toothpaste each time you see a peppy new commercial with scads of pearly-toothed actors; you don't change your political affiliation each time a candidate looks into the camera and declares sincerely that he or she deserves your vote. Many people in your life indulge in **persuasion**—deliberate efforts to change your attitudes. For persuasion to take place, certain conditions must be met. Let's explore some of those conditions.

To begin, let's review the **elaboration likelihood model**, a theory of persuasion that defines how likely it is that people will focus their cognitive processes to elaborate on a persuasive message (Petty & Briñol, 2008; Petty et al., 2005). This model makes a critical distinction between *central* and *peripheral routes* to persuasion. The central route represents circumstances in which people think carefully about a persuasive communication so that attitude change depends on the strength of the arguments. This careful thought is called *high* elaboration. When someone is trying to convince you that gasoline should

persuasion Deliberate efforts to change attitudes.

elaboration likelihood model A theory of persuasion that defines how likely it is that people will focus their cognitive processes to elaborate upon a message and therefore follow the central and peripheral routes to persuasion.

Why do advertisers pay celebrities to endorse their products?

ACCOUNT NOW" (Vishwanath et al., 2011). The researchers asked the undergraduates a series of questions to determine what factors prompted the students to engage in more elaboration with respect to the message. The analyses found, for example, that students who perceived the message as having more personal relevance were likely to have engaged in greater elaboration. On the other hand, people who focused on superficial cues (like the capital letters conveying urgency) were more likely to have been persuaded by the phishing messages.

These results remind you why phishing can be successful: When people focus on superficial features—this message is URGENT—rather than engaging critical thought about a request, they may unwittingly abet the theft of their personal information. Next time you get phished, analyze the message to see what its authors have done to keep your attention tightly focused on superficial cues.

There are many circumstances in life in which you probably want to resist having your attitudes changed. The elaboration likelihood model suggests that you'll often need to expend some effort to avoid being persuaded. Consider a study in which a researcher asked students to read an essay that argued that college vacations should be shortened to just one month (Burkley, 2008). The essay suggested, for example, that such a change would allow students to graduate more rapidly. Before reading the essay, some participants engaged in a separate task in which they spent five minutes listing thoughts that came to mind—but they were under explicit instructions *not* to think about a white bear. After doing that task, the participants gave attitude ratings that were more favorable toward the idea of one-month vacations than did control participants. It seemed that the effort they expended trying not to think about white bears had depleted the mental resources they needed to resist the essay's arguments. In your own life, when you know that you're going to face a persuasive appeal, you should try to ensure that you are ready to engage your full mental effort.

cost $8 a gallon, you are likely to process the information in this careful fashion. The peripheral route represents circumstances in which people do not focus critically on the message but respond to superficial cues in the situation. When an attractive model is placed in front of the product someone wishes you to buy, the seller is hoping you'll avoid critical thought. That absence of critical thought is called *low* elaboration. The central or peripheral route that people take depends in large part on their *motivation* with respect to the message: Are they willing and able to think carefully about the persuasive content; will they engage in high or low elaboration?

If you take a close look at the messages that surround you, you will quickly come to the conclusion that advertisers, for example, often count on you to take the peripheral route. Why do advertisers pay celebrities to sell their products? Do you really believe that Hollywood actors worry enormously about which long-distance phone service will produce bigger savings? Presumably, the advertisers hope that you won't evaluate the arguments too closely—instead, they hope you'll let yourself be persuaded by your general feelings of warmth toward the actor hawking the product.

Now ask yourself this question: Under what circumstances are you likely to feel sufficiently motivated to take the central route to persuasion? Researchers have undertaken an enormous amount of research to address that question (Petty et al., 2005). Let's consider a study that looked at the likelihood of elaboration in the context of phishing.

Persuasion by Your Own Actions

The last section described factors that influence people's ability to change others' attitudes. However, there are forces at work in a number of circumstances that cause people to bring about their *own* attitude change. Imagine a situation in which you've vowed not to eat any extra calories. You arrive at work, and there's a cake for your boss's birthday. You consume a piece. Did you break your vow? That is, should you have a negative attitude about your own behavior? Aren't you likely to think what you did was OK? Why? Let's consider two analyses of self-persuasion, *cognitive dissonance theory* and *self-perception theory*.

Cognitive Dissonance Theory　One of the most common assumptions in the study of attitudes is that people like to believe that their attitudes remain consistent over time. This striving for consistency was explored within the field of social psychology in the theory of *cognitive dissonance*, as developed by **Leon Festinger** (1957). **Cognitive dissonance** is the state of conflict someone experiences *after* making a decision, taking an action, or being exposed to information that is contrary to prior beliefs, feelings, or values. Suppose, for example, you

If you have an e-mail account, you almost certainly have been phished: You have received messages that have deceptively attempted to obtain personal information from you. Phishing is an exercise in persuasion. The phishers want to get you to believe that the request for information is genuine. A team of researchers collected data from undergraduates whose whole campus had received phishing e-mails with alarmist prose like "VERIFY YOUR UNIVERSITY EMAIL

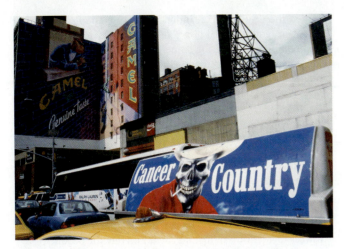

What messages might you give yourself to reduce cognitive dissonance if you were aware of the adverse effects of smoking but continued to smoke?

chose to buy a car against a friend's advice. Why might you be overly defensive about the car? It is assumed that when a person's cognitions about his or her behavior and relevant attitudes are dissonant—they do not follow one to the next—an aversive state arises that the person is motivated to reduce. Dissonance-reducing activities modify this unpleasant state. In the case of your car, being defensive—overstating its value—makes you feel better about going against your friend's advice. (Dissonance also might lead you to think less well of your friend.) 👁

Dissonance has motivational force—it impels you to take action to reduce the unpleasant feeling (Wood, 2000). The motivation to reduce dissonance increases with the magnitude of the dissonance created by a cognitive inconsistency. In other words, the stronger the dissonance, the greater the motivation to reduce it. In a classic dissonance experiment, college students told a lie to other students and came to believe in their lie when they got a small, rather than a large, reward for doing so.

Featured Study

Stanford students participated in a very dull task and were then asked (as a favor to the experimenter because his assistant hadn't shown up) to lie to another participant by saying that the task had been fun and interesting. Half the participants were paid $20 to tell the lie; the others were paid only $1. The $20 payment was sufficient external justification for lying, but the $1 payment was an inadequate justification. The people who were paid $1 were left with dissonant cognitions: "The task was dull" and "I chose to lie by telling another student it was fun and interesting without a good reason for doing so."

To reduce their dissonance, these $1 participants changed their evaluations of the task. They later expressed the belief that they found "it really was fun and interesting—I might like to do it again." In comparison, the participants who lied for $20 did not change their evaluations—the task was still a bore; they had only lied "for the money" (Festinger & Carlsmith, 1959).

As this experiment shows, under conditions of high dissonance, an individual acts to justify his or her behavior after the fact and engages in self-persuasion.

Hundreds of experiments and field studies have shown the power of cognitive dissonance to change attitudes and behavior (Cooper, 2007). Recently, however, researchers have begun to question whether dissonance effects generalize to other cultures. Consider again the way the concept of *self* changes from culture to culture. As noted earlier, North Americans typically view themselves as *independent,* distinct from others in the environment; members of Asian cultures typically view themselves as *interdependent,* fundamentally interconnected with others. Does the cultural concept of the self affect the experience of cognitive dissonance?

Featured Study

Groups of Canadian and Japanese participants examined a list of entrées for a Chinese restaurant (Hoshino-Browne et al., 2005). Out of a list of 25 dishes, they chose the 10 that they most liked (in one condition) or that they thought a friend would most like (in a second condition). Next, they rank-ordered those 10 dishes from most to least desirable—again, with respect either to their own or to a friend's preferences. The experimenters then asked the participants to choose between two coupons for free food. The coupons named the participants' fifth- and sixth-ranked choices (for them or their friend). Finally, participants were asked to go through and rate their top 10 choices once again. How might those ratings change from the first to the second time? According to dissonance theory, when you make a tough choice—like the one between your fifth- and sixth-ranked alternatives—you should adjust your attitudes to feel better about the outcome of the choice: "If I chose kung pao chicken [originally no. 5], it really must be a better choice than mu shu pork [originally no. 6]." However, cross-cultural research on the self suggests that Canadian participants should experience more dissonance with respect to their own choices (because of their independent senses of self), whereas Japanese participants should experience more dissonance with respect to their choices for their friends (because of their interdependent senses of self). The data confirmed those expectations: Canadian participants' attitudes changed considerably more for self-judgments; Japanese participants' attitudes changed considerably more for friend judgments.

This research suggests that people experience cognitive dissonance—they seek to maintain consistency within their self-concept—in ways that are specific to their particular senses of self. If you are ever in circumstances in which you must make decisions jointly with members of other cultures, you will want to reflect on the culture's impact on the way you all think and act after the decision has been made.

Self-Perception Theory Dissonance theory describes one way in which people, at least in Western cultures, allow their behaviors ("I chose that CD") to have an impact on their attitudes ("I must like it much better than my other option").

👁 **Watch** the **Video** *Cognitive Dissonance: Need to Justify Our Actions* on **MyPsychLab**

cognitive dissonance The theory that the tension-producing effects of incongruous cognitions motivate individuals to reduce such tension.

Self-perception theory, developed by Daryl Bem (1972), identifies other circumstances in which behaviors inform attitudes. According to **self-perception theory**, you infer what your internal states (beliefs, attitudes, motives, and feelings) are or should be by perceiving how you are acting now and recalling how you have acted in the past in a given situation. You use that self-knowledge to reason backward to the most likely causes or determinants of your behavior. For example, the self-perceiver responds to the question, "Do you like psychology?" by saying, "Sure, I'm taking the basic course and it's not required, I do all the readings, I pay attention during lectures, and I'm getting a good grade in the course." In other words, you answer a question about personal preferences by a behavioral description of relevant actions and situational factors—rather than undertaking an intense search of thoughts and feelings.

One flaw in the process of gaining self-knowledge through self-perception is that people can be insensitive about the extent to which their behavior is influenced by situational forces. You can see this if we return a final time to the College Bowl experiment. Recall that the participants who labored unsuccessfully as contestants rated their own general knowledge relatively low. Imagine what it must have been like to be in their position. Over and over you would hear yourself saying, "I don't know the answer to that question." Can you see how observation of this behavior—the process of self-perception—could give rise to a negative self-evaluation?

Let's return to the attitudes you might express toward yourself if you eat a slice of cake at your boss's birthday party. According to dissonance theory, you need to resolve the inconsistency between your vow ("I won't consume any extra calories") and your behavior (eating a piece of cake). There are many things you can do to avoid feeling bad: Perhaps you'd reason, "I can't afford to have my boss be angry at me by declining a piece of cake." Similarly, according to self-perception theory, you look at your behavior to calculate your attitude. If you think, "Because I ate cake, my boss's birthday must have been very important," you'll also escape any negative impact on your self-esteem. Self-persuasion can sometimes be useful!

Compliance

So far, this section has discussed what attitudes are and how they might be changed. It should be clear to you, however, that most often what people want you to do is change your *behavior*: People wish to bring about **compliance**—a change in behavior consistent with their direct requests. When advertisers spend a lot of money for TV commercials, they don't want you just to feel good about their products—they want you to march into a store and buy them. Similarly, doctors want you to follow their medical advice. Social psychologists have extensively

....

self-perception theory The idea that people observe themselves to figure out the reasons they act as they do; people infer what their internal states are by perceiving how they are acting in a given situation.

compliance A change in behavior consistent with a communication source's direct requests.

reciprocity norm Expectation that favors will be returned—if someone does something for another person, that person should do something in return.

studied the way in which individuals bring about compliance with their requests (Cialdini, 2009; Cialdini & Goldstein, 2004). This section will describe some of those techniques and note how wily salespeople often use them to get you to do things you might not otherwise have done.

Reciprocity One of the rules that dominates human experience is that when someone does something for you, you should do something for that person as well—this is called the **reciprocity norm**. Laboratory research has shown that even very small favors can lead participants to do much larger favors in return (Regan, 1971). Salespeople use reciprocity against you by appearing to do you a favor: "I'll tell you what, I'll take $5 off the price" or "Here's a free sample just for agreeing to talk to me today." This strategy puts you in a position of psychological distress if you don't return the favor and buy the product.

Another compliance technique that arises from the reciprocity norm has often been called the *door-in-the-face technique:* When people say "no" to a large request, they will often say "yes" to a more moderate request. For example, in one experiment, students were asked to spend two hours every week for two years as counselors for juvenile delinquents. They all said "no." Next, they were asked if they would serve as chaperones for some of the delinquents on a trip to the zoo. When they had previously said "no" to the large request, 50 percent of the students agreed to this smaller request. When a different group of students was approached, who had never been asked the large request, only 17 percent of them agreed to serve as chaperones (Cialdini et al., 1975). How does this technique invoke the reciprocity norm? When people making requests go from the large to the moderate request, they have done something for you: Now you must do something for them—or risk violating the norm. You agree to the smaller request!

Consistency and Commitment The door-in-the-face technique moves you from a large to a moderate request. Salespeople also know that people like to appear *consistent* in their behavior: So, if they can get you to *commit* yourself to some small concession, they can probably also get you to commit to something larger. In experiments, people who agreed to small requests (for example, signing petitions) were more likely subsequently to agree to a bigger request (for example, putting large signs on their lawn) (Freedman & Fraser, 1966). This is often called the *foot-in-the-door technique:* Once people get a foot in the door, they can use your sense of commitment to increase your later compliance. This strategy works because your original behavior makes you think about yourself in a particular way. You want your subsequent behavior to be consistent with that self-image.

Let's consider another compliance technique that also takes advantage of people's need to feel consistent. The technique has been called *foot-in-the-mouth:* By getting people to answer a simple initial question, you can raise the probability that they'll comply with a subsequent request.

At some point, you have probably answered your phone and discovered that the caller wanted you to answer a few survey questions. Did you comply with the request? A pair of researchers studied the impact of foot-in-the-mouth in this situation (Meineri & Guéguen, 2011). They placed telephone calls to about 1,800 participants. In one condition, the call began with an initial question, "Hello, I'm a student at the technical college in Vannes. I hope I'm not disturbing you, am I?" The caller waited for a "yes" or "no" response, and then asked the participants whether they would complete the survey. In this condition, 25.2 percent of the participants agreed to do so. In another condition, the caller asked participants to complete the survey without the initial question. Under those circumstances, the rate of compliance was 17.3 percent.

If you are in the business of getting people to complete surveys, you'd probably be happy to improve your compliance rate 8 percent just by adding an initial question!

In explaining these compliance techniques, this section has provided a couple of examples of things you might *want* to do: You might want to volunteer your time or sign petitions for good causes. However, you can see that much of the time people use these techniques to get you to do things you probably *wouldn't* want to do. How can you defend yourself against wily salespeople and their kin? Try to catch them using these strategies—and resist their efforts. Your knowledge of social psychology can make you an all-around wiser consumer.

This section has described attitudes and behaviors and the relationships between them. However, we have not yet touched on circumstances in which attitudes in the form of *prejudice* may lead to destructive behaviors. We turn now to the topic of prejudice and document both how it comes about and procedures that may be effective to reduce or eliminate it.

Stop *and* Review

① What three components define attitudes?
② What cognitive process discriminates the central and peripheral routes to persuasion?
③ Why does culture have an impact on processes of cognitive dissonance?
④ Why does the door-in-the-face technique engage the reciprocity norm?

CRITICAL THINKING Recall the study in which experimental participants filled out a questionnaire about their attitudes toward blood donation. Why was it important that people were randomly assigned to the experimental and control groups?

✔—Study and Review on MyPsychLab

PREJUDICE

Of all human weaknesses, none is more destructive to the dignity of the individual and the social bonds of humanity than prejudice. Prejudice is the prime example of social reality gone awry—a situation created in the minds of people that can demean and destroy the lives of others. **Prejudice**

What can you do if you want to increase the probability that your neighbors will recycle?

is a learned attitude toward a target object, involving negative feelings (dislike or fear), negative beliefs (stereotypes) that justify the attitude, and a behavioral intention to avoid, control, dominate, or eliminate those in the target group. Nazi leaders, for example, passed laws to enforce their prejudiced beliefs that Jews were subhuman and trying to bring about the downfall of Aryan culture. A false belief qualifies as prejudice when it resists change even in the face of appropriate evidence of its falseness. People display prejudice, for example, when they assert that African Americans are all lazy despite their hardworking African American colleagues. Prejudiced attitudes serve as biasing filters that influence the way individuals are perceived and treated once they are categorized as members of a target group. ◉

Social psychology has always put the study of prejudice high on its agenda in an effort to understand its complexity and persistence and to develop strategies to change prejudiced attitudes and discriminatory behavior (Allport, 1954; Nelson, 2006). In fact, the Supreme Court's 1954 decision to outlaw segregated public education was, in part, based on research, presented in federal court by social psychologist **Kenneth Clark**, that showed the negative impact on Black children of their separate and unequal education (Clark & Clark, 1947). This section will describe the progress social psychologists have made in their efforts to understand the origins and effects of prejudice, as well as their efforts to help reverse its effects.

Origins of Prejudice

One of the sad truths from the study of prejudice is that it is easy to get people to show negative attitudes toward people

◉ **Watch** the **Video** *Classic Footage of Gordon Allport on Personality Traits* on **MyPsychLab**

prejudice A learned attitude toward a target object, involving negative affect (dislike or fear), negative beliefs (stereotypes) that justify the attitude, and a behavioral intention to avoid, control, dominate, or eliminate the target object.

who do not belong to the same "group." **Social categorization** is the process by which people organize their social environment by categorizing themselves and others into groups. The simplest and most pervasive form of categorizing consists of an individual determining whether people are like him or her. This categorization develops from a "me versus not me" orientation to an "us versus them" orientation: People divide the world into **in-groups**—the groups with which they identify as members—and **out-groups**—the groups with which they do not identify.

The most minimal of distinctive cues is sufficient to give people strong feelings of in-groups and out-groups. **Henry Tajfel** and his colleagues (Tajfel et al., 1971) invented a paradigm that demonstrated the impact of what they called *minimal groups*. In one study, students provided estimates of the number of dots in a series of patterns projected on a movie screen. The students were told that, based on their performance, they were "dot overestimators" or "dot underestimators." In reality, the researchers randomly assigned the students to those two groups. Next, each student had the opportunity to allocate monetary rewards to the members of the two groups. The students consistently gave greater rewards to the people who they believed shared their dot-estimating tendencies.

Studies of this type illustrate how very easy it is to generate an **in-group bias:** With only a minimal cue to group identity, people begin to favor the members of their own group over the members of other groups (Nelson, 2006). Many experiments have examined the consequences of in-group versus out-group status (Brewer, 2007; Hewstone et al., 2002). This research points to the conclusion that, for the most part, people show favoritism toward those people who are members of their own group rather than bias against members of the other group. For example, people typically rate members of their in-group more highly (on pleasantness, diligence, and so on) than they do members of the out-group. However, that's because they have positive feelings toward the in-group and neutral feelings toward the out-group. Thus, one can have an in-group bias without also having the negative feelings that constitute prejudice.

Unfortunately, in some circumstances people's feelings about out-groups are guided by learned prejudices. In those cases, in-group bias may become more purposeful. Prejudice easily leads to **racism**—discrimination against people based on their skin color or ethnic heritage—and **sexism**—discrimination against people based on their sex. In contemporary times, people are often reluctant to admit to having racist or sexist attitudes. Instead people may express what have been called *modern racism* and *modern sexism*. Measures of modern racism, for example, include statements such as "Blacks are demanding

How does prejudice arise, and why is it so difficult to eradicate?

too much from the rest of society" and "Over the past few years, Blacks have gotten more economically than they deserve" (Henry & Sears, 2002).

You have seen so far that people's categorization of the world into "us" and "them" can swiftly lead to prejudice. Let's look at the way in which prejudice functions through applications of stereotypes.

Effects of Stereotypes

We can use the power of social categorization to explain the origins of many types of prejudice. To explain how prejudice affects day-to-day interactions, we must explore the memory structures that provide important support for prejudice, stereotypes. **Stereotypes** are generalizations about a group of people in which the same characteristics are assigned to all members of a group. You are no doubt familiar with a wide range of stereotypes. What beliefs do you have about men and women? Jews, Muslims, and Christians? Asians, African Americans, Native Americans, Hispanics, and Whites? How do those beliefs affect your day-to-day interactions with members of those groups? Do you avoid members of some of these groups based on your beliefs?

Because stereotypes so powerfully encode *expectations,* they frequently contribute to the types of situations described earlier in this chapter, in which people construct their own social reality. Consider the potential role stereotypes play to generate judgments about what "exists" in the environment. People are prone to fill in "missing data" with information from their stereotypes: "I'm not going to get in a car with Hiroshi—all Asians are terrible drivers." Those same powerful expectations may cause people to engage in a process called *behavioral confirmation:* Their own actions toward an out-group individual create a context in which the individual will produce behaviors consistent with the stereotype (Klein & Snyder, 2003). If,

....

social categorization The process by which people organize the social environment by categorizing themselves and others into groups.

in-group A group with which people identify as members.

out-group A group with which people do not identify.

in-group bias People's tendency to favor members of their own group over members of other groups.

racism Discrimination against people based on their skin color or ethnic heritage.

sexism Discrimination against people because of their sex.

stereotype Generalization about a group of people in which the same characteristics are assigned to all members of a group.

for example, someone were noticeably anxious when driving with an Asian friend, that friend might drive less well as a consequence. In addition, to maintain consistency, people are likely to discount information that is inconsistent with their stereotyped beliefs. For example, in one study students read an excerpt from an introductory psychology text that talked about the biological origins of sexual orientation (Boysen & Vogel, 2007). Participants with negative initial attitudes toward homosexuality did not find the text persuasive with respect to the legitimacy of homosexuality. This experiment suggests why information alone can typically not reduce prejudice: People tend to devalue information that is inconsistent with their prior stereotype. (A later section will discuss more successful methods for overcoming prejudice.)

You might also recall another effect of stereotypes that you met in the context of intelligence testing. Recall that Chapter 9 discussed racial differences among IQ scores. That section reviewed evidence that members of stereotyped groups experience *stereotype threat* when they are placed in situations to which negative aspects of stereotypes are relevant. Stereotype threat produces a context in which people are not able to make efficient use of their mental resources (Schmader et al., 2008). Although researchers first explored this concept in circumstances of intellectual performance, they have now demonstrated that there is potential for negative effects wherever stereotypes apply. For example, one study examined how a group of women who rated themselves as above-average athletes performed on a golf task (Stone & McWhinnie, 2008). Some of the women were told only that the task was a test of "natural ability." Others were told, in addition, that the task had previously yielded differences between men and women. The instructions continued, "So even though there may be gender differences on this test, we ask that you give 100 percent effort on the task so we can accurately measure your natural skills" (p. 448). Despite this request for 100 percent effort, the women who were reminded about gender differences needed more strokes to complete the eight holes of the golf course. This result illustrates how stereotype threat can impair people's performance across several life domains.

This discussion has focused on circumstances in which people are likely to be aware that they harbor prejudice or endorse stereotypes. We turn now to demonstrations that people may often have prejudice of which they are unaware.

Implicit Prejudice

Take a moment to examine your feelings toward members of groups that you consider as "out-groups" for you. How would we determine if you have prejudice toward those groups? Explicit measures of prejudice directly ask, "How do you feel about this group?" However, social psychologists have argued that negative attitudes often exist as **implicit prejudice**, outside of conscious awareness. Researchers have developed methods to measure implicit prejudice and have demonstrated how it functions to change people's behavior. 👁

The *implicit association test* (IAT) was introduced 25 years ago and remains a prominent measure of implicit prejudice (Greenwald et al., 1998). The IAT determines how quickly people put different concepts into the same categories. Imagine, for example, you are asked to sit in front of a computer and view photographs of thin or overweight people as well as

pleasant and unpleasant words. On one trial, you are asked to press one key if you see a thin person or a pleasant word and a different key if you see an obese person or an unpleasant word. On a second trial, you are asked to press one key if you see an obese person or a pleasant word and a different key if you see a thin person or an unpleasant word. Suppose that you respond more quickly when the task unites obese photos and unpleasant words. That pattern would suggest that you have implicit prejudice toward obese people (because you find it relatively easy to associate them with negative concepts). Researchers have used the IAT in a number of domains, including race, sexuality, and religion. The IAT often reveals prejudice that would not be socially acceptable. For example, students who took an IAT concerning disability displayed implicit prejudice toward people with four different categories of disability—people with alcoholism, mental illness, cancer, and paraplegia (Vaughn et al., 2011).

Research with the IAT regularly identifies people whose explicit attitudes do not show prejudice, but whose automatic responses suggest that they hold negative attitudes toward an out-group (Greenwald et al., 2002). Often the implicit attitudes allow better predictions of people's behavior than explicit measures (Greenwald et al., 2009). Let's look at a study in which managers' implicit prejudice had an impact on their interview decisions. 📷

The study focused on 153 managers who were involved in assessing job applications to invite candidates for interviews (Agerström & Rooth, 2011). The managers were unaware that they were part of a study. As they reviewed applicants as part of their normal responsibilities, they saw two applications that presented candidates who were equally qualified. However, one application included a photograph of an obese individual whereas the other application showed a normal-weight individual. The managers all completed measures of their explicit attitudes toward hiring obese people as well as an IAT measure in the same domain. Overall, the managers invited 7 percent fewer of the obese applicants for interviews. In addition, the managers with greater prejudice as revealed by the IAT were the least likely to invite obese applications for interviews. Explicit measures of prejudice were not correlated with the managers' behavior.

As a second example, let's consider a study that used the IAT to measure racial bias (Stanley et al., 2011). Participants played a game that allowed them to express their trust toward partners. Participants who showed the most pro-White bias in their IAT demonstrated the least trust toward Black partners. Participants' explicit attitudes did not predict their patterns of trust.

These examples suggest that people whose explicit beliefs are not prejudiced may nonetheless produce automatic acts of prejudice by virtue of implicit attitudes. The evidence confirms that prejudice is easy to create and has broad consequences.

....

👁 **Watch** the **Video** *Black Doll White Doll* on **MyPsychLab**

📷 **Simulate** the **Experiment** *Black* on **MyPsychLab**

implicit prejudice Prejudice that exists outside an individual's conscious awareness.

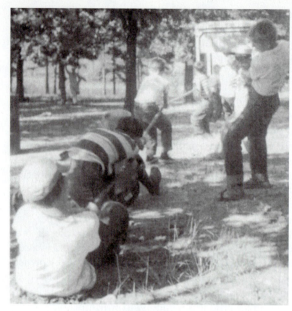

a & b In the intergroup competition phase of the Robbers Cave experiment, the "Eagles" and "Rattlers" pulled apart—but in the end, they pulled together. What general conclusions about contact and prejudice can be drawn from this study?

Even so, from the earliest days of social psychology, researchers have attempted to reverse the march of prejudice. Let's now sample some of those efforts.

Reversing Prejudice

One of the classic studies in social psychology was also the first demonstration that arbitrary "us" versus "them" divisions could lead to great hostility. In the summer of 1954, **Muzafer Sherif** and his colleagues (1961/1988) brought two groups of boys to a summer camp at Robbers Cave State Park in Oklahoma. The two groups were dubbed the "Eagles" and the "Rattlers." Each group forged its own camp bonds—for example, the boys hiked, swam, and prepared meals together—in ignorance of the other group for about a week. The groups' introduction to each other consisted of a series of competitive activities like baseball, football, and a tug-of-war. From this beginning, the rivalry between the groups grew violent. Group flags were burned, cabins were ransacked, and a near-riotlike food fight broke out. What could be done to reduce this animosity?

The experimenters tried a propaganda approach, by complimenting each group to the other. That did not work. The experimenters tried bringing the groups together in noncompetitive circumstances. That did not work either. Hostility seethed even when the groups were just watching a movie in the same place. Finally, the experimenters hit on a solution. What they did was to introduce problems that could be solved only through *cooperative action* on *shared goals*. For example, the experimenters arranged for the camp truck to break down.

Both groups of boys were needed to pull it back up a steep hill. In the face of mutual dependence, hostility faded away. In fact, the boys started to make "best friends" across group boundaries.

The Robbers Cave experiment disproved the idea that simple contact between hostile groups alone will reduce prejudice (Allport, 1954). The boys did not like each other any better just by being in each others' company. Instead, the experiment provided evidence for the **contact hypothesis**—a program combating prejudice must foster personal interaction (Pettigrew, 2008).

Researchers have carried out studies around the world to determine what types of contact between people lead to reduced prejudice. A review of 515 studies on the contact hypothesis strongly supported the conclusion that contact with out-group members lowers prejudice (Pettigrew et al., 2011). Recent research has tried to determine whether contact has an impact among people whose personalities particulary predispose them to express prejudice (Hodson, 2011). Let's consider a study that provides cause for optimism.

Featured Study

People who are highly authoritarian tend to be uncritical of authority and feel aggression toward people who violate norms. They also tend to express high levels of prejudice. Researchers wished to determine whether intergroup contact could, even so, reduce prejudice among authoritarians (Dhont & Van Hiel, 2009). In the study, 215 Belgian adults provided self-ratings of their authoritarianism as well as the amount of contact they had had with immigrants and their level of racism. The researchers' analyses demonstrated an overall positive correlation between authoritarianism and racism: The higher the level of authoritarianism, the greater the racism. However, even in that context, the contact hypothesis was supported. Specifically, among people who were high in authoritarianism,

----

contact hypothesis The prediction that contact between groups will reduce prejudice only if the contact includes features such as cooperation toward shared goals.

those with the most intergroup contact expressed lower levels of racism.

This study shows that intergroup contact can benefit even individuals who are inclined to be intolerant.

Research on the contact hypothesis emphasizes the particular importance for intergroup friendships for prejudice reduction (Davies et al., 2011). In fact, people's prejudice is reduced even when the contact is *indirect*—when it's just the case that they have in-group friends who have out-group friends (Pettigrew et al., 2007). Why are both direct and indirect friendships so effective? Friendships allow people to learn to take the perspective of out-group members and empathize with them. Friendships also reduce the anxiety associated with out-group contacts and make the out-group seem less threatening (Pettigrew, 2008).

Let's take a moment to consider an application of this research in an academic setting. Social psychologist **Elliot Aronson** and his colleagues (1978) developed a program anchored in the contact philosophy to tackle prejudice in newly desegregated classrooms in Texas and California. The research team created conditions in which fifth-grade students had to depend on one another rather than compete against one another to learn required material. In a strategy known as the *jigsaw technique,* each pupil is given part of the total material to master and then share with other group members. Performance is evaluated on the basis of the overall group presentation. Thus every member's contribution is essential and valued. Aronson and his colleagues found that interracial conflict decreased in classrooms in which jigsawing united formerly hostile White, Latino, and African American students into common-fate teams (Aronson, 2002; Aronson & Gonzalez, 1988).

Social psychology has no great solution to end prejudice all at once. It does, however, provide a set of ideas to eliminate prejudice's worst effects slowly but surely, in each small locality. It is worth taking a moment to contemplate the prejudices you have enforced or endured—to see how you might begin to make adjustments in your own small locality.

We have just considered circumstances in which psychological forces drive individuals apart. We now examine the opposite situations in which people are drawn together in relationships of liking and loving.

Stop *and* Review

① How does in-group bias affect ratings of in- and out-group members?
② How does the process of behavioral confirmation support stereotypes?
③ What has research demonstrated about the impact of contact between members of different groups?

CRITICAL THINKING   Recall the study that looked at implicit prejudice toward obese individuals. Why was it important that the participants were unaware that they were part of a study?

✔•⌐**Study** and **Review** on **MyPsychLab**

SOCIAL RELATIONSHIPS

How do you choose the people with whom you share your life? Why do you seek the company of your friends? Why are there some people for whom your feelings move beyond friendship to feelings of romantic love? Social psychologists have developed a variety of answers to these questions of *interpersonal attraction*. (But don't worry, no one yet has taken all the mystery out of love!)

Liking

Have you ever stopped to examine how and why you acquired each of your friends? The first part of this answer is straightforward: People tend to become attracted to others with whom they are in close *proximity*—you see and meet them because they live or work near you. This factor probably requires little explanation, but it might be worth noting that there is a general tendency for people to like objects and people just by virtue of *mere exposure*: As Chapter 12 explained, the more you are exposed to something or someone, the more you like it (Zajonc, 1968). This mere exposure effect means that, on the whole, you will come to like more and more the people who are nearby. Many people now maintain relationships over networks of computers. Although a friend may be geographically quite distant, daily messages appearing on a computer screen can make the person seem psychologically very close. Let's look now at other factors that can lead to attraction and liking.

Physical Attractiveness   For better or worse, *physical attractiveness* often plays a role in the kindling of friendship. Let's consider a laboratory demonstration of that force at work.

Participants viewed a series of 60 photographs of attractive and unattractive individuals with whom they were unacquainted (Lemay et al., 2010). For each photograph, the participants made judgments of the pictured individual's personality traits on dimensions such as kindness, generosity, and warmth. The participants also indicated how much they were motivated to get to know each individual by responding to statements such as, "Based on your first impression, to what extent would you like or dislike this person?" (p. 342). With only the photographs as the basis of their judgments, the participants credited the attractive individuals with more positive personality traits. They also indicated greater motivation to become socially engaged with the attractive individuals.

Featured Study

There is a strong stereotype in Western culture that physically attractive people are also good in other ways. A review of a large number of studies documented the impact of physical attractiveness on a whole range of judgments (Langlois et al., 2000). For example, people rate both children and adults as more socially competent when they are attractive. In addition, attractive children receive higher competence ratings in school, and attractive adults receive higher competence ratings in their occupations.

Why does physical attractiveness lead to liking? Evolutionary theorists have suggested that attractiveness judgments arise from the psychological mechanisms humans have evolved to choose a mate (Gallup & Frederick, 2010). On this view, a "judgment of attractiveness is the response in a receiver to a variety of traits reliably associated with fitness, such as helath, reproductive value, and, possibly, heritable genetic quality" (Penton-Voak, 2011, p. 177). Research from the evolutionary perspective has often focused on facial attractiveness (Little et al., 2011). Consider **Figure 16.5**. Which face do you find more attractive? Most people prefer the symmetrical face. Evolutionary psychologists argue that symmetry is a product of successful development; departures from symmetry suggest difficulties over the course of development. For that reason, asymmetry suggests a lack of genetic fitness. People also typically find average faces (that is, faces that represent the mathematical average for a population) more attractive than faces that depart from the average (Rhodes, 2006). On the evolutionary perspective, unusual features may signal a history of difficulty over development and, therefore, again, a lack of genetic fitness. This analysis suggests that some judgments of liking are a product of the evolutionary imperative toward successful mating.

Even if evolution explains responses to physical attractiveness, cultures still differ in the extent to which attractiveness affects everyday judgments. For example, students at universities in Ghana and the United States viewed the same photographs of attractive and unattractive people (Anderson et al., 2008). They provided ratings of each photograph for several personality traits (such as trustworthy, stable, sensitive, and strong). As you can see in **Figure 16.6**, participants from Ghana made nearly the same attributions to attractive and unattractive photographs. Participants from the United States made less positive attributions to the unattractive photographs. This finding echoes other results you've seen in which people with different cultural construals of the self—independent for the United States and interdependent for Ghana—provide different interpersonal judgments.

Similarity A famous adage on *similarity* suggests that "birds of a feather flock together." Is this correct? Research evidence

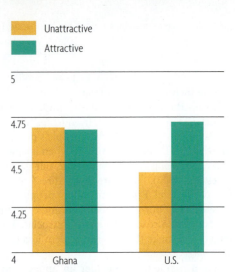

FIGURE 16.6 Cross-Cultural Trait Judgments for Attractive and Unattractive Individuals

Participants in Ghana and the United States made trait judgments based on photographs of attractive and unattractive individuals. Participants from Ghana made nearly the same attributions to attractive and unattractive photographs. U.S. participants made less positive attributions to the unattractive photographs.

From Anderson, S. L., Adams, G., & Plaut, V. C., *Journal of Personality and Social Psychology*, 95, 2008. Copyright © 2008 American Psychological Association. Reprinted with permission.

suggests that, under many circumstances, the answer is yes. Similarity on dimensions such as beliefs, attitudes, and values fosters friendship. Why might that be so? People who are similar to you can provide a sense of personal validation because a similar person makes you feel that the attitudes, for example, you hold dear are, in fact, the right ones (Byrne & Clore, 1970). Furthermore, dissimilarity often leads to strong repulsion (Chen & Kenrick, 2002). When you discover that someone holds opinions that are different from yours, you may evoke from memory past instances of interpersonal friction. That will motivate you to stay away—and if you stay away from dissimilar people, only the similar ones will be left in your pool of friends. Even 3-year-old children show an impact of similarity on liking, suggesting that we start to recognize "birds of a feather" at a very young age (Fawcett & Markson, 2010).

Similarity appears to play a role in allowing friendships to endure over time. Consider a study that began in 1983, when researchers assessed similarity between 45 pairs of friends (Ledbetter et al., 2007). In 2002, 58 of the 90 original participants provided information about the state of their friendships after the passage of 19 years. The participants indicated, for example, how much contact they still had with each other. The results suggested that those pairs that had been more similar in 1983 were also more likely to remain in contact in 2002. It's also important to note that, just as similarity may lead to attraction, attraction can lead to perceptions of similarity: People tend to believe that the people they like are more similar than they really are. In one study, students rated themselves and cross-sex friends on the same set of personality traits (Morry, 2007). The students rated their friends as being more similar to them than their friends' self-reports indicated they actually were.

FIGURE 16.5 Which Face Is More Attractive?

Face (a) is symmetrical; face (b) is asymmetrical.

Little, A. C., Jones, B. C., & DeBruine, L. M. (2011). Facial attractiveness: Evolutionary based research. *Philosohical Transactions of the Royal Society B, 366*, 1638–1659

Reciprocity Finally, you tend to like people whom you believe like you. Do you recall the discussion of salespeople's use of *reciprocity*? The rule that you should give back what you receive applies to friendship as well. People give back "liking" to people whom they believe have given "liking" to them (Whitchurch et al., 2011). People assume that those who express liking for them are going to act in a trustworthy fashion in future interactions; these expectations of trust provide the basis for the reciprocation of liking (Montoya & Insko, 2008). Furthermore, because of the way your beliefs can affect your behaviors, believing that someone likes or dislikes you can help bring that relationship about (Curtis & Miller, 1986). Can you predict how you would act toward someone you believe likes you? Toward someone you believe dislikes you? Suppose you act with hostility toward someone you think doesn't like you. Do you see how your belief could become a self-fulfilling prophecy?

The evidence this section has reviewed suggests that most of your friends will be people you encounter frequently, and people with whom you share the bonds of similarity and reciprocity. But what have researchers found about more intense relationships people call "loving"?

Loving

Many of the same forces that lead to liking also get people started on the road to love—in most cases, you will first like the people you end up loving. (However, some people report loving certain relatives that they don't particularly like as individuals.) What special factors have social psychologists learned about loving relationships?

The Experience of Love What does it mean to experience *love*? Take a moment to think how you would define this important concept. Do you think your definition would agree with your friends' definitions? Researchers have tried to answer this question in a variety of ways, and some consistency has emerged (Reis & Aron, 2008). People's conceptualizations of love cluster into three dimensions (Aron & Westbay, 1996):

- *Passion*—sexual passion and desire
- *Intimacy*—honesty and understanding
- *Commitment*—devotion and sacrifice

Would you characterize all your loving relationships as including all three dimensions? You're probably thinking, "not *all* of them." In fact, it is important to make a distinction between "loving" someone and being "in love" with someone (Meyers & Berscheid, 1997). Most people report themselves to "love" a larger category of people than the group with whom they are "in love"—who among us hasn't been heartbroken to hear the words, "I love you, but I'm not *in* love with you"? Being "in love" implies something more intense and special—this is the type of experience that includes sexual passion. ✳

Let's make one more distinction. Many loving relationships start out with a period of great intensity and absorption, which is called *passionate* love. Over time, there is a tendency for relationships to migrate toward a state of lesser intensity but greater intimacy, called *companionate love* (Berscheid &

✳ **Explore** the **Concept** *Passionate Love Scale* on **MyPsychLab**

Companionate feelings for someone you were once passionate about do not signal "falling out of love": On the contrary, they are a natural outgrowth of romance and a vital ingredient to most long-term partnerships.

Walster, 1978). When you find yourself in a loving relationship, you may do well to anticipate that transition—so that you don't misinterpret a natural change as a process of falling "out of love." In fact, people who report higher levels of companionate love also generally experience greater satisfaction with their lives (Kim & Hatfield, 2004). Even so, the decline of passionate love may not be as dramatic as the stereotype of long-committed couples suggests. Researchers find a reasonable level of passionate love as much as 30 years into a relationship (Aron & Aron, 1994). When you enter a loving relationship, you can have high hopes that the passion will endure in some form, even as the relationship grows to encompass other needs.

Note that experiences of romantic relationships are also influenced by cultural expectations (Wang & Mallinckrodt, 2006). At various moments, this chapter has alluded to the cultural dimension of independence versus interdependence: Cultures with independent construals of self value the person over the collective; interdependent cultures put greater value on shared cultural goals rather than on individual ones. How does this apply to your love life? If you choose a life partner based on your own feelings of love, you are showing preference for your personal goals; if you choose a partner with an eye to how that individual will mesh with your family's structure and concerns, you are being more attuned to collective goals. In fact, when asked what factors mattered most to their experiences of falling in love, people from the United States and China tend to rate different factors as most important (Riela et al., 2010). For example, U.S. citizens were more likely to emphasize appearance and similarity; Chinese citizens were more likely to emphasize the responses of family and friends to the potential romantic partner. Cross-cultural research also suggests that

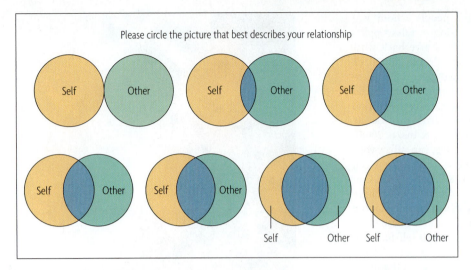

Please circle the picture that best describes your relationship

FIGURE 16.7 The Inclusion of Other in the Self (IOS) Scale

If you are in a romantic relationship, which diagram best captures the interdependence of you and your partner? Research with the IOS scale suggests that people who most perceive the other as included with the self are most likely to stay committed to their relationships.

From Aron, A., Aron, E. N., & Smollan, D., IOS Scale, *Journal of Personality and Social Psychology*. Vol 63(4), Oct 1992, 596–612. Copyright © 1992 by the American Psychological Association. Reproduced with permission.

members of interdependent cultures put less emphasis on love as the defining feature of a relationship (Dion & Dion, 1996). Consider the question, "If a man (woman) had all the other qualities you desired, would you marry this person if you were not in love with him (her)?" Only 3.5 percent of a sample of male and female undergraduates in the United States answered yes; 49 percent of a comparable group of students in India answered yes (Levine et al., 1995).

What Factors Allow Relationships to Last? It seems likely that everyone reading this text—and certainly everyone *writing* this text—has been in a relationship that didn't last. What happened? Or, to put the question in a more positive light, what can researchers say about the types of situations, and people in those situations, that are more likely to lead to long-term loving relationships?

One theory conceptualizes people in close relationships as having a feeling that the "other" is included in their "self" (Aron et al., 2004). Consider the series of diagrams given in **Figure 16.7**. Each of the diagrams represents a way you could conceptualize a close relationship. If you are in a romantic

relationship, can you say which of the diagrams seems to capture most effectively the extent of interdependence between you and your partner? Research has shown that people who perceive the most overlap between self and other—those people who come to view the other as included within the self—are most likely to remain committed to their relationships over time (Aron et al., 1992; Aron & Fraley, 1999).

Researchers have also been interested in understanding individual differences in people's ability to sustain loving relationships over an extended period of time. In recent years, attention has often focused on *adult attachment style* (Fraley et al., 2005; Fraley & Shaver, 2000). Recall from Chapter 10 the importance of the quality of a child's attachment to his or her parents for smooth social development. Researchers began to wonder how much impact that early attachment might have later in life, as the children grew up to have committed relationships and children of their own.

What are the types of attachment styles? **Table 16.1** provides three statements about close relationships (Hazan & Shaver, 1987; Shaver & Hazan, 1994). Please take a moment to note which statement fits you best. When asked which of these statements best describes them, the majority of people (55 percent) choose the first statement; this is a *secure* attachment style. Sizable minorities select the second statement (25 percent, an *avoidant* style) and the third (20 percent, an *anxious-ambivalent* style). Attachment style has proven to be an accurate predictor of relationship quality (Mikulincer et al., 2002; Nosko et al., 2011). Compared with individuals who chose the other two styles, securely attached individuals had the most enduring romantic relationships as adults.

This section has considered some of the factors that influence whether people enter into relationships with each other. Let's turn now to the types of behaviors that emerge within the context of those relationships.

Table 16.1 • Styles of Adult Attachment for Close Relationships

Statement 1:

I find it relatively easy to get close to others and am comfortable depending on them. I don't often worry about being abandoned or about someone getting too close to me.

Statement 2:

I am somewhat uncomfortable being close to others; I find it difficult to trust them completely, difficult to allow myself to depend on them. I am nervous when anyone gets too close; and, often, love partners want me to be more intimate than I feel comfortable being.

Statement 3:

I find that others are reluctant to get as close as I would like. I often worry that my partner doesn't really love me or won't want to stay with me. I want to get very close to my partner, and this sometime scares people away.

Stop *and* Review

① What effect does similarity have on liking?

② What three dimensions define love?

③ Which adult attachment style is generally associated with the highest-quality relationships?

Psychology in Your Life

IN WHAT WAYS ARE YOU LIKE A CHAMELEON?

Here's something you may have noticed: When you interact with other people, you are quite likely to find yourself mimicking them in certain ways. You may, for example, unconsciously match your friends' speech patterns and accents. Social psychologists Tanya Chartrand and John Bargh (1999) labeled this type of mimicry the *chameleon effect.* Chameleons automatically change their color to blend in with their environment. Chartrand and Bargh suggested that humans also automatically adjust their behavior to blend with the people around them.

In their original demonstration of the chameleon effect, Chartrand and Bargh had pairs of people interact to describe photographs. However, one member of each pair was actually a confederate of the researchers. Chartrand and Bargh instructed the confederates to perform one of two motor gestures while describing the photographs: Either they rubbed their faces or they shook one foot. If people act like chameleons, we would expect that the experimental participants would mimic those motor gestures. That's exactly what happened. Participants were considerably more likely to rub their faces or shake their feet when the confederates performed those actions.

Chartrand and Bargh speculated that this form of mimicry functions as a type of "social glue." By producing identical motor gestures, people make themselves more similar to the other individuals around them. Recall from the discussion of social relationships that similarity increases liking. For that reason, Chartrand and Bargh hypothesized that people whose gestures were mimicked by a partner would like that partner better. To test that hypothesis, Chartrand and Bargh conducted a second study in which they instructed their confederates to subtly mimic the actions of the experimental participants. Compared to members of the control group, whose gestures were not mimicked, the mimicked participants consistently reported liking the confederates better. Importantly, only one of the 37 participants was aware of having been mimicked. This strongly suggests that the chameleon effect operates outside of conscious awareness.

Even so, these results might lead you to wonder whether you could do better in some social circumstances by consciously mimicking others' behavior. To address this question, researchers provided explicit instructions to a subset of students who were about to carry out a negotiation: "Successful negotiators recommend that you should mimic the mannerisms of your negotiation partner to get a better deal. For example, when the other person rubs his/her face, you should too. If he/she leans back or leans forward in the chair, you should too. However, they say it is very important that you mimic subtly enough that the other person does not notice what you are doing, otherwise this technique completely backfires" (Maddux et al., 2008, p. 463). The students who received these instructions consistently scored more points in the negotiation than their peers who were not encouraged to mimic.

Now that you know about the chameleon effect, do you think you will be more aware of how mimicry affects your social relationships?

CRITICAL THINKING Recall the study that examined participants' judgments of attractive and unattractive individuals. Why was it important that the participants did not know the individuals in the photographs?

 Study and **Review** on **MyPsychLab**

AGGRESSION, ALTRUISM, AND PROSOCIAL BEHAVIOR

If you spend a few minutes reviewing the daily news, you'll almost certainly get reports on the extremes of human behavior: You'll learn both about situations in which people have done each other harm and those in which people have done each other good. This section considers the factors that yield both types of behavior. We begin with acts of **aggression:** People's behaviors that cause psychological or physical harm to other individuals. Psychologists try to understand the causes of aggression with the goal of using that knowledge to help reduce societal levels of aggression. We then turn our attention to the positive extreme: The **prosocial behaviors** that people carry out with the goal of helping other people. A particular focus will be on **altruism**—the prosocial behaviors people carry out without considering their own safety or interests. The section discusses some personal and situational factors that change the likelihood of these helping behaviors.

aggression Behaviors that cause psychological or physical harm to another individual.

prosocial behavior Behavior that is carried out with the goal of helping other people.

altruism Prosocial behaviors a person carries out without considering his or her own safety or interests.

Individual Differences in Aggression

One major fact of research on aggression is that some people are consistently more aggressive than others. Why might that be so? One type of research has examined genetic contributions to individual differences in rates of aggression. These studies typically demonstrate a strong genetic component for aggressive behavior (Yeh et al., 2010). For example, identical twins consistently show higher correlations for aggressiveness than do fraternal twins (Haberstick et al., 2006).

Researchers have also focused attention on differences in brain function that may mark a predisposition toward aggressive behavior. As you saw in Chapter 12, several brain structures, such as the amygdala and portions of cortex, play roles in the expression and regulation of emotion. With respect to aggression, it is critical that brain pathways function effectively so that individuals can control the expression of negative emotion. If, for example, people experience inappropriate levels of activation in the amygdala, they may not be able to inhibit the negative emotions that lead to aggressive behaviors (Siever, 2008).

Attention has also focused on the neurotransmitter serotonin. Research suggests that inappropriate levels of serotonin may impair the brain's ability to regulate negative emotions and impulsive behavior (Siever, 2008). For example, one study demonstrated that men with higher life histories of aggression showed decreased response in the serotonin system to a drug (fenfluramine) that typically has a considerable impact on that system (Manuck et al., 2002). Recall from Chapters 3 and 14 that researchers have begun to explore consequences of variations in the actual genes that underlie serotonin function. In this study as well, the researchers showed that a particular genetic variation was likely to affect serotonin function in a way that put people at risk for high levels of aggressive behavior.

Personality research on aggression has pointed to the importance of differentiating categories of aggressive behaviors: People with different personality profiles are likely to engage in different types of aggression. One important distinction separates *impulsive aggression* from *instrumental aggression* (Little et al., 2003; Ramírez & Andreu, 2006). **Impulsive aggression** is produced in reaction to situations and is emotion driven: People respond with aggressive acts in the heat of the moment. If you see people get into a fistfight after a car accident, that is impulsive aggression. **Instrumental aggression** is goal directed (the aggression serves as the *instrument* for some goal) and cognition based: People carry out acts of aggression, with premeditated thought, to achieve specific aims. If you see someone knock an elderly woman down to steal her purse, that is instrumental aggression. Research has confirmed that those individuals with high propensities toward one or the other of these types of violence have distinct sets of personality traits (Caprara et al., 1996). For example, individuals who reported a propensity toward impulsive aggression

Why do some types of day-to-day experiences make even the calmest people contemplate aggressive acts?

were likely, in general, to be characterized as high on the factor of *emotional responsivity*. That is, they were likely, in general, to report highly emotional responses to a range of situations. By contrast, individuals who reported a propensity toward instrumental aggression were likely to score high on the factor of *positive evaluation of violence*. These individuals believed that many forms of violence are justified, and they also did not accept moral responsibility for aggressive behaviors. You learn from this analysis that not all types of aggression arise from the same underlying personality factors.

Most people are not at the extremes of aggression: They do not lose their tempers at the least infraction or purposefully commit acts of violence. Even so, in some situations, even the most mild-mannered individuals will perform aggressive acts. Let's look now at the types of situations that may often provide the triggering conditions for aggression.

Situational Influences on Aggression

Take a moment now to think back to the last time you engaged in aggressive behavior. It may not have been physical aggression: You may just have been verbally abusive toward some other individual, with the intent of causing psychological distress. How would you explain why that particular situation gave rise to aggression?

Consider a situation in which other people made it impossible for you complete some important task. Did you reach a breaking point? This general relationship is captured by the **frustration-aggression hypothesis** (Dollard et al., 1939). According to this hypothesis, *frustration* occurs in situations in which people are prevented or blocked from attaining their goals; a rise in frustration then leads to a greater probability of aggression. The link between frustration and aggression has obtained a high level of empirical support (Berkowitz, 1993, 1998). For example, children who are frustrated in their expectation that they will be allowed to play with highly attractive toys act aggressively toward those toys when they finally have an opportunity to play (Barker et al., 1941).

Researchers have used this relationship to explain aggression at both the personal and societal levels. Consider an analysis that examined the relationship between San Francisco's unemployment rate and the rate at which people in that

....

impulsive aggression Cognition-based and goal-directed aggression carried out with premeditated thought, to achieve specific aims.

instrumental aggression Cognition-based and goal-directed aggression carried out with premeditated thought, to achieve specific aims.

frustration-aggression hypothesis According to this hypothesis, frustration occurs in situations in which people are prevented or blocked from attaining their goals; a rise in frustration then leads to a greater probability of aggression.

city were committed for being "dangerous to others" (Catalano et al., 1997, 2002). The researchers found that violence increased as unemployment increased, but only to a certain point. When unemployment got too high, violence began to fall again. Why might that be? The researchers speculated that people's fears that they too might lose their jobs helped inhibit frustration-driven tendencies toward violence. This study suggests how individual and societal forces interact to produce a net level of violence. We can predict a certain level of aggression based on the frustration each individual experiences in an economy with rising unemployment. However, as people realize that expressions of aggression may imperil their own employment, violence is inhibited. You can probably recognize these forces in your day-to-day experiences: There are many situations in which you might feel sufficiently frustrated to express aggression, but you also understand that an expression of aggression will work against your long-term best interest.

It's not going to surprise you that *direct provocation* will also give rise to aggression. That is, when someone behaves in a way that makes you angry or upset—and you think that behavior was intentional—you are more likely to respond with some form of physical or verbal aggression (Johnson & Rule, 1986). The effects of direct provocation are consistent with the general idea that situations that produce negative affect will lead to aggression. The intentionality of the act matters because you are less likely to interpret an unintentional act in a negative way. Consider a study that focused on fourth-grade children (Nelson et al., 2008). The researchers asked the children to read scenarios and make judgments about the actors' intentions. For example, in one scenario the children were meant to imagine that a peer's basketball rolled under their feet and caused them to fall during a race. The children indicated whether they believed the peer's actions were intentional or accidental. The researchers also gathered information about the extent of the children's actual physical aggression in the classroom. The two types of data revealed interesting relationships. For example, the boys who perceived the most hostile intent in scenarios like the basketball example were also the most physically aggressive. These data remind you why it matters how people construct social reality: When people interpret ambiguous situations as provocations, they are more likely to respond with aggression.

Our focus has been on aspects of particular situations that bring about aggression. In addition, broader social norms also affect the likelihood that people will display aggression (Leung & Cohen, 2011). Recall the research discussed in Chapter 6 suggesting that children very readily adapt aggressive behaviors from watching adult models. For example, children who watched adult models punching, hitting, and kicking a large plastic BoBo doll later showed a greater frequency of the same behaviors than did children in control conditions who had not observed the aggressive models (Bandura et al., 1963). Chapter 6 also suggested that television in the United States beams an enormous number of aggressive models directly into children's homes—exposure to violence is highly related to adult levels of aggression (Huesmann et al., 2003). 👁

Researchers have developed the *general aggression model* to explain the relationship between exposure to violent media (television, movies, and so on) and aggressive behavior

(DeWall et al., 2011). This model suggests that people acquire a general set of aggression-related knowledge structures through their experiences of media violence: On this view, "each violent media episode is essentially one more trial to learn that the world is a dangerous place, that aggression is an appropriate way to deal with conflict and anger, and that aggression works" (Bushman & Anderson, 2002, p. 1680). Consider a study that examined the short-term impact of violent video games.

Researchers recruited college undergraduates who had limited prior experience with violent video games (Engelhardt et al., 2011). In the first phase of the study, participants were randomly assigned to play either violent video games (for example, Grand Theft Auto: Vice City) or nonviolent video games (for example, MVP Baseball 2004) for 25 minutes. In the second phase, participants viewed neutral photographs (for example, a man on a bicycle) and violent photographs (for example, a man holding a gun in another man's mouth) while the researchers recorded their brain activity. Ordinarily, people produce a particular brain response known as a P3 when they view violent images. However, the participants who had played violent video games showed a relatively small P3 resopnse, suggesting that the violent game play had desensitized them to violent images. In the study's third phase, the participants had the opportunity to express aggression against an opponent by setting the loudness and length of blasts of noise. Participants whose brain activity showed the greatest desensitization to violent images also expressed the most aggression by choosing louder and longer blasts of noise.

This study illustrates how quickly violent video games can change people's tendency toward aggressive behavior. A large-scale analysis that examined data from a large number of experiments involving 130,296 participants reached the strong conclusion that playing violent video games puts people at risk for aggressive behavior (Anderson et al., 2010). As the researchers noted, "It is not surprising that when the game involves rehearsing aggressive and violent thoughts and actions, such deep game involvement results in antisocial effects on the player" (p. 171).

You can choose whether you wish to play violent video games. However, for many people, exposure to violence is

Why should parents worry that children who play violent video games may be prone to more real-world aggression?

👁 **Watch the Video** *Violence and Video Games: Douglas Gentile* on **MyPsychLab** outside of their control. Children may be exposed to aggressive acts in their homes (Evans et al., 2008). In addition, many children in the United States grow up in inner-city communities in which violence is daily and chronic (Berkowitz, 2003; Salzinger et al., 2006). Researchers have only begun to explore the consequences of exposure to violence for children's mental health and their inclination to aggressive behavior (Lambert et al., 2010; Spano et al., 2012).

This section has described too many reasons why people might engage in aggressive behavior. Fortunately, people are also well prepared to provide help to others. We turn now to the roots of helping behavior.

The Roots of Prosocial Behavior

In May 2008, an earthquake measuring 8.0 on the Richter scale struck China's Sichuan province. The media was full of images of the devastation the earthquake caused. However, the media also provided images of people risking their lives to save others. People from China and other parts of the world converged on Sichuan province with the hope of finding and aiding survivors. We see similar acts of heroism for other crises. For example, a group of Japanese citizens over the age of 60 volunteered themselves after the March 2011 disaster at the Fukushima nuclear plant; they wished to save younger volunteers from the danger of the radiation.

How can we explain why people engage in prosocial behaviors? Researcher **C. Daniel Batson** (1994) suggests that there are four forces that prompt people to act for the public good:

- *Altruism.* Acting in response to a motive to benefit others, as in the case of the driver who saved another person's life.
- *Egoism.* Performing prosocial behaviors ultimately in one's own self-interest; someone might perform a helping behavior to receive a similar favor in return (for example, compliance with a request) or to receive a reward (for example, money or praise).
- *Collectivism.* Performing prosocial behaviors to benefit a particular group; people might perform helping behaviors to improve circumstances for their families, fraternities or sororities, political parties, and so on.
- *Principlism.* Performing prosocial behaviors to uphold moral principles; someone might act in a prosocial manner because of a religious or civic principle.

You can see how each of these motives might apply in different situations.

The same prosocial behavior can serve more than one motive. For example, many colleges and universities now encourage students to participate in *service learning*: "an educational assignment in which students meet the academic learning goals of a course through an experience working on behalf of others" (Jay, 2008, p. 255). For example, in one service learning project students in an introductory course on gerontology assisted a county agency to gather information about legal issues relevant to older adults (Anstee et al., 2008). Because participation in this project enhanced students' educational experience, we might count this as an instance of egoism (that is, the student's reward is greater learning). However, their participation also provided benefits to older adults

What prosocial motive explains why people band together to protect the environment?

and to the county agency, so we might also count this instance of service learning as collectivism. In fact, educators who support service learning often hope that the values service learning instills will lead students to undertake a lifetime of prosocial behavior (Tomkovick et al., 2008).

Among these motives for prosocial behavior, the existence of altruism has sometimes been controversial. To understand why, you must think back to the discussion of evolutionary forces presented in earlier chapters. According to the evolutionary perspective, the main goal of life is to reproduce so that one can pass on one's genes. How, in that context, does altruism make sense? Why should you risk your life to aid others? There are two answers to this question, depending on whether the "others" are family members or strangers.

For family members, altruistic behaviors make some sense because—even if you imperil your own survival—you aid the general survival of your gene pool (Burnstein, 2005). Researchers have examined the extent to which genetic overlap influences people's altruistic behaviors.

Participants in an experiment had the opportunity to earn money for themselves and for relatives with whom they had 50 percent genetic overlap (for example, siblings and parents), 25 percent overlap (for example, grandparents, aunts, and nephews), or 12.5 percent overlap (as with cousins) (Madsen et al., 2007). However, to earn the money, the participants had to remain in a painful physical position: The longer they remained in the position, the more money they made for themselves or for their relatives. The participants returned to the laboratory over several days so that the researchers could complete the test for each relatedness category. Participants did not know how long they had held the painful position until the end of each trial. The results demonstrated a clear impact of genetic overlap. On the whole, the greater the genetic overlap, the longer the participants endured the pain. The researchers demonstrated much the same pattern with university students in London and with two South African Zulu populations.

Because the participants endured pain to provide funds to their relatives, their behavior meets the criteria for altruism. Other

Featured Study

What social forces prompt people—like rescue workers after the deadly earthquake in China's Sichuan Province—to put their lives in jeopardy for the sake of others?

research suggests that people are most willing to help individuals to whom they feel emotionally close, including their circle of friends (Korchmaros & Kenny, 2006; Stewart-Williams, 2007). For most people, their closest emotional attachments are also to their closest kin. Thus patterns of helping based on emotional closeness indirectly help people's gene pools to survive.

But how about nonkin? The focus on emotional closeness suggests why people might engage in altruistic behaviors toward their closest friends. But why, for example, would older adults in Japan risk their lives to save the lives of others? To explain altruism toward acquaintances and strangers, theorists have explored the concept of **reciprocal altruism** (Trivers, 1971). This concept suggests that people perform altruistic behaviors because they, in some sense, expect that others will perform altruistic behaviors for them: I will save you when you are drowning with the expectation that you would save me, in the future, when I am drowning. Note, however, that the concept of reciprocal altruism cannot explain all facets of cooperation in social species. For example, the older adults in Japan surely didn't expect that the stranger would perform a similarly altruistic act in return. To explain acts of this sort, researchers suggest that *indirect reciprocity* is at work: People perform altruistic behaviors because they believe that, in the future, they will become the recipients of altruistic acts. To put it somewhat more plainly, "I scratch your back, and someone else will scratch mine" (Nowak & Sigmund, 2005, p. 1291).

There is also often a social component when people perform altruistic behaviors toward nonkin. The *empathy-altruism hypothesis* suggests a particular relationship: When you feel empathy—feelings of emotional identification—toward another individual, those feelings evoke an altruistic motive to provide help (Batson, 1991). Research supports this hypothesis. For example, in one study the researchers asked participants to allocate raffle tickets either to a whole group or to individuals within the group (Batson et al., 1999). In one condition of the experiment, the participants read an autobiographical message from someone they were led to believe was a group member; the message revealed that that person had just been dumped by a longtime romantic partner. When participants experienced empathy, they gave extra tickets to the dumped individual. Across humans and other species,

researchers have demonstrated quite general links between empathy and altruism (de Waal, 2008).

This section has reviewed several reasons why people might engage in prosocial and altruistic behaviors. The next section describes a classic program of research that demonstrated fully how much people's willingness to help—their ability to follow through on prosocial motives—depends on characteristics of the situation.

The Effects of the Situation on Prosocial Behavior

This program of research began with news reports of a tragedy. The *New York Times* reported that 38 respectable, law-abiding citizens in Queens, New York, had watched the murder of Kitty Genovese. According to a book that further fleshed out the story, the New Yorkers watched from the safety of their apartment windows while, for more than half an hour, a killer stalked and stabbed Genovese in three separate attacks (Rosenthal, 1964). These news reports suggested that only one witness called the police after the woman was dead. Contemporary analyses suggest that these early accounts were largely inaccurate (Manning et al., 2007). For example, police records indicate that far fewer than 38 people witnessed the events and that, given the way the events unfolded, it would have been virtually impossible for any one witness to have seen them all. The police were almost certainly called after the first attack. Finally, Genovese was still alive when the police arrived.

These vast inaccuracies do not change the impact of the original newspaper account. Genovese's murder—in the way that it was narrated—shocked a nation that could not accept the idea of such apathy or hard-heartedness on the part of its responsible citizenry. News reports continue to provide less disputed accounts of circumstances in which bystanders failed to intervene. For example, in 2009, passersby watched while a German businessman was murdered by two teenagers (Fischer et al., 2011). In response to such news reports, social psychologists have asked important questions: Is it fair to pin the label of "apathy" or "hard-hearted" on bystanders? Or can we explain their inaction in terms of situational forces?

To make the case for situational forces, **Bibb Latané** and **John Darley** (1970) carried out a classic series of studies. Their goal was to demonstrate that **bystander intervention**—people's willingness to help strangers in distress—was very sensitive to precise characteristics of the situation. They ingeniously created in the laboratory an experimental analogue of the bystander-intervention situation. 👁

Featured Study

The participants were male college students (Darley & Latané, 1968). Each student, placed in a room by himself with an intercom, was led to believe that he was communicating with one or more students in an adjacent room. During the course of a discussion about personal problems, he heard what sounded

👁 **Watch** the **Video** *Prosocial Behavior* on **MyPsychLab**

reciprocal altruism The idea that people perform altruistic behaviors because they expect that others will perform altruistic behaviors for them in turn.

bystander intervention Willingness to assist a person in need of help.

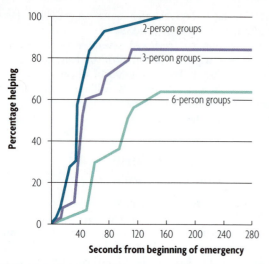

FIGURE 16.8 Bystander Intervention in an Emergency

The more people present, the less likely that any one bystander will intervene. Bystanders act most quickly in two-person groups.

From Darley & Latané, *Journal of Personality and Social Psychology, 8*(4), 1968. Copyright © 1968 American Psychological Association. Reprinted with permission.

like one of the other students having an epileptic seizure and gasping for help. During the "seizure," it was impossible for the participant to talk to the other students or to find out what, if anything, they were doing about the emergency. The dependent variable was the speed with which the participant reported the emergency to the experimenter.

It turned out that the likelihood of intervention depended on the number of bystanders the participant thought were present. The more people he thought were present, the slower he was in reporting the seizure, if he did so at all. As you can see in **Figure 16.8***, everyone in a two-person situation intervened within 160 seconds, but nearly 40 percent of those who believed they were part of a larger group never bothered to inform the experimenter that another student was seriously ill.*

This result arises from a **diffusion of responsibility.** When more than one person *could* help in an emergency situation, people often assume that someone else *will* or *should* help—so they back off and don't get involved.

Researchers continue to explore the features of situations that affect the likelihood that bystanders will intervene. One important variable is the seriousness of the emergency: The presence of other witnesses matters far less in dangerous situations (Fischer et al., 2011). Consider a study in which participants believed they were watching a real interaction between a man and a woman in which the man began to threaten the woman (Fischer et al., 2006). In the *low physical danger* version, the man was skinny and not very frightening; in the *high*

potential danger version, the man was large and physically intimidating. With low physical threat to the woman, participants went to help the woman 50 percent of the time when they were alone but only 6 percent of the time when there was a second bystander. When the danger was high, participants intervened 44 perecent of the time when they were alone but also 40 percent of the time when there was a second bystander. We might still wish that the partipicants had gone to the woman's rescue more often! However, this study provides hope that when you really need help, bystanders will provide it.

The exact nature of the emergency likely matters, in part, because evident danger makes it harder for bystanders to ignore what's happening. In many real-life circumstances, people who are pursuing their own agendas—they may, for example, be on their way to work or an appointment—may not even notice that there is a situation in which they can help. In one classic experiment, students at the Princeton Theological Seminary thought they were going to be evaluated on their sermons, one of which was to be about the parable of the Good Samaritan—a New Testament figure who takes time to help a man lying injured by the roadside (Darley & Batson, 1973). On their way to the sermon, the seminarians passed a man who lay slumped in a doorway, coughing and groaning. Among the seminarians who had been made to believe they were late for their sermon, only 10 percent helped. If they were on time, 45 percent helped the stranger. The most bystander intervention came from those who were early—63 percent of these seminarians acted as Good Samaritans. Once again, you see how aspects of the situation explain people's behavior.

Given what you've learned, what might you do if you find yourself in an emergency? You need to help bystanders pay attention and overcome the diffusion of responsibility. Point directly toward someone and say, "You! I need your help." In one classic study, New Yorkers watched as a thief snatched a portable radio from a beach blanket when the owner left it for a few minutes (Moriarty, 1975). The would-be theft victim (the experimenter's accomplice) asked the soon-to-be observer of the crime either, "Do you have the time?" or "Will you please keep an eye on my bag (radio) while I'm gone?" The first interaction elicited no personal responsibility, and the bystanders simply stood by idly as the thefts unfolded. However, of those who agreed to watch the victim's property, almost every bystander intervened. They called for help, and some even tackled the runaway thief on the beach. This experiment suggests that the act of requesting a favor forges a special human bond that involves other people in ways that materially change the situation.

This section has discussed prosocial behaviors—those circumstances in which people come to each others' aid. People have several motives that explain prosocial behaviors. However, as you have seen quite often in this chapter, the social situation has a large impact on the extent to which people will act on those motives.

diffusion of responsibility In emergency situations, the larger the number of bystanders, the less responsibility any one of the bystanders feels to help.

Stop and Review

① Why do researchers believe that genetic factors play a role in aggression?

② What is the relationship between frustration and aggression?

HOW CAN YOU GET PEOPLE TO VOLUNTEER?

Suppose you become a leader in an organization. It's very likely that you'll want to recruit volunteers to help with the organization's activities. To do so, it should help to have an understanding of why people undertake volunteer work and what sustains their interest in the work.

Let's begin with the question of why people volunteer. Researchers have identified several motives that prompt people to get involved (Mannino et al., 2011; Omoto & Snyder, 2002). For example, people volunteer to express personal values related to altruism, to expand their range of experiences, and to strengthen social relationships. If volunteer positions do not meet these needs, people may not wish to participate. To recruit volunteers, you may need to understand the motives of the people you wish to attract.

Once people begin to volunteer, what leads them to remain in their positions over time? To answer this question, researchers have engaged in longitudinal studies. For example, one study followed 238 volunteers in Florida over the course of a year (Davis et al., 2003). The volunteers participated in organizations such as the St. Petersburg Free Clinic and the Center against Spouse Abuse. One of the most important factors that influenced the participants' satisfaction as volunteers was the amount of distress they experienced in their volunteer positions. Although this result may not surprise you, it leads to important practical advice. The researchers note that attention should be given to "training methods that would prepare volunteers for distressing situations or provide them with strategies for coping with the distress they do experience" (p. 259).

Another study of 302 volunteers at a hospice in the southeastern United States focused on individual differences in the extent to which people view "volunteer" as an important social role (Finkelstein et al., 2005). This study addressed the hypothesis that those people for whom the role of volunteer was most part of their personal identity would also be most likely to continue volunteer work. Participants indicated the extent to which the social role mattered by responding to statements such as "Volunteering for hospice is an important part of who I am." Consistent with their expectations, the researchers found a positive correlation between the strength of role identity and the length of time people continued to volunteer. These results, once again, lead to concrete advice: "Once an individual begins volunteering, retention efforts might focus on cultivating a volunteer role identity. . . . Items (e.g., T-shirts, license plate holders) that allow volunteers to be recognized publicly for their contributions can help strengthen role identity" (p. 416).

This research allows you to contemplate your own behavior. What motives apply to your experiences of volunteering? Are you ready to cope with distress? To what extent do you embrace "volunteer" as a respected social role? You can address these questions to increase the personal and societal benefits of your volunteer activities.

- Why is it appropriate to use longitudinal designs to study volunteer behaviors?
- Why might T-shirts and license plate holders help strengthen role identity?

---

③ What is meant by reciprocal altruism?
④ Why does diffusion of responsibility occur?

CRITICAL THINKING Recall the experiment that assessed the impact of violent video games. Why was it important that participants believed the task in which they provided endings for stories was unrelated to their video game playing?

✓ **Study** and **Review** on **MyPsychLab**

A PERSONAL ENDNOTE

We have come to the end of our journey through *Psychology and Life*. As you think back, I hope you will realize just how much you have learned on the way. Yet we have barely scratched the surface of the excitement and challenges that await the student of psychology. I hope you will pursue your interest in psychology and that you may even go on to contribute to this dynamic enterprise as a scientific researcher or a clinical practitioner or by applying psychological knowledge to the solution of social and personal problems.

Playwright Tom Stoppard reminds us that "every exit is an entry somewhere else." I believe that the entry into the next phase of your life will be facilitated by what you have learned from *Psychology and Life* and from your introductory psychology course. In that next journey, may you infuse new life into the psychology of human endeavors while strengthening the connections among all the people you encounter.

Richard Gerrig

Recapping Main Points

Constructing Social Reality

- Each person constructs his or her own social reality.
- Social perception is influenced by beliefs and expectations.
- Attribution theory describes the judgments people make about the causes of behaviors.
- Several biases, such as the fundamental attribution error, self-serving biases, and self-fulfilling prophecies, can creep into attributions and other judgments and behaviors.

The Power of the Situation

- Being assigned to play a social role, even in artificial settings, can cause individuals to act contrary to their beliefs, values, and dispositions.
- Social norms shape the attitudes and behaviors of group members.
- Classic research by Sherif and Asch illustrated the informational and normative forces that lead to conformity.
- Minority influence may arise as a consequence of informational influence.
- Milgram's studies on obedience are a powerful testimony to the influence of the situational factors that can lead ordinary people to sanction and participate in organized aggression.

Attitudes, Attitude Change, and Action

- Attitudes are positive or negative evaluations of objects, events, or ideas.
- Not all attitudes accurately predict behaviors; they must be highly accessible or highly stable.
- According to the elaboration likelihood model, the central route to persuasion relies on careful analyses of arguments, whereas the peripheral route relies on superficial features of persuasive situations.
- Dissonance theory and self-perception theory consider attitude formation and change that arise from behavioral acts.
- To bring about compliance, people can exploit reciprocity, consistency, and commitment.

Prejudice

- Even arbitrary, minimal cues can yield prejudice when they define an in-group and an out-group.
- Stereotypes affect the way in which people evaluate behaviors and information in the world.
- Implicit prejudice often has an impact on people's behavior.
- Researchers have eliminated some of the effects of prejudice by creating situations in which members of different groups must cooperate to reach shared goals.
- Cross-cultural studies also suggest that friendship plays an important role in eliminating prejudice.

Social Relationships

- Interpersonal attraction is determined in part by proximity, physical attractiveness, similarity, and reciprocity.
- Frustration relationships are defined with respect to passion, intimacy, and commitment.
- A culture's attachment style affects the quality of relationships.

Aggression, Altruism, and Prosocial Behavior

- Individual differences in aggressive behavior reflect genetics, brain function, and personality profiles.
- Frustration and provocation can lead to aggression
- Cultures provide different norms for aggressive behavior.
- Researchers have tried to explain why people engage in prosocial behaviors, particularly altruistic behaviors that do not serve their own interests.
- Evolutionary explanations focus on kinship and reciprocity.
- Bystander intervention studies show that situations largely determine who is likely or unlikely to help in emergencies.

KEY TERMS

aggression (p. 473)
altruism (p. 473)
attitude (p. 460)
attribution theory (p. 448)
bystander intervention (p. 477)
cognitive dissonance (p. 463)
compliance (p. 464)
conformity (p. 454)
contact hypothesis (p. 468)
covariation model (p. 448)
diffusion of responsibility (p. 478)
elaboration likelihood model (p. 461)
frustration-aggression hypothesis (p. 474)
fundamental attribution error (FAE)
 (p. 448)

group polarization (p. 457)
groupthink (p. 457)
implicit prejudice (p. 467)
impulsive aggression (p. 474)
informational influence (p. 454)
in-group (p. 466)
in-group bias (p. 466)
instrumental aggression (p. 474)
norm crystallization (p. 454)
normative influence (p. 454)
out-group (p. 466)
persuasion (p. 461)
prejudice (p. 465)
prosocial behavior (p. 473)
racism (p. 466)

reciprocal altruism (p. 477)
reciprocity norm (p. 464)
rule (p. 451)
self-fulfilling prophecy (p. 450)
self-perception theory (p. 464)
self-serving bias (p. 449)
sexism (p. 466)
social categorization (p. 466)
social cognition (p. 447)
social norm (p. 453)
social perception (p. 448)
social psychology (p. 447)
social role (p. 451)
stereotype (p. 466)

1. Grace wants to help her friend Charlie avoid the fundamental attribution error. She suggests that he focus on _____ causes of behaviors.
   a. situational
   b. dispositional
   c. distinctive
   d. consistent

2. Which of these statements is *not* consistent with a self-serving bias?
   a. I lost because the other guy was probably cheating.
   b. I lost because it was too hot in the room.
   c. I won because I'm a genius.
   d. I won because I got lucky.

3. Self-fulfilling prophecies may be modest with teachers in classrooms because
   a. most students perform better than their teachers expect them to perform.
   b. teachers usually have accurate expectations about how students will perform.
   c. teachers rarely have expectations about students.
   d. students do not allow teachers to treat them differently from their classmates.

4. In the Stanford Prison Experiment, the guards often abused the prisoners. This result suggests that
   a. people seek situations in which they can indulge their aggressive impulses.
   b. some people are born to play the role of guards.
   c. only aggressive people are willing to assume the role of prison guard.
   d. social roles have an important influence on how people behave.

5. Solomon Asch's experiments on conformity demonstrate the impact of _____ in group situations.
   a. norm crystallization
   b. social rules
   c. normative influence
   d. informational influence

6. In Milgram's experiments on obedience, many people protested that they didn't want to give any more shocks. After that happened,
   a. the experimenter told them the study was over.
   b. most participants asked to leave the experiment.
   c. most participants continued to administer shocks.
   d. the experimenter asked to decrease shocks.

7. When a company hires a celebrity to endorse a product, it is likely hoping that most consumers will follow the _____ route to persuasion and engage in _____ elaboration.
   a. peripheral; low
   b. central; high
   c. peripheral; high
   d. central; low

8. Sam chooses desserts for himself and for his friend Randy. Both desserts turn out to be duds. If Sam has a(n) _____ sense of self, you'd expect him to experience the most cognitive dissonance with respect to the dessert he chose for _____.
   a. independent; Randy
   b. interdependent; himself
   c. interdependent; Randy
   d. dependent; himself

9. Oliver is trying to change his friend Stan's stereotype that women aren't as funny as men. They watch a TV special with a series of women doing comedy routines. Do you think Stan's stereotype will change?
   a. Yes, because he will appreciate Oliver's effort on his behalf.
   b. No, because he will discount information that is inconsistent with his stereotype.
   c. No, because he will convince Stan that the stereotype is true.
   d. Yes, because he will learn a new stereotype from the TV special.

10. Which of these statements suggests that Carmen is exploiting similarity to get Perry to like her more?
    a. "Did you know that we're both Libras?"
    b. "I really enjoy spending time with you."
    c. "Would you like me to get you the newspaper?"
    d. "Your new haircut looks terrific."

11. Which statement is *not* correct?
    a. Companionate love is associated with life satisfaction.
    b. Most relationships have more passionate love at the outset.
    c. Companionate love is characterized by less intensity but greater intimacy.
    d. There is little passionate love in long-term relationships.

12. During a job interview, Juliet subtly mimicked the interviewer's gestures. It sounds like Juliet was trying to use _____ to improve the likelihood that she would get the job.
    a. norm crystallization
    b. the reciprocity norm
    c. the chameleon effect
    d. cognitive dissonance

13. According to the frustration-aggression hypothesis, in which of these situations is Brett most likely to act in an aggressive fashion?
    a. Brett has an important job interview, but he's stuck in a traffic jam.
    b. Brett's girlfriend yelled at him all morning for being mean to her.
    c. Brett hates the song playing on his car radio.
    d. Brett thinks his boss has been monitoring the websites he visits.

14. With respect to bystander intervention, it is typically least important that bystanders must
    a. notice danger in the emergency.
    b. label events as an emergency.
    c. feel responsibility in the situation.
    d. consider themselves to be helpful people.

15. If you want to increase the likelihood that people will continue to volunteer in the future, which of these measures would you *not* want to try?
    a. Give T-shirts to identify people as volunteers.
    b. Have people start to volunteer as a mandatory assignment.
    c. Help people cope with distressing aspects of the volunteer work.
    d. Determine the motives people have for volunteering.

ESSAY QUESTIONS

1. What properties of attitudes increase the correlations between attitudes and behaviors?

2. How do stereotypes affect behavior?

3. What situational factors affect the likelihood that people will engage in prosocial behaviors?

Answer Appendix

Stop and Review Answers

CHAPTER 1

Stop and Review (What Makes Psychology Unique? p. 5)

1. Psychology is the *scientific* study of the *behavior* of *individuals* and their *mental* processes.
2. The four goals are to describe, explain, predict, and control behavior.
3. Researchers regularly try to explain behaviors by identifying underlying causes; successful causal explanations often allow accurate predictions.

Stop and Review (The Evolution of Modern Psychology, p. 13)

1. Structuralism tries to understand mental experiences as the combination of basic components. Functionalism focuses on the purposes of behavioral acts.
2. Wooley argued that sex differences do not reflect natural ability but, rather, differences in men's and women's social experiences.
3. The psychodynamic perspective focuses on powerful, instinctive forces, and the behaviorist perspective focuses on how consequences shape behaviors.
4. Researchers in cognitive neuroscience combine the cognitive and biological perspectives to understand the brain bases of mental activities such as memory and language.
5. The evolutionary perspective focuses on the features that all people share as a consequence of human evolution. The sociocultural perspective focuses on the differences brought about by cultures, against that shared evolutionary background.

Stop and Review (What Psychologists Do, p. 15)

1. Research provides new insights that psychologists then try to apply in real-world settings.
2. Psychologists are most employed in academic settings (e.g., colleges and universities) and hospitals and other human services.

Stop and Review (How to Use This Text, p. 17)

1. You must be actively involved in the course by developing your own understanding of what you hear in lectures and read in the text.
2. In the *Question* phase you invent questions that direct your attention while you are reading; in the *Read* phase you read the material with an eye to answering your questions.

3. When you attempt to recite explicit answers to questions, you obtain concrete evidence of what you know and what you don't know.

CHAPTER 2

Stop and Review (The Process of Research, p. 28)

1. Theories attempt to explain phenomena. Those explanations should generate new hypotheses—testable consequences of a theory.
2. Researchers can standardize their procedures and provide operational definitions for their variables.
3. Researchers use double-blind controls so that the expectations they bring to the research setting cannot have an impact on their studies' results.
4. When an experiment has a within-subjects design, each participant serves as his or her own control.
5. A correlation coefficient indicates the extent to which two variables are related—it does not give any indication of why that relationship exists.

Stop and Review (Psychological Measurement, p. 32)

1. If a measure is reliable, it means that it yields a comparable value when researchers use it repeatedly. However, that value might still not accurately reflect the psychological variable that the researcher is after. That's why shoe size would be a reliable but not a valid measure of happiness.
2. Interviewers seek to create a context in which people are willing to provide information through self-reports that might be highly personal or sensitive.
3. The researcher is engaged in naturalistic observation of the children's behavior.

Stop and Review (Ethical Issues in Human and Animal Research, p. 34)

1. Research participants must have the opportunity to understand their rights and responsibilities before they choose to engage in an experiment.
2. During debriefing, participants have an opportunity to learn something new about the psychological phenomena that were the topic of the study. In addition, through debriefing researchers can ensure that participants do not leave the study upset or confused.
3. The three Rs are reduce, replace, and refine.

CHAPTER 3

Stop and Review (Heredity and Behavior, p. 53)

1. The Grants observed that, as a result of changes in the environment, sometimes big-beaked finches were able to survive and reproduce, whereas at other times small-beaked finches were able to survive and reproduce.
2. The genotype is the underlying genetic material that helps determine the phenotype, which is the observable characteristics of an organism.
3. Two critical advances were bipedalism and encephalization.
4. Heritability is a measure of the relative influence of genetics in determining an organism's constellation of traits and behaviors.

Stop and Review (The Nervous System in Action, p. 60)

1. In general, the dendrites receive incoming signals. The soma integrates information from the many dendrites and passes that information along to the axon.
2. The all-or-none law suggests that, once the threshold for firing has been reached, the strength of an action potential is constant.
3. Neurotransmitters are released into synapses when synaptic vesicles rupture; the neurotransmitters then bind to receptor molecules on the receiving neuron.
4. GABA is the brain's most common inhibitory neurotransmitter.

Stop and Review (Biology and Behavior, p. 75)

1. fMRI allows researchers to make claims about both structures and functions.
2. The autonomic nervous system is divided into the sympathetic and parasympathetic divisions.
3. The amygdala plays a role in emotional control and the formation of emotional memories.
4. Most people show greater right-hemisphere activity when they make judgments about spatial relationships and facial expressions.
5. The pituitary gland produces hormones that influence the activity of all the other endocrine glands.
6. Neurogenesis is the creation of new neurons.

CHAPTER 4

Stop and Review (Sensory Knowledge of the World, p. 85)

1. The proximal stimulus is the optical image on the retina.
2. Psychophysics is the study of the relationship between physical stimuli and the psychological experience of those stimuli.
3. An absolute threshold is defined as the stimulus level at which a sensory signal is detected half the time.
4. Judgments are affected both by sensory processes and observers' biases.
5. A difference threshold is the smallest physical difference between two stimuli that observers can recognize.
6. Transduction is the conversion of one form of physical energy into another form.

Stop and Review (The Visual System, p. 93)

1. Accommodation is the process by which the thickness of the lens changes so that focus is achieved on both near and far objects.

2. The fovea is 100 percent cones.
3. Complex cells respond to bars in particular orientations, but those bars must also be moving.
4. This experience is explained by opponent-process theory.

Stop and Review (Hearing, p. 98)

1. You perceive sounds with different frequencies as having different pitches.
2. Hair cells transform the mechanical vibrations of the basilar membrane into nerve impulses.
3. Place theory associates pitch perception with the location of stimulation on the basilar membrane.
4. The sound should reach your right ear before it reaches your left ear.

Stop and Review (Your Other Senses, p. 102)

1. Nerve impulses convey odor information to the olfactory bulb.
2. The basic taste qualities are sweet, sour, bitter, saline, and umami.
3. You have separate types of receptors that encode information about warmth and coolness.
4. The vestibular sense provides information about how the body is oriented in space with respect to gravity.
5. Gate-control theory attempts to explain how experiences of pain are affected by psychological context.

Stop and Review (Organizational Processes in Perception, p. 112)

1. Sometimes stimulus features in the environment—like the abrupt change of a spotlight from red to green—will capture your attention.
2. People tend to fill in small gaps to experience objects as wholes.
3. When someone is walking toward you, the size of the man's image on your retina expands.
4. The angle of convergence is larger when an object is closer to you.
5. Shape constancy is your ability to perceive the true shape of an object even as the shape of the retinal image changes.

Stop and Review (Identification and Recognition Processes, p. 116)

1. People use their knowledge of sounds and words to restore information that is missing from the auditory signal.
2. A stimulus is ambiguous when more than one object or event in the environment could give rise to the same proximal stimulus.
3. A set is a temporary readiness to perceive or react to a stimulus in a particular way.

CHAPTER 5

Stop and Review (The Contents of Consciousness, p. 124)

1. A memory is preconscious when it is not currently part of the content of consciousness but could easily become so.
2. Freud suggested that if some ideas or motives are sufficiently threatening they become repressed into the unconscious.
3. Researchers ask experimental participants to report their thoughts while they carry out particular tasks.

Stop and Review (The Functions of Consciousness, p. 125)

1. Consciousness allows you to make explicit decisions about what information you should attempt to commit to memory.

2. A cultural construction of reality is a way of thinking about the world that is shared by most members of a particular group of people.
3. People generally need to use conscious attention to search for objects with a combination of features.

Stop and Review (Sleep and Dreams, p. 133)

1. You experience jet lag because your internal circadian rhythm is out of phase with the temporal environment.
2. Early in the night you experience relatively more NREM sleep; late in the night you experience relatively more REM sleep.
3. Sleep serves the functions of conservation and memory consolidation.
4. Sleep apnea is a sleep disorder in which a person stops breathing while asleep.
5. The latent content is the underlying meaning that has been hidden by the mind's censors.

Stop and Review (Altered States of Consciousness, p. 136)

1. Early twin studies suggested that hypnotizability has a genetic component; researchers have begun to identify specific genes that might underlie this impact.
2. Some people practice concentrative meditation, whereas others practice mindfulness meditation.

Stop and Review (Mind-Altering Drugs, p. 141)

1. Drug tolerance is the circumstance in which an individual requires greater doses of a drug to yield the same effect.
2. Drugs like heroin bind to the same receptor sites as the brain's endogenous opiates.
3. Nicotine is an example of a stimulant.

CHAPTER 6

Stop and Review (The Study of Learning, p. 147)

1. The learning-performance distinction acknowledges that people's behaviors might not always reflect everything they have learned.
2. He argued that people's private experiences were too subjective to be studied with scientific rigor.
3. Behavior analysts attempt to discover regularities in learning that occur in all types of animal species.
4. Habituation is a decrease in an organism's behavioral response when a stimulus occurs repeatedly.

Stop and Review (Classical Conditioning: Learning Predictable Signals, p. 156)

1. Classical conditioning begins with behaviors (such as salivation) that are reflex responses to unconditioned stimuli (such as the presentation of food powder).
2. The UCS is the unconditioned stimulus that produces a response prior to conditioning; the CS is the conditioned stimulus that produces a response as a result of conditioning.
3. Stimulus discrimination means that the organism has learned to produce a conditioned response to a more narrow range of conditioned stimuli than would otherwise be the case.
4. It's not enough for the CS and UCS to occur close together in time; the UCS must be contingent upon—be predictable from—the CS.
5. The CR is the body's compensatory response to the drug's effects.

6. Taste aversion will develop with only one pairing of the CS and UCS and with a long lag between the CS and UCS. It will often be permanent after one experience.

Stop and Review (Operant Conditioning: Learning about Consequences, p. 166)

1. The law of effect states that a response followed by satisfying consequences becomes more probable and a response followed by dissatisfying consequences becomes less probable.
2. Reinforcement makes behaviors more likely; punishment makes behaviors less likely.
3. Animals learn that behaviors will have consequences (reinforcement or punishment) only in the context of particular stimuli—those stimuli are the discriminative stimuli.
4. In FR schedules, a reinforcer is delivered each time the organism has made a fixed number of responses. In FI schedules, a reinforcer is delivered when the organism makes the first response after a fixed amount of time.
5. Shaping is a method that allows an organism to learn a behavior through successive approximations.
6. Instinctual drift is the tendency, over time, for learned behaviors to drift toward instinctual behaviors.

Stop and Review (Cognitive Influences on Learning, p. 170)

1. Tolman concluded that his rats developed cognitive maps for the layouts in the mazes.
2. Pigeons can learn to peck a circle on which a color had changed.
3. Vicarious reinforcement occurs when an individual's behavior becomes more probable after he or she observes other people's behaviors being reinforced.
4. Research suggests that children who observe a large number of aggressive acts may learn to be aggressive themselves.

CHAPTER 7

Stop and Review (What Is Memory? p. 177)

1. Explicit uses of memory involve conscious effort, whereas implicit uses of memory do not.
2. Your skill relies more on procedural memory.
3. Because you've previously encoded and stored your password, it's most likely your problem is with retrieval.

Stop and Review (Memory Use for the Short Term, p. 182)

1. Comparisons of the whole- and partial-report procedures indicate that people have very brief access to all the information in a display.
2. Researchers believe that the capacity of STM is in the range of three to five items.
3. Chunking is the process of reconfiguring items into meaningful groups.
4. Working memory includes the phonological loop, the visuospatial sketchpad, the central executive, and the episodic buffer.

Stop and Review (Long-Term Memory: Encoding and Retrieval, p. 191)

1. Recognition generally provides more retrieval cues.
2. This would be an example of the primacy effect in serial recall.

3. Transfer-appropriate processing suggests that memory is best when the type of processing carried out at encoding matches the type of processing carried out at retrieval.

4. These circumstances provide an example of retroactive interference because new information has made it harder to remember older information.

5. Beginning with hydrogen, you would associate each element with a position along a familiar route.

6. Judgments of learning are people's estimates of how well they have learned information.

Stop and Review (Structures in Long-Term Memory, p. 200)

1. Concepts are the mental representations of the categories you form.

2. The exemplar theory claims that people categorize new objects by comparing them to the exemplars they have stored in memory.

3. Bartlett identified the processes of leveling, sharpening, and assimilating.

4. Loftus and her colleagues demonstrated that people will include incorrect postevent information when they attempt to remember events.

Stop and Review (Biological Aspects of Memory, p. 203)

1. Lashley concluded that the engram did not exist in any localized regions but was widely distributed throughout the brain.

2. Research suggests that important aspects of implicit memory will often be spared for individuals who have amnesia for explicit memories.

3. PET scans reveal that different areas of the brain are disproportionately active for encoding and retrieval—left prefrontal cortex for encoding and right prefrontal cortex for retrieval.

CHAPTER 8

Stop and Review (Studying Cognition, p. 210)

1. Donders's goal was to determine the speed of mental processes by inventing tasks that differed only by specific processes.

2. Serial processes take place one after the other; parallel processes overlap in time.

3. Automatic processes do not generally require attentional resources.

Stop and Review (Language Use, p. 220)

1. The cooperative principle specifies some of the dimensions speakers should consider to design an utterance for a particular listener.

2. Spoonerisms are more likely when the sound exchange yields real words.

3. When representations include more information than the propositions provided by a text, you can conclude that people have encoded inferences.

4. Humans can produce and understand utterances with complex grammatical structures.

5. Linguistic relativity is the idea that the structure of the language people speak has an impact on the way in which they think about the world.

Stop and Review (Visual Cognition, p. 222)

1. The consistency of the rate of mental rotation suggests that the processes of mental rotation are very similar to those of physical rotation.

2. Brain-imaging research suggests large amount of overlap between the brain regions that people use for perception and the regions people use when they create visual images.

3. Research suggests that you find it easier to say what is in front of you, rather than behind you, in the mental scene.

Stop and Review (Problem Solving and Reasoning, p. 230)

1. An algorithm is a step-by-step procedure that guarantees a correct answer for a particular type of problem.

2. You have overcome functional fixedness if you have been able to find a new function for an object that you previously associated with a different purpose.

3. Ideas or products are often considered creative when they are both novel and appropriate to the circumstances.

4. When people succumb to the belief-bias effect, they have judged conclusions based on their real-world believability rather than on their logical relationship to premises.

5. People often engage in inductive reasoning by forming analogies between the features of current circumstances and past experiences in memory.

Stop and Review (Judgment and Decision Making, p. 236)

1. Heuristics provide people with the shortcuts that allow them to make frequent and rapid judgments.

2. It's likely that you would use the anchoring heuristic—by starting at a plausible anchor (e.g., 100 years old) and adjusting from there.

3. Frames play a large role because they determine, for example, whether people think about the gains or losses associated with particular circumstances.

4. When making a decision, satisficers often choose the first option that is good enough; maximizers keep evaluating options, trying to find the absolute best one.

CHAPTER 9

Stop and Review (What Is Assessment? p. 243)

1. Galton suggested that differences in intelligence could be measured objectively.

2. The researcher should determine whether scores on the measure allow for accurate predictions of relevant future outcomes.

3. Norms enable researchers to understand the scores of particular individuals in the context of a broader population's scores.

Stop and Review (Intelligence Assessment, p. 248)

1. The original measure of IQ was mental age divided by chronological age.

2. Wechsler added performance subtests to his IQ measure.

3. Diagnosis of intellectual disability focuses on both IQ and adaptive skills.

4. The three dimensions are ability, creativity, and task commitment.

Stop and Review (Theories of Intelligence, p. 250)

1. Because Spearman demonstrated that people's performance on a variety of intelligence tests was highly correlated, he concluded that there was a factor of general intelligence.

2. Sternberg proposed that people have analytical, creative, and practical intelligence.

3. Gardner defined "spatial" intelligence as the ability to perceive the visual–spatial world and transform one's initial perceptions—these abilities are relevant to sculpture.

Stop and Review (The Politics of Intelligence, p. 256)

1. Goddard and others suggested that IQ tests be used to exclude some immigrants as mentally inferior.
2. Heritability estimates do not allow for comparisons between groups of individuals.
3. Research has demonstrated that people who experience quality preschool programs have higher measured IQs and are more likely to graduate from regular high schools and have better-paying jobs.

Stop and Review (Assessment and Society, p. 257)

1. If members of particular groups generally test less well than others, that pattern might prevent equal access to jobs.
2. In many school districts, support is based on test scores—forcing teachers to cover only material that will be tested.
3. When tests are used without flexibility to label people as belonging to certain academic or social tracks, those labels can have broad consequences.

CHAPTER 10

Stop and Review (Studying Development, p. 263)

1. Developmental age is the chronological age at which most people are able to achieve a particular physical or mental accomplishment.
2. To study individual differences, researchers often measure variation (on some dimension) among people at one age and then reexamine the same participants later in life to examine the consequences of that variation.
3. For some cross-sectional analyses, researchers have to rule out the possibility that what appear to be age-related changes are really differences brought about by the time at which individuals were born.

Stop and Review (Physical Development across the Life Span, p. 269)

1. Compared to their noncrawling peers, children who have begun to crawl experience fear on the "deep" end of the visual cliff.
2. Recent studies indicate that the brain continues to mature during adolescence, particularly in areas such as the frontal lobes.
3. As people age, the lenses in their eyes often become yellowed, which is thought to be responsible for diminished color vision.

Stop and Review (Cognitive Development across the Life Span, p. 274)

1. Assimilation allows children to fit new information to old schemes; accommodation changes schemes to fit new information.
2. A child who can overcome centration is able to ignore surface aspects of a problem to show deeper understanding of a domain such as number or liquid quantity.
3. By inventing more subtle measures of infants' knowledge, researchers have been able to demonstrate that children show evidence of object permanence by age 4 months.
4. Vygotsky emphasized the importance of the social context in the way that children's cognitive development unfolds.
5. Research suggests that people's processing speed slows down as they age.

Stop and Review (Acquiring Language, p. 278)

1. When talking to infants and children, adults tend to slow down, use exaggerated, high-pitched intonation, and produce shorter utterances with simpler structures.
2. Children form hypotheses for the meanings of new words. On some occasions, their hypotheses are broader than the adult category.
3. Deaf children who have not been exposed to either a spoken language or a formal signed language will sometimes begin to use their own signed languages that share structural features with real languages.
4. If a child is overregularizing English past-tense constructions, you would expect to hear him or her say words like *doed* and *breaked* rather than *did* and *broke*.

Stop and Review (Social Development across the Life Span, p. 288)

1. Erikson suggested that the crisis of intimacy versus isolation comes into focus during early adulthood.
2. Research suggests that children who have secure attachments at early ages are, for example, more popular and less socially anxious later in life.
3. Parenting styles are defined by the dimensions of the parent's demandingness and the parent's responsiveness.
4. Adolescents experience peer relationships at the levels of friendships, cliques, and crowds.
5. The birth of a child often has a negative impact on marital satisfaction.

Stop and Review (Sex and Gender Differences, p. 290)

1. Sex differences emerge from biological differences between men and women; gender differences emerge from cultural constructions of different roles for men and women.
2. Research suggests that women show more activity in brain areas related to the processing of emotion.
3. Young children prefer the company of peers of the same sex.

Stop and Review (Moral Development, p. 293)

1. The three major levels are preconventional morality, conventional morality, and principled morality.
2. Gilligan argued that men are more focused on justice, whereas women are more focused on caring for others.
3. People may bring concerns related to autonomy, community, and divinity.

CHAPTER 11

Stop and Review (Understanding Motivation, p. 302)

1. You would probably draw some inference about why the student was running, which relates to the idea that motivational concepts can be links between public acts and private states.
2. Homeostasis reflects a state of equilibrium with respect to biological states.
3. Research demonstrated a good deal of variability in behavior between cultures—arguing against biological instincts.
4. Heider made a distinction between dispositional and situational forces as explanations for outcomes.
5. Attachment needs relate to people's needs to belong, to affiliate with others, to love, and to be loved.

Stop and Review (Eating, p. 307)

1. Sensory-specific satiety is the circumstance in which an individual has become satiated with respect to a particular flavor of food.

2. The dual-center model suggested that the VMH was the "satiety center." However, more recent research suggests that the role of the VMH depends on the type of food.

3. Restrained eaters habitually maintain a low-calorie diet until they become disinhibited, at which point they often will indulge in high-calorie binges.

4. Bulimia nervosa is characterized by the behaviors of binging and purging.

Stop and Review (Sexual Behaviors, p. 315)

1. In most nonhuman species, all members of the species follow the same predictable pattern of sexual behavior.

2. Masters and Johnson identified the phases of excitement, plateau, orgasm, and resolution.

3. Because men can impregnate several women in the same period of time, but women can have only one pregnancy at a time, men seek more sexual partners.

4. Sexual scripts are socially learned programs that define appropriate forms of sexual activity.

5. Concordance rates are higher for MZ twins than for DZ twins, supporting the claim that homosexuality has a genetic component.

Stop and Review (Motivation for Personal Achievement, p. 319)

1. Need for achievement reflects individual differences in the value people place on planning and working toward goals.

2. People make attributions along the dimensions of internal versus external, global versus specific, and stable versus unstable.

3. Expectancy theory proposes that workers are motivated when they expect their effort and performance will yield desirable outcomes.

CHAPTER 12

Stop and Review (Emotions, p. 332)

1. Cross-cultural research suggests there are seven facial expressions that people generally recognize around the world.

2. The autonomous nervous system plays an important role to bring about the physiological aspects of emotions—such as a racing heart and sweaty palms.

3. The Cannon–Bard theory suggests that an emotion stimulus produces concurrently arousal and an emotional feeling.

4. People in negative moods tend to process information in a more detailed and effortful fashion than people in positive moods.

5. Research suggests that good social relationships are the single most important source of happiness.

Stop and Review (Stress and Living, p. 345)

1. The three stages of the GAS are the alarm reaction, resistance, and exhaustion.

2. Participants in the 1990s reported more life-change units, suggesting that they were generally experiencing more stress than people in the 1960s.

3. In general, daily hassles have a negative impact on well-being, and daily pleasures have a positive impact.

4. When people engage in emotion-focused coping, they engage in activities that make them feel better but do not directly change the stressor.

5. When people do not believe they have control over a stressful situation, they are at risk for poor physical and psychological adjustment.

6. People are able to identify positive changes that arise from negative life events.

Stop and Review (Health Psychology, p. 353)

1. Research comparing MZ and DZ twins for the similarity of their tobacco use indicates that there is a genetic component to people's smoking behaviors.

2. Successful AIDS interventions must provide information, instill motivation, and teach behavioral skills.

3. To produce the relaxation response, people must find a quiet environment in which they can rest in a comfortable position with their eyes closed and use a repetitive mental device.

4. Researchers who study psychoneuroimmunology seek to understand how psychological states have an impact on the immune system.

5. The aspect of Type A personality that puts people at risk for illness is hostility.

6. Job burnout is a state of emotional exhaustion, depersonalization, and reduced sense of personal accomplishment.

CHAPTER 13

Stop and Review (Type and Trait Personality Theories, p. 362)

1. Neuroticism is defined as a dimension from stable, calm, and contented versus anxious, unstable, and temperamental.

2. To assess the heritability of traits, researchers have conducted studies that compare the trait similarity of monozygotic and dizygotic twins.

3. The consistency paradox refers to finding that people often give consistent personality descriptions for individuals even though the individuals' behavior is not consistent across situations.

Stop and Review (Psychodynamic Theories, p. 368)

1. The individual might engage in oral behaviors such as smoking or overeating; the individual might be overly passive or gullible.

2. The ego is guided by the reality principle to put reasonable choices before the id's demands for pleasure.

3. Leon might be using the defense mechanism of projection—he projects his own motives onto other people.

4. Adler suggested that people are driven to overcome feelings of inferiority.

Stop and Review (Humanistic Theories, p. 369)

1. Self-actualization is a person's constant striving to reach his or her inherent potential.

2. Humanistic theories focus on people's innate qualities, which influence their behaviors.

3. A psychobiography uses psychological theories to give a coherent account of the way in which an individual's life unfolds.

Stop and Review (Social-Learning and Cognitive Theories, p. 374)

1. People who have an external locus of control orientation believe that rewards are largely contingent on environmental factors.

2. Mischel's theory focuses on encodings, expectancies and beliefs, affects, goal and values, and competencies and self-regulatory plans.

3. According to Bandura, the individual's characteristics, the individual's behavior, and the environment all interact to influence and modify the other components.

Stop and Review (Self Theories, p. 378)

1. Self-esteem is a generalized evaluation of the self.
2. Self-handicapping applies to circumstances in which people engage in behaviors that allow them to attribute their failures to causes besides lack of ability.
3. People who have interdependent construals of self experience themselves as one element of a larger social structure.

Stop and Review (Comparing Personality Theories, p. 379)

1. Some theories explain individual differences by focusing on each person's genetic endowment, whereas other theories make reference to the life experiences that have shaped individual personalities.
2. Freud's theory stresses the way in which events in early childhood—the past—affect an adult's personality.
3. The relevant dimension of personality theories is consciousness versus unconsciousness.

Stop and Review (Assessing Personality, p. 382)

1. Each of the MMPI's 10 clinical scales is intended to differentiate people who have a specific clinical disorder from those who do not.
2. The NEO-PI measures the five personality traits defined by the five-factor model of personality.
3. Clinicians assess Rorschach responses for location, content, and determinants.

CHAPTER 14

Stop and Review (The Nature of Psychological Disorders, p. 392)

1. The most relevant criteria appear to be "distress or disability" (that is, Jerry's fear causes him personal distress) and "maladaptiveness" (that is, Jerry's fear prevents him from easily pursuing his goals).
2. Classification can provide a common shorthand language, an understanding of causality, and a treatment plan.
3. Behaviors are interpreted in different ways in different cultures—the same behaviors may seem "normal" or "abnormal" in different cultural contexts.

Stop and Review (Anxiety Disorders, p. 397)

1. People who suffer from phobias experience irrational fears in situations that are not objectively dangerous.
2. Obsessions are thoughts, whereas compulsions are acts.
3. Research suggests that the evolutionary history of the human species leaves people "prepared" to experience phobias with respect to certain stimuli.
4. People who are high on anxiety sensitivity are more likely to believe that bodily symptoms will have harmful consequences.

Stop and Review (Mood Disorders, p. 402)

1. Bipolar disorder is characterized by periods of severe depression alternating with manic episodes.
2. The cognitive triad refers to negative views of the person him- or herself, negative views of ongoing experiences, and negative views of the future.
3. Research suggests that women are more likely than men to ruminate on their problems, which has the result of increasing negative feelings.

4. Adolescents are at risk for suicide attempts when they feel depressed, hopeless, or isolated and have negative self-concepts.

Stop and Review (Somatoform and Dissociative Disorders, p. 405)

1. Howard's case fits the definition of hyponchondriasis.
2. Dissociative amnesia is an inability to recall important personal experiences, caused by psychological factors in the absence of any organic dysfunction.
3. Research suggests that nearly all the individuals who develop DID have undergone some form of physical or psychological abuse.

Stop and Review (Schizophrenic Disorders, p. 410)

1. Social withdrawal and flattened emotions are negative symptoms of schizophrenia.
2. Delusions of persecution or grandeur are symptoms of the paranoid type of schizophrenic disorder.
3. Research suggests that patients who return to families with high expressed emotion are more likely to experience relapses.

Stop and Review (Personality Disorders, p. 413)

1. People with borderline personality disorder have an intense fear of being abandoned.
2. People with borderline personality disorder have experienced substantially more childhood sexual abuse.
3. Antisocial personality disorder is characterized by both impulsive behaviors and a disregard for safety, which creates a risk for suicide.

Stop and Review (Psychological Disorders of Childhood, p. 414)

1. ADHD is characterized by degrees of inattention and hyperactivity-impulsivity that are inconsistent with children's levels of development.
2. Many parents start to have concerns only when children fail to meet developmental norms for social interaction or language use starting in the second year.
3. Researchers have suggested that children with autistic disorder fail to develop a standard theory of mind.

Stop and Review (The Stigma of Mental Illness, p. 415)

1. Negative attitudes about mental illnesses place people apart as unacceptable.
2. When people enter into treatment, they must often publicly acknowledge that they have a mental illness, creating a context for stigma.
3. Research suggests that contact with people who have mental illnesses serves to reduce stigma.

CHAPTER 15

Stop and Review (The Therapeutic Context, p. 422)

1. The goals of the process are to reach a diagnosis, propose a probable etiology, make a prognosis, and carry out a treatment.
2. Psychoanalysts have completed postgraduate training in the Freudian approach to therapy.
3. Research suggests that therapists with greater cultural competence achieve better therapeutic outcomes.

4. Substantial numbers of patients who are released from psychiatric institutions are readmitted after a short amount of time.

Stop and Review (Psychodynamic Therapies, p. 425)

1. Psychodynamic therapy is also known as insight therapy because a central goal is to guide a patient toward insights into the relationships between present symptoms and past conflicts.
2. Transference refers to circumstances in which a patient develops an emotional reaction toward the therapist that often represents an emotional conflict from the patient's life.
3. Klein believed that the death instinct precedes sexual awareness and leads to an innate aggressive impulse.

Stop and Review (Behavior Therapies, p. 430)

1. Treatments using counterconditioning attempt to replace a maladaptive response (such as fear) with a healthy response (such as relaxation).
2. Typically, clinicians use prizes to provide positive reinforcement for desirable behaviors (such as remaining drug free).
3. Generalization techniques attempt to preserve the positive changes of therapy over time.

Stop and Review (Cognitive Therapies, p. 432)

1. The underlying assumption of cognitive therapy is that abnormal behavior patterns and emotional distress arise from problems in what and how people think.
2. RET suggests that irrational beliefs lead to maladaptive emotional responses.
3. A goal of cognitive behavioral therapy is to change people's behaviors—it is important that they believe they have the efficacy to perform adaptive behaviors.

Stop and Review (Humanistic Therapies, p. 434)

1. The goal of the human-potential movement was to enhance individuals' potential toward greater levels of performance and greater richness of experience.
2. A client-centered therapist establishes a setting with unconditional positive regard—nonjudgmental acceptance and respect for the client.
3. In Gestalt therapy, clients imagine that a feeling, person, object, or situation is occupying an empty chair; they talk to the chair's "occupant" to work through issues in their lives.

Stop and Review (Group Therapies, p. 436)

1. Group therapy gives participants an opportunity to understand that the types of problems they have may actually be quite common.
2. The goal of couple therapy is often to help partners clarify and improve the quality of their interactions.
3. Internet self-help groups are particularly valuable for individuals with mobility issues, who otherwise might not have access to these groups.

Stop and Review (Biomedical Therapies, p. 439)

1. Atypical antipsychotic drugs help alleviate the symptoms of schizophrenia without causing severe problems in motor control.
2. SNRIs inhibit the reuptake of both serotonin and norepinephrine.
3. The procedure fundamentally alters personalities: People become less emotional, but they also lose their sense of self.
4. When people undergo the rTMS procedure, repeated pulses of magnetic stimulation are focused on their brains.

Stop and Review (Treatment Evaluation and Prevention Strategies, p. 442)

1. The meta-analyses suggest that many standard treatments for depression (such as cognitive behavioral therapy and drug therapy) provide relief beyond a placebo treatment.
2. Research has demonstrated that, in general, more positive therapeutic alliances bring about more relief from psychological disorders.
3. The goal of primary prevention is to implement programs that lower the probability that individuals will experience mental illnesses.

CHAPTER 16

Stop and Review (Constructing Social Reality, p. 451)

1. Kelley suggested that people assess distinctiveness, consistency, and consensus when they make attributions.
2. Students are likely to take responsibility for successes and explain away failures—this pattern might prompt them, for example, not to change their study habits when they do poorly on an exam.
3. In most classrooms, teachers have accurate information about their students' potential, which limits the possibility of self-fulfilling prophecies.

Stop and Review (The Power of the Situation, p. 460)

1. The Stanford Prison Experiment demonstrated how quickly people take up the patterns of behaviors that are defined by social roles.
2. Because people want to be liked, accepted, and approved of by others, groups are able to have normative influence.
3. Minorities are able to exert informational influence—they can have an impact because of majority group members' desire to be correct.
4. When a group's joint decision is more extreme than group members would have made on their own, it suggests that processes of group polarization have been at work.
5. Psychiatrists' predictions vastly underestimated the number of people who would continue to administer shocks up to very high levels.

Stop and Review (Attitudes, Attitude Change, and Action, p. 465)

1. Attitudes include cognitive, affective, and behavioral components.
2. The central route to persuasion is marked by high elaboration—careful thought about the persuasive material.
3. Because dissonance reduction reflects the impulse to be self-consistent, cross-cultural differences in sense of self affect the situations in which people experience dissonance.
4. When people make reductions from large to medium requests, they have done something for you. The reciprocity norm requires that you do something for them—by agreeing to their smaller request.

Stop and Review (Prejudice, p. 469)

1. In the absence of prejudice, people most often have positive feelings toward in-group members and neutral feelings toward out-group members.
2. People often interact with people in ways that do not allow them to behave in ways that disconfirm stereotypes.
3. Research suggests that contact with out-groups members consistently reduces prejudice.

1. People tend to like more those individuals who are similar to them.
2. The three dimensions that characterize love are passion, intimacy, and commitment.
3. People with secure attachment styles tend to have the most enduring romantic relationships as adults.

Stop and Review (Aggression, Altruism, and Prosocial Behavior, p. 478)

1. Researchers have used twin studies to demonstrate that identical twins have a higher concordance for forms of antisocial and aggressive behavior than do fraternal twins.

2. When people are frustrated in pursuit of their goals, they are more likely to engage in aggression.
3. Reciprocal altruism is the idea that people perform altruistic behaviors because they expect, in return, to be the recipients of such behaviors.
4. When groups of people witness an emergency, members of the group most often assume that someone else has taken the responsibility to provide assistance.

Practice Test Answers

CHAPTER 1	CHAPTER 3	CHAPTER 5	CHAPTER 7
1. b	1. c	1. a	1. b
2. b	2. b	2. d	2. c
3. c	3. d	3. d	3. a
4. a	4. d	4. d	4. a
5. b	5. c	5. b	5. b
6. c	6. d	6. d	6. d
7. d	7. c	7. b	7. b
8. b	8. b	8. a	8. a
9. c	9. b	9. a	9. b
10. c	10. a	10. b	10. d
11. d	11. c	11. d	11. a
12. a	12. a	12. c	12. a
13. a	13. a	13. c	13. b
14. b	14. b	14. a	14. c
15. a	15. d	15. d	15. d

CHAPTER 2	CHAPTER 4	CHAPTER 6	CHAPTER 8
1. a	1. b	1. b	1. c
2. c	2. b	2. a	2. c
3. b	3. a	3. b	3. b
4. d	4. b	4. d	4. a
5. a	5. d	5. b	5. d
6. b	6. d	6. a	6. b
7. d	7. b	7. c	7. c
8. c	8. c	8. d	8. a
9. b	9. a	9. d	9. a
10. d	10. c	10. c	10. a
11. d	11. a	11. d	11. c
12. c	12. d	12. b	12. b
13. a	13. c	13. c	13. d
14. b	14. c	14. a	14. a
15. c	15. a	15. a	15. a

CHAPTER 9

1. d
2. a
3. b
4. d
5. b
6. b
7. c
8. a
9. c
10. b
11. a
12. d
13. c
14. a
15. b

CHAPTER 10

1. c
2. a
3. d
4. b
5. d
6. a
7. d
8. c
9. d
10. d
11. b
12. a
13. c
14. d
15. b

CHAPTER 11

1. c
2. d
3. c
4. d
5. a
6. b
7. b
8. d
9. c
10. b
11. b
12. a
13. c
14. d
15. a

CHAPTER 12

1. a
2. a
3. c
4. c
5. c
6. c
7. d
8. b
9. c
10. a
11. b
12. a
13. d
14. b
15. d

CHAPTER 13

1. b
2. a
3. c
4. c
5. a
6. d
7. c
8. a
9. a
10. c
11. b
12. a
13. d
14. b
15. b

CHAPTER 14

1. d
2. a
3. a
4. d
5. b
6. c
7. d
8. b
9. c
10. b
11. a
12. d
13. d
14. a
15. c

CHAPTER 15

1. a
2. b
3. d
4. c
5. d
6. b
7. c
8. b
9. a
10. c
11. a
12. d
13. a
14. c
15. d

CHAPTER 16

1. a
2. d
3. b
4. d
5. c
6. c
7. a
8. c
9. b
10. a
11. d
12. c
13. a
14. d
15. b

Glossary

abnormal psychology The area of psychological investigation concerned with understanding the nature of individual pathologies of mind, mood, and behavior.

absolute threshold The minimum amount of physical energy needed to produce a reliable sensory experience; operationally defined as the stimulus level at which a sensory signal is detected half the time.

accommodation The process by which the ciliary muscles change the thickness of the lens of the eye to permit variable focusing on near and distant objects.

accommodation According to Piaget, the process of restructuring or modifying cognitive structures so that new information can fit into them more easily; this process works in tandem with assimilation.

acquisition The stage in a classical conditioning experiment during which the conditioned response is first elicited by the conditioned stimulus.

action potential The nerve impulse activated in a neuron that travels down the axon and causes neurotransmitters to be released into a synapse.

acute stress A transient state of arousal with typically clear onset and offset patterns.

addiction A condition in which the body requires a drug in order to function without physical and psychological reactions to its absence; often the outcome of tolerance and dependence.

aggression Behaviors that cause psychological or physical harm to another individual.

agoraphobia An extreme fear of being in public places or open spaces from which escape may be difficult or embarrassing.

AIDS Acronym for acquired immune deficiency syndrome, a syndrome caused by a virus that damages the immune system and weakens the body's ability to fight infection.

algorithm A step-by-step procedure that always provides the right answer for a particular type of problem.

all-or-none law The rule that the size of the action potential is unaffected by increases in the intensity of stimulation beyond the threshold level.

altruism Prosocial behaviors a person carries out without considering his or her own safety or interests.

amacrine cell One of the cells that integrate information across the retina; rather than sending signals toward the brain, amacrine cells link bipolar cells to other bipolar cells and ganglion cells to other ganglion cells.

ambiguity Property of perceptual object that may have more than one interpretation.

amnesia A failure of memory caused by physical injury, disease, drug use, or psychological trauma.

amygdala The part of the limbic system that controls emotion, aggression, and the formation of emotional memory.

analytic psychology A branch of psychology that views the person as a constellation of compensatory internal forces in a dynamic balance.

anchoring heuristic An insufficient adjustment up or down from an original starting value when judging the probable value of some event or outcome.

anorexia nervosa An eating disorder in which an individual weighs less than 85 percent of her or his expected weight but still expresses intense fear of becoming fat.

anterograde amnesia An inability to form explicit memories for events that occur after the time of physical damage to the brain.

anticipatory coping Efforts made in advance of a potentially stressful event to overcome, reduce, or tolerate the imbalance between perceived demands and available resources.

antisocial personality disorder A disorder characterized by stable patterns of irresponsible or unlawful behavior that violates social norms.

anxiety An intense emotional response caused by the preconscious recognition that a repressed conflict is about to emerge into consciousness.

anxiety disorder Mental disorder marked by psychological arousal, feeling of tension, and intense apprehension without apparent reason.

archetype A universal, inherited, primitive, and symbolic representation of a particular experience or object.

assimilation According to Piaget, the process whereby new cognitive elements are fitted in with old elements or modified to fit more easily; this process works in tandem with accommodation.

association cortex The parts of the cerebral cortex in which many high-level brain processes occur.

attachment Emotional relationship between a child and the regular caregiver.

attention A state of focused awareness on a subset of the available perceptual information.

attention-deficit hyperactivity disorder (ADHD) A disorder of childhood characterized by inattention and hyperactivity-impulsivity.

attitude The learned, relatively stable tendency to respond to people, concepts, and events in an evaluative way.

attribution Judgment about the causes of outcomes.

attribution theory A social–cognitive approach to describe the ways the social perceiver uses information to generate causal explanations.

audience design The process of shaping a message depending on the audience for which it is intended.

auditory cortex The area of the temporal lobes that receives and processes auditory information.

auditory nerve The nerve that carries impulses from the cochlea to the cochlear nucleus of the brain.

autistic disorder A developmental disorder characterized by severe disruption of children's ability to form social bonds and use language.

automatic process Process that does not require attention; it can often be performed along with other tasks without interference.

autonomic nervous system (ANS) The subdivision of the peripheral nervous system that controls the body's involuntary motor responses by connecting the sensory receptors to the central nervous system (CNS) and the CNS to the smooth muscle, cardiac muscle, and glands.

availability heuristic A judgment based on the information readily available in memory.

aversion therapy A type of behavioral therapy used to treat individuals attracted to harmful stimuli; an attractive stimulus is paired with a noxious stimulus in order to elicit a negative reaction to the target stimulus.

avoidance conditioning A form of learning in which animals acquire responses that allow them to avoid aversive stimuli before they begin.

axon The extended fiber of a neuron through which nerve impulses travel from the soma to the terminal buttons.

basic level The level of categorization that can be retrieved from memory most quickly and used most efficiently.

basilar membrane A membrane in the cochlea that, when set into motion, stimulates hair cells that produce the neural effects of auditory stimulation.

behavior The actions by which an organism adjusts to its environment.

behavior analysis The area of psychology that focuses on the environmental determinants of learning and behavior.

behavior modification The systematic use of principles of learning to increase the frequency of desired behaviors and/or decrease the frequency of problem behaviors.

behavior therapy See behavior modification.

behavioral data Observational reports about the behavior of organisms and the conditions under which the behavior occurs or changes.

behavioral measure Overt actions or reaction that is observed and recorded, exclusive of self-reported behavior.

behavioral neuroscience A multidisciplinary field that attempts to understand the brain processes that underlie behavior.

behaviorism A scientific approach that limits the study of psychology to measurable or observable behavior.

behaviorist perspective The psychological perspective primarily concerned with observable behavior that can be objectively recorded and with the relationships of observable behavior to environmental stimuli.

belief-bias effect A situation that occurs when a person's prior knowledge, attitudes, or values distort the reasoning process by influencing the person to accept invalid arguments.

between-subjects design A research design in which different groups of participants are randomly assigned to experimental conditions or to control conditions.

binge eating disorder An eating disorder characterized by out-of-control binge eating without subsequent purges.

binocular depth cue Depth cue that uses information from both eyes.

biofeedback A self-regulatory technique by which an individual acquires voluntary control over nonconscious biological processes.

biological perspective The approach to identifying causes of behavior that focuses on the functioning of the genes, the brain, the nervous system, and the endocrine system.

biomedical therapy Treatment for a psychological disorder that alters brain functioning with chemical or physical interventions such as drug therapy, surgery, or electroconvulsive therapy.

biopsychosocial model A model of health and illness that suggests links among the nervous system, the immune system, behavioral styles, cognitive processing, and environmental domains of health.

bipolar cell Nerve cell in the visual system that combines impulses from many receptors and transmits the results to ganglion cells.

bipolar disorder A mood disorder characterized by alternating periods of depression and mania.

blind spot The region of the retina where the optic nerve leaves the back of the eye; no receptor cells are present in this region.

borderline personality disorder A disorder defined by instability and intensity in personal relationships as well as turbulent emotions and impulsive behaviors.

bottom-up processing Perceptual analyses based on the sensory data available in the environment; results of analysis are passed upward toward more abstract representations.

brain stem The brain structure that regulates the body's basic life processes.

brightness The dimension of color space that captures the intensity of light.

Broca's area The region of the brain that translates thoughts into speech or signs.

bulimia nervosa An eating disorder characterized by binge eating followed by measures to purge the body of excess calories.

bystander intervention Willingness to assist a person in need of help.

Cannon–Bard theory of emotion A theory stating that an emotional stimulus produces two co-occurring reactions—arousal and experience of emotion—that do not cause each other.

case study Intensive observation of a particular individual or small group of individuals.

catharsis The process of expressing strongly felt but usually repressed emotions.

central nervous system (CNS) The part of the nervous system consisting of the brain and spinal cord.

centration Preoperational children's tendency to focus their attention on only one aspect of a situation and disregard other relevant aspects.

cerebellum The region of the brain attached to the brain stem that controls motor coordination, posture, and balance as well as the ability to learn control of body movements.

cerebral cortex The outer surface of the cerebrum.

cerebral hemispheres The two halves of the cerebrum, connected by the corpus callosum.

cerebrum The region of the brain that regulates higher cognitive and emotional functions.

child-directed speech A form of speech addressed to children that includes slower speed, distinctive intonation, and structural simplifications.

chronic stress A continuous state of arousal in which an individual perceives demands as greater than the inner and outer resources available for dealing with them.

chronological age The number of months or years since an individual's birth.

chunking The process of taking single items of information and recoding them on the basis of similarity or some other organizing principle.

circadian rhythm A consistent pattern of cyclical body activities, usually lasting 24 to 25 hours and determined by an internal biological clock.

classical conditioning A type of learning in which a behavior (conditioned response) comes to be elicited by a stimulus (conditioned stimulus) that has acquired its power through an association with a biologically significant stimulus (unconditioned stimulus).

client The term used by clinicians who think of psychological disorders as problems in living, and not as mental illnesses, to describe those being treated.

client-centered therapy A humanistic approach to treatment that emphasizes the healthy psychological growth of the individual based on the assumption that all people share the basic tendency of human nature toward self-actualization.

clinical psychologist An individual who has earned a doctorate in psychology and whose training is in the assessment and treatment of psychological problems.

clinical social worker A mental health professional whose specialized training prepares him or her to consider the social context of people's problems.

cochlea The primary organ of hearing; a fluid-filled coiled tube located in the inner ear.

cognition Processes of knowing, including attending, remembering, and reasoning; also the content of the processes, such as concepts and memories.

cognitive appraisal theory of emotion A theory stating that the experience of emotion is the joint effect of physiological arousal and cognitive appraisal, which serves to determine how an ambiguous inner state of arousal will be labeled.

cognitive behavioral therapy A therapeutic approach that combines the cognitive emphasis on thoughts and attitudes with the behavioral emphasis on changing performance.

cognitive development The development of processes of knowing, including imagining, perceiving, reasoning, and problem solving.

cognitive dissonance The theory that the tension-producing effects of incongruous cognitions motivate individuals to reduce such tension.

cognitive map A mental representation of physical space.

cognitive neuroscience A multidisciplinary field that attempts to understand the brain processes that underlie higher cognitive functions in humans.

cognitive perspective The perspective on psychology that stresses human thought and the processes of knowing, such as attending, thinking, remembering, expecting, solving problems, fantasizing, and consciousness.

cognitive process One of the higher mental processes, such as perception, memory, language, problem solving, and abstract thinking.

cognitive psychology The study of higher mental processes such as attention, language use, memory, perception, problem solving, and thinking.

cognitive science The interdisciplinary field of study of the approach systems and processes that manipulate information.

cognitive therapy A type of psychotherapeutic treatment that attempts to change feelings and behaviors by changing the way a client thinks about or perceives significant life experiences.

collective unconscious The part of an individual's unconscious that is inherited, evolutionarily developed, and common to all members of the species.

common factors The components that psychotherapies share that contribute to therapeutic effectiveness.

comorbidity The experience of more than one disorder at the same time.

comparative cognition The study of the development of cognitive abilities across species and the continuity of abilities from nonhuman to human animals.

complementary colors Colors opposite each other on the color circle; when additively mixed, they create the sensation of white light.

compliance A change in behavior consistent with a communication source's direct requests.

computerized axial tomography (CT or CAT) A technique that uses narrow beams of X-rays passed through the brain at several angles to assemble complete brain images.

concept Mental representation of a kind or category of items and ideas.

conditioned reinforcer In classical conditioning, a formerly neutral stimulus that has become a reinforcer.

conditioned response (CR) In classical conditioning, a response elicited by some previously neutral stimulus that occurs as a result of pairing the neutral stimulus with an unconditioned stimulus.

conditioned stimulus (CS) In classical conditioning, a previously neutral stimulus that comes to elicit a conditioned response.

cone One of the photoreceptors concentrated in the center of the retina that are responsible for visual experience under normal viewing conditions for all experiences of color.

conformity The tendency for people to adopt the behaviors, attitudes, and values of other members of a reference group.

confounding variable A stimulus other than the variable an experimenter explicitly introduces into a research setting that affects a participant's behavior.

consciousness A state of awareness of internal events and the external environment.

conservation According to Piaget, the understanding that physical properties do not change when nothing is added or taken away, even though appearances may change.

consistency paradox The observation that personality ratings across time and among different observers are consistent while behavior ratings across situations are not consistent.

construct validity The degree to which a test adequately measures an underlying construct.

contact comfort Comfort derived from an infant's physical contact with the mother or caregiver.

contact hypothesis The prediction that contact between groups will reduce prejudice only if the contact includes features such as cooperation toward shared goals.

content validity The extent to which a test adequately measures the full range of the domain of interest.

contingency management A general treatment strategy involving changing behavior by modifying its consequences.

control group A group in an experiment that is not exposed to a treatment or does not experience a manipulation of the independent variable.

control procedure Consistent procedure for giving instructions, scoring responses, and holding all other variables constant except those being systematically varied.

controlled process Process that requires attention; it is often difficult to carry out more than one controlled process at a time.

convergence The degree to which the eyes turn inward to fixate on an object.

convergent thinking An aspect of creativity characterized by the ability to gather together different sources of information to solve a problem.

conversion disorder A disorder in which psychological conflict or stress brings about loss of motor or sensory function.

coping The process of dealing with internal or external demands that are perceived to be threatening or overwhelming.

corpus callosum The mass of nerve fibers connecting the two hemispheres of the cerebrum.

correlation coefficient (r) A statistic that indicates the degree of relationship between two variables.

correlational method Research methodology that determines to what extent two variables, traits, or attributes are related.

counseling psychologist Psychologist who specializes in providing guidance in areas such as vocational selections, school problems, drug abuse, and marital conflict.

counterconditioning A technique used in therapy to substitute a new response for a maladaptive one by means of conditioning procedures.

countertransference Circumstances in which a psychoanalyst develops personal feelings about a client because of perceived similarity of the client to significant people in the therapist's life.

covariation model A theory that suggests that people attribute a behavior to a causal factor if that factor was present whenever the behavior occurred but was absent whenever it didn't occur.

creativity The ability to generate ideas or products that are both novel and appropriate to the circumstances.

criterion-related validity The degree to which test scores indicate a result on a specific measure that is consistent with some other criterion of the characteristic being assessed.

cross-sectional design A research method in which groups of participants of different chronological ages are observed and compared at a given time.

crystallized intelligence The facet of intelligence involving the knowledge a person has already acquired and the ability to access that knowledge; measures by vocabulary, arithmetic, and general information tests.

cutaneous senses The skin senses that register sensations of pressure, warmth, and cold.

dark adaptation The gradual improvement of the eyes' sensitivity after a shift in illumination from light to near darkness.

date rape Unwanted sexual violation by a social acquaintance in the context of a consensual dating situation.

debriefing A procedure conducted at the end of an experiment in which the researcher provides the participant with as much information about the study as possible and makes sure that no participant leaves feeling confused, upset, or embarrassed.

decision making The process of choosing between alternatives; selecting or rejecting available options.

declarative memory Memory for information such as facts and events.

deductive reasoning A form of thinking in which one draws a conclusion that is intended to follow logically from two or more statements or premises.

deinstitutionalization The movement to treat people with psychological disorders in the community rather than in psychiatric hospitals.

delusion False or irrational belief maintained despite clear evidence to the contrary.

dendrite One of the branched fibers of neurons that receive incoming signals.

dependent variable In an experimental setting, a variable that the researcher measures to assess the impact of a variation in an independent variable.

depressant Drug that depresses or slows down the activity of the central nervous system.

descriptive statistics Statistical procedures that are used to summarize sets of scores with respect to central tendencies, variability, and correlations.

determinism The doctrine that all events—physical, behavioral, and mental—are determined by specific causal factors that are potentially knowable.

developmental age The chronological age at which most children show a particular level of physical or mental development.

developmental psychology The branch of psychology concerned with interaction between physical and psychological processes and with stages of growth from conception throughout the entire life span.

diathesis-stress hypothesis A hypothesis about the cause of certain disorders, such as schizophrenia, that suggests that genetic factors predispose an individual to a certain disorder but that environmental stress factors must impinge in order for the potential risk to manifest itself.

difference threshold The smallest physical difference between two stimuli that can still be recognized as a difference;

operationally defined as the point at which the stimuli are recognized as different half of the time.

diffusion of responsibility In emergency situations, the larger the number of bystanders, the less responsibility any one of the bystanders feels to help.

discriminative stimulus Stimulus that acts as a predictor of reinforcement, signaling when particular behaviors will result in positive reinforcement.

dissociative amnesia The inability to remember important personal experiences, caused by psychological factors in the absence of any organic dysfunction.

dissociative disorder A personality disorder marked by a disturbance in the integration of identity, memory, or consciousness.

dissociative fugue A disorder characterized by a flight from home or work accompanied by a loss of ability to recall the personal past.

dissociative identity disorder (DID) A dissociative mental disorder in which two or more distinct personalities exist within the same individual; formerly known as multiple personality disorder.

distal stimulus In the processes of perception, the physical object in the world, as contrasted with the proximal stimulus, the optical image on the retina.

divergent thinking An aspect of creativity characterized by an ability to produce unusual but appropriate responses to problems.

DNA (deoxyribonucleic acid) The physical basis for the transmission of genetic information.

double-blind control An experimental technique in which biased expectations of experimenters are eliminated by keeping both participants and experimental assistants unaware of which participants have received which treatment.

dream analysis The psychoanalytic interpretation of dreams used to gain insight into a person's unconscious motives or conflicts.

dream work In Freudian dream analysis, the process by which the internal censor transforms the latent content of a dream into manifest content.

drive Internal state that arises in response to a disequilibrium in an animal's physiological needs.

DSM-IV-TR The current diagnostic and statistical manual of the American Psychological Association that classifies, defines, and describes mental disorders.

ego The aspect of personality involved in self-preservation activities and in directing instinctual drives and urges into appropriate channels.

egocentrism In cognitive development, the inability of a young child at the preoperational stage to take the perspective of another person.

ego defense mechanism Mental strategy (conscious or unconscious) used by the ego to defend itself against conflicts experienced in the normal course of life.

elaboration likelihood model A theory of persuasion that defines how likely it is that people will focus their cognitive processes to elaborate upon a message and therefore follow the central and peripheral routes to persuasion.

elaborative rehearsal A technique for improving memory by enriching the encoding of information.

electroconvulsive therapy (ECT) The use of electroconvulsive shock as an effective treatment for severe depression.

electroencephalogram (EEG) A recording of the electrical activity of the brain.

embryonic stage The second stage of prenatal development, lasting from the third through eighth week after conception.

emotion A complex pattern of changes, including physiological arousal, feelings, cognitive processes, and behavioral reactions, made in response to a situation perceived to be personally significant.

emotional intelligence Type of intelligence defined as the abilities to perceive, appraise, and express emotions accurately and appropriately, to use emotions to facilitate thinking, to understand and analyze emotions, to use emotional knowledge effectively, and to regulate one's emotions to promote both emotional and intellectual growth.

emotion regulation The processes through which people change the intensity and duration of the emotions they experience.

encoding The process by which a mental representation is formed in memory.

encoding specificity The principle that subsequent retrieval of information is enhanced if cues received at the time of recall are consistent with those present at the time of encoding.

endocrine system The network of glands that manufacture and secrete hormones into the bloodstream.

engram The physical memory trace for information in the brain.

episodic memory Long-term memory for an autobiographical event and the context in which it occurred.

equity theory A cognitive theory of work motivation that proposes that workers are motivated to maintain fair and equitable relationships with other relevant persons; also, a model that postulates that equitable relationships are those in which the participants' outcomes are proportional to their inputs.

escape conditioning A form of learning in which animals acquire a response that will allow them to escape from an aversive stimulus.

estrogen The female sex hormone, produced by the ovaries, that is responsible for the release of eggs from the ovaries as well as for the development and maintenance of female reproductive structures and secondary sex characteristics.

etiology The causes of, or factors related to, the development of a disorder.

evolutionary perspective The approach to psychology that stresses the importance of behavioral and mental adaptiveness, based on the assumption that mental capabilities evolved over millions of years to serve particular adaptive purposes.

evolutionary psychology The study of behavior and mind using the principles of evolutionary theory.

excitatory input Information entering a neuron that signals it to fire.

exemplar Member of a category that people have encountered.

expectancy The extent to which people believe that their behaviors in particular situations will bring about rewards.

expectancy effect Result that occurs when a researcher or observer subtly communicates to participants the kind of behavior he or she expects to find, thereby creating that expected reaction.

expectancy theory A cognitive theory of work motivation that proposes that workers are motivated when they expect their efforts and job performance to result in desired outcomes.

experimental group A group in an experiment that is exposed to a treatment or experiences a manipulation of the independent variable.

experimental method Research methodology that involves the manipulation of independent variables to determine their effects on the dependent variables.

explicit use of memory Conscious effort to encode or recover information through memory processes.

exposure therapy A behavioral technique in which clients are exposed to the objects or situations that cause them anxiety.

extinction In conditioning, the weakening of a conditioned association in the absence of a reinforcer or unconditioned stimulus.

fear A rational reaction to an objectively identified external danger that may induce a person to flee or attack in self-defense.

fetal stage The third stage of prenatal development, lasting from the ninth week through birth of the child.

fight-or-flight response A sequence of internal activities triggered when an organism is faced with a threat; prepares the body for combat and struggle or for running away to safety; recent evidence suggests that the response is characteristic only of males.

five-factor model A comprehensive descriptive personality system that maps out the relationships among common traits, theoretical concepts, and personality scales; informally called the Big Five.

fixation A state in which a person remains attached to objects or activities more appropriate for an earlier stage of psychosexual development.

fixed-interval (FI) schedule A schedule of reinforcement in which a reinforcer is delivered for the first response made after a fixed period of time.

fixed-ratio (FR) schedule A schedule of reinforcement in which a reinforcer is delivered for the first response made after a fixed number of responses.

flashbulb memory People's vivid and richly detailed memory in response to personal or public events that have great emotional significance.

fluid intelligence The aspect of intelligence that involves the ability to see complex relationships and solve problems.

formal assessment The systematic procedures and measurement instruments used by trained professionals to assess an individual's functioning, aptitudes, abilities, or mental states.

fovea Area of the retina that contains densely packed cones and forms the point of sharpest vision.

frame A particular description of a choice; the perspective from which a choice is described or framed affects how a decision is made and which option is ultimately exercised.

free association The therapeutic method in which a patient gives a running account of thoughts, wishes, physical sensations, and mental images as they occur.

frequency distribution A summary of how frequently each score appears in a set of observations.

frequency theory The theory that a tone produces a rate of vibration in the basilar membrane equal to its frequency, with the result that pitch can be coded by the place at which activation occurs.

frontal lobe Region of the brain located above the lateral fissure and in front of the central sulcus; involved in motor control and cognitive activities.

frustration-aggression hypothesis According to this hypothesis, frustration occurs in situations in which people are prevented or blocked from attaining their goals; a rise in frustration then leads to a greater probability of aggression.

functional fixedness An inability to perceive a new use for an object previously associated with some other purpose; adversely affects problem solving and creativity.

functional MRI (fMRI) A brain-imaging technique that combines benefits of both MRI and PET scans by detecting magnetic changes in the flow of blood to cells in the brain.

functionalism The perspective on mind and behavior that focuses on the examination of their functions in an organism's interactions with the environment.

fundamental attribution error (FAE) The dual tendency of observers to underestimate the impact of situational factors and to overestimate the influence of dispositional factors on a person's behavior.

g According to Spearman, the factor of general intelligence underlying all intelligent performance.

ganglion cell Cell in the visual system that integrates impulses from many bipolar cells in a single firing rate.

gate-control theory A theory about pain modulation that proposes that certain cells in the spinal cord act as gates to interrupt and block some pain signals while sending others to the brain.

gender A psychological phenomenon that refers to learned sex-related behaviors and attitudes of males and females.

gender identity One's sense of maleness or femaleness; usually includes awareness and acceptance of one's biological sex.

gender stereotype Belief about attributes and behaviors regarded as appropriate for males and females in a particular culture.

gene The biological unit of heredity; discrete section of a chromosome responsible for transmission of traits.

general adaptation syndrome (GAS) The pattern of nonspecific adaptational physiological mechanisms that occurs in response to continuing threat by almost any serious stressor.

generalized anxiety disorder An anxiety disorder in which an individual feels anxious and worried most of the time for at least six months when not threatened by any specific danger or object.

generativity A commitment beyond one's self and one's partner to family, work, society, and future generations; typically, a crucial state in development in one's 30s and 40s.

genetics The study of the inheritance of physical and psychological traits from ancestors.

genome The genetic information for an organism, stored in the DNA of its chromosomes.

genotype The genetic structure an organism inherits from its parents.

germinal stage The first two weeks of prenatal development following conception.

Gestalt psychology A school of psychology that maintains that psychological phenomena can be understood only when viewed as organized, structured wholes, not when broken down into primitive perceptual elements.

Gestalt therapy Therapy that focuses on ways to unite mind and body to make a person whole.

glia The cells that hold neurons together and facilitate neural transmission, remove damaged and dead neurons, and prevent poisonous substances in the blood from reaching the brain.

goal-directed attention A determinant of why people select some parts of sensory input for further processing; it reflects the choices made as a function of one's own goals.

group polarization The tendency for groups to make decisions that are more extreme than the decisions that would be made by the members acting alone.

groupthink The tendency of a decision-making group to filter out undesirable input so that a consensus may be reached, especially if it is in line with the leader's viewpoint.

gustation The sense of taste.

habituation A decrease in a behavioral response when a stimulus is presented repeatedly.

hallucination False perception that occurs in the absence of objective stimulation.

hallucinogen Drug that alters cognitions and perceptions and causes hallucinations.

health A general condition of soundness and vigor of body and mind; not simply the absence of illness or injury.

health promotion The development and implementation of general strategies and specific tactics to eliminate or reduce the risk that people will become ill.

health psychology The field of psychology devoted to understanding the ways people stay healthy, the reasons they become ill, and the ways they respond when they become ill.

heredity The biological transmission of traits from parents to offspring.

heritability The relative influence of genetics—versus environment—in determining patterns of behavior.

heritability estimate A statistical estimate of the degree of inheritance of a given trait or behavior, assessed by the degree of similarity between individuals who vary in their extent of genetic similarity.

heuristic Cognitive strategies, or "rules of thumb," often used as shortcuts in solving a complex inferential task.

hierarchy of needs Maslow's view that basic human motives form a hierarchy and that the needs at each level of the hierarchy must be satisfied before the next level can be achieved; these needs progress from basic biological needs to the need for self-actualization.

hippocampus The part of the limbic system that is involved in the acquisition of explicit memory.

HIV Human immunodeficiency virus, a virus that attacks white blood cells (T lymphocytes) in human blood, thereby weakening the functioning of the immune system; HIV causes AIDS.

homeostasis Constancy or equilibrium of the internal conditions of the body.

horizontal cell One of the cells that integrate information across the retina; rather than sending signals toward the brain, horizontal cells connect receptors to each other.

hormone One of the chemical messengers, manufactured and secreted by the endocrine glands, that regulate metabolism and influence body growth, mood, and sexual characteristics.

hozho A Navajo concept referring to harmony, peace of mind, goodness, ideal family relationships, beauty in arts and crafts, and health of body and spirit.

hue The dimension of color space that captures the qualitative experience of the color of light.

human behavior genetics The area of study that evaluates the genetic component of individual differences in behaviors and traits.

humanistic perspective A psychological model that emphasizes an individual's phenomenal world and inherent capacity for making rational choices and developing to maximum potential.

human-potential movement The therapy movement that encompasses all those practices and methods that release the potential of the average human being for greater levels of performance and greater richness of experience.

hypnosis An altered state of awareness characterized by deep relaxation, susceptibility to suggestions, and changes in perception, memory, motivation, and self-control.

hypnotizability The degree to which an individual is responsive to standardized hypnotic suggestion.

hypochondriasis A disorder in which individuals are preoccupied with having or getting physical ailments despite reassurances that they are healthy.

hypothalamus The brain structure that regulates motivated behavior (such as eating and drinking) and homeostasis.

hypothesis A tentative and testable explanation of the relationship between two (or more) events or variables; often stated as a prediction that a certain outcome will result from specific conditions.

iconic memory Memory system in the visual domain that allows large amounts of information to be stored for very brief durations.

id The primitive, unconscious part of the personality that represents the internalization of society's values, standards, and morals.

identification and recognition Two ways of attaching meaning to percepts.

illusion An experience of a stimulus pattern in a manner that is demonstrably incorrect but shared by others in the same perceptual environment.

implicit prejudice Prejudice that exists outside an individual's conscious awareness.

implicit uses of memory Availability of information through memory processes without conscious effort to encode or recover information.

imprinting A primitive form of learning in which some infant animals physically follow and form an attachment to the first moving object they see and/or hear.

impulsive aggression Cognition-based and goal-directed aggression carried out with premeditated thought, to achieve specific aims.

inattentional blindness People's failure to perceive objects when their attention is focused elsewhere.

incentive External stimulus or reward that motivates behavior although it does not relate directly to biological needs.

independent construal of self Conceptualization of the self as an individual whose behavior is organized primarily by reference to one's own thoughts, feelings, and actions, rather than by reference to the thoughts, feelings, and actions of others.

independent variable In an experimental setting, a variable that the researcher manipulates with the expectation of having an impact on values of the dependent variable.

inductive reasoning A form of reasoning in which a conclusion is made about the probability of some state of affairs, based on the available evidence and past experience.

infant-directed speech A form of speech addressed to infants that includes slower speed, distinctive intonation, and structural simplifications.

inference Missing information filled in on the basis of a sample of evidence or on the basis of prior beliefs and theories.

inferential statistics Statistical procedures that allow researchers to determine whether the results they obtain support their hypotheses or can be attributed just to chance variation.

informational influence Group effects that arise from individuals' desire to be correct and right and to understand how best to act in a given situation.

informed consent The process through which individuals are informed about experimental procedures, risks, and benefits before they provide formal consent to become research participants.

in-group A group with which people identify as members.

in-group bias People's tendency to favor members of their own group over members of other groups.

inhibitory input Information entering a neuron that signals it not to fire.

insanity The legal (not clinical) designation for the state of an individual judged to be legally irresponsible or incompetent.

insight Circumstances of problem solving in which solutions suddenly come to mind.

insight therapy A technique by which the therapist guides a patient toward discovering insights between present symptoms and past origins.

insomnia The chronic inability to sleep normally; symptoms include difficulty in falling asleep, frequent waking, inability to return to sleep, and early-morning awakening.

instinct Preprogrammed tendency that is essential to a species's survival.

instinctual drift The tendency for learned behavior to drift toward instinctual behavior over time.

instrumental aggression Cognition-based and goal-directed aggression carried out with premeditated thought, to achieve specific aims.

intellectual disability Condition in which individuals have IQ scores of 70 to 75 or below and also demonstrate limitations in the ability to bring adaptive skills to bear on life tasks.

intelligence The global capacity to profit from experience and to go beyond given information about the environment.

intelligence quotient (IQ) An index derived from standardized tests of intelligence; originally obtained by dividing an individual's mental age by chronological age and then multiplying by 100; now directly computed as an IQ test score.

interdependent construal of self Conceptualization of the self as part of an encompassing social relationship; recognizing that one's behavior is determined, contingent on, and, to a large extent organized by what the actor perceived to be the thoughts, feelings, and actions of others.

internal consistency A measure of reliability; the degree to which a test yields similar scores across its different parts, such as odd versus even items.

internalization According to Vygotsky, the process through which children absorb knowledge from the social context.

interneuron Brain neuron that relays messages from sensory neurons to other interneurons or to motor neurons.

intimacy The capacity to make a full commitment—sexual, emotional, and moral—to another person.

introspection Individuals' systematic examination of their own thoughts and feelings.

ion channel A portion of neurons' cell membranes that selectively permits certain ions to flow in and out.

James–Lange theory of emotion A peripheral-feedback theory of emotion stating that an eliciting stimulus triggers a behavioral response that sends different sensory and motor feedback to the brain and creates the feeling of a specific emotion.

job burnout The syndrome of emotional exhaustion, depersonalization, and reduced personal accomplishment, often experienced by workers in high-stress jobs.

judgment The process by which people form opinions, reach conclusions, and make critical evaluations of events and people based on available material; also, the product of the mental activity.

just noticeable difference (JND) The smallest difference between two sensations that allows them to be discriminated.

kinesthetic sense The sense concerned with bodily position and movement of the body parts relative to one another.

language-making capacity The innate guidelines or operating principles that children bring to the task of learning a language.

language production What people say, sign, and write, as well as the processes they go through to produce these messages.

latent content In Freudian dream analysis, the hidden meaning of a dream.

law of effect A basic law of learning that states that the power of a stimulus to evoke a response is strengthened when the response is followed by a reward and weakened when it is not followed by a reward.

learned helplessness A general pattern of nonresponding in the presence of noxious stimuli that often follows after an organism has previously experienced noncontingent, inescapable aversive stimuli.

learning A process based on experience that results in a relatively permanent change in behavior or behavioral potential.

learning disorder A disorder defined by a large discrepancy between individuals' measured IQ and their actual performance.

learning-performance distinction The difference between what has been learned and what is expressed in overt behavior.

lens The flexible tissue that focuses light on the retina.

lesion Injury to or destruction of brain tissue.

levels-of-processing theory A theory that suggests that the deeper the level at which information was processed, the more likely it is to be retained in memory.

libido The psychic energy that drives individuals toward sensual pleasures of all types, especially sexual ones.

life-change unit (LCU) In stress research, the measure of the stress levels of different types of changes experienced during a given period.

lightness constancy The tendency to perceive the whiteness, grayness, or blackness of objects as constant across changing levels of illuminations.

limbic system The region of the brain that regulates emotional behavior, basic motivational urges, and memory, as well as major physiological functions.

linguistic relativity The hypothesis that the structure of the language an individual speaks has an impact on the way in which that individual thinks about the world.

locus of control People's general expectancy about the extent to which the rewards they obtain are contingent on their own actions or on environmental factors.

longitudinal design A research design in which the same participants are observed repeatedly, sometimes over many years.

long-term memory (LTM) Memory processes associated with the preservation of information for retrieval at any later time.

loudness A perceptual dimension of sound influenced by the amplitude of a sound wave; sound waves in large amplitudes are generally experienced as loud and those with small amplitudes as soft.

lucid dreaming The theory that conscious awareness of dreaming is a learnable skill that enables dreamers to control the direction and content of their dreams.

magnetic resonance imaging (MRI) A technique for brain imaging that scans the brain using magnetic fields and radio waves.

major depressive disorder A mood disorder characterized by intense feelings of depression over an extended time, without the manic high phase of bipolar depression.

manic episode A component of bipolar disorder characterized by periods of extreme elation, unbounded euphoria without sufficient reason, and grandiose thoughts or feelings about personal abilities.

manifest content In Freudian dream analysis, the surface content of a dream, which is assumed to mask the dream's actual meaning.

maturation The continuing influence of heredity throughout development, the age-related physical and behavioral changes characteristic of a species.

mean The arithmetic average of a group of scores; the most commonly used measure of central tendency.

measure of central tendency A statistic, such as a mean, median, or mode, that provides one score as representative of a set of observations.

measure of variability A statistic, such as a range or standard deviation, that indicates how tightly the scores in a set of observations cluster together.

median The score in a distribution above and below which lie 50 percent of the other scores; a measure of central tendency.

meditation A form of consciousness alteration designed to enhance self-knowledge and well-being through reduced self-awareness.

medulla The region of the brain stem that regulates breathing, waking, and heartbeat.

memory The mental capacity to encode, store, and retrieve information.

menarche The onset of menstruation.

mental age In Binet's measure of intelligence, the age at which a child is performing intellectually, expressed in terms of the average age at which normal children achieve a particular score.

mental set The tendency to respond to a new problem in the manner used to respond to a previous problem.

meta-analysis A statistical technique for evaluating hypotheses by providing a formal mechanism for detecting the general conclusions found in data from many different experiments.

metamemory Implicit or explicit knowledge about memory abilities and effective memory strategies; cognition about memory.

mirror neuron Neuron that responds when an individual observes another individual performing a motor action.

mnemonic Strategy or device that uses familiar information during the encoding of new information to enhance subsequent access to the information in memory.

mode The score appearing most frequently in a set of observations; a measure of central tendency.

monocular depth cue Depth cue that uses information from only one eye.

mood disorder A mood disturbance such as severe depression or depression alternating with mania.

morality A system of beliefs and values that ensures that individuals will keep their obligations to others in society and will behave in ways that do not interfere with the rights and interests of others.

motion parallax A source of information about depth in which the relative distances of objects from a viewer determine the amount and direction of their relative motion in the retinal image.

motivation The process of starting, directing, and maintaining physical and psychological activities; includes mechanisms involved in preferences for one activity over another and the vigor and persistence of responses.

motor cortex The region of the cerebral cortex that controls the action of the body's voluntary muscles.

motor neuron Neuron that carries messages away from the central nervous system toward the muscles and glands.

myelin sheath Insulating material that surrounds axons and increases the speed of neural transmission.

narcolepsy A sleep disorder characterized by an irresistible compulsion to sleep during the daytime.

natural selection Darwin's theory that favorable adaptations to features of the environment allow some members of a species to reproduce more successfully than others.

naturalistic observation A research technique in which unobtrusive observations are made of behaviors that occur in natural environments.

need for achievement (n Ach) An assumed basic human need to strive for achievement of goals that motivates a wide range of behavior and thinking.

negative punishment A behavior is followed by the removal of an appetitive stimulus, decreasing the probability of that behavior.

negative reinforcement A behavior is followed by the removal of an aversive stimulus, increasing the probability of that behavior.

neurogenesis The creation of new neurons.

neuromodulator Any substance that modifies or modulates the activities of the postsynaptic neuron.

neuron A cell in the nervous system specialized to receive, process, and/or transmit information to other cells.

neuroscience The scientific study of the brain and of the links between brain activity and behavior.

neurotic disorder Mental disorder in which a person does not have signs of brain abnormalities and does not display grossly irrational thinking or violate basic norms but does experience subjective distress; a category dropped from *DSM-III*.

neurotransmitter Chemical messenger released from a neuron that crosses the synapse from one neuron to another, stimulating the postsynaptic neuron.

nightmare A frightening dream that usually wakes up the sleeper.

nonconscious Not typically available to consciousness or memory.

non-REM (NREM) sleep The period during which a sleeper does not show rapid eye movement; characterized by less dream activity than during REM sleep.

norm Standard based on measurement of a large group of people; used for comparing the scores of an individual with those of others within a well-defined group.

norm crystallization The convergence of the expectations of a group of individuals into a common perspective as they talk and carry out activities together.

normal curve The symmetrical curve that represents the distribution of scores on many psychological attributes; allows researchers to make judgments of how unusual an observation or result is.

normative influence Group effects that arise from individuals' desire to be liked, accepted, and approved of by others.

normative investigation Research effort designed to describe what is characteristic of a specific age or developmental stage.

object permanence The recognition that objects exist independently of an individual's action or awareness; an important cognitive acquisition of infancy.

observational learning The process of learning new responses by watching the behavior of another.

observer bias The distortion of evidence because of the personal motives and expectations of the viewer.

obsessive-compulsive disorder (OCD) A mental disorder characterized by obsessions—recurrent thoughts, images, or impulses that recur or persist despite efforts to suppress them—and compulsions—repetitive, purposeful acts performed according to certain rules or in a ritualized manner.

occipital lobe Rearmost region of the brain; contains primary visual cortex.

olfaction The sense of smell.

olfactory bulb The center where odor-sensitive receptors send their signals, located just below the frontal lobes of the cortex.

operant Behavior emitted by an organism that can be characterized in terms of the observable effects it has on the environment.

operant conditioning Learning in which the probability of a response is changed by a change in its consequences.

operant extinction When a behavior no longer produces predictable consequences, it returns to the level of occurrence it had before operant conditioning.

operational definition A definition of a variable or condition in terms of the specific operation or procedure used to determine its presence.

opponent-process theory The theory that all color experiences arise from three systems, each of which includes two "opponent" elements (red versus green, blue versus yellow, and black versus white).

optic nerve The axons of the ganglion cells that carry information from the eye toward the brain.

organizational psychologist Psychologist who studies various aspects of the human work environment, such as communication among employees, socialization or enculturation of workers, leadership, job satisfaction, stress and burnout, and overall quality of life.

out-group A group with which people do not identify.

overregularization A grammatical error, usually appearing during early language development, in which rules of the language are applied too widely, resulting in incorrect linguistic forms.

pain The body's response to noxious stimuli that are intense enough to cause, or threaten to cause, tissue damage.

panic disorder An anxiety disorder in which sufferers experience unexpected, severe panic attacks that begin with a feeling of intense apprehension, fear, or terror.

parallel processes Two or more mental processes that are carried out simultaneously.

parasympathetic division The subdivision of the autonomic nervous system that monitors the routine operation of the body's internal functions and conserves and restores body energy.

parental investment The time and energy parents must spend raising their offspring.

parenting style The manner in which parents rear their children; an authoritative parenting style, which balances demandingness and responsiveness, is seen as the most effective.

parietal lobe Region of the brain behind the frontal lobe and above the lateral fissure; contains somatosensory cortex.

partial reinforcement effect The behavioral principle that states that responses acquired under intermittent reinforcement are more difficult to extinguish than those acquired with continuous reinforcement.

participant modeling A therapeutic technique in which a therapist demonstrates the desired behavior and a client is aided, through supportive encouragement, to imitate the modeled behavior.

pastoral counselor A member of a religious order who specializes in the treatment of psychological disorders, often combining spirituality with practical problem solving.

patient The term used by those who take a biomedical approach to the treatment of psychological problems to describe the person being treated.

perceived control The belief that one has the ability to make a difference in the course of the consequences of some event or experience; often helpful in dealing with stressors.

perception The processes that organize information in the sensory image and interpret it as having been produced by properties of objects or events in the external, three-dimensional world.

perceptual constancy The ability to retain an unchanging percept of an object despite variations in the retinal image.

perceptual organization The processes that put sensory information together to give the perception of a coherent scene over the whole visual field.

peripheral nervous system (PNS) The part of the nervous system composed of the spinal and cranial nerves that connect the body's sensory receptors to the CNS and the CNS to the muscles and glands.

personality The psychological qualities of an individual that influence a variety of characteristic behavior patterns across different situations and over time.

personality disorder A chronic, inflexible, maladaptive pattern of perceiving, thinking, and behaving that seriously impairs an individual's ability to function in social or other settings.

personality inventory A self-report questionnaire used for personality assessment that includes a series of items about personal thoughts, feelings, and behaviors.

persuasion Deliberate efforts to change attitudes.

phenotype The observable characteristics of an organism, resulting from the interaction between the organism's genotype and its environment.

pheromone Chemical signal released by an organism to communicate with other members of the species; pheromones often serve as long-distance sexual attractors.

phi phenomenon The simplest form of apparent motion, the movement illusion in which one or more stationary lights going on and off in succession are perceived as a single moving light.

phobia A persistent and irrational fear of a specific object, activity, or situation that is excessive and unreasonable, given the reality of the threat.

phoneme Minimal unit of speech in any given language that makes a meaningful difference in speech and production and reception; ; r and l are two distinct phonemes in English but variations of one in Japanese.

photoreceptor Receptor cell in the retina that is sensitive to light.

physical development The bodily changes, maturation, and growth that occur in an organism starting with conception and continuing across the life span.

physiological dependence The process by which the body becomes adjusted to or dependent on a drug.

pitch Sound quality of highness or lowness; primarily dependent on the frequency of the sound wave.

pituitary gland Located in the brain, the gland that secretes growth hormone and influences the secretion of hormones by other endocrine glands

place theory The theory that different frequency tones produce maximum activation at different locations along the basilar membrane, with the result that pitch can be coded by the place at which activation occurs.

placebo control An experimental condition in which treatment is not administered; it is used in cases where a placebo effect might occur.

placebo effect A change in behavior in the absence of an experimental manipulation.

placebo therapy A therapy interdependent of any specific clinical procedures that results in client improvement.

plasticity Changes in the performance of the brain; may involve the creation of new synapses or changes in the function of existing synapses.

polygenic trait Characteristic that is influenced by more than one gene.

pons The region of the brain stem that connects the spinal cord with the brain and links parts of the brain to one another.

population The entire set of individuals to which generalizations will be made based on an experimental sample.

positive psychology A movement within psychology that applies research to provide people with the knowledge and skills that allow them to experience fulfilling lives.

positive punishment A behavior is followed by the presentation of an aversive stimulus, decreasing the probability of that behavior.

positive reinforcement A behavior is followed by the presentation of an appetitive stimulus, increasing the probability of that behavior.

positron emission tomography (PET) scan Brain image produced by a device that obtains detailed pictures of activity in the living brain by recording the radioactivity emitted by cells during different cognitive or behavioral activities.

posttraumatic stress disorder (PTSD) An anxiety disorder characterized by the persistent reexperience of traumatic events through distressing recollections, dreams, hallucinations, or dissociative flashbacks; develops in response to rapes, life-threatening events, severe injury, and natural disasters.

preconscious memory Memory that is not currently conscious but that can easily be called into consciousness when necessary.

prefrontal lobotomy An operation that severs the nerve fibers connecting the frontal lobes of the brain with the diencephalon, especially those fibers in the thalamic and hypothalamic areas; best known form of psychosurgery.

prejudice A learned attitude toward a target object, involving negative affect (dislike or fear), negative beliefs (stereotypes) that justify the attitude, and a behavioral intention to avoid, control, dominate, or eliminate the target object.

primacy effect Improved memory for items at the start of a list.

primary reinforcer Biologically determined reinforcer, such as food and water.

priming In the assessment of implicit memory, the advantage conferred by prior exposure to a word or situation.

proactive interference Circumstances in which past memories make it more difficult to encode and retrieve new information.

problem solving Thinking that is directed toward solving specific problems and that moves from an initial state to a goal state by means of a set of mental operations.

problem space The elements that make up a problem: the initial state, the incomplete information or unsatisfactory conditions the person starts with; the goal state, the set of information or state the person wishes to achieve; and the set of operations, the steps the person takes to move from the initial state to the goal state.

procedural memory Memory for how things get done; the way perceptual, cognitive, and motor skills are acquired, retained, and used.

projective test A method of personality assessment in which an individual is presented with a standardized set of ambiguous, abstract stimuli and asked to interpret their meanings; the individual's responses are assumed to reveal inner feelings, motives, and conflicts.

prosocial behavior Behavior that is carried out with the goal of helping other people.

prototype The most representative example of a category.

proximal stimulus The optical image on the retina; contrasted with the distal stimulus, the physical object in the world.

psychiatrist An individual who has obtained an MD degree and also has completed postdoctoral specialty training in mental and emotional disorders; a psychiatrist may prescribe medications for the treatment of psychological disorders.

psychic determinism The assumption that mental and behavioral reactions are determined by previous experiences.

psychoactive drug Chemical that affects mental processes and behavior by temporarily changing conscious awareness of reality.

psychoanalysis The form of psychodynamic therapy developed by Freud; an intensive prolonged technique for exploring unconscious motivations and conflicts in neurotic, anxiety-ridden individuals.

psychoanalyst An individual who has earned either a PhD or an MD degree and has completed postgraduate training in the Freudian approach to understanding and treating mental disorders.

psychobiography The use of psychological (especially personality) theory to describe and explain an individual's course through life.

psychodynamic personality theory Theory of personality that shares the assumption that personality is shaped by and behavior is motivated by inner forces.

psychodynamic perspective A psychological model in which behavior is explained in terms of past experiences and motivational forces; actions are viewed as stemming from inherited instincts, biological drives, and attempts to resolve conflicts between personal needs and social requirements.

psychological assessment The use of specified procedures to evaluate the abilities, behaviors, and personal qualities of people.

psychological dependence The psychological need or craving for a drug.

psychological diagnosis The label given to psychological abnormality by classifying and categorizing the observed behavior pattern into an approved diagnostic system.

psychology The scientific study of the behavior of individuals and their mental processes.

psychometric function A graph that plots the percentage of detections of a stimulus (on the vertical axis) for each stimulus intensity on the horizontal positions of corresponding images in the two eyes.

psychometrics The field of psychology that specializes in mental testing.

psychoneuroimmunology The research area that investigates interactions between psychological processes, such as responses to stress, and the functions of the immune system.

psychopathological functioning Disruptions in emotional, behavioral, or thought processes that lead to personal distress or block one's ability to achieve important goals.

psychopharmacology The branch of psychology that investigates the effects of drugs on behavior.

psychophysics The study of the correspondence between physical simulation and psychological experience.

psychosocial stage Proposed by Erik Erikson, one of the successive developmental stages that focus on an individual's orientation toward the self and others; these stages incorporate both the sexual and social aspects of a person's developmental and the social conflicts that arise from the interaction between the individual and the social environment.

psychosomatic disorder Physical disorder aggravated by or primarily attributable to prolonged emotional stress or other psychological causes.

psychosurgery A surgical procedure performed on brain tissue to alleviate a psychological disorder.

psychotherapy Any of a group of therapies, used to treat psychological disorders, that focus on changing faulty behaviors, thoughts, perceptions, and emotions that may be associated with specific disorders.

psychotic disorder Severe mental disorder in which a person experiences impairments in reality testing manifested through thought, emotional, or perceptual difficulties; no longer used as diagnostic category after *DSM–III*.

puberty The process through which sexual maturity is attained.

punisher Any stimulus that, when made contingent on a response, decreases the probability of that response.

pupil The opening at the front of the eye through which light passes.

racism Discrimination against people based on their skin color or ethnic heritage.

random assignment A procedure by which participants have an equal likelihood of being assigned to any condition within an experiment.

random sampling A procedure that ensures that every member of a population has an equal likelihood of participating in an experiment.

range The difference between the highest and the lowest scores in a set of observations; the simplest measure of variability.

rapid eye movement (REM) A behavioral sign of the phase of sleep during which the sleeper is likely to be experiencing dreamlike mental activity.

rational-emotive therapy (RET) A comprehensive system of personality change based on changing irrational beliefs that cause undesirable, highly charged emotional reactions such as severe anxiety.

reasoning The process of thinking in which conclusions are drawn from a set of facts; thinking directed toward a given goal or objective.

recall A method of retrieval in which an individual is required to reproduce the information previously presented.

recency effect Improved memory for items at the end of a list.

receptive field The area of the visual field to which a neuron in the visual system responds.

reciprocal altruism The idea that people perform altruistic behaviors because they expect that others will perform altruistic behaviors for them in turn.

reciprocal determinism A concept of Albert Bandura's social-learning theory that refers to the notion that a complex reciprocal interaction exists among the individual, his or her behavior, and environmental stimuli and that each of these components affects the others.

reciprocity norm Expectation that favors will be returned—if someone does something for another person, that person should do something in return.

recognition A method of retrieval in which an individual is required to identify stimuli as having been experienced before.

reconstructive memory The process of putting information together based on general types of stored knowledge in the absence of a specific memory representation.

reflex An unlearned response elicited by specific stimuli that have biological relevance for an organism.

refractory period The period of rest during which a new nerve impulse cannot be activated in a segment of an axon.

reinforcement contingency A consistent relationship between a response and the changes in the environment that it produces.

reinforcer Any stimulus that, when made contingent on a response, increases the probability of that response.

relaxation response A condition in which muscle tension, cortical activity, heart rate, and blood pressure decrease and breathing slows.

reliability The degree to which a test produces similar scores each time it is used; stability or consistency of the scores produced by an instrument.

repetitive transcranial magnetic stimulation (rTMS) A technique for producing temporary inactivation of brain areas using repeated pulses of magnetic stimulation.

representative sample A subset of a population that closely matches the overall characteristics of the population with respect to the distribution of males and females, racial and ethnic groups, and so on.

representativeness heuristic A cognitive strategy that assigns an object to a category on the basis of a few characteristics regarded as representative of that category.

repression The basic defense mechanism by which painful or guilt-producing thoughts, feelings, or memories are excluded from conscious awareness.

resistance The inability or unwillingness of a patient in psychoanalysis to discuss certain ideas, desires, or experiences.

response bias The systematic tendency as a result of nonsensory factors for an observer to favor responding in a particular way.

resting potential The polarization of cellular fluid within a neuron, which provides the capability to produce an action potential.

reticular formation The region of the brain stem that alerts the cerebral cortex to incoming sensory signals and is responsible for maintaining consciousness and awakening from sleep.

retina The layer at the back of the eye that contains photoreceptors and converts light energy to neutral responses.

retinal disparity The displacement between the horizontal positions of corresponding images in the two eyes.

retrieval The recovery of stored information from memory.

retrieval cue Internally or externally generated stimulus available to help with the retrieval of a memory.

retroactive interference Circumstances in which the formation of new memories makes it more difficult to recover older memories.

retrograde amnesia An inability to retrieve memories from the time before physical damage to the brain.

rod One of the photoreceptors concentrated in the periphery of the retina that is most active in dim illumination; rods do not produce sensation of color.

rule Behavioral guideline for acting in a certain way in a certain situation.

sample A subset of a population selected as participants in an experiment.

saturation The dimension of color space that captures the purity and vividness of color sensations.

schedule of reinforcement In operant conditioning, a pattern of delivering and withholding reinforcement.

schema General conceptual framework, or cluster of knowledge, regarding objects, people, and situations; knowledge package that encodes generalizations about the structure of the environment.

scheme Piaget's term for a cognitive structure that develops as infants and young children learn to interpret the world and adapt to their environment.

schizophrenic disorder Severe form of psychopathology characterized by the breakdown of integrated personality functioning, withdrawal from reality, emotional distortions, and disturbed thought processes.

scientific method The set of procedures used for gathering and interpreting objective information in a way that minimizes error and yields dependable generalizations.

selective optimization with compensation A strategy for successful aging in which one makes the most gains while minimizing the impact of losses that accompany normal aging.

self-actualization A concept in personality psychology referring to a person's constant striving to realize his or her potential and to develop inherent talents and capabilities.

self-concept A person's mental model of his or her typical behaviors and unique qualities.

self-efficacy The set of beliefs that one can perform adequately in a particular situation.

self-esteem A generalized evaluative attitude toward the self that influences both moods and behavior and that exerts a powerful effect on a range of personal and social behaviors.

self-fulfilling prophecy A prediction made about some future behavior or event that modifies interactions so as to produce what is expected.

self-handicapping The process of developing, in anticipation of failure, behavioral reactions and explanations that minimize ability deficits as possible attributions for the failure.

self-perception theory The idea that people observe themselves to figure out the reasons they act as they do; people infer what their internal states are by perceiving how they are acting in a given situation.

self-report measure A self-behavior that is identified through a participant's own observations and reports.

self-serving bias An attributional bias in which people tend to take credit for their successes and deny responsibility for their failures.

semantic memory Generic, categorical memory, such as the meaning of words and concepts.

sensation The process by which stimulation of a sensory receptor gives rise to neutral impulses that result in an experience, or awareness, of conditions inside or outside the body.

sensitization An increase in behavioral response when a stimulus is presented repeatedly.

sensory adaptation A phenomenon in which receptor cells lose their power to respond after a period of unchanged stimulation; allows a more rapid reaction to new sources of information.

sensory neuron Neuron that carries messages from sense receptors toward the central nervous system.

sensory receptor Specialized cell that converts physical signals into cellular signals that are processed by the nervous system.

serial position effect A characteristic of memory retrieval in which the recall of beginning and end items on a list is often better than recall of items appearing in the middle.

serial processes Two or more mental processes that are carried out in order, one after the other.

set A temporary readiness to perceive or react to a stimulus in a particular way.

sex chromosome Chromosome that contains the genes that code for the development of male or female characteristics.

sex difference One of the biologically based characteristics that distinguish males from females.

sexism Discrimination against people because of their sex.

sexual arousal The motivational state of excitement and tension brought about by physiological and cognitive reactions to erotic stimuli.

sexual script Socially learned program of sexual responsiveness.

shape constancy The ability to perceive the true shape of an object despite variations in the size of the retinal image.

shaping by successive approximations A behavioral method that reinforces responses that successively approximate and ultimately match the desired response.

short-term memory (STM) Memory processes associated with preservation of recent experiences and with retrieval of information from long-term memory; short-term memory is of limited capacity and stores information for only a short length of time without rehearsal.

signal detection theory A systematic approach to the problem of response bias that allows an experimenter to identify and separate the roles of sensory stimuli and the individual's criterion level in producing the final response.

significant difference A difference between experimental groups or conditions that would have occurred by chance less than an accepted criterion; in psychology, the criterion most often used is a probability of less than 5 times out of 100, or $p < .05$.

size constancy The ability to perceive the true size of an object despite variations in the size of its retinal image.

sleep apnea A sleep disorder of the upper respiratory system that causes the person to stop breathing while asleep.

sleep terrors Episodes in which sleepers wake up suddenly in an extreme state of arousal and panic.

social categorization The process by which people organize the social environment by categorizing themselves and others into groups.

social cognition The process by which people select, interpret, and remember social information.

social development The ways in which individuals' social interactions and expectations change across the life span.

social learning theory The learning theory that stresses the role of observation and the imitation of behaviors observed in others.

social norm The expectation a group has for its members regarding acceptable and appropriate attitudes and behaviors.

social perception The process by which a person comes to know or perceive the personal attributes.

social phobia A persistent, irrational fear that arises in anticipation of a public situation in which an individual can be observed by others.

social psychology The branch of psychology that studies the effect of social variables on individual behavior, attitudes, perceptions, and motives; also studies group and intergroup phenomena.

social role A socially defined pattern of behavior that is expected of a person who is functioning in a given setting or group.

social support Resources, including material aid, socioemotional support, and informational aid, provided by others to help a person cope with stress.

socialization The lifelong process whereby an individual's behavioral patterns, values, standards, skills, attitudes, and motives are shaped to conform to those regarded as desirable in a particular society.

sociobiology A field of research that focuses on evolutionary explanations for the social behavior and social systems of humans and other animal species.

sociocultural perspective The psychological perspective that focuses on cross-cultural differences in the causes and consequences of behavior.

soma The cell body of a neuron, containing the nucleus and cytoplasm.

somatic nervous system The subdivision of the peripheral nervous system that connects the central nervous system to the skeletal muscles and skin.

somatization disorder A disorder characterized by unexplained physical complaints in several categories over many years.

somatoform disorder A disorder in which people have physical illnesses or complaints that cannot be fully explained by actual medical conditions.

somatosensory cortex The region of the parietal lobes that processes sensory input from various body areas.

somnambulism A disorder that causes sleepers to leave their beds and wander while still remaining asleep; also known as sleepwalking.

sound localization The auditory processes that allow the spatial origins of environmental sounds.

specific phobia Phobia that occurs in response to a specific type of object or situation.

spontaneous recovery The reappearance of an extinguished conditioned response after a rest period.

spontaneous-remission effect The improvement of some mental patients and clients in psychotherapy without any professional intervention; a baseline criterion against which the effectiveness of therapies must be assessed.

standard deviation (SD) The average difference of a set of scores from their mean; a measure of variability.

standardization A set of uniform procedures for treating each participant in a test, interview, or experiment, or for recording data.

stereotype Generalization about a group of people in which the same characteristics are assigned to all members of a group.

stereotype threat The threat associated with being at risk for confirming a negative stereotype of one's group.

stigma The negative reaction of people to an individual or group because of some assumed inferiority or source of difference that is degraded.

stimulant Drug that causes arousal, increased activity, and euphoria.

stimulus discrimination A conditioning process in which an organism learns to respond differently to stimuli that differ from the conditioned stimulus on some dimension.

stimulus generalization The automatic extension of conditioned responding to similar stimuli that have never been paired with the unconditioned stimulus.

stimulus-driven attention A determinant of why people select some parts of sensory input for further processing; occurs when features of stimuli—objects in the environment—automatically capture attention, independent of the local goals of a perceiver.

storage The retention of encoded material over time.

stress The pattern of specific and nonspecific responses an organism makes to stimulus events that disturb its equilibrium and tax or exceed its ability to cope.

stress moderator variable Variable that changes the impact of a stressor on a given type of stress reaction.

stressor An internal or external event or stimulus that induces stress.

structuralism The study of the structure of mind and behavior; the view that all human mental experience can be understood as a combination of simple elements or events.

subjective well-being Individuals' overall evaluation of life satisfaction and happiness.

superego The aspect of personality that represents the internalization of society's values, standards, and morals.

sympathetic division The subdivision of the autonomic nervous system that deals with emergency response and the mobilization of energy.

synapse The gap between one neuron and another.

synaptic transmission The relaying information from one neuron to another across the synaptic gap.

systematic desensitization A behavioral therapy technique in which a client is taught to prevent the arousal of anxiety by confronting the feared stimulus while relaxed.

taste-aversion learning A biological constraint on learning in which an organism learns in one trial to avoid a food whose ingestion is followed by illness.

temperament A child's biologically based level of emotional and behavioral response to environmental events.

temporal distinctiveness The extent to which a particular item stands out from or is distinct from other items in time.

temporal lobe Region of the brain found below the lateral fissure; contains auditory cortex.

tend-and-befriend response A response to stressors that is hypothesized to be typical for females; stressors prompt females to protect their offspring and join social groups to reduce vulnerability.

teratogen Environmental factors such as diseases and drugs that cause structural abnormalities in a developing fetus.

terminal button A bulblike structure at the branched ending of an axon that contains vesicles filled with neurotransmitters.

terror management theory A theory proposing that self-esteem helps people cope with the inevitability of death.

test–retest reliability A measure of the correlation between the scores of the same people on the same test given on two different occasions

testosterone The male sex hormone, secreted by the testes, that stimulates production of sperm and is also responsible for the development of male secondary sex characteristics.

thalamus The brain structure that relays sensory impulses to the cerebral cortex.

Thematic Apperception Test (TAT) A projective test in which pictures of ambiguous scenes are presented to an individual, who is encouraged to generate stories about them.

theory An organized set of concepts that explains a phenomenon or set of phenomena.

theory of mind The ability to explain and predict other people's behavior based on an understanding of their mental states.

think-aloud protocol Report made by an experimental participant of the mental processes and strategies he or she uses while working on a task.

three-term contingency The means by which organisms learn that, in the presence of some stimuli but not others, their behavior is likely to have a particular effect on the environment.

timbre The dimension of auditory sensation that reflects the complexity of a sound wave.

tolerance A situation that occurs with continued use of a drug in which an individual requires greater dosages to achieve the same effect.

top-down processing Perceptual processes in which information from an individual's past experience, knowledge, expectations, motivations, and background influence the way a perceived object is interpreted and classified.

trait Enduring personal quality or attribute that influences behavior across situations.

transduction Transformation of one form of energy into another; for example, light is transformed into neutral impulses.

transfer-appropriate processing The perspective that suggests that memory is best when the type of processing carried out at encoding matches the processes carried out at retrieval.

transference The process by which a person in psychoanalysis attaches to a therapist feelings formerly held toward some significant person who figured into past emotional conflict.

trichromatic theory The theory that there are three types of color receptors that produce the primary color sensations of red, green, and blue.

two-factor theory of emotion The theory that emotional experiences arise from autonomic arousal and cognitive appraisal.

Type A behavior pattern A complex pattern of behaviors and emotions that includes excessive emphasis on competition, aggression, impatience, and hostility; hostility increases the risk of coronary heart disease.

Type B behavior pattern As compared to Type A behavior pattern, a less competitive, less aggressive, less hostile pattern of behavior and emotion.

unconditional positive regard Complete love and acceptance of an individual by another person, such as a parent for a child, with no conditions attached.

unconditioned response (UCR) In classical conditioning, the response elicited by an unconditioned stimulus without prior training or learning.

unconditioned stimulus (UCS) In classical conditioning, the stimulus that elicits an unconditioned response.

unconscious The domain of the psyche that stores repressed urges and primitive impulses.

validity The extent to which a test measures what it was intended to measure.

variable In an experimental setting, a factor that varies in amount and kind.

variable-interval (VI) schedule A schedule of reinforcement in which a reinforcer is delivered for the first response made after a variable period of time whose average is predetermined.

variable-ratio (VR) schedule A schedule of reinforcement in which a reinforcer is delivered for the first response made after a variable number of responses whose average is predetermined.

vestibular sense The sense that tells how one's own body is oriented in the world with respect to gravity.

visual cortex The region of the occipital lobes in which visual information is processed.

volley principle An extension of frequency theory, which proposes that when peaks in a sound wave come too frequently for a single neuron to fire at each peak, several neurons fire as a group at the frequency of the stimulus tone.

Weber's law An assertion that the size of a difference threshold is proportional to the intensity of the standard stimulus.

wellness Optimal health, incorporating the ability to function fully and actively over the physical, intellectual, emotional, spiritual, social, and environmental domains of health.

Wernicke's area A region of the brain that allows fluent speech production and comprehension.

wisdom Expertise in the fundamental pragmatics of life.

within-subjects design A research design that uses each participant as his or her own control; for example, the behavior of an experimental participant before receiving treatment might be compared to his or her behavior after receiving treatment.

working memory A memory resource that is used to accomplish tasks such as reasoning and language comprehension; consists of the phonological loop, visuospatial sketchpad, central executive, and episodic buffer.

zygote The single cell that results when a sperm fertilizes an egg.

References

Abrahamsen, R., Baad-Hansen, L., Zachariae, R., & Svensson, P. (2011). Effect of hypnosis on pain and blink reflexes in patients with painful temporomandibular disorders. *The Clinical Journal of Pain, 27*, 344–351.

Abramson, L. Y., Seligman, M. E. P., & Teasdale, J. D. (1978). Learned helplessness in humans: Critique and reformulation. *Journal of Abnormal Psychology, 87*, 32–48, 49–74.

Adams, J. L. (1986). *Conceptual blockbusting* (3rd ed.). New York: Norton.

Adams, J. S. (1965). Inequity in social exchange. In L. Berkowitz (Ed.), *Advances in experimental social psychology* (Vol. 2, pp. 267–299). New York: Academic Press.

Adams, R. E., & Laursen, B. (2007). The correlates of conflict: Disagreement is not necessarily detrimental. *Journal of Family Psychology, 21*, 445–458.

Adaval, R., & Wyer, R. S., Jr. (2011). Conscious and nonconscious comparisons with price anchors: Effects on willingness to pay for related and unrelated products. *Journal of Marketing Research, 48*, 355–365.

Ader, R., & Cohen, N. (1981). Conditioned immunopharmacological responses. In R. Ader (Ed.), *Psychoneuroimmunology* (pp. 281–319). New York: Academic Press.

Ader, R., & Cohen, N. (1993). Psychoneuroimmunology: Conditioning and stress. *Annual Review of Psychology, 44*, 53–85.

Adler, A. (1929). *The practice and theory of individual psychology.* New York: Harcourt, Brace & World.

Adolph, K. E., Karasik, L. B., & Tamis-LeMonda, C. S. (2010). Motor skill. In M. Bornstein (Ed.), *Handbook of cultural developmental science* (pp. 61–88). New York: Psychology Press.

Adolphs, R., & Damasio, A. R. (2001). The interaction of affect and cognition: A neurobiological perspective. In J. P. Forgas (Ed.), *Handbook of affect and social cognition* (pp. 27–49). Mahwah, NJ: Erlbaum.

Agerström, J., & Rooth, D.-O. (2011). The role of automatic obesity stereotypes in real hiring discrimination. *Journal of Applied Psychology, 96*, 790–805.

Ainsworth, M. D. S., Blehar, M., Waters, E., & Wall, S. (1978). *Patterns of attachment.* Hillsdale, NJ: Erlbaum.

Akechi, T., Okuyama, T., Endo, C., Sagawa, R., Uchida, M., Nakaguchi, T., Sakamoto, M., Komatsu, H., Ueda, R., Wada, M., & Furukawa, T. A. (2010). Anticipatory nausea among ambulatory cancer patients undergoing chemotherapy: Prevalence, associated factors, and impact on quality of life. *Cancer Science, 101*, 2596–2600.

Akinbami, L. J., Liu, X., Pastor, P. N., & Reuben, C. A. (2011). Attention deficit hyperactivity disorder among children aged 5–17 years in the United States, 1998–2009. *NCHS data brief* (no. 70). Hyattsville, MD: National Center for Health Statistics. Retrieved from www.cdc.gov/nchs/data/databriefs/db70.pdf.

Akmajian, A., Demers, R. A., Farmer, A. K., & Harnish, R. M. (1990). *Linguistics.* Cambridge, MA: The MIT Press.

Albarracín, D., Durantini, M. R., Earl, A., Gunnoe, J. B., & Leeper, J. (2008). Beyond the most willing audiences: A meta-intervention to increase exposure to HIV-prevention programs by vulnerable populations. *Health Psychology, 27*, 638–644.

Allan, C. A., Forbes, E. A., Strauss, B. J. G., & McLachlan, R. I. (2008). Testosterone therapy increases sexual desire in ageing men with low-normal testosterone levels and symptoms of androgen deficiency. *International Journal of Impotence Research, 20*, 396–401.

Allen, J. P., Porter, M. R., & McFarland, F. C. (2006). Leaders and followers in adolescent close relationships: Susceptibility to peer influence as a predictor of risky behavior, friendship instability, and depression. *Development and Psychopathology, 18*, 155–172.

Allport, G. W. (1937). *Personality: A psychological interpretation.* New York: Holt, Rinehart & Winston.

Allport, G. W. (1954). *The nature of prejudice.* Cambridge, MA: Addison-Wesley.

Allport, G. W. (1961). *Pattern and growth in personality.* New York: Holt, Rinehart & Winston.

Allport, G. W. (1966). Traits revisited. *American Psychologist, 21*, 1–10.

Allport, G. W., & Odbert, H. S. (1936). Trait-names, a psycholexical study. *Psychological Monographs, 47*(1, Whole No. 211).

Almeida, L. S., Prieto, M. D., Ferreira, A. I., Bermejo, M. R., Ferrando, M., & Ferrándiz, C. (2010). Intelligence assessment: Gardner multiple intelligence theory as an alternative. *Learning and Individual Differences, 20*, 225–230.

Aly, M., Knight, R. T., & Yonelinas, A. P. (2010). Faces are special but not too special: Spared face recognition in amnesia is based on familiarity. *Neuropsychologia, 48*, 3941–3948.

Alzheimer's Association. (2011). *2011 Alzheimer's disease facts and figures.* Retrieved from www.alz.org/downloads/Facts_Figures_2011.pdf.

Amaral, D. G., Schumann, C. M., & Nordahl, C. W. (2008). Neuroanatomy of autism. *Trends in Neurosciences, 31*, 137–145.

Amato, P. R. (2010). Research on divorce: Continuing trends and new developments. *Journal of Marriage and Family, 72*, 650–666.

American Association on Intellectual and Developmental Disabilities. (2010). *Intellectual disability: Definition, classification, and systems of supports* (11th ed.). Washington, DC: American Association on Intellectual and Developmental Disabilities.

American Psychological Association. (2002). Ethical principles of psychologists and code of conduct. *American Psychologist, 57*, 1060–1073.

American Psychological Association. (2011). Summary report of journal operations, 2010. *American Psychologist, 66*, 405–406.

Anderson, C. A., Shibuya, A., Ihori, N., Swing, E. L., Bushman, B. J., Sakamoto, A., Rothstein, H. R., & Saleem, M. (2010). Violent video game effects on aggression, empathy, and prosocial behavior in Eastern and Western countries. *Psychological Bulletin, 136*, 151–173.

Anderson, S. L., Adams, G., & Plaut, V. C. (2008). The cultural grounding of personal relationship: The importance of attractiveness in everyday life. *Journal of Personality and Social Psychology, 95*, 352–368.

Andrews-Hanna J. R., Mackiewicz Seghete, K. L., Claus, E. D., Burgess, G. C., Ruzic, L., & Banich, M. T. (2011). Cognitive control in adolescence: Neural underpinnings and relation to self-report behaviors. *PLoS ONE, 6*, e21598.

Andreyeva, T., T., Long, M. W., & Brownell, K. D. (2010). The impact of food prices on consumption: A systematic review of research on the price elasticity of demand for food. *American Journal of Public Health, 100*, 216–222.

Anstee, J. L. K., Harris, S. G., Pruitt, K. D., & Sugar, J. A. (2008). Service-learning projects in an undergraduate gerontology course: A six-stage model and application. *Educational Gerontology, 34*, 595–609.

Anthony, D. B., Holmes, J. G., & Wood, J. V. (2007). Social acceptance and self-esteem: Tuning the sociometer to interpersonal value. *Journal of Personality and Social Psychology, 92*, 1024–1039.

Appleby, D. C. (2006). Defining, teaching, and assessing critical thinking in introductory psychology. In D. S. Dunn & S. L. Chew (Eds.), *Best practices for teaching introduction to psychology* (pp. 57–69). Mahwah, NJ: Erlbaum.

Arendt, J. (2010). Shift work: Coping with the biological clock. *Occupational Medicine, 60,* 10–20.

Arendt, J., & Skene, D. J. (2005). Melatonin as a chronobiotic. *Sleep Medicine Reviews, 9,* 25–39.

Arnett, J. J. (1999). Adolescent storm and stress reconsidered. *American Psychologist, 54,* 317–326.

Arnett, J. J. (2008). The neglected 95%: Why American psychology needs to become less American. *American Psychologist, 63,* 602–614.

Arnon, Z., Maoz, G., Gazit, T., & Klein, E. (2011). Rorschach indicators of PTSD: A retrospective study. *Rorschachiana, 32,* 5–26.

Aron, A., & Aron, E. N. (1994). Love. In A. L. Weber & J. H. Harvey (Eds.), *Perspectives on close relationships* (pp. 131–152). Boston: Allyn & Bacon.

Aron, A., & Fraley, B. (1999). Relationship closeness as including other in the self: Cognitive underpinnings and measures. *Social Cognition, 17,* 140–160.

Aron, A., & Westbay, L. (1996). Dimensions of the prototype of love. *Journal of Personality and Social Psychology, 70,* 535–551.

Aron, A., Aron, E. N., & Smollan, D. (1992). Inclusion of other in the self scale and the structure of interpersonal closeness. *Journal of Personality and Social Psychology, 63,* 596–612.

Aron, A., Mashek, D., McLaughlin-Volpe, T., Wright, S., Lewandowski, G., & Aron, E. N. (2004). Including close others in the cognitive structure of self. In M. W. Baldwin (Ed.), *Interpersonal cognition* (pp. 206–232). New York: Guilford Press.

Aronson, E. (2002). Building empathy, compassion, and achievement in the jigsaw classroom. In J. Aronson (Ed.), *Improving academic achievement: Impact of psychological factors on education* (pp. 209–225). San Diego, CA: Academic Press.

Aronson, E., & Gonzalez, A. (1988). Desegregation jigsaw, and the Mexican-American experience. In P. A. Katz & D. Taylor (Eds.), *Towards the elimination of racism: Profiles in controversy.* New York: Plenum Press.

Aronson, E., Blaney, N., Stephan, C., Sikes, J., & Snapp, M. (1978). *The jigsaw classroom.* Beverly Hills, CA: Sage.

Asch, S. E. (1940). Studies in the principles of judgments and attitudes: II. Determination of judgments by group and by ego standards. *Journal of Social Psychology, 12,* 433–465.

Asch, S. E. (1952). *Social psychology.* Englewood Cliffs, NJ: Prentice Hall.

Asch, S. E. (1955). Opinions and social pressure. *Scientific American, 193*(5), 31–35.

Asch, S. E. (1956). Studies of independence and conformity: A minority of one against a unanimous majority. *Psychological Monographs, 70*(9, Whole No. 416), www.nsf.gov/statistics/nsf11306/.

Auvray, M., Gallace, A., & Spence, C. (2011). Tactile short-term memory for stimuli presented on the fingertips and across the rest of the surface of the body. *Attention, Perception, & Psychophysics, 73,* 1227–1241.

Ayduk, O., Rodriguez, M. L., Mischel, W., Shoda, Y., & Wright, J. (2007). Verbal intelligence and self-regulatory competencies: Joint predictors of boys' aggression. *Journal of Research in Personality, 41,* 374–388.

Ayllon, T., & Michael, J. (1959). The psychiatric nurse as a behavioral engineer. *Journal of the Experimental Analysis of Behavior, 2,* 323–334.

Baars, B. J. (1992). A dozen completing-plans techniques for inducing predictable slips in speech and action. In B. J. Baars (Ed.), *Experimental slips and human error: Exploring the architecture of volition* (pp. 129–150). New York: Plenum Press.

Baars, B. J., Motley, M. T., & MacKay, D. G. (1975). Output editing for lexical status in artificially elicited slips of the tongue. *Journal of Verbal Learning and Verbal Behavior, 14,* 382–391.

Baas, M., De Creu, C. K. W., & Nijstad, B. A. (2008). A meta-analysis of 25 years of mood-creativity research: Hedonic tone, activation, or regulatory focus? *Psychological Bulletin, 134,* 779–806.

Back, M. D., Schmukle, S. C., & Egloff, B. (2008). How extraverted is honey. bunny77@hotmail.de? *Journal of Research in Personality, 42,* 1116–1122.

Baddeley, A. D. (2002). Is working memory still working? *European Psychologist, 7,* 85–97.

Baddeley, A. D. (2003). Working memory: Looking back and looking forward. *Nature Reviews Neuroscience, 4,* 829–839.

Badzakova-Trajov, G., Häberling, I. S., Roberts, R. P., & Corballis, M. C. (2010). Cerebral asymmetries: Complementary and independent processes. *PLoS ONE, 5,* e9862.

Bahrick, H. P., Bahrick, P. O., & Wittlinger, R. P. (1975). Fifty years of memory for names and faces: A cross-sectional approach. *Journal of Experimental Psychology: General, 104,* 54–75.

Bailey, B. A., & Sokol, R. J. (2008). Pregnancy and alcohol use: Evidence and recommendations for prenatal care. *Clinical Obstetrics and Gynecology, 51,* 436–444.

Bakken, T. E., Bloss, C. S., Roddey, C., Joyner, A. H., Rimol, L. M., Djurovic, S., Melle, I., Sundet, K., Agartz, I., Andreassen, O. A., Dale, A. M., & Schork, N. J. (2011). Association of genetic variants on 15q12 with cortical thickness and cognition in schizophrenia. *Archives of General Psychiatry, 68,* 781–790.

Balch, R. W., & Taylor, D. (2002). Making sense of the Heaven's Gate suicides. In D. G. Bromley & J. G. Melton (Eds.), *Cults, religion, and violence* (pp. 209–228). Cambridge, UK: Cambridge University Press.

Balsam, K. F., Beauchaine, T. P., Rothblum, E. D., & Solomon, S. E. (2008). Three-year follow-up of same-sex couples who had civil unions in Vermont, same-sex couples not in civil unions, and heterosexual married couples. *Developmental Psychology, 44,* 102–116.

Baltes, P. B. (1993). The aging mind: Potential and limits. *The Gerontologist, 33,* 580–594.

Baltes, P. B., Smith, J., & Staudinger, U. M. (1992). Wisdom and successful aging. In T. B. Sonderegger (Ed.), *The Nebraska Symposium on Motivation: Vol. 39. The psychology of aging* (pp. 123–167). Lincoln: University of Nebraska Press.

Bandelow, B., Krause, J., Wedekind, D., Broocks, A., Hajak, G., & Rüther, E. (2005). Early traumatic life events, parental attitudes, family history, and birth risk factors in patients with borderline personality disorder and healthy controls. *Psychiatry Research, 134,* 169–179.

Bandura, A. (1970). Modeling therapy. In W. S. Sahakian (Ed.), *Psychopathology today: Experimentation, theory and research.* Itasca, IL: Peacock.

Bandura, A. (1977). *Social learning theory.* Englewood Cliffs, NJ: Prentice-Hall.

Bandura, A. (1986). *Social foundations of thought and action: A social cognitive theory.* Englewood Cliffs, NJ: Prentice-Hall.

Bandura, A. (1992). Exercise of personal agency through the self-efficacy mechanism. In R. Schwarzer (Ed.), *Self-efficacy: Thought control of action* (pp. 3–38). Washington, DC: Hemisphere.

Bandura, A. (1997). *Self-efficacy: The exercise of control.* New York: Freeman.

Bandura, A. (1999). Social cognitive theory of personality. In L. A. Pervin & O. P. John (Eds.), *Handbook of personality: Theory and research* (2nd ed., pp. 154–196). New York: Guilford Press.

Bandura, A. (2006). Toward of psychology of human agency. *Perspectives on Psychological Science, 1,* 164–180.

Bandura, A., Ross, D., & Ross, S. A. (1963). Imitation of film-mediated aggressive models. *Journal of Abnormal and Social Psychology, 66,* 3–11.

Banks, S., & Dinges, D. F. (2007). Behavioral and physiological consequences of sleep restriction. *Journal of Clinical Sleep Medicine, 3,* 519–528.

Banyai, E. I., & Hilgard, E. R. (1976). Comparison of active-alert hypnotic induction with traditional relaxation induction. *Journal of Abnormal Psychology, 85,* 218–224.

Barak, A., Boniel-Nissim, M., & Suler, J. (2008). Fostering empowerment in online support groups. *Computers in Human Behavior, 24,* 1867–1883.

Bárez, M., Blasco, T., Fernández-Castro, J., & Viladrich, C. (2007). A structural model of the relationships between perceived control and the adaptation to illness in women with breast cancer. *Journal of Psychosocial Oncology, 25,* 21–43.

Bar-Hillel, M., & Neter, E. (1993). How alike is it versus how likely is it: A disjunction fallacy in probability judgments. *Journal of Personality and Social Psychology, 65,* 1119–1131.

Barkataki, I., Kumari, V., Das, M., Taylor, P., & Sharma, T. (2006). Volumetric structural brain abnormalities in men with schizophrenia and antisocial personality disorder. *Behavioural Brain Research, 169,* 239–247.

Barker, R., Dembo, T., & Lewin, D. (1941). Frustration and aggression: An experiment with young children. *University of Iowa Studies in Child Welfare, 18*(1).

Baron-Cohen, S. (2008). Theories of the autistic mind. *The Psychologist, 21,* 112–116.

Barrett, L. F., Tugade, M. M., & Engle, R. W. (2004). Individual differences in working memory capacity and dual-process theories of mind. *Psychological Bulletin, 130,* 553–573.

Barrett, M. S., Chua, W.-J., Crits-Christoph, P., Gibbons, M. B., & Thompson, D. (2008). Early withdrawal from mental health treatment: Implications for psychotherapy practice. *Psychotherapy Theory, Research, Practice, Training, 45,* 247–267.

Bartlett, F. C. (1932). *Remembering: A study in experimental and social psychology.* Cambridge, UK: Cambridge University Press.

Bartoshuk, L. M. (1993). The biological basis of food perception and acceptance. *Food Quality and Preference, 4,* 21–32.

Bartoshuk, L. M., & Beauchamp, G. K. (1994). Chemical senses. *Annual Review of Psychology, 45,* 419–449.

Bartz, J. A., Zaki, J., Bolger, N., & Ochsner, K. N. (2011). Social effects of oxytocin in humans: Context and person matter. *Trends in Cognitive Sciences, 15,* 301–309.

Basso, E. B. (1987). The implications of a progressive theory of dreaming. In B. Tedlock (Ed.), *Dreaming: Anthropological and psychological interpretations* (pp. 86–104). Cambridge, UK: Cambridge University Press.

Bastardi, A., Uhlmann, E. L., & Ross, L. (2011). Wishful thinking: Belief, desire, and the motivated evaluation of scientific evidence. *Psychological Science, 22,* 731–732.

Bastien, C. H. (2011). Insomnia: Neurophysiological and neuropsychological approaches. *Neuropsychology Review, 21,* 22–40.

Batson, C. D. (1991). *The altruism question: Toward a social-psychological answer.* Hillsdale, NJ: Erlbaum.

Batson, C. D. (1994). Why act for the public good? Four answers. *Personality and Social Psychology Bulletin, 20,* 603–610.

Batson, C. D., Ahmad, N., Yin, J., Bedell, S. J., Johnson, J. W., Templin, C. M., & Whiteside, A. (1999). Two threats to the common good: Self-interested egoism and empathy-induced altruism. *Personality and Social Psychology Bulletin, 25,* 3–16.

Baum, J. R., Bird, B. J., & Singh, S. (2011). The practical intelligence of entrepreneurs: Antecedents and a link with new venture growth. *Personnel Psychology, 64,* 397–425.

Baumeister, R. F., Campbell, J. D., Krueger, J. I., & Vohs, K. D. (2003). Does high self-esteem cause better performance, interpersonal success, happiness, or healthy lifestyles? *Psychological Science in the Public Interest, 4,* 1–44.

Baumgartner, T., Heinrichs, M., Vonlanthen, A., Fischbacher, U., & Fehr, E. (2008). Oxytocin shapes the neural circuitry of trust and trust adaptation in humans. *Neuron, 58,* 639–650.

Bauminger, N., Finzi-Dottan, R., Chason, S., & Har-Even, D. (2008). Intimacy in adolescent friendship: The roles of attachment, coherence, and self-disclosure. *Journal of Social and Personal Relationships, 25,* 409–428.

Bayley, N. (1956). Individual patterns of development. *Child Development, 27,* 45–74.

Beauchamp, G. K., & Mennella, J. A. (2011). Flavor perception in human infants: Development and functional significance. *Digestion, 83,* 1–6.

Beck, A. T. (1967). *Depression: Clinical, experimental, and theoretical Aspects.* New York: Harper & Row.

Beck, A. T. (1976). *Cognitive therapy and emotional disorders.* New York: International Universities Press.

Beck, A. T., & Emery, G. (1985). *Anxiety disorders and phobias: A cognitive perspective.* New York: Basic Books.

Beck, A. T., & Rush, A. J. (1989). Cognitive therapy. In H. I. Kaplan & B. Sadock (Eds.), *Comprehensive textbook of psychiatry* (Vol. 5). Baltimore: Williams & Wilkins.

Beck, A. T., Rush, A. J., Shaw, B. F., & Emery, G. (1979). *Cognitive therapy of depression.* New York: Guilford Press.

Beck, H. P., Levinson, S., & Irons, G. (2009). Finding Little Albert. *American Psychologist, 64,* 605–614.

Becker, S. W., & Eagly, A. H. (2004). The heroism of women and men. *American Psychologist, 59,* 163–178.

Beer, J. S. (2002). Implicit self-theories of shyness. *Journal of Personality and Social Psychology, 83,* 1009–1024.

Behne, T., Liszkowski, U., Carpenter, M., & Tomasello, M. (2012). Twelve-month-olds' comprehension and production of pointing. *British Journal of Developmental Psychology,* in press.

Bell, D. C. (2001). Evolution of parental caregiving. *Personality and Social Psychology Review, 5,* 216–229.

Bellebaum, C., & Daum, I. (2011). Mechanisms of cerebellar involvement in associate learning. *Cortex, 47,* 128–136.

Belsky, J., Vandell, D. L., Burchinal, M., Clarke-Stewart, K. A., McCartney, K., Owen, M. T., & The NICHD Early Child Care Research Network. (2007). Are there long-term effects of early child care? *Child Development, 78,* 681–701.

Bem, D. (2000). The exotic-becomes-erotic theory of sexual orientation. In J. Bancroft (Ed.), *The role of theory in sex research* (pp. 67–81). Bloomington: Indiana University Press.

Bem, D. J. (1972). Self-perception theory. In L. Berkowitz (Ed.), *Advances in experimental social psychology* (Vol. 6, pp. 1–62). New York: Academic Press.

Bem, D. J. (1996). Exotic becomes erotic: A developmental theory of sexual orientation. *Psychological Review, 103,* 320–335.

Bem, S. L. (1974). The measurement of psychological androgyny. *Journal of Consulting and Clinical Psychology, 42,* 155–162.

Bem, S. L. (1981). *The Bem Sex Role Inventory: Professional manual.* Palo Alto, CA: Consulting Psychology Press.

Benedict, R. (1938). Continuities and discontinuities in cultural conditioning. *Psychiatry, 1,* 161–167.

Benedict, R. (1959). *Patterns of culture.* Boston: Houghton Mifflin.

Benenson, J. F., & Heath, A. (2006). Boys withdraw from one-on-one interactions, whereas girls withdraw more in groups. *Developmental Psychology, 42,* 272–282.

Benenson, J. F., Apostoleris, N. H., & Parnass, J. (1997). Age and sex differences in dyadic and group interaction. *Developmental Psychology, 33,* 538–543.

Benight, C. C., Cieslak, R., Molton, I. R., & Johnson, L. E. (2008). Self-evaluative appraisals of coping capability and posttraumatic distress following motor vehicle accidents. *Journal of Consulting and Clinical Psychology, 76,* 677–685.

Benish, S. G., Quintant, S., & Wampold, B. E. (2011). Culturally adapted psychotherapy and the legitimacy of myth: A direct-comparison meta-analysis. *Journal of Counseling Psychology, 58,* 279–289.

Benjamin, L. T., Jr. (2007). *A brief history of modern psychology.* Malden, MA: Blackwell.

Benjet, C., & Kazdin, A. E. (2003). Spanking children: The controversies, findings, and new directions. *Clinical Psychology Review, 23,* 197–224.

Bennett, D. S., Bendersky, M., & Lewis, M. (2008). Children's cognitive ability from 4 to 9 years old as a function of prenatal cocaine exposure, environmental risk, and maternal verbal intelligence. *Developmental Psychology, 44,* 919–928.

Benson, H. (2000). *The relaxation response* (Updated ed.). New York: HarperCollins.

Berenson, K. R., Downey, G., Rafaeli, E., Coifman, K. G., & Paquin, N. L. (2011). The rejection-rage contingency in borderline personality disorder. *Journal of Abnormal Psychology, 120*, 681–690.

Berger, T., Hold, E., & Caspar, F. (2009). Internet-based treatment for social phobia: A randomized control trial. *Journal of Clinical Psychology, 65*, 1021–1035.

Bering, J. M., & Bjorklund, D. F. (2007). The serpent's gift: Evolutionary psychology and consciousness. In P. D. Zelazo, M. Moscovitch, & E. Thompson (Eds.), *The Cambridge handbook of consciousness* (pp. 597–629). New York: Cambridge University Press.

Berkowitz, L. (1993). *Aggression: Its causes, consequences, and control.* New York: McGraw-Hill.

Berkowitz, L. (1998). Affective aggression: The role of stress, pain, and negative affect. In R. G. Geen & E. Donnerstein (Eds.), *Human aggression: Theories, research, and implications for public policy* (pp. 49–72). San Diego, CA: Academic Press.

Berkowitz, S. J. (2003). Children exposed to community violence: The rationale for early intervention. *Clinical Child and Family Psychology Review, 6*, 293–302.

Berlin, B., & Kay, P. (1969). *Basic color terms: Their universality and evolution.* Berkeley: University of California Press.

Berlyne, D. E. (1960). *Conflict, arousal, and curiosity.* New York: McGraw-Hill.

Bernal, G., Jiménez-Chafey, M. I., & Domenech Rodríguez, M. M. (2009). Cultural adaptation of treatments: A resource for considering culture in evidence-based practice. *Professional Psychology: Research and Practice, 40*, 361–368.

Bernard, L. L. (1924). *Instinct.* New York: Holt, Rinehart & Winston.

Berscheid, E., & Walster, E. H. (1978). *Interpersonal attraction* (2nd ed.). Reading, MA: Addison-Wesley.

Bersoff, D. N. (Ed.) (2008). *Ethical conflicts in psychology* (4th ed.). Washington, DC: American Psychological Association.

Bialystok, E., & Craik, F. I. M. (2010). Cognitive and linguistic processing in the bilingual mind. *Current Directions in Psychological Science, 19*, 19–23.

Bialystok, E., & Shapero, D. (2005). Ambiguous benefits: The effect of bilingualism on reversing ambiguous figures. *Developmental Science, 8*, 595–604.

Bialystok, E., Luk, G., Peets, K. F., & Yang, S. (2010). Receptive vocabulary differences in monolingual and bilingual children. *Bilingualism: Language and Cognition, 13*, 525–531.

Biederman, J., Faraone, S. V., & Monteaux, M. C. (2002). Differential effect of environmental adversity by gender: Rutter's index of adversity in a group of boys and girls with and without ADHD. *American Journal of Psychiatry, 159*, 1556–1562.

Biehl, M., Matsumoto, D., Ekman, P., Hearn, V., Heider, K., Kudoh, T., & Ton, V. (1997). Matsumoto and Ekman's Japanese and Caucasian facial expressions of emotion (JACFEE): Reliability data and cross-national differences. *Journal of Nonverbal Behavior, 21*, 3–21.

Biel, M. B., Preselow, E., Mulcare, L., Case, B. G., & Fieve, R. (2007). Continuation versus discontinuation of lithium in recurrent bipolar illness: A naturalistic study. *Bipolar Disorders, 9*, 435–442.

Bielak, A. A. M., Hughes, T. F., Small, B. J., & Dixon, R. A. (2007). It's never too late to engage in lifestyle activities: Significant concurrent but not change relationships between lifestyle activities and cognitive speed. *Journal of Gerontology: Psychological Sciences, 62B*, P331–P339.

Bierbach, D., Kronmarck, C., Hennige-Schulz, C., Stadler, S., & Plath, M. (2011). Sperm competition risk affects male mate choice copying. *Behavioral Ecology and Sociobiology, 65*, 1699–1707.

Billings, A. G., & Moos, R. H. (1982). Family environments and adaptation: A clinically applicable typology. *American Journal of Family Therapy, 20*, 26–38.

Binet, A. (1911). *Les idées modernes sur les enfants.* Paris: Flammarion.

Biss, R. K., & Hasher, L. (2011). Delighted and distracted: Positive affect increases priming for irrelevant information. *Emotion, 11*, 1474–1478.

Bjorvatn, B., Grønli, J., & Pallesen, S. (2010). Prevalence of different parasomnias in the general population. *Sleep Medicine, 11*, 1031–1034.

Blagrove, M., Henley-Einion, J., Barnett, A., Edwards, D., & Seage, C. H. (2011). A replication of the 5–7 day dream-lag effect with comparisons of dreams to future events as control for baseline matching. *Consciousness and Cognition, 20*, 384–391.

Blatter, K., & Cajochen, C. (2007). Circadian rhythms in cognitive performance: Methodologocial constrains, protocols, theoretical underpinnings. *Physiology & Behavior, 90*, 196–208.

Bleuler, M. (1978). The long-term course of schizophrenic psychoses. In L. C. Wynne, R. L. Cromwell, & S. Mattysse (Eds.), *The nature of schizophrenia: New approaches to research and treatment* (pp. 631–636). New York: Wiley.

Blond, A. (2008). Impacts of exposure to images of ideal bodies on male body dissatisfaction: A review. *Body Image, 5*, 244–250.

Blos, P. (1965). *On adolescence: A psychoanalytic interpretation.* New York: The Free Press.

Blumberg, H. P., Leung, H. C., Skudlarski, P., Lacadie, C. M., Fredericks, C. A., Harris, B. C., Charney, D. S., Gore, J. C., Krystal, J. H., & Peterson, B. S. (2003). A functional magnetic resonance imaging study of bipolar disorder. *Archives of General Psychiatry, 60*, 601–609.

Blustein, D. L. (2008). The role of work in psychological health and well-being: A conceptual, historical, and public policy perspective. *American Psychologist, 63*, 228–240.

Boardman, J. D., Saint Onge, J. M., Haberstick, B. C., Timberlake, D. S., & Hewitt, J. K. (2008). Do schools moderate the genetic determinants of smoking? *Behavioral Genetics, 38*, 234–246.

Bock, K. (1990). Structure in language: Creating form in talk. *American Psychologist, 45*, 1221–1236.

Bock, K., Dell, G. S., Chang, F., & Onishi, K. H. (2007). Persistent structural priming from language comprehension to language production. *Cognition, 104*, 437–458.

Bogle, K. A. (2008). *Hooking up: Sex, dating, and relationships on campus.* New York: New York University Press.

Bohannon, J. N. III, Gratz, S., & Cross, V. S. (2007). The effects of affect and input source on flashbulb memories. *Applied Cognitive Psychology, 21*, 1023–1036.

Bohlin, G., Hagekull, B., & Rydell, A.-M. (2000). Attachment and social functioning: A longitudinal study from infancy to middle childhood. *Social Development, 9*, 24–39.

Bohner, G., & Dickel, N. (2011). Attitudes and attitude change. *Annual Review of Psychology, 62*, 391–417.

Bolden, L., & Wicks, M. N. (2005). Length of stay, admission types, psychiatric diagnoses, and the implications of stigma in African Americans in the nationwide inpatient sample. *Issues in Mental Health Nursing, 26*, 1043–1059.

Bolhuis, J. J., & Honey, R. C. (1998). Imprinting, learning and development: From behaviour to brain and back. *Trends in Neurosciences, 21*, 306–311.

Bolino, M. C., & Turnley, W. H. (2008). Old faces, new places: Equity theory in cross-cultural contexts. *Journal of Organizational Behavior, 29*, 29–50.

Bolton, D., & Perrin, S. (2008). Evaluation of exposure with response-prevention for obsessive compulsive disorder in childhood and adolescence. *Journal of Behavior Therapy and Experimental Psychiatry, 39*, 11–22.

Bolton, J. M., Belik, S.-L., Enns, M. W., Cox, B. J., & Sareen, J. (2008). Exploring the correlates of suicide attempts among individuals with major depressive disorder: Findings from the national epidemiologic survey on alcohol and related conditions. *The Journal of Clinical Psychiatry, 69*, 1139–1149.

Bonanno, G. A., Pat-Horenczyk, R., & Noll, J. (2011). Coping flexibility and trauma: The perceived ability to cope with trauma (PACT) scale. *Psychological Trauma: Theory, Research, Practice, and Policy, 3*, 117–129.

Bond, C. F., Jr., Pitre, U., & van Leeuwen, M. D. (1991). Encoding operations and the next-in-line effect. *Personality and Social Psychology Bulletin, 17,* 435–441.

Borges, N. J., Manuel, R. S., Elam, C. L., & Jones, B. J. (2010). Differences in motives between Millennial and Generation X medical students. *Medical Education, 44,* 570–576.

Bornstein, M. H., & Arterberry, M. E. (2003). Recognition, discrimination and categorization of smiling by 5-month-old infants. *Developmental Science, 6,* 585–599.

Bornstein, R. F., Becker-Matero, N., Winarick, D. J., & Reichman, A. L. (2010). Interpersonal dependency in borderline personality disorder: Clinical context and empirical evidence. *Journal of Personality Disorders, 24,* 109–127.

Botella, C., Bretón-López, J., Quero, S., Baños, R., & García-Palacios, A. (2010). Treating cockroach phobia with augmented reality. *Behavior Therapy, 41,* 401–413.

Bouchard, T. J. Jr., & Loehlin, J. C. (2001). Genes, evolution, and personality. *Behavior Genetics, 31,* 243–273.

Bouris, A., Guilamo-Ramos, V., Pickard, A., Shiu, C., Loosier, P. S., Dittus, P., Gloppen, K., & Waldmiller, J. M. (2010). A systematic review of parental influences on the health and well-being of lesbian, gay, and bisexual youth: Time for a new public health research and practice agenda. *The Journal of Primary Prevention, 31,* 273–309.

Bourque, F., van der Ven, E., & Malla, A. (2011). A meta-analysis of the risk for psychotic disorders among first- and second-generation immigrants. *Psychological Medicine, 41,* 897–910.

Bovbjerg, D. H. (2006). The continuing problem of post chemotherapy nausea and vomiting: Contributions of classical conditioning. *Autonomic Neuroscience: Basic and Clinical, 129,* 92–98.

Bowden, E. M., & Beeman, M. J. (2003). Normative data for 144 compound remote associates problem. *Behavior Research Methods, Instruments, and Computers, 35,* 634–639.

Bowlby, J. (1969). *Attachment and loss, Vol 1. Attachment.* New York: Basic Books.

Bowlby, J. (1973). *Attachment and loss, Vol 2. Separation, anxiety and anger.* London: Hogarth.

Boyd, J. E., Katz, E. P., Link, B. G., & Phelan, J. C. (2010). The relationship of multiple aspects of stigma and personal contact with someone hospitalized for mental illness, in a nationally representative sample. *Social Psychiatry and Psychiatric Epidemiology, 45,* 1063–1070.

Boyd, R. C., Diamond, G. S., & Bourolly, J. N. (2006). Developing a family-based depression prevention program in urban community mental health clinics: A qualitative investigation. *Family Process, 45,* 187–203.

Boysen, G. A., & Vogel, D. L. (2007). Biased assimilation and attitude polarization in response to learning about biological explanations of homosexuality. *Sex Roles, 57,* 755–762.

Brainerd, C. J. (1996). Piaget: A centennial celebration. *Psychological Science, 7,* 191–195.

Branje, S. J. T., Frijns, T., Finkenaer, C., Engels, R., & Meeus, W. (2007). You are my best friend: Commitment and stability in adolescents' same-sex friendships. *Personal Relationships, 14,* 587–603.

Brans, R. G. H., van Haren, N. E. M., van Baal, C. M., Schnack, H. G., Kahn, R. S., & Hulshoff, H. E. (2008). Heritability of changes in brain volume over time in twin pairs discordant for schizophrenia. *Archives of General Psychiatry, 65,* 1259–1268.

Braun, K. A., Ellis, R., & Loftus, E. F. (2002). Make my memory: How advertising can change our memories of the past. *Psychology & Marketing, 19,* 1–23.

Brechwald, W. A., & Prinstein, M. J. (2011). Beyond homophily: A decade of advances in understanding peer influence processes. *Journal of Research on Adolescence, 21,* 166–179.

Breland, K., & Breland, M. (1951). A field of applied animal psychology. *American Psychologist, 6,* 202–204.

Breland, K., & Breland, M. (1961). A misbehavior of organisms. *American Psychologist, 16,* 681–684.

Brennan, S. E., & Hanna, J. E. (2009). Partner-specific adaptation in dialog. *Topics in Cognitive Science, 1,* 274–291.

Breslin, P. A. S., & Spector, A. C. (2008). Mammalian taste perception. *Current Biology, 18,* R148–R155.

Brewer, M. B. (2007). The importance of being *we:* Human nature and intergroup relations. *American Psychologist, 62,* 728–738.

Bridge, J. A., & Barbe, R. P. (2004). Reducing hospital readmission in depression and schizophrenia: Current evidence. *Current Opinion in Psychiatry, 17,* 505–511.

Bridge, J. A., Iyengar, S., Salary, C. B., Barbe, R. P., Birmaher, B., Pincus, H. A., Ren, L., & Brent, D. A. (2007). Clinical response and risk for reported suicidal ideation and suicide attempts in pediatric antidepressant treatment: A meta-analysis of randomized controlled trials. *JAMA, 297,* 1683–1696.

Brody, N. (2003). Construct validation of the Sternberg Triarchic Abilities Test: Comment and reanalysis. *Intelligence, 31,* 319–329.

Bronfenbrenner, U. (Ed.) (2004). *Making human beings human: Bioecological perspectives on human development.* Thousand Oaks, CA: Sage Publications.

Brown, F. B., & Klute, C. (2003). Friendships, cliques, and crowds. In G. R. Adams & M. D. Berzonsky (Eds.), *Blackwell handbooks of developmental psychology* (pp. 330–348). Malden, MA: Blackwell Publishing.

Brown, R. (1976). Reference: In memorial tribute to Eric Lenneberg. *Cognition, 4,* 125–153.

Brown, R. (1986). *Social psychology: The second edition.* New York: The Free Press.

Brown, R. J. (2004). Psychological mechanisms in medically unexplained symptoms: An integrative conceptual model. *Psychological Bulletin, 130,* 793–812.

Brown, R., & Kulik, J. (1977). Flashbulb memories. *Cognition, 5,* 73–99.

Brumm, V. L., & Grant, M. L. (2010). The role of intelligence in phenylketonuria: A review of research and management. *Molecular Genetics and Metabolism, 99,* S18–S21.

Bruni, O., Ferri, R., Novelli, L., Finotti, E., Miano, S., & Guilleminault, C. (2008). NREM sleep instability in children with sleep terrors: The role of slow wave activity interruptions. *Clinical Neurophysiology, 119,* 985–992.

Brunyé, T. T., Rapp, D. N., & Taylor, H. A. (2008). Representational flexibility and specificity following spatial descriptions of real-world environments. *Cognition, 108,* 418–443.

Brysbaert, M., & Rastle, K. (2009). *Historical and conceptual issues in psychology.* Harlow, England: Pearson.

Büchel, C., Brassen, S., Yacubian, J., Kalisch, R., & Sommer, T. (2011). Ventral striatal signal changes represent missed opportunities and predict future choice. *NeuroImage, 57,* 1124–1130.

Buchler, N. E. G., & Reder, L. M. (2007). Modeling age-related memory deficits: A two-parameter solution. *Psychology and Aging, 22,* 104–121.

Buckworth, J., Lee, R. E., Regan, G., Schneider, L. K., & DiClemente, C. C. (2007). Decomposing intrinsic and extrinsic motivation for exercise: Application to stages of motivational readiness. *Psychology of Sport and Exercise, 8,* 441–461.

Buckworth, J., Lee, R. E., Regan, G., Schneider, L. K., & DiClemente, C. C. (2007). Decomposing intrinsic and extrinsic motivation for exercise: Application to stages of motivational readiness. *xi,* 441–461.

Buffardi, L. E., & Campbell, W. K. (2008). Narcissism and social networking web sites. *Personality and Social Psychology Bulletin, 34,* 1303–1314.

Burgard, M., & Mitchell, J. E. (2000). Group cognitive behavioral therapy for buying disorder. In A. L. Benson (Ed.), *I shop therefore I am: Compulsive buying and the search for self* (pp. 367–397). Northvale, NJ: Jason Aronson.

Burger, J. M. (2009). Replicating Milgram: Would people still obey today? *American Psychologist, 64,* 1–11.

Burkley, E. (2008). The role of self-control in resistance to persuasion. *Personality and Social Psychology Bulletin, 34,* 419–431.

Burnett, R. C., Medin, D. L., Ross, N. O., & Blok, S. V. (2005). Ideal is typical. *Canadian Journal of Experimental Psychology, 59,* 3–10.

Burnstein, E. (2005). Altruism and genetic relatedness. In D. M. Buss (Ed.), *The handbook of evolutionary psychology* (pp. 528– 551). Hoboken, NJ: Wiley.

Bushman, B. J., & Anderson, C. J. (2002). Violent video games and hostile expectations: A test of the general aggression model. *Personality and Social Psychology Bulletin, 28,* 1679–1686.

Buss, D. M. (2008). Evolutionary psychology: *The new science of mind* (3rd ed.). Boston, MA: Allyn & Bacon.

Buss, D. M. (2009). How can evolutionary psychology successfully explain personality and individual differences? *Perspectives on Psychological Science, 4,* 359–366.

Bustillo, J. R., Chen, H., Gasparovic, C., Mullins, P., Caprihan, A., Qualls, C., Apfeldorf, W., Lauriello, J., & Posse, S. (2011). Glutamate as a marker of cognitive function in schizophrenia: A proton spectroscopic imaging study at 4 Tesla. *Biological Psychiatry, 69,* 19–27.

Butcher, J. N. (2010). Personality assessment from the nineteenth to the early twenty-first century: Past achievements and contemporary challenges. *Annual Review of Clinical Psychology, 6,* 1–20.

Butcher, J. N., Graham, J. R., Ben-Porath, Y. S., Tellegen, A., Dahlstrom, W. G., & Kaemmer, B. (2001). *Minnesota Multiphasic Personality Inventory-2 (MMPI-2): Manual for administration and scoring* (2nd ed.). Minneapolis: University of Minnesota Press.

Butcher, J. N., Mineka, S., & Hooley, J. M. (2008). *Abnormal Psychology* (13th ed.). Boston, MA: Allyn & Bacon.

Bykov, K. M. (1957). *The cerebral cortex and the internal organs.* New York: Academic Press.

Byrne, D., & Clore, G. L. (1970). A reinforcement model of evaluative processes. *Personality: An International Journal, 1,* 103–128.

Cahill, L., Uncapher, M., Kilpatrick, L., Alkire, M. T., & Turner, J. (2004). Sex-related hemispheric lateralization of amygdala function in emotionally influenced memory: An fMRI investigation. *Learning & Memory, 11,* 261–266.

Calati, R., De Ronchi, D., Bellini, M., & Serretti, A. (2011). The 5-HTTLPR polymorphism and eating disorders: A meta-analysis. *International Journal of Eating Disorders, 44,* 191–199.

Cameron, C. L., Cella, D. C., Herndon, E. E., II, Kornblith, A. B., Zucerkman, E., Henderson, E., Weiss, R. B., Cooper, M. R., Silver, R. T., Leone, L., Canellos, G. P., Peterson, B. A., & Holland, J. C. (2001). Persistent symptoms among survivors of Hodgkin's disease: An explanatory model based on classical conditioning. *Health Psychology, 20,* 71–75.

Campbell, I., Mill, J., Uher, R., & Schmidt. (2011). Eating disorders, gene-environment interactions and epigentics. *Neuroscience and Biobehavioral Reviews, 35,* 784–793.

Camras, L A., & Shutter, J. M. (2010). Emotional facial expressions in infancy. *Emotion Review, 2,* 120–129.

Camras, L. A., Oster, H., Bakeman, R., Meng, Z., Ujiie, T., & Campos, J. L. (2007). Do infants show distinct negative facial expressions for fear and anger? Emotional expression in 11-month-old European American, Chinese, and Japanese infants. *Infancy, 11,* 131–155.

Canli, T., Desmond, J. E., Zhao, Z., & Gabrieli, J. D. E. (2002a). Sex differences in the neural basis of emotional memories. *Proceedings of the National Academy of Sciences, 99,* 10789–10794.

Canli, T., Desmond, J. E., Zhao, Z., Glover, G., & Gabrieli, J. D. E. (1998). Hemispheric asymmetry for emotional stimuli detected with fMRI. *NeuroReport, 9,* 3233–3239.

Canli, T., Sivers, H., Whitfield, S. L., Gotlib, I. H., & Gabrieli, J. D. E. (2002b). Amygdala response to happy faces as a function of extraversion. *Science, 296,* 2191.

Cannon, W. B. (1927). The James–Lange theory of emotion: A critical examination and an alternative theory. *American Journal of Psychology, 39,* 106–124.

Cannon, W. B. (1929). *Bodily changes in pain, hunger, fear, and rage* (2nd ed.). New York: Appleton-Century-Crofts.

Cannon, W. B. (1934). Hunger and thirst. In C. Murchison (Ed.), *A handbook of general experimental psychology.* Worcester, MA: Clark University Press.

Cannon, W. B., & Washburn, A. L. (1912). An explanation of hunger. *American Journal of Physiology, 29,* 441–454.

Cantlon, J. F., Pinel, P., Dehaene, S., & Pelphrey, K. A. (2011). Cortical representations of symbols, objects, and faces are pruned back during early childhood. *Cerebral Cortex, 21,* 191–199.

Cantor, N., & Kihlstrom, J. R. (1987). *Personality and social intelligence.* Englewood Cliffs, NJ: Prentice Hall.

Cappelletti, M., Fregni, F., Shapiro, K., Pascual-Leone, A., & Caramazza, A. (2008). Processing nouns and verbs in the left frontal cortex: A transcranial magnetic stimulation study. *Journal of Cognitive Neuroscience, 20,* 707–720.

Caprara, G. V., Barbaranelli, C., & Zimbardo, P. G. (1996). Understanding the complexity of human aggression: Affective, cognitive, and social dimensions of individual differences in propensity toward aggression. *European Journal of Personality, 10,* 133–155.

Carey, S. (1978). The child as word learner. In M. Hale, J. Bresnan, & G. A. Miller (Eds.), *Linguistic theory and psychological reality* (pp. 265–293). Cambridge, MA: MIT Press.

Carleton, A., Accolla, R., & Simon, S. A. (2010). Coding in the mammalian gustatory system. *Trends in Neurosciences, 33,* 326–334.

Carlson, E. A. (2004). *Mendel's legacy: The origin of classical genetics.* Cold Spring Harbor, NY: Cold Spring Harbor Laboratory Press.

Carroll, M. E., & Overmier, J. B. (Eds.). (2001). *Animal research and human health: Advancing human welfare through behavioral science.* Washington, DC: American Psychological Association.

Carstensen, L. L., Turan, B., Scheibe, S., Ram, N., Ersner-Hershfield, H., Samanez-Larkin, G. R., Brooks, K. P., & Nesselroade, J. R. (2011). Emotional experience improves with age: Evidence based on over 10 years of experience sampling. *Psychology and Aging, 26,* 21–33.

Carter, S. J., & Cassaday, H. J. (1998). State-dependent retrieval and chlorpheniramine. *Human Psychopharmacology, 13,* 513–523.

Carvalho, J. P., & Hopko, D. R. (2011). Behavioral theory of depression: Reinforcement as a mediating variable between avoidance and depression. *Journal of Behavior Therapy and Experimental Psychiatry, 42,* 154–162.

Carver, C. S., Johnson, S. L., Joorman, J., LeMoult, J., & Cuccaro, M. L. (2011). Childhood adversity interacts separately with 5-HTTLPR and BDNF to predict lifetime depression diagnosis. *Journal of Affective Disorders, 132,* 89–93.

Carver, C. S., Scheier, M. F., & Segerstrom, S. C. (2010). Optimism. *Clinical Psychology Review, 30,* 879–889.

Casey, B. J., Getz, S., & Galvan, A. (2008). The adolescent brain. *Developmental Review, 28,* 62–77.

Caspi, A., Hariri, A. R., Holmes, A., Uher, R., & Moffitt, T. E. (2010). Genetic sensitivity to the environment: The case of the serotonin transporter gene and its implications for studying complex diseases and traits. *American Journal of Psychiatry, 167,* 509–527.

Cassel, J.-C., Riegert, C., Rutz, S., Koenig, J., Rothmaier, K., Cosquer, B., Lazarus, C., Birthelmer, A., Jeltsch, H., Jones, B. C., & Jackisch, R. (2005). Ethanol, 3,4-methylenedioxymethamphetamine (Ecstasy) and their combination: Long-term behavioral, neurochemical and neuropharmacological effects in the rat. *Neuropsychopharmacology, 30,* 1870–1882.

Cassin, S. E., von Ranson, K. M., Heng, K., Brar, J., & Wojtowica, A. E. (2008). Adapted motivational interviewing for women with binge eating disorder: A randomized controlled trial. *Psychology of Addictive Behaviors, 22,* 417–425.

Catalano, R., Novaco, R. W., & McConnell, W. (2002). Layoffs and violence revisited. *Aggressive Behavior, 28,* 233–247.

Catalano, R., Novaco, R., & McConnell, W. (1997). A model of the net effect of job loss on violence. *Journal of Personality and Social Psychology, 72,* 1440–1447.

Cattell, R. B. (1963). Theory of fluid and crystallized intelligence: A critical experiment. *Journal of Educational Psychology, 54,* 1–22.

Cattell, R. B. (1979). *Personality and learning theory.* New York: Springer.

Centers for Disease Control and Prevention (2011). *Tobacco-related mortality.* Retrieved from www.cdc.gov/tobacco/data_statistics/fact_sheets/health_effects/tobacco_related_mortality.

Centers for Disease Control and Prevention. (2009, December 18). Prevalence of autism spectrum disorders—Autism and Developmental Disabilities Monitoring Network, United States, 2006. *Morbidity and Mortality Weekly Report, 58,* 1–24. Retrieved from ftp://ftp.cdc.gov/pub/publications/mmwr/ss/SS5810.pdf.

Ceschi, G., van der Linden, M., Dunker, D., Perroud, A., & Brédart, S. (2003). Further exploration memory bias in compulsive washers. *Behaviour Research and Therapy, 41,* 737–748.

Chan, M. Y. T., Cross-Mellor, S. K., Kavaliers, M., & Ossenkopp, K.-P. (2009). Lipopolysaccharide (LPS) blocks the acquisition of LiCl-induced gaping in a rodent model of anticipatory nausea. *Neuroscience Letters, 450,* 301–305.

Charlton, R. E., Barrick, T. R., Markus, H. S., & Morris, R. G. (2010). The relationship between episodic long-term memory and white matter integrity in normal aging. *Neuropsychologia, 48,* 114–122.

Chartrand, T. L., & Bargh, J. A. (1999). The chameleon effect: The perception-behavior link and social interaction. *Journal of Personality and Social Psychology, 76,* 893–910.

Chase, W. G., & Ericsson, K. A. (1981). Skilled memory. In J. R. Anderson (Ed.), *Cognitive skills and their acquisition.* Hillsdale, NJ: Erlbaum.

Chen, F. F., & Kenrick, D. T. (2002). Repulsion or attraction? Group membership and assumed attitude similarity. *Journal of Personality and Social Psychology, 83,* 111–125.

Chen, S., Boucher, H. C., & Tapias, M. P. (2006). The relational self revealed: Integrative conceptualization and implications for interpersonal life. *Psychological Bulletin, 132,* 151–179.

Cheng, P. W., & Holyoak, K. J. (1985). Pragmatic reasoning schemas. *Cognitive Psychology, 17,* 391–416.

Chida, Y., & Steptoe, A. (2009). The association of anger and hostility with future coronary heart disease. *Journal of the American College of Cardiology, 53,* 936–946.

Child Welfare Information Gateway. (2011). *Foster Care Statistics 2009.* Retrieved from www.childwelfare.gov/pubs/factsheets/foster.pdf.

Cho, S., Holyoak, K. J., & Cannon, T. D. (2007). Analogical reasoning in working memory: Resources shared among relational integration, interference resolution, and maintenance. *Memory & Cognition, 35,* 1445–1455.

Choi-Kahn, L. W., Zanarini, M. C., Frankenburg, F. R., Fitzmaurice, G. M., & Reich, D. B. (2010). A longitudinal study of the 10-year course of interpersonal features in borderline personality disorder. *Journal of Personality Disorders, 24,* 365–376.

Chomsky, N. (1965). *Aspects of a theory of syntax.* Cambridge, MA: MIT Press.

Chomsky, N. (1975). *Reflections on language.* New York: Pantheon Books.

Chorover, S. (1981, June). Organizational recruitment in "open" and "closed" social systems: A neuropsychological perspective. Conference paper presented at the Center for the Study of New Religious Movements, Berkeley, CA.

Christensen, A. J., & Johnson, J. A. (2002). Patient adherence with medical treatment regimens: An interactive approach. *Current Directions in Psychological Science, 11,* 94–97.

Christensen, A. J., Howren, M. B., Hillis, S. L., Kaboli, P., Carter, B. L., Cvengros, J. A., Wallston, K. A., & Rosenthal, G. E. (2010). Patient and physician beliefs about control over health: Association of symmetrical beliefs with medication regimen. *Journal of General Internal Medicine, 25,* 397–402.

Christensen, A., Atkins, D. C., Yi, J., Baucom, D. H., & George, W. H. (2006). Couple and individual adjustment for 2 years following a randomized clinical trial comparing traditional versus integrative behavioral couple therapy. *Journal of Consulting and Clinical Psychology, 74,* 1180–1191.

Christensen, B. T., & Schunn, C. D. (2007). The relationship of analogical distance to analogical function and preinventive structure: The case of engineering design. *Memory & Cognition, 35,* 29–38.

Christopoulou, F. D., & Kiortsis, D. N. (2011). An overview of the metabolic effects of rimonabant in randomized controlled trials: Potential for other cannabinoid 1 receptor blockers in obesity. *Journal of Clinical Pharmacy and Therapeutics, 36,* 10–18.

Chun, M. M., Golomb, J. D., & Turk-Browne, N. B. (2011). A taxonomy of external and internal attention. *Annual Review of Psychology, 62,* 73–101.

Cialdini, R. B. (2009). *Influence: Science and practice* (5th ed.). Boston, MA: Allyn & Bacon.

Cialdini, R. B., & Goldstein, N. J. (2004). Social influence: Compliance and conformity. *Annual Review of Psychology, 55,* 591–621.

Cialdini, R. B., Vincent, J. E., Lewis, S. K., Catalan, J., Wheeler, D., & Darby, B. L. (1975). Reciprocal concessions procedure for inducing compliance: The door-in-the-face technique. *Journal of Personality and Social Psychology, 31,* 206–215.

Clamp, M., Fry, B., Kamal, M., Xie, X., Cuff, J., Lin, M. F., Kellis, M., Lindblad-Toh, K., & Lander, E. S. (2007). Distinguishing protein-coding and noncoding genes in the human genome. *PNAS, 104,* 19428–19433.

Clapper, J. R., Moreno-Sanz, G., Russo, R., Guijarro, A., Vacondio, F., Duranti, A., Tontini, A., Sanchini, S., Sciolino, N. F., Spradley, J. M., Hohmann, A. G., Caglignano, A., Mor, M. Tarzia, G., & Piomelli, D. (2010). Anandamide suppresses pain initiation through a peripheral endocannabinoid mechanism. *Nature Neuroscience, 13,* 1265–1270.

Clark, E. V. (2003). *First language acquisition.* Cambridge, UK: Cambridge University Press.

Clark, H. H., & Clark, E. V. (1977). *Psychology and language: An introduction to psycholinguistics.* New York: Harcourt Brace Jovanovich.

Clark, K., & Clark, M. (1947). Racial identification and preference in Negro children. In T. M. Newcomb & E. L. Hartley (Eds.), *Readings in social psychology* (pp. 169–178). New York: Holt.

Clark, M. D., & Carroll, M. H. (2008). Acquaintance rape scripts of women and men: Similarities and differences. *Sex Roles, 58,* 616–625.

Clarke-Stewart, A., & Alhusen, V. D. (2005). *What we know about childcare.* Cambridge, MA: Harvard University Press.

Clarke-Stewart, K. A. (1993). *Daycare.* Cambridge, MA: Harvard University Press.

Clore, G. L., & Huntsinger, J. R. (2007). How emotions inform judgment and regulate thought. *Trends in Cognitive Sciences, 11,* 393–399.

Coates, T. J., & Szekeres, G. (2004). A plan for the next generation of HIV prevention research: Seven key policy investigative challenges. *American Psychologist, 59,* 747–757.

Coe, C. L. (1999). Psychosocial factors and psychoneuroimmunology within a lifespan perspective. In D. P. Keating & C. Hertzman (Eds.), *Developmental health and the wealth of nations: Social, biological, and educational dynamics* (pp. 201–219). New York: Guilford Press.

Cohen, A., & Avrahami, A. (2005). Soccer fans' motivation as a predictor of participation in soccer-related activities: An empirical examination in Israel. *Social Behavior and Personality, 33,* 419–434.

Cohen, P., Chen, H., Gordon, K., Johnson, J., Brook, J., & Kasen, S. (2008). Socioeconomic background and the developmental course of schizotypal and borderline personality disorder symptoms. *Development and Psychopathology, 20,* 633–650.

Cojan, Y., Waber, L., Carruzzo, A., & Vuilleumier, P. (2009). Motor inhibition in hysterical conversion disorder. *NeuroImage, 47,* 1026–1037.

Cole, D. A., Ciesla, J. A., Dallaire, D. H., Jacquez, F. M., Pineda, A. Q., LaGrange, B., Truss, A. E., Folmer, A. S., Tilghman-Osborne, C., & Felton, J. W. (2008). Emergence of attributional style and its relation to depressive symptoms. *Journal of Abnormal Psychology, 117,* 16–31.

Collins, C. J., Hanges, P. J., & Locke, E. A. (2004). The relationship of achievement motivation to entrepreneurial behavior: A meta-analysis. *Human Performance, 17,* 95–117.

Collins, G. T., Truong, Y. N.-T., Levant, B., Chen, J., Wang, S., & Woods, J. H. (2011). Behavioral sensitization to cocaine in rats: Evidence for temporal differences in dopamine D_3 and D_2 receptor sensitivity. *Psychopharmacology, 215,* 609–620.

Collins, W. A., Maccoby, E. E., Steinberg, L., Hetherington, E. M., & Bornstein, M. H. (2000). Contemporary research on parenting: The case for nature and nurture. *American Psychologist, 55,* 218–232.

Colloca, L., & Miller, F. G. (2011). Role of expectations in health. *Current Opinion in Psychiatry, 24,* 149–155.

Conger, R. D., Conger, K. J., & Martin, M. J. (2010). Socioeconomic status, family processes, and individual development. *Journal of Marriage and Family, 72,* 685–704.

Conway, A. R., Kane, M. J., Bunting, M. F., Hambrick, D. Z., Wilhelm, O., & Engle, R. W. (2005). Working memory span tasks: A methodological review and user's guide. *Psychonomic Bulletin & Review, 12,* 769–786.

Conway, B. R., Chatterjee, S., Field, G. D., Horwitz, G. D., Johnson, E. N., Koida, K., & Mancuso, K. (2010). Advances in color science: From retina to behavior. *The Journal of Neuroscience, 30,* 14955–14963.

Cooper, J. (2007). *Cognitive dissonance: Fifty years of a classic theory.* Thousand Oaks, CA: Sage Publications.

Cooper, J. O., Heron, T. E., & Heward, W. L. (2007). *Applied behavior analysis.* Upper Saddle River, NJ: Prentice-Hall.

Coren, S., Ward, L. M., & Enns, J. T. (1999). *Sensation and perception* (5th ed.). Fort Worth, TX: Harcourt Brace.

Corley, M., Brocklehurst, P. H., & Moat, H. S. (2011). Error biases in inner and overt speech: Evidence from tongue twisters. *Journal of Experimental Psychology: Learning, Memory, and Cognition, 37,* 162–175.

Cornelis, M. C., Monda, K. L., Yu, K., Paynter, N., Azzato, E. M., Bennett, S. N., Berndt, S. I., Boerwinkle, E., Chanock, S., Chatterjee, N., Couper, D., Curhan, G., Heiss, G., Hu, F. B., Hunter, D. J., Jacobs, K., Jensen, M. K., Kraft, P., Landi, M. T., Nettleton, J. A., Purdue, M. P., Rajaraman, P., Rimm, E. B., Rose, L. M., Rothman, N., Silverman, D., Stolzenberg-Solomon, R., Subar, A., Yeager, M., Chasman, D. I., van Dam, R. M., & Caporaso, N. E. (2011). Genome-wide meta-analysis identifies regions on 7p21 (*AHR*) and 15q24 (*CYP1A2*) as determinants of habitual caffeine consumption. *PLoS Genetics, 7,* e10002033.

Coslett, H. B., & Lie, G. (2008). Simultanagnosia: When a rose is not red. *Journal of Cognitive Neuroscience, 20,* 36–48.

Costa, P. T. Jr., & McCrae, R. R. (1985). *The NEO Personality Inventory manual.* Odessa, FL: Psychological Assessment Resources.

Cota, D., Marsicano, G., Lutz, B., Vicennati, V. Stalla, G. K., Pasquali, R., & Pagotto, U. (2003). Endogenous cannabinoid system as a modulator of food intake. *International Journal of Obesity, 27,* 289–301.

Cota, D., Tschöp, M. H., Horvath, T. L., & Levine, A. S. (2006). Cannabinoids, opioidis and eating behavior: The molecular face of hedonism? *Brain Research Reviews, 51,* 85–107.

Council, J. R., & Green, J. P. (2004). Examining the absorption-hypnotizability link: The roles of acquiescence and consistency motivation. *International Journal of Clinical and Experimental Hypnosis, 52,* 364–377.

Cousins, D. A., & Young, A. H. (2007). The armamentarium of treatments for bipolar disorder: A review of the literature. *International Journal of Neuropsychopharmacology, 10,* 411–431.

Couture, S., & Penn, D. (2003). Interpersonal contact and the stigma of mental illness: A review of the literature. *Journal of Mental Health, 12,* 291–306.

Cowan, C. P., & Cowan, P. (2000). *When partners become parents: The big life change for couples.* Mahwah, NJ: Erlbaum.

Cowan, N. (2001). The magical number 4 in short-term memory: A reconsideration of mental storage capacity. *Behavioral and Brain Sciences, 24,* 87–185.

Cowan, W. M. (1979, September). The development of the brain. *Scientific American, 241,* 106–117.

Cowles, J. T. (1937). Food tokens as incentives for learning by chimpanzees. *Comparative Psychology Monographs, 74,* 1–96.

Cox, J. J., Reimann, F. Nicholas, A. K., Thornton, G., Roberts, E., Springell, K., Karbani, G., Jafri, H., Mannan, J., Raashid, Y., Al-Gazali, L., Hamamy, H., Valente, E. M., Gorman, S., Williams, R., McHale, D. P., Wood, J. N., Gribble, F. M., & Woods, C. G. (2006). An SCN9A channelopathy causes congenital inability to experience pain. *Nature, 444,* 894–898.

Craig, L. A., Hong, N. S., & McDonald, R. J. (2011). Revisiting the cholinergic hypothesis in the development of Alzheimer's disease. *Neuroscience and Biobehavioral Reviews, 35,* 1397–1409.

Craik, F. I. M., & Lockhart, R. S. (1972). Levels of processing: A framework for memory research. *Journal of Verbal Learning and Verbal Behavior, 11,* 671–684.

Crane, J., Keough, M., Murphy, P., Burrage, & L., Hutchens, D. (2011). Effects of environmental tobacco smoke on perinatal outcomes: A retrospective cohort study. *BJOG, 118,* 865–871.

Crano, W. D., & Prislin, R. (2006). Attitudes and persuasion. *Annual Review of Psychology, 57,* 345–374.

Croarkin, P. E., Levinson, A. J., & Daskalakis, Z. J. (2011). Evidence for GABA-ergic inhibitory deficits in major depressive disorder. *Neuroscience and Biobehavioral Reviews, 35,* 818–825.

Crocco, M. S., & Costigan, A. T. (2007). The narrowing of curriculum and pedagogy in the age of accountability: Urban educators speak out. *Urban Education, 42,* 512–535.

Cross, S. E., Hardin, E. E., & Gercek-Swing, B. (2011). The what, how, why, and where of self-construal. *Personality and Social Psychology Review, 15,* 142–179.

Cryder, C. H., Kilmer, R. P., Tedeschi, R. G., & Calhoun, L. G. (2006). An exploratory study of posttraumatic growth in children following a natural disaster. *American Journal of Orthopsychiatry, 76,* 65–69.

Curci, A., & Luminet, O. (2006). Follow-up of a cross-national comparison on flashbulb and event memory for the September 11th attacks. *Memory, 14,* 329–344.

Curtis, R. C., & Miller, K. (1986). Believing another likes or dislikes you: Behaviors making the beliefs come true. *Journal of Personality and Social Psychology, 51,* 284–290.

Cutajar, M. C., Mullen, P. E., Ogloff, J. R. P., Thomas, S. D., Wells, D. L., & Spataro, J. (2010). Psychopathology in a large cohort of sexually abused children followed up to 43 years. *Child Abuse & Neglect, 34,* 813–822.

Czeisler, C. A., Duffy, J. F., Shanahan, T. L., Brown, E. N., Mitchell, J. F., Rimmer, D. W., Ronda, J. M., Silva, E. J., Allan, J. S., Emens, J. S., Dijk, D. J., & Kronauer, R. E. (1999). Stability, precision, and near-24-hour period of the human circadian pacemaker. *Science, 284,* 2177–2181.

Daddis, C. (2011). Desire for increased autonomy and adolescents' perceptions of peer autonomy: "Everyone else can; why can't I?" *Child Development, 82,* 1310–1326.

Daffner, K. R., Chong, H., Sun, X., Tarbi, E. C., Riis, J. L., McGinnis, S. M., & Holcomb, P. J. (2011). Mechanisms underlying age- and performance-related differences in working memory. *Journal of Cognitive Neuroscience, 23,* 1298–1314.

Dagan, M., Sanderman, R., Schokker, M. C., Wiggers, T., Baas, P. C., van Haastert, M., & Hagedoorn, M. (2011). Spousal support and changes in distress over time in couples coping with cancer: The role of personal control. *Journal of Family Psychology, 25,* 31–318.

Dailey, M. N., Joyce, C., Lyons, M. J., Kamachi, M., Ishi, H., Gyoba, J., Cottrell, G. W. (2010). Evidence and a computational explanation of cultural differences in facial expression recognition. *Emotion, 10*, 874–893.

Daley, C. E., & Onwuegbuzie, A. J. (2011). Race and intelligence. In R. J. Sternberg & S. B. Kaufman (Eds.), *The Cambridge handbook of intelligence* (pp. 293–306). New York: Cambridge University Press.

Danese, A., Moffitt, T. E., Harrington, H., Milne, B. J., Polanczyk, G., Pariante, C. M., Poulton, R., & Caspi, A. (2009). Adverse childhood experiences and adult risk factors for age-related disease. *Archives of Pediatric & Adolescent Medicine, 163*, 1135–1143.

Darley, J. M., & Batson, C. D. (1973). From Jerusalem to Jericho: A study of situational and dispositional variables in helping behavior. *Journal of Personality and Social Psychology, 27*, 100–108.

Darling, N., & Steinberg, L. (1993). Parenting style as context: An integrative model. *Psychological Bulletin, 113*, 487–496.

Darnon, C., Butera, F., Mugny, G., Quiamzade, A., & Hulleman, C. S. (2009). "Too complex for me!" Why do performance-approach and performance-avoidance goals predict exam performance? *European Journal of Psychology of Education, 24*, 423–434.

Darwin, C. (1965). *The expression of emotions in man and animals.* Chicago: University of Chicago Press. (Original work published 1872)

Daskalakis, Z. J., Levinson, A. J., & Fitzgerald, P. B. (2008). Repetitive transcranial magnetic stimulation for major depressive disorder: A review. *Canadian Journal of Psychiatry, 53*, 555–566.

Davidson, R. J., Jackson D.C., & Kalin, N. H. (2000). Emotion, plasticity, context, and regulation: Perspectives for affective neuroscience. *Psychological Bulletin, 126*, 890–909.

Davies, K., Tropp, L. R., Aron, A., Pettigrew, T. F., & Wright, S. C. (2011). Cross-group friendships and intergroup attitudes: A meta-analytic review. *Personality and Social Psychology Review, 15*, 332–351.

Davis, J. L., Byrd, P., Rhudy, J. L., & Wright, D. C. (2007). Characteristics of chronic nightmares in a trauma-exposed treatment-seeking sample. *Dreaming, 17*, 187–198.

Davis, M. H., Hall, J. A., & Meyer, M. (2003). The first year: Influences on the satisfaction, involvement, and persistence of new community volunteers. *Personality and Social Psychology Bulletin, 29*, 248–260.

Davison, S. L., & Davis, S. R. (2011). Androgenic hormones and aging— The link with female sexual function. *Hormones and Behavior, 59*, 745–753.

Dawson, L. L., & Hennebry, J. (2003). New religions and the Internet: Recruiting in a new public space. In L. L. Dawson (Ed.), *Cults and new religious movements* (pp. 271–291). Oxford, UK: Blackwell.

De Pascalis, V, Cacace, I., & Massicolle, F. (2008). Focused analgesia in waking and hypnosis: Effects on pain, memory, and somatosensory event-related potentials. *Pain, 134*, 197–208.

de Ridder, D., Geenen, R., Kuijer, R., & van Middendorp, H. (2008). Psychological adjustment to chronic disease. *The Lancet, 372*, 246–255.

de Rivera, J. (1997). The construction of false memory syndrome: The experience of retractors. *Psychological Inquiry, 8*, 271–292.

De Santis, M., Cavaliere, A. F., Straface, G., & Caruso, A. (2006). Rubella infection in pregnancy. *Reproductive Toxicology, 21*, 390–398.

De Valois, R. L., & Jacobs, G. H. (1968). Primate color vision. *Science, 162*, 533–540.

de Waal, F. B. M. (2008). Putting the altruism back into altruism: The evolution of empathy. *Annual Review of Psychology, 59*, 279–300.

Deary, I. J. (2008). Why do intelligent people live longer? *Nature, 456*, 175–176.

Deary, I. J., Batty, G. D., Pattie, A., & Gale, C. R. (2008). More intelligent, more dependable children live longer: A 55-year longitudinal study of a representative sample of the Scottish nation. *Psychological Science, 19*, 874–880.

Deary, I. J., Penke, L., & Johnson, W. (2010a). The neuroscience of human intelligence differences. *Nature Reviews Neuroscience, 11*, 201–211.

Deary, I. J., Weiss, A., & Batty, G. D. (2010b). Intelligence, personality, and health outcomes. *Psychological Science in the Public Interest, 11*, 53–79.

Deaux, K., Bikmen, N., Gilkes, A., Ventuneac, A., Joseph, Y., Payne, Y. A., & Steele, C. A. (2007). Becoming American: Stereotype threat effects in Afro-Caribbean immigrant groups. *Social Psychology Quarterly, 70*, 384–404.

DeBraganza, N., & Hausenblas, H. A. (2010). Media exposure of the ideal physique on women's body dissatisfaction and mood. *Journal of Black Studies, 40*, 700–716.

DeCasper, A. J., & Prescott, P. A. (1984). Human newborns' perception of male voices: Preference, discrimination, and reinforcing value. *Developmental Psychology, 17*, 481–491.

Degnan, K. A., Hane, A. A., Henderson, H. A., Moas, O. L., Reeb-Sutherland, B. C., & Fox, N. A. (2011). Longitudinal stability of temperamental exuberance and social-emotional outcomes in early childhood. *Developmental Psychology, 47*, 765–780.

Del Giudice, M. (2011). Alone in the dark? Modeling the conditions for visual experience in human fetuses. *Developmental Psychobiology, 53*, 214–219.

DeLamater, J. D., & Sill, M. (2005). Sexual desire in later life. *The Journal of Sex Research, 42*, 138–149.

Dell, G. S. (2004). Speech errors in language production: Neuropsychological and connectionist perspectives. In B. H. Ross (Ed.), *The psychology of learning and motivation* (Vol. 44, pp. 63–108). New York: Elsevier.

DePaulo, B. M., Lindsay, J. J., Malone, B. E., Muhlenbruck, L., Charlton, K., & Cooper, H. (2003). Cues to deception. *Psychological Bulletin, 129*, 74–118.

Derntl, B., Finkelmeyer, A., Eickhoff, S., Kellermann, T., Falkenberg, D. I., Schneider, F., & Habel, U. (2010). Multidimensional assessment of empathic abilities: Neural correlates and gender differences. *Psychoneuroendocrinology, 35*, 67–82.

Després, J.-P., Golay, A., & Sjöström, L. (2005). Effects of rimonabant on metabolic risk factors in overweight patients with dyslipidemia. *The New England Journal of Medicine, 353*, 2121–2134.

Deutsch, D., Henthorn, T., & Lapidis, R. (2011). Illusory transformation from speech to song. *Journal of the Acoustical Society of America, 129*, 2245–2252.

Dew, J., & Wilcox, W. B. (2011). If momma ain't happy: Explaining declines in marital satisfaction among new mothers. *Journal of Marriage and Family, 73*, 1–12.

Dew, M. A., Hoch, C. C., Buysse, D. J., Monk, T. H., Begley, A. E., Houck, P. R., Hall, M., Kupfer, D. J., & Reynolds, C. F. (2003). Healthy older adults' sleep predicts all-cause mortality at 4 to 19 years of follow-up. *Psychosomatic Medicine, 65*, 63–73.

DeWall, C. N., Anderson, C. A., & Bushman, B. J. (2011). The general aggression model: Theoretical extensions to violence. *Psychology of Violence, 1*, 245–258.

Dewey, J. (1896). The reflex arc concept in psychology. *Psychological Review, 3*, 357–370.

Dewsbury, D. A. (1981). Effects of novelty on copulatory behavior: The Coolidge effect and related phenomena. *Psychological Bulletin, 89*, 464–482.

Dhawan, N., Roseman, I. J., Naidu, R. K., Thapa, K., & Rettek, S. I. (1995). Self-concepts across two cultures: India and the United States. *Journal of Cross-Cultural Psychology, 26*, 606–621.

Dhont, K., & Van Hiel, A. (2009). We must not be enemies: Interracial contact and the reduction of prejudice among authoritarians. *Personality and Individual Differences, 46*, 172–177.

Di Biasi, M., & Dani, J. A. (2011). Reward, addiction, withdrawal to nicotine. *Annual Review of Neuroscience, 34*, 105–130.

Di Marzo, V., & Cristino, L. (2008). Why endocannabinoids are not all alike. *Nature Neuroscience, 11*, 124–126.

Diamond, S., Schensul, J. J., Snyder, L. B., Bermudez, A., D'Alessandro, N., & Morgan, D. S. (2009). Building Xperience: A multilevel alcohol and drug prevention intervention. *American Journal of Community Psychology*, *43*, 292–312.

Dickens, W. T., & Flynn, J. R. (2006). Black Americans reduce the racial IQ gap: Evidence from standardization samples. *Psychological Science, 17*, 913–920.

Dickerson, F. B., Tenhula, W. N., & Green-Paden, L. D. (2005). The token economy for schizophrenia: Review of the literature and recommendations for future research. *Schizophrenia Research, 75*, 405–416.

Dickinson, C. A., & Intraub, H. (2008). Transsaccadic representation of layout: What is the time course of boundary extension? *Journal of Experimental Psychology: Human Perception and Performance, 34*, 543–555.

Diekelmann, S., & Born, J. (2010). The memory function of sleep. *Nature Reviews Neuroscience, 11*, 114–126.

Diener, E., Ng, W., Harter, J., & Arora, R. (2010). Wealth and happiness across the world: Material prosperity predicts life evaluation, whereas psychological prosperity predicts positive feeling. *Journal of Personality and Social Psychology, 99*, 52–61.

DiGrande, L., Neria, Y., Brackbill, R. M., Pulliam, P., & Galea, S. (2011). Long-term posttraumatic stress symptoms among 3,271 civilian survivors of the September 11, 2001, terrorist attacks on the World Trade Center. *American Journal of Epidemiology, 173*, 271–281.

Dillworth, T., & Jensen, M. P. (2010). The role of suggestions in hypnosis for chronic pain: A review of the literature. *The Open Pain Journal, 3*, 39–51.

DiMatteo, M. R. (2004). Social support and patient adherence to medical treatment: A meta-analysis. *Health Psychology, 23*, 207–218.

DiMatteo, M. R., Haskard, K. B., & Williams, S. L. (2007). Health beliefs, disease severity, and patient adherence: A meta-analysis. *Medical Care, 45*, 521–528.

Dimidjian, S., Barrera, M., Jr., Martell, C., Muñoz, R. F., & Lewinsohn, P. M. (2011). The origins and current status of behavioral activation treatments for depression. *Annual Review of Clinical Psychology, 7*, 1–38.

Dion, K. K., & Dion, K. L. (1996). Cultural perspectives on romantic love. *Personal Relationships, 3*, 5–17.

Dirkzwager, A. J. E., Bramsen, I., & van der Ploeg, H. M. (2003). Social support, coping, life events, and posttraumatic stress symptoms among former peacekeepers: A prospective study. *Personality and Individual Differences, 34*, 1545–1559.

Dishion, T. J., & Tipsord, J. M. (2011). Peer contagion in child and adolescent social and emotional development. *Annual Review of Psychology, 62*, 189–214.

Disner, S. G., Beevers, C. G., Haigh, E. A., & Beck, A. T. (2011). Neural mechanisms of the cognitive model of depression. *Nature Reviews Neuroscience, 12*, 467–477.

Distel, M. A., Trull, T. J., Derom, C. A., Thiery, E. W., Grimmer, M. A., Martin, N. G., Willemsen, G., & Boomsma, D. I. (2008). Heritability of borderline personality disorder features is similar across three countries. *Psychological Medicine, 38*, 1219–1229.

Dixon, R. A. (2003). Themes in the aging of intelligence: Robust decline with intriguing possibilities. In R. J. Sternberg, J. Lautrey, & T. I. Lubart (Eds.), *Models of intelligence: International perspectives* (pp. 151–167). Washington, DC: American Psychological Association.

Dixon, R. A., & de Frias, C. M. (2004). The Victoria longitudinal study: From characterizing cognitive aging to illustrating changes in memory compensation. *Aging Neuropsychology and Cognition, 11*, 346–376.

Do, A. M., Rupert, A. V., & Wolford, G. (2008). Evaluations of pleasurable experiences: The peak-end rule. *Psychonomic Bulletin & Review, 15*, 96–98.

Docherty, N. M., St-Hilaire, A., Aakre, J. M., & Seghers, J. P. (2009). Life events and high-trait reactivity together predict psychotic symptom increases in schizophrenia. *Schizophrenia Bulletin 35*, 638–645.

Dollard, J., Doob, L. W., Miller, N., Mower, O. H., & Sears, R. R. (1939). *Frustration and aggression*. New Haven: Yale University Press.

Domhoff, G. W. (2005). Refocusing the neurocognitive approach to dreams: A critique of the Hobson versus Solms debate. *Dreaming, 15*, 3–20.

Domhoff, G. W. (2011). The neural substrate for dreaming: Is it a subsystem of the default network? *Consciousness and Cognition, 20*, 1163–1174.

Donnellan, M. B., Trzesniewski, K. H., Conger, K. J., & Conger, R. D. (2007). A three-wave longitudinal study of self-evaluations during young adulthood. *Journal of Research in Personality, 41*, 453–472.

Donnellan, M. B., Trzesniewski, K. H., Robins, R. W., Moffitt, T. E., & Caspi, A. (2005). Low self-esteem is realted to aggression, antisocial behavior, and delinquency. *Psychological Science, 16*, 328–335.

Donovan, W., Leavitt, L., Taylor, N., & Broder, J. (2007). Maternal sensitivity, mother-infant 9-month interaction, infant attachment status: Predictors of mother-toddler interaction at 24 months. *Infant Behavior & Development, 30*, 336–352.

Douglas, K. S., & Skeem, J. L. (2005). Violence risk assessment: Getting specific about being dynamic. *Psychology, Public Policy, and Law, 11*, 347–383.

DSM-IV. (1994). *Diagnostic and statistical manual of mental disorders* (4th ed.). Washington, DC: American Psychiatric Association.

DSM-IV-TR. (2000). *Diagnostic and statistical manual of mental disorders* (4th ed., Text revision). Washington, DC: American Psychiatric Association.

Du Mont, J., Macdonald, S., Rotbard, N., Bainbridge, D., Asllani, E., Smith, N., & Cohen, M. M. (2010). Drug-assisted sexual assault in Ontario, Canada: Toxicological and DNA findings. *Journal of Forensic and Legal Medicine, 17*, 333–338.

Dube, C., Rotello, C. M., & Heit, E. (2010). Assessing the belief bias effect with ROCs: It's a response bias effect. *Psychological Review, 117*, 931–863.

DuBois, P. H. (1970). *A history of psychological testing*. Boston: Allyn & Bacon.

Dudycha, G. J. (1936). An objective study of punctuality in relation to personality and achievement. *Archives of Psychology, 204*, 1–53.

Duncker, D. (1945). On problem solving. *Psychological Monographs, 58* (No. 270).

Durkin, S. J., & Paxton, S. J. (2002). Predictors of vulnerability to reduced body image satisfaction and psychological well-being in response to exposure to idealized female media images in adolescent girls. *Journal of Psychosomatic Research, 53*, 995–1005.

Dutton, D. G., & Aron, A. P. (1974). Some evidence for heightened sexual attraction under conditions of high anxiety. *Journal of Personality and Social Psychology, 30*, 510–517.

Dweck, C. S. (1975). The role of expectations and attributions in the alleviation of learned helplessness. *Journal of Personality and Social Psychology, 31*, 674–685.

Dweck, C. S. (1999). *Self-theories: Their role in motivation, personality, and development*. Philadelphia: Psychology Press.

Dykas, M. J., & Cassidy, J. (2011). Attachment and the the processing of social information across the life span: Theory and evidence. *Psychological Bulletin, 137*, 19–46.

Eastwick, P. W., Eagly, A. H., Glick, P., Johannesen-Schmidt, M. C., Fiske, S. T., Blum, A. M. B., Eckes, T., Freiburger, P., Huang, L.-L., Fernández, M. L., Manganelli, A. M., Pek, J. C. X., Rodríguez Castro, Y., Sakalli-Ugurlu, N., Six-Materna, I., & Volpato, C. (2006). Is traditional gender ideology associated with sex-typed mate preferences? A test in nine nations. *Sex Roles, 54*, 603–614.

Ebbinghaus, H. (1964). *Memory: A contribution to experimental psychology*. New York: Dover. (Original work published 1885)

Ebbinghaus, H. (1973). *Psychology: An elementary text-book*. New York: Arno Press. (Original work published 1908)

Edin, K., & Kissane, R. J. (2010). Poverty and the American family: A decade in review. *Journal of Marriage and Family, 72*, 460–479.

Edvardsen, J., Torgersen, S., Røysamb, E., Lygren, S., Skre, I., Onstad, S., & Øien, P. A. (2008). Heritability of bipolar spectrum disorders. Unity or heterogeneity. *Journal of Affective Disorders, 106,* 229–240.

Eich, T. S., & Metcalfe, J. (2009). Effects of the stress of marathon running on implicit and explicit memory. *Psychonomic Bulletin & Review, 16,* 475–479.

Ein-Dor, T., Mikulincer, M., Doron, G., & Shaver, P. R. (2010). The attachment paradox: How can so many of (the insecure ones) have no adaptive advantages? *Perspectives on Psychological Science, 5,* 123–141.

Ekman, P. (1984). Expression and the nature of emotion. In K. R. Scherer & P. Ekman (Eds.), *Approaches to emotion.* Hillsdale, NJ: Erlbaum.

Ekman, P. (1994). Strong evidence for universals in facial expressions: A reply to Russell's mistaken critique. *Psychological Bulletin, 115,* 268–287.

Ekman, P., & Friesen, W. V. (1971). Constants across cultures in the face and emotion. *Journal of Personality and Social Psychology, 17,* 124–129.

Ekman, P., & Friesen, W. V. (1986). A new pan-cultural facial expression of emotion. *Motivation and Emotion, 10,* 159–168.

Elbert, T., Pantev, C., Wienbruch, C., Rockstroh, B., & Taub, E. (1995). Increased cortical representation of the fingers of the left hand in string players. *Science, 270,* 305–307.

Elfenbein, H. A., Beaupre, M., Levesque, M., & Hess, U. (2007). Toward a dialect theory: Cultural differences in the expression and recognition of posed facial expressions. *Emotion, 7,* 131–146.

Elkins, I. J., Malone, S., Keyes, M., Iacono, W. G., McGue, M. (2011). The impact of attention-deficit/hyperactivity disorder on preadolescent adjustment may be greater for girls than for boys. *Journal of Clinical Child & Adolescent Psychology, 40,* 532–545.

Ellenstein, A., Kranick, S. M., & Hallet, M. (2011). An update on psychogenic movement disorders. *Current Neurology and Neuroscience Reports, 11,* 396–403.

Elliot, A. J., & McGregor, H. A. (2001). A 2x2 achievement goal framework. *Journal of Personality and Social Psychology, 80,* 501–519.

Ellis, A. (1962). *Reason and emotion in psychotherapy.* New York: Lyle Stuart.

Ellis, A. (1995). *Better, deeper, and more enduring brief therapy: The rational emotive behavior therapy approach.* New York: Brunner/Mazel.

Elms, A. C. (1988). Freud as Leonardo: Why the first psychobiography went wrong. *Journal of Personality, 56,* 19–40.

Elsabagh, S., Hartley, D. E., Ali, O., Williamson, E. M., & File, S. E. (2005). Differential cognitive effects of *Ginkgo biloba* after acute and chronic treatment in healthy young volunteers. *Psychopharmacology, 179,* 437–446.

Endler, N. S., Macrodimitris, S. D., & Kocovski, N. L. (2000). Controllability in cognitive and interpersonal tasks: Is control good for you? *Personality & Individual Differences, 29,* 951–962.

Endress, A. D., Cahill, D., Block, S., Watumull, J., & Hauser, M. D. (2009). Evidence of an evolutionary precursor to human language affixation in a non-human primate. *Biology Letters, 5,* 749–751.

Engelhardt, C. R., Bartholow, B. D., Kerr, G. T., & Bushman, B. J. (2011). This is your brain on violent video games: Neural desensitization to violence predicts increased aggression following violent video game exposure. *Journal of Experimental Social Psychology, 47,* 1033–1036.

Epley, N., & Gilovich, T. (2006). The anchoring-and-adjustment heuristic. *Psychological Science, 17,* 311–318.

Erikson, E. (1963). *Childhood and society.* New York: Norton.

Eshbaugh, E. M., & Gute, G. (2008). Hookups and sexual regret among college women. *The Journal of Social Psychology, 148,* 77–89.

Espelage, D. L., Aragon, S. R., Birkett, M., & Koenig, B. W. (2008). Homophobic teasing, psychological outcomes, and sexual orientation among high school students: What influence do parents and schools have? *School Psychology Review, 37,* 202–216.

Evans, A. D., & Lee, K. (2011). Verbal deception from late childhood to middle adolescence and its relation to executive functioning skills. *Developmental Psychology, 47,* 1108–1116.

Evans, E., Hawton, K., Rodham, K., & Deeks, J. (2005). The prevalence of suicidal phenomena in adolescents: A systematic review of population-based studies. *Suicide and Life Threatening Behavior, 35,* 239–250.

Evans, S. E., Davies, C., & DiLillo, D. (2008). Exposure to domestic violence: A meta-analysis of child and adolescent outcomes. *Aggression and Violent Behavior, 13,* 131–140.

Everett, D. L. (2005). Cultural constraints on grammar and cognition in Pirahã. *Current Anthropology, 46,* 621–646.

Everett, G. E., Hupp, S. D. A., & Olmi, D. J. (2010). Time-out with parents: A descriptive analysis of 30 years of research. *Education and Treatment of Children, 33,* 235–259.

Everett, G. E., Olmi, D. J., Edwards, R. P., Tingstrom, D. H., Sterling-Turner, H. E., & Christ, T. J. (2007). An empirical investigation of time-out with and without escape extinction to treat escape-maintained noncompliance. *Behavior Modification, 31,* 412–434.

Evers, C., Stok, F. M., & de Ridder, D. T. D. (2010). Feeding your feelings: Emotion regulations strategies and emotional eating. *Personality and Social Psychology Bulletin, 36,* 792–804.

Exner, J. E. Jr. (1974). *The Rorschach: A comprehensive system.* New York: Wiley.

Exner, J. E. Jr. (2003). *The Rorschach: A comprehensive system* (4th ed.). New York: Wiley.

Exner, J. E. Jr., & Weiner, I. B. (1994). *The Rorschach: A comprehensive system: Vol. 3. Assessment of children and adolescents* (2nd ed.). New York: Wiley.

Eysenck, H. J. (1952). The effects of psychotherapy: An evaluation. *Journal of Consulting Psychology, 16,* 319–324.

Eysenck, H. J. (1973). *The inequality of man.* London: Temple Smith.

Eysenck, H. J. (1990). Biological dimensions of personality. In L. A. Pervin (Ed.), *Handbook of personality theory and research* (pp. 244–276). New York: Guilford Press.

Fabian, J. M. (2006). A literature review of the utility of selected violence and sexual violence risk assessment instruments. *The Journal of Psychiatry & Law, 34,* 307–350.

Fagan, J. F., & Holland, C. R. (2007). Racial equality in intelligence: Predictions from a theory of intelligence as processing. *Intelligence, 35,* 319–334.

Fahey, C. D., & Zee, P. C. (2006). Circadian rhythm sleep disorders and phototherapy. *Psychiatric Clinics of North America, 29,* 989–1007.

Fan, F., Zhang, Y., Yang, Y., Mo, L., & Liu, X. (2011). Symptoms of posttraumatic stress disorder, depression, and anxiety among adolescents following the 2008 Wenchuan earthquake in China. *Journal of Traumatic Stress, 24,* 44–53.

Fantegrossi, W. E., Murnane, K. S., & Reissig, C. J. (2008). The behavioral pharmacology of hallucinogens. *Biochemical Pharmacology, 75,* 17–33.

Fantz, R. L. (1963). Pattern vision in newborn infants. *Science, 140,* 296–297.

Farmer, T. A., Anderson, S. E., & Spivey, M. J. (2007). Gradiency and visual context in syntactic garden-paths. *Journal of Memory and Language, 57,* 570–595.

Fattore, L., Spano, M. S., Deiana, S., Melis, V., Cossu, G., Fadda, P. & Fratta, W. (2007). An endocannabinoid mechanism in relapse to drug seeking: A review of animal studies and clinical perspectives. *Brain Research Reviews, 53,* 1–16.

Fausey, C. M., & Boroditsky, L. (2011). Who dunnit? Cross-linguistic differences in eye-witness memory. *Psychonomic Bulletin & Review, 18,* 150–157.

Fawcett, C. A., & Markson, L. (2010). Similarity predicts liking in 3-year-old children. *Journal of Experimental Child Psychology, 105,* 345–358.

Fawcett, J. M., Russell, E. M., Peace, K. A., & Christie, J. (2012). Of guns and geese: A meta-analytic review of the "weapon focus" literature. *Psychology, Crime & Law*, in press.

Fazio, R. H., & Roskos-Ewoldsen, D. R. (2005). Acting as we feel: When and how attitudes guide behavior. In T. C. Brock & M. C. Green (Eds.), *Persuasion: Psychological insights and perspectives* (2nd ed., pp. 41–62). Thousand Oaks, CA: Sage.

Feather, N. T. (1961). The relationship of persistence at a task to expectation of success and achievement related motives. *Journal of Abnormal and Social Psychology, 63,* 552–561.

Fechner, G. T. (1966). *Elements of psychophysics* (H. E. Adler, Trans.). New York: Holt, Rinehart & Winston. (Original work published 1860)

Federal Interagency Forum on Aging-Related Statistics. (2010). *Older Americans 2010: Key indicators of well-being.* Retrieved from www.agingstats.gov/agingstatsdotnet/Main_Site/Data/2010_Documents/Docs/OA_2010.pdf.

Feldman, D. H. (2004). Piaget's stages: The unfinished symphony of cognitive development. *New Ideas in Psychology, 22,* 175–231.

Fernández-Dávila, P., Salazar, X., Cáceres, C. F., Maiorana, A., Kegeles, S., Coates, T. J., & Martinez, J. (2008). Compensated sex and sexual risk: Sexual, social and economic interactions between homosexually- and heterosexually-identified men of low income in two cities of Peru. *Sexualities, 11,* 352–374.

Ferrari, M. C. O., & Chivers, D. P. (2008). Cultural learning of predator recognition in mixed-species assemblages of frogs: The effect of tutor-to-observer ratio. *Animal Behaviour, 75,* 1921–1925.

Ferster, C. B., & Skinner, B. F. (1957). *Schedules of reinforcement.* New York: Appleton-Century-Crofts.

Festinger, L. (1957). *A theory of cognitive dissonance.* Stanford, CA: Stanford University Press.

Festinger, L., & Carlsmith, J. M. (1959). Cognitive consequences of forced compliance. *Journal of Abnormal and Social Psychology, 58,* 203–211.

Fillmore M. T., Blackburn, J. S., & Harrison, E. L. R. (2008). Acute disinhibiting effects of alcohol as a factor in risky driving behavior. *Drug and Alcohol Dependence, 95,* 97–106.

Fink, P., Hansen, M. S., & Oxhøj, M. L. (2004). The prevalence of somatoform disorders among internal medical inpatients. *Journal of Psychosomatic Research, 56,* 413–418.

Finkelstein, M. A., Penner, L. A., & Brannick, M. T. (2005). Motive, role identity, and prosocial personality as predictors of volunteer activity. *Social Behavior and Personality, 33,* 403–418.

Finn, B. (2010). Ending on a high note: Adding a better end to effortful study. *Journal of Experimental Psychology: Learning, Memory, and Cognition, 36,* 1548–1553.

Finn, J., & Steele, T. (2010). Online self-help/mutual aid groups in mental health practice. In L. D. Brown & S. Wituk (Eds.), *Mental health self-help* (pp. 87–105). New York: Springer.

Fiore, M. C., Jaén, C. R., & Baker, T. B. (2008). *Treating tobacco use and dependence: 2008 update.* Rockville, MD: U.S. Department of Health and Human Services. Public Health Service.

Fischer, P., Greitemeyer, T., Pollozek, F., & Frey, D. (2006). The unresponsive bystander: Are bystanders more responsive in dangerous emergencies? *European Journal of Social Psychology, 36,* 267–278.

Fischer, P., Krueger, J. I., Greitemeyer, T., Vogrincic, C., Kastenmüller, A., Frey, D., Heene, M., Wicher, M., & Kainbacher, M. (2011). The bystander-effect: A meta-analytic review on bystander intervention in dangerous and non-dangerous emergencies. *Psychological Bulletin, 137,* 517–537.

Fisher, B. S., Cullen, F. T., & Turner, M. G. (2000). *The sexual victimization of college women.* Washington, DC: National Institute of Justice.

Fitch, W. T. (2011). Unity and diversity in human language. *Philosophical Transactions of the Royal Society B, 366,* 376–388.

Fitzgerald, T. D., Hunter, P. V., Hadjistavropoulos, T., & Koocher, G. P. (2010). Ethical and legal considerations for Internet-based psychotherapy. *Cognitive Behaviour Therapy, 39,* 173–187.

Fitzpatrick, B. M., Fordyce, J. A., & Gavrilets, S. (2008). What, if anything, is sympatric speciation? *Journal of Evolutionary Biology, 21,* 1452–1459.

Flavell, J. H. (1985). *Cognitive development* (2nd ed.). Englewood Cliffs, NJ: Prentice Hall.

Flavell, J. H. (1996). Piaget's legacy. *Psychological Science, 7,* 200–203.

Fleer, M., & Hedegaard, M. (2010). Children's development as participation in everyday practices across different institutions. *Mind, Culture, and Activity, 17,* 149–168.

Foa, E. B., & Riggs, D. S. (1995). Posttraumatic stress disorder following assault: Theoretical considerations and empirical findings. *Current Directions in Psychological Science, 4,* 61–65.

Folkard, S. (2008). Do permanent night workers show circadian adjustment? A review based on endogenous melatonin rhythm. *Chronobiology International, 25,* 215–224.

Folkman, S. (1984). Personal control and stress and coping processes: A theoretical analysis. *Journal of Personality and Social Psychology, 46,* 839–852.

Forbey, J. D., Lee, T. T. C., & Handel, R. W. (2010). Correlates of the MMPI-2 in a college setting. *Psychological Assessment, 22,* 737–744.

Ford, C. S., & Beach, F. A. (1951). *Patterns of sexual behavior.* New York: Harper & Row.

Forgas, J. P. (2008). Affect and cognition. *Perspectives on Psychological Science, 3,* 94–101.

Forgas, J. P., & East, R. (2008). On being happy and gullible: Mood effects on skepticism and detection of deception. *Journal of Experimental Social Psychology, 44,* 1362–1367.

Förster, J., Friedman, R. S., & Liberman, N. (2004). Temporal construal effects on abstract and concrete thinking: Consequences for insight and creative cognition. *Journal of Personality and Social Psychology, 87,* 177–189.

Försterling, F. (2001). *Attributions: An introduction to theories, research and applications.* New York: Psychology Press.

Fortin, A., LeFebvre, M. B., & Ptito, M. (2010). Traumatic brain injury and olfactory deficits: The tale of two smell tests! *Brain Injury, 24,* 27–33.

Foster, R. G., & Wulff, K. (2005). The rhythm of rest and excess. *Nature Reviews Neuroscience, 6,* 407–414.

Foucault, M. (1975). *The birth of the clinic.* New York: Vintage Books.

Foulkes, D. (1962). Dream reports from different states of sleep. *Journal of Abnormal and Social Psychology, 65,* 14–25.

Fournier, J. C., DeRubeis, R. J., Hollon, S. D., Dimidjian, S., Amsterdam, J. D., Shelton, R. C., & Fawcett, J. (2010). Antidepressant drug effects and depression severity: A patient-level meta-analysis. *Journal of the American Medical Association, 303,* 47–53.

Fowler, H. (1965). *Curiosity and exploratory behavior.* New York: Macmillan.

Fox, M. C., Ericsson, K. A., & Best, R. (2011). Do procedures for verbal reporting of thinking have to be reactive? A meta-analysis and recommendations for best reporting methods. *Psychological Bulletin, 137,* 316–344.

Frager, R., & Fadiman, J. (1998). *Personality and personal growth.* New York: Longman.

Fraley, R. C., & Shaver, P. R. (2000). Adult romantic attachment: Theoretical developments, emerging controversies, and unanswered questions. *Review of General Psychology, 4,* 132–154.

Fraley, R. C., Brumbaugh, C. C., & Marks, M. J. (2005). The evolution and function of adult attachment: A comparative and phylogenetic analysis. *Journal of Personality and Social Psychology, 89,* 731–746.

Frank, J. D., & Frank, J. B. (1991). *Persuasion and healing: A comparative study of psychotherapy* (3rd ed.). Baltimore: Johns Hopkins University Press.

Frank, M. C., Everett, D. L., Fedorenko, E., & Gibson, E. (2008). Number as a cognitive technology: Evidence from the Pirahã language and cognition. *Cognition, 108,* 819–824.

Frank, M. E., & Nowlis, G. H. (1989). Learned aversions and taste qualities in hamsters. *Chemical Senses, 14,* 379–394.

Franklin, A., Giannakidou, A., & Goldin-Meadow, S. (2011). Negation, questions, and structure building in a homesign system. *Cognition, 118,* 398–416.

Franklin, N., & Tversky, B. (1990). Searching imagined environments. *Journal of Experimental Psychology: General, 119,* 63–76.

Frans, Ö., Rimmö, P. A., Åberg, L., & Fredrikson, M. (2005). Trauma exposure and post-traumatic stress disorder in the general population. *Acta Psychiatrica Scandinavica, 111,* 291–299.

Fraser, L. M., O'Carroll, R. E., & Ebmeier, K. P. (2008). The effect of electro-convulsive therapy on autobiographical memory: A systematic review. *The Journal of ECT, 24,* 10–17.

Freedman, J. L., & Fraser, S. C. (1966). Compliance without pressure: The foot-in-the-door technique. *Journal of Personality and Social Psychology, 4,* 195–202.

Frenda, S. J., Nichols, R. M., & Loftus, E. F. (2011). Current issues and advances in misinformation research. *Current Directions in Psychological Science, 20,* 20–23.

Freud, A. (1946). *The ego and the mechanisms of defense.* New York: International Universities Press.

Freud, A. (1958). Adolescence. *Psychoanalytic Study of the Child, 13,* 255–278.

Freud, S. (1923). *Introductory lectures on psychoanalysis* (J. Riviera, Trans.). London: Allen & Unwin.

Freud, S. (1957). Leonardo da Vinci and a memory of his childhood. In J. Strachey (Ed. and Trans.), *The standard edition of the complete psychological works of Sigmund Freud* (Vol. 11, pp. 59–137). London: Hogarth Press. (Original work published 1910)

Freud, S. (1965). *The interpretation of dreams.* New York: Avon. (Original work published 1900)

Freund, A. M., & Baltes, P. B. (1998). Selection, optimization, and compensation as strategies of life management: Correlations with subjective indicators of successful aging. *Psychology and Aging, 13,* 531–543.

Friedman, B. H. (2010). Feelings and the body: The Jamesian perspective on autonomic specificity of emotion. *Biological Psychology, 84,* 383–393.

Friedman, M., & Rosenman, R. F. (1974). *Type A behavior and your heart.* New York: Knopf.

Friend, R., Rafferty, Y., & Bramel, D. (1990). A puzzling misinterpretation of the Asch "conformity" study. *European Journal of Social Psychology, 20,* 29–44.

Friesen, C. A., & Kammrath, L. K. (2011). What it pays to know about a close other: The value of if-then personality knowledge in close relationships. *Psychological Science, 22,* 567–571.

Fromkin, V. A. (Ed.). (1980). *Errors in linguistic performance: Slips of the tongue, pen, and hand.* New York: Academic Press.

Furley, P., Memmert, D., & Heller, C. (2010). The dark side of visual awareness in sport: Inattentional blindness in a real-world basketball task. *Attention, Perception, and Psychophysics, 72,* 1327–1337.

Galati, A., & Brennan, S. E. (2010). Attenuating information in spoken communication: For the speaker, or for the addressee? *Journal of Memory and Language, 62,* 35–51.

Gale, C. R., Batty, G. D., & Deary, I. J. (2008). Locus of control at age 10 years and health outcomes and behaviors at age 30 years: The 1970 British Cohort Study. *Psychosomatic Medicine, 70,* 397–403.

Galesic, M., & Garcia-Retamero, R. (2011). Do low-numeracy people avoid shared decision making? *Health Psychology, 30,* 336–341.

Gallace, A., & Spence, C. (2010). The science of interpersonal touch: An overview. *Neuroscience and Biobehavioral Reviews, 34,* 246–259.

Gallup, G. G., Jr., & Frederick, D. A. (2010). The science of sex appeal: An evolutionary perspective. *Review of General Psychology, 14,* 240–250.

Galton, F. (1907). *Inquiries into human faculty and its development.* London: Dent Publishers. (Original work published 1883)

Ganis, F., Thompson, W. L., & Kosslyn, S. M. (2004). Brain areas underlying visual imagery and visual perception: An fMRI study. *Cognitive Brain Research, 20,* 226–241.

Ganis, G., Rosenfeld, J. P., Meixner, J., Kievit, R. A., & Schendan, H. E. (2011). Lying in the scanner: Covert countermeasures disrupt deception detection by functional magnetic resonance imaging. *NeuroImage, 55,* 312–319.

Ganor-Stern, D., Tzelgov, J., & Ellenbogen, R. (2007). Automaticity and two-digit numbers. *Journal of Experimental Psychology: Human Perception and Performance, 33,* 483–496.

Gao, Q., & Horvath, T. L. (2007). Neurobiology of feeding and energy expenditure. *Annual Review of Neuroscience, 30,* 367–398.

Garb, H. N., Wood, J. M., Lilienfeld, S. O., & Nezworski, M. T. (2005). Roots of the Rorschach controversy. *Clinical Psychology Review, 25,* 97–118.

Garcia, J. (1990). Learning without memory. *Journal of Cognitive Neuroscience, 2,* 287–305.

Garcia, J., & Koelling, R. A. (1966). The relation of cue to consequence in avoidance learning. *Psychonomic Science, 4,* 123–124.

Gardner, H. (1999). *The disciplined mind.* New York: Simon & Schuster.

Gardner, H. (2006). *Multiple intelligences: New Horizons.* New York: Basic books.

Gardner, R. A., & Gardner, B. T. (1969). Teaching sign language to a chimpanzee. *Science, 165,* 664–672.

Garrison, M. M., Liekweg, K., & Christakis, D. A. (2011). Media use and child sleep: The impact of content, timing, and environment. *Pediatrics, 128,* 29–35.

Gatchel, R. J., Peng, Y. B., Peters, M. D., Fuchs, P. N., & Turk, D. C. (2007). The biopsychosocial approach to chronic pain: Scientific advances in future directions. *Psychological Bulletin, 133,* 581–624.

Gaultney, J. F. (2010). The prevalence of sleep disorders in college students: Impact on academic performance. *Journal of American College Health, 59,* 91–97.

Gautron, L., & Elmquist, J. K. (2011). Sixteen years and counting: An update on leptin in energy balance. *The Journal of Clinical Investigation, 121,* 2087–2093.

Gauvain, M., Beebe, H., & Zhao, S. (2011). Applying the cultural approach to cognitive development. *Journal of Cognition and Development, 12,* 121–133.

Gazzaniga, M. (1970). *The bisected brain.* New York: Appleton-Century-Crofts.

Gazzaniga, M. S. (1985). *The social brain.* New York: Basic Books.

Geraerts, E., Schooler, J. W., Merckelbach, H., Jelicic, M., Hauer, B. J. A., & Ambadar, Z. (2007). The reality of recovered memories: Corroborating continuous and discontinuous memories of childhood sexual abuse. *Psychological Science, 18,* 564–568.

Gergen, K. J., Gulerce, A., Lock, A., & Misra, G. (1996). Psychological science in a cultural context. *American Psychologist, 51,* 496–503.

Gershoff, E. T., & Bitensky, S. H. (2007). The case against corporal punishment for children: Converging evidence from social science research and international human rights law and implications for U. S. public policy. *Psychology, Public Policy, and Law, 13,* 231–272.

Gibbons, A. (2007). Food for thought. *Science, 316,* 1558–1560.

Gibbons, M. B. C., Crits-Christoph, P., & Hearon, B. (2008). The empirical status of psychodynamic therapies. *Annual Review of Clinical Psychology, 4,* 93–108.

Gibbs, J. C., Basinger, K. S., Grime, R. L., & Snarey, J. R. (2007). Moral judgment development across culture: Revisiting Kohlberg's universality claims. *Developmental Review, 27,* 443–500.

Gibson, E. J., & Walk, R. D. (1960). The "visual cliff." *Scientific American, 202,* 64–71.

Gibson, J. J. (1979). *An ecological approach to visual perception.* Boston: Houghton Mifflin.

Giesbrecht, T., Lynn, S. J., Lilienfeld, S. O., & Merckelbach, H. (2008). Cognitive processes in dissociation: An analysis of core theoretical assumptions. *Psychological Bulletin, 134,* 617–647.

Gigerenzer, G., & Gaissmaier, W. (2011). Heuristic decision making. *Annual Review of Psychology, 62,* 451–482.

Gilbert, D. T., Morewedge, C. K., Risen, J. L., & Wilson, T. D. (2004). Looking forward to looking backward: The misprediction of regret. *Psychological Science, 15*, 346–350.

Gilligan, C. (1982). *In a different voice: Psychological theory and women's development.* Cambridge, MA: Harvard University Press.

Gilovich, T. (1991). *How we know what isn't so: The fallibility of human reason in everyday life.* New York: The Free Press.

Glasman, L. R., & Albarracín, D. (2006). Forming attitudes that predict behavior: A meta-analysis of the attitude-behavior relation. *Psychological Bulletin, 132*, 778–822.

Gleaves, D. H., May, M. C., & Cardeña, E. (2001). An examination of the diagnostic validity of dissociative identity disorder. *Clinical Psychology Review, 21*, 577–608.

Goddard, A. W., Ball, S. G., Martinez, J., Robinson, M. J., Yang, C. R., Russell, J. M., & Shekhar, A. (2010). Current perspectives of the roles of the central norepinephrine system in anxiety and depression. *Depression and Anxiety, 27*, 339–250.

Goddard, H. H. (1914). *The Kallikak family: A study of the heredity of feeblemindedness.* New York: Macmillan.

Godden, D. R., & Baddeley, A. D. (1975). Context-dependent memory in two natural environments: On land and under water. *British Journal of Psychology, 66*, 325–331.

Godin, G., Sheeran, P., Conner, M., & Germain, M. (2008). Asking questions changes behavior: Mere measurement effects on frequency of blood donation. *Health Psychology, 27*, 179–184.

Goldberg, A. E., & Perry-Jenkins, M. (2007). The division of labor and perceptions of parental roles: Lesbian couples across the transition to parenthood. *Journal of Social and Personal Relationships, 24*, 297–318.

Goldberg, A. E., & Sayer, A. (2006). Lesbian couples' relationship quality across the transition to parenthood. *Journal of Marriage and Family, 68*, 87–100.

Goldfried, M. R. (2003). Cognitive-behavior therapy: Reflections on the evolution of a therapeutic orientation. *Cognitive Therapy and Research, 27*, 53–69.

Goldfried, M. R., & Davila, J. (2005). The role of relationship and technique in therapeutic change. *Psychotherapy: Theory, Research, Practice, Training, 42*, 421–430.

Goldin-Meadow, S. (2003). *The resilience of language: What gesture creation in deaf children can tell us about how all children learn language.* New York: Psychology Press.

Goldin-Meadow, S., & Mylander, C. (1990). Beyond the input given: The child's role in the acquisition of language. *Language, 66*, 323–355.

Goldrick, M., & Larson, M. (2008). Phonotactic probability influences speech production. *Cognition, 107*, 1155–1164.

Goldstein, D., Hahn, C. S., Hasher, L., Wiprzycka, U. J., & Zelazo, P. D. (2007). Time of day, intellectual performance, and behavioral problems in morning versus evening type adolescents: Is there a synchrony effect? *Personality and Individual Differences, 42*, 431–440.

Goldstein, R. B., Compton, W. M., Pulay, A. J., Ruan, W. J., Pickering, R. P., Stinson, F. S., & Grant, B. F. (2007). Antisocial behavioral syndromes and DSM-IV drug use disorders in the United States: Results from the National Epidemiologic Survey on Alcohol and Related Conditions. *Drug and Alcohol Dependence, 90*, 145–158.

Goldstrom, I. D., Campbell, J., Rogers, J. A., Lambert, D. B., Blacklow, B., Henderson, M. J., & Manderscheid, R. W. (2006). National estimates for mental health support groups, self-help organizations, and consumer-operated services. *Administration and Policy in Mental Health and Mental Health Services Research, 33*, 92–103.

Golombok, S., Rust, J., Zervoulis, K., Croudace, T., Golding, J., & Hines, M. (2008). Developmental trajectories of sex-typed behavior in boys and girls: A longitudinal general population study of children aged 2.5–8 years. *Child Development, 79*, 1583–1593.

Goodheart, C. D., Kadzin, A. E., & Sternberg, R. J. (2006). *Evidence-based psychotherapy: Where practice and research meet.* Washington, DC: American Psychological Association.

Goonawardena, A. V., Riedel, G., & Hampson, R. E. (2011). Cannabinoids alter spontaneous firing, bursting, and cell synchrony of hippocampal principal cells. *Hippocampus, 21*, 520–531.

Gorchoff, S. M., John, O. P., & Helson, R. (2008). Contextualizing change in marital satisfaction during middle age: An 18-year longitudinal study. *Psychological Science, 19*, 1194–1200.

Gordon, P. (2004). Numerical cognition without words: Evidence from Amazonia. *Science, 306*, 496–499.

Gotlib, I. H., & Hamilton, J. P. (2008). Neuroimaging and depression: Current status and unresolved issues. *Current Directions in Psychological Science, 17*, 159–163.

Gottesman, I. I. (1991). *Schizophrenia genesis: The origins of madness.* New York: Freeman.

Gottfredson, L. S. (1997). Mainstream science on intelligence: An editorial with 52 signatories, history, and bibliography. *Intelligence, 24*, 13–23.

Gottfredson, L. S. (2002). Where and why g matters: Not a mystery. *Human Performance, 15*, 25–46.

Gottfredson, L. S. (2003). Dissecting practical intelligence theory: Its claims and evidence. *Intelligence, 31i*, 343–397.

Gouin, J.-P., Kielcolt-Glaser, J. K., Malarkey, W. B., & Glaser, R. (2008). The influence of anger expression on wound healing. *Brain, Behavior, and Immunity, 22*, 699–708.

Granic, I., & Patterson, G. R. (2006). Toward a comprehensive model of antisocial development: A dynamic systems approach. *Psychological Review, 113*, 101–131.

Grant, P. R., & Grant, B. R. (2006). Evolution of character displacement in Darwin's finches. *Science, 313*, 224–226.

Grant, P. R., & Grant, B. R. (2008). *How and why species multiply.* Princeton, NJ: Princeton University Press.

Gray, M. R., & Steinberg, L. (1999). Unpacking authoritative parenting: Reassessing a multidimensional construct. *Journal of Marriage and the Family, 61*, 574–587.

Graziano, M., & Sigman, M. (2008). The dynamics of sensory buffers: Geometric, spatial, and experience-dependent shaping of iconic memory. *Journal of Vision, 8*, 1–13.

Greaves, N., Prince, E., Evans, D. W., & Charman, T. (2006). Repetitive and ritualistic behaviour in children with Prader-Willi syndrome and children with autism. *Journal of Intellectual Disability Research, 50*, 92–100.

Green, D. M., & Swets, J. A. (1966). *Signal detection theory and psychophysics.* New York: Wiley.

Greenberg, J. (2008). Understanding the vital human quest for self-esteem. *Perspectives on Psychological Science, 3*, 48–55.

Greenberg, J., Kosloff, S., Solomon, S., Cohen, F., & Landau, M. (2010). Toward understanding the fame game: The effect of mortality salience on the appeal of fame. *Self and Identity, 9*, 1–18.

Greenberg, S. T., & Schoen, E. G. (2008). Males and eating disorders: Gender-based therapy for eating disorder recovery. *Professional Psychology: Research and Practice, 39*, 464–471.

Greene, J. D., Morelli, S. A., Lowenberg, K., Nystrom, L. E., & Cohen, J. D. (2008). Cognitive load selectively interferes with utilitarian moral judgment. *Cognition, 107*, 1144–1154.

Greenfield, P. M. (1997). You can't take it with you: Why ability assessments don't cross cultures. *American Psychologist, 52*, 1115–1124.

Greenwald, A. G., McGhee, D. E., & Schwartz, J. L. K. (1998). Measuring individual differences in implicit cognition: The Implicit Association Test. *Journal of Personality and Social Psychology, 74*, 1464–1480.

Greenwald, A. G., Poehlman, T. A., Uhlmann, E., & Banaji, M. R. (2009). Understanding and using the Implicit Association Test: III. Meta-analysis of predictive validity. *Journal of Personality and Social Psychology, 97*, 17–41.

Gregory, R. (1966). *Eye and brain*. New York: McGraw-Hill.

Greven, C. U., Rijsdijk, F. V., & Plomin, R. (2011). A twin study of ADHD symptoms in early adolescence: Hyperactivity-impulsivity and inattentiveness show substantial genetic overlap but also genetic specificity. *Journal of Abnormal Child Psychology, 39*, 265–275.

Grice, H. P. (1968). Utterer's meaning, sentence-meaning, and word-meaning. *Foundations of Language, 4*, 1–18.

Grice, H. P. (1975). Logic and conversation. In P. Cole & J. L. Morgan (Eds.), *Syntax and semantics: Vol. 3. Speech acts* (pp. 41–58). New York: Academic Press.

Grilo, C. M., Hrabosky, J. I., White, M., Allison, K. C., Stunkard, A. J., & Masheb, R. M. (2008). Overvaluation of shape and weight in binge eating disorder and overweight controls: Refinement of a diagnostic construct. *Journal of Abnormal Psychology, 117*, 414–419.

Groh, D. R., Jason, L. A., & Keys, C. B. (2008). Social network variables in alcoholics anonymous: A literature review. *Clinical Psychology Review, 28*, 430–450.

Guérard, K., Neath, I., Surprenant, A. M., & Tremblay, S. (2010). Distinctiveness in serial memory for spatial information. *Memory & Cognition, 38*, 83–91.

Guéraud, S., Tapiero, I., & O'Brien, E. J. (2008). Context and the activation of predictive inferences. *Psychonomic Bulletin & Review, 15*, 351–356.

Guido, M. E., Garbarino-Pico, E., Contin, M. A., Valdez, D. J., Nieto, P. S., Verra, D. M., Acosta-Rodriguez, V. A., de Zavalía, N., & Rosenstein, R. E. (2010). Inner retinal circadian clocks and non-visual photoreceptors: Novel players in the circadian system. *Progress in Neurobiology, 92*, 484–504.

Guilleminault, C., Poyares, D., Aftab, F., & Palombini, L. (2001). Sleep and wakefulness in somnambulism: A spectral analysis study. *Journal of Psychosomatic Research, 51*, 411–416.

Gupta, R. Koscik, T. R., Bechara, A., & Tranel, D. (2011). The amygdala and decision-making. *Neuropsychologia, 49*, 760–765.

Gutierrez, P. M., Watkins, R., & Collura, D. (2004). Suicide risk screening in an urban high school. *Suicide and Life-Threatening Behavior, 34*, 421–428.

Gyurak, A., Gross, J. J., & Etkin, A. (2011). Explicit and implicit emotion regulation: A dual-process framework. *Cognition and Emotion, 25*, 400–412.

Haas, S. M., & Stafford, L. (2005). Maintenance behaviors in same-sex and marital relationships: A matched sample comparison. *Journal of Family Communication, 5*, 43–60.

Haberstick, B. C., Schmitz, S., Young, S. E., & Hewitt, J. K. (2006). Genes and developmental stability of aggressive behavior: Problems at home and school in a community sample of twins aged 7–12. *Behavior Genetics, 36*, 809–819.

Habib, R., Nyberg, L., & Tulving, E. (2003). Hemispheric asymmetries of memory: the HERA model revisited. *TRENDS in Cognitive Sciences, 7*, 241–245.

Hackman, D. A., Farah, M. J., & Meaney, M. J. (2010). Socioeconomic status and the brain: Mechanistic insights from human and animal research. *Nature Reviews Neuroscience, 11*, 651–659.

Haidt, J. (2007). The new synthesis in moral psychology. *Science, 316*, 998–1002.

Haier, R. J., Jung, R. E., Yeo, R. A., Head, K., & Alkire, M. T. (2004). Structural variation and general intelligence. *NeuroImage, 23*, 425–433.

Hajcak, G., & Olvet, D. M. (2008). The persistence of attention to emotion: Brain potentials during and after picture presentation. *Emotion, 8*, 250–255.

Hall, G. S. (1904). *Adolescence: Its psychology and its relations to physiology, anthropology, sociology, sex, crime, religion and education* (Vols. 1 and 2). New York: D. Appleton.

Hall, J. S. (2004). *Roadblocks on the journey of psychotherapy*. Lanham, MD: Jason Aronson.

Hamilton, N. A., Gallagher, M. W., Preacher, K. J., Stevens, N., Nelson, C. A., Karlson, C., & McCurdy, D. (2007). Insomnia and well-being. *Journal of Consulting and Clinical Psychology, 75*, 939–946.

Hamlin, J. K., Hallinan, E. V., & Woodward, A. L. (2008). Do as I do: 7-month-old infants selectively reproduce other's goals. *Developmental Science, 11*, 487–494.

Han, J.-S. (2011). Acupuncture analgesia: Areas of consensus and controversy. *Pain, 152*, S41–S48.

Harati, H., Majchrzak, M., Cosquer, B., Galani, R., Kelche, C., Cassel, J.-C., & Barbelivien, A. (2011). Attention and memory in aged rats: Impact of lifelong environmental enrichment. *Neurobiology of Aging, 32*, 718–736.

Harbluk, J. L., Noy, Y. I., Trbovich, P. L., & Eizenman, M. (2007). An on-road assessment of cognitive distraction: Impacts on drivers' visual behavior and braking performance. *Accident Analysis and Prevention, 39*, 372–379.

Harder, J. W. (1991). Equity theory versus expectancy theory: The case of major league baseball free agents. *Journal of Applied Psychology, 76*, 458–464.

Hardy, J., & Selkoe, D. J. (2002). The amyloid hypothesis of Alzheimer's disease: Progress and problems on the road to therapeutics. *Science, 297*, 353–356.

Harlow, H. F. (1958). The nature of love. *American Psychologist, 13*, 673–685.

Harlow, H. F., & Zimmerman, R. R. (1958). The development of affectional responses in infant monkeys. *Proceedings of the American Philosophical Society, 102*, 501–509.

Harlow, H. F., & Zimmerman, R. R. (1959). Affectional responses in the infant monkey. *Science, 130*, 421–432.

Harlow, J. M. (1868). Recovery from the passage of an iron bar through the head. *Publications of the Massachusetts Medical Society, 2*, 327–347.

Hart, J. T. (1965). Memory and the feeling-of-knowing experience. *Journal of Educational Psychology, 56*, 208–216.

Hartley, C. A., Fischl, B., & Phelps, E. A. (2011). Brain structure correlates of individual differences in the acquisition and inhibition of conditioned fear. *Cerebral Cortex 21*, 1954–1962.

Hartshorne, H., & May, M. A. (1928). *Studies in the nature of character: Vol. 1. Studies in deceit*. New York: Macmillan.

Hartwig, M., & Bond, C. F., Jr. (2011). Why do lie-catchers fail? A lens model meta-analysis of human lie judgments. *Psychological Bulletin, 137*, 643–659.

Haselton, M. G., & Gildersleeve, K. (2011). Can men detect ovulation? *Current Directions in Psychological Science, 20*, 87–92.

Hasson, U., Furman, O., Clark, D., Dudai, Y., & Davachi, L. (2008). Enhanced intersubject correlations during movie viewing correlate with successful episodic encoding. *Neuron, 57*, 452–462.

Hastorf, A. H., & Cantril, H. (1954). They saw a game: A case study. *Journal of Abnormal and Social Psychology, 49*, 129–134.

Hatcher, C., & Himelstein, P. (Eds.). (1996). *The handbook of Gestalt therapy*. Northvale, NJ: Jason Aronson.

Hathaway, S. R., & McKinley, J. C. (1940). A multiphasic personality schedule (Minnesota): I. Construction of the schedule. *Journal of Psychology, 10*, 249–254.

Hathaway, S. R., & McKinley, J. C. (1943). *Minnesota Multiphasic Inventory manual*. New York: Psychological Corporation.

Hauser, R. M., & Palloni, A. (2011). Adolescent IQ and survival in the Wisconsin longitudinal study. *The Journals of Gerontology: Series B, 66*, i91–i101.

Hayes, J. A., Gelso, C. J., & Hummel, A. M. (2011). Managing countertransference. *Psychotherapy, 48*, 88–97.

Hazan, C., & Shaver, P. (1987). Romantic love conceptualized as an attachment process. *Journal of Personality and Social Psychology, 52*, 511–524.

Hearst, E. (1988). Fundamentals of learning and conditioning. In R. C. Atkinson, R. J. Herrnstein, G. Lindzey, & R. D. Luce (Eds.), *Stevens'* handbook of experimental psychology: Vol. 2. Learning and cognition (2nd ed., pp. 3–109). New York: Wiley.

Heatherington, L., & Lavner, J. A. (2008). Coming to terms with coming out: Review and recommendations for family systems-focused research. *Journal of Family Psychology, 22*, 329–343.

Heider, F. (1958). *The psychology of interpersonal relationships.* New York: Wiley.

Hektner, J. M., Schmidt, J. A., Csikszentmihaly, M. (2007). *Experience sampling method: Measuring the quality of everyday life.* Thousand Oaks, CA: Sage.

Helgeson, V. S., Reynolds, K. A., & Tomich, P. L. (2006). A meta-analytic review of benefit finding and growth. *Journal of Consulting and Clinical Psychology, 74*, 797–816.

Helms, J. E. (2006). Fairness is not validity or cultural bias in racial-group assessment: A quantitative perspective. *American Psychologist, 61*, 845–859.

Hendriksen, E. S., Pettifor, A., Lee, S.-J., Coates, T. J., & Rees, H. V. (2007). Predictors of condom use among young adults in South Africa: The reproductive health and HIV research unit national youth survey. *American Journal of Public Health, 97*, 1241–1248.

Hendry, A. P., Huber, S. K., De León, L. F., Herrel, A., & Podos, J. (2009). Disruptive selection in a bimodal population of Darwin's finches. *Proceedings of the Royal Society B, 276*, 753–759.

Henneberger, C., & Rusakov, D. A. (2010). Synaptic plasticity and Ca^{2+} signaling in astrocytes. *Neuron Glia Biology, 6*, 141–146.

Hennessey, B. A., & Amabile, T. M. (2010). Creativity. *Annual Review of Psychology, 61*, 569–598.

Henningsen, D. D., Henningsen, M. L. M., Eden, J., & Cruz, M. G. (2006). Examining the symptoms of groupthink and retrospective sensemaking. *Small Group Research, 37*, 36–64.

Henry, P. J., & Sears, D. O. (2002). The symbolic racism 2000 scale. *Political Psychology, 2*, 253–283.

Herbers, J. E., Cutuli, J. J., Lafavor, T. L., Vrieze, D., Leibel, C., Obradović, J., & Masten, A. S. (2011). Direct and indirect effects of parenting on academic functioning of young homeless children. *Early Education and Development, 22*, 77–104.

Herbst, C., Baier, B., Tolasch, T., & Steidle, J. L. M. (2011). Demonstration of sex pheromones in the predaceous diving beetle *Rhantus suturalis* (MacLeay 1825) (Dytiscidae). *Chemoecology, 21*, 19–23.

Herek, G. M. (2002). Gender gaps in public opinion about lesbians and gay men. *Public Opinion Quarterly, 66*, 40–66.

Herek, G. M. (2006). Legal recognition of same-sex relationships in the United States: A social science perspective. *American Psychologist, 61*, 607–621.

Herman, C. P., Roth, D. A., & Polivy, J. (2003). Effects of the presence of others on food intake: A normative investigation. *Psychological Bulletin, 129*, 873–886.

Hernnstein, R. J., & Murray, C. (1994). *The bell curve.* New York: The Free Press.

Hersh, S. M. (1971). *My Lai 4: A report on the massacre and its aftermath.* New York: Random House.

Hertwig, R., Herzog, S. M., Schooler, L. J., & Reimer, T. (2008). Fluency heuristic: A model of how the mind exploits a by-product of information retrieval. *Journal of Experimental Psychology: Learning, Memory, and Cognition, 34*, 1191–1206.

Hertzog, C. (2011). Intelligence in adulthood. In R. J. Sternberg & S. B. Kaufman (Eds.), *The Cambridge handbook of intelligence* (pp. 174–190). New York: Cambridge University Press.

Hertzog, C., Kramer, A. F., Wilson, R. S., & Lindenberger, U. (2008). Enrichment efforts on adult cognitive development: Can the functional capacity of older adults be preserved and enhanced? *Psychological Science in the Public Interest, 9*, 1–49.

Hess, T. M. (2005). Memory and aging in context. *Psychological Bulletin, 131*, 383–406.

Hess, T. M., & Hinson, J. T. (2006). Age-related variation in the influences of aging sterotypes on memory in adulthood. *Psychology and Aging, 21*, 621–625.

Hess, U., & Thibault, P. (2009). Darwin and emotional expression. *American Psychologist, 64*, 120–128.

Hettema, J. M., Prescott, C. A., Myerse, J. M., Neale, M. C., & Kendler, K. S. (2005). The structure of genetic and environmental risk factors for anxiety disorders in men and women. *Archives of General Psychiatry, 62*, 182–189.

Hewstone, M., Rubin, M., & Willis, H. (2002). Intergroup bias. *Annual Review of Psychology, 53*, 575–604.

Higgins, E. T., & Pittman, T. S. (2008). Motives of the *human* animal: Comprehending, managing, and sharing inner states. *Annual Review of Psychology, 59*, 361–385.

Hilsenroth, M. J., Charnas, J. W., Zodan, J., & Streiner, D. L. (2007). Criterion-based training for Rorschach scoring. *Training and Education in Professional Psychology, 1*, 125–134.

Hines, M. (2011). Gender development and the human brain. *Annual Review of Neuroscience, 34*, 69–88.

Hinshaw, S. P., & Stier, A. (2008). Stigma as related to mental disorders. *Annual Review of Clinical Psychology, 4*, 367–393.

Hobara, M. (2005). Beliefs about appropriate pain behavior: Cross-cultural and sex differences between Japanese and Euro-Americans. *European Journal of Pain, 9*, 389–393.

Hobson, J. A. (1988). *The dreaming brain.* New York: Basic Books.

Hobson, J. A., & McCarley, R. W. (1977). The brain as a dream state generator: An activation-synthesis hypothesis of the dream process. *American Journal of Psychiatry, 134*, 1335–1348.

Hodgkinson, G. P., & Healey, M. P. (2008). Cognition in organizations. *Annual Review of Psychology, 59*, 387–417.

Hodson, G. (2011). Do ideologically intolerant people benefit from intergroup contact? *Current Directions in Psychological Science, 20*, 154–159.

Hoekstra, R. A., Bartels, M., & Boomsma, D. I. (2007). Longitudinal genetic study of verbal and nonverbal IQ from early childhood to young adulthood. *Learning and Individual Differences, 17*, 97–114.

Hoffman, E. J., & Mathew, S. J. (2008). Anxiety disorders: A comprehensive review of pharmacotherapies. *Mount Sanai Journal of Medicine, 75*, 248–262.

Hoffmann, A. A., & Willi, Y. (2008). Detecting genetic responses to environmental change. *Nature Reviews Genetics, 9*, 421–432.

Holahan, C. K., & Sesrs, R. R. (1995). *The gifted group in later maturity.* Stanford, CA: Stanford University Press.

Holen, M. C., & Oaster, T. R. (1976). Serial position and isolation effects in a classroom lecture simulation. *Journal of Educational Psychology, 68*, 723–725.

Hollins, M. (2010). Somesthetic senses. *Annual Review of Psychology, 61*, 243–271.

Hollon, S. D., Stewart, M. O., & Strunk, D. (2006). Enduring effects for cognitive behavior therapy in the treatment of depression and anxiety. *Annual Review of Psychology, 57*, 285–315.

Hollon, S. D., Thase, M. E., & Markowitz, J. C. (2002). Treatment and prevention of depression. *Psychological Science in the Public Interest, 3*, 39–77.

Holmes, T. H., & Rahe, R. H. (1967). The social readjustment rating scale. *Journal of Psychosomatic Research, 11*(2), 213–218.

Homer, B. D., Solomon, T. M., Moeller, R. W., Mascia, A., DeRaleau, L., & Halktis, P. N. (2008). Methamphetamine abuse and impairment of social functioning: A review of the underlying neurphysiological causes and behavioral implications. *Psychological Bulletin, 134*, 301–310.

Hooley, J. M. (2007). Expressed emotion and relapse of psychopathology. *Annual Review of Clinical Psychology, 3*, 329–352.

Horgen, K. B., & Brownell, K. D. (2002). Comparison of price change and health message interventions in promoting healthy food choices. *Health Psychology, 21,* 505–512.

Horney, K. (1937). *The neurotic personality of our time.* New York: Norton.

Horney, K. (1939). *New ways in psychoanalysis.* New York: Norton.

Horney, K. (1945). *Our inner conflicts: A constructive theory of neurosis.* New York: Norton.

Horney, K. (1950). *Neurosis and human growth.* New York: Norton.

Horowitz, A., Brennan, M., & Reinhardt, J. P. (2005). Prevalence and risk factors for self-reported visual impairment among middle-aged and older adults. *Research on Aging, 27,* 307–326.

Horton, J. E., Crawford, H. J., Harrington, G., & Downs, J. H. III. (2004). Increased anterior corpus callosum size associated positively with hypnotizability and the ability to control pain. *Brain, 127,* 1741–1747.

Horton, W. S. (2007). The influence of partner-specific memory associations on language production: Evidence from picture naming. *Language and Cognitive Processes, 22,* 1114–1139.

Horton, W. S., & Gerrig, R. J. (2005). The impact of memory demands on audience design during language production. *Cognition, 96,* 127–142.

Horvath, A. O., Del Re, A. C., Flückiger, C., & Symonds, D. (2011). Alliance in individual psychotherapy. *Psychotherapy, 48,* 9–16.

Horwitz, A. V., Widom, C. S., McLaughlin, J., & White, H. R. (2001). The impact of abuse and neglect on adult mental health: A prospective study. *Journal of Health and Social Behavior, 42,* 184–201.

Hoshino-Browne, E., Zanna, A. S., Spencer, S. J., Zanna, M. P., Kitayama, S., & Lackenbauer, S. (2005). On the cultural guises of cognitive dissonance: The case of Easterners and Westerners. *Journal of Personality and Social Psychology, 89,* 294–310.

Hosp, J. L., Hosp, M. A., & Dole, J. K. (2011). Potential bias in predictive validity of universal screening measures across disaggregation subgroups. *School Psychology Review, 40,* 108–131.

Houlihan, D., Schwartz, C., Miltenberger, R., & Heuton, D. (1993). The rapid treatment of a young man's balloon (noise) phobia using in vivo flooding. *Journal of Behavior Therapy and Experimental Psychiatry, 24,* 233–240.

Howe, C. Q., & Purves, D. (2005). The Müller-Lyer illusion explained by the statistics of image-source relationships. *PNAS, 102,* 1234–1239.

Howell, R. T., & Howell, C. J. (2008). The relation of economic status to subjective well-being in developing countries: A meta-analysis. *Psychological Bulletin, 134,* 536–560.

Hu, A. W.-L., & Tang, L.-R. (2010). Factors motivating sports broadcast viewership with fan identification as a mediator. *Social Behavior and Personality, 38,* 681–690.

Hublin, C., Partinen, M., Koskenvuo, M., & Kaprio, J. (2007). Sleep and mortality: A population-based 22-year follow-up study. *Sleep, 30,* 1245–1253.

Hudson, J. I., Hiripi, E., Pope, H. G. Jr., & Kessler, R. C. (2007). The prevalence and correlates of eating disorders in the national comorbidity survey replication. *Biological Psychiatry, 61,* 348–358.

Hudson, J. L., Flannery-Schroeder, E., & Kendall, P. (2004). Primary prevention of anxiety disorders. In D. J. A. Dozois, & K. S. Dobson (Eds.), *The prevention of anxiety and depression: Theory, research, and practice* (pp. 101–130). Washington, DC: American Psychological Association.

Huesmann, L. R., Moise-Titus, J., Podolski, C. L., & Eron, L. D. (2003). Longitudinal relations between children's exposure to TV violence and their aggressive and violent behavior in young adulthood: 1977–1992. *Developmental Psychology, 39,* 201–221.

Huizink, A. C., & Mulder, E. J. H. (2006). Maternal smoking, drinking or cannabis use during pregnancy and neurobehavioral and cognitive functioning in human offspring. *Neuroscience and Biobehavioral Reviews, 30,* 24–41.

Hull, C. L. (1943). *Principles of behavior: An introduction to behavior theory.* New York: Appleton-Century-Crofts.

Hull, C. L. (1952). *A behavior system: An introduction to behavior theory concerning the individual organism.* New Haven, CT: Yale University Press.

Humphreys, K. R., Menzies, H., & Lake, J. K. (2010). Repeated speech errors: Evidence for learning. *Cognition, 117,* 151–165.

Hunt, E., & Carlson, J. (2007). Considerations relating to the study of group differences in intelligence. *Perspectives on Psychological Science, 2,* 194–213.

Hurvich, L., & Jameson, D. (1974). Opponent processes as a model of neural organization. *American Psychologist, 29,* 88–102.

Hyde, J. S., Mezulis, A. H., & Abramson, L. Y. (2008). The ABCs of depression: Integrating affective, biological, and cognitive models to explain the emergence of the gender difference in depression. *Psychological Review, 115,* 291–313.

Hyland, M. E., Whalley, B., & Geraghty, A. W. A. (2007). Dispositional predictors of placebo responding: A motivational interpretation of flower essence and gratitude therapy. *Journal of Psychosomatic Research, 62,* 331–340.

Imada, T., & Ellsworth, P. C. (2011). Proud Americans and lucky Japanese: Cultural differences in appraisal and corresponding emotion. *Emotion, 11,* 329–345.

Imel, Z. E., Baldwin, S., Atkins, D. C., Owen, J., Baardseth, T., & Wampold, B. E. (2011). Racial/ethnic disparities in therapist effectiveness: A conceptualization and initial study of cultural competence. *Journal of Counseling Psychology, 58,* 290–298.

Ingram, A., Saling, M. M., & Schweitzer, I. (2008). Cognitive side effects of brief pulse electroconvulsive therapy: A review. *The Journal of ECT, 24,* 3–9.

Insko, C. A., Thibaut, J. W., Moehle, D., Wilson, M., Diamond, W. D., Gilmore, R., Solomon, M. R., & Lipsitz, A. (1980). Social evolution and the emergence of leadership. *Journal of Personality and Social Psychology, 39,* 431–448.

Ireland, M. E., Slatcher, R. B., Eastwick, P. W., Scissors, L. E., Finkel, E. J., & Pennebaker, J. W. (2011). Language style matching predicts relationship initiation and stability. *Psychological Science, 22,* 39–44.

Irvine, J. T. (1990). Registering affect: Heteroglossia in the linguistic expression of emotion. In C. A. Lutz & L. Abu-Lughod (Eds.), *Language and the politics of emotions* (pp. 126–161). Cambridge, UK: Cambridge University Press.

IsHak, W. W., Kahloon, M., & Fakhry, H. (2011). Oxytocin role in enhancing well-being: A literature review. *Journal of Affective Disorders, 130,* 1–9.

Ives-Deliperi, V. L., Solms, M., & Meintjes, E. M. (2011). The neural substrates of mindfulness: An fMRI investigation. *Social Neuroscience, 6,* 231–242.

Iyengar, S. S., Wells, R. E. & Schwartz, B. (2006). Doing better but feeling worse: Looking for the "best" job undermines satisfaction. *Psychological Science, 17,* 143–150.

Izard, C. E. (1993). Four systems for emotion activation: Cognitive and noncognitive processes. *Psychological Review, 100,* 68–90.

Izard, C. E. (1994). Innate and universal facial expressions: Evidence from developmental and cross-cultural research. *Psychological Bulletin, 115,* 288–299.

Jack, R. E., Blais, C., Scheepers, C., Schyns, P. G., & Caldara, R. (2009). Cultural confusions show that facial expressions are not universal. *Current Biology, 19,* 1543–1548.

Jack, R.E., Caldara, R. & Schyns, P.G. (2012). Internal representations reveal cultural diversity in expectations of facial expressions of emotion. *Journal of Experimental Psychology: General,* in press.

Jackson, V. A., Mack, J., Matsuyama, R., Lakoma, M. D., Sullivan A. M., Arnold, R. M., Weeks, J. C., & Block, S. D. (2008). A qualitative study of oncologists' approaches to end-of-life care. *Journal of Palliative Medicine, 11,* 893–906.

Jacob, B. R., & Levitt, S. D. (2003). Rotten apples: An investigation of the prevalence and predictors of teacher cheating. *The Quarterly Journal of Economics, 118,* 843–877.

Jacobs, R. C., & Campbell, D. T. (1961). The perpetuation of an arbitrary tradition through several generations of a laboratory microculture. *Journal of Abnormal and Social Psychology, 62,* 649–658.

Jaffee, S., & Hyde, J. S. (2000). Gender differences in moral orientation: A meta-analysis. *Psychological Bulletin, 126,* 703–726.

Jager, G., de Win, M. M. L., van der Tweel, I., Schilt, T., Kahn, R. S., van den Brink, W., van Ree, J. M., & Ramsey, N. F. (2008). Assessment of cognitive brain function in ecstasy users and contributions of other drugs of abuse: Results from an fMRI study. *Neuropsychopharmacology, 33,* 247–258.

Jahnke, J. C. (1965). Primacy and recency effects in serial-position curves of immediate recall. *Journal of Experimental Psychology, 70,* 130–132.

Jain, S., Mills, P. J., von Känel, R., Hong, S., & Dimsdale, J. E. (2007). Effects of perceived stress and uplifts on inflammation and coagulability. *Psychophysiology, 44,* 154–160.

James, W. (1882). Subjective effects of nitrous oxide. *Mind, 7,* 186–208.

James, W. (1892). *Psychology.* New York: Holt.

James, W. (1950). *The principles of psychology* (2 vols.). New York: Holt, Rinehart & Wilson. (Original work published 1890)

Janis, I. (1982). *Groupthink* (2nd ed.). Boston: Houghton Mifflin.

Janis, I. L., & Frick, F. (1943). The relationship between attitudes toward conclusions and errors in judging logical validity of syllogisms. *Journal of Experimental Psychology, 33,* 73–77.

Janofsky, J. S., Dunn, M. H., Roskes, E. J., Briskin, J. K., & Rudolph, M. S. L. (1996). Insanity defense pleas in Baltimore city: An analysis of outcome. *American Journal of Psychiatry, 153,* 1464–1468.

Janowitz, H. D., & Grossman, M. I. (1950). Hunger and appetite: Some definitions and concepts. *Journal of the Mount Sinai Hospital, 16,* 231–240.

January, D., & Kako, E. (2007). Re-evaluating evidence for linguistic relativity: Reply to Boroditsky (2001). *Cognition, 104,* 417–426.

Jara, C., Popp, R., Zulley, J., Hajcak, G., & Geisler, P. (2011). Determinants of depressive symptoms in narcoleptic patients with and without cataplexy. *The Journal of Nervous and Mental Disease, 199,* 329–334.

Jasper, F., & Witthöft, M. (2011). Health anxiety and attentional bias: The time course of vigilance and avoidance in light of pictorial illness information. *Journal of Anxiety Disorders, 25,* 1131–1138.

Javdani, S., Sadeh, N., & Verona, E. (2011). Suicidality as a function of impulsivity, callous-unemotional traits, and depressive symptoms in youth. *Journal of Abnormal Psychology, 120,* 400–413.

Jay, G. (2008). Service learning, multiculturalism, and the pedagogies of difference. *Pedagogy, 8,* 255–281.

Jedrej, M. C. (1995). *Ingessana: The religious institutions of a people of the Sudan–Ethiopia borderland.* Leiden: Brill.

Jensen, A. R. (1962). Spelling errors and the serial position effect. *Journal of Educational Psychology, 53,* 105–109.

Jensen, L. A. (2008). Through two lenses: A cultural-developmental approach to moral psychology. *Developmental Review, 28,* 289–315.

Jo, H., Chen, Y. J., Chua, S. C., Jr., Talmage, D. A., & Role, L. W. (2005). Integration of endocannabinoid and leptin signaling in an appetite-related neural circuit. *Neuron, 48,* 1055–1066.

Johnson, T. E., & Rule, B. G. (1986). Mitigating circumstances, information, censure, and aggression. *Journal of Personality and Social Psychology, 50,* 537–542.

Johnson-Laird, P. N., & Wason, P. C. (1977). A theoretical analysis of insight into a reasoning task. In P. N. Johnson-Laird & P. C. Wason (Eds.), *Thinking* (pp. 143–157). Cambridge, UK: Cambridge University Press.

Joly, M., & Zimmermann, E. (2011). Do solitary foraging animals plan their routes? *Biology Letters, 7,* 638–640.

Jones, E. (1953). *The life and works of Sigmund Freud.* New York: Basic Books.

Jones, M. C. (1924). A laboratory study of fear: The case of Peter. *Pedagogical Seminary and Journal of Genetic Psychology, 31,* 308–315.

Jose, P. E., & Brown, I. (2008). When does the gender difference in rumination begin? Gender and age differences in the use of rumination by adolescents. *Journal of Youth and Adolescence, 37,* 180–192.

Jowkar-Baniani, F., & Schmuckler, M. A. (2011). Picture perception in infants: Generalization from two-dimensional to three-dimensional displays. *16,* 211–226.

Jung, C. G. (1959). The concept of the collective unconscious. In *The archetypes and the collective unconscious, collected works* (Vol. 9, Part 1, pp. 54–74.). Princeton, NJ: Princeton University Press. (Original work published 1936)

Jung, C. G. (1973). *Memories, dreams, reflections* (rev. ed., A. Jaffe, Ed.). New York: Pantheon Books.

Jusczyk, P. W. (2003). Chunking language input to find patterns. In D. H. Rakison & L. M. Oakes (Eds.), *Early category and concept development.* London: Oxford University Press.

Jusczyk, P. W., & Aslin, R. N. (1995). Infants' detection of the sound patterns of words in fluent speech. *Cognitive Psychology, 29,* 1–23.

Jussim, L., & Harber, K. D. (2005). Teacher expectations and self-fulfilling prophecies: Knowns and unknowns, resolved and unresolved controversies. *Personality and Social Psychology Review, 9,* 131–155.

Kabat-Zinn, J. (1990). *Full catastrophe living: Using the wisdom of your body and mind to face stress, pain, and illness.* New York: Dell.

Kadden, R. M., & Litt, M. D. (2011). The role of self-efficacy in the treatment of substance abuse disorders. *Addictive Behaviors, 36,* 1120–1126.

Kagan, J., & Snidman, N. (1991). Infant predictors of inhibited and uninhibited profiles. *Psychological Science, 2,* 40–44.

Kahneman, D. (1992). Reference points, anchors, norms, and mixed feelings. *Organizational Behavior and Human Decision Processes, 51,* 296–312.

Kahneman, D., & Frederick, S. (2002). Representativeness revisited: Attribute substitution in intuitive judgment. In T. Gilovich, D. Griffin, & D. Kahneman (Eds.), *Heuristics and biases: The psychology of intuitive judgment* (pp. 49–81). Cambridge, UK: Cambridge University Press.

Kahneman, D., & Tversky, A. (1973). On the psychology of prediction. *Psychological Review, 80,* 237–251.

Kallmann, F. J. (1946). The genetic theory of schizophrenia: An analysis of 691 schizophrenic index families. *American Journal of Psychiatry, 103,* 309–322.

Kalueff, A. V., & Nutt, D. J. (2007). Role of GABA in anxiety and depression. *Depression and Anxiety, 24,* 495–517.

Kamin, L. J. (1969). Predictability, surprise, attention, and conditioning. In B. A. Campbell & R. M. Church (Eds.), *Punishment and aversive behavior* (pp. 279–296). New York: Appleton-Century-Crofts.

Kandler, C., Bleidorn, W., Riemann, R., Spinath, F. M., Thiel, W., & Angleitner, A. (2010). Sources of cumulative continuity in personality: A longitudinal multiple-rater twin study. *Journal of Personality and Social Psychology, 98,* 995–1008.

Kaplan, C. A., & Simon, H. A. (1990). In search of insight. *Cognitive Psychology, 22,* 374–419.

Kapur, V. K. (2010). Obstructive sleep apnea: Diagnosis, epidemiology, and economics. *Respiratory Care, 55,* 1155–1167.

Káradóttir, R., Hamilton, N. B., Bakiri, Y., & Attwell, D. (2008). Spiking and nonspiking classes of oligodendrocyte precursor glia in CNS white matter. *Nature Neuroscience, 11,* 450–456.

Karavasilis, L., Doyle, A. B., & Markiewicz, D. (2003). Associations between parenting style and attachment to mother in middle childhood and adolescence. *International Journal of Behavioral Development, 27,* 153–164.

Karg, K., Burmeister, M., Shedden, K., & Sen, S. (2011). The serotonin transporter promoter variant (5-HTTLPR), stress, and depression meta-analysis revisited. *Archives of General Psychiatry, 68,* 444–454.

Karpicke, J. D., & Blunt, J. R. (2011). Retrieval practice produces more learning than elaborative studying with concept mapping. *Science, 331,* 772–775.

Kassebaum, N. L. (1994). Head Start: Only the best for America's children. *American Psychologist, 49,* 1123–1126.

Kazdin, A. E. (2008). Evidence-based treatment and practice: New opportunities to bridge clinical research and practice, enhance the knowledge base, and improve patient care. *American Psychologist, 63,* 146–159.

Keller, M. C., & Miller, G. (2006). Resolving the paradox of common, harmful, an heritable mental disorders: Which evolutionary genetic models work best? *Behavioral and Brain Sciences, 29,* 385–452.

Kelley, H. H. (1967). Attribution theory in social psychology. In D. Levine (Ed.), *Nebraska symposium on motivation* (Vol. 15). Lincoln: University of Nebraska Press.

Kellner, C. H., Knapp, R., Husain, M. M., Rasmussen, K., Samplson, S., Cullum, M., McClintock, S. M., Tobias, K. G., Martino, C., Mueller, M., Bailine, S. H., Fink, M., & Petrides, G. (2010). Bifrontal, bitemporal and right unilateral placement in ECT: Randomised trial. *The British Journal of Psychiatry, 196,* 226–234.

Kellough, J. L., Beevers, C. G., Ellis, A. J., & Wells, T. T. (2008). Time course of selective attention in clinically depressed young adults: An eye tracking study. *Behaviour Research and Therapy, 46,* 1238–1243.

Keltner, N. L, & Boschini, D. J. (2009). Electroconvulsive therapy. *Perspectives in Psychiatric Care, 45,* 66–70.

Kempermann, G. (2008). The neurogenic reserve hypothesis: What is adult hippocampus neurogenesis good for? *Trends in Neurosciences, 31,* 163–169.

Kendler, K. S., Gatz, M., Gardner, C. O., & Pedersen, N. L. (2006). A Swedish national twin study of lifetime major depression. *American Journal of Psychiatry, 163,* 109–114.

Kendler, K. S., Kuhn, J. W., & Prescott, C. A. (2004). Childhood sexual abuse, stressful life events and risk for major depression in women. *Psychological Medicine, 34,* 1475–1482.

Kendler, K. S., Thornton, L. M., Gilman, S. E., & Kessler, R. C. (2000a). Sexual orientation in a U.S. national sample of twin and nontwin sibling pairs. *American Journal of Psychiatry, 157,* 1843–1846.

Kennedy, R. E., & Craighead, W. E. (1988). Differential effects of depression and anxiety on recall of feedback in a learning task. *Behavior Therapy, 19,* 437–454.

Keren, G. (2007). Framing, intentions, and trust-choice incompatibility. *Organizational Behavior and Human Decision Processes, 103,* 238–255.

Kermer, D. A., Driver-Linn, E., Wilson, T. D., & Gilbert, D. T. (2006). Loss aversion is an affective forecasting error. *Psychological Science, 17,* 649–653.

Kerr, N. L., & Tindale, R. S. (2004). Group performance and decision making. *Annual Review of Psychology, 55,* 625–655.

Kesebir, P., & Diener, E. (2008). In pursuit of happiness: Empirical answers to philosophical questions. *Perspectives on Psychological Science, 3,* 117–125.

Keshavan, M. S., Nasrallah, H. A., & Tandon, R. (2011). Schizophrenia, "Just the facts" 6. Moving ahead with the schizophrenia concept: From the elephant to the mouse. *Schizophrenia Research, 127,* 3–13.

Keshavan, M. S., Tandon, R., Boutros, N. N., & Nasrallah, H. A. (2008). Schizophrenia, "Just the Facts": What we know in 2008. Part 3: Neurobiology. *Schizophrenia Research, 106,* 89–107.

Kessler, R. C., Adler, L., Barkley, R., Biederman, J., Conners, C. K., Demler, O., Faraone, S. V., Greenhill, L. L., Howes, M. J., Secnik, K., Spencer, T., Ustun, T. B., Walters, E. E., & Zaslavsky, A. M. (2006a). The prevalence and correlates of adult ADHD in the United States: Results form the National Comorbidity Survey Replication. *American Journal of Psychiatry, 163,* 716–723.

Kessler, R. C., Berglund, P., Demler, O., Jin, R., Merikangas, K. R., & Walters, E. E. (2005a). Lifetime prevalence and age-of-onset distributions of *DSM-IV* disorders in the National Comorbidity Survey Replication. *Archives of General Psychiatry, 62,* 593–602.

Kessler, R. C., Chiu, W. T., Demler, O., & Walters, E. E. (2005b). Prevalence, severity, and comorbidity of 12-month *DSM-IV* disorders in the National Comorbidity Survey Replication. *Archives of General Psychiatry, 62,* 617–627.

Kessler, R. C., Chiu, W. T., Jin. R., Ruscio, A. M., Shear, K., & Walters, E. E. (2006b). The epidemiology of panic attacks, panic disorder, and agoraphobia in the National Comorbidity Survey Replication. *Archives of General Psychiatry, 63,* 415–424.

Kessler, R. C., McGonagle, K. A., Zhao, S., Nelson, C. B., Hughes, M., Eshleman, S., Wittchen, H. U., & Kendler, K. S. (1994). Lifetime and 12-month prevalence of *DSM-III-R* psychiatric disorders in the United States. *Archives of General Psychiatry, 51,* 8–19.

Kettenmann, H., & Verkhratsky, A. (2008). Neuroglia: The 150 years after. *Trends in Neuroscience, 31,* 653–659.

Kiecolt-Glaser, J. K., Marucha, P. T., Malarkey, P. T., Mercado, A. M., & Glaser, R. (1995). Slowing of wound healing by psychological stress. *Lancet, 346,* 1194–1196.

Kihlstrom, J. F. (2007). Consciousness in hypnosis. In P. D. Zelazo, M. Moscovitch, & E. Thompson (Eds.), *The Cambridge handbook of consciousness* (pp. 445–479). New York: Cambridge University Press.

Kihlstrom, J. F., & Cantor, N. (2000). Social intelligence. In R. J. Sternberg (Ed.), *Handbook of intelligence* (pp. 359–369). New York: Cambridge University Press.

Kilmer, R. P., & Gil-Rivas, V. (2010). Exploring posttraumatic growth in children impacted by Hurricane Katrina: Correlates of the phenomenon and developmental considerations. *Child Development, 81,* 1211–1227.

Kilpatrick, L A., Suyenobu, B. Y., Smith, S. R., Bueller, J. A., Goodman, T., Creswell, J. D., Tillisch, K., Mayer, E. A., & Naliboff, B. D. (2011). Impact of mindfulness-based stress reduction training on intrinsic brain connectivity. *NeuroImage, 56,* 290–298.

Kim, C.-H., Chang, J. W., Koo, M.-S., Kim, J. W., Suh, H. S., Park, I. H., & Lee, H. S. (2003). *Acta Psychatrica Scandinavica, 107,* 283–290.

Kim, H. S., Sherman, D. K., & Taylor, S. E. (2008). Culture and social support. *American Psychologist, 63,* 518–526.

Kim, J., & Hatfield, E. (2004). Love types and subjective well-being: A cross-cultural study. *Social Behavior and Personality, 32,* 173–182.

Kim, M. J., Loucks, R. A., Palmer, A. L., Brown, A. C., Solomon, K. M., Marchante, A. N., & Whalen, P. J. (2011). The structural and functional complexity of the amygdala: From normal emotion to pathological anxiety. *Behavioural Brain Research, 223,* 403–410.

Kim, Y.-K. (Ed.) (2009). *Handbook of behavior genetics.* New York: Springer.

King, D. B., Viney, W., & Woody, W. D. (2009). *A History of psychology: Ideas and context* (4th ed.). Boston: Allyn & Bacon.

Kingdom, F. A. A. (2011). Lightness, brightness and transparency: A quarter century of new ideas, captivating demonstrations and unrelenting controversy. *Vision Research, 51,* 652–673.

Kinsey, A. C., Martin, C. E., & Pomeroy, W. B. (1948). *Sexual behavior in the human male.* Philadelphia: Saunders.

Kinsey, A. C., Pomeroy, W. B., Martin, C. E., & Gebhard, R. H. (1953). *Sexual behavior in the human female.* Philadelphia: Saunders.

Kintsch, W. (1974). *The representation of meaning in memory.* Hillsdale, NJ: Erlbaum.

Kirschner, F., Paas, F., Kirschner, P. A., & Janssen, J. (2011). Differential effects of problem-solving demands on individual and collaborative learning outcomes. *Learning and Instruction, 21,* 587–599.

Kirschner, S. M., & Galperin, G. J. (2001). Psychiatric defenses in New York County: Pleas and results. *Journal of the American Academy of Psychiatry and the Law, 29,* 194–201.

Kisilevsky, B. S., Hains, S. M. J., Brown, C. A., Lee, C. T., Cowperthwaite, B., Stutzman, S. S., Swansburg, M. L., Lee, L., Xie, X., Huang, H., Ye, H.-H., Zhang, K., & Wang, Z. (2009). Fetal sensitivity to properties of maternal speech and language. *Infant Behavior and Development, 32,* 59–71.

Kissane, D. W., Grabsch, B., Clarke, D. M., Christie, G., Clifton, D., Gold, S., Hill, C., Morgan, A., McDermott, F., & Smith, G. C. (2004). Supportive-expressive group therapy: The transformation of existential ambivalence into creative living while enhancing adherence to anticancer therapies. *Psycho-Oncology, 13,* 755–768.

Kitamura, C., Thanavishuth, C., Burnham, D., & Luksaneeyanawin, S. (2002). Universality and specificity in infant-directed speech: Pitch modifications as a function of infant age and sex in a tonal and nontonal language. *Infant Behavior & Development, 24,* 372–392.

Kitayama, S., & Uskul, A. K. (2011). Culture, mind, and the brain: Current evidence and future directions. *Annual Review of Psychology, 62,* 419–449.

Kitayama, S., Markus, H. R., & Lieberman, C. (1995). The collective construction of self-esteem: Implications for culture, self, and emotion. In J. A. Russell, J. Fernandez-Dols, T. Manstead, & J. Wellenkamp (Eds.), *Everyday conceptions of emotion* (pp. 523–550). Dordrecht: Kluwer.

Klatt, K. P., & Morris, E. K. (2001). The Premack principle, response deprivation, and establishing operations. *The Behavior Analyst, 24,* 173–180.

Kleider, H. M., Parrott, D. J., & King, T. Z. (2010). Shooting behaviour: How working memory and negative emotionality influence police officer shoot decisions. *Applied Cognitive Psychology, 24,* 707–717.

Klein, M. (1975). *The writings of Melanie Klein* (Vols. 1–4). London: Hogarth Press and the Institute of Psychoanalysis.

Klein, O., & Snyder, M. (2003). Stereotypes and behavioral confirmation: From interpersonal to intergroup perspectives. In M. P. Zanna (Ed.), *Advances in experimental social psychology* (Vol. 35, pp. 153–234). New York: Academic Press.

Klump, K. L., Burt, A., McGue, M., & Iacono, W. G. (2007). Changes in genetic and environmental influences on disordered eating across adolescence. *Archives of General Psychiatry, 64,* 1409–1415.

Knickmeyer, R., Baron-Cohen, S., Raggatt, P., & Taylor, K. (2005). Foetal testosterone, social relationships, and restricted interests in children. *Journal of Child Psychology and Psychiatry, 46,* 198–210.

Knobloch, L. K., Miller, L. E., Bond, B. J., & Mannone, S. E. (2007). Relational uncertainty and message processing in marriage. *Communication Monographs, 74,* 154–180.

Kobiella, A., Grossmann, T., Reid, V. M., & Striano, T. (2008). The discrimination of angry and fearful facial expressions in 7-month-old infants: An event-related potential study. *Cognition and Emotion, 22,* 133–146.

Kochanska, G., Kim, S., Barry, R. A., & Philibert, R. A. (2011). Children's genotypes interact with maternal responsive care in predicting children's competence: Diathesis-stress or differential susceptibility? *Development and Psychopathology, 23,* 605–616.

Koffka, K. (1935). *Principles of Gestalt psychology.* New York: Harcourt Brace.

Kohlberg, L. (1964). Development of moral character and moral ideology. In M. L. Hoffman & L. W. Hoffman (Eds.), *Review of child development research* (Vol. 1). New York: Russell Sage Foundation.

Kohlberg, L. (1981). *The philosophy of moral development.* New York: Harper & Row.

Köhler, W. (1947). *Gestalt psychology.* New York: Liveright.

Kohn, N., Kellermann, T., Gur, R. C., Schneider, F., & Habel, U. (2011). Gender differences in the neural correlates of humor processing: Implications for different processing modes. *Neuropsychologia, 49,* 888–897.

Konen, C. S., & Kastner, S. (2008). Two hierarchically organized neural systems for object information in human visual cortex. *Nature Neuroscience, 11,* 224–231.

Kong, L. L., Allen, J. J. B., & Glisky, E. L. (2008). Interidentity memory transfer in dissociative identity disorder. *Journal of Abnormal Psychology, 117,* 686–692.

Korchmaros, J. D., & Kenny, D. A. (2006). An evolutionary and close-relationship model of helping. *Journal of Social and Personal Relationships, 23,* 21–43.

Koriat, A., & Fischhoff, B. (1974). What day is today? An inquiry into the process of time orientation. *Memory & Cognition, 2,* 201–205.

Kotovsky, K., Hayes, J. R., & Simon, H. A. (1985). Why are some problems hard? Evidence from Tower of Hanoi. *Cognitive Psychology, 17,* 248–294.

Kounios, J., Fleck, J. I., Green, D. L., Payne, L., Stevenson, J. L., Bowdend, E. M., Jung-Beeman, M. (2008). The origins of insight in resting-state brain activity. *Neuropsychologia, 46,* 281–291.

Krahé, B., Bieneck, S., & Scheinberger-Olwig, R. (2007). Adolescents' sexual scripts: Schematic representations of consensual and nonconsensual heterosexual interactions. *Journal of Sex Research, 44,* 316–327.

Krämer, N. C., & Winter, S. (2008). Impression management 2.0: The relationship of self-esteem, extraversion, self- efficacy, and self-presentation within social networking sites. *Journal of Media Psychology, 20,* 106–116.

Krebs, D. L. (2008). Morality: An evolutionary account. *Perspectives on Psychological Science, 3,* 149–172.

Kristensen, P., & Bjerkedal, T. (2007). Explaining the relation between birth order and intelligence. *Science, 316,* 1717.

Krohne, H. W., & Slangen, K. E. (2005). Influence of social support on adaptation to surgery. *Health Psychology, 24,* 101–105.

Kronenfeld, L. W., Reba-Harrelson, L., Von Holle, A., Reyes, M. L., & Bulik, C. M. (2010). Ethnic and racial differences in body size perception and satisfaction. *Body Image, 7,* 131–136.

Kross, E., Berman, M. G., Mischel, W., Smith, E. E., & Wager, T. D. (2011). Social rejection shares somatosensory representations with physical pain. *Proceedings of the National Academy of Sciences, 108,* 6270–6275.

Krueger, J., & Stanke, D. (2001). The role of self-referent and other-referent knowledge in perceptions of group characteristics. *Personality & Social Psychology Bulletin, 27,* 878–888.

Kruger, J., Wirtz, D., & Miller, D. T. (2005). Counterfactual thinking and the first instinct fallacy. *Journal of Personality and Social Psychology, 88,* 725–735.

Kruglanski, A. W., & Gigerenzer, G. (2011). Intuitive and deliberate judgments are based on common principles. *Psychological Review, 118,* 97–109.

Kuhn, M. H., & McPartland, T. S. (1954). An empirical investigation of self-attitudes. *American Sociological Review, 19,* 68–76.

Kuipers, E., Onwumere, J., & Bebbington, P. (2010). Cognitive model of caregiving in psychosis. *The British Journal of Psychiatry, 196,* 259–265.

Kujawski, J. H., & Bower, T. G. R. (1993). Same-sex preferential looking during infancy as a function of abstract representation. *British Journal of Developmental Psychology, 11,* 201–209.

Kuppens, P., Realo, A., & Diener, E. (2008). The role of positive and negative emotions in life satisfaction judgment across nations. *Journal of Personality and Social Psychology, 95,* 66–75.

Kyriacou, C. P., & Hastings, M. H. (2010). Circadian clocks: Genes, sleep, and cognition. *Trends in Cognitive Sciences, 14,* 259–267.

LaBerge, S. (2007). Lucid dreaming. In D. Barret & P. McNamara (Eds.), *The new science of dreaming: Vol 2. Content, recall, and personality correlates* (pp. 307–328). Westport, CT: Praeger.

LaBerge, S., & Levitan, L. (1995). Validity established of DreamLight cues for eliciting lucid dreaming. *Dreaming: Journal of the Association for the Study of Dreams, 5,* 159–168.

Laborde, S., Brüll, A., Weber, J., & Anders, L. S. (2011). Trait emotional intelligence in sports: A protective role against stress through heart rate variability? *Personality and Individual Differences, 51,* 23–27.

Lachman, M. E. (2004). Development in midlife. *Annual Review of Psychology, 55,* 305–331.

Lamb, R. J., Morral, A. R., Kirby, K. C., Javors, M. A., Galbicka, G., & Iguchi, M. (2007). Contingencies for change in complacent smokers. *Experimental and Clinical Psychopharmacology, 15,* 245–255.

Lambert, S. F., Nylund-Gibson, K., Copeland-Linder, N., & Ialongo, N. S. (2010). Patterns of community violence exposure during adolescence. *American Journal of Community Psychology, 46,* 289–302.

Lambert, T. A., Kahn, A. S., & Apple, K. J. (2003). Pluralistic ignorance and hooking up. *The Journal of Sex Research, 40,* 129–133.

Lammers, J., Stoker, J. I., Jordan, J., Pollmann, M., & Stapel, D. A. (2011). Power increases infidelity among men and women. *Psychological Science, 22,* 1191–1197.

Lampinen, J. M., Copeland, S. M., & Neuschatz, J. S. (2001). Recollections of things schematic: Room schemas revisited. *Journal of Experimental Psychology: Learning, Memory, and Cognition, 27,* 1211–1222.

Lander, E. S., & Weinberg, R. A. (2000). Genomics: Journey to the center of biology. *Science, 287,* 1777–1782.

Langlois, J. H., Kalakanis, L., Rubenstein, A. J., Larson, A., Hallam, M., & Smoot, M. (2000). Maxims or myths of beauty? A meta-analytic and theoretical review. *Psychological Bulletin, 126,* 390–423.

Långström, N., Rahman, Q., Carlström, E., & Lichstenstein, P. (2010). Genetic and environmental effects on same-sex sexual behavior: A population study of twins in Sweden. *Archives of Sexual Behavior, 39,* 75–80.

Langton, S. R. H., Law, A. S., Burton, A. M., & Schweinberger, S. R. (2008). Attention capture by faces. *Cognition, 107,* 330–342.

Lashley, K. S. (1929). *Brain mechanisms and intelligence.* Chicago: University of Chicago Press.

Lashley, K. S. (1950). In search of the engram. In *Physiological mechanisms in animal behavior: Symposium of the Society for Experimental Biology* (pp. 454–482). New York: Academic Press.

Latané, B., & Darley, J. M. (1970). *The unresponsive bystander: Why doesn't he help?* New York: Appleton-Century-Crofts.

Lau, J. Y. F., & Eley, T. C. (2008). Attributional style as a risk marker of genetic effects for adolescent depressive symptoms. *Journal of Abnormal Psychology, 117,* 849–859.

Lawrence, E., Nylen, K., & Cobb, R. J. (2007). Prenatal expectations and marital satisfaction over the transition to parenthood. *Journal of Family Psychology, 21,* 155–164.

Lawyer, S., Resnick, H., Bakanic, V., Burkett, T., & Kilpatrick, D. (2010). Forcible, drug-facilitated, and incapacitated rape and sexual assault among undergraduate women. *Journal of American College Health, 58,* 453–460.

Lay, C. H. (1986). At last my research article on procrastination. *Journal of Research in Personality, 20,* 474–495.

Lazarus, R. S. (1981, July). Little hassles can be hazardous to your health. *Psychology Today,* pp. 58–62.

Lazarus, R. S. (1984a). On the primacy of cognition. *American Psychologist, 39,* 124–129.

Lazarus, R. S. (1984b). Puzzles in the study of daily hassles. *Journal of Behavioral Medicine, 7,* 375–389.

Lazarus, R. S. (1991). Cognition and motivation in emotion. *American Psychologist, 46,* 352–367.

Lazarus, R. S. (1993). From psychological stress to the emotions: A history of changing outlooks. *Annual Review of Psychology, 44,* 1–21.

Lazarus, R. S. (1995). Vexing research problems inherent in cognitive-mediational theories of emotion—and some solutions. *Psychological Inquiry, 6,* 183–196.

Lazarus, R. S., & Folkman, S. (1984). *Stress, appraisal, and coping.* New York: Springer.

Lazarus, R. S., & Lazarus, B. N. (1994). *Passion and reason: Making sense of our emotions.* New York: Oxford University Press.

Lea, V. (2004). Mēbengokre ritual wailing and flagellation: A performative outlet for emotional self-expression. *Indiana, 21,* 113–125.

Lecci, L., & Myers, B. (2008). Individual differences in attitudes relevant to juror decision making: Development and validation of the Pretrial Juror Attitude Questionnaire (PJAQ). *Journal of Applied Social Psychology, 38,* 2010–2038.

Ledbetter, A. M., Griffin, E., & Sparks, G. S. (2007). Forecasting "friends forever": A longitudinal investigation of sustained closeness between best friends. *Personal Relationships, 14,* 343–350.

Lee, H. S., & Holyoak, K. J. (2008). The role of causal models in analogical inference. *Journal of Experimental Psychology: Learning, Memory, and Cognition, 34,* 1111–1122.

Lee, K. (2011). Impacts of the duration of head start enrollment on children's academic outcomes: Moderation effects of family risk factors and early outcomes. *Journal of Community Psychology, 39,* 698–716.

Lee, M., Zimbardo, P., & Bertholf, M. (1977, November). Shy murderers. *Psychology Today,* pp. 68–70, 76, 148.

Lee, S. A. S., & Davis, B. L. (2010). Segmental distribution patterns of English infant- and adult-directed speech. *Journal of Child Language, 37,* 767–791.

Lee, S.-H., Földy, C., & Soltesz, I. (2010). Distinct endocannabinoid control of GABA release at perisomatic and dendritic synapses in the hippocampus. *The Journal of Neuroscience, 30,* 7993–8000.

Leekam, S. R., Prior, M. R., & Uljarevic, M. (2011). Restricted and repetitive behaviors in autism spectrum disorders: A review of research in the last decade. *Psychological Bulletin, 137,* 562–593.

Leen-Feldner, E. W., Feldner, M. T., Reardon, L. E., Babson, K. A., & Dixon, L. (2008). Anxiety sensitivity and posttraumatic stress among traumatic event-exposed youth. *Behaviour Research and Therapy, 46,* 548–556.

Legate, N., Ryan, R. M., & Weinstein, N. (2012). Is coming out always a "good thing"? Exploring the relations of autonomy support, outness, and wellness for lesbian, gay, and bisexual individuals. *Social Psychological and Personality Science,* in press.

Legrand, D. (2007). Pre-reflective self-as-subject from experiential and empirical perspectives. *Consciousness and Cognition, 16,* 583–599.

Leiter, M. P., & Maslach, C. (2005). *Banishing burnout: Six strategies for improving your relationship with work.* San Francisco: Jossey-Bass.

Lemay, E. P., Jr., Clark, M. S., & Greenberg, A. (2010). What is beautiful is good because what is beautiful is desired: Physical attractiveness stereotyping as projection of personal goals. *Personality and Social Psychology Bulletin, 36,* 339–353.

Lenroot, R. K., & Giedd, J. N. (2010). Sex differences in the adolescent brain. *Brain and Cognition, 72,* 46–55.

Lenroot, R. K., Gogtay, N., Greenstein, D. K., Wells, E. M., Gregory L. Wallace, G. L., Clasen, L. V., Blumenthal, J. D., Lerch, J., Zijdenbos, A. P., Evans, A. C., Thompson, P. M., & Giedda, J. N. (2007). Sexual dimorphism of brain developmental trajectories during childhood and adolescence. *NeuroImage, 36,* 1065–1073.

Lenzenweger, M. F., Lane, M. C., Loranger, A. W., & Kessler, R. C. (2007). *DSM-IV* personality disorders in the National Comorbidity Survey Replication. *Biological Psychiatry, 62,* 553–564.

Lesku, J. A., Bark, R. J., Martinez-Gonzalez, D., Rattenborg, N. C., Amlaner, C. J., & Lima, S. L. (2008). Predator-induced plasticity in sleep architecture in wild-caught Norway rats (*Rattus norvegicus*). *Behavioural Brain Research, 189,* 298–305.

Leucht, S., Barnes, T. R. E., Kissling, W., Engel, R. R., Correll, C., & Kane, J. M. (2003). Relapse prevention in schizophrenia with new-generation antipsychotics: A systematic review and exploratory meta-analysis of randomized, controlled trials. *American Journal of Psychiatry, 160,* 1209–1222.

Leuner, B., & Gould, E. (2010). Structural plasticity and hippocampal function. *Annual Review of Psychology, 61,* 111–140.

Leung, A. K.-Y., & Chiu, C-Y. (2010). Multicultural experiences, idea receptiveness, and creativity. *Journal of Cross-Cultural Psychology, 41,* 723–741.

Leung, A. K.-Y., & Cohen, D. (2011). Within- and between-culture variation: Individual differences and the cultural logics of honor, face, and dignity cultures. *Journal of Personality and Social Psychology, 100,* 507–526.

Levenson, R. W., Ekman, P., Heider, K., & Friesen, W. V. (1992). Emotion and autonomic nervous system activity in the Minangkabau of West Sumatra. *Journal of Personality and Social Psychology, 62,* 972–988.

Leventhal, A. M., Martin, R. L., Seals, R. W., Tapia, E., & Rehm, L. P. (2007). Investigating the dynamics of affect: Psychological mechanisms of affective habituation to pleasurable stimuli. *Motivation and Emotion, 31,* 145–157.

Leventhal, H. (1980). Toward a comprehensive theory of emotion. In L. Berkowitz (Ed.), *Advances in experimental social psychology* (Vol. 13, pp. 139–207). New York: Academic Press.

Levine, R., Sato, S., Hashimoto, T., & Verma, J. (1995). Love and marriage in eleven cultures. *Journal of Cross-Cultural Psychology, 26,* 544–571.

Lew, A. R. (2011). Looking beyond boundaries: Time to put landmarks back on the cognitive map? *Psychological Bulletin, 137,* 484–507.

Lewin, K. (1936). *Principles of topological psychology.* New York: McGraw-Hill.

Lewis, R. J., Derlega, V. J., Clarke, E. G., & Kuang, J. C. (2006). Stigma consciousness, social constraints, and lesbian well-being. *Journal of Counseling Psychology, 53,* 48–56.

Li, J.-Y., Christophersen, M. S., Hall, V., Soulet, D., & Brundin, P. (2008). Critical issues of clinical human embryonic stem cell therapy for brain repair. *Trends in Neurosciences, 31,* 146–153.

Li, X., Sundquist, J., & Sundquist, K. (2011). Sibling risk of anxiety disorders based on hospitalizations in Sweden. *Psychiatry and Clinical Neurosciences, 65,* 233–238.

Liao, H.-L., Liu, S.-H., Pi, S.-M. (2011). Modeling motivations for blogging: An expectancy theory analysis. *Social Behavior and Personality, 39,* 251–264.

Licata, S. C., & Rowlett, J. K. (2008). Abuse and dependence liability of benzodiazepine-type drugs: GABA$_A$ receptor modulation and beyond. *Pharmacology, Biochemistry and Behavior, 90,* 74–89.

Lietzén, R., Virtanen, P., Kivimäki, M., Sillanmäki, L., Vahtera, J., & Koskenvuo, M. (2011). Stressful life events and the onset of asthma. *European Respiratory Journal, 37,* 1360–1365.

Lilienfeld, S. O., & Lynn, S. J. (2003). Dissociative identity disorder: Multiple personalities, multiple controversies. In S. O. Lilienfeld, S. J. Lynn, & J. M. Lohr (Eds.), *Science and pseudoscience in clinical psychology* (pp. 109–142). New York: Guilford Press.

Lilienfeld, S. O., Wood, J. M., & Garb, H. N. (2001). The scientific status of projective techniques. *Psychological Science in the Public Interest, 1,* 27–66.

Lin, H., Tian, W., Chen, C., Liu, T., Tsai, S., & Lee, H. (2006). The association between readmission rates and length of stay for schizophrenia: A 3-year population based study. *Schizophrenia Research, 83,* 211–214.

Lindau, S. T., Schumm, L. P., Laumann, E. O., Levinson, W., O'Muircheartaigh, C. A., & Waite, L. J. (2007). A study of sexuality and health among older adults in the United States. *The New England Journal of Medicine, 357,* 762–775.

Link, B. G., Struening, E. L., Rahav, M., Phelan, J. C., & Nuttbrock, L. (1997). On stigma and its consequences: Evidence from a longitudinal study of men with dual diagnoses of mental illness and substance abuse. *Journal of Health and Social Behavior, 38,* 177–190.

Linnman, C., Rougemont-Bücking, A., Beucke, J. C., Zeffiro, T. A., & Milad, M. R. (2011). Unconditioned responses and functional fear networks in human classical conditioning. *Behavioural Brain Research, 221,* 237–245.

Lisanby, S. H. (2007). Electroconvulsive therapy for depression. *New England Journal of Medicine, 357,* 1939–1945.

Little, T. D., Jones, S. M., Henrich, C. C., & Hawley, P. H. (2003). Disentangling the "whys" from the "whats" of aggressive behavior. *International Journal of Behavioral Development, 27,* 122–123.

Littlewood, R. A., Venable, P. A., Carey, M. P., & Blair D. C. (2008). The association of benefit finding to psychosocial and health behavior adaptation among HIV+ men and women. *Journal of Behavioral Medicine, 31,* 145–155.

Liu, J. H., & Latané, B. (1998). Extremitization of attitudes: Does thought- and discussion-induced polarization cumulate? *Basic and Applied Social Psychology, 20,* 103–110.

Livesley, W. J., & Lang, K. L. (2005). Differentiating normal, abnormal, and disordered personality. *European Journal of Personality, 19,* 257–268.

Livingston, J. D., & Boyd, J. E. (2010). Correlates and consequences of internalized stigma for people living with mental illness: A systematic review and meta-analysis. *Social Science & Medicine, 71,* 2150–2161.

Lobbestael, J., Arntz, A., & Bernstein, D. P. (2010). Disentangling the relationship between different types of childhood maltreatment and personality disorders. *Journal of Personality Disorders, 24,* 285–295.

Lobo, I. A., & Harris, R. A. (2008). GABA$_A$ receptors and alcohol. *Pharmacology, Biochemistry and Behavior, 90,* 90–94.

LoBue, V., & DeLoache, J. (2008). Detecting the snake in the grass: Attention to fear-relevant stimuli by adults and young children. *Psychological Science, 19,* 284–289.

LoBue, V., Coan, J. A., Thrasher, C., & DeLoache, J. S. (2011). Prefrontal asymmetry and parent-rated temperament in infants. *PLOSone, 6,* e22694.

Locher, P., Frens, J., & Overbeeke, K. (2008). The influence of induced positive affect and design experience on aesthetic responses to new product designs. *Psychology of Aesthetics, Creativity, and the Arts, 2,* 1–7.

Lockhart, R. S., & Craik, F. I. M. (1990). Levels of processing: A retrospective commentary on a framework for memory research. *Canadian Journal of Psychology, 44,* 87–122.

Loftus, E. F. (1979). *Eyewitness testimony.* Cambridge, MA: Harvard University Press.

Loftus, E. F., & Palmer, J. C. (1974). Reconstruction of automobile destruction: An example of the interaction between language and memory. *Journal of Verbal Learning and Verbal Behavior, 13,* 585–589.

Loftus, E. F., Miller, D. G., & Burns, H. J. (1978). Semantic integration of verbal information into a visual memory. *Journal of Experimental Psychology: Human Learning and Memory, 4,* 19–31.

Lohmann, R. I. (2010). How evaluating dreams makes history: Asabano examples. *History & Anthropology, 21,* 227–249.

London, B., Nabet, B., Fisher, A. R., White, B., Sammel, M. D., & Doty, R. L. (2008). Predictors of prognosis in patients with olfactory disturbance. *Annals of Neurology, 63,* 159–166.

Loomis, A. L., Harvey, E. N., & Hobart, G. A. (1937). Cerebral states during sleep as studied by human brain potentials. *Journal of Experimental Psychology, 21,* 127–144.

Lord, C. G., Paulson, R. M., Sia, T. L., Thomas, J. C., & Lepper, M. R. (2004). Houses built on sand: Effects of exemplar stability on susceptibility to attitude change. *Journal of Personality and Social Psychology, 87,* 733–749.

Lourenço, O., & Machado, A. (1996). In defense of Piaget's theory: A reply to 10 common criticisms. *Psychological Review, 103,* 143–164.

Louw, M. E. (2010). Dreaming up futures: Dream omens and magic in Bishkek. *History & Anthropology, 21,* 277–292.

Lovibond, S. H., Adams, M., & Adams, W. G. (1979). The effects of three experimental prison environments on the behavior of nonconflict volunteer subjects. *Australian Psychologist, 14,* 273–285.

Luborsky, L., & Barrett, M. S. (2006). The history and empirical status of key psychoanalytic concepts. *Annual Review of Clinical Psychology, 2,* 1–19.

Lucas, R. E. (2007). Adaptation and the set-point model of subjective well-being: Does happiness change after major life events? *Current Directions in Psychological Science, 16,* 75–79.

Luchins, A. S. (1942). Mechanization in problem solving. *Psychological Monographs, 54* (No. 248).

Luijk, M. P. C. M., Tharner, A., Bakermans-Kranenburg, M. J., van IJzendoorn, M. H., Jaddoe, V. W. V., Hofman, A., Verhulst, F. C., &

Tiemeier, H. (2011). The association between parenting and attachment security is moderated by a polymorphism of the mineralocorticoid receptor gene: Evidence for differential susceptibility. *Biological Psychology, 88,* 37–40.

Lumpkin, E. A., & Caterina, M. J. (2007). Mechanisms of sensory transduction in the skin. *Nature, 445,* 858–865.

Lynch, D. J., McGrady, A., Alvarez, E., & Forman, J. (2005). Recent life changes and medical utilization in an academic family practice. *The Journal of Nervous and Mental Disease, 193,* 633–635.

Lynch, W. C., Heil, D. P., Wagner, E., & Havens, M. D. (2008). Body dissatisfaction mediates the association between body mass index and risky weight control behaviors among White and Native American adolescent girls. *Appetite, 51,* 210–213.

Lynn, S. J., & Kirsch, I. (2006). *Essentials of clinical hypnosis: An evidence-based approach.* Washington, DC: American Psychological Association.

Lynn, S. J., Lock, T., Loftus, E. F., Krackow, E., & Lilienfeld, S. O. (2003). The remembrance of things past: Problematic memory recovery techniques in psychotherapy. In S. O. Lilienfeld, S. J. Lynn, & J. M. Lohr (Eds.), *Science and pseudoscience in clinical psychology* (pp. 205–239). New York: Guilford Press.

Lyubomirsky, S., King, L., & Diener, E. (2005). The benefits of frequent positive affect: Does happiness lead to success? *Psychological Bulletin, 131,* 803–855.

Ma, V., & Schoeneman, T. J. (1997). Individualism versus collectivism: A comparison of Kenyan and American self-concepts. *Basic and Applied Social Psychology, 19,* 261–273.

Macaluso, M., Kalia, R., Ali, F., & Khan, A. Y. (2010). The role of benzodiazepines in the treatment of anxiety disorders: A clinical review. *Psychiatric Annals, 40,* 605–610.

Macchi Cassia, V., Turati, C., & Simion, F. (2004). Can a nonspecific bias toward top-heavy patterns explain newborns' face preference? *Psychological Science, 15,* 379–383.

Maccoby, E. E. (2002). Gender and group processes: A developmental perspective. *Current Directions in Psychological Science, 11,* 54–58.

Maccoby, E. E., & Martin, J. A. (1983). Socialization in the context of the family: Parent–child interaction. In E. M. Hetherington (Ed.), *Handbook of child psychology: Vol. 4. Socialization, personality, and social development* (pp. 1–101). New York: Wiley.

MacDonald, G., & Leary, M. R. (2005). Why does social exclusion hurt? The relationship between social and physical pain. *Psychological Bulletin, 131,* 202–223.

Machado, M., & Einarson, T. R. (2010). Comparison of SSRIs and SNRIs in major depressive disorder: A meta-analysis of head-to-head randomized clinical trials. *Journal of Clinical Pharmacy and Therapeutics, 35,* 177–188.

MacKay, D. G., James, L. E., Hadley, C. B., & Fogler, K. A. (2011). Speech errors of amnesic H.M.: Unlike everyday slips-of-the-tongue. *Cortex, 47,* 377–408.

MacKay, D. G., James, L. E., Taylor, J. K., & Marian, D. E. (2007). Amnesic H.M. exhibits parallel deficits and sparing in language and memory: Systems versus binding theory accounts. *Language and Cognitive Processes, 22,* 377–452.

Mackinnon, S. P., Jordan, C. H., & Wilson, A. E. (2011). Birds of a feather sit together: Physical similarity predicts seating choice. *Personality and Social Psychology Bulletin, 37,* 879–892.

Macknik, S. L., King. M., Randi, J., Robbins, A., Teller, Thompson, J., & Martinez-Conde, S. (2008). Attention and awareness in stage magic: Turning tricks into research. *Nature Research Neuroscience,*

Macmillan, M. (2008). Phineas Gage—Unravelling the myth. *Psychologist, 21,* 828–831.

MacSweeney, M., Capek, C. M., Campbell, R., & Woll, B. (2008). The signing brain: The neurobiology of sign language. *Trends in Cognitive Sciences, 12,* 432–440.

Maddux, W. W., Mullen, E., & Galinsky, A. D. (2008). Chameleons bake bigger pies and take bigger pieces: Strategic behavioral mimicry facilitates negotiation outcomes. *Journal of Experimental Social Psychology, 44,* 461–468.

Maddux, W. W., Yang, H., Falk, C., Adam, H., Adair, W., Endo, Y., Carmon, Z., & Heine, S. J. (2010). For whom is parting with possessions more painful? Cultural differences in the endowment effect. *Psychological Science, 21,* 1910–1917.

Madon, S., Guyll, M., Buller, A. A., Scherr, K. C., Willard, J., & Spoth, R. (2008). The mediation of mothers' self-fulfilling effects on their children's alcohol use: Self-verification, informational conformity, and modeling processes. *Journal of Personality and Social Psychology, 95,* 369–384.

Madsen, E. A., Tunney, R. J., Gieldman, G., Plotkin, H. C., Dunbar, R. I. M., Richardson, J.-M., & McFarland, D. (2007). Kinship and altruism: A cross-cultural experimental study. *British Journal of Psychology, 98,* 339–359.

Maguen, S., Floyd, F. J., Bakeman, R., & Armistead, L. (2002). Developmental milestones and disclosure of sexual orientation among gay, lesbian, and bisexual youths. *Applied Developmental Psychology, 23,* 219–233.

Mahon, B. Z., & Caramazza, A. (2011). What drives the organization of object knowledge in the brain? *Trends in Cognitive Sciences, 15,* 97–103.

Maier, N. R. F. (1931). Reasoning in humans: II. The solution of a problem and its appearance in consciousness. *Journal of Comparative Psychology, 12,* 181–194.

Maier, S. F., & Seligman, M. E. P. (1976). Learned helplessness: Theory and evidence. *Journal of Experimental Psychology, 105,* 3–46.

Mailis-Gagnon, A., & Nicholson, K. (2011). On the nature of nondermatomal somatosensory deficits. *The Clinical Journal of Pain, 27,* 76–84.

Ma-Kellams, C., & Blascovich, J. (2011). Culturally divergent responses to mortality salience. *Psychological Science, 22,* 1019–1024.

Male, L. H., & Smulders, T. V. (2007). Memory for food caches: Not just retrieval. *Behavioral Ecology, 18,* 456–459.

Malinowski, B. (1927). *Sex and repression in savage society.* London: Routledge & Kegan Paul.

Manber, R., Kraemer, H. C., Arnow, B. A., Trivedi, M. H., Rush, A. J., Thase, M. E., Rothbaum, B. O., Klein, D. N., Kocsis, J. H., Gelenberg, A. J., & Keller, M. E. (2008). Faster remission of chronic depression with combined psychotherapy and medication than with each therapy alone. *Journal of Consulting and Clinical Psychology, 76,* 459–467.

Mandel, D. R., Jusczyk, P. W., & Pisoni, D. B. (1995). Infants' recognition of the sound patterns of their own names. *Psychological Science, 5,* 314–317.

Manning, R., Levine, M., & Collins, A. (2007). The Kitty Genovese murder and the social psychology of helping: The parable of the 38 witnesses. *American Psychologist, 62,* 555–562.

Mannino, C. A., Snyder, M., & Omoto, A. M. (2011). Why do people get involved? Motivations for volunteerism and other forms of social action. In D. Dunning (Ed.), *Social motivation* (pp. 127–146). New York: Psychology Press.

Manoussaki, D., Chadwick, R. S., Ketten, D. R., Arruda, J., Dimitriadis, E. K., & O'Malley, J. T. (2008). *Proceedings of the National Academy of Sciences, 105,* 6162–6166.

Manuck, S. B., Flory, J. D., Muldoon, M. F., & Ferrell, R. E. (2002). Central nervous system serotonergic responsivity and aggressive disposition in men. *Physiology & Behavior, 77,* 705–709.

Marcia, J. E. (1966). Development and validation of ego-identity status. *Journal of Personality and Social Psychology, 3,* 551–558.

Marcia, J. E. (1980). Identity in adolescence. In J. Adelson (Ed.), *Handbook of adolescent psychology* (pp. 159–187). New York: Wiley.

Marcus, A. D. (1990, December 3). Mists of memory cloud some legal proceedings. *Wall Street Journal,* p. B1.

Mares, M. L., & Woodard, E. (2005). Positive effects of television on children's social interactions: A meta-analysis. *Media Psychology, 7,* 301–322.

Mark, T. L., Levit, K. R., Buck, J. A., Coffey, R. M., & Vandivort-Warren, R. (2007). Mental health treatment expenditure trends, 1986–2003. *Psychiatric Services, 58,* 1041–1048.

Markman, K. D., Lindberg, M. J., Kray, L. J., & Galinsky, A. D. (2007). Implications of counterfactual structure for creative generation and analytic problem solving. *Personality and Social Psychology Bulletin, 33,* 312–324.

Markou, A. (2007). Metabotropic glutamate receptor antagonists: Novel therapeutics for nicotine dependence and depression? *Biological Psychiatry, 61,* 17–22.

Markus, H. R., & Kitayama, S. (1991). Culture and the self: Implications for cognition, emotion, and motivation. *Psychological Review, 98,* 224–253.

Markus, H. R., Mullally, P. R., & Kitayama, S. (1997). Selfways: Diversity in modes of cultural participation. In U. Neisser & D. A. Jopling (Eds.), *The conceptual self in context* (pp. 13–61). Cambridge, UK: Cambridge University Press.

Markus, H. R., Uchida, Y., Omoregie, H., Townsend, S. S. M. & Kitayama, S. (2006). Going for the gold: Models of agency in Japanese and American contexts. *Psychological Science, 17,* 103–112.

Marshal, M. P., Dietz, L. J., Friedman, M. S., Stall, R., Smith, H. A., McGinley, J., Thoma, B., Murray, P. J., D'Augelli, A. R., & Brent, D. A. (2011). Suicidality and depression disparities between sexual minority and heterosexual youth: A meta-analytic review. *Journal of Adolescent Health, 49,* 115–123.

Marshall, G. D., & Zimbardo, P. G. (1979). Affective consequences of inadequately explained physiological arousal. *Journal of Personality and Social Psychology, 37,* 970–988.

Martin, C. L., & Ruble, D. N. (2010). Patterns of gender development. *Annual Review of Psychology, 61,* 353–381.

Martin, L. T., Burns, R. M., & Schonlau, M. (2010). Mental disorders among gifted and nongifted youth. A selected review of the epidemiologic literature. *Gifted Child Quarterly, 54,* 31–41.

Martínez-Taboas, A., Canino, G., Wang, M. Q., Garcías, P., & Bravo, M. (2006). Prevalence of victimization correlates of pathological dissociation in a community sample of youths. *Journal of Traumatic Stress, 19,* 439–448.

Martin-Fardon, R., Lorentz, C. U., Stuempfig, N. D., & Weiss, F. (2005). Priming with BTCP, a dopamine reuptake blocker, reinstates cocaine-seeking and enhances cocaine cue-induced reinstatement. *Pharmacology, Biochemistry, and Behavior, 92,* 46–54.

Maslach, C. (1979). Negative emotional biasing of unexplained arousal. *Journal of Personality and Social Psychology, 37,* 953–969.

Maslach, C., & Leiter, M. (2008). Early predictors of job burnout and engagement. *Journal of Applied Psychology, 93,* 498–512.

Maslow, A. H. (1968). *Toward a psychology of being* (2nd ed.). Princeton, NJ: Van Nostrand.

Maslow, A. H. (1970). *Motivation and personality* (rev. ed.). New York: Harper & Row.

Mason, L. E. (1997, August 4). Divided she stands. *New York,* pp. 42–49.

Mason, R. A., & Just, M. A. (2007). Lexical ambiguity in sentence comprehension. *Brain Research, 1146,* 115–127.

Mason, T. B. A. II, & Pack, A. I. (2007). Pediatric parasomnias. *Sleep, 30,* 141–151.

Masten, A. S. (2011). Resilience in children threatened by extreme adversity: Frameworks for research, practice, and translational synergy. *Development and Psychopathology, 23,* 493–506.

Masters, W. H., & Johnson, V. E. (1966). *Human sexual response.* Boston: Little, Brown.

Masters, W. H., & Johnson, V. E. (1970). *Human sexual inadequacy.* Boston: Little, Brown.

Masters, W. H., & Johnson, V. E. (1979). *Homosexuality in perspective.* Boston: Little, Brown.

Mather, M., & Sutherland, M. R. (2011). Arousal-based competition in perception and memory. *Perspectives on Psychological Science, 6,* 114–133.

Matson, J. L., & Boisjoli, J. A. (2009). The token economy for children with intellectual disability and/or autism: A review. *Research in Developmental Disabilities, 30,* 240–248.

Maxwell, J. C. (2005). Party drugs: Properties, prevalence, patterns, and problems. *Substance Abuse & Misuse, 40,* 1203–1240.

Maxwell, J. S., & Davidson, R. J. (2007). Emotion as motion: Asymmetries in approach and avoidant actions. *Psychological Science, 18,* 1113–1119.

May, R. (1975). *The courage to create.* New York: Norton.

Mayer, J. D., Roberts, R. D., & Barsade, S. G. (2008a). Human abilities: Emotional intelligence. *Annual Review of Psychology, 59,* 507–536.

Mayer, J. D., Salovey, P., & Caruso, D. R. (2008b). Emotional intelligence: New ability or eclectic traits. *American Psychologist, 63,* 503–517.

Maynard, A. E. (2008). What we thought we knew and how we came to know it: Four decades of cross-cultural research from a Piagetian point of view. *Human Development, 51,* 56–65.

McAdams, D. P. (1988). Biography, narrative, and lives: An introduction. *Journal of Personality, 56,* 1–18.

McAdams, D. P., & Olson, B. D. (2010). Personality development: Continuity and change over the life course. *Annual Review of Psychology, 61,* 517–542.

McAdams, D. P., Bauer, J. J., Sakaeda, A. R., Anyidoho, N. A., Machado, M. A., Magrino-Failla, K., White, K. W., & Pals, J. L. (2006). Continuity and change in the life story: A longitudinal study of autobiographical memories in emerging adulthood. *Journal of Personality, 74,* 1371–1400.

McAllister, H. A. (1996). Self-serving bias in the classroom: Who shows it? Who knows it? *Journal of Educational Psychology, 88,* 123–131.

McCabe, C., & Rolls, E. T. (2007). Umami: A delicious flavor formed by convergence of taste and olfactory pathways in the human brain. *European Journal of Neuroscience, 25,* 1855–1864.

McClelland, D. C. (1961). *The achieving society.* Princeton, NJ: Van Nostrand.

McClelland, D. C. (1971). *Motivational trends in society.* Morristown, NJ: General Learning Press.

McClelland, D. C., Atkinson, J. W., Clark, R. A., & Lowell, E. L. (1953). *The achievement motive.* New York: Appleton-Century-Crofts.

McClelland, D. C., Atkinson, J. W., Clark, R. A., & Lowell, E. L. (1976). *The achievement motive* (2nd ed.). New York: Irvington.

McCrae, R. R., & Costa, P. T., Jr. (2008). The five-factor theory of personality. In O. P. John, R. W. Robins, & L. A. Pervin (Eds.), *The handbook of personality: Theory and research* (3rd ed., 159–181). New York: Guilford Press.

McCrae, R. R., Costa, P. T. Jr., & Martin, T. A. (2005). The NEO-PI-3: A more readable revised NEO Personality Inventory. *Journal of Personality Assessment, 84,* 261–270.

McCrae, R. R., Costa, P. T. Jr., Martin, T. A., Oryol, V. E., Rukavishnikov, A. A., Senin, I. G., Hřebíčková, M., & Urbánek, T. (2004). Consensual validation of personality traits across cultures. *Journal of Research in Personality, 38,* 179–201.

McCrae, R. R., Kurtz, J. E., Yamagata, S., & Terracciano, A. (2011). Internal consistency, retest reliability, and their implications for personality scale validity. *Personality and Social Psychology Review, 15,* 28–50.

McCrae, R. R., Scally, M., Terracciano, A., Abecasis, G. R., & Costa, P. T., Jr. (2010). An alternative to the search for single polymorphisms: Toward molecular personality scales for the five-factor model. *Journal of Personality and Social Psychology, 99,* 1014–1024.

McCrae, S. M., & Hirt, E. R. (2001). The role of ability judgments in self-handicapping. *Personality & Social Psychology Bulletin, 27,* 1378–1389.

McCrae, S. M., Hirt, E. R., & Milner, B. J. (2008). She works hard for the money: Valuing effort underlies gender differences in behavioral self-handicapping. *Journal of Experimental Social Psychology, 44*, 292–311.

McDaniel, M. A., Agarwal, P. K., Huelser, B. J., McDermott, K. B., & Roediger, H. L., III. (2011). Test-enhanced learning in a middle school science classroom: The effects of quiz frequency and placement. *Journal of Educational Psychology, 103*, 399–414.

McGlone, F., & Reilly, D. (2010). The cutaneous sensory system. *Neuroscience and Biobehavioral Reviews, 34*, 148–159.

McGovern, K., & Baars, B. J. (2007). Cognitive theories of consciousness. In P. D. Zelazo, M. Moscovitch, & E. Thompson (Eds.), *The Cambridge handbook of consciousness* (pp. 177–205). New York: Cambridge University Press.

McGrath, M. P., & Zook, J. M. (2011). Maternal control of girls versus boys: Relations to empathy and persuasive style with peers. *Journal of Child and Family Studies, 20*, 57–65.

McGregor, H. A., & Elliot, A. J. (2002). Achievement goals as predictors of achievement-relevant processes prior to task engagement. *Journal of Educational Psychology, 94*, 381–395.

McGue, M., Elkins, I., Walden, B., & Iacono, W. G. (2005). Perceptions of the parent-adolescent relationship: A longitudinal investigation. *Developmental Psychology, 41*, 971–984.

McHale, S. M., Crouter, A. C., & Whiteman, S. D. (2003). The family contexts of gender development in childhood and adolescence. *Social Development, 12*, 125–148.

McLeod, B. D., Wood, J. J., & Avny, S. B. (2011). Parenting and child anxiety disorders. In D. McKay & E. A. Storch (Eds.), *Handbook of child and adolescent anxiety disorders* (pp. 213–228). New York: Springer.

McLeskey, J., Landers, E., Williamson, P., & Hoppey, D. (2011). Are we moving toward educating students with disabilities in less restrictive settings? *Journal of Special Education, 26*, 60–66.

McNamara, D. S., & Magliano, J. (2009). Toward a comprehensive model of comprehension. In B. H. Ross (Ed.), *The psychology of learning and motivation* (Vol. 51, pp. 298–384). Burlington, MA: Academic Press.

McNeil, B. J., Pauker, S. G., Sox, H. C., Jr., & Tversky, A. (1982). On the elicitation of preferences for alternative therapies. *New England Journal of Medicine, 306*, 1259–1262.

McRae, K., Hughes, B., Chopra, S., Gabrieli, J. D. E., Gross, J. J., & Ochsner, K. N. (2010). The neural bases of distraction and reappraisal. *Journal of Cognitive Neuroscience, 22*, 248–262.

Mead, M. (1928). *Coming of age in Samoa.* New York: Morrow.

Mead, M. (1939). *From the South Seas: Studies of adolescence and sex in primitive societies.* New York: Morrow.

Meador, B. D., & Rogers, C. R. (1979). Person-centered therapy. In R. J. Corsini (Ed.), *Current psychotherapies* (2nd ed., pp. 131–184). Itasca, IL: Peacock.

Meeus, W. (2011). The study of adolescent identity formation 2000–2010: A review of longitudinal research. *Journal of Research on Adolescence, 21*, 75–94.

Meichenbaum, D. (1977). *Cognitive-behavior modification: An integrative approach.* New York: Plenum.

Meichenbaum, D. (1985). *Stress inoculation training.* New York: Pergamon Press.

Meichenbaum, D. (1993). Changing conceptions of cognitive behavior modification: Retrospect and prospect. *Journal of Consulting and Clinical Psychology, 61*, 202–204.

Meineri, S., & Guéguen, N. (2011). "I hope I'm not disturbing you, am I?" Another operationalization of the foot-in-the-mouth paradigm. *Journal of Applied Social Psychology, 41*, 965–975.

Melzack, R. (1973). *The puzzle of pain.* New York: Basic Books.

Melzack, R. (1980). Psychological aspects of pain. In J. J. Bonica (Ed.), *Pain.* New York: Raven Press.

Melzack, R. (2005). Evolution of the neuromatrix theory of pain. *Pain Practice, 5*, 85–94.

Mendelson, J. R., & Rajan, R. (2011). Cortical effects of aging and hearing loss. In J. A. Winer & C. E. Schreiner (Eds.), *The auditory cortex* (pp. 493–501). New York: Springer.

Menzel, R., Kirbach, A., Haass, W.-D., Fischer, B., Fuchs, J., Koblofsky, M., Lehmann, K., Reiter, L., Meyer, H., Nguyen, H., Jones, S., Norton, P., & Greggers, U. (2011). A common frame of reference for learned and communicated vectors in honeybee navigation. *Current Biology, 21*, 645–650.

Mercadillo, R. E., Díaz, J. L., Pasaye, E. H., & Barrios, F. A. (2011). Perception of suffering and compassion experience: Brain gender disparities. *Brain and Cognition, 76*, 5–14.

Mercer, S. (2012). Dispelling the myth of the natural-born linguist. *ELT Journal, 66*, 22–29.

Merton, R. K. (1957). *Social theory and social structures.* New York: The Free Press.

Mesquita, B., & Leu, J. (2007). The cultural psychology of emotion. In S. Kitayama & D. Cohen (Eds.), *Handbook of cultural psychology* (pp. 734–759). New York: Guilford Press.

Metcalfe, J. (2009). Metacognitive judgments and control of study. *Current Directions in Psychological Science, 18*, 159–163.

Meyer, R. G. (2003). *Case studies in abnormal behavior* (6th ed.). Boston: Allyn & Bacon.

Meyers, S. A., & Berscheid, E. (1997). The language of love: The difference a preposition makes. *Personality and Social Psychology Bulletin, 23*, 347–362.

Michalski, R. L., & Shackelford, T. K. (2010). Evolutionary personality psychology: Reconciling human nature and individual differences. *Personality and Individual Differences, 48*, 509–516.

Miklowitz, D. J., & Tompson, M. C. (2003). Family variables and interventions in schizophrenia. In G. P. Sholevar & L. D. Schwoeri (Eds.), *Textbook of family and couples therapy: Clinical applications* (pp. 585–617). Washington, DC: American Psychiatric Publishing.

Mikulincer, M., Florian, V., Cowan, P. A., & Cowan, C. P. (2002). Attachment security in couple relationships: A systematic model and its implications for family dynamics. *Family Process, 41*, 405–434.

Milar, K. S. (2000). The first generation of women psychologists and the psychology of women. *American Psychologist, 55*, 616–619.

Milgram, S. (1965). Some conditions of obedience and disobedience to authority. *Human Relations, 18*, 56–76.

Milgram, S. (1974). Obedience to authority. New York: Harper & Row.

Miller, G. A. (1956). The magic number seven plus or minus two: Some limits in our capacity for processing information. *Psychological Review, 63*, 81–97.

Miller, G. A. (1969). Psychology as a means of promoting human welfare. *American Psychologist, 24*, 1063–1075.

Miller, J. G. (1984). Culture and the development of everyday social explanation. *Journal of Personality and Social Psychology, 46*, 961–978.

Miller, J. G., Bersoff, D. M., & Harwood, R. L. (1990). Perceptions of social responsibilities in India and in the United States: Moral imperatives or personal decisions? *Journal of Personality and Social Psychology, 58*, 33–47.

Miller, K. A., Fisher, P. A., Fetrow, B., & Jordan, K. (2006). Trouble on the journey home: Reunification failures in foster care. *Children and Youth Services Review, 28*, 260–274.

Miller, M. A., & Rahe, R. H. (1997). Life changes scaling for the 1990s. *Journal of Psychosomatic Research, 43*, 279–292.

Miller, N. E. (1978). Biofeedback and visceral learning. *Annual Review of Psychology, 29*, 373–404.

Miller, S. L., & Maner, J. K. (2011). Ovulation as a male mating prime: Subtle signs of women's fertility influence men's mating cognition and behavior. *Journal of Personality and Social Psychology, 100*, 295–308.

Miniño, A. M., Xu, J., & Kochanek, K. D. (2010). Deaths: Preliminary data for 2008. *National Vital Statistics Reports, 59*, 1–52.

Mischel, W. (1968). *Personality and assessment.* New York: Wiley.

Mischel, W. (1973). Toward a cognitive social learning reconceptualization of personality. *Psychological Review, 80*, 252–283.

Mischel, W. (2004). Toward an integrative science of the person. *Annual Review of Psychology, 55*, 1–22.

Mischel, W., & Shoda, Y. (1995). A cognitive-affective system theory of personality: Reconceptualizing situations, dispositions, dynamics, and invariance in personality structure. *Psychological Review, 102*, 246–268.

Mischel, W., & Shoda, Y. (1999). Integrating dispositions and processing dynamics within a unified theory of personality: The cognitive-affective personality system. In L. A. Pervin & O. P. John (Eds.), *Handbook of personality: Theory and research* (2nd ed., pp. 197–218). New York: Guilford Press.

Mishra, J., & Backlin, W. (2007). The effects of altering environmental and instrumental context on the performance of memorized music. *Psychology of Music, 35*, 1–20.

Mitchell, K. J., & Johnson, M. K. (2009). Source monitoring 15 years later: What have we learned from fMRI about the neural mechanisms of source memory? *Psychological Bulletin, 135*, 638–677.

Miyashita, T., Kubik, S., Lewandowski, G., & Guzowski, J. F. (2008). Networks of neurons, networks of genes: An integrated view of memory consolidation. *Neurobiology of Learning and Memory, 89*, 269–284.

Modirrousta, M., & Fellows, L. K. (2008). Medial prefrontal cortex plays a critical and selective role in "feeling of knowing" meta-memory judgments. *Neuropsychologia, 46*, 2958–2965.

Mogil, J. S., Davis, K. D., & Derbyshire, S. W. (2010). The necessity of animal models in pain research. *Pain, 151*, 12–17.

Mohamed, F. B., Faro, S. H., Gordon, N. J., Platek, S. M., Ahmad, H., & Williams, J. M. (2006). Brain mapping of deception and truth telling about an ecologically valid situation: Functional MR imaging and polygraph investigation—initial experience. *Radiology, 238*, 679–688.

Möller, J.-J., Baldwin, D. S., Goodwin, G., Kasper, S., Okasha, A., Stein, D. J., Tandon, R., Versiani, M., & the WPA section on Pharmacopsychiatry. (2008). Do SSRIs or antidepressants in general increase suicidality? WPA Section on Pharmacopsychiatry: Consensus statement. *European Archives of Psychiatry and Clinical Neuroscience, 258* (Suppl. 3), 3–23.

Moncrieff, R. W. (1951). *The chemical senses.* London: Leonard Hill.

Montanari, S. (2010). Translation equivalents and the emergence of multiple lexicons in early trilingual development. *First Language, 30*, 102–125.

Montoya, R. M., & Insko, C. A. (2008). Toward a more complete understanding of the reciprocity of liking effect. *European Journal of Social Psychology, 38*, 477–498.

Morawska, A., & Sanders, M. (2011). Parental use of time out revisited: A useful or harmful parenting strategy? *Journal of Child and Family Studies, 20*, 1–8.

Morgado-Bernal, I. (2011). Learning and memory consolidation: Linking molecular and behavioral data. *Neuroscience, 176*, 12–19.

Morgan, A. H., Hilgard, E. R., & Davert, E. C. (1970). The heritability of hypnotic susceptibility of twins: A preliminary report. *Behavior Genetics, 1*, 213–224.

Moriarty, T. (1975). Crime, commitment and the responsive bystander: Two field experiments. *Journal of Personality and Social Psychology, 31*, 370–376.

Morin, S. F., & Rothblum, E. D. (1991). Removing the stigma: Fifteen years of progress. *American Psychologist, 46*, 947–949.

Morling, B., & Lamoreaux, M. (2008). Measuring culture outside the head: A meta-analysis of individualism-collectivism in cultural products. *Personality and Social Psychology Review, 12*, 199–221.

Morris, J. A., Jordan, C. L., & Breedlove, S. M. (2004). Sexual differentiation of the vertebrate nervous system. *Nature Neuroscience, 7*, 1034–1039.

Morris, T., Moore, M., & Morris, F. (2011). Stress and chronic illness: The case of diabetes. *Journal of Adult Development, 18*, 70–80.

Morry, M. M. (2007). The attraction-similarity hypothesis among cross-sex friends: Relationship satisfaction, perceived similarities, and self-serving perceptions. *Journal of Social and Personal Relationships, 24*, 117–138.

Moscovici, S. (1976). *Social influence and social change.* New York: Academic Press.

Moscovici, S. (1980). Toward a theory of conversion behavior. In L. Berkowitz (Ed.), *Advances in experimental social psychology* (Vol. 13, pp. 209–239). New York: Academic Press.

Moscovici, S. (1985). Social influence and conformity. In G. Lindzey & E. Aronson (Eds.), *The handbook of social psychology* (3rd ed., pp. 347–412). New York: Random House.

Moscovici, S., & Faucheux, C. (1972). Social influence, conformity bias, and the study of active minorities. In L. Berkowitz (Ed.), *Advances in experimental social psychology* (Vol. 6). New York: Academic Press.

Moskowitz, G. B. (2004). *Social cognition: Understanding self and others.* New York: Guilford Press.

Motherwell, L., & Shay, J. J. (2005). (Eds.). *Complex dilemmas in group therapy.* New York: Brunner-Routledge.

Moulson, M. C., Fox, N. A., Zeanah, C. H., & Nelson, C. A. (2009). Early adverse experiences and the neurobiology of facial emotion processing. *Developmental Psychology, 45*, 17–30.

Moulton, E. A., Schmahmann, J. D., Becerra, L., & Borsook, D. (2010). The cerebellum and pain: Passive integrator or active participator? *Brain Research Reviews, 65*, 14–27.

Mueller, A., Mueller, U., Silbermann, A., Reinecker, H., Bleich, S., Mitchell, J. E., & de Zwaan, M. (2008). A randomized, controlled trial of group cognitive-behavioral therapy for compulsive buying disorder: Posttreatment and 6-month follow-up results. *Journal of Clinical Psychiatry, 69*, 1131–1138.

Mulvaney, M. K., & Mebert, C. J. (2007). Parental corporal punishment predicts behavior problems in early childhood. *Journal of Family Psychology, 21*, 389–397.

Munafò, M. R., & Flint, J. (2011). Dissecting the genetic architecture of human personality. *Trends in Cognitive Sciences, 15*, 395–400.

Munafò, M. R., & Johnstone, E. C. (2008). Genes and cigarette smoking. *Addiction, 103*, 893–904.

Murayama, K., Elliot, A. J., & Yamagata, S. (2011). Separation of performance-approach and performance-avoidance achievement goals: A broader analysis. *Journal of Educational Psychology, 103*, 238–256.

Murdoch, B. E. (2010). The cerebellum and language: Historical perspective and review. *Cortex, 46*, 858–868.

Murphy, G. L. (2002). *The big book of concepts.* Cambridge, MA: MIT Press.

Murphy, K. J., Troyer, A. K., Levine, B., & Moscovitch, M. (2008). Episodic, but not semantic, autobiographical memory is reduced in amnestic mild cognitive impairment. *Neuropsychologia, 46*, 3116–3123.

Murty, V. P., Ritchey, M., Adcock, R. A., & LaBar, K. S. (2011). Reprint of: fMRI studies of successful emotional memory encoding: A quantitative meta-analysis. *Neuropsychologia, 49*, 695–705.

Musewicz, J., Marczyk, G., Knauss, L., & York, D. (2009). Current assessment practice, personality measurement, and Rorschach usage by psychologists. *Journal of Personality Assessment, 91*, 453–461.

Mussweiler, T., & Bodenhausen, G. V. (2002). I know you are, but what am I? Self-evaluative consequences of judging in-group and out-group members. *Journal of Personality and Social Psychology, 82*, 19–32.

Myers, K. M., Carlezon, W. A., Jr., & Davis, M. (2011). Glutamate receptors in extinction and extinction-based therapies for psychiatric illness. *Neuropsychopharmacology, 36*, 274–293.

Nadel, L., & Hardt, O. (2011). Update on memory systems and processes. *Neuropsychopharmacology, 36,* 251–273.

Narayan, V. M., Narr, K. L., Phillips, O. R., Thompson, P. M. Toga, A. W., Szeszko, P. R. (2008). Greater regional cortical gray matter thickness in obsessive-compulsive disorder. *NeuroReport, 19,* 1551–1555.

Nash, J. R., Sargent, P. A., Rabiner, E. A., Hood, S. D., Argyropoulos, S. V., Potokar, J. P., Grasby, P. M., & Nutt, D. J. (2008). Serotonin 5-HT$_{1A}$ receptor binding in people with panic disorder: Positron emission tomography study. *The British Journal of Psychiatry, 193,* 229–234.

National Science Foundation, Division of Science Resources Statistics. (2010). *Doctorate Recipients from U.S. Universities: 2009.* Special Report NSF 11-306. Arlington, VA. Available at http://www.nsf.gov/statistics/nsf11306/.

Neath, I., & Crowder, R. G. (1990). Schedules of presentation and temporal distinctiveness in human memory. *Journal of Experimental Psychology: Learning, Memory, and Cognition, 16,* 316–327.

Neath, I., & Surprenant, A. M. (2003). *Human memory: An introduction to research, data, and theory* (2nd ed.). Belmont, CA: Wadsworth.

Neath, I., Brown, G. D. A., McCormack, T., Chater, N., & Freeman, R. (2006). Distinctiveness models of memory and absolute identification: Evidence for local, not global, effects. *Quarterly Journal of Experimental Psychology, 59,* 121–135.

Neider, M., Pace-Schott, E. F., Forselius, E., Pittman, B., & Morgan, P. T. (2011). Lucid dreaming and ventromedial versus dorsolateral prefrontal task performance. *Consciousness and Cognition, 20,* 234–244.

Neiss, M. B., Sedikides, C., & Stevenson, J. (2006). Genetic influences on level and stability of self-esteem. *Self and Identity, 5,* 247–266.

Neisser, U. (1967). *Cognitive psychology.* New York: Appleton-Century-Crofts.

Neitz, J., & Neitz, M. (2011). The genetics of normal and defective color vision. *Vision Research, 51,* 633–651.

Nelson, D. A., Mitchell, C., & Yang, C. (2008). Intent attributions and aggression: A study of children and their parents. *Journal of Abnormal Child Psychology, 36,* 793–806.

Nelson, T. D. (2006). *The psychology of prejudice* (2nd ed.). Boston: Allyn & Bacon.

Nes, R. B., Røysamb, E., Tambs, K., Harris, J. R., & Reichborn-Kjennerud, T. (2006). Subjective well-being: Genetic and environmental contributions to stability and change. *Psychological Medicine, 36,* 1033–1042.

Nettelbeck, T., & Wilson, C. (2005). Intelligence and IQ: What teachers should know. *Educational Psychology, 25,* 609–630.

Nettle, D. (2006). The evolution of personality variation in humans and other animals. *American Psycholgist, 61,* 622–631.

Neubauer, A. C., & Fink, A. (2009). Intelligence and neural efficiency. *Neuroscience and Biobehavioral Reviews, 33,* 1004–1023.

Nevéus, T., Cnattingius, S., Olsson, U., & Hetta, J. (2001). Sleep habits and sleep problems among a community sample of schoolchildren. *Acta Paediatr, 90,* 1450–1455.

Newcomb, T. M. (1929). *The consistency of certain extrovert-introvert behavior traits in 50 problem boys* (Contributions to Education, No. 382). New York: Columbia University Press.

Newell, A., & Simon, H. A. (1972). *Human problem solving.* Englewood Cliffs, NJ: Prentice Hall.

Newman, D. A., & Lyon, J. S. (2009). Recruitment efforts to reduce adverse impact: Targeted recruiting for personality, cognitive ability, and diversity. *Journal of Applied Psychology, 94,* 298–317.

Newman, G. E., Keil, F. C., Kuhlmeier, V. A., & Wynn, K. (2010). Early understandings of the link between agents and order. *PNAS, 107,* 17140–17145.

Niaura, R., Todaro, J. F., Stroud, L., Spiro, A., III, Ward, K. D., & Weiss, S. (2002). Hostility, the metabolic syndrome, and incident coronary heart disease. *Health Psychology, 21,* 588–593.

Niccols, A. (2007). Fetal alcohol syndrome and the developing socio-emotional brain. *Brain and Cognition, 65,* 135–142.

NICHD Early Child Care Research Network. (1997). The effects of infant child care on infant-mother attachment security: Results of the NICHD Study of Early Child Care. *Child Development, 68,* 860–879.

NICHD Early Child Care Research Network. (2006). Infant-mother attachment classification: Risk and protection in relation to changing maternal caregiving quality. *Developmental Psychology, 42,* 38–58.

Nielsen, B. D., Pickett, C. L., & Simonton, D. K. (2008). Conceptual versus experimental creativity: Which works best on convergent and divergent thinking tasks? *Psychology of Aesthetics, Creativity, and the Arts, 2,* 131–138.

Nielsen, S. F., Hjorthøj, C. R., Erlangsen, A., & Nordentoft, M. (2011). Psychiatric disorders and mortality among people in homeless shelters in Denmark: A nationwide register-based cohort study. *Lancet, 377,* 2205–2214.

Nielsen, T. A., & Stenstrom, P. (2005). What are the memory sources of dreaming? *Nature, 437,* 1286–1289.

Nigg, C. R., Borrelli, B., Maddock, J., & Dishman, R. K. (2008). A theory of physical activity maintenance. *Applied Psychology: An International Review, 57,* 544–560.

Nir, Y., & Tononi, G. (2010). Dreaming and the brain: From phenomenology to neurophysiology. *Trends in Cognitive Sciences, 14,* 88–100.

Nock, M. K., Borges, G., Bromet, E. J., Cha, C. B., Kessler, R. C., & Lee, S. (2008). Suicide and suicidal behavior. *Epidemiologic Reviews, 30,* 133–154.

Nooteboom, S., & Quené, H. (2008). Self-monitoring and feedback: A new attempt to find the main cause of lexical bias in phonological speech errors. *Journal of Memory and Language, 58,* 837–861.

Norcross, J. C., Karpiak, C. P., & Lister, K. M. (2005). What's an integrationist? A study of self-identified and (occasionally) eclectic psychologists. *Journal of Clinical Psychology, 61,* 1587–1594.

Norman, G. J., Velicer, W. F., Fava, J. L., & Prochaska, J. O. (1998). Dynamic topology clustering within the stages of change for smoking cessation. *Addictive Behaviors, 23,* 139–153.

Norman, G. J., Velicer, W. F., Fava, J. L., & Prochaska, J. O. (2000). Cluster subtypes within stage of change in a representative sample of smokers. *Addictive Behaviors, 25,* 183–204.

Norman, W. T. (1963). Toward an adequate taxonomy of personality attributes: Replicated factor structure in peer nomination personality ratings. *Journal of Abnormal and Social Psychology, 66,* 574–583.

Norman, W. T. (1967). *2,800 personality trait descriptors: Normative operating characteristics for a university population* (Research Rep. No. 083101-T). Ann Arbor: University of Michigan Press.

Nosko, A., T., T.-T., Lawford, H., & Pratt, M. W. (2011). How do I love thee? Let me count the ways: Parenting during adolescence, attachment styles, and romantic narratives in emerging adulthood. *Developmental Psychologyi, 47,* 645–657.

Nosofsky, R. M. (2011). The generalized context model: An exemplar model of classification. In E. M. Pothos & A. J. Wills (Eds.), *Formal approaches in categorization* (pp. 18–39). New York: Cambridge University Press.

Novick, L. R., & Bassok, M. (2005). Problem solving. In K. J. Holyoak & R. G. Morrison (Eds.), *Cambridge handbook of thinking and reasoning* (pp. 321–349). New York: Cambridge University Press.

Nowak, M. A., & Sigmund, K. (2005). Evolution of indirect reciprocity. *Nature, 437,* 1291–1298.

Nrugham, L., Larsson, B., & Sund, A. M. (2008). Predictors of suicidal acts across adolescence: Influences of family, peer and individual factors. *Journal of Affective Disorders, 109,* 35–45.

Nutt, R. L., & Stanton, M. (2011). Family psychology specialty practice. *Couple and Family Psychology: Research and Practice, 1,* 92–105.

Ogden, C. L., & Carroll, M. D. (2010). *Prevalence of overweight, obesity, and extreme obesity among adults: United States, trends 1960–1962 through 2007–2008*. National Center for Health Statistics. Retrieved from www.cdc.gov/nchs/data/hestat/obesity_adult_07_08/obesity_adult_07_08.pdf.

Öhman, A., & Mineka, S. (2001). Fears, phobias, and preparedness: Toward an evolved module of fear and fear learning. *Psychological Review, 108,* 483–522.

Olsson, I. A. S., Hansen, A. K., & Sandøe, P. (2007). Ethics and refinement in animal research. *Science, 317,* 1680.

Oman, D., Hedberg, J., & Thoresen, C. E. (2006). Passage meditation reduces perceived stress in health professionals: A randomized, controlled trial. *Journal of Consulting and Clinical Psychology, 74,* 714–719.

Omoto, A. M., & Snyder, M. (2002). Considerations of community: The context and process of volunteerism. *American Behavioral Scientist, 45,* 846–867.

Oppenheimer, D. M., & Frank, M. C. (2008). A rose in any other font would not smell as sweet: Effects of perceptual fluency on categorization. *Cognition, 106,* 1178–1194.

Opton, E. M. Jr. (1970). Lessons of My Lai. In N. Sanford & C. Comstock (Eds.), *Sanctions for evil.* San Francisco: Jossey-Bass.

Opton, E. M. Jr. (1973). "It never happened and besides they deserved it." In W. E. Henry & N. Stanford (Eds.), *Sanctions for evil* (pp. 49–70). San Francisco: Jossey-Bass.

Orban, G. A., van Essen, D., & Vandeuffel, W. (2004). Comparative mapping of higher areas in monkeys and humans. *Trends in Cognitive Science, 8,* 315–324.

Orth, U., Robins, R. W., & Roberts, B. W. (2008). Low self-esteem prospectively predicts depression in adolescence and young adulthood. *Journal of Personality and Social Psychology, 95,* 695–708.

Ossenkopp, K.-P., Biagi, E., Cloutier, C. J., Chan, M. Y. T., Kavaliers, M., & Cross-Mellor, S. K. (2011). Acute corticosterone increases conditioned spontaneous orofacial behaviors but fails to influence dose related LiCl-induced conditioned "gaping" responses in a rodent model of anticipatory nausea. *European Journal of Pharmacology, 660,* 358–362.

Ozer, D. J., & Reise, S. P. (1994). Personality assessment. *Annual Review of Psychology, 45,* 357–388.

Packer, I. K. (2008). Specialized practice in forensic psychology: Opportunities and obstacles. *Professional Psychology: Research and Practice, 39,* 245–249.

Pagel, J. F. (2008). The burden of obstructive sleep apnea and associated excessive sleepiness. *Journal of Family Practice, 57,* S3–S8.

Pagnoni, G., & Cekic, M. (2007). Age effects on gray matter volume and attentional performance in Zen meditation. *Neurobiology of Aging, 28,* 1623–1627.

Paivio, A. (2006). *Mind and its evolution: A dual coding theoretical interpretation.* Mahwah, NJ: Lawrence Erlbaum Associates, Inc.

Paller, K. A., & Voss, J. L. (2004). Memory reactivation and consolidation during sleep. *Learning & Memory, 11,* 664–670.

Pandi-Perumal, S. R., Srinivasan, V., & Spence, D. W., & Cardinali, D. P. (2007). Rold of the melatonin system in the control of sleep: Therapeutic implications. *CNS Drugs, 21,* 995–1018.

Papafragou, A., Li, P., Choi, Y., & Han, C.-H. (2007). Evidentiality in language and cognition. *Cognition, 103,* 253–299.

Paris, J. (2003). *Personality disorders over time: Precursors, course, and outcome.* Washington, DC: American Psychiatric Publishing.

Parker, A. M., Bruine de Bruin, W., & Fischhoff, B. (2007). Maximizers versus satisficers: Decision-making styles, competence, and outcomes. *Judgment and Decision Making, 2,* 342–350.

Parr, W. V., & Siegert, R. (1993). Adults' conceptions of everyday memory failures in others: Factors that mediate the effects of target age. *Psychology and Aging, 8,* 599–605.

Parrino, L., Milioli, G., De Paolis, F., Grassi, A., & Terzano, M. G. (2009). Paradoxical insomnia: The role of CAP and arousals in sleep misperception. *Sleep Medicine, 10,* 1139–1145.

Paterson, H. M., Kemp, R. I., & Ng, J. R. (2011). Combating co-witness contamination: Attempting to decrease the negative effects of discussion on eye-witness memory. *Applied Cognitive Psychology, 25,* 43–52.

Patson, N. D., & Warren, T. (2011). Building complex reference objects from dual sets. *Journal of Memory and Language, 64,* 443–459.

Paus, T. (2005). Mapping brain maturation and cognitive development during adolescence. *Trends in Cognitive Sciences, 9,* 60–68.

Pavlov, I. P. (1927). *Conditioned reflexes* (G. V. Anrep, Trans.). London: Oxford University Press.

Pavlov, I. P. (1928). *Lectures on conditioned reflexes: Twenty-five years of objective study of higher nervous activity (behavior of animals)* (Vol. 1, W. H. Gantt, Trans.). New York: International Publishers.

Peck, D. F. (2010). The therapist-client relationship, computerized self-help and active therapy ingredients. *Clinical Psychology and Psychotherapy, 17,* 147–153.

Peckham, A. D., McHugh, K., & Otto, M. W. (2010). A meta-analysis of the magnitude of biased attention in depression. *Depression and Anxiety, 27,* 1135–1142.

Pedersen, A. F., Zachariae, R., & Bovbjerg, D. H. (2009). Psychological stress and antibody response to influenza vaccination: A meta-analysis. *Brain, Behavior, and Immunity, 23,* 427–433.

Penick, S., Smith, G., Wienske, K., & Hinkle, L. (1963). An experimental evaluation of the relationship between hunger and gastric motility. *American Journal of Physiology, 205,* 421–426.

Penke, L., Denissen, J. J. A., & Miller, G. F. (2007). The evolutionary genetics of personality. *European Journal of Personality, 21,* 549–587.

Pennebaker, J. W. (1990). *Opening up: The healing power of confiding in others.* New York: Morrow.

Pennebaker, J. W. (1997). Writing about emotional experiences as a therapeutic process. *Psychological Science, 8,* 162–166.

Penton-Voak, I. (2011). In retreat from nature? Successes and concerns in Darwinian approaches to facial attractiveness. *Journal of Evolutionary Psychology, 2011,* 173–193.

Perahia, D. G. S., Pritchett, Y. L., Kajdasz, D. K., Bauer, M., Jain, R., Russell, J. M., Walker, D. J., Spencer, K. A., Froud, D. M., Raskin, J., & Thase, M. E. (2008). A randomized, double-blind comparison of duloxetine and venlafaxine in the treatment of patients with major depressive disorder. *Journal of Psychiatric Research, 42,* 22–34.

Perls, F. S. (1969). *Gestalt therapy verbatim.* Lafayette, CA: Real People Press.

Perrin, P. B., Heesacker, M., Tiegs, T. J., Swan, L. K., Lawrence, A. W., Jr., Smith, M. B., Carrillo, R. J., Cawood, R. L., & Mejia-Millan, C. M. (2011). Aligning Mars and Venus: The social construction and instability of gender differences in romantic relationships. *Sex Roles, 64,* 613–628.

Perry, D. G., & Pauletti, R. E. (2011). Gender and adolescent development. *Journal of Research on Adolescence, 21,* 61–74.

Peters, E., Västfjäll, D., Slovic, P., Mertz, C. K., Mazzocco, K., & Dickert, S. (2006). Numeracy and decision making. *Psychological Science, 17,* 407–413.

Peterson, C., & Seligman, M. E. P. (1984). Causal explanations as a risk factor for depression: Theory and evidence. *Psychological Review, 91,* 347–374.

Peterson, C., & Vaidya, R. S. (2001). Explanatory style, expectations, and depressive symptoms. *Personality and Individual Differences, 31,* 1217–1223.

Peterson, H. M., & Kemp, R. I. (2006). Co-witness talk: A survey of eyewitness discussion. *Psychology Crime & Law, 12,* 181–191.

Peterson, L. R., & Peterson, M. J. (1959). Short-term retention of individual verbal items. *Journal of Experimental Psychology, 58,* 193–198.

Petrie, K. J., Booth, R. J., & Pennebaker, J. W. (1998). The immunological effects of thought suppression. *Journal of Personality and Social Psychology, 75,* 1264–1272.

Petrie, K. J., Fontanilla, I., Thomas, M. G., Booth, R. J., & Pennebaker, J. W. (2004). Effect of written emotional expression on immune function in patients with human immunodeficiency virus infection: A randomized trial. *Psychosomatic Medicine, 66,* 272–275.

Petry, N. M., & Roll, J. M. (2011). Amount of earnings during prize contingency management treatment is associated with posttreatment abstinence outcomes. *Experimental and Clinical Psychopharmacology, 19,* 445–450.

Pettigrew, T. F. (2008). Future directions for intergroup contact theory and research. *International Journal of Intercultural Relations, 32,* 187–199.

Pettigrew, T. F., Christ, O., Wagner, U., & Stellmacher, J. (2007). Direct and indirect intergroup contact effects on prejudice: A normative interpretation. *International Journal of Intercultural Relations, 31,* 41–425.

Pettigrew, T. F., Tropp, L. R., Wagner, U., & Christ, O. (2011). Recent advances in intergroup contact theory. *International Journal of Intercultural Relations, 35,* 271–280.

Petty, R. E., & Briñol, P. (2008). Persuasion: From single to multiple to meta-cognitive processes. *Perspectives on Psychological Sciences, 3,* 137–147.

Petty, R. E., Cacioppo, J. T., Strathman, A. J., & Priester, J. R. (2005). To think or not to think: Exploring two routes to persuasion. In T. C. Brock & M. C. Green (Eds.), *Persuasion: Psychological insights and perspectives* (2nd ed., pp. 81–116). Thousand Oaks, CA: Sage.

Pfeiffer, P. N., Heisler, M., Piette, J. D., Rogers, M. A. M., & Valenstein, M. (2011). Efficacy of peer support interventions for depression: A meta-analysis. *General Hospital Psychiatry, 33,* 29–36.

Phillips, M. C., Meek, S. W., & Vendemia, J. M. C. (2011). Understanding the underlying structure of deceptive behaviors. *Personality and Individual Differences, 50,* 783–789.

Piaget, J. (1929). *The child's conception of the world.* New York: Harcourt, Brace.

Piaget, J. (1954). *The construction of reality in the child.* New York: Basic Books.

Piaget, J. (1965). *The moral judgment of the child* (M. Gabain, Trans.). New York: Macmillan.

Piaget, J. (1977). *The development of thought: Equilibrium of cognitive structures.* New York: Viking Press.

Piccione, C., Hilgard, E. R., & Zimbardo, P. G. (1989). On the degree of stability of measured hypnotizability over a 25-year period. *Journal of Personality and Social Psychology, 56,* 289–295.

Pickel, K. L. (2009). The weapon focus effect on memory for female versus male perpetrators. *Memory, 17,* 664–678.

Pietrzak, R. H., Goldstein, R. B., Southwick, S. M., & Grant, B. F. (2011). Prevalence and Axis I comorbidity of full and partial posttraumatic stress disorder in the United States: Results from wave 2 of the national epidemiological survey on alcohol and related conditions. *Journal of Anxiety Disorders, 25,* 456–465.

Pischke, C. R., Scherwitz, L., Weidner, G., & Ornish, D. (2008). Long-term effects of lifestyle changes on well-being and cardiac variables among coronary heart disease patients. *Health Psychology, 27,* 584–592.

Plaks, J., Levy, S. R., & Dweck, C. (2009). Lay theories of personality: Cornerstones of meaning in social cognition. *Social and Personality Psychology Compass, 3,* 1069–1081.

Plomin, R., & Petrill, S. A. (1997). Genetics and intelligence: What's new? *Intelligence, 24,* 53–77.

Plomin, R., & Spinath, F. M. (2004). Intelligence: Genetics, genes, and genomics. *Journal of Personality and Social Psychology, 86,* 112–129.

Podell, J. L., & Kendall, P. C. (2011). Mothers and fathers in family cognitive-behavioral therapy for anxious youth. *Journal of Child and Family Studies, 20,* 182–195.

Poelmans, G., Pauls, D. L., Buitelaar, J. K., & Franke, B. (2011). *American Journal of Psychiatry, 168,* 365–377.

Polivy, J., & Herman, C. P. (1999). Distress and eating: Why do dieters overeat? *International Journal of Eating Disorders, 26,* 153–164.

Polivy, J., Herman, C. P., & Deo, R. (2010). Getting a bigger slice of the pie. Effects on eating and emotion in restrained and unrestrained eaters. *Appetite, 55,* 426–430.

Pollo, A., Carlino, E., & Benedetti, F. (2011). Placebo mechanisms across different conditions: From the clinical setting to physical performance. *Philosophical Transactions of the Royal Society B, 366,* 1790–1798.

Porter, L. W., & Lawler, E. E. (1968). *Managerial attitudes and performance.* Homewood, IL: Irwin.

Posada, R., & Wainryb, C. (2008). Moral development in a violent society: Columbian children's judgments in the context of survival and revenge. *Child Devleopment, 79,* 882–898.

Poucet, B. (1993). Spatial cognitive maps in animals: New hypotheses on their structure and neural mechanisms. *Psychological Review, 100,* 163–182.

Poulin, S. R., Maguire, M., Metraux, S., & Culhane, D. P. (2010). Service use and costs for persons experiencing chronic homelessness in Philadelphia: A population-based study. *Psychiatric Services, 61,* 1093–1098.

Poulin-Dubois, D., Blaye, A., Coutya, J., & Bialystok, E. (2011). The effects of bilingualism on toddlers' executive functioning. *Journal of Experimental Child Psychology, 108,* 567–579.

Powell, R. A. (2011). Little Albert, lost or found: Further difficulties with the Douglas Merritte hypothesis. *History of Psychology, 14,* 106–107.

Powers, M. B., & Emmelkamp, P. M. G. (2008). Virtual reality exposure therapy for anxiety disorders: A meta-analysis. *Journal of Anxiety Disorders, 22,* 561–569.

Powley, T. (1977). The ventromedial hypothalamic syndrome, satiety, and a cephalic phase hypothesis. *Psychological Review, 84,* 89–126.

Prangnell, S. J. (2010). Behavioural interventions for self injurious behaviour: A review of recent evidence (1998–2008). *British Journal of Learning Disabilities, 38,* 259–270.

Premack, D. (1965). Reinforcement theory. In D. Levine (Ed.), *Nebraska symposium on motivation* (pp. 128–180). Lincoln: University of Nebraska Press.

Premack, D. (1971). Language in chimpanzee? *Science, 172,* 808–822.

Pressman, L. J., Loo, S. K., Carpenter, E. M., Asarnow, J. R., Lynn, D., McCracken, J. T., McGough, J. J., Lubke, G. H., Yang, M. H., & Smalley, S. L. (2006). Relationship of family environment and parental psychiatric diagnosis to impairment in ADHD. *Journal of the American Academy of Child and Adolescent Psychiatry, 45,* 346–354.

Preusse, F., van der Meer, E., Deshpande, G., Krueger, F., & Wartenburger, I. (2011). Fluid intelligence allows flexilble recruitment of the parieto-frontal network in analogical reasoning. *Frontiers in Human Neuroscience, 5,* Article 22.

Prosser, D., Johnson, S., Kuipers, E., Szmukler, G., Bebbington, P., & Thornicroft, G. (1997). Perceived sources of work stress and satisfaction among hospital and community mental health staff, and their relation to mental health, burnout, and job satisfaction. *Journal of Psychosomatic Research, 43,* 51–59.

Pyszczynski, T., Greenberg, J., Solomon, S., Arndt, J., & Schimel, J. (2004). Why do people need self-esteem? A theoretical and empirical review. *Psychological Bulletin, 130,* 435–468.

Quine, W. V. O. (1960). *Word and object.* Cambridge, MA: The MIT Press.

Quittner, A. L., Modi, A., Lemanek, K. L., Ievers-Landis, C. E., & Rapoff, M. A. (2008). Evidence-based assessment of adherence to medical treatments in pediatric psychology. *Journal of Pediatric Psychology, 33,* 916–936.

Radke, A. K., Rothwell, P. E., & Gewirtz, J. C. (2011). An anatomical basis for opponent processes mechanisms of opiate withdrawal. *The Journal of Neuroscience, 31,* 7533–7539.

Radua, J., van den Heuvel, O. A., Surguladze, S., & Mataix-Cols, D. (2010). Meta-analytical comparison of voxel-based morphometry studies in obsessive compulsive disorder vs. other anxiety disorders. *Archives of General Psychiatry, 67*, 701–711.

Radvansky, G. A. (2006). *Human memory.* Boston: Allyn & Bacon.

Rahman, Q., & Wilson, G. D. (2003). Born gay? The psychobiology of human sexual orientation. *Personality and Individual Differences, 34*, 1337–1382.

Rahman, R. A., & Melinger, A. (2007). When bees hamper the production of honey: Lexical interference from associates in speech production. *Journal of Experimental Psychology: Learning, Memory, and Cognition, 33*, 604–614.

Raizen, D. M., & Wu, M. N. (2011). Genome-wide association studies of sleep disorders. *Chest, 139*, 446–452.

Ramachandran, V. S. (2011). *The tell-tale brain.* New York: Norton.

Ramachandrappa, S., & Farooqi, I. S. (2011). Genetic approaches to understanding human obesity. *The Journal of Clinical Investigation, 121*, 2080–2086.

Ramirez, G., & Beilock, S. L. (2011). Writing about testing worries boosts exam performance in the classroom. *Science, 331*, 211–213.

Ramírez, J. M., & Andreu, J. M. (2006). Aggression, and some related psychological constructs (anger, hostility, and impulsivity): Some comments from a research project. *Neuroscience and Biobehavioral Reviews, 30*, 276–291.

Rapoport, J. L. (1989, March). The biology of obsessions and compulsions. *Scientific American*, pp. 83–89.

Rasmussen, T., & Milner, B. (1977). The role of early left-brain injury in determining lateralization of cerebral speech functions. *Annals of the New York Academy of Sciences, 299*, 355–369.

Ratcliff, R., & McKoon, G. (1978). Priming in item recognition: Evidence for the propositional structure of sentences. *Journal of Verbal Learning and Verbal Behavior, 17*, 403–418.

Rau, H., Bührer, M., & Wietkunat, R. (2003). Biofeedback of R-wave-to-pulse interval normalizes blood pressure. *Applied Psychophysiology and Biofeedback, 28*, 37–46.

Rawson, R. A., Maxwell, J., & Rutkowski, B. (2007). OxyContin abuse: Who are the users? *The American Journal of Psychiatry, 164*, 1634–1636.

Ray, W. J., Keil, A., Mikuteit, A., Bongartz, W., & Elbert, T. (2002). High resolution EEG indicators of pain responses in relation to hypnotic susceptibility and suggestion. *Biological Psychology, 60*, 17–36.

Recanzone, G. H., & Sutter, M. L. (2008). The biological basis of audition. *Annual Review of Psychology, 59*, 119–142.

Recipients from U.S. Universities: 2009. Special Report NSF 11–306. Arlington, VA. Available

Regan, R. T. (1971). Effects of a favor and liking on compliance. *Journal of Experimental Social Psychology, 7*, 627–639.

Reis, H. T., & Aron, A. (2008). Love: What is it, why does it matter, and how does it operate? *Perspectives on Psychological Science, 3*, 80–86.

Reis, S. M., & Renzulli, J. S. (2010). Is there still a need for gifted education? An examination of current research. *Learning and Individual Differences, 20*, 308–317.

Remick, A. K., Polivy, J., & Pliner, P. (2009). Internal and external moderators of the effect of variety on food intake. *Psychological Bulletin, 135*, 434–451.

Renzulli, J. S. (2005). The three-ring conception of giftedness: A developmental model for promoting creative productivity. In R. J. Sternberg & J. E. Davidson (Eds.), *Conceptions of giftedness* (2nd ed., pp. 246–279). New York: Cambridge University Press.

Rescorla, R. A. (1966). Predictability and number of pairings in Pavlovian fear conditioning. *Psychonomic Science, 4*, 383–384.

Rescorla, R. A. (1988). Pavlovian conditioning: It's not what you think it is. *American Psychologist, 43*, 151–160.

Reyna, V. R., Nelson, W. L., Han, P. K., & Dieckmann, N. F. (2009). How numeracy influences risk comprehension and medical decision making. *Psychological Bulletin, 135*, 943–973.

Reynolds, J. S., & Perrin, N. A. (2004). Mismatches in social support and psychosocial adjustment. *Health Psychology, 23*, 425–430.

Rhodes, G. (2006). The evolutionary psychology of facial beauty. *Annual Review of Psychology, 57*, 199–226.

Rhodes, M. G., & Tauber, S. K. The influence of delaying judgments of learning on metacognitve accuracy: A meta-analytic review. *Psychological Bulletin, 137*, 131–148.

Ribeiro, S. C., Kennedy, S. E., Smith, Y. R., Stohler, C. S., & Zubieta, J. K. (2005). Interface of physical and emotional stress regulation through the endogenous opioid system and μ-opioid receptors. *Progress in Neuro-Psychopharmacology & Biological Psychiatry, 29*, 1264–1280.

Richards, D. (2009). Features and benefits of online counselling: Trinity College online mental health community. *British Journal of Guidance and Counselling, 37*, 231–242.

Rief, W., & Broadbent, E. (2007). Explaining medically unexplained symptoms—models and mechanisms. *Clinical Psychology Review, 27*, 821–841.

Riela, S., Rodriguez, G., Aron, A., Xu, Xiaomeng, & Acevedo, B. P. (2010). Experiences of falling in love: Investigating culture, ethnicity, gender, and speed. *Journal of Social and Personal Relationships, 27*, 473–493.

Riley, B. (2011). Genetic studies of schizophrenia. In J. D. Clelland (Ed.), *Genomics, proteomics, and the nervous system* (pp. 333–380). New York: Springer.

Rinck, M. (2008). Spatial situation models and narrative comprehension. In M. A. Gluck, J. R. Anderson, & S. M. Kosslyn (Eds.), *Memory and mind: A festschrift for Gordon H. Bower* (pp. 359–370). Mahwah, NJ: Erlbaum.

Ritchie, P. L.-J. (2010). Annual report of the International Union of Psychological Science (IUPsyS). *International Journal of Psychology, 45*, 398–404.

Rizolatti, G., & Sinigaglia, C. (2010). The functional role of the parieto-frontal mirror circuit: Interpretations and misinterpretations. *Nature Reviews Neuroscience, 11*, 264–274.

Roberson, D., Davidoff, J., Davies, I. R. L., & Shapiro, L. R. (2005). Color categories: Evidence for the cultural relativity hypothesis. *Cognitive Psychology, 50*, 378–411.

Robert, G., & Zadra, A. (2008). Measuring nightmare and bad dream frequency: Impact of retrospective and prospective instruments. *Journal of Sleep Research, 17*, 132–139.

Roberts, A., Cash, T. F., Feingold, A., & Johnson, B. T. (2006). Are Black–White differences in females' body dissatisfaction decreasing? A meta-analytic review. *Journal of Consulting and Clinical Psychology, 74*, 1121–1131.

Rodd, J. M., Longe, O. A., Randall, B., & Tyler, L. K. (2010). The functional organisation of the fronto-temporal language system: Evidence from syntactic and semantic ambiguity. *Neuropsychologia, 48*, 1324–1335.

Rodriguez, E. T., & Tamis-LeMonda, C. S. (2011). Trajectories of the home learning environment across the first 5 years: Associations with children's vocabulary and literacy skills at prekindergarten. *Child Development, 82*, 1058–1075.

Roediger, H. L., III. (2008). Relativity of remembering: Why the laws of memory vanished. *Annual Review of Psychology, 59*, 225–254.

Roediger, H. L., III., & Butler, A. C. (2011). The critical role of retrieval practice in long-term retention. *Trends in Cognitive Sciences, 15*, 20–27.

Roediger, H. L., III., & Karpicke, J. D. (2006). Test-enhanced learning: Taking memory tests improves long-term retention. *Psychological Science, 17*, 249–255.

Roenneberg, T., Kuehnle, T., Juda, M., Kantermann, T., Allebrandt, K., Gordijn, M., & Merrow, M. (2007). Epidemiology of the human circadian clock. *Sleep Medicine Reviews, 11*, 429–438.

Roese, N. J., & Summerville, A. (2005). What we regret most . . . and why. *Personality and Social Psychology Bulletin, 31*, 1273–1285.

Rogers, C. R. (1947). Some observations on the organization of personality. *American Psychologist, 2,* 358–368.

Rogers, C. R. (1951). *Client-centered therapy.* Boston: Houghton Mifflin Company.

Rogers, C. R. (1951). *Client-centered therapy: Its current practice, implications and theory.* Boston: Houghton Mifflin.

Rogers, C. R. (1959). A theory of therapy, personality, and interpersonal relationships, as developed in the client-centered framework. In S. Koch (Ed.), *Psychology: A study of a science* (Vol. 3). New York: McGraw-Hill.

Rogers, C. R. (1977). *On personal power: Inner strength and its revolutionary impact.* New York: Delacorte.

Rogoff, B. (1990). *Apprenticeship in thinking: Cognitive development in social context.* New York: Oxford University Press.

Rohrer, J. H., Baron, S. H., Hoffman, E. L., & Swinder, D. V. (1954). The stability of autokinetic judgment. *Journal of Abnormal and Social Psychology, 49,* 595–597.

Roid, G. (2003). *Stanford-Binet intelligence scale* (5th ed.). Itasca, IL: Riverside Publishing.

Roisman, G. I., Clausell, E., Holland, A., Fortuna, K., & Elieff, C. (2008). Adult romantic relationships as contexts of human development: A multimethod comparison among same-sex couples with opposite-sex dating, engaged, and married dyads. *Developmental Psychology, 44,* 91–101.

Romer, M., Lehrner, J., Wymelbeke, V. V., Jiang, T., Deecke, L. & Brondel, L. (2006). Does modification of olfacto-gustatory stimulation diminish sensory-specific satiety in humans? *Physiology & Behavior, 87,* 469–477.

Rorschach, H. (1942). *Psychodiagnostics: A diagnostic test based on perception.* New York: Grune & Stratton.

Rosch, E. H. (1973). Natural categories. *Cognitive Psychology, 4,* 328–350.

Rosch, E. H. (1978). Principles of categorization. In E. Rosch & B. B. Lloyd (Eds.), *Cognition and categorization* (pp. 27–48). Hillsdale, NJ: Erlbaum.

Rosch, E. H., Mervis, C. B., Gray, W. D., Johnson, D. M., & Boyes-Braem, P. (1976). Basic objects in natural categories. *Cognitive Psychology, 8,* 382–439.

Rosch, E., & Mervis, C. B. (1975). Family resemblances: Studies in the internal structure of categories. *Cognitive Psychology, 7,* 573–605.

Roscoe, J. A., Morrow, G. R., Aapro, M. S., Molassiotis, A., & Olver, I. (2011). Anticipatory nausea and vomiting. *Supportive Care in Cancer, 19,* 1533–1538.

Rose, A. J., & Rudolph, K. D. (2006). A review of sex- differences in peer relationship processes: Potential trade-offs for the emotional and behavioral development of girls and boys. *Psychological Bulletin, 132,* 98–131.

Rose, M. E., & Grant, J. E. (2008). Pharmacotherapy for methamphetamine dependence: A review of the pathophysiology of methamphetamine addiction and the theoretical basis and efficacy of pharmacotherapeutic interventions. *Annals of Clinical Psychiatry, 20,* 145–155.

Rosenhan, D. L. (1973). On being sane in insane places. *Science, 179,* 250–258.

Rosenhan, D. L. (1975). The contextual nature of psychiatric diagnoses. *Journal of Abnormal Psychology, 84,* 462–474.

Rosenthal, A. M. (1964). *Thirty-eight witnesses.* New York: McGraw-Hill.

Rosenthal, R., & Fode, K. L. (1963). The effect of experimenter bias on the performance of the albino rat. *Behavioral Science, 8,* 183–189.

Rosenthal, R., & Jacobson, L. F. (1968). *Pygmalion in the classroom: Teacher expectations and intellectual development.* New York: Holt.

Rosenzweig, M. R. (1996). Aspects of the search for neural mechanisms of memory. *Annual Review of Psychology, 47,* 1–32.

Rosenzweig, M. R. (1999). Effects of differential experience on brain and cognition throughout the life span. In S. H. Broman & J. M. Fletcher (Eds.), *The changing nervous system: Neurobehavioral consequences of early brain disorders* (pp. 25–50). New York: Oxford University Press.

Ross, C. A. (2009). Errors of logic and scholarship concerning dissociative identity disorder. *Journal of Child Sexual Abuse, 18,* 221–231.

Ross, L. (1977). The intuitive psychologist and his shortcomings. In L. Berkowitz (Ed.), *Advances in experimental social psychology* (Vol. 10, pp. 173–220). New York: Academic Press.

Ross, L. (1988). Situational perspectives on the obedience experiments. [Review of the obedience experiments: A case study of controversy in social science]. *Contemporary Psychology, 33,* 101–104.

Ross, L., & Nisbett, R. E. (1991). *The person and the situation: Perspectives of social psychology.* New York: McGraw-Hill.

Ross, L., Amabile, T., & Steinmetz, J. (1977). Social roles, social control and biases in the social perception process. *Journal of Personality and Social Psychology, 37,* 485–494.

Ross, W. (2011). Ethical issues involved in online counseling. *Journal of Psychological Issues in Organizational Culture, 2,* 54–66.

Rothbart, M. K. (2007). Temperament, development, and personality. *Current Directions in Psychological Science, 16,* 207–212.

Rothbaum, B. O., Anderson, P., Zimand, E., Hodges, L., Lang, D., & Wilson, J. (2006). Virtual reality exposure therapy and standard (in vivo) exposure therapy in the treatment of fear of flying. *Behavior Therapy, 37,* 80–90.

Rothman, D. J. (1971). *The discovery of the asylum: Social order and disorder in the new republic.* Boston: Little, Brown.

Rothrauff, T., & Cooney, T. M. (2008). The role of generativity in psychological well-being: Does it differ for childless adults and parents? *Journal of Adult Development, 15,* 148–159.

Rotter, J. B. (1954). *Social learning and clinical psychology.* Englewood Cliffs, NJ: Prentice-Hall.

Rotter, J. B. (1966). Generalized expectancies for internal versus external locus of control of reinforcement. *Psychological Monographs, 80* (Whole No. 609).

Rouse, S. V., Greene, R. L., Butcher, J. N., Nichols, D. S., & Williams, C. L. (2008). What do the MMPI-2 Restructured Clinical Scales reliably measure? Answers from multiple research settings. *Journal of Personality Assessment, 90,* 435–442.

Roussi, P. (2002). Discriminative facility in perceptions of control and its relation to psychological distress. *Anxiety, Stress, & Coping: An International Journal, 15,* 179–191.

Roussi, P., Krikeli, V., Hatzidimitriou, C., & Koutri, I. (2007). Patterns of coping, flexibility in coping and psychological distress in women diagnosed with breast cancer. *Cognitive Therapy and Research, 31,* 97–109.

Rozin, P., & Fallon, A. E. (1987). A perspective on disgust. *Psychological Review, 94,* 23–41.

Rozin, P., Millman, L., & Nemeroff, C. (1986). Operation of the laws of sympathetic magic in disgust and other domains. *Journal of Personality and Social Psychology, 50,* 703–712.

Rubin, D. C., & Kontis, T. C. (1983). A schema for common cents. *Memory & Cognition, 11,* 335–341.

Ruby, M. B., Dunn, E. W., Perrino, A., Gillis, R., & Viel, S. (2011). The invisible benefits of exercise. *Health Psychology, 30,* 67–74.

Ruch, R. (1937). *Psychology and life.* Glenview, IL: Scott, Foresman.

Rucklidge, J. J. (2010). Gender differences in attention-deficit/hyperactivity disorder. *Psychiatric Clinics of North America, 33,* 357–373.

Rudd, M. D., Berman, A. L., Joiner, T. E. Jr., Nock, M. K., Silverman, M. M., Mandrusiak, M., Van Orden, K., & Witte, T. (2006). Warning signs for suicide: Theory, research, and clinical applications. *Suicide and Life-Threatening Behavior, 36,* 255–262.

Ruitenbeek, H. M. (1973). *The first Freudians.* New York: Jason Aronson.

Ruiz, J. R., Labayen, I., Ortega, F. B., Legry, V., Moreno, L. A., Dallongeville, J., Martínez-Gómez, D., Bokor, S., Manios, Y., Ciarapica, D., Gottrand, F., De Henauw, S., Molnár, D., Sjöström, M., & Meirhaeghe, A. (2010). Attenuation of the effect of the *FTO* rs9939609 polymorphism on total and central body fat by physical activity in adolescents. *Archives of Pediatric & Adolescent Medicine, 164,* 328–333.

Rule, N. O., & Ambady, N. (2008). The face of success: Inferences from chief executive officers' appearance predict company profits. *Psychological Science, 19,* 109–111.

Rule, N. O., Rosen, K. S., Slepian, M. L., & Ambady, N. (2011). Mating interest improves women's accuracy in judging male sexual orientation. *Psychological Science, 22,* 881–886.

Rummel-Kluge, C., Komossa, K., Schwarz, S., Hunger, H., Schmid, F., Lobos, C. A., Kissling, W., Davis, J. M., & Leucht, S. (2010). Head-to-head comparisons of metabolic side effects of second generation antipsychotics in the treatment of schizophrenia: A systematic review. *Schizophrenia Research, 123,* 225–233.

Runco, M. A. (1991). *Divergent thinking.* Norwood, NJ: Ablex.

Runco, M. A. (2007). *Creativity: Theories and themes: Research, development, and practice.* San Diego, CA: Elsevier Academic Press.

Ruscio, A. M. Brown, T. A., Chiu, W. T., Sareen, J., Stein, M. B., & Kessler, R. C. (2008). Social fears and social phobia in the USA: Results from the National Comorbidity Survey Replication. *Psychological Medicine, 38,* 15–28.

Rutter, P. A., & Behrendt, A. E. (2004). Adolescent suicide risk: Four psychosocial factors. *Adolescence, 39,* 295–302.

Ryder, R. D. (2006). Speciesism in the laboratory. In P. Singer (Ed.), *In defense of animals: The second wave.* Oxford, UK: Blackwell.

Sachdev, P., Mondraty, N., Wen, W., & Gulliford, K. (2008). Brains of anorexia nervosa patients process self-images differently from non-self-images: An fMRI study. *Neuropsychologia, 46,* 2161–2168.

Sachdeva, S., Singh, P., & Medin, D. (2011). Culture and the quest for universal principles of moral reasoning. *International Journal of Psychology, 46,* 161–176.

Sack, R. L. (2010). Jet lag. *The New England Journal of Medicine, 362,* 440–447.

Saffran, J., Hauser, M., Seibel, R., Kapfhamer, J., Tsao, F., & Cushman, F. (2008). Grammatical pattern learning by human infants and cotton-top tamarin monkeys. *Cognition, 107,* 479–500.

Sai, F. Z. (2005). The role of the mother's voice in developing mother's face preference: Evidence for intermodal perceptional at birth. *Infant and Child Development, 14,* 29–50.

Salihu, H. M., & Wilson, R. E. (2007). Epidemiology of prenatal smoking and perinatal outcomes. *Early Human Development, 83,* 713–720.

Salthouse, T. A. (2006). Mental exercise and mental aging: Evaluating the validity of the "use it or lose it" hypothesis. *Perspectives on Psychological Science, 1,* 68–87.

Salvy, S.-J., Jarrin, D., Paluch, R., Irfan, N., & Pliner, P. (2007). Effects of social influence on eating in couples, friends and strangers. *Appetite, 49,* 92–99.

Salvy, S.-J., Kieffer, E., & Epstein, L. H. (2008). Effects of social context on overweight and normal-weight children's food selection. *Eating Behaviors, 9,* 190–196.

Salzinger, S., Ng-Mak, D. S., Feldman, R. S., Kam, C. M., & Rosario, M. (2006). Exposure to community violence: Processes that increase the risk for inner-city middle school children. *Journal of Early Adolescence, 26,* 232–266.

Samuel, A. G. (1997). Lexical activation produces potent phonemic percepts. *Cognitive Psychology, 32,* 97–127.

Samuel, A. G. (2011). Speech perception. *Annual Review of Psychology, 62,* 49–72.

Samuelson, M., Foret, M., Baim, M., Lerner, J., Fricchione, G., Benson, H., Dusek, J., & Yeung, A. (2010). Exploring the effectiveness of a comprehensive mind–body intervention for medical symptom relief. *The Journal of Alternative and Complementary Medicine, 16,* 187–192.

Sanderson, C. A., Rahm, K. B., & Beigbeder, S. A. (2005). The link between pursuit of intimacy goals and satisfaction in close same-sex friendships: An examination of the underlying processes. *Journal of Social and Personal Relationships, 22,* 75–98.

Sandrini, M., Umiltà, C., & Rusconi, E. (2011). The use of transcranial magnetic stimulation in cognitive neuroscience: A new synthesis of methodological issues. *Neuroscience and Biobehavioral Reviews, 35,* 516–536.

Sandstrom, M. J., & Cramer, P. (2003). Girls' use of defense mechanisms following peer rejection. *Journal of Personality, 71,* 605–627.

Santhi, N., Aeschbach, D., Horowitz, T. S., & Czeisler, C. A. (2008). The impact of sleep timing and bright light exposure on attentional impairment during night work. *Journal of Biological Rhythms, 23,* 341–352.

Santiago, C. D., Wadsworth, M. E., & Stump, J. (2011). Socioeconomic status, neighborhood disadvantage, and poverty-related stress: Prospective effects on psychological syndromes among diverse low-income families. *Journal of Economic Psychology, 32,* 218–230.

Sapir, E. (1964). *Culture, language, and personality.* Berkeley: University of California Press. (Original work published 1941)

Sargent, J. D., Tanski, S., Stoolmiller, M., & Hanewinkel, R. (2010). Using sensation seeking to target adolescents for substance use interventions. *Addiction, 105,* 506–514.

Satir, V. (1967). *Conjoint family therapy* (rev. ed.). Palo Alto, CA: Science and Behavior Books.

Savage-Rumbaugh, S., Shanker, S. G., & Taylor, T. J. (1998). *Apes, language, and the human mind.* New York: Oxford University Press.

Savic, I., & Lindström, P. (2008). PET and MRI show differences in cerebral asymmetry and functional connectivity between homo- and heterosexual subjects. *PNAS, 105,* 9403–9408.

Schachter, S. (1971a). *Emotion, obesity and crime.* New York: Academic Press.

Schalock, R. L., Luckasson, R. A., & Shogren, K. A. (2007). The renaming of *mental retardation*: Understanding the change to the term *intellectual disability*. *Intellectual and Developmental Disabilities, 45,* 116–124.

Schank, R. C., & Abelson, R. P. (1977). *Scripts, plans, goals, and understanding.* Hillsdale, NJ: Erlbaum.

Schachter, S. (1971b). Some extraordinary facts about obese humans and rats. *American Psychologist, 26,* 129–144.

Scherr, K. C., Madon, S., Guyll, M., Willard, J., & Spoth, R. (2011). Self-verification as a mediator of mothers' self-fulfilling effects on adolescents' educational attainment. *Personality and Social Psychology Bulletin, 37,* 587–600.

Schick, B., Marschark, M., & Spencer, P. E. (Eds.) (2006). *Advances in the sign language development of deaf children.* New York: Oxford University Press.

Schlitz, M. (1997). *Dreaming for the community: Subjective experience and collective action among the Anchuar Indians of Ecuador.* Research proposal. Marin, CA: Institute of Noetic Sciences.

Schloeg, H., Percik, R., Horstmann, A., Villringer, A., & Stumvoloo, M. (2011). Peptide hormones regulating appetite—focus on neuroimaging studies. *Diabetes/Metabolism Research and Reviews, 27,* 104–112.

Schlosser, D. A., Zinberg, J. L., Loewy, R. L., Casey-Cannon, S., O'Brien, M. P., Bearden, C. E., Vinogradov, S., & Cannon, T. D. (2010). Predicting the longitudinal effects of the family environment on prodromal symptoms and functioning in patients at-risk for psychosis. *Schizophrenia Research, 118,* 69–75.

Schmader, T., Johns, M., & Forbes, C. (2008). An integrated process model of stereotype threat effects on performance. *Psychological Review, 115,* 336–356.

Schmitt, D. P. (2003). Universal sex differences in desire for sexual variety: Tests from 52 nations, 6 continents, and 13 islands. *Journal of Personality and Social Psychology, 85,* 85–104.

Schmitt, D. P., Allik, J., McCrae, R. R., & Benet-Martinez, V. (2007). The geographic distribution of Big Five personality traits: Patterns and profiles of human self-description across 56 nations. *Journal of Cross-Cultural Psychology, 38,* 173–212.

Schneider, K., & May, R. (1995). *The psychology of existence: An integrative, clinical perspective.* New York: McGraw-Hill.

Scholz, U., Schüz, B., Ziegelmann, J., Lippke, S., & Schwarzer, R. (2008). Beyond behavioural intentions: Planning mediates between intentions and physical activity. *British Journal of Health Psychology, 13*, 479–494.

Schousboe, K., Visscher, P. M., Erbas, B., Kyvik, K. O., Hopper, J. L., Henriksen, J. E., Heitmann, B. L., & Sørensen, T. I. A. (2004). Twin study of genetic and environmental influences on adult body size, shape, and composition. *International Journal of Obesity, 28*, 39–48.

Schredl, M., & Erlacher, D. (2008). Relation between waking sport activities, reading, and dream content in sports students and psychology students. *The Journal of Psychology, 142*, 267–275.

Schredl, M., & Reinhard, I. (2011). Gender differences in nightmare frequency: A meta-analysis. *Sleep Medicine Reviews, 15*, 115–121.

Schueller, S. M. (2009). Promoting wellness: Integrating community and positive psychology. *Journal of Community Psychology, 37*, 922–937.

Schutter, D. J. L. G. (2008). Antidepressant efficacy of high-frequency transcranial magnetic stimulation over the left dorsolateral prefrontal cortex in double-blind sham-controlled designs: A meta-analysis. *Psychological Medicine*

Schwab, C., Bugnyar, T., Schloegl, C., & Kotrschal, K. (2008). Enhanced social learning between siblings in common ravens, *Corvus corax. Animal Behaviour, 75*, 501–508.

Schwartz, B., Ward, A., Monterosso, J., Lyubomirsky, S., White, K., & Lehman, D. R. (2002). Maximizing versus satisficing: Happiness is a matter of choice. *Journal of Personality and Social Psychology, 83*, 1178–1197.

Schwarzkopf, D. S., Sterzer, P., & Rees, G. (2011). Decoding of coherent but not incoherent motion signals in early dorsal visual cortex. *NeuroImage, 56*, 688–698.

Schweinhart, L. J. (2004). *The High/Scope Perry preschool study through age 40: Summary, conclusions, and frequently asked questions.* Retrieved from www.highscope.org/Research/PerryProject/PerryAge40SumWeb.pdf.

Sciutto, M. J., & Eisenberg, M. (2007). Evaluating the evidence for and against the overdiagnosis of ADHD. *Journal of Attention Disorders, 11*, 106–113.

Scott, D., Scott, L. M., & Goldwater, B. (1997). A performance improvement program for an international-level track and field athlete. *Journal of Applied Behavior Analysis, 30*, 573–575.

Scull, A. (1993). *A most solitary of afflictions: Madness and society in Britain 1700–1900.* London: Yale University Press.

Seal, D. S., Smith, M., Coley, B., Perry, J., & Gamez, M. (2008). Urban heterosexual couples' sexual scripts for three shared sexual experiences. *Sex Roles, 58*, 626–638.

Seamon, J. G., Philbin, M. M., & Harrison, L G. (2006). Do you remember proposing marriage to the Pepsi machine? False recollections from a campus walk. *Psychonomic Bulletin & Review, 13*, 752–756.

Sear, R., & Mace, R. (2008). Who keeps children alive? A review of the effects of kin on child survival. *Evolution and Human Behavior, 29*, 1–18.

Searle, J. R. (1979). Literal meaning. In J. R. Searle (Ed.), *Expression and meaning* (pp. 117–136). Cambridge, UK: Cambridge University Press.

Sedikides, C., & Gregg, A. P. (2008). Self-enhancement: Food for thought. *Perspectives on Psychological Science, 3*, 102–116.

Segerstrom, S. C. (2005). Optimism and immunity: Do positive thoughts always lead to positive effects? *Brain, Behavior, and Immunity, 19*, 195–200.

Segerstrom, S. C. (2006). How does optimism suppress immunity? Evaluation of three affective pathways. *Health Psychology, 25*, 653–657.

Segerstrom, S. C. (2007). Stress, energy, and immunity. *Current Directions in Psychological Science, 16*, 326–330.

Seidenberg, M. S., & Petitto, L. A. (1979). Signing behavior in apes: A critical review. *Cognition, 7*, 177–215.

Selfridge, O. G. (1955). Pattern recognition and modern computers. *Proceedings of the Western Joint Computer Conference.* New York: Institute of Electrical and Electronics Engineers.

Seligman, M. E. P. (1975). *Helplessness: On depression, development, and death.* San Francisco: Freeman.

Seligman, M. E. P., & Maier, S. F. (1967). Failure to escape traumatic shock. *Journal of Experimental Psychology, 74*, 1–9.

Seligman, M. E. P., Steen, T. A., Park, N., & Peterson, C. (2005). Positive psychology progress: Empirical validation of interventions. *American Psychologist, 60*, 410–421.

Selye, H. (1976a). *Stress in health and disease.* Reading, MA: Butterworth.

Selye, H. (1976b). *The stress of life* (2nd ed.). New York: McGraw-Hill.

Serpell, R. (2000). Intelligence and culture. In R. J. Sternberg (Ed.), *Handbook of intelligence* (pp. 549–577). Cambridge, UK: Cambridge University Press.

Sevdalis, N., & Harvey, N. (2007). Biased forecasting of postdecisional affect. *Psychological Science, 18*, 678–681.

Severson, K. (2011, July 6). Systematic cheating is found in Atlanta's school system. *The New York Times*, p. A13.

Shapley, R., & Hawken, M. J. (2011). Color in the cortex: Single- and double-opponent cells. *Vision Research, 51*, 701–717.

Shaver, P. R., & Hazan, C. (1994). Attachment. In A. L. Weber & J. H. Harvey (Eds.), *Perspectives on close relationships* (pp. 110– 130). Boston: Allyn & Bacon.

Shaw, K. L., & Mullen, S. P. (2011). Genes versus phenotypes in the study of speciation. *Genetica, 139*, 649–661.

Shaw, P., Greenstein, D., Lerch, J., Clasen, L. Lenroot, R., Gogtay, N., Evans, A., Rapoport, J., & Giedd, J. (2006). Intellectual ability and cortical development in children and adolescents. *Nature, 440*, 676–679.

Shedler, J. (2010). The efficacy of psychodynamic therapy. *American Psychologist, 65*, 98–109.

Shepard, R. N. (1978). Externalization of mental images and the act of creation. In B. S. Randhawa & W. E. Coffman (Eds.), *Visual learning, thinking, and communicating.* New York: Academic Press.

Sheppard, L. D., & Vernon, P. A. (2008). Intelligence and speed of information-processing: A review of 50 years of research. *Personality and Individual Differences, 44*, 535–551.

Sherif, C. W. (1981, August). *Social and psychological bases of social psychology.* The G. Stanley Hall Lecture on social psychology, presented at the annual convention of the American Psychological Association, Los Angeles, 1961.

Sherif, M. (1935). A study of some social factors in perception. *Archives of Psychology, 27*(187).

Sherif, M., Harvey, O. J., White, B. J., Hood, W. R., & Sherif, C. W. (1988). *The Robbers Cave experiment: Intergroup conflict and cooperation.* Middletown, CT: Wesleyan University Press. (Original work published 1961)

Sherwood, C. C., Subiaul, F., & Zawidzki, T. W. (2008). A natural history of the human mind: Tracing evolutionary changes in brain and cognition. *Journal of Anatomy, 212*, 426–454.

Shevlin, M., Houston, J. E., Dorahy, M. J., & Adamson, G. (2008). Cumulative traumas and psychosis: An analysis of the National Comorbidity Study and the British Psychiatric Morbidity Survey. *Schizophrenia Bulletin, 34*, 193–199.

Shi, J., Gershon, E. S., & Liu, C. (2008). Genetic associations with schizophrenia: Meta-analyses of 12 candidate genes. *Schizophrenia Research, 104*, 96–107.

Shields, D. C., Asaad, W., Eskandar, E. N., Jain, F. A., Cosgrove, G. R., Flahtery, A. W., Cassem, E. H., Prince, B. H., Rauch, S. L., & Dougherty, D. D. (2008). Prospective assessment of stereotactic ablative surgery for intractable major depression. *Biological Psychiatry, 64*, 449–454.

Shiffrin, R. M. (2003). Modeling memory and perception. *Cognitive Science, 27*, 341–378.

Shiffrin, R. M., & Schneider, W. (1977). Controlled and automatic human information processing: II. Perceptual learning, automatic attending, and a general theory. *Psychological Review, 84*, 127–190.

Shih, J. H., Eberhart, N. K., Hammen, C. L., & Brennan, P. A (2006). Differential exposure and reactivity to interpersonal stress predict sex differences in adolescent depression. *Journal of Clinical Child and Adolescent Psychology, 35,* 103–115.

Shmueli-Goetz, Y., Target, M., Fonagy, P., & Datta, A. (2008). The child attachment interview: A psychometric study of reliability and discriminant validity. *Developmental Psychology, 44,* 939–956.

Shneidman, E. S. (1987, March). At the point of no return. *Psychology Today,* pp. 54–59.

Shoda, Y., Mischel, W., & Wright, J. C. (1993a). The role of situational demands and cognitive competencies in behavior organization and personality coherence. *Journal of Personality and Social Psychology, 65,* 1023–1035.

Shuwairi, S. M., Albert, M. K., & Johnson, S. P. (2007). Discrimination of possible and impossible objects in infancy. *Psychological Science, 18,* 303–307.

Sia, T. L., Lord, C. G., Blessum, K. A., Ratcliff, C. D., & Lepper, M. R. (1997). Is a rose always a rose? The role of social category exemplar change in attitude stability and attitude-behavior consistency. *Journal of Personality and Social Psychology, 72,* 501–514.

Siegel, J. M. (2009). Sleep viewed as a state of adaptive inactivity. *Nature Reviews Neuroscience, 10,* 747–753.

Siegel, P. H., Schraeder, M., & Morrison, R. (2008). A taxonomy of equity factors. *Journal of Applied Social Psychology, 38,* 61–75.

Siegel, S. (1984). Pavlovian conditioning and heroin overdose: Reports by overdose victims. *Bulletin of the Psychonomic Society, 22,* 428–430.

Siegel, S. (2005). Drug tolerance, drug addiction, and drug anticipation. *Current Directions in Psychological Science, 14,* 296–300.

Siegel, S., Hinson, R. E., Krank, M. D., & McCully, J. (1982). Heroin "overdose" death: The contribution of drug-associated environmental cues. *Science, 216,* 436–437.

Siever, L. J. (2008). Neurobiology of aggression and violence. *American Journal of Psychiatry, 165,* 429–442.

Sigmon, S. T., Pells, J. J., Edenfield, T. M., Hermann, B. A., Scharter, J. G., LaMattina, S. M., & Boulard, N. E. (2007). Are we there yet? A review of gender comparisons in three behavioral journals through the 20th century. *Behavior Therapy, 38,* 333–339.

Silva, S., Martins, Y., Matias, A., & Blickstein, I. (2011). Why are monozygotic twins different? *Journal of Perinatal Medicine, 39,* 195–202.

Silventoinen, K., Pietiläinen, K. H., Tynelius, P., Sørensen, T. I. A., Kaprio, J., & Rasmussen, F. (2007). Genetic and environmental factors in relative weight from birth to age 18: The Swedish young male twins study. *International Journal of Obesity, 31,* 615–621.

Silventoinen, K., Posthuma, D., van Beijsterveldt, T., Bartels, M., Boomsma, D. I. (2006). Genetic contributions to the association between height and intelligence: Evidence from Dutch twin data from childhood to middle age. *Genes, Brain and Behavior, 5,* 585–595.

Simmons, J. A., Ferragamo, M. J., & Moss, C. F. (1998). Echo-delay resolution in sonar images of the big brown bat, *Eptesicus fuscus. Proceedings of the National Academy of Sciences of the United States, 95,* 12647–12652.

Simon, H. A. (1973). The structure of ill-structured problems. *Artificial Intelligence, 4,* 181–202.

Simons, D. J., & Ambinder, M. S. (2005). Change blindness: Theory and consequences. *Current Directions in Psychological Science, 14,* 44–48.

Simons, D. J., & Chabris, C. F. (1999). Gorillas in our midst: Sustained inattentional blindness for dynamic events. *Perception, 28,* 1059–1074.

Simons, D. J., & Levin, D. T. (1998). Failure to detect changes to people during a real-world interaction. *Psychonomic Bulletin & Review, 5,* 644–649.

Simons-Morton, B. G., Ouimet, M. C., Zhang, Z., Klauer, S. E., Lee, S. E., Wang, J., Chen, R., Albert, P., & Dingus, T. A. (2011). The effect of passengers and risk-taking friends on risky driving and crashes/near crashes among novice teenagers. *Journal of Adolescent Health, 49,* 587–593.

Sinaceur, M., Thomas-Hunt, M. C., Neale, M. A., O'Neill, O. A., & Haag, C. (2010). Accuracy and perceived expert status in group decisions: When minority members make majority members more accurate privately. *Personality and Social Psychology Bulletin, 36,* 423–437.

Singer, L. T., Arendt, R., Minnes, S., Farkas, K., Salvator, A., Kirchner, H. L., & Kliegman, R. (2002). Cognitive and motor outcomes of cocaine-exposed infants. *Journal of the American Medical Association, 287,* 1952–1960.

Singh, G. K., Kogan, M. D., & van Dyck, P. C. (2010). Changes in state-specific childhood obesity and overweight prevalence in the United States from 2003 to 2007. *Archives of Pediatric & Adolescent Medicine, 164,* 598–607.

Singh, J. P., Grann, M., & Fazel, S. (2011). A comparative study of violence risk assessment tools: A systematic review and metaregression analysis of 68 studies involving 25,980 participants. *Clinical Psychology Review, 31,* 599–513.

Sinigaglia, C., & Rizzolatti, G. (2011). Through the looking glass: Self and others. *Consciousness and Cognition, 20,* 64–74.

Sireteanu, R. (1999). Switching on the infant brain. *Science, 286,* 59–61.

Skinner, B. F. (1938). *The behavior of organisms.* New York: Appleton-Century-Crofts.

Skinner, B. F. (1953). *Science and human behavior.* New York: Macmillan.

Skinner, B. F. (1957). *Verbal behavior.* New York: Appleton-Century-Crofts.

Skinner, B. F. (1966). What is the experimental analysis of behavior? *Journal of the Experimental Analysis of Behavior, 9,* 213–218.

Skinner, B. F. (1990). Can psychology be a science of mind? *American Psychologist, 45,* 1206–1210.

Slivia, P. J. (2008). Discernment and creativity: How well can people identify their most creative ideas? *Psychology of Aesthetics, Creativity, and the Arts, 2,* 139–146.

Sloane, R. B., Staples, F. R., Cristol, A. H., Yorkston, N. J., & Whipple, K. (1975). *Psychotherapy versus behavior therapy.* Cambridge, MA: Harvard University Press.

Slobin, D. I. (1985). Crosslinguistic evidence for the language-making capacity. In D. Slobin (Ed.), *The crosslinguistic study of language acquisition: Vol. 2. Theoretical issues* (pp. 1157–1256). Hillsdale, NJ: Erlbaum.

Slovic, P., Monahan, J., & MacGregor, D. G. (2000). Violence risk assessment and risk communication: The effects of using actual cases, providing instruction, and employing probability versus frequency formats. *Law and Human Behavior, 24,* 271–296.

Smetana, J. G., Campione-Barr, N., & Metzger, A. (2006). Adolescent development in interpersonal and societal contexts. *Annual Review of Psychology, 57,* 255–284.

Smith, A. R., Hawkeswood, S. E., Bodell, L. P., & Joiner, T. E. (2011). Muscularity versus leanness: An examination of body ideals and predictors of disordered eating in heterosexual and gay college students. *Body Image, 8,* 232–236.

Smith, J., & Baltes, P. B. (1990). Wisdom-related knowledge: Age/cohort differences in response to life-planning problems. *Developmental Psychology, 26,* 494–505.

Smith, M., Hopkins, D., Peveler, R. C., Holt, R. I. G., Woodward, M., & Ismail K. (2008). First- v. second-generation antipsychotics and risk for diabetes in schizophrenia: Systematic review and meta-analysis. *The British Journal of Psychiatry, 192,* 406–411.

Smith, P. L., Smith, J. C., & Houpt, T. A. (2010). Interactions of temperatures and taste in conditioned aversions. *Physiology & Behavior, 99,* 324–333.

Smith, S. J., Axelton, A. M., & Saucier, D. A. (2009). The effects of contact on sexual prejudice: A meta-analysis. *Sex Roles, 61,* 178–191.

Smith, T. B., Domenech Rodríguez, M., & Bernal, G. (2011). Culture. *Journal of Clinical Psychology: In Session, 67,* 166–175.

Smith, T. W., & Ruiz, J. M. (2002). Psychosocial influences on the development and course of coronary heart disease: Current status and implications for research and practice. *Journal of Consulting and Clinical Psychology, 70,* 548–568.

Smoller, J. W., Biederman, J., Arbeitman, L., Doyle, A. E., Fagerness, J., Perlis, R. H., Sklar, P., & Faraone, S. V. (2006). Association between the

5HT1B receptor gene (*HTR1B*) and the inattentive subtype of ADHD. *Biological Psychiatry, 59,* 460–467.

Sniehotta, F. F., Scholz, U., & Schwarzer, R. (2006). Action plans and coping plans for physical exercise: A longitudinal study in cardiac rehabilitation. *British Journal of Health Psychology, 11,* 23–37.

Snowden, L. R., & Yamada, A.-M. (2005). Cultural differences in access to care. *Annual Review of Clinical Psychology, 1,* 143–166.

Snyder, D. K., & Balderrama-Durbin, C. (2012). Integrative approaches to couple therapy: Implications for clinical practice and research. *Behavior Therapy,* in press.

Soderstrom, M. (2007). Beyond babytalk: Re-evaluating the nature and content of speech input to preverbal infants. *Developmental Review, 27,* 501–532.

Solberg Nes, L., Evans, D. R., & Segerstrom, S. C. (2009). Optimism and college retention: Mediation by motivation, performance, and adjustment. *Journal of Applied Social Psychology, 39,* 1887–1912.

Solomon, A. (2001). *The noonday demon.* New York: Scribner.

Song, J. Y., Demuth, K., & Morgan, J. (2010). Effects of the acoustic properties of infant-directed speech on infant word recognition. *Journal of the Acoustical Society of America, 128,* 389–400.

Sörqvist, P., Haling, N., & Hygge, S. (2010). Individual differences in susceptibility to the effects of speech on reading comprehension. *Applied Cognitive Psychology, 24,* 67–76.

Soska, K. C., & Johnson, S. P. (2008). Development of three-dimensional object completion in infancy. *Child Development, 79,* 1230–1236.

Spano, R., Pridemore, W. A., & Bolland, J. (2012). Are exposure to violence and violent behavior precursors for initiation of gun carrying for poor, urban minority youth? *Journal of Interpersonal Violence, 27,* 158–176.

Spearman, C. (1927). *The abilities of man.* New York: Macmillan.

Spence, I., & Feng, J. (2010). Video games and spatial cognition. *Review of General Psychology, 14,* 92–104.

Spence, M. J., & DeCasper, A. J. (1987). Prenatal experience with low-frequency maternal-voice sounds influences neonatal perception of maternal voice samples. *Infant Behavior and Development, 10,* 133–142.

Spence, M. J., & Freeman, M. S. (1996). Newborn infants prefer the maternal low-pass filtered voice, but not the maternal whispered voice. *Infant Behavior and Development, 19,* 199–212.

Sperling, G. (1960). The information available in brief visual presentations. *Psychological Monographs, 74,* 1–29.

Sperling, G. (1963). A model for visual memory tasks. *Human Factors, 5,* 19–31.

Sperry, R. W. (1968). Mental unity following surgical disconnection of the cerebral hemispheres. *The Harvey Lectures,* Series 62. New York: Academic Press.

Spiers, H. J., & Maguire, E. A. (2007). Decoding human brain activity during real-world experiences. *Trends in Cognitive Sciences, 11,* 356–365.

Spitz, R. A., & Wolf, K. (1946). Anaclitic depression. *Psychoanalytic Study of Children, 2,* 313–342.

Squire, L. R., & Wixted, J. T. (2011). The cognitive neuroscience of human memory since H. M. *Annual Review of Neuroscience, 34,* 259–288.

Stafford, B. L., Balda, R. P., & Kamil, A. C. (2006). Does seed-caching experience affect spatial memory performance by pinyon jays? *Ethology, 112,* 1202–1208.

Stagnitti, M. N. (2007). *Trends in the use and expenditures for the therapeutic class prescribed psychotherapeutic agents and a subclasses, 1997 and 2004.* Rockville, MD: Agency for Healthcare Research and Quality. Retrieved from www.meps.ahrq.gov/mepsweb/data_files/publications/st163/stat163.pdf.

Stahr, B., Cushing, D., Lane, K., & Fox, J. (2006). Efficacy of a function-based intervention in decreasing off-task behavior exhibited by a student with ADHD. *Journal of Positive Behavior Interventions, 8,* 201–211.

Stanley, D. A., Sokol-Hessner, P., Banaji, M. R., & Phelps, E. A. (2011). Implicit race attitudes predict trustworthiness judgments and economic trust decisions. *PNAS, 108,* 7710–7715.

Stanley, D., Phelps, E., & Banaji, M. (2008). The neural basis of implicit attitudes. *Current Directions in Psychological Science, 17,* 164–170.

Stanojevic, M., Kurjak, A., Salihagić-Kadić, A., Vasilj, O., Miskovic, B., Shaddad, A. N., Ahmed, B., & Tomasović, S. (2011). Neurobehavioral continuity from fetus to neonate. *Journal of Perinatal Medicine, 39,* 171–177.

Starace, F., Massa, A., Amico, K. R., & Fisher, J. D. (2006). Adherence to antiretroviral therapy: An empirical test of the information-motivation-behavioral skills model. *Health Psychology, 25,* 153–162.

Staudinger, U. M., & Glück, J. (2011). Psychological wisdom research: Commonalities and differences in a growing field. *Annual Review of Psychology, 62,* 215–241.

Steele, C. M. (1997). A threat in the air: How stereotypes shape intellectual identity and performance. *American Psychologist, 6,* 613–629.

Steele, C. M., & Aronson, J. (1995). Stereotype threat and the intellectual test performance of African Americans. *Journal of Personality and Social Psychology, 69,* 797–811.

Steele, C. M., & Aronson, J. (1998). Stereotype threat and the test performance of academically successful African Americans. In C. Jencks & M. Phillips (Eds.), *The Black–White test score gap* (pp. 401–427). Washington, DC: Brookings Institution Press.

Stein, M. B., Jang, K. L., Taylor, S., Vernon, P. A., & Livesley, W. J. (2002). Genetic and environmental influences on trauma exposure and post-traumatic stress disorder symptoms: A twin study. *American Journal of Psychiatry, 159,* 1675–1681.

Steinberg, L. (2008). A social neuroscience perspective on adolescent risk-taking. *Developmental Review, 28,* 78–106.

Stepanova, E. V., Strube, M. J., & Hetts, J. J. (2009). They saw a triple lutz: Bias and perception in American and Russian newspaper coverage of the 2002 Olympic figure skating scandal. *Journal of Applied Social Psychology, 39,* 1763–1784.

Stern, W. (1914). The psychological methods of testing intelligence. *Educational Psychology Monographs* (No. 13).

Sternberg, R. J. (1986). *Intelligence applied.* San Diego: Harcourt Brace Jovanovich.

Sternberg, R. J. (1999). The theory of successful intelligence. *Review of General Psychology, 3,* 292–316.

Sternberg, R. J. (2006). The Rainbow Project: Enhancing the SAT through assessments of analytical, practical, and creative skills. *Intelligence, 34,* 321–350.

Sternberg, R. J. (2007). Who are the bright children? The cultural context of being and acting intelligent. *Educational Researcher, 36,* 148–155.

Sternberg, R. J. (2010). Assessment of gifted students for identification purposes: New techniques for a new millennium. *Learning and Individual Differences, 20,* 327–336.

Sternberg, R. J., & Grigorenko, E. L. (2007). The difficulty of escaping preconceptions in writing an article about the difficulty of escaping preconceptions: Commentary on Hunt and Carlson (2007). *Perspectives on Psychological Science, 2,* 221–226.

Sternberg, R. J., Grigorenko, E. L., & Kidd, K. K. (2005). Intelligence, race, and genetics. *American Psychologist, 60,* 46–59.

Sternthal, M. J., Slopen, N., & Williams, D. R. (2011). Racial disparities in health: How much does stress really matter? *Du Bois Review, 8,* 95–113.

Stewart, D. E., & Yuen, T. (2011). A systematic review of resilience in the physically ill. *Psychosomatics, 52,* 199–209.

Stewart, S. A. (2005). The effects of benzodiazepines on cognition. *Journal of Clinical Psychiatry, 66* (Suppl. 2), 9–13.

Stewart, W. H., Jr., & Roth, P. L. (2007). A meta-analysis of achievement motivation differences between entrepreneurs and managers. *Journal of Small Business Management, 45*, 401–421.

Stewart-Williams, S. (2007). Altruism among kin vs. nonkin: Effects of cost of help and reciprocal exchange. *Evolution and Human Behavior, 28*, 193–198.

Stiles, J., & Jernigan, T. L. (2010). The basics of brain development. *Neuropsychology Review, 20*, 327–348.

Stocco, A., Lebiere, C., & Anderson, J. R. (2010). Conditional routing of information in the cortex: A model of the basal ganglia's role in cognitive coordination. *Psychological Review, 117*, 541–574.

Stockhorst, U., Steingrueber, H.-J., Enck, P., & Klosterhalfen, S. (2006). Pavlovian conditioning of nausea and vomiting. *Autonomic Neuroscience: Basic and Clinical, 129*, 50–57.

Stone, J., & McWhinnie, C. (2008). Evidence that blatant versus subtle stereotype threat cues impact performance through dual processes. *Journal of Experimental Social Psychology, 44*, 445–452.

Storbeck, J., & Clore, G. L. (2007). On the interdependence of cognition and emotion. *Cognition and Emotion, 21*, 1212–1237.

Strayer, D. L., Drews, R. A., & Johnston, W. A. (2003). Cell phone-induced failures of visual attention during simulated driving. *Journal of Experimental Psychology: Applied, 9*, 23–32.

Strayer, D. L., Watson, J. M., & Drews, F. A. (2011). Cognitive distraction while multitasking in the automobile. In B. H. Ross (Ed.), *The psychology of learning and motivation* (Vol. 54, pp. 29–58). Burlington, MA: Academic Press.

Striegel-Moore, R. H., & Franko, D. L. (2008). Should binge eating disorder be included in *DSM-V*? A critical review of the state of the evidence. *Annual Review of Clinical Psychology, 4*, 305–324.

Striegel-Moore, R. H., Dohm, F. A., Kraemer, H. C., Taylor, C. B., Daniels, S., Crawford, P. B., & Schreiber, G. B. (2003). Eating disorders in White and Black women. *American Journal of Psychiatry, 160*, 1326–1331.

Striegel-More, R. H., & Bulik, C. M. (2007). Risk factors for eating disorders. *American Psychologist, 62*, 181–198.

Subotnik, K. L., Nuechterlein, K. H., Ventura, J., Gitlin, M. J., Marder, S., Mintz, J., Hellemann, G. S., Thornton, L. A., & Singh, I. R. (2011). Risperidone nonadherence and return of positive symptoms in the early course of schizophrenia. *American Journal of Psychiatry, 168*, 286–292.

Substance Abuse and Mental Health Service Administration (SAMHSA). (2010). *Results from the 2009 national survey on drug use and health: Volume I. Summary of national findings.* Available at www.oas.samhsa.gov/.

Sue, S. (2006). Cultural competency: From philosophy to research and practice. *Journal of Community Psychology, 34*, 237–245.

Sulem, P., Gudbjartsson, D. F., Geller, F., Prokopenko, Feenstra, B., Aben, K. K. H., Franke, B., den Heijer, M., Kovacs, P., Stumvoll, M., Mägi, R., Yanek, L. R., Becker, L. C., Boyd, H. A., Stacey, S. N., Walters, G. B., Jonasdottir, A., Thorleifsson, G., Holm, H., Gudjonsson, S. A., Rafnar, T., Björnsdottir, G., Becker, D. M., Melbye, M., Kong, A., Tönjes, A., Thorgeirsson, T., Thorsteinsdottir, U., Kiemeney, L. A., & Stefansson, K. (2011). Sequence variants at CYP1A1–CYP1A2 and AHR associate with coffee consumption. *Human Molecular Genetics, 20*, 2071–2077.

Sullivan, H. S. (1953). *The interpersonal theory of psychiatry.* New York: Norton.

Summerville, A., & Roese, N. J. (2008). Dare to compare: Fact-based versus simulation-based comparison in daily life. *Journal of Experimental Social Psychology, 44*, 664–671.

Swann, W. B., Chang-Schneider, C., & McClarty, K. L. (2007). Do people's self-views matter? Self-concept and self-esteem in everyday life. *American Psychologist, 62*, 84–94.

Swazey, J. P. (1974). *Chlorpromazine in psychiatry: A study of therapeutic innovation.* Cambridge, MA: MIT Press.

Swogger, M. T., Conner, K. R., Meldrum, S. C., & Caine, E. D. (2009). Dimensions of psychopathy in relation to suicidal and self-injurious behavior. *Journal of Personality Disorders, 23*, 201–210.

Szasz, T. S. (1974). *The myth of mental illness* (rev. ed.). New York: Harper & Row.

Szasz, T. S. (2004). *Faith in freedom: Libertarian principles and psychiatric practices.* Somerset, NJ: Transaction Publishers.

Szekely, A., Loránd, E., Kovacs-Nagy, R., Bányai, E. I., Gosi-Greguss, A. C., Varga, K., Halmai, Z., Ronai, Z., & Sasvari-Szekely, M. (2010). Association between hypnotizability and the catechol-o-methyltransferase (COMT) polymorphism. *International Journal of Clinical and Experimental Hypnosis, 58*, 301–315.

Taatgen, N. A., & Lee, F. J. (2003). Production compilation: A simple mechanism to model complex skill acquisition. *Human Factors, 45*, 61–76.

Taatgen, N. A., Huss, D., Dickison, D., & Anderson, J. R. (2008). The acquisition of robust and flexible cognitive skills. *Journal of Experimental Psychology: General, 137*, 548–565.

Tacon, A. M., McComb, J., Caldera, Y., & Randolph, P. Mindfulness meditation, anxiety reduction, and heart disease: A pilot study. *Family and Community Health, 26*, 25–33.

Tajfel, H., Billig, M., Bundy, R., & Flament, C. (1971). Social categorization and intergroup behavior. *European Journal of Social Psychology, 1*, 149–178.

Talarico, J. M., & Rubin, D. C. (2003). Confidence, not consistency, characterizes flashbulb memories. *Psychological Science, 14*, 455–461.

Talarico, J. M., & Rubin, D. C. (2007). Flashbulb memories are special after all; in phenomenology, not accuracy. *Applied Cognitive Psychology, 21*, 527–578.

Tan, K. R., Rudolph, U., & Lüscher, C. (2011). Hooked on benzodiazepines: $GABA_A$ receptor subtypes and addiction. *Trends in Neurosciences, 34*, 188–197.

Tandon, R., Keshavan, M. S., & Nasrallah, H. A. (2008). Schizophrenia, "Just the Facts": What we know in 2008. 2. Epidemiology and etiology. *Schizophrenia Research, 102*, 1–18.

Tanofsky-Kraff, M., Wilfley, D. E., & Spurrell, E. (2000). Impact of interpersonal and ego-related stress on restrained eaters. *International Journal of Eating Disorders, 27*, 411–418.

Tarbox, S. I., & Pogue-Geile, M. F. (2008). Development of social functioning in preschizophrenic children and adolescents: A systematic review. *Psychological Bulletin, 34*, 561–583.

Tay, L., & Diener, E. (2011). Needs and subjective well-being around the world. *Journal of Personality and Social Psychology, 101*, 354–365.

Taylor, C. T., Bomyea, J., & Amir, N. (2010). Attentional bias away from positive social information mediates the link between social anxiety and anxiety vulnerability to a social stressor. *Journal of Anxiety Disorders, 24*, 403–408.

Taylor, S. E. (2006). Tend and befriend: Biobehavioral bases of affiliation under stress. *Current Directions in Psychological Science, 15*, 273–277.

Taylor, S. E., Klein, L. C., Lewis, B. P., Gruenewald, T. L., Gurung, R. A. R., & Updegraff, J. A. (2000). Biobehavioral responses to stress in females: Tend-and-befriend, not fight-or-flight. *Psychological Review, 107*, 411–429.

Tedeschi, R. G., & Calhoun, L. G. (2004). Posttraumatic growth: Conceptual foundations and empirical evidence. *Psychological Inquiry, 15*, 1–18.

Tedlock, B. (1992). The role of dreams and visionary narratives in Mayan cultural survival. *Ethos, 20*, 453–476.

Tellegen, A. & Ben-Porath, Y. S. (2008). *MMPI-2-RF Technical Manual.* Minneapolis: University of Minnesota Press.

Templin, M. (1957). Certain language skills in children: Their development and interrelationships. *Institute of Child Welfare Monograph*, Series No. 26. Minneapolis: University of Minnesota Press.

Teplin, L. A., McClelland, G. M., Abram, K. M., & Weiner, D. A. (2005). Crime victimization in adults with severe mental illness. *Archives of General Psychiatry, 62*, 911–921.

Terman, L. M. (1916). *The measurement of intelligence*. Boston: Houghton Mifflin.

Terman, L. M., & Merrill, M. A. (1937). *Measuring intelligence*. Boston: Houghton Mifflin.

Terman, L. M., & Merrill, M. A. (1960). *The Stanford-Binet intelligence scale*. Boston: Houghton Mifflin.

Terman, L. M., & Merrill, M. A. (1972). *Stanford-Binet intelligence scale—manual for the third revision, Form L-M*. Boston: Houghton Mifflin.

Thase, M. E., & Denko, T. (2008). Pharmacotherapy of mood disorders. *Annual Review of Clinical Psychology, 4*, 53–91.

Thiessen, E. D., Hill, E. A., & Saffran, J. R. (2005). Infant-directed speech facilitates word segmentation. *Infancy, 7*, 53–71.

Thoma, N. C., & Cecero, J. J. (2009). Is integrative use of techniques in psychotherapy the exception or the rule? Results of a national survey of doctoral-level practitioners. *Psychotherapy Theory, Research, Practice, Teaching, 46*, 405–417.

Thomas, A., & Chess, S. (1977). *Temperament and development*. New York: Brunner/Mazel.

Thomas, E. L., & Robinson, H. A. (1972). *Improving reading in every class: A sourcebook for teachers*. Boston: Allyn & Bacon.

Thomas, M. L. (2011). Detection of female mating status using chemical signals and cues. *Biological Reviews, 86*, 1–13.

Thompson, P. M., Vidal, C., Giedd, J. N., Gochman, P., Blumenthal, J., Nicolson, R., Toga, A. W., & Rapoport, J. L. (2001). Mapping adolescent brain change reveals dynamic wave of accelerated gray matter loss in very early-onset schizophrenia. *PNAS, 98*, 11650–11655.

Thompson, R. J., Mata, J., Jaeggi, S. M., Buschkuehl, M., Jonides, J., & Gotlib, I. H. (2011). Concurrent and prospective relations between attention to emotion and affect intensity: An experience sampling study. *Emotion, 11*, 1489–1494.

Thompson, W. L., Kosslyn, S. M., Hoffman, M. S., & van der Koolj, K. (2008). Inspecting visual mental images: Can people "see" implicit properties as easily in imagery and perception? *Memory & Cognition, 36*, 1024–1032.

Thomson, D. R., Milliken, B., & Smilek, D. (2010). Long-term conceptual implicit memory: A decade of evidence. *Memory & Cognition, 38*, 42–46.

Thorndike, E. L. (1898). Animal intelligence. *Psychological Review Monograph Supplement, 2*(4, Whole No. 8).

Thorndike, R. L., Hagen, E. P., & Sattler, J. M. (1986). *Stanford-Binet intelligence scale* (4th ed.). Chicago: Riverside.

Thorne, B. M., & Henley, T. B. (2005). *Connections in the history and systems of psychology* (3rd ed.). Boston: Houghton Mifflin.

Thorpe, S. K. S., Holder, R. L., & Crompton, R. H. (2007). Origin of human bipedalism as an adaptation for locomotion on flexible branches. *Science, 316*, 1328–1331.

Tice, D. M., & Baumeister, R. F. (1997). Longitudinal study of procrastination, performance, stress, and health: The costs and benefits of dawdling. *Psychological Science, 8*, 454–458.

Tiger, J. H., & Hanley, G. P. (2006). Using reinforcer pairing and fading to increase the milk consumption of a preschool child. *Journal of Applied Behavior Analysis, 39*, 399–403.

Timmann, D., Drepper, J., Frings, M., Maschke, M., Richter, S., Gerwig, M., & Kolb, F. P. (2010). The human cerebellum contributes to motor, emotional and cognitive associative learning. A review. *Cortex, 46*, 845–857.

Titchener, E. B. (1910). *A textbook of psychology*. New York: Macmillan.

Toblin, R. L., Mack, K. A., Pervenn, G., & Paulozzi, L. J. (2011). A population-based survey of chronic pain and its treatment with prescription drugs. *Pain, 152*, 1249–1255.

Todrank, J., & Bartoshuk, L. M. (1991). A taste illusion: Taste sensation localized by touch. *Physiology & Behavior, 50*, 1027–1031.

Tolman, E. C. (1948). Cognitive maps in rats and men. *Psychological Review, 55*, 189–208.

Tolman, E. C., & Honzik, C. H. (1930). "Insight" in rats. *University of California Publications in Psychology, 4*, 215–232.

Tomasello, M. (2008). *Origins of human communication*. Cambridge, MA: MIT Press.

Tomkins, S. (1962). *Affect, imagery, consciousness* (Vol. 1). New York: Springer.

Tomkins, S. (1981). The quest for primary motives: Biography and autobiography of an idea. *Journal of Personality and Social Psychology, 41*, 306–329.

Tomkovick, C., Lester, S. W., Flunker, L., & Wells, T. A. (2008). Linking collegiate service-learning to future volunteerism: Implications for nonprofit organizations. *Nonprofit Management and Leadership, 19*, 3–26.

Tong, S. T., Van Der Heide, B., Langwell, L., & Walther, J. B. (2008). Too much of a good thing? The relationship between number of friends and interpersonal impressions on Facebook. *Journal of Computer-Mediated Communication, 13*, 531–549.

Torgersen, S., Lygren, S., Øien, P. A., Skre, I., Onstad, S., Edvardsen, J., Tambs, K., & Kringlen, E. (2000). A twin study of personality disorders. *Comprehensive Psychiatry, 41*, 416–425.

Torrance, E. P. (1974). *The Torrance tests of creative thinking: Technical-norms manual*. Bensenville, IL: Scholastic Testing Services.

Tran, V., Wiebe, D. J., Fortenberry, K. T., Butler, J. M., & Berg, C. A. (2011). Benefit finding, affective reactions to diabetes stress, and diabetes management among early adolescents. *Health Psychology, 30*, 212–219.

Trautner, H. M., Ruble, D. N., Cyphers, L., Kirsten, B., Behrendt, R., & Hartmann, P. (2005). Rigiditiy and flexibility of gender stereotypes in childhood: Developmental or differential? *Infant and Child Development, 14*, 365–381.

Trescot, A. M., Datta, S., Lee, M., & Hansen, H. (2008). Opiod pharmacology. *Pain Physician, 11*, S133–S153.

Triandis, H. C. (1990). Cross-cultural studies of individualism and collectivism. In J. Berman (Ed.), *Nebraska Symposium on Motivation, 1989* (pp. 41–133). Lincoln: University of Nebraska Press.

Triandis, H. C. (1994). *Culture and social behavior*. New York: McGraw-Hill.

Triandis, H. C. (1995). *Individualism and collectivism*. Boulder, CO: Westview.

Trivers, R. L. (1971). The evolution of reciprocal altruism. *Quarterly Review of Biology, 46*, 35–57.

Troisi, J. D., & Gabriel, S. (2011). Chicken soup really is good for the soul: "Comfort food" fulfills the need to belong. *Psychological Science, 22*, 747–753.

Tryon, G. S., & Winograd, G. (2011). Goal consensus and collaboration. *Psychotherapy, 48*, 50–57.

Tryon, W. W. (2008). Whatever happened to symptom substitution? *Clinical Psychology Review, 28*, 963–968.

Trzesniewski, K. H., Donnellan, M. B., Moffitt, T. E., Robins, R. W., Poulton, R., & Caspi, A. (2006). Low self-esteem during adolescence predicts poor health, criminal behavior, and limited economic prospects during adulthood. *Developmental Psychology, 42*, 381–390.

Tsakaris, M., Carpenter, L., James, D., & Fotopoulou, A. (2010). Hands only illusion: Multisensory integration elicits sense of ownership for body parts but not for non-corporeal objects. *Experimental Brain Research, 204*, 343–352.

Tucker-Drob, E., Rhemtulla, M., Harden, K. P., Turkheimer, E., & Fask, D. (2011). Emergence of a gene x socioeconomic status on infant mental ability between 10 months and 2 years. *Psychological Science, 22*, 125–133.

Tulving, E. (1972). Episodic and semantic memory. In E. Tulving & W. Donaldson (Eds.), *Organization of memory*. New York: Academic Press.

Tulving, E., & Thomson, D. M. (1973). Encoding specificity and retrieval processes in episodic memory. *Psychological Review, 80*, 352–373.

Tun, P. A., & Lachman, M. E. (2010). The association between computer use and cognition across adulthood: Use it so you won't lose it? *Psychology and Aging, 25*, 560–568.

Tupes, E. G., & Christal, R. C. (1961). *Recurrent personality factors based on trait ratings* (Tech. Rep. No. ASD-TR-61-97). Lackland Air Force Base, TX: U.S. Air Force.

Turkeltaub, P. E., Messing, S., Norise, C., & Hamilton, R. H. (2011). Are networks for residual language function and recovery consistent across aphasic patients? *Neurology, 76,* 1726-1734.

Turner, C. F., Villarroel, M. A., Chromy, J. R., Eggleston, E., & Rogers, S. M. (2005). Same-gender sex among U.S. adults: Trends across the twentieth century and during the 1990s. *Public Opinion Quarterly, 69,* 439-462.

Turner, M. E., & Pratkanis, A. R. (1998). A social identity maintenance model of groupthink. *Organizational Behavior and Human Decision Processes, 73,* 210-235.

Turner, M. L., & Engle, R. W. (1989). Is working memory capacity task dependent? *Journal of Memory and Language, 28,* 127-154.

Tversky, A., & Kahneman, D. (1973). Availability: A heuristic for judging frequency and probability. *Cognitive Psychology, 5,* 207-232.

Twenge, J. M., Campbell, W. K., & Foster, C. A. (2003). Parenthood and marital satisfaction: A meta-analytic review. *Journal of Marriage and Family, 65,* 574-583.

U.S. Census Bureau (2008). 2007 American community survey. Retrieved from www.census.gov/acs/www/index.html.

U.S. Census Bureau (2011). America's families and living arrangements: 2010. Retrieved from www.census.gov/population/www/socdemo/hh-fam/cps2010.html.

U.S. Department of Agriculture. (2010). Dietary guidelines for Americans 2010. Retrieved from www.health.gov/dietaryguidelines/dga2010/DietaryGuidelines2010.pdf.

U.S. Department of Health and Human Services. (2010). Child maltreatment 2009. Retrieved from www.acf.hhs.gov/programs/cb/pubs/cm09/cm09.pdf.

U.S. Department of Health and Human Services. (2010). Trends in the prevalence of sexual behaviors. Retrieved from www.cdc.gov/HealthyYouth/yrbs/pdf/us_sexual_trend_yrbs.pdf.

Uher, R., Caspi, A., Houts, R., Sugden, K., Williams, B., Poulton, R., & Moffitt, T. E. (2011). Serotonin transporter gene moderates childhood maltreatment's effects on persistent but not single-episode depression: Replications and implications for resolving inconsistent results. *Journal of Affective Disorders, 135,* 56-65.

Ullman, S. E., Filipas, H. H., Townsend, S. M., & Starzynski, L. L. (2007). Psychosocial correlates of PTSD symptom severity in sexual assault survivors. *Journal of Traumatic Stress, 20,* 821-831.

Underwood, B. J. (1948). Retroactive and proactive inhibition after five and forty-eight hours. *Journal of Experimental Psychology, 38,* 28-38.

Underwood, B. J. (1949). Proactive inhibition as a function of time and degree of prior learning. *Journal of Experimental Psychology, 39,* 24-34.

Undorf, M., & Erdfelder, E. (2011). Judgments of learning reflect encoding fluency: Conclusive evidence for the ease-of-processing hypothesis. *Journal of Experimental Psychology: Learning, Memory, and Cognition, 37,* 1264-1269.

Unsworth, N., Spillers, G. J., & Brewer, G. A. (2012). Dynamics of context-dependent recall: An examination of internal and external context change. *Journal of Memory and Language, 66,* 1-16.

Urban, J., Carlson, E., Egeland, B., & Stroufe, L. A. (1991). Patterns of individual adaptation across childhood. *Development and Psychopathology, 3,* 445-460.

van der Sluis, S., Willemsen, G., de Geus, E. J. C., Boomsma, D. I., & Posthuma, D. (2008). Gene-environment interaction in adults' IQ scores: Measures of past and present environment. *Behavior Genetics, 38,* 348-360.

van Dijk, E., & Zeelenberg, M. (2005). On the psychology of "if only": Regret and the comparison between factual and counterfactual outcomes. *Organizational Behavior and Human Decision Processes, 97,* 152-160.

van Soelen, I. L. C., Brouwer, R. M., van Leeuwen, M., Kahn, R. S., Hulshoff Pol, H. E., & Boomsma, D. I. (2011). Heritability of verbal and performance intelligence in a pediatric longitudinal sample. *Twin Research and Human Genetics, 14,* 119-128.

van Tol, M.-J., van der Wee, N. J. A., van den Heuvel, O. A., Nielen, M. M. A., Demenescu, L. R., Aleman, A., Renken, R., van Buchem, M. A., Zitman, F. G., & Veltman, D. J. (2010). Regional brain volume in depression and anxiety disorders. *Archives of General Psychiatry, 67,* 1002-1011.

Van Zeijl, J., Mesman, J., Van IJzendoorn, M. H., Bakermans-Kranenburg, M. J., Juffer, F., Stolk, M. N., Koot, H. M., & Alink, L. R. A. (2006). Attachment-based intervention for enhancing sensitive discipline in mothers of 1- to 3-year-old children at risk for externalizing behavior problems: A randomized controlled trial. *Journal of Consulting and Clinical Psychology, 74,* 994-1005.

Vandell, D. L., Belsky, J., Burchinal, M., Steinberg, L., Vandergrift, N., & NICHD Early Child Care Research Network. (2010). Do effects of early child care extend to age 15 years? Results from the NICHD study of early child care and youth development. *Child Development, 81,* 737-756.

Vanden Bogaerde, A., & De Raedt, R. (2011). The moderational role of anxiety sensitivity in flight phobia. *Journal of Anxiety Disorders, 25,* 422-426.

Vartanian, L. R., Herman, C. P., & Wansink, B. (2008). Are we aware of the external factors that influence our food intake? *Health Psychology, 27,* 533-538.

Vaughn, E. D., Thomas, A., & Doyle, A. L. (2011). The multiple disability implicit association test: Psychometric analysis of a multiple administration IAT measure. *Rehabilitation Counselling Bulletin, 54,* 223-235.

Velicer, W. F., Redding, C. A., Sun, X., & Prochaska, J. O. (2007). Demographic variables, smoking variables, and outcome across five studies. *Health Psychology, 26,* 278-287.

Vemuri, V. K., Janero, R., & Makriyannis, A. (2008). Pharmacotherapeutic targeting of the endocannabinoid system: Drugs for obesity and the metabolic syndrome. *Physiology & Behavior, 93,* 671-686.

Vezina, P., McGehee, D. S., & Green, W. N. (2007). Exposure to nicotine and sensitization of nicotine-induced behaviors. *Progress in Neuro-Psychopharmacology & Biological Psychiatry, 31,* 1625-1638.

Viding, E., Blair, J. R., Moffitt, T. E., & Plomin, R. (2005). Evidence for substantial genetic risk for psychopathy in 7-year-olds. *Journal of Child Psychology and Psychiatry, 46,* 592-597.

Vieland, V. J., Hallmayer, J., Huang, Y., Pagnamenta, A. T., Pinto, D. Khan, H., Monaco, A. P., Paterson, A. D., Scherer, S. W., Sutcliffe, J. S., Szatmari, P., & The Autism Genome Project (AGP). (2011). Novel method for combined linkage and genome-wide association analysis finds evidence of distinct genetic architecture for two subtypes of autism. *Journal of Neurodevelopmental Disorders, 3,* 113-123.

Vignoles, V. L., Regalia, C., Manzi, C., Golledge, J., & Scabini, E. (2006). Beyond self-esteem: Influence of multiple motives on identity construction. *Journal of Personality and Social Psychology, 90,* 308-333.

Vink, J. M., Staphorsius, A. S., & Boomsma, D. I. (2009). A genetic analysis of coffee consumption in a sample of Dutch twins. *Twin Research and Human Genetics, 12,* 127-131.

Vishwanath, A., Herath, T., Chen, R., Wang, J., & Rao, H. R. (2011). Why do people get phished? Testing individual differences in phishing vulnerability within an integrated information processing model. *Decision Support Systems, 51,* 576-586.

Visser, B. A., Ashton, M. C., & Vernon, P. A. (2006). Beyond *g*: Putting multiple intelligences theory to the test. *Intelligence, 34,* 487-502.

Vocks, S., Busch, M., Grönemeyer, D., Schulte, D., Herpertz, S., & Suchan, B. (2010). Differential neuronal responses to the self and others in the extrastriate body area (EBA) and the fusiform body area. *Cognitive, Affective, and Behavioral Neuroscience, 10,* 422-429.

Vohs, K. D., & Schooler, J. W. (2008). The value of believing in free will: Encouraging a belief in determinism increases cheating. *Psychological Science, 19,* 49–54.

Von Oorsouw, W. M. W. J., Israel, M. L., von Heyn, R. E., & Duker, P. C. (2008). Side effects of contingent shock treatment. *Research in Developmental Disabilities, 29,* 513–523.

Vonnegut, M. (1975). *The Eden express.* New York: Bantam.

Voorspoels, W., Vanpaemel, W., & Storms, G. (2008). Exemplars and prototypes in natural language concepts: A typicality-based evaluation. *Psychonomic Bulletin & Review, 15,* 630–637.

Voss, J. L., & Paller, K. A. (2008). Brain substrates of implicit and explicit memory: The importance of concurrently acquired neural signals of both memory types. *Neuropsychologia, 46,* 3021–3029.

Voss, U., Holzmann, R., Tuin, I., & Hobson, J. A. (2009). Lucid dreaming: A state of consciousness with features of both waking and non-lucid dreaming. *Sleep, 32,* 1191–1200.

Vroom, V. H. (1964). *Work and motivation.* New York: Wiley.

Vu, H., Kellas, G., Metcalf, K., & Herman, R. (2000). The influence of global discourse on lexical ambiguity resolution. *Memory & Cognition, 28,* 236–252.

Vuong, M., Brown-Welty, S., & Tracz, S. (2010). The effects of self-efficacy on academic success of first-generation college sophomore students. *Journal of College Student Development, 51,* 50–64.

Wade, T. D., Tiggemann, M., Bulik, C. M., Fairburn, C. G., Wray, N. R., & Martin, N. G. (2008). Shared temperament risk factors for anorexia nervosa: A twin study. *Psychosomatic Medicine, 70,* 239–244.

Wallach, M. A., & Kogan, N. (1965). *Modes of thinking in young children.* New York: Holt, Rinehart & Winston.

Wallis, D. J., & Hetherington, M. M. (2004). Stress and eating: The effects of ego-threat and cognitive demand on food intake in restrained and emotional eaters. *Appetite, 43,* 39–46.

Walton, G. M., & Cohen, G. L. (2007). A question of belonging: Race, social fit, and achievement. *Journal of Personality and Social Psychology, 92,* 82–96.

Walton, G. M., & Cohen, G. L. (2011). A brief social-belonging intervention improves academic and health outcomes of minority students. *Science, 331,* 1447–1451.

Wampold, B. E. (2001). *The great psychotherapy debate: Models, methods, and findings.* Mahwah, NJ: Erlbaum.

Wang, C., & Mallinckrodt, B. S. (2006). Differences between Taiwanese and U.S. cultural beliefs about ideal adult attachment. *Journal of Counseling Psychology, 53,* 192–204.

Wang, P. S., Berglund, P., Olfson, M., Pincus, H. A., Wells, K. B., & Kessler, R. C. (2005). Failure and delay in initial treatment contact after first onset of mental disorders in the national comorbidity survey replication. *Archives of General Psychiatry, 62,* 603–613.

Wang, S., Baillargeon, R., & Brueckner, L. (2004). Young infants' reasoning about hidden objects: Evidence from violation-of-expectation tasks with test trials only. *Cognition, 93,* 167–198.

Wang, S.-H., & Morris, R. G. M. (2010). Hippocampal-neocortical interactions in memory formation, consolidation, and reconsolidation. *Annual Review of Psychology, 61,* 49–79.

Warren, C. S. (2008). The influence of awareness and internalization of Western appearance ideals on body dissatisfaction in Euro-American and Hispanic males. *Psychology of Men & Masculinity, 9,* 257–266.

Warren, R. M. (1970). Perceptual restoration of missing speech sounds. *Science, 167,* 392–393.

Wasserman, E. A., & Young, M. E. (2010). Same-different discrimination: The keel and backbone of thought and reasoning. *Journal of Experimental Psychology: Animal Behavior Processes, 36,* 3–22.

Wasserman, E. A., & Zentall, T. R. (Eds.). (2006). *Comparative cognition: Experimental explorations of animal intelligence.* New York: Oxford University Press.

Waters, N. L., & Hans, V. P. (2009). A jury of one: Opinion formation, conformity, and dissent on juries. *Journal of Empirical Legal Studies, 6,* 513–540.

Watson, J. B. (1913). Psychology as the behaviorist views it. *Psychological Review, 20,* 158–177.

Watson, J. B. (1919). *Psychology from the standpoint of a behaviorist.* Philadelphia: Lippincott.

Watson, J. B. (1924). *Behaviorism.* New York: Norton.

Watson, J. B., & Rayner, R. (1920). Conditioned emotional reactions. *Journal of Experimental Psychology, 3,* 1–14.

Wax, M. L. (2004). Dream sharing as social practice. *Dreaming, 14,* 83–93.

Wechsler, D. (2002). *WPPSI-III manual.* San Antonio, TX: Psychological Corporation.

Wechsler, D. (2003). *WISC-IV manual.* San Antonio, TX: Psychological Corporation.

Wechsler, D. (2008). *Wechsler Adult Intelligence Scale—Fourth Edition.* San Antonio, TX: Pearson.

Weeks, J. W., Heimberg, R. G., Rodebaugh, T. L., & Norton, P. J. (2008). Exploring the relationship between fear of positive evaluation and social anxiety. *Journal of Anxiety Disorders, 22,* 386–400.

Weidner, R., & Find, G. R. (2007). The neural mechanisms underlying the Müller-Lyer illusion and its interaction with visuospatial judgments. *Cerebral Cortex, 17,* 878–884.

Weinberger, L. E., Sreenivasan, S., Garrick, T., & Osran, H. (2005). The impact of surgical castration on sexual recidivism risk among sexually violent predatory offenders. *The Journal of the American Academy of Psychiatry and the Law, 33,* 16–36.

Weinfield, N. S., Ogawa, J. R., & Sroufe, L. A. (1997). Early attachment as a pathway to adolescent peer competence. *Journal of Research on Adolescence, 7,* 241–265.

Weiss, A., Bates, T. C., & Luciano, M. (2008). Happiness is a personal(ity) thing: The genetics of personality and well-being in a representative sample. *Psychological Science, 19,* 205–210.

Weissenborn, R., & Duka, T. (2000). State-dependent effects of alcohol on explicit memory: The role of semantic associations. *Psychopharmacology, 149,* 98–106.

Welborn, B. L., Papademetris, X., Reis, D. L., Rajeevan, N., Bloise, S. M., & Gray, J. R. (2009). Variation in orbitofrontal cortex volume: Relation to sex, emotion regulation and affect. *Social Cognitive and Affective Neuroscience, 4,* 328–339.

Wellman, H. M., Fang, F., & Peterson, C. C. (2011). Sequential progressions in a theory-of-mind scale: Longitudinal perspectives. *Child Development, 82,* 780–792.

Wells, G. L., & Loftus, E. F. (2003). Eyewitness memory for people and events. In A. M. Goldstein (Ed.), *Handbook of psychology: Forensic psychology* (Vol. 11, pp. 149–160). New York: Wiley.

Werker, J. F. (1991). The ontogeny of speech perception. In I. G. Mattingly & M. Studdert-Kennedy (Eds.), *Modularity and the motor theory of speech perception* (pp. 91–109). Hillsdale, NJ: Erlbaum.

Werker, J. F., & Lalond, F. M. (1988). Cross-language speech perception: Initial capabilities and developmental change. *Developmental Psychology, 24,* 672–683.

Werker, J. F., & Tees, R. C. (1999). Influences on infant speech processing: Toward a new synthesis. *Annual Review of Psychology, 50,* 509–535.

Wertheimer, M. (1923). Untersuchungen zur lehre von der gestalt, II. *Psychologische Forschung, 4,* 301–350.

West, M. L., Yanos, P. T., Smith, S. M., Roe, D., & Lysaker, P. H. (2011). Prevalence of internalized stigma among persons with severe mental illness. *Stigma Research and Action, 1,* 54–59.

Wever, E. G. (1949). *Theory of hearing.* New York: Wiley.

Whitbourne, S. K., Sneed, J. R., & Sayer, A. (2009). Psychological development from college through midlife: A 34-year sequential study. *Developmental Psychology, 45,* 1328–1340.

Whitchurch, E. R., Wilson, T. D., & Gilbert, D. T. (2011). "He loves me, he loves me not...": Uncertainty can increase romantic attraction. *Psychological Science, 22,* 172–175.

Whorf, B. L. (1956). In J. B. Carroll (Ed.), *Language, and reality: Selected writings of Benjamin Lee Whorf.* Cambridge, MA: MIT Press.

Widom, C. S., Dutton, M. A., Czaja, S. J., & DuMont, K. A. (2005). Development and validation of a new instrument to assess lifetime trauma and victimization history. *Journal of Traumatic Stress, 18,* 519–531.

Wiggins, J. S. (1973). *Personality and prediction: Principles of personality assessment.* Reading, MA: Addison-Wesley.

Wilhelm, I., Diekelmann, S., Molzow, I., Ayoub, A., Mölle, M., & Born, J. (2011). Sleep selectively enhances memory expected to be of future relevance. *The Journal of Neuroscience, 31,* 1563–1569.

Wilkinson, S. (2010). *Choosing tomorrow's children: The ethics of selective reproduction.* Oxford: Oxford University Press.

Windy, D., & Ellis, A. (1997). *The practice of rational emotive behavior therapy.* New York: Springer.

Winter, D. G. (2010). Why achievement motivation predicts success in business but failure in politics: The importance of personal control. *Journal of Personality, 78,* 1637–1667.

Witherington, D. C., Campos, J. J., Anderson, D. I., Lejeune, L., & Seah, E. (2005). Avoidance of heights on the visual cliff in newly walking infants. *Infancy, 7,* 285–298.

Witt, J. K., & Proffitt, D. R. (2005). See the ball, hit the ball: Apparent ball size is correlated with batting average. *Psychological Science, 16,* 937–938.

Wittmann, M., Dinich, J., Merrow, M., & Roenneberg, T. (2006). Social jetlag: Misalignment of biological and social time. *Chronobiology International, 23,* 497–509.

Wittmann, M., Paulus, M., & Roenneberg, T. (2010). Decreased psychological well-being in late "chronotypes" is mediated by smoking and alcohol consumption. *Substance Use & Misuse, 45,* 15–30.

Wolcott, S., & Strapp, C. M. (2002). Dream recall frequency and dream detail as mediated by personality, behavior, and attitude. *Dreaming, 12,* 27–44.

Wolf, H. (2011). Odometry and insect navigation. *The Journal of Experimental Biology, 214,* 1629–1641.

Wolfe, J. M. (2003). Moving towards solutions to some enduring controversies in visual search. *Trends in Cognitive Science, 7,* 70–76.

Wolfe, J. M., Friedman-Hill, S. R., & Bilsky, A. B. (1994). Parallel processing of part-whole information in visual search tasks. *Perception & Psychophysics, 55,* 537–550.

Wolmer, L., Hamiel, D., & Laor, N. (2011). Preventing children's stress after disaster with teacher-based intervention: A controlled study. *Journal of the Academy of Child & Adolescent Psychiatry, 50,* 340–348.

Wolpe, J. (1958). *Psychotherapy by reciprocal inhibition.* Stanford, CA: Stanford University Press.

Wolpe, J. (1973). *The practice of behavior therapy* (2nd ed.). New York: Pergamon Press.

Wong, S. C. P., & Gordon, A. (2006). The validity and reliability of the violence risk scale: A treatment-friendly violence risk assessment tool. *Psychology, Public Policy, and Law, 12,* 279–309.

Wood, E., Desmarais, S., & Gugula, S. (2002). The impact of parenting experience of gender stereotyped toy play of children. *Sex Roles, 47,* 39–49.

Wood, J. M., Bootzin, R. R., Rosenhan, D., Nolen-Hoeksema, S., & Jourden, F. (1992). Effects of the 1989 San Francisco earthquake on frequency and content of nightmares. *Journal of Abnormal Psychology, 101,* 219–224.

Wood, S. J., Pantelis, C., Velakoulis, D., Yücel, M., Fornito, A., & McGorry, P. D. (2008). Progressive changes in the development toward schizophrenia: Studies in subjects at increased symptomatic risk. *Schizophrenia Bulletin, 34,* 322–329.

Wood, W. (2000). Attitude change: Persuasion and social influence. *Annual Review of Psychology, 51,* 539–570.

Wood, W., Lundgren, S., Ouellette, J. A., Busceme, S., & Blackstone, T. (1994). Minority influence: A meta-analytic review of social influence processes. *Psychological Bulletin, 115,* 323–345.

Woolf, C. J. (2011). Central sensitization: Implications for diagnosis and treatment of pain. *Pain, 152,* S2–S15.

Woolley, H. T. (1910). Psychological literature: A review of the recent literature on the psychology of sex. *Psychological Bulletin, 7,* 335–342.

Workman, B. (1990, December 1). Father guilty of killing daughter's friend, in '69. *San Francisco Examiner-Chronicle,* pp. 1, 4.

World Health Orgnization. (2008). The global burden of disease: 2004 update. Retrieved from www.who.int/healthinfo/global_burden_disease/GBD_report_2004update_full.pdf.

Wright, A. A., Katz, J. S., Magnotti, J., Elmore, L. C., Babb, S., & Alwin, S. (2010). Testing pigeon memory in a change detection task. *Psychonomic Bulletin & Review, 17,* 243–249.

Wright, L. B., Gregoski, M. J., Tingen, M. S., Barnes, V. A., & Treiber, F. A. (2011). Impact of stress reduction interventions on hostility and ambulatory systolic blood pressure in African American adolescents. *Journal of Black Psychology, 37,* 210–233.

Wright, M., Creed, P., & Zimmer-Gembeck, M. J. (2010). The development and initial validation of a brief daily hassles scale suitable for use with adolescents. *European Journal of Psychological Assessment, 26,* 220–226.

Wu, G. F., & Alvarez, E. (2011). The immunopathophysiology of multiple sclerosis. *Neurologic Clinics, 29,* 257–278.

Wyble, B., Potter, M. C., Bowman, H., & Nieuwenstein, M. (2011). Attentional episodes in visual perception. *Journal of Experimental Psychology: General, 140,* 488–505.

Yaeger, D. S., Trzesniewski, K. H., Tirri, K., Nokelainen, P., & Dweck, C. S. (2011). Adolescents' implicit theories predict desire for vengeance after peer conflict: Correlational and experimental evidence. *Developmental Psychology, 47,* 1090–1107.

Yamagata, S., Suzuki, A., Ando, J., Ono, Y., Kijima, N., Yoshimura, K., Osendorf, F., Angleitner, A., Riemann, R., Spinath, F. M., Livesley, W. J., & Jang, K. L. (2006). Is the genetic structure of human personality universal? A cross-cultural twin study from North America, Europe, and Asia. *Journal of Personality and Social Psychology, 90,* 987–998.

Yang, C. Y., Kim, S. J., & Lee, S. G. (2011). Identification and field evaluation of the sex pheromone of *Synanthedon bicingulata* (Staudinger). *Journal of Chemical Ecology, 37,* 398–402.

Yang, M., Wong, S. C. P., & Coid, J. (2010). The efficacy of violence prediction: A meta-analytic comparison of nine risk assessment tools. *Psychological Bulletin, 136,* 740–767.

Yegneswaran, B., & Shapiro, C. (2007). Do sleep deprivation and alcohol have the same effects of psychomotor performance? *Journal of Psychosomatic Medicine, 63,* 569–572.

Yeh, M. T., Coccaro, E. F., & Jacobson, K. C. (2010). Multivariate behavior genetic analyses of aggressive behavior subtypes. *Behavior Genetics, 40,* 603–617.

You, D., Maeda, Y., & Bebeau, M. J. (2011). Gender differences in moral sensitivity: A meta-analysis. *Ethics & Behavior, 21,* 262–282.

Youman, K., Drapalski, A., Stuewig, J., Bagley, K., & Tangney, J. (2010). Race differences in psychopathology and disparities in treatment seeking: Community and jail-based treatment-seeking patterns. *Psychological Services, 7,* 11–26.

Zacher, H., Rosing, K., Henning, T., & Frese, M. (2011). Establishing the next generation at work: Leader generativity as a moderator of the relationship between leader age, leader-member exchange, and leadership success. *Psychology and Aging, 26,* 241–252.

Zahn-Waxler, C., Shirtcliff, E. A., & Marceau, K. (2008). Disorders of childhood and adolescence: Gender and psychopathology. *Annual Review of Clinical Psychology, 4,* 275–303.

Zajacova, A., Lynch, M. S., & Espenshade, J. T. (2005). Self-efficacy, stress, and academic success in college. *Research in Higher Education, 46,* 677–706.

Zajonc, R. B. (1968). Attitudinal effects of mere exposure. *Journal of Personality and Social Psychology. Monograph Supplement, 9*(2, Part 2), 1–27.

Zajonc, R. B. (2000). Feeling and thinking: Closing the debate over the independence of affect. In J. P. Forgas (Ed.), *Feeling and thinking: The role of affect in social cognition* (pp. 31–58). New York: Cambridge University Press.

Zajonc, R. B. (2001). Mere exposure: A gateway to the subliminal. *Current Directions in Psychological Science, 10,* 224–228.

Zeanah, C. H., Smyke, A. T., Koga, S. F., & Carlson, E. (2005). Attachment in institutionalized and community children in Romania. *Child Development, 76,* 1015–1028.

Zeidner, M., & Shani-Zinovich, I. (2011). Do academically gifted and nongifted students differ on the Big-Five and adaptive status? Some recent data and conclusions. *Personality and Individual Differences, 51,* 566–570.

Zeineh, M. M., Engel, S. A., Thompson, P. M., & Bookheimer, S. Y. (2003). Dynamics of the hippocampus during encoding and retrieval of face-name pairs. *Science, 299,* 577–580.

Zelazo, P. D., Helwig, C. C., & Lau, A. (1996). Intention, act, and outcome in behavioral prediction and moral judgment. *Child Development, 67,* 2478–2492.

Zenderland, L. (1998). *Measuring minds: Henry Herbert Goddard and the origins of American intelligence testing.* Cambridge, UK: Cambridge University Press.

Zhai, F., Brooks-Gunn, J., & Waldfogel, J. (2011). Head Start and urban children's school readiness: A birth cohort study in 18 cities. *Developmental Psychology, 47,* 134–152.

Zheng, Z. Z., MacDonald, E. N., Munchall, K. G., & Johnsrude, I. S. (2011). Perceiving a stranger's voice as being one's own: A "rubber voice" illusion? *PLoS ONE, 6(4),* e18655.

Zimbardo, P. G. (2007). *The Lucifer effect: Understanding how good people turn evil.* New York: Random House.

Zimbardo, P. G., & Montgomery, K. D. (1957). The relative strengths of consummatory responses in hunger, thirst, and exploratory drive. *Journal of Comparative and Physiological Psychology, 50,* 504–508.

Zimbardo, P. G., & Radl, S. L. (1999). *The shy child* (2nd ed.). Los Altos, CA: Malor Press.

Zimmerman, B. J., Bandura, A., & Martinez-Pons, M. (1992). Self-motivation for academic attainment: The role of self-efficacy beliefs and personal goal setting. *American Educational Research Journal, 29,* 663–676.

Zuckerman, M. (2007). *Sensation seeking and risky behavior.* Washington, DC: American Psychological Association.

Zwaigenbaum, L., Bryson, S., Rogers, T., Roberts, W., Brian, J., & Szatmari, P. (2005). Behavioral manifestations of autism in the first year of life. *International Journal of Developmental Neuroscience, 23,* 143–152.

Name Index

Aapro, M. S., 157
Abecasis, G. R., 331, 360
Abelson, R. P., 194
Aben, K. K. H., 52, 53
Åberg, L., 395
Abrahamsen, R., 235
Abram, K. M., 422
Abramson, L. Y., 400
Accolla, R., 99
Acevedo, B. P., 471
Acosta-Rodriguez, V. A., 126
Adair, W., 76
Adam, H., 76
Adams, G., 470
Adams, J. L., 221, 225
Adams, J. S., 318
Adams, M., 452
Adams, R. E., 285
Adams, W. G., 452
Adamson, G., 410
Adaval, R., 233
Adcock, R. A., 68
Ader, R., 350
Adler, A., 367
Adler, L., 413
Adolph, K. E., 266
Adolphs, R., 68
Aeschbach, D., 126
Aftab, F., 130
Agartz, I., 408
Agarwal, P. K., 199
Agerström, J., 467
Ahmad, H., 219
Ahmad, N., 477
Ahmed, B., 263
Ainsworth, M., 282
Ainsworth, M. D. S., 282
Akechi, T., 157
Akinbami, L. J., 413
Akmajian, A., 214
Albarracín, D., 348, 461
Albert, M. K., 265
Albert, P., 286
Aleman, A., 396
Al-Gazali, L., 102
Alhusen, V. D., 286
Ali, F., 438
Ali, O., 26
Alink, L. R. A., 283
Alkire, M. T., 257, 289
Allan, C. A., 309
Allan, J. S., 126

Allebrandt, K., 133
Allen, J. J. B., 405
Allen, J. P., 286
Allik, J., 359
Allison, K. C., 393
Allport, G., 357, 358
Allport, G. W., 357, 359, 465
Almeida, L. S., 249
Alvarez, E., 58, 337
Alwin, S., 168, 340
Aly, M., 202
Alzheimer's Association, 202
Amabile, T., 448
Amabile, T. M., 225, 227
Amaral, D. G., 414
Amato, P. R., 288
Ambadar, Z., 425
Ambady, N., 28, 311
American Association
   on Intellectual and
   Developmental
   Disabilities, 246
American Psychological
   Association, 33
Amico, K. R., 348
Amir, N., 397
Amlaner, C. J., 128
Amsterdam, J. D., 437, 442
Anders, L. S., 250
Anderson, C. A., 475
Anderson, C. J., 475
Anderson, D. I., 265
Anderson, J. R., 175, 176
Anderson, P., 427
Anderson, S. E., 216
Anderson, S. L., 470
Ando, J., 360
Andreassen, O. A., 408
Andreu, J. M., 474
Andrews-Hanna J. R., 267
Andreyeva, T., 304
Angleitner, A., 360
Anstee, J. L. K., 476
Anthony, D. B., 375
Anyidoho, N. A., 369
Apfeldorf, W., 59
Apostoleris, N. H., 290
Apple, K. J., 312, 313
Appleby, D. C., 6
Aragon, S. R., 314
Arbeitman, L., 413
Arendt, J., 126

Arendt, R., 264
Argyropoulos, S. V., 396
Aristotle, 6
Armistead, L., 314
Armstrong, L., 299
Arndt, J., 375
Arnett, J. J., 12, 285
Arnold, B., 177
Arnold, R. M., 353
Arnon, Z., 382
Arnow, B. A., 440, 441
Arntz, A., 413
Aron, A., 469, 471, 472
Aron, A. P., 329
Aron, E. N., 471, 472
Aronson, E., 469
Aronson, J., 255
Arora, R., 332
Arruda, J., 95
Arterberry, M. E., 324
Asaad, W., 439
Asarnow, J. R., 413
Asch, S., 455
Asch, S. E., 455, 456
Ashton, M. C., 249
Aslin, R. N., 276
Asllani, E., 139
Atkins, D. C., 421, 435
Atkinson, J. W., 315, 316
Attwell, D., 56
The Autism Genome Project
   (AGP), 414
Avny, S. B., 435
Avrahami, A., 344
Axelton, A. M., 315
Ayduk, O., 371, 372
Ayoub, A., 128
Azzato, E. M., 52

Baad-Hansen, L., 235
Baardseth, T., 421
Baars, B. J., 123, 125, 213, 366
Baas, M., 330
Baas, P. C., 344
Babb, S., 168, 340
Babson, K. A., 397
Back, M. D., 379
Backlin, W., 185
Baddeley, A., 181
Baddeley, A. D., 181, 185
Badzakova-Trajov, G., 73
Bagley, K., 421

Bahrick, H. P., 274
Bahrick, P. O., 274
Baier, B., 99, 308
Bailey, B. A., 264
Bailine, S. H., 439
Baillargeon, R., 271
Baim, M., 349
Bainbridge, D., 139
Bakanic, V., 139
Bakeman, R., 314, 324
Baker, T. B., 347
Bakermans-Kranenburg,
   M. J., 283
Bakiri, Y., 56
Bakken, T. E., 408
Balch, R. W., 456
Balda, R. P., 167
Balderrama-Durbin, C., 435
Baldwin, D. S., 438
Baldwin, S., 421
Ball, S. G., 60
Balsam, K. F., 287
Baltes, M., 293
Baltes, P., 293
Baltes, P. B., 274, 293, 294
Banaji, M., 461
Banaji, M. R., 467
Bandelow, B., 412
Bandura, A., 168, 169, 372,
   373, 428, 432, 475
Banich, M. T., 267
Banks, S., 128
Baños, R., 427
Banyai, E. I., 134
Barak, A., 435
Barbaranelli, C., 474
Barbe, R. P., 422, 438
Barbelivien, A., 75
Bárez, M., 343
Bargh, J., 473
Bargh, J. A., 473
Bar-Hillel, M., 232
Bark, R. J., 128
Barkataki, I., 408
Barker, R., 474
Barkley, R., 413
Barnes, T. R. E., 437
Barnes, V. A., 352
Barnett, A., 132
Baron, S. H., 455
Baron-Cohen, S., 289, 414
Barrera, M., Jr., 399

Barrett, L. F., 210
Barrett, M. S., 423, 441
Barrick, T. R., 274
Barrios, F. A., 292
Barry, R. A., 324
Barsade, S. G., 250
Bartels, M., 252, 253
Bartholow, B. D., 475
Bartlett, F., 196
Bartlett, F. C., 196
Bartoshuk, L. M., 99, 111
Bartz, J. A., 61
Basinger, K. S., 292
Basso, E. B., 131
Bassok, M., 225
Bastardi, A., 29
Bastien, C. H., 129
Bates, T. C., 331
Batson, C. D., 476, 477, 478
Batty, G. D., 247, 351, 370
Baucom, D. H., 435
Bauer, J. J., 369
Bauer, M., 438
Baum, J. R., 249
Baumeister, R. F., 338, 376
Baumgartner, T., 61
Bauminger, N., 285
Bayley, N., 265
Beach, F. A., 308
Bearden, C. E., 410
Beauchaine, T. P., 287
Beauchamp, G. K., 99
Beaupre, M., 325
Bebbington, P., 352, 410
Bebeau, M. J., 292
Becerra, L., 68
Bechara, A., 68
Beck, A., 399
Beck, A. T., 396, 399, 430, 431
Beck, H. P., 153
Becker, D. M., 52, 53
Becker, L. C., 52, 53
Becker, S. W., 31
Becker-Matero, N., 411
Bedell, S. J., 477
Beebe, H., 273
Beeman, M. J., 226
Beer, J. S., 362
Beevers, C. G., 399, 400
Begley, A. E., 127
Behne, T., 272
Behrendt, A. E., 402
Behrendt, R., 289
Beigbeder, S. A., 372
Beilock, S. L., 181
Belik, S.-L., 401
Bell, D. C., 310
Bellebaum, C., 68
Bellini, M., 306
Belsky, J., 286
Bem, D., 314
Bem, D. J., 314, 464

Bem, S. L., 39
Bendersky, M., 246, 264
Benedetti, F., 60, 102
Benedict, R., 285, 300
Benenson, J. F., 290
Benet-Martinez, V., 359
Benight, C. C., 432
Benish, S. G., 421
Benjamin, L. T., Jr., 8
Benjet, C., 162
Bennett, D. S., 246, 264
Bennett, S. N., 52
Ben-Porath, Y. S., 380, 381
Benson, H., 349
Berenson, K. R., 411
Berg, C. A., 344
Berger, T., 442
Berglund, P., 386, 389, 392,
    394, 397, 398, 399, 414, 421
Bering, J. M., 124
Berkowitz, L., 474
Berkowitz, S. J., 476
Berlin, B., 218
Berlyne, D. E., 300
Berman, A. L., 402
Berman, M. G., 103
Bermejo, M. R., 249
Bermudez, A., 442
Bernal, G., 421
Bernard, L. L., 300
Berndt, S. I., 52
Bernstein, D. P., 413
Berscheid, E., 471
Bersoff, D. M., 293
Bersoff, D. N., 32
Bertholf, M., 38
Best, R., 123, 225
Beucke, J. C., 153
Biagi, E., 157
Bialystok, E., 279
Biederman, J., 413
Biehl, M., 325
Biel, M. B., 438
Bielak, A. A. M., 273
Bieneck, S., 312
Bierbach, D., 309
Bikmen, N., 255, 256
Billig, M., 466
Billings, A. G., 341
Bilsky, A. B., 125
Binet, A., 243
Bird, B. J., 249
Birkett, M., 314
Birmaher, B., 438
Birthelmer, A., 141
Biss, R. K., 330
Bitensky, S. H., 162
Bjerkedal, T., 253
Bjorklund, D. F., 124
Björnsdottir, G., 52, 53
Bjorvatn, B., 130
Blackburn, J. S., 140

Blacklow, B., 435
Blackstone, T., 457
Blagrove, M., 132
Blair, J. R., 412
Blair D. C., 344
Blais, C., 325
Blaney, N., 469
Blasco, T., 343
Blascovich, J., 377
Blatter, K., 126, 133
Blaye, A., 279
Blehar, M., 282
Bleich, S., 431, 432
Bleidorn, W., 360
Blessum, K. A., 461
Bleuler, M., 408
Blickstein, I., 52
Block, S., 218
Block, S. D., 353
Bloise, S. M., 289
Blok, S. V., 193
Blond, A., 307
Blos, P., 285
Bloss, C. S., 408
Blum, A. M. B., 311
Blumberg, H. P., 399
Blumenthal, J., 409
Blumenthal, J. D., 289
Blunt, J. R., 199
Blustein, D. L., 318
Boardman, J. D., 346
Bock, K., 8, 213
Bodell, L. P., 307
Bodenhausen, G. V., 375
Boerwinkle, E., 52
Bogle, K. A., 312
Bohannon, J. N. III, 197
Bohlin, G., 282
Bohner, G., 461
Boisjoli, J. A., 162, 429
Bokor, S., 304
Bolden, L., 421
Bolger, N., 61
Bolhuis, J. J., 281
Bolino, M. C., 318
Bolland, J., 476
Bolton, D., 427
Bolton, J. M., 401
Bomyea, J., 397
Bonanno, G. A., 341
Bond, B. J., 23
Bond, C. F., Jr., 190, 219
Bongartz, W., 135
Boniel-Nissim, M., 435
Boomsma, D. I., 52, 252, 253
Booth, R. J., 350, 366
Bootzin, R. R., 130
Borges, G., 401
Borges, N. J., 382
Born, J., 128
Bornstein, M. H., 282, 324
Bornstein, R. F., 411

Boroditsky, L., 219
Borrelli, B., 348
Borsook, D., 68
Boschini, D. J., 439
Botella, C., 427
Bouchard, T. J., Jr., 360
Boucher, H. C., 375
Boulard, N. E., 421
Bouris, A., 314
Bourolly, J. N., 441
Bourque, F., 410
Boutros, N. N., 408
Bovbjerg, D. H., 157, 350
Bowden, E. M., 226
Bowdend, E. M., 73
Bower, T. G. R., 289
Bowlby, J., 281, 284
Bowman, H., 209
Boyd, H. A., 52, 53
Boyd, J. E., 415
Boyd, R. C., 441
Boyes-Braem, P., 193
Boysen, G. A., 467
Brackbill, R. M., 338, 395
Brainerd, C. J., 269
Bramel, D., 456
Bramsen, I., 343
Branje, S. J. T., 285
Brannick, M. T., 479
Brans, R. G. H., 408
Brar, J., 432
Brassen, S., 235
Braun, K. A., 196
Bravo, M., 405, 406
Brechwald, W. A., 285
Brédart, S., 397
Breedlove, S. M., 289
Breland, K., 166
Breland, M., 166
Brennan, M., 268
Brennan, P. A., 400
Brennan, S. E., 211, 213
Brent, D. A., 402, 438
Breslin, P. A. S., 99
Bretón-López, J., 427
Brewer, G. A., 185
Brewer, M. B., 466
Brian, J., 414
Bridge, J. A., 422, 438
Briñol, P., 460
Briskin, J. K., 390
Broadbent, E., 207
Broca, P., 62
Brocklehurst, P. H., 213
Broder, J., 282
Brody, N., 249
Bromet, E. J., 401
Brondel, L., 303
Bronfenbrenner, U., 261
Broocks, A., 412
Brook, J., 412
Brooks, K. P., 288

Folkman, S., 340, 341
Folmer, A. S., 317
Fonagy, P., 282
Fontanilla, I., 350, 351, 366
Forbes, C., 467
Forbes, E. A., 309
Forbey, J. D., 381
Ford, C. S., 308
Fordyce, J. A., 49
Foret, M., 349
Forgas, J. P., 330
Forman, J., 337
Fornito, A., 409
Forselius, E., 132
Förster, J., 228
Försterling, F., 448
Fortenberry, K. T., 344
Fortin, A., 98
Fortuna, K., 287
Foster, C. A., 287
Foster, R. G., 128
Fotopoulou, A., 111
Foucault, M., 422
Foulkes, D., 130
Fournier, J. C., 437, 442
Fowler, H., 300
Fox, J., 206
Fox, M. C., 123, 225
Fox, N. A., 281, 284
Frager, R., 368, 425
Fraley, B., 472
Fraley, R. C., 472
Frank, J. B., 440
Frank, J. D., 440
Frank, M. C., 218, 231
Frank, M. E., 99
Franke, B., 52, 53, 413
Frankenburg, F. R., 412
Franklin, A., 277
Franklin, N., 221
Franko, D. L., 393
Frans, Ö., 395
Fraser, L. M., 439
Fraser, S. C., 464
Fratta, W., 138
Frederick, D. A., 470
Frederick, S., 232
Fredericks, C. A., 399
Fredrikson, M., 395
Freedman, J. L., 464
Freeman, M. S., 264
Freeman, R., 185
Fregni, F., 62
Freiburger, P., 311
Frenda, S. J., 199
Frens, J., 123
Frese, M., 288
Freud, A., 285
Freud, S., 9, 131, 369, 425
Freund, A. M., 293
Frey, D., 477, 478
Fricchione, G., 349

Frick, F., 228
Friedman, B. H., 329
Friedman, M., 351
Friedman, M. S., 402
Friedman, R. S., 228
Friedman-Hill, S. R., 125
Friend, R., 456
Friesen, C. A., 361
Friesen, W. V., 324, 325, 327
Frijns, T., 285
Fromkin, V. A., 213
Froud, D. M., 438
Fry, B., 52
Fuchs, J., 167
Fuchs, P. N., 102
Furley, P., 122
Furman, O., 203
Furukawa, T. A., 157

Gabriel, S., 6
Gabrieli, J. D. E., 327, 331, 359, 360
Gage, P., 62
Gaissmaier, W., 230, 231
Galani, R., 75
Galati, A., 213
Galbicka, G., 429
Gale, C. R., 247, 370
Galea, S., 338, 395
Galesic, M., 35
Galinsky, A. D., 228, 473
Gallace, A., 101
Gallagher, M. W., 129
Gallup, G. G., Jr., 470
Galperin, G. J., 390
Galton, F., 240, 241
Galvan, A., 268, 285
Gamez, M., 312
Ganis, F., 221
Ganis, G., 219
Ganor-Stern, D., 210
Gao, Q., 303
Garb, H. N., 382
Garbarino-Pico, E., 126
Garcia, J., 155, 156
García-Palacios, A., 427
Garcia-Retamero, R., 35
Garcías, P., 405, 406
Gardner, B. T., 217
Gardner, C. O., 399
Gardner, H., 249, 250
Gardner, R. A., 217
Garrick, T., 309
Garrison, M. M., 27
Gasparovic, C., 59
Gatchel, R. J., 102
Gatz, M., 399
Gaultney, J. F., 28
Gautron, L., 304
Gauvain, M., 273
Gavrilets, S., 49
Gazit, T., 382

Gazzaniga, M., 71
Gazzaniga, M. S., 72
Gebhard, R. H., 312
Geenen, R., 339
Geisler, P., 129
Gelenberg, A. J., 440, 441
Geller, F., 52, 53
Gelso, C. J., 424
George, W. H., 435
Geraerts, E., 425
Geraghty, A. W. A., 440
Gercek-Swing, B., 377
Gergen, K. J., 12
Germain, M., 461
Gerrig, R. J., 212
Gershoff, E. T., 162
Gershon, E. S., 408
Getz, S., 268, 285
Gewirtz, J. C., 138
Giannakidou, A., 277
Gibbons, A., 50
Gibbons, M. B., 441
Gibbons, M. B. C., 425
Gibbs, J. C., 292
Gibson, E., 218, 265
Gibson, E. J., 265
Gibson, J. J., 106
Giedd, J., 257
Giedd, J. N., 289, 409
Gieldman, G., 476
Giesbrecht, T., 405
Gigerenzer, G., 125, 230, 231
Gilbert, D. T., 333, 471
Gildersleeve, K., 311
Gilkes, A., 255, 256
Gilligan, C., 292
Gillis, R., 26
Gilman, S. E., 314
Gilmore, R., 455
Gilovich, T., 233, 449
Gil-Rivas, V., 345
Gitlin, M. J., 437
Glaser, R., 350
Glasman, L. R., 461
Gleaves, D. H., 405
Glick, P., 311
Glisky, E. L., 405
Gloppen, K., 314
Glover, G., 327
Glück, J., 273
Gochman, P., 409
Goddard, A. W., 60
Goddard, H., 251
Goddard, H. H., 251
Godden, D. R., 185
Godin, G., 461
Gogtay, N., 257, 289
Golay, A., 138
Gold, S., 436
Goldberg, A. E., 287
Goldfried, M. R., 419, 431, 441, 442

Golding, J., 290
Goldin-Meadow, S., 277
Goldrick, M., 213
Goldstein, D., 133
Goldstein, N. J., 464
Goldstein, R. B., 395, 412
Goldstrom, I. D., 435
Goldwater, B., 165
Golledge, J., 375
Golomb, J. D., 103, 210
Golombok, S., 290
Gonzalez, A., 469
Goodheart, C. D., 441
Goodman, T., 136
Goodwin, G., 438
Goonawardena, A. V., 137
Gorchoff, S. M., 288
Gordijn, M., 133
Gordon, A., 16
Gordon, K., 412
Gordon, N. J., 219
Gordon, P., 218
Gore, J. C., 399
Gorman, S., 102
Gosi-Greguss, A. C., 134
Gotlib, I. H., 123, 359, 399
Gottesman, I., 408
Gottesman, I. I., 408
Gottfredson, L. S., 243, 255
Gottfresdon, L. S., 249
Gottrand, F., 304
Gouin, J.-P., 350
Gould, E., 75
Grabsch, B., 436
Graham, J. R., 380
Granic, I., 162
Grann, M., 16
Grant, B. F., 395, 412
Grant, B. R., 48
Grant, J. E., 140
Grant, M. L., 246
Grant, P. R., 48
Grasby, P. M., 396
Grassi, A., 129
Gratz, S., 197
Gray, J. R., 289
Gray, M. R., 282
Gray, W. D., 193
Greaves, N., 414
Green, D. L., 73
Green, D. M., 83
Green, J. P., 134
Green, W. N., 141
Greenberg, A., 469
Greenberg, J., 375, 376
Greenberg, S. T., 421
Greene, J. D., 125
Greene, R. L., 381
Greenfield, P. M., 255
Greenhill, L. L., 413
Green-Paden, L. D., 162, 429
Greenstein, D., 257

Kalia, R., 438
Kalin, N. H., 327
Kalisch, R., 235
Kallmann, F. J., 408
Kalueff, A. V., 59
Kam, C. M., 476
Kamachi, M., 325
Kamal, M., 52
Kamil, A. C., 167
Kamin, L. J., 152
Kammrath, L. K., 361
Kandler, C., 360
Kane, J. M., 437
Kane, M. J., 182
Kantermann, T., 133
Kapfhamer, J., 218
Kaplan, C. A., 225
Kaprio, J., 128, 304
Kapur, V. K., 130
Káradóttir, R., 56
Karasik, L. B., 266
Karavasilis, L., 283
Karbani, G., 102
Karg, K., 403
Karlson, C., 129
Karpiak, C. P., 419
Karpicke, J. D., 199
Kasen, S., 412
Kasper, S., 438
Kassebaum, N. L., 254
Kastenmüller, A., 477, 478
Kastner, S., 88
Katz, E. P., 415
Katz, J. S., 168, 340
Kavaliers, M., 157
Kay, P., 218
Kazdin, A. E., 162, 441
Kegeles, S., 348
Keil, A., 135
Keil, F. C., 272
Kelche, C., 75
Kellas, G., 123
Keller, M. C., 52
Keller, M. E., 289, 440, 441
Kellermann, T., 289
Kelley, H., 448
Kelley, H. H., 448
Kellis, M., 52
Kellner, C. H., 439
Kellough, J. L., 400
Keltner, N. L., 439
Kemp, R. I., 200
Kempermann, G., 75
Kendall, P., 441
Kendall, P. C., 435
Kendler, K. S., 314, 396, 399, 400
Kennedy, R. E., 399
Kennedy, S. E., 205
Kenny, D. A., 477
Kenrick, D. T., 470
Keough, M., 264

Keren, G., 234
Kermer, D. A., 333
Kerr, G. T., 475
Kerr, N. L., 457
Kesebir, P., 287, 331, 332
Keshavan, M. S., 60, 406, 408, 410, 437
Kessler, R. C., 306, 314, 386, 389, 392, 393, 394, 397, 398, 399, 400, 401, 411, 412, 413, 414, 421
Ketten, D. R., 95
Kettenmann, H., 56
Keyes, M., 413
Keys, C. B., 435
Khan, A. Y., 438
Khan, H., 414
Kidd, K. K., 253
Kiecolt-Glaser, J. K., 350
Kieffer, E., 308
Kielcolt-Glaser, J. K., 350
Kiemeney, L. A., 52, 53
Kievit, R. A., 219
Kihlstrom, J. F., 134, 372
Kihlstrom, J. R., 372
Kijima, N., 360
Kilmer, R. P., 345
Kilpatrick, D., 139
Kilpatrick, L., 289
Kilpatrick, L. A., 136
Kim, C.-H., 439
Kim, H. S., 343
Kim, J., 471
Kim, J. W., 439
Kim, M. J., 327
Kim, S., 324
Kim, S. J., 99, 308
Kim, Y.-K., 51
King, D. B., 7
King, L., 340
King, M., 106
King, T. Z., 182
Kingdom, F. A. A., 110
Kinsey, A., 312
Kinsey, A. C., 312
Kintsch, W., 216
Kiortsis, D. N., 138
Kirbach, A., 167
Kirby, K. C., 429
Kirchner, H. L., 264
Kirsch, I., 134
Kirschner, F., 225
Kirschner, P. A., 225
Kirschner, S. M., 390
Kirsten, B., 289
Kisilevsky, B. S., 265
Kissane, D. W., 436
Kissane, R. J., 278
Kissling, W., 437
Kitamura, C., 276
Kitayama, S., 76, 376, 377, 449, 463

Kivimäki, M., 337
Klatt, K. P., 163
Klauer, S. E., 286
Kleider, H. M., 182
Klein, D. N., 440, 441
Klein, E., 382
Klein, L. C., 335
Klein, M., 424
Klein, O., 466
Kliegman, R., 264
Klosterhalfen, S., 157
Klump, K. L., 306
Klute, C., 285
Knapp, R., 439
Knauss, L., 381
Knickmeyer, R., 289
Knight, R. T., 202
Knobloch, L. K., 23
Kobiella, A., 324
Koblofsky, M., 167
Kochanek, K. D., 401
Kochanska, G., 324
Kocovski, N. L., 343
Kocsis, J. H., 440, 441
Koelling, R. A., 155
Koenig, B. W., 314
Koenig, J., 141
Koffka, K., 104
Koga, S. F., 285
Kogan, M. D., 304
Kogan, N., 226
Kohlberg, L., 291
Köhler, W., 104
Kohn, N., 289
Koida, K., 93
Komatsu, H., 157
Komossa, K., 437
Konen, C. S., 88
Kong, A., 52, 53
Kong, L. L., 405
Kontis, T. C., 194
Koo, M.-S., 439
Koocher, G. P., 442
Koot, H. M., 283
Korchmaros, J. D., 477
Koriat, A., 185
Kornblith, A. B., 157
Koscik, T. R., 68
Koskenvuo, M., 128, 337
Kosloff, S., 376
Kosslyn, S. M., 221
Kotovsky, K., 225
Kotrschal, K., 168
Kounios, J., 73
Koutri, I., 341
Kovacs, P., 52, 53
Kovacs-Nagy, R., 134
Krackow, E., 425
Kraemer, H. C., 306, 440, 441
Kraepelin, E., 388
Kraft, P., 52
Krahé, B., 312

Kramer, A. F., 273
Krämer, N. C., 379
Kranick, S. M., 404
Krank, M. D., 155
Krause, J., 412
Kray, L. J., 228
Krebs, D. L., 291
Krikeli, V., 341
Kringlen, E., 412
Kristensen, P., 253
Krohne, H. W., 343
Kronauer, R. E., 126
Kronmarck, C., 309
Kross, E., 103
Krueger, F., 257
Krueger, J., 375
Krueger, J. I., 376, 477, 478
Kruger, J., 231
Kruglanski, A. W., 125
Krystal, J. H., 399
Kuang, J. C., 315
Kubik, S., 74
Kudoh, T., 325
Kuehnle, T., 133
Kuhlmeier, V. A., 272
Kuhn, J. W., 400
Kuhn, M. H., 377
Kuijer, R., 339
Kuipers, E., 352, 410
Kujawski, J. H., 289
Kulik, J., 197
Kumari, V., 408
Kupfer, D. J., 127
Kuppens, P., 331
Kurjak, A., 263
Kurtz, J. E., 381
Kyriacou, C. P., 126
Kyvik, K. O., 304

LaBar, K. S., 68
Labayen, I., 304
LaBerge, S., 132
Laborde, S., 250
Lacadie, C. M., 399
Lachman, M. E., 261, 273
Lackenbauer, S., 463
Lafavor, T. L., 342
LaGrange, B., 317
Lake, J. K., 213
Lakoma, M. D., 353
Lalond, F. M., 275
LaMattina, S. M., 421
Lamb, R. J., 429
Lambert, D. B., 435
Lambert, S. F., 476
Lambert, T. A., 312, 313
Lammers, J., 311
Lamoreaux, M., 449
Lampinen, J. M., 195
Landau, M., 376
Lander, E. S., 51, 52
Landers, E., 246

Rayner, R., 153
Realo, A., 331
Reardon, L. E., 397
Recanzone, G. H., 97
Redding, C. A., 347
Reder, L. M., 274
Reeb-Sutherland, B. C., 281
Rees, G., 106
Rees, H. V., 348
Regalia, C., 375
Regan, G., 348
Regan, R. T., 464
Rehm, L. P., 146
Reich, D. B., 412
Reichborn-Kjennerud, T., 331
Reichman, A. L., 411
Reid, V. M., 324
Reilly, D., 100
Reimann, F., 102
Reimer, T., 231
Reinecker, H., 431, 432
Reinhard, I., 130
Reinhardt, J. P., 268
Reis, D. L., 289
Reis, H. T., 471
Reis, S. M., 247
Reise, S. P., 359
Reissig, C. J., 60, 137
Reiter, L., 167
Remick, A. K., 303
Ren, L., 438
Renken, R., 396
Renzulli, J. S., 246, 247
Rescorla, R., 151
Rescorla, R. A., 151, 152
Resnick, H., 139
Rettek, S. I., 377
Reuben, C. A., 413
Reyna, V. R., 35
Reynolds, C. F., 127
Reynolds, J. S., 343
Reynolds, K. A., 344
Rhemtulla, M., 254
Rhodes, G., 470
Rhodes, M. G., 191
Rhudy, J. L., 130
Ribeiro, S. C., 205
Richards, D., 442
Richardson, J.-M., 476
Riedel, G., 137
Rief, W., 207
Riegert, C., 141
Riela, S., 471
Riemann, R., 360
Riggs, D. S., 339
Riis, J. L., 209
Rijsdijk, F. V., 413
Riley, B., 408
Rimm, E. B., 52
Rimmer, D. W., 126
Rimmö, P. A., 395
Rimol, L. M., 408

Rinck, M., 221
Risen, J. L., 333
Ritchey, M., 68
Ritchie, P. L.-J., 15
Rizolatti, G., 56
Robbins, A., 106
Robert, G., 130
Roberts, A., 306
Roberts, B. W., 375
Roberts, E., 102
Roberts, R. D., 250
Roberts, R. P., 73
Roberts, W., 414
Robins, R. W., 375
Robinson, H. A., 17
Robinson, M. J., 60
Rockstroh, B., 75, 76
Rodd, J. M., 216
Roddey, C., 408
Rodebaugh, T. L., 394
Rodham, K., 402
Rodriguez, E. T., 261
Rodriguez, G., 471
Rodriguez, M. L., 371, 372
Rodríguez Castro, Y., 311
Roe, D., 415
Roediger, H. L., 199
Roediger, H. L., III., 119, 175,
    187, 199
Roenneberg, T., 133
Roese, N. J., 123, 235
Rogers, C., 10, 368
Rogers, C. R., 368, 433
Rogers, J. A., 435
Rogers, M. A. M., 436
Rogers, S. M., 313
Rogers, T., 414
Rogoff, B., 273
Rohrer, J. H., 455
Roid, G., 244
Roisman, G. I., 287
Role, L. W., 303
Roll, J. M., 429
Rolls, E. T., 99
Romer, M., 303
Ronai, Z., 134
Ronda, J. M., 126
Rooth, D.-O., 467
Rorschach, H., 381
Rosario, M., 476
Rosch, E., 193
Rosch, E. H., 193, 194
Roscoe, J. A., 157
Rose, A. J., 290
Rose, L. M., 52
Rose, M. E., 140
Roseman, I. J., 377
Rosen, K. S., 311
Rosenfeld, J. P., 219
Rosenhan, D., 130, 387
Rosenhan, D. L., 387

Rosenman, R. F., 351
Rosenstein, R. E., 126
Rosenthal, A. M., 477
Rosenthal, G. E., 349
Rosenthal, R., 25, 450
Rosenzweig, M., 74
Rosenzweig, M. R., 74
Rosing, K., 288
Roskes, E. J., 390
Roskos-Ewoldsen, D. R., 461
Ross, C. A., 405
Ross, D., 168, 475
Ross, L., 29, 448, 459
Ross, N. O., 193
Ross, S. A., 168, 475
Ross, W., 442
Rotbard, N., 139
Rotello, C. M., 228
Roth, D. A., 308
Roth, P. L., 316
Rothbart, M. K., 281
Rothbaum, B. O., 427, 440, 441
Rothblum, E. D., 287, 314
Rothmaier, K., 141
Rothman, D. J., 422
Rothman, N., 52
Rothrauff, T., 288
Rothstein, H. R., 475
Rothwell, P. E., 138
Rotter, J., 370
Rotter, J. B., 301, 370
Rougemont-Bücking, A., 153
Rouse, S. V., 381
Roussi, P., 341, 343
Rowlett, J. K., 139
Røysamb, E., 331, 399
Rozin, P., 153
Ruan, W. J., 412
Rubenstein, A. J., 469
Rubin, D. C., 194, 197, 198
Rubin, M., 466
Ruble, D. N., 289
Ruby, M. B., 26
Ruch, R., 251
Rucklidge, J. J., 413
Rudd, M. D., 402
Rudolph, K. D., 290
Rudolph, M. S. L., 390
Rudolph, U., 438
Ruitenbeek, H. M., 424
Ruiz, J. M., 352
Ruiz, J. R., 304
Rukavishnikov, A. A., 381
Rule, B. G., 475
Rule, N. O., 28, 311
Rummel-Kluge, C., 437
Runco, M. A., 226
Rupert, A. V., 233
Rusakov, D. A., 56
Rusconi, E., 62
Rush, A. J., 431, 440, 441

Russell, E. M., 331
Russell, J. M., 60, 438
Russo, R., 138
Rust, J., 290
Rüther, E., 412
Rutkowski, B., 137
Rutter, P. A., 402
Rutz, S., 141
Ruzic, L., 267
Ryan, R. M., 315
Rydell, A.-M., 282
Ryder, R. D., 33

Sachdev, P., 306
Sachdeva, S., 292
Sack, R. L., 126
Sadeh, N., 412
Saffran, J., 218
Saffran, J. R., 276
Sagawa, R., 157
Sai, F. Z., 265
Saint Onge, J. M., 346
Sakaeda, A. R., 369
Sakalli-Ugurlu, N., 311
Sakamoto, A., 475
Sakamoto, M., 157
Salary, C. B., 438
Salazar, X., 348
Saleem, M., 475
Salihagić-Kadić, A., 263
Salihu, H. M., 264
Saling, M. M., 439
Salovey, P., 250
Salthouse, T. A., 273
Salvator, A., 264
Salvy, S.-J., 308
Salzinger, S., 476
Samanez-Larkin, G. R., 288
Sammel, M. D., 99
Samplson, S., 439
Samuel, A. G., 114
Samuelson, M., 349
Sanchini, S., 138
Sanderman, R., 344
Sanders, M., 163
Sanderson, C. A., 372
Sandøe, P., 33
Sandrini, M., 62
Sandstrom, M. J., 366
Santhi, N., 126
Santiago, C. D., 339
Sapir, E., 218
Sareen, J., 394, 401
Sargent, J. D., 347
Sargent, P. A., 396
Sasvari-Szekely, M., 134
Satir, V., 435
Sato, S., 472
Sattler, J. M., 244
Saucier, D. A., 315
Savage-Rum, S., 217
Savage-Rumbaugh, S., 217

Warren, R. M., 114
Warren, T., 216
Wartenburger, I., 257
Washburn, A. L., 303
Washburn, M. F., 8
Wason, P. C., 229
Wasserman, E. A., 167, 168
Waters, E., 282
Waters, N. L., 456
Watkins, R., 402
Watson, J., 10, 146
Watson, J. B., 146, 153
Watson, J. M., 113
Watumull, J., 218
Wax, M. L., 131
Weber, E., 84
Weber, J., 244, 250
Wechsler, D., 244
Wedekind, D., 412
Weeks, J. C., 353
Weeks, J. W., 394
Weidner, G., 352
Weidner, R., 111
Weinberg, R. A., 51
Weinberger, L. E., 309
Weiner, D. A., 422
Weiner, I. B., 381
Weinfield, N. S., 282
Weinstein, N., 315
Weiss, A., 247, 331, 351
Weiss, F., 140
Weiss, R. B., 157
Weiss, S., 351
Weissenborn, R., 185
Welborn, B. L., 289
Wellman, H. M., 272
Wells, D. L., 284
Wells, E. M., 289
Wells, G. L., 198
Wells, K. B., 398, 421
Wells, R. E., 235, 236
Wells, T. A., 476
Wells, T. T., 400
Wen, W., 306
Werker, J., 275
Werker, J. F., 275
Wernicke, C., 69
Wertheimer, M., 7, 104
West, M. L., 415
Westbay, L., 471
Wever, E. G., 96
Whalen, P. J., 327
Whalley, B., 440
Wheeler, D., 464
Whipple, K., 426
Whitbourne, S. K., 288
Whitchurch, E. R., 471
White, B., 99
White, B. J., 468
White, H. R., 412
White, K., 235
White, K. W., 369

White, M., 393
Whiteman, S. D., 290
Whiteside, A., 477
Whitfield, S. L., 359
Whorf, B. L., 218
Wicher, M., 477, 478
Wicks, M. N., 421
Widom, C. S., 395, 412
Wiebe, D. J., 344
Wienbruch, C., 75, 76
Wienske, K., 303
Wiesel, T., 89
Wietkunat, R., 349
Wiggers, T., 344
Wiggins, J. S., 240
Wilcox, W. B., 287
Wilfley, D. E., 305
Wilhelm, I., 128
Wilhelm, O., 182
Wilkinson, S., 53
Willard, J., 451
Willemsen, G., 253
Willi, Y., 48
Williams, B., 403
Williams, C. L., 381
Williams, D. R., 339
Williams, J. M., 219
Williams, R., 102
Williams, S. L., 349
Williamson, E. M., 26
Williamson, P., 246
Willis, H., 466
Wilson, A. E., 31
Wilson, C., 255
Wilson, G. D., 314
Wilson, J., 427
Wilson, M., 455
Wilson, R. E., 264
Wilson, R. S., 273
Wilson, T. D., 333, 471
Winarick, D. J., 411
Windy, D., 431
Winograd, G., 441
Winter, D. G., 316
Winter, S., 379
Wiprzycka, U. J., 133
Wirtz, D., 231
Witherington, D. C., 265
Wittchen, H. U., 400
Witte, T., 402
Witthöft, M., 404
Wittlinger, R. P., 274
Wittmann, M., 133
Wixted, J. T., 201
Wojtowica, A. E., 432
Wolcott, S., 132
Wolf, H., 99
Wolf, K., 284
Wolfe, J. M., 125
Wolford, G., 233
Woll, B., 73
Wolmer, L., 342

Wolpe, J., 426, 427
Wong, S. C. P., 16
Wood, E., 290
Wood, J. J., 435
Wood, J. M., 130, 382
Wood, J. N., 102
Wood, J. V., 375
Wood, S. J., 409
Wood, W., 457, 463
Woodard, E., 169
Woods, C. G., 102
Woods, J. H., 140
Woods, T., 253
Woodward, A. L., 272
Woodward, M., 437
Woody, W. D., 7
Wooley, H. T., 9
Woolf, C. J., 146
Workman, B., 425
World Health Organization, 398
Wray, N. R., 306
Wright, A. A., 168, 340
Wright, D. C., 130
Wright, J., 371, 372
Wright, J. C., 371
Wright, L. B., 352
Wright, M., 168, 340
Wright, S., 472
Wright, S. C., 469
Wu, G. F., 58
Wu, M. N., 129
Wulff, K., 128
Wundt, W., 6
Wyble, B., 209
Wyer, R. S., Jr., 233
Wymelbeke, V. V., 303
Wynn, K., 272

Xie, X., 52, 265
Xu, J., 401
Xu, Xiaomeng, 471

Yacubian, J., 235
Yamada, A.-M., 421
Yamagata, S., 318, 360, 381
Yanek, L. R., 52, 53
Yang, C., 475
Yang, C. R., 60
Yang, C. Y., 99, 308
Yang, H., 76
Yang, M., 16
Yang, M. H., 413
Yang, S., 279
Yang, Y., 395
Yanos, P. T., 415
Ye, H.-H., 265
Yeager, D. S., 362
Yeager, M., 52
Yegneswaran, B., 128
Yeh, M. T., 474
Yeo, R. A., 257
Yeung, A., 349

Yi, J., 435
Yin, J., 477
Yonelinas, A. P., 202
York, D., 381
Yorkston, N. J., 426
Yoshimura, K., 360
You, D., 292
Youman, K., 421
Young, A. H., 438
Young, M. E., 168
Young, S. E., 474
Young, Sir Thomas, 92
Yu, K., 52
Yücel, M., 409
Yuen, T., 342

Zachariae, R., 235, 350
Zacher, H., 288
Zadra, A., 130
Zahn-Waxler, C., 413
Zajacova, A., 373
Zajonc, R. B., 330, 469
Zaki, J., 61
Zanarini, M. C., 412
Zanna, A. S., 463
Zanna, M. P., 463
Zaslavsky, A. M., 413
Zawidzki, T. W., 50
Zeanah, C. H., 284, 285
Zee, P. C., 126
Zeelenberg, M., 235
Zeffiro, T. A., 153
Zeidner, M., 247
Zelazo, P. D., 133
Zenderland, L., 251
Zentall, T. R., 167
Zervoulis, K., 290
Zhai, F., 254
Zhang, K., 265
Zhang, Y., 395
Zhang, Z., 286
Zhao, S., 273, 400
Zhao, Z., 327
Zheng, Z. Z., 111
Ziegelmann, J., 348
Zijdenbos, A. P., 289
Zimand, E., 427
Zimbardo, P., 38
Zimbardo, P. G., 4, 134, 299, 330, 452, 474
Zimmer-Gembeck, M. J., 168, 340
Zimmerman, R. R., 283
Zimmermann, E., 167
Zinberg, J. L., 410
Zitman, F. G., 396
Zodan, J., 382
Zook, J. M., 31
Zubieta, J. K., 205
Zucerkman, E., 157
Zuckerman, M., 347
Zulley, J., 129
Zwaigenbaum, L., 414

Subject Index

process for including disorders in, 393
versions of, 388–389
Dual-center model of eating, 303
Dynamic factors, 16

Eardrum, 95
Ears. *See* Hearing
Eating, 302–307
brain control of, 303
central responses and, 303
culture and, 304
obesity/overweight and, 304–305
oral gratification and, 364
peripheral responses and, 302–303
physiology of, 302–303
in presence of others, 308
psychology of, 304–307
social context of, 308
Eating disorders, 305–307, 392
in *DSM-IV-TR (Diagnostic and Statistical Manual of Mental Disorders)*, 393
Echolocation, 97, 98
Ecstasy, 137, 140
The Eden Express (Vonnegut), 406
Education
and cognition, 273
intellectual disability and, 246
progressive education, 8
EEG (electroencephalogram), 63
sleep cycles and, 126–127
Effexor, 438
Ego, 365
psychoanalysis and, 423
psychological disorders and, 391
repression and, 365–366
Egocentrism, 270
Ego defense mechanisms, 365–366
Ego integrity *vs.* despair stage, 280
Egoism, 476
Ego-overcontrol scale, 39
Eidetic imagery, 178
Elaboration likelihood model, 461
Elaborative rehearsal, 190
exam-preparation and, 192
Elavil, 437
Electroconvulsive therapy (ECT), 439
Electromagnetic spectrum, 90, 91
E-mail
and personality, 379
psychotherapists using, 442
Embrainment, 76
Embryonic stage, 263
Emergency, bystander intervention in, 478
Emergency reaction system, 334–335
Emotional deficits, 400

Emotional intelligence, 249–250
Emotional reactivity and schizophrenia, 410
Emotional responsivity, 474
Emotion-focused coping with stress, 341
Emotion regulation, 331
Emotions, 323–326
adaptive functions of, 323
amygdala and, 68
antisocial personality disorder and, 412
Cannon–Bard theory of central neural processes, 328
classical conditioning and, 153–154
cognitive appraisal theories of, 328–330
culture and, 323–326
health and, 350
impact of, 330–331
innate responses, 323–324
James-Lange theory of emotion, 327
learned helplessness and, 400
physiology of, 326–327
predicting future emotions, 333
schizophrenia and, 406, 410
subjective well-being, 331–332
theories of, 326–330
two-factor theory of, 328
Empathy-altruism hypothesis, 477
Empiricist view, 6
Empty chair technique, 434
Empty nest situation, 288
Encephalization, 50
Encoding
brain activity for, 202
in cognitive-affective personality theory, 371
context and, 184–187
and long-term memory, 182
processes of, 187–188
serial position effect, 185–187
and short-term memory, 176
Encoding specificity, 184
exam-preparation and, 192
Endocannabinoids, 137, 138
Endocrine system, 73–74
list of glands and hormones, 74
Endogenous morphine, 138
Endorphins, 60, 102
opiates and, 138
Engram, 200
Entrepreneurs, 316
Environment. *See also* Nature *vs.* nurture
borderline personality disorders and, 412
consciousness and, 124

intelligence quotient (IQ) and, 253–255
plasticity of brain and, 74
schizophrenia and, 409–410
Epilepsy, 71
Epinephrine and stress response, 334
Episodic buffer, 181
Episodic memories, 183
Equilibrium and motivation, 299
Equity theory, 318
Erogenous zones, 101
Eros drive, 363
Adler, Alfred and, 367
Erotic stimuli, 309
Escape conditioning, 159
Esteem. *See* Self-esteem
Estrogen, 74, 308
Ethics
of animal research, 33–34
intelligence assessment and, 256–257
and research, 32–34
Etiology, 390–392, 419
Eugenics movement, 241
Eustress, 333, 344
Evening people, 133
Evolution, 47–50
adolescence and, 267–268
cultural evolution, 50
human evolution, 50
language and, 217–218
personality traits and, 360
of sexual behaviors, 310–312
Evolutionary perspective, 11–12
and aggression, 13
Evolutionary psychology, 51
Excitatory inputs, 56, 57
Excitement phase of sexual arousal, 310
Exemplars, 195
Exercise. *See* Physical exercise
Exhaustion from stress, 336
Existentialist approaches, 433
Expectancy
in cognitive-affective personality theory, 371
effects, 25
outcome-based expectancies, 374
in Rotter's personality theory, 370
theory, 319
Expectations
influence of, 114–116
and motivation, 300–301
and self-fulfilling prophecies, 450–451
Experience
deductive reasoning and, 229
eyewitness memory and, 199
learning and, 145

German measles. *See* Rubella
Germinal stage, 263
Gestalt psychology, 7
    perceptual grouping and, 104
Gestalt therapy, 434
GHB, 137, 139
Giftedness, 246–247
Glia, 56
Glial cells (glia), 56
Global-specific explanatory style, 400
Glutamate, 59
Goal-directed attention, 103
Goals
    in cognitive-affective personality
        theory, 371
    of psychology, 3–5
    of therapies, 419
Goal state of problem, 224
Gonads, 308
Good continuation, law of, 105
Good Samaritan parable, 478
Graduate Record Examination, 24
Grammar, 275
    acquisition of, 277
    operating principles for, 277
Grandeur, delusions of, 407
Graphs, 40–41
Griots, 325
Group decision-making, 457–458
Group polarization, 457
Group therapies, 434–436
    community support groups,
        435–436
Groupthink, 457–458
Guilty conditions, 219
Gustation, 99

Habitats, 48
Habitual criminal murderers, 38
Habituation, 146
Hair cells of ear, 95
Haldol, 437
Hallucinations, 111
    hallucinogenic drugs and, 137
    methamphetamines and, 140
    and narcolepsy, 129
    and schizophrenia, 406
Hallucinogenic drugs, 137
Haloperidol, 437
Hammer of ear, 95, 96
Happiness, 331, 332
    steps for, 353
Harmony and health, 345
Hashish, 137
Head Start program, 254
Health. *See also* Treatment
    AIDS and, 347–348
    biopsychosocial model of, 345–348
    cigarette smoking and, 346–347

defined, 345
job burnout and health care
    system, 352–353
optimism and, 352
personality and, 351–352
promotion of, 346
psychological impact on
    outcomes, 350–351
science, 3
self-esteem and, 375
steps for better health, 353
traditional health practices, 345
Health psychology, 323, 345–353
    exercise and, 348
Hearing, 93–98
    in adulthood, 268
    auditory cortex and, 70
    of infants, 264
    physiology of, 95–98
    sound localization, 97–98
    structure of ear, 96
Heart disease, 351
Heaven's Gate cult, 456
Hemispheric lateralization, 71–73
Hereditary Genius (Galton), 240
Heredity, 51
Heritability. *See also* Genetics
    and behavior, 47–53
    estimate, 252, 253
    and intelligence quotient (IQ),
        251–253
    measuring, 52–53
    of personality traits, 360
Heroin, 137–138
    classical conditioning and, 155
Hertz (Hz), 93
    pitch and, 94
Heuristics, 225
    anchoring heuristic, 233–234
    availability heuristic, 231–232
    and judgment, 230–234
    representativeness heuristic,
        232–233
Hierarchy
    and long-term memory, 193–194
    of needs (Maslow), 301–302
High/Scope Perry program, 254
High self-esteem, 375
Hippocampus, 68
    dreams and, 132
    memory and, 201
    neurogenesis in, 75
Histograms, 41
History of psychology, 5–8
    women researchers, 8–9
HIV/AIDS, 347–348
    emotional writing and, 350, 351
    psychological impact on
        outcomes, 350–351

HMOs (health maintenance
    organizations) and drug
    therapies, 436
HMS *Beagle*, 47
Holistic view, 10
    of personality, 369
Homelessness, 422
Homeostasis, 68, 299
Homo erectus, 50
Homophobia, 314
Homo sapiens, 50
Homosexuality, 287, 313–315.
    See also Prejudice
    awareness of, 314
    nature *vs.* nurture and, 313–314
    society and, 314–315
    suicide and, 402
Hooking up, 312, 313
Horizontal cells, 87
Hormones, 73–74
    sexual arousal and, 308
Hostility
    and health, 351–352
    NEO-PI dimension for, 381
Hot/spicy foods, 99
Hozho concept, 345
Hue, 91
Human behavior genetics, 51
Human deprivation, 284
Human development. *See*
    Development
Human Genome Project (HGP), 52, 53
Humanistic perspective, 10
    and aggression, 13
    of personality, 368–370
Humanistic therapies, 419, 432–434
    client-centered therapy, 433–434
    Gestalt therapy, 434
Human-potential
    movement, 433
Hunger and marijuana, 138
Hunger center, 303
Hyperactivity-impulsivity, 413
Hypercomplex cells, 89
Hypnosis, 133–135
    effects of, 134–135
Hypnotic induction, 134
Hypnotizability, 134
Hypochondriasis, 380, 402–404
Hypomania, 380
Hyposmia, 98
Hypothalamus, 68
    eating and, 303
    and endocrine system, 74
    stress response and, 327, 334
Hypotheses, 22
    with behavior measures, 31
    perceptual processes and, 81
    and word meanings, 276

Ion channels, 57
Ions, 56–57
Iraq, Abu Ghraib prison, 453
Iris of eye, 85
Irrationality, 387
Isolation, 365
    methamphetamines and, 140
    suicide and, 402

James-Lange theory of emotion, 327
Jealousy
    and schizophrenia, 407
Jet lag, 126
Job burnout, 352–353
Judgment, 230–236
    anchoring heuristic, 233–234
    availability heuristic, 231–232
    defined, 230
    heuristics and, 230–234
    representativeness heuristic,
      232–233
    self-efficacy judgments, 373
Just noticeable difference (JND), 84

Kahneman, Daniel, 231
Kinesthetic intelligence, 249, 250
Kinesthetic senses, 101
Knowledge. *See also* Intelligence
    procedural knowledge, 274
Korsakoff's syndrome, 201

Labels, effect of, 386–387
Language, 211–220. *See also*
    Grammar; Words
    acquisition of, 274–278
    ambiguity, resolving, 214–216
    audience design and, 211–212
    autistic disorder and, 413–414
    Broca's aphasia, 71
    cognitive perspective and, 11
    community membership and, 212
    and culture, 218–220
    errors in speech, 212–214
    and evolution, 50, 217–218
    Grice's maxims in production,
      211, 212
    hemispheric lateralization and,
      72–73
    lying, 219
    -making capacity, 277
    meanings of words, learning, 276
    operating principles for, 277
    perceiving speech and words, 275
    production, 211–214
    propositions, 216
    representations and, 216
    and schizophrenia, 406
    speech execution and errors,
      212–214

structure of, 275
thought and, 218–220
unconscious processes and, 123
understanding, 214–217
Language style matching, 23, 28
Latent content
    to behavior, 364
    of dreams, 131, 423
Lateral hypothalamus (LH), 303
Lawful patterns, 22
Law of closure, 105
Law of common fate, 105
Law of effect, 157
Law of good continuation, 105
Law of proximity, 105
Law of similarity, 105
Learned helplessness, 400
Learning. *See also* Social learning
    biology and, 166
    change and, 145–146
    cognitive influences on, 167–170
    cognitive maps, 167
    comparative cognition, 167–168
    defined, 145
    disorders, 245, 246
    habituation and, 146
    instinctual drift, 166
    observational learning, 168–170
    sensitization and, 146
    taste-aversion learning, 155
Learning-performance distinction, 145
Learning theories of personality,
    370–374
Left visual field, 71, 72
Legal system, psychology and, 16
Lens of eye, 85, 86
Leptin, 303, 304
Lesbians. *See* Homosexuality
Lesions, 62
Levels of analysis, 3, 4
Levels-of-processing theory, 187
Lexical ambiguity, 214, 215
Lexical meaning, 275
Libido, 363
Lieben und Arbeiten, 286
Life-change units (LCUs), 337
Life events
    and schizophrenia, 410
    and stress reactions, 337–338
    and subjective well-being, 331–332
Life span contextualism, 273
Life span development. *See*
    Development
Life stories, 369
Light and circadian rhythms, 126
Lightness constancy, 110–111
Liking, 469–471
Limbic system, 68
    and adolescence, 267

cingulotomy, 438–439
    and emotions, 327
Linear perspective, 108
Linguistic intelligence, 249, 250
Linguistic relativity, 218, 219
Literacy, 35
Lithium salts, 438
Little Albert experiment, 153, 396
Liver and stress response, 334
Lobotomy, 438
Locomotion sequence, 266, 267
Locus of control, 371
Logical intelligence, 249, 250
Logic and deductive reasoning,
    227–229
Longitudinal design, 261–262
Long-term memory, 177
    dimensions of, 184
    hierarchies and, 193–194
    representations, using, 194–196
    schemas and, 194
    structures in, 192–200
Loudness, 94
Loving, 471–472
Low self-esteem, 375
LSD (lysergic acid diethylamide),
    60, 137
Lucid dreaming, 132
Lying, 219
    and antisocial personality
      disorder, 412

Maintenance rehearsal, 180
Maladaptiveness, 386–387
Mandala, 367
Manic depression. *See* Bipolar
    disorder
Manic episodes, 398
Manifest content
    to behavior, 364
    of dreams, 131, 423
MAO (monoamine oxidase)
    inhibitors, 437
Marcia, James, 285
Marijuana, 137, 138
    state-dependent memory and, 185
Marriage
    and divorce, 288
    and young adulthood, 287
Masculinity-femininity scale
    MMPI-2, 380
Maslow's hierarchy of needs, 301–302
Mastery goals, 318
Material me, 374
Mathematical intelligence, 249
Maturation, 265
Maximizers, 235
Mayan culture and dreams, 131
McNaughton rule, 390

MDMA (Ecstasy), 137, 140
Mean, 41–42
Measles. *See* Rubella
Measurement, 28–32. *See also*
Statistics
behavioral measures, 30–32
of heritability, 52–53
reliability and, 30
self-report measures, 30
validity and, 30
Measures of central tendency, 41–42
Media
and aggression, 475
observational learning and,
168–170
Median, 41
Medical students' disease, 392
Meditation, 135–136, 349, 350
Medulla, 67
Meissner corpuscles, 100
Melatonin, 126
Memory. *See also* Encoding; Implicit
memory; Long-term memory;
Metamemory; Reconstructive
memory; Retrieval; Short-term
memory
amnesia, 201
amygdala and, 68
availability heuristic and, 231–232
biological aspects of, 200–203
brain imaging and, 202–203
categories, using, 194–196
cognitive maps and, 167
context and encoding, 184–187
declarative memory, 175
defined, 174
disorders, 201–202
distortions, 196
engram, 200
episodic memories, 183
exam-preparation and, 192
exemplars and, 195
explicit memory, 174–175
eyewitness memory, 198–200
flashbulb memories, 197–198
forgetting, 188–189
functions of, 174–176
iconic memory, 177–178
implicit memory, 174–175
improving, 189–190
interference and, 189
internal working model, 282
and older adults, 274
preconscious memories, 121, 122
propositions and, 216
psychoanalysis and, 423
repressed/recovered memories, 425
span, 179
Men. *See* Gender

Menarche, 267
Menopause, 268
Menstruation, 267
Mental age, 243
Mental hospitals, history of, 422
Mental illness. *See also* Psychological
disorders
drug therapies for, 437
Mental processes, 2
Mental representations, 176
Mental resources, 208–210
Mental retardation, 246
Mental rotation, 220
Mental set, 116, 230
Mere exposure effect, 330
Merkel disks, 100
Meta-analysis, 440
Metamemory, 190–191
exam preparation and, 192
prefrontal cortex and, 202
Methamphetamines, 137, 140
Method of loci, 190, 191
Middle ear, 95
Mimicry, 473
Mind-altering drugs, 136–141
Mindfulness meditation, 135
Minimal groups, 466
Minority influence and conformity,
456–457
Mirror neuron, 56
Misattribution, 329
Misinformation effect, 199
MMPI (Minnesota Multiphasic
Personality Inventory), 39, 380–381
content scales for MMPI-2, 380
MMPI-2, 380–381
Mnemonics, 190
exam-preparation and, 192
Mode, 41
Modern racism, 466
Modern sexism, 466
Monocular depth cues, 108
Monozygotic (MZ) twins, 52. *See also*
Twin studies
Mood disorders. *See also* Bipolar
disorder; Depression
behavioral perspective on, 399
biology and, 399
causes of, 399–400
characteristics of, 398
cognitive perspective on, 399–400
dopamine and, 60
major depressive disorder, 397–398
norepinephrine and, 60
psychodynamic model of, 399
suicide, 401–402
Moods, 323
impact of, 330–331
self-esteem and, 375

Moral development, 290–293
culture and, 290–293
gender and, 290–293
Morality, 290
Moral reasoning, 290–293
Moral standards, 292
abnormality and, 387
Morbidity, 389
Morning people, 133
Morphemes, 275
Morphine, 60, 102, 137
Mortality frame, 234
Motion cues, 107–108
Motion parallax, 108
Motion perception, 106
Motion sickness, 101
Motivation. *See also* Eating
academic achievement and, 318
cognitive approaches to, 300–301
dissonance and, 463
expectations and, 300–301
functions of concepts, 298–299
hierarchy of needs and, 301–302
learned helplessness and, 400
observational learning and, 169
possible selves and, 375
for prosocial behavior, 476
sources of, 299–301
Motivational deficits, 400
Motor cortex, 69, 70
Motor neurons, 54, 55
Motor set, 116
MRI (magnetic resonance imaging),
63–64. *See also* Functional MRI
(fMRI)
Müller-Lyer illusion, 111, 112
Multiple intelligences theory, 249–250
Multiple interpretations, 115
Multiple personality disorder, 405
Multiple sclerosis (MS), 58
Murder, 38
Muscles and motor cortex, 69–70
Musical intelligence, 249, 250
Mutual support groups, 435
Myelin sheath, 55, 56
damage to, 58
My Lai massacre, 458

Naloxone, 60
Naming explosion phase, 276
Nanometers, 90–91
Narcolepsy, 129
Narratives, 369
National Comorbidity Study
(NCS), 389
on depression, 398
Nativist view, 6
Naturalistic observations, 31
Naturalist intelligence, 249, 250

Photoreceptors, 86
Physical aggression, 474
Physical attractiveness, 469–470
Physical development, 263–269
 in adolescence, 266–268
 in adulthood, 268
 in childhood, 265–266
 of infants, 264–265
 prenatal development, 263
Physical exercise
 health psychology and, 348
Physiological dependence, 137
Pinna, 95
Pitch, 94
 perception theories, 95–97
Pituitary gland, 74
 and stress response, 334–335
Placebo effect, 25
 controls, 26
 hypnosis and, 134
Placebo therapy, 440
Place recognition, 88
Place theory, 96
Planning function of consciousness, 124
Plaques, 202
Plasticity, 74–75
Plateau phase of sexual arousal, 310
Plurals, rules for, 277–278
Poggendorf illusion, 112
Polarized cells, 57
Polygenic traits, 52
Pons, 67
Ponzo illusion, 108, 109
Populations, 26
 variations in, 48
Positive correlations, 27, 28
Positive evaluation of violence, 474
Positive psychology, 331
Positive punishers, 160
Positive reinforcement/reinforcers, 159
 response deprivation and, 163
 strategies, 428–429
Positive transference, 424
Positron emission tomography (PET)
 scans, 63
Possible selves, 375
Posterior parahippocampal gyrus
 (pPHG), 202, 203
Posterior pituitary gland, 74
Postevent information, 198, 199
Posttraumatic growth, 345
Posttraumatic stress disorder. See
 PTSD (posttraumatic stress
 disorder)
Potassium and action potentials, 56
Poverty
 intelligence quotient (IQ) and, 253
 social development and, 278
Power of the situation, 451–460

PQ4R (Preview, Question, Read,
 Reflect, Recite, Review)
 technique, 17
Practical intelligence, 249
Practice index, 376
Pragmatics, 275
Preconscious memories, 121, 122
Preconventional morality, 292
Predictability. See Contingency
Predictions, 4–5
Preferences and classical
 conditioning, 153–154
Prefrontal cortex, and memory, 202
Prefrontal lobotomy, 438
Pregnancy
 intellectual disability and, 246
 teratogens and, 264
Prejudice, 465–469
 implicit prejudice, 467–468
 origins of, 465–466
 reversing, 468–469
 stereotypes and, 466–467
Premature infants, 130
Prenatal development, 263
Preoperational stage, 270
Preparedness hypothesis, 395
Preschool Activities Inventory
 (PSAI), 290
Pressure on skin, 100
*Pretrial Juror Attitude Questionnaire
 (PJAQ)*, 242
Prevention strategies, 441–442
Primacy effect, 185
Primary appraisal of stress, 340
Primary colors, 93
Primary prevention, 441
Primary reinforcers, 162
Priming and implicit memory,
 187–188
Principled morality, 292
Principle of contrast, 276
Principles of Physiological Psychology
 (Wundt), 6–7
The Principles of Psychology (James), 7
Principlism, 476
Proactive interference, 189
Problem-directed coping with
 stress, 341
Problem solving, 223–227
 analogical problem solving, 229
 functional fixedness and, 225
 improving, 225
 inductive reasoning and, 229
Problem spaces, 224
Procedural knowledge, 274
Procedural memory, 175
Procrastination, 338
Production of language, 211–214
Prognosis, 419

Progressive education, 8
Projection, 365, 366
Projective test for personality,
 381–382
Propositions and language, 216
Prosocial behavior, 473–478
 bystander intervention, 477–478
 observational learning and,
 168–169
 situational effects on, 477–478
 volunteering, 479
Prototypes and memory, 195
Provocation and aggression, 475
Proximal stimulus, 80–82
Proximity, law of, 105
Prozac, 60, 437, 438
Psilocybe mushrooms, 136
Psychedelics, 137
Psychiatrists, 420
Psychic determinism, 364
Psychic energy, 363
Psychoactive drugs, 136. *See also*
 Drugs
Psychoanalysis, 423
Psychoanalysts, 420, 423
Psychobiography, 369
Psychodynamic model, 9–10, 391
 and aggression, 13
 and anxiety disorders, 396
 and mood disorders, 399
 of personality, 363–368
 for therapies, 419
Psychodynamic therapy, 422–425
 later therapies, 424–425
Psychological assessment, 240
Psychological dependence, 137
Psychological diagnosis, 388, 419
Psychological disorders. *See also
 specific types*
 abnormal, labeling behavior as,
 386–387
 ADHD (attention deficit
 hyperactivity disorder), 413
 behavioral model, 391
 biological approaches, 391
 of children, 413–414
 classifying, 388–390
 cognitive perspective on, 391
 dissociative disorders, 404–405
 etiology of, 390–392
 history of classification, 388
 and homelessness, 422
 interactionist perspective, 391
 nature of, 386–392
 nature *vs.* nurture, explaining, 403
 objectivity and, 387–388
 panic disorder, 392–393
 phobias, 393–394
 prevention strategies, 441–442

Spontaneous recovery
   in classical conditioning, 150
   in operant conditioning, 160
Spontaneous-remission effect, 440
Spoonerisms, 213
SSRIs (selective serotonin reuptake
   inhibitors), 437
Stability *vs.* instability, 316
Stable–unstable explanatory style, 400
Standard deviation (SD), 42
Standardization
   and assessment, 242–243
   and objectivity challenge, 23
Stanford-Binet Intelligence Scale,
   43, 244
Stanford Hypnotic Susceptibility
   Scale, 134
Stanford Prison Experiment, 451–453
Stanford Shyness Survey, 39
State-dependent memory, 185
Static factors, 16
Statistical rarity, 387
Statistical significance, 43–44
Statistics
   analyzing data, 38–45
   correlation, 43
   descriptive statistics, 40–43
   frequency distributions, 40
   graphs, 40–41
   inferential statistics, 39, 44
   measures of central tendency,
      41–42
   misleading results, 45
   normal curve, 43
   psychometric theories and, 248
   statistical significance, 43–44
   variability, measures of, 42–43
Stealing and antisocial personality
   disorder, 412
Stem cells, 74
Stereotypes
   gender stereotypes, 289–290
   of passionate love, 471
   prejudice and, 466–467
   of sexual behavior, 308
Stereotype threat, 255–256, 467
Stigma of mental illness, 414–415
Stimulants, 140–141
   medical uses of, 137
Stimulus
   absolute thresholds, 82–83
   categorization, 208
   distal stimulus, 80–82
   generalization, 150–151
   just noticeable difference (JND), 84
   proximal stimulus, 80–82
Stimulus discrimination, 151
   and operant conditioning, 160, 161
Stimulus-driven attention, 103–104

Stimulus–response (S–R)
   connection, 157
Stirrup of ear, 95, 96
St. Mary of Bethlehem, 422
Storage, 176
   episodic buffer, 181
Storm and stress of adolescence, 285
Strange Situation Test, 282
Stress, 332. *See also* Chronic stress
   appraisal of, 340–341
   benefit finding, 344
   coping with, 340–344
   daily hassles and, 339–340
   dissociative disorders and, 405
   general adaptation syndrome
      (GAS) and, 335–336
   inoculation, 342
   moderator variables, 341
   modifying cognitive strategies,
      342–343
   physiological stress reactions,
      333–336
   positive effects of, 344–345
   procrastination and, 338
   psychological stress reactions,
      336–340
   and psychosomatic disorders, 336
   resilience and, 342
   schizophrenia and, 409–410
   self-statements and coping, 342, 343
   social support and, 343–344
   tend-and-befriend response, 335
   traumatic events and, 338
Stressors, 333
   controllable/uncontrollable
      stressors, 341
Striatum and memory, 201
Strobe lights, 106
Strokes
   brain plasticity and, 75
   prenatal strokes, 264
Structural ambiguity, 214
Structuralism, 7
Study strategies and techniques,
   16–17
Subfields of psychology, 14–15
Subjective well-being, 331–332
Subjectivity, 4
Sublimation, 365
Substance abuse, 136. *See also*
   Alcohol; Drugs
   disorders, 392
Subtractive color mixture, 92
Success, attributions for, 316–317
Successful aging, 293
Sucking reflex, 264
Sudden murderers, 38
Suicide, 401–402
   homosexuality and, 314

Suicide cults, 456
Sunlight, 91
Superego, 365
   psychoanalysis and, 423
   psychological disorders and, 391
Superior temporal gyrus (STG),
   202, 203
Supertasters, 99, 100
Survey research, self-reports, 30
Survival
   consciousness and, 124
   of the fittest, 49
   perception and, 80
Syllogisms, 227, 228
Symbolic modeling therapy, 428
Sympathetic division, 65
Sympathetic nervous system, 66
   and emotions, 326
Symptom substitution, 426
Synapses, 58
Synaptic cleft, 59
Synaptic transmission, 58–59
Synaptic vesicles, 59
Syntax, 275
Syphilis, 246
Systematic desensitization, 427

Tardive dyskinesia, 437
Taste, 99–100
   hot/spicy foods and, 99
   receptors, 99–100
Taste-aversion learning, 155
Taste buds, 99
Telegraphic speech, 277
Television. *See* Media
Temperament, 281
   parenting styles and, 282–284
Temperature, sensitivity to, 100–101
Temporal distinctiveness, 185
Temporal integration, 105–106
Temporal lobe, 69
Temporal parietal junction (TPJ),
   202, 203
Temporal pole (TP), 202, 203
Tend-and-befriend
   response, 335
Tension
   motivation and reduction of, 299
   systems, 363
Teonanacatl, 136
Teratogens, 264
Terminal buttons, 54, 55
Terror management theory, 375,
   376, 377
Tertiary prevention, 441–442
Testes, 74
Testing effect, 199
Testosterone, 74, 289
   sexual arousal and, 309

Ventricles of brain and schizophrenia, 408, 409
Ventromedial hypothalamus (VMH), 303
Verbal Behavior (Skinner), 11
Vestibular senses, 101
Viagra, 312
Vicarious punishment, 168
Vicarious reinforcement, 168
Victimization and dissociative symptoms, 405, 406
Video games and aggression, 475
Violence. *See* Aggression and violence
Violence Risk Scale (VRS), 16
Virtual reality techniques, 427
Visual cliff research, 265, 266
Visual cognition, 220–222
    brain and, 222
    in infants, 265
    mental rotation, 220
    visual representations, 221
Visual cortex, 70, 88
Visual imagination, 221
Visual memory, 177
Visual pathways to cortex, 89
Visual system, 85–93. *See also* Blindness; Retina
    accommodation process, 86
    in adulthood, 268
    blind spot, 87–88
    brain processes, 88–90
    color, seeing, 90–93

of infants, 265
neural pathways for, 71
structures of eye, 85
visual cortex and, 70, 88
Visuospatial sketchpad, 181
Vitreous humor, 85
Volley principle, 96
Volunteering, 479
Vomiting and opiate addiction, 138
Vonnegut, Mark, 406
Vulnerability, NEO-PI dimension for, 381

Warm fibers, 101
Wason selection task, 229
Wavelengths of light, 90–92
Wealth
    intelligence quotient (IQ) and, 253
    subjective well-being and, 332
Weber's law, 84
Wechsler Adult Intelligence Scale (WAIS), 244
Wechsler Intelligence Scale for Children—Fourth Edition (WISC-IV), 244
Wechsler Preschool and Primary Scale of Intelligence—Third Edition (WPPSI-III), 244
Well-being, subjective, 331–332
Well-defined problem, 224
Wellness, 346. *See also* Health
Wernicke's area, 69

WHO (World Health Organization)
    depression, study on, 398
Whole-report procedure, 178, 179
Wisdom, 274
Wish-fulfillment, 131
Withdrawal-related emotional responses, 327, 360
Withdrawal symptoms, 137
Within-subjects design, 26
Wolof people, Senegal, 325
Womb envy, 367
Women. *See* Gender
Woodworth Personal Data Sheet, 380
Words
    meanings, learning, 276
Work and organizational psychology, 317–319
Working memory, 180–182
World Trade Center attacks. *See* September 11th attacks
World War I, intelligence assessment in, 244

Xanax, 59, 139, 438
X chromosome, 51
    color blindness and, 92

Y chromosome, 51
Young-Helmholtz trichromatic theory, 93
Youth suicide, 401–402

Zöllner illusion, 112
Zygotes, 263

Credits

Chapter 1

Photos: CO: p. 1: © Form Advertising/Alamy; p. 3, topleft: Copyright © Myrleen Ferguson Cate/PhotoEdit; p. 3, topright: © Tony Savino/The Image Works; p. 3, bottomleft: Copyright © David Young-Wolff/PhotoEdit; p. 3, bottomright: © Michael Schwarz/The Image Works; p. 5: Copyright © Jeff Greenberg/PhotoEdit; p. 7: © INTERFOTO/Alamy; p. 8: Copyright © Michael Newman/PhotoEdit; p. 8: Archives of the History of American Psychology, The Center for the History of Psychology–The University of Akron; p. 9: ZUMA Press/Newscom; p. 10: Courtesy of Prof. Ben Harris, University of New Hampshire; p. 11: Michael Rougier/Time & Life Pictures/Getty Images; p. 12: Wolfgang Kaehler/Glow Images; p. 15: Copyright © David Kelly Crow/PhotoEdit.

Figure: Fig 1.1: © INTERFOTO/Alamy.

Chapter 2

Photos: CO: p. 20: © Exactostock/SuperStock; p. 22: AP Photo/Amy Sancetta; p. 24: Copyright © Michael Newman/Photo Edit; p. 27: © Luca DiCecco/Alamy; p. 29: © David Young-Wolff/Alamy; p. 30: © Spencer Grant/Alamy; p. 31: Copyright © Bill Aron/Photo Edit; p. 32, topleft: AVAVA/Shutterstock.com; p. 32, bottomleft: Zagibalov Aleksandr/Shutterstock.com; p. 32, topright: Zurijeta/Shutterstock.com; p. 32, bottomright: © Brigitte Sporrer/Christine Schneider/Alamy; p. 34, top: Richard T. Nowitz/Photo Researchers, Inc.; p. 34, bottom: © Pixelstock/Alamy.

Figure: Fig 2.2: Data from Kathlee D. Vohs and Jonathan W. Schooler, "The value of believing in free will: Encouraging a belief in determinism increases cheating," Psychological Science, January 1, 2008, pp. 49–54. © 2008 by the Association for Psychological Science.

Chapter 3

Photos: CO: p. 46: © Mads Abildgaard/iStockphoto.com; p. 47: © Blend Images/Alamy; p. 48: SPL/Photo Researchers, Inc.; p. 52: Custom Medical Stock Photo/Newscom; p. 54: Don W. Fawcett/Photo Researchers, Inc.; p. 60: AP Photo/Joe Marquette; p. 62: Collection of Jack and Beverly Wilgus; p. 63, bottom: © Jiang Jin/SuperStock; p. 63, top: © BanksPhotos/iStockphoto.com; p. 64: © Mike Hill/Alamy; p. 72: Will & Deni McIntyre/Photo Researchers, Inc.

Figures: Fig 3.2, top: © Friedrich Saurer/Alamy; Fig 3.2, middle: Pascal Goetgheluck/Photo Researchers, Inc.; Fig 3.2, bottom: Daniel Sambraus/Photo Researchers, Inc.; Fig 3.3: From Lefton, Lester A.; Brannon, Linda, Psychology, 8th Edition © 2003. Printed and electronically reproduced by permission of Pearson Education Inc., Upper Saddle River, New Jersey; Fig 3.4: Data from Grazyna Kochanska, Sanghag Kim, Robin A. Barry and Robert A. Philibert, "Children's genotypes interact with maternal responsive care in predicting children's competence," Development and Psychopathology, May 23, 2011, pp. 605–616; Fig 3.8: From Lefton, Lester A.; Brannon, Linda, Psychology, 8th Edition © 2003. Printed and electronically reproduced by permission of Pearson Education Inc., Upper Saddle River, New Jersey; Fig 3.11: Reprinted by permission of Richard McAnulty; Fig 3.17: Lilienfeld, Scott O.; Lynn, Steven J.; Namy, Laura L.; Woolf, Nancy J, Psychology: From Inquiry to Understanding, 1st Edition, © 2009. Printed and electronically reproduced by permission of Pearson Education Inc., Upper Saddle River, New Jersey; Fig 3.21: Zimbardo, Philip G.; Johnson, Robert L.; McCann, Vivian, Psychology: Core Concepts, 6th Edition. © 2009. Printed and electronically reproduced by permission of Pearson Education Inc., Upper Saddle River, New Jersey.

Chapter 4

Photos: CO: p. 79: Meg Takamura/Getty Images; p. 80: Karen H. Ilagan/Shutterstock.com; p. 84: © Christophe Viseux/Alamy; p. 94: © imagebroker/Alamy; p. 97: © Corbis Flirt/Alamy; p. 97: © Juniors Bildarchiv/Alamy; p. 99: ©Norbert Schwerin/The Image Works; p. 101, top: © Aflo Foto Agency/Alamy; p. 101, bottom: © Kelley.garner | Dreamstime.com; p. 102: ©Fujifotos/The Image Works; p. 106, bottom: © Corbis Bridge/Alamy.

Figures: Fig 4.10: From Lilienfeld, Scott O.; Lynn, Steven J.; Namy, Laura L; Woolf, Nancy J., Psychology: From Inquiry to Understanding, 2nd Ed., © 2011. Reprinted and electronically reproduced by permission of Pearson Education, Inc., Upper Saddle River, New Jersey; Fig 4.12: From Vocks, S., Busch, M., Grönemeyer, D., Schulte, D., Herpertz, S., & Suchan, B. (2010). Differential neuronal responses to the self and others in the extrastriate body area (EBA) and the fusiform body area. Cognitive, Affective, and Behavioral Neuroscience, 10, 422–429. Courtesy of Springer; Fig 4.13: From Wade, Carole; Tavris, Carol, Psychology, 10th Edition, © 2011. Reprinted and electronically reproduced by permission of Pearson Education, Inc., Upper Saddle River, New Jersey; Fig 4.14: Reprinted from Color workbook, 3rd Edition by Becky Koenig. Prentice-Hall, 2003–2009. Reprinted by permission of the author; Fig 4.23, left: Photos from the lab of Linda Bartoshuk; Fig 4.23, right: Photos from the lab of Linda Bartoshuk; Fig 4.26: Federico Veronesi/Gallo Images/Getty Images; Fig 4.28: From Ciccarelli, Saundra K; White, J. Noland, Psychology, 3rd Edition, © 2012. Reprinted and electronically reproduced by permission· of Pearson Education, Inc., Upper Saddle River, New Jersey; Fig 4.29: © moodboard/Corbis; Fig 4.31, top: Igumnova Irina/Shutterstock.com; Fig 4.31, bottom: Yuri Samsonov/Shutterstock.com; Fig 4.35: © Todd Ivins/Alamy; p. 116: Reprinted by permission of Sylvia Rock.

Chapter 5

Photos: CO: p. 120: Matthias Heitmann/Lifesize/Getty Images; p. 121: Copyright © David Young-Wolff/PhotoEdit; p. 122, top: © Peter Casolino/Alamy; p. 122, middle: © Nick Gregory/Alamy; p. 122, bottom: © Juniors Bildarchiv/Alamy; p. 129, left: Copyright © Spencer Grant/PhotoEdit; p. 129, right: Copyright © Spencer Grant/PhotoEdit; p. 130: © Janine Wiedel Photolibrary/Alamy; p. 135: © Denkou Images/Alamy; p. 139, bottom: Doug Menuez/Photodisc/Getty Images; p. 139, top: © ACE STOCK LIMITED/Alamy; p. 140: Multnomah County Sheriff/Splash/Newscom;

Figures: Fig 5.1: Data from Jeremy M. Wolfs, "Parallel processing of part-whole information in visual search tasks" Perception & Psychophysics, 55 (1995), 537–550; Fig 5.3: From Carlson, Neil R., Physiology of Behavior, 11th Ed., © 2013. Reproduced and Electronically reproduced by permission of Pearson Education, Inc., Upper Saddle River, New Jersey; Fig 5.4: Data from "Ontogenetic development of the human sleep-dream cycle" by Howard P. Roffwarg, Joseph N. Muzio and William C. Dement, Science, April 29, 1966.

Chapter 6

Photos: CO: p. 144: Andersen Ross/Blend Images/Getty Images; p. 145: © London Entertainment/Alamy; p. 146: Sam Falk/Photo Researchers, Inc.; p. 147: © RIA Novosti/Alamy; p. 151: © Richard Heinzen/SuperStock; p. 153: Courtesy of Prof. Ben Harris, University of New Hampshire; p. 154, left: Image Courtesy of The Advertising Archives; p. 154, right: Image Courtesy of The Advertising Archives;

p. 156, left: Courtesy of Stuart R. Ellins Ph.D.; p. 156, right: Courtesy of Stuart R. Ellins Ph.D.; p. 159: © Paul Kuroda/SuperStock; p. 161, top: Oleksiy Mark/Shutterstock.com; p. 161, second from top: Katariina Järvinen/Shutterstock.com; p. 161, middle: Vlue/Shutterstock.com; p. 161, second from middle: Eric Gevaert/Shutterstock.com; p. 161, bottom: Copyright © Cindy Charles/PhotoEdit; p. 165: Rita Nannini/ Photo Researchers, Inc.; p. 166: Bodil1955/Shutterstock.com; p. 168, left: Courtesy of Albert Bandura; p. 168, middle: Courtesy of Albert Bandura; p. 168, right: Courtesy of Albert Bandura.

Figures: Fig 6.4: From Baron, Robert A., Psychology, 5th Edition., © 2001. Printed and electronically reproduced by permission of Pearson Education Inc., Upper Saddle River, New Jersey; Fig 6.5: Data from Siegel, S., Hearst, E., George, N., & O'Neal, E. (1968). Generalization gradients obtained from individual subjects following classical conditioning. Journal of Experimental Psychology, 78, 171–174.

Chapter 7

Photos: CO: p. 173: James Hardy/Altopress/Newscom; p. 174: ROSLAN RAHMAN/AFP/Getty Images/Newscom; p. 176: Copyright © Michael Newman/PhotoEdit; p. 179: © Ocean/Corbis; p. 181: © Design Pics Inc./Alamy; p. 183: © Frank Chmura/Alamy; p. 184: Copyright © Jeff Greenberg/PhotoEdit; p. 185: Spencer Grant/Photo Researchers, Inc; p. 190: © dbimages/Alamy; p. 193: © MBI/Alamy; p. 197: © Imageshop/Alamy; p. 198: Copyright © Lon C. Diehl/PhotoEdit.

Figures: Fig 7.11: From Baron, Robert A., Psychology, 5th Edition, © 2001. Printed and electronically reproduced by permission of Pearson Education Inc., Upper Saddle River, New Jersey; Fig 7.16: From Jennifer M. Talarico and David C. Rubin, "Confidence, not consistency, characterizes flashbulb memories" Psychological Science 14, pp. 445–461, copyright © 2003 the Association for Psychological Science. Reprinted by permission of Sage Publications; Fig 7.18: Reprinted from Trends in Cognitive Sciences 7(6), Reza Habib, Lars Nyberg, Endel Tulving, "Hemispheric asymmetries of memory: The HERA model revisited," pp. 241–245, © 2003, with permission from Elsevier.

Chapter 8

Photos: CO: p. 206: Philippe Garo/Photo Researchers, Inc.; p. 210: Copyright © David Young-Wolff/PhotoEdit; p. 216: Pressurepics/ Shutterstock.com; p. 218, top: Copyright © Robin Nelson/Photo Edit; p. 218, bottom: REUTERS/Beawiharta Beawiharta; p. 230: © Juice Images/Alamy; p. 233: Copyright © Dennis MacDonald/Photo Edit; p. 234: Thinkstock/Comstock Images/Getty Images.

Figures and Cartoon: Fig 8.1: From Solso, Robert L., Cognitive Psychology, 3rd Edition, © 1991. Printed and electronically reproduced by permission of Pearson Education Inc., Upper Saddle River, New Jersey; Fig 8.10: Reprinted from Cognitive Brain Research, 20, G. Ganis et al., "Brain areas underlying visual mental imagery and visual perception: An fMRI study," pp. 226–241, copyright © 2004, with permission from Elsevier; Fig 8.12: Data from How to Solve Problems: Elements of a Theory of Problems and Problem Solving, by Wickelgren, Wayne. Copyright 1974; Fig 8.13: Data from How to Solve Problems: Elements of a Theory of Problems and Problem Solving, by Wickelgren, Wayne. Copyright 1974; Fig 8.15 Top: Julija Sapic/Shutterstock.com; Fig 8.15 bottom: Dariush M./Shutterstock.com; p. 233: © ScienceCartoonsPlus .com; Fig 8.18: From Buchel, C., Brassen, S., Yacubian, J., Kalisch, R" & Sommer, T. (2011). Ventral striatal signal changes represent missed opportunities and predict future choice. NeuroImage, 57, 1124–1130. Courtesy of Elsevier.

Chapter 9

Photos: CO: p. 239: © Image Source/Alamy; p. 240: SPL/Photo Researchers, Inc.; p. 242: © Image Source/Alamy; p. 243: © Tetra Images/Alamy; p. 251: akg-images/Newscom; p. 252: © INTERFOTO/ Alamy; p. 253: Debby Wong/Shutterstock.com; p. 254, top: © Bettmann/ CORBIS; p. 254, bottom: © Blend Images/Alamy; p. 256: Comstock/ Getty Images.

Figures and Tables: Fig 9.2: From Craig, Grace J.; Dunn, Wendy L., Understanding Human Development, 2nd Edition, © 2010. Printed and electronically reproduced by permission of Pearson Education Inc., Upper Saddle River, New Jersey; Fig 9.3: Reprinted by permission of the author; Fig 9.5: From Lifetime Effects: The High/Scope Perry Preschool Study Through Age 40 (p. 196) by Lawrence J. Schweinhart, JU. Montie, Z. Xiang, W.S. Barnett, C.R. Belfield & M. Nores, Ypsilanti, MI: HighScope Press. © 2005 HighScope Educational Research Foundation. Used with permission; Fig 9.6: Based on Kay Deaux, Nida Bikmen, Alwyn Gilkes, Ana Ventuneac, Yvanne Joseph, Yasser A. Payne and Claude M. Steele, "Becoming American: Stereotype threat effects in Afro-Caribbean immigrant groups," Social Psychological Quarterly, 70, pp. 384–404, copyright © 2007 by the American Sociological Association; Table 9.3: From Sternberg, R. J. 1986. Intelligence applied. San Diego: Harcourt Brace Jovanovich. Reprinted by permission of the author; Table 9.4: From Kosslyn, Stephen M.; Rosenberg, Robin S., Introducing psychology: Brain, Person, Group, 4th Edition, © 2011. Reprinted and Electronically reproduced by permission of Pearson Education, Inc., Upper Saddle River, New Jersey.

Chapter 10

Photos: CO: p. 260: Mike Bluestone/Photo Researchers, Inc.; p. 262, left: © Science and Society/SuperStock; p. 262, middle: © MARKA/ Alamy; p. 262, right: © Michael Cullen/Alamy; p. 263, top: © Images. com/Alamy; p. 263, bottom: © Peter Cavanagh/Alamy; p. 264: Dr G. Moscoso/Photo Researchers, Inc.; p. 265, top: ©Elizabeth Crews/ The Image Works; p. 265, bottom: ©Alan Carey/The Image Works; p. 268: Copyright © Robert W. Ginn/PhotoEdit; p. 270, left: Doug Goodman/Photo Researchers, Inc.; p. 270, right: Doug Goodman/ Photo Researchers, Inc.; p. 274: © Gallo Images/Alamy; p. 277: © DPA/ The Image Works; p. 282: Photo by Nina Leen/Time Life Pictures/Getty Images; p. 282: © Blue Jean Images/Alamy; p. 285: Martin Rogers/Getty Images; p. 288, top: © Fancy Collection/SuperStock; p. 288, bottom: Stockbyte/Getty Images; p. 290: © Asia Images Group Pte Ltd/Alamy; p. 291: Copyright © Michael Newman/PhotoEdit.

Figures and Tables: Fig 10.3: From "Sequential progressions in a theory -of-mind scale: Longitudinal perspectives" by Henry M. Wellman, Fuxi Fang, and Candida C. Peterson, Child Development, 82, pp. 780–79, copyright © 2011 Society for Research in Child Development. Reprinted by permission of John Wiley and Sons; Fig 10.12: From "Longitudinal general population study of sex-typed behavior in boys and girls: A longitudinal general population study of children aged 2.5–8 years" by Susan Golombok, John Rust, Karyofyllis Zervoulis, Tim Croudace, Jean Golding and Melissa Hines, Child Development, September 1, 2008, pp. 1583–1593, copyright © 2008 by the Society for Research in Child Development. Reprinted by permission of John Wiley and Sons; Table 10.6: From Morris, Charles G.; Maisto, Albert A., Understanding Psychology, 9th Ed., © 2010. Reprinted the Electronically reproduced by permission of Pearson Education, Inc., Upper Saddle River, New Jersey.

Chapter 11

Photos: CO: p. 297: © Ben Radford/Corbis; p. 298: © SuperStock/ Alamy; p. 299: AP Photo/Peter Dejong; p. 300: Tim_Booth/Shutterstock .com; p. 301: Copyright © Robin Nelson/Photo Edit; p. 307, left: Graham Whitby/ZUMAPRESS/Newscom; p. 307, right: © Mary Evans Picture Library/Alamy; p. 309, top: D. Kucharski & K. Kucharska/Shutterstock .com; p. 309, bottom: © Bettmann/CORBIS; p. 311: ©Bill Bachmann/The Image Works; p. 312: © Chris Rout/Alamy; p. 313: Carolyn A. McKeone/ Photo Researchers, Inc.; p. 315: Poulsons Photography/Shutterstock .com; p. 319: © DG Photography/Alamy.

Figures: Fig 11.5: From Nicholas O. Rule, Katherine S. Rosen, Michael L. Slepian, Nalini Ambady, "Mating interest improves women's accuracy in judging male sexual orientation," Psychological Science, 22, pp. 881–886, copyright © 2011 the Association for Psychological Science. Reprinted by permission of Sage Publications; Fig 11.6: Data from "Pluralistic ignorance and hooking up" by Tracy A. Lambert, Arnold S. Kahn and Kevin J. Apple, Journal of Sex Research 40(2),

2003, pp. 129–133. reprinted by permission of Taylor & Francis Group, http://www.informaworld.com; Fig 11.7: Data from Gregory M. Herek, "Gender Gaps in Public Opinion about Lesbians and Gay Men," Public Opinion Quarterly, 66 (2002) pp. 40–66.

Chapter 12

Photos: CO: p. 322: © FogStock/Alamy; p. 324, topleft: © NMPFT/SSPL/The Image Works; p. 324, topright: © NMPFT/SSPL/The Image Works; p. 324, bottom: AP Photos/Imperial Household Agency, HO; p. 326, left: © Jon Burbank/The Image Works; p. 326, right: AP Photo/Kathy Willens; p. 327, left: cynoclub/Shutterstock.com; p. 327, right: James L. Davidson/Shutterstock.com; p. 329: © Action Plus Sports Images/Alamy; p. 330: © UpperCut Images/Alamy; p. 333: Copyright © Robert Brenner/PhotoEdit; p. 337: © Corbis Flirt/Alamy; p. 339, top: © Stacy Walsh Rosenstock/Alamy; p. 339, bottom: © Gerald Holubowicz/Alamy; p. 342: Copyright © Bill Aron/PhotoEdit; p. 344: © Corbis RF/Alamy; p. 346: © Chris Howes/Wild Places Photography/Alamy; p. 347: © Jesse Reardon/Twila Reardon/Corbis; p. 350: © Novarc Images/Alamy; p. 353: Samuel Ashfield/Photo Researchers, Inc.

Figures: Fig 12.2–4: From Ciccarelli, Saundra; White, J. Noland, Psychology, 3rd Edition, © 2012. Printed and electronically reproduced by permission of Pearson Education Inc., Upper Saddle River, New Jersey; Fig 12.10: Data from figure "Viral Load" in "Effect of written emotional expression on immune function in patients with human immunodeficiency virus infection: A randomized trial" by Keith J. Petrie, Iris Fontanilla, Mark G. Thomas, Roger J. Booth, and James W. Pennebaker, Psychosomatic Medicine 66(2), March 2004; Fig 12.12: Data from Suzanne C. Segerstrom, "Stress, energy and immunity: An Ecological view," Current directions in Psychological Science, December 1, 2007, © 2007 by the Association for Psychological Science.

Chapter 13

Photos: CO: p. 356: © Oliver Furrer/Alamy; p. 358, left: © UK History/Alamy; p. 358, middle: ZUMA Press/Newscom; p. 358, right: vipflash/Shutterstock.com; p. 360: © prettyfoto/Alamy; p. 361, left: Maugli/Shutterstock.com; p. 361, right: Fotoksa/Shutterstock.com; p. 364: Plush Studios/Blend Images/Getty Images; p. 367, bottom: © James Ingram/Alamy; p. 367, top: © Jim Holden/Alamy; p. 368: © Corbis Premium RF/Alamy; p. 370: © Blend Images/Alamy; p. 372: Copyright © Michael Newman/PhotoEdit; p. 376: © moodboard/Alamy; p. 377: © paul prescott/Alamy.

Figures and Tables: Fig 13.2: Andresr/Shutterstock.com; Fig 13.3: From "Amygdala response to happy faces as a function of extraversion" by Turhan Canli, Heidi Sivers, Susan L. Whitfield, Ian H. Gotlib, and john D.E. Gabrieli, Science, June 1, 2002. Reprinted with permission from AAAS; Fig 13.5: Data from O. Ayduk, M. L. Rodriguez, W. Mischel, Y. Shoda, & J. Wright. Verbal intelligence & self-regulatory competencies, Journal of Research in Personality (41): 374–388, Copyright © 2007; Fig 13.8: Data from S. M. McCrae, E. R. Hirt, & B. J. Milner, She works hard for the money, Journal of Experimental Social Psychology (44): 292–311, © 2008; Fig 13.9: Data from Christine Ma-Kellams and Jim Blascovich, "Culturally divergent responses to mortality salience," Psychological Science, August 1, 2011, copyright © 2011 Association for Psychological Science; Fig 13.11: Reprinted by permission of the publishers from Thematic Apperception Test by Henry A. Murray, Card 12F, Cambridge, Mass.: Harvard University Press, Copyright © 1943 by the President and Fellows of Harvard College, copyright © renewed 1971 by Henry A. Murray; Table 13.7: Excerpted from the MMPI(R)-2 (Minnesota Mulitphasic Personality Inventory(R)-2) Manual for Administration, Scoring and Interpretation, Revised Edition. Copyright © 2001 by the Regents of the University of Minnesota. All rights reserved. Used by permission of the University of Minnesota Press. "MMPI" and "Minnesota Multiphasic Personality Inventory" are trademarks owned by the Regents of the University of Minnesota; Table 13.8: Excerpted from the MMPI(R)-2 (Minnesota Mulitphasic Personality Inventory(R)-2) Manual for Administration, Scoring and Interpretation, Revised Edition. Copyright © 2001 by the Regents of the University of Minnesota. All rights reserved. Used by permission of the University of Minnesota Press. "MMPI" and "Minnesota Multiphasic Personality Inventory" are trademarks owned by the Regents of the University of Minnesota.

Chapter 14

Photos: CO: p. 385: © Blend Images/Alamy; p. 386: © B Christopher/Alamy; p. 388: Photograph courtesy of the Peabody Essex Museum, Salem, Massachusetts; p. 390: ZUMA Press/Newscom; p. 394: © David J. Green—lifestyle themes/Alamy; p. 395: topseller/Shutterstock.com; p. 397: © Kuttig—People—2/Alamy; p. 398: © dieKleinert/SuperStock; p. 401: Copyright © Bill Aron/PhotoEdit; p. 402: DFree/Shutterstock.com; p. 404: © Blend Images/Alamy; p. 407: Getty Images; p. 412: © Bob Ingelhart/iStockphoto.com; p. 414: © Adriane Moll/Corbis.

Figures: Fig 14.2: Data from Behaviour Research and Therapy 46(11), Kellough, J. L., Beevers, C. G., Ellis, A.J., Wells, T. T. "Time course of selective attention in clinically depressed young adults," pp. 1238–1243, 2008; Fig 14.3: Data from Jose, P. E. & Grown, I. "When does the gender difference in rumination begin?" Journal of Youth and Adolescence 37(2), 2008, 180–192. Excerpt: From Vivian Ann Conan, "Divided She Stands." Originally appeared in New York Magazine August 4, 1997 under the pseudonym Laura Emily Mason. Reprinted by permission of the author; Fig 14.4: Data from Martinez-Taboas, A. et al. (2006). "Prevalence of victimization correlates of pathological dissociation in a community sample of youths," Journal of Traumatic Stress, 19, 439–448; Fig 14.5, top: Dr. E. Fuller Torrey and Dr. Weinberger/National Institute of Mental Health; Fig 14.5, bottom: "Mapping adolescent brain change reveals dynamic wave of accelerated gray matter loss in very early-onset schizophrenia". PNAS, 98, 11650–11655. Thompson, P. M., VIdeal, C., Geidd, J. N., Gochman, P., Blumenthal, J., Nicolson, R., Toga, A. W., & Rapport, J. Copyright 2001 National Academy of Sciences, U.S.A.; Fig 14.8: Data from Docherty, N. M. et al. (2008). "Life events and high-trait reactivity together predict psychotic symptom increases in schizophrenia" Schizophrenia Bulletin, 35(3). Reprinted by permission of Oxford University Press.

Chapter 15

Photos: CO: p. 418: Grantpix/Photo Researchers, Inc.; p. 420: © Guido Schiefer/Alamy; p. 421: © Everett Collection Inc/Alamy; p. 423: © Prisma Bildagentur AG/Alamy; p. 424: Wellcome Library, London; p. 426: Copyright © David Young-Wolff/PhotoEdit; p. 428, left: © Bob Mahoney/The Image Works; p. 428, right: ©Bob Mahoney/The Image Works; p. 431: © Datacraft—QxQ images/Alamy; p. 433: Copyright © Tony Freeman/Photo Edit; p. 434: © Bill Bachmann/Alamy; p. 436: Chris Gallagher/Photo Researchers, Inc.; p. 439, left: Will & Deni McIntyre/Photo Researchers, Inc.; p. 439, right: Will McIntyre/Photo Researchers, Inc.; p. 441: Jeffrey Greenberg/Photo Researchers, Inc.

Figures and Tables: Fig 15.1: Albert Bandura, from "Modeling Therapy." Reprinted by permission of Albert Bandura; Table 15.1: From Hall, J. S. (2004). Roadblocks on the journey of psychotherapy. Lanham, MD: Jason Aronson, pp. 73–74. Reprinted by permission; Table 15.4: Reprinted by permission of Natalie Rogers, executor of the Estate of Carl Rogers; Table 15.2: From Butcher, James N.; Mineka, Susan; Hooley, Jill M., Abnormal Psychology, 13th Ed., © 2007. Reprinted and electronically reproduced by permission of Pearson Education, Inc., Upper Saddle River, New Jersey.

Chapter 16

Photos: CO: p. 446: © Tetra Images/Alamy; p. 447: © Homer Sykes Archive/Alamy; p. 450: AJPhoto/Photo Researchers, Inc.; p. 451: © Inmagine/Alamy; p. 452, topleft: Philip G. Zimbardo, Inc., Department of Psychology, Stanford University; p. 452, topright: Philip G. Zimbardo, Inc., Department of Psychology, Stanford University; p. 452, bottomleft: Philip G. Zimbardo, Inc., Department of Psychology, Stanford University; p. 452, bottomright: Philip G. Zimbardo, Inc., Department of Psychology, Stanford University; p. 453: AP Photo; p. 454: © Juice Images/Corbis; p. 457: YOUN JAE-WOOK/AFP/Newscom; p. 458,